Oxford
French
Minidictionary

FOURTH EDITION

French–English
English–French

Français–Anglais
Anglais–Français

Daniel Sterlin-Altman

OXFORD
UNIVERSITY PRESS

OXFORD

UNIVERSITY PRESS

Great Clarendon Street, Oxford OX2 6DP

Oxford University Press is a department of the University of Oxford.
It furthers the University's objective of excellence in research, scholarship,
and education by publishing worldwide in

Oxford New York

Auckland Cape Town Dar es Salaam Hong Kong Karachi Kuala Lumpur
Madrid Melbourne Mexico City Nairobi New Delhi Shanghai Taipei
Toronto

With offices in

Argentina Austria Brazil Chile Czech Republic France Greece
Guatemala Hungary Italy Japan South Korea Poland Portugal
Singapore Switzerland Thailand Turkey Ukraine Vietnam

Oxford is a registered trade mark of Oxford University Press
in the UK and in certain other countries

Published in the United States
by Oxford University Press Inc., New York

British Library Cataloguing in Publication Data

Data available

Library of Congress Cataloging in Publication Data
Data available

ISBN 978-0-19-861045-8

10 9 8 7 6 5 4

Typeset by Interactive Sciences Ltd, Gloucester
Printed in Italy
by Legoprint S.p.A.

Contents/Table des matières

Contributors/Collaborateurs

Fourth Edition/Quatrième édition

Nicholas Rollin
Jean Benoit Ormal-Grenon

Data capture/Saisie des données
Susan Wilkin

Proofreaders/Correcteurs
Isabelle Stables-Lemoine
Meic Haines
Mary O'Neill

Third Edition/Troisième édition

Isabelle Stables-Lemoine
Marianne Chalmers
Rosalind Combley
Catherine Roux
Laura Wedgeworth

Phrasefinder/Mini guide de conversation
Hélène Haenen
Neil and Roswitha Morris

First and Second Edition/Première et deuxième éditions

Michael Janes
Dora Latiri-Carpenter
Edwin Carpenter

Introduction

This new edition of the *Oxford French Minidictionary* has been designed to be a practical reference tool for the student, adult learner, traveller and business professional. It provides user-friendly treatment of core vocabulary across a broad spectrum of written and spoken language.

Enhanced coverage

The wordlist has been revised to reflect recent additions to both languages. The *Phrasefinder* has been expanded and enables the user to communicate in commonly encountered situations such as travel, shopping, eating out and organizing leisure activities.

The more complex grammatical words, or *function words*, are given special treatment in highlighted entries to make them easily accessible. All verbs in the French-English section are cross-referenced to the verb tables at the end of the book. Here information is given on regular, irregular and reflexive verbs as well as the translation of French verb tenses.

Easy reference

The dictionary layout has been designed to be clear, streamlined and easy to use. Bullet points separate each new part of speech within an entry. Nuances of meaning or usage are pinpointed by semantic indicators or by typical collocates with which the headword frequently occurs. Extra help is given with symbols to mark the register of language. A boxed exclamation mark ▣ indicates colloquial language and a cross ▣ indicates slang.

The pronunciation of French is given in the International Phonetic Alphabet. Irregular parts of French verbs appear as headwords with a cross-reference to the main entry of the verb.

Introduction

Cette nouvelle édition de l'*Oxford French Minidictionary* a été conçue comme un outil de référence practique destiné aux étudiants, aux touristes et aux professionnels. Il offre un traitement convivial du vocabulaire de base représentatif de la langue écrite et parlée.

Une édition augmentée

La nomenclature a été revisée de façon à refléter les récents apports de vocabulaire dans les deux langues. La partie centrale intitulée *Mini guide de conversation* aidera l'utilisateur à communiquer dans les situations les plus courantes telles que le voyage, le shopping, les sorties au restaurant ou les loisirs.

Les mots grammaticaux, qui forment les structures de base des deux langues, font l'objet d'une présentation distincte qui les rend rapidement accessibles, les choix de traduction et des exemples étant clairement signalés. De courtes notes d'usage indiquent les pièges éventuels. Une liste de verbes irréguliers anglais se trouve à la fin de l'ouvrage.

Une consulatation facilitée

La présentation du dictionnaire a été conçue de façon à être claire, simplifiée et à faciliter la consultation de l'ouvrage. Des *puces* séparent chaque nouvelle partie du discours à l'intérieur d'une entrée, ce qui facilite leur repérage. Les nuances de sens ou d'usage sont marquées au moyen d'indicateurs sémantiques ou par des collocateurs types avec lesquels le mot s'emploie fréquemment, guidant ainsi rapidement l'utilisateur à la traduction appropriée. Un point d'exclamation **!** indique un niveau de langue familier et une croix **⊠** indique un niveau argotique.

Les symboles utilisés pour la prononciation sont ceux de l'Alphabet Phonétique International. Les pluriels irréguliers ainsi que les conjugaisons ou les formes du comparatif et du superlatif irrégulières anglaises sont indiqués entre parenthèses.

Pronunciation of French

Vowels

a	*as in* patte	/pat/		ɑ	*as in* pâte	/pɑt/
ã	clan	/klɑ̃/		e	dé	/de/
ɛ	belle	/bɛl/		ɛ̃	lin	/lɛ̃/
ə	demain	/dəmɛ̃/		i	gris	/gʀi/
o	gros	/gʀo/		ɔ	corps	/kɔʀ/
ɔ̃	long	/lɔ̃/		œ	leur	/lœʀ/
œ̃	brun	/bʀœ̃/		ø	deux	/dø/
u	fou	/fu/		y	pur	/pyʀ/

Semi-Vowels

j	*as in* fille	/fij/
ɥ	huit	/ɥit/
w	oui	/wi/

Consonants

Aspiration of 'h'
Where it is impossible to make a liaison this is indicated by /'/ immediately after the slash e.g. *haine* /'ɛn/.

b	*as in* bal	/bal/		ŋ	*as in* camping	/kɑ̃piŋ/
d	dent	/dɑ̃/		p	porte	/pɔʀt/
f	foire	/fwaʀ/		ʀ	rire	/ʀiʀ/
g	gomme	/gɔm/		s	sang	/sɑ̃/
k	clé	/kle/		ʃ	chien	/ʃjɛ̃/
l	lien	/ljɛ̃/		t	train	/tʀɛ̃/
m	mer	/mɛʀ/		v	voile	/vwal/
n	nage	/naʒ/		z	zèbre	/zɛbʀ/
ɲ	oignon	/ɲɔ̃/		ʒ	jeune	/ʒœn/

La prononciation de l'anglais

Voyelles et diphtongues

iː	see	ɔː	saw	eɪ	page	ɔɪ	join
ɪ	sit	ʊ	put	əʊ	home	ɪə	near
e	ten	uː	too	aɪ	five	eə	hair
æ	hat	ʌ	cup	aɪə	fire	ʊə	poor
ɑː	arm	ɜː	fur	aʊ	now		
ɒ	got	ə	ago	aʊə	flour		

Consonnes

p	pen	tʃ	chin	s	so	n	no
b	bad	dʒ	June	z	zoo	ŋ	sing
t	tea	f	fall	ʃ	she	l	leg
d	dip	v	voice	ʒ	measure	r	red
k	cat	θ	thin	h	how	j	yes
g	got	ð	then	m	man	w	wet

L'accent d'intensité

L'accent d'intensité est indiqué au moyen du signe / ' /, placé devant la syllabe qu'il affecte.

Aa

a /a/ ➡AVOIR **5**.

à /a/
● *préposition*

à+le = au
à+les = aux

····▸ (avec verbe de mouvement) to.

····▸ (pour indiquer où l'on se trouve) ~ **la maison** at home; ~ **Nice** in Nice.

····▸ (âge, date, heure) ~ **l'âge de...** at the age of...; **au XIXe siècle** in the 19th century; ~ **deux heures** at two o'clock.

····▸ (description) with; **aux yeux verts** with green eyes.

····▸ (appartenance) ~ **qui est ce stylo?** whose pen is this?; **c'est** ~ **vous?** is this yours?

····▸ (avec nombre) ~ **90 km/h** at 90 km per hour; ~ **10 minutes d'ici** 10 minutes from here; **des tomates** ~ **2 euros le kilo** tomatoes at 2 euros a kilo; **un timbre** ~ **2 euros** a 2-euro stamp; **nous avons fait le travail** ~ **deux** two of us did the work; **mener 5** ~ **4** to lead 5 (to) 4.

····▸ (avec être) **c'est** ~ **moi** it's my turn; **je suis** ~ **vous tout de suite** I'll be with you in a minute; **c'est** ~ **toi de décider** it's up to you to decide.

····▸ (hypothèse) ~ **ce qu'il paraît** apparently; ~ **t'entendre** to hear you talk.

····▸ (exclamatif) ~ **ta santé!** cheers!; ~ **demain/bientôt!** see you tomorrow/soon!

····▸ (moyen) ~ **la main** by hand; ~ **vélo** by bike; ~ **pied** on foot; **chauffage au gaz** gas heating.

abaissement /abɛsmɑ̃/ *nm* (de taux, de prix) cut; (de seuil) lowering.

abaisser /abese/ **1** *vt* lower; (*levier*) pull *ou* push down; (fig) humiliate. □ **s'~** *vpr* go down, drop; (fig) demean oneself; **s'~ à** stoop to.

abandon /abɑ̃dɔ̃/ *nm* abandonment; (de personne) desertion; (de course) withdrawal; (naturel) abandon; **à l'~** in a state of neglect.

abandonner /abɑ̃dɔne/ **1** *vt* abandon; (*épouse, cause*) desert; (renoncer à) give up, abandon; (céder) give (**à** to); (course) withdraw from; (Ordinat) abort. □ **s'~ à** *vpr* give oneself up to.

abasourdir /abazuʀdiʀ/ **2** *vt* stun.

abat-jour /abaʒuʀ/ *nm inv* lampshade.

abats /aba/ *nmpl* offal.

abattement /abatmɑ̃/ *nm* dejection; (faiblesse) exhaustion; (Comm) reduction; (fig) ~ **fiscal** tax allowance.

abattre /abatʀ/ **11** *vt* knock down; (*arbre*) cut down; (*animal*) slaughter; (*avion*) shoot down; (affaiblir) weaken; (démoraliser) demoralize; **ne pas se laisser** ~ not let things get one down. □ **s'~** *vpr* come down, fall (down).

abbaye /abei/ *nf* abbey.

a

abbé /abe/ nm priest; (supérieur d'une abbaye) abbot.

abcès /apsɛ/ nm abscess.

abdiquer /abdike/ **1** vt/i abdicate.

abdomen /abdɔmɛn/ nm abdomen.

abdominal (pl **-aux**) /abdɔminal/ adj abdominal. **abdominaux** nmpl (Sport) stomach exercises.

abeille /abɛj/ nf bee.

aberrant, ∼e /abɛʀɑ̃, -t/ adj absurd.

abêtir /abetiʀ/ **2** vt turn into a moron.

abîme /abim/ nm abyss.

abîmer /abime/ **1** vt damage, spoil. □ s'∼ vpr get damaged ou spoilt.

ablation /ablasjɔ̃/ nf removal.

aboiement /abwamɑ̃/ nm bark, barking; ∼s barking.

abolir /abɔliʀ/ **2** vt abolish.

abondance /abɔ̃dɑ̃s/ nf abundance; (prospérité) affluence. **abondant, ∼e** adj abundant, plentiful.

abonder /abɔ̃de/ **1** vi abound (en in); ∼ dans le sens de qn agree wholeheartedly with sb.

abonné, ∼e /abɔne/ nm, f (lecteur) subscriber; (voyageur, spectateur) season-ticket holder.

abonnement /abɔnmɑ̃/ nm (à un journal) subscription; (de bus, Théât) season-ticket; (au gaz) standing charge.

abonner (s') /(s)abɔne/ **1** vpr subscribe (à to).

abord /abɔʀ/ nm access; ∼s surroundings; d'∼ first.

abordable /abɔʀdabl/ adj (prix) affordable; (personne) approachable; (texte) accessible.

aborder /abɔʀde/ **1** vt approach; (lieu) reach; (problème) tackle. ● vi reach land.

aborigène /abɔʀiʒɛn/ nm aborigine.

aboutir /abutiʀ/ **2** vi succeed, achieve a result; ∼ à end (up) in, lead to; n'∼ à rien come to nothing.

aboutissement /abutismɑ̃/ nm outcome; (de carrière, d'évolution) culmination.

aboyer /abwaje/ **31** vi bark.

abrégé /abʀeʒe/ nm summary.

abréger /abʀeʒe/ **14 40** vt (texte) shorten, abridge; (mot) abbreviate, shorten; (visite) cut short.

abreuver /abʀœve/ **1** vt water; (fig) overwhelm (de with). □ s'∼ vpr drink.

abréviation /abʀevjasjɔ̃/ nf abbreviation.

abri /abʀi/ nm shelter; à l'∼ under cover; (en lieu sûr) safe; à l'∼ de sheltered from; se mettre à l'∼ take shelter.

abricot /abʀiko/ nm apricot.

abriter /abʀite/ **1** vt shelter; (recevoir) house. □ s'∼ vpr (take) shelter.

abrupt, ∼e /abʀypt/ adj steep, sheer; (fig) abrupt.

abruti, ∼e /abʀyti/ nm, f □ idiot.

absence /apsɑ̃s/ nf absence; **il a des ∼s** sometimes his mind goes blank.

absent, ∼e /apsɑ̃, -t/ adj (personne) absent, away; (chose) missing; **il est toujours ∼** he's still away; **d'un air ∼** absently. ● nm, f absentee.

absenter (s') /(s)apsɑ̃te/ **1** vpr go ou be away; (sortir) go out, leave.

absolu, ∼e /apsɔly/ adj absolute.

absorbant, ∼e /apsɔʀbɑ̃, -t/ adj

(*travail*) absorbing; (*matière*) absorbent.

absorber /apsɔʀbe/ **1** vt absorb; **être absorbé par qch** be engrossed in sth.

abstenir (s') /(s)apstəniʀ/ **58** vpr abstain; **s'~ de** refrain from.

abstrait, ~e /apstʀɛ, -t/ adj & nm abstract.

absurde /apsyʀd/ adj absurd.

abus /aby/ nm abuse, misuse; (*injustice*) abuse; **~ de confiance** breach of trust.

abuser /abyze/ **1** vt deceive. ● vi go too far; **~ de** abuse, misuse; (*profiter de*) take advantage of; (*alcool*) overindulge in. □ **s'~** vpr be mistaken.

abusif, -ive /abyzif, -v/ adj excessive; (*impropre*) wrong; (*injuste*) unfair.

académie /akademi/ nf academy; (*circonscription*) local education authority.

Académie française A scholarly body composed of 40 life members selected on the basis of their contribution to scholarship or literature. It monitors developments in the French language and rules on French usage, as encoded in the *Dictionnaire de l'Académie française* (which is not always taken seriously by the public at large).

acajou /akaʒu/ nm mahogany.

accablant, ~e /akablɑ̃, -t/ adj (*chaleur*) oppressive; (*fait, témoignage*) damning.

accabler /akable/ **1** vt overwhelm; **~ d'impôts** burden with taxes; **~ d'injures** heap insults upon.

accéder /aksede/ **14** vi **~ à** (*lieu*) reach; (*pouvoir, trône*) accede to; (*requête*) grant; (Ordinat) access; **~ à la propriété** become a homeowner.

accélérateur /akseleʀatœʀ/ nm accelerator.

accélérer /akselere/ **14** vt/i accelerate. □ **s'~** vpr speed up.

accent /aksɑ̃/ nm accent; (*sur une syllabe*) stress, accent; **mettre l'~ sur** stress; **~ aigu/grave/circonflexe** acute/grave/circumflex accent.

accentuer /aksɑ̃tɥe/ **1** vt (*lettre, syllabe*) accent; (fig) emphasize, accentuate. □ **s'~** vpr become more pronounced, increase.

accepter /aksɛpte/ **1** vt accept; **~ de faire** agree to do.

accès /aksɛ/ nm access; (*porte*) entrance; (*de fièvre*) bout; (*de colère*) fit; (*d'enthousiasme*) burst; (Ordinat) access; **les ~ de** (*voies*) the approaches to; **facile d'~** easy to get to.

accessoire /akseswaʀ/ adj secondary, incidental. ● nm accessory; (Théât) prop.

accident /aksidɑ̃/ nm accident; **~ de train/d'avion** train/plane crash; **par ~** by accident. **accidenté, ~e** adj (*personne*) injured (in an accident); (*voiture*) damaged; (*terrain*) uneven, hilly. **accidentel, ~le** adj accidental.

acclamer /aklame/ **1** vt cheer, acclaim.

accommoder /akɔmɔde/ **1** vt adapt (à to); (*cuisiner*) prepare; (*assaisonner*) flavour. □ **s'~ de** vpr make the best of.

accompagnateur, -trice /akɔ̃paɲatœʀ, -tʀis/ nm, f (Mus) accompanist; (*guide*) guide; **~ d'enfants** accompanying adult.

a **accompagner** /akɔ̃paɲe/ **1** vt accompany. □ **s'~ de** vpr be accompanied by.

accomplir /akɔ̃pliʀ/ **2** vt carry out, fulfil. □ **s'~** vpr take place, happen; (vœu) be fulfilled.

accord /akɔʀ/ nm agreement; (harmonie) harmony; (Mus) chord; **être d'~** agree (**pour** to); **se mettre d'~** come to an agreement, agree; **d'~!** all right [1], OK!

accorder /akɔʀde/ **1** vt grant; (couleurs) match; (Mus) tune; (attribuer) (valeur, importance) assign. □ **s'~** vpr (se mettre d'accord) agree; (s'octroyer) allow oneself; **s'~ avec** (s'entendre avec) get on with.

accotement /akɔtmɑ̃/ nm verge; **~ non stabilisé** soft verge.

accouchement /akuʃmɑ̃/ nm childbirth; (travail) labour.

accoucher /akuʃe/ **1** vi give birth (**de** to); (être en travail) be in labour. ● vt deliver. **accoucheur** nm **médecin ~** obstetrician.

accoudoir /akudwaʀ/ nm arm-rest.

accoupler /akuple/ **1** vt (Tech) couple. □ **s'~** vpr mate.

accourir /akuʀiʀ/ **20** vi run up.

accoutumance /akutymɑ̃s/ nf familiarization; (Méd) addiction.

accoutumer /akutyme/ **1** vt accustom. □ **s'~** vpr get accustomed.

accro /akʀo/ nmf [1] (drogué) addict; (amateur) fan.

accroc /akʀo/ nm tear, rip; (fig) hitch.

accrochage /akʀɔʃaʒ/ nm hanging; hooking; (Auto) collision; (dispute) clash; (Mil) encounter.

accrocher /akʀɔʃe/ **1** vt (suspendre) hang up; (attacher) hook, hitch; (déchirer) catch; (heurter) hit; (attirer) attract. □ **s'~** vpr cling, hang on (**à** to); (se disputer) clash.

accroissement /akʀwasmɑ̃/ nm increase (**de** in).

accroître /akʀwɑtʀ/ **24** vt increase. □ **s'~** vpr increase.

accroupir (s') /(s)akʀupiʀ/ **2** vpr squat.

accru, ~e /akʀy/ adj increased, greater.

accueil /akœj/ nm reception, welcome.

accueillant, ~e /akœjɑ̃, -t/ adj friendly, welcoming.

accueillir /akœjiʀ/ **25** vt receive, welcome; (film, livre) receive; (prendre en charge) (réfugiés, patients) take care of, cater for.

accumuler /akymyle/ **1** vt (énergie) store up; (capital) accumulate. □ **s'~** vpr (neige, ordures) pile up; (dettes) accrue.

accusation /akyzasjɔ̃/ nf accusation; (Jur) charge; **l'~** (magistrat) the prosecution.

accusé, ~e /akyze/ adj marked. ● nm, f defendant, accused.

accuser /akyze/ **1** vt accuse (**de** of); (blâmer) blame (**de** for); (Jur) charge (**de** with); (fig) emphasize; **~ réception de** acknowledge receipt of.

acharné, ~e /aʃaʀne/ adj relentless, ferocious. **acharnement** nm (énergie) furious energy; (ténacité) determination.

acharner (s') /(s)aʃaʀne/ **1** vpr persevere; **s'~ sur** set upon; (poursuivre) hound; **s'~ à faire** (s'évertuer) try desperately; (s'obstiner) keep on doing.

achat /aʃa/ nm purchase; **~s** shopping; **faire l'~ de** buy; **faire des ~s** do some shopping.

acheminer /aʃ(ə)mine/ **1** vt dispatch, convey; (*courrier*) handle. □ **s'~ vers** *vpr* head for.

acheter /aʃ(ə)te/ 6 *vt* buy; **~ qch à qn** (pour lui) buy sth for sb; (chez lui) buy sth from sb. **acheteur, -euse** *nm, f* buyer; (client de magasin) shopper.

achèvement /aʃɛvmɑ̃/ *nm* completion.

achever /aʃ(ə)ve/ 6 *vt* finish (off). □ **s'~** *vpr* end.

acide /asid/ *adj* acid, sharp. ● *nm* acid.

acier /asje/ *nm* steel.

acné /akne/ *nf* acne.

acompte /akɔ̃t/ *nm* deposit, part-payment.

à-côté (*pl* **~s**) /akote/ *nm* side issue; **~s** (*argent*) extras.

acoustique /akustik/ *nf* acoustics (+ *sg*). ● *adj* acoustic.

acquéreur /akerœr/ *nm* purchaser, buyer.

acquérir /akerir/ 7 *vt* acquire, gain; (*biens*) purchase, acquire.

acquis, ~e /aki, -z/ *adj* acquired; (*fait*) established; **tenir qch pour ~** take sth for granted. ● *nm* experience. **acquisition** *nf* acquisition; purchase.

acquitter /akite/ 1 *vt* acquit; (*dette*) settle. □ **s'~ de** *vpr* (*promesse*) fulfil; (*devoir*) discharge.

âcre /akr/ *adj* acrid.

acrobatie /akrobasi/ *nf* acrobatics (+ *pl*); **~ aérienne** aerobatics (+ *pl*).

acte /akt/ *nm* act, action, deed; (*Théât*) act; (*Jur*) deed; **~ de naissance/mariage** birth/marriage certificate; **~s** (compte rendu) proceedings; **prendre ~ de** note.

acteur /aktœr/ *nm* actor.

actif, -ive /aktif, -v/ *adj* active; (*population*) working. ● *nm* (Comm) assets; **avoir à son ~** have to one's

credit *ou* name.

action /aksjɔ̃/ *nf* action; (Comm) share; (Jur) action; (effet) effect; (initiative) initiative. **actionnaire** *nmf* shareholder.

activer /aktive/ 1 *vt* speed up; (*feu*) boost. □ **s'~** *vpr* hurry up; (s'affairer) be very busy.

activité /aktivite/ *nf* activity; **en ~** (*volcan*) active; (*fonctionnaire*) working; (*usine*) in operation.

actrice /aktris/ *nf* actress.

actualité /aktyalite/ *nf* topicality; **l'~** current affairs; **les ~s** news; **d'~** topical.

actuel, ~le /aktyɛl/ *adj* current, present; (d'actualité) topical. **actuellement** *adv* currently, at the present time.

acupuncture /akypɔ̃ktyr/ *nf* acupuncture.

adaptateur /adaptatœr/ *nm* (Électr) adapter.

adapter /adapte/ 1 *vt* adapt; (fixer) fit. □ **s'~** *vpr* adapt (oneself); (Tech) fit.

additif /aditif/ *nm* (note) rider; (substance) additive.

addition /adisjɔ̃/ *nf* addition; (au café) bill; (US) check. **additionner** 1 *vt* add; (totaliser) add (up).

adepte /adɛpt/ *nmf* follower; (d'activité) enthusiast.

adéquat, ~e /adekwa, -t/ *adj* suitable; (suffisant) adequate.

adhérent, ~e /aderɑ̃, -t/ *nm, f* member.

adhérer /adere/ 14 *vi* adhere, stick (à to); **~ à** (club) be a member of; (s'inscrire à) join.

adhésif, -ive /adezif, -v/ *adj* adhesive; **ruban ~** sticky tape.

adhésion /adezjɔ̃/ *nf* membership; (soutien) support.

adieu (*pl* **~x**) /adjø/ *interj & nm*

goodbye, farewell.

adjectif /adʒɛktif/ nm adjective.

adjoint, ~e /adʒwɛ̃, -t/ nm, f assistant; **~ au maire** deputy mayor. ● adj assistant.

adjuger /adʒyʒe/ **40** vt award; (aux enchères) auction. □ **s'~** vpr take (for oneself).

ADM abrév fpl (armes de destruction massive) WMD.

admettre /admɛtʀ/ **42** vt let in, admit; (tolérer) allow; (reconnaître) admit, acknowledge; (candidat) pass.

administrateur, -trice /administʀatœʀ, -tʀis/ nm, f administrator, director; (jur) trustee; **~ de site Internet** Webmaster.

administratif, -ive /administʀatif, -v/ adj administrative; (document) official. **administration** nf administration; (gestion) management; **l'A~** Civil Service.

administrer /administʀe/ **1** vt run, manage; (justice, biens, antidote) administer.

admirateur, -trice /admiʀatœʀ, -tʀis/ nm, f admirer.

admiration /admiʀasjɔ̃/ nf admiration.

admirer /admiʀe/ **1** vt admire.

admission /admisjɔ̃/ nf admission.

ADN abrév m (acide désoxyribonucléique) DNA.

adolescence /adɔlesɑ̃s/ nf adolescence. **adolescent, ~e** nm, f adolescent, teenager.

adopter /adɔpte/ **1** vt adopt. **adoptif, -ive** adj (enfant) adopted; (parents) adoptive.

adorer /adɔʀe/ **1** vt love; (plus fort) adore; (Relig) worship, adore.

adosser /adose/ **1** vt lean (à, contre against). □ **s'~** vpr lean

back (à, contre against).

adoucir /adusiʀ/ **2** vt soften; (boisson) sweeten; (chagrin) ease. □ **s'~** vpr soften; (chagrin) ease; (temps) become milder. **adoucissant** nm (fabric) softener.

adresse /adʀɛs/ nf address; (habileté) skill; **~ électronique** email address.

adresser /adʀese/ **1** vt send; (écrire l'adresse sur) address; (remarque) address; **~ la parole à** speak to. □ **s'~ à** vpr address; (aller voir) (personne) go and ask ou see; (bureau) enquire at; (viser, intéresser) be directed at.

adroit, ~e /adʀwa, -t/ adj skilful, clever.

ADSL abrév m (asymmetrical digital subscriber line) ADSL.

adulte /adylt/ nmf adult. ● adj adult; (plante, animal) fully grown.

adultère /adyltɛʀ/ adj adulterous. ● nm adultery.

adverbe /advɛʀb/ nm adverb.

adversaire /advɛʀsɛʀ/ nmf opponent, adversary.

aérer /aeʀe/ **1** vt air; (texte) space out. □ **s'~** vpr get some air.

aérien, ~ne /aeʀjɛ̃, -jɛn/ adj air; (photo) aerial; (câble) overhead.

aérobic /aeʀɔbik/ nm aerobics (+ sg).

aérogare /aeʀɔgaʀ/ nf air terminal.

aéroglisseur /aeʀɔglisœʀ/ nm hovercraft.

aérogramme /aeʀɔgʀam/ nm airmail letter; (US) aerogram.

aéronautique /aeʀɔnotik/ adj aeronautical. ● nf aeronautics (+ sg).

aéroport /aeʀɔpɔʀ/ nm airport.

aérospatial, ~e (mpl **-iaux**) /aeʀɔspasjal, -jo/ adj aerospace.

affaiblir /afeblir/ **2** vt weaken.
□ **s'~** vpr get weaker.

affaire /afɛʀ/ nf affair, matter; (Jur) case; (histoire, aventure) affair; (occasion) bargain; (entreprise) business; (transaction) deal; (question, problème) matter; **~s** (Comm) business; (Pol) affairs; (problèmes personnels) business; (effets personnels) things; **c'est mon ~** that's my business; **avoir ~ à** deal with; **ça fera l'~** that will do the job; **ça fera leur ~** that's just what they need; **tirer qn d'~** help sb out of a tight spot; **se tirer d'~** get out of trouble.

affairé, ~e /afeʀe/ adj busy.

affaisser (s') /(s)afese/ **1** vpr (terrain, route) sink, subside; (poutre) sag; (personne) collapse.

affamé, ~e /afame/ adj starving.

affectation /afɛktasjɔ̃/ nf (nomination) (à une fonction) appointment; (dans un lieu) posting; (de matériel, d'argent) allocation; (comportement) affectation.

affecter /afɛkte/ **1** vt (feindre) affect; (toucher, affliger) affect; (destiner) assign; (nommer) appoint, post.

affectif, -ive /afɛktif, -v/ adj emotional.

affection /afɛksjɔ̃/ nf affection; (maladie) complaint.

affectueux, -euse /afɛktɥø, -z/ adj affectionate.

affichage /afiʃaʒ/ nm billposting; (électronique) display.

affiche /afiʃ/ nf (public) notice; (publicité) poster; (Théât) bill; **être à l'~** (film) be showing; (pièce) be on.

afficher /afiʃe/ **1** vt (annonce) put up; (événement) announce; (sentiment) display; (Ordinat) display.

affirmatif, -ive /afiʀmatif, -v/ adj affirmative. **affirmation** nf assertion.

affirmer /afiʀme/ **1** vt assert; (soutenir) maintain.

affligé, ~e /afliʒe/ adj distressed; **~ de** afflicted with.

affluer /aflye/ **1** vi flood in; (sang) rush.

affolant, ~e /afɔlɑ̃, -t/ adj alarming.

affoler /afɔle/ **1** vt throw into a panic. □ **s'~** vpr panic.

affranchir /afʀɑ̃ʃiʀ/ **2** vt stamp; (à la machine) frank; (esclave) emancipate; (fig) free. **affranchissement** nm (tarif) postage.

affreux, -euse /afʀø, -z/ adj (laid) hideous; (mauvais) awful.

affrontement /afʀɔ̃tmɑ̃/ nm confrontation.

affronter /afʀɔ̃te/ **1** vt confront. □ **s'~** vpr confront each other.

affûter /afyte/ **1** vt sharpen.

afin /afɛ̃/ prép & conj **~ de faire** in order to do; **~ que** so that.

africain, ~e /afʀikɛ̃, -ɛn/ adj African. **A~, ~e** nm, f African.

Afrique /afʀik/ nf Africa; **~ du Sud** South Africa.

agacer /agase/ **10** vt irritate, annoy.

âge /aʒ/ nm age; (vieillesse) (old) age; **quel ~ avez-vous?** how old are you?; **~ adulte** adulthood; **~ mûr** maturity; **d'un certain ~** middle-aged.

âgé, ~e /aʒe/ adj elderly; **~ de cinq ans** five years old.

agence /aʒɑ̃s/ nf agency, bureau, office; (succursale) branch; **~ d'interim** employment agency; **~ de voyages** travel agency; **~ publicitaire** advertising agency.

agenda /aʒɛ̃da/ nm diary; **~ élec-**

a tronique electronic organizer.

agent /aʒɑ̃/ nm agent; (fonctionnaire) official; ~ **(de police)** policeman; ~ **de change** stockbroker; ~ **commercial** sales representative.

agglomération /aglomerasjɔ̃/ nf town, built-up area.

aggraver /agrave/ **1** vt aggravate, make worse. □ s'~ vpr get worse.

agile /aʒil/ adj agile, nimble.

agir /aʒir/ **2** vi act; (se comporter) behave; (avoir un effet) work, take effect. □ s'~ de vpr (être nécessaire) **il s'agit de faire** we/you etc. must do; (être question de) **il s'agit de faire** it is a matter of doing; **dans ce livre il s'agit de** this book is about; **dont il s'agit** in question; **il s'agit de ton fils** it's about your son; **de quoi s'agit-il?** what is it about?

agitation /aʒitasjɔ̃/ nf bustle; (trouble) agitation; (malaise social) unrest.

agité, ~e /aʒite/ adj restless, fidgety; (troublé) agitated; (mer) rough.

agiter /aʒite/ **1** vt (bras, mouchoir) wave; (liquide, boîte) shake; (troubler) agitate; (discuter) debate. □ s'~ vpr bustle about; (enfant) fidget; (foule, pensées) stir.

agneau (pl ~x) /aɲo/ nm lamb.

agrafe /agraf/ nf hook; (pour papiers) staple. **agrafeuse** nf stapler.

agrandir /agrɑ̃dir/ **2** vt enlarge; (maison) extend. □ s'~ vpr expand, grow. **agrandissement** nm extension; (de photo) enlargement.

agréable /agreabl/ adj pleasant.

agréé, ~e /agree/ adj (agence) authorized; (nourrice, médecin) registered; (matériel) approved.

agréer /agree/ **19** vt accept; ~ **à**

please; **veuillez ~, Monsieur, mes salutations distinguées** (personne non nommée) yours faithfully; (personne nommée) yours sincerely.

agrégation /agregasjɔ̃/ nf highest examination for recruitment of teachers. **agrégé, ~e** nm, f teacher (who has passed the agrégation).

agrément /agremɑ̃/ nm charm; (plaisir) pleasure; (accord) assent.

agresser /agrese/ **1** vt attack; (pour voler) mug.

agressif, -ive /agresif, -v/ adj aggressive. **agression** nf attack; (pour voler) mugging; (Mil) aggression.

agricole /agrikɔl/ adj agricultural; (ouvrier, produit) farm. **agriculteur, -trice** nm, f farmer. **agriculture** nf agriculture, farming.

agripper /agripe/ **1** vt grab. □ s'~ vpr cling (à to).

agroalimentaire /agroalimɑ̃tɛr/ nm food industry.

agrumes /agrym/ nmpl citrus fruit(s).

ai /e/ →**avoir** **5**.

aide /ɛd/ nf help, assistance; (en argent) aid; **à l'~ de** with the help of; **venir en ~ à** help; ~ **à domicile** carer, home help; ~ **familiale** mother's help; ~ **sociale** social security; (US) welfare. ● nmf assistant. **aide-éducateur, -trice** nm, f classroom assistant. **aide-mémoire** nm inv handbook of key facts.

aider /ede/ **1** vt/i help, assist; (subventionner) aid, give aid to; ~ **à faire** help to do. □ s'~ de vpr use.

aïeul, ~e /ajœl/ nm, f grandparent.

aigle /ɛgl/ nm eagle.

aigre /ɛgr/ adj sour, sharp; (fig) sharp.

aigrir /egrir/ **2** vt embitter. □ s'~ vpr turn sour; (personne) become embittered.

aigu, ~ë /egy/ adj (douleur, problème) acute; (objet) sharp; (voix) shrill; (Mus) high-(pitched); (accent) acute.

aiguille /eguij/ nf needle; (de montre) hand; (de balance) pointer; **~ à tricoter** knitting needle.

aiguilleur /eguijœr/ nm pointsman; **~ du ciel** air traffic controller.

aiguiser /eg(ɥ)ize/ ❶ vt sharpen; (fig) stimulate.

ail (pl ~s ou aulx) /aj, o/ nm garlic.

aile /ɛl/ nf wing.

ailier /elje/ nm winger; (US) end.

aille /aj/ →ALLER ❽.

ailleurs /ajœr/ adv elsewhere, somewhere else; **d'~** besides, moreover; **nulle part ~** nowhere else; **par ~** moreover, furthermore; **partout ~** everywhere else.

aimable /ɛmabl/ adj kind.

aimant /ɛmɑ̃/ nm magnet.

aimer /eme/ ❶ vt like; (d'amour) love; **j'aimerais faire** I'd like to do; **~ bien** quite like; **~ mieux** ou **autant** prefer.

aîné, ~e /ene/ adj eldest; (de deux) elder. ● nm, f eldest (child); (premier de deux) elder (child); **~s** elders; **il est mon ~** he is older than me ou my senior.

ainsi /ɛ̃si/ adv like this, thus; (donc) so; **et ~ de suite** and so on; **pour ~ dire** so to speak, as it were; **~ que** as well as; (comme) as.

air /ɛr/ nm air; (mine) look, air; (mélodie) tune; **~ conditionné** air-conditioning; **avoir l'~** look, appear; **avoir l'~ de** to look like; **avoir l'~ de faire** appear to be doing; **en l'~** (up) in the air; (promesses) empty; **prendre l'~** get some fresh air.

aire /ɛr/ nf area; **~ d'atterrissage** landing-strip; **~ de pique-nique**

picnic area; **~ de repas** rest area; **~ de services** (motorway) services.

aisance /ɛzɑ̃s/ nf ease; (richesse) affluence.

aise /ɛz/ nf joy; **à l'~** (sur un siège) comfortable; (pas gêné) at ease; (fortuné) comfortably off; **mal à l'~** uncomfortable; ill at ease; **aimer ses ~s** like one's creature comforts; **mettre qn à l'~** put sb at ease; **se mettre à l'~** make oneself comfortable.

aisé, ~e /eze/ adj easy; (fortuné) well-off.

aisselle /ɛsɛl/ nf armpit.

ait /ɛ/ →AVOIR ❺.

ajourner /aʒurne/ ❶ vt postpone; (débat, procès) adjourn.

ajout /aʒu/ nm addition.

ajouter /aʒute/ ❶ vt add (à to); **~ foi à** lend credence to. □ **s'~** vpr be added.

ajuster /aʒyste/ ❶ vt adjust; (cible) aim at; (adapter) fit; **~ son coup** aim one's aim.

alarme /alarm/ nf alarm; **donner l'~** raise the alarm.

alarmer /alarme/ ❶ vt alarm. □ **s'~** vpr become alarmed (de at).

Albanie /albani/ nf Albania.

alcool /alkɔl/ nm alcohol; (eau de vie) brandy; **~ à brûler** methylated spirit. **alcoolique** adj & nmf alcoholic. **alcoolisé, ~e** adj (boisson) alcoholic. **alcoolisme** nm alcoholism.

alcootest /alkɔtɛst/ nm breath test; (appareil) Breathalyser®.

aléa /alea/ nm hazard. **aléatoire** adj unpredictable, uncertain; (Ordinat) random.

alentours /alɑ̃tur/ nmpl surroundings; **aux ~ de** (de lieu) around; (de chiffre, date) about, around.

alerte /alɛrt/ adj (personne) alert;

algèbre | allocation

(vif) lively. ● *nf* alert; ∼ **à la bombe** bomb scare. **alerter** **1** *vt* alert.

algèbre /alʒɛbʀ/ *nf* algebra.

Algérie /alʒeʀi/ *nf* Algeria.

algue /alg/ *nf* seaweed; **les** ∼**s** (Bot) algae.

aliéné, ∼**e** /aljene/ *nm, f* insane person.

aliéner /aljene/ **14** *vt* alienate; (céder) give up. □ **s'**∼ *vpr* alienate.

aligner /aliɲe/ **1** *vt* (objets) line up, make lines of; (chiffres) string together; ∼ **sur** bring into line with. □ **s'**∼ *vpr* line up; **s'**∼ **sur** align oneself on.

aliment /alimɑ̃/ *nm* food.

alimentaire /alimɑ̃tɛʀ/ *adj* (industrie) food; (habitudes) dietary; **produits** ∼**s** foodstuffs.

alimentation /alimɑ̃tasjɔ̃/ *nf* feeding, supply(ing); (régime) diet; (aliments) food; **magasin d'**∼ grocery shop *ou* store.

alimenter /alimɑ̃te/ **1** *vt* feed; (fournir) supply; (fig) sustain. □ **s'**∼ *vpr* eat.

allaiter /alɛte/ *vt* (bébé) breastfeed; (US) nurse; (animal) suckle.

allée /ale/ *nf* path, lane; (menant à une maison) drive(way); (dans un cinéma, magasin) aisle; (rue) road; ∼**s et venues** comings and goings.

allégé, ∼**e** /aleʒe/ *adj* diet; (beurre, yaourt) low-fat.

alléger /aleʒe/ **14** **40** *vt* make lighter; (fardeau, chargement) lighten; (fig) (souffrance) alleviate.

allégresse /alegʀɛs/ *nf* gaiety, joy.

alléguer /alege/ **14** *vt* (exemple) invoke; (prétexter) allege.

Allemagne /alman/ *nf* Germany.

allemand, ∼**e** /almɑ̃, -d/ *adj* German. ● *nm* (Ling) German. **A**∼, ∼**e** *nm, f* German.

aller /ale/ **8**

● *verbe auxiliaire*

····▸ **je vais l'appeler** I'm going to call him; **j'allais partir** I was about to leave; **va savoir** who knows?; ∼ **en s'améliorant** be improving.

● *verbe intransitif*

····▸ (se déplacer) go; **allons-y!** let's go!; **allez!** come on!

····▸ (se porter) **comment allezvous?, comment ça va?** how are you?; **ça va (bien)** I'm fine; **qu'est-ce qui ne va pas?** what's the matter?; **ça ne va pas la tête?** **1** are you mad? **1**.

····▸ (mettre en valeur) ∼ **à qn** suit sb; **ça te va bien** it really suits you.

····▸ (convenir) **ça va ma coiffure?** is my hair OK?; **ça ne va pas du tout** that's no good at all.

□ **s'en aller** *verbe pronominal*

····▸ go; **va-t'en!** go away!; **ça ne s'en va pas** (tache) it won't come out.

● *nom masculin*

····▸ outward journey; ∼ **(simple)** single (ticket); (US) one-way (ticket); ∼ **retour** return (ticket); (US) round trip (ticket); **à l'**∼ on the way out.

allergie /alɛʀʒi/ *nf* allergy. **allergique** *adj* allergic (à to).

alliance /aljɑ̃s/ *nf* alliance; (bague) wedding-ring; (mariage) marriage.

allier /alje/ **45** *vt* combine; (Pol) ally. □ **s'**∼ *vpr* combine; (Pol) form an alliance; (famille) become related (à to).

allô /alo/ *interj* hallo, hello.

allocation /alɔkasjɔ̃/ *nf* allowance; ~ **chômage** unemployment benefit; ~**s familiales** family allowance.

allonger /alɔ̃ʒe/ 40 vt lengthen; (bras, jambe) stretch (out); (coucher) lay down. □ **s'**~ vpr get longer; (s'étendre) lie down; (s'étirer) stretch (oneself) out.

allouer /alwe/ 1 vt allocate; (prêt) grant.

allumer /alyme/ 1 vt (bougie, gaz) light; (lampe, appareil) turn on; (pièce) switch the light(s) on in; (fig) arouse. □ **s'**~ vpr (lumière, appareil) come on.

allumette /alymɛt/ nf match.

allure /alyʀ/ nf speed, pace; (démarche) walk; (apparence) appearance; **à toute** ~ at full speed; **avoir de l'**~ have style; **avoir des** ~**s de** look like; **avoir une drôle d'**~ be funny-looking.

allusion /alyzjɔ̃/ nf allusion (à to); (implicite) hint (à at); **faire** ~ **à** allude to; hint at.

alors /alɔʀ/ adv (à ce moment-là) then; (de ce fait) so; (dans ce cas-là) then; **ça** ~! welll; **et** ~? so what? ● conj ~ **que** (pendant que) while; (tandis que) when, whereas.

alouette /alwɛt/ nf lark.

alourdir /aluʀdiʀ/ 2 vt weigh down; (rendre plus important) increase.

aloyau (pl ~**x**) /alwajo/ nm sirloin.

Alpes /alp/ nfpl **les** ~ the Alps.

alphabet /alfabɛ/ nm alphabet. **alphabétique** adj alphabetical.

alphabétiser /alfabetize/ 1 vt teach to read and write.

alpiniste /alpinist/ nmf mountaineer.

altérer /alteʀe/ 14 vt (fait, texte) distort; (abîmer) spoil; (donner soif à) make thirsty. □ **s'**~ vpr deteriorate.

alternance /alternɑ̃s/ nf alternation; **en** ~ alternately.

altitude /altityd/ nf altitude, height.

amabilité /amabilite/ nf kindness.

amaigrir /amegʀiʀ/ 2 vt make thin(ner).

amande /amɑ̃d/ nf almond; (d'un fruit à noyau) kernel.

amant /amɑ̃/ nm lover.

amarre /amaʀ/ nf (mooring) rope; ~**s** moorings.

amas /amɑ/ nm heap, pile.

amasser /amase/ 1 vt amass, gather; (empiler) pile up. □ **s'**~ vpr pile up; (gens) gather.

amateur /amatœʀ/ nm amateur; ~ **de** lover of; **d'**~ amateur; (péj) amateurish.

ambassade /ɑ̃basad/ nf embassy. **ambassadeur, -drice** nm, f ambassador.

ambiance /ɑ̃bjɑ̃s/ nf atmosphere. **ambiant, ~e** adj surrounding.

ambigu, ~ë /ɑ̃bigy/ adj ambiguous.

ambitieux, -ieuse /ɑ̃bisjø, -z/ adj ambitious. **ambition** nf ambition.

ambulance /ɑ̃bylɑ̃s/ nf ambulance.

ambulant, ~e /ɑ̃bylɑ̃, -t/ adj itinerant, travelling.

âme /ɑm/ nf soul; ~ **sœur** soul mate.

amélioration /ameljɔʀasjɔ̃/ nf improvement.

améliorer /ameljɔʀe/ 1 vt improve. □ **s'**~ vpr improve.

aménagement /amenaʒmɑ̃/ nm (de magasin) fitting out; (de grenier) conversion; (de territoire) development; (de cuisine) equipping.

aménager /amenaʒe/ **40** vt (magasin) fit out; (transformer) convert; (territoire) develop; (cuisine) equip.

amende /amɑ̃d/ nf fine; **faire ∼ honorable** make amends.

amener /am(ə)ne/ **6** vt bring; (causer) bring about; **∼ qn à faire** cause sb to do. □ **s'∼** vpr **1** turn up.

amer, -ère /amɛʀ/ adj bitter.

américain, ∼e /amerikɛ̃, -ɛn/ adj American. **A∼, ∼e** nm, f American.

Amérique /amerik/ nf America; **∼ centrale/latine** Central/Latin America; **∼ du Nord/Sud** North/ South America.

amertume /amɛʀtym/ nf bitterness.

ami, ∼e /ami/ nm, f friend; (amateur) lover; **un ∼ des bêtes** an animal lover. ● adj friendly.

amiable /amjabl/ adj amicable; **à l'∼** (divorcer) by mutual consent; (se séparer) on friendly terms; (séparation) amicable.

amical, ∼e (mpl **-aux**) /amikal, -o/ adj friendly.

amiral (pl **-aux**) /amiʀal, -o/ nm admiral.

amitié /amitje/ nf friendship; **∼s** (en fin de lettre) kind regards; **prendre qn en ∼** take a liking to sb.

amnistie /amnisti/ nf amnesty.

amoindrir /amwɛ̃dʀiʀ/ **2** vt reduce.

amont: en **∼** /ɑ̃namɔ̃/ loc upstream.

amorcer /amɔʀse/ **10** vt start; (hameçon) bait; (pompe) prime; (arme à feu) arm.

amortir /amɔʀtiʀ/ **2** vt (choc) cushion; (bruit) deaden; (dette) pay off; **∼ un achat** make a purchase pay for itself.

amortisseur /amɔʀtisœʀ/ nm shock absorber.

amour /amuʀ/ nm love; **pour l'∼ de** for the sake of.

amoureux, -euse /amuʀø, -z/ adj (personne) in love; (relation, regard) loving; (vie) love; **∼ de qn** in love with sb. ● nm, f lover.

amour-propre /amuʀpʀɔpʀ/ nm self-esteem.

amphithéâtre /ɑ̃fiteatʀ/ nm amphitheatre; (d'université) lecture hall.

ampleur /ɑ̃plœʀ/ nf extent, size; (de vêtement) fullness; **prendre de l'∼** spread, grow.

amplifier /ɑ̃plifje/ **45** vt amplify; (fig) expand, develop. □ **s'∼** vpr (son) grow; (scandale) intensify.

ampoule /ɑ̃pul/ nf (électrique) bulb; (sur la peau) blister; (Méd) phial, ampoule.

amusant, ∼e /amyzɑ̃, -t/ adj (blague) funny; (soirée) enjoyable, entertaining.

amuse-gueule /amyzgœl/ nm inv cocktail snack.

amusement /amyzmɑ̃/ nm amusement; (passe-temps) entertainment.

amuser /amyze/ **1** vt amuse; (détourner l'attention) distract. □ **s'∼** vpr enjoy oneself; (jouer) play.

amygdale /amidal/ nf tonsil.

an /ɑ̃/ nm year; **avoir dix ∼s** be ten years old; **un garçon de deux ∼s** a two-year-old boy; **à soixante ∼s** at the age of sixty; **les moins de dix-huit ∼s** under eighteens.

analogie /analɔʒi/ nf analogy.

analogue /analɔg/ adj similar, analogous (à to).

analphabète /analfabɛt/ adj & nmf illiterate.

analyse /analiz/ *nf* analysis; (Méd) test. **analyser** ◼ *vt* analyse; (Méd) test.

ananas /anana(s)/ *nm* pineapple.

anarchie /anaʀʃi/ *nf* anarchy.

anatomie /anatɔmi/ *nf* anatomy.

ancêtre /ɑ̃sɛtʀ/ *nm* ancestor.

anchois /ɑ̃ʃwa/ *nm* anchovy.

ancien, ~ne /ɑ̃sjɛ̃, -jɛn/ *adj* old; (de jadis) ancient; (meuble) antique; (précédent) former, ex-, old; (dans une fonction) senior; **~ combattant** veteran. ● *nm, f* senior; (par l'âge) elder. **anciennement** *adv* formerly. **ancienneté** *nf* age, seniority.

ancre /ɑ̃kʀ/ *nf* anchor; **jeter/lever l'~** cast/weigh anchor.

andouille /ɑ̃duj/ *nf* sausage (filled with chitterlings); (idiot ◼) fool; **faire l'~** fool around.

âne /ɑn/ *nm* donkey, ass; (imbécile ◼) dimwit ◼.

anéantir /aneɑ̃tiʀ/ ◼ *vt* destroy; (exterminer) annihilate; (accabler) overwhelm.

anémie /anemi/ *nf* anaemia.

ânerie /ɑnʀi/ *nf* stupid remark.

anesthésie /anɛstezi/ *nf* (opération) anaesthetic.

ange /ɑ̃ʒ/ *nm* angel; **aux ~s** in seventh heaven.

angine /ɑ̃ʒin/ *nf* throat infection.

anglais, ~e /ɑ̃glɛ, -z/ *adj* English. ● *nm* (Ling) English. **A~, ~e** *nm, f* Englishman, Englishwoman.

angle /ɑ̃gl/ *nm* angle; (coin) corner.

Angleterre /ɑ̃glətɛʀ/ *nf* England.

anglophone /ɑ̃glɔfɔn/ *adj* English-speaking. ● *nmf* English speaker.

angoissant, ~e /ɑ̃gwasɑ̃, -t/ *adj* alarming; (effrayant) harrowing.

angoisse /ɑ̃gwas/ *nf* anxiety. **angoissé, ~e** *adj* anxious. **angoisser**

◼ *vi* worry.

animal (*pl* **-aux**) /animal, -o/ *nm* animal; **~ familier, ~ de compagnie** pet. ● *adj* (*mpl* **-aux**) animal.

animateur, -trice /animatœʀ, -tʀis/ *nm, f* organizer, leader; (TV) host, hostess.

animation /animasjɔ̃/ *nf* liveliness; (affairement) activity; (au cinéma) animation; (activité dirigée) organized activity.

animé, ~e /anime/ *adj* lively; (affairé) busy; (être) animate.

animer /anime/ ◼ *vt* liven up; (débat, atelier) lead; (spectacle) host; (pousser) drive; (encourager) spur on. □ **s'~** *vpr* liven up.

anis /ani(s)/ *nm* (Culin) aniseed; (Bot) anise.

anneau (*pl* **~x**) /ano/ *nm* ring; (de chaîne) link.

année /ane/ *nf* year; **~ bissextile** leap year; **~ civile** calendar year.

annexe /anɛks/ *adj* (document) attached; (question) related; (bâtiment) adjoining. ● *nf* (bâtiment) annexe; (US) annex; (document) appendix; (électronique) attachment. **annexer** ◼ *vt* annex; (document) attach.

anniversaire /anivɛʀsɛʀ/ *nm* birthday; (d'un événement) anniversary. ● *adj* anniversary.

annonce /anɔ̃s/ *nf* announcement; (publicitaire) advertisement; (indice) sign.

annoncer /anɔ̃se/ ◼◼ *vt* announce; (prédire) forecast; (être l'indice de) herald. □ **s'~** *vpr* (crise, tempête) be brewing; **s'~ bien/mal** look good/bad. **annonceur** *nm* advertiser.

annuaire /anɥɛʀ/ *nm* year-book; **~ (téléphonique)** (telephone) directory.

annuel, ~le /anɥɛl/ *adj* annual,

a yearly.

annulation /anylasjɔ̃/ *nf* cancellation; (de sanction, loi) repeal; (de mesure) abolition.

annuler /anyle/ **1** *vt* cancel; (contrat) nullify; (jugement) quash; (loi) repeal. □ **s'~** *vpr* cancel each other out.

anodin, ~e /anɔdɛ̃, -in/ *adj* insignificant; (sans risques) harmless, safe.

anonymat /anɔnima/ *nm* anonymity; **garder l'~** remain anonymous. **anonyme** *adj* anonymous.

anorexie /anɔrɛksi/ *nf* anorexia.

anormal, ~e (*mpl* **-aux**) /anɔrmal, -o/ *adj* abnormal.

anse /ɑ̃s/ *nf* handle; (baie) cove.

Antarctique /ɑ̃tarktik/ *nm* Antarctic.

antenne /ɑ̃tɛn/ *nf* aerial; (US) antenna; (d'insecte) antenna; (succursale) agency; (Mil) outpost; **à l'~** on the air; **~ chirurgicale** mobile emergency unit; **~ parabolique** satellite dish.

antérieur, ~e /ɑ̃terjœr/ *adj* previous, earlier; (placé devant) front; **~ à** prior to.

antiaérien, ~ne /ɑ̃tiaerjɛ̃, -ɛn/ *adj* anti-aircraft; **abri ~** air-raid shelter.

antiatomique /ɑ̃tiatɔmik/ *adj* **abri ~** nuclear fall-out shelter.

antibiotique /ɑ̃tibjɔtik/ *nm* antibiotic.

anticipation /ɑ̃tisipasjɔ̃/ *nf* **d'~** (livre, film) science fiction; **par ~** in advance.

anticiper /ɑ̃tisipe/ **1** *vt* **~ (sur)** anticipate; (effectuer à l'avance) bring forward.

anticorps /ɑ̃tikɔr/ *nm* antibody.

antidater /ɑ̃tidate/ **1** *vt* backdate, antedate.

antigel /ɑ̃tiʒɛl/ *nm* antifreeze.

Antilles /ɑ̃tij/ *nfpl* **les ~** the West Indies.

antipathique /ɑ̃tipatik/ *adj* unpleasant.

antiquaire /ɑ̃tikɛr/ *nmf* antique dealer.

antiquité /ɑ̃tikite/ *nf* (objet) antique; **l'A~** antiquity.

antisémite /ɑ̃tisemit/ *adj* anti-Semitic.

antiseptique /ɑ̃tisɛptik/ *adj & nm* antiseptic.

antivirus /ɑ̃tivirys/ *nm inv* (Ordinat) antivirus software.

antivol /ɑ̃tivɔl/ *nm* anti-theft device; (Auto) steering lock.

anxiété /ɑ̃ksjete/ *nf* anxiety.

anxieux, -ieuse /ɑ̃ksjø, -z/ *adj* anxious. ● *nm, f* worrier.

août /u(t) / *nm* August.

apaiser /apeze/ **1** *vt* calm down; (colère, militant) appease; (douleur) soothe; (faim) satisfy. □ **s'~** *vpr* (tempête) die down.

apathie /apati/ *nf* apathy. **apathique** *adj* apathetic.

apercevoir /apɛrsəvwar/ **52** *vt* see. □ **s'~ de** *vpr* notice; **s'~ que** notice ou realize that.

aperçu /apɛrsy/ *nm* (échantillon) glimpse, taste; (intuition) insight.

apéritif /aperitif/ *nm* aperitif, drink.

aphte /aft/ *nm* mouth ulcer.

apitoyer /apitwaje/ **31** *vt* move (to pity). □ **s'~** *vpr* **s'~ sur (le sort de) qn** feel sorry for sb.

aplanir /aplanir/ **2** *vt* level; (fig) iron out.

aplatir /aplatir/ **2** *vt* flatten (out). □ **s'~** *vpr* (s'immobiliser) flatten oneself.

aplomb /aplɔ̃/ nm balance; (fig) self-confidence; **d'~** (en équilibre) steady; **je ne suis pas bien d'~** I don't feel very well.

apogée /apoʒe/ nm peak.

apologie /apɔlɔʒi/ nf panegyric.

apostrophe /apɔstʀɔf/ nf apostrophe; (remarque) remark.

apothéose /apoteoz/ nf high point; (d'événement) grand finale.

apparaître /apaʀɛtʀ/ 18 vi appear; **il apparaît que** it appears that.

appareil /apaʀɛj/ nm device; (électrique) appliance; (Anat) system; (téléphone) phone; (avion) plane; (Culin) mixture; (système administratif) apparatus; **~ (dentaire)** brace; (dentier) dentures; **~ (photo)** camera; **c'est Gabriel à l'~** it's Gabriel on the phone; **~ auditif** hearing aid; **~ électroménager** household electrical appliance.

appareiller /apaʀeje/ 1 vi (navire) cast off, put to sea.

apparemment /apaʀamɑ̃/ adv apparently.

apparence /apaʀɑ̃s/ nf appearance; **en ~** outwardly; (apparemment) apparently.

apparent, ~e /apaʀɑ̃, -t/ adj apparent; (visible) conspicuous.

apparenté, ~e /apaʀɑ̃te/ adj related; (semblable) similar.

apparition /apaʀisjɔ̃/ nf appearance; (spectre) apparition.

appartement /apaʀtəmɑ̃/ nm flat; (US) apartment.

appartenir /apaʀtəniʀ/ 58 vi belong (à to); **il lui appartient de** it is up to him to.

appât /apɑ/ nm bait; (fig) lure.

appauvrir /apovʀiʀ/ 2 vt impoverish. □ **s'~** vpr become

impoverished.

appel /apɛl/ nm call; (jur) appeal; (supplique) appeal, plea; (Mil) call-up; (US) draft; **faire ~** appeal; **faire ~ à** (recourir à) call on; (invoquer) appeal to; (évoquer) call up; (exiger) call for; **faire l'~** (Scol) call the register; (Mil) take a roll-call; **~ d'offres** (Comm) invitation to tender; **faire un ~ de phares** flash one's headlights.

appeler /aple/ 33 vt call; (téléphoner) phone, call; (nécessiter) call for; **en ~ à** appeal to; **appelé à** (destiné) destined for. □ **s'~** vpr be called; **il s'appelle Tim** his name is Tim ou he is called Tim.

appellation /apelasjɔ̃/ nf name, designation.

appendice /apɛ̃dis/ nm appendix. **appendicite** nf appendicitis.

appesantir /apəzɑ̃tiʀ/ 2 vt weigh down. □ **s'~** vpr grow heavier; **s'~ sur** dwell upon.

appétissant, ~e /apetisɑ̃, -t/ adj appetizing.

appétit /apeti/ nm appetite; **bon ~!** enjoy your meal!

applaudir /aplodiʀ/ 2 vt/i applaud. **applaudissements** nmpl applause.

application /aplikasjɔ̃/ nf (soin) care; (de loi) (respect) application; (mise en œuvre) implementation; (Ordinat) application program.

appliqué, ~e /aplike/ adj (travail) painstaking; (sciences) applied; (élève) hard-working.

appliquer /aplike/ 1 vt apply; (loi) enforce. □ **s'~** vpr apply oneself (à to), take great care (à faire to do); **s'~ à** (concerner) apply to.

appoint /apwɛ̃/ nm support; **d'~** extra; **faire l'~** give the correct money.

apport /apɔʀ/ nm contribution.

apporter /apɔʀte/ **1** vt bring; (aide, précision) give; (causer) bring about.

appréciation /apʀesjasjɔ̃/ nf estimate, evaluation; (de monnaie) appreciation; (jugement) assessment.

apprécier /apʀesje/ **45** vt appreciate; (évaluer) assess; (objet) value, appraise.

appréhender /apʀeɑ̃de/ **1** vt dread, fear; (arrêter) apprehend.

apprendre /apʀɑ̃dʀ/ **50** vt learn; (être informé de) hear, learn; (de façon indirecte) hear of; ~ qch à qn teach sb sth; (informer) tell sb sth; ~ à faire learn to do sth; ~ à qn à faire teach sb to do; ~ que learn that; (être informé) hear that.

apprenti, ~e /apʀɑ̃ti/ nm, f apprentice. **apprentissage** nm apprenticeship; (d'un sujet) learning.

apprêter /apʀete/ **1** vt prepare; (bois) prime; (mur) size. □ s'~ à vpr prepare to.

apprivoiser /apʀivwaze/ **1** vt tame.

approbation /apʀɔbasjɔ̃/ nf approval.

approchant, ~e /apʀɔʃɑ̃, -t/ adj close, similar.

approcher /apʀɔʃe/ **1** vt (objet) move near(er) (de to); (personne) approach; ~ de get nearer ou closer to. ● vi approach. □ s'~ de vpr approach, move near(er) to.

approfondir /apʀɔfɔ̃diʀ/ **2** vt deepen; (fig) (sujet) go into sth in depth; (connaissances) improve.

approprié, ~e /apʀɔpʀije/ adj appropriate.

approprier (s') /(s)apʀɔpʀije/ **45** vpr appropriate.

approuver /apʀuve/ **1** vt approve; (trouver louable) approve of; (soutenir) agree with.

approvisionner /apʀɔvizjɔne/ **1** vt supply (en with); (compte en banque) pay money into. □ s'~ vpr stock up.

approximatif, -ive /apʀɔksimatif, -v/ adj approximate.

appui /apɥi/ nm support; (de fenêtre) sill; (pour objet) rest; à l'~ de in support of; **prendre ~ sur** lean on.

appui-tête (pl appuis-tête) /apɥitɛt/ nm headrest.

appuyer /apɥije/ **31** vt lean, rest; (presser) press; (soutenir) support, back. ● vi ~ sur press (on); (fig) stress. □ s'~ sur vpr lean on; (compter sur) rely on.

après /apʀɛ/ prép after; (au-delà de) after, beyond; ~ avoir fait after doing; ~ tout after all; ~ coup after the event; (en imitant) from; ~ (selon) according to; (adapté de) based on. ● adv after (wards); (plus tard) later; **le bus d'~** the next bus. ● conj ~ qu'il est parti after he left. **après-demain** adv the day after tomorrow. **après-guerre** (pl ~s) nm ou f postwar period. **après-midi** (pl inv) nm ou f inv afternoon. **après-rasage** (pl ~s) nm aftershave. **après-shampooing** nm conditioner. **après-ski** nm inv moon boot. **après-vente** adj inv aftersales.

a priori /apʀijɔʀi/ adv (à première vue) offhand, on the face of it; (sans réfléchir) out of hand. ● nm preconception.

à-propos /apʀopo/ nm timing, timeliness; (fig) presence of mind.

apte /apt/ adj capable (à of); (ayant les qualités requises) suitable (à for); (en état) fit (à for).

aptitude /aptityd/ nf aptitude,

ability.

aquarelle /akwaʀɛl/ nf watercolour.

aquatique /akwatik/ adj aquatic; (Sport) water.

arabe /aʀab/ adj Arab; (Ling) Arabic; (désert) Arabian. ● nm (Ling) Arabic. **A~** nmf Arab.

Arabie /aʀabi/ nf **~ Saoudite** Saudi Arabia.

arachide /aʀaʃid/ nf groundnut; **huile d'~** groundnut oil.

araignée /aʀeɲe/ nf spider.

arbitraire /aʀbitʀɛʀ/ adj arbitrary.

arbitre /aʀbitʀ/ nm referee; (au cricket, tennis) umpire; (expert) arbiter; (Jur) arbitrator. **arbitrer 1** vt (match) referee, umpire; (Jur) arbitrate in.

arbre /aʀbʀ/ nm tree; (Tech) shaft.

arbuste /aʀbyst/ nm shrub.

arc /aʀk/ nm (arme) bow; (courbe) curve; (voûte) arch; **~ de cercle** arc of a circle.

arc-en-ciel (pl **arcs-en-ciel**) /aʀkɑ̃sjɛl/ nm rainbow.

arche /aʀʃ/ nf arch; **~ de Noé** Noah's ark.

archéologie /aʀkeɔlɔʒi/ nf archaeology.

archevêque /aʀʃəvɛk/ nm archbishop.

architecte /aʀʃitɛkt/ nmf architect. **architecture** nf architecture.

Arctique /aʀktik/ nm Arctic.

ardent, ~e /aʀdɑ̃, -t/ adj burning; (passionné) ardent; (foi) fervent. **ardeur** nf ardour; (chaleur) heat.

ardoise /aʀdwaz/ nf slate; **~ électronique** notepad computer.

arène /aʀɛn/ nf arena; **~s** amphitheatre; (pour corridas) bullring.

arête /aʀɛt/ nf (de poisson) bone; (bord) ridge.

argent /aʀʒɑ̃/ nm money; (métal) silver; **~ comptant** cash; **prendre pour ~ comptant** take at face value; **~ de poche** pocket money.

argenté, ~e /aʀʒɑ̃te/ adj silver(y); (métal) (silver-)plated.

argenterie /aʀʒɑ̃tʀi/ nf silverware.

Argentine /aʀʒɑ̃tin/ nf Argentina.

argile /aʀʒil/ nf clay.

argot /aʀgo/ nm slang.

argument /aʀgymɑ̃/ nm argument; **~ de vente** selling point. **argumenter 1** vi argue.

aristocratie /aʀistɔkʀasi/ nf aristocracy.

arithmétique /aʀitmetik/ nf arithmetic. ● adj arithmetical.

armature /aʀmatyʀ/ nf framework; (de tente) frame.

arme /aʀm/ nf arm, weapon; **~ à feu** firearm; **~s** (blason) coat of arms; **~s de destruction massive** weapons of mass destruction.

armée /aʀme/ nf army; **~ de l'air** Air Force; **~ de terre** Army.

armer /aʀme/ **1** vt arm; (fusil) cock; (navire) equip; (renforcer) reinforce; (Photo) wind on. □ **s'~ de** vpr arm oneself with.

armoire /aʀmwaʀ/ nf cupboard; (penderie) wardrobe; (US) closet; **~ à pharmacie** medicine cabinet.

armure /aʀmyʀ/ nf armour.

arnaque /aʀnak/ nf **1** swindling; **c'est de l'~** it's a swindle **1**.

arobas(e) /aʀɔbas, aʀɔbaz/ nm at sign.

aromate /aʀɔmat/ nm herb, spice.

aromatisé, ~e /aʀɔmatize/ adj flavoured.

arôme /aʀom/ nm aroma; (additif) flavouring.

arpenter /aʀpɑ̃te/ **1** vt pace up and down; (terrain) survey.

arqué /arke/ adj arched; (*jambes*) bandy.

arrache-pied: d'~ /daraʃpje/ loc relentlessly.

arracher /araʃe/ **1** vt pull out ou off; (*plante*) pull up; (*cheveux, page*) tear ou pull out; (*par une explosion*) blow off; ~ à (*enlever à*) snatch from; (*fig*) force ou wrest from. □ **s'~ qch** vpr fight over sth.

arranger /arɑ̃ʒe/ **40** vt arrange, fix up; (*réparer*) put right; (*régler*) sort out; (*convenir à*) suit. □ **s'~** vpr (*se mettre d'accord*) come to an arrangement; (*se débrouiller*) manage (*pour* to).

arrestation /arɛstasjɔ̃/ nf arrest.

arrêt /arɛ/ nm stopping; (*de combats*) cessation; (*de production*) halt; (*lieu*) stop; (*pause*) pause; (*Jur*) ruling; **aux ~s** (Mil) under arrest; **à l'~** (*véhicule*) stationary; (*machine*) idle; **faire un ~** (make a) stop; **sans ~** (*sans escale*) nonstop; (*sans interruption*) constantly; ~ **maladie** sick leave; ~ **de travail** (*grève*) stoppage; (*Méd*) sick leave.

arrêté /arɛte/ nm order; ~ **municipal** bylaw.

arrêter /arɛte/ **1** vt stop; (*date*) fix; (*appareil*) turn off; (*renoncer à*) give up; (*appréhender*) arrest. ● vi stop. □ **s'~** vpr stop; **s'~ de faire** stop doing.

arrhes /ar/ nfpl deposit; **verser des ~** pay a deposit.

arrière /arjɛr/ adj inv back, rear. ● nm back; rear; (*football*) back; **à l'~** in ou au the back; **en ~** behind; (*marcher, tomber*) backwards; **en ~ de** behind. **arrière-boutique** (*pl* ~**s**) nf back room (of the shop). **arrière-garde** (*pl* ~**s**) nf rearguard. **arrière-goût** (*pl* ~**s**) nm aftertaste. **arrière-grand-mère** (*pl* ~**s**) nf **arrière-**

grands-mères nf great-grandmother. **arrière-grand-père** (*pl* **arrière-grands-pères**) nm great-grandfather. **arrière-pays** nm inv backcountry. **arrière-pensée** (*pl* ~**s**) nf ulterior motive. **arrière-plan** nm (*pl* ~**s**) background.

arrimer /arime/ **1** vt secure; (*cargaison*) stow.

arrivage /arivaʒ/ nm consignment.

arrivée /arive/ nf arrival; (*Sport*) finish.

arriver /arive/ **1** vi (*aux être*) arrive, come; (*réussir*) succeed; (*se produire*) happen; ~ **à** (*atteindre*) reach; ~ **à faire** manage to do; **je n'arrive pas à faire** I can't do; **en ~ à faire** get to the stage of doing; **il arrive que** it happens that; **il lui arrive de faire** he (sometimes) does.

arriviste /arivist/ nmf go-getter, self-seeker.

arrondir /arɔ̃dir/ **2** vt (make) round; (*somme*) round off. □ **s'~** vpr become round(ed).

arrondissement /arɔ̃dismɑ̃/ nm district.

Arrondissement A subdivision of a *département*. Each *arrondissement* has a *sous-préfet* representing the state administration at local level. In Paris, Lyons and Marseilles, an *arrondissement* is a sub-division of the commune, and has its own *maire* and local council. ⓘ

---

arroser /aroze/ **1** vt water; (*repas*) wash down (with a drink); (*rôti*) baste; (*victoire*) drink to. **arrosoir** nm watering can.

art /ar/ nm art; (*don*) knack (**de** faire of doing); ~**s et métiers** arts and crafts; **~s ménagers** home economics (+ sg).

artère /aʀtɛʀ/ nf artery; **(grande) ~** main road.

arthrite /aʀtʀit/ nf arthritis.

arthrose /aʀtʀoz/ nf osteoarthritis.

artichaut /aʀtiʃo/ nm artichoke.

article /aʀtikl/ nm article; (Comm) item, article; **l'~ de la mort** at death's door; **~ de fond** feature (article); **~s de voyage** travel goods.

articulation /aʀtikylasjɔ̃/ nf articulation; (Anat) joint.

articuler /aʀtikyle/ **1** vt articulate; (structurer) structure; (assembler) connect (**sur** to).

artificiel, ~le /aʀtifisjɛl/ adj artificial.

artisan /aʀtizɑ̃/ nm artisan, craftsman; **l'~ de** (fig) the architect of.

artisanal, ~e (mpl **~aux**) /aʀtizanal/ adj craft; (méthode) traditional; (amateur) home-made; **de fabrication ~e** hand-made, hand-crafted.

artiste /aʀtist/ nmf artist. **artistique** adj artistic.

as[1] /a/ ➡AVOIR **5**.

as[2] /ɑs/ nm ace.

ascenseur /asɑ̃sœʀ/ nm lift; (US) elevator.

ascension /asɑ̃sjɔ̃/ nf ascent; **l'A~** Ascension.

asiatique /azjatik/ adj Asian. **A~** nmf Asian.

Asie /azi/ nf Asia.

asile /azil/ nm refuge; (Pol) asylum; (pour malades, vieillards) home; **~ de nuit** night shelter.

aspect /aspɛ/ nm appearance; (facettes) aspect; (perspective) side; **à l'~ de** at the sight of.

asperge /aspɛʀʒ/ nf asparagus.

asperger /aspɛʀʒe/ **40** vt spray.

asphyxier /asfiksje/ **45** vt (personne) asphyxiate; (entreprise, réseau) paralyse. □ **s'~** vpr suffocate; gas oneself; (entreprise, réseau) become paralysed.

aspirateur /aspiʀatœʀ/ nm vacuum cleaner.

aspirer /aspiʀe/ **1** vt inhale; (liquide) suck up. ● vi **~ à** aspire to.

aspirine® /aspiʀin/ nf aspirin.

assainir /asɛniʀ/ **2** vt clean up.

assaisonnement /asɛzɔnmɑ̃/ nm seasoning.

assassin /asasɛ̃/ nm murderer; (Pol) assassin. **assassiner** **1** vt murder; (Pol) assassinate.

assaut /aso/ nm assault, onslaught; **donner l'~ à, prendre d'~** storm.

assemblage /asɑ̃blaʒ/ nm assembly; (combinaison) collection; (Tech) joint.

assemblée /asɑ̃ble/ nf meeting; (gens réunis) gathering; (Pol) assembly.

Assemblée nationale The lower house of the French parliament, in which 577 *députés* are elected for a five-year term. *Députés* sit in parties in the semi-circular chamber, with the most left-wing to the extreme left and the most right-wing to the extreme right. The *Assemblée nationale* passes laws, votes on the Budget, and questions ministers.

---

assembler /asɑ̃ble/ **1** vt assemble, put together; (réunir) gather. □ **s'~** vpr gather, assemble.

asseoir /aswaʀ/ **9** vt sit (down),

seat; (*bébé, malade*) sit up; (affermir) establish; (baser) base. □ **s'~** *vpr* sit (down).

assez /ase/ *adv* (suffisamment) enough; (plutôt) quite, fairly; ~ **grand/rapide** big/fast enough (**pour** to); ~ **de** enough; **j'en ai** (~ **de**) I've had enough (of).

assidu, ~**e** /asidy/ *adj* (zélé) assiduous; (régulier) regular; ~ **auprès de** attentive to. **assiduité** *nf* assiduousness, regularity.

assiéger /asjeʒe/ **14 40** *vt* besiege.

assiette /asjɛt/ *nf* plate; (équilibre) seat; ~ **anglaise** assorted cold meats; ~ **creuse/plate** soup-/dinner-plate; **ne pas être dans son** ~ feel out of sorts.

assigner /asiɲe/ **1** *vt* assign; (limite) fix.

assimilation /asimilasjɔ̃/ *nf* assimilation; (comparaison) likening, comparison.

assimiler /asimile/ **1** *vt* ~ **à** liken to; (classer) class as. □ **s'~** *vpr* assimilate; (être comparable) be comparable (**à** to).

assis, ~**e** /asi, -z/ *adj* sitting (down), seated. ● →**ASSEOIR 9**.

assise /asiz/ *nf* (base) foundation; ~**s** (tribunal) assizes; (congrès) conference, congress.

assistance /asistɑ̃s/ *nf* audience; (aide) assistance; **l'A~** (publique) welfare services.

assistant, ~**e** /asistɑ̃, -t/ *nm, f* assistant; (Scol) foreign language assistant; ~**s** (spectateurs) members of the audience; ~**e sociale** social worker; ~ **personnel numérique** personal digital assistant, PDA.

assister /asiste/ **1** *vt* assist; ~ **à** attend, be (present) at; (accident) witness; **assisté par ordinateur** computer-assisted.

association /asɔsjasjɔ̃/ *nf* association.

associé, ~**e** /asɔsje/ *nm, f* partner, associate. ● *adj* associate.

associer /asɔsje/ **45** *vt* associate; (mêler) combine (**à** with); ~ **qn à** (*projet*) involve sb in; (*bénéfices*) give sb a share of. □ **s'~** *vpr* (sociétés, personnes) become associated, join forces (**à** with); (s'harmoniser) combine (**à** with); **s'~ à** (*joie, opinion de qn*) share; (*projet*) take part in.

assommer /asɔme/ **1** *vt* knock out; (animal) stun; (fig) overwhelm; (ennuyer **1**) bore.

Assomption /asɔ̃psjɔ̃/ *nf* Assumption.

assortiment /asɔrtimɑ̃/ *nm* assortment.

assortir /asɔrtir/ **2** *vt* match (**à** with, to); ~ **de** accompany with. □ **s'~** *vpr* match; **s'~ à qch** match sth.

assoupir (**s'**) /(s)asupir/ **2** *vpr* doze off; (s'apaiser) subside.

assouplir /asuplir/ **2** *vt* make supple; (fig) make flexible.

assourdir /asurdir/ **2** *vt* (personne) deafen; (bruit) muffle.

assouvir /asuvir/ **2** *vt* satisfy.

assujettir /asyʒetir/ **2** *vt* subjugate, subdue; ~ **à** subject to.

assumer /asyme/ **1** *vt* assume; (coût) meet; (accepter) come to terms with, accept.

assurance /asyrɑ̃s/ *nf* (self-) assurance; (garantie) assurance; (contrat) insurance; ~**s sociales** social insurance; ~ **automobile/maladie** car/health insurance.

assuré, ~**e** /asyre/ *adj* certain, assured; (sûr de soi) confident, assured. ● *nm, f* insured party.

assurer /asyre/ **1** *vt* ensure;

(fournir) provide; (exécuter) carry out; (Comm) insure; (stabiliser) steady; (*frontières*) make secure; ~ **à qn que** assure sb that; ~ **qn de** assure sb of; ~ **la gestion/défense de** manage/defend. □ **s'**~ *vpr* take out insurance; **s'**~ **de/que** make sure of/that; **s'**~ **qch** (se procurer) secure sth. **assureur** *nm* insurer.

astérisque /asterisk/ *nm* asterisk.

asthmatique /asmatik/ *adj & nmf* asthmatic.

asthme /asm/ *nm* asthma.

asticot /astiko/ *nm* maggot.

astreindre /astrɛ̃dr/ 22 *vt* ~ **qn à qch** force sth on sb; ~ **qn à faire** force sb to do.

astrologie /astrɔlɔʒi/ *nf* astrology. **astrologue** *nmf* astrologer.

astronaute /astrɔnot/ *nmf* astronaut.

astronomie /astrɔnɔmi/ *nf* astronomy.

astuce /astys/ *nf* smartness; (truc) trick; (plaisanterie) wisecrack.

astucieux, -ieuse /astysjø, -z/ *adj* smart, clever.

atelier /atalje/ *nm* (local) workshop; (de peintre) studio; (séance de travail) workshop.

athée /ate/ *nmf* atheist. ● *adj* atheistic.

athlète /atlɛt/ *nmf* athlete. **athlétisme** *nm* athletics.

Atlantique /atlãtik/ *nm* Atlantic (Ocean).

atmosphère /atmɔsfɛʀ/ *nf* atmosphere.

atomique /atɔmik/ *adj* atomic; (énergie, centrale) nuclear.

atomiseur /atɔmizœr/ *nm* spray.

atout /atu/ *nm* trump (card); (avantage) asset.

atroce /atrɔs/ *adj* atrocious.

attabler (s') /(s)atable/ 1 *vpr* sit down at table.

attachant, ~**e** /ataʃɑ̃, -t/ *adj* charming.

attache /ataʃ/ *nf* (agrafe) fastener; (lien) tie.

attaché, ~**e** /ataʃe/ *adj* être ~ **à** (aimer) be attached to. ● *nm, f* (Pol) attaché.

attacher /ataʃe/ 1 *vt* tie (up); (ceinture, robe) fasten; (bicyclette) lock; ~ **à** (attribuer à) attach to. ● *vi* (Culin) stick. □ **s'**~ *vpr* fasten, do up; **s'**~ **à** (se lier à) become attached to; (se consacrer à) apply oneself to.

attaquant, ~**e** /atakɑ̃, -t/ *nm, f* attacker; (au football) striker; (au football américain) forward.

attaque /atak/ *nf* attack; ~ **(cérébrale)** stroke; **il va en faire une** ~ he'll have a fit; ~ **à main armée** armed attack.

attaquer /atake/ 1 *vt* attack; (banque) raid. ● *vi* attack. □ **s'**~ **à** *vpr* attack; (*problème, sujet*) tackle.

attardé, ~**e** /atarde/ *adj* backward; (idées) outdated; (en retard) late.

attarder (s') /(s)atarde/ 1 *vpr* linger.

atteindre /atɛ̃dʀ/ 22 *vt* reach; (blesser) hit; (affecter) affect.

atteint, ~**e** /atɛ̃, -t/ *adj* ~ **de** suffering from.

atteinte /atɛ̃t/ *nf* attack (à on); **porter** ~ **à** attack; (droit) infringe.

atteler /atle/ 38 *vt* (cheval) harness; (remorque) couple. □ **s'**~ **à** *vpr* get down to.

attelle /atɛl/ *nf* splint.

attenant, ~**e** /atnɑ̃, -t/ *adj* ~ **(à)** adjoining.

attendant: en ~ /ɑ̃natɑ̃dɑ̃/ *loc* meanwhile.

attendre /atɑ̃dʀ/ **3** vt wait for; (bébé) expect; (être le sort de) await; (escompter) expect; ~ **que qn fasse** wait for sb to do. ● vi wait; (au téléphone) hold. □ **s'~ à** vpr expect.

attendrir /atɑ̃dʀiʀ/ **2** vt move (to pity). □ **s'~** vpr be moved to pity.

attendu[1] /atɑ̃dy/ prép given, considering; ~ **que** considering that.

attendu[2], ~**e** /atɑ̃dy/ adj (escompté) expected; (espéré) long-awaited.

attentat /atɑ̃ta/ nm assassination attempt; ~ **(à la bombe)** (bomb) attack.

attente /atɑ̃t/ nf wait(ing); (espoir) expectations (+ pl).

attenter /atɑ̃te/ **1** vi ~ **à** make an attempt on; (fig) violate.

attentif, -ive /atɑ̃tif, -v/ adj attentive; (scrupuleux) careful; ~ **à** mindful of; (soucieux) careful of.

attention /atɑ̃sjɔ̃/ nf attention; (soin) care; ~ **(à)!** watch out (for)!; **faire** ~ **à** (écouter) pay attention to; (prendre garde à) watch out for; (prendre soin de) take care of; **faire** ~ **à faire** be careful to do. **attentionné, ~e** adj considerate.

attentisme /atɑ̃tism/ nm wait-and-see policy.

atténuer /atenye/ **1** vt (violence) reduce; (critique) tone down; (douleur) ease; (faute) mitigate. □ **s'~** vpr subside.

atterrir /ateʀiʀ/ **2** vi land. **atterrissage** nm landing.

attestation /atɛstasjɔ̃/ nf certificate.

attester /atɛste/ **1** vt testify to; ~ **que** testify that.

attirant, ~e /atiʀɑ̃, -t/ adj attractive.

attirer /atiʀe/ **1** vt draw, attract;

(causer) bring. □ **s'~** vpr bring upon oneself; (amis) win.

attiser /atize/ **1** vt (feu) poke; (sentiment) stir up.

attitré, ~e /atitʀe/ adj accredited; (habituel) usual, regular.

attitude /atityd/ nf attitude; (maintien) bearing.

attraction /atʀaksjɔ̃/ nf attraction.

attrait /atʀɛ/ nm attraction.

attraper /atʀape/ **1** vt catch; (corde, main) catch hold of; (habitude, accent) pick up; (maladie) catch; **se faire** ~ **1** get told off.

attrayant, ~e /atʀɛjɑ̃, -t/ adj attractive.

attribuer /atʀibye/ **1** vt allocate; (prix) award; (imputer) attribute. □ **s'~** vpr claim (for oneself). **attribution** nf awarding, allocation.

attrouper (s') /(s)atʀupe/ **1** vpr gather.

au /o/ ➞**À**.

aubaine /obɛn/ nf godsend, opportunity.

aube /ob/ nf dawn, daybreak.

auberge /obɛʀʒ/ nf inn; ~ **de jeunesse** youth hostel.

aubergine /obɛʀʒin/ nf aubergine; (US) eggplant.

aucun, ~e /okœ̃, okyn/ adj (dans une phrase négative) no, not any; (positif) any. ● pron (dans une phrase négative) none, not any; (positif) any; ~ **des deux** neither of the two; **d'~s** some. **aucunement** adv not at all, in no way.

audace /odas/ nf daring; (impudence) audacity.

audacieux, -ieuse /odasjø, -z/ adj daring.

au-delà /od(a)la/ adv beyond. ● prép ~ **de** beyond.

au-dessous /od(ə)su/ adv below.
● prép ~ de below; (couvert par)
under.

au-dessus /od(ə)sy/ adv above.
● prép ~ de above.

au-devant /od(ə)vã/ prép aller ~
de qn go to meet sb; aller ~ des
désirs de qn anticipate sb's wishes.

audience /odjãs/ nf audience;
(d'un tribunal) hearing; (succès, attention) success.

audimat® /odimat/ nm l'~ the
TV ratings.

audiovisuel, ~le /odjovizɥɛl/ adj
audio-visual.

auditeur, -trice /oditœr, -tris/
nm, f listener.

audition /odisjɔ̃/ nf hearing;
(Théât, Mus) audition.

auditoire /oditwar/ nm audience.

augmentation /ogmɑ̃tasjɔ̃/ nf
increase; ~ (de salaire) (pay) rise;
(US) raise.

augmenter /ogmɑ̃te/ **1** vt/i increase; (employé) give a pay rise ou
raise to.

augure /ogyr/ nm (devin) oracle;
être de bon/mauvais ~ be a
good/ bad sign.

aujourd'hui /oʒurdɥi/ adv today.

auparavant /oparavã/ adv
(avant) before; (précédemment)
previously; (en premier lieu) beforehand.

auprès /opRɛ/ prép ~ de (à côté
de) beside, next to; (comparé à)
compared with; **s'excuser/se plaindre** ~ **de** apologize/complain to.

auquel /okɛl/ ➡LEQUEL.

aura, aurait /ora, orɛ/ ➡AVOIR **5**.

aurore /orɔr/ nf dawn.

aussi /osi/ adv (également) too,
also, as well; (dans une comparaison) as; (si, tellement) so; ~ **bien
que** as well as. ● conj (donc) so,

consequently.

aussitôt /osito/ adv immediately;
~ **que** as soon as, the moment; ~
arrivé as soon as he arrived.

austère /ostɛr/ adj austere.

Australie /ostrali/ nf Australia.

australien, ~ne /ostraljɛ̃, -ɛn/
adj Australian. **A~,** ~**ne** nm, f Australian.

autant /otã/ adv (travailler, manger)
as much (**que**) as; ~ **(de)** (quantité) as much (**que** as); (nombre) as
many (**que** as); (tant) so much, so
many (**que** as); en avoir had better do;
d'~ plus que all the more than; **en
faire** ~ do the same; **pour** ~ for
all that.

autel /otɛl/ nm altar.

auteur /otœr/ nm author; **l'~ du
crime** the perpetrator of the crime.

authentifier /otãtifje/ **45** vt au-
thenticate.

authentique /otãtik/ adj authentic.

auto /oto/ nf car; ~ **tamponneuse**
dodgem, bumper car.

autobus /otobys/ nm bus.

autocar /otokar/ nm coach.

autochtone /otɔktɔn/ nmf native.

autocollant, ~e /otɔkɔlã, -t/
self-adhesive. ● nm sticker.

autodidacte /otodidakt/ nmf self-
taught person.

auto-école (pl ~s) /otoekɔl/ nf
driving school.

automate /otomat/ nm automa-
ton, robot.

automatique /otomatik/ adj
automatic.

automatisation /otomatizasjɔ̃/
nf automation.

automne /otɔn/ nm autumn;
(US) fall.

automobile /otɔmɔbil/ adj

motor, car; (US) automobile. ● *nf* (motor) car; **l'~** the motor industry; (Sport) motoring. **automobiliste** *nmf* motorist.

autonome /otɔnɔm/ *adj* autonomous; (Ordinat) stand-alone.

autoradio /otɔʀadjo/ *nm* car radio.

autorisation /otɔʀizasjɔ̃/ *nf* permission, authorization; (permis) permit.

autorisé, ~e /otɔʀize/ *adj* (opinions) authoritative; (approuvé) authorized.

autoriser /otɔʀize/ **1** *vt* authorize, permit; (rendre possible) allow (of); (donner un droit) **~ qn à faire** entitle sb to do.

autoritaire /otɔʀitɛʀ/ *adj* authoritarian.

autorité /otɔʀite/ *nf* authority; **faire ~** be authoritative.

autoroute /otɔʀut/ *nf* motorway; (US) highway; **~ de l'information** (Ordinat) superhighway.

auto-stop /otostɔp/ *nm* hitchhiking; **faire de l'~** hitch-hike; **prendre qn en ~** give a lift to sb.

autour /otuʀ/ *adv* around; **tout ~** all around. ● *prép* **~** de around.

autre /otʀ/ *adj* other; **un ~ jour/livre** another day/book; **~ chose** something/somewhere else; **quelqu'un/rien d'~** somebody/nothing else; **quoi d'~?** what else?; **d'~ part** on the other hand; (de plus) moreover, besides; **vous ~s Anglais** you English. ● *pron* **un ~, une ~** another (one); **l'~** the other (one); **les ~s** the others; (autrui) others; **d'~s** (some) others; **l'un l'~** each other; **l'un et l'~** both of them; **d'un jour à l'~** (bientôt) any day now; **entre ~s** among other things.

autrefois /otʀəfwa/ *adv* in the past; (précédemment) formerly.

autrement /otʀəmɑ̃/ *adv* differently; (sinon) otherwise; (plus 🔟) far more; **~ dit** in other words.

Autriche /otʀiʃ/ *nf* Austria.

autrichien, ~ne /otʀiʃjɛ̃, -jɛn/ *adj* Austrian. **A~, ~ne** *nm, f* Austrian.

autruche /otʀyʃ/ *nf* ostrich.

autrui /otʀɥi/ *pron* others, other people.

aux /o/ ➡**À**.

auxiliaire /oksiljɛʀ/ *adj* auxiliary. ● *nmf* (assistant) auxiliary. ● *nm* (Gram) auxiliary.

auxquels, -quelles /okɛl/ ➡**LEQUEL**.

aval: en ~ /ãnaval/ *loc* downstream.

avaler /avale/ **1** *vt* swallow.

avance /avɑ̃s/ *nf* advance; (sur concurrent) lead; **~ (de fonds)** advance; **à l'~** in advance; **d'~** already; **en ~** (montre) fast; **en (~ sur)** (menant) ahead (of).

avancement /avɑ̃smɑ̃/ *nm* promotion.

avancé, ~e /avɑ̃se/ *adj* advanced.

avancer /avɑ̃se/ 🔟 *vi* move forward, advance; (travail) make progress; (montre) be fast; (faire saillie) jut out. ● *vt* move forward; (dans le temps) bring forward; (argent) advance; (montre) put forward. □ **s'~** *vpr* move forward, advance; (se hasarder) commit oneself.

avant /avɑ̃/ *nm* front; (Sport) forward. ● *adj inv* front. ● *prép* before; **~ de faire** before doing; **en ~ de** in front of; **~ peu** shortly; **~ tout** above all. ● *adv* (dans le temps) before, beforehand; (d'abord) first; **en ~** (dans l'espace) forward(s); (dans le temps) ahead; **le bus d'~** the previous bus. ● *conj* ~ **que** before; ~ **qu'il (ne) fasse** before he does.

avantage /avɑ̃taʒ/ *nm* advantage; (Comm) benefit.

avantager /avɑ̃taʒe/ **40** *vt* favour; (*embellir*) show off to advantage.

avantageux, -euse /avɑ̃taʒø, -z/ *adj* advantageous, favourable; (*prix*) attractive.

avant-bras /avɑ̃bʀa/ *nm inv* forearm.

avant-centre (*pl* **avants-centres**) /avɑ̃sɑ̃tʀ/ *nm* centre forward.

avant-coureur (*pl* ~**s**) /avɑ̃kuʀœʀ/ *adj* precursory, fore-shadowing.

avant-dernier, -ière (*pl* ~**s**) /avɑ̃dɛʀnje, -jɛʀ/ *adj* & *nm, f* last but one.

avant-goût (*pl* ~**s**) /avɑ̃gu/ *nm* foretaste.

avant-hier /avɑ̃tjɛʀ/ *adv* the day before yesterday.

avant-poste (*pl* ~**s**) /avɑ̃pɔst/ *nm* outpost.

avant-première (*pl* ~**s**) /avɑ̃pʀəmjɛʀ/ *nf* preview.

avant-propos /avɑ̃pʀɔpo/ *nm inv* foreword.

avare /avaʀ/ *adj* miserly; ~ **de** sparing with. ● *nmf* miser.

avarié, ~e /avaʀje/ *adj* (*aliment*) spoiled.

avatar /avataʀ/ *nm* misfortune.

avec /avɛk/ *prép* with. ● *adv* **1** with it ou them.

avènement /avɛnmɑ̃/ *nm* advent; (*d'un roi*) accession.

avenir /avniʀ/ *nm* future; **à l'**~ in future; **d'**~ with (future) prospects.

aventure /avɑ̃tyʀ/ *nf* adventure; (*sentimentale*) affair. **aventureux, -euse** *adj* adventurous; (*hasardeux*)

risky.

avérer (s') /(s)aveʀe/ **14** *vpr* prove (to be).

averse /avɛʀs/ *nf* shower.

avertir /avɛʀtiʀ/ **2** *vt* inform; (*mettre en garde, menacer*) warn. **avertissement** *nm* warning.

avertisseur /avɛʀtisœʀ/ *nm* alarm; (Auto) horn; ~ **d'incendie** fire-alarm; ~ **lumineux** warning light.

aveu (*pl* ~**x**) /avø/ *nm* confession; **de l'**~ **de** by the admission of.

aveugle /avœgl/ *adj* blind. ● *nmf* blind man, blind woman.

aviateur, -trice /avjatœʀ, -tʀis/ *nm, f* aviator.

aviation /avjasjɔ̃/ *nf* flying; (*industrie*) aviation; (Mil) air force.

avide /avid/ *adj* greedy (**de** for); (*anxieux*) eager (**de** for); ~ **de faire** eager to do.

avion /avjɔ̃/ *nm* plane, aeroplane, aircraft; (US) airplane; ~ **à réaction** jet.

aviron /aviʀɔ̃/ *nm* oar; **l'**~ (Sport) rowing.

avis /avi/ *nm* opinion; (*conseil*) advice; (*renseignement*) notification; (Comm) advice; **à mon** ~ in my opinion; **changer d'**~ change one's mind; **être d'**~ **que** be of the opinion that; ~ **au lecteur** foreword.

avisé, ~e /avize/ *adj* sensible; **être bien/mal** ~ **de** be well-/ill-advised to.

aviser /avize/ **1** *vt* advise, notify. ● *vi* decide what to do. □ **s'**~ **de** *vpr* suddenly realize; **s'**~ **de faire** take it into one's head to do.

avocat, ~e /avɔka, -t/ *nm, f* barrister; (US) attorney; (fig) advocate; ~ **de la défense** counsel for the defence. ● *nm* (*fruit*) avocado (pear).

avoine /avwan/ *nf* oats (+ *pl*).

a

b

avoir /avwaʀ/ 5

● *verbe auxiliaire*

⋯▸ have; **il nous a appelés hier** he called us yesterday.

● *verbe transitif*

⋯▸ (possession) have (got).

⋯▸ (obtenir) get; (au téléphone) get through to.

⋯▸ (duper) 1 have; **on m'a eu!** I've been had!

⋯▸ ~ **chaud/faim** be hot/hungry.

⋯▸ ~ **dix ans** be ten years old.

● **avoir à** *verbe + préposition*

⋯▸ to have to; **j'ai beaucoup à faire** I have a lot to do; **tu n'as qu'à leur écrire** all you have to do is write to them.

● **en avoir pour** *verbe + préposition*

⋯▸ **j'en ai pour une minute** I will only be a minute; **j'en ai eu pour 100 euros** it cost me 100 euros.

● **il y a** *verbe impersonnel*

⋯▸ there is; (pluriel) there are; **qu'est-ce qu'il y a?** what's the matter?; **il est venu il y a cinq ans** he came here five years ago; **il y a au moins 5 km jusqu'à la gare** it's at least 5 km to the station.

● *nom masculin*

⋯▸ (dans un magasin) credit note.

⋯▸ (biens) asset (+ *pl*).

avortement /avɔʀtəmɑ̃/ *nm* (Méd) abortion.

avorter /avɔʀte/ 1 *vi* (projet) abort; **(se faire)** ~ have an abortion.

avoué, ~e /avwe/ *adj* avowed.
● *nm* solicitor; (US) attorney.

avouer /avwe/ 1 *vt* (amour, ignorance) confess; (crime) confess to, admit. ● *vi* confess.

avril /avʀil/ *nm* April.

axe /aks/ *nm* axis; (essieu) axle; (d'une politique) main line(s), basis; ~ **(routier)** main road.

ayant /ɛjɑ̃/ →**AVOIR** 5

azote /azɔt/ *nm* nitrogen.

azur /azyʀ/ *nm* sky-blue.

Bb

baba /baba/ *nm* ~ **(au rhum)** (rum) baba; **en rester** ~ 1 be flabbergasted.

babillard /babijaʀ/ *nm* ~ **électronique** (Internet) bulletin board system, BBS.

babines /babin/ *nfpl* **se lécher les** ~ lick one's chops.

babiole /babjɔl/ *nf* trinket.

bâbord /bɑbɔʀ/ *nm* port (side).

baby-foot /babifut/ *nm inv* table football.

bac /bak/ *nm* (Scol) →**BACCALAURÉAT**; (bateau) ferry; (récipient) tub; (plus petit) tray.

baccalauréat /bakalɔʀea/ *nm* school leaving certificate.

Baccalauréat Known informally as *le bac*, the *Baccalauréat* is an examination taken in the final year of the *lycée* (*la terminale*). Students sit exams in a broad range of subjects in a particular category: the *bac* S emphasises science subjects, for example, while the *bac* L has a literary bias.

bâche /baʃ/ *nf* tarpaulin.

bachelier, -ière /baʃəlje, -jɛʀ/ *nm, f* holder of the *baccalauréat*.

bachoter /baʃɔte/ **1** *vi* cram (for an exam).

bâcler /bɑkle/ **1** *vt* botch (up).

bactérie /bakteʀi/ *nf* bacterium; **∼s** bacteria.

badaud, ∼e /bado, -d/ *nm, f* onlooker.

badigeonner /badiʒɔne/ **1** *vt* whitewash; (barbouiller) daub.

badiner /badine/ **1** *vi* banter.

baffe /baf/ *nf* **1** slap.

baffle /bafl/ *nm* speaker.

bafouiller /bafuje/ **1** *vt/i* stammer.

bagage /bagaʒ/ *nm* bag; (connaissances) knowledge; **∼s** luggage; **∼ à main** hand luggage.

bagarre /bagaʀ/ *nf* fight.

bagatelle /bagatɛl/ *nf* trifle; (somme) trifling amount.

bagnard /baɲaʀ/ *nm* convict.

bagnole /baɲɔl/ *nf* **1** car.

bague /bag/ *nf* (bijou) ring.

baguette /bagɛt/ *nf* stick; (de chef d'orchestre) baton; (chinoise) chopstick; (pain) baguette; **∼ magique** magic wand; **∼ de tambour** drumstick.

baie /bɛ/ *nf* (Géog) bay; (fruit) berry; **∼ (vitrée)** picture window; (Ordinat) bay.

baignade /bɛɲad/ *nf* swimming.

baigner /beɲe/ **1** *vt* bathe; (enfant) bath. ● *vi* **∼ dans l'huile** swim in grease. □ **se ∼** *vpr* have a swim. **baigneur, -euse** *nm, f*

swimmer.

baignoire /bɛɲwaʀ/ *nf* bath(tub).

bail (*pl* **baux**) /baj, bo/ *nm* lease.

bâiller /bɑje/ **1** *vi* yawn; (être ouvert) gape.

bailleur /bajœʀ/ *nm* **∼ de fonds** (Comm) sleeping partner.

bain /bɛ̃/ *nm* bath; (baignade) swim; **prendre un ∼ de soleil** sunbathe; **∼ de bouche** mouthwash; **être dans le ∼** (fig) be in the swing of things; **se remettre dans le ∼** get back into the swing of things; **prendre un ∼ de foule** mingle with the crowd.

bain-marie (*pl* **bains-marie**) /bɛ̃maʀi/ *nm* double boiler.

baiser /beze/ **1** *vt* (main) kiss; ✗ screw ✗. ● *nm* kiss.

baisse /bɛs/ *nf* fall, drop; **être en ∼** be going down.

baisser /bese/ **1** *vt* lower; (radio, lampe) turn down. ● *vi* (niveau) go down, fall; (santé, forces) fail. □ **se ∼** *vpr* bend down.

bal (*pl* **∼s**) /bal/ *nm* dance; (habillé) ball; (lieu) dance-hall; **∼ costumé** fancy-dress ball.

balade /balad/ *nf* stroll; (en auto) drive.

balader /balade/ **1** *vt* take for a stroll. □ **se ∼** *vpr* (à pied) (go for a) stroll; (en voiture) go for a drive; (voyager) travel.

baladeur /baladœʀ/ *nm* personal stereo.

balafre /balafʀ/ *nf* gash; (cicatrice) scar.

balai /balɛ/ *nm* broom.

balance /balɑ̃s/ *nf* scales (+ *pl*); **la B∼** Libra.

balancer /balɑ̃se/ **10** *vt* swing; (doucement) sway; (lancer **1**) chuck!; (se débarrasser de **1**) chuck out **1**. ● *vi* sway. □ **se ∼** *vpr* swing;

sway; **s'en ~** 1 not to give a damn 1.

b **balancier** /balɑ̃sje/ *nm* (d'horloge) pendulum; (d'équilibriste) pole.

balançoire /balɑ̃swaʀ/ *nf* swing.

balayage /balɛjaʒ/ *nm* sweeping; (cheveux) highlights.

balayer /baleje/ 31 *vt* sweep (up); (vent) sweep away; (se débarrasser de) sweep aside.

balbutiement /balbysimɑ̃/ *nm* stammering; **les ~s** (fig) the first steps.

balcon /balkɔ̃/ *nm* balcony; (Théât) dress circle.

baleine /balɛn/ *nf* whale.

balise /baliz/ *nf* beacon; (bouée) buoy; (Auto) (road) sign. **baliser** 1 *vt* mark out (with beacons); (route) signpost; (sentier) mark out.

balivernes /balivɛʀn/ *nfpl* nonsense.

ballant, ~e /balɑ̃, -t/ *adj* dangling.

balle /bal/ *nf* (projectile) bullet; (Sport) ball; (paquet) bale.

ballerine /balʀin/ *nf* (danseuse) ballerina; (chaussure) ballet pump.

ballet /balɛ/ *nm* ballet.

ballon /balɔ̃/ *nm* (Sport) ball; **~ (de baudruche)** balloon; **~ de football** football.

ballonné, ~e /balɔne/ *adj* bloated.

balnéaire /balneɛʀ/ *adj* seaside.

balourd, ~e /baluʀ, -d/ *nm, f* oaf. ● *adj* uncouth.

balustrade /balystʀad/ *nf* railing.

ban /bɑ̃/ *nm* round of applause; **~s** (de mariage) banns; **mettre au ~** de cast out from.

banal, ~e (*mpl* **~s**) /banal/ *adj* commonplace, banal.

banane /banan/ *nf* banana.

banc /bɑ̃/ *nm* bench; (de poissons)

shoal; **~ des accusés** dock; **~ d'essai** (test) testing ground.

bancaire /bɑ̃kɛʀ/ *adj* (secteur) banking; (chèque) bank.

bancal, ~e (*mpl* **~s**) /bɑ̃kal/ *adj* wobbly; (solution) shaky.

bande /bɑ̃d/ *nf* (groupe) gang; (de papier) strip; (rayure) stripe; (de film) reel; (pansement) bandage; **~ dessinée** comic strip; **~ (magnétique)** tape; **~ sonore** sound-track.

Bande dessinée More than just a comic book, this form of popular literature (known as the *neuvième art*) plays a significant cultural role in France and is celebrated annually at the Festival d'Angoulême. Cartoon characters such as *Astérix*, *Lucky Luke* and *Tintin* are household names, and older *BD* are often collectors' items.

---

bande-annonce (*pl* **bandes-annonces**) /bɑ̃danɔ̃s/ *nf* trailer.

bandeau (*pl* **~x**) /bɑ̃do/ *nm* headband; (sur les yeux) blindfold; **~ publicitaire** (Ordinat) banner.

bander /bɑ̃de/ 1 *vt* bandage; (arc) bend; (muscle) tense; **~ les yeux à** blindfold.

banderole /bɑ̃dʀɔl/ *nf* banner.

bandit /bɑ̃di/ *nm* bandit. **banditisme** *nm* crime.

bandoulière: en ~ /ɑ̃bɑ̃duljɛʀ/ *loc* across one's shoulder.

banlieue /bɑ̃ljø/ *nf* suburbs; **de ~** suburban. **banlieusard, ~e** *nm, f* (suburban) commuter.

bannir /baniʀ/ 2 *vt* banish.

banque /bɑ̃k/ *nf* bank; (activité) banking; **~ de données** databank.

banqueroute /bɑ̃kʀut/ *nf* bankruptcy.

banquet /bɑ̃kɛ/ nm banquet.

banquette /bɑ̃kɛt/ nf seat.

banquier, -ière /bɑ̃kje, -jɛʁ/ nm, f banker.

baptême /batɛm/ nm baptism, christening. **baptiser** ❶ vt baptize, christen; (nommer) call.

bar /baʁ/ nm (lieu) bar.

baragouiner /baʁagwine/ ❶ vt/i gabble; (langue) speak a few words of.

baraque /baʁak/ nf hut, shed; (maison ⑤) house.

baratin /baʁatɛ̃/ nm ⑤ sweet ou smooth talk.

barbare /baʁbaʁ/ adj barbaric.
● nmf barbarian.

barbe /baʁb/ nf beard; **~ à papa** candy-floss; (US) cotton candy; **quelle ~!** ⑤ what a drag! ⑤.

barbelé /baʁbəle/ adj fil **~** barbed wire.

barber /baʁbe/ ❶ vt ⑤ bore.

barboter /baʁbɔte/ ❶ vi (dans l'eau) paddle, splash. ● vt (voler ⑤) pinch.

barbouiller /baʁbuje/ ❶ vt (souiller) smear (de with); **tu es tout barbouillé** your face is all dirty; **être barbouillé** feel queasy.

barbu, ~e /baʁby/ adj bearded.

barème /baʁɛm/ nm list, table; (échelle) scale.

baril /baʁil/ nm barrel.

bariolé, ~e /baʁjɔle/ adj multicoloured.

baromètre /baʁɔmɛtʁ/ nm barometer.

baron, ~ne /baʁɔ̃, -ɔn/ nm, f baron, baroness.

barque /baʁk/ nf (small) boat.

barrage /baʁaʒ/ nm dam; (sur route) roadblock.

barre /baʁ/ nf bar; (trait) line, stroke; (Naut) helm; **~ de boutons** (Ordinat) toolbar.

barreau (pl **~x**) /baʁo/ nm bar; (d'échelle) rung; **le ~** (Jur) the bar.

barrer /baʁe/ ❶ vt block; (porte) bar; (rayer) cross out; (Naut) steer. □ **se ~** vpr ⑤ leave.

barrette /baʁɛt/ nf (hair) slide.

barrière /baʁjɛʁ/ nf (porte) gate; (clôture) fence; (obstacle) barrier.

bar-tabac (pl **bars-tabac**) /baʁtaba/ nm café (selling stamps and cigarettes).

bas, basse /bɑ, bɑs/ adj (niveau, table) low; (action) base; **au ~ mot** at the lowest estimate; **en ~ âge** young; **~ morceaux** (viande) cheap cuts. ● nm bottom; (chaussette) stocking; **~ de laine** (fig) nest-egg. ● adv low; **en ~** down below; (dans une maison) downstairs; **en ~ de la page** at the bottom of the page; **plus ~** further ou lower down; **mettre ~** give birth (to). **bas de casse** nm inv lower case. **bas-côté** (pl **~s**) nm (de route) verge; (US) shoulder.

bascule /baskyl/ nf (balance) scales (+ pl); **cheval/fauteuil à ~** rocking-horse/-chair.

basculer /baskyle/ ❶ vi topple over; (benne) tip up.

base /bɑz/ nf base; (fondement) basis; (Pol) rank and file; **~** basic. **base de données** nf database.

baser /bɑze/ ❶ vt base. □ **se ~ sur** vpr go by.

bas-fonds /bɑfɔ̃/ nmpl (eau) shallows; (fig) dregs.

basilic /bazilik/ nm basil.

basilique /bazilik/ nf basilica.

basque /bask/ adj Basque. **B~** nmf Basque.

basse /bɑs/ ➜**BAS**.

basse-cour (*pl* **basses-cours**) /baskuʀ/ *nf* farmyard.

b **bassesse** /bases/ *nf* baseness; (action) base act.

bassin /basɛ̃/ *nm* (pièce d'eau) pond; (de piscine) pool; (Géog) basin; (Anat) pelvis; (plat) bowl; ~ **houiller** coalfield.

bassine /basin/ *nf* bowl.

basson /basɔ̃/ *nm* bassoon.

bas-ventre (*pl* ~**s**) /bavɑ̃tʀ/ *nm* lower abdomen.

bat /ba/ →**BATTRE** 🔟.

bataille /bataj/ *nf* battle; (fig) fight.

bâtard, ~**e** /bɑtaʀ, -d/ *adj* (*solution*) hybrid. ● *nm, f* bastard.

bateau (*pl* ~**x**) /bato/ *nm* boat; ~ **pneumatique** rubber dinghy. **bateau-mouche** (*pl* **bateaux-mouches**) *nm* sightseeing boat.

bâti, ~**e** /bati/ *adj* **bien** ~ wellbuilt.

bâtiment /batimɑ̃/ *nm* building; (industrie) building trade; (navire) vessel.

bâtir /batiʀ/ 🔟 *vt* build.

bâton /batɔ̃/ *nm* stick; **conversation à** ~**s rompus** rambling conversation; ~ **de rouge** lipstick.

battant /batɑ̃/ *nm* (vantail) flap; **porte à deux** ~**s** double door.

battement /batmɑ̃/ *nm* (de cœur) beat(ing); (temps) interval; (Mus) beat.

batterie /batʀi/ *nf* (Mil, Électr) battery; (Mus) drums; ~ **de cuisine** pots and pans.

batteur /batœʀ/ *nm* (Mus) drummer; (Culin) whisk.

battre /batʀ/ 🔟 *vt/i* beat; (cartes) shuffle; (Culin) whisk; (l'emporter sur) beat; ~ **des ailes** flap its wings; ~ **des mains** clap; ~ **des paupières** blink; ~ **en retraite** beat

a retreat; ~ **la semelle** stamp one's feet; ~ **son plein** be in full swing. □ **se** ~ *vpr* fight.

baume /bom/ *nm* balm.

bavard, ~**e** /bavaʀ, -d/ *adj* talkative. ● *nm, f* chatterbox.

bavardage /bavaʀdaʒ/ *nm* chatter, gossip. **bavarder** 🔟 *vi* chat; (jacasser) chatter, gossip.

bave /bav/ *nf* dribble, slobber; (de limace) slime. **baver** 🔟 *vi* dribble, slobber. **baveux**, **-euse** *adj* dribbling; (*omelette*) runny.

bavoir /bavwaʀ/ *nm* bib.

bavure /bavyʀ/ *nf* smudge; (erreur) blunder; ~ **policière** police blunder.

bazar /bazaʀ/ *nm* bazaar; (objets 🔟) clutter.

BCBG *abrév mf* (**bon chic bon genre**) posh.

BD *abrév f* (**bande dessinée**) comic strip.

béant, ~**e** /beɑ̃, -t/ *adj* gaping.

béat, ~**e** /bea, -t/ *adj* (hum) blissful; ~ **d'admiration** wide-eyed with admiration.

beau (**bel** *before vowel or mute h*), **belle** (*mpl* ~**x**) /bo, bɛl/ *adj* beautiful; (*femme*) beautiful; (*homme*) handsome; (*temps*) fine, nice. ● *nm* beauty. ● *adv* **il fait** ~ the weather is nice; **au** ~ **milieu** right in the middle; **bel et bien** well and truly; **de plus belle** more than ever; **faire le** ~ sit up and beg; **on a** ~ **essayer/insister** however much one tries/insists.

beaucoup /boku/ *adv* a lot, very much; ~ **de** (nombre) many; (quantité) lots of; **pas** ~ **(de)** not many; (quantité) not much; ~ **plus/mieux** much more/better; ~ **trop** far too much; **de** ~ by far.

beau-fils (*pl* **beaux-fils**) /bofis/

nm (remariage) stepson.

beau-frère (*pl* beaux-frères) /bofʀɛʀ/ *nm* brother-in-law.

beau-père (*pl* beaux-pères) /bopɛʀ/ *nm* father-in-law; (remariage) stepfather.

beauté /bote/ *nf* beauty; **finir en** ~ end magnificently.

beaux-arts /bozaʀ/ *nmpl* fine arts.

beaux-parents /bopaʀɑ̃/ *nmpl* parents-in-law.

bébé /bebe/ *nm* baby.
bébé-éprouvette (*pl* **bébés-éprouvette**) *nm* test-tube baby.

bec /bɛk/ *nm* beak; (de théière) spout; (de casserole) lip; (bouche 🔲) mouth; ~ **de gaz** gas street-lamp.

bécane /bekan/ *nf* 🔲 bike.

bêche /bɛʃ/ *nf* spade.

bégayer /begeje/ 🔢 *vt/i* stammer.

bègue /bɛg/ *nmf* stammerer. ● *adj* **être** ~ stammer.

bégueule /begœl/ *adj* prudish.

beige /bɛʒ/ *adj & nm* beige.

beignet /bɛɲɛ/ *nm* fritter.

bel /bɛl/ ➡BEAU.

bêler /bele/ 🔢 *vi* bleat.

belette /bəlɛt/ *nf* weasel.

belge /bɛlʒ/ *adj* Belgian. **B**~ *nmf* Belgian.

Belgique /bɛlʒik/ *nf* Belgium.

bélier /belje/ *nm* ram; **le B**~ Aries.

belle /bɛl/ ➡BEAU.

belle-fille (*pl* belles-filles) /bɛlfij/ *nf* daughter-in-law; (remariage) stepdaughter.

belle-mère (*pl* belles-mères) /bɛlmɛʀ/ *nf* mother-in-law; (remariage) stepmother.

belle-sœur (*pl* belles-sœurs) /bɛlsœʀ/ *nf* sister-in-law.

belliqueux, -euse /belikø, -z/ *adj*

warlike.

bémol /bemɔl/ *nm* (Mus) flat.

bénédiction /benediksjɔ̃/ *nf* blessing.

bénéfice /benefis/ *nm* (gain) profit; (avantage) benefit.

bénéficiaire /benefisjɛʀ/ *nmf* beneficiary.

bénéficier /benefisje/ 🔢 *vi* ~ **de** benefit from; (jouir de) enjoy, have.

bénéfique /benefik/ *adj* beneficial.

Bénélux /benelyks/ *nm* Benelux.

bénévole /benevɔl/ *adj* voluntary.

bénin, -igne /benɛ̃, -iɲ/ *adj* minor; (tumeur) benign.

bénir /beniʀ/ 🔢 *vt* bless. **bénit, ~e** *adj* (eau) holy; (pain) consecrated.

benjamin, ~e /bɛ̃ʒamɛ̃, -in/ *nm, f* youngest child.

benne /bɛn/ *nf* (de grue) scoop; ~ **à ordures** (camion) waste disposal truck; (conteneur) skip; ~ **(basculante)** dump truck.

béquille /bekij/ *nf* crutch; (de moto) stand.

berceau (*pl* ~**x**) /bɛʀso/ *nm* (de bébé, civilisation) cradle.

bercer /bɛʀse/ 🔢 *vt* (balancer) rock; (apaiser) lull; (leurrer) delude.

béret /beʀɛ/ *nm* beret.

berge /bɛʀʒ/ *nf* (bord) bank.

berger, -ère /bɛʀʒe, -ɛʀ/ *nm, f* shepherd, shepherdess.

berne: en ~ /ābɛʀn/ *loc* at halfmast.

berner /bɛʀne/ 🔢 *vt* fool.

besogne /bəzɔɲ/ *nf* task, job.

besoin /bəzwɛ̃/ *nm* need; **avoir** ~ **de** need; **au** ~ if need be; **dans le** ~ in need.

bestiole /bɛstjɔl/ *nf* 🔲 bug.

bétail /betaj/ *nm* livestock.

bête /bɛt/ *adj* stupid. ● *nf* animal;

~ **noire** pet hate; ~ **sauvage** wild beast; **chercher la petite** ~ **be** overfussy.

bêtise /betiz/ nf stupidity; (action) stupid thing.

béton /betõ/ nm concrete; ~ **armé** reinforced concrete; **en** ~ (mur) concrete; (argument 🔲) watertight. **bétonnière** nf concrete mixer.

betterave /bɛtʀav/ nf beet; ~ **rouge** beetroot.

beugler /bøgle/ 🔲 vi bellow; (radio) blare out.

beur /bœʀ/ nmf & adj 🔲 second-generation North African living in France.

beurre /bœʀ/ nm butter. **beurré, ~e** adj buttered; 🔲 drunk. **beurrier** nm butter-dish.

bévue /bevy/ nf blunder.

biais /bjɛ/ nm (moyen) way; **par le** ~ **de** by means of; **de** ~, **en** ~ at an angle.

bibelot /biblo/ nm ornament.

biberon /bibʀõ/ nm (feeding) bottle; **nourrir au** ~ bottle-feed.

bible /bibl/ nf bible; **la B**~ the Bible.

bibliographie /biblijɔgʀafi/ nf bibliography.

bibliothécaire /biblijɔtekɛʀ/ nmf librarian.

bibliothèque /biblijɔtɛk/ nf library; (meuble) bookcase.

bic® /bik/ nm biro®.

bicarbonate /bikaʀbɔnat/ nm ~ **(de soude)** bicarbonate (of soda).

biceps /bisɛps/ nm biceps.

biche /biʃ/ nf doe; **ma** ~ darling.

bichonner /biʃɔne/ 🔲 vt pamper.

bicyclette /bisiklɛt/ nf bicycle.

bide /bid/ nm (ventre 🔲) paunch; (échec 🔲) flop.

bidet /bidɛ/ nm bidet.

bidon /bidõ/ nm can; (plus grand) drum; (ventre 🔲) belly; **c'est du** ~**!** it's a load of hogwash 🔲. ● adj inv 🔲 phoney.

bidonville /bidõvil/ nm shanty town.

bidule /bidyl/ nm 🔲 thing.

Biélorussie /bjelɔʀysi/ nf Byelo-russia.

bien /bjɛ̃/ adv well; (très) quite, very; ~ **des** (nombre) many; **tu as** ~ **de la chance** you are very lucky; **j'aimerais** ~ I would like to; **ce n'est pas** ~ **de** it is not nice to; ~ **sûr** of course. ● nm good; (patrimoine) possession; ~**s de consommation** consumer goods. ● adj inv good; (passable) all right; (en forme) well; (à l'aise) comfortable; (beau) attractive; (respectable) nice, respectable. ● conj ~ **que** (al-)though; ~ **que ce soit** although it is. **bien-aimé, ~e** adj & nm, f beloved. **bien-être** nm wellbeing.

bienfaisance /bjɛ̃fəzɑ̃s/ nf charity; **fête de** ~ charity event. **bienfaisant, ~e** adj beneficial.

bienfait /bjɛ̃fɛ/ nm (kind) favour; (avantage) beneficial effect. **bienfaiteur, -trice** nm, f benefactor.

bien-pensant, ~e /bjɛ̃pɑ̃sɑ̃, -t/ adj right-thinking.

bienséance /bjɛ̃seɑ̃s/ nf propriety.

bientôt /bjɛ̃to/ adv soon; **à** ~ see you soon.

bienveillance /bjɛ̃vɛjɑ̃s/ nf kind-(li)ness.

bienvenu, ~e /bjɛ̃vny/ adj welcome. ● nm, f **être le** ~, **être la** ~**e** be welcome.

bienvenue /bjɛ̃vny/ nf welcome; **souhaiter la** ~ **à** welcome.

bière /bjɛʀ/ nf beer; (cercueil) coffin; ~ **blonde** lager; ~ **brune** ≈

b

stout; ~ **pression** draught beer.

bifteck /biftɛk/ *nm* steak.

bifurquer /bifyʀke/ **1** *vi* branch off, fork.

bigarré, ~e /bigaʀe/ *adj* motley.

bigoudi /bigudi/ *nm* curler.

bijou (*pl* ~x) /biʒu/ *nm* jewel; ~x **en or** gold jewellery. **bijouterie** *nf* (boutique) jewellery shop; (Comm) jewellery. **bijoutier, -ière** *nm, f* jeweller.

bilan /bilɑ̃/ *nm* outcome; (d'une catastrophe) (casualty) toll; (Comm) balance sheet; **faire le ~ de** assess; ~ **de santé** check-up.

bile /bil/ *nf* bile; **se faire de la ~** 🔄 worry.

bilingue /bilɛ̃g/ *adj* bilingual.

billard /bijaʀ/ *nm* billiards (+ *pl*); (table) billiard-table.

bille /bij/ *nf* (d'enfant) marble; (de billard) billiard-ball.

billet /bijɛ/ *nm* ticket; (lettre) note; (article) column; ~ **(de banque)** (bank) note; ~ **de 50 euros** 50-euro note.

billetterie /bijɛtʀi/ *nf* cash dispenser.

billion /biljɔ̃/ *nm* billion; (US) trillion.

bimensuel, ~le /bimɑ̃sɥɛl/ *adj* fortnightly, bimonthly.

binette /binɛt/ *nf* hoe; (visage) face; (Internet) smiley.

biochimie /bjoʃimi/ *nf* biochemistry.

biodégradable /bjodegʀadabl/ *adj* biodegradable.

biographie /bjogʀafi/ *nf* biography.

biologie /bjolɔʒi/ *nf* biology. **biologique** *adj* biological; (*produit*) organic.

bioterrorisme /bjotɛʀɔʀism/ *nm* bioterrorism.

bis /bis/ *nm & interj* encore.

biscornu, ~e /biskɔʀny/ *adj* crooked; (bizarre) cranky 🔄.

biscotte /biskɔt/ *nf* continental toast.

biscuit /biskɥi/ *nm* biscuit; (US) cookie; ~ **salé** cracker; ~ **de Savoie** sponge-cake.

bise /biz/ *nf* 🔄 kiss; (vent) north wind.

bison /bizɔ̃/ *nm* buffalo.

Bison Futé Devised by the   *i*
French traffic information
service, *Bison Futé* reports
on travel conditions nationally and
recommends alternative routes (*les
itinéraires 'bis'*) for travellers wishing to avoid traffic jams. *Bison Futé*
traffic tips are made known
through the media and appear on
road signs in yellow on a green
background.

---

bisou /bizu/ *nm* 🔄 kiss.

bistro(t) /bistʀo/ *nm* 🔄 café, bar.

bit /bit/ *nm* (Ordinat) bit.

bitume /bitym/ *nm* asphalt.

bizarre /bizaʀ/ *adj* odd, strange. **bizarrerie** *nf* peculiarity.

blafard, ~e /blafaʀ, -d/ *adj* pale.

blague /blag/ *nf* 🔄 joke; **sans ~!** no kidding! 🔄.

blaguer /blage/ **1** 🔄 *vi* joke.

blaireau (*pl* ~x) /blɛʀo/ *nm* shaving-brush; (animal) badger.

blâmer /blame/ **1** *vt* criticize.

blanc, blanche /blɑ̃, blɑ̃ʃ/ *adj* white; (*papier, page*) blank. ● *nm* white; (espace) blank; ~ **d'œuf** egg white; ~ **de poireau** white part of the leek; ~ **(de poulet)** chicken breast; **le ~ (linge)** whites; **laisser en ~** leave blank. **B~, Blanche** *nm,* f white man, white woman. **blanche** nf (Mus) minim.

b blanchiment /blɑ̃ʃimɑ̃/ nm (d'argent) laundering.

blanchir /blɑ̃ʃiʀ/ 2 vt whiten; (personne: fig) clear; (argent) launder; (Culin) blanch; ~ **(à la chaux)** whitewash. ● vi turn white.

blanchisserie /blɑ̃ʃisʀi/ nf laundry.

blason /blazɔ̃/ nm coat of arms.

blasphème /blasfɛm/ nm blasphemy.

blé /ble/ nm wheat.

blême /blɛm/ adj pallid.

blessant, ~e /blesɑ̃, -t/ adj hurtful.

blessé, ~e /blese/ nm, f casualty, injured person.

blesser /blese/ 1 vt injure, hurt; (par balle) wound; (offenser) hurt. □ **se** ~ vpr injure ou hurt oneself. **blessure** nf wound.

bleu, ~e /blø/ adj blue; (Culin) very rare; ~ **marine/turquoise** navy blue/turquoise; **avoir une peur** ~**e** be scared stiff. ● nm blue; (contusion) bruise; ~ **(de travail)** overalls (+ pl).

bleuet /bløɛ/ nm cornflower.

blindé, ~e /blɛ̃de/ adj armoured; (fig) immune **(contre** to); **porte** ~**e** security car. ● nm armoured car, tank.

blinder /blɛ̃de/ 1 vt armour; (fig) harden.

bloc /blɔk/ nm block; (de papier) pad; **serrer à** ~ tighten hard; **en** ~ (matériau) in a block; (nier) outright.

blocage /blɔkaʒ/ nm (des prix) freeze, freezing; (des roues) locking; (Psych) block.

bloc-notes (pl **blocs-notes**) /blɔknɔt/ nm note-pad.

blocus /blɔkys/ nm blockade.

blond, ~e /blɔ̃, -d/ adj fair, blond. ● nm, f fair-haired man, fairhaired woman.

bloquer /blɔke/ 1 vt block; (porte, machine) jam; (roues) lock; (prix, crédits) freeze. □ **se** ~ vpr jam; (roues) lock; (freins) jam; (ordinateur) crash; **bloqué par la neige** snowbound.

blottir (se) /(sə)blɔtiʀ/ 2 vpr snuggle, huddle **(contre** against).

blouse /bluz/ nf overall. **blouse blanche** nf white coat.

blouson /bluzɔ̃/ nm jacket, blouson.

bluffer /blœfe/ 1 vt/i bluff.

bobine /bɔbin/ nf (de fil, film) reel; (Électr) coil.

bobo /bɔbo/ nm 1 sore, cut; **avoir** ~ have a pain.

bocal (pl **-aux**) /bɔkal, -o/ nm jar.

bœuf (pl ~s) /bœf, bø/ nm bullock; (US) steer; (viande) beef; ~**s** oxen.

bogue /bɔg/ nm (Ordinat) bug.

bohème /bɔɛm/ adj & nmf bohemian.

boire /bwaʀ/ 12 vt/i (personne, plante) drink; (argile) soak up; ~ **un coup** 1 have a drink.

bois /bwa/ →**BOIRE** 12. ● nm (matériau, forêt) wood; **de** ~, **en** ~ wooden. ● nmpl (de cerf) antlers.

boiseries /bwazʀi/ nfpl panelling.

boisson /bwasɔ̃/ nf drink.

boit /bwa/ →**BOIRE** 12.

boîte /bwat/ nf box; (de conserves) tin, can; (entreprise 1) firm; **en** ~ tinned, canned; ~ **à gants** glove compartment; ~ **aux lettres** letterbox; ~ **aux lettres électronique** mailbox; ~ **de nuit** night-club; ~ **postale** post-office box; ~ **de vitesses** gear box.

boiter /bwate/ **1** vi limp. **boiteux, -euse** adj lame; (raisonnement) shaky.

boîtier /bwatje/ nm case.

bol /bɔl/ nm bowl; ~ **d'air** a breath of fresh air; **avoir du** ~! be lucky.

bolide /bɔlid/ nm racing car.

Bolivie /bɔlivi/ nf Bolivia.

bombardement /bɔ̃bardəmɑ̃/ nm bombing; shelling.

bombarder /bɔ̃barde/ **1** vt bomb; (par obus) shell; ~ **qn de** (fig) bombard sb with. **bombardier** nm (Aviat) bomber.

bombe /bɔ̃b/ nf bomb; (atomiseur) spray, aerosol.

bombé, ~e /bɔ̃be/ adj rounded; (route) cambered.

bon, bonne /bɔ̃, bɔn/ adj good; (qui convient) right; ~ **à/pour** (approprié) it to/for; **bonne année** happy New Year; ~ **anniversaire** happy birthday; ~ **appétit/voyage** enjoy your meal/trip; **bonne chance/nuit** good luck/night; ~ **sens** common sense; **bonne femme** (péj) woman; **de bonne heure** early; **à quoi** ~? what's the point? ● adv **sentir** ~ smell nice; **tenir** ~ stand firm; **il fait** ~ the weather is mild. ● interj right, well. ● nm (billet) voucher, coupon; ~ **de commande** order form; **pour de bon** for good. **bonne** nf (domestique) maid.

bonbon /bɔ̃bɔ̃/ nm sweet; (US) candy.

bonbonne /bɔ̃bɔn/ nf demijohn; (de gaz) cylinder.

bond /bɔ̃/ nm leap; **faire un** ~ (de surprise) jump.

bonde /bɔ̃d/ nf plug; (trou) plughole.

bondé, ~e /bɔ̃de/ adj packed.

bondir /bɔ̃diʀ/ **2** vi leap; (de surprise) jump.

bonheur /bɔnœʀ/ nm happiness; (chance) (good) luck; **au petit** ~ haphazardly; **par** ~ luckily.

bonhomme (pl **bonshommes**) /bɔnɔm, bɔzɔm/ nm fellow; ~ **de neige** snowman. ● adj inv good-hearted.

bonifier (se) /(sə)bɔnifje/ **45** vpr improve.

bonjour /bɔ̃ʒuʀ/ nm & interj hallo, hello, good morning or afternoon.

bon marché /bɔ̃maʀʃe/ adj inv cheap. ● adv cheap (ly)

bonne /bɔn/ ➞BON.

bonne-maman (pl **bonnes-mamans**) /bɔnmamɑ̃/ nf **1** granny.

bonnement /bɔnmɑ̃/ adv **tout** ~ quite simply.

bonnet /bɔnɛ/ nm hat; (de soutien-gorge) cup; ~ **de bain** swimming cap. **bonneterie** nf hosiery.

bonsoir /bɔ̃swaʀ/ nm good evening; (en se couchant) good night.

bonté /bɔ̃te/ nf kindness.

bonus /bɔnys/ nm (Auto) no-claims bonus.

boots /buts/ nmpl ankle boots.

bord /bɔʀ/ nm edge; (rive) bank; **à** (~ **de**) on board; **au** ~ **de la mer** at the seaside; **au** ~ **des larmes** on the verge of tears; ~ **de la route** road-side.

bordeaux /bɔʀdo/ adj inv maroon. ● nm inv Bordeaux.

bordel /bɔʀdɛl/ nm brothel; (désordre **1**) shambles.

border /bɔʀde/ **1** vt line, border; (tissu) edge; (personne, lit) tuck in.

bordereau (pl ~**x**) /bɔʀdəʀo/ nm (document) slip.

bordure /bɔʀdyʀ/ nf border; **en** ~

de on the edge of.

borgne /bɔʀɲ/ adj one-eyed.

borne /bɔʀn/ nf boundary marker; (pour barrer le passage) bollard; ∼ **(kilométrique)** ≈ milestone; ∼**s** limits.

borné, ∼**e** /bɔʀne/ adj (esprit) narrow; (personne) narrow minded.

borner (se) /(sə)bɔʀne/ **1** vpr confine oneself (à to).

bosniaque /bɔsnjak/ adj Bosnian. B∼ nmf Bosnian.

Bosnie /bɔsni/ nf Bosnia.

bosse /bɔs/ nf bump; (de chameau) hump; **avoir la** ∼ **de** 🔟 have a gift for; **avoir roulé sa** ∼ have been around. **bosselé**, ∼**e** adj dented; (terrain) bumpy.

bosser /bɔse/ **1** vi 🔟 work (hard).

bossu, ∼**e** /bɔsy/ adj hunchbacked. ● nm, f hunchback.

botanique /bɔtanik/ nf botany.● adj botanical.

botte /bɔt/ nf boot; (de fleurs, légumes) bunch; (de paille) bundle, bale; ∼**s de caoutchouc** wellingtons.

botter /bɔte/ **1** vt 🔟 **ça me botte** I like the idea.

bottin® /bɔtɛ̃/ nm phone book.

bouc /buk/ nm (billy-)goat; (barbe) goatee; ∼ **émissaire** scapegoat.

boucan /bukɑ̃/ nm 🔟 din.

bouche /buʃ/ nf mouth; (lèvres) lips; ∼ **bée** open-mouthed; ∼ **d'égout** manhole; ∼ **d'incendie** (fire)hydrant; ∼ **de métro** entrance to the underground ou subway (US). **bouche-à-bouche** nm inv mouth-to-mouth resuscitation. **bouche-à-oreille** nm inv word of mouth.

bouché, ∼**e** /buʃe/ adj (profession, avenir) oversubscribed; (stupide) péj) stupid.

bouchée /buʃe/ nf mouthful.

boucher¹ /buʃe/ **1** vt block; (bouteille) cork. □ **se** ∼ vpr get blocked; **se** ∼ **le nez** hold one's nose.

boucher², -**ère** /buʃe, -ɛʀ/ nm, f butcher. **boucherie** nf butcher's (shop); (carnage) butchery.

bouchon /buʃɔ̃/ nm stopper; (en liège) cork; (de stylo, tube) cap; (de pêcheur) float; (embouteillage) traffic jam; ∼ **de cérumen** plug of earwax.

boucle /bukl/ nf (de ceinture) buckle; (de cheveux) curl; (forme) loop; ∼ **d'oreille** earring. **bouclé**, ∼**e** adj (cheveux) curly.

boucler /bukle/ **1** vt fasten; (enfermer 🔟) shut up; (encercler) seal off; (budget) balance; (terminer) finish off. ● vi curl.

bouclier /buklije/ nm shield.

bouddhiste /budist/ adj & nmf Buddhist.

bouder /bude/ **1** vi sulk. ● vt stay away from.

boudin /budɛ̃/ nm black pudding.

boue /bu/ nf mud.

bouée /bwe/ nf buoy; ∼ **de sauvetage** lifebuoy.

boueux, -**euse** /buø, -z/ adj muddy.

bouffe /buf/ nf 🔟 food, grub.

bouffée /bufe/ nf puff, whiff; (d'orgueil) fit; ∼ **de chaleur** (Méd) hot flush.

bouffi, ∼**e** /bufi/ adj bloated.

bouffon, ∼**e** /bufɔ̃, -ɔn/ adj farcical. ● nm buffoon.

bougeoir /buʒwaʀ/ nm candlestick.

bougeotte /buʒɔt/ nf **avoir la** ∼ 🔟 have the fidgets.

bouger /buʒe/ **40** vt/i move. □ **se** ∼ vpr 🔟 move.

bougie /buʒi/ nf candle; (Auto)

spark(ing)-plug.

bouillant, ~e /bujã, -t/ adj boiling; (très chaud) boiling hot.

bouillie /buji/ nf (pour bébé) baby cereal; (péj) mush; **en ~** crushed, mushy.

bouillir /bujiʀ/ 🔢 vi boil; (fig) seethe; **faire ~** boil.

bouilloire /bujwaʀ/ nf kettle.

bouillon /bujɔ̃/ nm (de cuisson) stock; (potage) broth.

bouillonner /bujɔne/ 🔢 vi bubble.

bouillotte /bujɔt/ nf hot-water bottle.

boulanger, -ère /bulãʒe, -ɛʀ/ nm, f baker. **boulangerie** nf bakery. **boulangerie-pâtisserie** nf bakery (selling cakes and pastries).

boule /bul/ nf ball; **~s** (jeu) boules; **jouer aux ~s** play boules; **une ~ dans la gorge** a lump in one's throat; **~ de neige** snowball.

> **Boules** A form of bowls, played on rough, dry ground with metal balls. The aim is to throw the balls to land as near as possible to a smaller target ball called the co-chonnet. In the South of France, boules is often called pétanque.

bouleau (pl **~x**) /bulo/ nm (silver) birch.

boulet /bulɛ/ nm (de forçat) ball and chain; **~ (de canon)** cannonball; **~ de charbon** coal nut.

boulette /bulɛt/ nf (de pain, papier) pellet; (bévue) blunder; **~ de viande** meat ball.

boulevard /bulvaʀ/ nm boulevard.

bouleversant, ~e /bulvɛʀsã, -t/ adj deeply moving. **bouleverse-**

ment nm upheaval. **bouleverser** vt turn upside down; (pays, plans) disrupt; (émouvoir) upset.

boulimie /bulimi/ nf bulimia.

boulon /bulɔ̃/ nm bolt.

boulot, ~te /bulo, -ɔt/ adj (rond 🔢) dumpy. ● nm (travail 🔢) work.

boum /bum/ nm & interj bang. ● nf (fête 🔢) party.

bouquet /bukɛ/ nm (de fleurs) bunch, bouquet; (d'arbres) clump; **c'est le ~!** 🔢 that's the last straw!

bouquin /bukɛ̃/ nm 🔢 book. **bouquiner** 🔢 vt/i 🔢 read. **bouquiniste** nmf second-hand bookseller.

bourbier /buʀbje/ nm mire; (fig) tangle.

bourde /buʀd/ nf blunder.

bourdon /buʀdɔ̃/ nm bumble bee. **bourdonnement** nm buzzing.

bourg /buʀ/ nm (market) town (centre), village centre.

bourgeois, ~e /buʀʒwa, -z/ adj & nm,f middle-class (person); (péj) bourgeois. **bourgeoisie** nf middle class(es).

bourgeon /buʀʒɔ̃/ nm bud.

bourgogne /buʀgɔɲ/ nm Burgundy.

bourlinguer /buʀlɛ̃ge/ 🔢 vi 🔢 travel about.

bourrage /buʀaʒ/ nm **~ de crâne** brainwashing.

bourratif, -ive /buʀatif, -v/ adj stodgy.

bourreau (pl **~x**) /buʀo/ nm executioner; **~ de travail** (fig) workaholic.

bourrelet /buʀlɛ/ nm weather strip, draught excluder; (de chair) roll of fat.

bourrer /buʀe/ 🔢 vt cram (de with); (pipe) fill; **~ de** (nourriture) stuff with; **~ de coups** thrash; **~**

le crâne à qn brainwash sb. **bourrique** /buʀik/ nf donkey; 🔟 pig-headed person.

bourru, ~e /buʀy/ adj gruff.

bourse /buʀs/ nf purse; (subvention) grant; **la B~** the Stock Exchange.

boursier, -ière /buʀsje, -jɛʀ/ adj (valeurs) Stock Exchange. ● nm, f grant holder.

boursoufler /buʀsufle/ 🔟 vt (visage) cause to swell; (peinture) blister.

bousculade /buskylad/ nf crush; (précipitation) rush. **bousculer** 🔟 vt (pousser) jostle; (presser) rush; (renverser) knock over.

bousiller /buzije/ 🔟 vt 🔟 wreck.

boussole /busɔl/ nf compass.

bout /bu/ nm end; (de langue, bâton) piece; (morceau) bit; **à ~** exhausted; **à ~ de souffle** out of breath; **à ~ portant** point-blank; **au ~ de** (après) after; **venir à ~ de** (finir) manage to finish; **d'un ~ à l'autre** throughout; **au ~ du compte** in the end; **~ filtre** filtertip.

bouteille /butɛj/ nf bottle; **~ d'oxygène** oxygen cylinder.

boutique /butik/ nf shop; (de mode) boutique.

bouton /butɔ̃/ nm button; (sur la peau) spot, pimple; (pousse) bud; (de porte, radio) knob; **~ de manchette** cuff-link. **boutonner** 🔟 vt button (up). **boutonnière** nf buttonhole. **bouton-pression** (pl **boutons-pression**) nm press-stud; (US) snap.

bouture /butyʀ/ nf cutting.

bovin, ~e /bɔvɛ̃, -in/ adj bovine. **bovins** nmpl cattle (pl).

box (pl ~ ou **boxes**) /bɔks/ nm lock-up garage; (de dortoir) cubicle;

(d'écurie) (loose) box; (Jur) dock.

boxe /bɔks/ nf boxing.

boyau (pl ~x) /bwajo/ nm gut; (corde) string; (galerie) gallery; (de bicyclette) tyre; (US) tire.

boycotter /bɔjkɔte/ 🔟 vt boycott.

BP abrév f (**boîte postale**) PO Box.

bracelet /bʀaslɛ/ nm bracelet; (de montre) watchstrap.

braconnier /bʀakɔnje/ nm poacher.

brader /bʀade/ 🔟 vt sell off. **braderie** nf clearance sale.

braguette /bʀagɛt/ nf fly.

braille /bʀaj/ nm & adj Braille.

brailler /bʀaje/ 🔟 vt/i bawl.

braise /bʀɛz/ nf embers (+ pl).

braiser /bʀeze/ 🔟 vt (Culin) braise.

brancard /bʀakaʀ/ nm stretcher; (de charrette) shaft.

branche /bʀɑ̃ʃ/ nf branch.

branché, ~e /bʀɑ̃ʃe/ adj 🔟 trendy.

branchement /bʀɑ̃ʃmɑ̃/ nm connection. **brancher** vt (prise) plug in; (à un réseau) connect.

brandir /bʀadiʀ/ 2️⃣ vt brandish.

branler /bʀale/ 🔟 vi be shaky.

braquer /bʀake/ 🔟 vt (arme) aim; (regard) fix; (roue) turn; (banque: 🔟) hold up; **~ qn contre** turn sb against. ● vi (Auto) turn (the wheel). □ **se ~** vpr dig one's heels in.

bras /bʀa/ nm arm; (de rivière) branch; (Tech) arm; **~ dessus ~ dessous** arm in arm; **~ droit** right hand man; **~ de mer** sound; **en ~ de chemise** in one's shirt-sleeves. ● nmpl (fig) labour, hands.

brasier /bʀazje/ nm blaze.

brassard /bʀasaʀ/ nm armband.

brasse /bʀas/ nf breast-stroke; **~ papillon** butterfly (stroke).

brasser /bʀase/ **1** *vt* mix; (*bière*) brew; (*affaires*) handle a lot of.
brasserie *nf* brewery; (*café*) brasserie.

brave /bʀav/ *adj* (*bon*) good; (*valeureux*) brave. **braver 1** *vt* defy.

bravo /bʀavo/ *interj* bravo. ● *nm* cheer.

bravoure /bʀavuʀ/ *nf* bravery.

break /bʀɛk/ *nm* estate car; (US) station-wagon.

brebis /bʀəbi/ *nf* ewe.

brèche /bʀɛʃ/ *nf* gap, breach; **être sur la ~** be on the go.

bredouille /bʀəduj/ *adj* empty-handed.

bredouiller /bʀəduje/ **1** *vt/i* mumble.

bref, brève /bʀɛf, -v/ *adj* short, brief. ● *adv* in short; **en ~** in short.

Brésil /bʀezil/ *nm* Brazil.

Bretagne /bʀətaɲ/ *nf* Brittany.

bretelle /bʀətɛl/ *nf* (*de sac, maillot*) strap; (*d'autoroute*) access road; **~s** (*pour pantalon*) braces; (US) suspenders.

breton, ~ne /bʀətɔ̃, -ɔn/ *adj* & *nm* (Ling) Breton. **B~, ~ne** *nm, f* Breton.

breuvage /bʀœvaʒ/ *nm* beverage.

brève /bʀɛv/ →**BREF.**

brevet /bʀəvɛ/ *nm* **~ (d'invention)** patent; (*diplôme*) diploma.

breveté, ~e /bʀəvte/ *adj* patented.

bribes /bʀib/ *nfpl* scraps.

bricolage /bʀikɔlaʒ/ *nm* do-it yourself (jobs).

bricole /bʀikɔl/ *nf* trifle.

bricoler /bʀikɔle/ **1** *vi* do DIY; (US) fix things, tinker with.

bricoleur, -euse /bʀikɔlœʀ, -øz/ *nm, f* handyman, handywoman.

bride /bʀid/ *nf* bridle.

bridé, ~e /bʀide/ *adj* **yeux ~s** slanting eyes.

brider /bʀide/ **1** *vt* (*cheval*) bridle; (fig) keep in check.

brièvement /bʀijɛvmɑ̃/ *adv* briefly.

brigade /bʀigad/ *nf* (*de police*) squad; (Mil) brigade; (fig) team. **brigadier** *nm* (*de gendarmerie*) sergeant.

brigand /bʀigɑ̃/ *nm* robber.

brillant, ~e /bʀijɑ̃, -t/ *adj* (*couleur*) bright; (*luisant*) shiny; (*remarquable*) brilliant. ● *nm* (*éclat*) shine; (*diamant*) diamond.

briller /bʀije/ **1** *vi* shine.

brimade /bʀimad/ *nf* vexation.
brimer 1 *vt* bully, harass; **se sentir brimé** feel put down.

brin /bʀɛ̃/ *nm* (*de muguet*) sprig; (*d'herbe*) blade; (*de paille*) wisp; **un ~ de** (un peu) a bit of.

brindille /bʀɛ̃dij/ *nf* twig.

brioche /bʀijɔʃ/ *nf* brioche, sweet bun; (*ventre* 🄸) paunch.

brique /bʀik/ *nf* brick.

briquet /bʀikɛ/ *nm* (cigarette-)lighter.

brise /bʀiz/ *nf* breeze.

briser /bʀize/ **1** *vt* break. □ **se ~** *vpr* break.

britannique /bʀitanik/ *adj* British. **B~** *nmf* Briton; **les B~s** the British.

brocante /bʀɔkɑ̃t/ *nf* bric-à-brac trade; (*marché*) flea market.

broche /bʀɔʃ/ *nf* brooch; (Culin) spit; **à la ~** spit-roasted.

broché, ~e /bʀɔʃe/ *adj* paperback.

brochet /bʀɔʃɛ/ *nm* pike.

brochette /bʀɔʃɛt/ *nf* skewer.

brochure /bʀɔʃyʀ/ *nf* brochure, booklet.

broder /bʀɔde/ **1** *vt/i* embroider.

broderie nf embroidery.

broncher /bʀɔ̃ʃe/ **1** vi sans ~ without turning a hair.

bronchite /bʀɔ̃ʃit/ nf bronchitis.

bronze /bʀɔ̃z/ nm bronze.

bronzé, ~e /bʀɔ̃ze/ adj (sun-)tanned.

bronzer /bʀɔ̃ze/ **1** vi (personne) get a (sun-)tan.

brosse /bʀɔs/ nf brush; ~ à dents toothbrush; ~ à habits clothes brush; en ~ (coiffure) in a crew cut.

brosser /bʀɔse/ **1** vt brush; (fig) paint. □ se ~ vpr se ~ les dents/les cheveux brush one's teeth/hair.

brouette /bʀuɛt/ nf wheelbarrow.

brouhaha /bʀuaa/ nm hubbub.

brouillard /bʀujaʀ/ nm fog.

brouille /bʀuj/ nf quarrel.

brouiller /bʀuje/ **1** vt (vue) blur; (œufs) scramble; (amis) set at odds; ~ les pistes cloud the issue. □ se ~ vpr (ciel) cloud over; (amis) fall out.

brouillon, ~ne /bʀujɔ̃, -ɔn/ adj untidy. ● nm (rough) draft.

brousse /bʀus/ nf la ~ the bush.

brouter /bʀute/ **1** vt/i graze.

broyer /bʀwaje/ **31** vt crush; (moudre) grind.

bru /bʀy/ nf daughter-in-law.

bruine /bʀɥin/ nf drizzle.

bruissement /bʀɥismã/ nm rustling.

bruit /bʀɥi/ nm noise; ~ de couloir (fig) rumour.

bruitage /bʀɥitaʒ/ nm sound effects.

brûlant, ~e /bʀylã, -t/ adj burning (hot); (sujet) red-hot; (passion) fiery.

brûlé /bʀyle/ nm burning; ça sent le ~ I can smell something burning. ● →BRÛLER **1**.

brûler /bʀyle/ **1** vt/i burn; (es-

sence) use (up); (cierge) light (à to); ~ un feu (rouge) jump the lights; ~ d'envie de faire be longing to do. □ se ~ vpr burn oneself.

brûlure /bʀylyʀ/ nf burn; ~s d'estomac heartburn.

brume /bʀym/ nf mist. **brumeux, -euse** adj misty; (esprit) hazy.

brun, ~e /bʀœ̃, -yn/ adj brown, dark. ● nm brown. ● nm, f dark haired person. **brunir** **2** vi turn brown; (bronzer) get a tan.

brushing /bʀœʃiŋ/ nm blow-dry.

brusque /bʀysk/ adj (personne) abrupt; (geste) violent; (soudain) sudden.

brusquer /bʀyske/ **1** vt be abrupt with; (précipiter) rush.

brut, ~e /bʀyt/ adj (diamant) rough; (champagne) dry; (pétrole) crude; (Comm) gross.

brutal, ~e /bʀytal, -o/ adj (mpl -aux) brutal. **brutalité** nf brutality.

brute /bʀyt/ nf brute.

Bruxelles /bʀysɛl/ npr Brussels.

bruyant, ~e /bʀɥijã, -t/ adj noisy.

bruyère /bʀyjɛʀ/ nf heather.

bu /by/ →BOIRE **1**.

bûche /byʃ/ nf log; ~ de Noël Christmas log; ramasser une ~ **1** fall.

bûcher /byʃe/ **1** vt/i **1** slog away (at) **1**. ● nm (supplice) stake.

bûcheron /byʃʀɔ̃/ nm lumberjack.

budget /bydʒɛ/ nm budget. **budgétaire** adj budgetary.

buée /bɥe/ nf condensation.

buffet /byfɛ/ nm sideboard; (table garnie) buffet.

buffle /byfl/ nm buffalo.

buisson /bɥisɔ̃/ nm bush.

buissonnière /bɥisɔnjɛʀ/ adj faire l'école ~ play truant.

bulbe /bylb/ nm bulb.

bulgare /bylgaʀ/ *adj & nm* Bulgarian. **B∼** *nmf* Bulgarian.

Bulgarie /bylgaʀi/ *nf* Bulgaria.

bulldozer /byldozɛʀ/ *nm* bulldozer.

bulle /byl/ *nf* bubble.

bulletin /byltɛ̃/ *nm* bulletin, report; (Scol) report; ∼ **d'information** news bulletin; ∼ **météorologique** weather report; ∼ **(de vote)** ballot-paper; ∼ **de salaire** pay-slip.

buraliste /byʀalist/ *nmf* tobacconist.

bureau (*pl* ∼**x**) /byʀo/ *nm* office; (meuble) desk; (comité) board; ∼ **d'études** design office; ∼ **de poste** post office; ∼ **de tabac** tobacconist's (shop); ∼ **de vote** polling station.

bureaucrate /byʀokʀat/ *nmf* bureaucrat. **bureaucratie** *nf* bureaucracy. **bureaucratique** *adj* bureaucratic.

bureautique /byʀotik/ *nf* office automation.

burlesque /byʀlɛsk/ *adj* (histoire) ludicrous; (film) farcical.

bus /bys/ *nm* bus.

business /biznɛs/ *nm inv* (affaires commerciales) business; (affaires privées) affairs.

buste /byst/ *nm* bust.

but /by(t)/ *nm* target; (dessein) aim, goal; (football) goal; **avoir pour** ∼ **de** aim to; **de** ∼ **en blanc** point-blank; **dans le** ∼ **de** with the intention of; **aller droit au** ∼ go straight to the point.

butane /bytan/ *nm* butane, Calor gas®.

buté, -e /byte/ *adj* obstinate.

buter /byte/ **1** *vi* ∼ **contre** knock against; (problème) come up against. ● *vt* antagonize. □ **se** ∼ *vpr* (s'entêter) become obstinate.

buteur /bytœʀ/ *nm* (au football) striker.

butin /bytɛ̃/ *nm* booty, loot.

butte /byt/ *nf* mound; **en** ∼ **à** exposed to.

buvard /byvaʀ/ *nm* blotting-paper.

buvette /byvɛt/ *nf* (refreshment) bar.

buveur, -euse /byvœʀ, -øz/ *nm, f* drinker.

Cc

c' /s/ ➤**CE**.

ça /sa/

● *pronom démonstratif*

⋯▸ (sujet) it; that; ∼ **flotte** it floats; ∼ **suffit!** that's enough!; ∼ **y est!** that's it!; ∼ **sent le brûlé** there's a smell of burning; ∼ **va?** how are things?

⋯▸ (objet) (proche) this; (plus éloigné) that; **c'est** ∼ that's right.

⋯▸ (dans expressions) **où** ∼? where?; **quand** ∼? when?; **et avec** ∼? anything else?

çà /sa/ *adv* ∼ **et là** here and there.

cabane /kaban/ *nf* hut; (à outils) shed.

cabaret /kabaʀɛ/ *nm* cabaret.

cabillaud /kabijo/ *nm* cod.

cabine /kabin/ *nf* (à la piscine) cubicle; (de bateau) cabin; (de camion) cab; (d'ascenseur) cage; ∼ **d'essayage** fitting room; ∼ **de pilotage** cockpit; ∼ **de plage** beach hut; ~ **(téléphonique)** phone booth, phone box.

cabinet /kabinɛ/ nm (de médecin) surgery; (US) office; (d'avocat) office; (clientèle) practice; (cabinet collectif) firm; (Pol) Cabinet; (pièce) room; ~**s** (toilettes) toilet; (US) bathroom; ~ **de toilette** bathroom.

câble /kabl/ nm cable; (corde) rope; (TV) cable TV. **câbler** vt ❶ cable; (TV) install cable television in.

cabosser /kabose/ ❶ vt dent.

cabotage /kabotaʒ/ nm coastal navigation.

cabrer (se) /(sə)kabʀe/ ❶ vpr (cheval) rear; se ~ **contre** rebel against.

cabriole /kabʀijol/ nf faire des ~s caper about.

cacahuète /kakawɛt/ nf peanut.

cacao /kakao/ nm cocoa.

cachalot /kaʃalo/ nm sperm whale.

cache /kaʃ/ nm mask. ● nf hiding place; ~ **d'armes** arms cache.

cache-cache /kaʃkaʃ/ nm inv hide-and-seek.

cache-nez /kaʃne/ nm inv scarf.

cacher /kaʃe/ ❶ vt hide, conceal (à from). □ **se** ~ vpr hide; (se trouver caché) be hidden.

cachet /kaʃɛ/ nm (de cire) seal; (à l'encre) stamp; (de la poste) postmark; (comprimé) tablet; (d'artiste) fee; (chic) style, cachet.

cachette /kaʃɛt/ nf hiding-place; **en** ~ in secret.

cachot /kaʃo/ nm dungeon.

cachottier, -ière /kaʃɔtje, -jɛʀ/ adj secretive.

cacophonie /kakɔfɔni/ nf cacophony.

cactus /kaktys/ nm cactus.

cadavérique /kadaveʀik/ adj (teint) deathly pale.

cadavre /kadavʀ/ nm corpse; (de victime) body.

caddie /kadi/ nm (de supermarché®) trolley; (au golf) caddie.

cadeau (pl ~**x**) /kado/ nm present, gift; **faire un** ~ **à qn** give sb a present.

cadenas /kadna/ nm padlock.

cadence /kadɑ̃s/ nf rhythm, cadence; (de travail) rate; **en** ~ in time; (marcher) in step.

cadet, ~te /kadɛ, -t/ adj youngest; (entre deux) younger. ● nm, f youngest (child); younger (child).

cadran /kadʀɑ̃/ nm dial; ~ **solaire** sundial.

cadre /kadʀ/ nm frame; (lieu) setting; (milieu) surroundings; (limites) scope; (contexte) framework; **dans le** ~ **de** (à l'occasion de) on the occasion of; (dans le contexte de) in the framework of. ● nm (personne) executive; **les** ~**s** the managerial staff.

cadrer /kadʀe/ ❶ vi ~ **avec** tally with. ● vt (photo) centre.

cafard /kafaʀ/ nm (insecte) cockroach; **avoir le** ~ ❶ be down in the dumps.

café /kafe/ nm coffee; (bar) café; ~ **crème** espresso with milk; ~ **en grains** coffee beans; ~ **au lait** white coffee.

cafetière /kaftjɛʀ/ nf coffee-pot; ~ **électrique** coffee machine.

cage /kaʒ/ nf cage; ~ **d'ascenseur** lift shaft; ~ **d'escalier** stairwell; ~ **thoracique** rib cage.

cageot /kaʒo/ nm crate.

cagibi /kaʒibi/ nm storage room.

cagneux, -euse /kaɲø, -z/ adj **avoir les genoux** ~ be knock-kneed.

cagnotte /kaɲɔt/ nf kitty.

cagoule /kagul/ nf hood; (passe-montagne) balaclava.

cahier /kaje/ nm notebook; (Scol) exercise book; ~ **de textes** homework notebook; ~ **des charges** (Tech) specifications (+ pl).

cahot /kao/ nm bump, jolt. **cahoteux, -euse** adj bumpy.

caïd /kaid/ nm ❶ big shot.

caille /kaj/ nf quail.

cailler /kaje/ ❶ vi curdle; **ça caille** ❶ it's freezing. □ **se** ~ vpr (sang) clot; (lait) curdle. **caillot** nm (blood) clot.

caillou (pl ~x) /kaju/ nm stone; (galet) pebble.

caisse /kɛs/ nf crate, case; (tiroir, machine) till; (guichet) cash desk; (au supermarché) check-out; (bureau) office; (Mus) drum; ~ **enregistreuse** cash register; ~ **d'épargne** savings bank; ~ **de retraite** pension fund. **caissier, -ière** nf, f cashier.

cajoler /kaʒɔle/ ❶ vt coax.

calcaire /kalkɛʀ/ adj (sol) chalky; (eau) hard.

calciné, ~e /kalsine/ adj charred.

calcul /kalkyl/ nm calculation; (Scol) arithmetic; (différentiel) calculus; ~ **biliaire** gallstone.

calculatrice /kalkylatʀis/ nf calculator. **calculer** ❶ vt calculate. **calculette** nf (pocket) calculator.

cale /kal/ nf wedge; (pour roue) chock; (de navire) hold; ~ **sèche** dry dock.

calé, ~e /kale/ adj ❶ clever.

caleçon /kalsɔ̃/ nm boxer shorts (+ pl); underpants (+ pl); (de femme) leggings.

calembour /kalɑ̃buʀ/ nm pun.

calendrier /kalɑ̃dʀije/ nm calendar; (fig) schedule, timetable.

calepin /kalpɛ̃/ nm notebook.

caler /kale/ ❶ vt wedge. ● vi stall; (abandonner ❶) give up.

calfeutrer /kalføtʀe/ ❶ vt (fissure) stop up; (porte) draught proof.

calibre /kalibʀ/ nm calibre; (d'un œuf, fruit) grade.

calice /kalis/ nm (Relig) chalice; (Bot) calyx.

califourchon: à ~ /akalifuʀʃɔ̃/ loc astride.

câlin, ~e /kɑlɛ̃, -in/ adj (regard, ton) affectionate; (personne) cuddly.

calmant /kalmɑ̃/ nm sedative.

calme /kalm/ adj calm. ● nm peace; calm; (maîtrise de soi) composure; **du** ~! calm down!

calmer /kalme/ ❶ vt (personne) calm down; (situation) defuse; (douleur) ease; (soif) quench. □ **se** ~ vpr (personne, situation) calm down; (agitation, tempête) die down; (douleur) ease.

calomnie /kalɔmni/ nf (orale) slander; (écrite) libel. **calomnier** ⓯ vt slander; libel. **calomnieux, -ieuse** adj slanderous; libellous.

calorie /kalɔʀi/ nf calorie.

calque /kalk/ nm tracing; (papier) ~ tracing paper; (fig) exact copy. **calquer** /kalke/ ❶ vt trace; (fig) copy; ~ **qch sur** model sth on.

calvaire /kalvɛʀ/ nm (croix) Calvary; (fig) suffering.

calvitie /kalvisi/ nf baldness.

camarade /kamaʀad/ nmf friend; (Pol) comrade; ~ **de jeu** playmate. **camaraderie** nf friendship.

cambouis /kɑ̃bwi/ nm dirty oil.

cambrer /kɑ̃bʀe/ ❶ vt arch. □ **se** ~ vpr arch one's back.

cambriolage /kɑ̃bʀijɔlaʒ/ nm burglary. **cambrioler** ❶ vt burgle.

cambrioleur, -euse nm, f burglar.
camelot /kamlo/ nm ① street vendor.
camelote /kamlɔt/ nf ① junk.
caméra /kamera/ nf (cinéma, télévision) camera.
caméscope® /kameskɔp/ nm camcorder.
camion /kamjɔ̃/ nm lorry, truck. **camion-citerne** (pl **camions-citernes**) nm tanker. **camionnage** nm haulage. **camionnette** nf van. **camionneur** nm lorry ou truck driver; (entrepreneur) haulage contractor.
camisole /kamizɔl/ nf ~ **(de force)** straitjacket.
camoufler /kamufle/ ① vt camouflage.
camp /kɑ̃/ nm camp; (Sport, Pol) side.
campagnard, ~e /kɑ̃paɲar, -d/ adj country. ● nm, f countryman, countrywoman.
campagne /kɑ̃paɲ/ nf country; countryside; (Mil, Pol) campaign.
campement /kɑ̃pmɑ̃/ nm camp, encampment.
camper /kɑ̃pe/ ① vi camp. ● vt (esquisser) sketch. ❑ **se ~** vpr plant oneself. **campeur, -euse** nm, f camper.
camping /kɑ̃piŋ/ nm camping; **faire du ~** go camping; **(terrain de)** ~ campsite. **camping-car** (pl ~**s**) nm camper-van; (US) motorhome. **camping-gaz®** nm inv (réchaud) camping stove.
Canada /kanada/ nm Canada.
canadien, ~ne /kanadjɛ̃, -ɛn/ adj Canadian. **C~, ~ne** nm, f Canadian. **canadienne** nf (veste) fur-lined jacket; (tente) ridge tent.
canaille /kanaj/ nf rogue.
canal (pl **-aux**) /kanal, -o/ nm (arti-

ficiel) canal; (bras de mer) channel; (Tech, TV) channel; (moyen) channel; **par le ~ de** through. **canalisation** nf (tuyaux) mains (+ pl). **canaliser** ① vt (eau) canalize; (fig) channel.
canapé /kanape/ nm sofa.
canard /kanar/ nm duck; (journal ①) rag.
canari /kanari/ nm canary.
cancans /kɑ̃kɑ̃/ nmpl ① gossip.
cancer /kɑ̃sɛr/ nm cancer; **le C~** Cancer. **cancéreux, -euse** adj cancerous. **cancérigène** adj carcinogenic.
cancre /kɑ̃kr/ nm dunce.
candeur /kɑ̃dœr/ nf ingenuousness.
candidat, ~e /kɑ̃dida, -t/ nm, f (à un examen, Pol) candidate; (à un poste) applicant, candidate (à for).
candidature /kɑ̃didatyr/ nf application; (Pol) candidacy; **poser sa ~ à un poste** apply for a job.
candide /kɑ̃did/ adj ingenuous.
cane /kan/ nf (female) duck. **caneton** nm duckling.
canette /kanɛt/ nf (bouteille) bottle; (boîte) can.
canevas /kanva/ nm canvas; (ouvrage) tapestry; (plan) framework, outline.
caniche /kaniʃ/ nm poodle.
canicule /kanikyl/ nf scorching heat; (vague de chaleur) heatwave.
canif /kanif/ nm penknife.
canine /kanin/ nf canine (tooth).
caniveau (pl ~**x**) /kanivo/ nm gutter.
cannabis /kanabis/ nm cannabis.
canne /kan/ nf (walking) stick; ~ **à pêche** fishing rod; ~ **à sucre** sugar cane.
cannelle /kanɛl/ nf cinnamon.

cannibale /kanibal/ adj & nmf cannibal.

canoë /kanɔe/ nm canoe; (Sport) canoeing.

canon /kanɔ̃/ nm (big) gun; (ancien) cannon; (d'une arme) barrel; (principe, règle) canon.

canot /kano/ nm dinghy, (small) boat; ~ **de sauvetage** lifeboat; ~ **pneumatique** rubber dinghy. **canotier** nm boater.

cantatrice /kɑ̃tatris/ nf opera singer.

cantine /kɑ̃tin/ nf canteen.

cantique /kɑ̃tik/ nm hymn.

cantonner /kɑ̃tɔne/ **1** vt (Mil) billet. □ **se** ~ **dans** vpr confine oneself to.

canular /kanylar/ nm hoax.

caoutchouc /kautʃu/ nm rubber; (élastique) rubber band; ~ **mousse** foam rubber.

cap /kap/ nm cape, headland; (direction) course; (obstacle) hurdle; **franchir le** ~ **de la cinquantaine** pass the fifty mark; **mettre le** ~ **sur** steer a course for.

capable /kapabl/ adj capable (**de** of); ~ **de faire** able to do, capable of doing.

capacité /kapasite/ nf ability; (contenance, potentiel) capacity.

cape /kap/ nf cape; **rire sous** ~ laugh up one's sleeve.

capillaire /kapilɛr/ adj (lotion, soins) hair; (**vaisseau**) ~ capillary.

capitaine /kapitɛn/ nm captain.

capital, ~**e** (mpl -**aux**) /kapital,-o/ adj key, crucial, fundamental; (peine, lettre) capital. ● nm (pl -**aux**) (Comm) capital; (fig) stock; **capitaux** (Comm) capital; **capital-risque** venture capital; **capital-risqueur** venture capitalist. **capitale** nf (ville, lettre) capital.

capitalisme /kapitalism/ nm capitalism.

capitonné, ~**e** /kapitɔne/ adj padded.

capituler /kapityle/ **1** vi capitulate.

caporal (pl -**aux**) /kapɔral, -o/ nm corporal.

capot /kapo/ nm (Auto) bonnet; (US) hood.

capote /kapɔt/ nf (Auto) hood; (US) top; (préservatif **1**) condom. **capoter** /kapɔte/ **1** vi overturn; (fig) collapse.

câpre /kɑpr/ nf (Culin) caper.

caprice /kapris/ nm whim; (colère) tantrum; **faire un** ~ throw a tantrum. **capricieux, -ieuse** adj capricious; (appareil) temperamental.

Capricorne /kaprikɔrn/ nm **le** ~ Capricorn.

capsule /kapsyl/ nf capsule; (de bouteille) cap.

capter /kapte/ **1** vt (eau) collect; (émission) get; (signal) pick up; (fig) win, capture.

captif, -ive /kaptif, -v/ adj & nm, f captive.

captiver /kaptive/ **1** vt captivate.

capturer /kaptyre/ **1** vt capture.

capuche /kapyʃ/ nf hood. **capuchon** nm hood; (de stylo) cap.

car /kar/ conj because, for. ● nm coach; (US) bus.

carabine /karabin/ nf rifle.

caractère /karaktɛr/ nm (lettre) character; (nature) nature; ~**s d'imprimerie** block letters; **avoir bon/mauvais** ~ be good-natured/bad-tempered; **avoir du** ~ have character.

caractériel, ~**le** /karakterjel/ adj (trait) character; (enfant) disturbed.

caractériser /karakterize/ **1** vt

characterize. □ **se ~ par** *vpr* be characterized by. **caractéristique** *adj & nf* characteristic.

carafe /karaf/ *nf* carafe.

Caraïbes /karaib/ *nfpl* **les ~** the Caribbean.

carambolage /kaʀɑ̃bɔlaʒ/ *nm* pile-up.

caramel /kaʀamɛl/ *nm* caramel; (bonbon) toffee.

carapace /kaʀapas/ *nf* shell.

caravane /kaʀavan/ *nf* (Auto) caravan; (US) trailer; (convoi) caravan.

carbone /kaʀbɔn/ *nm* carbon; (papier) **~** carbon (paper). **carboniser** **1** *vt* burn to ashes.

carburant /kaʀbyʀɑ̃/ *nm* (motor) fuel.

carburateur /kaʀbyʀatœʀ/ *nm* carburettor; (US) carburetor.

carcan /kaʀkɑ̃/ *nm* constraints (+ *pl*).

carcasse /kaʀkas/ *nf* (squelette) carcass; (armature) frame; (de voiture) shell.

cardiaque /kaʀdjak/ *adj* heart.
● *nmf* heart patient.

cardinal, ~e /kaʀdinal, -o/ (*mpl* **-aux**) *adj & nm* cardinal.

Carême /kaʀɛm/ *nm* **le ~** Lent.

carence /kaʀɑ̃s/ *nf* shortcomings (+ *pl*); inadequacy; (Méd) deficiency; (absence) lack.

caresse /kaʀɛs/ *nf* caress; (à un animal) stroke. **caresser** **1** *vt* caress, stroke; (espoir) cherish.

cargaison /kaʀɡɛzɔ̃/ *nf* cargo.

cargo /kaʀɡo/ *nm* cargo boat.

caricature /kaʀikatyʀ/ *nf* caricature.

carie /kaʀi/ *nf* (trou) cavity; **la ~** (dentaire) tooth decay.

carillon /kaʀijɔ̃/ *nm* chimes (+ *pl*);

(horloge) chiming clock.

caritatif, -ive /kaʀitatif, -v/ *adj* **association caritative** charity.

carnage /kaʀnaʒ/ *nm* carnage.

carnassier, -ière /kaʀnasje, -jɛʀ/ *adj* carnivorous.

carnaval (*pl* **~s**) /kaʀnaval/ *nm* carnival.

carnet /kaʀnɛ/ *nm* notebook; (de tickets, timbres) book; **~ d'adresses** address book; **~ de chèques** chequebook.

carotte /kaʀɔt/ *nf* carrot.

carpe /kaʀp/ *nf* carp.

carré, ~e /kaʀe/ *adj* (forme, mesure) square; (fig) straightforward; **un mètre ~** one square metre.
● *nm* square; (de terrain) patch.

carreau (*pl* **~x**) /kaʀo/ *nm* (window) pane; (par terre, au mur) tile; (dessin) check; (aux cartes) diamonds (+ *pl*); **à ~x** (tissu) check(ed); (papier) squared.

carrefour /kaʀfuʀ/ *nm* crossroads (+ *sg*).

carrelage /kaʀlaʒ/ *nm* tiling; (sol) tiles.

carrément /kaʀemɑ̃/ *adv* (complètement) completely; (stupide, dangereux) downright; (dire) straight out; **elle a ~ démissionné** she went straight ahead and resigned.

carrière /kaʀjɛʀ/ *nf* career; (terrain) quarry.

carrossable /kaʀɔsabl/ *adj* suitable for vehicles.

carrosse /kaʀɔs/ *nm* (horse-drawn) coach.

carrosserie /kaʀɔsʀi/ *nf* (Auto) body(work).

carrure /kaʀyʀ/ *nf* shoulders; (fig) necessary qualities, calibre.

cartable /kaʀtabl/ *nm* satchel.

carte /kaʀt/ *nf* card; (Géog) map;

(Naut) chart; (au restaurant) menu; ~**s** (jeu) cards; **à la** ~ (*manger*) à la carte; (*horaire*) personalized; **donner** ~ **blanche à** give a free hand to; ~ **bleue**® credit card; ~ **de crédit** credit card; ~ **de fidélité** loyalty card; ~ **grise** (car) registration document; ~ **d'identité** identity card; ~ **magnétique** swipe card; ~ **de paiement** debit card; ~ **postale** postcard; ~ **à puce** smart card; ~ **de séjour** resident's permit; ~ **des vins** wine list; ~ **visite** (business) card; ~ **vitale** social insurance smart card.

> **Carte d'identité** Not to be confused with a passport, this is a proof of identity carried by French citizens. It is issued by the *préfecture* and is valid for ten years. Though not compulsory, it is used to guarantee payments by cheque and is accepted as a travel document within the EU.

cartilage /kaʀtilaʒ/ *nm* cartilage.

carton /kaʀtɔ̃/ *nm* cardboard; (*boîte*) (cardboard) box; ~ **à dessin** portfolio; **faire un** ① do well.

cartonné, ~e /kaʀtɔne/ *adj* **livre** ~ hardback.

cartouche /kaʀtuʃ/ *nf* cartridge; (*de cigarettes*) carton. **cartouchière** *nf* cartridge-belt.

cas /kɑ/ *nm* case; **au** ~ **où** in case; ~ **urgent** emergency; **en aucun** ~ on no account; **en** ~ **de** in the event of, in case of; **en tout** ~ in any case; (*du moins*) at least; **faire** ~ **de** set great store by; ~ **de conscience** moral dilemma.

casanier, -ière /kazanje, -jɛʀ/ *adj* home-loving.

cascade /kaskad/ *nf* waterfall; (au

cinéma) stunt; (fig) spate, series (+ *sg*).

cascadeur, -euse /kaskadœʀ, -øz/ *nm, f* stuntman, stuntwoman.

case /kɑz/ *nf* hut; (*de damier*) square; (compartiment) pigeonhole; (sur un formulaire) box.

caser /kaze/ ① *vt* ① (mettre) put; (*loger*) put up; (dans un travail) find a job for; (marier: péj) marry off.

caserne /kazɛʀn/ *nf* barracks; ~ **de sapeurs-pompiers** fire station.

casier /kazje/ *nm* pigeon-hole, compartment; (à bouteilles, chaussures) rack; ~ **judiciaire** criminal record.

casque /kask/ *nm* (de motard) crash helmet; (de cycliste) cycle helmet; (chez le coiffeur) (hair-)drier; ~ (à écouteurs) headphones; ~ **anti-bruit** ear defenders; ~ **de protection** safety helmet.

casquette /kaskɛt/ *nf* cap.

cassant, ~e /kasɑ̃, -t/ *adj* brittle; (brusque) curt.

cassation /kasasjɔ̃/ *nf* **cour de** ~ appeal court.

casse /kas/ *nf* (objets) breakages; (lieu) breaker's yard; **mettre à la** ~ scrap.

① **casse-cou** /kasku/ *nmf inv* daredevil.

casse-croûte /kaskʀut/ *nm inv* snack.

casse-noix /kasnwa/ *nm inv* nutcrackers (+ *pl*).

casse-pieds /kaspje/ *nmf inv* ① pain (in the neck) ①.

casser /kase/ ① *vt* break; (annuler) annul; ~ **les pieds à qn** ① annoy sb. ● *vi* break. □ **se** ~ *vpr* break; (partir) ① ① leave.

casserole /kasʀɔl/ *nf* saucepan.

casse-tête /kastɛt/ *nm inv* (problème) headache; (jeu) brain teaser.

cassette /kasɛt/ *nf* casket; (de magnétophone) cassette, tape; (de vidéo) video tape; **~ audio numérique ~** digital audio tape.

cassis /kasi(s)/ *nm inv* blackcurrant.

cassure /kasyʀ/ *nf* break.

castor /kastɔʀ/ *nm* beaver.

castration /kastʀasjɔ̃/ *nf* castration.

catalogue /katalɔg/ *nm* catalogue.

catalyseur /katalizœʀ/ *nm* catalyst; (Auto) catalytic convertor.

catastrophe /katastʀɔf/ *nf* disaster, catastrophe. **catastrophique** *adj* catastrophic.

catch /katʃ/ *nm* (all-in) wrestling.

catéchisme /kateʃism/ *nm* catechism.

catégorie /kategɔʀi/ *nf* category. **catégorique** *adj* categorical.

cathédrale /katedʀal/ *nf* cathedral.

catholique /katɔlik/ *adj* Catholic; **pas très ~** a bit fishy.

catimini: en ~ /ãkatimini/ *loc* on the sly.

cauchemar /koʃmaʀ/ *nm* nightmare.

cause /koz/ *nf* cause; (raison) reason; (Jur) case; **à ~ de** because of; **en ~** (en jeu, concerné) involved; **pour ~ de** on account of; **mettre en ~** implicate; **remettre en ~** call into question.

causer /koze/ **1** *vt* cause; (discuter de **1**) ~ **travail** talk shop; ~ **de** talk about. ● *vi* chat. **causerie** *nf* talk.

causette /kozɛt/ *nf* (Internet) chat; **faire la ~** have a chat.

caution /kosjɔ̃/ *nf* surety; (Jur) bail; (appui) backing; (garantie) deposit; **libéré sous ~** released on bail. **cautionner** **1** *vt* guarantee;

(soutenir) back.

cavalcade /kavalkad/ *nf* stampede, rush.

cavalier, -ière /kavalje, -jɛʀ/ *adj* offhand; **allée cavalière** bridle path. ● *nm, f* rider; (pour danser) partner. ● *nm* (aux échecs) knight.

cave /kav/ *nf* cellar. ● *adj* sunken.

caveau (*pl* **~x**) /kavo/ *nm* vault.

caverne /kavɛʀn/ *nf* cave.

CCP *abrév m* (**compte chèque postal**) post office account.

CD *abrév m* (**compact disc**) CD.

CD-ROM *abrév m inv* (**compact disc read only memory**) CD-ROM.

ce, c', cet, cette (*pl* **ces**)
/sə, s, sɛt, se/

c' before e. **cet** before vowel or mute h.

● **ce, cet, cette** (*pl* **ces**) *adjectif démonstratif*

····▸ this; (plus éloigné) that; **ces** these; (plus éloigné) those; **cette nuit** (passée) last night; (à venir) tonight.

● **ce, c'** *pronom démonstratif*

····▸ **c'est** it's ou it is; **c'est un policier** he's a policeman; ~ **sont eux qui l'ont fait** they did it; **qui est- ~?** who is it?

····▸ **ce que/qui** what; ~ **que je ne comprends pas** what I don't understand; **elle est venue,** ~ **qui est étonnant** she came, which is surprising; ~ **que tu as de la chance!** how lucky you are! **tout ~ qu'elle trouve/peut** everything she finds/can

CE *abrév f* (**Communauté européenne**) EC.

ceci /səsi/ *pron* this.

cécité /sesite/ nf blindness.

céder /sede/ **14** vt give up; ~ **le passage** give way; (vendre) sell. ● vi (se rompre) give way; (se soumettre) give in.

cédérom /sederɔm/ nm CD-ROM.

cédille /sedij/ nf cedilla.

cèdre /sɛdʀ/ nm cedar.

CEI abrév f (**Communauté des États indépendants**) CIS.

ceinture /sɛtyʀ/ nf belt; (taille) waist; ~ **de sauvetage** lifebelt; ~ **de sécurité** seatbelt.

cela /səla/ pron it, that; (pour désigner) that; ~ **va de soi** it is obvious; ~ **dit/fait** having said/done that.

célèbre /selɛbʀ/ adj famous. **célébrer** **14** vt celebrate. **célébrité** nf fame; (personne) celebrity.

céleri /sɛlʀi/ nm (en branches) celery. **céleri-rave** (pl **célerisraves**) nm celeriac.

célibat /seliba/ nm celibacy; (état) single status.

célibataire /selibatɛʀ/ adj single. ● nm bachelor. ● nf single woman.

celle, celles /sɛl/ ➞**CELUI.**

cellulaire /selylɛʀ/ adj cell; **emprisonnement** ~ solitary confinement; **fourgon** ou **voiture** ~ prison van; **téléphone** ~ cellular phone.

cellule /selyl/ nf cell; ~ **souche** stem cell.

celui, celle (pl **ceux, celles**) /səlɥi, sɛl, sø/ pron the one; ~ **de mon ami** my friend's; ~**-ci** this (one); ~**-là** that one; **ceux-ci** these (ones); **ceux-là** those (ones).

cendre /sɑ̃dʀ/ nf ash.

cendrier /sɑ̃dʀije/ nm ashtray.

censé, ~e /sɑ̃se/ adj **être** ~ **faire** be supposed to do.

censeur /sɑ̃sœʀ/ nm censor; (Scol)

administrator in charge of discipline.

censure /sɑ̃syʀ/ nf censorship. **censurer** **1** vt censor; (critiquer) censure.

cent /sɑ̃/ adj (a) hundred; **20 pour** ~ 20 per cent. ● n (quantité) hundred; ~ **un** a hundred and one;)centième d'euro) cent.

centaine /sɑ̃tɛn/ nf hundred; **une** ~ (**de**) (about) a hundred.

centenaire /sɑ̃tnɛʀ/ nm (anniversaire) centenary.

centième /sɑ̃tjɛm/ adj & nmf hundredth.

centimètre /sɑ̃timɛtʀ/ nm centimetre; (ruban) tape-measure.

central, ~e (mpl **-aux**) /sɑ̃tʀal,-o/ adj central. ● nm (pl **-aux**) ~ (**téléphonique**) (telephone) exchange. **centrale** nf power-station.

centre /sɑ̃tʀ/ nm centre; ~ **commercial** shopping centre; (US) mall; ~ **d'appels** call centre; ~ **de formation** training centre; ~ **hospitalier** hospital. **centrer** **1** vt centre. **centre-ville** (pl **centres-villes**) nm town centre.

centuple /sɑ̃typl/ nm **le** ~ **de** a hundred times; **au** ~ a hundredfold.

cep /sɛp/ nm vine stock.

cépage /sepaʒ/ nm grape variety.

cèpe /sɛp/ nm cep.

cependant /səpɑ̃dɑ̃/ adv however.

céramique /seʀamik/ nf ceramic; (art) ceramics (+ sg).

cercle /sɛʀkl/ nm circle; (cerceau) hoop; (association) society, club; ~ **vicieux** vicious circle.

cercueil /sɛʀkœj/ nm coffin.

céréale /seʀeal/ nf cereal; ~**s** (Culin) (breakfast) cereal.

cérébral, ~e (mpl **-aux**) /seʀebʀal, -o/ adj cerebral.

cérémonie /seʀemɔni/ nf ceremony; **sans ~s** (repas) informal; (recevoir) informally.

cerf /sɛʀ/ nm stag.

cerfeuil /sɛʀfœj/ nm chervil.

cerf-volant (pl **cerfs-volants**) /sɛʀvɔlɑ̃/ nm kite.

cerise /s(ə)ʀiz/ nf cherry. **cerisier** nm cherry tree.

cerner /sɛʀne/ **1** vt surround; (question) define; **avoir les yeux cernés** have rings under the eyes.

certain, ~e /sɛʀtɛ̃, -ɛn/ adj certain; (sûr) certain, sure (**de** of; **que** that); **d'un ~ âge** no longer young; **un ~ temps** some time. **certainement** adv (probablement) most probably; (avec certitude) certainly. **certains, -es** pron some people.

certes /sɛʀt/ adv (sans doute) admittedly; (bien sûr) of course.

certificat /sɛʀtifika/ nm certificate.

certifier /sɛʀtifje/ **45** vt certify; **~ qch à qn** assure sb of sth; **copie certifiée conforme** certified true copy.

certitude /sɛʀtityd/ nf certainty.

cerveau (pl **~x**) /sɛʀvo/ nm brain.

cervelle /sɛʀvɛl/ nf (Anat) brain; (Culin) brains.

ces /se/ ➡CE.

césarienne /sezaʀjɛn/ nf Caesarean (section).

cesse /sɛs/ nf **n'avoir de ~ que** have no rest until; **sans ~** constantly, incessantly.

cesser /sese/ **1** vt stop; **~ de faire** stop doing. ● vi cease; **faire ~** put an end to.

cessez-le-feu /seselfø/ nm inv ceasefire.

cession /sesjɔ̃/ nf transfer.

c'est-à-dire /setadiʀ/ conj that

is (to say).

cet, cette /sɛt/ ➡CE.

ceux /sø/ ➡CELUI.

chacun, ~e /ʃakœ̃, -yn/ pron each (one), every one; (tout le monde) everyone; **~ d'entre nous** each (one) of us.

chagrin /ʃagʀɛ̃/ nm sorrow; **avoir du ~** be sad.

chahut /ʃay/ nm row, din.

chahuter /ʃayte/ **1** vi make a row. ● vt (enseignant) be rowdy with; (orateur) heckle.

chaîne /ʃɛn/ nf chain; (de télévision) channel; **~ (d'assemblage)** assembly line; **~s** (Auto) snow chains; **~ de montagnes** mountain range; **~ de montage/fabrication** assembly/production line; **~ hi-fi** hi-fi system; **~ laser** CD player; **en ~** (accidents) multiple; (réaction) chain. **chaînette** nf (small) chain. **chaînon** nm link.

chair /ʃɛʀ/ nf flesh; **bien en ~** plump; **en ~ et en os** in the flesh; **à saucisses** sausage meat; **la ~ de poule** goose pimples. ● adj inv **(couleur) ~** flesh-coloured.

chaire /ʃɛʀ/ nf (d'église) pulpit; (Univ) chair.

chaise /ʃɛz/ nf chair; **~ longue** deckchair.

châle /ʃɑl/ nm shawl.

chaleur /ʃalœʀ/ nf heat; (moins intense) warmth; (d'un accueil, d'une couleur) warmth. **chaleureux, -euse** adj warm.

chalumeau (pl **~x**) /ʃalymo/ nm blowtorch.

chalutier /ʃalytje/ nm trawler.

chamailler (se) /(sə)ʃamaje/ **1** vpr squabble.

chambre /ʃɑ̃bʀ/ nf (bed) room; (Pol, Jur) chamber; **faire ~ à part** sleep in separate rooms; **~ à air**

inner tube; ~ **d'amis** spare *ou* guest room; ~ **de commerce (et d'industrie)** Chamber of Commerce; ~ **à coucher** bedroom; ~ **à un lit/deux lits** single/twinroom; ~ **pour deux personnes** double room; ~ **forte** strong-room; ~ **d'hôte** bed and breakfast, B and B. **chambrer 1** *vt* (vin) bring to room temperature.

chameau (*pl* ~**x**) /ʃamo/ *nm* camel.

chamois /ʃamwa/ *nm* chamois.

champ /ʃã/ *nm* field; ~ **de bataille** battlefield; ~ **de courses** racecourse; ~ **de tir** firing range.

champêtre /ʃãpɛtʀ/ *adj* rural.

champignon /ʃãpiɲɔ̃/ *nm* mushroom; (moisissure) fungus; ~ **de Paris** button mushroom.

champion, -ne /ʃãpjɔ̃, -ɔn/ *nm, f* champion. **championnat** *nm* championship.

chance /ʃãs/ *nf* (good) luck; (possibilité) chance; **avoir de la** ~ be lucky; **quelle** ~! what luck!

chanceler /ʃãsle/ **38** *vi* stagger; (fig) falter, waver.

chancelier /ʃãsəlje/ *nm* chancellor.

chanceux, -euse /ʃãsø, -z/ *adj* lucky.

chandail /ʃãdaj/ *nm* sweater.

chandelier /ʃãdəlje/ *nm* candlestick.

chandelle /ʃãdɛl/ *nf* candle; **dîner aux** ~**s** candlelight dinner.

change /ʃãʒ/ *nm* (foreign) exchange; (taux) exchange rate.

changement /ʃãʒmã/ *nm* change; ~ **de vitesse** (dispositif) ears.

changer /ʃãʒe/ **40** *vt* change; ~ **qch de place** move sth; (échanger) change (**pour, contre** for); ~ **de nom/voiture** change one's name/

car; ~ **de place/train** change places/trains; ~ **de direction** change direction; ~ **d'avis** *ou* **d'idée** change one's mind; ~ **de vitesse** change gear. **□ se** ~ *vpr* change, get changed.

chanson /ʃãsɔ̃/ *nf* song.

chant /ʃã/ *nm* singing; (chanson) song; (Relig) hymn.

chantage /ʃãtaʒ/ *nm* blackmail.

chanter /ʃãte/ **1** *vt* sing; **si cela vous chante 1** if you feel like it. ● *vi* sing; **faire** ~ (délit) blackmail. **chanteur, -euse** *nm, f* singer.

chantier /ʃãtje/ *nm* building site; ~ **naval** shipyard; **mettre en** ~ get under way, start.

chaos /kao/ *nm* chaos.

chaparder /ʃapaʀde/ **1** *vt* **1** pinch **1**, filch.

chapeau (*pl* ~**x**) /ʃapo/ *nm* hat; ~! well done!

chapelet /ʃaplɛ/ *nm* rosary; (fig) string.

chapelle /ʃapɛl/ *nf* chapel.

chapelure /ʃaplyʀ/ *nf* (Culin) breadcrumbs.

chaperonner /ʃapʀɔne/ **1** *vt* chaperone.

chapiteau (*pl* ~**x**) /ʃapito/ *nm* marquee; (de cirque) big top; (de colonne) capital.

chapitre /ʃapitʀ/ *nm* chapter; (fig) subject.

chaque /ʃak/ *adj* every, each.

char /ʃaʀ/ *nm* (Mil) tank; (de carnaval) float; (charrette) cart; (dans l'antiquité) chariot.

charabia /ʃaʀabja/ *nm* **1** gibberish.

charade /ʃaʀad/ *nf* riddle.

charbon /ʃaʀbɔ̃/ *nm* coal; (Méd) anthrax; ~ **de bois** charcoal.

charcuterie /ʃaʀkytʀi/ *nf* pork

butcher's shop; (aliments) (cooked) pork meats. **charcutier, -ière** *nm, f* pork butcher.

chardon /ʃaʀdɔ̃/ *nm* thistle.

charge /ʃaʀʒ/ *nf* load, burden; (Mil, Électr, Jur) charge; (responsabilité) responsibility; **avoir qn à ~** be responsible for; **~s** expenses; (de locataire) service charges; **être à la ~ de** (*personne*) be the responsibility of; (*frais*) be payable by; **~s sociales** social security contributions; **prendre en ~** take charge of.

chargé, ~e /ʃaʀʒe/ *adj* (*véhicule*) loaded; (*journée, emploi du temps*) busy; (*langue*) coated. ● *nm, f* **~ de mission** head of mission; **~ d'affaires** chargé d'affaires; **~ de cours** lecturer.

chargement /ʃaʀʒəma/ *nm* loading; (objets) load.

charger /ʃaʀʒe/ 40 *vt* load; (Ordinat, Photo) load; (attaquer) charge; (*batterie*) charge; **~ qn de** (*fardeau*) weigh sb down with; (*tâche*) entrust sb with; **~ qn de faire** make sb responsible for doing. ● *vi* (attaquer) charge. □ **se ~ de** *vpr* take charge *ou* care of.

chariot /ʃaʀjo/ *nm* (à roulettes) rolley; (US) cart; (charrette) cart.

charitable /ʃaʀitabl/ *adj* charitable.

charité /ʃaʀite/ *nf* charity; **faire la ~ à** give (money) to.

charlatan /ʃaʀlatã/ *nm* charlatan.

charmant, ~e /ʃaʀmã, -t/ *adj* charming.

charme /ʃaʀm/ *nm* charm; (qui envoûte) spell. **charmer** 1 *vt* charm. **charmeur, -euse** *nm, f* charmer.

charnel, ~le /ʃaʀnɛl/ *adj* carnal.

charnière /ʃaʀnjɛʀ/ *nf* hinge; **à la ~ de** at the meeting point between.

charnu, ~e /ʃaʀny/ *adj* plump, fleshy.

charpente /ʃaʀpãt/ *nf* framework; (carrure) build.

charpentier /ʃaʀpãtje/ *nm* carpenter.

charrette /ʃaʀɛt/ *nf* cart.

charrue /ʃaʀy/ *nf* plough.

chasse /ʃas/ *nf* hunting; (au fusil) shooting; (*recherche*) chase; (recherche) hunt(ing); **~ (d'eau)** (toilet) flush; **~ sous-marine** harpoon fishing.

chasse-neige /ʃasnɛʒ/ *nm inv* snowplough.

chasser /ʃase/ 1 *vt* hunt; (au fusil) shoot; (*faire partir*) chase away; (*odeur, employé*) get rid of. ● *vi* go hunting; (au fusil) go shooting.

chasseur, -euse /ʃasœʀ, -øz/ *nm, f* hunter. ● *nm* bellboy; (US) bellhop; (avion) fighter plane.

châssis /ʃasi/ *nm* frame; (Auto) chassis.

chasteté /ʃastəte/ *nf* chastity.

chat¹ /ʃa/ *nm* cat; (mâle) tomcat.

chat² /tʃat/ *nm* (Internet) chat.

châtaigne /ʃatɛɲ/ *nf* chestnut. **châtaignier** *nm* chestnut tree. **châtain** *adj* chestnut (brown).

château (*pl* **~x**) /ʃato/ *nm* castle; (manoir) manor; **~ d'eau** water tower; **~ fort** fortified castle.

châtiment /ʃatimã/ *nm* punishment.

chaton /ʃatɔ̃/ *nm* (chat) kitten.

chatouillement /ʃatujmã/ *nm* tickling. **chatouiller** 1 *vt* tickle. **chatouilleux, -euse** *adj* ticklish; (susceptible) touchy.

châtrer /ʃatʀe/ 1 *vt* castrate; (chat) neuter.

chatte /ʃat/ *nf* female cat.

chaud, ~e /ʃo, -d/ adj warm; (brûlant) hot; (vif: fig) warm. ● nm heat; **au ~** in the warm(th); **avoir ~** be warm; be hot; **il fait ~** it is warm; it is hot; **pour te tenir ~** to keep you warm. **chaudement** adv warmly; (disputé) hotly.

chaudière /ʃodjɛʀ/ nf boiler.

chaudron /ʃodʀɔ̃/ nm cauldron.

chauffage /ʃofaʒ/ nm heating; ~ **central** central heating.

chauffard /ʃofaʀ/ nm (péj) reckless driver.

chauffer /ʃofe/ **1** vt/i heat (up); (moteur, appareil) overheat. □ **se ~** vpr warm oneself (up).

chauffeur /ʃofœʀ/ nm driver; (aux gages de qn) chauffeur.

chaume /ʃom/ nm (de toit) thatch.

chaussée /ʃose/ nf road (way).

chausse-pied /ʃospje/ (pl ~s) /ʃospje/ nm shoehorn.

chausser /ʃose/ **1** vt (chaussures) put on; (enfant) put shoes on (to). ● vi ~ **bien** (aller) fit well; ~ **du 35** take a size 35 shoe. □ **se ~** vpr put one's shoes on.

chaussette /ʃosɛt/ nf sock.

chausson /ʃosɔ̃/ nm slipper; (de bébé) bootee; ~ **de danse** ballet shoe; ~ **aux pommes** apple turnover.

chaussure /ʃosyʀ/ nf shoe; ~ **de ski** ski boot; ~ **de marche** hiking boot.

chauve /ʃov/ adj bald.

chauve-souris (pl **chauves-souris**) /ʃovsuʀi/ nf bat.

chauvin, ~e /ʃovɛ̃, -in/ adj chauvinistic. ● nm, f chauvinist.

chavirer /ʃaviʀe/ **1** vt (bateau) capsize; (objets) tip over.

chef /ʃɛf/ nm leader, head; (supérieur) boss, superior; (Culin) chef; (de tribu) chief; **architecte en ~**

chief ou head architect; ~ **d'accusation** (Jur) charge; ~ **d'équipe** foreman; (Sport) captain; ~ **d'État** head of State; ~ **de famille** head of the family; ~ **de file** (Pol) leader; ~ **de gare** stationmaster; ~ **d'orchestre** conductor; ~ **de service** department head; ~ **de train** guard; (US) conductor.

chef-d'œuvre (pl **chefs-d'œuvre**) /ʃɛdœvʀ/ nm masterpiece.

chef-lieu (pl **chefs-lieux**) /ʃɛfljø/ nm county town, administrative centre.

chemin /ʃəmɛ̃/ nm road; (étroit) lane; (de terre) track; (pour piétons) path; (passage) way; (direction, trajet) way; **avoir du ~ à faire** have a long way to go; ~ **de fer** railway; **par ~ de fer** by rail; ~ **de halage** towpath; ~ **vicinal** country lane.

cheminée /ʃəmine/ nf chimney; (intérieure) fireplace; (encadrement) mantelpiece; (de bateau) funnel.

cheminot /ʃəmino/ nm railwayman; (US) railroad man.

chemise /ʃəmiz/ nf shirt; (dossier) folder; (de livre) jacket; ~ **de nuit** nightdress. **chemisette** nf shortsleeved shirt. **chemisier** nm blouse.

chêne /ʃɛn/ nm oak.

chenil /ʃəni(l)/ nm (pension) kennels (+ sg).

chenille /ʃənij/ nf caterpillar; **véhicule à ~s** tracked vehicle.

cheptel /ʃɛptɛl/ nm livestock.

chèque /ʃɛk/ nm cheque; ~ **sans provision** bad cheque; ~ **de voyage** traveller's cheque. **chéquier** nm chequebook.

cher, chère /ʃɛʀ/ adj (coûteux) dear, expensive; (aimé) dear; (dans la correspondance) dear. ● adv (coûter, payer) a lot (of money); (en importance) dearly. ● *nm, f* **mon ~, ma chère** my dear.

chercher /ʃɛʀʃe/ **1** *vt* look for; (*aide, paix, gloire*) seek; **aller ~** go and get *ou* fetch, go for; **~ à faire** attempt to do; **~ la petite bête** be finicky.

chercheur, -euse /ʃɛʀʃœʀ, -øz/ *nm, f* research worker.

chèrement /ʃɛʀmɑ̃/ *adv* dearly.

chéri, ~e /ʃeʀi/ *adj* beloved. ● *nm, f* darling.

chérir /ʃeʀiʀ/ **2** *vt* cherish.

chétif, -ive /ʃetif, -v/ *adj* puny.

cheval (*pl* **-aux**) /ʃəval, -o/ *nm* horse; **à ~** on horseback; **à ~ sur** astride, straddling; **faire du ~** go horse-riding.

chevalerie /ʃəvalʀi/ *nf* chivalry.

chevalet /ʃəvalɛ/ *nm* easel; (*de menuisier*) trestle.

chevalier /ʃəvalje/ *nm* knight.

chevalière /ʃəvaljɛʀ/ *nf* signet ring.

cheval-vapeur (*pl* **chevaux-vapeur**) /ʃəvalvapœʀ/ *nm* horsepower.

chevaucher /ʃəvoʃe/ **1** *vt* sit astride. □ **se ~** *vpr* overlap.

chevelu, ~e /ʃəvly/ *adj* (*péj*) long-haired; (Bot) hairy.

chevelure /ʃəvlyʀ/ *nf* hair.

chevet /ʃəvɛ/ *nm* **au ~ de** at the bedside of; **livre de ~** bedside book.

cheveu (*pl* **~x**) /ʃəvø/ *nm* (*poil*) air; **~x** (*chevelure*) hair; **avoir les ~x longs** have long hair.

cheville /ʃəvij/ *nf* ankle; (*fiche*) peg, pin; (*pour mur*) (wall) plug.

chèvre /ʃɛvʀ/ *nf* goat.

chevreuil /ʃəvʀœj/ *nm* roe (deer); (Culin) venison.

chevron /ʃəvʀɔ̃/ *nm* (*poutre*)

rafter; **à ~s** herringbone.

chez /ʃe/ *prép* (*au domicile de*) at the house of; (*parmi*) among; (*dans le caractère de*) in; (*dans l'œuvre de*) in; **aller ~ qn** go to sb's house; **~ le boucher** at *ou* to the butcher's; **~ soi** at home; **rentrer ~ soi** go home. **chez-soi** *nm inv* home.

chic /ʃik/ *adj inv* smart; (*gentil*) kind. ● *nm* style; **avoir le ~ pour** have a knack for; **~ (alors)!** great!

chicane /ʃikan/ *nf* double bend; **chercher ~ à qn** pick a quarrel with sb.

chiche /ʃiʃ/ *adj* mean (**de** with); **~ que je le fais!** **1** I bet you I can do it.

chichis /ʃiʃi/ *nmpl* **1** fuss.

chicorée /ʃikɔʀe/ *nf* (*frisée*) endive; (*à café*) chicory.

chien /ʃjɛ̃/ *nm* dog; **~ d'aveugle** guide dog; **~ de garde** watch-dog. **chienne** *nf* dog, bitch.

chiffon /ʃifɔ̃/ *nm* rag; (*pour nettoyer*) duster; **~ humide** damp cloth. **chiffonner** **1** *vt* crumple; (*préoccuper* **1**) bother.

chiffre /ʃifʀ/ *nm* figure; (*numéro*) number; (*code*) code; **~s arabes/romains** Arabic/Roman numerals; **~s** (*statistiques*) statistics; **~ d'affaires** turnover.

chiffrer /ʃifʀe/ **1** *vt* put a figure on, assess; (*texte*) encode. □ **se ~ à** *vpr* come to.

chignon /ʃiɲɔ̃/ *nm* bun, chignon.

Chili /ʃili/ *nm* Chile.

chimère /ʃimɛʀ/ *nf* fantasy.

chimie /ʃimi/ *nf* chemistry. **chimique** *adj* chemical. **chimiste** *nmf* chemist.

chimpanzé /ʃɛ̃pɑ̃ze/ *nm* chimpanzee.

Chine /ʃin/ *nf* China.

chinois, ~e /ʃinwa, -z/ adj Chinese. ● nm (Ling) Chinese. **C**~, ~**e** nm, f Chinese.

chiot /ʃjo/ nm pup(py).

chipoter /ʃipɔte/ **1** vi (manger) pick at one's food; (discuter) quibble.

chips /ʃips/ nf inv crisp; (US) chip.

chirurgie /ʃiryRʒi/ nf surgery; ~ **esthétique** plastic surgery. **chirurgien** nm surgeon.

chlore /klɔR/ nm chlorine.

choc /ʃɔk/ nm (heurt) impact, shock; (émotion) shock; (collision) crash; (affrontement) clash; (Méd) shock; **sous le** ~ in shock.

chocolat /ʃɔkɔla/ nm chocolate; (à boire) drinking chocolate; ~ **au lait** milk chocolate; ~ **chaud** hot chocolate; ~ **noir** plain ou dark chocolate.

chœur /kœR/ nm (antique) chorus; (chanteurs, nef) choir; **en** ~ in chorus.

choisir /ʃwaziR/ **2** vt choose, select.

choix /ʃwa/ nm choice, selection; **fromage ou dessert au** ~ a choice of cheese ou dessert; **de** ~ choice; **de premier** ~ top quality.

chômage /ʃomaʒ/ nm unemployment; **au** ~, **en** ~ unemployed; **mettre en** ~ **technique** lay off.

chômeur, -euse /ʃomœR, -øz/ nm, f unemployed person; **les** ~**s** the unemployed.

choquer /ʃɔke/ **1** vt shock; (commotionner) shake.

choral, ~e (mpl ~s) /kɔRal/ adj choral. **chorale** nf choir, choral society.

chorégraphie /kɔRegRafi/ nf choreography.

choriste /kɔRist/ nmf (à l'église)

chorister; (à l'opéra) member of the chorus ou choir.

chose /ʃoz/ nf thing; **(très) peu de** ~ nothing much; **pas grand** ~ not much.

chou (pl ~**x**) /ʃu/ nm cabbage; ~ **(à la crème)** cream puff; ~ **de Bruxelles** Brussels sprout; **mon petit** ~ **1** my dear.

chouchou, ~**te** /ʃuʃu, -t/ nm, f (de professeur) pet; (du public) darling.

choucroute /ʃukRut/ nf sauerkraut.

chouette /ʃwɛt/ nf owl. ● adj **1** super.

chou-fleur (pl **choux-fleurs**) /ʃuflœR/ nm cauliflower.

choyer /ʃwaje/ **31** vt pamper.

chrétien, ~**ne** /kRetjɛ̃, -jɛn/ adj & nm, f Christian.

Christ /kRist/ nm **le** ~ Christ.

chrome /kRom/ nm chromium, chrome.

chromosome /kRomozom/ nm chromosome.

chronique /kRonik/ adj chronic. ● nf (rubrique) column; (nouvelles) news; (annales) chronicle.

chronologique /kRonolɔʒik/ adj chronological.

chronomètre /kRonometR/ nm stopwatch. **chronométrer** **14** vt time.

chrysanthème /kRizɑ̃tɛm/ nm chrysanthemum.

chuchoter /ʃyʃote/ **1** vt/i whisper.

chut /ʃyt/ interj shh, hush.

chute /ʃyt/ nf fall; (déchet) offcut; ~ **(d'eau)** waterfall; ~ **de pluie** rainfall; ~ **des cheveux** hair loss; ~ **des ventes** ~ drop in sales; ~ **de 5%** drop. **chuter** **1** vi fall.

Chypre /ʃipr/ nf Cyprus.

ci /si/ adv here; **~-gît** here lies; **cet homme-~** this man; **ces maisons-~** these houses.

ci-après /siaprε/ adv below.

cible /sibl/ nf target.

ciboulette /sibulεt/ nf (Culin) chives (+ pl).

cicatrice /sikatris/ nf scar.

cicatriser /sikatrize/ **1** vt heal. □ **se ~** vpr heal.

ci-dessous /sidəsu/ adv below.

ci-dessus /sidəsy/ adv above.

cidre /sidr/ nm cider.

ciel (pl **cieux**, **ciels**) /sjεl, sjø/ nm sky; (Relig) heaven; **cieux** (Relig) heaven.

cierge /sjεrʒ/ nm (church) candle.

cigale /sigal/ nf cicada.

cigare /sigar/ nm cigar.

cigarette /sigarεt/ nf cigarette.

cigogne /sigɔɲ/ nf stork.

ci-joint /siʒwε̃/ adv enclosed.

cil /sil/ nm eyelash.

cime /sim/ nf peak, tip.

ciment /simɑ̃/ nm cement.

cimetière /simtjεr/ nm cemetery, graveyard; **~ de voitures** breaker's yard.

cinéaste /sineast/ nmf film-maker.

cinéma /sinema/ nm cinema; (US) movie theater. **cinémathèque** nf film archive; (salle) film theatre. **cinématographique** adj cinema.

cinéphile /sinefil/ nmf film lover.

cinglant, ~e /sε̃glɑ̃, -t/ adj (vent) biting; (remarque) scathing.

cinglé /sε̃gle/ adj **1** crazy.

cinq /sε̃k/ adj & nm five.

cinquante /sε̃kɑ̃t/ adj & nm fifty.

cinquième /sε̃kjεm/ adj & nmf fifth.

Cinquième République
As established by the constitution of 1958 and still in force today, the *Cinquième République* refers to the system of government established by Charles de Gaulle, enshrining a strong executive and institutions to guarantee stability.

cintre /sε̃tr/ nm coat-hanger; (Archit) curve.

cirage /siraʒ/ nm polish.

circoncision /sirkɔ̃sizjɔ̃/ nf circumcision.

circonflexe /sirkɔ̃flεks/ adj circumflex.

circonscription /sirkɔ̃skripsjɔ̃/ nf district; **~ électorale** constituency; (US) district; (de conseiller, maire) ward.

circonscrire /sirkɔ̃skrir/ **30** vt (incendie, épidémie) contain; (sujet) define.

circonspect, ~e /sirkɔ̃spεkt/ adj circumspect.

circonstance /sirkɔ̃stɑ̃s/ nf circumstance; (situation) situation; (occasion) occasion; **~s atténuantes** mitigating circumstances.

circuit /sirkɥi/ nm circuit; (trajet) tour, trip.

circulaire /sirkylεr/ adj & nf circular.

circulation /sirkylasjɔ̃/ nf circulation; (de véhicules) traffic.

circuler /sirkyle/ **1** vi (se répandre, être distribué) circulate; (aller d'un lieu à un autre) get around; (en voiture) travel; (piéton) walk; (être en service) (bus, train) run; **faire ~** (badauds) move on; (rumeur) spread.

cire /sir/ nf wax.

ciré /sire/ nm oilskin.

cirer /siʀe/ **1** vt polish.

cirque /siʀk/ nm circus; (arène) amphitheatre; (désordre: fig) chaos; **faire le ~l** make a racket 🅣.

ciseau (pl ~x) /sizo/ nm chisel; ~x scissors.

ciseler /sizle/ **6** vt chisel.

citadelle /sitadɛl/ nf citadel.

citadin, ~e /sitadɛ̃, -in/ nm, f city-dweller. ● adj city.

citation /sitasjɔ̃/ nf quotation; (Jur) summons.

cité /site/ nf city; (logements) housing estate; ~ **universitaire** (university) halls of residence.

citer /site/ **1** vt quote, cite; (Jur) summon.

citerne /sitɛʀn/ nf tank.

citoyen, ~ne /sitwajɛ̃, -ɛn/ nm, f citizen.

citron /sitʀɔ̃/ nm lemon; ~ **vert** lime. **citronnade** nf lemon squash, (still) lemonade.

citrouille /sitʀuj/ nf pumpkin.

civet /sivɛ/ nm stew; ~ **de lièvre** jugged hare.

civière /sivjɛʀ/ nf stretcher.

civil, ~e /sivil/ adj civil; (non militaire) civilian; (poli) civil. ● nm civilian; **dans le ~** in civilian life; **en ~** in plain clothes.

civilisation /sivilizasjɔ̃/ nf civilization.

civiliser /sivilize/ **1** vt civilize. □ **se ~** vpr become civilized.

civique /sivik/ adj civic.

clair, ~e /klɛʀ/ adj clear; (éclairé) light, bright; (couleur) light; **le plus ~ de** most of. ● adv clearly; **il faisait ~** it was already light. ● nm ~ **de lune** moonlight; **tirer une histoire au ~** get to the bottom of things. **clairement** adv clearly.

clairière /klɛʀjɛʀ/ nf clearing.

clairsemé, ~e /klɛʀsəme/ adj sparse.

clamer /klame/ **1** vt proclaim.

clameur /klamœʀ/ nf clamour.

clan /klɑ̃/ nm clan.

clandestin, ~e /klɑ̃dɛstɛ̃, -in/ adj secret; (journal) underground; (immigration, travail) illegal; **passager ~** stowaway.

clapier /klapje/ nm (rabbit) utch.

clapoter /klapɔte/ **1** vi lap.

claquage /klakaʒ/ nm strained muscle; **se faire un ~** pull a muscle.

claque /klak/ nf slap.

claquer /klake/ **1** vi bang; (porte) slam, bang; (fouet) crack; (se casser 🅣) conk out; (mourir 🅣) snuff it!; ~ **des doigts** snap one's fingers; ~ **des mains** clap one's hands; **il claque des dents** his teeth are chattering. ● vt (porte) slam, bang; (dépenser 🅣) blow; (fatiguer 🅣) tire out.

claquettes /klakɛt/ nfpl tap-dancing.

clarifier /klaʀifje/ **45** vt clarify.

clarinette /klaʀinɛt/ nf clarinet.

clarté /klaʀte/ nf light, brightness; (netteté) clarity.

classe /klas/ nf class; (salle: Scol) classroom; (cours) class, lesson; **aller en ~** to go to school; **faire la ~** teach; ~ **ouvrière/moyenne** working/middle class.

classement /klasmɑ̃/ nm classification; (d'élèves) grading; (de documents) filing; (rang) place, grade; (de coureur) placing.

classer /klase/ **1** vt classify; (par mérite) grade; (papiers) file; (Jur) (affaire) close. □ **se ~** vpr rank.

classeur /klasœʀ/ nm (meuble) filing cabinet; (chemise) file; (à anneaux) ring binder.

classification /klasifikasjɔ̃/ nf

classification.

classique /klasik/ *adj* classical; (de qualité) classic; (habituel) classic, standard. ● *nm* classic; (auteur) classical author.

clavecin /klavsɛ̃/ *nm* harpsichord.

clavicule /klavikyl/ *nf* collarbone.

clavier /klavje/ *nm* keyboard; ~ **numérique** keypad.

clé, clef /kle/ *nf* key; (outil) spanner; (Mus) clef; ~ **anglaise** (monkey-)wrench; ~ **de contact** ignition key; ~ **à molette** adjustable spanner; ~ **de voûte** keystone. ● *adj inv* key.

clémence /klemɑ̃s/ *nf* (de climat) mildness; (indulgence) leniency.

clergé /klɛʀʒe/ *nm* clergy.

clérical, ~e (*mpl* -**aux**) /kleʀikal, -o/ *adj* clerical.

clic /klik/ *nm* (Ordinat) click.

cliché /kliʃe/ *nm* cliché; (Photo) negative.

client, ~e /klijɑ̃, -t/ *nm, f* customer; (d'un avocat) client; (d'un médecin) patient; (d'hôtel) guest; (de taxi) passenger.

clientèle /klijɑ̃tɛl/ *nf* customers, clientele; (d'un avocat) clients, practice; (d'un médecin) patients, practice; (soutien) custom.

cligner /kliɲe/ **1** *vi* ~ **des yeux** blink; ~ **de l'œil** wink.

clignotant /kliɲɔtɑ̃/ *nm* (Auto) indicator, turn.

clignoter /kliɲɔte/ **1** *vi* blink; (lumière) flicker; (comme signal) flash.

climat /klima/ *nm* climate.

climatisation /klimatizasjɔ̃/ *nf* air-conditioning.

clin d'œil /klɛ̃dœj/ *nm* wink; **en un ~** in a flash.

clinique /klinik/ *adj* clinical. ● *nf* (private) clinic.

clinquant, ~e /klɛ̃kɑ̃, -t/ *adj* showy.

clip /klip/ *nm* video.

cliquer /klike/ **1** *vi* (Ordinat) click (**sur** on).

cliqueter /klikte/ **38** *vi* (couverts) clink; (clés, monnaie) jingle; (ferraille) rattle. **cliquetis** *nm* clink(ing), jingle, rattle.

clivage /klivaʒ/ *nm* divide.

clochard, ~e /klɔʃaʀ, -d/ *nm, f* tramp.

cloche /klɔʃ/ *nf* bell; (imbécile 🗓) idiot; ~ **à fromage** cheese-cover.

cloche-pied: à ~ /aklɔʃpje/ *loc* **sauter à ~** hop on one leg.

clocher /klɔʃe/ *nm* bell-tower; (pointu) steeple; **de ~** parochial.

cloison /klwazɔ̃/ *nf* partition; (fig) barrier.

cloître /klwatʀ/ *nm* cloister. **cloîtrer (se)** **1** *vpr* shut oneself away.

clonage /klɔnaʒ/ *nm* cloning.

cloner /klone/ **1** *vt* clone.

cloque /klɔk/ *nf* blister.

clos, ~e /klo, -z/ *adj* closed.

clôture /klotyʀ/ *nf* fence; (fermeture) closure; (de magasin, bureau) closing; (de débat, liste) close; (en Bourse) close of trading. **clôturer** **1** *vt* enclose, fence in; (festival, séance) close.

clou /klu/ *nm* nail; (furoncle) boil; (de spectacle) star attraction; **les ~s** (passage) pedestrian crossing; (US) crosswalk.

clouer /klue/ **1** *vt* nail down; (fig) pin down; **être cloué au lit** be confined to one's bed; ~ **le bec à qn** shut sb up.

clouté, ~e /klute/ *adj* studded; **passage ~** pedestrian crossing; (US) crosswalk.

CMU *abrév f* free health care for

people on low incomes.

coaliser (se) /(sə)kɔalize/ **1** *vpr* join forces.

coalition /kɔalisjɔ̃/ *nf* coalition.

cobaye /kɔbaj/ *nm* guinea-pig.

cocaïne /kɔkain/ *nf* cocaine.

cocasse /kɔkas/ *adj* comical.

coccinelle /kɔksinɛl/ *nf* ladybird; (US) ladybug.

cocher /kɔʃe/ **1** *vt* tick (off), check. ● *nm* coachman.

cochon, ~e /kɔʃɔ̃, -ɔn/ *nm, f* (personne 🖪) pig. ● *adj* 🖪 filthy. ● *nm* pig. **cochonnerie** *nf* (saleté 🖪) filth; (marchandise 🖪) rubbish, junk.

cocon /kɔkɔ̃/ *nm* cocoon.

cocorico /kɔkɔriko/ *nm* cock-a-doodle-doo.

cocotier /kɔkɔtje/ *nm* coconut palm.

cocotte /kɔkɔt/ *nf* (marmite) casserole; ~ **minute®** pressure-cooker; **ma ~** 🖪 my dear.

cocu, ~e /kɔky/ *nm, f* 🖪 deceived husband, deceived wife.

code /kɔd/ *nm* code; ~s dipped headlights; **se mettre en ~s** dip one's headlights; ~ **(à) barres** bar code; ~ **confidentiel (d'instruction)** PIN number; ~ **postal** post code; (US) zip code; ~ **de la route** Highway Code. **coder** 🖪 *vt* code, encode.

coéquipier, -ière /kɔekipje, -jɛʀ/ *nm, f* team mate.

cœur /kœʀ/ *nm* heart; (aux cartes) hearts (+ *pl*); ~ **d'artichaut** artichoke heart; ~ **de palmier** palm heart; **à ~ ouvert** (*opération*) open-heart; (*parler*) freely; **avoir bon** ~ be kind-hearted; **de bon** ~ willingly; (*rire*) heartily; **par** ~ by heart; **avoir mal au** ~ feel sick *ou* nauseous; **je veux en avoir le** ~

net I want to be clear in my own mind (about it).

coffre /kɔfʀ/ *nm* chest; (pour argent) safe; (Auto) boot; (US) trunk. **coffre-fort** (*pl* **coffres-forts**) *nm* safe.

coffret /kɔfʀɛ/ *nm* casket, box; (de livres, cassettes) boxed set.

cogner /kɔɲe/ **1** *vt/i* knock. □ **se** ~ *vpr* knock oneself; **se** ~ **la tête** bump one's head.

cohabiter /kɔabite/ **1** *vi* live together.

cohérent, ~e /kɔeʀɑ̃, -t/ *adj* coherent; (homogène) consistent.

cohue /kɔy/ *nf* crowd.

coi, ~te /kwa, -t/ *adj* silent.

coiffe /kwaf/ *nf* headgear.

coiffer /kwafe/ **1** *vt* do the hair of; (*chapeau*) put on; (surmonter) cap; ~ **qn d'un chapeau** put a hat on sb; **coiffé de** wearing; **être bien/mal coiffé** have tidy/untidy hair. □ **se** ~ *vpr* do one's hair.

coiffeur, -euse /kwafœʀ, -øz/ *nm, f* hairdresser. **coiffeuse** *nf* dressing-table.

coiffure /kwafyʀ/ *nf* hairstyle; (métier) hairdressing; (chapeau) hat.

coin /kwɛ̃/ *nm* corner; (endroit) spot; (cale) wedge; **au ~ du feu** by the fireside; **dans le ~** locally; **du** ~ local.

coincer /kwɛ̃se/ **10** *vt* jam; (caler) wedge; (attraper) catch. □ **se** ~ *vpr* get jammed.

coïncidence /kɔɛ̃sidɑ̃s/ *nf* coincidence.

coing /kwɛ̃/ *nm* quince.

coït /kɔit/ *nm* intercourse.

col /kɔl/ *nm* collar; (de bouteille) neck; (de montagne) pass; ~ **blanc** white-collar worker; ~ **roulé** polo-neck; (US) turtle-neck; ~ **de l'utérus** cervix; **se casser le ~ du**

fémur break one's hip.

colère /kɔlɛʀ/ nf anger; (accès) fit of anger; **en ~** angry; **se mettre en ~** lose one's temper; **faire une ~** throw a tantrum.

coléreux, -euse /kɔleʀø, -z/ adj quick-tempered.

colin /kɔlɛ̃/ nm (merlu) hake; (lieu noir) coley.

colique /kɔlik/ nf diarrhoea; (Méd) colic.

colis /kɔli/ nm parcel.

collaborateur, -trice /kɔlabɔʀatœʀ, -tʀis/ nm, f collaborator; (journaliste) contributor; (collègue) colleague.

collaboration /kɔlabɔʀasjɔ̃/ nf collaboration (à on); (à ouvrage, projet) contribution (à to).

collaborer /kɔlabɔʀe/ **1** vi collaborate (à on); **~ à** (journal) contribute to.

collant, ~e /kɔlɑ̃, -t/ adj (mouillant) kin-tight; (poisseux) sticky. ●nm (bas) tights; (US) panty hose.

colle /kɔl/ nf glue; (en pâte) paste; (problème ①) poser; (Scol ①) detention.

collecter /kɔlɛkte/ **1** vt collect.

collectif, -ive /kɔlɛktif, -v/ adj collective; (billet, voyage) group.

collection /kɔlɛksjɔ̃/ nf collection; (ouvrages) series (+ sg); (du même auteur) set. **collectionner** **1** vt collect. **collectionneur, -euse** nm, f collector.

collectivité /kɔlɛktivite/ nf community; **~ locale** local authority.

collège /kɔlɛʒ/ nm secondary school (up to age 15); (US) junior high school; (assemblée) college. **collégien, ~ne** nm, f schoolboy, schoolgirl.

collègue /kɔlɛg/ nmf colleague.

coller /kɔle/ **1** vt stick; (avec colle

liquide) glue; (affiche) stick up; (mettre ①) stick; (par une question ①) stump; (Scol ①) **se faire ~** get a detention; **je me suis fait ~ en maths** I failed ou flunked maths. ●vi stick (à to); (être collant) be sticky; **~ à** (convenir à) fit, correspond to.

collet /kɔlɛ/ nm (piège) snare; **~ monté** prim and proper; **mettre la main au ~ de qn** collar sb.

collier /kɔlje/ nm necklace; (de chien) collar.

colline /kɔlin/ nf hill.

collision /kɔlizjɔ̃/ nf (choc) collision; (lutte) clash; **entrer en ~ (avec)** collide (with).

collyre /kɔliʀ/ nm eye drops (+ pl).

colmater /kɔlmate/ **1** vt plug, seal.

colombe /kɔlɔ̃b/ nf dove.

Colombie /kɔlɔ̃bi/ nf Colombia.

colon /kɔlɔ̃/ nm settler.

colonel /kɔlɔnɛl/ nm colonel.

colonie /kɔlɔni/ nf colony; **~ de vacances** children's holiday camp.

Colonie de vacances A holiday village or summer camp where children take part in a variety of outdoor activities. Originally set up to give poorer children a means of getting out into the countryside, they are still largely state-subsidized. Colloquially they are referred to as *la/une colo*.

colonne /kɔlɔn/ nf column; **~ vertébrale** spine; **en ~ par deux** in double file.

colorant /kɔlɔʀɑ̃/ nm colouring.

colorier /kɔlɔʀje/ **45** vt colour (in).

colosse /kɔlɔs/ nm giant.

colza /kɔlza/ nm rape(-seed).

coma /kɔma/ *nm* coma; **dans le ~** in a coma.

combat /kɔ̃ba/ *nm* fight; (Sport) match; **~s** fighting. **combatif, -ive** *adj* eager to fight; (*esprit*) fighting.

combattre /kɔ̃batʀ/ **11** *vt/i* fight.

combien /kɔ̃bjɛ̃/ *adv* **~ (de)** quantité) how much; (nombre) how many; (temps) how long; **~ il a changé!** (comme) how he has changed!; **~ y a-t-il d'ici à...?** how far is it to...?; **on est le ~ aujourd'hui?** what's the date today?

combinaison /kɔ̃binɛzɔ̃/ *nf* combination; (de femme) slip; (bleu de travail) boiler suit; (US) overalls; **~ d'aviateur** flying-suit; **~ de plongée** wetsuit.

combine /kɔ̃bin/ *nf* trick; (fraude) fiddle; (intrigue) scheme.

combiné /kɔ̃bine/ *nm* (de téléphone) receiver, handset.

combiner /kɔ̃bine/ **11** *vt* (réunir) combine; (calculer) devise; **~ de faire** plan to do.

comble /kɔ̃bl/ *adj* packed. ● *nm* height; **~s** (mansarde) attic, loft; **c'est le ~!** that's the (absolute) limit!

combler /kɔ̃ble/ **11** *vt* fill; (perte, déficit) make good; (désir) fulfil; **~ qn de cadeaux** lavish gifts on sb.

combustible /kɔ̃bystibl/ *nm* fuel.

comédie /kɔmedi/ *nf* comedy; (histoire) fuss; **~ musicale** musical; **jouer la ~** put on an act. **comédien, ~ne** *nm, f* actor,actress.

comestible /kɔmɛstibl/ *adj* edible.

comète /kɔmɛt/ *nf* comet.

comique /kɔmik/ *adj* comical, funny; (genre) comic. ● *nm* (acteur) comic; (comédie) comedy; (côté drôle) comical aspect.

commandant /kɔmɑ̃dɑ̃/ *nm*

commander; (dans l'armée de terre) major; **~ (de bord)** captain; **~ en chef** Commander-in-Chief.

commande /kɔmɑ̃d/ *nf* (Comm) order; (Tech) control; **~s** (d'avion) controls.

commandement /kɔmɑ̃dmɑ̃/ *nm* command; (Relig) commandment.

commander /kɔmɑ̃de/ **11** *vt* command; (acheter) order; (étude, œuvre d'art) commission; **~ à** (maîtriser) control; **~ à qn de** command sb to. ● *vi* be in command.

comme /kɔm/ *adv* **~ c'est bon!** it's so good!; **~ il est mignon!** isn't he sweet! ● *conj* (dans une comparaison) as; (dans une équivalence, illustration) like; (en tant que) as; (puisque) as, since; (au moment où) as; **vif ~ l'éclair** as quick as a flash; **travailler ~ sage-femme** work as a midwife; **~ ci ~ ça** so-so; **~ il faut** properly; **~ pour faire** as if to do; **jolie ~ tout** as pretty as anything; **qu'est-ce qu'il y a ~ légumes?** what is there in the way of vegetables?

commencer /kɔmɑ̃se/ **10** *vt/i* begin, start; **~ à faire** begin ou start to do.

comment /kɔmɑ̃/ *adv* how; **~?** (répétition) pardon?; (surprise) what?; **~ est-il?** what is he like?; **le ~ et le pourquoi** the whys and wherefores.

commentaire /kɔmɑ̃tɛʀ/ *nm* comment; (d'un texte, événement) commentary. **commentateur, -trice** *nm, f* commentator.

commenter /kɔmɑ̃te/ **11** *vt* comment on; (film, visite) provide a commentary for; (radio,TV) commentate.

commérages /kɔmeʀaʒ/ *nmpl*

gossip.

commerçant, ~e /kɔmɛʀsɑ̃, -t/ adj (rue) shopping; (personne) business-minded. ● nm, f shopkeeper.

commerce /kɔmɛʀs/ nm trade, commerce; (magasin) business; **faire du** ~ be in business; ~ **électrique** e-commerce.

commercial, ~e (mpl -iaux) kɔmɛʀsjal, -jo/ adj commercial. **commercialiser** 🔟 vt market.

commettre /kɔmɛtʀ/ 🔁 vt commit.

commis /kɔmi/ nm (de magasin) assistant; (de bureau) clerk.

commissaire /kɔmisɛʀ/ nm commissioner; (Sport) steward; ~ **(de police)** (police) superintendent. **commissaire-priseur** (pl **commissaires-priseurs**) nm auctioneer.

commissariat /kɔmisaʀja/ nm ~ **(de police)** police station.

commission /kɔmisjɔ̃/ nf commission; (course) errand; (message) message; ~s shopping.

commode /kɔmɔd/ adj handy, convenient; (facile) easy; **il n'est pas** ~ he's a difficult customer. ● nf chest (of drawers). **commodité** nf convenience.

commotion /kɔmosjɔ̃/ nf ~ **(cérébrale)** concussion.

commun, ~e /kɔmœ̃, -yn/ adj common; (effort, action) joint; (frais, pièce) shared; **en** ~ jointly; **avoir** ou **mettre en** ~ share; **le** ~ **des mortels** ordinary mortals. **communal**, ~e (mpl -aux) adj of the commune, local.

communauté /kɔmynote/ nf community.

commune /kɔmyn/ nf (circonscription, collectivité) commune.

Commune The smallest administrative unit in France, headed by a *maire* and a *conseil municipal*. Each village, town and city is a *commune*, of which there are 36,000 throughout the country.

communicatif, -ive /kɔmynikatif, -v/ adj (personne) talkative; (gaieté) infectious.

communication /kɔmynikasjɔ̃/ nf communication; (téléphonique) call; ~s (relations) relations (+ pl); **voies** ou **moyens de** ~ communications (+ pl).

communier /kɔmynje/ 🔂 vi (Relig) receive communion; (fig) commune.

communiqué /kɔmynike/ nm statement; (de presse) communiqué.

communiquer /kɔmynike/ 🔟 vt pass on, communicate; (date, décision) announce. ● vi communicate. □ **se** ~ **à** vpr spread to.

communiste /kɔmynist/ adj & nmf communist.

commutateur /kɔmytatœʀ/ nm (Électr) switch.

compagne /kɔ̃paɲ/ nf companion.

compagnie /kɔ̃paɲi/ nf company; **tenir** ~ **à** keep company; **en** ~ **de** together with; ~ **aérienne** airline.

compagnon /kɔ̃paɲɔ̃/ nm companion.

comparable /kɔ̃paʀabl/ adj comparable (à to). **comparaison** nf comparison; (littéraire) simile.

comparaître /kɔ̃paʀɛtʀ/ 🔢 vi (Jur) appear (devant before).

comparatif, -ive /kɔ̃paʀatif, -v/ adj & nm comparative.

comparer /kɔ̃paʀe/ 🔟 vt compare (à with). □ se ~ vpr compare oneself; (être comparable) be comparable.

compartiment /kɔ̃paʀtimɑ̃/ nm compartment.

comparution /kɔ̃paʀysjɔ̃/ nf (Jur) appearance.

compas /kɔ̃pa/ nm (pair of) compasses; (boussole) compass.

compassion /kɔ̃pasjɔ̃/ nf compassion.

compatible /kɔ̃patibl/ adj compatible.

compatir /kɔ̃patiʀ/ [2] vi sympathize; ~ à share in.

compatriote /kɔ̃patʀijɔt/ nmf compatriot.

compensation /kɔ̃pɑ̃sasjɔ̃/ nf compensation. **compenser** [1] vt compensate for, make up for.

compère /kɔ̃pɛʀ/ nm accomplice.

compétence /kɔ̃petɑ̃s/ nf competence; (fonction) domain, sphere; entrer dans les ~s de qn be in sb's domain. **compétent, ~e** adj competent.

compétition /kɔ̃petisjɔ̃/ nf competition; (sportive) event; de ~ competitive.

complaire (se) /(sə)kɔ̃plɛʀ/ vpr se ~ dans delight in.

complaisance /kɔ̃plɛzɑ̃s/ nf kindness; (indulgence) indulgence.

complément /kɔ̃plemɑ̃/ nm supplement; (Gram) complement; ~ (d'objet) (Gram) object; ~ d'information further information. **complémentaire** adj complementary; (renseignements) supplementary.

complet, -ète /kɔ̃plɛ, -t/ adj complete; (train, hôtel) full. ● nm suit.

compléter /kɔ̃plete/ [14] vt complete; (agrémenter) complement. □ se ~ vpr complement each other.

complexe /kɔ̃plɛks/ adj com-

plex. ● nm (sentiment, bâtiments) complex.

complexé, ~e /kɔ̃plekse/ adj être ~ have a lot of hang-ups.

complice /kɔ̃plis/ nm accomplice.

compliment /kɔ̃plimɑ̃/ nm compliment; ~s (félicitations) compliments, congratulations.

compliquer /kɔ̃plike/ [1] vt complicate. □ se ~ vpr become complicated.

complot /kɔ̃plo/ nm plot.

comportement /kɔ̃pɔʀtəmɑ̃/ nm behaviour; (de joueur, voiture) performance.

comporter /kɔ̃pɔʀte/ [1] vt (être composé de) comprise; (inclure) include; (risque) entail. □ se ~ vpr behave; (joueur, voiture) perform.

composant /kɔ̃pozɑ̃/ nm component.

composé, ~e /kɔ̃poze/ adj composite; (salade) mixed; (guindé) affected. ● nm compound.

composer /kɔ̃poze/ [1] vt make up, compose; (chanson, visage) compose; (numéro) dial; (page) typeset. ● vi (transiger) compromise. □ se ~ de vpr be made up ou composed of. **compositeur, -trice** nm, f (Mus) composer.

composter /kɔ̃pɔste/ [1] vt (billet) punch.

compote /kɔ̃pɔt/ nf stewed fruit; ~ de pommes stewed apples.

compréhensible /kɔ̃pʀeɑ̃sibl/ adj understandable; (intelligible) comprehensible.

compréhensif, -ive /kɔ̃pʀeɑ̃sif, -v/ adj understanding.

compréhension /kɔ̃pʀeɑ̃sjɔ̃/ nf understanding, comprehension.

comprendre /kɔ̃pʀɑ̃dʀ/ [50] vt understand; (comporter) comprise, be made up of. □ se ~

vpr (*personnes*) understand each other; **ça se comprend** that is understandable.

compresse /kɔ̃pʀɛs/ *nf* compress.

comprimé /kɔ̃pʀime/ *nm* tablet.

comprimer /kɔ̃pʀime/ **1** *vt* compress; (*réduire*) reduce.

compris, **~e** /kɔ̃pʀi, -z/ *adj* included; (d'accord) agreed; **~ entre** (contained) between; **service (non) ~** service (not) included; **tout ~** (all) inclusive; **y ~** including.

compromettre /kɔ̃pʀɔmɛtʀ/ 42 *vt* compromise. **compromis** *nm* compromise.

comptabilité /kɔ̃ptabilite/ *nf* accountancy; (*comptes*) accounts; (*service*) accounts department.

comptable /kɔ̃tabl/ *adj* accounting. ● *nmf* accountant.

comptant /kɔ̃tɑ̃/ *adv* (*payer*) (in) cash; (*acheter*) for cash.

compte /kɔ̃t/ *nm* count; (*facture, comptabilité*) account; (*nombre exact*) right number; **~ bancaire, ~ en banque** bank account; **prendre qch en ~, tenir ~ de qch** take sth into account; **se rendre ~ de** realize; **demander/rendre des ~s** ask for/give an explanation; **à bon ~** cheaply; **s'en tirer à bon ~** get off lightly; **travailler à son ~** be self-employed; **faire le ~ de** count; **pour le ~ de** on behalf of; **sur le ~ de** about; **au bout du ~** all things considered; **~ à rebours** countdown.

compte-gouttes /kɔ̃tgut/ *nm inv* (Méd) dropper; **au ~** (fig) in dribs and drabs.

compter /kɔ̃te/ **1** *vt* count; (*prévoir*) allow, reckon on; (*facturer*) charge for; (*avoir*) have; (*classer*) consider; **~ faire** intend to do. ● *vi* (*calculer, importer*) count; **~ avec** reckon with; **~ parmi** (*figurer*) be

considered among; **~ sur** rely on, count on.

compte(-)rendu /kɔ̃tʀɑ̃dy/ *nm* report; (de film, livre) review.

compteur /kɔ̃tœʀ/ *nm* meter; **~ de vitesse** speedometer.

comptine /kɔ̃tin/ *nf* nursery rhyme.

comptoir /kɔ̃twaʀ/ *nm* counter; (de café) bar.

comte /kɔ̃t/ *nm* count.

comté /kɔ̃te/ *nm* county.

comtesse /kɔ̃tɛs/ *nf* countess.

con, **~ne** /kɔ̃, kɔn/ *adj* 🗶 bloody stupid 🗶. ● *nm, f* 🗶 bloody fool 🗶.

concentrer /kɔ̃sɑ̃tʀe/ **1** *vt* concentrate. □ **se ~** *vpr* be concentrated.

concept /kɔ̃sɛpt/ *nm* concept.

concerner /kɔ̃sɛʀne/ **1** *vt* concern; **en ce qui me concerne** as far as I am concerned.

concert /kɔ̃sɛʀ/ *nm* concert; **de ~** in unison.

concerter /kɔ̃sɛʀte/ **1** *vt* organize, prepare. □ **se ~** *vpr* confer.

concession /kɔ̃sesjɔ̃/ *nf* concession; (terrain) plot.

concevoir /kɔ̃svwaʀ/ 52 *vt* (*imaginer, engendrer*) conceive; (*comprendre*) understand; (*élaborer*) design.

concierge /kɔ̃sjɛʀʒ/ *nmf* caretaker.

concilier /kɔ̃silje/ 45 *vt* reconcile. □ **se ~** *vpr* (*s'attirer*) win (over).

concis, **~e** /kɔ̃si, -z/ *adj* concise.

conclure /kɔ̃klyʀ/ 18 *vt* conclude; **~ à** conclude in favour of. ● *vi* **~ en faveur de/contre** find in favour of/against. **conclusion** *nf* conclusion.

concombre /kɔ̃kɔ̃bʀ/ *nm* cucumber.

concordance /kɔ̃kɔʀdɑ̃s/ *nf* agreement.

concourir /kɔ̃kuRiR/ **20** *vi* compete. ● *vt* ~ **à** contribute towards.

concours /kɔ̃kuR/ *nm* competition; (examen) competitive examination; (aide) help; (de circonstances) combination.

concret, -ète /kɔ̃kRɛ, -t/ *adj* concrete.

concrétiser /kɔ̃kRetize/ **1** *vt* give concrete form to. □ **se** ~ *vpr* materialize.

conçu, ~e /kɔ̃sy/ *adj* **bien/mal** ~ well/badly designed.

concubinage /kɔ̃kybinaʒ/ *nm* cohabitation; **vivre en** ~ live together, cohabit.

concurrence /kɔ̃kyRɑ̃s/ *nf* competition; **faire** ~ **à** compete with; **jusqu'à** ~ **de** up to a limit of.

concurrencer /kɔ̃kyRɑ̃se/ **10** *vt* compete with.

concurrent, ~e /kɔ̃kyRɑ̃, -t/ *nm, f* competitor; (Scol) candidate. ● *adj* rival.

condamnation /kɔ̃danasjɔ̃/ *nf* condemnation; (peine) sentence; ~ **centralisée des portières** central locking. **condamné, ~e** *nm, f* condemned man, condemned woman. **condamner** **1** *vt* (censurer, obliger) condemn; (Jur) sentence; (porte) block up.

condition /kɔ̃disjɔ̃/ *nf* condition; ~**s** (prix) terms; **à** ~ **de** ou **que** provided (that); **sans** ~ unconditional(ly); **sous** ~ conditionally.

conditionnel, ~le /kɔ̃disjɔnɛl/ *adj* conditional. ● *nm* conditional (tense).

conditionnement /kɔ̃disjɔnmɑ̃/ *nm* conditioning; (emballage) packaging.

condoléances /kɔ̃dɔleɑ̃s/ *nfpl* condolences.

conducteur, -trice /kɔ̃dyktœR,

-tRis/ *nm, f* driver.

conduire /kɔ̃dɥiR/ **17** *vt* take (à to); (guider) lead; (Auto) drive; (affaire) conduct; ~ **à** (faire aboutir) lead to. ● *vi* drive. □ **se** ~ *vpr* behave.

conduit /kɔ̃dɥi/ *nm* duct.

conduite /kɔ̃dɥit/ *nf* conduct, behaviour; (Auto) driving; (tuyau) pipe; **voiture avec** ~ **à droite** right-hand drive car.

confection /kɔ̃fɛksjɔ̃/ *nf* making; **de** ~ ready-made; **la** ~ the clothing industry.

conférence /kɔ̃feRɑ̃s/ *nf* conference; (exposé) lecture; ~ **au sommet** summit meeting. **conférencier, -ière** *nm, f* lecturer.

confesser /kɔ̃fese/ **1** *vt* confess. □ **se** ~ *vpr* go to confession.

confiance /kɔ̃fjɑ̃s/ *nf* trust; **avoir** ~ **en** trust.

confiant, ~e /kɔ̃fjɑ̃, -t/ *adj* (assuré) confident; (sans défiance) trusting.

confidence /kɔ̃fidɑ̃s/ *nf* confidence.

confidentiel, ~le /kɔ̃fidɑ̃sjɛl/ *adj* confidential.

confier /kɔ̃fje/ **45** *vt* ~ **à qn** entrust sb with; ~ **un secret à qn** tell sb a secret. □ **se** ~ **à** *vpr* confide in.

configuration /kɔ̃figyRasjɔ̃/ *nf* configuration.

configurer /kɔ̃figyRe/*vt* configure.

confiner /kɔ̃fine/ **1** *vt* confine; ~ **à** border on. □ **se** ~ *vpr* confine oneself (à, dans to).

confirmation /kɔ̃fiRmasjɔ̃/ *nf* confirmation. **confirmer** **1** *vt* confirm.

confiserie /kɔ̃fizRi/ *nf* sweet shop; ~**s** confectionery.

confisquer /kɔ̃fiske/ **1** *vt* confiscate.

confit, ~e /kɔ̃fi, -t/ adj candied;
(fruits) crystallized. ● nm ~ de canard confit of duck.

confiture /kɔ̃fityr/ nf jam.

conflit /kɔ̃fli/ nm conflict.

confondre /kɔ̃fɔdr/ **3** vt confuse,
mix up; (étonner) confound. □ se
~ vpr merge; se ~ en excuses
apologize profusely.

conforme /kɔ̃fɔrm/ adj être ~ à
comply with; (être en accord) be in
keeping with.

conformer /kɔ̃fɔrme/ **1** vt adapt.
□ se ~ à vpr conform to.

conformité /kɔ̃fɔrmite/ nf compliance, conformity; **agir en** ~ **avec**
act in accordance with.

confort /kɔ̃fɔr/ nm comfort; **tout**
~ with all mod cons. **confortable**
adj comfortable.

confrère /kɔ̃frɛr/ nm colleague.

confronter /kɔ̃frɔ̃te/ **1** vt confront; (textes) compare. □ se ~ à
vpr be confronted with.

confus, ~e /kɔ̃fy, -z/ adj confused;
(gêné) embarrassed.

congé /kɔ̃ʒe/ nm holiday; (arrêt
momentané) time off, leave; (avis
de départ) notice; **en** ~ on holiday
ou leave; ~ **de maladie/maternité**
sick/maternity leave; **jour de** ~ day
off; **prendre** ~ **de** take one's
leave of.

congédier /kɔ̃ʒedje/ **45** vt dismiss.

congélateur /kɔ̃ʒelatœr/ nm
freezer.

congeler /kɔ̃ʒle/ **6** vt freeze.

congère /kɔ̃ʒɛr/ nf snowdrift.

congrès /kɔ̃grɛ/ nm conference;
(Pol) congress.

conjoint, ~e /kɔ̃ʒwɛ̃, -t/ nm, f
spouse. ● adj joint.

conjonctivite /kɔ̃ʒɔ̃ktivit/ nf
conjunctivitis.

conjoncture /kɔ̃ʒɔ̃ktyr/ nf situation; (économique) economic
climate.

conjugaison /kɔ̃ʒygɛzɔ̃/ nf conjugation.

conjugal, ~e (mpl -aux) /kɔ̃ʒygal,
-o/ adj conjugal, married.

conjuguer /kɔ̃ʒyge/ **1** vt (Gram)
conjugate; (efforts) combine. □ se
~ (Gram) be conjugated; (fac-
teurs) be combined.

conjurer /kɔ̃ʒyre/ **1** vt (éviter)
avert; (implorer) beg.

connaissance /kɔnɛsɑ̃s/ nf knowledge; (personne) acquaintance; ~s
(science) knowledge; **faire la** ~ **de**
meet; (apprécier une personne) get
to know; **perdre/reprendre** ~
lose/regain consciousness; **sans** ~
unconscious.

connaisseur /kɔnɛsœr/ nm expert, connoisseur.

connaître /kɔnɛtr/ **18** vt know;
(difficultés, faim, succès) experience;
faire ~ make known. □ se ~ vpr
(se rencontrer) meet; **s'y** ~ **en**
know (all) about.

connecter /kɔnɛkte/ **1** vt connect; **être/ne pas être connecté** be
on-/off-line. □ se ~ à vpr (Ordinat)
log on to.

connerie /kɔnri/ nf ☒ **faire une**
~ do something stupid; **dire des**
~s talk rubbish.

connexion /kɔnɛksjɔ̃/ nf (Ordinat)
connection.

connu, ~e /kɔny/ adj well-known.

conquérant, ~e /kɔkerɑ̃, -t/ nm,
f conqueror.

conquête /kɔkɛt/ nf conquest.

consacrer /kɔsakre/ **1** vt devote;
(Relig) consecrate; (sanctionner)
sanction. □ se ~ à vpr devote oneself to.

conscience /kɔsjɑ̃s/ nf conscience; (perception) awareness; (de collectivité) conscience; **avoir/prendre ~ de** be/become aware of; **perdre/reprendre ~** lose/regain consciousness; **avoir bonne/mauvaise ~** have a clear/guilty conscience.

conscient, ~e /kɔ̃sjɑ̃, -t/ adj conscious; **~ de** aware ou conscious of.

conseil /kɔ̃sɛj/ nm (piece) of advice; (assemblée) council, committee; (séance) meeting; (personne) consultant; **~ d'administration** board of directors; **~ en gestion** management consultant; **~ des ministres** Cabinet; **~ municipal** town council.

conseiller[1] /kɔ̃seje/ **1** vt advise; **~ à qn** advise sb to; **~ qch à qn** recommend sth to sb.

conseiller,[2] -ère /kɔ̃seje, -jɛʀ/ nm, f adviser, counsellor; **~ municipal** town councillor; **~ d'orientation** careers adviser.

consentement /kɔ̃sɑ̃tmɑ̃/ nm consent.

conséquence /kɔ̃sekɑ̃s/ nf consequence; **en ~** (il convient) accordingly; **en ~ (de quoi)** as a result of which.

conséquent, ~e /kɔ̃sekɑ̃, -t/ adj consistent, logical; (important) substantial; **par ~** consequently, therefore.

conservateur, -trice /kɔ̃sɛʀvatœʀ, -tʀis/ adj conservative. ● nm, f (Pol) conservative; (de musée) curator. ● nm preservative.

conservation /kɔ̃sɛʀvasjɔ̃/ nf preservation; (d'espèce, patrimoine) conservation.

conservatoire /kɔ̃sɛʀvatwaʀ/ nm academy.

conserve /kɔ̃sɛʀv/ nf tinned ou canned food; **en ~** tinned, canned; **boîte de ~** tin, can.

conserver /kɔ̃sɛʀve/ **1** vt keep; (en bon état) preserve; (Culin) preserve. □ **se ~** vpr (Culin) keep.

considérer /kɔ̃sideʀe/ **14** vt consider; (respecter) esteem; **~ comme** consider to be.

consigne /kɔ̃siɲ/ nf (de gare) left-luggage office; (US) baggage checkroom; (somme) deposit; (ordres) orders; **~ automatique** left-luggage lockers; (US) baggage lockers.

consistance /kɔ̃sistɑ̃s/ nf consistency; (fig) substance, weight. **consistant**, ~e adj solid; (épais) thick.

consister /kɔ̃siste/ **1** vi **~ en/dans** consist of/in; **~ à faire** consist in doing.

consoler /kɔ̃sɔle/ **1** vt console. □ **se ~** vpr find consolation; **se ~ de qch** get over sth.

consolider /kɔ̃sɔlide/ **1** vt strengthen; (fig) consolidate.

consommateur, -trice /kɔ̃sɔmatœʀ, -tʀis/ nm, f (Comm) consumer; (dans un café) customer.

consommation /kɔ̃sɔmasjɔ̃/ nf consumption; (accomplissement) consummation; (boisson) drink; **de ~** (Comm) consumer.

consommer /kɔ̃sɔme/ **1** vt consume, use; (manger) eat; (boire) drink; (mariage) consummate. □ **se ~** vpr (être mangé) be eaten; (être utilisé) be used.

consonne /kɔ̃sɔn/ nf consonant.

constat /kɔ̃sta/ nm (official) report; **~ (à l'amiable)** accident report drawn up by those involved.

constatation /kɔ̃statasjɔ̃/ nf observation, statement of fact. **constater** **1** vt note, notice; (certifier) certify.

consternation /kɔ̃stɛʀnasjɔ̃/ nf dismay.

constipé, ~e /kõstipe/ adj constipated; (fig) uptight.

constituer /kõstitɥe/ **1** vt (composer) make up, constitute; (organiser) form; (être) constitute; **constitué de** made up of. □ se ~ vpr se ~ **prisonnier** give oneself up.

constitution /kõstitysjõ/ nf formation, setting up; (Pol, Méd) constitution.

constructeur /kõstryktœr/ nm manufacturer, builder.

construction /kõstryksjõ/ nf building; (structure, secteur) construction; (fabrication) manufacture.

construire /kõstrɥir/ **17** vt build; (système, phrase) construct.

consulat /kõsyla/ nm consulate.

consultation /kõsyltasjõ/ nf consultation; (réception: Méd) surgery; (US) office; **heures de** ~ surgery ou office (US) hours.

consulter /kõsylte/ **1** vt consult. ● vi (médecin) hold surgery, see patients. □ se ~ vpr consult together.

contact /kõtakt/ nm contact; (toucher) touch; **au** ~ **de** on contact with; (personne) by contact with, by seeing; **mettre/couper le** ~ (Auto) switch on/off the ignition; **prendre** ~ **avec** get in touch with. **contacter** **1** vt contact.

contagieux, -ieuse /kõtaʒjø, -z/ adj contagious.

conte /kõt/ nm tale; ~ **de fées** fairy tale.

contempler /kõtãple/ **1** vt contemplate.

contemporain, ~e /kõtãpɔrɛ̃, -ɛn/ adj & nmf contemporary.

contenance /kõt(ə)nɑ̃s/ nf (volume) capacity; (allure) bearing; **perdre** ~ lose one's composure.

contenir /kõt(ə)nir/ **58** vt contain; (avoir une capacité de) hold. □ se

~ vpr contain oneself.

content, ~e /kõtã, -t/ adj pleased, happy (**de** with); ~ **de faire** pleased ou happy to do.

contenter /kõtãte/ **1** vt satisfy. □ se ~ **de** vpr content oneself with.

contenu /kõt(ə)ny/ nm (de récipient) contents (+ pl); (de texte) content.

conter /kõte/ **1** vt tell, relate.

contestation /kõtɛstasjõ/ nf dispute; (opposition) protest.

contester /kõtɛste/ **1** vt question, dispute; (s'opposer) protest against. ● vi protest.

conteur, -euse /kõtœr, -øz/ nm, f storyteller.

contigu, ~ë /kõtigy/ adj adjacent (**à** to).

continent /kõtinã/ nm continent.

continu, ~e /kõtiny/ adj continuous.

continuer /kõtinɥe/ **1** vt continue, go on; ~ **à** ou **de faire** carry on ou go on ou continue doing.

contorsionner (se) /(se) kõtɔrsjɔne/ **1** vpr wriggle.

contour /kõtur/ nm outline, contour; ~s (d'une route) twists and turns, bends.

contourner /kõturne/ **1** vt go round, by-pass; (difficulté) get round.

contraceptif, -ive /kõtrasɛptif, -v/ adj contraceptive. ● nm contraceptive. **contraception** nf contraception.

contracter /kõtrakte/ **1** vt (maladie) contract; (dette) incur; (muscle) tense; (assurance) take out. □ se ~ vpr contract.

contractuel, ~le /kõtraktɥel/ nm, f (agent) traffic warden.

contradictoire /kõtradiktwar/

adj contradictory; (*débat*) open.

contraignant, ~e /kɔ̃tʀɛɲɑ̃, -t/ *adj* restricting.

contraindre /kɔ̃tʀɛ̃dʀ/ **22** *vt* force, compel (**à faire** to do).

contrainte /kɔ̃tʀɛ̃t/ *nf* constraint.

contraire /kɔ̃tʀɛʀ/ *adj* opposite; ~ **à** contrary to. ● *nm* opposite; **au** ~ on the contrary; **au** ~ **de** unlike.

contrarier /kɔ̃tʀaʀje/ **45** *vt* annoy; (*projet, volonté*) frustrate; (*chagriner*) upset.

contraste /kɔ̃tʀast/ *nm* contrast.

contrat /kɔ̃tʀa/ *nm* contract.

contravention /kɔ̃tʀavɑ̃sjɔ̃/ *nf* (parking) ticket; **en** ~ in breach (**à** of).

contre /kɔ̃tʀ(ə)/ *prép* against; (*en échange de*) for; **par** ~ on the other hand; **tout** ~ close by.

contre-attaque (*pl* ~**s**) *nf* counterattack. **contre-attaquer** **1** *vt* counter-attack. **contre-balancer** **10** *vt* counterbalance.

contrebande /kɔ̃tʀəbɑ̃d/ *nf* contraband; **faire la** ~ **de** smuggle.

contrebas: en ~ /ɑ̃kɔ̃tʀəba/ *loc* below.

contrebasse /kɔ̃tʀəbas/ *nf* double bass.

contrecœur: à ~ /akɔ̃tʀəkœʀ/ *loc* reluctantly.

contrecoup /kɔ̃tʀəku/ *nm* effects, repercussions.

contredire /kɔ̃tʀədiʀ/ **37** *vt* contradict. □ **se** ~ *vpr* contradict oneself.

contrée /kɔ̃tʀe/ *nf* region; (*pays*) land.

contrefaçon /kɔ̃tʀəfasɔ̃/ *nf* (*objet imité*, action) forgery.

contre-indiqué, ~e /kɔ̃tʀɛ̃dike/ *adj* (Méd) contra-indicated; (*déconseillé*) not recommended.

contre-jour: à ~ /akɔ̃tʀəʒuʀ/ *loc* against the light.

contrepartie /kɔ̃tʀəpaʀti/ *nf* compensation; **en** ~ in exchange, in return.

contreplaqué /kɔ̃tʀəplake/ *nm* plywood.

contresens /kɔ̃tʀəsɑ̃s/ *nm* misinterpretation; (*absurdité*) nonsense; **à** ~ the wrong way.

contretemps /kɔ̃tʀətɑ̃/ *nm* hitch; **à** ~ (fig) at the wrong time.

contribuable /kɔ̃tʀibɥabl/ *nmf* taxpayer.

contribuer /kɔ̃tʀibɥe/ **1** *vt* contribute (**à** to, towards).

contrôle /kɔ̃tʀol/ *nm* (*maîtrise*) control; (*vérification*) check; (*des prix*) control; (*poinçon*) hallmark; (Scol) test; ~ **continu** continuous assessment; ~ **des changes** exchange control; ~ **des naissances** birth control; ~ **de soi-même** self-control; ~ **technique (des véhicules)** MOT (test).

contrôler /kɔ̃tʀole/ **1** *vt* (*vérifier*) check; (*surveiller, maîtriser*) control. □ **se** ~ *vpr* control oneself.

contrôleur, -**euse** /kɔ̃tʀolœʀ, -øz/ *nm, f* inspector.

convaincre /kɔ̃vɛ̃kʀ/ **59** *vt* convince; ~ **qn de faire** persuade sb to do.

convalescence /kɔ̃valesɑ̃s/ *nf* convalescence; **être en** ~ be convalescing.

convalescent, ~e /kɔ̃valesɑ̃, -t/ *adj, nm, f* convalescent.

convenable /kɔ̃vnabl/ *adj* (*correct*) decent, proper; (*approprié*) suitable; (*acceptable*) reasonable, acceptable.

convenance /kɔ̃vnɑ̃s/ *nf* **à ma** ~ to my satisfaction; **les** ~**s** convention.

convenir /kɔ̃vniʀ/ **58** *vt/i* be suitable; ~ **à** suit; ~ **que** admit that;

$\sim$ **de qch** (avouer) admit sth; (s'accorder sur) agree on sth; $\sim$ **de faire** agree to do; **il convient de it** is advisable to; (selon les bienséances) it would be right to.

convention /kɔ̃vɑ̃sjɔ̃/ *nf* agreement, convention; (clause) article, clause; $\sim$**s** (convenances) conventions; **de** $\sim$ conventional; $\sim$ **collective** industrial agreement.

convenu, ~e /kɔ̃vny/ *adj* agreed.

conversation /kɔ̃vɛʀsasjɔ̃/ *nf* conversation.

convertir /kɔ̃vɛʀtiʀ/ **2** *vt* convert (à to; en into). □ **se** $\sim$ *vpr* be converted, convert.

conviction /kɔ̃viksjɔ̃/ *nf* conviction; **avoir la** $\sim$ **que** be convinced that.

convivial, ~e (*mpl* **-iaux**) /kɔ̃vivjal, -jo/ *adj* convivial; (Ordinat) user-friendly.

convocation /kɔ̃vɔkasjɔ̃/ *nf* (Jur) summons; (d'une assemblée) convening; (document) notification to attend.

convoi /kɔ̃vwa/ *nm* convoy; (train) train; $\sim$ **(funèbre)** funeral procession.

convoquer /kɔ̃vɔke/ **1** *vt* (assemblée) convene; (personne) summon; **être convoqué pour un entretien** be called for interview.

coopération /kɔɔpeʀasjɔ̃/ *nf* cooperation; (Mil) civilian national service abroad.

coordination /kɔɔʀdinasjɔ̃/ *nf* coordination. **coordonnées** *nfpl* (adresse) address and telephone number.

copain /kɔpɛ̃/ *nm* friend; (petit ami) boyfriend.

copie /kɔpi/ *nf* copy; (Scol) paper; $\sim$ **d'examen** exam paper *ou* script; $\sim$ **de sauvegarde** back-up copy.

copier /kɔpje/ **45** *vt/i* copy; $\sim$ **sur** (Scol) copy *ou* crib from.

copieux, -ieuse /kɔpjø, -z/ *adj* copious.

copine /kɔpin/ *nf* friend; (petite amie) girlfriend.

coq /kɔk/ *nm* cockerel.

coque /kɔk/ *nf* shell; (de bateau) hull.

coquelicot /kɔkliko/ *nm* poppy.

coqueluche /kɔklyʃ/ *nf* whooping cough.

coquet, ~te /kɔkɛ, -t/ *adj* flirtatious; (élégant) pretty; (somme **1**) tidy.

coquetier /kɔktje/ *nm* eggcup.

coquillage /kɔkijaʒ/ *nm* shellfish; (coquille) shell.

coquille /kɔkij/ *nf* shell; (faute) misprint; $\sim$ **Saint-Jacques** scallop.

coquin, ~e /kɔkɛ̃, -in/ *adj* mischievous. ● *nm, f* rascal.

cor /kɔʀ/ *nm* (Mus) horn; (au pied) corn.

corail (*pl* **-aux**) /kɔʀaj, -o/ *nm* coral.

corbeau (*pl* **~x**) /kɔʀbo/ *nm* (oiseau) crow.

corbeille /kɔʀbɛj/ *nf* basket; $\sim$ **à papier** waste-paper basket.

corbillard /kɔʀbijaʀ/ *nm* hearse.

cordage /kɔʀdaʒ/ *nm* rope; $\sim$**s** (Naut) rigging.

corde /kɔʀd/ *nf* rope; (d'arc, de violon) string; $\sim$ **à linge** washing line; $\sim$ **à sauter** skipping-rope; $\sim$ **raide** tightrope; $\sim$**s vocales** vocal cords.

cordon /kɔʀdɔ̃/ *nm* string, cord; $\sim$ **de police** police cordon.

cordonnier /kɔʀdɔnje/ *nm* cobbler.

Corée /kɔʀe/ *nf* Korea.

coriace /kɔʀjas/ *adj* tough.

corne /kɔrn/ nf horn.

corneille /kɔrnɛj/ nf crow.

cornemuse /kɔrnəmyz/ nf bagpipes (+ pl).

corner /kɔrne/ **1** vt (page) turn down the corner of; **page cornée** dog-eared page. ● vi (Auto) hoot, honk.

cornet /kɔrnɛ/ nm (paper) cone; (crème glacée) cornet, cone.

corniche /kɔrniʃ/ nf cornice; (route) cliff road.

cornichon /kɔrniʃɔ̃/ nm gherkin.

corporel, ~le /kɔrpɔrɛl/ adj bodily; (châtiment) corporal.

corps /kɔr/ nm body; (Mil) corps; **combat à ~** hand-to-hand combat; **~ électoral** electorate; **~ enseignant** teaching profession.

correct, ~e /kɔrɛkt/ adj proper, correct; (exact) correct.

correcteur, -trice /kɔrɛktœr, -tris/ nm, f (d'épreuves) proofreader; (Scol) examiner; **~ liquide** correction fluid; **~ d'orthographe** spell-checker.

correction /kɔrɛksjɔ̃/ nf correction; (d'examen) marking, grading; (punition) beating.

correspondance /kɔrɛspɔ̃dɑ̃s/ nf correspondence; (de train, d'autobus) connection; **vente par ~** mail order; **faire des études par ~** do a correspondence course.

correspondant, ~e /kɔrɛspɔ̃dɑ̃, -t/ adj corresponding. ● nm, f correspondent; penfriend; (au téléphone) **votre ~** the person you are calling.

correspondre /kɔrɛspɔ̃dr/ **3** vi (s'accorder, écrire) correspond; (chambres) communicate. ● v + prép **~ à** (être approprié à) match, suit; (équivaloir à) correspond to. □ **se ~** vpr correspond.

corrida /kɔrida/ nf bullfight.

corriger /kɔriʒe/ **40** vt correct; (devoir) mark, grade, correct; (punir) beat; (guérir) cure.

corsage /kɔrsaʒ/ nm bodice; (chemisier) blouse.

corsaire /kɔrsɛr/ nm pirate.

Corse /kɔrs/ nf Corsica. ● nmf Corsican. **corse** adj Corsican.

corsé, ~e /kɔrse/ adj (vin) fullbodied; (café) strong; (scabreux) racy; (problème) tough.

cortège /kɔrtɛʒ/ nm procession; **~ funèbre** funeral procession.

corvée /kɔrve/ nf chore.

cosmonaute /kɔsmɔnot/ nmf cosmonaut.

cosmopolite /kɔsmɔpɔlit/ adj cosmopolitan.

cosse /kɔs/ nf (de pois) pod.

cossu, ~e /kɔsy/ adj (gens) well-to-do; (demeure) opulent.

costaud, ~e /kɔsto, -d/ **1** adj strong. ● nm strong man.

costume /kɔstym/ nm suit; (Théât) costume.

cote /kɔt/ nf (classification) mark; (en Bourse) quotation; (de cheval) odds (**de** on); (de candidat, acteur) rating; **~ d'alerte** danger level; **avoir la ~** be popular.

côte /kot/ nf (littoral) coast; (pente) hill; (Anat) rib; (Culin) chop; **~ à ~** side by side; **la C~ d'Azur** the (French) Riviera.

côté /kote/ nm side; (direction) way; **à ~** nearby; **voisin d'à ~** next-door neighbour; **à ~ de** next to; (comparé à) compared to; **à ~ de la cible** wide of the target; **aux ~s de** by the side of; **de ~** (regarder) sideways; (sauter) to one side; **mettre de ~** put aside; **de ce ~** this way; **de chaque ~** on each side; **de tous les ~s** on every side;

(partout) everywhere; **du ~ de** (vers) towards; **(proche de)** near.

côtelette /kotlɛt/ nf chop.

coter /kote/ **1** vt (Comm) quote; **coté en Bourse** listed on the Stock Exchange; **très coté** highly rated.

cotiser /kotize/ **1** vi pay one's contributions (**à** to); (**à un club**) pay one's subscription. □ **se ~** vpr club together.

coton /kotõ/ nm cotton; **~ hydrophile** cotton wool.

cou /ku/ nm neck.

couchant /kuʃɑ̃/ nm sunset.

couche /kuʃ/ nf layer; (de peinture) coat; (de bébé) nappy; (US) diaper; **~s** (Méd) childbirth; **~s sociales** social strata.

coucher /kuʃe/ **1** vt put to bed; (loger) put up; (étendre) lay down; **~ (par écrit)** set down. ● vi sleep. □ **se ~** vpr go to bed; (s'étendre) lie down; (soleil) set. ● nm **~ de soleil** sunset.

couchette /kuʃɛt/ nf (de train) couchette; (Naut) berth.

coude /kud/ nm elbow; (de rivière, chemin) bend; **~ à ~** side by side.

cou-de-pied (pl **cous-de-pied**) /kudpje/ nm instep.

coudre /kudʀ/ **19** vt/i sew.

couette /kwɛt/ nf duvet, quilt.

couler /kule/ **1** vi flow; run; (fromage, nez) run; (fuir) leak; (bateau) sink; (entreprise) go under; **faire ~ un bain** run a bath. ● vt (bateau) sink; (sculpture, métal) cast. □ **se ~** vpr slip (**dans** into).

couleur /kulœʀ/ nf colour; (de peinture) paint; (aux cartes) suit; **~s** (teint) colour; **de ~** (homme, femme) coloured; **en ~s** (télévision, film) colour.

couleuvre /kulœvʀ/ nf grass snake.

coulisse /kulis/ nf (de tiroir) runner; **à ~** (porte, fenêtre) sliding; **~s** (Théât) wings; **dans les ~s** (fig) behind the scenes.

couloir /kulwaʀ/ nm corridor; (Sport) lane; **~ de bus** bus lane.

coup /ku/ nm blow; (choc) knock; (Sport) stroke; (de crayon, chance, cloche) stroke; (de fusil, pistolet) shot; (fois) time; (aux échecs) move; **donner un ~ de pied/poing à** kick/punch; **à ~ sûr** definitely; **après ~** after the event; **boire un ~** I have a drink; **~ sur ~** in rapid succession; **du ~** as a result; **d'un seul ~** in one go; **du premier ~** first go; **sale ~** dirty trick; **sous le ~ de la fatigue/colère** out of tiredness/anger; **sur le ~** instantly; **tenir le ~** hold out; **manquer son ~** I blow it!; **~ de chiffon** wipe (with a rag); **~ de coude** nudge; **~ de couteau** stab; **~ d'envoi** kickoff; **~ d'État** (Pol) coup; **~ franc** free kick; **~ de main** helping hand; **~ d'œil** glance; **~ de soleil** sunburn; **~ de téléphone** telephone call; **~ de vent** gust of wind.

coupable /kupabl/ adj guilty.

coupe /kup/ nf cup; (de champagne) goblet; (à fruits) dish; (de vêtement) cut; (dessin) section; **~ de cheveux** haircut.

couper /kupe/ **1** vt cut; (arbre) cut down; (arrêter) cut off; (voyage) break up; (appétit) take away; (vin) water down; **~ par** take a short cut via; **~ la parole à qn** cut sb short. ● vi cut. □ **se ~** vpr cut oneself; **se ~ le doigt** cut one's finger; (routes) intersect; **se ~ de** cut oneself off from.

couple /kupl/ nm couple; (d'animaux) pair.

coupure /kupyʀ/ nf cut; (billet de banque) note; (de presse) cutting;

(pause, rupture) break; (~ **de cou-rant**) power cut.

cour /kuʀ/ nf (court) yard; (du roi) court; (tribunal) court; (de récréation) playground; ~ **martiale** court-martial; **faire la** ~ **à** court.

courageux, -euse /kuʀaʒø, -z/ adj courageous.

couramment /kuʀamɑ̃/ adv frequently; (parler) fluently.

courant, ~e /kuʀɑ̃, -t/ adj standard, ordinary; (en cours) current. ● nm current; (de mode, d'idées) trend; ~ **d'air** draught; **dans le** ~ **de** in the course of; **être/mettre au** ~ know/tell about; (à jour) be/bring up to date on.

courbature /kuʀbatyʀ/ nf ache; **avoir des** ~s be stiff, ache.

courber /kuʀbe/ **1** vt bend.

coureur, -euse /kuʀœʀ, -øz/ nm, f (Sport) runner; ~ **automobile** racing driver; ~ **cycliste** racing cyclist. ● nm womanizer.

courgette /kuʀʒɛt/ nf courgette; (US) zucchini.

courir /kuʀiʀ/ **20** vi run; (se hâter) rush; (nouvelles) go round; ~ **après qn/qch** chase after sb/ sth. ● vt (risque) run; (danger) face; (épreuve sportive) run ou compete in; (fréquenter) do the rounds of; (filles) chase (after).

couronne /kuʀɔn/ nf crown; (de fleurs) wreath.

couronnement /kuʀɔnmɑ̃/ nm coronation, crowning; (fig) crowning achievement.

courriel /kuʀjɛl/ nm email.

courrier /kuʀje/ nm post, mail; (à écrire) letters; ~ **du cœur** problem page; ~ **électronique** email.

cours /kuʀ/ nm (leçon) class; (série de leçons) course; (prix) price; (cote) de valeur, denrée) price; (de

devises) exchange rate; (déroulement, d'une rivière) course; (allée) avenue; **au** ~ **de** in the course of; **avoir** ~ (monnaie) be legal tender; (fig) be current; (Scol) have a lesson; ~ **d'eau** river, stream; ~ **du soir** evening class; ~ **particulier** private lesson; ~ **magistral** (Univ) lecture; **en** ~ current; (travail) in progress; **en** ~ **de route** along the way.

course /kuʀs/ nf running; (épreuve de vitesse) race; (activité) racing; (entre rivaux: fig) race; (de projectile) flight; (voyage) journey; (commission) errand; ~s (achats) shopping; (de chevaux) races; **faire la** ~ **avec qn** race sb.

coursier, -ière /kuʀsje, -jɛʀ/ nm, f messenger.

court, ~e /kuʀ, -t/ adj short. ● adv short; **à** ~ **de** short of; **pris de** ~ caught unawares. ● nm ~ **(de tennis)** (tennis) court.

courtier, -ière /kuʀtje, -jɛʀ/ nm, f broker.

courtiser /kuʀtize/ **1** vt woo, court.

courtois, ~e /kuʀtwa, -z/ adj courteous. **courtoisie** nf courtesy.

cousin, ~e /kuzɛ̃, -in/ nm, f cousin; ~ **germain** first cousin.

coussin /kusɛ̃/ nm cushion.

coût /ku/ nm cost; **le** ~ **de la vie** the cost of living.

couteau (pl ~**x**) /kuto/ nm knife; ~ **à cran d'arrêt** flick knife.

coûter /kute/ **1** vt/i cost; **coûte que coûte** at all costs; **au prix coûtant** at cost (price).

couture /kutyʀ/ nf sewing; (métier) dressmaking; (points) seam. **couturier** nm fashion designer. **couturière** nf dressmaker.

couvée /kuve/ *nf* brood.

couvent /kuvã/ *nm* convent.

couver /kuve/ **1** *vt* (*œufs*) hatch; (*personne*) overprotect, pamper; (*maladie*) be coming down with, be sickening for. ● *vi* (*feu*) smoulder; (*mal*) be brewing.

couvercle /kuvɛʀkl/ *nm* (de marmite, boîte) lid; (qui se visse) screwtop.

couvert, ~e /kuvɛʀ, -t/ *adj* covered (**de** with); (habillé) covered up; (ciel) overcast. ● *nm* (à table) place setting; (prix) cover charge; ~s (couteaux etc.) cutlery; **mettre le** ~ la lay the table; (abri) cover; **à** ~ (Mil) under cover; **à** ~ **de** (fig) safe from.

couverture /kuvɛʀtyʀ/ *nf* cover; (de lit) blanket; (toit) roofing; (dans la presse) coverage; ~ **chauffante** electric blanket.

couvre-feu (*pl* ~**x**) /kuvʀəfø/ *nm* curfew.

couvre-lit (*pl* ~**s**) /kuvʀəli/ *nm* bedspread.

couvrir /kuvʀiʀ/ **21** *vt* cover. □ **se** ~ *vpr* (s'habiller) wrap up; (se coiffer) put one's hat on; (ciel) become overcast.

covoiturage /kɔvwatyʀaʒ/ *nm* car sharing.

cracher /kʀaʃe/ **1** *vi* spit; (radio) crackle. ● *vt* spit (out); (fumée) belch out.

crachin /kʀaʃɛ̃/ *nm* drizzle.

craie /kʀe/ *nf* chalk.

craindre /kʀɛ̃dʀ/ **22** *vt* be afraid of, fear; (être sensible à) be easily damaged by.

crainte /kʀɛ̃t/ *nf* fear (**pour** for); **de** ~ **de/que** for fear of/that.

craintif, **-ive** *adj* timid.

crampon /kʀãpõ/ *nm* (de chaussure) stud.

cramponner (se) /(sə)kʀãpɔne/ **1** *vpr* **se** ~ **à** cling to.

cran /kʀã/ *nm* (entaille) notch; (trou) hole; (courage **1**) guts **1**, courage; ~ **de sûreté** safety catch.

crâne /kʀɑn/ *nm* skull.

crapaud /kʀapo/ *nm* toad.

craquer /kʀake/ **1** *vi* crack, snap; (plancher) creak; (couture) split; (fig) (personne) break down; (céder) give in. ● *vt* (allumette) strike; (vêtement) split.

crasse /kʀas/ *nf* grime.

cravache /kʀavaʃ/ *nf* (horse) whip.

cravate /kʀavat/ *nf* tie.

crayon /kʀejõ/ *nm* pencil; ~ **de couleur** coloured pencil; ~ **à bille** ballpoint pen; ~ **optique** light pen.

créateur, **-trice** /kʀeatœʀ, -tʀis/ *adj* creative. ● *nm, f* creator, designer.

crèche /kʀɛʃ/ *nf* day nursery, crèche; (Relig) crib.

crédit /kʀedi/ *nm* credit; (somme allouée) funds; **à** ~ on credit; **faire** ~ give credit (**à** to).

créer /kʀee/ **15** *vt* create; (produit) design; (société) set up.

crémaillère /kʀemajɛʀ/ *nf* pendre la ~ have a housewarming party.

crème /kʀɛm/ *adj inv* cream. ● *nm* (café) ~ espresso with milk. ● *nf* cream; (dessert) cream dessert; ~ **anglaise** egg custard; ~ **fouettée** whipped cream; ~ **pâtissière** confectioner's custard. **crémerie** *nf* dairy. **crémeux**, **-euse** *adj* creamy. **crémier**, **-ière** *nm, f* dairyman, dairywoman.

créneau (*pl* ~**x**) /kʀeno/ *nm* (trou, moment) slot, window; (dans le marché) gap; **faire un** ~ to parallel-park.

crêpe /krɛp/ nf (galette) pancake. ● nm (tissu) crêpe; (matière) crêpe (rubber).

crépitement /krepitmã/ nm crackling; (d'huile) sizzling.

crépuscule /krepyskyl/ nm twilight, dusk.

cresson /krəsɔ̃/ nm (water) cress.

crête /krɛt/ nf crest; (de coq) comb.

crétin, ~e /kretɛ̃, -in/ nm, f 🗊 moron 🗊.

creuser /krøze/ 🗊 vt dig; (évider) hollow out; (fig) go into in depth. □ se ~ vpr (écart) widen; se ~ (la cervelle) 🗊 rack one's brains.

creux, -euse /krø, -z/ adj hollow; (heures) off-peak. ● nm hollow; (de l'estomac) pit; **dans le ~ de la main** in the palm of the hand.

crevaison /krəvɛzɔ̃/ nf puncture.

crevasse /krəvas/ nf crack; (de glacier) crevasse; (de la peau) chap.

crevé, ~e /krəve/ adj 🗊 worn out.

crever /krəve/ 🗊 vt burst; (pneu) puncture, burst; (exténuer 🗊) exhaust; (œil) put out. ● vi (pneu, sac) burst; (mourir 🗊) die.

crevette /krəvɛt/ nf ~ **grise** shrimp; ~ **rose** prawn.

cri /kri/ nm cry; (de douleur) scream, cry; **pousser un ~** cry out, scream.

criard, ~e /krijar, -d/ adj (couleur) garish; (voix) shrill.

crier /krije/ 45 vi (fort) shout, cry (out); (de douleur) scream; (grincer) creak. ● vt (ordre) shout (out).

crime /krim/ nm crime; (meurtre) murder.

criminel, ~le /kriminɛl/ adj criminal. ● nm, f criminal; (assassin) murderer.

crinière /krinjɛr/ nf mane.

crise /kriz/ nf crisis; (Méd) attack; (de colère) fit; ~ **cardiaque** heart attack; ~ **de foie** bilious attack; ~ **de nerfs** hysterics (+ pl).

crisper /krispe/ 🗊 vt tense; (énerver 🗊) irritate. □ se ~ vpr tense; (mains) clench.

critère /kritɛr/ nm criterion.

critique /kritik/ adj critical. ● nf criticism; (article) review; (commentateur) critic; **la ~** (personnes) the critics. **critiquer** 🗊 vt criticize.

Croate /krɔat/ adj Croatian. **C~** nmf Croatian.

Croatie /krɔasi/ nf Croatia.

croche /krɔʃ/ nf quaver.

croche-pied /krɔʃpje/ (pl **~s**) /krɔʃpje/ nm 🗊 **faire un ~ à** trip up.

crochet /krɔʃɛ/ nm hook; (détour) detour; (signe) (square) bracket; (tricot) crochet; **faire au ~** crochet.

crochu, ~e /krɔʃy/ adj hooked.

crocodile /krɔkɔdil/ nm crocodile.

croire /krwar/ 23 vt believe (à, en in); (estimer) think, believe (que that). ● vi believe.

croisade /krwazad/ nf crusade.

croisement /krwazmã/ nm crossing; (fait de passer à côté de) passing; (carrefour) crossroads.

croiser /krwaze/ 🗊 vt (bateau) cruise. ● vi (passant, véhicule) pass; ~ **les bras** fold one's arms; ~ **les jambes** cross one's legs; (animaux) crossbreed. □ se ~ vpr (véhicules, piétons) pass each other; (lignes) cross. **croisière** nf cruise.

croissance /krwasãs/ nf growth.

croissant, ~e /krwasã, -t/ adj growing. ● nm crescent; (pâtisserie) croissant.

croix /krwa/ nf cross; ~ **gammée** swastika; **C~-Rouge** Red Cross.

croquant, ~e /krɔkã, -t/ adj crunchy.

croque-monsieur /kʀɔkməsjø/ *nm inv* toasted ham and cheese sandwich.

croque-mort (*pl* ~**s**) /kʀɔkmɔʀ/ *nm* undertaker.

croquer /kʀɔke/ **1** *vt* crunch; (dessiner) sketch; **chocolat à** ~ plain chocolate. ● *vi* be crunchy.

croquis /kʀɔki/ *nm* sketch.

crotte /kʀɔt/ *nf* dropping.

crotté, ~e /kʀɔte/ *adj* muddy.

crottin /kʀɔtɛ̃/ *nm* (horse) dropping.

croupir /kʀupiʀ/ **2** *vi* stagnate.

croustillant, ~e /kʀustijɑ̃, -t/ *adj* crispy; (*pain*) crusty; (fig) spicy.

croûte /kʀut/ *nf* crust; (de fromage) rind; (de plaie) scab; **en** ~ (Culin) in pastry.

croûton /kʀutɔ̃/ *nm* (bout de pain) crust; (avec potage) croûton.

CRS *abrév m* (**Compagnie républicaine de sécurité**) French riot police; **un** ~ a member of the French riot police.

cru[1] /kʀy/ →CROIRE 23.

cru[2], **~e** /kʀy/ *adj* raw; (lumière) harsh; (*propos*) crude. ● *nm* vineyard; (vin) vintage wine.

crû /kʀy/ →CROÎTRE 24.

cruauté /kʀyote/ *nf* cruelty.

cruche /kʀyʃ/ *nf* jug, pitcher.

crucial, ~e (*mpl* **-iaux**) /kʀysjal, -jo/ *adj* crucial.

crudité /kʀydite/ *nf* (de langage) crudeness; **~s** (Culin) raw vegetables.

crue /kʀy/ *nf* rise in water level; **en** ~ in spate.

crustacé /kʀystase/ *nm* shellfish.

cube /kyb/ *nm* cube. ● *adj* (mètre) cubic.

cueillir /kœjiʀ/ 25 *vt* pick, gather; (*personne* 🔢) pick up.

cuiller, cuillère /kɥijɛʀ/ *nf* spoon; ~ **à soupe** soup spoon; (mesure) tablespoonful.

cuir /kɥiʀ/ *nm* leather; ~ **chevelu** scalp.

cuire /kɥiʀ/ 17 *vt* cook; ~ **(au four)** bake. ● *vi* cook; **faire** ~ cook.

cuisine /kɥizin/ *nf* kitchen; (art) cookery, cooking; (aliments) food; **faire la** ~ cook.

cuisiner /kɥizine/ **1** *vt* cook; (interroger 🔢) grill. ● *vi* cook.

cuisinier, -ière /kɥizinje, -jɛʀ/ *nm, f* cook. **cuisinière** *nf* (appareil) cooker, stove.

cuisse /kɥis/ *nf* thigh; (de poulet) thigh; (de grenouille) leg.

cuisson /kɥisɔ̃/ *nf* cooking.

cuit, ~e /kɥi, -t/ *adj* cooked; **bien** ~ well done *ou* cooked; **trop** ~ overdone.

cuivre /kɥivʀ/ *nm* copper; ~ **(jaune)** brass; **~s** (Mus) brass.

cul /ky/ *nm* (derrière 🔢) backside, bottom, arse 🔢.

culbuter /kylbyte/ **1** *vi* (personne) tumble; (objet) topple (over). ● *vt* knock over.

culminer /kylmine/ **1** *vi* reach its highest point *ou* peak.

culot /kylo/ *nm* (audace 🔢) nerve, cheek; (Tech) base.

culotte /kylɔt/ *nf* (de femme) pants (+ *pl*), knickers (+ *pl*); (US) panties (+ *pl*); ~ **de cheval** riding breeches; **en** ~ **courte** in short trousers.

culpabilité /kylpabilite/ *nf* guilt.

culte /kylt/ *nm* cult, worship; (religion) religion; (office protestant) service.

cultivateur, -trice /kyltivatœʀ, -tʀis/ *nm, f* farmer.

cultiver /kyltive/ **1** *vt* cultivate; (*plantes*) grow.

culture /kyltyʀ/ *nf* cultivation; (de plantes) growing; (agriculture) farming; (éducation) culture; (connaissances) knowledge; **~s** (terrains) lands under cultivation; **~ physique** physical training.

culturel, ~le /kyltyʀɛl/ *adj* cultural.

cumuler /kymyle/ **1** *vt* accumulate; (*fonctions*) hold concurrently.

cure /kyʀ/ *nf* (course of) treatment.

curé /kyʀe/ *nm* (parish) priest.

cure-dent (*pl* **~s**) /kyʀdɑ̃/ *nm* toothpick.

curer /kyʀe/ **1** *vt* clean. □ **se ~** *vpr* **se ~ les dents/ongles** clean one's teeth/nails.

curieux, -ieuse /kyʀjø, -z/ *adj* curious. ● *nm, f* (badaud) onlooker.

curiosité /kyʀjozite/ *nf* curiosity; (objet) curio; (spectacle) unusual sight.

curriculum vitae /kyʀikylɔm vite/ *nm inv* curriculum vitae; (US) résumé.

curseur /kyʀsœʀ/ *nm* cursor.

cutané, ~e /kytane/ *adj* skin.

cuve /kyv/ *nf* vat; (à mazout, eau) tank.

cuvée /kyve/ *nf* (de vin) vintage.

cuvette /kyvɛt/ *nf* bowl; (de lavabo) (wash) basin; (des cabinets) pan, bowl.

CV *abrév m* (**curriculum vitae**) CV.

cyberbranché, ~e /sibɛʀbʀɑ̃ʃe/ *adj* cyberwired.

cybercafé /sibɛʀkafe/ *nm* cybercafe.

cyberespace /sibɛʀɛspas/ *nm* cyberspace.

cybernaute /sibɛʀnot/ *nmf* Netsurfer.

cybernétique /sibɛʀnetik/ *nf* cybernetics (+ *pl*).

cyclisme /siklism/ *nm* cycling.

cycliste /siklist/ *nmf* cyclist. ● *nm* cycling shorts. ● *adj* cycle.

cyclone /siklon/ *nm* cyclone.

cygne /siɲ/ *nm* swan.

cynique /sinik/ *adj* cynical. ● *nm* cynic.

Dd

d' /d/ ⇒DE.

d'abord /dabɔʀ/ *adv* first; (au début) at first.

dactylo /daktilo/ *nf* typist. **dactylographier** **45** *vt* type.

dada /dada/ *nm* hobby-horse.

daim /dɛ̃/ *nm* (fallow) deer; (cuir) suede.

dallage /dalaʒ/ *nm* paving. **dalle** *nf* slab.

daltonien, ~ne /daltɔnjɛ̃, -ɛn/ *adj* colour-blind.

dame /dam/ *nf* lady; (cartes, échecs) queen; **~s** (jeu) draughts; (US) checkers.

damier /damje/ *nm* draught board; (US) checker-board; **à ~** chequered.

damner /dane/ **1** *vt* damn.

dandiner (se) /(sə)dɑ̃dine/ **1** *vpr* waddle.

Danemark /danmaʀk/ *nm* Denmark.

danger /dɑ̃ʒe/ *nm* danger; **en ~** in danger; **mettre en ~** endanger.

dangereux, -euse /dɑ̃ʒ(ə)ʀø, -z/ *adj* dangerous.

danois, ~e /danwa, -z/ *adj* Danish. ● *nm* (Ling) Danish. **D~, ~e** *nm, f* Dane.

dans | débit

78

dans /dɑ̃/ *prép* in; (mouvement) into; (à l'intérieur de) inside, in; être ∼ **un avion** be on a plane; ∼ **dix jours** in ten days' time; **boire** ∼ **un verre** drink out of a glass; ∼ **les 10 euros** about 10 euros.

danse /dɑ̃s/ *nf* dance; (art) dancing.

danser /dɑ̃se/ **1** *vt/i* dance. **danseur, -euse** *nm, f* dancer.

darne /daʀn/ *nf* steak (of fish).

date /dat/ *nf* date; ∼ **limite** deadline; ∼ **limite de vente** sell-by date; ∼ **de péremption** use-by date.

dater /date/ **1** *vt/i* date; **à** ∼ **de** as from.

datte /dat/ *nf* (fruit) date.

daube /dob/ *nf* casserole.

dauphin /dofɛ̃/ *nm* (animal) dolphin.

davantage /davɑ̃taʒ/ *adv* more; (plus longtemps) longer; ∼ **de** more; **je n'en sais pas** ∼ that's as much as I know.

de, d' /də, d/

d' before vowel or mute h.

● **préposition**

····▸ of; **le livre** ∼ **mon ami** my friend's book; **un pont** ∼ **fer** an iron bridge.

····▸ (provenance) from.

····▸ (temporel) from; ∼ **8 heures à 10 heures** from 8 till 10.

····▸ (mesure, manière) **dix mètres** ∼ **haut** ten metres high; **pleurer** ∼ **rage** cry with rage.

····▸ (agent) by; **un livre** ∼ **Marcel Aymé** a book by Marcel Aymé.

● **de, de l', de la, du**, (*pl* **des**) *déterminant*

····▸ some; **du pain** (some) bread; **des fleurs** (some) flowers; **je ne bois jamais** ∼ **vin** I never drink wine.

de + le = du
de + les = des

dé /de/ *nm* (à jouer) dice; (à coudre) thimble; ∼s (jeu) dice.

débâcle /debɑkl/ *nf* (Géog) breaking up; (Mil) rout.

déballer /debale/ **1** *vt* unpack; (révéler) spill out.

débarbouiller /debaʀbuje/ *vt* wash the face of. □ **se** ∼ *vpr* wash one's face.

débarcadère /debaʀkadɛʀ/ *nm* landing-stage.

débardeur /debaʀdœʀ/ *nm* (vêtement) tank top.

débarquement /debaʀkəmɑ̃/ *nm* disembarkation. **débarquer** **1** *vt/i* disembark, land; (arriver 🔢) turn up.

débarras /debaʀa/ *nm* junk room; **bon** ∼! good riddance!

débarrasser /debaʀase/ **1** *vt* clear (**de** of); ∼ **qn de** relieve sb of; (défaut, ennemi) rid sb of. □ **se** ∼ **de** *vpr* get rid of.

débat /deba/ *nm* debate.

débattre /debatʀ/ **11** *vt* debate. ● *vi* ∼ **de** discuss. □ **se** ∼ *vpr* struggle (to get free).

débauche /deboʃ/ *nf* debauchery; (fig) profusion.

débaucher /deboʃe/ **1** *vt* (licencier) lay off; (distraire) tempt away.

débile /debil/ *adj* weak; 🔢 stupid. ● *nmf* moron 🔢.

débit /debi/ *nm* (rate of) flow; (élocution) delivery; (de compte) debit; ∼ **de tabac** tobacconist's shop; ∼ **de boissons** bar; **haut** ∼

broadband.

débiter /debite/ **1** vt (compte) debit; (fournir) produce; (vendre) sell; (dire: péj) spout; (couper) cut up.

débiteur, -trice /debitœR, -tRis/ nm, f debtor. ● adj (compte) in debit.

déblayer /debleje/ **31** vt clear.

déblocage /deblɔkaʒ/ nm (de prix) deregulating. **débloquer** **1** vt (prix, salaires) unfreeze.

déboiser /debwaze/ **1** vt clear (of trees).

déboîter /debwate/ **1** vi (véhicule) pull out. ● vt (membre) dislocate.

débordement /debɔrdəmã/ nm (de joie) excess.

déborder /debɔrde/ **1** vi overflow. ● vt (dépasser) extend beyond; ~ de (joie etc.) be brimming over with.

débouché /debuʃe/ nm opening; (carrière) prospect; (Comm) outlet; (sortie) end, exit.

déboucher /debuʃe/ **1** vt (bouteille) uncork; (évier) unblock. ● vi come out (de from); ~ sur (rue) lead into.

débourser /deburse/ **1** vt pay out.

debout /dəbu/ adv standing; (levé, éveillé) up; être ~, se tenir ~ be standing, stand; se mettre ~ stand up.

déboutonner /debutɔne/ **1** vt unbutton. □ se ~ vpr unbutton oneself; (vêtement) come undone.

débrancher /debrãʃe/ **1** vt (prise) unplug; (système) disconnect.

débrayer /debreje/ **31** vi (Auto) declutch; (faire grève) stop work.

débris /debri/ nmpl fragments; (détritus) rubbish (+ sg); debris.

débrouillard, ~e /debrujar, -d/ adj **1** resourceful.

débrouiller /debruje/ **1** vt disentangle; (problème) solve. □ se ~ vpr manage.

début /deby/ nm beginning; faire ses ~s (en public) make one's début; à mes ~s when I started out. **débutant, ~e** nm, f beginner. **débuter** **1** vi begin; (dans un métier etc.) start out.

déca /deka/ nm **1** decaf.

deçà: en ~ /ãdəsa/ loc this side. ● prép en ~ de this side of.

décacheter /dekaʃte/ **6** vt open.

décade /dekad/ nf ten days; (décennie) decade.

décadent, ~e /dekadã, -t/ adj decadent.

décalage /dekalaʒ/ nm (écart) gap; ~ horaire time difference. **décaler** **1** vt shift.

décalquer /dekalke/ **1** vt trace.

décamper /dekãpe/ **1** vi clear off.

décanter /dekãte/ vt allow to settle. □ se ~ vpr settle.

décapant /dekapã/ nm chemical agent; (pour peinture) paint stripper. ● adj (humour) caustic.

décapotable /dekapɔtabl/ adj convertible.

décapsuleur /dekapsylœR/ nm bottle-opener.

décédé, ~e /desede/ adj deceased. **décéder** **14** vi die.

déceler /desle/ **6** vt detect; (démontrer) reveal.

décembre /desãbr/ nm December.

décemment /desamã/ adv decently. **décence** nf decency. **décent, ~e** adj decent.

décennie /deseni/ nf decade.

décentralisation /desã tralizasjɔ̃/ nf decentralization. **décentraliser** **1** vt decentralize.

déception /desɛpsjɔ̃/ *nf* disappointment.

décerner /desɛʁne/ **1** *vt* award.

décès /desɛ/ *nm* death.

décevant, ~e /des(ə)vɑ̃, -t/ *adj* disappointing. **décevoir** **52** *vt* disappoint.

déchaîner /deʃene/ **1** *vt* (*enthousiasme*) rouse. □ **se ~** *vpr* go wild.

décharge /deʃaʁʒ/ *nf* (*de fusil*) discharge; **~ électrique** electric shock; **~ publique** municipal dump.

décharger /deʃaʁʒe/ **40** *vt* unload; **~ qn de** relieve sb from. □ **se ~** *vpr* (*batterie, pile*) go flat.

déchausser (se) /(sə)deʃose/ *vpr* take off one's shoes; (*dent*) work loose.

dèche /dɛʃ/ *nf* **1** **dans la ~** broke.

déchéance /deʃeɑ̃s/ *nf* decay.

déchet /deʃɛ/ *nm* (*reste*) scrap; (*perte*) waste; **~s** (*ordures*) refuse.

déchiffrer /deʃifʁe/ **1** *vt* decipher.

déchiqueter /deʃikte/ **38** *vt* tear to shreds.

déchirement /deʃiʁmɑ̃/ *nm* heartbreak; (*conflit*) split.

déchirer /deʃiʁe/ **1** *vt* (*par accident*) tear; (*lacérer*) tear up; (*arracher*) tear off *ou* out; (*diviser*) tear apart. □ **se ~** *vpr* tear. **déchirure** *nf* tear.

décibel /desibɛl/ *nm* decibel.

décidément /desidemɑ̃/ *adv* really.

décider /deside/ **1** *vt* decide on; (*persuader*) persuade; **~ que/de** decide that/to; **~ de qch** decide on sth. □ **se ~** *vpr* make up one's mind (**à** to).

décimal, ~e (*mpl* **~aux**) /desimal, -o/ *adj* & *nf* decimal.

décisif, -ive /desizif, -v/ *adj* decisive.

décision /desizjɔ̃/ *nf* decision.

déclaration /deklaʁasjɔ̃/ *nf* declaration; (*commentaire politique*) statement; **~ d'impôts** tax return.

déclarer /deklaʁe/ **1** *vt* declare; (*naissance*) register; **déclaré coupable** found guilty; **~ forfait** (*Sport*) withdraw. □ **se ~** *vpr* (*feu*) break out.

déclencher /deklɑ̃ʃe/ **1** *vt* (*Tech*) set off; (*conflit*) spark off; (*avalanche*) start; (*rire*) provoke. □ **se ~** *vpr* (*Tech*) go off. **déclencheur** *nm* (*Photo*) shutter release.

déclic /deklik/ *nm* click.

déclin /deklɛ̃/ *nm* decline.

déclinaison /deklinɛzɔ̃/ *nf* (*Ling*) declension.

décliner /dekline/ **1** *vt* (*refuser*) decline; (*dire*) state; (*Ling*) decline.

décocher /dekɔʃe/ *vt* (*coup*) fling; (*regard*) shoot.

décollage /dekɔlaʒ/ *nm* take-off.

décoller /dekɔle/ **1** *vt* unstick. ● *vi* (*avion*) take off. □ **se ~** *vpr* come off.

décolleté, ~e /dekɔlte/ *adj* low-cut. ● *nm* low neckline.

décolorer /dekɔlɔʁe/ **1** *vt* fade; (*cheveux*) bleach. □ **se ~** *vpr* fade.

décombres /dekɔ̃bʁ/ *nmpl* rubble.

décommander /dekɔmɑ̃de/ **1** *vt* cancel.

décomposer /dekɔ̃poze/ **1** *vt* break up; (*substance*) decompose. □ **se ~** *vpr* (*pourrir*) decompose.

décompte /dekɔ̃t/ *nm* deduction; (*détail*) breakdown.

décongeler /dekɔ̃ʒle/ **6** *vt* thaw.

déconseillé, ~e /dekɔ̃seje/ *adj* not recommended, inadvisable.

déconseiller /dekɔ̃seje/ **1** *vt* ~

qch à qn advise sb against sth.

décontracté, ~e /dekɔ̃trakte/ *adj* relaxed.

déconvenue /dekɔ̃vny/ *nf* disappointment.

décor /dekɔr/ *nm* (paysage) scenery; (de cinéma, théâtre) set; (cadre) setting; (de maison) décor.

décoratif, -ive /dekɔratif, -v/ *adj* decorative.

décorateur, -trice /dekɔratœr, -tris/ *nm, f* (de cinéma) set designer. **décoration** *nf* decoration. **décorer** **1** *vt* decorate.

décortiquer /dekɔrtike/ **1** *vt* shell; (fig) dissect.

découdre (se) /(sə)dekudr/ **19** *vpr* come unstitched.

découler /dekule/ **1** *vi* ~ **de** follow from.

découper /dekupe/ **1** *vt* cut up; (viande) carve; (détacher) cut out.

découragement /dekuraʒmɑ̃/ *nm* discouragement.

décourager /dekuraʒe/ **40** *vt* discourage. □ **se** ~ *vpr* become discouraged.

décousu, ~e /dekuzy/ *adj* (vêtement) which has come unstitched; (idées) disjointed.

découvert, ~e /dekuver, -t/ *adj* (tête) bare; (terrain) open. ● *nm* (de compte) overdraft; **à** ~ exposed; (fig) openly.

découverte /dekuvert/ *nf* discovery; **à la** ~ **de** in search of.

découvrir /dekuvrir/ **21** *vt* discover; (voir) see; (montrer) reveal. □ **se** ~ *vpr* (se décoiffer) take one's hat off; (ciel) clear.

décrasser /dekrase/ **1** *vt* clean.

décrépit, ~e /dekrepi, -t/ *adj* decrepit. **décrépitude** *nf* decay.

décret /dekrɛ/ *nm* decree. **décréter** **14** *vt* order; (dire) declare.

décrié, ~e /dekrije/ *adj* criticized.

décrire /dekrir/ **30** *vt* describe.

décroché, ~e /dekrɔʃe/ *adj* (téléphone) off the hook.

décrocher /dekrɔʃe/ **1** *vt* unhook; (obtenir **1**) get. ● *vi* (abandonner **1**) give up; ~ **(le téléphone)** pick up the phone.

décroître /dekrwatr/ **24** *vi* decrease.

déçu, ~e /desy/ *adj* disappointed.

décupler /dekyple/ **1** *vt/i* increase tenfold.

dédaigner /dedɛɲe/ **1** *vt* scorn. **dédain** /dedɛ̃/ *nm* scorn.

dédale /dedal/ *nm* maze.

dedans /dədɑ̃/ *adv & nm* inside; **en** ~ on the inside.

dédicacer /dedikase/ **10** *vt* dedicate; (signer) sign.

dédier /dedje/ **45** *vt* dedicate.

dédommagement /dedɔmaʒmɑ̃/ *nm* compensation. **dédommager** **40** *vt* compensate (de for).

déduction /dedyksjɔ̃/ *nf* deduction; ~ **d'impôts** tax deduction.

déduire /deduir/ **17** *vt* deduct; (conclure) deduce.

déesse /deɛs/ *nf* goddess.

défaillance /defajɑ̃s/ *nf* (panne) failure; (évanouissement) blackout. **défaillant, ~e** *adj* (système) faulty; (personne) faint.

défaire /defɛr/ **33** *vt* undo; (valise) unpack; (démonter) take down. □ **se** ~ *vpr* come undone; **se** ~ **de** rid oneself of.

défait, ~e /defɛ, -t/ *adj* (cheveux) ruffled; (visage) haggard; (nœud) undone. **défaite** *nf* defeat.

défaitiste /defetist/ *adj & nmf* defeatist.

défalquer /defalke/ **1** *vt* (somme)

deduct.

défaut /defo/ *nm* fault, defect; (d'un verre, diamant, etc.) flaw; (pénurie) shortage; **à ~ de** for lack of; **pris en ~** caught out; **faire ~** (*argent etc.*) be lacking; **par ~** (Jur) in one's absence; **~ de paiement** non-payment.

défavorable /defavɔʀabl/ *adj* unfavourable.

défavoriser /defavɔʀize/ **1** *vt* discriminate against.

défectueux, -euse /defɛktɥø, -z/ *adj* faulty, defective.

défendre /defɑ̃dʀ/ **3** *vt* defend; (interdire) forbid; **~ à qn de** forbid sb to. □ **se ~** *vpr* defend oneself; (se protéger) protect oneself; (se débrouiller) manage; **se ~ de** (refuser) refrain from.

défense /defɑ̃s/ *nf* defence; **~ de fumer** no smoking; (d'éléphant) tusk. **défenseur** *nm* defender. **défensif, -ive** *adj* defensive.

déferler /defɛʀle/ **1** *vi* (vagues) break; (violence) erupt.

défi /defi/ *nm* challenge; (provocation) defiance; **mettre au ~** challenge.

déficience /defisjɑ̃s/ *nf* deficiency. **déficient, ~e** *adj* deficient.

déficit /defisit/ *nm* deficit. **déficitaire** *adj* in deficit.

défier /defje/ **45** *vt* challenge; (braver) defy.

défilé /defile/ *nm* procession; (Mil) parade; (fig) (continual) stream; (Géog) gorge; **~ de mode** fashion parade.

défiler /defile/ **1** *vi* march; (visiteurs) stream; (images) flash by; (chiffres, minutes) add up. □ **se ~** *vpr* **1** sneak off.

défini, ~e /defini/ *adj* (Ling) definite.

définir /definiʀ/ **2** *vt* define.

définitif, -ive /definitif, -v/ *adj* final, definitive; **en définitive** in the end.

définition /definisjɔ̃/ *nf* definition; (de mots croisés) clue.

définitivement /definitivmɑ̃/ *adv* definitively, permanently.

déflagration /deflagʀasjɔ̃/ *nf* explosion.

déflation /deflasjɔ̃/ *nf* deflation. **déflationniste** *adj* deflationary.

défoncé, ~e /defɔ̃se/ *adj* (terrain) full of potholes; (siège) broken; (drogué: ▯) high.

défoncer /defɔ̃se/ **10** *vt* (porte) break down; (mâchoire) break. □ **se ~** *vpr* **1** to give one's all.

déformation /defɔʀmasjɔ̃/ *nf* distortion. **déformer** **1** *vt* put out of shape; (faits, pensée) distort.

défouler (se) /(sa)defule/ **1** *vpr* let off steam.

défrayer /defʀeje/ **31** *vt* (payer) pay the expenses of; **~ la chronique** be the talk of the town.

défricher /defʀiʃe/ **1** *vt* clear.

défroisser /defʀwase/ **1** *vt* smooth out.

défunt, ~e /defœ̃, -t/ *adj* (mort) late. ● *nm, f* deceased.

dégagé, ~e /degaʒe/ *adj* (ciel) clear; (front) bare; **d'un ton ~** casually.

dégagement /degaʒmɑ̃/ *nm* clearing; (football) clearance.

dégager /degaʒe/ **40** *vt* (exhaler) give off; (désencombrer) clear; (faire ressortir) bring out; (ballon) clear. □ **se ~** *vpr* free oneself; (ciel, rue) clear; (odeur) emanate.

dégarnir (se) /(sa)degaʀniʀ/ **2** *vpr* clear, empty; (personne) be going bald.

dégâts /dega/ *nmpl* damage (+ sg).

dégel | délégué

dégel /deʒɛl/ *nm* thaw. **dégeler** 🖸 *vi* thaw (out).

dégénéré, ~e /deʒenere/ *adj & nm,f* degenerate.

dégivrer /deʒivre/ 🛈 *vt* (Auto) de-ice; (*réfrigérateur*) defrost.

déglinguer /deglɛ̃ge/ 🛈 🛈 *vt* bust. □ **se ~** *vpr* break down.

dégonflé, ~e /degɔ̃fle/ *adj* (*pneu*) flat; (*lâche* 🛈) yellow.

dégonfler /degɔ̃fle/ 🛈 *vt* deflate. ● *vi* (*blessure*) go down. □ **se ~** *vpr* 🛈 chicken out.

dégouliner /deguline/ 🛈 *vi* trickle.

dégourdi, ~e /degurdi/ *adj* smart.

dégourdir /degurdir/ 🛽 *vt* (*membre, liquide*) warm up. □ **se ~** *vpr* **se ~ les jambes** stretch one's legs.

dégoût /degu/ *nm* disgust.

dégoûtant, ~e /degutã, -t/ *adj* disgusting.

dégoûter /degute/ 🛈 *vt* disgust; **~ qn de qch** put sb off sth.

dégradant, ~e /degradã, -t/ *adj* degrading.

dégradation /degradasjɔ̃/ *nf* damage; **commettre des ~s** cause damage.

dégrader /degrade/ 🛈 *vt* (*abîmer*) damage. □ **se ~** *vpr* (*se détériorer*) deteriorate.

dégrafer /degrafe/ 🛈 *vt* unhook.

degré /dəgre/ *nm* degree; (*d'escalier*) step.

dégressif, -ive /degresif, -v/ *adj* graded; **tarif ~** tapering charge.

dégrèvement /degrɛvmã/ *nm* **~ fiscal** *ou* **d'impôts** tax reduction.

dégringolade /degrɛ̃gɔlad/ *nf* tumble.

dégringoler /degrɛ̃gɔle/ 🛈 *vi* tumble. ● *vt* (*escalier*) rush down.

dégrossir /degrosir/ 🛽 *vt* (*bois*) trim; (*projet*) rough out.

déguerpir /degɛrpir/ 🛽 *vi* clear off.

dégueulasse /degœlas/ *adj* 🗵 disgusting, lousy.

dégueuler /degœle/ 🛈 *vt* 🗵 throw up.

déguisement /degizmã/ *nm* (de carnaval) fancy dress; (pour duper) disguise.

déguiser /degize/ 🛈 *vt* dress up; (pour duper) disguise. □ **se ~** *vpr* (au carnaval etc.) dress up; (pour duper) disguise oneself.

déguster /degyste/ 🛈 *vt* taste, sample; (savourer) enjoy.

dehors /dəɔr/ *adv* **en ~ de** outside; (hormis) apart from; **jeter/mettre ~** throw/put out. ● *nm* outside. ● *nmpl* (aspect de qn) exterior.

déjà /deʒa/ *adv* already; (avant) before, already.

déjeuner /deʒœne/ 🛈 *vi* have lunch; (le matin) have breakfast. ● *nm* lunch; **petit ~** breakfast.

delà /dəla/ *adv & prép* **au ~ (de)** **par ~** beyond.

délai /dele/ *nm* time-limit; (attente) wait; (sursis) extension (of time); **sans ~** immediately; **dans un ~ de 2 jours** within 2 days; **finir dans les ~s** finish within the deadline; **dans les plus brefs ~s** as soon as possible.

délaisser /delese/ 🛈 *vt* (négliger) neglect.

délassement /delasmã/ *nm* relaxation.

délation /delasjɔ̃/ *nf* informing.

délavé, ~e /delave/ *adj* faded.

délayer /deleje/ 🛽 *vt* mix (with liquid); (idée) pad out.

délecter (se) /(sə)delɛkte/ 🛈 *vpr* **se ~ de** delight in.

délégué, ~e /delege/ *nm, f*

delegate.

délibéré, ~e /delibere/ adj deliberate; (résolu) determined.

délicat, ~e /delika, -t/ adj delicate; (plein de tact) tactful. **délicatesse** nf delicacy; (tact) tact. **délicatesses** nfpl (kind) attentions.

délice /delis/ nm delight. **délicieux**, **-ieuse** adj (au goût) delicious; (charmant) delightful.

délier /delje/ 45 vt untie; (délivrer) free. □ se ~ vpr come untied.

délimiter /delimite/ 1 vt determine, demarcate.

délinquance /delɛ̃kɑ̃s/ nf delinquency. **délinquant**, ~e adj & nm, f delinquent.

délirant, ~e /delirɑ̃, -t/ adj delirious; (frénétique) frenzied; ▣ wild.

délire /delir/ nm delirium; (fig) frenzy. **délirer** 1 vi be delirious (de with); ▣ be off one's rocker ▣.

délit /deli/ nm offence.

délivrance /delivrɑ̃s/ nf release; (soulagement) relief; (remise) issue. **délivrer** 1 vt free, release; (pays) liberate; (remettre) issue.

déloyal, ~e (mpl **-aux**) /delwajal, -jo/ adj disloyal; (procédé) unfair.

deltaplane /dɛltaplan/ nm hang-glider.

déluge /delyʒ/ nm downpour; **le D~** the Flood.

démagogie /demagɔʒi/ nf demagogy. **démagogue** nmf demagogue.

demain /dəmɛ̃/ adv tomorrow.

demande /dəmɑ̃d/ nf request; ~ d'emploi job application; ~ en mariage marriage proposal.

demander /dəmɑ̃de/ 1 vt ask for; (chemin, heure) ask; (nécessiter) require; ~ que/si ask that/if; ~ qch à qn ask sb sth; ~ à qn de ask sb to; ~ en mariage propose to. □ se ~ vpr se ~ si/où wonder if/where.

demandeur, **-euse** /dəmɑ̃dœr, -øz/ nm, f ~ **d'emploi** job seeker; ~ **d'asile** asylum-seeker.

démangeaison /demɑ̃ʒezɔ̃/ nf itch(ing).

démanteler /demɑ̃tle/ 6 vt break up.

démaquillant /demakijɑ̃/ nm make-up remover. **démaquiller** (se) vpr remove one's make-up.

démarchage /demarʃaʒ/ nm door-to-door selling.

démarche /demarʃ/ nf walk, gait; (procédé) step.

démarcheur, **-euse** /demarʃœr, -øz/ nm, f (door-to-door) canvasser.

démarrage /demaraʒ/ nm start.

démarrer /demare/ 1 vi (moteur) start (up); (partir) move off; (fig) get moving. ● vt ▣ get moving.

démarreur /demarœr/ nm starter.

démêlant /demelɑ̃/ nm conditioner. **démêler** 1 vt disentangle.

déménagement /demenaʒmɑ̃/ nm move; (transport) removal.

déménager /demenaʒe/ 40 vi move (house). ● vt (meubles) remove.

déménageur /demenaʒœr/ nm removal man.

démence /demɑ̃s/ nf insanity.

démener (se) /(sə)demne/ 6 vpr move about wildly; (fig) put oneself out.

dément, ~e /demɑ̃, -t/ adj insane. ● nm, f lunatic.

démenti /demɑ̃ti/ nm denial.

démentir /demɑ̃tir/ 46 vt deny; (contredire) refute; ~ que deny that.

démerder (se) /(sə)demɛrde/ 1 vpr ▣ manage.

démettre /demɛtʀ/ 42 vt (*poignet etc.*) dislocate; ~ **qn de** relieve sb of. □ **se ~ de** *vpr* resign (de from).

demeure /dəmœʀ/ nf residence; **mettre en ~ de** order to.

demeurer /dəmœʀe/ 1 vi live; (*rester*) remain.

demi, ~e /dəmi/ adj half(-). ● nm, f half. ● nm (*bière*) (half-pint) glass of beer; (football) half-back. ● adv **à ~** half; (*ouvrir, fermer*) halfway; **à la ~e** at half past; **une heure et ~e** an hour and a half; (à l'horloge) half past one; **une ~-journée-livre** half a day/pound. **demi-cercle** (*pl* ~**s**) nm semicircle. **demi-finale** (*pl* ~**s**) nf semifinal. **demi-frère** (*pl* ~**s**) nm half-brother, stepbrother. **demi-heure** (*pl* ~**s**) nf half-hour, half an hour. **demi-litre** (*pl* ~**s**) nm half a litre. **demi-mesure** (*pl* ~**s**) nf half-measure. **à demi mot** adv without having to express every word. **demi-pension** nf half-board. **demi-queue** nm boudoir grand piano.

demi-sel adj inv slightly salted.

demi-sœur (*pl* ~**s**) nf half-sister, stepsister.

démission /demisjɔ̃/ nf resignation.

demi-tarif (*pl* ~**s**) /dəmitaʀif/ nm half-fare.

demi-tour (*pl* ~**s**) /dəmituʀ/ nm about turn; (Auto) U-turn; **faire ~** turn back.

démocrate /demɔkʀat/ nmf democrat. ● adj democratic. **démocratie** nf democracy.

démodé, ~e /demode/ adj old-fashioned.

demoiselle /dəmwazɛl/ nf young lady; (*célibataire*) single lady; ~ **d'honneur** bridesmaid.

démolir /demɔliʀ/ 2 vt demolish.

démon /demɔ̃/ nm demon; **le D~**

the Devil. **démoniaque** adj fiendish.

démonstration /demɔ̃stʀasjɔ̃/ nf demonstration; (de force) show.

démonter /demɔ̃te/ 1 vt take apart, dismantle; (*installation*) take down; (fig) disconcert. □ **se ~** *vpr* come apart.

démontrer /demɔ̃tʀe/ 1 vt demonstrate; (indiquer) show.

démoraliser /demɔʀalize/ 1 vt demoralize.

démuni, ~e /demyni/ adj impoverished; ~ **de** without.

démunir /demyniʀ/ 2 vt ~ **de** deprive of. □ **se ~ de** *vpr* part with.

dénaturer /denatyʀe/ 1 vt (*faits*) distort.

dénigrement /denigʀəmɑ̃/ nm denigration.

dénivellation /denivelasjɔ̃/ nf (pente) slope.

dénombrer /denɔ̃bʀe/ 1 vt count.

dénomination /denɔminasjɔ̃/ nf designation.

dénommé, ~e /denɔme/ nm, f **le ~ X** the said X.

dénoncer /denɔ̃se/ 10 vt denounce. □ **se ~** *vpr* give oneself up. **dénonciateur, -trice** nm, f informer.

dénouement /denumɑ̃/ nm outcome; (Théât) dénouement.

dénouer /denwe/ 1 vt undo. □ **se ~** *vpr* (*nœud*) come undone.

dénoyauter /denwajote/ 1 vt stone.

denrée /dɑ̃ʀe/ nf ~ **alimentaire** foodstuff.

dense /dɑ̃s/ adj dense. **densité** nf density.

dent /dɑ̃/ nf tooth; **faire ses ~s** teethe; ~ **de lait** milk tooth; ~ **de sagesse** wisdom tooth; (de roue) cog. **dentaire** adj dental.

denté, ~e /dɑ̃te/ adj (roue) toothed

dentelé, ~e /dɑ̃tle/ adj jagged.

dentelle /dɑ̃tɛl/ nf lace.

dentier /dɑ̃tje/ nm dentures (+ pl), false teeth (+ pl).

dentifrice /dɑ̃tifʁis/ nm toothpaste.

dentiste /dɑ̃tist/ nmf dentist.

dentition /dɑ̃tisjɔ̃/ nf teeth, dentition.

dénudé, ~e /denyde/ adj bare.

dénué, ~e /denye/ adj ~ de devoid of.

dénuement /denymɑ̃/ nm destitution.

déodorant /deodoʁɑ̃/ nm deodorant.

dépannage /depanaʒ/ nm repair; (Ordinat) troubleshooting. **dépanner** 1 vt repair; (fig) help out. **dépanneuse** nf breakdown lorry.

dépareillé, ~e /depaʁeje/ adj odd, not matching.

départ /depaʁ/ nm departure; (Sport) start; **au ~ de Nice** from Nice; **au ~** (d'abord) at first.

département /depaʁtəmɑ̃/ nm department.

Département An administrative unit, of which there are 96 in Metropolitan France, most are named after rivers or mountains within their borders. Each *département* has a number which appears as the first two digits in postcodes for addresses within the *département* and as the final two-digit number in vehicle registration numbers. See ▸**RÉGION**.

---

dépassé, ~e /depase/ adj outdated.

dépasser /depase/ 1 vt go past, pass; (véhicule) overtake; (excéder) exceed; (rival) surpass; **ça me dépasse** 1 it's beyond me. ● vi stick out.

dépaysement /depeizmɑ̃/ nm change of scenery; (désagréable) disorientation.

dépêche /depɛʃ/ nf dispatch.

dépêcher /depeʃe/ 1 vt dispatch. □ **se** ~ vpr hurry (up).

dépendance /depɑ̃dɑ̃s/ nf dependence; (à une drogue) dependency; (bâtiment) outbuilding.

dépendre /depɑ̃dʁ/ 3 vt take down. ● vi depend (~ de on); ~ **de** (appartenir à) belong to.

dépens /depɑ̃/ nmpl **aux** ~ **de** at the expense of.

dépense /depɑ̃s/ nf expense; expenditure.

dépenser /depɑ̃se/ 1 vt/i spend; (énergie etc.) use up. □ **se** ~ vpr get some exercise.

dépérir /depeʁiʁ/ 2 vi wither.

dépêtrer (se) /(sə)depetʁe/ 1 vpr get oneself out (**de** of).

dépeupler /depœple/ 1 vt depopulate. □ **se** ~ vpr become depopulated.

déphasé, ~e /defazo/ adj 1 out of step.

dépilatoire /depilatwaʁ/ adj & nm depilatory.

dépistage /depistaʒ/ nm screening. **dépister** 1 vt detect; (criminel) track down.

dépit /depi/ nm resentment; **par** ~ out of pique; **en** ~ **de** despite; **en** ~ **du bon sens** in a very illogical way. **dépité**, ~e adj vexed.

déplacé, ~e /deplase/ adj (remarque) uncalled for.

déplacement /deplasmɑ̃/ nm

(voyage) trip.

déplacer /deplase/ **10** vt move.
□ **se ~** vpr move; (voyager) travel.

déplaire /deplɛʀ/ **47** vi **~ à** (irriter) displease; **ça me déplaît** I don't like it.

déplaisant, ~e /deplɛzɑ̃, -t/ adj unpleasant, disagreeable.

dépliant /deplijɑ̃/ nm leaflet.

déplier /deplije/ **45** vt unfold.

déploiement /deplwamɑ̃/ nm (démonstration) display; (militaire) deployment.

déplorable /deplɔʀabl/ adj deplorable. **déplorer** **1** vt (trouver regrettable) deplore; (mort) lament.

déployer /deplwaje/ **31** vt (ailes, carte) spread; (courage) display; (armée) deploy.

déportation /depɔʀtasjɔ̃/ nf (en 1940) internment in a concentration camp.

déposer /depoze/ **1** vt put down; (laisser) leave; (passager) drop; (argent) deposit; (plainte) lodge; (armes) lay down. ● vi (Jur) testify. □ **se ~** vpr settle.

dépositaire /depozitɛʀ/ nmf (Comm) agent.

déposition /depozisjɔ̃/ nf (Jur) statement.

dépôt /depo/ nm (entrepôt) warehouse; (d'autobus) depot; (particules) deposit; (garantie) deposit; **laisser en ~** give for safe keeping; **~ légal** formal deposit of a publication with an institution.

dépouille /depuj/ nf skin, hide; (~ mortelle) mortal remains.

dépouiller /depuje/ **1** vt (courrier) open; (scrutin) count; (écorcher) skin; **~ qn de** strip sb of.

dépourvu, ~e /depuʀvy/ adj **~ de** devoid of; **prendre au ~** catch unawares.

déprécier /depʀesje/ **45** vt depreciate. □ **se ~** vpr depreciate.

déprédations /depʀedasjɔ̃/ nfpl damage (+ sg).

dépression /depʀesjɔ̃/ nf depression; **~ nerveuse** nervous breakdown.

déprimer /depʀime/ **1** vt depress.

---

depuis /dəpɥi/

● préposition

····▸ (point de départ) since; **~ quand attendez-vous?** how long have you been waiting?

····▸ (durée) for; **~ toujours** always; **~ peu** recently.

● adverbe

····▸ since; **il a eu une attaque le mois dernier, ~ nous sommes inquiets** he had a stroke last month and we've been worried ever since.

● **depuis que** conjonction

····▸ since, ever since; **Sophie a beaucoup changé depuis que Camille est née** Sophie has changed a lot since Camille was born.

---

député /depyte/ nm ≈ Member of Parliament.

déraciné, -e /deʀasine/ nm, f rootless person.

déraillement /deʀajmɑ̃/ nm derailment.

dérailler /deʀaje/ **1** vi be derailed; (fig **11**) be talking nonsense; **faire ~** derail. **dérailleur** nm (de vélo) derailleur.

déraisonnable /deʀezɔnabl/ adj unreasonable.

dérangement /deʀɑ̃ʒmɑ̃/ nm bother; (désordre) disorder, upset;

en ~ out of order; **les** ~s the fault reporting service.

déranger /deʀɑ̃ʒe/ **40** vt (gêner) bother, disturb; (dérégler) upset, disrupt. □ **se** ~ vpr (aller) go; (fig) put oneself out; **ça te dérangerait de...?** would you mind...?

dérapage /deʀapaʒ/ nm skid. **déraper** **1** vi skid; (fig) (prix) get out of control.

déréglé, ~e /deʀegle/ adj (vie) dissolute; (estomac) upset; (mécanisme) (that is) not running properly.

dérégler /deʀegle/ **14** vt make go wrong. □ **se** ~ vpr go wrong.

dérision /deʀizjɔ̃/ nf mockery; **tourner en** ~ ridicule.

dérive /deʀiv/ nf aller à la ~ drift.

dérivé /deʀive/ nm by-product.

dériver /deʀive/ **1** vi (bateau) drift; ~ **de** stem from.

dermatologie /dɛʀmatɔlɔʒi/ nf dermatology.

dernier, -ière /dɛʀnje, -jɛʀ/ adj last; (nouvelles, mode) latest; (étage) top. ● nm, f last (one); **ce** ~ the latter; **le** ~ **de mes soucis** the least of my worries.

dernièrement /dɛʀnjɛʀmɑ̃/ adv recently.

dérober /deʀɔbe/ **1** vt steal. □ **se** ~ vpr slip away; **se** ~ **à** (obligation) shy away from.

dérogation /deʀɔgasjɔ̃/ nf special authorization.

déroger /deʀɔʒe/ **40** vi ~ **à** depart from.

déroulement /deʀulmɑ̃/ nm (d'une action) development.

dérouler /deʀule/ **1** vt (fil etc.) unwind. □ **se** ~ vpr unwind; (avoir lieu) take place; (récit, paysage) unfold.

déroute /deʀut/ nf (Mil) rout.

dérouter /deʀute/ **1** vt disconcert.

derrière /dɛʀjɛʀ/ prép & adv behind. ● nm back, rear; (postérieur **1**) behind **1**; **de** ~ (fenêtre) back, rear; (pattes) hind.

des /de/ →**DE**.

dès /dɛ/ prép (right) from; ~ **lors** from then on; ~ **que** as soon as.

désabusé, ~e /dezabyze/ adj disillusioned.

désaccord /dezakɔʀ/ nm disagreement.

désaffecté, ~e /dezafɛkte/ adj disused.

désagréable /dezagʀeabl/ adj unpleasant.

désagrément /dezagʀemɑ̃/ nm annoyance, inconvenience.

désaltérer (se) /(sə)dezalteʀe/ **14** vpr quench one's thirst.

désamorcer /dezamɔʀse/ **10** vt (situation, obus) defuse.

désapprobation /dezapʀɔbasjɔ̃/ nf disapproval. **désapprouver** **1** vt disapprove of.

désarçonner /dezaʀsɔne/ **1** vt throw.

désarmement /dezaʀməmɑ̃/ nm (Pol) disarmament.

désarroi /dezaʀwa/ nm distress.

désastre /dezastʀ/ nm disaster. **désastreux, -euse** adj disastrous.

désavantage /dezavɑ̃taʒ/ nm disadvantage. **désavantager** **40** vt put at a disadvantage.

désaveu (pl ~**x**) /dezavø/ nm denial. **désavouer** **1** vt deny.

descendance /desɑ̃dɑ̃s/ nf descent; (enfants) descendants (+ pl). **descendant, ~e** nm, f descendant.

descendre /desɑ̃dʀ/ **3** vi (aux être) go down; (venir) come down; (passager) get off ou out; (nuit) fall;

~ **à pied** walk down; ~ **par l'ascenseur** take the lift down; ~ **de** (être issu de) be descended from; ~ **à l'hôtel** go to a hotel; ~ **dans la rue** (Pol) take to the streets. ● vt (aux avoir) (escalier etc.) go ou come down; (objet) take down; (abattre [1]) shoot down.

descente /desɑ̃t/ nf descent; (à ski) downhill; (raid) raid; **dans la ~** going downhill; ~ **de lit** bedside rug.

descriptif, -ive /dɛskriptif, -v/ adj descriptive. **description** nf description.

désemparé, ~e /dezɑ̃pare/ adj distraught.

désendettement /dezɑ̃dɛtmɑ̃/ nm reduction of the debt.

déséquilibré, ~e /dezekilibre/ adj unbalanced; [1] crazy. ● nm, f lunatic. **déséquilibrer** [1] vt throw off balance.

désert, ~e /dezɛr, -t/ adj deserted. ● nm desert.

déserter /dezɛrte/ [1] vt/i desert. **déserteur** nm deserter.

désertique /dezɛrtik/ adj desert.

désespérant, ~e /dezɛsperɑ̃, -t/ adj utterly disheartening.

désespéré, ~e /dezɛspere/ adj in despair; (état, cas) hopeless; (effort) desperate.

désespérer /dezɛspere/ [14] vt drive to despair. ● vi despair, lose hope; ~ **de** despair of. □ se ~ vpr despair.

désespoir /dezɛspwar/ nm despair; **en ~ de cause** as a last resort.

déshabillé, ~e /dezabije/ adj undressed. ● nm négligee.

déshabiller /dezabije/ [1] vt undress. □ se ~ vpr get undressed.

désherbant /dezɛrbɑ̃/ nm

weedkiller.

déshérité, ~e /dezerite/ adj (région) deprived; (personne) the underprivileged.

déshériter /dezerite/ [1] vt disinherit.

déshonneur /dezɔnœr/ nm disgrace.

déshonorer /dezɔnɔre/ [1] vt dishonour.

déshydrater /dezidrate/ [1] vt dehydrate. □ se ~ vpr get dehydrated.

désigner /dezine/ [1] vt (montrer) point to ou out; (élire) appoint; (signifier) designate.

désillusion /dezilyzjɔ̃/ nf disillusionment.

désinence /dezinɑ̃s/ nf (Gram) ending.

désinfectant /dezɛ̃fɛktɑ̃/ nm disinfectant. **désinfecter** [1] vt disinfect.

désintéressé, ~e /dezɛ̃terese/ adj (personne, acte) selfless.

désintéresser (se) /(sə)dezɛ̃terese/ [1] vpr **se ~ de** lose interest in.

désintoxiquer /dezɛ̃tɔksike/ [1] vt detoxify; **se faire ~** to undergo detoxification.

désinvolte /dezɛ̃vɔlt/ adj casual. **désinvolture** nf casualness.

désir /dezir/ nm wish, desire; (convoitise) desire.

désirer /dezire/ [1] vt want; (sexuellement) desire; **vous désirez?** what would you like?

désireux, -euse /deziro, -z/ adj ~ **de faire** anxious to do.

désistement /dezistəmɑ̃/ nm withdrawal.

désobéir /dezɔbeir/ [2] vi (~ à) disobey. **désobéissant, ~e** adj disobedient.

désobligeant, ~e /dezɔbliʒɑ̃, -t/ adj disagreeable, unkind.

désodorisant /dezɔdɔrizɑ̃/ nm air freshener.

désodoriser /dezɔdɔrize/ **1** vt freshen up.

désœuvré, ~e /dezœvre/ adj at a loose end. **désœuvrement** nm lack of anything to do.

désolation /dezɔlasjɔ̃/ nf distress.

désolé, ~e /dezɔle/ adj (au regret) sorry; (région) desolate.

désoler /dezɔle/ **1** vt distress. □ **se ~** vpr be upset (**de qch** about sth).

désopilant, ~e /dezɔpilɑ̃, -t/ adj hilarious.

désordonné, ~e /dezɔrdɔne/ adj untidy; (mouvements) uncoordinated.

désordre /dezɔrdr/ nm untidiness; (Pol) disorder; **en ~** untidy.

désorganiser /dezɔrganize/ **1** vt disorganize.

désorienter /dezɔrjɑ̃te/ **1** vt disorient.

désormais /dezɔrmɛ/ adv from now on.

desquels, desquelles /dekɛl/ ➞LEQUEL.

dessécher /deseʃe/ **1** vt dry out. □ **se ~** vpr dry out, become dry; (plante) wither.

dessein /desɛ̃/ nm intention; **à ~** intentionally.

desserrer /desere/ **1** vt loosen; **il n'a pas desserré les dents** he never once opened his mouth. □ **se ~** vpr come loose.

dessert /desɛr/ nm dessert; **en ~** for dessert.

desservir /deservir/ **46** vt/i (débarrasser) clear away; (autobus) serve.

dessin /desɛ̃/ nm drawing; (motif) design; (discipline) art; (contour) outline; **~ animé** (cinéma) cartoon; **~ humoristique** cartoon.

dessinateur, -trice /desinatœr, -tris/ nm, f artist; (industriel) draughtsman.

dessiner /desine/ **1** vt/i draw; (fig) outline. □ **se ~** vpr appear, take shape.

dessoûler /desule/ **1** vt/i sober up.

dessous /dəsu/ adv underneath. ● nm underside, underneath. ● nmpl underwear; **les ~ d'une histoire** what is behind a story; **du ~** bottom; (voisins) downstairs; **en ~, par-~** underneath. **dessous-de-plat** nm inv (heat resistant) table-mat. **dessous-de-table** nm inv backhander. **dessous-de-verre** nm inv coaster.

dessus /dəsy/ adv on top (of it), on it. ● nm top; **du ~** top; (voisins) upstairs; **avoir le ~** get the upper hand. **dessus-de-lit** nm inv bedspread.

déstabiliser /destabilize/ **1** vt destabilize, unsettle.

destin /dɛstɛ̃/ nm (sort) fate; (avenir) destiny.

destinataire /dɛstinatɛr/ nmf addressee.

destination /dɛstinasjɔ̃/ nf destination; (fonction) purpose; **vol à ~ de** flight to.

destinée /dɛstine/ nf destiny.

destiner /dɛstine/ **1** vt **~ à** intend for; (vouer) destine for; **le commentaire m'est destiné** this comment is aimed at me; **être destiné à faire** to be intended to do; (obligé) be destined to do; **se ~ à** vpr (carrière) intend to take up.

destituer /dɛstitɥe/ **1** vt discharge.

destructeur, -trice /dɛstryktœʀ, -tʀis/ *adj* destructive. **destruction** *nf* destruction.

désuet, -ète /dezɥɛ, -t/ *adj* outdated.

détachant /detaʃɑ̃/ *nm* stain remover.

détacher /detaʃe/ **1** *vt* untie; (ôter) remove, detach; (déléguer) second. □ **se** ~ *vpr* come off, break away; (nœud etc.) come undone; (ressortir) stand out.

détail /detaj/ *nm* detail; (de compte) breakdown; (Comm) retail; **au** ~ (vendre etc.) retail; **de** ~ (prix etc.) retail; **en** ~ in detail; **entrer dans les** ~s go into detail.

détaillant, ~e /detajɑ̃, -t/ *nm, f* retailer.

détaillé, ~e /detaje/ *adj* detailed.

détailler /detaje/ **1** *vt* (rapport) detail; ~ **ce que qn fait** scrutinize what sb does.

détaler /detale/ **22** *vi* **1** bolt.

détartrant /detaʀtʀɑ̃/ *nm* descaler.

détecter /detɛkte/ **1** *vt* detect. **détecteur** *nm* detector.

détective /detɛktiv/ *nm* detective.

déteindre /detɛ̃dʀ/ **1** *vi* (dans l'eau) run (**sur** on to); (au soleil) fade; ~ **sur** (fig) rub off on.

détendre /detɑ̃dʀ/ **3** *vt* slacken; (ressort) release; (personne) relax. □ **se** ~ *vpr* (ressort) slacken; (personne) relax. **détendu, ~e** *adj* (calme) relaxed.

détenir /det(ə)niʀ/ **58** *vt* hold; (secret, fortune) possess.

détente /detɑ̃t/ *nf* relaxation; (Pol) détente; (saut) spring; (gâchette) trigger; **être lent à la** ~ **1** be slow on the uptake.

détenteur, -trice /detɑ̃tœʀ, -tʀis/ *nm, f* holder.

détention /detɑ̃sjɔ̃/ *nf* detention; ~ **provisoire** custody.

détenu, ~e /detny/ *nm, f* prisoner.

détergent /detɛʀʒɑ̃/ *nm* detergent.

détérioration /deteʀjɔʀasjɔ̃/ *nf* deterioration; (dégât) damage.

détériorer /deteʀjɔʀe/ **1** *vt* damage. □ **se** ~ *vpr* deteriorate.

détermination /detɛʀminasjɔ̃/ *nf* determination. **déterminé, ~e** *adj* (résolu) determined; (précis) definite. **déterminer** **1** *vt* determine.

déterrer /deteʀe/ **1** *vt* dig up.

détestable /detɛstabl/ *adj* (caractère, temps) foul.

détester /detɛste/ **1** *vt* hate. □ **se** ~ *vpr* hate each other.

détonation /detɔnasjɔ̃/ *nf* explosion, detonation.

détour /detuʀ/ *nm* (crochet) detour; (fig) roundabout means; (virage) bend.

détournement /detuʀnəmɑ̃/ *nm* hijack(ing); (de fonds) embezzlement.

détourner /detuʀne/ **1** *vt* (attention) divert; (tête, yeux) turn away; (avion) hijack; (argent) embezzle. □ **se** ~ **de** *vpr* stray from.

détraquer /detʀake/ **1** *vt* make go wrong; (estomac) upset. □ **se** ~ *vpr* (machine) go wrong.

détresse /detʀɛs/ *nf* distress; **dans la** ~, **en** ~ in distress.

détritus /detʀity(s)/ *nmpl* rubbish (+ sg).

détroit /detʀwa/ *nm* strait.

détromper /detʀɔ̃pe/ **1** *vt* set straight. □ **se** ~ *vpr* **détrompe-toi!** you'd better think again!

détruire /detʀɥiʀ/ **17** *vt* destroy.

dette /dɛt/ *nf* debt.

deuil /dœj/ *nm* (période) mourning; (décès) bereavement; **porter le** ~

be in mourning; **faire son ~ de qch** give sth up as lost.

deux /dø/ adj & nm two; **~ fois** twice; **tous (les ~)** both.

deuxième adj & nmf second. **deux-pièces** nm inv (maillot de bain) two-piece; (logement) two-room flat.

deux-points nm inv (Gram) colon.

deux-roues nm inv two-wheeled vehicle.

dévaliser /devalize/ **1** vt rob, clean out.

dévalorisant, ~e /devalɔrizɑ̃, -t/ adj demeaning.

dévaloriser /devalɔrize/ **1** vt (monnaie) devalue. □ **se ~** vpr (personne) put oneself down.

dévaluation /devalɥasjɔ̃/ nf devaluation.

dévaluer /devalɥe/ **1** vt devalue. □ **se ~** vpr devalue.

devancer /dəvɑ̃se/ **10** vt be ou go ahead of; (arriver) arrive ahead of; (prévenir) anticipate.

devant /d(ə)vɑ̃/ prép in front of; (distance) ahead of; (avec mouvement) past; (en présence de) in front of; (face à) in the face of; **avoir du temps ~ soi** have plenty of time. ● adv in front; (à distance) ahead; **de ~** front; **prendre les ~s** take the initiative.

devanture /dəvɑ̃tyʀ/ nf shop front; (vitrine) shop window.

développement /devlɔpmɑ̃/ nm development; (de photos) developing.

développer /devlɔpe/ **1** vt develop. □ **se ~** vpr (corps, talent) develop; (entreprise) grow, expand.

devenir /dəvniʀ/ **58** vi (aux être) become; **qu'est-il devenu?** what has become of him?

dévergondé, ~e /devɛʀgɔ̃de/ adj & nm,f shameless (person).

déverser /devɛʀse/ **1** vt (liquide)

pour; (ordures, pétrole) dump. □ **se ~** vpr (rivière) flow; (égout, foule) pour.

dévêtir /devetiʀ/ **61** vt undress. □ **se ~** vpr get undressed.

déviation /devjasjɔ̃/ nf diversion.

dévier /devje/ **45** vt divert; (coup) deflect. ● vi (ballon, balle) veer; (personne) deviate.

devin /dəvɛ̃/ nm soothsayer.

deviner /dəvine/ **1** vt guess; (apercevoir) distinguish.

devinette /dəvinɛt/ nf riddle.

devis /dəvi/ nm estimate, quote.

dévisager /devizaʒe/ **40** vt stare at.

devise /dəviz/ nf motto; **~s** (monnaie) (foreign) currency.

dévisser /devise/ **1** vt unscrew.

dévitaliser /devitalize/ **1** vt (dent) carry out root canal treatment on.

dévoiler /devwale/ **1** vt reveal.

devoir /dəvwaʀ/ **26**

● verbe auxiliaire

····▸ **~ faire** (obligation, hypothèse) must do; (nécessité) have got to do; **je dois dire que...** I have to say that...; **il a dû partir** (nécessité) he had to leave; (hypothèse) he must have left.

····▸ (prévision) **je devais lui dire** I was to tell her; **elle doit rentrer bientôt** she's due back soon.

····▸ (conseil) **tu devrais** you should.

● verbe transitif

····▸ (argent, excuses) owe; **combien je vous dois?** (en achetant) how much is it?

□ **se devoir** verbe pronominal

····▸ **je me dois de le faire** it's my duty to do it.

● *nom masculin*

····▸ duty; **faire son ~** do one's duty.

····▸ (Scol) **~ (surveillé)** test; **les ~s** homework (+ *sg*); **faire ses ~s** do one's homework.

dévorer /devɔʀe/ **1** *vt* devour.

dévot, ~e /devo, -ɔt/ *adj* devout.

dévoué, ~e /devwe/ *adj* devoted. **dévouement** *nm* devotion.

dévouer (se) /(sə)devwe/ **1** *vpr* devote oneself (à to); (se sacrifier) sacrifice oneself.

dextérité /deksteʀite/ *nf* skill.

diabète /djabɛt/ *nm* diabetes. **diabétique** *adj* & *nmf* diabetic.

diable /djabl/ *nm* devil.

diagnostic /djagnɔstik/ *nm* diagnosis. **diagnostiquer** **1** *vt* diagnose.

diagonal, ~e /djagɔnal, -o/ *adj* diagonal. **diagonale** *nf* diagonal; **en ~** diagonally.

diagramme /djagʀam/ *nm* diagram; (graphique) graph.

dialecte /djalɛkt/ *nm* dialect.

dialogue /djalɔg/ *nm* dialogue. **dialoguer** **1** *vi* have talks, enter into a dialogue.

diamant /djamɑ̃/ *nm* diamond.

diamètre /djamɛtʀ/ *nm* diameter.

diapositive /djapozitiv/ *nf* slide.

diarrhée /djaʀe/ *nf* diarrhoea.

dictateur /diktatœʀ/ *nm* dictator.

dicter /dikte/ **1** *vt* dictate. **dictée** *nf* dictation.

dictionnaire /diksjɔnɛʀ/ *nm* dictionary.

dicton /diktɔ̃/ *nm* saying.

dièse /djɛz/ *nm* (Mus) sharp.

diesel /djezɛl/ *nm* & *adj inv* diesel.

diète /djɛt/ *nf* restricted diet.

diététicien, ~ne /djetetisjɛ̃, -ɛn/ *nm, f* dietician.

diététique /djetetik/ *nf* dietetics. ● *adj* **produit** *ou* **aliment ~** dietary product; **magasin ~** health food shop *ou* store.

dieu (*pl* **~x**) /djø/ *nm* god; **D~** God.

diffamation /difamasjɔ̃/ *nf* slander; (par écrit) libel. **diffamer** **1** *vt* slander; (par écrit) libel.

différé: en ~ /ɑ̃difeʀe/ *loc* (émission) pre-recorded.

différemment /difeʀamɑ̃/ *adv* differently.

différence /difeʀɑ̃s/ *nf* difference; **à la ~ de** unlike.

différencier /difeʀɑ̃sje/ **45** *vt* differentiate. □ **se ~** *vpr* differentiate oneself; **se ~ de** (différer de) differ from.

différend /difeʀɑ̃/ *nm* difference (of opinion).

différent, ~e /difeʀɑ̃, -t/ *adj* different (de from).

différer /difeʀe/ **14** *vt* postpone. ● *vi* differ (de from).

difficile /difisil/ *adj* difficult; (exigeant) fussy. **difficilement** *adv* with difficulty.

difficulté /difikylte/ *nf* difficulty; **faire des ~s** raise objections.

diffus, ~e /dify, -z/ *adj* diffuse.

diffuser /difyze/ **1** *vt* (émission) broadcast; (nouvelle) spread; (lumière, chaleur) diffuse; (Comm) distribute. **diffusion** *nf* broadcasting; diffusion; distribution.

digérer /diʒeʀe/ **14** *vt* digest; (endurer □) stomach. **digeste** *adj* digestible.

digestif, -ive /diʒɛstif, -v/ *adj* digestive. ● *nm* after-dinner liqueur.

digital, ~e (*mpl* **-aux**) /diʒital, -o/

adj digital.

digne /diɲ/ *adj* (noble) dignified; (approprié) worthy; ~ **de** worthy of; ~ **de foi** trustworthy.

digue /dig/ *nf* dyke; (US) dike.

dilater /dilate/ **1** *vt* dilate. □ **se** ~ *vpr* dilate; (estomac) distend.

dilemme /dilɛm/ *nm* dilemma.

dilettante /diletɑ̃t/ *nmf* amateur.

diluant /dilɥɑ̃/ *nm* thinner.

diluer /dilɥe/ **1** *vt* dilute.

dimanche /dimɑ̃ʃ/ *nm* Sunday.

dimension /dimɑ̃sjɔ̃/ *nf* (taille) size; (mesure) dimension; (aspect) dimension.

diminuer /diminɥe/ **1** *vt* reduce, decrease; (plaisir, courage) dampen; (dénigrer) diminish. ● *vi* (se réduire) decrease; (faiblir) (bruit, flamme) die down; (ardeur) cool. **diminutif** *nm* diminutive; (surnom) pet name. **diminution** *nf* decrease (de in); (réduction) reduction; (affaiblissement) diminishing.

dinde /dɛ̃d/ *nf* turkey.

dîner /dine/ **1** *vi* have dinner. ● *nm* dinner.

dingue /dɛ̃g/ *adj* **1** crazy.

dinosaure /dinozɔʀ/ *nm* dinosaur.

diphtongue /diftɔ̃g/ *nf* diphthong.

diplomate /diplɔmat/ *nmf* diplomat. ● *adj* diplomatic. **diplomatique** /diplɔmatik/ *adj* diplomatic.

diplôme /diplom/ *nm* certificate, diploma; (Univ) degree. **diplômé, ~e** *adj* qualified.

dire /diʀ/ **27** *vt* say; (secret, vérité, heure) tell; (penser) think; ~ **que** say that; ~ **à qn que** tell sb that; ~ **à qn de** tell sb to; **ça me dit de faire** I feel like doing; **on dirait que** it would seem that, it seems that; **dis/dites donc!** hey! □ **se** ~ *vpr* (mot) be said; (penser) tell oneself;

(se prétendre) claim to be. ● *nm* **au** ~ **de, selon les** ~**s de** according to.

direct, ~e /diʀɛkt/ *adj* direct. ● *nm* (train) express train; **en** ~ (émission) live.

directeur, -trice /diʀɛktœʀ, -tʀis/ *nm, f* director; (chef de service) manager, manageress; (de journal) editor; (d'école) headteacher; (US) principal; ~ **de banque** bank manager; ~ **commercial** sales manager; ~ **des ressources humaines** human resources manager.

direction /diʀɛksjɔ̃/ *nf* (sens) direction; (de société) management; (Auto) steering; **en** ~ **de** (going) to.

dirigeant, ~e /diʀiʒɑ̃, -t/ *nm, f* (Pol) leader; (Comm) manager. ● *adj* (classe) ruling.

diriger /diʀiʒe/ **40** *vt* (service, école, parti, pays) run; (entreprise, usine) manage; (travaux) supervise; (véhicule) steer; (orchestre) conduct; (braquer) aim; (tourner) turn. □ **se** ~ *vpr* (s'orienter) find one's way; **se** ~ **vers** head for, make for.

dis /di/ ➡ DIRE **27**.

discernement /disɛʀnəmɑ̃/ *nm* discernment.

disciplinaire /disiplinɛʀ/ *adj* disciplinary. **discipline** *nf* discipline.

discontinu, ~e /diskɔ̃tiny/ *adj* intermittent.

discordant, ~e /diskɔʀdɑ̃, -t/ *adj* discordant.

discothèque /diskɔtɛk/ *nf* record library; (boîte de nuit) disco(thèque).

discours /diskuʀ/ *nm* speech; (propos) views.

discret, -ète /diskʀɛ, -t/ *adj* discreet.

discrétion /diskʀesjɔ̃/ *nf* discretion; **à ~** (*vin*) unlimited; (*manger, boire*) as much as one desires.

discrimination /diskʀiminasjɔ̃/ *nf* discrimination. **discriminatoire** *adj* discriminatory.

disculper /diskylpe/ **1** *vt* exonerate. □ **se ~** *vpr* vindicate oneself.

discussion /diskysjɔ̃/ *nf* discussion; (*querelle*) argument.

discutable /diskytabl/ *adj* debatable; (*critiquable*) questionable.

discuter /diskyte/ **1** *vt* discuss; (*contester*) question. ● *vi* (*parler*) talk; (*répliquer*) argue; **~ de** discuss.

disette /dizɛt/ *nf* food shortage.

disgrâce /disgʀɑs/ *nf* disgrace.

disgracieux, -ieuse /disgʀasjø, -z/ *adj* ugly, unsightly.

disjoindre /diʒwɛ̃dʀ/ **22** *vt* take apart. □ **se ~** *vpr* come apart.

disloquer /dislɔke/ **1** *vt* (*membre*) dislocate; (*machine*) break (apart). □ **se ~** *vpr* (*parti, cortège*) break up; (*meuble*) come apart.

disparaître /dispaʀɛtʀ/ **18** *vi* disappear; (*mourir*) die; **faire ~** get rid of. **disparition** *nf* disappearance; (*mort*) death.

disparate /dispaʀat/ *adj* illassorted.

disparu, ~e /dispaʀy/ *adj* missing. ● *nm, f* missing person; (*mort*) dead person.

dispensaire /dispãsɛʀ/ *nm* clinic.

dispense /dispãs/ *nf* exemption.

dispenser /dispãse/ **1** *vt* exempt (*de* from). □ **se ~ de** *vpr* avoid.

disperser /dispɛʀse/ **1** *vt* (*éparpiller*) scatter; (*répartir*) disperse. □ **se ~** *vpr* disperse.

disponibilité /disponibilite/ *nf* availability. **disponible** *adj* available.

dispos, ~e /dispo, -z/ *adj* frais et

~ fresh and alert.

disposé, ~e /dispoze/ *adj* **bien/ mal ~** in a good/bad mood; **~ à** prepared to; **~ envers** disposed towards.

disposer /dispoze/ **1** *vt* arrange; **~ à** (*engager à*) incline to. ● *vi* **~ de** have at one's disposal. □ **se ~ à** *vpr* prepare to.

dispositif /dispozitif/ *nm* device; (*ensemble de mesures*) operation.

disposition /dispozisjɔ̃/ *nf* arrangement, layout; (*tendance*) tendency; **~s** (*humeur*) mood; (*préparatifs*) arrangements; (*mesures*) measures; (*aptitude*) aptitude; **mettre à la ~ de** place ou put at the disposal of.

disproportionné, ~e /dis pʀopɔʀsjone/ *adj* disproportionate; **~ à** out of proportion with.

dispute /dispyt/ *nf* quarrel.

disputer /dispyte/ **1** *vt* (*match*) play; (*course*) run in; (*prix*) fight for; (*gronder* [T]) tell off. □ **se ~** *vpr* quarrel; (*se battre pour*) fight over; (*match*) be played.

disquaire /diskɛʀ/ *nmf* record dealer.

disque /disk/ *nm* (Mus) record; (Sport) discus; (*cercle*) disc, disk; (Ordinat) disk; **~ compact** compact disc; **~ dur** hard disk; **~ optique compact** CD-ROM; **~ souple** floppy disk.

disquette /diskɛt/ *nf* floppy disk, diskette; **~ de sauvegarde** backup disk.

disséminer /disemine/ **1** *vt* spread, scatter.

dissertation /disɛʀtasjɔ̃/ *nf* essay, paper.

disserter /disɛʀte/ **1** *vi* **~ sur** speak about; (*par écrit*) write about.

dissident, ~e /disidã, -t/ *adj* &

nm, f dissident.

dissimulation /disimylasjɔ̃/ *nf* concealment; (fig) deceit.

dissimuler /disimyle/ **1** *vt* conceal (à from). □ se ~ *vpr* conceal oneself.

dissipé, ~e /disipe/ *adj* (élève) unruly.

dissiper /disipe/ **1** *vt* (fumée, crainte) dispel; (fortune) squander; (personne) distract. □ se ~ *vpr* disappear; (élève) grow restless.

dissolvant /disɔlvɑ̃/ *nm* solvent; (pour ongles) nail polish remover.

dissoudre /disudR/ **53** *vt* dissolve. □ se ~ *vpr* dissolve.

dissuader /disɥade/ **1** *vt* dissuade (de from).

dissuasion /disɥazjɔ̃/ *nf* dissuasion; force de ~ deterrent force.

distance /distɑ̃s/ *nf* distance; (écart) gap; à ~ at ou from a distance.

distancer /distɑ̃se/ **10** *vt* outdistance.

distendre /distɑ̃dR/ **3** *vt* (estomac) distend; (corde) stretch.

distinct, ~e /distɛ̃(kt), -ɛkt/ *adj* distinct.

distinctif, **-ive** /distɛ̃ktif, -v/ *adj* (trait) distinctive; (signe, caractère) distinguishing.

distinction /distɛ̃ksjɔ̃/ *nf* distinction; (récompense) honour.

distinguer /distɛ̃ge/ **1** *vt* distinguish.

distraction /distRaksjɔ̃/ *nf* absent-mindedness; (passe-temps) entertainment, leisure; (détente) recreation.

distraire /distRER/ **29** *vt* amuse; (rendre inattentif) distract; ~ qn de qch take sb's mind off sth. □ se ~ *vpr* amuse oneself.

distrait, ~e /distRe, -t/ *adj* absent-minded; (élève) inattentive.

distrayant, ~e /distRejɑ̃, -t/ *adj* entertaining.

distribuer /distRibɥe/ **1** *vt* hand out, distribute; (répartir) distribute; (tâches, rôles) allocate; (cartes) deal; (courrier) deliver.

distributeur /distRibytœR/ *nm* (Auto, Comm) distributor; ~ (automatique) vending-machine; ~ de billets (de banque) cash dispenser.

distribution /distRibysjɔ̃/ *nf* distribution; (du courrier) delivery; (acteurs) cast; (secteur) retailing.

district /distRikt/ *nm* district.

dit[1], **dites** /di, dit/ ➔DIRE **27**.

dit[2], ~e /di, dit/ *adj* (décidé) agreed; (surnommé) known as.

diurne /djyRn/ *adj* diurnal; (activité) daytime.

divagations /divagasjɔ̃/ *nfpl* ravings.

divergence /diveRʒɑ̃s/ *nf* divergence. **divergent**, ~e *adj* divergent. **diverger** **40** *vi* diverge.

divers, ~e /diveR, -s/ *adj* (varié) diverse; (différent) various; (frais) miscellaneous; **dépenses** ~es sundries. **diversifier** **45** *vt* diversify.

diversité /diveRsite/ *nf* diversity, variety.

divertir /diveRtiR/ **2** *vt* amuse, entertain. □ se ~ *vpr* amuse oneself; (passer du bon temps) enjoy oneself. **divertissement** *nm* amusement, entertainment.

dividende /dividɑ̃d/ *nm* dividend.

divin, ~e /divɛ̃, -in/ *adj* divine. **divinité** *nf* divinity.

diviser /divize/ **1** *vt* divide. □ se ~ *vpr* become divided; se ~ par sept be divisible by seven. **division** *nf* division.

divorce /divɔRs/ *nm* divorce.

divorcé, ~e /divɔRse/ *adj*

divorced. ● nm, f divorcee.

divorcer /divɔʀse/ **10** vi (d'avec) divorce.

dix /dis/ (/di/ before consonant, /diz/ before vowel) adj & nm ten.

dix-huit /dizɥit/ adj & nm eighteen.

dixième /dizjɛm/ adj & nmf tenth.

dix-neuf /diznœf/ adj & nm nineteen.

dix-sept /disɛt/ adj & nm seventeen.

docile /dɔsil/ adj docile.

docteur /dɔktœʀ/ nm doctor.

doctorat /dɔktɔʀa/ nm doctorate, PhD.

document /dɔkymɑ̃/ nm document. **documentaire** adj & nm documentary.

documentaliste /dɔkymɑ̃talist/ nmf information officer; (Scol) librarian.

documentation /dɔkymɑ̃tasjɔ̃/ nf information, literature; **centre de ~** resource centre.

documenté, ~e /dɔkymɑ̃te/ adj well-documented.

documenter /dɔkymɑ̃te/ **1** vt provide with information. □ **se ~** vpr collect information.

dodo /dodo/ nm faire ~ (langage enfantin) sleep.

dodu, ~e /dɔdy/ adj plump.

dogmatique /dɔgmatik/ adj dogmatic. **dogme** nm dogma.

doigt /dwa/ nm finger; **un ~ de** a drop of; **montrer qch du ~** point at sth; **à deux ~s de** a hair's breadth away from; **~ de pied** toe. **doigté** nm (Mus) fingering, touch; (diplomatie) tact.

dois, doit /dwa/ ➡DEVOIR 26.

doléances /dɔleɑ̃s/ nfpl grievances.

dollar /dɔlaʀ/ nm dollar.

domaine /dɔmɛn/ nm estate, domain; (fig) domain, field.

domestique /dɔmɛstik/ adj domestic. ● nmf servant. **domestiquer** **1** vt domesticate.

domicile /dɔmisil/ nm home; **à ~** at home; (livrer) to the home.

domicilié, ~e /dɔmisilje/ adj resident; **être ~ à Paris** live ou be resident in Paris.

dominant, ~e /dɔminɑ̃, -t/ adj dominant. **dominante** nf dominant feature.

dominer /dɔmine/ **1** vt dominate; (surplomber) tower over, dominate; (sujet) master; (peur) overcome. ● vi dominate; (équipe) be in the lead; (prévaloir) stand out.

domino /dɔmino/ nm domino.

dommage /dɔmaʒ/ nm (tort) harm; (~s) (dégâts) damage; **c'est ~** it's a pity ou shame; **quel ~** what a pity ou shame. **dommages-intérêts** nmpl (Jur) damages.

dompter /dɔ̃te/ **1** vt tame. **dompteur, -euse** nm, f tamer.

DOM-TOM /dɔmtɔm/ abrév mpl (départements et territoires d'outre-mer) French overseas departments and territories.

don /dɔ̃/ nm (cadeau, aptitude) gift. **donateur, -trice** nm, f donor. **donation** nf donation.

donc /dɔ̃k/ conj so, then; (par conséquent) so, therefore; **quoi ~?** what did you say?; **tiens ~!** fancy that!

donjon /dɔ̃ʒɔ̃/ nm (tour) keep.

donné, ~e /dɔne/ adj (fixé) given; (pas cher **1**) dirt cheap; **étant ~ que** given that.

donnée /dɔne/ nf (élément d'information) fact; **~s** data.

donner /dɔne/ **1** vt give; (vieilles

affaires) give away; (*distribuer*) give out; (*fruits, résultats*) produce; (*film*) show; (*pièce*) put on; **ça donne soif/faim** it makes one thirsty/hungry; **~ qch à réparer** take sth to be repaired; **~ lieu à** give rise to. ● *vi* **~ sur** look out on to; **~ dans** tend towards. □ **se ~ à** *vpr* devote oneself to; **se ~ du mal** go to a lot of trouble (**pour faire** to do).

dont /dɔ̃/
● *pronom*
····➤ (*personne*) **la fille ~ je te parlais** the girl I was telling you about; **l'homme ~ la fille a dit...** the man whose daughter said...
····➤ (*chose*) **which, l'affaire ~ il parle** the matter which he is referring to; **la manière ~ elle parle** the way she speaks; **ce ~ il parle** what he's talking about.
····➤ (*provenance*) from which.
····➤ (*parmi lesquels*) **deux personnes ~ toi** two people, one of whom is you; **plusieurs thèmes ~ l'identité et le racisme** several topics including identity and racism.

dopage /dɔpaʒ/ *nm* (*de cheval*) doping; (*d'athlète*) illegal drug-use.

doper /dɔpe/ **1** *vt* dope. □ **se ~** *vpr* take drugs.

doré, ~e /dɔre/ *adj* (*couleur d'or*) golden; (*qui rappelle de l'or*) gold; (*avec de l'or*) gilt; **la jeunesse ~e** gilded youth.

dorénavant /dɔrenavɑ̃/ *adv* henceforth.

dorer /dɔre/ **1** *vt* gild; (*Culin*) brown.

dormir /dɔrmir/ **46** *vi* sleep; (*être endormi*) be asleep; **~ debout** be asleep on one's feet; **une histoire à ~ debout** a cock-and-bull story.

dortoir /dɔrtwar/ *nm* dormitory.

dorure /dɔryr/ *nf* gilding.

dos /do/ *nm* back; (*de livre*) spine; **à ~ de** riding on; **au ~ de** (*chèque*) on the back of; **de ~** from behind; **~ crawlé** backstroke.

dosage /dozaʒ/ *nm* (*mélange*) mixture; (*quantité*) amount; (*proportions*) dose. **dose** *nf* dose. **doser** **1** *vt* measure out; (*contrôler*) use in a controlled way.

dossier /dɔsje/ *nm* (*documents*) file; (*Jur*) case; (*de chaise*) back; (*TV, presse*) special feature.

dot /dɔt/ *nf* dowry.

douane /dwan/ *nf* customs. **douanier, -ière** /dwanje, -jɛr/ *adj* customs. ● *nm* customs officer.

double /dubl/ *adj & adv* double. ● *nm* (*copie*) duplicate; (*sosie*) double; **le ~ (de)** twice as much *ou* as many (as); **le ~ messieurs** the men's doubles.

double-cliquer /dublklike/ **1** *vt* double-click.

doubler /duble/ **1** *vt* double; (*dépasser*) overtake; (*vêtement*) line; (*film*) dub; (*classe*) repeat; (*cap*) round. ● *vi* double.

doublure /dublyr/ *nf* (*étoffe*) lining; (*acteur*) understudy.

douce /dus/ →**DOUX**.

doucement /dusmã/ *adv* gently; (*sans bruit*) quietly; (*lentement*) slowly.

douceur /dusœr/ *nf* (*mollesse*) softness; (*de climat*) mildness; (*de personne*) gentleness; (*friandise*) sweet; (US) candy; **en ~** smoothly.

douche /duʃ/ *nf* shower.

doucher (se) /duʃe/ **1** *vpr* have

ou take a shower.

doudoune /dudun/ *nf* **1** down jacket.

doué, **~e** /dwe/ *adj* gifted; **~ de** endowed with.

douille /duj/ *nf* (Électr) socket.

douillet, **~te** /duje, -t/ *adj* cosy, comfortable; (*personne*: péj) soft.

douleur /dulœr/ *nf* pain; (*chagrin*) sorrow, grief. **douloureux**, **-euse** *adj* painful.

doute /dut/ *nm* doubt; **sans ~** no doubt; **sans aucun ~** without doubt.

douter /dute/ **1** *vt* **~ de** doubt; **~ que** doubt that. ● *vi* doubt. □ **se ~ de** *vpr* suspect; **je m'en doutais** I thought so.

douteux, **-euse** /dutø, -z/ *adj* dubious, doubtful.

Douvres /duvr/ *npr* Dover.

doux, **douce** /du, dus/ *adj* (*moelleux*) soft; (*sucré*) sweet; (*clément, pas fort*) mild; (*pas brusque, bienveillant*) gentle.

douzaine /duzen/ *nf* about twelve; (*douze*) dozen; **une ~ d'œufs** a dozen eggs.

douze /duz/ *adj* & *nm* twelve. **douzième** *adj* & *nmf* twelfth.

doyen, **~ne** /dwajɛ̃, -ɛn/ *nm, f* dean; (*en âge*) most senior person.

dragée /draʒe/ *nf* sugared almond.

draguer /drage/ **1** *vt* (*rivière*) dredge; (*filles* **1**) chat up.

drainer /drene/ **1** *vt* drain.

dramatique /dramatik/ *adj* dramatic; (*tragique*) tragic. ● *nf* (television) drama.

dramatiser /dramatize/ **1** *vt* dramatize.

dramaturge /dramatyrʒ/ *nmf* dramatist.

drame /dram/ *nm* (*genre*) drama;

(*pièce*) play; (*événement tragique*) tragedy.

drap /dra/ *nm* sheet; (*tissu*) (woollen) cloth.

drapeau (*pl* **~x**) /drapo/ *nm* flag.

drap-housse (*pl* **draps-housses**) /drauss/ *nm* fitted sheet.

dressage /dresaʒ/ *nm* training; (*compétition équestre*) dressage.

dresser /drese/ **1** *vt* put up, erect; (*tête*) raise; (*animal*) train; (*liste, plan*) draw up; **~ l'oreille** prick up one's ears. □ **se ~** *vpr* (*bâtiment*) stand; (*personne*) draw oneself up. **dresseur**, **-euse** *nm, f* trainer.

dribbler /drible/ **1** *vi* (Sport) dribble.

drive /drajv/ *nm* (Ordinat) drive.

drogue /drɔg/ *nf* drug; **la ~** drugs.

drogué, **~e** /drɔge/ *nm, f* drug addict.

droguer /drɔge/ **1** *vt* (*malade*) drug heavily; (*victime*) drug. □ **se ~** *vpr* take drugs.

droguerie /drɔgri/ *nf* hardware shop. **droguiste** *nmf* owner of a hardware shop.

droit, **~e** /drwa, -t/ *adj* (*contraire de gauche*) right; (*non courbe*) straight; (*loyal, honnête*) upright; **angle ~** right angle. ● *adv* straight. ● *nm* right; **~(s)** (*taxe*) duty; **le ~** (Jur) law; **avoir ~ à** be entitled to; **avoir le ~ de** be allowed to; **être dans son ~** be in the right; **~ d'auteur** copyright; **~ d'inscription** registration fee; **~s d'auteur** royalties.

droite /drwat/ *nf* (*contraire de gauche*) right; **à ~** on the right; (*direction*) (to the) right; **la ~** the right (side); (Pol) the right (wing); (*ligne*) straight line. **droitier**, **-ière** *adj* right-handed.

drôle /dʀol/ adj (amusant) funny; (bizarre) funny, odd. **drôlement** adv funnily; (très 11) really.

dru, ~e /dʀy/ adj thick; **tomber** ~ fall thick and fast.

drugstore /dʀœgstɔʀ/ nm drugstore.

DTD abrév m (**document type definition**) DTD.

du /dy/ →DE.

dû, due /dy/ adj due. ● nm due; (argent) dues; ~ **à** due to. ● →DE VOIR 26.

duc, duchesse /dyk, dyʃɛs/ nm, f duke, duchess.

duo /dɥo/ nm (Mus) duet; (fig) duo.

dupe /dyp/ nf dupe.

duplex /dyplɛks/ nm split-level apartment; (US) duplex; (émission) link-up.

duplicata /dyplikata/ nm inv duplicate.

duquel /dykɛl/ →LEQUEL.

dur, ~e /dyʀ/ adj hard; (sévère) harsh, hard; (viande) tough; (col, brosse) stiff; ~ **d'oreille** hard of hearing. ● adv hard. ● nm, f tough nut 11; (Pol) hardliner.

durable /dyʀabl/ adj lasting.

durant /dyʀɑ̃/ prép (au cours de) during; (avec mesure de temps) for; ~ **des heures** for hours; **des heures** ~ for hours and hours.

durcir /dyʀsiʀ/ 2 vt harden. ● vi (terre) harden; (ciment) set; (pain) go hard. □ **se** ~ vpr harden.

durée /dyʀe/ nf length; (période) duration; **de courte** ~ short-lived; **pile longue** ~ long-life battery.

durer /dyʀe/ 11 vi last.

dureté /dyʀte/ nf hardness; (sévérité) harshness.

duvet /dyvɛ/ nm down; (sac) sleeping-bag.

DVD abrév m (**digital versatile disc**) DVD.

dynamique /dinamik/ adj dynamic.

dynamite /dinamit/ nf dynamite.

dynamo /dinamo/ nf dynamo.

....

Ee

....

eau (pl ~x) /o/ nf water; ~ **courante** running water; ~ **de mer** seawater; ~ **de source** spring water; ~ **douce/salée** fresh/salt water; ~ **de pluie** rainwater; ~ **potable** drinking water; ~ **de Javel** bleach; ~ **minérale** mineral water; ~ **gazeuse** sparkling water; ~ **plate** still water; ~ **de toilette** eau de toilette; ~x **usées** dirty water; ~x **et forêts** forestry commission (+ sg); **tomber à l'**~ (fig) fall through; **prendre l'**~ take in water. **eau-de-vie** (pl **eaux-de-vie**) nf brandy.

ébahi, ~e /ebai/ adj dumbfounded.

ébauche /eboʃ/ nf (dessin) sketch; (fig) attempt.

ébéniste /ebenist/ nm cabinetmaker.

éblouir /ebluiʀ/ 2 vt dazzle.

éboueur /ebwœʀ/ nm dustman.

ébouillanter /ebujɑ̃te/ 11 vt scald.

éboulement /ebulmɑ̃/ nm landslide.

ébouriffé, ~e /eburife/ adj dishevelled.

ébrécher /ebreʃe/ 14 vt chip.

ébruiter /ebruite/ 11 vt spread

about. □ **s'~** vpr get out.

ébullition /ebylisjɔ̃/ nf boiling; **en ~** boiling.

écaille /ekaj/ nf (de poisson) scale; (de peinture, roc) flake; (matière) tortoiseshell.

écarlate /ekaʀlat/ adj scarlet.

écarquiller /ekaʀkije/ **1** vt **~ les yeux** open one's eyes wide.

écart /ekaʀ/ nm gap; (de prix) difference; (embardée) swerve; **~ de conduite** lapse in behaviour; **être à l'~** be isolated; **se tenir à l'~ de** stand apart from; (fig) keep out of the way of.

écarté, ~e /ekaʀte/ adj (lieu) remote; **les jambes ~es** (with) legs apart; **les bras ~s** with one's arms out.

écarter /ekaʀte/ **1** vt (séparer) move apart; (membres) spread; (branches) part; (éliminer) dismiss; **~ qch de** move sth away from; **~ qn de** keep sb away from. □ **s'~** vpr (s'éloigner) move away; (quitter son chemin) move aside; **s'~ de** stray from.

ecchymose /ekimoz/ nf bruise.

écervelé, ~e /esɛʀvale/ adj scatterbrained. ● nm, f scatterbrain.

échafaudage /eʃafodaʒ/ nm scaffolding; (amas) heap.

échalote /eʃalɔt/ nf shallot.

échancré /eʃɑ̃kʀe/ adj lowcut.

échange /eʃɑ̃ʒ/ nm exchange; **en ~ (de)** in exchange (for). **échanger** **40** vt exchange (**contre** for).

échangeur /eʃɑ̃ʒœʀ/ nm (Auto) interchange.

échantillon /eʃɑ̃tijɔ̃/ nm sample.

échappatoire /eʃapatwaʀ/ nf way out.

échappement /eʃapmɑ̃/ nm exhaust.

échapper /eʃape/ **1** vi **~ à** escape; (en fuyant) escape (from); **~ des mains** de slip out of the hands of; **ça m'a échappé** (fig) it just slipped out; **l'~ belle** have a narrow ou lucky escape. □ **s'~** vpr escape.

écharde /eʃaʀd/ nf splinter.

écharpe /eʃaʀp/ nf scarf; (de maire) sash; **en ~ (bras)** in a sling.

échasse /eʃas/ nf stilt.

échauffement /eʃofmɑ̃/ nm (Sport) warm-up.

échauffer /eʃofe/ **1** vt heat; (fig) excite. □ **s'~** vpr warm up.

échéance /eʃeɑ̃s/ nf due date (for payment); (délai) deadline; (obligation) (financial) commitment.

échéant: le cas ~ /ləkazeʃeɑ̃/ loc if need be.

échec /eʃɛk/ nm failure; **~s** (jeu) chess; **~ et mat** checkmate.

échelle /eʃɛl/ nf ladder; (dimension) scale.

échelon /eʃlɔ̃/ nm rung; (hiérarchique) grade; (niveau) level.

échevelé, ~e /eʃəvle/ adj dishevelled.

écho /eko/ nm echo; **~s** (dans la presse) gossip.

échographie /ekɔgʀafi/ nf (ultrasound) scan.

échouer /eʃwe/ **1** vi (bateau) run aground; (ne pas réussir) fail; **~ à un examen** fail an exam. ● vt (bateau) ground. □ **s'~** vpr run aground.

échu, ~e /eʃy/ adj (délai) expired.

éclabousser /eklabuse/ **1** vt splash.

éclair /eklɛʀ/ nm (flash of) lightning; (fig) flash; (gâteau) éclair. ● adj inv (visite) brief.

éclairage /eklɛʀaʒ/ nm lighting.

éclaircie /eklɛrsi/ nf sunny interval.

éclaircir /eklɛrsir/ **2** vt lighten; (mystère) clear up. □ **s'~** vpr (ciel) clear; (mystère) become clearer. **éclaircissement** nm clarification.

éclairer /eklere/ **1** vt light (up); (personne) (fig) enlighten; (situation) throw light on. ● vi give light. □ **s'~** vpr become clearer.

éclaireur, -euse /eklerœr, -øz/ nm, f (boy) scout, (girl) guide.

éclat /ekla/ nm fragment; (de lumière) brightness; (splendeur) brilliance; **~ de rire** burst of laughter.

éclatant, ~e /eklatɑ̃, -t/ adj brilliant; (soleil) dazzling.

éclater /eklate/ **1** vi burst; (explosion) go off; (verre) shatter; (guerre) break out; (groupe) split up; **~ de rire** burst out laughing.

éclipse /eklips/ nf eclipse.

éclosion /eklozjɔ̃/ nf hatching, opening.

écluse /eklyz/ nf (de canal) lock.

écœurant, ~e /ekœrɑ̃, -t/ adj (gâteau) sickly; (fig) disgusting. **écœurer** **1** vt sicken.

éco-guerrier, -ière /ekogɛrje, jɛr/ nmf eco-warrior.

école /ekɔl/ nf school; **~ maternelle/primaire/secondaire** nursery/primary/secondary school; **~ normale** teachers' training college. **écolier, -ière** nm, f schoolboy, schoolgirl.

écologie /ekɔlɔʒi/ nf ecology. **écologique** adj ecological, green. **écologiste** nmf (chercheur) ecologist; (dans l'âme) environmentalist; (Pol) Green.

économie /ekɔnɔmi/ nf economy; (discipline) economics; **~s** (argent) savings; **une ~ de** (gain) a saving of. **économique** adj (Pol) economic;

(bon marché) economical.

économiser /ekɔnɔmize/ **1** vt/i save.

écorce /ekɔrs/ nf bark; (de fruit) peel.

écorcher /ekɔrʃe/ **1** vt (genou) graze; (animal) skin. □ **s'~** vpr graze oneself. **écorchure** nf graze.

écossais, ~e /ekɔsɛ, -z/ adj Scottish. **É~, ~e** nm, f Scot.

Écosse /ekɔs/ nf Scotland.

écoulement /ekulmɑ̃/ nm flow.

écouler /ekule/ **1** vt dispose of, sell. □ **s'~** vpr (liquide) flow; (temps) pass.

écourter /ekurte/ **1** vt shorten.

écoute /ekut/ nf listening; **à l'~ (de)** listening in (to); **heures de grande ~** prime time; **~s téléphoniques** phone tapping.

écouter /ekute/ **1** vt listen to. ● vi listen; **~ aux portes** eavesdrop. **écouteur** nm earphones (+ pl); (de téléphone) receiver.

écran /ekrɑ̃/ nm screen; **~ total** sun-block.

écraser /ekraze/ **1** vt crush; (piéton) run over; (cigarette) stub out. □ **s'~** vpr crash (contre into).

écrémé, ~e /ekreme/ adj skimmed; **demi-~** semi-skimmed.

écrevisse /ekrəvis/ nf crayfish.

écrier (s') /(s)ekrije/ **45** vpr exclaim.

écrin /ekrɛ̃/ nm case.

écrire /ekrir/ **30** vt/i write; (orthographier) spell. □ **s'~** vpr (mot) be spelt.

écrit /ekri/ nm document; (examen) written paper; **par ~** in writing.

écriteau (pl **~x**) /ekrito/ nm notice.

écriture /ekrityr/ nf writing; **~s**

(Comm) accounts.

écrivain /ekʁivɛ̃/ *nm* writer.

écrou /ekʁu/ *nm* (Tech) nut.

écrouler (s') /(s)ekʁule/ **1** *vpr* collapse.

écru, ~e /ekʁy/ *adj* (couleur) natural; (tissu) raw.

écueil /ekœj/ *nm* reef; (fig) danger.

éculé, ~e /ekyle/ *adj* (soulier) worn at the heel; (fig) well-worn.

écume /ekym/ *nf* foam; (Culin) scum.

écumer /ekyme/ **1** *vt* skim. ● *vi* foam.

écureuil /ekyʁœj/ *nm* squirrel.

écurie /ekyʁi/ *nf* stable.

écuyer, -ère /ekɥije, -jɛʁ/ *nm, f* (horse) rider.

eczéma /ɛgzema/ *nm* eczema.

EDF *abrév f* (Électricité de France) French electricity board.

édifice /edifis/ *nm* building.

édifier /edifje/ **45** *vt* construct; (porter à la vertu) edify.

Édimbourg /edɛ̃buʁ/ *npr* Edinburgh.

édit /edi/ *nm* edict.

éditer /edite/ **1** *vt* publish; (annoter) edit. **éditeur, -trice** *nm, f* publisher; (réviseur) editor.

édition /edisjɔ̃/ *nf* (activité) publishing; (livre, disque) edition.

éditique /editik/ *nf* electronic publishing.

éditorial, ~e (*pl* **-iaux**) /editɔʁjal, -jo/ *adj & nm* editorial.

édredon /edʁədɔ̃/ *nm* eiderdown.

éducateur, -trice /edykatœʁ, -tʁis/ *nm, f* youth worker.

éducatif, -ive /edykatif, -v/ *adj* educational.

éducation /edykasjɔ̃/ *nf* (façon d'élever) upbringing; (enseignement) education; (manières) manners; **~ physique** physical education.

éduquer /edyke/ **1** *vt* (élever) bring up; (former) educate.

effacé, ~e /efase/ *adj* (modeste) unassuming.

effacer /efase/ **10** *vt* (gommer) rub out; (à l'écran) delete; (souvenir) erase. □ **s'~** *vpr* fade; (s'écarter) step aside.

effarer /efaʁe/ **1** *vt* alarm; **être effaré** be astounded.

effaroucher /efaʁuʃe/ **1** *vt* scare away.

effectif, -ive /efɛktif, -v/ *adj* effective. ● *nm* (d'école) number of pupils; **~s** numbers. **effectivement** *adv* effectively; (en effet) indeed.

effectuer /efɛktɥe/ **1** *vt* carry out, make.

efféminé, ~e /efemine/ *adj* effeminate.

effervescent, ~e /efɛʁvesɑ̃, -t/ *adj* **comprimé ~** effervescent tablet.

effet /efɛ/ *nm* effect; (impression) impression; **~s** (habits) clothes, things; **sous l'~ d'une drogue** under the influence of drugs; **en ~** indeed; **faire de l'~** have an effect, be effective; **faire bon/ mauvais ~** make a good/bad impression; **ça fait un drôle d'~** it feels strange.

efficace /efikas/ *adj* effective; (personne) efficient. **efficacité** *nf* effectiveness; (de personne) efficiency.

effleurer /eflœʁe/ **1** *vt* touch lightly; (sujet) touch on; **ça ne m'a pas effleuré** it did not cross my mind.

effondrement /efɔ̃dʁəmɑ̃/ *nm* collapse. **effondrer (s')** **1** *vpr* collapse.

efforcer (s') /(s)efɔʁse/ **10** *vpr* try (hard) (**de** to).

effort /efɔʀ/ nm effort.

effraction /efʀaksjɔ̃/ nf **entrer par** ~ break in.

effrayant, ~e /efʀejɑ̃, -t/ adj frightening; (fig) frightful.

effrayer /efʀeje/ **31** vt frighten; (décourager) put off. □ **s'**~ vpr be frightened.

effréné, ~e /efʀene/ adj wild.

effriter (s') /(s)efʀite/ **1** vpr crumble.

effroi /efʀwa/ nm dread.

effronté, ~e /efʀɔ̃te/ adj cheeky. ● nm, f cheeky boy, cheeky girl.

effroyable /efʀwajabl/ adj dreadful.

égal, ~e (mpl **-aux**) /egal, -o/ adj equal; (surface, vitesse) even. ● nm, f equal; **ça m'est/lui est** ~ it is all the same to me/him; **sans** ~ matchless; **d'**~ **à** ~ between equals. **également** adv equally; (aussi) as well. **égaler** **1** vt equal.

égaliser /egalize/ **1** vt/i (Sport) equalize; (niveler) level out; (cheveux) trim.

égalitaire /egalitɛʀ/ adj egalitarian.

égalité /egalite/ nf equality; (de surface) evenness; **être à** ~ be level.

égard /egaʀ/ nm consideration; ~s respect (+ sg); **par** ~ **pour** out of consideration for; **à cet** ~ in this respect; **à l'**~ **de** with regard to; (envers) towards.

égarer /egaʀe/ **1** vt mislay; (tromper) lead astray. □ **s'**~ vpr get lost; (se tromper) go astray.

égayer /egeje/ **31** vt (personne) cheer up; (pièce) brighten up.

église /egliz/ nf church.

égoïsme /egoism/ nm selfishness, egoism.

égoïste /egoist/ adj selfish. ● nmf

egoist.

égorger /egɔʀʒe/ **40** vt slit the throat of.

égout /egu/ nm sewer.

égoutter /egute/ **1** vt drain. □ **s'**~ vpr (vaisselle) drain; (lessive) drip dry. **égouttoir** nm draining-board.

égratigner /egʀatiɲe/ **1** vt scratch. **égratignure** nf scratch.

Égypte /eʒipt/ nf Egypt.

éjecter /eʒɛkte/ **1** vt eject.

élaboration /elabɔʀasjɔ̃/ nf elaboration. **élaborer** **1** vt elaborate.

élan /elɑ̃/ nm (animal) moose; (Sport) run-up; (vitesse) momentum; (fig) surge.

élancé, ~e /elɑ̃se/ adj slender.

élancement /elɑ̃smɑ̃/ nm twinge.

élancer (s') /(s)elɑ̃se/ **10** vpr leap forward, dash; (arbre, édifice) soar.

élargir /elaʀʒiʀ/ **2** vt (route) widen; (connaissances) broaden. □ **s'**~ vpr (famille) expand; (route) widen; (écart) increase; (vêtement) stretch.

élastique /elastik/ adj elastic. ● nm elastic band; (tissu) elastic.

électeur, -trice /elɛktœʀ, -tʀis/ nm, f voter. **élection** nf election. **électoral, ~e** (mpl **-aux**) (réunion) election. **électorat** nm electorate, voters (+ pl).

électricien, ~ne /elɛktʀisjɛ̃, ɛn/ nm, f electrician. **électricité** nf electricity.

électrifier /elɛktʀifje/ **45** vt electrify.

électrique /elɛktʀik/ adj electric; (installation) electrical.

électrocuter /elɛktʀokyte/ **1** vt electrocute.

électroménager /elɛktʀomenaʒe/ nm **l'**~ household

appliances (+ pl).

électron /elɛktʀɔ̃/ nm electron. **électronicien, ~ne** nm, f electronics engineer.

électronique /elɛktʀɔnik/ adj electronic. ● nf electronics.

élégance /elegɑ̃s/ nf elegance. **élégant, ~e** adj elegant.

élément /elemɑ̃/ nm element; (meuble) unit. **élémentaire** adj elementary.

éléphant /elefɑ̃/ nm elephant.

élevage /ɛlvaʒ/ nm (stock-) breeding.

élévation /elevasjɔ̃/ nf rise; (hausse) rise; (plan) elevation; ~ de terrain rise in the ground.

élève /elɛv/ nmf pupil.

élevé, ~e /ɛlve/ adj high; (noble) elevated; **bien ~** well-mannered.

élever /ɛlve/ 6 vt (lever) raise; (enfants) bring up, raise; (animal) breed. □ s'~ vpr rise; (dans le ciel) soar up; s'~ à amount to. **éleveur, -euse** nm, f (stock-)breeder.

éligible /eliʒibl/ adj eligible.

élimination /eliminasjɔ̃/ nf elimination.

éliminatoire /eliminatwaʀ/ adj qualifying. ● nf (Sport) heat.

éliminer /elimine/ 1 vt eliminate.

élire /eliʀ/ 39 vt elect.

elle /ɛl/ pron she; (complément) her; (chose) it. **elle-même** pron herself; itself. **elles** pron they; (complément) them. **elles-mêmes** pron themselves.

élocution /elɔkysjɔ̃/ nf diction.

éloge /elɔʒ/ nm praise; **faire l'~ de** praise; **~s** praise (+ sg).

éloigné, ~e /elwaɲe/ adj distant; ~ de far away from; **parent ~** distant relative.

éloigner /elwaɲe/ 1 vt take away

ou remove (**de** from); (visite) put off. □ s'~ vpr go ou move away (**de** from); (affectivement) become estranged (**de** from).

élongation /elɔ̃gasjɔ̃/ nf strained muscle.

éloquent, ~e /elɔkɑ̃, -t/ adj eloquent.

élu, ~e /ely/ adj elected. ● nm, f (Pol) elected representative.

élucider /elyside/ 1 vt elucidate.

éluder /elyde/ 1 vt evade.

Élysée The palais de l'Élysée is the official residence of the Président de la République, not far from the Champs Élysées in central Paris. The word Élysée is often used to refer to the president's office. See ▷MATIGNON.

émacié, ~e /emasje/ adj emaciated.

e-mail /imel/ nm email; **envoyer un ~** a qn email sb.

émail (pl **-aux**) /emaj, -o/ nm enamel.

émanciper /emɑ̃sipe/ 1 vt emancipate. □ s'~ vpr become emancipated.

émaner /emane/ 1 vi emanate.

emballage /ɑ̃balaʒ/ nm (dur) packaging; (souple) wrapping.

emballer /ɑ̃bale/ 1 vt pack; (en papier) wrap; **ça ne m'emballe pas** 1 I'm not really taken by it. □ s'~ vpr (moteur) race; (cheval) bolt; (personne) get carried away; (prices) shoot up.

embarcadère /ɑ̃baʀkadɛʀ/ nm landing-stage.

embarcation /ɑ̃baʀkasjɔ̃/ nf boat.

embardée /ɑ̃baʀde/ nf swerve.

embarquement /ãbaʀkəmã/ *nm* (de passagers) boarding; (de fret) loading.

embarquer /ãbaʀke/ **1** *vt* take on board; (*frêt*) load; (emporter 🄸) cart off. ● *vi* board. ☐ **s'~** *vpr* board; **s'~ dans** embark upon.

embarras /ãbaʀa/ *nm* (gêne) embarrassment; (difficulté) difficulty.

embarrasser /ãbaʀase/ **1** *vt* (encombrer) clutter (up); (fig) embarrass. ☐ **s'~ de** *vpr* burden oneself with.

embauche /ãboʃ/ *nf* hiring. **embaucher** **1** *vt* hire, take on.

embaumer /ãbome/ **1** *vt* (*pièce*) fill; (*cadavre*) embalm. ● *vi* be fragrant.

embellir /ãbeliʀ/ **2** *vt* make more attractive; (*récit*) embellish.

embêtant, ~e /ãbɛtã, -t/ *adj* 🄸 annoying.

embêter /ãbete/ **1** *vt* bother. ☐ **s'~** *vpr* be bored.

emblée: d'~ /dãble/ *loc* right away.

emblème /ãblɛm/ *nm* emblem.

emboîter /ãbwate/ **1** *vt* fit together; **~ le pas à qn** (imiter) follow suit. ☐ **s'~ dans** fit into.

embonpoint /ãbõpwɛ̃/ *nm* stoutness.

embourber (s') /(s)ãbuʀbe/ **1** *vpr* get stuck in the mud; (fig) get bogged down.

embouteillage /ãbutɛjaʒ/ *nm* traffic jam.

emboutir /ãbutiʀ/ **2** *vt* (Auto) crash into.

embraser (s') /(s)ãbʀaze/ **1** *vpr* catch fire.

embrasser /ãbʀase/ **1** *vt* kiss; (adopter, contenir) embrace. ☐ **s'~** *vpr* kiss.

embrayage /ãbʀɛjaʒ/ *nm* clutch. **embrayer** 🄸 *vi* engage the clutch.

embrouiller /ãbʀuje/ **1** *vt* confuse; (*fils*) tangle. ☐ **s'~** *vpr* become confused.

embryon /ãbʀijõ/ *nm* embryo.

embûches /ãbyʃ/ *nfpl* traps.

embuer(s') /(s)ãbɥe/ **1** *vpr* mist up.

embuscade /ãbyskad/ *nf* ambush.

émeraude /ɛmʀod/ *nf* emerald.

émerger /emɛʀʒe/ 🄸 *vi* emerge; (fig) stand out.

émeri /ɛmʀi/ *nm* emery.

émerveillement /emɛʀvɛjmã/ *nm* amazement, wonder.

émerveiller /emɛʀveje/ **1** *vt* fill with wonder. ☐ **s'~** *vpr* marvel at.

émetteur /emɛtœʀ/ *nm* transmitter.

émettre /emɛtʀ/ 🄸 *vt* (son) produce; (message) send out; (timbre, billet) issue; (opinion) express.

émeute /emøt/ *nf* riot.

émietter /emjete/ **1** *vt* crumble. ☐ **s'~** *vpr* crumble.

émigrant, ~e /emigʀã, -t/ *nm, f* emigrant. **émigration** *nf* emigration. **émigrer** **1** *vi* emigrate.

émincer /emɛ̃se/ 🄸 *vt* cut into thin slices.

éminent, ~e /eminã, -t/ *adj* eminent.

émissaire /emisɛʀ/ *nm* emissary.

émission /emisjõ/ *nf* (programme) programme; (de chaleur, gaz) emission; (de timbre) issue.

emmagasiner /ãmagazine/ **1** *vt* store.

emmanchure /ãmãʃyʀ/ *nf* armhole.

emmêler /ãmele/ **1** *vt* tangle. ☐ **s'~** *vpr* get mixed up.

emménager /ɑ̃menaʒe/ **40** vi
move in; ~ **dans** move into.

emmener /ɑ̃mne/ **6** vt take;
(comme prisonnier) take away.

emmerder /ɑ̃mɛʀde/ **1** ⊠ vt ~
qn get on sb's nerves. □ **s'~** vpr be
bored.

emmitoufler /ɑ̃mitufle/ **1** vt
wrap up warmly. □ **s'~** vpr wrap
oneself up warmly.

émoi /emwa/ nm turmoil; (plaisir)
excitement.

émotif, -ive /emotif, -v/ adj emotional. **émotion** nf emotion; (peur)
fright. **émotionnel, ~le** adj emotional.

émousser /emuse/ **1** vt blunt.

émouvant, ~e /emuvɑ̃, -t/ adj
moving.

empailler /ɑ̃paje/ **1** vt stuff.

empaqueter /ɑ̃pakte/ **38** vt
package.

emparer (s') /(s)ɑ̃paʀe/ vpr
s'~ de get hold of.

empêchement /ɑ̃pɛʃmɑ̃/ nm
avoir un ~ to be held up.

empêcher /ɑ̃pɛʃe/ **1** vt prevent;
~ **de faire** prevent ou stop (from)
doing; **(il) n'empêche que** still.
□ **s'~** vpr **il ne peut pas s'en ~** he
cannot help it.

empereur /ɑ̃pʀœʀ/ nm emperor.

empester /ɑ̃pɛste/ **1** vt stink out;
(essence) stink of. ● vi stink.

empêtrer (s') /(s)ɑ̃petʀe/ **1** vpr
become entangled.

empiéter /ɑ̃pjete/ **14** vi ~ **sur** encroach upon.

empiffrer (s') /(s)ɑ̃pifʀe/ **1** vpr
1 stuff oneself.

empiler /ɑ̃pile/ **1** vt pile up.
□ **s'~** vpr pile up.

empire /ɑ̃piʀ/ nm empire.

emplacement /ɑ̃plasmɑ̃/ nm site.

emplâtre /ɑ̃plɑtʀ/ nm (Méd)
plaster.

emploi /ɑ̃plwa/ nm (travail) job;
(embauche) employment; (utilisation) use; **un ~ de chauffeur** a job
as a driver; ~ **du temps** timetable.
employé, ~e nm, f employee.

employer /ɑ̃plwaje/ **31** vt (personne) employ; (utiliser) use. □ **s'~**
vpr be used; **s'~ à** devote oneself
to. **employeur, -euse** nm, f employer.

empoigner /ɑ̃pwaɲe/ **1** vt grab.
□ **s'~** vpr come to blows.

empoisonnement
/ɑ̃pwazɔnmɑ̃/ nm poisoning.

empoisonner /ɑ̃pwazɔne/ **1** vt
poison; (embêter **1**) annoy. □ **s'~**
vpr to poison oneself.

emporter /ɑ̃pɔʀte/ **1** vt take
(away); (entraîner) sweep away; (arracher) tear off. □ **s'~** vpr lose
one's temper; **l'~** get the upper
hand (**sur** of); **plat à ~** take-away.

empoté, ~e /ɑ̃pɔte/ adj clumsy.

empreinte /ɑ̃pʀɛ̃t/ nf mark; ~
(digitale) fingerprint; ~ **de pas**
footprint.

empressé, ~e /ɑ̃pʀese/ adj eager,
attentive.

empresser (s') /(s)ɑ̃pʀese/ **1**
vpr **s'~ de** hasten to; **s'~ auprès
de** be attentive to.

emprise /ɑ̃pʀiz/ nf influence.

emprisonnement /ɑ̃pʀizɔnmɑ̃/
nm imprisonment. **emprisonner** **1**
vt imprison.

emprunt /ɑ̃pʀɛ̃/ nm loan; **faire
un ~** take out a loan.

emprunté, ~e /ɑ̃pʀɛ̃te/ adj
awkward.

emprunter /ɑ̃pʀɛ̃te/ **1** vt borrow (**à** from); (route) take; (fig) assume. **emprunteur, -euse** nm, f
borrower.

ému, ~e /emy/ adj moved; (intimidé) nervous.

émule /emyl/ nmf imitator.

---

en /ã/

> Pour les expressions comme en principe, en train de, s'en aller, etc. ➡ **principe, train, aller,** etc.

● préposition

····➤ (lieu) in.

····➤ (avec mouvement) to.

····➤ (temps) in.

····➤ (manière, état) in; ~ **faisant** by ou while doing; **je t'appelle ~ rentrant** I will call you when I get back.

····➤ (en qualité de) as.

····➤ (transport) by.

····➤ (composition) made of; **table ~ bois** wooden table.

● pronom

····➤ **en avoir/vouloir** have/want some; **ne pas ~ avoir/vouloir** not have/want any; **j'~ ai deux** I've got two; **prends-~** plu**sieurs** take several; **il m'~ reste un** I have one left; **j'~ suis content** I am pleased with him/her/it/them; **je m'~ souviens** I remember it.

····➤ ~ **êtes-vous sûr?** are you sure?

encadrement /ãkadʀəmã/ nm framing; (de porte) frame. **encadrer** 🔳 vt frame; (entourer d'un trait) circle; (superviser) supervise.

encaisser /ãkese/ 🔳 vt (argent) collect; (chèque) cash; (coups 🔳) take.

encart /ãkaʀ/ nm ~ **publicitaire** (advertising) insert.

en-cas /ãkɑ/ nm (stand-by) snack.

encastré, ~e /ãkastʀe/ adj built-in.

encaustique /ãkostik/ nf wax polish.

enceinte /ãsɛ̃t/ adj f pregnant; ~ **de 3 mois** 3 months pregnant. ● nf enclosure; ~ **(acoustique)** speaker.

encens /ãsã/ nm incense.

encercler /ãseʀkle/ 🔳 vt surround.

enchaînement /ãʃɛnmã/ nm (suite) chain; (d'idées) sequence.

enchaîner /ãʃene/ 🔳 vt chain (up); (phrases) link (up). ● vi continue. □ **s'~** vpr follow on.

enchanté, ~e /ãʃãte/ adj (ravi) delighted. **enchanter** 🔳 vt delight; (ensorceler) enchant.

enchère /ãʃeʀ/ nf bid; **mettre** ou **vendre aux ~** sell by auction.

enchevêtrer /ãʃəvetʀe/ 🔳 vt tangle. □ **s'~** vpr become tangled.

enclave /ãklav/ nf enclave.

enclencher /ãklãʃe/ 🔳 vt engage.

enclin, ~e /ãklɛ̃, -in/ adj ~ **à** inclined to.

enclos /ãklo/ nm enclosure.

enclume /ãklym/ nf anvil.

encoche /ãkɔʃ/ nf notch.

encolure /ãkɔlyʀ/ nf neck.

encombrant, ~e /ãkɔ̃bʀã, -t/ adj cumbersome.

encombre /ãkɔ̃bʀ/ nm sans ~ without any problems.

encombrement /ãkɔ̃bʀəmã/ nm (Auto) traffic congestion; (volume) bulk.

encombrer /ãkɔ̃bʀe/ 🔳 vt clutter (up); (obstruer) obstruct. □ **s'~ de** vpr burden oneself with.

encontre: à l'~ de /alãkɔ̃tʀədə/ loc against.

encore /ãkɔʀ/ adv (toujours) still; (de nouveau) again; (de plus) more;

(aussi) also; ~ **plus grand** even larger; ~ **un café** another coffee; **pas** ~ not yet; **si** ~ if only; **et puis quoi** ~? 🔟 what next?

encouragement /ãkuraʒmã/ nm encouragement. **encourager** 🐵 vt encourage.

encourir /ãkuRiR/ 🔟 vt incur.

encrasser /ãkRase/ 🔟 vt clog up (with dirt).

encre /ãkR/ nf ink. **encrier** nm ink-well.

encyclopédie /ãsiklɔpedi/ nf encyclopaedia.

endettement /ãdɛtmã/ nm debt.

endetter /ãdɛte/ 🔟 vt put into debt. □ **s'**~ vpr get into debt.

endiguer /ãdige/ 🔟 vt dam; (fig) curb.

endimanché, ~e /ãdimãʃe/ adj in one's Sunday best.

endive /ãdiv/ nf chicory.

endoctriner /ãdɔktRine/ 🔟 vt indoctrinate.

endommager /ãdɔmaʒe/ 🐵 vt damage.

endormi, ~e /ãdɔRmi/ adj asleep; (apathique) sleepy.

endormir /ãdɔRmiR/ 🐵 vt send to sleep; (médicalement) put to sleep; (duper) dupe (**avec** with). □ **s'**~ vpr fall asleep.

endosser /ãdose/ 🔟 vt (vêtement) put on; (assumer) take on; (Comm) endorse.

endroit /ãdRwa/ nm place; (de tissu) right side; **à l'**~ the right way round; **par** ~**s** in places.

enduire /ãdɥiR/ 🔟 vt coat. **enduit** nm coating.

endurance /ãdyRãs/ nf endurance. **endurant, ~e** adj tough.

endurcir /ãdyRsiR/ 🔟 vt strengthen. □ **s'**~ vpr become

hard (hardened).

endurer /ãdyRe/ 🔟 vt endure.

énergétique /enɛRʒetik/ adj energy; (food) high-calorie. **énergie** nf energy; (Tech) power. **énergique** adj energetic.

énervant, ~e /enɛRvã, -t/ adj irritating, annoying.

énerver /enɛRve/ 🔟 vt irritate. □ **s'**~ vpr get worked up.

enfance /ãfãs/ nf childhood; **la petite** ~ infancy.

enfant /ãfã/ nmf child. **enfantillage** nm childishness. **enfantin, ~e** adj simple, easy; (puéril) childish; (jeu, langage) children's.

enfer /ãfɛR/ nm (Relig) Hell; (fig) hell.

enfermer /ãfɛRme/ 🔟 vt shut up. □ **s'**~ vpr shut oneself up.

enfiler /ãfile/ 🔟 vt (aiguille) thread; (vêtement) slip on; (rue) take.

enfin /ãfɛ̃/ adv (de soulagement) at last; (en dernier lieu) finally; (résignation, conclusion) well; ~ **presque** well nearly.

enflammé, ~e /ãflame/ adj (Méd) inflamed; (discours) fiery; (lettre) passionate.

enflammer /ãflame/ 🔟 vt set fire to. □ **s'**~ vpr catch fire.

enfler /ãfle/ 🔟 vt (histoire) exaggerate. ● vi (partie du corps) swell (up); (mer) swell; (rumeur, colère) spread. □ **s'**~ vpr (colère) mount; (rumeur) grow.

enfoncer /ãfɔse/ 🔟 vt (épingle) push ou drive in; (chapeau) push down; (porte) break down. ● vi sink. □ **s'**~ vpr sink (**dans** into).

enfouir /ãfwiR/ 🔟 vt bury.

enfourcher /ãfuRʃe/ 🔟 vt mount.

enfreindre /ãfRɛdR/ 🔟 vt infringe, break.

enfuir (s') /(s)ɑ̃fɥiʀ/ **35** vpr run away.

enfumé, ~e /ɑ̃fyme/ adj filled with smoke.

engagé, ~e /ɑ̃ɡaʒe/ adj committed.

engagement /ɑ̃ɡaʒmɑ̃/ nm (promesse) promise; (Pol, Comm) commitment.

engager /ɑ̃ɡaʒe/ **40** vt (lier) bind, commit; (embaucher) take on; (commencer) start; (introduire) insert; (investir) invest. □ **s'~** vpr (promettre) commit oneself; (commencer) start; (soldat) enlist; (concurrent) enter; **s'~ à faire** undertake to do; **s'~ dans** (voie) enter.

engelure /ɑ̃ʒlyʀ/ nf chilblain.

engendrer /ɑ̃ʒɑ̃dʀe/ **1** vt (causer) generate.

engin /ɑ̃ʒɛ̃/ nm device; (véhicule) vehicle; (missile) missile.

engloutir /ɑ̃ɡlutiʀ/ **2** vt swallow (up).

engouement /ɑ̃ɡumɑ̃/ nm passion.

engouffrer /ɑ̃ɡufʀe/ **1** vt **1** gobble up. □ **s'~ dans** vpr rush in.

engourdir /ɑ̃ɡuʀdiʀ/ **2** vt numb. □ **s'~** vpr go numb.

engrais /ɑ̃ɡʀɛ/ nm manure; (chimique) fertilizer.

engrenage /ɑ̃ɡʀənaʒ/ nm gears (pl); (fig) spiral.

engueuler /ɑ̃ɡœle/ **1** **✗** vt shout at. □ **s'~** vpr have a row.

enhardir (s') /(s)ɑ̃aʀdiʀ/ **2** vpr become bolder.

énième /enjɛm/ adj umpteenth.

énigmatique /enigmatik/ adj enigmatic. **énigme** nf enigma; (devinette) riddle.

enivrer /ɑ̃nivʀe/ **1** vt intoxicate. □ **s'~** vpr get intoxicated.

enjambée /ɑ̃ʒɑ̃be/ nf stride. **enjamber** **1** vt step over; (pont) span.

enjeu (pl **~x**) /ɑ̃ʒø/ nm stake.

enjoué, ~e /ɑ̃ʒwe/ adj cheerful.

enlacer /ɑ̃lase/ **10** vt entwine.

enlèvement /ɑ̃lɛvmɑ̃/ nm (de colis) removal; (d'ordures) collection; (rapt) kidnapping.

enlever /ɑ̃lve/ **6** vt remove (à from); (vêtement) take off; (tache, organe) take out, remove; (kidnapper) kidnap; (gagner) win.

enliser (s') /(s)ɑ̃lize/ **1** vpr get bogged down.

enneigé, ~e /ɑ̃neʒe/ adj snow-covered.

ennemi, ~e /ɛnmi/ adj & nm enemy; **~ de** (fig) hostile to.

ennui /ɑ̃nɥi/ nm problem; (tracas) boredom; **s'attirer des ~s** run into trouble.

ennuyer /ɑ̃nɥije/ **31** vt bore; (irriter) annoy; (préoccuper) worry; **si cela ne t'ennuie pas** if you don't mind. □ **s'~** vpr get bored.

ennuyeux, -euse /ɑ̃nɥijø, -z/ adj boring; (fâcheux) annoying.

énoncé /enɔ̃se/ nm wording; text; (Gram) utterance.

énoncer /enɔ̃se/ **10** vt express, state.

enorgueillir (s') /(s)ɑ̃nɔʀɡœjiʀ/ **2** vpr **s'~ de** pride oneself on.

énorme /enɔʀm/ adj enormous.

enquête /ɑ̃kɛt/ nf (Jur) investigation, inquiry; (sondage) survey; **mener l'~** lead the inquiry. **enquêter** **1** vi **~ (sur)** investigate. **enquêteur, -euse** nm, f investigator.

enquiquinant, ~e /ɑ̃kikinɑ̃, -t/ adj **1** irritating.

enraciné, ~e /ɑ̃ʀasine/ adj deep rooted.

enragé, ~e /ɑ̃ʀaʒe/ adj furious; (chien) rabid; (fig) fanatical.

enrager /ɑ̃ʀaʒe/ **40** vi be furious; faire ~ qn annoy sb.

enregistrement /ɑ̃ʀ(ə)ʒistʀəmɑ̃/ nm recording; (des bagages) check-in. **enregistrer** **1** vt (Mus, TV) record; (mémoriser) take in; (bagages) check in.

enrhumer (s') /(s)ɑ̃ʀyme/ **1** vpr catch a cold.

enrichir /ɑ̃ʀiʃiʀ/ **2** vt enrich. □ s'~ vpr grow rich(er). **enrichissant**, ~e adj (expérience) rewarding.

enrober /ɑ̃ʀɔbe/ **1** vt coat (de with).

enrôler /ɑ̃ʀole/ **1** vt recruit. □ s'~ vpr enlist, enrol.

enroué, ~e /ɑ̃ʀwe/ adj hoarse.

enrouler /ɑ̃ʀule/ **1** vt wind, wrap. □ s'~ vpr wind; s'~ dans une couverture roll oneself up in a blanket.

ensanglanté, ~e /ɑ̃sɑ̃glɑ̃te/ adj bloodstained.

enseignant, ~e /ɑ̃sɛɲɑ̃, -t/ nm, f teacher. ● adj teaching.

enseigne /ɑ̃sɛɲ/ nf sign.

enseignement /ɑ̃sɛɲəmɑ̃/ nm (profession) teaching; (instruction) education.

enseigner /ɑ̃sɛɲe/ **1** vt/i teach; ~ qch à qn teach sb sth.

ensemble /ɑ̃sɑ̃bl/ adv together. ● nm group; (Mus) ensemble; (vêtements) outfit; (cohésion) unity; (maths) set; dans l'~ on the whole; d'~ (idée) general; l'~ de (totalité) all of, the whole of.

ensevelir /ɑ̃səvliʀ/ **2** vt bury.

ensoleillé, ~e /ɑ̃sɔleje/ adj sunny.

ensorceler /ɑ̃sɔʀsale/ **38** vt bewitch.

ensuite /ɑ̃sɥit/ adv next, then; (plus tard) later.

ensuivre (s') /(s)ɑ̃sɥivʀ/ **57** vpr follow; **et tout ce qui s'ensuit** and all the rest of it.

entaille /ɑ̃taj/ nf cut; (profonde) gash; (encoche) notch.

entamer /ɑ̃tame/ **1** vt start; (inciser) cut into; (ébranler) shake.

entasser /ɑ̃tase/ **1** vt (livres) pile; (argent) hoard; (personnes) cram (dans into). □ s'~ vpr (objets) pile up (dans into); (personnes) squeeze (dans into).

entendement /ɑ̃tɑ̃dmɑ̃/ nm understanding; **ça dépasse l'~** it's beyond belief.

entendre /ɑ̃tɑ̃dʀ/ **3** vt hear; (comprendre) understand; (vouloir dire) mean; ~ parler de hear of; ~ dire que hear that. □ s'~ vpr (être d'accord) agree; s'~ (bien) get on (avec with); cela s'entend of course.

entendu, ~e /ɑ̃tɑ̃dy/ adj (convenu) agreed; (sourire, air) knowing; **bien** ~ of course; (c'est) ~! all right!

entente /ɑ̃tɑ̃t/ nf understanding; **bonne** ~ good relationship.

enterrement /ɑ̃tɛʀmɑ̃/ nm funeral.

enterrer /ɑ̃tere/ **1** vt bury.

en-tête /ɑ̃tɛt/ nm heading; **à** ~ headed.

entêté, ~e /ɑ̃tete/ adj stubborn. **entêtement** nm stubbornness. **entêter (s')** **1** vpr persist (à, dans in).

enthousiasme /ɑ̃tuzjasm/ nm enthusiasm. **enthousiasmer** **1** vt fill with enthusiasm. **enthousiaste** adj enthusiastic.

enticher (s') /(s)ɑ̃tiʃe/ **1** vpr s'~ de become infatuated with.

entier, **-ière** /ɑ̃tje, -jɛʀ/ adj whole; (absolu) absolute; (entêté) unyielding. ● nm whole; **en** ~ entirely.

entonnoir /ɑ̃tɔnwaʀ/ nm funnel; (trou) crater.

entorse /ɑ̃tɔʀs/ nf sprain; (fig) ~ à (loi) infringement of.

entortiller /ɑ̃tɔʀtije/ **1** vt wind, wrap (**autour** around); (duper **1**) get round.

entourage /ɑ̃tuʀaʒ/ nm circle of family and friends; (bordure) surround.

entouré, ~e /ɑ̃tuʀe/ adj (personne) supported.

entourer /ɑ̃tuʀe/ **1** vt surround (**de** with); (réconforter) rally round; ~ **qch de mystère** shroud sth in mystery.

entracte /ɑ̃tʀakt/ nm interval.

entraide /ɑ̃tʀɛd/ nf mutual aid.

entraider (s') /ɑ̃tʀede/ **1** vpr help each other.

entrain /ɑ̃tʀɛ̃/ nm zest, spirit.

entraînement /ɑ̃tʀɛnmɑ̃/ nm (Sport) training.

entraîner /ɑ̃tʀene/ **1** vt (emporter) carry away; (provoquer) lead to; (Sport) train; (actionner) drive. □ **s'**~ vpr train. **entraîneur** nm trainer.

entrave /ɑ̃tʀav/ nf hindrance. **entraver 1** vt hinder.

entre /ɑ̃tʀ(ə)/ prép between; (parmi) among(st); ~ **autres** among other things; **l'un d'**~ **nous/eux** one of us/them.

entrebâillé, ~e /ɑ̃tʀəbaje/ adj ajar, half-open.

entrechoquer (s') /(s)ɑ̃tʀə ʃɔke/ **1** vpr knock against each other.

entrecôte /ɑ̃tʀəkot/ nf rib steak.

entrecouper /ɑ̃tʀəkupe/ **1** vt ~ **de** intersperse with.

entrecroiser (s') /(s)ɑ̃tʀə kʀwaze/ **1** vpr (routes) intertwine.

entrée /ɑ̃tʀe/ nf entrance; (vesti-

bule) hall; (accès) admission, entry; (billet) ticket; (Culin) starter; (Ordinat) **tapez sur E**~ press Enter; **'**~ **interdite'** 'no entry'.

entrejambes /ɑ̃tʀəʒɑ̃b/ nm crotch.

entremets /ɑ̃tʀəmɛ/ nm dessert.

entremise /ɑ̃tʀəmiz/ nf intervention; **par l'**~ **de** through.

entreposer /ɑ̃tʀəpoze/ **1** vt store.

entrepôt /ɑ̃tʀəpo/ nm warehouse.

entreprenant, ~e /ɑ̃tʀəpʀənɑ̃, -t/ adj (actif) enterprising; (séducteur) forward.

entreprendre /ɑ̃tʀəpʀɑ̃dʀ/ **50** vt start on, undertake; (personne) buttonhole; ~ **de faire** undertake to do.

entrepreneur /ɑ̃tʀəpʀənœʀ/ nm (de bâtiment) contractor; (chef d'entreprise) firm manager.

entreprise /ɑ̃tʀəpʀiz/ nf (projet) undertaking; (société) firm, business, company.

entrer /ɑ̃tʀe/ **1** vi (aux être) go in, enter; (venir) come in, enter; ~ **dans** go ou come into, enter; (club) join; ~ **en collision** collide (**avec** with); **faire** ~ (personne) show in; **laisser** ~ let in; ~ **en guerre** go to war. ● vt (données) enter.

entre-temps /ɑ̃tʀətɑ̃/ adv meanwhile.

entretenir /ɑ̃tʀət(ə)niʀ/ **58** vt (appareil) maintain; (vêtement) look after; (alimenter) (feu) keep going; (amitié) keep alive; ~ **qn de** converse with sb about. □ **s'**~ vpr speak (**de** about; **avec** to). **entretien** nm maintenance; (discussion) talk; (pour un emploi) interview.

entrevoir /ɑ̃tʀəvwaʀ/ **63** vt make out; (brièvement) glimpse.

entrevue /ɑ̃tʀəvy/ nf meeting.

entrouvert, ~e /ɑ̃truvɛr, -t/ *adj* ajar, half-open.

énumération /enymerasjɔ̃/ *nf* enumeration. **énumérer** 14 *vt* enumerate.

envahir /ɑ̃vair/ 2 *vt* invade, overrun; (*douleur, peur*) overcome.

enveloppe /ɑ̃vlɔp/ *nf* envelope; (*emballage*) wrapping; ~ **budgétaire** budget. **envelopper** 1 *vt* wrap (up); (*fig*) envelop.

envergure /ɑ̃vɛrgyr/ *nf* wingspan; (*importance*) scope; (*qualité*) calibre.

envers /ɑ̃vɛr/ *prép* toward(s), to. ● *nm* (de tissu) wrong side; **à l'~** (*tableau*) upside down; (*devant derrière*) back to front; (*chaussette*) inside out.

envie /ɑ̃vi/ *nf* urge; (*jalousie*) envy; **avoir ~ de qch** feel like sth; **avoir ~ de faire** want to do; (*moins urgent*) feel like doing; **faire ~ à qn** make sb envious.

envier /ɑ̃vje/ 45 *vt* envy. **envieux, -ieuse** *adj* envious.

environ /ɑ̃virɔ̃/ *adv* about.

environnant, ~e /ɑ̃virɔnɑ̃, -t/ *adj* surrounding.

environnement /ɑ̃virɔnmɑ̃/ *nm* environment.

environs /ɑ̃virɔ̃/ *nmpl* vicinity; **aux ~ de** (*lieu*) in the vicinity of; (*heure*) round about.

envisager /ɑ̃vizaʒe/ 40 *vt* consider; (*imaginer*) envisage; ~ **de faire** consider doing.

envoi /ɑ̃vwa/ *nm* dispatch; (*paquet*) consignment; **faire un ~** send; **coup d'~** (Sport) kick-off.

envoler (s') /(s)ɑ̃vɔle/ 1 *vpr* fly away; (*avion*) take off; (*papiers*) blow away.

envoyé, ~e /ɑ̃vwaje/ *nm, f* envoy; ~ **spécial** special correspondent.

envoyer /ɑ̃vwaje/ 32 *vt* send; (*lancer*) throw.

éolienne /eɔljɛn/ *nf* windmill; **ferme d'~s** wind farm.

épais, ~se /epɛ, -s/ *adj* thick. **épaisseur** *nf* thickness.

épaissir /epesir/ 2 *vt/i* thicken. □ **s'~** *vpr* thicken; (*mystère*) deepen.

épanoui, ~e /epanwi/ *adj* (*personne*) beaming, radiant.

épanouir (s') /(s)epanwir/ 2 *vpr* (*fleur*) open out; (*visage*) beam; (*personne*) blossom. **épanouissement** *nm* (*éclat*) blossoming, full bloom.

épargne /eparɲ/ *nf* savings. **épargner** /eparɲe/ 1 *vt/i* save; (*ne pas tuer*) spare; ~ **qch à qn** spare sb sth.

éparpiller /eparpije/ 1 *vt* scatter. □ **s'~** *vpr* scatter; (*fig*) dissipate one's efforts.

épars, ~e /epar, -s/ *adj* scattered.

épatant, ~e /epatɑ̃, -t/ *adj* 1 amazing.

épaule /epol/ *nf* shoulder.

épave /epav/ *nf* wreck.

épée /epe/ *nf* sword.

épeler /ɛple/ 6 *vt* spell.

éperdu, ~e /epɛrdy/ *adj* wild, frantic.

éperon /eprɔ̃/ *nm* spur.

éphémère /efemɛr/ *adj* ephemeral.

épi /epi/ *nm* (de blé) ear; (*mèche*) tuft of hair; ~ **de maïs** corn cob.

épice /epis/ *nf* spice. **épicé,** ~e *adj* spicy.

épicerie /episri/ *nf* grocery shop; (*produits*) groceries. **épicier, -ière** *nm, f* grocer.

épidémie /epidemi/ *nf* epidemic.

épiderme /epidɛrm/ *nm* skin.

épier /epje/ 45 *vt* spy on.

épilepsie /epilɛpsi/ nf epilepsy. **épileptique** adj & nmf epileptic.

épiler /epile/ **1** vt remove unwanted hair from; (sourcils) pluck.

épilogue /epilɔg/ nm epilogue; (fig) outcome.

épinard /epinaʀ/ ~s spinach (+ sg).

épine /epin/ nf thorn, prickle; (d'animal) prickle, spine; ~ dorsale backbone. **épineux, -euse** adj thorny.

épingle /epɛ̃gl/ nf pin; ~ de nourrice, ~ de sûreté safety-pin.

épisode /epizod/ nm episode; à ~s serialized.

épitaphe /epitaf/ nf epitaph.

épluche-légumes /eplyʃlegym/ nm inv (potato) peeler.

éplucher /eplyʃe/ **1** vt peel; (examiner: fig) scrutinize.

épluchure /eplyʃyʀ/ nf ~s peelings.

éponge /epɔ̃ʒ/ nf sponge. **éponger** **40** vt (liquide) mop up; (surface, front) mop; (fig) (dettes) wipe out.

épopée /epope/ nf epic.

époque /epɔk/ nf time, period; à l'~ at the time; d'~ period.

épouse /epuz/ nf wife.

épouser /epuze/ **1** vt marry; (forme, idée) adopt.

épousseter /epuste/ **38** vt dust.

épouvantable /epuvɑ̃tabl/ adj appalling.

épouvantail /epuvɑ̃taj/ nm scarecrow.

épouvante /epuvɑ̃t/ nf terror. **épouvanter** **1** vt terrify.

époux /epu/ nm husband; les ~ the married couple.

éprendre (s') /(s)epʀɑ̃dʀ/ **50** vpr s'~ de fall in love with.

épreuve /epʀœv/ nf test; (Sport)

event; (malheur) ordeal; (Photo, d'imprimerie) proof; mettre à l'~ put to the test.

éprouver /epʀuve/ **1** vt (ressentir) experience; (affliger) distress; (tester) test.

éprouvette /epʀuvɛt/ nf test tube.

EPS abrév f (**éducation physique et sportive**) PE.

épuisé, ~e /epɥize/ adj exhausted; (livre) out of print. **épuisement** nm exhaustion.

épuiser /epɥize/ **1** vt (fatiguer, user) exhaust. □ s'~ vpr become exhausted.

épuration /epyʀasjɔ̃/ nf purification; (Pol) purge. **épurer** **1** vt purify; (Pol) purge.

équateur /ekwatœʀ/ nm equator.

équilibre /ekilibʀ/ nm balance; être ou se tenir en ~ (personne) balance; (objet) be balanced. **équilibré, ~e** adj well-balanced.

équilibrer /ekilibʀe/ **1** vt balance. □ s'~ vpr balance each other.

équilibriste /ekilibʀist/ nmf acrobat.

équipage /ekipaʒ/ nm crew.

équipe /ekip/ nf team; ~ de nuit/ jour night/day shift.

équipé, ~e /ekipe/ adj equipped; cuisine ~e fitted kitchen.

équipement /ekipmɑ̃/ nm equipment; ~s (installations) amenities, facilities.

équiper /ekipe/ **1** vt equip (de with). □ s'~ vpr equip oneself.

équipier, -ière /ekipje, -jɛʀ/ nm, f team member.

équitable /ekitabl/ adj fair.

équitation /ekitasjɔ̃/ nf (horse-)riding.

équivalence /ekivalɑ̃s/ nf equivalence. **équivalent, ~e** *adj* equivalent.

équivaloir /ekivalwaʀ/ **60** *vi* à be equivalent to.

équivoque /ekivɔk/ *adj* equivocal; (louche) questionable. ● *nf* ambiguity.

érable /eʀabl/ *nm* maple.

érafler /eʀafle/ **1** *vt* scratch. **éraflure** *nf* scratch.

éraillé, ~e /eʀaje/ *adj* (voix) raucous.

ère /eʀ/ *nf* era.

éreintant, ~e /eʀɛ̃tɑ̃, -t/ *adj* exhausting. **éreinter (s')** **1** *vpr* wear oneself out.

ériger /eʀiʒe/ **40** *vt* erect. □ **s'~ en** *vpr* set (oneself) up as.

éroder /eʀɔde/ **1** *vt* erode. **érosion** *nf* erosion.

errer /eʀe/ **1** *vi* wander.

erreur /eʀœʀ/ *nf* mistake, error; **dans l'~** mistaken; **par ~** by mistake; **~ judiciaire** miscarriage of justice.

erroné, ~e /eʀɔne/ *adj* erroneous.

érudit, ~e /eʀydi, -t/ *adj* scholarly. ● *nm, f* scholar.

éruption /eʀypsjɔ̃/ *nf* eruption; (Méd) rash.

es /ɛ/ →**ÊTRE** **4**.

escabeau (*pl* **~x**) /ɛskabo/ *nm* step-ladder.

escadron /ɛskadʀɔ̃/ *nm* (Mil) company.

escalade /ɛskalad/ *nf* climbing; (Pol, Comm) escalation. **escalader** **1** *vt* climb.

escale /ɛskal/ *nf* (d'avion) stopover; (port) port of call; **faire ~ à** (avion, passager) stop over at; (navire, passager) put in at.

escalier /ɛskalje/ *nm* stairs (+ *pl*); **~ mécanique** ou **roulant** escalator.

escalope /ɛskalɔp/ *nf* escalope.

escargot /ɛskaʀgo/ *nm* snail.

escarpé, ~e /ɛskaʀpe/ *adj* steep.

escarpin /ɛskaʀpɛ̃/ *nm* court shoe; (US) pump.

escient: à bon ~ /abɔ̃sesjã/ *loc* wisely.

esclandre /ɛsklɑ̃dʀ/ *nm* scene.

esclavage /ɛsklavaʒ/ *nm* slavery. **esclave** *nmf* slave.

escompte /ɛskɔ̃t/ *nm* discount. **escompter** **1** *vt* expect; (Comm) discount.

escorte /ɛskɔʀt/ *nf* escort.

escrime /ɛskʀim/ *nf* fencing.

escroc /ɛskʀo/ *nm* swindler.

escroquer /ɛskʀɔke/ **1** *vt* swindle; **~ qch à qn** swindle sb out of sth. **escroquerie** *nf* swindle.

espace /ɛspas/ *nm* space; **~s verts** gardens and parks.

espacer /ɛspase/ **10** *vt* space out. □ **s'~** *vpr* become less frequent.

espadrille /ɛspadʀij/ *nf* rope sandal.

Espagne /ɛspaɲ/ *nf* Spain.

espagnol, ~e /ɛspaɲɔl/ *adj* Spanish. ● *nm* (Ling) Spanish. **E~, ~e** *nm, f* Spaniard.

espèce /ɛspɛs/ *nf* kind, sort; (race) species; **en ~s** (argent) in cash; **~ d'idiot!** **1** you idiot! **1**.

espérance /ɛspeʀɑ̃s/ *nf* hope.

espérer /ɛspeʀe/ **14** *vt* hope for; **faire/que** hope to do/that. ● *vi* hope.

espiègle /ɛspjɛgl/ *adj* mischievous.

espion, ~ne /ɛspjɔ̃, -ɔn/ *nm, f* spy. **espionnage** *nm* espionage, spying. **espionner** **1** *vt* spy (on).

espoir /ɛspwaʀ/ *nm* hope; **reprendre ~** feel hopeful again.

esprit /ɛspʀi/ *nm* (intellect) mind; (humour) wit; (fantôme) spirit; (ambiance) atmosphere; **perdre l'~** lose one's mind; **reprendre ses ~s** come to; **faire de l'~** try to be witty.

esquimau, **~de** (mpl **~x**) /ɛskimo, -d/ nm, f Eskimo.

esquinter /ɛskɛ̃te/ **1** vt **1** ruin.

esquisse /ɛskis/ nf sketch; (fig) outline.

esquiver /ɛskive/ **1** vt dodge. □ **s'~** vpr slip away.

essai /esɛ/ nm (épreuve) test, trial; (tentative) try; (article) essay; (au rugby) try; **~s** (Auto) qualifying round (+ sg); **à l'~** on trial.

essaim /esɛ̃/ nm swarm.

essayage /esɛjaʒ/ nm fitting; **salon d'~** fitting room.

essayer /eseje/ **31** vt/i try; (vêtement) try (on); (voiture) try (out); **~ de faire** try to do.

essence /esɑ̃s/ nf (carburant) petrol; (nature, extrait) essence; **~ sans plomb** unleaded petrol.

essentiel, **~le** /esɑ̃sjɛl/ adj essential. ● nm **l'~** the main thing; (quantité) the main part.

essieu (pl **~x**) /esjø/ nm axle.

essor /esɔR/ nm expansion; **prendre son ~** expand.

essorage /esɔRaʒ/ nm spin drying.

essorer /esɔRe/ **1** vt (linge) spin-dry; (en tordant) wring.

essoreuse /esɔRøz/ nf spin-drier; **~ à salade** salad spinner.

essoufflé, **~e** /esufle/ adj out of breath.

essuie-glace /esɥiglas/ nm inv windscreen wiper.

essuie-mains /esɥimɛ̃/ nm inv hand-towel.

essuie-tout /esɥitu/ nm inv kitchen paper.

essuyer /esɥije/ **31** vt wipe; (subir)

suffer. □ **s'~** vpr dry ou wipe oneself.

est[1] /ɛ/ ➡**ÊTRE** **4**.

est[2] /ɛst/ nm east. ● adj inv east; (partie) eastern; (direction) easterly.

estampe /ɛstɑ̃p/ nf print.

esthète /ɛstɛt/ nmf aesthete.

esthéticienne /ɛstetisjɛn/ nf beautician.

esthétique /ɛstetik/ adj aesthetic.

estimation /ɛstimasjɔ̃/ nf (de coûts) estimate; (valeur) valuation.

estime /ɛstim/ nf esteem.

estimer /ɛstime/ **1** vt (tableau) value; (calculer) estimate; (respecter) esteem; (considérer) consider (que that).

estival, **~e** (mpl **-aux**) /ɛstival, -o/ adj summer. **estivant**, **~e** nm, f summer visitor.

estomac /ɛstɔma/ nm stomach.

estomaqué, **~e** /ɛstɔmake/ adj **1** stunned.

Estonie /ɛstɔni/ nf Estonia.

estrade /ɛstrad/ nf platform.

estragon /ɛstragɔ̃/ nm tarragon.

estropié, **~e** /ɛstRɔpje/ nm, f cripple. ● adj crippled.

estuaire /ɛstɥɛR/ nm estuary.

et /e/ conj and; **~ moi?** what about me?; **~ alors?** so what?

étable /etabl/ nf cow-shed.

établi, **~e** /etabli/ adj established; **un fait bien ~** a well-established fact. ● nm work-bench.

établir /etablir/ **2** vt establish; (liste, facture) draw up; (personne, camp, record) set up. □ **s'~** vpr (personne) settle; **s'~ à son compte** set up on one's own.

établissement /etablismɑ̃/ nm (entreprise) organization; (institution) establishment; **~ scolaire** school.

étage /etaʒ/ nm floor, storey; (de fusée) stage; **à l'~** upstairs; **au premier ~** on the first floor.

étagère /etaʒɛʀ/ nf shelf; (meuble) shelving unit.

étain /etɛ̃/ nm pewter.

étais, était /etɛ/ →ÊTRE 4.

étalage /etalaʒ/ nm display; (vitrine) shop-window; **faire ~ de** flaunt. **étalagiste** nmf window-dresser.

étaler /etale/ 1 vt spread; (journal) spread (out); (pâte) roll out; (exposer) display; (richesse) flaunt. □ **s'~** vpr (prendre de la place) spread out; (tomber 1) fall flat; **s'~ sur** (paiement) be spread over.

étalon /etalɔ̃/ nm (cheval) stallion; (modèle) standard.

étanche /etɑ̃ʃ/ adj watertight; (montre) waterproof.

étancher /etɑ̃ʃe/ 1 vt (soif) quench.

étang /etɑ̃/ nm pond.

étant /etɑ̃/ →ÊTRE 4.

étape /etap/ nf stage; (lieu d'arrêt) stopover; (fig) stage.

état /eta/ nm state; (liste) statement; (métier) profession; **en bon/mauvais ~** in good/bad condition; **en ~ de** in a position to; **en ~ de marche** in working order; **faire ~ de** (citer) mention; **être dans tous ses ~s** be in a state; **~ civil** civil status; **~ des lieux** inventory of fixtures. **État** nm State.

état-major (pl **états-majors**) /etamaʒɔʀ/ nm (officiers) staff (+ pl).

États-Unis /etazyni/ nmpl **~ (d'Amérique)** United States (of America).

étau (pl **~x**) /eto/ nm vice.

étayer /eteje/ 31 vt prop up.

été[1] /ete/ →ÊTRE 4.

été[2] /ete/ nm summer.

éteindre /etɛ̃dʀ/ 27 vt (feu) put out; (lumière, radio) turn off. □ **s'~** vpr (feu, lumière) go out; (appareil) go off; (mourir) die. **éteint, ~e** adj (feu) out; (volcan) extinct.

étendard /etɑ̃daʀ/ nm standard.

étendre /etɑ̃dʀ/ 3 vt (nappe) spread (out); (bras, jambes) stretch (out); (linge) hang out; (agrandir) extend. □ **s'~** vpr (s'allonger) lie down; (se propager) spread; (plaine) stretch; **s'~ sur** (sujet) dwell on.

étendu, ~e /etɑ̃dy/ adj extensive. **étendue** nf area; (d'eau) stretch; (importance) extent.

éternel, ~le /etɛʀnɛl/ adj (vie) eternal; (fig) endless.

éterniser (s') /(s)etɛʀnize/ 1 vpr (durer) drag on.

éternité /etɛʀnite/ nf eternity.

éternuement /etɛʀnymɑ̃/ nm sneeze. **éternuer** 1 vi sneeze.

êtes /ɛt/ →ÊTRE 4.

éthique /etik/ adj ethical. ● nf ethics (+ sg).

ethnie /ɛtni/ nf ethnic group. **ethnique** adj ethnic.

étincelant, ~e /etɛ̃slɑ̃, -t/ adj sparkling. **étinceler** 38 vi sparkle. **étincelle** nf spark.

étiqueter /etikte/ 40 vt label. **étiquette** nf label; (protocole) etiquette.

étirer /etire/ 1 vt stretch. □ **s'~** vpr stretch.

étoffe /etɔf/ nf fabric.

étoffer /etɔfe/ 1 vt expand. □ **s'~** vpr fill out.

étoile /etwal/ nf star; **à la belle ~** in the open; **~ filante** shooting star; **~ de mer** starfish.

étonnant, ~e /etɔnɑ̃, -t/ adj (curieux) surprising; (formidable) amazing. **étonnement** nm surprise; (plus fort) amazement.

étonner /etɔne/ **1** vt amaze.
□ **s'~** vpr be amazed (**de** at).

étouffant, ~e /etufɑ̃, -t/ adj
stifling.

étouffer /etufe/ **1** vt/i suffocate;
(sentiment, révolte) stifle; (feu)
smother; (bruit) muffle; **on étouffe**
it is stifling. □ **s'~** vpr suffocate; (en
mangeant) choke.

étourderie /eturdəri/ nf thoughtlessness; (acte) careless mistake.

étourdi, ~e /eturdi/ adj absent-
minded. ● nm, f scatterbrain.

étourdir /eturdir/ **2** vt stun; (fatiguer) make sb's head spin. **étour-
dissant, ~e** adj stunning.

étourneau (pl ~**x**) /eturno/ nm
starling.

étrange /etrɑ̃ʒ/ adj strange.

étranger, -ère /etrɑ̃ʒe, -ɛr/ adj
(inconnu) strange, unfamiliar; (d'un
autre pays) foreign. ● nm, f foreigner; (inconnu) stranger; **à l'~**
abroad; **de l'~** from abroad.

étrangler /etrɑ̃gle/ **1** vt strangle;
(col) throttle. □ **s'~** vpr choke.

être /ɛtr/ **4**
● verbe auxiliaire
····▸ (du passé) have; **elle est
partie/venue hier** she left/came
yesterday.
····▸ (de la voix passive) be.
● verbe intransitif (aux avoir)
····▸ be; **~ médecin** be a doctor;
je suis à vous I'm all yours; **j'en
suis à me demander si...** I'm
beginning to wonder whether...;
qu'en est-il de...? what's the
news about...?
····▸ (appartenance) be, belong to.
····▸ (heure, date) be; **nous sommes le 3 mars** it's March 3.

····▸ (aller) be; **je n'y ai jamais
été** I've never been; **il a été le
voir** he went to see him.
····▸ **c'est** it is or it's; **c'est moi
qui l'ai fait** I did it; **est-ce que
tu veux du thé?** do you want
some tea?
● nom masculin
····▸ being; **~ humain** human
being.
····▸ (personne) person; **un ~
cher** a loved one.

étreindre /etrɛ̃dr/ **22** vt embrace.
étreinte nf embrace.

étrennes /etrɛn/ nfpl (New Year's)
gift (+ sg); (argent) money.

étrier /etrije/ nm stirrup.

étriqué, ~e /etrike/ adj tight.

étroit, ~e /etrwa, -t/ adj narrow;
(vêtement) tight; (liens, surveillance)
close; **à l'~** cramped. **étroitement**
adv closely. **étroitesse** nf nar-
rowness.

étude /etyd/ nf study; (enquête)
survey; (bureau) office; (salle d')~
(Scol) prep room; **à l'~** under consideration; **faire des ~s (de)** study;
il n'a pas fait d'~s he didn't go to
university; **~ de marché** market research.

étudiant, ~e /etydjɑ̃, -t/ nm, f
student.

étudier /etydje/ **45** vt/i study.

étui /etɥi/ nm case.

étuve /etyv/ nf steam room.

eu, ~e /y/ ➞AVOIR **5**.

euro /øro/ nm euro.

Europe /ørɔp/ nf Europe.

européen, ~ne /ørɔpeɛ̃, -ɛɛn/ adj
European. **E~, ~ne** nm, f European.

euthanasie /øtanazi/ nf euthanasia.

eux /ø/ pron they; (complément)
them. **eux-mêmes** pron themselves.

évacuation /evakyasjɔ̃/ nf evacuation; (d'eaux usées) discharge. **évacuer** 1 vt evacuate.

évadé, ~e adj escaped. ● nm, f escaped prisoner. **évader (s')** 1 vpr escape.

évaluation /evalyasjɔ̃/ nf assessment. **évaluer** 1 vt assess.

évangile /evɑ̃ʒil/ nm gospel; **l'É~** the Gospel.

évanouir (s') /(s)evanwir/ 2 vpr faint; (disparaître) vanish.

évaporation /evaporasjɔ̃/ nf evaporation. **évaporer (s')** 1 vpr evaporate.

évasif, -ive /evazif, -v/ adj evasive.

évasion /evazjɔ̃/ nf escape.

éveil /evɛj/ nm awakening; **en ~** alert.

éveillé, ~e /eveje/ adj awake; (intelligent) alert.

éveiller /eveje/ 1 vt awake(n); (susciter) arouse. □ **s'~** vpr awake.

événement /evenmɑ̃/ nm event.

éventail /evɑ̃taj/ nm fan; (gamme) range.

éventrer /evɑ̃tre/ 1 vt (sac) rip open.

éventualité /evɑ̃tɥalite/ nf possibility; **dans cette ~** in that event.

éventuel, ~le /evɑ̃tɥɛl/ adj possible. **éventuellement** adv possibly.

évêque /evɛk/ nm bishop.

évertuer (s') /(s)evɛrtɥe/ 1 vpr **s'~ à** struggle hard to.

éviction /eviksjɔ̃/ nf eviction.

évidemment /evidamɑ̃/ adv obviously; (bien sûr) of course.

évidence /evidɑ̃s/ nf obviousness; (fait) obvious fact; **être en ~** be conspicuous; **mettre en ~** (fait) highlight. **évident,** ~e adj obvious, evident.

évier /evje/ nm sink.

évincer /evɛ̃se/ 10 vt oust.

éviter /evite/ 1 vt avoid (de faire doing); **~ qch à qn** (dérangement) save sb sth.

évocateur, -trice /evokatœr, -tris/ adj evocative. **évocation** nf evocation.

évolué, ~e /evɔlɥe/ adj highly developed.

évoluer /evɔlɥe/ 1 vi evolve; (situation) develop; (se déplacer) glide. **évolution** nf evolution; (d'une situation) development.

évoquer /evɔke/ 1 vt call to mind, evoke.

exacerber /ɛgzasɛrbe/ 1 vt exacerbate.

exact, ~e /ɛgza(kt), -akt/ adj (précis) exact, accurate; (juste) correct; (personne) punctual. **exactement** adv exactly. **exactitude** nf exactness; punctuality.

ex æquo /ɛgzeko/ adv être ~ tie (avec qn with sb).

exagération /ɛgzaʒerasjɔ̃/ nf aggeration. **exagéré,** ~e adj excessive.

exagérer /ɛgzaʒere/ 14 vt/i exaggerate; (abuser) go too far.

exalté, ~e /ɛgzalte/ nm, f fanatic. **exalter** 1 vt excite; (glorifier) exalt.

examen /ɛgzamɛ̃/ nm examination; (Scol) exam. **examinateur, -trice** nm, f examiner. **examiner** 1 vt examine.

exaspération /ɛgzasperasjɔ̃/ nf exasperation. **exaspérer** 14 vt exasperate.

exaucer /ɛgzose/ 10 vt grant; (personne) grant the wish(es) of.

excédent /ɛksedɑ̃/ nm surplus; **~ de bagages** excess luggage; **~ de la balance commerciale** trade surplus. **excédentaire** adj excess, surplus.

excéder /ɛksede/ **14** vt (dépasser) exceed; (agacer) irritate.

excellence /ɛksɛlɑ̃s/ nf excellence. **excellent, ~e** adj excellent. **exceller 1** vi excel (**dans** in).

excentricité /ɛksɑ̃tʀisite/ nf eccentricity. **excentrique** adj & nmf eccentric.

excepté, ~e /ɛksɛpte/ adj & prép except.

excepter /ɛksɛpte/ **1** vt except.

exception /ɛksɛpsjɔ̃/ nf exception; **à l'~ de** except for; **d'~** exceptional; **faire ~** be an exception. **exceptionnel, ~le** adj exceptional. **exceptionnellement** adv exceptionally.

excès /ɛksɛ/ nm excess; **~ de vitesse** speeding. **excessif, -ive** /ɛksesif, -v/ adj excessive.

excitant, ~e /ɛksitɑ̃, -t/ adj stimulating; (palpitant) exciting. ● nm stimulant.

exciter /ɛksite/ **1** vt excite; (irriter) get excited. □ **s'~** vpr get excited.

exclamer (s') /(s)ɛksklame/ **1** vpr exclaim.

exclure /ɛksklyʀ/ **16** vt exclude; (expulser) expel; (empêcher) preclude.

exclusif, -ive /ɛksklyzif, -v/ adj exclusive.

exclusion /ɛksklyzjɔ̃/ nf exclusion.

exclusivité /ɛksklyzivite/ nf (Comm) exclusive rights (+ pl); **projeter en ~** show exclusively.

excursion /ɛkskyʀsjɔ̃/ nf excursion; (à pied) hike.

excuse /ɛkskyz/ nf excuse; **~s** apology (+ sg); **faire des ~s** apologize.

excuser /ɛkskyze/ **1** vt excuse; **excusez-moi** excuse me. □ **s'~** vpr apologize (**de** for).

exécrable /ɛgzekʀabl/ adj dreadful. **exécrer 14** vt loathe.

exécuter /ɛgzekyte/ **1** vt carry out, execute; (Mus) perform; (tuer) execute.

exécutif, -ive /ɛgzekytif, -v/ adj & nm (Pol) executive.

exécution /ɛgzekysjɔ̃/ nf execution; (Mus) performance.

exemplaire /ɛgzɑ̃plɛʀ/ adj exemplary. ● nm copy.

exemple /ɛgzɑ̃pl/ nm example; **par ~** for example; **donner l'~** set an example.

exempt, ~e /ɛgzɑ̃, -t/ adj **~ de** exempt (**de** from).

exempter /ɛgzɑ̃te/ **1** vt exempt (**de** from). **exemption** nf exemption.

exercer /ɛgzɛʀse/ **10** vt exercise; (influence, contrôle) exert; (former) train, exercise; **~ un métier** have a job; **~ le métier de...** work as a... □ **s'~** vpr practise.

exercice /ɛgzɛʀsis/ nm exercise; (de métier) practice; **en ~** in office; (médecin) in practice.

exhaler /ɛgzale/ **1** vt emit.

exhaustif, -ive /ɛgzostif, -v/ adj exhaustive.

exhiber /ɛgzibe/ **1** vt exhibit.

exhorter /ɛgzɔʀte/ **1** vt exhort (**à** to).

exigeant, ~e /ɛgziʒɑ̃, -t/ adj demanding; **être ~ avec qn** demand a lot of sb. **exigence** nf demand. **exiger 40** vt demand.

exigu, ~ë /ɛgzigy/ adj tiny.

exil /ɛgzil/ nm exile. **exilé, ~e** nm, f exile.

exiler /ɛgzile/ **1** vt exile. □ **s'~** vpr go into exile.

existence /ɛgzistɑ̃s/ nf existence.

exister **1** vi exist.

exode /ɛgzɔd/ nm exodus.

exonérer /ɛgzɔnere/ **14** vt exempt (**de** from).

exorbitant, ~**e** /ɛgzɔrbitã, -t/ adj exorbitant.

exorciser /ɛgzɔrsize/ **1** vt exorcize.

exotique /ɛgzɔtik/ adj exotic.

expansé, ~**e** /ɛkspãse/ adj (Tech) expanded.

expansif, -ive /ɛkspãsif, -v/ adj expansive. **expansion** nf expansion.

expatrié, ~**e** /ɛkspatrije/ nm, f expatriate.

expectative /ɛkspɛktativ/ nf **être dans l'**~ wait and see.

expédient /ɛkspedjã/ nm expedient; **vivre d'**~**s** live by one's wits; **user d'**~**s** resort to expedients.

expédier /ɛkspedje/ **45** vt send, dispatch; (*tâche* **1**) polish off. **expéditeur, -trice** nm, f sender.

expéditif, -ive /ɛkspeditif, -v/ quick.

expédition /ɛkspedisjɔ̃/ nf (envoi) dispatching; (voyage) expedition.

expérience /ɛksperjãs/ nf experience; (scientifique) experiment.

expérimental, ~**e** (mpl **-aux**) /ɛksperimãtal, o/ adj experimental. **expérimentation** nf experimentation. **expérimenté,** ~**e** adj experienced. **expérimenter** **1** vt test, experiment with.

expert, ~**e** /ɛkspɛr, -t/ adj expert. ● nm expert; (*d'assurances*) adjuster. **expert-comptable** (pl **experts-comptables**) nm accountant.

expertise /ɛkspɛrtiz/ nf valuation; (de dégâts) assessment. **expertiser** **1** vt value; (dégâts) assess.

expier /ɛkspje/ **45** vt atone for.

expiration /ɛkspirasjɔ̃/ nf expiry.

expirer /ɛkspire/ **1** vi breathe out; (finir, mourir) expire.

explicatif, -ive /ɛksplikatif, -v/ adj explanatory.

explication /ɛksplikasjɔ̃/ nf explanation; (fig) discussion; ~ **de texte** (Scol) literary commentary.

explicite /ɛksplisit/ adj explicit.

expliquer /ɛksplike/ **1** vt explain. □ **s'**~ vpr explain oneself; (discuter) discuss things; (être explicable) be understandable.

exploit /ɛksplwa/ nm exploit.

exploitant, ~**e** /ɛksplwatã, -t/ nm, f ~ **(agricole)** farmer.

exploitation /ɛksplwatasjɔ̃/ nf exploitation; (d'entreprise) running; (ferme) farm.

exploiter /ɛksplwate/ **1** vt exploit; (ferme) run; (mine) work.

explorateur, -trice /ɛksplɔratœr, -tris/ nm, f explorer. **exploration** nf exploration. **explorer** **1** vt explore.

exploser /ɛksploze/ **1** vi explode; **faire** ~ explode; (bâtiment) blow up.

explosif, -ive /ɛksplozif, -v/ adj & nm explosive. **explosion** nf explosion.

exportateur, -trice /ɛkspɔrtatœr, -tris/ nm, f exporter. ● adj exporting. **exportation** nf export. **exporter** **1** vt export.

exposant, ~**e** /ɛkspozã, -t/ nm, f exhibitor.

exposé, ~**e** /ɛkspoze/ nm talk (**sur** on); (d'une action) account; **faire l'**~ **de la situation** give an account of the situation. ● adj ~ **au nord** facing north.

exposer /ɛkspoze/ **1** vt display, show; (expliquer) explain; (soumettre, mettre en danger) expose (à to); (*vie*) endanger. □ **s'~ à** *vpr* expose oneself to.

exposition /ɛkspozisjɔ̃/ *nf* (d'art) exhibition; (de faits) exposition; (géographique) aspect.

exprès¹ /ɛksprɛ/ *adv* specially; (délibérément) on purpose.

exprès², -esse /ɛksprɛs/ *adj* express.

express /ɛksprɛs/ *adj & nm inv* (café) ~ espresso; (train) ~ fast train.

expressif, -ive /ɛksprɛsif, -v/ *adj* expressive. **expression** *nf* expression.

exprimer /ɛksprime/ **1** *vt* express. □ **s'~** *vpr* express oneself.

expulser /ɛkspylse/ **1** *vt* expel; (*locataire*) evict; (*joueur*) send off. **expulsion** *nf* (d'élève) expulsion; (de locataire) eviction; (d'immigré) deportation.

exquis, ~e /ɛkski, -z/ *adj* exquisite.

extase /ɛkstɑz/ *nf* ecstasy.

extasier (s') /(s)ɛkstɑzje/ **45** *vpr* **s'~ sur** be ecstatic about.

extensible /ɛkstɑ̃sibl/ *adj* (tissu) stretch.

extension /ɛkstɑ̃sjɔ̃/ *nf* extension; (expansion) expansion.

exténuer /ɛkstenye/ **1** *vt* exhaust.

extérieur, ~e /ɛksterjœr/ *adj* outside; (*signe, gaieté*) outward; (*politique*) foreign. ● *nm* outside, (*de personne*) exterior; à l'~ (de) outside. **extérioriser** **1** *vt* show, externalize.

extermination /ɛkstɛrminasjɔ̃/ *nf* extermination. **exterminer** **1** *vt* exterminate.

externe /ɛkstɛrn/ *adj* external. ● *nmf* (Scol) day pupil.

extincteur /ɛkstɛ̃ktœr/ *nm* fire extinguisher.

extinction /ɛkstɛ̃ksjɔ̃/ *nf* extinction; **avoir une ~ de voix** have lost one's voice.

extorquer /ɛkstɔrke/ **1** *vt* extort.

extra /ɛkstra/ *adj inv* first-rate. ● *nm inv* (repas) (special) treat.

extraction /ɛkstraksjɔ̃/ *nf* extraction.

extrader /ɛkstrade/ **1** *vt* extradite.

extraire /ɛkstrɛr/ **29** *vt* extract. **extrait** *nm* extract.

extraordinaire /ɛkstraɔrdinɛr/ *adj* extraordinary.

extravagance /ɛkstravagɑ̃s/ *nf* extravagance. **extravagant, ~e** *adj* extravagant.

extraverti, ~e /ɛkstraverti/ *nm, f* extrovert.

extrême /ɛkstrɛm/ *adj & nm* extreme. **extrêmement** *adv* extremely.

Extrême-Orient /ɛkstrɛmɔrjɑ̃/ *nm* Far East.

extrémiste /ɛkstremist/ *nmf* extremist.

extrémité /ɛkstremite/ *nf* end; (mains, pieds) extremity.

exubérance /ɛgzyberɑ̃s/ *nf* exuberance. **exubérant, ~e** *adj* exuberant.

Ff

F *abrév* franc *f* (**franc, francs**) franc, francs.

fabricant, ~e /fabrikɑ̃, -t/ *nm, f* manufacturer. **fabrication** *nf* making; manufacture.

fabrique /fabrik/ *nf* factory. **fabriquer** **1** *vt* make; (industriellement) manufacture; (fig) make up.

fabuler /fabyle/ **1** *vi* fantasize.

fabuleux, -euse /fabylø, -z/ *adj* fabulous.

fac /fak/ *nf* **1** university.

façade /fasad/ *nf* front; (fig) façade.

face /fas/ *nf* face; (d'un objet) side; **en** (~ **de**), **d'en** ~ opposite; **en** ~ **de** (figé) faced with; ~ **à** facing; (fig) faced with; **faire** ~ **à** face. **face-à-face** *nm inv* (débat) one-to-one debate.

fâcher /faʃe/ **1** *vt* anger; **fâché** angry; (désolé) sorry. □ **se** ~ *vpr* get angry; (se brouiller) fall out.

facile /fasil/ *adj* easy; (caractère) easygoing.

facilité /fasilite/ *nf* easiness; (aisance) ease; (aptitude) ability; ~**s** (possibilités) facilities, opportunities; ~**s d'importation** import opportunities; ~**s de paiement** easy terms.

faciliter /fasilite/ **1** *vt* facilitate, make easier.

façon /fasɔ̃/ *nf* way; (de vêtement) cut; **de cette** ~ in this way; **de** ~ **à** so as to; **de toute** ~ anyway; ~**s** (chichis) fuss; **faire des** ~**s** stand on ceremony; **sans** ~**s** (repas) informal; (personne) unpretentious. **façonner** **1** *vt* shape; (faire) make.

fac-similé (*pl* ~**s**) /faksimile/ *nm* facsimile.

facteur, -trice /faktœr, -tris/ *nm, f* postman, postwoman. ● *nm* (élément) factor.

facture /faktyr/ *nf* bill; (Comm) invoice; ~ **détaillée** itemized bill. **facturer** **1** *vt* invoice. **facturette** *nf* credit card slip.

facultatif, -ive /fakyltatif, -v/ *adj* optional.

faculté /fakylte/ *nf* faculty; (possi-

bilité) power; (Univ) faculty.

fade /fad/ *adj* insipid.

faible /fɛbl/ *adj* weak; (espoir, quantité, écart) slight; (revenu, intensité) low; ~ **d'esprit** feeble-minded. ● *nm* (personne) weakling; (penchant) weakness. **faiblesse** *nf* weakness. **faiblir** **2** *vi* weaken.

faïence /fajɑ̃s/ *nf* earthenware.

faillir /fajir/ **2** *vi* **j'ai failli acheter** I almost bought.

faillite /fajit/ *nf* bankruptcy; (fig) collapse.

faim /fɛ̃/ *nf* hunger; **avoir** ~ be hungry; **rester sur sa** ~ (fig) be left wanting more.

fainéant, ~**e** /feneɑ̃, -t/ *adj* idle. ● *nm, f* idler.

---

faire /fɛr/ **33**

➡ Pour les expressions comme **faire attention, faire la cuisine,** etc. ➡ **attention, cuisine** etc.

● *verbe transitif*

••••▶ (préparer, créer) make; ~ **une tarte/une erreur** make a tart/a mistake.

••••▶ (se livrer à une activité) do; ~ **du droit** do law; ~ **du foot/ du violon** play football/the violin; **qu'est-ce qu'elle fait?** (dans la vie) what does she do?; (en ce moment précis) what is she doing?

••••▶ (dans les calculs, mesures, etc.) **10 et 10 font** 20 and 10 make 20; **ça fait 25 euros** that's 25 euros; ~ **60 kilos** weigh 60 kilos; **il fait 1,75 m** he's 1.75 m tall.

••••▶ (dans les expressions de temps) **ça fait une heure que** j'attends I have been waiting for an hour.

····▸ (imiter) ∼ **le clown** act the clown; **faire le malade** pretend to be ill.

····▸ (parcourir) ∼ **10 km** do ou cover 10 km; ∼ **les musées** go round the museums.

····▸ (entraîner, causer) **ça ne fait rien** it doesn't matter; **l'accident a fait 8 morts** 8 people died in the accident.

····▸ (dire) say; **'excusez-moi', fit-elle** 'excuse me', she said.

● *verbe auxiliaire*

····▸ (faire + infinitif + qn) make; ∼ **pleurer qn** make sb cry.

····▸ (faire + infinitif + qch) have, get; ∼ **réparer sa voiture** have ou get one's car mended.

····▸ (ne faire que + infinitif) (continuellement) **ne** ∼ **que pleurer** do nothing but cry; (seulement) **je ne fais qu'obéir** I'm only following orders.

● *verbe intransitif*

····▸ (agir) do, act; ∼ **vite** act quickly; **fais comme tu veux** do as you please; **fais comme chez toi** make yourself at home.

····▸ (paraître) look; ∼ **joli** look pretty; **ça fait cher** it's expensive.

····▸ (en parlant du temps) **il fait chaud/gris** it's hot/overcast.

□ **se faire** *verbe pronominal*

····▸ (obtenir, confectionner) make; **se** ∼ **des amis** make friends; **se** ∼ **un thé** make (oneself) a cup of tea.

····▸ (se faire + infinitif) **se** ∼ **gronder** be scolded; **se** ∼ **couper les cheveux** have one's hair cut.

····▸ (devenir) **il se fait tard** it's getting late.

····▸ (être d'usage) **ça ne se fait pas** it's not the done thing.

····▸ (emploi impersonnel) **comment se fait-il que tu sois ici?** how come you're here?

····▸ □ **se faire à** get used to; **je ne m'y fais pas** I can't get used to it.

····▸ □ **s'en faire** worry; **ne t'en fais pas** don't worry.

① Lorsque **faire** remplace un verbe plus précis, on traduira quelquefois par ce dernier: **faire une visite** pay a visit, **faire un nid** build a nest.

faire-part /fɛʀpaʀ/ *nm inv* announcement.

fais /fɛ/ ➟**FAIRE** 33.

faisan /fəzɑ̃/ *nm* pheasant.

faisceau (*pl* ∼**x**) /fɛso/ *nm* (rayon) beam; (fagot) bundle.

fait, ∼**e** /fɛ, fɛt/ *adj* done; (*fromage*) ripe; ∼ **pour** made for; **tout** ∼ ready made; **c'est bien** ∼ **pour toi** it serves you right. ● *nm* fact; (événement) event; **au** ∼ **(de)** informed (of); **de ce** ∼ therefore; **du** ∼ **de** on account of; ∼ **divers** (trivial) news item; ∼ **nouveau** new development; **prendre qn sur le** ∼ catch sb in the act. ● ➟**FAIRE** 33.

faîte /fɛt/ *nm* top; (fig) peak.

faites /fɛt/ ➟**FAIRE** 33.

falaise /falɛz/ *nf* cliff.

falloir /falwaʀ/ 34 *vi* **il faut qch/qn** we/you *etc.* need sth/sb; **il lui faut du pain** he needs bread; **il faut rester** we/you *etc.* have to ou must stay; **il faut que j'y aille** I have to ou must go; **il faudrait que tu partes** you should leave; **il aurait fallu le faire** we/you *etc.* should have done it; **comme il faut** (*manger, se tenir*) properly; (*personne*) respectable, proper. □ **s'en ~** *vpr* **il s'en est fallu de peu qu'il gagne** he nearly won; **il s'en faut de beaucoup que je sois** I am far from being.

falsifier /falsifje/ 45 *vt* falsify; (*signature, monnaie*) forge.

famé, ~e /fame/ *adj* **mal ~** disreputable, seedy.

fameux, -euse /famø, -z/ *adj* famous; (excellent 1) first-rate.

familial, ~e (*mpl* **-iaux**) /familjal, -jo/ *adj* family.

familiale /familjal/ *nf* estate car; (US) station wagon.

familiariser /familjarize/ 1 *vt* familiarize (**avec** with). □ **se ~** *vpr* familiarize oneself.

familier, -ière /familje, -jɛR/ *adj* familiar; (*amical*) informal.

famille /famij/ *nf* family; **en ~** with one's family.

famine /famin/ *nf* famine.

fanatique /fanatik/ *adj* fanatical. ● *nmf* fanatic.

fanfare /fɑ̃faR/ *nf* brass band; (*musique*) fanfare.

fantaisie /fɑ̃tezi/ *nf* imagination, fantasy; (*caprice*) whim; (**de**) ~ (*boutons etc.*) fancy. **fantaisiste** *adj* unorthodox; (*personne*) eccentric.

fantasme /fɑ̃tasm/ *nm* fantasy.

fantastique /fɑ̃tastik/ *adj* fantastic.

fantôme /fɑ̃tom/ *nm* ghost; **cabinet(-)~** (Pol) shadow cabinet.

faon /fɑ̃/ *nm* fawn.

FAQ *abrév f* (**Foire aux questions**) (Internet) FAQ, Frequently Asked Questions.

farce /faRs/ *nf* (practical) joke; (Théât) farce; (*hachis*) stuffing.

farcir /faRsiR/ 2 *vt* stuff.

fard /faR/ *nm* make-up; ~ **à paupières** eye-shadow; **piquer un ~** blush.

fardeau (*pl* ~**x**) /faRdo/ *nm* burden.

farfelu, ~e /faRfəly/ *adj* & *nm,f* eccentric.

farine /faRin/ *nf* flour. **farineux, -euse** *adj* floury. **farineux** *nmpl* starchy food.

farouche /faRuʃ/ *adj* shy; (*peu sociable*) unsociable; (*violent*) fierce.

fascicule /fasikyl/ *nm* (brochure) booklet; (*partie d'un ouvrage*) fascicule.

fasciner /fasine/ 1 *vt* fascinate.

fascisme /faʃism/ *nm* fascism.

fasse /fas/ ➔**FAIRE** 33.

fast-food /fastfud/ *nm* fast-food place.

fastidieux, -ieuse /fastidjø, -z/ *adj* tedious.

fatal, ~e (*mpl* ~**s**) /fatal/ *adj* inevitable; (*mortel*) fatal. **fatalité** *nf* (*destin*) fate.

fatigant, ~e /fatigɑ̃, -t/ *adj* tiring; (*ennuyeux*) tiresome.

fatigue /fatig/ *nf* fatigue, tiredness.

fatigué, ~e /fatige/ *adj* tired.

fatiguer /fatige/ 1 *vt* tire; (*yeux, moteur*) strain. ● *vi* (*moteur*) labour. □ **se ~** *vpr* get tired, tire (**de** of).

faubourg /fobuR/ *nm* suburb.

faucher /foʃe/ 1 *vt* (*herbe*) mow; (*voler* 1) pinch; ~ **qn** (*véhicule, tir*) mow sb down.

faucon /fokɔ̃/ *nm* falcon, hawk.

faudra, faudrait /fodRa, fodRɛ/ ➔**FALLOIR** 34.

faufiler (se) /(sə)fofile/ 1 *vpr* edge one's way, squeeze.

faune /fon/ *nf* wildlife, fauna.

faussaire /fosɛʀ/ nmf forger.

fausse /fos/ →**FAUX**².

fausser /fose/ **1** vt buckle; (fig) distort; ~ **compagnie à qn** give sb the slip.

faut /fo/ →**FALLOIR 34**.

faute /fot/ nf mistake; (responsabilité) fault; (délit) offence; (péché) sin; **en** ~ at fault; ~ **de** for want of; ~ **de quoi** failing which; **sans** ~ without fail; ~ **de frappe** typing error; ~ **de goût** bad taste; ~ **professionnelle** professional misconduct.

fauteuil /fotœj/ nm armchair; (de président) chair; (Théât) seat; ~ **roulant** wheelchair.

fautif, -ive /fotif, -v/ adj guilty; (faux) faulty. ● nm, f guilty party.

fauve /fov/ adj (couleur) fawn, tawny. ● nm wild cat.

faux¹ /fo/ nf scythe.

faux², fausse /fo, fos/ adj false; (falsifié) fake, forged; (numéro, calcul) wrong; (voix) out of tune; **c'est** ~**l** that is wrong!; ~ **témoignage** perjury; **faire** ~ **bond à qn** stand sb up; **fausse couche** miscarriage; ~ **frais** incidental expenses. ● adv (chanter) out of tune. ● nm forgery. **faux-filet** (pl ~**s**) nm sirloin.

faveur /favœʀ/ nf favour; **de** ~ (régime) preferential; **en** ~ **de** in favour of.

favorable /favɔʀabl/ adj favourable.

favori, ~te /favɔʀi, -t/ adj & nm,f favourite. **favoriser 1** vt favour.

fax /faks/ nm fax. **faxer 1** vt fax.

fébrile /febʀil/ adj feverish.

fécond, ~e /fekɔ̃, -d/ adj fertile. **féconder 1** vt fertilize. **fécondité** nf fertility.

fédéral, ~e (mpl -**aux**) /federal, -o/ adj federal. **fédération** nf federation.

fée /fe/ nf fairy. **féerie** nf magical spectacle. **féerique** adj magical.

feindre /fɛ̃dʀ/ **22** vt feign; ~ **de** pretend to.

fêler /fele/ **1** vt crack. □ **se** ~ vpr crack.

félicitations /felisitasjɔ̃/ nfpl congratulations (**pour** on). **féliciter 1** vt congratulate (**de** on).

félin, ~e /felɛ̃, -in/ adj & nm feline.

femelle /fəmɛl/ adj & nf female.

féminin, ~e /feminɛ̃, -in/ adj feminine; (sexe) female; (mode, équipe) women's. ● nm feminine. **féministe** nmf feminist.

femme /fam/ nf woman; (épouse) wife; ~ **au foyer** housewife; ~ **de chambre** chambermaid; ~ **de ménage** cleaning lady.

fémur /femyʀ/ nm thigh-bone.

fendre /fɑ̃dʀ/ **3** vt (couper) split; (fissurer) crack. □ **se** ~ vpr crack.

fenêtre /fənɛtʀ/ nf window.

fenouil /fənuj/ nm fennel.

fente /fɑ̃t/ nf (ouverture) slit, slot; (fissure) crack.

féodal, ~e (mpl -**aux**) /feodal, -o/ adj feudal.

fer /fɛʀ/ nm iron; ~ (**à repasser**) iron; ~ **à cheval** horseshoe; ~ **de lance** spearhead; ~ **forgé** wrought iron.

fera, ferait /fəʀa, fəʀɛ/ →**FAIRE 33**.

férié, ~e /feʀje/ adj **jour** ~ public holiday.

ferme /fɛʀm/ nf farm; (maison) farm(house); ~ **éolienne** wind farm. ● adj firm. ● adv (travailler) hard.

fermé, ~e /fɛʀme/ adj closed; (gaz, radio) off.

fermenter /fɛʀmɑ̃te/ **1** vi ferment.

fermer /fɛʀme/ **1** vt/i close, shut;

(cesser d'exploiter) close ou shut down; (gaz, robinet) turn off. □ se ~ vpr close, shut.

fermeté /fɛʀməte/ nf firmness.

fermeture /fɛʀmətyʀ/ nf closing; (dispositif) catch; ~ **annuelle** annual closure; ~ **éclair®** zip(-fastener); (US) zipper.

fermier, -ière /fɛʀmje, -ɛʀ/ adj farm. ● nm farmer. **fermière** nf farmer's wife.

féroce /feʀɔs/ adj ferocious.

ferraille /feʀɑj/ nf scrap-iron.

ferrer /feʀe/ **1** vt (cheval) shoe.

ferroviaire /feʀɔvjɛʀ/ adj rail(way).

ferry /feʀi/ nm ferry.

fertile /fɛʀtil/ adj fertile; ~ **en** (fig) rich in. **fertiliser** **1** vt fertilize. **fertilité** nf fertility.

fervent, ~e /fɛʀvɑ̃, -t/ adj fervent. ● nm, f enthusiast (**de** of).

fesse /fɛs/ nf buttock. **fessée** nf spanking, smack.

festin /fɛstɛ̃/ nm feast.

festival (pl ~s) /fɛstival/ nm festival.

fêtard, ~e /fɛtaʀ, -d/ nm, f **1** party animal.

fête /fɛt/ nf holiday; (religieuse) feast; (du nom) name-day; (réception) party; (en famille) celebration; (foire) fair; (folklorique) festival; ~ **des Mères** Mother's Day; ~ **foraine** fun-fair; **faire la** ~ live it up; **les** ~**s** (de fin d'année) the Christmas season. **fêter** **1** vt celebrate; (personne) give a celebration for.

fétiche /fetiʃ/ nm fetish; (fig) mascot.

feu¹ (pl ~x) /fø/ nm fire; (lumière) light; (de réchaud) burner; **à** ~ **doux/vif** on a low/high heat; ~ **rouge/vert/orange** red/green/amber light; **aux** ~**x, tournez à**

droite turn right at the traffic lights; **avez-vous du** ~**?** (pour cigarette) have you got a light?; **au** ~**!** fire!; **mettre le** ~ **à** set fire to; **prendre** ~ catch fire; **jouer avec le** ~ play with fire; **ne pas faire long** ~ not last; ~ **d'artifice** firework display; ~ **de joie** bonfire; ~ **de position** sidelight.

feu² /fø/ adj inv (mort) late.

feuillage /fœjaʒ/ nm foliage.

feuille /fœj/ nf leaf; (de papier) sheet; (formulaire) form; ~ **d'impôts** tax return; ~ **de paie** payslip.

feuilleté, ~e /fœjte/ adj **pâte** ~**e** puff pastry. ● nm savoury pasty.

feuilleter /fœjte/ **1** vt leaf through.

feuilleton /fœjtɔ̃/ nm (à suivre) serial; (histoire complète) series.

feutre /føtʀ/ nm felt; (chapeau) felt hat; (crayon) felt-tip (pen).

fève /fɛv/ nf broad bean.

février /fevʀije/ nm February.

fiable /fjabl/ adj reliable.

fiançailles /fjɑ̃saj/ nfpl engagement.

fiancé, ~e /fjɑ̃se/ adj engaged. ● nm fiancé. **fiancée** nf fiancée. **fiancer (se)** **10** vpr become engaged (**avec** to).

fibre /fibʀ/ nf fibre; ~ **de verre** fibreglass.

ficeler /fisle/ **38** vt tie up.

ficelle /fisɛl/ nf string.

fiche /fiʃ/ nf (index) card; (formulaire) form, slip; (Électr) plug.

ficher¹ /fiʃe/ **1** vt (enfoncer) drive (**dans** into).

ficher² /fiʃe/ **1** **1** vt (faire) do; (donner) give; (mettre) put; **le camp** clear off. □ se ~ **de** vpr make fun of; **il s'en fiche** he couldn't care less.

fichier /fiʃje/ nm file.

fichu, ~e /fiʃy/ adj 🔼 (mauvais) rotten; (raté) done for; **mal ~** terrible.

fictif, -ive /fiktif, -v/ adj fictitious. **fiction** nf fiction.

fidèle /fidɛl/ adj faithful. ● nmf (client) regular; (Relig) believer; **~s** (à l'église) congregation. **fidélité** nf fidelity.

fier¹, fière /fjɛʀ/ adj proud (**de** of).

fier²(se) /(sə)fje/ 🔼 vpr **se ~ à** trust.

fierté /fjɛʀte/ nf pride.

fièvre /fjɛvʀ/ nf fever; **avoir de la ~** have a temperature; **~ aphteuse** foot-and-mouth disease. **fiévreux, -euse** /fjevʀø, -z/ adj feverish.

figer /fiʒe/ 🔼 vi (graisse) congeal; (sang) clot; **figé sur place** frozen to the spot. □ **se ~** vpr (personne, sourire) freeze; (graisse) congeal; (sang) clot.

figue /fig/ nf fig.

figurant, ~e /figyʀɑ̃, -t/ nm, f (au cinéma) extra.

figure /figyʀ/ nf face; (forme, personnage) figure; (illustration) picture.

figuré, ~e /figyʀe/ adj (sens) figurative.

figurer /figyʀe/ 🔼 vi appear. ● vt represent. □ **se ~** vpr imagine.

fil /fil/ nm thread; (métallique, électrique) wire; (de couteau) edge; (à coudre) cotton; **au ~ de** with the passing of; **au ~ de l'eau** with the current; **~ de fer** wire; **au bout du ~** 🔼 on the phone.

file /fil/ nf line; (voie: Auto) lane; **~ (d'attente)** queue; (US) line; **en ~ indienne** in single file.

filer /file/ 🔼 vt spin; (suivre) shadow; **~ qch à qn** 🔼 slip sb sth. ● vi (bas) ladder, run; (liquide) run;

(aller vite 🔼) speed along, fly by; (partir 🔼) dash off; (disparaître 🔼) **~ entre les mains** slip through one's fingers; **~ doux** do as one's told.

filet /filɛ/ nm net; (d'eau) trickle; (de viande) fillet; **~ (à bagages)** (luggage) rack; **~ à provisions** string bag (for shopping).

filiale /filjal/ nf subsidiary (company).

filière /filjɛʀ/ nf (official) channels; (de trafiquants) network; **passer par** ou **suivre la ~** (employé) work one's way up.

fille /fij/ nf girl; (opposé à fils) daughter. **fillette** nf little girl.

filleul /fijœl/ nm godson.

filleule /fijœl/ nf god-daughter.

film /film/ nm ~ **d'épouvante/muet/parlant** horror/ silent/talking film; ~ **dramatique** drama. **filmer** 🔼 vt film.

filon /filɔ̃/ nm (Géol) seam; (travail lucratif 🔼) money spinner; **avoir trouvé le bon ~** be onto a good thing.

fils /fis/ nm son.

filtre /filtʀ/ nm filter. **filtrer** 🔼 vt/i filter; (personne) screen.

fin¹ /fɛ̃/ nf end; **à la ~** finally; **en ~ de compte** all things considered; **~ de semaine** weekend; **mettre ~ à** put an end to; **prendre ~** come to an end.

fin², ~e /fɛ̃, fin/ adj fine; (tranche, couche) thin; (taille) slim; (plat) exquisite; (esprit, vue) sharp; **~es herbes** mixed herbs. ● adv (couper) finely.

final, ~e (mpl **-aux**) /final, -o/ adj final.

finale /final/ nm (Mus) finale. ● nf (Sport) final; (Gram) final syllable. **finalement** adv finally; (somme toute) after all. **finaliste** nmf finalist.

finance /finɑ̃s/ nf finance. **financer** 🔟 vt finance.

financier, -ière /finɑ̃sje, -jɛʀ/ adj financial. ● nm financier.

finesse /fines/ nf fineness; (de taille) slimness; (acuité) sharpness; ∼s (de langue) niceties.

finir /finiʀ/ 🔟 vt/i finish, end; (arrêter) stop; (manger) finish (up); **en** ∼ **avec** have done with; ∼ **par faire** end up doing; **ça va mal** ∼ it will turn out badly.

finlandais, ∼e /fɛ̃lɑ̃dɛ, -z/ adj Finnish. **F∼, ∼e** nm, f Finn.

Finlande /fɛ̃lɑ̃d/ nf Finland.

finnois, ∼e /finwa/ adj Finnish. ● nm (Ling) Finnish.

firme /fiʀm/ nf firm.

fisc /fisk/ nm tax authorities. **fiscal, ∼e** /fiskal/ (mpl **-aux**) adj tax, fiscal. **fiscalité** nf tax system.

fissure /fisyʀ/ nf crack.

FIV abrév f (**fécondation in vitro**) IVF.

fixe /fiks/ adj fixed; (stable) steady; **à heure** ∼ at a set time; **menu à prix** ∼ set menu. ● nm basic pay.

fixer /fikse/ 🔟 vt fix; ∼ **(du regard)** stare at; **être fixé** (personne) have made up one's mind. ◻ **se** ∼ vpr (s'attacher) be attached; (s'installer) settle down.

flacon /flakɔ̃/ nm bottle.

flagrant, ∼e /flagʀɑ̃, -t/ adj flagrant, blatant; **en** ∼ **délit** in the act.

flair /flɛʀ/ nm (sense of) smell; (fig) intuition.

flamand, ∼e /flamɑ̃, -d/ adj Flemish. ● nm (Ling) Flemish. **F∼, ∼e** nm, f Fleming.

flamant /flamɑ̃/ nm flamingo.

flambeau (pl ∼x) /flɑ̃bo/ nm

torch.

flambée /flɑ̃be/ nf blaze; (fig) explosion.

flamber /flɑ̃be/ 🔟 vi blaze; (prix) shoot up. ● vt (aiguille) sterilize; (volaille) singe.

flamme /flam/ nf flame; (fig) ardour; **en** ∼s ablaze.

flan /flɑ̃/ nm custard tart.

flanc /flɑ̃/ nm side; (d'animal, d'armée) flank.

flâner /flɑne/ 🔟 vi stroll. **flânerie** nf stroll.

flanquer /flɑ̃ke/ 🔟 vt flank; (jeter 🔟) chuck; (donner 🔟) give; ∼ **à la porte** kick out.

flaque /flak/ nf (d'eau) puddle; (de sang) pool.

flash (pl ∼**es**) /flaʃ/ nm (Photo) flash; (information) news flash; ∼ **publicitaire** commercial.

flatter /flate/ 🔟 vt flatter. ◻ **se** ∼ **de** vpr pride oneself on.

flatteur, -euse /flatœʀ, -øz/ adj flattering. ● nm, f flatterer.

fléau (pl ∼**x**) /fleo/ nm (désastre) scourge; (personne) pest.

flèche /flɛʃ/ nf arrow; (de clocher) spire; **monter en** ∼ spiral; **partir en** ∼ shoot off.

flécher /fleʃe/ 🔝 vt mark ou signpost (with arrows). **fléchette** nf dart.

fléchir /fleʃiʀ/ 🔟 vt bend; (personne) move, sway. ● vi (faiblir) weaken; (prix) fall; (poutre) sag, bend.

flemme /flɛm/ nf 🔟 laziness; **j'ai la** ∼ **de faire** I can't be bothered doing.

flétrir (se) /(sə)fletʀiʀ/ 🔟 vpr (plante) wither; (fruit) shrivel; (beauté) fade.

fleur /flœʀ/ nf flower; **à** ∼ **de terre/d'eau** just above the ground/

water; **à ~s** flowery; **~ de l'âge** prime of life; **en ~** in flower.

fleurir /flœriʀ/ **2** vi flower; (arbre) blossom; (fig) flourish. ● vt decorate with flowers. **fleuriste** nmf florist.

fleuve /flœv/ nm river.

flic /flik/ nm **①** cop.

flipper /flipœʀ/ nm pinball (machine).

flirter /flœʀte/ **1** vi flirt.

flocon /flɔkɔ̃/ nm flake.

flore /flɔʀ/ nf flora.

florissant, ~e /flɔʀisɑ̃, -t/ adj flourishing.

flot /flo/ nm flood, stream; **être à ~** be afloat; **les ~s** the waves.

flottant, ~e /flɔtɑ̃, -t/ adj (vêtement) loose; (indécis) indecisive.

flotte /flɔt/ nf fleet; (pluie **①**) rain; (eau **①**) water.

flottement /flɔtmɑ̃/ nm (incertitude) indecision.

flotter /flɔte/ **1** vi float; (drapeau) flutter; (nuage, parfum, pensées) drift; (pleuvoir **①**) rain. **flotteur** nm float.

flou, ~e /flu/ adj out of focus; (fig) vague.

fluctuer /flyktɥe/ **1** vi fluctuate.

fluet, ~te /flɥɛ, -t/ adj thin.

fluide /flɥid/ adj & nm fluid.

fluor /flyɔʀ/ nm (pour les dents) fluoride.

fluorescent, ~e /flyɔʀesɑ̃, -t/ adj fluorescent.

flûte /flyt/ nf flute; (verre) champagne glass.

fluvial, ~e (mpl **-iaux**) /flyvjal, -jo/ adj river.

flux /fly/ nm flow; **~ et reflux** ebb and flow.

FM abrév f (**frequency modulation**) FM.

fœtus /fetys/ nm foetus.

foi /fwa/ nf faith; **être de bonne/ mauvaise ~** be acting in good/bad faith; **ma ~!** well (indeed)!

foie /fwa/ nm liver.

foin /fwɛ̃/ nm hay.

foire /fwaʀ/ nf fair; **faire la ~ ①** live it up.

fois /fwa/ nf time; **une ~** once; **deux ~** twice; **à la ~** at the same time; **des ~** (parfois) sometimes; **une ~ pour toutes** once and for all.

fol /fɔl/ ➡**FOU.**

folie /fɔli/ nf madness; (bêtise) foolish thing, folly; **faire une ~, faire des ~s** be extravagant.

folklore /fɔlklɔʀ/ nm folklore. **folklorique** adj folk; **①** eccentric.

folle /fɔl/ ➡**FOU.**

foncé, ~e /fɔ̃se/ adj dark.

foncer /fɔ̃se/ **10** vt darken. ● vi (s'assombrir) darken; (aller vite **①**) dash along; **~ sur ①** charge at.

foncier, -ière /fɔ̃sje, -jɛʀ/ adj fundamental; (Comm) real estate.

fonction /fɔ̃ksjɔ̃/ nf function; (emploi) position; **~s** (obligations) duties; **en ~ de** according to; **~ publique** civil service; **voiture de ~** company car. **fonctionnaire** nmf civil servant. **fonctionnement** nm working.

fonctionner /fɔ̃ksjɔne/ **1** vi work; **faire ~** work.

fond /fɔ̃/ nm bottom; (de salle, magasin, etc.) back; (essentiel) basis; (contenu) content; (plan) background; (Sport) long-distance running; **à ~** thoroughly; **au ~** basically; **de ~** (bruit) background; **de ~ en comble** from top to bottom; **au ou dans le ~** really; **de ~ de teint** foundation, make-up base.

fondamental, ~e (mpl **-aux**) /fɔ̃damɑ̃tal, -o/ adj fundamental.

fondateur, -trice /fɔ̃datœr, -tris/ *nm, f* founder. **fondation** *nf* foundation.

fonder /fɔ̃de/ **1** *vt* found; (baser) base (**sur** on); (**bien**) **fondé** wellfounded. □ **se ~ sur** *vpr* be guided by, be based on.

fonderie /fɔ̃dri/ *nf* foundry.

fondre /fɔ̃dr/ **3** *vt/i* melt; (dans l'eau) dissolve; (mélanger) merge; **faire ~** melt; dissolve; **~ en larmes** burst into tears; **~ sur** swoop on. □ **se ~** *vpr* merge.

fonds /fɔ̃/ *nm* fund; **~ de commerce** business. ● *nmpl* (capitaux) funds.

fondu, ~e /fɔ̃dy/ *adj* melted; (métal) molten.

font /fɔ̃/ ➡ **FAIRE** 33.

fontaine /fɔ̃tɛn/ *nf* fountain; (source) spring.

fonte /fɔ̃t/ *nf* melting; (fer) cast iron; **~ des neiges** thaw.

foot /fut/ *nm* **1** football.

football /futbol/ *nm* football.

footing /futiŋ/ *nm* jogging.

forain /fɔrɛ̃/ *nm* fairground entertainer; **marchand ~** stallholder.

forçat /fɔrsa/ *nm* convict.

force /fɔrs/ *nf* force; (physique) strength; (hydraulique etc.) power; **~s** (physiques) strength; **à ~ de** by sheer force of; **de ~, par la ~** by force; **~ de dissuasion** deterrent; **~ de frappe** strike force, deterrent; **~ de l'âge** prime of life; **~s de l'ordre** police (force) ; **~s de marché** market forces.

forcé, ~e /fɔrse/ *adj* forced; (inévitable) inevitable; **c'est ~ qu'il fasse** **1** he's bound to do. **forcément** *adv* necessarily; (évidemment) obviously.

forcené, ~e /fɔrsəne/ *adj* frenzied. ● *nm, f* maniac.

forcer /fɔrse/ **10** *vt* force (**à faire** to do); (voix) strain; **~ la dose** **1** overdo it. ● *vi* force; (exagérer) overdo it. □ **se ~** *vpr* force oneself.

forer /fɔre/ **1** *vt* drill.

forestier, -ière /fɔrɛstje, -jɛr/ *adj* forest. ● *nm, f* forestry worker.

forêt /fɔrɛ/ *nf* forest.

forfait /fɔrfɛ/ *nm* (Comm) (prix fixe) fixed price; (offre promotionnelle) package. **forfaitaire** *adj* (*prix*) fixed.

forger /fɔrʒe/ **40** *vt* forge; (inventer) make up.

forgeron /fɔrʒərɔ̃/ *nm* blacksmith.

formaliser (se) /(sə)fɔrmalize/ **1** *vpr* take offence (**de** at).

formalité /fɔrmalite/ *nf* formality.

format /fɔrma/ *nm* format. **formater** **1** *vt* (Ordinat) format.

formation /fɔrmasjɔ̃/ *nf* formation; (professionnelle) training; (culture) education; **~ permanente** ou **continue** continuing education.

forme /fɔrm/ *nf* form; (contour) shape, form; **~s** (de femme) figure; **être en ~** be in good shape, be on form; **en ~ de** in the shape of, be on form; **en bonne et due ~** in due form.

formel, ~le /fɔrmɛl/ *adj* formal; (catégorique) positive.

former /fɔrme/ **1** *vt* form; (instruire) train. □ **se ~** *vpr* form.

formidable /fɔrmidabl/ *adj* fantastic.

formulaire /fɔrmylɛr/ *nm* form.

formule /fɔrmyl/ *nf* formula; (expression) expression; (feuille) form; **~ de politesse** polite phrase, letter ending. **formuler** **1** *vt* formulate.

fort, ~e /fɔr, -t/ *adj* strong; (grand) big; (*pluie*) heavy; (*bruit*) loud; (*pente*) steep; (*élève*) clever; **au plus ~ de** at the height of; **c'est une ~e tête** she/he's headstrong. ● *adv*

(*frapper*) hard; (*parler*) loud; (très) very; (beaucoup) very much. ● *nm* (atout) strong point; (Mil) fort.

fortifiant /fɔʀtifjɑ̃/ *nm* tonic. **fortifier** 45 *vt* fortify.

fortune /fɔʀtyn/ *nf* fortune; de ~ (improvisé) makeshift; faire ~ make one's fortune.

forum /fɔʀɔm/ *nm* forum; ~ de discussion (Internet) newsgroup.

fosse /fos/ *nf* pit; (tombe) grave; ~ d'orchestre orchestra pit; ~ septique septic tank.

fossé /fose/ *nm* ditch; (fig) gulf; ~ numérique digital divide.

fossette /fosɛt/ *nf* dimple.

fossile /fosil/ *nm* fossil.

fou (**fol** *before vowel or mute h*), **folle** /fu, fɔl/ *adj* mad; (course, regard) wild; (énorme 1) tremendous; ~ de crazy about; le ~ rire the giggles. ● *nm* madman; (bouffon) jester. **folle** *nf* madwoman.

foudre /fudʀ/ *nf* lightning.

foudroyant, ~e /fudʀwajɑ̃, -t/ *adj* (mort, maladie) violent.

foudroyer /fudʀwaje/ 31 *vt* (orage) strike; (maladie etc.) strike down; ~ qn du regard look daggers at sb.

fouet /fwɛ/ *nm* whip; (Culin) whisk.

fougère /fuʒɛʀ/ *nf* fern.

fougue /fug/ *nf* ardour. **fougueux, -euse** *adj* ardent.

fouille /fuj/ *nf* search; (Archéol) excavation.

fouiller /fuje/ 1 *vt/i* search; (creuser) dig; ~ dans (tiroir) rummage through.

fouillis /fuji/ *nm* jumble.

foulard /fular/ *nm* scarf.

foule /ful/ *nf* crowd; une ~ de (fig) a mass of.

foulée /fule/ *nf* stride; il l'a fait dans la ~ he did it while he was at ou about it.

fouler /fule/ 1 *vt* (raisin) press; (sol) set foot on; ~ qch aux pieds trample sth underfoot; (fig) ride roughshod over sth. □ se ~ le poignet/le pied sprain one's wrist/foot; ne pas se ~ 1 not strain oneself.

four /fur/ *nm* oven; (de potier) kiln; (Théât) flop; ~ à micro-ondes microwave oven; ~ crématoire crematorium.

fourbe /furb/ *adj* deceitful.

fourche /furʃ/ *nf* fork; (à foin) pitchfork. **fourchette** *nf* fork; (Comm) bracket, range.

fourgon /furgɔ̃/ *nm* van.

fourmi /furmi/ *nf* ant; avoir des ~s have pins and needles.

fourmiller /furmije/ 1 *vi* swarm (de with).

fourneau (*pl* ~x) /furno/ *nm* stove.

fourni, ~e /furni/ *adj* (épais) thick.

fournir /furnir/ 2 *vt* supply, provide; (client) supply; (effort) put in; ~ à qn supply sb with. □ se ~ chez *vpr* shop at.

fournisseur /furnisœr/ *nm* supplier; ~ d'accès à l'Internet Internet service provider.

fourniture /furnityr/ *nf* supply.

fourrage /furaʒ/ *nm* fodder.

fourré, ~e /fure/ *adj* (vêtement) fur-lined; (gâteau etc.) filled (with jam, cream, etc.). ● *nm* thicket.

fourre-tout /furtu/ *nm inv* (sac) holdall.

fourreur /furœr/ *nm* furrier.

fourrière /furjɛr/ *nf* (lieu) pound.

fourrure /furyr/ *nf* fur.

foutre /futr/ 3 *vt* 🗙= **ficher²** 1.

foutu | free-lance

foutu, ~e /futy/ *adj* ⊠ = **fichu**.

foyer /fwaje/ *nm* home; (âtre) hearth; (club) club; (d'étudiants) hostel; (Théât) foyer; (Photo) focus; (centre) centre.

fracas /fraka/ *nm* din; (de train) roar; (d'objet qui tombe) crash. **fracassant**, ~e *adj* (bruyant) deafening; (violent) shattering.

fraction /fraksjɔ̃/ *nf* fraction.

fracture /fraktyr/ *nf* fracture; ~ **du poignet** fractured wrist.

fragile /fraʒil/ *adj* fragile; (peau) sensitive; (cœur) weak. **fragilité** *nf* fragility.

fragment /fragmɑ̃/ *nm* bit, fragment. **fragmenter** 1 *vt* split, fragment.

fraîchement /frɛʃmɑ̃/ *adv* (récemment) freshly; (avec froideur) coolly. **fraîcheur** *nf* coolness; (nouveauté) freshness. **fraîchir** 2 *vi* freshen, become colder.

frais[1], **fraîche** /frɛ, -ʃ/ *adj* fresh; (temps, accueil) cool; (peinture) wet; ~ **et dispos** fresh; **il fait** ~ it is cool. ● *adv* (récemment) newly, freshly. ● *nm* **mettre au** ~ put in a cool place; **prendre le** ~ get some fresh air.

frais[2] /frɛ/ *nmpl* expenses; (droits) fees; **aux** ~ **de** at the expense of; **faire des** ~ spend a lot of money; ~ **généraux** (Comm) overheads, running expenses; ~ **de scolarité** school fees.

fraise /frɛz/ *nf* strawberry. **fraisier** *nm* strawberry plant; (gâteau) strawberry gateau.

framboise /frɑ̃bwaz/ *nf* raspberry. **framboisier** *nm* raspberry bush.

franc, franche /frɑ̃, -ʃ/ *adj* frank; (regard) direct; (cassure) clean; (net) clear; (libre) free; (véritable) downright. ● *nm* franc.

français, ~e /frɑ̃sɛ, -z/ *adj* French. ● *nm* (Ling) French. **F~**, ~e *nm, f* Frenchman, Frenchwoman.

France /frɑ̃s/ *nf* France.

franchement /frɑ̃ʃmɑ̃/ *adv* frankly; (nettement) clearly; (tout à fait) really.

franchir /frɑ̃ʃir/ 2 *vt* (obstacle) get over; (distance) cover; (limite) exceed; (traverser) cross.

franchise /frɑ̃ʃiz/ *nf* (qualité) frankness; (Comm) franchise; (exemption) exemption; ~ **douanière** exemption from duties.

franc-maçon (*pl* **francs-maçons**) /frɑ̃masɔ̃/ *nm* Freemason. **franc-maçonnerie** *nf* Freemasonry.

franco /frɑ̃ko/ *adv* postage paid.

francophone /frɑ̃kɔfɔn/ *adj* French-speaking. ● *nmf* French speaker.

franc-parler /frɑ̃parle/ *nm inv* outspokenness.

frange /frɑ̃ʒ/ *nf* fringe.

frappe /frap/ *nf* (de texte) typing.

frappé, ~e /frape/ *adj* chilled.

frapper /frape/ 1 *vt/i* strike; (battre) hit, strike; (monnaie) mint; (à la porte) knock, bang; **frappé de panique** panic-stricken.

fraternel, ~le /fraternɛl/ *adj* brotherly. **fraternité** *nf* brotherhood.

fraude /frod/ *nf* fraud; (à un examen) cheating; **passer qch en** ~ smuggle sth in. **frauder** 1 *vt/i* cheat. **frauduleux**, **-euse** *adj* fraudulent.

frayer /freje/ 31 *vt* open up. □ **se** ~ *vpr* **se** ~ **un passage** force one's way (à travers, dans) through).

frayeur /frejœr/ *nf* fright.

fredonner /frədɔne/ 1 *vt* hum.

free-lance /frilɑ̃s/ *adj* & *nmf* freelance.

freezer /fʀizœʀ/ nm freezer.

frein /fʀɛ̃/ nm brake; **mettre un ~** à curb; **~ à main** hand brake.

freiner /fʀene/ **1** vt slow down; (modérer, enrayer) curb. ● vi (Auto) brake.

frêle /fʀɛl/ adj frail.

frelon /fʀəlɔ̃/ nm hornet.

frémir /fʀemiʀ/ **2** vi shudder, shake; (feuille, eau) quiver.

frêne /fʀɛn/ nm ash.

frénésie /fʀenezi/ nf frenzy. **frénétique** adj frenzied.

fréquemment /fʀekamɑ̃/ adv frequently. **fréquence** nf frequency. **fréquent, ~e** adj frequent. **fréquentation** nf frequenting.

fréquentations /fʀekɑ̃tasjɔ̃/ nfpl acquaintances; **avoir de mauvaises ~** keep bad company.

fréquenter /fʀekɑ̃te/ **1** vt frequent; (école) attend; (personne) see.

frère /fʀɛʀ/ nm brother.

fret /fʀɛt/ nm freight.

friand, ~e /fʀijɑ̃, -d/ adj **~ de** very fond of.

friandise /fʀijɑ̃diz/ nf sweet; (US) candy; (gâteau) cake.

fric /fʀik/ nm 🔟 money.

friction /fʀiksjɔ̃/ nf friction; (massage) rub-down.

frigidaire ® /fʀiʒideʀ/ nm refrigerator.

frigo /fʀigo/ nm 🔟 fridge. **frigorifique** adj (vitrine etc.) refrigerated.

frileux, -euse /fʀilø, -z/ adj sensitive to cold.

frime /fʀim/ nf 🔟 **c'est de la ~** it's all pretence; **pour la ~** for show.

frimousse /fʀimus/ nf face.

fringale /fʀɛ̃gal/ nf 🔟 ravenous appetite.

fringant, ~e /fʀɛ̃gɑ̃, -t/ adj dashing.

fringues /fʀɛ̃g/ nfpl 🔟 gear.

friper /fʀipe/ **1** vt crumple, crease. □ se **~** vpr crumple, crease.

fripon, ~ne /fʀipɔ̃, -ɔn/ nm, f rascal. ● adj mischievous.

fripouille /fʀipuj/ nf rogue.

frire /fʀiʀ/ 🔠 vt/i fry; **faire ~** fry.

frise /fʀiz/ nf frieze.

friser /fʀize/ **1** vt/i (cheveux) curl; (personne) curl the hair of; **frisé** curly.

frisson /fʀisɔ̃/ nm (de froid) shiver; (de peur) shudder. **frissonner** **1** vi shiver; shudder.

frit, ~e /fʀi, -t/ adj fried.

frite /fʀit/ nf chip; **avoir la ~** 🔟 feel good.

friteuse /fʀitøz/ nf chip pan; (électrique) (deep) fryer.

friture /fʀityʀ/ nf fried fish; (huile) (frying) oil ou fat.

frivole /fʀivɔl/ adj frivolous.

froid, ~e /fʀwa, -d/ adj & nm cold; **avoir/prendre ~** be/catch cold; **il fait ~** it is cold. **froidement** adv coldly; (calculer) coolly. **froideur** nf coldness.

froisser /fʀwase/ **1** vt crumple; (fig) offend. □ se **~** vpr crumple; (fig) take offence; **se ~ un muscle** strain a muscle.

frôler /fʀole/ **1** vt brush against, skim; (fig) come close to.

fromage /fʀɔmaʒ/ nm cheese. **fromager, -ère** /fʀɔmaʒe, -ɛʀ/ adj cheese. ● nm, f (fabricant) cheesemaker; (marchand) cheesemonger.

froment /fʀɔmɑ̃/ nm wheat.

froncer /fʀɔ̃se/ 🔟 vt gather; **~ les sourcils** frown.

front /fʀɔ̃/ nm forehead; (Mil, Pol) front; **de ~** at the same time; (de face) head-on; (côte à côte) abreast; **faire ~ à** face up to. **frontal, ~e** (*mpl* **-aux**) *adj* frontal; (Ordinat) front-end.

frontalier, -ière /fʀɔtalje, -jɛʀ/ *adj* border; **travailleur ~** commuter from across the border.

frontière /fʀɔtjɛʀ/ *nf* border, frontier.

frottement /fʀɔtmɑ̃/ *nm* rubbing; (Tech) friction. **frotter** 🔟 *vt/i* rub; (*allumette*) strike.

frottis /fʀɔti/ *nm* **~ vaginal** cervical smear.

frousse /fʀus/ *nf* 🔟 fear; **avoir la ~** 🔟 be scared.

fructifier /fʀyktifje/ *vi* **faire ~** put to work.

fructueux, -euse /fʀyktɥø, -z/ *adj* fruitful.

frugal, ~e (*mpl* **-aux**) /fʀygal, -o/ *adj* frugal.

fruit /fʀɥi/ *nm* fruit; **des ~s** (some) fruit; **~s de mer** seafood. **fruité, ~e** *adj* fruity.

frustrant, ~e /fʀystʀɑ̃, -t / *adj* frustrating. **frustrer** 🔟 *vt* frustrate.

fuel /fjul/ *nm* fuel oil.

fugitif, -ive /fyʒitif, -v/ *adj* (*passager*) fleeting. ● *nm, f* fugitive.

fugue /fyg/ *nf* (Mus) fugue; **faire une ~** run away.

fuir /fɥiʀ/ 🔞 *vi* flee, run away; (*eau, robinet, etc.*) leak; **en ~** on the run; **mettre en ~** put to flight; **prendre la ~** take flight. ● *vt* (quitter) flee; (*éviter*) shun.

fuite /fɥit/ *nf* flight; (de liquide, d'une nouvelle) leak; **en ~** on the run; **mettre en ~** put to flight; **prendre la ~** take flight.

fulgurant, ~e /fylgyʀɑ̃, -t/ *adj* (*vitesse*) lightning.

fumé, ~e /fyme/ *adj* (*poisson, verre*) smoked.

fumée /fyme/ *nf* smoke; (vapeur) steam.

fumer /fyme/ 🔟 *vt/i* smoke.

fumeur, -euse /fymœʀ, -øz/ *nm, f* smoker; **zone non-~s** no smoking area.

fumier /fymje/ *nm* manure.

funambule /fynɑ̃byl/ *nmf* tightrope walker.

funèbre /fynɛbʀ/ *adj* funeral; (fig) gloomy.

funérailles /fyneʀaj/ *nfpl* funeral.

funéraire /fyneʀɛʀ/ *adj* funeral.

funeste /fynɛst/ *adj* fatal.

fur: au ~ et à mesure /ofyʀeaməzyʀ/ *loc* as one goes along, progressively; **au ~ et à mesure que** as.

furet /fyʀɛ/ *nm* ferret.

fureur /fyʀœʀ/ *nf* fury; (passion) passion; **avec ~** furiously; passionately; **mettre en ~** infuriate; **faire ~** be all the rage.

furieux, -ieuse /fyʀjø, -z/ *adj* furious.

furoncle /fyʀɔ̃kl/ *nm* boil.

furtif, -ive /fyʀtif, -v/ *adj* furtive.

fuseau (*pl* **~x**) /fyzo/ *nm* ski trousers; (pour filer) spindle; **~ horaire** time zone.

fusée /fyze/ *nf* rocket.

fusible /fyzibl/ *nm* fuse.

fusil /fyzi/ *nm* rifle, gun; (de chasse) shotgun; **~ mitrailleur** machine-gun.

fusion /fyzjɔ̃/ *nf* fusion; (Comm) merger. **fusionner** 🔟 *vt/i* merge.

fut /fy/ **⇒ÊTRE** 🔟.

fût /fy/ *nm* (tonneau) barrel; (d'arbre) trunk.

futé, ~e /fyte/ *adj* cunning.

futile /fytil/ *adj* futile.

futur, ~e /fytyʀ/ *adj* future; **~e femme/maman** wife-/mother-to-be. ● *nm* future.

fuyant, ~e /fɥijɑ̃, -t/ *adj* (front,

ligne) receding; (*personne*) evasive.
fuyard, ~e /fɥijaʀ, -d/ *nm, f*
runaway.

. . . .

Gg

. . . .

gabardine /ɡabaʀdin/ *nf* raincoat.
gabarit /ɡabaʀi/ *nm* size; (*patron*)
template; (*fig*) calibre.
gâcher /ɡɑʃe/ **1** *vt* (*gâter*) spoil;
(*gaspiller*) waste.
gâchette /ɡɑʃɛt/ *nf* trigger.
gâchis /ɡɑʃi/ *nm* waste.
gaffe /ɡaf/ *nf* **1** blunder; **faire** ~
be careful (à of).
gage /ɡaʒ/ *nm* security; (*de bonne
foi*) pledge; (*de jeu*) forfeit; ~**s** (*salaire*) wages; **en** ~ **de** as a token
of; **mettre en** ~ pawn; **tueur à** ~**s**
hired killer.
gageure /ɡaʒyʀ/ *nf* challenge.
gagnant, ~e /ɡaɲɑ̃, -t/ *adj* winning. ● *nm, f* winner.
gagne-pain /ɡaɲpɛ̃/ *nm inv* job.
gagner /ɡaɲe/ **1** *vt* (*match, prix*)
win; (*argent, pain*) earn; (*terrain*)
gain; (*temps*) save; (*atteindre*) reach;
(*convaincre*) win over; ~ **sa vie**
earn one's living. ● *vi* win;
(*fig*) gain.
gai, ~e /ɡe/ *adj* cheerful; (*ivre*)
merry. **gaiement** *adv* cheerfully.
gaieté *nf* cheerfulness.
gain /ɡɛ̃/ *nm* (*salaire*) earnings;
(*avantage*) gain; (*économie*) saving;
~**s** (*Comm*) profits; (*au jeu*)
winnings.
gaine /ɡɛn/ *nf* (*corset*) girdle; (*étui*)
sheath.
galant, ~e /ɡalɑ̃, -t/ *adj* courte-

ous; (*amoureux*) romantic.
galaxie /ɡalaksi/ *nf* galaxy.
gale /ɡal/ *nf* (*de chat etc.*) mange.
galère /ɡalɛʀ/ *nf* (*navire*) galley;
c'est la ~! **1** what an ordeal!
galérer /ɡaleʀe/ **14** *vi* **1** (*peiner*)
have a hard time.
galerie /ɡalʀi/ *nf* gallery; (*Théât*)
circle; (*de voiture*) roof-rack; ~
marchande shopping arcade.
galet /ɡalɛ/ *nm* pebble.
galette /ɡalɛt/ *nf* flat cake; ~ **des
Rois** Twelfth Night cake.
Galles /ɡal/ *nfpl* **le pays de** ~
Wales.
gallois, ~e /ɡalwa, -z/ *adj* Welsh.
● *nm* (*Ling*) Welsh. **G**~, ~e, *nm, f*
Welshman, Welshwoman.
galon /ɡalɔ̃/ *nm* braid; (*Mil*) stripe;
prendre du ~ be promoted.
galop /ɡalo/ *nm* canter; **aller au** ~
canter; **grand** ~ gallop; ~ **d'essai**
trial run. **galoper** **1** *vi* (*cheval*) canter; (*au grand galop*) gallop; (*personne*) run.
galopin /ɡalɔpɛ̃/ *nm* **1** rascal.
gambader /ɡɑ̃bade/ **1** *vi* leap
about.
gamelle /ɡamɛl/ *nf* (*de soldat*)
mess kit; (*d'ouvrier*) lunch-box.
gamin, ~e /ɡamɛ̃, -in/ *adj* childish;
(*air*) youthful. ● *nm, f* **1** kid.
gamme /ɡam/ *nf* (*Mus*) scale;
(*série*) range; **haut de** ~
up-market, top of the range; **bas
de** ~ down-market, bottom of the
range.
gang /ɡɑ̃ɡ/ *nm* **1** gang.
ganglion /ɡɑ̃ɡlijɔ̃/ *nm* ganglion.
gangster /ɡɑ̃ɡstɛʀ/ *nm* gangster;
(*escroc*) crook.
gant /ɡɑ̃/ *nm* glove; ~ **de ménage**
rubber glove; ~ **de toilette** face-
flannel, face-cloth.

garage /gaʀaʒ/ *nm* garage. **gara-giste** *nmf* garage owner; (employé) car mechanic.

garant, ~e /gaʀɑ̃, -t/ *nm*, *f* guarantor. ● *adj* **se porter** ~ **de** vouch for.

garanti, ~e /gaʀɑ̃ti/ *adj* guaranteed.

garantie /gaʀɑ̃ti/ *nf* guarantee; ~s (de police d'assurance) cover. **garantir** 2 *vt* guarantee; (protéger) protect (**de** from).

garçon /gaʀsɔ̃/ *nm* boy; (jeune homme) young man; (célibataire) bachelor; ~ (**de café**) waiter; ~ **d'honneur** best man. **garçonnière** *nf* bachelor flat.

garde[1] /gaʀd/ *nf* guard; (d'enfants, de bagages) care; (service) guard (duty); (infirmière) nurse; **de** ~ on duty; ~ **à vue** (police) custody; **mettre en** ~ warn; **prendre** ~ be careful (**à** of); (**droit de**) ~ custody (**de** of).

garde[2] /gaʀd/ *nm* guard; (de propriété, parc) warden; ~ **champêtre** village policeman; ~ **du corps** bodyguard.

garde-à-vous /gaʀdavu/ *nm inv* (Mil) **se mettre au** ~ stand to attention.

garde-chasse (*pl* ~s) /gaʀdə-ʃas/ *nm* gamekeeper.

garde-manger /gaʀdmɑ̃ʒe/ *nm inv* meat safe; (placard) larder.

garder /gaʀde/ 1 *vt* (conserver, maintenir) keep on; (vêtement) keep on; (surveiller) look after; (défendre) guard; ~ **le lit** stay in bed. □ **se** ~ *vpr* (denrée) keep; **se** ~ **de faire** be careful not to do.

garderie /gaʀdəʀi/ *nf* day nursery.

garde-robe (*pl* ~s) /gaʀdəʀɔb/ *nf* wardrobe.

gardien, ~ne /gaʀdjɛ̃, -ɛn/ *nm*, *f* (de locaux) security guard; (de pri-son, réserve) warden; (d'immeuble) caretaker; (de musée) attendant; (de zoo) keeper; (de traditions) guardian; ~ **de but** goalkeeper; ~ **de la paix** policeman; ~ **de nuit** night watchman; **gardienne d'enfants** childminder.

gare /gaʀ/ *nf* (Rail) station; ~ **routière** coach station; (US) bus station. ● *interj* ~ (**à toi**) watch out!

garer /gaʀe/ 1 *vt* park. □ **se** ~ *vpr* park; (s'écarter) move out of the way.

gargouille /gaʀguj/ *nf* waterspout; (sculptée) gargoyle. **gargouiller** 1 *vi* gurgle; (stomach) rumble.

garni, ~e /gaʀni/ *adj* (plat) served with vegetables; **bien** ~ (rempli) well-filled.

garnir /gaʀniʀ/ 2 *vt* (remplir) fill; (décorer) decorate; (couvrir) cover; (doubler) line; (Culin) garnish. **garniture** *nf* (légumes) vegetables; (ornement) trimming; (de voiture) trim.

gars /ga/ *nm* 1 lad; (adulte) guy, bloke.

gas-oil /gazwal/ *nm* diesel (oil).

gaspillage /gaspijaʒ/ *nm* waste. **gaspiller** 1 *vt* waste.

gastrique /gastʀik/ *adj* gastric.

gastronome /gastʀɔnɔm/ *nmf* gourmet.

gâteau (*pl* ~x) /gɑto/ *nm* cake; ~ **sec** biscuit; (US) cookie; **un papa** ~ a doting dad.

gâter /gɑte/ 1 *vt* spoil. □ **se** ~ *vpr* (viande) go bad; (dent) rot; (temps) get worse.

gâterie /gɑtʀi/ *nf* little treat.

gâteux, **-euse** /gɑtø, -z/ *adj* senile.

gauche /goʃ/ *adj* left; (maladroit) awkward. ● *nf* left; **à** ~ on the left; (direction) (to the) left; **la** ~ the left (side); (Pol) the left (wing).

gaucher, -ère /goʃe, -ɛʀ/ adj left handed.

gaufre /gofʀ/ nf waffle. **gaufrette** nf wafer.

gaulois, ~e /golwa, -z/ adj Gallic; (fig) bawdy. **G~, ~e** m, f Gaul.

gaver /gave/ **1** vt force-feed; (fig) cram. □ **se ~ de** vpr gorge oneself with; (fig) devour.

gaz /gaz/ nm inv gas; **~ d'échappement** exhaust fumes; **~ lacrymogène** tear-gas.

gaze /gaz/ nf gauze.

gazer /gaze/ **1** vt **1** ça gaze? how's things?

gazette /gazɛt/ nf newspaper.

gazeux, -euse /gazø, -z/ adj (boisson) fizzy; (eau) sparkling.

gazoduc /gazɔdyk/ nm gas pipeline.

gazon /gazɔ̃/ nm lawn, grass.

gazouiller /gazuje/ **1** vi (oiseau) chirp; (bébé) babble.

GDF abrév m (**Gaz de France**) French gas board.

géant, ~e /ʒeɑ̃, -t/ adj giant. ● nm giant. **géante** nf giantess.

geindre /ʒɛ̃dʀ/ **22** vi groan, moan.

gel /ʒɛl/ nm frost; (produit) gel; (Comm) freeze; **~ coiffant** hair gel.

gelée /ʒ(ə)le/ nf frost; (Culin) jelly; **~ blanche** hoarfrost.

geler /ʒale/ **6** vt/i freeze; **on gèle** (on a froid) it's freezing; **il** ou **ça gèle** (il fait froid) it's freezing.

gélule /ʒelyl/ nf (Méd) capsule.

Gémeaux /ʒemo/ nmpl Gemini.

gémir /ʒemiʀ/ **2** vi groan.

gênant, ~e /ʒenɑ̃, -t/ adj embarrassing; (irritant) annoying; (incommode) cumbersome.

gencive /ʒɑ̃siv/ nf gum.

gendarme /ʒɑ̃daʀm/ nm police-

man, gendarme. **gendarmerie** nf police force; (local) police station.

gendre /ʒɑ̃dʀ/ nm son-in-law.

gène /ʒɛn/ nm gene.

gêne /ʒɛn/ nf discomfort; (confusion) embarrassment; (dérangement) trouble, inconvenience; (pauvreté) poverty.

gêné, ~e /ʒene/ adj embarrassed; (désargenté) short of money.

généalogie /ʒenealɔʒi/ nf genealogy.

gêner /ʒene/ **1** vt bother, disturb; (troubler) embarrass; (entraver) block; (faire mal) hurt.

général, ~e (mpl **-aux**) /ʒeneʀal, -o/ adj general; **en ~** in general. ● nm (pl **-aux**) general.

généralement /ʒeneʀalmɑ̃/ adv generally.

généraliser /ʒeneʀalize/ **1** vt make general. ● vi generalize. □ **se ~** vpr become widespread ou general.

généraliste /ʒeneʀalist/ nmf general practitioner, GP.

généralité /ʒeneʀalite/ nf general point.

génération /ʒeneʀasjɔ̃/ nf generation.

généreux, ~euse /ʒeneʀø, -z/ adj generous.

générique /ʒeneʀik/ nm (au cinéma) credits. ● adj generic.

générosité /ʒeneʀozite/ nf generosity.

génétique /ʒenetik/ adj genetic. ● nf genetics.

Genève /ʒənɛv/ npr Geneva.

génial, ~e (mpl -iaux) /ʒenjal, -jo/ adj brilliant; (fantastique 🛈) fantastic.

génie /ʒeni/ nm genius; ~ civil civil engineering.

génital, ~e (mpl -aux) /ʒenital, -o/ adj genital.

génocide /ʒenɔsid/ nm genocide.

génoise /ʒenwaz/ nf sponge (cake).

génome /ʒenom/ nm genome.

génothèque /ʒenɔtɛk/ nf gene bank.

genou (pl ~x) /ʒənu/ nm knee; être à ~x be kneeling.

genre /ʒɑ̃r/ nm sort, kind; (Gram) gender; (allure) **avoir bon/mauvais** ~ to look nice/disreputable; (comportement) **c'est bien son** ~ it's just like him/her.

gens /ʒɑ̃/ nmpl people.

gentil, ~le /ʒɑ̃ti, -j/ adj kind, nice; (sage) good. **gentillesse** nf kindness. **gentiment** adv kindly.

géographie /ʒeɔgrafi/ nf geography.

geôlier, -ière /ʒolje, -jɛr/ nm, f gaoler, jailer.

géologie /ʒeɔlɔʒi/ nf geology.

géomètre /ʒeɔmɛtr/ nm surveyor.

géométrie /ʒeɔmetri/ nf geometry. **géométrique** adj geometric.

gérance /ʒerɑ̃s/ nf management.

gérant, ~e /ʒerɑ̃, -t/ nm, f manager, manageress; ~ **d'immeuble** landlord's agent.

gerbe /ʒɛrb/ nf (de fleurs) bunch, bouquet; (d'eau) spray; (de blé) sheaf.

gercer /ʒɛrse/ 🔟 vt chap; **avoir les lèvres gercées** have chapped lips. ● vi become chapped. **gerçure** nf crack, chap.

gérer /ʒere/ 🔢 vt manage, run;

(traiter: fig) (crise, situation) handle.

germe /ʒɛrm/ nm germ; ~s **de soja** bean sprouts.

germer /ʒɛrme/ 🔟 vi germinate.

gestation /ʒɛstasjɔ̃/ nf gestation.

geste /ʒɛst/ nm gesture.

gesticuler /ʒɛstikyle/ 🔟 vi gesticulate.

gestion /ʒɛstjɔ̃/ nf management. **gestionnaire** nmf administrator.

ghetto /ɡeto/ nm ghetto.

gibier /ʒibje/ nm (animaux) game.

giboulée /ʒibule/ nf shower.

gicler /ʒikle/ 🔟 vi squirt; **faire** ~ squirt.

gifle /ʒifl/ nf slap in the face. **gifler** 🔟 vt slap.

gigantesque /ʒigɑ̃tɛsk/ adj gigantic.

gigot /ʒigo/ nm leg (of lamb).

gigoter /ʒigote/ 🔟 vi wriggle; (nerveusement) fidget.

gilet /ʒile/ nm waistcoat; (cardigan) cardigan; ~ **de sauvetage** life jacket.

gingembre /ʒɛ̃ʒɑ̃br/ nm ginger.

girafe /ʒiraf/ nf giraffe.

giratoire /ʒiratwar/ adj sens ~ roundabout.

girofle /ʒirɔfl/ nm clou de ~ clove.

girouette /ʒirwɛt/ nf weathercock, weathervane.

gisement /ʒizmɑ̃/ nm deposit.

gitan, ~e /ʒitɑ̃, -an/ nm, f gypsy.

gîte /ʒit/ nm (maison) home; (abri) shelter; ~ **rural** holiday cottage.

givre /ʒivr/ nm frost; (sur pare-brise) ice.

givré, ~e /ʒivre/ adj 🛈 crazy.

glace /glas/ nf ice; (crème) icecream; (vitre) window; (miroir) mirror; (verre) glass.

glacé, ~e /glase/ adj (vent, accueil) icy; (hands) frozen; (gâteau) iced.

glacer /glase/ 10 vt freeze; (gâteau, boisson) chill; (pétrifier) chill. □ se ~ vpr freeze.

glacier /glasje/ nm (Géog) glacier; (vendeur) ice-cream seller. **glacière** nf coolbox. **glaçon** nm ice-cube.

glaïeul /glajœl/ nm gladiolus.

glaise /glɛz/ nf clay.

gland /glɑ̃/ nm acorn; (ornement) tassel.

glande /glɑ̃d/ nf gland.

glander /glɑ̃de/ 1 vi 1 laze around.

glaner /glane/ 1 vt glean.

glauque /glok/ adj (fig) murky; (street) squalid.

glissade /glisad/ nf (jeu) slide; (dérapage) skid.

glissant, ~e /glisɑ̃, -t/ adj slippery.

glissement /glismɑ̃/ nm sliding; gliding; (fig) shift; ~ de terrain landslide.

glisser /glise/ 1 vi slide; (être glissant) be slippery; (sur l'eau) glide; (déraper) slip; (véhicule) skid. ● vt (objet) slide (dans into); (remarque) slip in. □ se ~ vpr slip (dans into).

glissière /glisjɛʀ/ nf slide; porte à ~ sliding door; ~ de sécurité (Auto) crash-barrier; fermeture à ~ zip.

global, ~e (mpl -aux) /glɔbal, -o/ adj (entier, général) overall. **globalement** adv as a whole.

globe /glɔb/ nm globe; ~ oculaire eyeball; ~ terrestre globe.

globule /glɔbyl/ nm (du sang) corpuscle.

gloire /glwaʀ/ nf glory, fame. **glorieux**, **-ieuse** adj glorious. **glorifier** 45 vt glorify.

glose /gloz/ nf gloss.

glossaire /glɔsɛʀ/ nm glossary.

gloussement /glusmɑ̃/ nm chuckle; (de poule) cluck.

glouton, ~ne /glutɔ̃, -ɔn/ adj gluttonous. ● nm, f glutton.

gluant, ~e /glyɑ̃, -t/ adj sticky.

glucose /glykoz/ nm glucose.

glycérine /gliseʀin/ nf glycerin(e).

GO abrév fpl (**grandes ondes**) long wave.

goal /gol/ nm 1 goalkeeper.

gobelet /gɔblɛ/ nm cup; (en verre) tumbler.

gober /gɔbe/ 1 vt swallow (whole); **je ne peux pas le ~** 1 I can't stand him.

goéland /gɔelɑ̃/ nm (sea)gull.

gogo: à ~ /agogo/ loc 1 galore, in abundance.

goinfre /gwɛ̃fʀ/ nm (glouton 1) pig. **goinfrer (se)** 1 vpr 1 stuff oneself (**de** with).

golf /gɔlf/ nm golf; (terrain) golf course.

golfe /gɔlf/ nm gulf.

gomme /gɔm/ nf rubber; (US) eraser; (résine) gum. **gommer** 1 vt rub out.

gond /gɔ̃/ nm hinge; **sortir de ses** ~s 1 go mad.

gondoler (se) /(sa)gɔ̃dɔle/ 1 vpr (bois) warp; (métal) buckle.

gonflé, ~e /gɔ̃fle/ adj swollen; **il est** ~ 1 he's got a nerve.

gonflement /gɔ̃flemɑ̃/ nm swelling.

gonfler /gɔ̃fle/ 1 vt (ballon, pneu) pump up, blow up; (augmenter) increase; (exagérer) inflate. ● vi swell.

gorge /gɔʀʒ/ nf throat; (poitrine) breast; (vallée) gorge.

gorgée /gɔʀʒe/ nf sip, gulp.

gorger /gɔʁʒe/ 40 vt fill (**de** with); **gorgé de** full of. □ **se** ~ vpr gorge oneself (**de** with).

gorille /gɔʁij/ nm gorilla; (garde 1) bodyguard.

gosier /gozje/ nm throat.

gosse /gɔs/ nmf 1 kid.

gothique /gɔtik/ adj Gothic.

goudron /gudʁɔ̃/ nm tar. **goudronner** 1 vt tarmac.

gouffre /gufʁ/ nm abyss, gulf.

goujat /guʒa/ nm lout, boor.

goulot /gulo/ nm neck; **boire au** ~ drink from the bottle.

goulu, ~**e** /guly/ adj gluttonous. ● nm, f glutton.

gourde /guʁd/ nf (à eau) flask; (idiot 1) fool.

gourer (se) /(sə)guʁe/ 1 vpr 1 make a mistake.

gourmand, ~**e** /guʁmɑ̃, -d/ adj greedy. ● nm, f glutton.

gourmandise /guʁmɑ̃diz/ nf greed; ~**s** sweets.

gourmet /guʁmɛ/ nm gourmet.

gourmette /guʁmɛt/ nf chain bracelet.

gousse /gus/ nf ~ **d'ail** clove of garlic.

goût /gu/ nm taste; (gré) liking; **prendre** ~ **à** develop a taste for; **avoir bon** ~ (aliment) taste nice; (personne) have good taste; **donner du** ~ **à** give flavour.

goûter /gute/ 1 vt taste; (apprécier) enjoy; ~ **à** ou **de** taste. ● vi have tea. ● nm tea, snack.

goutte /gut/ nf drop; (Méd) gout. **goutte-à-goutte** nm inv drip. **goutter** 1 vi drip.

gouttière /gutjɛʁ/ nf gutter.

gouvernail /guvɛʁnaj/ nm rudder; (barre) helm.

gouvernement /guvɛʁnəmɑ̃/ nm government.

gouverner /guvɛʁne/ 1 vt/i govern; (dominer) control. **gouverneur** nm governor.

GPS abrév m (**global positioning system**) GPS.

grâce /gʁɑs/ nf (charme) grace; (faveur) favour; (clémence) grace; (Jur) pardon; (Relig) grace; ~ **à** thanks to; **rendre** (~**s**) **à** give thanks to.

gracier /gʁasje/ 45 vt pardon.

gracieusement /gʁasjøzmɑ̃/ adv gracefully; (gratuitement) free (of charge).

gracieux, -ieuse /gʁasjø, -z/ adj graceful.

grade /gʁad/ nm rank; **monter en** ~ be promoted.

gradin /gʁadɛ̃/ nm tier, step; **en** ~**s** terraced; **les** ~**s** terraces.

gradué, ~**e** /gʁadɥe/ adj graded, graduated; **verre** ~ measuring jug.

graffiti /gʁafiti/ nmpl graffiti.

grain /gʁɛ̃/ nm grain; (Naut) squall; ~ **de beauté** beauty spot; ~ **de café** coffee bean; ~ **de poivre** pepper corn; ~ **de raisin** grape.

graine /gʁɛn/ nf seed.

graisse /gʁɛs/ nf fat; (lubrifiant) grease. **graisser** 1 vt grease. **graisseux, -euse** adj greasy.

grammaire /gʁam(m)ɛʁ/ nf grammar.

gramme /gʁam/ nm gram.

grand, ~**e** /gʁɑ̃, -d/ adj big, large; (haut) tall; (intense, fort) great; (brillant) great; (principal) main; (plus âgé) big, elder; (adulte) grown-up; **au** ~ **air** in the open air; **au** ~ **jour** in broad daylight; (fig) in the open; **en** ~**e partie** largely; ~**e banlieue** outer suburbs; ~ **ensemble** housing estate; ~**es lignes** (Rail) main lines; ~ **magasin** department store; ~**e personne**

g

grown-up; ~ **public** general public; ~**e surface** hypermarket; ~**es vacances** summer holidays. ● *adv* (*ouvrir*) wide; ~ **ouvert** wide open; **voir** ~ think big. ● *nm, f* (*adulte*) grown-up; (*enfant*) big boy, big girl; (Scol) senior.

grand-chose /grɑ̃ʃoz/ *pron* **pas** ~ not much, not a lot.

Grande-Bretagne /grɑ̃dbrətaɲ/ *nf* Great Britain.

Grande école A prestigious tertiary institution to which admission is usually by competitive examination or *concours*. Places are much sought after as they generally guarantee more promising career prospects than the standard universities. Many *grandes écoles* specialize in particular disciplines or fields of study, e.g. *ENA* (public administration), *Sciences Po* (political science), etc.

grandeur /grɑ̃dœr/ *nf* greatness; (dimension) size; **folie des** ~**s** delusions of grandeur.

grandir /grɑ̃dir/ **2** *vi* grow; (*bruit*) grow louder. ● *vt* (*talons*) make taller; (*loupe*) magnify.

grand-mère (*pl* **grands-mères**) /grɑ̃mɛr/ *nf* grandmother.

grand-père (*pl* **grands-pères**) /grɑ̃pɛr/ *nm* grandfather.

grands-parents /grɑ̃parɑ̃/ *nmpl* grandparents.

grange /grɑ̃ʒ/ *nf* barn.

granulé /granyle/ *nm* granule.

graphique /grafik/ *adj* graphic; (Ordinat) graphics; **informatique** ~ computer graphics. ● *nm* graph.

graphologie /grafɔlɔʒi/ *nf* graphology.

grappe /grap/ *nf* cluster; ~ **de**

raisin bunch of grapes.

gras, ~**se** /grɑ, -s/ *adj* (gros) fat; (*aliment*) fatty; (surface, peau, cheveux) greasy; (épais) thick; (caractères) bold; **faire la** ~**se matinée** sleep late. ● *nm* (Culin) fat.

gratifiant, ~**e** /gratifjɑ̃, -t/ *adj* gratifying; (*travail*) rewarding.

gratifier /gratifje/ **45** *vt* favour, reward (**de** with).

gratin /gratɛ̃/ *nm* gratin (baked dish with cheese topping); (élite 🏷) upper crust.

gratis /gratis/ *adv* free.

gratitude /gratityd/ *nf* gratitude.

gratte-ciel /gratsjɛl/ *nm inv* skyscraper.

gratter /grate/ **1** *vt/i* scratch; (avec un outil) scrape; **ça me gratte** 🏷 it itches. □ se ~ *vpr* scratch oneself; **se** ~ **la tête** scratch one's head.

gratuiciel /gratɥisjɛl/ *nm* (Internet) freeware.

gratuit, ~**e** /gratɥi, -t/ *adj* free; (*acte*) gratuitous. **gratuitement** *adv* free (of charge).

grave /grav/ *adj* (maladie, accident, problème) serious; (solennel) grave; (voix) deep; (accent) grave. **gravement** *adv* seriously; gravely.

graver /grave/ **1** *vt* engrave; (sur bois) carve; (Ordinat) burn.

graveur /gravœr/ *nm* (Ordinat) burner.

gravier /gravje/ *nm* **du** ~ gravel.

gravité /gravite/ *nf* gravity.

graviter /gravite/ **1** *vi* revolve.

gravure /gravyr/ *nf* engraving; (de tableau, photo) print, plate.

gré /gre/ *nm* (volonté) will; (goût) taste; **à son** ~ (agir) as one likes; **de bon** ~ willingly; **bon** ~ **mal** ~ like it or not; **je vous en saurais** ~ I'd be grateful for that.

grec, ~que /gʀɛk/ adj Greek. ● nm (Ling) Greek. **G~, ~que** nm, f Greek.

Grèce nf /gʀɛs/ Greece.

greffe /gʀɛf/ nf graft; (d'organe) transplant. **greffer 1** vt graft; transplant.

greffier, -ière /gʀefje, -jɛʀ/ nm, f clerk of the court.

grêle /gʀɛl/ adj (maigre) spindly; (voix) shrill. ● nf hail.

grêler /gʀele/ vi hail; **il grêle** it's hailing. **grêlon** nm hailstone.

grelot /gʀəlo/ nm (little) bell.

grelotter /gʀəlɔte/ 1 vi shiver.

grenade /gʀənad/ nf (fruit) pomegranate; (explosif) grenade.

grenat /gʀəna/ adj inv dark red.

grenier /gʀənje/ nm attic; (pour grain) loft.

grenouille /gʀənuj/ nf frog.

grès /gʀɛ/ nm sandstone; (poterie) stoneware.

grésiller /gʀezije/ 1 vi sizzle; (radio) crackle.

grève /gʀɛv/ nf (rivage) shore; (cessation de travail) strike; **faire ~, être en ~** on strike; **se mettre en ~** go on strike. **gréviste** nmf striker.

gribouiller /gʀibuje/ 1 vt/i scribble.

grief /gʀijɛf/ nm grievance.

grièvement /gʀijɛvmɑ̃/ adv seriously.

griffe /gʀif/ nf claw; (de couturier) label; **coup de ~** scratch.

griffé, ~e /gʀife/ adj (vêtement, article) designer.

griffer /gʀife/ 1 vt scratch, claw.

grignoter /gʀiɲɔte/ 1 vt/i nibble.

gril /gʀil/ nm (de cuisinière) grill; (plaque) grill pan.

grillade /gʀijad/ nf (viande) grill.

grillage /gʀijaʒ/ nm wire netting.

grille /gʀij/ nf railings; (portail) (metal) gate; (de fenêtre) bars; (de cheminée) grate; (fig) grid. **grille-pain** nm inv toaster.

griller /gʀije/ 1 vt (pain) toast; (viande) grill; (ampoule) blow; (feu rouge) go through; (appareil) burn out. ● vi (ampoule) blow; (Culin) **faire ~** (viande) grill; (pain) toast.

grillon /gʀijɔ̃/ nm cricket.

grimace /gʀimas/ nf (funny) face; (de douleur, dégoût) grimace; **faire des ~** make faces; **faire la ~** pull a face, grimace.

grimper /gʀɛ̃pe/ 1 vi climb; **~ sur** ou **dans un arbre** climb a tree.

grincement /gʀɛ̃smɑ̃/ nm creak(ing).

grincer /gʀɛ̃se/ 10 vi creak; **~ des dents** grind one's teeth.

grincheux, -euse /gʀɛ̃ʃø, -z/ adj grumpy.

grippe /gʀip/ nf influenza, flu.

grippé, ~e /gʀipe/ adj **être ~** have (the) flu; (mécanisme) be seized up ou jammed.

gris, ~e /gʀi, -z/ adj grey; (saoul) tipsy.

grivois, ~e /gʀivwa, -z/ adj bawdy.

grog /gʀɔg/ nm hot toddy.

grogner /gʀɔɲe/ 1 vi (animal) growl; (personne) grumble.

grognon /gʀɔɲɔ̃/ adj grumpy.

groin /gʀwɛ̃/ nm snout.

gronder /gʀɔ̃de/ 1 vi (tonnerre, volcan) rumble; (chien) growl; (conflit) be brewing. ● vt scold.

groom /gʀum/ nm bellboy.

gros, ~se /gʀo, -s/ adj big, large; (gras) fat; (important) big; (épais) thick; (lourd) heavy; (buveur, fu-

meur) heavy; ~ **bonnet** 🔲 bigwig; ~ **lot** jackpot; ~ **mot** swear word; ~ **plan** close-up; ~**se caisse** bass drum; ~ **titre** headline. ● *nm, f* fat man, fat woman. ● *adv* (*écrire*) big; (*risquer, gagner*) a lot. ● *nm* **le ~ de** the bulk of; **de ~** (Comm) wholesale; **en ~** roughly; (Comm) wholesale.

groseille /gʀozɛj/ *nf* redcurrant; ~ **à maquereau** gooseberry.

grossesse /gʀosɛs/ *nf* pregnancy.

grosseur /gʀosœʀ/ *nf* (*volume*) size; (*enflure*) lump.

grossier, -ière /gʀosje, -jɛʀ/ *adj* (*sans finesse*) coarse, rough; (*rudimentaire*) crude; (*vulgaire*) coarse; (*impoli*) rude; (*erreur*) gross. **grossièrement** *adv* (*sommairement*) roughly; (*vulgairement*) coarsely.

grossièreté *nf* coarseness; crudeness; rudeness; (*mot*) rude word.

grossir /gʀosiʀ/ 🔢 *vt* (*faire augmenter*) increase, boost; (*agrandir*) enlarge; (*exagérer*) exaggerate; ~ **les rangs** *ou* **la foule** swell the ranks. ● *vi* (*personne*) put on weight; (*augmenter*) grow.

grossiste /gʀosist/ *nmf* wholesaler.

grosso modo /gʀosomodo/ *adv* roughly.

grotesque /gʀotɛsk/ *adj* grotesque; (*ridicule*) ludicrous.

grotte /gʀot/ *nf* cave; grotto.

grouiller /gʀuje/ 🔢 *vi* swarm; ~ **de** be swarming with.

groupe /gʀup/ *nm* group; (Mus) group, band; ~ **électrogène** generating set; ~ **scolaire** school; ~ **de travail** working party.

groupement /gʀupmɑ̃/ *nm* grouping.

grouper /gʀupe/ 🔢 *vt* put together. □ **se ~** *vpr* group (together).

grue /gʀy/ *nf* (*machine, oiseau*) crane.

gruyère /gʀyjɛʀ/ *nm* gruyère (cheese).

gué /ge/ *nm* ford; **passer** *ou* **traverser à ~** ford.

guenon /gənɔ̃/ *nf* female monkey.

guépard /gepaʀ/ *nm* cheetah.

guêpe /gɛp/ *nf* wasp.

guère /gɛʀ/ *adv* **ne ~** hardly; **il n'y a ~ d'espoir** there is no hope; **elle n'a ~ dormi** she didn't sleep much, she hardly slept.

guérilla /geʀija/ *nf* guerrilla warfare; (*groupe*) guerillas.

guérir /geʀiʀ/ 🔢 *vt* (*personne, maladie, mal*) cure (**de** of); (*plaie, membre*) heal. ● *vi* get better; (*blessure*) heal; ~ **de** recover from. **guérison** *nf* curing; healing; (*de personne*) recovery.

guerre /gɛʀ/ *nf* war; **en ~** at war; **faire la ~** wage war (**à** against); ~ **civile** civil war; ~ **mondiale** world war.

guerrier, -ière /geʀje, -jɛʀ/ *adj* warlike. ● *nm, f* warrior.

guet /gɛ/ *nm* watch; **faire le ~** be on the watch. **guet-apens** (*pl* **guets-apens**) *nm* ambush.

guetter /gete/ 🔢 *vt* watch; (*attendre*) watch out for.

gueule /gœl/ *nf* mouth; (*figure* 🔲) face; **ta ~!** shut up!; ~ **de bois** 🔲 hangover.

gueuleton /gœltɔ̃/ *nm* 🔲 blowout, slap-up meal.

gui /gi/ *nm* mistletoe.

guichet /giʃɛ/ *nm* window, counter; (*de gare*) ticket-office; (Théât) box-office; **jouer à ~s fermés** (*pièce*) be sold out; ~ **automatique** cash dispenser.

guide /gid/ *nm* guide. ● *nf* (*fille scout*) girl guide.

guider /gide/ **1** vt guide.

guidon /gidɔ̃/ nm handlebars.

guignol /giɲɔl/ nm puppet; (personne) clown; (spectacle) puppet-show.

guillemets /gijmɛ/ nmpl quotation marks, inverted commas; **entre ~** in inverted commas.

guillotine /gijɔtin/ nf guillotine.

guimauve /gimov/ nf marshmallow; **c'est de la ~ 1** it's slushy ou schmaltzy **1**.

guindé, ~e /gɛ̃de/ adj stiff, formal; (style) stilted.

guirlande /girlɑ̃d/ nf garland; tinsel.

guitare /gitar/ nf guitar.

gym /ʒim/ nf gymnastics; (Scol) physical education, PE.

gymnase /ʒimnɑz/ nm gym(nasium). **gymnastique** nf gymnastics.

gynécologie /ʒinekɔlɔʒi/ nf gynaecology.

● ●

Hh

● ●

habile /abil/ adj skilful, clever.

habillé, ~e /abije/ adj (vêtement) smart; (soirée) formal.

habillement /abijmɑ̃/ nm clothing.

habiller /abije/ **1** vt dress (de in); (équiper) clothe; (recouvrir) cover (de with). □ s'~ vpr get dressed; (élégamment) dress up.

habit /abi/ nm (de personnage) outfit; (de cérémonie) tails; **~s** clothes.

habitant, ~e /abitɑ̃, -t/ nm, f (de maison, quartier) resident; (de pays) inhabitant.

habitat /abita/ nm (mode de peuplement) settlement; (conditions) housing.

habitation /abitasjɔ̃/ nf (logement) house.

habité, ~e /abite/ adj (terre) inhabited.

habiter /abite/ **1** vi live. ● vt live in.

habitude /abityd/ nf habit; **avoir l'~ de** be used to; **d'~** usually; **comme d'~** as usual.

habitué, ~e /abitɥe/ nm, f (client) regular.

habituel, ~le /abitɥɛl/ adj usual. **habituellement** adv usually.

habituer /abitɥe/ **1** vt **~ qn à** get sb used to. □ s'~ **à** vpr get used to.

hache /'aʃ/ nf axe.

haché, ~e /'aʃe/ adj (viande) minced; (phrases) jerky.

hacher /'aʃe/ **1** vt mince; (au couteau) chop.

hachis /'aʃi/ nm minced meat; (US) ground meat; **~ Parmentier** ≈ shepherd's pie.

hachisch /'aʃiʃ/ nm hashish.

hachoir /'aʃwar/ nm (appareil) mincer; (couteau) chopper; (planche) chopping board.

haie /'ɛ/ nf hedge; **course de ~s** hurdle race.

haillon /'ajɔ̃/ nm rag.

haine /'ɛn/ nf hatred.

haïr /'air/ **38** vt hate.

hâlé, ~e /'ɑle/ adj (sun-)tanned.

haleine /alɛn/ nf breath; **travail de longue ~** long job.

haleter /'alte/ **6** vi pant.

hall /'ol/ nm hall; (de gare) concourse.

halle /'al/ *nf* market hall; ∼**s** covered market.

halte /'alt/ *nf* stop; **faire** ∼ stop. ● *interj* stop; (Mil) halt.

haltère /alter/ *nm* dumbbell; **faire des** ∼**s** to do weightlifting.

hameau (*pl* ∼**x**) /'amo/ *nm* hamlet.

hameçon /amsɔ̃/ *nm* hook.

hanche /'ɑ̃ʃ/ *nf* hip.

handicap /'ɑ̃dikap/ *nm* handicap. **handicapé, ∼e** *adj* & *nm, f* disabled (person).

hangar /'ɑ̃gar/ *nm* shed; (pour avions) hangar.

hanter /'ɑ̃te/ **1** *vt* haunt.

hantise /'ɑ̃tiz/ *nf* dread; **avoir la** ∼ **de** dread.

hardi, ∼e /'ardi/ *adj* bold.

hareng /'arɑ̃/ *nm* herring.

hargne /'arɲ/ *nf* (aggressive) bad temper.

haricot /'ariko/ *nm* bean; ∼ **vert** French bean; (US) green bean.

harmonie /armɔni/ *nf* harmony. **harmonieux, -ieuse** *adj* harmonious.

harmoniser /armɔnize/ **1** *vt* harmonize. □ **s'**∼ *vpr* harmonize.

harnacher /arnaʃe/ **1** *vt* harness.

harnais /'arnɛ/ *nm* harness.

harpe /'arp/ *nf* harp.

harpon /'arpɔ̃/ *nm* harpoon.

hasard /'azar/ *nm* chance; (coïncidence) coincidence; **les** ∼**s de** the fortunes of; **au** ∼ (choisir etc.) at random; (flâner) aimlessly. **hasardeux, -euse** *adj* risky.

hasarder /'azarde/ **1** *vt* risk; (remarque) venture.

hâte /'at/ *nf* haste; **à la** ∼, **en** ∼ hurriedly; **avoir** ∼ **de** look forward to.

hâter /'ate/ **1** *vt* hasten. □ **se** ∼ *vpr* hurry (**de** to).

hâtif, -ive /'atif, -v/ *adj* hasty; (précoce) early.

hausse /'os/ *nf* rise (**de** in); ∼ **des prix** price rise; **en** ∼ rising.

hausser /'ose/ **1** *vt* raise; (épaules) shrug.

haut, ∼e /'o, 'ot/ *adj* high; (de taille) tall; **à voix** ∼**e** aloud; ∼ **en couleur** colourful; **plus** ∼ higher up; (dans un texte) above; **en** ∼ **lieu** in high places. ● *adv* high; **tout** ∼ out loud. ● *nm* top; **des** ∼**s et des bas** ups and downs; **en** ∼ (regarder) up; (à l'étage) upstairs; **en** ∼ **de** at the top (of).

hautbois /'obwa/ *nm* oboe.

haut-de-forme /'odfɔrm/ (*pl* **hauts-de-forme**) *nm* top hat.

hauteur /'otœr/ *nf* height; (colline) hill; (arrogance) haughtiness; **être à la** ∼ **de** be up to it; **à la** ∼ **de** (*ville*) near; **être à la** ∼ **de la situation** be equal to the situation.

haut-le-cœur /'olkœr/ *nm inv* nausea.

haut-parleur (*pl* ∼**s**) /'oparlœr/ *nm* loudspeaker.

havre /'avr/ *nm* haven (**de** of).

hayon /'ajɔ̃/ *nm* (Auto) hatchback.

hebdomadaire /ɛbdɔmader/ *adj* & *nm* weekly.

hébergement /eberʒemɑ̃/ *nm* accommodation.

héberger /eberʒe/ **40** *vt* (*ami*) put up; (*réfugiés*) take in.

hébreu (*pl* ∼**x**) /ebrø/ *am* Hebrew. ● *nm* (Ling) Hebrew; **c'est de l'**∼! it's all Greek to me!

Hébreu (pl ~x) /ebʀø/ nm Hebrew; **les** ~x the Hebrews.

hécatombe /ekatɔ̃b/ nf slaughter.

hectare /ɛktaʀ/ nm hectare (= 10,000 square metres).

hélas /'elɑs/ interj alas. ● adv sadly.

hélice /elis/ nf propeller.

hélicoptère /elikɔptɛʀ/ nm helicopter.

helvétique /ɛlvetik/ adj Swiss.

hématome /ematom/ nm bruise.

hémorragie /emɔʀaʒi/ nf haemorrhage.

hémorroïdes /emɔʀɔid/ nfpl piles, haemorrhoids.

hennir /'eniʀ/ ② vi neigh.

hépatite /epatit/ nf hepatitis.

herbe /ɛʀb/ nf grass; (Méd, Culin) herb; **en** ~ in the blade; (fig) budding.

héréditaire /eʀediteʀ/ adj hereditary.

hérédité /eʀedite/ nf heredity.

hérisser /'eʀise/ ① vt bristle; ~ **qn** (fig) ruffle sb. □ **se** ~ vpr bristle.

hérisson /'eʀisɔ̃/ nm hedgehog.

héritage /eʀitaʒ/ nm inheritance; (spirituel) heritage.

hériter /eʀite/ ① vt/i inherit (**de** from); ~ **de qch** inherit sth. **héritier, -ière** nm, f heir, heiress.

hermétique /ɛʀmetik/ adj airtight; (fig) unfathomable.

hernie /'ɛʀni/ nf hernia.

héroïne /eʀɔin/ nf (femme) heroine; (drogue) heroin.

héroïque /eʀɔik/ adj heroic.

héros /'eʀo/ nm hero.

hésiter /ezite/ ① vi hesitate (**à** to); **j'hésite** I'm not sure.

hétérogène /eteʀɔʒɛn/ adj heterogeneous.

hétérosexuel, ~le /eteʀɔsɛksɥɛl/ nm/f & adj hetero-sexual.

hêtre /'ɛtʀ/ nm beech.

heure /œʀ/ nf time; (soixante minutes) hour; **quelle** ~ **est-il?** what time is it?; **il est dix** ~**s** it is ten o'clock; **à l'**~ (venir, être) on time; **d'**~ **en** ~ by the hour; **toutes les deux** ~**s** every two hours; ~ **de pointe** rush-hour; ~ **de cours** (Scol) period; ~ **indue** ungodly hour; ~**s creuses** off peak periods; ~**s supplémentaires** overtime.

heureusement /œʀøzmɑ̃/ adv fortunately, luckily.

heureux, -euse /œʀø, -z/ adj happy; (chanceux) lucky, fortunate.

heurt /'œʀ/ nm collision; (conflit) clash; **sans** ~ smoothly.

heurter /'œʀte/ ① vt (cogner) hit; (mur) bump into, hit; (choquer) offend. □ **se** ~ **à** vpr bump into, hit; (fig) come up against.

hexagone /ɛgzagon/ nm hexagon; **l'**~ France.

hiberner /ibɛʀne/ ① vi hibernate.

hibou (pl ~x) /'ibu/ nm owl.

hier /jɛʀ/ adv yesterday; ~ **soir** last night, yesterday evening.

hiérarchie /'jeʀaʀʃi/ nf hierarchy.

hilare /ilaʀ/ adj (visage) merry; **être** ~ be laughing.

hindou, ~e /ɛ̃du/ adj & nm, f Hindu. **H~, ~e** nm, f Hindu.

hippique /ipik/ adj equestrian; **le concours** ~ showjumping.

hippodrome /ipodʀom/ nm racecourse.

hippopotame /ipopotam/ nm hippopotamus.

hirondelle /iʀɔ̃dɛl/ nf swallow.

hisser /'ise/ ① vt hoist, haul. □ **se** ~ vpr heave oneself up.

histoire /istwaʀ/ nf (récit) story; (étude) history; (affaire) business;

~(s) /ʃiʃi/ (chichis) fuss; (ennuis) trouble.

historique /istɔrik/ adj historical.

hiver /ivεʀ/ nm winter. **hivernal, ~e** (mpl **-aux**) adj winter; (glacial) wintry.

H.L.M. abbrév m ou f (**habitation à loyer modéré**) block of council flats; (US) low-rent apartment building.

hocher /ɔʃe/ vt **1** ~ **la tête** (pour dire oui) nod; (pour dire non) shake one's head.

hochet /ɔʃε/ nm rattle.

hockey /ɔkε/ nm hockey; ~ **sur glace** ice hockey.

hollandais, ~e /ɔlɑ̃dε, -z/ adj Dutch. ● nm (Ling) Dutch. **H~, ~e** nm, f Dutchman, Dutchwoman.

Hollande /ɔlɑ̃d/ nf Holland.

homard /ɔmaʀ/ nm lobster.

homéopathie /ɔmeopati/ nf homoeopathy.

homicide /ɔmisid/ nm homicide; ~ **involontaire** manslaughter.

hommage /ɔmaʒ/ nm tribute; ~**s** (salutations) respects; **rendre** ~ **à** pay tribute to.

homme /ɔm/ nm man; (espèce) man (kind); ~ **d'affaires** business-man; ~ **de la rue** man in the street; ~ **d'État** statesman; ~ **politique** politician.

homogène /ɔmɔʒεn/ adj homogeneous.

homonyme /ɔmɔnim/ nm (personne) namesake.

homosexualité /ɔmɔsεksɥalite/ nf homosexuality.

homosexuel, ~le /ɔmɔsεksɥεl/ adj & nm, f homosexual.

Hongrie /ˈɔ̃gʀi/ nf Hungary.

hongrois, ~e /ˈɔ̃gʀwa, -z/ adj Hungarian. ● nm (Ling) Hungarian. **H~, ~e** nm, f Hungarian.

honnête /ɔnεt/ adj honest; (juste) fair. **honnêteté** nf honesty.

honneur /ɔnœʀ/ nm honour; (mérite) credit; **d'**~ (invité, place) of honour; **en l'**~ **de** in honour of; **en quel** ~? **1** why?; **faire** ~ **à** (équipe, famille) bring credit to.

honorable /ɔnɔʀabl/ adj honourable; (convenable) respectable.

honoraire /ɔnɔʀεʀ/ adj honorary. **honoraires** nmpl fees.

honorer /ɔnɔʀe/ vt honour; (faire honneur à) do credit to.

honte /ˈɔ̃t/ nf shame; **avoir** ~ **be** ashamed (**de** of); **faire** ~ **à** make ashamed. **honteux, -euse** adj (personne) ashamed (**de** of); (action) shameful.

hôpital (pl **-aux**) /ɔpital, -o/ nm hospital.

hoquet /ˈɔkε/ nm **le** ~ (the) hiccups.

horaire /ɔʀεʀ/ adj hourly. ● nm timetable; ~ **libres** flexitime.

horizon /ɔʀizɔ̃/ nm horizon; (Fig) outlook.

horizontal, ~e (mpl **-aux**) /ɔʀizɔ̃tal, -o/ adj horizontal.

horloge /ɔʀlɔʒ/ nf clock.

hormis /ˈɔʀmi/ prép save.

hormonal, ~e (mpl **-aux**) /ɔʀmɔnal, -o/ adj hormonal, hormone.

hormone /ɔʀmɔn/ nf hormone.

horreur /ɔʀœʀ/ nf horror; **avoir** ~ **de** hate.

horrible /ɔʀibl/ adj horrible.

horrifier /ɔʀifje/ **45** vt horrify.

hors /ˈɔʀ/ prép ~ **de** outside, (avec mouvement) out of; ~ **d'atteinte** out of reach; ~ **d'haleine** out of breath; ~ **de prix** extremely expensive; ~ **pair** outstanding; ~ **de soi** beside oneself. **hors-bord** nm inv speedboat. **hors-d'œuvre** nm inv hors-d'œuvre. **hors-jeu** adj inv off-side. **hors-la-loi** nm inv outlaw. **hors-piste** nm off-piste skiing. **hors-taxe** adj inv duty-free.

horticulteur, -trice /ɔrtikyltœr, -tris/ nm, f horticulturist.

hospice /ɔspis/ nm home.

hospitalier, -ière /ɔspitalje, -jɛr/ adj hospitable; (Méd) hospital. **hospitaliser** 1 vt take to hospital. **hospitalité** nf hospitality.

hostile /ɔstil/ adj hostile. **hostilité** nf hostility.

hôte /ot/ nm (maître) host; (invité) guest.

hôtel /otɛl/ nm hotel; ~ (particulier) (private) mansion; ~ de ville town hall.

hôtelier, -ière /otəlje, -jɛr/ adj hotel. ● nm, f hotel keeper. **hôtellerie** nf hotel business.

hôtesse /otɛs/ nf hostess; ~ de l'air stewardess.

hotte /'ɔt/ nf basket; ~ aspirante extractor (hood), (US) ventilator.

houblon /'ublɔ̃/ nm le ~ hops.

houille /'uj/ nf coal; ~ blanche hydroelectric power.

houle /'ul/ nf swell. **houleux, -euse** adj (mer) rough; (débat) stormy.

housse /'us/ nf cover; ~ de siège seat cover.

houx /'u/ nm holly.

huées /'ɥe/ nfpl boos. **huer** 1 vt boo.

huile /ɥil/ nf oil; (personne 1) bigwig. **huiler** 1 vt oil. **huileux, -euse** adj oily.

huis /'ɥi/ nm à ~ clos in camera.

huissier /ɥisje/ nm (Jur) bailiff; (portier) usher.

huit /'ɥi(t)/ adj eight; ~ jours a week; lundi en ~ a week on Mon-

day. ● nm eight. **huitième** adj & nmf eighth.

huître /ɥitr/ nf oyster.

humain, ~e /ymɛ̃, -ɛn/ adj human; (compatissant) humane. **humanitaire** adj humanitarian. **humanité** nf humanity.

humble /œbl/ adj humble.

humeur /ymœr/ nf mood; (tempérament) temper; **de bonne/mauvaise ~** in a good/bad mood.

humide /ymid/ adj damp; (chaleur, climat) humid; (lèvres, yeux) moist. **humidité** nf humidity.

humilier 45 vt humiliate.

humoristique /ymɔristik/ adj humorous.

humour /ymur/ nm humour; **avoir de l'~** have a sense of humour.

hurlement /'yrləmã/ nm howl(ing). **hurler** 1 vt/i howl.

hutte /'yt/ nf hut.

hydratant, ~e /idratã, -t/ adj (lotion) moisturizing.

hydravion /idravjɔ̃/ nm seaplane.

hydroélectrique /idroelɛktrik/ adj hydroelectric.

hydrogène /idrɔʒɛn/ nm hydrogen.

hygiène /iʒjɛn/ nf hygiene. **hygiénique** adj hygienic.

hymne /imn/ nm hymn; ~ national national anthem.

hyperlien /iperljɛ̃/ nm (Internet) hyperlink.

hypermarché /ipermarʃe/ nm (supermarché) hypermarket.

hypertension /ipertãsjɔ̃/ nf high blood-pressure.

hypertexte /ipertɛkst/ nm (Internet) hypertext.

hypnotiser /ipnotize/ 1 vt hypnotize.

hypocrisie /ipɔkrizi/ *nf* hypocrisy.

hypocrite /ipɔkʀit/ *adj* hypocritical. ● *nmf* hypocrite.

hypothèque /ipɔtɛk/ *nf* mortgage.

hypothèse /ipɔtɛz/ *nf* hypothesis.

hystérie /isteʀi/ *nf* hysteria.

Ii

ici /isi/ *adv* (dans l'espace) here; (dans le temps) now; **d'~ demain** by tomorrow; **d'~ là** in the meantime; **d'~ peu** shortly; **même** in this very place; **jusqu'~** until now; (dans le passé) until then.

idéal, ~e (*mpl* **-aux**) /ideal, -o/ *adj* & *nm* ideal. **idéaliser** 🔟 *vt* idealize.

idée /ide/ *nf* idea; (esprit) mind; **avoir dans l'~ de faire** plan to do; **il ne me viendrait jamais à l'~ de faire** it would never occur to me to do; **~ fixe** obsession; **~ reçue** conventional opinion.

identification /idɑ̃tifikasjɔ̃/ *nf* identification. **identifier** 45 *vt*, **s'identifier** *vpr* identify (à with).

identique /idɑ̃tik/ *adj* identical.

identité /idɑ̃tite/ *nf* identity.

idéologie /ideɔlɔʒi/ *nf* ideology.

idiome /idjom/ *nm* idiom.

idiot, ~e /idjo, -ɔt/ *adj* idiotic. ● *nm, f* idiot. **idiotie** /idjosi/ *nf* idiocy; (acte, parole) idiotic thing.

idole /idɔl/ *nf* idol.

if /if/ *nm* yew.

ignare /iɲaʀ/ *adj* ignorant. ● *nmf* ignoramus.

ignoble /iɲɔbl/ *adj* vile.

ignorance /iɲɔʀɑ̃s/ *nf* ignorance.

ignorant, ~e /iɲɔʀɑ̃, -t/ *adj* ignorant. ● *nm, f* ignoramus.

ignorer /iɲɔʀe/ 🔟 *vt* not know; **je l'ignore** I don't know; (personne) ignore.

il /il/ *pron* (personne, animal familier) he; (chose, animal) it; (impersonnel) it; **~ est vrai que** it is true that; **~ neige/pleut** it is snowing/raining; **~ y a** there is; (pluriel) there are; (temps) ago; (durée) for; **~ y a 2 ans** 2 years ago; **~ y a plus d'une heure que j'attends** I've been waiting for over an hour.

île /il/ *nf* island; **~ déserte** desert island; **~s anglo-normandes** Channel Islands; **~s Britanniques** British Isles.

illégal, ~e (*mpl* **~aux**) /ilegal, -o/ *adj* illegal.

illégitime /ileʒitim/ *adj* illegitimate.

illettré, ~e /iletʀe/ *adj* & *nm, f* illiterate.

illicite /ilisit/ *adj* illicit; (Jur) unlawful.

illimité, ~e /ilimite/ *adj* unlimited.

illisible /ilizibl/ *adj* illegible; (livre) unreadable.

illogique /ilɔʒik/ *adj* illogical.

illuminé, ~e /ilymine/ *adj* lit up; (monument) floodlit.

illusion /ilyzjɔ̃/ *nf* illusion; **se faire des ~s** delude oneself. **Illusoire** *adj* illusory.

illustre /ilystʀ/ *adj* illustrious.

illustré, ~e /ilystʀe/ *adj* illustrated. ● *nm* comic.

illustrer /ilystʀe/ 🔟 *vt* illustrate. □ **s'~** *vpr* become famous.

îlot /ilo/ *nm* islet; (de maisons) block.

ils /il/ *pron* they.

image /imaʒ/ *nf* picture; (métaphore) image; (reflet) reflection. **imagé**, ~e adj full of imagery.

imaginaire /imaʒinɛʀ/ adj imaginary. **imaginatif, -ive** adj imaginative. **imagination** nf imagination.

imaginer /imaʒine/ **1** vt imagine; (inventer) think up. □ **s'~** vpr (se représenter) imagine (que that); (croire) think (que that).

imbécile /ɛ̃besil/ adj idiotic. ● nmf idiot.

imbiber /ɛ̃bibe/ **1** vt soak (de with). □ **s'~** vpr become soaked (de with).

imbriqué, ~e /ɛ̃bʀike/ adj (lié) interlinked, interlocking; (tuiles) overlapping.

imbu, ~e /ɛ̃by/ adj ~ de full of.

imitateur, -trice /imitatœʀ, -tʀis/ nm, f imitator; (comédien) impersonator. **imiter** **1** vt imitate; (personnage) impersonate; (signature) forge; (faire comme) do the same as.

immatriculation /imatʀikylasjɔ̃/ nf registration.

immatriculer /imatʀikyle/ **1** vt register; **se faire ~** register; **faire ~ une voiture** have a car registered.

immédiat, ~e /imedja, -t/ adj immediate. ● nm **dans l'~** for the time being.

immense /imɑ̃s/ adj huge, immense.

immerger /imɛʀʒe/ **40** vt immerse. □ **s'~** vpr immerse oneself (dans in).

immeuble /imœbl/ nm block of flats, building; ~ **de bureaux** office building ou block.

immigrant, ~e /imigʀɑ̃, -t/ adj & nm, f immigrant. **immigration** nf immigration. **immigré**, ~e adj &

nm, f immigrant. **immigrer** **1** vi immigrate.

imminent, ~e /iminɑ̃, -t/ adj imminent.

immobile /imɔbil/ adj still, motionless.

immobilier, -ière /imɔbilje, -jɛʀ/ adj property; **agence immobilière** estate agent's office; (US) real estate office; **agent ~** estate agent; (US) real estate agent. ● nm **l'~** property; (US) real estate.

immobiliser /imɔbilize/ **1** vt immobilize; (stopper) stop. □ **s'~** vpr stop.

immonde /imɔ̃d/ adj filthy.

immoral, ~e (mpl **-aux**) /imɔʀal, -o/ adj immoral.

immortel, ~le /imɔʀtɛl/ adj immortal.

immuable /imɥabl/ adj unchanging.

immuniser /imynize/ **1** vt immunize; **immunisé contre** (à l'abri de) immune to. **immunité** nf immunity.

impact /ɛ̃pakt/ nm impact.

impair, ~e /ɛ̃pɛʀ/ adj (numéro) odd. ● nm blunder, faux pas.

imparfait, ~e /ɛ̃paʀfɛ, -t/ adj & nm imperfect.

impasse /ɛ̃pas/ nf (rue) dead end; (situation) deadlock.

impatient, ~e /ɛ̃pasjɑ̃, -t/ adj impatient.

impatienter /ɛ̃pasjɑ̃te/ **1** vt annoy. □ **s'~** vpr get impatient (contre qn with sb).

impayé, ~e /ɛ̃peje/ adj unpaid.

impeccable /ɛ̃pekabl/ adj (propre) impeccable, spotless; (soigné) perfect.

impensable /ɛ̃pɑ̃sabl/ adj unthinkable.

impératif, -ive /ɛ̃peratif, -v/ adj imperative. ● nm (Gram) imperative; (contrainte) imperative; ~s (exigences) requirements, demands (**de** of).

impératrice /ɛ̃peratris/ nf empress.

impérial, ~e (mpl -iaux) /ɛ̃perjal, -jo/ adj imperial.

impérieux, -ieuse /ɛ̃perjø, -z/ adj imperious; (pressant) pressing.

imperméable /ɛ̃permeabl/ adj impervious (**à** to); (manteau, tissu) waterproof. ● nm raincoat.

impersonnel, ~le /ɛ̃personel/ adj impersonal.

impertinent, ~e /ɛ̃pertinɑ̃, -t/ adj impertinent.

imperturbable /ɛ̃pertyrbabl/ adj unshakeable, unruffled.

impétueux, -euse /ɛ̃petɥø, -z/ adj impetuous.

impitoyable /ɛ̃pitwajabl/ adj merciless.

implant /ɛ̃plɑ̃/ nm implant.

implanter /ɛ̃plɑ̃te/ **1** vt establish, set up. □ **s'~** vpr become established.

implication /ɛ̃plikasjɔ̃/ nf (conséquence) implication; (participation) involvement.

impliquer /ɛ̃plike/ **1** vt (mêler) implicate (**dans** in); (signifier) imply, mean (**que** that); (nécessiter) involve (**de faire** doing).

implorer /ɛ̃plɔre/ **1** vt implore, beg for.

impoli, ~e /ɛ̃pɔli/ adj impolite, rude.

importance /ɛ̃pɔrtɑ̃s/ nf importance; (taille) size; (ampleur) extent; **sans ~** unimportant.

important, ~e /ɛ̃pɔrtɑ̃, -t/ adj important; (en quantité) considerable, sizeable, big; (air) self-important. ● nm **l'~** the important thing.

importateur, -trice /ɛ̃pɔrtatœr, -tris/ nm, f importer. ● adj importing. **importation** nf import.

importer /ɛ̃pɔrte/ **1** vt (Comm) import. ● vi matter, be important (**à** to); **il importe que** it is important that; **n'importe, peu importe** it does not matter; **n'importe comment** anyhow; **n'importe où** anywhere; **n'importe qui** anybody; **n'importe quoi** anything.

importun, ~e /ɛ̃pɔrtœ̃, -yn/ adj troublesome. ● nm, f nuisance.

imposer /ɛ̃poze/ **1** vt impose (**à** on); (taxer) tax; **en ~ à qn** impress sb. □ **s'~** vpr (action) be essential; (se faire reconnaître) stand out; (s'astreindre à) **s'~ de faire** force oneself to do.

imposition /ɛ̃pozisjɔ̃/ nf taxation; **~ des mains** laying-on of hands.

impossible /ɛ̃posibl/ adj impossible. ● nm **faire l'~** do one's utmost.

impôt /ɛ̃po/ nm tax; **~s** (contributions) tax(ation), taxes; **~ sur le revenu** income tax.

impotent, ~e /ɛ̃potɑ̃, -t/ adj disabled.

imprécis, ~e /ɛ̃presi, -z/ adj imprecise.

imprégner /ɛ̃preɲe/ **14** vt fill (**de** with); (imbiber) impregnate (**de** with). □ **s'~ de** vpr (fig) immerse oneself in.

impression /ɛ̃presjɔ̃/ nf impression; (de livre) printing. **impressionnant, ~e** adj impressive; (choquant) disturbing. **impressionner** **1** vt impress; (choquer) disturb.

imprévisible /ɛ̃previzibl/ adj unpredictable.

imprévu, ~e /ɛ̃prevy/ adj unexpected. ● *nm* unexpected incident; **sauf** ~ unless anything unexpected happens.

imprimante /ɛ̃pʀimɑ̃t/ *nf* (Ordinat) printer; ~ **à jet d'encre** ink-jet printer; ~ **(à) laser** laser printer.

imprimé /ɛ̃pʀime/ **1** *vt* print; (marquer) imprint. **imprimerie** *nf* (art) printing; (lieu) printing works. **imprimeur** *nm* printer.

improbable /ɛ̃pʀɔbabl/ *adj* unlikely, improbable.

impropre /ɛ̃pʀɔpʀ/ *adj* incorrect; ~ **à** unfit for.

improviste: à l'~ /alɛ̃pʀɔvist/ *loc* unexpectedly.

imprudence /ɛ̃pʀydɑ̃s/ *nf* carelessness; (acte) careless action.

imprudent, ~e /ɛ̃pʀydɑ̃, -t/ *adj* careless; **il est ~ de** it is unwise to.

impudent, ~e /ɛ̃pydɑ̃, -t/ *adj* impudent.

impuissant, ~e /ɛ̃pɥisɑ̃, -t/ *adj* helpless; (Méd) impotent; ~ **à faire** powerless to do.

impulsif, -ive /ɛ̃pylsif, -v/ *adj* impulsive. **impulsion** *nf* (poussée, influence) impetus; (instinct, mouvement) impulse.

impur, ~e /ɛ̃pyʀ/ *adj* impure.

imputer /ɛ̃pyte/ **1** *vt* ~ **à** attribute, to impute to.

inabordable /inabɔʀdabl/ *adj* (prix) prohibitive.

inacceptable /inaksɛptabl/ *adj* unacceptable.

inactif, -ive /inaktif, -v/ *adj* inactive.

inadapté, ~e /inadapte/ *adj* maladjusted; *nm, f* (Psych) maladjusted person.

inadmissible /inadmisibl/ *adj* unacceptable.

inadvertance /inadvɛʀtɑ̃s/ *nf* **par** ~ by mistake.

inanimé, ~e /inanime/ *adj* (évanoui) unconscious; (mort) lifeless; (matière) inanimate.

inaperçu, ~e /inapɛʀsy/ *adj* unnoticed.

inapte /inapt/ *adj* unsuited (à to); ~ **à faire** incapable of doing; ~ **au service militaire** unfit for military service.

inattendu, ~e /inatɑ̃dy/ *adj* unexpected.

inaugurer /inogyʀe/ **1** *vt* inaugurate.

incapable /ɛ̃kapabl/ *adj* incapable (**de qch** of sth); ~ **de faire** unable to do, incapable of doing. ● *nmf* incompetent.

incapacité /ɛ̃kapasite/ *nf* inability, incapacity; **être dans l'~ de faire** be unable to do.

incarcérer /ɛ̃kaʀseʀe/ **14** *vt* imprison, incarcerate.

incarnation /ɛ̃kaʀnasjɔ̃/ *nf* embodiment, incarnation. **incarné, ~e** *adj* (ongle) ingrowing.

incassable /ɛ̃kasabl/ *adj* unbreakable.

incendiaire /ɛ̃sɑ̃djɛʀ/ *adj* incendiary; (propos) inflammatory. ● *nmf* arsonist.

incendie /ɛ̃sɑ̃di/ *nm* fire; ~ **criminel** arson. **incendier** **45** *vt* set fire to.

incertain, ~e /ɛ̃sɛʀtɛ̃, -ɛn/ *adj* uncertain; (contour) indistinct; (temps) unsettled. **incertitude** *nf* uncertainty.

inceste /ɛ̃sɛst/ *nm* incest.

incidence /ɛ̃sidɑ̃s/ *nf* effect.

incident /ɛ̃sidɑ̃/ *nm* incident; ~ **technique** technical hitch.

incinérer /ɛ̃sineʀe/ **14** *vt* incinerate; (mort) cremate.

inciser /ɛ̃size/ **1** *vt* make an incision in; (*abcès*) lance. **incisif, -ive** *adj* incisive. **incision** *nf* incision; (d'*abcès*) lancing.

incitation /ɛ̃sitasjɔ̃/ *nf* (Jur) incitement (**à** to); (encouragement) incentive. **inciter** **1** *vt* incite (**à** to); (encourager) encourage.

inclinaison /ɛ̃klinɛzɔ̃/ *nf* incline; (de la tête) tilt.

inclination /ɛ̃klinasjɔ̃/ *nf* (penchant) inclination; (geste) (du buste) bow; (de la tête) nod.

incliner /ɛ̃kline/ **1** *vt* tilt, lean; (courber) bend; (inciter) encourage (**à** to); **~ la tête** (approuver) nod; (révérence) bow. ● *vi* **~ à** be inclined to. □ **s'~** *vpr* lean forward; (se courber) bow down (**devant** before); (céder) give in, yield (**devant** to); (*chemin*) slope.

inclure /ɛ̃klyʀ/ **16** *vt* include; (enfermer) enclose; **jusqu'au lundi inclus** up to and including Monday.

incohérence /ɛ̃kɔeʀɑ̃s/ *nf* incoherence; (contradiction) discrepancy. **incohérent, ~e** *adj* incoherent, inconsistent.

incolore /ɛ̃kɔlɔʀ/ *adj* colourless; (*verre*) clear.

incommoder /ɛ̃kɔmɔde/ **1** *vt* inconvenience, bother.

incompatible /ɛ̃kɔ̃patibl/ *adj* incompatible.

incompétent, ~e /ɛ̃kɔ̃petɑ̃, -t/ *adj* incompetent.

incomplet, -ète /ɛ̃kɔ̃plɛ, -t/ *adj* incomplete.

incompréhension /ɛ̃kɔ̃pʀeɑ̃sjɔ̃/ *nf* lack of understanding.

incompris, ~e /ɛ̃kɔ̃pʀi, -z/ *adj* misunderstood.

inconcevable /ɛ̃kɔ̃svabl/ *adj* inconceivable.

incongru, ~e /ɛ̃kɔ̃gʀy/ *adj* unseemly.

inconnu, ~e /ɛ̃kɔny/ *adj* unknown (**à** to). ● *nm, f* stranger. ● *nm* **l'~** the unknown.

inconscience /ɛ̃kɔ̃sjɑ̃s/ *nf* unconsciousness; (folie) madness.

inconscient, ~e /ɛ̃kɔ̃sjɑ̃, -t/ *adj* unconscious (**de** of); (fou) mad. ● *nm* (Psych) subconscious.

incontestable /ɛ̃kɔ̃tɛstabl/ *adj* indisputable.

incontrôlable /ɛ̃kɔ̃tʀolabl/ *adj* unverifiable; (non maîtrisé) uncontrollable.

inconvenant, ~e /ɛ̃kɔ̃vnɑ̃, -t/ *adj* improper.

inconvénient /ɛ̃kɔ̃venjɑ̃/ *nm* disadvantage, drawback; (objection) objection.

incorporer /ɛ̃kɔʀpɔʀe/ **1** *vt* incorporate; (Culin) blend (**à** into); (Mil) enlist.

incorrect, ~e /ɛ̃kɔʀɛkt/ *adj* (faux) incorrect; (malséant) improper; (impoli) impolite; (déloyal) unfair.

incrédule /ɛ̃kʀedyl/ *adj* incredulous.

incriminer /ɛ̃kʀimine/ **1** *vt* (*personne*) incriminate; (*conduite, action*) attack.

incroyable /ɛ̃kʀwajabl/ *adj* incredible.

incruster /ɛ̃kʀyste/ **1** *vt* inlay (**de** with).

incubateur /ɛ̃kybatœʀ/ *nm* incubator.

inculpation /ɛ̃kylpasjɔ̃/ *nf* charge (**de**, pour of); (personne) **nm, f** accused. **inculper** **1** *vt* charge (**de** with).

inculquer /ɛ̃kylke/ **1** *vt* instil (**à** into).

inculte /ɛ̃kylt/ *adj* uncultivated; (*personne*) uneducated.

incurver /ɛ̃kyʀve/ **1** *vt* curve, bend. □ **s'~** *vpr* curve, bend.

Inde /ɛ̃d/ nf India.

indécent, ~e /ɛ̃desɑ̃, -t/ adj indecent.

indécis, ~e /ɛ̃desi, -z/ adj (de nature) indecisive; (temporairement) undecided.

indéfini, ~e /ɛ̃defini/ adj (Gram) indefinite; (vague) undefined; (sans limites) indeterminate.

indemne /ɛ̃dɛmn/ adj unharmed.

indemniser /ɛ̃dɛmnize/ **1** vt compensate (**de** for).

indemnité /ɛ̃dɛmnite/ nf indemnity, compensation; (allocation) allowance; **~s de licenciement** redundancy payment.

indépendance /ɛ̃depɑ̃dɑ̃s/ nf independence. **indépendant, ~e** adj independent.

indéterminé, ~e /ɛ̃detɛrmine/ adj unspecified.

index /ɛ̃dɛks/ nm forefinger; (liste) index.

indicateur, -trice /ɛ̃dikatœr, -tris/ nm, f (police) informer. ● nm (livre) guide; (Tech) indicator.

indicatif, -ve /ɛ̃dikatif, -v/ adj indicative (**de** of). ● nm (à la radio) signature tune; (téléphonique) dialling code; (Gram) indicative.

indication /ɛ̃dikasjɔ̃/ nf indication; (renseignement) information; (directive) instruction.

indice /ɛ̃dis/ nm sign; (dans une enquête) clue; (des prix) index; (évaluation) rating; **~ d'écoute** audience ratings.

indifférence /ɛ̃difeʀɑ̃s/ nf indifference.

indifférent, ~e /ɛ̃difeʀɑ̃, -t/ adj indifferent (**à** to); **ça m'est ~** it makes no difference to me.

indigène /ɛ̃diʒɛn/ adj & nmf native, indigenous; (du pays) local. ● nmf native.

indigent, ~e /ɛ̃diʒɑ̃, -t/ adj destitute.

indigeste /ɛ̃diʒɛst/ adj indigestible. **indigestion** nf indigestion.

indigne /ɛ̃diɲ/ adj unworthy (**de** of); (acte) vile. **indigner (s')** **1** vpr become indignant (**de** at).

indiqué, ~e /ɛ̃dike/ adj (heure) appointed; (opportun) appropriate; (conseillé) recommended.

indiquer /ɛ̃dike/ **1** vt (montrer) show, indicate; (renseigner sur) point out, tell; (déterminer) give, state, appoint; **~ du doigt** point to ou out ou at.

indirect, ~e /ɛ̃dirɛkt/ adj indirect.

indiscipliné, ~e /ɛ̃disipline/ adj unruly.

indiscret, -ète /ɛ̃diskrɛ, -t/ adj (personne) inquisitive; (question) indiscreet.

indiscutable /ɛ̃diskytabl/ adj unquestionable.

indispensable /ɛ̃dispɑ̃sabl/ adj indispensable; **il est ~ qu'il vienne** it is essential that he comes.

individu /ɛ̃dividy/ nm individual.

individuel, ~le /ɛ̃dividɥɛl/ adj (pour une personne) individual; (qui concerne l'individu) personal; **chambre ~le** single room; **maison ~le** detached house.

indolore /ɛ̃dɔlɔr/ adj painless.

Indonésie /ɛ̃dɔnezi/ nf Indonesia.

indu, ~e /ɛ̃dy/ adj **à une heure ~e** at some ungodly hour.

induire /ɛ̃dɥir/ **17** vt infer (**de** from); (inciter) induce (**à faire** to do); **~ en erreur** mislead.

indulgence /ɛ̃dylʒɑ̃s/ nf indulgence; (du jury) leniency. **indulgent, ~e** adj indulgent; (clément) lenient.

industrialisé, ~e /ɛ̃dystrijalize/

adj industrialized.

industrie /ɛ̃dystʀi/ nf industry.

industriel, ~le /ɛ̃dystʀijɛl/ adj industrial. ● nm industrialist.

inédit, ~e /inedi, -t/ adj unpublished; (fig) original.

inefficace /inefikas/ adj (remède, mesure) ineffective; (appareil, système) inefficient.

inégal, ~e (mpl **-aux**) /inegal, -o/ adj unequal; (irrégulier) uneven. **inégalable** adj matchless. **inégalité** nf (injustice) inequality; (irrégularité) unevenness; (disproportion) disparity.

inéluctable /inelyktabl/ adj inescapable.

inepte /inɛpt/ adj inept, absurd.

inerte /inɛʀt/ adj inert; (immobile) lifeless; (sans énergie) apathetic. **inertie** nf inertia; (fig) apathy.

inespéré, ~e /inɛspeʀe/ adj unhoped for.

inestimable /inɛstimabl/ adj priceless; (aide) invaluable.

inexact, ~e /inɛgza(kt), -kt/ adj (imprécis) inaccurate; (incorrect) incorrect.

in extremis /inɛkstʀemis/ adv (par nécessité) as a last resort; (au dernier moment) at the last minute. ● adj last-minute.

infaillible /ɛ̃fajibl/ adj infallible.

infâme /ɛ̃fɑm/ adj vile.

infantile /ɛ̃fɑ̃til/ adj (puéril) infantile; (maladie) childhood; (mortalité) infant.

infarctus /ɛ̃faʀktys/ nm coronary, heart attack.

infatigable /ɛ̃fatigabl/ adj tireless.

infect, ~e /ɛ̃fɛkt/ adj revolting.

infecter /ɛ̃fɛkte/ **1** vt infect. □ s'~ vpr become infected. **infectieux, -ieuse** adj infectious.

infection nf infection.

inférieur, ~e /ɛ̃feʀjœʀ/ adj (plus bas) lower; (moins bon) inferior (à to); ~ à (plus petit que) smaller than; (plus bas que) lower than. ● nm, f inferior. **infériorité** nf inferiority.

infernal, ~e (mpl **-aux**) /ɛ̃fɛʀnal, -o/ adj infernal.

infester /ɛ̃fɛste/ **1** vt infest.

infidèle /ɛ̃fidɛl/ adj unfaithful (à to). **infidélité** nf unfaithfulness; (acte) infidelity.

infiltrer (s') /sɛ̃filtʀe/ **1** vpr s'~ (dans) (personnes, idées) infiltrate; (liquide) seep through.

infime /ɛ̃fim/ adj tiny, minute.

infini, ~e /ɛ̃fini/ adj infinite. ● nm infinity; à l'~ endlessly. **infiniment** adv l'~ infinity; une ~ de an endless number of.

infinitif /ɛ̃finitif/ nm infinitive.

infirme /ɛ̃firm/ adj disabled. ● nmf disabled person. **infirmerie** nf sickbay, infirmary. **infirmier** nm (male) nurse. **infirmière** nf nurse. **infirmité** nf disability.

inflammable /ɛ̃flamabl/ adj inflammable.

inflation /ɛ̃flasjɔ̃/ nf inflation.

infliger /ɛ̃fliʒe/ **40** vt inflict; (sanction) impose.

influence /ɛ̃flyɑ̃s/ nf influence. **influencer** **10** vt influence. **influent, ~e** adj influential.

influer /ɛ̃flye/ **1** vi ~ sur influence.

informateur, -trice /ɛ̃fɔʀmatœʀ, -tʀis/ nm, f informant; (pour la police) informer.

informaticien, ~ne /ɛ̃fɔʀmatisjɛ̃, -ɛn/ nm, f computer scientist.

information /ɛ̃fɔʀmasjɔ̃/ nf information; (Jur) inquiry; une ~ (some) information; (nouvelle) (some) news; les ~s the news.

informatique /ɛ̃fɔʀmatik/ nf computer science; (techniques) information technology. **informatiser 1** vt computerize.

informer /ɛ̃fɔʀme/ **1** vt inform (de about, of). □ **s'~** vpr enquire (de about).

inforoute /ɛ̃fɔʀut/ nf (Ordinat) information highway.

infortune /ɛ̃fɔʀtyn/ nf misfortune.

infraction /ɛ̃fʀaksjɔ̃/ nf offence; ~ à (loi, règlement) breach of.

infrastructure /ɛ̃fʀastʀyktyʀ/ nf infrastructure; (équipements) facilities.

infructueux, -euse /ɛ̃fʀyktɥø, -z/ adj fruitless.

infuser /ɛ̃fyze/ **1** vt/i infuse, brew. **infusion** nf herbal tea, infusion.

ingénier (s') /(s)ɛ̃ʒenje/ **45** vpr **s'~ à** strive to.

ingénieur /ɛ̃ʒenjœʀ/ nm engineer.

ingénieux, -ieuse /ɛ̃ʒenjø, -z/ adj ingenious. **ingéniosité** nf ingenuity.

ingénu, ~e /ɛ̃ʒeny/ adj naïve.

ingérence /ɛ̃ʒeʀɑ̃s/ nf interference.

ingérer (s') /sɛ̃ʒeʀe/ **14** vpr **s'~ dans** interfere in.

ingrat, ~e /ɛ̃gʀa, -t/ adj (personne) ungrateful; (travail) unrewarding, thankless; (visage) unattractive.

ingrédient /ɛ̃gʀedjɑ̃/ nm ingredient.

ingurgiter /ɛ̃gyʀʒite/ **1** vt swallow.

inhabité, ~e /inabite/ adj uninhabited.

inhabituel, ~le /inabitɥɛl/ adj unusual.

inhumain, ~e /inymɛ̃, -ɛn/ adj inhuman.

inhumation /inymasjɔ̃/ nf burial.

initial, ~e (mpl **-iaux**) /inisjal, -jo/ adj initial. **initiale** nf initial.

initialisation /inisjalizasjɔ̃/ nf (Ordinat) formatting. **initialiser 1** vt format.

initiation /inisjasjɔ̃/ nf initiation; (formation) introduction (à to); **cours d'~** introductory course.

initiative /inisjativ/ nf initiative.

initier /inisje/ **45** vt initiate (à into); (faire découvrir) introduce (à to). □ **s'~** vpr **s'~ à qch** learn sth.

injecter /ɛ̃ʒekte/ **1** vt inject; **injecté de sang** bloodshot. **injection** nf injection.

injure /ɛ̃ʒyʀ/ nf insult. **injurier 45** vt insult. **injurieux, -ieuse** adj insulting.

injuste /ɛ̃ʒyst/ adj unjust, unfair. **injustice** nf injustice.

inné, ~e /inne/ adj innate, inborn.

innocence /inɔsɑ̃s/ nf innocence.

innocent, ~e adj & nm, f innocent. **innocenter 1** vt clear, prove innocent.

innombrable /inɔ̃bʀabl/ adj countless.

innovateur, -trice /inɔvatœʀ, -tʀis/ nm, f innovator. **innovation** nf innovation. **innover 1** vi innovate.

inodore /inɔdɔʀ/ adj odourless.

inoffensif, -ive /inɔfɑ̃sif, -v/ adj harmless.

inondation /inɔ̃dasjɔ̃/ nf flood; (action) flooding.

inonder /inɔ̃de/ **1** vt flood; (mouiller) soak; (envahir) inundate (de with); **inondé de soleil** bathed in sunlight.

inopiné, ~e /inɔpine/ adj unexpected; (mort) sudden.

inopportun, ~e /inɔpɔʀtœ̃, -yn/ adj inopportune, ill-timed.

inoubliable /inublijabl/ adj unforgettable.

inouï, ~e /inwi/ adj incredible; (événement) unprecedented.

inox® /inɔks/ nm stainless steel.

inoxydable /inɔksidabl/ adj **acier** ~ stainless steel.

inqualifiable /ɛ̃kalifjabl/ adj unspeakable.

inquiet, -iète /ɛ̃kjɛ, -t/ adj worried. **inquiétant, ~e** adj worrying.

inquiéter /ɛ̃kjete/ **[14]** vt worry. **□ s'~** vpr worry (de about). **inquiétude** nf anxiety, worry.

insaisissable /ɛ̃sezisabl/ adj (personne) elusive; (nuance) indefinable.

insalubre /ɛ̃salybR/ adj unhealthy.

insatisfaisant, ~e /ɛ̃satisfəzɑ̃, -t/ adj unsatisfactory. **insatisfait, ~e** adj (mécontent) dissatisfied; (frustré) unfulfilled.

inscription /ɛ̃skRipsjɔ̃/ nf inscription; (immatriculation) enrolment.

inscrire /ɛ̃skRiR/ **[30]** vt write (down); (graver, tracer) inscribe; (personne) enrol; (sur une liste) put down. **□ s'~** vpr put one's name down; **s'~ à** (école) enrol at; (club, parti) join; (examen) enter for.

insecte /ɛ̃sɛkt/ nm insect.

insécurité /ɛ̃sekyRite/ nf insecurity.

insensé, ~e /ɛ̃sɑ̃se/ adj mad.

insensibilité /ɛ̃sɑ̃sibilite/ nf insensitivity. **insensible** adj insensitive (à to); (graduel) imperceptible.

insérer /ɛ̃seRe/ **[14]** vt insert. **□ s'~** vpr be inserted; **s'~ dans** be part of.

insigne /ɛ̃siɲ/ nm badge; **~s** (d'une fonction) insignia.

insignifiant, ~e /ɛ̃siɲifjɑ̃, -t/ adj insignificant.

insinuation /ɛ̃sinɥasjɔ̃/ nf

insinuation.

insinuer /ɛ̃sinɥe/ **[1]** vt insinuate. **□ s'~** vpr (socialement) ingratiate oneself (auprès de qn with sb); **s'~ dans** (se glisser) slip into; (idée, nuance) creep into.

insipide /ɛ̃sipid/ adj insipid.

insistance /ɛ̃sistɑ̃s/ nf insistence. **insistant, ~e** adj insistent.

insister /ɛ̃siste/ **[1]** vi insist (**pour faire** on doing); ~ **sur** stress.

insolation /ɛ̃sɔlasjɔ̃/ nf (Méd) sunstroke.

insolent, ~e /ɛ̃sɔlɑ̃, -t/ adj insolent.

insolite /ɛ̃sɔlit/ adj unusual.

insolvable /ɛ̃sɔlvabl/ adj insolvent.

insomnie /ɛ̃sɔmni/ nf insomnia.

insonoriser /ɛ̃sɔnɔRize/ **[1]** vt soundproof.

insouciance /ɛ̃susjɑ̃s/ nf lack of concern. **insouciant, ~e** adj carefree.

insoutenable /ɛ̃sutnabl/ adj unbearable; (argument) untenable.

inspecter /ɛ̃spɛkte/ **[1]** vt inspect. **inspecteur, -trice** nm, f inspector. **inspection** nf inspection.

inspiration /ɛ̃spiRasjɔ̃/ nf inspiration; (respiration) breath.

inspirer /ɛ̃spiRe/ **[1]** vt inspire; ~ **la méfiance à qn** inspire distrust in sb. ● vi breathe in. **□ s'~ de** vpr be inspired by.

instabilité /ɛ̃stabilite/ nf instability; unsteadiness. **instable** adj unstable; (temps) unsettled.

installation /ɛ̃stalasjɔ̃/ nf installation; (de local) fitting out; (de locataire) settling in. **installations** nfpl facilities.

installer /ɛ̃stale/ **[1]** vt install; (meuble) put in; (étagère) put up; (gaz, téléphone) connect; (équiper) fit out. □ **s'~** *vpr* settle (down); (emménager) settle in; **s'~ comme** set oneself up as.

instance /ɛ̃stɑ̃s/ *nf* authority; (prière) entreaty; **avec ~** with insistence; **en ~** pending; **en ~ de** in the course of, on the point of.

instant /ɛ̃stɑ̃/ *nm* moment, instant; **à l'~** this instant.

instantané, ~e /ɛ̃stɑ̃tane/ *adj* instantaneous; (café) instant.

instar: à l'~ de /alɛstaʁda/ *loc* like.

instaurer /ɛ̃stɔʁe/ **1** *vt* institute.

instigateur, -trice /ɛ̃stigatœʁ, -tʁis/ *nm, f* instigator.

instinct /ɛ̃stɛ̃/ *nm* instinct; **d'~** instinctively. **instinctif, -ive** *adj* instinctive.

instituer /ɛ̃stitɥe/ **1** *vt* establish.

institut /ɛ̃stity/ *nm* institute; **~ de beauté** beauty parlour.

instituteur, -trice /ɛ̃stitytœʁ, -tʁis/ *nm, f* primary-school teacher.

institution /ɛ̃stitysjɔ̃/ *nf* institution; (école) private school.

instructif, -ive /ɛ̃stʁyktif, -v/ *adj* instructive.

instruction /ɛ̃stʁyksjɔ̃/ *nf* (formation) education; (Mil) training; (document) directive; **~s** (ordres, mode d'emploi) instructions; (Ordinat) (énoncé) instruction; (pas de séquence) statement.

instruire /ɛ̃stʁɥiʁ/ **17** *vt* teach, educate; **~ de** inform of. □ **s'~** *vpr* learn, educate oneself; **s'~ de** enquire about. **instruit, ~e** *adj* educated.

instrument /ɛ̃stʁymɑ̃/ *nm* instrument; (outil) tool; (moyen: fig) instrument; **~ de gestion** management tool; **~s de bord** (Aviat) controls.

insu: à l'~ de /alɛ̃syda/ *loc* without the knowledge of.

insuffisance /ɛ̃syfizɑ̃s/ *nf* (pénurie) shortage; (médiocrité) inadequacy. **insuffisant, ~e** *adj* inadequate; (en nombre) insufficient.

insulaire /ɛ̃sylɛʁ/ *adj* island. ● *nmf* islander.

insuline /ɛ̃sylin/ *nf* insulin.

insulte /ɛ̃sylt/ *nf* insult. **insulter** **1** *vt* insult.

insupportable /ɛ̃sypɔʁtabl/ *adj* unbearable.

insurger (s') /(s)ɛ̃syʁʒe/ **40** *vpr* rebel.

intact, ~e /ɛ̃takt/ *adj* intact.

intangible /ɛ̃tɑ̃ʒibl/ *adj* intangible; (principe) inviolable.

intarissable /ɛ̃taʁisabl/ *adj* inexhaustible.

intégral, ~e (*mpl* **-aux**) /ɛ̃tegʁal, -o/ *adj* complete; (texte, édition) unabridged; (paiement) full, in full. **intégralement** *adv* in full. **intégralité** *nf* whole.

intègre /ɛ̃tɛgʁ/ *adj* upright.

intégrer /ɛ̃tegʁe/ **14** *vt* integrate. □ **s'~** *vpr* (personne) integrate; (maison) fit in.

intégriste /ɛ̃tegʁist/ *nmf* fundamentalist.

intégrité /ɛ̃tegʁite/ *nf* integrity.

intellect /ɛ̃telɛkt/ *nm* intellect. **intellectuel, ~le** *adj & nm, f* intellectual.

intelligence /ɛ̃teliʒɑ̃s/ *nf* intelligence; (compréhension) understanding; (complicité) agreement; **agir d'~ avec qn** act in agreement with sb. **intelligent, ~e** *adj* intelligent.

intempéries /ɛ̃tɑ̃peʁi/ *nfpl* severe weather.

intempestif, -ive /ɛ̃tɑ̃pestif, -v/ *adj* untimely.

i

intenable /ɛ̃tnabl/ adj unbearable; (enfant) impossible.

intendance /ɛ̃tɑ̃dɑ̃s/ nf (Scol) bursar's office.

intendant, ~e /ɛ̃tɑ̃dɑ̃, -t/ nm (Mil) quartermaster. ● nm, f (Scol) bursar.

intense /ɛ̃tɑ̃s/ adj intense; (circulation) heavy. **intensif, -ive** adj intensive. **intensité** nf intensity.

intenter /ɛ̃tɑ̃te/ **1** vt ~ un procès ou une action institute proceedings (à, contre against).

intention /ɛ̃tɑ̃sjɔ̃/ nf intention (de faire of doing); à l'~ de qn for sb. **intentionnel, ~le** adj intentional.

interactif, -ive /ɛ̃tɛʀaktif, -v/ adj (TV, vidéo) interactive.

interaction /ɛ̃tɛʀaksjɔ̃/ nf interaction.

intercaler /ɛ̃tɛʀkale/ **1** vt insert.

intercéder /ɛ̃tɛʀsede/ **14** vi intercede (en faveur de on behalf of).

intercepter /ɛ̃tɛʀsepte/ **1** vt intercept.

interdiction /ɛ̃tɛʀdiksjɔ̃/ nf ban; ~ de fumer no smoking.

interdire /ɛ̃tɛʀdiʀ/ **37** vt forbid; (officiellement) ban, prohibit; ~ à qn de faire forbid sb to do.

interdit, ~e /ɛ̃tɛʀdi, -t/ adj prohibited, forbidden; (étonné) dumbfounded.

intéressant, ~e /ɛ̃teʀesɑ̃, -t/ adj interesting; (avantageux) attractive.

intéressé, ~e /ɛ̃teʀese/ adj (en cause) concerned; (pour profiter) self-interested. ● nm, f person concerned.

intéresser /ɛ̃teʀese/ **1** vt interest; (concerner) concern. □ s'~ à vpr be interested in.

intérêt /ɛ̃teʀe/ nm interest; (égoïsme) self-interest; (~s) (Comm) interest; **vous avez ~** à it is in your interest to.

interface /ɛ̃tɛʀfas/ nf (Ordinat) interface.

intérieur, ~e /ɛ̃teʀjœʀ/ adj inner, inside; (mur, escalier) internal; (vol, politique) domestic; (vie, calme) inner. ● nm interior; (de boîte, tiroir) inside; à l'~ (de) inside; (fig) within. **intérieurement** adv inwardly.

intérim /ɛ̃teʀim/ nm interim; assurer l'~ deputize (de for); par ~ on an interim basis; **président par ~** acting president; **faire de l'~** temp.

intérimaire /ɛ̃teʀimɛʀ/ adj temporary, interim. ● nmf (secrétaire) temp; (médecin) locum.

interjection /ɛ̃tɛʀʒɛksjɔ̃/ nf interjection.

interlocuteur, -trice /ɛ̃tɛʀlɔkytœʀ, -tʀis/ nm, f son ~ the person one is speaking to.

interloqué, ~e /ɛ̃tɛʀlɔke/ adj être ~ be taken aback.

intermède /ɛ̃tɛʀmɛd/ nm interlude.

intermédiaire /ɛ̃tɛʀmedjɛʀ/ adj intermediate. ● nmf intermediary. ● nm sans ~ without an intermediary, direct; par l'~ de through.

interminable /ɛ̃tɛʀminabl/ adj endless.

intermittence /ɛ̃tɛʀmitɑ̃s/ nf par ~ intermittently.

internat /ɛ̃tɛʀna/ nm boarding-school.

international, ~e (mpl -aux) /ɛ̃tɛʀnasjɔnal, -o/ adj international.

internaute /ɛ̃tɛʀnot/ nmf (Ordinat) Netsurfer, Internet user.

interne /ɛ̃tɛʀn/ adj internal; (cours, formation) in-house. ● nmf (Scol) boarder; (Méd) house officer; (US) intern.

internement /ɛ̃tɛʀnəmɑ̃/ nm (Pol) internment. **interner 1** vt

(Pol) intern; (Méd) commit.

Internet /ɛtɛʀnɛt/ nm Internet; **sur ~ on the Internet.**

interpellation /ɛtɛʀpelasjɔ̃/ nf (Pol) questioning. **interpeller 1** vt shout to; (apostropher) shout at; (interroger) question.

interphone /ɛtɛʀfɔn/ nm intercom; (d'immeuble) entry phone.

interposer (s') /(s)ɛtɛʀpoze/ 1 vpr intervene.

interprétariat /ɛtɛʀpʀetaʀja/ nm interpreting. **interprétation** nf interpretation; (d'artiste) performance. **interprète** nmf interpreter; (artiste) performer. **interpréter 14** vt interpret; (jouer) play; (chanter) sing.

interrogateur, -trice /ɛtɛʀɔgatœʀ, -tʀis/ adj questioning. **interrogatif, -ive** adj interrogative. **interrogation** nf question; (action) questioning; (épreuve) test. **interrogatoire** nm interrogation. **interroger 40** vt question; (élève) test.

interrompre /ɛtɛʀɔ̃pʀ/ 3 vt break off, interrupt; (personne) interrupt. □ s'~ vpr break off. **interrupteur** nm switch. **interruption** nf interruption; (arrêt) break.

interurbain, ~e /ɛtɛʀyʀbɛ̃, -ɛn/ adj long-distance, trunk.

intervalle /ɛtɛʀval/ nm space; (temps) interval; **dans l'~ in the meantime.**

intervenir /ɛtɛʀvəniʀ/ 58 vi (agir) intervene (**auprès de qn** with sb); (survenir) occur, take place; (Méd) operate. **intervention** nf intervention; (Méd) operation.

intervertir /ɛtɛʀvɛʀtiʀ/ 2 vt invert; (rôles) reverse.

interview /ɛtɛʀvju/ nf interview. **interviewer 1** vt interview.

intestin /ɛtɛstɛ̃/ nm intestine.

intime /ɛtim/ adj intimate; (fête, vie) private; (dîner) quiet. ● nmf intimate friend.

intimider /ɛtimide/ 1 vt intimidate.

intimité /ɛtimite/ nf intimacy; (vie privée) privacy.

intituler /ɛtityle/ 1 vt call, entitle. □ s'~ vpr be called ou entitled.

intolérable /ɛtɔleʀabl/ adj intolerable. **intolérance** nf intolerance. **intolérant, ~e** adj intolerant.

intonation /ɛtɔnasjɔ̃/ nf intonation.

intox /ɛtɔks/ nf 1 brainwashing.

intoxication /ɛtɔksikasjɔ̃/ nf poisoning; (fig) brainwashing; **~ alimentaire** food poisoning. **intoxiquer 1** vt poison; (fig) brainwash.

intraitable /ɛtʀɛtabl/ adj inflexible.

Intranet /ɛtʀanɛt/ nm Intranet.

intransigeant, ~e /ɛtʀɑ̃ziʒɑ̃, -t/ adj intransigent.

intransitif, -ive /ɛtʀɑ̃zitif, -v/ adj intransitive.

intraveineux, -euse /ɛtʀavɛnø, -z/ adj intravenous.

intrépide /ɛtʀepid/ adj fearless.

intrigue /ɛtʀig/ nf intrigue; (scénario) plot.

intrinsèque /ɛtʀɛsɛk/ adj intrinsic.

introduction /ɛtʀɔdyksjɔ̃/ nf introduction; (insertion) insertion.

introduire /ɛtʀɔdɥiʀ/ 17 vt introduce, bring in; (insérer) put in, insert; **~ qn** show sb in. □ s'~ vpr get in; s'~ **dans** get into, enter.

introuvable /ɛtʀuvabl/ adj that cannot be found.

introverti, ~e /ɛtʀɔvɛʀti/ nm, f introvert. ● adj introverted.

i

intrus, ~e /ɛ̃try, -z/ nm, f intruder. **intrusion** nf intrusion.

intuitif, -ive /ɛ̃tɥitif, -iv/ adj intuitive. **intuition** nf intuition.

inusable /inyzabl/ adj hard-wearing.

inusité, ~e /inyzite/ adj little used.

inutile /inytil/ adj useless; (vain) needless. **inutilement** adv needlessly. **inutilisable** adj unusable.

invalide /ɛ̃valid/ adj & nmf disabled (person).

invariable /ɛ̃varjabl/ adj invariable.

invasion /ɛ̃vazjɔ̃/ nf invasion.

invectiver /ɛ̃vɛktive/ **1** vt abuse.

inventaire /ɛ̃vɑ̃tɛr/ nm inventory; (Comm) stocklist; **faire l'~** draw up an inventory; (Comm) do a stocktake.

inventer /ɛ̃vɑ̃te/ **1** vt invent. **inventeur, -trice** nm, f inventor. **inventif, -ive** adj inventive. **invention** nf invention.

inverse /ɛ̃vɛrs/ adj opposite; (ordre) reverse; **en sens ~** in ou from the opposite direction. ● nm reverse; **c'est l'~** it's the other way round. **inversement** adv conversely. **inverser** **1** vt reverse, invert.

investir /ɛ̃vɛstir/ **2** vt invest. **investissement** nm investment.

investiture /ɛ̃vɛstityr/ nf (de candidat) nomination; (de président) investiture.

invétéré, ~e /ɛ̃vetere/ adj inveterate; (menteur) compulsive; (enraciné) deep-rooted.

invisible /ɛ̃vizibl/ adj invisible.

invitation /ɛ̃vitasjɔ̃/ nf invitation. **invité, ~e** nm, f guest. **inviter** **1** vt invite (**à** to).

involontaire /ɛ̃vɔlɔ̃tɛr/ adj involuntary; (témoin, héros) unwitting.

invoquer /ɛ̃vɔke/ **1** vt call upon, invoke.

invraisemblable /ɛ̃vrɛsɑ̃blabl/ adj improbable, unlikely; (incroyable) incredible. **invraisemblance** nf improbability.

iode /jɔd/ nm iodine.

ira, irait /ira, irɛ/ →ALLER **8**.

Irak /irak/ nm Iraq.

Iran /irɑ̃/ nm Iran.

iris /iris/ nm iris.

irlandais, ~e /irlɑ̃dɛ, -z/ adj Irish. **I~, ~e** nm, f Irishman, Irishwoman. **Irlande** /irlɑ̃d/ nf Ireland.

IRM abrév m (imagerie par résonance magnétique) magnetic resonance imaging.

ironie /irɔni/ nf irony. **ironique** adj ironic.

irrationnel, ~le /irasjɔnɛl/ adj irrational.

irréalisable /irealizabl/ adj (idée, rêve) unachievable; (projet) unworkable.

irrécupérable /irekyperabl/ adj irretrievable; (capital) irrecoverable.

irréel, ~le /ireɛl/ adj unreal.

irréfléchi, ~e /irefleʃi/ adj thoughtless.

irrégulier, -ière /iregylje, -jɛr/ adj irregular.

irrémédiable /iremedjabl/ adj irreparable.

irremplaçable /irɑ̃plasabl/ adj irreplaceable.

irréparable /ireparabl/ adj (objet) beyond repair; (tort, dégâts) irreparable.

irréprochable /ireproʃabl/ adj flawless.

irrésistible /irezistibl/ adj irresistible; (drôle) hilarious.

irrésolu, ~e /irezɔly/ adj indecisive; (problème) unsolved.

irrespirable /iʀɛspiʀabl/ *adj* stifling.

irresponsable /iʀɛspɔ̃sabl/ *adj* irresponsible.

irrigation /iʀigasjɔ̃/ *nf* irrigation. **irriguer ① ** *vt* irrigate.

irritable /iʀitabl/ *adj* irritable.

irriter /iʀite/ **①** *vt* irritate. □ **s'~** *vpr* get annoyed (**de** at).

irruption /iʀypsjɔ̃/ *nf* faire ~ **dans** burst into.

Islam /islam/ *nm* Islam. **islamique** *adj* Islamic.

islamiste /islamist/ *adj* Islamist, Islamic; *n m/f* Islamist.

islandais, ~e /islɑ̃dɛ, -z/ *adj* Icelandic. ● *nm* (Ling) Icelandic. **I~, ~e** *nm, f* Icelander.

Islande /islɑ̃d/ *nf* Iceland.

isolant /izɔlɑ̃/ *nm* insulating material. **isolation** *nf* insulation.

isolé, ~e /izɔle/ *adj* isolated. **isolement** *nm* isolation.

isoler /izɔle/ **①** *vt* isolate; (Électr) insulate. □ **s'~** *vpr* isolate oneself.

isoloir /izɔlwaʀ/ *nm* polling booth.

Isorel ® /izɔʀɛl/ *nm* hardboard.

Israël /israɛl/ *nm* Israel. **israélien, ~ne** *adj* Israeli.

israélite /israelit/ *adj* Jewish. ● *nmf* Jew.

issu, ~e /isy/ *adj* être ~ **de** (*personne*) come from; (*résulter de*) result ou stem from.

issue /isy/ *nf* (sortie) exit; (résultat) outcome; (fig) solution; **à l'** ~ **de** at the conclusion of; ~ **de secours** emergency exit; **rue** ou **voie sans** ~ dead end.

Italie /itali/ *nf* Italy.

italien, ~ne /italjɛ̃, -ɛn/ *adj* Italian. ● *nm* (Ling) Italian. **I~, ~ne** *nm, f* Italian.

italique /italik/ *nm* italics.

itinéraire /itineʀɛʀ/ *nm* itinerary, route.

I.U.T. *abrév m* (**Institut universitaire de technologie**) university institute of technology.

I.V.G. *abrév f* (**interruption volontaire de grossesse**) abortion.

ivoire /ivwaʀ/ *nm* ivory.

ivre /ivʀ/ *adj* drunk. **ivresse** *nf* drunkenness; (fig) exhilaration. **ivrogne** *nmf* drunk(ard).

Jj

j' /ʒ/ →**je**.

jacinthe /ʒasɛ̃t/ *nf* hyacinth.

jadis /ʒadis/ *adv* long ago.

jaillir /ʒajiʀ/ **②** *vi* (*liquide*) spurt (out); (*lumière*) stream out; (*apparaître*) burst forth, spring out.

jalonner /ʒalɔne/ **①** *vt* mark (out).

jalousie /ʒaluzi/ *nf* jealousy; (store) (venetian) blind. **jaloux, -ouse** *adj* jealous.

jamais /ʒamɛ/ *adv* ever; **ne** ~ never; **il ne boit** ~ he never drinks; **à** ~ for ever; **si** ~ if ever.

jambe /ʒɑ̃b/ *nf* leg.

jambon /ʒɑ̃bɔ̃/ *nm* ham. **jambonneau** (*pl* ~**x**) *nm* knuckle of ham.

janvier /ʒɑ̃vje/ *nm* January.

Japon /ʒapɔ̃/ *nm* Japan.

japonais, ~e /ʒapɔnɛ, -z/ *adj* Japanese. ● *nm* (Ling) Japanese. **J~, ~e** *nm, f* Japanese.

japper /ʒape/ **①** *vi* yap.

jaquette /ʒakɛt/ *nf* (de livre, femme) jacket; (d'homme) morning coat.

jardin /ʒardɛ̃/ nm garden; ~ d'enfants nursery (school); ~ public public park. **jardinage** nm gardening. **jardiner 1** vi do some gardening, garden. **jardinier, -ière** nm, f gardener.

jardinière /ʒardinjɛr/ nf (meuble) plant-stand; ~ de légumes mixed vegetables.

jarretelle /ʒartɛl/ nf suspender; (US) garter.

jarretière /ʒartjɛr/ nf garter.

jatte /ʒat/ nf bowl.

jauge /ʒoʒ/ nf capacity; (de navire) tonnage; (compteur) gauge; ~ d'huile dipstick.

jaune /ʒon/ adj & nm yellow; (péj) scab; ~ d'œuf (egg) yolk; rire ~ give a forced laugh. **jaunir 1** vt/i turn yellow. **jaunisse** nf jaundice.

javelot /ʒavlo/ nm javelin.

jazz /dʒaz/ nm jazz.

J.C. abrév m (**Jésus-Christ**) 500 avant/après ~ 500 B.C./A.D.

je, j' /ʒə, ʒ/ pron I.

jean /dʒin/ nm jeans; un ~ a pair of jeans.

jet¹ /ʒɛ/ nm throw; (de liquide, vapeur) jet; ~ d'eau fountain.

jet² /dʒɛt/ nm (avion) jet.

jetable /ʒətabl/ adj disposable.

jetée /ʒəte/ nf pier.

jeter /ʒəte/ 38 vt throw; (au rebut) throw away; (regard, ancre, lumière) cast; (cri) utter; (bases) lay; ~ un coup d'œil have ou take a look (à at). □ se ~ vpr se ~ contre/dans crash ou bash into; se ~ dans (fleuve) flow into; se ~ sur (se ruer sur) rush at.

jeton /ʒətɔ̃/ nm token; (pour compter) counter; (au casino) chip.

jeu (pl ~x) /ʒø/ nm game; (amusement) play; (au casino) gambling; (Théât) acting; (série) set; (de lu-

mière, ressort) play; **en ~** (honneur) at stake; (forces) at work; ~ **de cartes** (paquet) pack of cards; ~d'échecs (boîte) chess set; ~ **de mots** pun; ~ **télévisé** tv game show; ~ **vidéo** video game; ~**x de grattage** scratch cards; **les** ~**x olympiques/paralympiques** the Olympic Games/Paralympic Games.

jeudi /ʒødi/ nm Thursday.

jeun: à ~ /aʒœ̃/ loc on an empty stomach.

jeune /ʒœn/ adj young; ~ **fille** girl; ~ **pousse** (Comm) start-up; ~**s mariés** newlyweds. ● nmf young person; **les** ~**s** young people.

jeûne /ʒøn/ nm fast.

jeunesse /ʒœnɛs/ nf youth; (apparence) youthfulness; **la** ~ (jeunes) the young.

joaillerie /ʒoajri/ nf jewellery; (magasin) jeweller's shop.

joie /ʒwa/ nf joy.

joindre /ʒwɛ̃dr/ 22 vt join (à to); (mains, pieds) put together; (efforts) combine; (contacter) contact; (dans une enveloppe) enclose. □ se ~ à vpr join.

joint, ~e /ʒwɛ̃, -t/ adj (efforts) joint; (pieds) together. ● nm joint; (de robinet) washer.

joli, ~e /ʒɔli/ adj pretty, nice; (somme, profit) nice; **c'est du** ~! (ironique) charming! **c'est bien ~ mais** that is all very well but.

joncher /ʒɔ̃ʃe/ 1 vt litter, be strewn over; **jonché de** littered with.

jonction /ʒɔ̃ksjɔ̃/ nf junction.

jongleur, -euse /ʒɔ̃glœr, øz/ nm, f juggler.

jonquille /ʒɔ̃kij/ nf daffodil.

joue /ʒu/ nf cheek.

jouer /ʒwe/ 1 vt/i play; (Théât) act; (au casino) gamble; (fonctionner) work; (*film, pièce*) put on; (*cheval*) back; (être important) count; ~ **à** (*jeu, Sport*) play; ~ **de** (*Mus*) play; ~ **la comédie** put on an act; **bien joué!** well done!

jouet /ʒwɛ/ *nm* toy; (*personne: fig*) plaything; (*victime*) victim.

joueur, -euse /ʒwœR, -øz/ *nm, f* player; (*parieur*) gambler.

joufflu, ~e /ʒufly/ *adj* chubby-cheeked; (*visage*) chubby.

jouir /ʒwiR/ **2** *vi* (*sexe*) come; ~ **de** (*droit, avantage*) enjoy; (*bien, concession*) enjoy the use of. **jouissance** *nf* pleasure; (*usage*) use (**de** qch of sth).

joujou (*pl* ~**x**) /ʒuʒu/ *nm* **1** toy.

jour /ʒuR/ *nm* day; (*opposé à nuit*) day (time); (*lumière*) daylight; (*aspect*) light; (*ouverture*) gap; **de nos** ~**s** nowadays; **du** ~ **au lendemain** overnight; **il fait** ~ it is daylight; **chômé ou férié** public holiday; ~ **de fête** holiday; ~ **ouvrable** ~ **de travail** working day; **mettre à** ~ update; **mettre au** ~ uncover; **au grand** ~ in the open; **donner le** ~ give birth; **voir le** ~ be born; **vivre au** ~ **le jour** live from day to day.

journal (*pl* -**aux**) /ʒuRnal, -o/ *nm* (news)paper; (*spécialisé*) journal; (*intime*) diary; (*à la radio*) news; ~ **de bord** log-book.

journalier, -ière /ʒuRnalje, -jɛR/ *adj* daily.

journalisme /ʒuRnalism/ *nm* journalism. **journaliste** *nmf* journalist.

journée /ʒuRne/ *nf* day.

jovial, ~e (*mpl* -**iaux**) /ʒɔvjal, -jo/ *adj* jovial.

joyau (*pl* ~**x**) /ʒwajo/ *nm* gem.

joyeux, -euse /ʒwajø, -z/ *adj* merry, joyful; ~ **anniversaire** happy birthday.

jubiler /ʒybile/ **1** *vi* be jubilant.

jucher /ʒyʃe/ **1** *vt* perch. □ **se** ~ *vpr* perch.

judaïsme /ʒydaism/ *nm* Judaism.

judiciaire /ʒydisjɛR/ *adj* judicial.

judicieux, -ieuse /ʒydisjø, -z/ *adj* judicious.

judo /ʒydo/ *nm* judo.

juge /ʒyʒ/ *nm* judge; (*arbitre*) referee; ~ **de paix** Justice of the Peace; ~ **de touche** linesman.

jugé: au ~ /oʒyʒe/ *loc* by guesswork.

jugement /ʒyʒmã/ *nm* judgement; (*criminel*) sentence.

juger /ʒyʒe/ **40** *vt/i* judge; (*estimer*) consider (**que** that); ~ **de** judge.

juguler /ʒygyle/ **1** *vt* stamp out; curb.

juif, -ive /ʒɥif, -v/ *adj* Jewish. ● *nm, f* Jew.

juillet /ʒɥijɛ/ *nm* July.

juin /ʒɥɛ̃/ *nm* June.

jumeau, -elle (*mpl* ~**x**) /ʒymo, -ɛl/ *adj & nm, f* twin. **jumeler** **38** *vt* (*villes*) twin.

jumelles /ʒymɛl/ *nfpl* binoculars.

jument /ʒymã/ *nf* mare.

junior /ʒynjɔR/ *adj & nmf* junior.

jupe /ʒyp/ *nf* skirt.

jupon /ʒypõ/ *nm* slip, petticoat.

juré, ~e /ʒyRe/ *nm, f* juror. ● *adj* sworn.

jurer /ʒyRe/ **1** *vt* swear (**que** that). ● *vi* (*pester*) swear; (*contraster*) clash (**avec** with).

juridiction /ʒyRidiksjõ/ *nf* jurisdiction; (*tribunal*) court of law.

juridique /ʒyRidik/ *adj* legal.

juriste /ʒyRist/ *nmf* legal expert.

juron /ʒyRõ/ *nm* swearword.

jury /ʒyRi/ *nm* (*Jur*) jury; (*examina-*

teurs) panel of judges.

jus /ʒy/ nm juice; (de viande) gravy; ~ **de fruit** fruit juice.

jusque /ʒysk(ə)/ prép jusqu'à (up) to, as far as; (temps) until, till; (limite) up to; (y compris) even; **jusqu'à ce que** until; **jusqu'à présent** until now; **jusqu'en** until; **jusqu'où?** how far?; ~ **dans**, ~ as far as.

juste /ʒyst/ adj fair, just; (légitime) just; (correct, exact) right; (vrai) true; (vêtement) tight; (quantité) on the short side; **le ~ milieu** the happy medium. ● adv rightly, correctly; (chanter) in tune; (seulement, exactement) just; (un peu) ~ (calculer, mesurer) a bit fine ou close; **au ~** exactly; **c'était ~** (presque raté) it was a close thing. **justement** adv (précisément) precisely; (à l'instant juste) (avec justesse) correctly; (légitimement) justifiably.

justesse /ʒystɛs/ nf accuracy; **de ~** just, narrowly.

justice /ʒystis/ nf justice; (autorités) law; (tribunal) court.

justifier /ʒystifje/ 45 vt justify. ● vi ~ **de** prove. □ **se** ~ vpr justify oneself.

juteux, -euse /ʒytø, -z/ adj juicy.

juvénile /ʒyvenil/ adj youthful; (délinquance, mortalité) juvenile.

....

Kk

....

kaki /kaki/ adj inv & nm khaki.

kangourou /kãguʀu/ nm kangaroo.

karaté /kaʀate/ nm karate.

kart /kaʀt/ nm go-cart.

kascher /kaʃɛʀ/ adj inv kosher.

kayak /kajak/ nm kayak.

képi /kepi/ nm kepi.

kermesse /kɛʀmɛs/ nf fête.

kidnapper /kidnape/ 1 vt kidnap.

kilo /kilo/ nm kilo.

kilogramme /kilɔgʀam/ nm kilogram.

kilométrage /kilɔmetʀaʒ/ nm ≈ mileage. **kilomètre** nm kilometre.

kinésithérapeute /kineziteʀapø t/ nmf physiotherapist. **kinésithérapie** nf physiotherapy.

kiosque /kjɔsk/ nm kiosk; ~ **à musique** bandstand.

kit /kit/ nm kit; ~ **mains libres** conducteur hands-free kit.

klaxon® /klaksɔn/ nm (Auto) horn. **klaxonner** 1 vi sound one's horn.

Ko abrév m (**kilo-octet**) (Ordinat) KB.

KO abrév m (**knock-out**) KO 🔟.

K-way® /kawɛ/ nm inv windcheater.

kyste /kist/ nm cyst.

....

Ll

....

l', la /l, la/ ➡**le**.

là /la/
● adverbe
···▸ (dans ce lieu) there; (ici) here; (chez soi) in; **c'est ~ que** this is where; ~ **où** where; **par** ~ (dans cette direction) this

way; (dans cette zone) around there; **de ~** hence.

····▸ (à ce moment) then; **c'est ~ que** that's when.

····▸ **cet homme-~** that man; **ces maisons-~** those houses.

● *interjection*

····▸ **~** [1] **c'est fini** there (now), it's all over!

là-bas /lɑbɑ/ *adv* there; (à l'endroit que l'on indique) over there.

label /label/ *nm* seal, label.

laboratoire /labɔʀatwaʀ/ *nm* laboratory.

laborieux, -ieuse /labɔʀjø, -z/ *adj* laborious; (*personne*) industrious; **classes laborieuses** working classes.

labour /labuʀ/ *nm* ploughing; (US) plowing. **labourer** [1] *vt* plough; (US) plow; (*déchirer*) rip at.

labyrinthe /labiʀɛ̃t/ *nm* maze, labyrinth.

lac /lak/ *nm* lake.

lacer /lase/ [10] *vt* lace up.

lacet /lasɛ/ *nm* (de chaussure) (shoe-)lace; (de route) sharp bend.

lâche /lɑʃ/ *adj* cowardly; (détendu) loose; (sans rigueur) lax. ● *nmf* coward.

lâcher /lɑʃe/ [1] *vt* let go of; (laisser tomber) drop; (abandonner) give up; (laisser) leave; (libérer) release; (*flèche, balle*) fire; (*juron, phrase*) come out with; (desserrer) loosen; **~ prise** let go. ● *vi* give way.

lâcheté /lɑʃte/ *nf* cowardice.

lacrymogène /lakʀimɔʒɛn/ *adj* **gaz ~** tear gas.

lacune /lakyn/ *nf* gap.

là-dedans /lad(ə)dɑ̃/ *adv* (près) in here; (plus loin) in there.

là-dessous /lad(ə)su/ *adv* (près)

under here; (plus loin) under there.

là-dessus /lad(ə)sy/ *adv* (sur une surface) on here; (plus loin) on there; (sur ce) with that; (quelque temps après) after that; **qu'avez-vous à dire ~?** what have you got to say about it?

ladite /ladit/ ➡**ledit**.

lagune /lagyn/ *nf* lagoon.

là-haut /lao/ *adv* (en hauteur) up here; (plus loin) up there; (à l'étage) upstairs.

laïc /laik/ *nm* layman.

laid, ~e /lɛ, lɛd/ *adj* ugly; (action) vile. **laideur** *nf* ugliness.

lainage /lɛnaʒ/ *nm* woollen garment.

laine /lɛn/ *nf* wool; **de ~** woollen.

laïque /laik/ *adj* (état, loi) secular; (habit, personne) lay; (école) nondenominational. ● *nmf* layman, laywoman.

laisse /lɛs/ *nf* lead, leash; **tenir en ~** keep on a lead.

laisser /lese/ [1] *vt* (déposer) leave, drop off; (confier) leave (**à qn** with sb); (abandonner) leave; (rendre) **~ qn perplexe/froid** leave sb puzzled/cold; **~ qch à qn** (céder, prêter) let sb have sth; (donner) (choix, temps) give sb sth. □ **se ~ persuader/insulter** let oneself be persuaded/insulted; **elle ne se laisse pas faire** she won't be pushed around; **laisse-toi faire** leave it to me/him/her etc.; **se ~ aller** let oneself go. ● **v aux ~ qn/qch faire** let sb/sth do; **laisse-moi faire** (ne m'aide pas) let me do it; (je m'en occupe) leave it to me; **laisse faire!** so what! **laisser-aller** *nm inv* carelessness; (dans la tenue) scruffiness. **laissez-passer** *nm inv* pass.

lait /lɛ/ *nm* milk; **~ longue conser-**

vation long-life ou UHT milk; **frère/ sœur de** ~ foster-brother/-sister.
laitage nm milk product. **laiterie** nf dairy. **laiteux, -euse** adj milky.

laitier, -ière /lɛtje, -jɛʀ/ adj dairy. ● nm, f (livreur) milkman, milkwoman.

laiton /lɛtɔ̃/ nm brass.

laitue /lety/ nf lettuce.

lama /lama/ nm llama.

lambeau (pl ~**x**) /lãbo/ nm shred; **en** ~**x** in shreds.

lame /lam/ nf blade; (lamelle) strip; (vague) wave; ~ **de fond** ground swell; ~ **de rasoir** razor blade.

lamentable /lamãtabl/ adj deplorable. **lamenter (se)** ▮ vpr moan (sur about, over).

lampadaire /lãpadɛʀ/ nm standard lamp; (de rue) street lamp.

lampe /lãp/ nf lamp; (ampoule) bulb; (de radio) valve; ~ **(de poche)** (US) flashlight; ~ **à souder** blowlamp; ~ **de chevet** bedside lamp; ~ **solaire**, ~ **à bronzer** sunlamp.

lance /lãs/ nf spear; (de tournoi) lance; (tuyau) hose; ~ **d'incendie** fire hose.

lancement /lãsmã/ nm throwing; (de navire, de missile, mise sur le marché) launch.

lance-missiles /lãsmisil/ nm inv missile launcher.

lance-pierres /lãspjɛʀ/ nm inv catapult.

lancer /lãse/ ▮ vt throw; (avec force) hurl; (navire, idée, artiste) launch; (émettre) give out; (regard) cast; (moteur) start. □ **se** ~ vpr (Sport) gain momentum; (se précipiter) rush; **se** ~ **dans** (explication) launch into; (passetemps) take up. ● nm throw; (action) throwing.

lancinant, -e /lãsinã, -t/ adj

(douleur) shooting; (problème) nagging.

landau /lãdo/ nm pram; (US) baby carriage.

lande /lãd/ nf heath, moor.

langage /lãgaʒ/ nm language; ~ **machine/de programmation** machine/programming language.

langouste /lãgust/ nf spiny lobster. **langoustine** nf Dublin Bay prawn.

langue /lãg/ nf (Anat) tongue; (Ling) language; **il m'a tiré la** ~ he stuck his tongue out at me; **de** ~ **anglaise** English-speaking; (journal) English-language; ~ **maternelle** mother tongue; ~ **vivante** modern language.

lanière /lanjɛʀ/ nf strap.

lanterne /lãtɛʀn/ nf lantern; (électrique) lamp; (de voiture) sidelight.

lapin /lapɛ̃/ nm rabbit; **poser un** ~ **à qn** ▮ stand sb up; **le coup du** ~ rabbit punch; (en voiture) whiplash injury.

lapsus /lapsys/ nm slip (of the tongue).

laque /lak/ nf lacquer; (pour cheveux) hairspray; (peinture) gloss paint.

laquelle /lakɛl/ ➡**LEQUEL.**

lard /laʀ/ nm streaky bacon.

large /laʀʒ/ adj wide, broad; (grand) large; (généreux) generous; **avoir les idées** ~**s** be broad-minded; ~ **d'esprit** broad-minded. ● adv (calculer, mesurer) on the generous side; **voir** ~ think big. ● nm **faire 10 cm de** ~ be 10 cm wide; **le** ~ (mer) the open sea; **au** ~ **de** (Naut) off. **largement** adv widely; (ouvrir) wide; (amplement) amply; (généreusement) generously; (au moins) easily.

largesse /laʀʒɛs/ nf generous gift.

largeur /laʀʒœʀ/ nf width, breadth; ~ **d'esprit** broad-mindedness.

larguer /laʀge/ **1** vt drop; ~ **les amarres** cast off.

larme /laʀm/ nf tear; (goutte **1**) drop; **en** ~**s** in tears.

larmoyant, ~e /laʀmwajɑ̃, -t/ adj full of tears. **larmoyer** **31** vi (yeux) water; (pleurnicher) whine.

larynx /laʀɛ̃ks/ nm larynx.

las, ~se /lɑ, lɑs/ adj weary.

lasagnes /lazaɲ/ nfpl lasagna.

laser /lazɛʀ/ nm laser.

lasser /lase/ **1** vt tire. □ **se** ~ vpr grow tired, get weary (**de** of).

latéral, ~e (mpl **-aux**) /lateʀal, -o/ adj lateral.

latin, ~e /latɛ̃, -in/ adj Latin. ● nm (Ling) Latin.

latte /lat/ nf lath; (de plancher) board; (de siège) slat; (de mur, plafond) lath.

lauréat, ~e /lɔʀea, -t/ adj prize-winning. ● nm, f prize-winner.

laurier /lɔʀje/ nm (Bot) laurel; (Culin) bay-leaves.

lavable /lavabl/ adj washable.

lavabo /lavabo/ nm wash-basin; ~**s** toilet(s).

lavage /lavaʒ/ nm washing; ~ **de cerveau** brainwashing.

lavande /lavɑ̃d/ nf lavender.

lave /lav/ nf lava.

lave-glace (pl ~**s**) /lavglas/ nm windscreen washer.

lave-linge /lavlɛ̃ʒ/ nm inv washing machine.

laver /lave/ **1** vt wash; ~ **qn de** (fig) clear sb of. □ **se** ~ vpr wash (oneself); **se** ~ **les mains** wash one's hands.

laverie /lavʀi/ nf ~ **(automatique)** launderette; (US) laundromat.

lave-vaisselle /lavvɛsɛl/ nm inv dishwasher.

laxatif, -ive /laksatif, -v/ adj & nm laxative.

layette /lejɛt/ nf baby clothes.

---

le, la, l' (pl **les**) /lə, la, l, le/

l' before vowel or mute h.

● **déterminant**

····▸ the.

····▸ (notion générale) **aimer la musique** like music; **l'amour** love.

····▸ (possession) **avoir les yeux verts** have green eyes; **il s'est cassé la jambe** he broke his leg.

····▸ (prix) **10 euros** ~ **kilo** 10 euros a kilo.

····▸ (temps) ~ **lundi** on Mondays; **tous les mardis** every Tuesday.

····▸ (avec nom propre) **les Dury** the Durys; **la reine Margot** Queen Margot; **la Belgique** Belgium.

····▸ (avec adjectif) the; **je veux la rouge** I want the red one; **les riches** the rich.

● **pronom**

····▸ (homme) him; (femme) her; (chose, animal) it; (au pluriel) them.

····▸ (remplaçant une phrase) **je te l'avais bien dit** I told you so; **je croyais aussi** I thought so too.

---

lécher /leʃe/ **14** vt lick; (flamme) lick; (mer) lap.

lèche-vitrines /lɛʃvitʀin/ nm inv **faire du** ~ go window-shopping.

leçon /ləsɔ̃/ nf lesson; **faire la** ~ **à** lecture sb; ~ **particulière** private lesson; ~**s de conduite**

driving lessons.

lecteur, -trice /lɛktœʀ, -tʀis/ nm, f reader; (Univ) foreign language assistant; ~ **de cassettes** cassette player; ~ **de disquettes** (disk) drive; ~ **laser** CD player; ~ **optique** optical scanner.

lecture /lɛktyʀ/ nf reading.

ledit, ladite (pl **lesdit(e)s**) /lədi, ladit, ledi(t)/ adj the aforementioned.

légal, ~e (mpl **-aux**) /legal, -o/ adj legal. **légaliser 1** vt legalize. **légalité** nf legality; (loi) law.

légendaire /leʒɑ̃dɛʀ/ adj legendary. **légende** nf (histoire, inscription) legend; (de carte) key; (d'illustration) caption.

léger, -ère /leʒe, -ɛʀ/ adj light; (bruit, faute, maladie) slight; (café, argument) weak; (imprudent) thoughtless; (frivole) fickle; **à la légère** thoughtlessly. **légèrement** adv lightly; (agir) thoughtlessly; (un peu) slightly. **légèreté** nf lightness; thoughtlessness.

légion /leʒjɔ̃/ nf legion.

> **Légion d'honneur** The system of honours awarded by the state for meritorious achievement. The *Président de la République* is the *Grand maître*. The basic rank is *Chevalier*. Holders of the *Légion d'honneur* are entitled to wear *une rosette* (a small red lapel ribbon).

légionellose /leʒjɔnelɔz/ nf (Méd) legionnaire's disease.

législatif, -ive /leʒislatif, -v/ adj legislative; **élections législatives** general election.

législature /leʒislatyʀ/ nf term of office.

légitime /leʒitim/ adj (Jur) legitim-

ate; (fig) rightful; **agir en état de** ~ **défense** act in self-defence. **légitimité** nf legitimacy.

legs /lɛg/ nm legacy; (d'effets personnels) bequest.

léguer /lege/ **14** vt bequeath.

légume /legym/ nm vegetable.

lendemain /lɑ̃dmɛ̃/ nm **le** ~ the next day; (fig) the future; **le** ~ **de** the day after; **le** ~ **matin/soir** the next morning/evening; **du jour au** ~ from one day to the next.

lent, ~e /lɑ̃, -t/ adj slow. **lentement** adv slowly. **lenteur** nf slowness.

lentille /lɑ̃tij/ nf (Culin) lentil; (verre) lens; ~**s de contact** contact lenses.

léopard /leɔpaʀ/ nm leopard.

lèpre /lɛpʀ/ nf leprosy.

lequel, laquelle (pl **lesquel(le)s**, **auquel** (pl **auxquel(le)s**), **duquel** (pl **desquel(le)s**) /lakɛl, lakɛl, lekɛl, okɛl, dykɛl, dekɛl/

à + lequel = auquel
à + lesquel(le)s = auxquel(le)s
de + lequel = duquel
de + lesquel(le)s = desquel(le)s

● **pronom**
····▸ (relatif) (personne) who; (complément indirect) whom; (autres cas) which; **l'ami auquel tu as écrit** the friend to whom you wrote; **les voisins chez lesquels Sophie est allée** the neighbours whose house Sophie went to.
····▸ (interrogatif) which; ~ **tu veux?** which one do you want?
● **adjectif**
····▸ **auquel cas** in which case.

les /le/ ➡**le.**

lesbienne /lɛsbjɛn/ nf lesbian.

léser /leze/ **14** vt wrong.

lésiner /lezine/ **1** vi ne pas ~ sur not stint on.

lessive /lesiv/ nf (poudre) washing-powder; (liquide) washing liquid; (linge, action) washing.

leste /lɛst/ adj agile, nimble; (grivois) coarse.

Lettonie /letɔni/ nf Latvia.

lettre /lɛtʀ/ nf letter; à la ~, au pied de la ~ literally; en toutes ~s in full; les ~s (Univ) (the) arts.

leucémie /løsemi/ nf leukaemia.

---

leur (pl ~s) /lœʀ/

● pronom personnel invariable

····▸ them; **donne-le** ~ give it to them; **je** ~ **fais confiance** I trust them.

● adjectif possessif

····▸ their; ~s **enfants** their children; à ~ **arrivée** when they arrived.

● **le leur, la leur,** (pl **les leurs**) pronom possessif

····▸ theirs; **chacun le** ~ one each; **je suis des** ~s I am one of them.

---

levain /ləvɛ̃/ nm leaven.

levé, ~e /ləve/ adj (debout) up.

levée /ləve/ nf (de peine, de sanctions) lifting; (de courrier) collection; (de troupes, d'impôts) levying.

lever /ləve/ **6** vt lift (up), raise; (interdiction) lift; (séance) close; (armée, impôts) levy. ● vi (pâte) rise. □ **se** ~ vpr get up; (soleil, rideau) rise; (jour) break. ● nm **au** ~ on getting up; ~ **du jour** daybreak; ~

de rideau (Théât) curtain (up); ~ du soleil sunrise.

levier /ləvje/ nm lever; ~ **de changement de vitesse** gear lever.

lèvre /lɛvʀ/ nf lip.

lévrier /levʀije/ nm greyhound.

levure /ləvyʀ/ nf yeast; ~ **chimique** baking powder.

lexique /lɛksik/ nm vocabulary; (glossaire) lexicon.

lézard /lezaʀ/ nm lizard.

lézarde /lezaʀd/ nf crack.

liaison /ljɛzɔ̃/ nf connection; (transport, Ordinat) link; (contact) contact; (Gram, Mil) liaison; (amoureuse) affair; **être en** ~ **avec** be in contact with; **assurer la** ~ **entre** liaise between.

liane /ljan/ nf creeper.

Liban /libɑ̃/ nm Lebanon.

libeller /libele/ **1** vt (chèque) write; (contrat) draw up; **libellé à l'ordre de** made out to.

libellule /libelyl/ nf dragonfly.

libéral, ~e (mpl **-aux**) /liberal, -o/ adj liberal; **les professions** ~es the professions.

libérateur, -trice /liberatœʀ, -tʀis/ adj liberating. ● nm, f liberator.

libération /liberasjɔ̃/ nf release; (de pays) liberation.

libérer /libere/ **14** vt (personne) free, release; (pays) liberate; free; (bureau, lieux) vacate; (gaz) release. □ **se** ~ vpr free oneself.

liberté /libɛʀte/ nf freedom, liberty; (loisir) free time; **être/mettre en** ~ be/set free; ~ **conditionnelle** parole; ~ **provisoire** provisional release (pending trial); ~ **surveillée** probation; ~s **publiques** civil liberties.

Libertel /libɛʀtɛl/ nm (Internet) Freenet.

libraire /libʀɛʀ/ nmf bookseller.

librairie /librɛri/ nf bookshop.

libre /libr/ adj free; (place, pièce) vacant, free; (passage) clear; (école) private (usually religious); **~ de qch/de faire** free from sth/to do.

libre-échange nm free trade. **libre-service** (pl **libres-services**) nm (magasin) self-service shop; (restaurant) self-service restaurant.

licence /lisãs/ nf licence; (Univ) degree.

licencié, ~e /lisãsje/ nm, f graduate; **~ ès lettres/sciences** Bachelor of Arts/Science.

licenciements /lisãsimã/ nm redundancy; (pour faute) dismissal. **licencier** 45 vt make redundant; (pour faute) dismiss.

licorne /likɔrn/ nf unicorn.

liège /ljɛʒ/ nm cork.

lien /ljɛ̃/ nm (rapport) link; (attache) bond, tie; (corde) rope; **~s affectifs/de parenté** emotional/family ties.

lier /lje/ 45 vt (up) bind; (relier) link; (engager, unir) bind; **~ conversation** strike up a conversation; **ils sont très liés** they are very close. □ **se ~ avec** vpr make friends with.

lierre /ljɛr/ nm ivy.

lieu (pl **~x**) /ljø/ nm place; **~x** (locaux) premises; (d'un accident) scene; **sur les ~x** at the scene; **au ~ de** instead of; **avoir ~** take place; **donner ~ à** give rise to; **tenir ~ de** serve as; **s'il y a ~** if necessary; **en premier ~** firstly; **en dernier ~** lastly; **~ commun** commonplace; **~ de rencontre** meeting place.

lièvre /ljɛvr/ nm hare.

lifting /liftiŋ/ nm face-lift.

ligne /liɲ/ nf line; (trajet) route; (de métro, train) line; (formes) lines;

(de femme) figure; **en ~** (joueurs) lined up; (au téléphone) on the phone; (Ordinat) on line; **~ spécialisée** (Internet) dedicated line.

ligoter /ligɔte/ 1 vt tie up.

ligue /lig/ nf league. **liguer (se)** 1 vpr join forces (contre against).

lilas /lila/ nm & a inv lilac.

limace /limas/ nf slug.

limande /limãd/ nf (poisson) dab.

lime /lim/ nf file; **~ à ongles** nail file.

limitation /limitasjõ/ nf limitation; **~ de vitesse** speed limit.

limite /limit/ nf limit; (délimiter) form the border of. □ **se ~** vpr limit oneself (à to).

limonade /limɔnad/ nf lemonade.

limpide /lɛ̃pid/ adj limpid, clear.

lin /lɛ̃/ nm (tissu) linen.

linge /lɛ̃ʒ/ nm linen; (lessive) washing; (torchon) cloth; **~ (de corps)** underwear. **lingerie** nf underwear. **lingette** nf wipe.

lingot /lɛ̃go/ nm ingot.

linguistique /lɛ̃gɥistik/ adj linguistic. ● nf linguistics.

lion /ljõ/ nm lion; **le L~** Leo. **lionceau** (pl **~x**) nm lion cub. **lionne** nf lioness.

liquidation /likidasjõ/ nf liquidation; (vente) (clearance) sale; **entrer en ~** go into liquidation.

liquide /likid/ adj liquid. ● nm (argent) **~** ready money; **payer en ~** pay cash; **~ de frein** brake fluid.

liquider /likide/ **1** vt liquidate; (vendre) sell.

lire /liʀ/ **39** vt/i read. ● nf lira.

lis¹ /lis/ →LIRE **39**.

lis² /lis/ nm (fleur) lily.

lisible /lizibl/ adj legible; (roman) readable.

lisière /lizjɛʀ/ nf edge.

lisse /lis/ adj smooth.

liste /list/ nf list; ~ d'attente waiting list; ~ électorale register of voters; être sur (la) ~ rouge be ex-directory.

listing /listiŋ/ nm printout.

lit /li/ nm bed; se mettre au ~ get into bed; ~ de camp camp-bed; ~ d'enfant cot; ~ d'une personne single bed; ~ de deux personnes, grand ~ double bed.

literie /litʀi/ nf bedding.

litière /litjɛʀ/ nf litter.

litige /litiʒ/ nm dispute.

litre /litʀ/ nm litre.

littéraire /literɛʀ/ adj literary; (études, formation) arts.

littéral, ~e (mpl ~aux) /literal, -o/ adj literal.

littérature /literatyʀ/ nf literature.

littoral (pl ~aux) /litɔral, -o/ nm coast.

Lituanie /lityani/ nf Lithuania.

livide /livid/ adj deathly pale.

livraison /livʀɛzɔ̃/ nf delivery.

livre /livʀ/ nf (monnaie, poids) pound. ● nm book; ~ de bord logbook; ~ de compte books; ~ de poche paperback.

livrer /livʀe/ **1** vt (Comm) deliver; (abandonner) give over (à to); (remettre) (coupable, document) hand over (à to); livré à soi-même left to oneself. □ se ~ vpr (se rendre)

give oneself up (à to); se ~ à (boisson, actes) indulge in; (ami) confide in.

livret /livʀɛ/ nm book; (Mus) libretto; ~ de caisse d'épargne savings book; ~ scolaire school report (book).

livreur, -euse /livʀœʀ, -øz/ nm, f delivery man, delivery woman.

local¹, ~e (mpl ~aux) /lɔkal, -o/ adj local.

local² (pl ~aux) /lɔkal, -o/ nm premises; locaux premises.

localement /lɔkalmɑ̃/ adv locally.

localisation /lɔkalizasjɔ̃/ nf localization.

localiser /lɔkalize/ **1** vt (repérer) locate; (circonscrire) localize.

locataire /lɔkatɛʀ/ nmf tenant; (de chambre) lodger.

location /lɔkasjɔ̃/ nf (de maison) renting; (de voiture, de matériel) hire, rental; (de place) booking, reservation; (par propriétaire) renting out; hiring out; en ~ (voiture) on hire, rented; (habiter) in rented accommodation.

locomotive /lɔkɔmɔtiv/ nf engine, locomotive.

locution /lɔkysjɔ̃/ nf phrase.

loft /lɔft/ nm loft (apartment).

loge /lɔʒ/ nf (de concierge, de franc-maçons) lodge; (d'acteur) dressing-room; (de spectateur) box.

logement /lɔʒmɑ̃/ nm accommodation; (appartement) flat; (habitat) housing.

loger /lɔʒe/ **40** vt (réfugié, famille) house; (ami) put up; (client) accommodate. ● vi live. □ se ~ vpr live; trouver à se ~ find accommodation; se ~ dans (balle) lodge itself in.

logiciel /lɔʒisjɛl/ nm software; ~

contributif shareware; ~ **d'application** application software; ~ **de groupe** groupware; ~ **de jeux** games software; ~ **de navigation** browser; ~ **public** freeware.

logique /lɔʒik/ adj logical. ● nf logic.

logis /lɔʒi/ nm dwelling.

logistique /lɔʒistik/ nf logistics.

loi /lwa/ nf law.

loin /lwɛ̃/ adv far (away); **au** ~ far away; **de** ~ from far away; (de beaucoup) by far; ~ **de là** far from it; **plus** ~ further; **il revient de** ~ (fig) he had a close shave.

lointain, ~e /lwɛtɛ̃, -ɛn/ adj distant. ● nm distance; **dans le** ~ in the distance.

loisir /lwazir/ nm (spare) time; ~s (temps libre) leisure, spare time; (distractions) leisure activities; **à** ~ at one's leisure; **avoir le** ~ **de faire** have time to do.

londonien, ~ne /lɔ̃dɔnjɛ̃, -ɛn/ adj London. **L~**, ~**ne** nm, f Londoner.

Londres /lɔ̃dr/ npr London.

long, **longue** /lɔ̃, lɔ̃g/ adj long; **à** ~ **terme** long-term; **être** ~ **à faire** be a long time doing. ● nm **de** ~ (mesure) long; **de** ~ **en large** back and forth; **(tout) le** ~ **de** (all) along. ● adv **en dire** ~ **sur qn/qch** say a lot about sb/sth; **en savoir plus** ~ **sur** know more about.

longer /lɔ̃ʒe/ 40 vt go along; (limiter) border.

longitude /lɔ̃ʒityd/ nf longitude.

longtemps /lɔ̃tɑ̃/ adv a long time; **avant** ~ before long; **trop** ~ too long; **ça prendra** ~ it will take a long time; **prendre plus** ~ **que prévu** take longer than anticipated.

longuement /lɔ̃gmɑ̃/ adv (longtemps) for a long time; (en

détail) at length.

longueur /lɔ̃gœr/ nf length; ~s (de texte) over-long parts; **à** ~ **de journée** all day long; **en** ~ lengthwise; ~ **d'onde** wavelength.

lopin /lɔpɛ̃/ nm ~ **de terre** patch of land.

loque /lɔk/ nf ~s rags; ~ **(humaine)** (human) wreck.

loquet /lɔkɛ/ nm latch.

lors de /lɔrdə/ prép (au moment de) at the time of; (pendant) during.

lorsque /lɔrsk(ə)/ conj when.

losange /lɔzɑ̃ʒ/ nm diamond.

lot /lo/ nm (portion) share; (aux enchères) lot; (Ordinat) batch; (destin) lot; **gagner le gros** ~ hit the jackpot.

loterie /lɔtri/ nf lottery.

lotion /losjɔ̃/ nf lotion.

lotissement /lɔtismɑ̃/ nm (à construire) building plot; (construit) (housing) development.

louable /luabl/ adj praiseworthy.

louange nf praise.

louche /luʃ/ adj shady, dubious. ● nf ladle.

loucher /luʃe/ vi squint.

louer /lwe/ 1 vt (approuver) praise (de for); (prendre en location) (maison) rent; (voiture, matériel) hire, rent; (place) book, reserve; (donner en location) (maison) rent out; (matériel) rent out, hire out; **à** ~ to let, for rent (US).

loufoque /lufɔk/ adj 1 crazy.

loup /lu/ nm wolf.

loupe /lup/ nf magnifying glass.

louper /lupe/ 1 vt 1 miss; (examen) flunk 1.

lourd, ~e /lur, -d/ adj heavy; (faute) serious; ~ **de dangers**

fraught with danger; **il fait** ∼ it's close ou muggy.

loutre /lutʀ/ *nf* otter.

louveteau (*pl* ∼**x**) /luvto/ *nm* wolf cub; (scout) Cub (Scout).

loyal, ∼**e** (*mpl* **-aux**) /lwajal, -o/ *adj* loyal, faithful; (*honnête*) fair. **loyauté** *nf* loyalty; fairness.

loyer /lwaje/ *nm* rent.

lu /ly/ →**LIRE** 39.

lubrifiant /lybʀifjɑ̃/ *nm* lubricant.

lucide /lysid/ *adj* lucid. **lucidité** *nf* lucidity.

lucratif, **-ive** /lykʀatif, -v/ *adj* lucrative; **à but non** ∼ non-profitmaking.

ludiciel /lydisjel/ *nm* (Ordinat) games software.

lueur /lɥœʀ/ *nf* (faint) light, glimmer; (fig) glimmer, gleam.

luge /lyʒ/ *nf* toboggan.

lugubre /lygybʀ/ *adj* gloomy.

---

lui /lɥi/

● *pronom*

····▸ (masculin) (sujet) he; ∼, **il est à l'étranger** he's abroad; **c'est** ∼ **l** it's him!; (objet) him; (animal) it; **c'est à** ∼ it's his; **elle conduit mieux que** ∼ she's a better driver than he is.

····▸ (féminin) her; **je** ∼ **ai annoncé** I told her.

····▸ (masculin/féminin) **donne-le-**∼ give it to him/her.

---

lui-même /lɥimɛm/ *pron* himself; (animal) itself.

luire /lɥiʀ/ 17 *vi* shine; (reflet humide) glisten; (reflet chaud, faible) glow.

lumière /lymjɛʀ/ *nf* light; ∼**s** (connaissances) knowledge; **faire**

(toute) la ∼ **sur une affaire** clear a matter up.

luminaire /lyminɛʀ/ *nm* lamp.

lumineux, **-euse** /lyminø, -z/ *adj* luminous; (éclairé) illuminated; (*rayon*) of light; (radieux) radiant; **source lumineuse** light source.

lunaire /lynɛʀ/ *adj* lunar.

lunatique /lynatik/ *adj* temperamental.

lunch /lœnʃ/ *nm* buffet lunch.

lundi /lœdi/ *nm* Monday.

lune /lyn/ *nf* moon; ∼ **de miel** honeymoon.

lunettes /lynɛt/ *nfpl* glasses; (de protection) goggles; ∼ **de ski/natation** ski/swimming goggles; ∼ **noires** dark glasses; ∼ **de soleil** sun-glasses.

lustre /lystʀ/ *nm* (éclat) lustre; (objet) chandelier.

lutin /lytɛ̃/ *nm* goblin.

lutte /lyt/ *nf* fight, struggle; (Sport) wrestling. **lutter** ❶ *vi* fight, struggle; (Sport) wrestle. **lutteur**, **-euse** *nm, f* fighter; (Sport) wrestler.

luxe /lyks/ *nm* luxury; **de** ∼ luxury; (produit) de luxe.

Luxembourg /lyksãbuʀ/ *nm* Luxemburg.

luxer (se) /(sə)lykse/ ❶ *vpr* se ∼ **le genou** dislocate one's knee.

luxueux, **-euse** /lyksɥø, -z/ *adj* luxurious.

lycée /lise/ *nm* (secondary) school. **lycéen**, ∼**ne** /liseɛ̃, ɛn/ *m, f* pupil (at secondary school).

lyophilisé, ∼**e** /ljɔfilize/ *adj* freeze-dried.

lyrique /liʀik/ *adj* (poésie) lyric; (passionné) lyrical; **artiste/théâtre** ∼ opera singer/house.

lys /lis/ *nm* lily.

Mm

m' /m/ →ME.

ma /ma/ →MON.

macabre /makabʀ/ adj macabre.

macadam /makadam/ nm Tarmac®.

macaron /makaʀɔ̃/ nm (gâteau) macaroon; (insigne) badge.

macédoine /masedwan/ nf mixed diced vegetables; ~ de fruits fruit salad.

macérer /maseʀe/ **14** vt/i soak; (dans du vinaigre) pickle.

mâcher /maʃe/ **1** vt chew; **ne pas ~ ses mots** not mince one's words.

machin /maʃɛ̃/ nm **1** (chose) thing; (dont on ne trouve pas le nom) whatsit **1**.

machinal, ~e (mpl -aux) /maʃinal, -o/ adj automatic. **machinalement** adv mechanically, automatically.

machination /maʃinasjɔ̃/ nf plot; **des ~s** machinations.

machine /maʃin/ nf machine; (d'un train, navire) engine; ~ à écrire typewriter; ~ à laver/coudre washing-/sewing-machine; ~ à sous fruit machine; (US) slot machine. **machine-outil** (pl **machines-outils**) nf machine tool. **machinerie** nf machinery.

machiniste /maʃinist/ nm (Théât) stage-hand; (conducteur) driver.

mâchoire /maʃwaʀ/ nf jaw.

mâchonner /maʃone/ **1** vt chew.

maçon /masɔ̃/ nm (entrepreneur) builder; (poseur de briques) bricklayer; (qui construit en pierre)

mason. **maçonnerie** nf (briques) brickwork; (pierres) stonework, masonry; (travaux) building.

madame (pl **mesdames**) /madam, medam/ nf (à une inconnue) (dans une lettre) **M~** Dear Madam; **bonjour**, ~ good morning; **mesdames et messieurs** ladies and gentlemen; (à une femme dont on connaît le nom) (dans une lettre) **Chère M~** Dear Mrs ou Ms X; **bonjour**, ~ good morning Mrs ou Ms X; **oui M~ le Ministre** yes Minister; (formule de respect) **oui M~** yes madam.

mademoiselle (pl **mesdemoiselles**) /madmwazɛl, medmwazɛl/ nf (à une inconnue) (dans une lettre) **M~** Dear Madam; **bonjour**, ~ good morning; **entrez mesdemoiselles** come in (ladies); (à une jeune fille dont on connaît le nom) (dans une lettre) **Chère M~** Dear Ms ou Miss X; **bonjour**, ~ good morning Miss ou Ms X.

magasin /magazɛ̃/ nm shop, store; (entrepôt) warehouse; (d'une arme) magazine; **en** ~ in stock.

magazine /magazin/ nm magazine; (émission) programme.

Maghreb /magʀɛb/ nm North Africa.

magicien, ~ne /maʒisjɛ̃, -ɛn/ nm, f magician.

magie /maʒi/ nf magic. **magique** adj magic; (mystérieux) magical.

magistral, ~e (mpl -aux) /maʒistʀal, -o/ adj masterly; (grand; hum) tremendous; **cours** ~ lecture.

magistrat /maʒistʀa/ nm magistrate.

magistrature /maʒistʀatyʀ/ nf judiciary; (fonction) public office.

magner (se) /(sə)maɲe/ **1** vpr **ⓧ** get a move on.

magnétique /maɲetik/ adj magnetic. **magnétiser** **1** vt magnetize. **magnétisme** nm magnetism.

magnétophone /maɲetɔfɔn/ nm tape recorder; (à cassettes) cassette recorder.

magnétoscope /maɲetɔskɔp/ nm video recorder.

magnificence /maɲifisɑ̃s/ nf magnificence. **magnifique** adj magnificent.

magot /mago/ nm **1** hoard (of money).

magouille /maguj/ nf **1** scheming, skulduggery.

magret /magʀɛ/ nm ~ de canard duck breast.

mai /mɛ/ nm May.

maigre /mɛgʀ/ adj thin; (viande) lean; (yaourt) low-fat; (fig) poor, meagre; **faire** ~ abstain from meat. **maigreur** nf thinness; leanness; (fig) meagreness.

maigrir /megʀiʀ/ **2** vi get thin(ner); (en suivant un régime) slim. ● vt make thin(ner).

maille /maj/ nf stitch; (de filet) mesh; ~ **qui file** ladder, run; **avoir** ~ **à partir avec qn** have a brush with sb.

maillet /majɛ/ nm mallet.

maillon /majɔ̃/ nm link.

maillot /majo/ nm (Sport) shirt, jersey; (~ **de corps**) vest; (US) undershirt; (~ **de bain**) (swimming) costume.

main /mɛ̃/ nf hand; **donner la** ~ **à qn** hold sb's hand; **se donner la** ~ hold hands; **en** ~s **propres** in person; **en bonnes** ~s in good hands; ~ **courante** handrail; **se faire la** ~ get the hang of it; **perdre la** ~ lose one's touch; **sous la** ~ to hand; **vol à** ~ **armée** armed robbery; **fait (à la)** ~ handmade; **haut**

les ~**s!** hands up! **main-d'œuvre** (pl **mains-d'œuvre**) nf labour; (ouvriers) labour force.

main-forte /mɛ̃fɔʀt/ nf inv **prêter** ~ **à qn** come to sb's aid.

maint, ~e /mɛ̃, mɛ̃t/ adj many a (+ sg); ~**s** many; **à** ~**es reprises** many times.

maintenant /mɛ̃t(ə)nɑ̃/ adv now; (de nos jours) nowadays; (l'époque actuelle) today.

maintenir /mɛ̃t(ə)niʀ/ **58** vt keep, maintain; (soutenir) support, hold up; (affirmer) maintain; (decision) stand by. ● **se** ~ vpr (tendance) persist; (prix, malade) remain stable.

maintien /mɛ̃tjɛ̃/ nm (attitude) bearing; (conservation) maintenance.

maire /mɛʀ/ nm mayor.

mairie /meʀi/ nf town hall; (administration) town council.

mais /mɛ/ conj but; ~ **oui** of course; ~ **non** of course not.

maïs /mais/ nm maize, corn; (Culin) sweetcorn.

maison /mezɔ̃/ nf house; (foyer) home; (immeuble) building; (de commerce) firm; **à la** ~ at home; **rentrer** ou **aller à la** ~ go home; ~ **des jeunes (et de la culture)** youth club; ~ **de repos** rest home; ~ **de convalescence** convalescent home; ~ **de retraite** old people's home; ~ **mère** parent company. ● adj inv (Culin) home-made.

Maison des jeunes et de la culture The *Maison des jeunes et de la culture* (MJC) is an organization which provides community arts, sports and leisure activities for young people. Attached to the Ministry of Sport, the MJC was founded in 1964 to

m

enable young people in rural communities to take part in cultural activities in winter.

maître, -esse /mɛtʀ, -ɛs/ adj (qui contrôle) **être ~ de soi** be one's own master; **~ de la situation** in control of the situation; (principal) (idée, qualité) key, main. ● nm, f (Scol) teacher; (d'animal) owner, master. ● nm (expert, guide) master; (dirigeant) leader; **~ de conférences** senior lecturer; **~ d'hôtel** head waiter; (domestique) butler. **maître-assistant, ~ e** (pl **maîtres-assistants**) nm, f lecturer. **maître-chanteur** (pl **maîtres-chanteurs**) nm blackmailer. **maître-nageur** (pl **maîtres-nageurs**) nm swimming instructor. **maîtresse** nf (amante) mistress.

maîtrise /mɛtʀiz/ nf mastery; (contrôle) control; (Mil) supremacy; (Univ) master's degree; (**~ de soi**) self-control.

maîtriser /mɛtʀize/ ⬛ vt (sujet, technique) master; (incendie, sentiment, personne) control. □ **se ~** vpr have self-control.

maïzena® /maizena / nf cornflour.

majesté /maʒɛste/ nf majesty.

majestueux, -euse /maʒɛstɥø, z/ adj majestic.

majeur, ~ e /maʒœʀ/ adj major, main; (Jur) of age; **en ~ e partie** mostly; **la ~ e partie** de most of. ● nm middle finger.

majoration /maʒɔʀasjɔ̃/ nf increase (de in). **majorer** ⬛ vt increase.

majoritaire /maʒɔʀitɛʀ/ adj majority; **être ~** be in the majority. **majorité** nf majority; **en ~** chiefly.

Majorque /maʒɔʀk/ nf Majorca.

majuscule /maʒyskyl/ adj capital. ● nf capital letter.

mal¹ /mal/ adv badly; (incorrectement) wrong(ly); **aller ~** (personne) be unwell; (affaires) go badly; **~ entendre/comprendre** not hear/understand properly; **~ en point** in a bad state; **pas ~** quite a lot. ● adj inv bad, wrong; **c'est ~** de it is wrong ou bad to; **ce n'est pas ~** 🔲 it's not bad; **Nick n'est pas ~** 🔲Nick is not bad-looking.

mal² (pl **maux**) /mal, mo/ nm evil; (douleur) pain, ache; (maladie) disease; (effort) trouble; (dommage) harm; (malheur) misfortune; **avoir ~ à la tête/à la gorge** have a headache/a sore throat; **avoir le ~ de mer/du pays** be seasick/homesick; **faire ~** hurt; **se faire ~** hurt oneself; **j'ai ~** it hurts; **faire du ~ à** hurt, harm; **se donner du ~ pour faire qch** go to a lot of trouble to do sth.

malade /malad/ adj sick, ill; (bras, œil) bad; (plante, poumons, côlon) diseased; **tomber ~** fall ill; (fou 🔲) mad. ● nmf sick person; (d'un médecin) patient; **~ mental** mentally ill person.

maladie /maladi/ nf illness, disease; (manie 🔲) mania.

maladif, -ive /maladif, -v/ adj sickly; (jalousie, peur) pathological.

maladresse /maladʀɛs/ nf clumsiness; (erreur) blunder.

maladroit, ~ e /maladʀwa, -t/ adj clumsy; (sans tact) tactless.

malaise /malɛz/ nm feeling of faintness; (gêne) uneasiness; (état de crise) unrest.

malaisé, ~ e /maleze/ adj difficult.

Malaisie /malɛzi/ nf Malaysia.

malaria /malaʀja/ nf malaria.

malaxer /malakse/ ⬛ vt (pétrir) knead; (mêler) mix.

malchance /malʃɑ̃s/ nf misfortune. **malchanceux, -euse** adj unlucky.

mâle /mɑl/ adj male; (viril) manly. ● nm male.

malédiction /malediksjɔ̃/ nf curse.

maléfice /malefis/ nm evil spell. **maléfique** adj evil.

malentendant, ~e /malɑ̃tɑ̃dɑ̃, -t/ adj hard of hearing.

malentendu /malɑ̃tɑ̃dy/ nm misunderstanding.

malfaçon /malfasɔ̃/ nf defect.

malfaisant, ~e /malfəzɑ̃, -t/ adj harmful; (personne) evil.

malfaiteur /malfɛtœr/ nm criminal.

malformation /malfɔrmasjɔ̃/ nf malformation.

malgré /malgre/ prép in spite of, despite; **~ tout** nevertheless.

malheur /malœr/ nm misfortune; (accident) accident; **par ~** unfortunately; **faire un ~** 🔢 be a big hit; **porter ~** be ou bring bad luck.

malheureusement /malœrøzmɑ̃/ adv unfortunately.

malheureux, -euse /malœrø, -z/ adj unhappy; (regrettable) unfortunate; (sans succès) unlucky; (insignifiant) paltry, pathetic. ● nm, f (poor) wretch.

malhonnête /malɔnɛt/ adj dishonest. **malhonnêteté** nf dishonesty.

malice /malis/ nf mischief; **sans ~** harmless; **avec ~** mischievously. **malicieux, -ieuse** adj mischievous.

malignité /malinite/ nf malignancy. **malin, -igne** adj clever, smart; (méchant) malicious; (tumeur) malignant; (difficile 🔢) difficult.

malingre /malɛ̃gr/ adj puny.

malle /mal/ nf (valise) trunk; (Auto) boot; (US) trunk.

mallette /malɛt/ nf (small) suitcase; (pour le bureau) briefcase.

malmener /malməne/ 🖪 vt manhandle; (fig) give a rough ride to.

malnutrition /malnytrisjɔ̃/ nf malnutrition.

malodorant, ~e /malɔdɔrɑ̃, -t/ adj smelly, foul-smelling.

malpoli, ~e /malpɔli/ adj rude, impolite.

malpropre /malprɔpr/ adj dirty.

malsain, ~e /malsɛ̃, -ɛn/ adj unhealthy.

malt /malt/ nm malt.

Malte /malt/ nf Malta.

maltraiter /maltrete/ 🚺 vt illtreat.

malveillance /malvɛjɑ̃s/ nf malice. **malveillant, ~e** adj malicious.

maman /mamɑ̃/ nf mum(my), mother; (US) mom(my).

mamelle /mamɛl/ nf teat.

mamelon /mamlɔ̃/ nm (Anat) nipple; (colline) hillock.

mamie /mami/ nf 🔢 granny.

mammifère /mamifɛr/ nm mammal.

manche /mɑ̃ʃ/ nf sleeve; (Sport, Pol) round. ● nm (d'un instrument) handle; **~ à balai** broomstick; (Aviat) joystick. **M~** nf **la M~** the Channel; **le tunnel sous la M~** the Channel tunnel.

manchette /mɑ̃ʃɛt/ nf cuff; (de journal) headline.

manchot, ~te /mɑ̃ʃo, -ɔt/ nm, f one-armed person; (sans bras) armless person. ● nm (oiseau) penguin.

mandarine /mɑ̃darin/ nf tangerine, mandarin (orange).

mandat /mɑ̃da/ nm (postal) money order; (Pol) mandate; (procuration) proxy; (de police) warrant; ~ **d'arrêt** arrest warrant.

mandataire /mɑ̃datɛʀ/ nm representative; (Jul) proxy.

manège /manɛʒ/ nm riding school; (à la foire) merry-go-round; (manœuvre) trick, ploy.

manette /manɛt/ nf lever; (de jeu) joystick.

mangeable /mɑ̃ʒabl/ adj edible.

mangeoire /mɑ̃ʒwaʀ/ nf trough; (pour oiseaux) feeder.

manger /mɑ̃ʒe/ 40 vt eat; (fortune) go through; (profits) eat away at; (économies) use up; (ronger) eat into. ● vi eat; **donner à** ~ **à** feed. ● nm food.

mangue /mɑ̃g/ nf mango.

maniable /manjabl/ adj easy to handle.

maniaque /manjak/ adj fussy. ● nmf fusspot; (fou) maniac; (fanatique) fanatic; **un** ~ **de l'ordre** a stickler for tidiness.

manie /mani/ nf habit; (marotte) obsession.

maniement /manimɑ̃/ nm handling. **manier** 45 vt handle.

manière /manjɛʀ/ nf way, manner; ~**s** (politesse) manners; (chichis) fuss; **à la** ~ **de** in the style of; **de** ~ **à** so as to; **de toute** ~ anyway, in any case.

maniéré, -e /manjeʀe/ adj affected.

manif /manif/ nf ⚀ demo.

manifestant, -e /manifɛstɑ̃, -t/ nm, f demonstrator.

manifestation /manifɛstasjɔ̃/ nf expression, manifestation; (de maladie, phénomène) appearance; (Pol) demonstration; (événement) event; ~ **culturelle** cultural event.

manifeste /manifɛst/ adj obvious. ● nm manifesto.

manifester /manifɛste/ ◗ vt show, manifest; (désir, crainte) express. ● vi (Pol) demonstrate. □ se ~ vpr (sentiment) show itself; (apparaître) appear; (répondre à un appel) come forward.

manigance /manigɑ̃s/ nf little plot. **manigancer** ⑩ vt plot.

manipulation /manipylasjɔ̃/ nf handling; (péj) manipulation.

manivelle /manivɛl/ nf handle, crank.

mannequin /mankɛ̃/ nm (personne) model; (statue) dummy.

manœuvrer /manœvʀe/ ◗ vt manoeuvre; (machine) operate. ● vi manoeuvre.

manoir /manwaʀ/ nm manor.

manque /mɑ̃k/ nm lack (de of); (lacune) gap; ~ **à gagner** loss of earnings; **en (état de)** ~ having withdrawal symptoms.

manqué, -e /mɑ̃ke/ adj (écrivain) failed; **garçon** ~ tomboy.

manquement /mɑ̃kmɑ̃/ nm ~ **à** breach of.

manquer /mɑ̃ke/ ◗ vt miss; (gâcher) spoil; ~ **à** (devoir) fail in; (gâcher) be short of, lack; **il/ça lui manque** he misses him/it; ~ **(de) faire** (faillir) nearly do; **ne manquez pas de** be sure to; ~ **à sa parole** break one's word. ● vi be short ou lacking; (être absent) be absent; (en moins, disparu) be missing; **il me manque 20 euros** I'm 20 euros short.

mansarde /mɑ̃saʀd/ nf attic (room).

manteau (pl ~**x**) /mɑ̃to/ nm coat.

manucure /manykyʀ/ nmf manicurist. ● nf (soins) manicure.

manuel, -le /manɥɛl/ adj manual. ● nm (livre) manual; (Scol) textbook.

manufacture /manyfaktyʀ/ nf factory; (fabrication) manufacture.
manufacturer 1 vt manufacture.

manuscrit, ~e /manyskʀi, -t/ adj handwritten. ● nm manuscript.

mappemonde /mapmɔ̃d/ nf world map; (sphère) globe.

maquereau (pl ~x) /makʀo/ nm (poisson) mackerel; 1 pimp.

maquette /makɛt/ nf (scale) model; ~ (de mise en page) paste-up.

maquillage /makijaʒ/ nm make-up.

maquiller /makije/ 1 vt make up; (truquer) doctor, fake. □ se ~ vpr make (oneself) up.

maquis /maki/ nm (paysage) scrub; (Mil) Maquis, underground.

maraîcher, -ère /maʀeʃe, -ɛʀ/ nm, f market gardener; (US) truck farmer.

marais /maʀɛ/ nm marsh.

marasme /maʀasm/ nm slump, stagnation; **dans le** ~ **in the** doldrums.

marbre /maʀbʀ/ nm marble.

marc /maʀ/ nm (eau-de-vie) marc; ~ **de café** coffee grounds.

marchand, ~e /maʀʃɑ̃, -d/ adj (valeur) market. ● nm, f trader; (de charbon, vins) merchant; ~ **de couleurs** ironmonger; (US) hardware merchant; ~ **de journaux** newsagent; ~ **de légumes** greengrocer; ~ **de poissons** fishmonger.

marchander /maʀʃɑ̃de/ 1 vt haggle over. ● vi haggle.

marchandise /maʀʃɑ̃diz/ nf goods.

marche /maʀʃ/ nf (démarche, trajet) walk; (rythme) pace; (Mil, Mus, Pol) march; (d'escalier) step; (Sport) walking; (de machine) operation, working; (de véhicule) running; **en**

~ (train) moving; (moteur, machine) running; **faire** ~ **arrière** (véhicule) reverse; **mettre en** ~ start (up); **se mettre en** ~ start moving.

marché /maʀʃe/ nm market; (contrat) deal; **faire son** ~ do one's shopping; ~ **aux puces** flea market; ~ **noir** black market.

marchepied /maʀʃəpje/ nm (de train, camion) step.

marcher /maʀʃe/ 1 vi walk; (poser le pied) tread (**sur** on); (aller) go; (fonctionner) work, run; (prospérer) go well; (film, livre) do well; (consentir 1) agree; **faire** ~ **qn** 1 pull sb's leg.

mardi /maʀdi/ nm Tuesday; **M** ~ **gras** Shrove Tuesday.

mare /maʀ/ nf (étang) pond; (flaque) pool.

marécage /maʀekaʒ/ nm marsh; (sous les tropiques) swamp.

maréchal (pl -aux) /maʀeʃal, -o/ nm field marshal.

maréchal-ferrant (pl -aux-ferrants /maʀeʃalferɑ̃/ nm blacksmith.

marée /maʀe/ nf tide; (poissons) fresh fish; ~ **haute/basse** high/ low tide; ~ **noire** oil slick.

marelle /maʀɛl/ nf hopscotch.

margarine /maʀgaʀin/ nf margarine.

marge /maʀʒ/ nf margin; **en** ~ **de** (à l'écart de) on the fringe(s) of; ~ **bénéficiaire** profit margin.

marginal, ~e (mpl -aux) /maʀʒinal, -o/ adj marginal. ● nm, f drop-out.

marguerite /maʀgəʀit/ nf daisy; (qui imprime) daisy-wheel.

mari /maʀi/ nm husband.

mariage /maʀjaʒ/ nm marriage; (cérémonie) wedding.

marié, ~e /maʀje/ adj married.

m

● *nm, f* (bride) groom, bride; **les ~s** the bride and groom.

Marianne The symbolic female figure often used to represent the French Republic. There are statues of her in public places all over France, always wearing the Phrygian bonnet, a pointed cap which became a symbol of liberty as represented by the 1789 Revolution. She also appears on the standard French postage stamp.

marier /maʀje/ **45** *vt* marry. □ se **~** *vpr* get married, marry; **se ~ avec** marry, get married to.

marin, ~e /maʀɛ̃, -in/ *adj* sea. ● *nm* sailor.

marine /maʀin/ *nf* navy; **~ marchande** merchant navy. ● *adj inv* navy (blue).

marionnette /maʀjɔnɛt/ *nf* puppet; (à fils) marionette.

maritalement /maʀitalmɑ̃/ *adv* (vivre) as husband and wife.

maritime /maʀitim/ *adj* maritime, coastal; (agent, compagnie) shipping.

marmaille /maʀmaj/ *nf* 🗣 brats.

marmelade /maʀməlad/ *nf* stewed fruit; **~ d'oranges** (orange) marmalade.

marmite /maʀmit/ *nf* (cooking-)pot.

marmonner /maʀmɔne/ **1** *vt* mumble.

marmot /maʀmo/ *nm* 🗣 kid.

Maroc /maʀɔk/ *nm* Morocco.

maroquinerie /maʀɔkinʀi/ *nf* (magasin) leather goods shop.

marquant, ~e /maʀkɑ̃, -t/ *adj* (remarquable) outstanding; (qu'on n'oublie pas) memorable.

marque /maʀk/ *nf* mark; (de produits) brand, make; (décompte) score; **à vos ~s!** (Sport) on your marks!; **de ~** (Comm) brand name; (fig) important; **~ de fabrique** trademark; **~ déposée** registered trademark.

marquer /maʀke/ **1** *vt* mark; (indiquer) show, say; (écrire) note down; (point, but) score; (joueur) mark; (influencer) leave its mark on; (exprimer) (volonté, sentiment) show. ● *vi* (laisser une trace) leave a mark; (événement) stand out; (Sport) score.

marquis, ~e /maʀki, -z/ *nm, f* marquis, marchioness.

marraine /maʀɛn/ *nf* godmother.

marrant, ~e /maʀɑ̃, -t/ *adj* 🗣 funny.

marre /maʀ/ *adv* **en avoir ~** 🗣 be fed up (de with).

marrer (se) /(sə)maʀe/ **1** *vpr* 🗣 laugh, have a (good) laugh.

marron /maʀɔ̃/ *nm* chestnut; (couleur) brown; (coup 🗣) thump; **~ d'Inde** horse chestnut. ● *adj inv* brown.

mars /maʀs/ *nm* March.

Marseillaise, la The popular name of the French national anthem, composed by Claude-Joseph Rouget de Lisle in 1792. It was adopted as a marching song by a group of Republican volunteers from Marseilles and became famous as they sang it on entering Paris.

marteau (pl ~x) /maʀto/ *nm* hammer; **~ (de porte)** (door) knocker; **~ piqueur** ou **pneumatique** pneumatic drill; **être ~** 🗣 be mad.

marteler /maʀtəle/ **6** *vt* hammer;

(*poings*, *talons*) pound; (*scander*) rap out.

martial, ~e (*mpl* **-iaux**) /marsjal, -jo/ *adj* military; (*art*) martial.

martien, ~ne /marsjɛ̃, -ɛn/ *adj* & *nm, f* Martian.

martyr, ~e /martir/ *nm, f* martyr. ● *adj* martyred; (*enfant*) battered.

martyre /martir/ *nm* (*Relig*) martyrdom; (*fig*) agony, suffering.

martyriser /martirize/ **1** *vt* (*Relig*) martyr; (*torturer*) torture; (*enfant*) batter.

marxisme /marksism/ *nm* Marxism. **marxiste** *adj* & *nmf* Marxist.

masculin, ~e /maskylɛ̃, -in/ *adj* masculine; (*sexe*) male; (*mode, équipe*) men's. ● *nm* masculine.

masochisme /mazoʃism/ *nm* masochism.

masochiste /mazoʃist/ *nmf* masochist. ● *adj* masochistic.

masque /mask/ *nm* mask; ~ **de beauté** face pack. **masquer** **1** *vt* (*cacher*) hide, conceal (**à** from); (*lumière*) block (off).

massacre /masakr/ *nm* massacre. **massacrer** **1** *vt* massacre; (*abîmer* **1**) ruin.

massage /masaʒ/ *nm* massage.

masse /mas/ *nf* (*volume*) mass; (*gros morceau*) lump, mass; (*outil*) sledge-hammer; **en ~** (*vendre*) in bulk; (*venir*) in force; **produire en ~** mass-produce; **la ~** (*foule*) the masses; **une ~ de** **1** masses of; **la ~ de** the majority of.

masser /mase/ **1** *vt* (*assembler*) assemble; (*pétrir*) massage. □ **se ~** *vpr* (*gens, foule*) mass.

massif, -ive /masif, -v/ *adj* massive; (*or, argent*) solid. ● *nm* (**de** *fleurs*) clump; (*parterre*) bed; (*Géog*) massif. **massivement** *adv* (*en masse*) in large numbers.

massue /masy/ *nf* club, bludgeon.

mastic /mastik/ *nm* putty; (*pour trous*) filler.

mastiquer /mastike/ **1** *vt* (*mâcher*) chew.

mat /mat/ *adj* (*couleur*) matt; (*bruit*) dull; (*teint*) olive; **être ~** (**aux échecs**) in checkmate.

mât /ma/ *nm* mast; (*pylône*) pole; ~ **de drapeau** flagpole.

match /matʃ/ *nm* match; (*US*) game; **faire ~ nul** tie, draw; ~ **aller** first leg; ~ **retour** return match.

matelas /matla/ *nm* mattress; ~ **pneumatique** air bed.

matelassé, ~e /matlase/ *adj* padded; (*tissu*) quilted.

matelot /matlo/ *nm* sailor.

mater /mate/ **1** *vt* (*révolte*) put down; (*personne*) bring into line.

matérialiser (se) /(sə)materjalize/ **1** *vpr* materialize.

matérialiste /materjalist/ *adj* materialistic. ● *nmf* materialist.

matériau (*pl* **~x**) /materjo/ *nm* material.

matériel, ~le /materjɛl/ *adj* material. ● *nm* equipment, materials; ~ **informatique** hardware.

maternel, ~le /matɛrnɛl/ *adj* maternal; (*comme d'une mère*) motherly. **maternelle** *nf* nursery school.

maternité /matɛrnite/ *nf* maternity hospital; (*état de mère*) motherhood; **de ~** maternity.

mathématicien, ~ne /matematisjɛ̃, -ɛn/ *nm, f* mathematician.

mathématique /matematik/ *adj* mathematical. **mathématiques** *nfpl* mathematics (+ *sg*).

maths /mat/ *nfpl* **1** maths (+ *sg*).

matière /matjɛʀ/ nf matter; (produit) material; (sujet) subject; en ~ de as regards; ~ plastique plastic; ~s grasses fat content; ~s premières raw materials.

matin /matɛ̃/ nm morning; de bon ~ early in the morning.

matinal, ~e (mpl -aux) /matinal, -o/ adj morning; (de bonne heure) early; être ~ be up early; (d'habitude) be an early riser.

matinée /matine/ nf morning; (spectacle) matinée.

matou /matu/ nm tomcat.

matraque /matʀak/ nf (de police) truncheon; (US) billy (club). matraquer 1 vt club, beat; (produit, chanson) plug.

matrimonial, ~e (mpl -iaux) /matʀimɔnjal, -jo/ adj matrimonial; agence ~ marriage bureau.

maturité /matyʀite/ nf maturity.

maudire 41 vt curse.

maudit, ~e /modi, -t/ adj 1 blasted, damned.

maugréer /mogʀee/ 15 vi grumble.

mausolée /mozole/ nm mausoleum.

maussade /mosad/ adj gloomy.

mauvais, ~e /mɔvɛ, -z/ adj bad; (erroné) wrong; (malveillant) evil; (désagréable) nasty, bad; (mer) rough; le ~ moment the wrong time; ~e herbe weed; ~e langue gossip; ~e passe tight spot; ~

traitements ill-treatment. ● adv (sentir) bad; il fait ~ the weather is bad. ● nm le bon et le ~ the good and the bad.

mauve /mov/ adj & nm mauve.

mauviette /movjɛt/ nf weakling, wimp.

maux /mo/ →MAL².

maximal, ~e (mpl -aux) /maksimal, -o/ adj maximum.

maxime /maksim/ nf maxim.

maximum /maksimɔm/ adj maximum. ● nm maximum; au ~ as much as possible; (tout au plus) at most; faire le ~ do one's utmost.

mazout /mazut/ nm (fuel) oil.

me, m' /mə, m/ pron me; (indirect) (to) me; (réfléchi) myself.

méandre /meɑ̃dʀ/ nm meander.

mec /mɛk/ nm 1 bloke, guy.

mécanicien, ~ne /mekanisjɛ̃, -jɛn/ nm, f mechanic. ● nm train driver.

mécanique /mekanik/ adj mechanical; (jouet) clockwork; problème ~ engine trouble. ● nf mechanics (+ sg); (mécanisme) mechanism. mécaniser 1 vt mechanize.

mécanisme /mekanism/ nm mechanism.

méchamment /meʃamɑ̃/ adv spitefully. méchanceté nf nastiness; (action) wicked action.

méchant, ~e /meʃɑ̃, -t/ adj (cruel) wicked; (désagréable, grave) nasty; (enfant) naughty; (chien) vicious; (sensationnel 1) terrific. ● nm, f (enfant) naughty child.

mèche /mɛʃ/ nf (de cheveux) lock; (de bougie) wick; (d'explosif) fuse; (outil) drill bit; de ~ avec in league with.

méconnaissable /mekɔnɛsabl/ adj unrecognizable.

méconnaître /mekɔnɛtʀ/ 18 vt

Matignon The Hôtel Matignon is the official residence and office of the French prime minister, situated in the rue de Varenne, Paris. The word Matignon is often used to refer to the prime minister's office. See ▷ÉLYSÉE

méconnu | mêler

misunderstand, misread; (mésestimer) underestimate.

méconnu, **~e** /mekɔny/ adj unrecognized; (artiste) neglected.

mécontent, **~e** /mekɔ̃tɑ̃, -t/ adj dissatisfied (**de** with); (irrité) annoyed (**de** at, with). **mécontentement** nm dissatisfaction; annoyance. **mécontenter 1** vt dissatisfy; (irriter) annoy.

médaille /medaj/ nf medal; (insigne) badge; (bijou) medallion. **médaillé**, **~e** nm, f medallist.

médaillon /medajɔ̃/ nm medallion; (bijou) locket.

médecin /medsɛ̃/ nm doctor.

médecine /medsin/ nf medicine.

média /medja/ nm medium; **les ~s** the media.

médiateur, **-trice** /medjatœr, -tris/ nm, f mediator.

médiatique /medjatik/ adj (événement, personnalité) media.

médical, **~e** (mpl **-aux**) /medikal, -o/ adj medical.

médicament /medikamɑ̃/ nm medicine, drug.

médico-légal, **~e** (mpl **-aux**) /medikɔlegal, -o/ adj forensic.

médiéval, **~e** (mpl **-aux**) /medjeval, -o/ adj medieval.

médiocre /medjɔkr/ adj mediocre, poor. **médiocrité** nf mediocrity.

médire /medir/ **37** vi **~ de** speak ill of, malign.

médisance /medizɑ̃s/ nf **~(s)** malicious gossip.

méditer /medite/ **1** vi meditate (**sur** on). ● vt contemplate; (paroles, conseils) mull over; **~ de** plan to.

Méditerranée /mediterane/ nf **la ~** the Mediterranean.

méditerranéen, **~ne** /mediterane, -ɛn/ adj Mediterranean.

médium /medjɔm/ nm (personne) medium.

méduse /medyz/ nf jellyfish.

meeting /mitiŋ/ nm meeting.

méfait /mefɛ/ nm misdeed; **les ~s de** (conséquences) the ravages of.

méfiance /mefjɑ̃s/ nf suspicion, distrust. **méfiant**, **~e** adj suspicious, distrustful.

méfier (se) /(sə)mefje/ **45** vpr be wary or careful; **se ~ de** distrust, be wary of.

mégaoctet /megaɔkte/ nm (Ordinat) megabyte.

mégère /meʒɛr/ nf (femme) shrew.

mégot /mego/ nm cigarette end.

meilleur, **~e** /mejœr/ adj (comparatif) better (**que** than); (superlatif) best; **le ~** the best book; **mon ~ ami** my best friend; **~ marché** cheaper. ● nm, f (one, **la ~e** the best; (one). ● adv (sentir) better; **il fait ~** the weather is better.

mél /mel/ nm email; **envoyer un ~** send an email.

mélancolie /melɑ̃kɔli/ nf melancholy.

mélange /melɑ̃ʒ/ nm mixture, blend.

mélanger /melɑ̃ʒe/ **40** vt mix; (thés, parfums) blend. □ **se ~** vpr mix; (thés, parfums) blend; (idées) get mixed up.

mélasse /melas/ nf black treacle; (US) molasses.

mêlée /mele/ nf free for all; (au rugby) scrum.

mêler /mele/ **1** vt mix (**à** with); (qualités) combine; (embrouiller) mix up; **~ qn à** (impliquer dans) involve sb in. □ **se ~** vpr mix; combine; **se ~ à** (se joindre à) mingle with; (participer à) join in; **se ~ de** meddle in; **mêle-toi de ce qui te regarde** mind your own business.

méli-mélo (*pl* **mélis-mélos**) /melimelo/ *nm* jumble.

mélo /melo/ 🔟 *nm* melodrama.
● *adj inv* slushy, schmaltzy 🔟.

mélodie /melɔdi/ *nf* melody. **mélodieux, -ieuse** *adj* melodious. **mélodique** *adj* melodic.

mélodramatique /melɔdʀa matik/ *adj* melodramatic. **mélodrame** /melɔdʀam/ *nm* melodrama.

mélomane /melɔman/ *nmf* music lover.

melon /mǝlɔ̃/ *nm* melon; **(chapeau)** ~ bowler (hat).

membrane /mãbʀan/ *nf* membrane.

membre /mãbʀ/ *nm* (Anat) limb; (adhérent) member.

même /mɛm/ *adj* same; **ce livre** ~ this very book; **la bonté** ~ kindness itself; **en ~ temps** at the same time. ● *pron* **le** ~, **la** ~ the same (one). ● *adv* even; **à** ~ (sur) directly on; **à** ~ **de** in a position to; **de** ~ (aussi) too; (de la même façon) likewise; **de** ~ **que** just as; ~ **si** even if.

mémé /meme/ *nf* 🔟 granny.

mémo /memo/ *nm* note, memo.

mémoire /memwaʀ/ *nm* (rapport) memorandum; (Univ) dissertation; ~**s** (souvenirs écrits) memoirs. ● *nf* memory; **à la** ~ **de** to the memory of; **de** ~ from memory; ~ **morte/vive** (Ordinat) ROM/RAM.

mémorable /memɔʀabl/ *adj* memorable.

menace /mǝnas/ *nf* threat. **menacer** 🔟 *vt* threaten (**de faire** to do).

ménage /menaʒ/ *nm* (couple) couple; (travail) housework; (fa-

mille) household; **se mettre en** ~ set up house.

ménagement /menaʒmã/ *nm* **avec** ~**s** gently; **sans** ~**s** (dire) bluntly; (jeter, pousser) roughly.

ménager¹, **-ère** /menaʒe, -ɛʀ/ *adj* household, domestic; **travaux** ~**s** housework.

ménager² /menaʒe/ 🔟 *vt* be gentle with, handle carefully; (utiliser) be careful with; (organiser) prepare (carefully); **ne pas** ~ **ses efforts** spare no effort.

ménagère /menaʒɛʀ/ *nf* housewife.

ménagerie /menaʒʀi/ *nf* menagerie.

mendiant, ~e /mãdjã, -t/ *nm, f* beggar.

mendier /mãdje/ 🔟 *vt* beg for.
● *vi* beg.

mener /mǝne/ 🔟 *vt* lead; (entreprise, pays) run; (étude, enquête) carry out; (politique) pursue; ~ **à** (accompagner à) take to; (faire aboutir) lead to; ~ **à bien** see through. ● *vi* lead.

méningite /menɛ̃ʒit/ *nf* meningitis.

menotte /mǝnɔt/ *nf* 🔟 hand; ~**s** handcuffs.

mensonge /mãsɔ̃ʒ/ *nm* lie; (action) lying. **mensonger, -ère** *adj* untrue, false.

mensualité /mãsɥalite/ *nf* monthly payment.

mensuel, ~le /mãsɥɛl/ *adj* monthly. ● *nm* monthly (magazine). **mensuellement** *adv* monthly.

mensurations /mãsyʀasjɔ̃/ *nfpl* measurements.

mental, ~e (*mpl* **-aux**) /mãtal, -o/ *adj* mental; **malade** ~ mentally ill person; **handicapé** ~ mentally handicapped person.

mentalité | messieurs

mentalité /mɑ̃talite/ nf mentality.

menteur, -euse /mɑ̃tœʀ, -øz/ nm, f liar. ● adj untruthful.

menthe /mɑ̃t/ nf mint.

mention /mɑ̃sjɔ̃/ nf mention; (annotation) note; (Scol) grade; **rayer la ~ inutile** delete as appropriate. **mentionner** 1 vt mention.

mentir /mɑ̃tiʀ/ 46 vi lie.

menton /mɑ̃tɔ̃/ nm chin.

menu, ~e /məny/ adj (petit) tiny; (fin) fine; (insignifiant) minor. ● adv (couper) fine. ● nm (carte) menu; (repas) meal; (Ordinat) menu; **~ déroulant** pull-down menu.

menuiserie /mənɥizʀi/ nf carpentry, joinery. **menuisier** nm carpenter, joiner.

méprendre (se) /(sə)mepʀɑ̃dʀ/ 50 vpr **se ~ sur** be mistaken about.

mépris /mepʀi/ nm contempt, scorn (**de** for); **au ~ de** regardless of.

méprisable /mepʀizabl/ adj contemptible, despicable.

méprise /mepʀiz/ nf mistake.

méprisant, ~e /mepʀizɑ̃, -t/ adj scornful. **mépriser** 1 vt scorn, despise.

mer /mɛʀ/ nf sea; (marée) tide; **en pleine ~** out at sea.

mercenaire /mɛʀsənɛʀ/ nm & a mercenary.

mercerie /mɛʀs(ə)ʀi/ nf haberdashery; (US) notions store. **mercier, -ière** nm, f haberdasher; (US) notions seller.

merci /mɛʀsi/ interj thank you, thanks (**de, pour** for); **~ beaucoup, ~ bien** thank you very much. ● nm thank you. ● nf mercy.

mercredi /mɛʀkʀədi/ nm Wednesday; **~ des Cendres** Ash Wednesday.

merde /mɛʀd/ nf ✕ shit ✕.

mère /mɛʀ/ nf mother; **~ de famille** mother.

méridional, ~e (mpl **-aux**) /meʀidjɔnal, -o/ adj southern. ● nm, f Southerner.

mérite /meʀit/ nm merit; **avoir du ~ à faire** deserve credit for doing.

mériter /meʀite/ 1 vt deserve; **~ d'être lu** be worth reading.

méritoire /meʀitwaʀ/ adj commendable.

merlan /mɛʀlɑ̃/ nm whiting.

merle /mɛʀl/ nm blackbird.

merveille /mɛʀvɛj/ nf wonder, marvel; **à ~** wonderfully; **faire des ~s** work wonders.

merveilleux, -euse /mɛʀvɛjø, -z/ adj wonderful, marvellous.

mes /me/ ➡MON.

mésange /mezɑ̃ʒ/ nf tit(mouse).

mésaventure /mezavɑ̃tyʀ/ nf misadventure; **par ~** by some misfortune.

mesdames /medam/ ➡MADAME.

mesdemoiselles /medmwazɛl/ ➡MADEMOISELLE.

mésentente /mezɑ̃tɑ̃t/ nf disagreement.

mesquin, ~e /mɛskɛ̃, -in/ adj mean-minded, petty; (chiche) mean. **mesquinerie** nf meanness.

message /mesaʒ/ nm message; **un ~ électronique** an email; **~ texte** text message.

messager, -ère /mesaʒe, -ɛʀ/ nm, f messenger. ● nm **~ de poche** pager.

messagerie /mesaʒʀi/ nf (transports) freight forwarding; (télécommunications) messaging; **~ électronique** electronic mail; **~ vocale** voice mail.

messe /mɛs/ nf (Relig) mass.

messieurs /mesjø/ ➡MONSIEUR.

mesure /məzyʀ/ nf measurement; (quantité, unité) measure; (disposition) measure, step; (cadence) time; **en ~** in time; (modération) moderation; **à ~ que** as; **dans la ~ où** in so far as; **dans une certaine ~** to some extent; **en ~ de** in a position to; **sans ~** to excess; **(fait) sur ~** made-to-measure.

mesuré, ~e /məzyʀe/ adj measured; (atttitude) moderate.

mesurer /məzyʀe/ **1** vt measure; (juger) assess; (argent, temps) ration. ● vi **~ 15 mètres de long** be 15 metres long. □ **se ~ avec** vpr pit oneself against.

met /mɛ/ →METTRE 42.

métal (pl **-aux**) /metal, -o/ nm metal. **métallique** adj (objet) metal; (éclat) metallic.

métallurgie /metalyʀʒi/ nf (industrie) metalworking industry.

métamorphoser /metamɔʀfoze/ **1** vt transform. □ **se ~** vpr be transformed; **se ~ en** metamorphose into.

métaphore /metafɔʀ/ nf metaphor.

météo /meteo/ nf (bulletin) weather forecast.

météore /meteɔʀ/ nm meteor.

météorologie /meteɔʀɔlɔʒi/ nf meteorology.

météorologique /meteɔʀɔlɔʒik/ adj meteorological; **conditions ~s** weather conditions.

méthode /metɔd/ nf method; (ouvrage) course, manual. **méthodique** adj methodical.

méticuleux, -euse /metikylø, -z/ adj meticulous.

métier /metje/ nm job; (manuel) trade; (intellectuel) profession; (expérience) experience, skill; **~ (à tisser)** loom; **remettre qch sur le ~** rework sth.

métis, ~se /metis/ adj mixed race. ● nm, f person of mixed race.

métrage /metʀaʒ/ nm length; **court ~** short (film); **long ~** feature-length film.

mètre /mɛtʀ/ nm metre; (règle) rule; **~ ruban** tape-measure.

métreur, -euse /metʀœʀ, -øz/ nm, f quantity surveyor.

métrique /metʀik/ adj metric.

métro /metʀo/ nm underground; (US) subway.

métropole /metʀɔpɔl/ nf metropolis; (pays) mother country. **métropolitain, ~e** adj metropolitan.

mets /mɛ/ nm dish. ● →METTRE 42.

mettable /metabl/ adj wearable.

metteur /metœʀ/ nm **~ en scène** director.

mettre /mɛtʀ/ 42 vt put; (radio, chauffage) put ou switch on; (réveil) set; (installer) put in; (revêtir) put on; (porter habituellement) (vêtement, lunettes) wear; (prendre) take; (investir, dépenser) put; (écrire) write, say; **elle a mis deux heures** it took her two hours; **~ la table** lay the table; **~ en question** question; **~ en valeur** highlight; (terrain) develop; **mettons que** let's suppose that. ● vi **~ bas** (animal) give birth. □ **se ~** vpr (vêtement, maquillage) put on; (se placer) (objet) go; (personne) (debout) stand; (assis) sit; (couché) lie; **se ~ en short** put shorts on; **se ~ debout** stand up; **se ~ au lit** go to bed; **se ~ à table** sit down at table; **se ~ en ligne** line up; **se ~ du sable dans les yeux** get sand in one's eyes; **se ~ au chinois/tennis** take up Chinese/tennis; **se ~ au travail** set to work; **se ~ à faire** start to do.

meuble /mœbl/ *nm* piece of furniture; **~s** furniture.

meublé /møble/ *nm* furnished flat.

meubler /møble/ **1** *vt* furnish; (fig) fill. □ **se ~** *vpr* buy furniture.

meugler /møgle/ **1** *vi* moo.

meule /møl/ *nf* millstone; **~ de foin** haystack.

meunier, -ière /mønje, -jɛʀ/ *nm, f* miller.

meurs, meurt /mœʀ/ **➡MOURIR** 43.

meurtre /mœʀtʀ/ *nm* murder.

meurtrier, -ière /mœʀtʀije, -jɛʀ/ *adj* deadly. ● *nm, f* murderer, murderess.

meurtrir /mœʀtʀiʀ/ **2** *vt* bruise.

meute /møt/ *nf* pack of hounds.

Mexique /mɛksik/ *nm* Mexico.

mi- /mi/ *préf* mid-, half-; **à mi-chemin** half-way; **à mi-pente** half-way up the hill; **à la mi-juin** in mid-June.

miauler /mjole/ **1** *vi* miaow.

micro /mikʀo/ *nm* microphone, mike; (Ordinat) micro.

microbe /mikʀɔb/ *nm* germ.

microfilm /mikʀofilm/ *nm* microfilm.

micro-onde /mikʀoɔd/ *nf* microwave; **un four à ~s** microwave (oven). **micro-ondes** *nm inv* microwave (oven).

micro-ordinateur (*pl* **~s**) /mikʀoɔʀdinatœʀ/ *nm* personal computer.

microphone /mikʀofɔn/ *nm* microphone.

microprocesseur /mikʀopʀosɛsœʀ/ *nm* microprocessor.

microscope /mikʀoskɔp/ *nm* microscope.

midi /midi/ *nm* twelve o'clock, mid-

day, noon; (déjeuner) lunch-time; (sud) south. **Midi** *nm* le M**~** the South of France.

mie /mi/ *nf* soft part (of the loaf); **un pain de ~** a sandwich loaf.

miel /mjɛl/ *nm* honey.

mielleux, -euse /mjɛlø, -z/ *adj* unctuous.

mien, ~ne /mjɛ̃, -ɛn/ *pron* le **~**, la **~ne**, les **~(ne)s** mine.

miette /mjɛt/ *nf* crumb; (fig) scrap; **en ~s** in pieces.

mieux /mjø/ *adj inv* better (que than); **le** *ou* **la** *ou* **les ~** (the) best. ● *nm* best; (progrès) improvement; **faire de son ~** do one's best; **le ~ serait de** the best thing would be to. ● *adv* better; **le** *ou* **la** *ou* **les ~** (de deux) the better; (de plusieurs) the best; **elle va ~** she is better; **j'aime ~ rester** I'd rather stay; **il vaudrait ~ partir** it would be best to leave; **tu ferais ~ de faire** you would be best to do.

mièvre /mjɛvʀ/ *adj* insipid.

mignon, ~ne /miɲɔ̃, -ɔn/ *adj* cute; (gentil) kind.

migraine /migʀɛn/ *nf* headache; (plus fort) migraine.

migration /migʀasjɔ̃/ *nf* migration.

mijoter /miʒɔte/ **1** *vt/i* simmer; (tramer 1) cook up.

mil /mil/ *nm* a thousand.

milice /milis/ *nf* militia.

milieu (*pl* **~x**) /miljø/ *nm* middle; (environnement) environment; (appartenance sociale) background; (groupe) circle; (voie) middle way; (criminel) underworld; **au ~ de** in the middle of; **en plein** *ou* **au beau ~ de** right in the middle (of).

militaire /militɛʀ/ *adj* military. ● *nm* soldier, serviceman.

militant, ~e /militɑ̃, -t/ *nm, f*

m

militant.

militer /milite/ **1** vi be a militant; ~ **pour** militate in favour of.

mille¹ /mil/ adj & nm inv a thousand; **deux** ~ two thousand; **mettre dans le** ~ (fig) hit the nail on the head.

mille² /mil/ nm ~ **(marin)** (nautical) mile.

millénaire /milenɛʀ/ nm millennium. ● adj a thousand years old.

mille-pattes /milpat/ nm inv centipede.

millésime /milezim/ nm date; (de vin) vintage.

millet /mijɛ/ nm millet.

milliard /miljaʀ/ nm thousand million, billion. **milliardaire** nmf multimillionaire.

millième /miljɛm/ adj & nmf thousandth.

millier /milje/ nm thousand; **un** ~ **(de)** about a thousand.

millimètre /milimɛtʀ/ nm millimetre.

million /miljɔ̃/ nm million; **deux** ~s **(de)** two million. **millionnaire** nmf millionaire.

mime /mim/ nmf mime-artist. ● nm (art) mime. **mimer** **1** vt mime; (imiter) mimic.

mimique /mimik/ nf expressions and gestures.

minable /minabl/ adj **1** (logement) shabby; (médiocre) pathetic, crummy.

minauder /minode/ **1** vi simper.

mince /mɛ̃s/ adj thin; (svelte) slim; (faible) (espoir, majorité) slim. ● interj **1** blast **1**, darn it **1**. **minceur** nf thinness; slimness.

mincir /mɛ̃siʀ/ **2** vi get slimmer; **ça te mincit** it makes you look slimmer.

mine /min/ nf expression; (allure) appearance; **avoir bonne** ~ look well; **faire** ~ **de** make as if to; (exploitation, explosif) mine; (de crayon) lead; ~ **de charbon** coalmine.

miner /mine/ **1** vt (saper) undermine; (garnir d'explosifs) mine.

minerai /minʀɛ/ nm ore.

minéral, ~**e** (mpl -**aux**) /mineʀal, -o/ adj mineral. ● nm (pl -**aux**) mineral.

minéralogique /mineʀalɔʒik/ adj **plaque** ~ numberplate; (US) license plate.

minet, ~**te** /minɛ, -t/ nm, f (chat **1**) pussy(cat).

mineur, ~**e** /minœʀ/ adj minor; (Jur) under age. ● nm, f (Jur) minor. ● nm (ouvrier) miner.

miniature /minjatyʀ/ nf & adj miniature.

minier, -ière /minje, -jɛʀ/ adj mining.

minimal, ~**e** (mpl -**aux**) /minimal, o/ adj minimal, minimum.

minime /minim/ adj minimal, minor. ● nmf (Sport) junior.

minimum /minimɔm/ adj minimum. ● nm minimum; **au** ~ (pour le moins) at the very least; **en faire un** ~ do as little as possible.

ministère /ministɛʀ/ nm ministry; (gouvernement) government; ~ **public** public prosecutor's office. **ministériel,** ~**le** adj ministerial, government.

ministre /ministʀ/ nm minister; (au Royaume-Uni) Secretary of State; (US) Secretary.

Minitel® /minitɛl/ nm Minitel (telephone videotext system).

minorer /minɔʀe/ **1** vt reduce.

minoritaire /minɔʀitɛʀ/ adj minority; **être** ~ be in the minority. **minorité** nf minority.

minuit /minɥi/ nm midnight.

minuscule /minyskyl/ adj minute. ● nf (lettre) ~ lower case.

minute /minyt/ nf minute; **'talons** ~' 'heels repaired while you wait'.

minuterie /minytʀi/ nf time-switch.

minutie /minysi/ nf meticulousness.

minutieux, -ieuse /minysjø, -z/ adj meticulous.

mioche /mjoʃ/ nm, f 🄵 kid.

mirabelle /miʀabɛl/ nf (mirabelle) plum.

miracle /miʀakl/ nm miracle; **par** ~ miraculously.

miraculeux, -euse /miʀakylø, -z/ adj miraculous.

mirage /miʀaʒ/ nm mirage.

mire /miʀ/ nf (fig) centre of attraction; (TV) test card.

mirobolant, ~e /miʀɔbɔlɑ̃, -t/ adj 🄵 marvellous.

miroir /miʀwaʀ/ nm mirror.

miroiter /miʀwate/ 🄵 vi shimmer, sparkle.

mis, ~e /mi, miz/ adj **bien** ~ well-dressed. ● → **METTRE** 🄸.

mise /miz/ nf (argent) stake; (tenue) attire; ~ **à feu** blast-off; ~ **au point** adjustment; (fig) clarification; ~ **de fonds** capital outlay; ~ **en garde** warning; ~ **en plis** set; ~ **en scène** direction.

miser /mize/ 🄵 vt (argent) bet, stake (**sur** on). ● vi ~ **sur** (parier) place a bet on; (compter sur) bank on.

misérable /mizeʀabl/ adj miserable, wretched; (indigent) destitute; (minable) seedy, squalid.

misère /mizɛʀ/ nf destitution;

(malheur) trouble, woe. **miséreux, -euse** nm, f destitute person.

miséricorde /mizeʀikɔʀd/ nf mercy.

missel /misɛl/ nm missal.

missile /misil/ nm missile.

mission /misjɔ̃/ nf mission. **missionnaire** nmf missionary.

missive /misiv/ nf missive.

mistral /mistʀal/ nm (vent) mistral.

mitaine /mitɛn/ nf fingerless mitt.

mite /mit/ nf (clothes-)moth.

mi-temps /mitɑ̃/ nf inv (arrêt) half-time; (période) half. ● nm inv part-time work; **à** ~ part-time.

miteux, -euse /mitø, -z/ adj shabby.

mitigé, ~e /mitiʒe/ adj (modéré) lukewarm; (succès) qualified.

mitonner /mitɔne/ 🄵 vt cook slowly with care; (fig) cook up.

mitoyen, ~ne /mitwajɛ̃, -ɛn/ adj **mur** ~ party wall.

mitrailler /mitʀaje/ 🄵 vt machine-gun; (fig) bombard.

mitraillette /mitʀajɛt/ nf sub-machine gun. **mitrailleuse** nf machine gun.

mi-voix: **à** ~ /amivwa/ loc in a low voice.

mixeur /miksœʀ/ nm liquidizer, blender; (batteur) mixer.

mixte /mikst/ adj mixed; (commission) joint; (école) coeducational; (peau) combination.

mobile /mɔbil/ adj mobile; (pièce) moving; (feuillet) loose. ● nm (art) mobile; (raison) motive.

mobilier /mɔbilje/ nm furniture.

mobilisation /mɔbilizasjɔ̃/ nf mobilization. **mobiliser** 🄵 vt mobilize.

mobilité /mɔbilite/ nf mobility.

m

mobylette® /mɔbilɛt/ nf moped.

moche /mɔʃ/ adj 🚹 (laid) ugly; (mauvais) lousy.

modalités /mɔdalite/ nfpl (conditions) terms; (façon de fonctionner) practical details.

mode /mɔd/ nf fashion; (coutume) custom; **à la ~** fashionable. ● nm method, mode; (genre) way; **~ d'emploi** directions (for use).

modèle /mɔdɛl/ adj model. ● nm model; (exemple) example; (Comm) (type) model; (taille) size; (style) style; **~ familial** family size; **~ réduit** (small-scale) model.

modeler /mɔdle/ 🔟 vt model (sur on). □ **se ~ sur** vpr model oneself on.

modem /mɔdɛm/ nm modem.

modérateur, -trice /mɔderatœʀ, -tʀis/ adj moderating. **modération** nf moderation.

modéré, ~e /mɔdeʀe/ adj & nm, f moderate.

modérer /mɔdeʀe/ 🔢 vt (propos) moderate; (désirs, sentiments) curb. □ **se ~** vpr restrain oneself.

moderne /mɔdɛʀn/ adj modern. **moderniser** 🚹 vt modernize.

modeste /mɔdɛst/ adj modest. **modestie** nf modesty.

modification /mɔdifikasjɔ̃/ nf modification.

modifier /mɔdifje/ 🔢 vt change, modify. □ **se ~** vpr change, alter.

modique /mɔdik/ adj modest.

modiste /mɔdist/ nf milliner.

moduler /mɔdyle/ 🚹 vt modulate; (adapter) adjust.

moelle /mwal/ nf marrow; **~ épinière** spinal cord; **~ osseuse** bone marrow.

moelleux, -euse /mwalø, -z/ adj soft; (onctueux) smooth.

mœurs /mœʀ(s)/ nfpl (morale) morals; (usages) customs; (manières) habits, ways.

moi /mwa/ pron me; (indirect) (to) me; (sujet) I. ● nm self.

moignon /mwaɲɔ̃/ nm stump.

moi-même /mwamɛm/ pron myself.

moindre /mwɛ̃dʀ/ adj (moins grand) lesser; **le** ou **la ~, les ~s** the slightest, the least.

moine /mwan/ nm monk.

moineau (pl **~x**) /mwano/ nm sparrow.

moins /mwɛ̃/ prép minus; (pour dire l'heure) to; **une heure ~ dix** ten to one. ● adv less (que than); **le** ou **la** ou **les ~** the least; **le ~ grand/haut** the smallest/lowest; **~ de** (avec un nom non dénombrable) less (que than); **~ de dix euros** less than ten euros; **~ de livres** fewer books; **au ~, du ~** at least; **à ~ que** unless; **de ~** less; **de ~ en ~** less and less; **en ~** less; (manquant) missing.

mois /mwa/ nm month.

moisi, ~e /mwazi/ adj mouldy. ● nm mould; **de ~** (odeur) musty. **moisir** 🔢 vi go mouldy. **moisissure** nf mould.

moisson /mwasɔ̃/ nf harvest.

moissonner /mwasɔne/ 🚹 vt harvest, reap. **moissonneur, -euse** nm, f harvester.

moite /mwat/ adj sticky, clammy.

moitié /mwatje/ nf half; (milieu) halfway mark; **s'arrêter à la ~** stop halfway through; **à ~ vide** half empty; **à ~ prix** (at) half-price; **la ~ de** half (of). **moitié-moitié** adv half-and-half.

mol /mɔl/ →MOU.

molaire /mɔlɛʀ/ nf molar.

molécule /mɔlekyl/ nf molecule.

molester /mɔlɛste/ ① vt man-handle, rough up.

molle /mɔl/ →**MOU**.

mollement /mɔlmɑ̃/ adv softly; (faiblement) feebly. **mollesse** nf softness; (faiblesse) feebleness; (apathie) listlessness.

mollet /mɔlɛ/ nm (de jambe) calf.

mollir /mɔliʀ/ ② vi soften; (céder) yield.

môme /mom/ nmf ① kid.

moment /mɔmɑ̃/ nm moment; (période) time; (petit) ~ short while; **au** ~ **où** when; **par** ~**s** now and then; **du** ~ **où** ou **que** (pourvu que) as long as, provided that; (puisque) since; **en ce** ~ at the moment.

momentané, ~e /mɔmɑ̃tane/ adj momentary. **momentanément** adv momentarily; (en ce moment) at present.

momie /mɔmi/ nf mummy.

mon, ma (before vowel or mute h) (pl **mes**) /mɔ̃, ma, mɔ̃, me/ adj my.

Monaco /mɔnako/ npr Monaco.

monarchie /mɔnaʀʃi/ nf monarchy.

monarque /mɔnaʀk/ nm monarch.

monastère /mɔnastɛʀ/ nm monastery.

monceau (pl ~**x**) /mɔ̃so/ nm heap, pile.

mondain, ~e /mɔ̃dɛ̃, -ɛn/ adj society, social.

monde /mɔ̃d/ nm world; **du** ~ (a lot of) people; (quelqu'un) somebody; **le (grand)** ~ (high) society; **se faire (tout) un** ~ **de qch** make a great deal of fuss about sth; **pas le moins du** ~ not in the least.

mondial, ~e (mpl **-iaux**) /mɔ̃djal, -jo/ adj world; (influence) worldwide.

mondialement adv the world over.

mondialisation /mɔ̃djalizasjɔ̃/ nf globalisation.

monétaire /mɔnetɛʀ/ adj monetary.

moniteur, -trice /mɔnitœʀ, -tʀis/ nm, f instructor; (de colonie de vacances) group leader; (US) (camp) counselor.

monnaie /mɔnɛ/ nf currency; (pièce) coin; (appoint) change; **faire la** ~ **de** get change for; **faire de la** ~ **à qn** give sb change; **menue** ou **petite** ~ small change.

monnayer /mɔneje/ ③ vt convert into cash.

monologue /mɔnɔlɔg/ nm monologue.

monoparental, ~e /mɔnɔpaʀɑ̃tal/ adj **famille** ~**e** single-parent family.

monopole /mɔnɔpɔl/ nm monopoly. **monopoliser** ① vt monopolize.

monospace /mɔnɔspas/ nm (Auto) people carrier.

monotone /mɔnɔtɔn/ adj monotonous. **monotonie** nf monotony.

Monseigneur (pl **Messeigneurs**) /mɔ̃sɛɲœʀ/ nm (à un duc, archevêque) Your Grace; (à un prince) Your Highness.

monsieur (pl **messieurs**) /məsjø, mesjø/ nm (à un inconnu) (dans une lettre) **M**~ Dear Sir; **bonjour**, ~ good morning; **mesdames et messieurs** ladies and gentlemen; (à un homme dont on connaît le nom) (dans une lettre) **Cher M**~ Dear Mr X; **bonjour**, ~ good morning Mr X; **M**~ **le curé** Father X; **oui M**~ **le ministre** yes Minister; (homme) man; (formule de respect) sir.

monstre /mɔ̃stʀ/ nm monster.
● adj ① colossal.

monstrueux, -euse /mɔ̃stʀyø, -z/

adj monstrous. **monstruosité** nf monstrosity.

mont /mɔ̃/ nm mountain; le ~ Everest Mount Everest; être toujours par ~s et par vaux be always on the move.

montage /mɔ̃taʒ/ nm (assemblage) assembly; (au cinéma) editing.

montagne /mɔ̃taɲ/ nf mountain; (région) mountains; ~s russes roller-coaster. **montagneux, -euse** adj mountainous.

montant, ~e /mɔ̃tɑ̃, -t/ adj rising; (col) high; (chemin) uphill. ● nm amount; (pièce de bois) upright.

mont-de-piété (pl **monts-de-piété**) /mɔ̃dpjete/ nm pawnshop.

monte-charge /mɔ̃tʃaʁʒ/ nm inv goods lift.

montée /mɔ̃te/ nf ascent, rise; (de prix) rise; (de coûts, risques) increase; (côte) hill.

monter /mɔ̃te/ **1** vt (aux. avoir) take up; (à l'étage) take upstairs; (escalier, rue, pente) go up; (assembler) assemble; (tente, échafaudage) put up; (col, manche) set in; (organiser) (pièce) stage; (société) set up; (attaque, garde) mount. ● vi (aux. être) go ou come up; (à l'étage) go ou come upstairs; (avion) climb; (route) go uphill, climb; (augmenter) rise; (marée) come up; ~ **sur** (trottoir, toit) get up on; (cheval, bicyclette) get on; ~ **à l'échelle/ l'arbre** climb the ladder/tree; ~ **dans** (voiture) get in; (train, bus, avion) get on; ~ **à bord** climb on board; ~ (**à cheval**) ride; ~ **à bicyclette/moto** ride a bike/ motorbike.

monteur, -euse /mɔ̃tœʁ, -øz/ nm, f (Tech) fitter; (au cinéma) editor.

montre /mɔ̃tʁ/ nf watch; faire ~ de show.

montrer /mɔ̃tʁe/ **1** vt show (à to); ~ **du doigt** point to. □ se ~ vpr show oneself; (être) be; (s'avérer) prove to be.

monture /mɔ̃tyʁ/ nf (cheval) mount; (de lunettes) frames (+ pl); (de bijou) setting.

monument /mɔnymɑ̃/ nm monument; ~ **aux morts** war memorial. **monumental** (mpl -**aux**) adj monumental.

moquer (se) /(sə)mɔke/ **1** vpr se ~ **de** make fun of; **je m'en moque** **1** I couldn't care less. **moquerie** nf mockery. **moqueur, -euse** adj mocking.

moquette /mɔkɛt/ nf fitted carpet; (US) wall-to-wall carpeting.

moral, ~e /mɔʁal/ (mpl -**aux**, -o/ adj moral. ● nm (pl -**aux**) morale; **ne pas avoir le** ~ feel down; **avoir le** ~ be in good spirits; **ça m'a remonté le** ~ it gave me a boost.

morale /mɔʁal/ nf moral code; (mœurs) morals; (de fable) moral; **faire la** ~ **à** lecture. **moralité** nf (de personne) morals (+ pl); (d'action, œuvre) morality; (de fable) moral.

moralisateur, -trice /mɔʁalizatœʁ, -tʁis/ adj moralizing.

morbide /mɔʁbid/ adj morbid.

morceau (pl ~**x**) /mɔʁso/ nm piece, bit; (de sucre) lump; (de viande) cut; (passage) passage; **manger un** ~ **1** have a bite to eat; **mettre en** ~**x** smash ou tear to bits.

morceler /mɔʁsəle/ **6** vt divide up.

mordant, ~e /mɔʁdɑ̃, -t/ adj scathing; (froid) biting. ● nm vigour, energy.

mordiller /mɔʁdije/ **1** vt nibble at.

mordre | mouiller

mordre /mɔʀdʀ/ **3** vi bite (**dans** into); ~ **sur** (ligne) go over; (territoire) encroach on; ~ **à l'hameçon** bite. ● vt bite.

mordu, ~e /mɔʀdy/ **1** nm, f fan. ● adj smitten; ~ **de** crazy about.

morfondre (se) /(sə)mɔʀfɔ̃dʀ/ **3** vpr wait anxiously; (languir) mope.

morgue /mɔʀg/ nf morgue, mortuary; (attitude) arrogance.

moribond, ~e /mɔʀibɔ̃, -d/ adj dying.

morne /mɔʀn/ adj dull.

morphine /mɔʀfin/ nf morphine.

mors /mɔʀ/ nm (de cheval) bit.

morse /mɔʀs/ nm (animal) walrus; (code) Morse code.

morsure /mɔʀsyʀ/ nf bite.

mort[1] /mɔʀ/ nf death.

mort[2]**, ~e** /mɔʀ, -t/ adj dead; ~ **de fatigue** dead tired. ● nm, f dead man, dead woman; **les ~s** the dead.

mortalité /mɔʀtalite/ nf mortality; (taux de) ~ death rate.

mortel, ~le /mɔʀtɛl/ adj mortal; (accident) fatal; (poison, silence) deadly. ● nm, f mortal. **mortellement** adv mortally.

mortifié, ~e /mɔʀtifje/ adj mortified.

mort-né, ~e /mɔʀne/ adj stillborn.

mortuaire /mɔʀtɥɛʀ/ adj (cérémonie) funeral.

morue /mɔʀy/ nf cod.

mosaïque /mozaik/ nf mosaic.

mosquée /mɔske/ nf mosque.

mot /mo/ nm word; (lettre, message) note; ~ **d'ordre** watchword; ~ **de passe** password; ~**s croisés** crossword (puzzle).

motard /mɔtaʀ/ nm biker; (policier) police motorcyclist.

moteur, -trice /mɔtœʀ, -tʀis/ adj (Méd) motor; (force) driving; **à 4 roues motrices** 4-wheel drive. ● nm engine, motor; **barque à ~** motor launch; ~ **de recherche** (Internet) search engine.

motif /mɔtif/ nm (raisons) grounds (+ pl); (cause) reason; (Jur) motive; (dessin) pattern.

motion /mosjɔ̃/ nf motion.

motivation /mɔtivasjɔ̃/ nf motivation. **motiver** **1** vt motivate.

moto /mɔto/ nf motor cycle. **motocycliste** nmf motorcyclist.

motorisé, ~e /mɔtɔʀize/ adj motorized.

motrice /mɔtʀis/ ➡**MOTEUR**.

motte /mɔt/ nf lump; (de beurre) slab; (de terre) clod; ~ **de gazon** turf.

mou /mu/ (before vowel or mute h), **molle** /mu, mɔl/ adj soft; (ventre) flabby; (sans conviction) feeble; (apathique) sluggish, listless. ● nm slack; **avoir du ~** be slack.

mouchard /muʃaʀ/ nm, f informer; (Scol) sneak.

mouche /muʃ/ nf fly; (de cible) bull's eye.

moucher (se) /(sə)muʃe/ **1** vpr blow one's nose.

moucheron /muʃʀɔ̃/ nm midge.

moucheté, ~e /muʃte/ adj speckled.

mouchoir /muʃwaʀ/ nm handkerchief, hanky; ~ **en papier** tissue.

moue /mu/ nf pout; **faire la ~** pout.

mouette /mwɛt/ nf (sea)gull.

moufle /mufl/ nf (gant) mitten.

mouillé, ~e /muje/ adj wet.

mouiller /muje/ **1** vt wet, make wet; ~ **l'ancre** drop anchor.

m

□ se ~ vpr get (oneself) wet.

moulage /mulaʒ/ nm cast.

moule /mul/ f (coquillage) mussel. ● nm mould; ~ à gâteau cake tin; ~ à tarte flan dish. **mouler 1** vt mould; (statue) cast.

moulin /mulɛ̃/ nm mill; ~ à café coffee grinder; ~ à poivre pepper mill; ~ à vent windmill.

moulinet /mulinɛ/ nm (de canne à pêche) reel; **faire des ~s avec qch** twirl sth around.

moulinette® /mulinɛt/ nf vegetable mill.

moulu, ~e /muly/ adj ground; (fatigué 1) worn out.

moulure /mulyr/ nf moulding.

mourant, ~e /murɑ̃, -t/ adj dying. ● nm, f dying person.

mourir /murir/ 43 vi (aux. être) die; ~ **d'envie de** be dying to; ~ **de faim** be starving; ~ **d'ennui** be dead bored.

mousquetaire /muskətɛr/ nm musketeer.

mousse /mus/ nf moss; (écume) froth, foam; (de savon) lather; (dessert) mousse; ~ à raser shaving foam. ● nm ship's boy.

mousseline /muslin/ nf muslin; (de soie) chiffon.

mousser /muse/ 1 vi froth, foam; (savon) lather. □ se ~ en vi froth, foam; (savon) lather.

mousseux, -euse /musø, -z/ adj frothy. ● nm sparkling wine.

mousson /musɔ̃/ nf monsoon.

moustache /mustaʃ/ nf moustache; ~s (d'animal) whiskers.

moustique /mustik/ nm mosquito.

moutarde /mutard/ nf mustard.

mouton /mutɔ̃/ nm sheep; (peau) sheepskin; (viande) mutton.

mouvant, ~e /muvɑ̃, -t/ adj chan-

ging; (terrain) shifting, unstable.

mouvement /muvmɑ̃/ nm movement; (agitation) bustle; (en gymnastique) exercise; (impulsion) impulse; (tendance) tend, tendency; **en ~** in motion.

mouvementé, ~e /muvmɑ̃te/ adj eventful.

moyen, ~ne /mwajɛ̃, -ɛn/ adj average; (médiocre) poor; **de taille moyenne** medium-sized. ● nm means, way; **~s** means; (dons) ability; **au ~ de** by means of; **il n'y a pas ~ de** it is not possible to. **Moyen Âge** nm Middle Ages (+ pl).

moyennant /mwajɛnɑ̃/ prép (pour) for; (grâce à) with.

moyenne /mwajɛn/ nf average; (Scol) pass-mark; **en ~** on average; **~ d'âge** average age. **moyennement** adv moderately.

Moyen-Orient /mwajɛnɔrjɑ̃/ nm Middle East.

moyeu (pl ~x) /mwajø/ nm hub.

mû, mue /my/ adj driven (**par** by).

mucoviscidose /mykɔvisidoz/ nf cystic fibrosis.

mue /my/ nf moulting; (de voix) breaking of the voice.

muer /mɥe/ 1 vi moult; (voix) break. □ se ~ en vi change into.

muet, ~te /mɥɛ, -t/ adj (Méd) dumb; (fig) speechless (**de** with); (silencieux) silent. ● nm, f mute.

mufle /myfl/ nm nose, muzzle; (personne 1) boor, lout.

mugir /myʒir/ 2 vi (vache) moo; (bœuf) bellow; (fig) howl.

muguet /mygɛ/ nm lily of the valley.

mule /myl/ nf (female) mule; (pantoufle) mule.

mulet /mylɛ/ nm (male) mule.

multicolore /myltikɔlɔr/ adj multicoloured.

multimédia /myltimedja/ adj &
nm multimedia.

multinational, ∼e (mpl **-aux**)
/myltinasjɔnal, -o/ adj multinational. **multinationale** nf multinational (company).

multiple /myltipl/ nm multiple.
● adj numerous, many; (naissances)
multiple.

multiplication /myltiplikasjɔ̃/ nf
multiplication.

multiplicité /myltiplisite/ nf
multiplicity.

multiplier /myltiplije/ 45 vt
multiply; (risques) increase. □ **se ∼**
vpr multiply; (accidents) be on the
increase; (difficultés) increase.

multitude /myltityd/ nf multitude, mass.

municipal, ∼e (mpl **-aux**)
/mynisipal, -o/ adj municipal; **conseil ∼** town council. **municipalité**
nf (ville) municipality; (conseil) town
council.

munir /mynir/ 2 vt ∼ **de** provide
with. □ **se ∼ de** vpr (apporter)
bring; (emporter) take.

munitions /mynisjɔ̃/ nfpl ammunition.

mur /myr/ nm wall; ∼ **du son**
sound barrier.

mûr, ∼e /myr/ adj ripe; (personne)
mature.

muraille /myrɑj/ nf (high) wall.

mural, ∼e (mpl **-aux**) /myral, -o/
adj wall; **peinture ∼e** mural.

mûre /myr/ nf blackberry.

mûrir /myrir/ 2 vi ripen; (abcès)
come to a head; (personne, projet)
mature. ● vt (fruit) ripen; (personne)
mature.

murmure /myrmyr/ nm murmur.

muscade /myskad/ nf **noix ∼**
nutmeg.

muscle /myskl/ nm muscle. **mus-**

clé, ∼e adj muscular. **musculaire**
adj muscular.

musculation /myskylasjɔ̃/ nf
bodybuilding.

musculature /myskylatyr/ nf
muscles (+ pl).

museau (pl ∼**x**) /myzo/ nm muzzle; (de porc) snout.

musée /myze/ nm museum; (de
peinture) art gallery.

muselière /myzaljɛr/ nf muzzle.

musette /myzɛt/ nf haversack.

muséum /myzeɔm/ nm natural
history museum.

musical, ∼e (mpl **-aux**) /myzikal,
-o/ adj musical.

musicien, ∼ne /myzisjɛ̃, -ɛn/ adj
musical. ● nm, f musician.

musique /myzik/ nf music; (orchestre) band.

must /myst/ nm 🗓 must.

musulman, ∼e /myzylmɑ̃, -an/
adj & nm, f Muslim.

mutation /mytasjɔ̃/ nf change;
(biologique) mutation; (d'un employé) transfer.

muter /myte/ 1 vt transfer. ● vi
mutate.

mutilation /mytilasjɔ̃/ nf mutilation. **mutiler** 1 vt mutilate. **mu-
tilé, ∼e** nm, f disabled person.

mutin, ∼e /mytɛ̃, -in/ adj mischievous. ● nm mutineer; (prisonnier) rioter.

mutinerie /mytinri/ nf mutiny;
(de prisonniers) riot.

mutisme /mytism/ nm silence.

mutuel, ∼le /mytɥɛl/ adj mutual.
mutuelle nf mutual insurance company. **mutuellement** adv mutually;
(l'un l'autre) each other.

myope /mjɔp/ adj short-sighted.
myopie nf short-sightedness.

myosotis /mjɔzɔtis/ nm

m

forget-me-not.

myrtille /mirtij/ nf bilberry, blueberry.

mystère /mistɛr/ nm mystery.

mystérieux, -ieuse /misterjø, -z/ adj mysterious.

mystification /mistifikasjɔ̃/ nf hoax.

mysticisme /mistisism/ nm mysticism.

mystique /mistik/ adj mystic(al). ● nmf mystic. ● nf mystique.

mythe /mit/ nm myth. **mythique** adj mythical.

mythologie /mitɔlɔʒi/ nf mythology.

. . . .

Nn

. . . .

n' /n/ ➡NE.

nacre /nakr/ nf mother-of-pearl.

nage /naʒ/ nf swimming; (manière) stroke; **traverser à la** ~ swim across; **en** ~ sweating.

nageoire /naʒwar/ nf fin; (de mammifère) flipper.

nager /naʒe/ vt/i swim. **nageur, -euse** nm, f swimmer.

naguère /nagɛr/ adv (autrefois) formerly.

naïf, -ive /naif, -v/ adj naïve.

nain, ~**e** /nɛ̃, nɛn/ nm, f & adj dwarf.

naissance /nɛsɑ̃s/ nf birth; **donner** ~ **à** give birth to; (fig) give rise to.

naître /nɛtr/ 44 vi be born; (résulter) arise (**de** from); **faire** ~ (susciter) give rise to.

naïveté /naivte/ nf naïvety.

nappe /nap/ nf tablecloth; (de pétrole, gaz) layer; ~ **phréatique** ground water.

napperon /naprɔ̃/ nm (cloth) tablemat.

narco-dollars /narkodɔlar/ nmpl drug money.

narcotique /narkɔtik/ adj & nm narcotic. **narco(-)trafiquant,** ~**e** (pl ~**s**) nm, f drug trafficker.

narguer /narge/ 1 vt taunt; (autorité) flout.

narine /narin/ nf nostril.

nasal, ~**e** (mpl -**aux**) /nazal, -o/ adj nasal.

naseau (pl ~**x**) /nazo/ nm nostril.

natal, ~**e** (mpl ~**s**) /natal/ adj native.

natalité /natalite/ nf birth rate.

natation /natasjɔ̃/ nf swimming.

natif, -ive /natif, -v/ adj native.

nation /nasjɔ̃/ nf nation.

national, ~**e** (mpl -**aux**) /nasjɔnal, -o/ adj national. **nationale** nf A road; (US) highway. **nationaliser** 1 vt nationalize.

nationalité /nasjɔnalite/ nf nationality.

natte /nat/ nf (de cheveux) plait; (US) braid; (tapis de paille) mat.

nature /natyr/ nf nature; ~ **morte** still life; **de** ~ **à** likely to; **payer en** ~ pay in kind. ● adj inv plain; (yaourt) natural; (thé) black.

naturel, ~**le** /natyrɛl/ adj natural. ● nm nature; (simplicité) naturalness; (Culin) **au** ~ plain; (thon) in brine. **naturellement** adv naturally; (bien sûr) of course.

naufrage /nofraʒ/ nm shipwreck; **faire** ~ be shipwrecked; (bateau) be wrecked.

nauséabond, ~**e** /nozeabɔ̃, -d/ adj nauseating.

nausée /noze/ *nf* nausea.

nautique /notik/ *adj* nautical; **sports** ~s water sports.

naval, ~e (*mpl* ~s) /naval/ *adj* naval; **chantier** ~ shipyard.

navet /navɛ/ *nm* turnip; (film: péj) flop; (US) turkey.

navette /navɛt/ *nf* shuttle (service); **faire la** ~ shuttle back and forth.

navigateur, **-trice** /navigatœr, -tris/ *nm, f* sailor; (qui guide) navigator; (Internet) browser. **navigation** *nf* navigation; (trafic) shipping; (Internet) browsing.

naviguer /navige/ **1** *vi* sail; (piloter) navigate; (Internet) browse; ~ **dans l'Internet** surf the Internet.

navire /navir/ *nm* ship.

navré, ~e /navre/ *adj* sorry (de to).

---

ne, **n'** /nə, n/

n' before vowel or mute h.

● *adverbe*

····▸ **je n'ai que 10 euros** I've only got 10 euros.

····▸ **tu n'avais qu'à le dire!** you only had to say so!

····▸ **je crains qu'il** ~ **parte** I am afraid he will leave.

> Pour les expressions comme **ne... guère**, **ne... jamais**, **ne... pas**, **ne... plus**, etc. ➡**guère, jamais, pas, plus,** etc.

---

né, ~e /ne/ *adj* born; ~e **Martin** née Martin; (dans composés) **dernier-**~ last-born. ● ➡**NAÎTRE** 44.

néanmoins /neɑ̃mwɛ̃/ *adv* nevertheless.

néant /neɑ̃/ *nm* nothingness; **réduire à** ~ (*effet, efforts*) negate, nullify; (*espoir*) dash; **'revenus:** ~' 'income: nil'.

nécessaire /nesesɛr/ *adj* necessary. ● *nm* (sac) bag; (trousse) kit; **le** ~ l'indispensable the necessities *ou* essentials; **faire le** ~ do what is necessary.

nécessité /nesesite/ *nf* necessity; **de première** ~ vital.

nécessiter /nesesite/ **1** *vt* necessitate.

néerlandais, ~e /neɛrlɑ̃dɛ, -z/ *adj* Dutch. ● *nm* (Ling) Dutch. **N**~, ~e *nm, f* Dutchman, Dutchwoman.

néfaste /nefast/ *adj* harmful (à to).

négatif, **-ive** /negatif, -v/ *adj & nm* negative.

négligé, ~e /neglize/ *adj* (*travail*) careless; (*tenue*) scruffy. ● *nm* (tenue) negligee.

négligent, ~e /neglizɑ̃, -t/ *adj* careless, negligent.

négliger /neglize/ **40** *vt* neglect; (ne pas tenir compte de) ignore, disregard; ~ **de faire** fail to do. □ **se** ~ *vpr* neglect oneself.

négoce /negɔs/ *nm* business, trade. **négociant**, ~e *nm, f* merchant.

négociation /negɔsjasjɔ̃/ *nf* negotiation. **négocier** 45 *vt/i* negotiate.

nègre /negr/ *adj* (*musique, art*) Negro. ● *nm* (écrivain) ghost writer.

neige /nɛʒ/ *nf* snow. **neiger** 40 *vi* snow.

nénuphar /nenyfar/ *nm* waterlily.

nerf /nɛr/ *nm* nerve; (vigueur) stamina; **être sur les** ~s be on edge.

nerveux, **-euse** /nɛrvø, -z/ *adj* nervous; (irritable) nervy; (*centre, cellule*) nerve; (*voiture*) responsive. **nervosité** *nf* nervousness; (irritabilité) touchiness.

net, **~te** /nɛt/ adj (clair, distinct) clear; (propre) clean; (notable marked; (soigné) neat; (prix, poids) net. ● **N~** nm (Ordinat) net. ● adv (s'arrêter) dead; (refuser) flatly; (parler) plainly; (se casser) cleanly; (tuer) outright. **nettement** adv (expliquer) clearly; (augmenter, se détériorer) markedly; (indiscutablement) distinctly, decidedly. **netteté** nf clearness.

netéconomie /nɛtekɔnɔmi/ nf e-economy.

nétiquette /netikɛt/ nf netiquette.

nettoyage /nɛtwajaʒ/ nm cleaning; ~ à sec dry-cleaning; **produit de ~** cleaner; ~ **ethnique** ethnic cleansing.

nettoyer /nɛtwaje/ [31] vt clean.

neuf¹ /nœf/ (/nœv/ before vowels and mute h) adj inv & nm nine.

neuf², **-euve** /nœf, -v/ adj new; tout ~ brand new. ● nm new; re-mettre à ~ brighten up; du ~ a new development; quoi de ~? what's new?

neutre /nøtR/ adj neutral; (Gram) neuter. ● nm (Gram) neuter.

neuve /nœv/ →NEUF².

neuvième /nœvjɛm/ adj & nm, f ninth.

neveu (pl ~x) /nəvø/ nm nephew.

névrose /nevRoz/ nf neurosis. **névrosé**, **~e** /-e/ adj & nm, f neurotic.

nez /ne/ nm nose; ~ à ~ face to face; ~ **retroussé** turned-up nose.

ni /ni/ conj neither, nor; ~ **grand ~ petit** neither big nor small; ~ l'un ~ l'autre ne fument neither (one nor the other) smokes; **sortir sans manteau ~ chapeau** go without a coat or hat; **elle n'a dit ~ oui ~ non** she didn't say either yes or no.

niais, **~e** /njɛ, -z/ adj silly.

niche /niʃ/ nf (de chien) kennel; (cavité) niche.

nicher /niʃe/ **1** vi nest. □ **se ~** vpr nest; (se cacher) hide.

nicotine /nikɔtin/ nf nicotine.

nid /ni/ nm nest; **faire un ~** build a nest. **nid-de-poule** (pl **nids-de-poule**) nm pot-hole.

nièce /njɛs/ nf niece.

nier /nje/ **45** vt deny.

nigaud, **~e** /nigo, -d/ nm, f fool.

nippon, **~e** /nipɔ̃, -ɔn/ adj Japanese. **N~**, **~ne** nm, f Japanese.

niveau (pl ~x) /nivo/ nm level; (compétence) standard; (étage) storey; (US) story; **au ~** up to standard; **mettre à ~** (Ordinat) up-grade; ~ **à bulle** (d'air) spirit level; ~ **de vie** standard of living.

niveler /nivle/ **6** vt level.

noble /nɔbl/ adj noble. ● nm, f nobleman, noblewoman. **noblesse** nf nobility.

noce /nɔs/ nf (fête ⚀) party; (invités) wedding guests; ~s wedding; **faire la ~** ⚀ live it up.

nocif, **-ive** /nɔsif, -v/ adj harmful.

nocturne /nɔktyRn/ adj nocturnal. ● nm (Mus) nocturne. ● nf (Sport) evening fixture; (de magasin) late-night opening.

Noël /nɔɛl/ nm Christmas.

nœud /nø/ nm (Naut) knot; (pour lier) knot; (pour orner) bow; ~s (fig) ties; ~ **coulant** slipknot, noose; ~ **papillon** bow-tie.

noir, **~e** /nwaR/ adj black; (obscur, sombre) dark; (triste) gloomy. ● nm black; (obscurité) dark; **travail au ~** moonlighting. ● nm, f (personne) Black.

noircir /nwaRsiR/ **2** vt blacken; ~ **la situation** paint a black picture of the situation. ● vi (banane) go black; (mur) get dirty; (métal) tarnish. □ **se** ~ vpr (ciel) darken.

noire /nwar/ nf (Mus) crotchet.

noisette /nwazɛt/ nf hazelnut; (de beurre) knob.

noix /nwa/ nf nut; (du noyer) walnut; (de beurre) knob; ~ **de cajou** cashew nut; ~ **de coco** coconut; **à la** ~ 🔢 useless.

nom /nɔ̃/ nm name; (Gram) noun; **au** ~ **de** on behalf of; (Gram) noun; **au** ~ **de** on behalf of; ~ **et prénom** full name; ~ **déposé** registered trademark; ~ **de famille** surname; ~ **de jeune fille** maiden name; ~ **de plume** pen name; ~ **propre** proper noun.

nomade /nɔmad/ adj nomadic; (worker, Internet) mobile. ● nmf nomad.

nombre /nɔ̃bʀ/ nm number; **au** ~ **de** (parmi) among; (l'un de) one of; **en (grand)** ~ in large numbers; **sans** ~ countless.

nombreux, -euse /nɔ̃bʀø, -z/ adj (en grand nombre) many, numerous; (important) large; **de** ~ **enfants** many children; **nous étions très** ~ there were a great many of us.

nombril /nɔ̃bʀil/ nm navel.

nomination /nɔminasjɔ̃/ nf appointment.

nommer /nɔme/ 🔢 vt name; (élire) to appoint; (à un poste) appoint; (à un lieu) post. □ **se** ~ vpr (s'appeler) be called.

non /nɔ̃/ adv no; (pas) not; ~ **(pas) que** not that; **il vient,** ~? he is coming, isn't he?; **moi** ~ **plus** neither am/do/can/etc. I. ● nm inv no.

non- /nɔ̃/ préf non-; ~**-fumeur** non-smoker.

nonante /nɔnɑ̃t/ adj & nm ninety.

non-sens /nɔ̃sɑ̃s/ nm inv absurdity.

nord /nɔʀ/ adj inv (façade, côte)

north; (frontière, zone) northern. ● nm north; **le** ~ **de l'Europe** northern Europe; **vent de** ~ northerly (wind); **aller vers le** ~ go north; **le Nord** the North; **du Nord** northern. **nord-est** nm north-east.

nordique /nɔʀdik/ adj Scandinavian.

nord-ouest /nɔʀwɛst/ nm north-west.

normal, ~**e** (mpl **-aux**) /nɔʀmal, -o/ adj normal. **normale** nf normality; (norme) norm; (moyenne) average.

normand, ~**e** /nɔʀmɑ̃, -d/ adj Norman. **N**~, ~**e** nm, f Norman.

Normandie /nɔʀmɑ̃di/ nf Normandy.

norme /nɔʀm/ nf norm; (de production) standard; ~**s de sécurité** safety standards.

Norvège /nɔʀvɛʒ/ nf Norway.

norvégien, ~**ne** /nɔʀveʒjɛ̃, -ɛn/ adj Norwegian. **N**~, ~**ne** nm, f Norwegian.

nos /no/ ➡**NOTRE**.

nostalgie /nɔstalʒi/ nf nostalgia; **avoir la** ~ **de son pays** be homesick. **nostalgique** adj nostalgic.

notaire /nɔtɛʀ/ nm notary public.

notamment /nɔtamɑ̃/ adv notably.

note /nɔt/ nf (remarque) note; (chiffrée) mark, grade; (facture) bill; (Mus) note; ~ **(de service)** memorandum.

noter /nɔte/ 🔢 vt note, notice; (écrire) note (down); (devoir) mark; (US) grade; **bien/mal noté** (employé) highly/poorly rated.

notice /nɔtis/ nf note; (mode d'emploi) instructions, directions.

notifier /nɔtifje/ 🔢 vt notify (à to).

notion /nɔsjɔ̃/ nf notion; **avoir des**

n

~ **de** have a basic knowledge of.

notoire /nɔtwaʀ/ *adj* well-known; (*criminel*) notorious.

notre (*pl* **nos**) /nɔtʀ, no/ *adj* our.

nôtre /notʀ/ *pron* **le** ou **la** ~, **les** ~**s** ours.

nouer /nwe/ **1** *vt* tie, knot; (*relations*) strike up.

nouille /nuj/ *nf* (Culin) noodle; **des** ~**s** noodles, pasta; (*idiot* **1**) idiot.

nounours /nunuʀs/ *nm* **1** teddy bear.

nourri, ~**e** /nuʀi/ *adj* **être logé** ~ have bed and board; ~ **au sein** breastfed.

nourrice /nuʀis/ *nf* childminder.

nourrir /nuʀiʀ/ **2** *vt* feed; (*espoir, crainte*) harbour; (*projet*) nurture; (*passion*) fuel. ● *vi* be nourishing. □ **se** ~ *vpr* eat; **se** ~ **de** feed on.

nourrissant, ~**e** *adj* nourishing.

nourrisson /nuʀisɔ̃/ *nm* infant.

nourriture /nuʀityʀ/ *nf* food.

nous /nu/ *pron* (*sujet*) we; (*complément*) us; (*indirect*) (to) us; (*réfléchi*) ourselves; (*l'un l'autre*) each other; **la voiture est à** ~ the car is ours. **nous-mêmes** *pron* ourselves.

nouveau (**nouvel** *before vowel or mute h*), **nouvelle** (*mpl* ~**x**) /nuvo, nuvɛl/ *adj* new; **nouvel an** new year; ~**x mariés** newly-weds; ~ **venu, nouvelle venue** newcomer. ● *nm, f* (*élève*) new boy, new girl. ● *nm* **du** ~ (*fait nouveau*) a new development; **de** ~, **à** ~ again. **nouveau-né** (*pl* ~**s**) *nm* newborn baby.

nouveauté /nuvote/ *nf* novelty; (*chose*) new thing; (*livre*) new publication; (*disque*) new release.

nouvelle /nuvɛl/ *nf* (*pièce of*) news; (*récit*) short story; ~**s** news.

Nouvelle-Zélande /nuvɛlzelɑ̃d/ *nf* New Zealand.

novembre /nɔvɑ̃bʀ/ *nm* November.

noyade /nwajad/ *nf* drowning.

noyau (*pl* ~**x**) /nwajo/ *nm* (de fruit) stone; (US) pit; (de cellule) nucleus; (groupe) group; (centre: fig) core.

noyer /nwaje/ **31** *vt* drown; (inonder) flood. □ **se** ~ *vpr* drown; (volontairement) drown oneself; **se** ~ **dans un verre d'eau** make a mountain out of a molehill. ● *nm* walnut-tree.

nu, ~**e** /ny/ *adj* (*corps, personne*) naked; (*mains, mur, fil*) bare; **à l'œil** ~ to the naked eye. ● *nm* nude; **mettre à** ~ expose.

nuage /nyaʒ/ *nm* cloud.

nuance /nɥɑ̃s/ *nf* shade; (de sens) nuance; (différence) difference.

nuancer **10** *vt* (*opinion*) qualify.

nucléaire /nykleɛʀ/ *adj* nuclear. ● *nm* **le** ~ nuclear energy.

nudisme /nydism/ *nm* nudism.

nudité /nydite/ *nf* nudity; (de lieu) bareness.

nuée /nɥe/ *nf* swarm, host.

nues /ny/ *nfpl* **tomber des** ~ be amazed; **porter qn aux** ~ praise sb to the skies.

nuire /nɥiʀ/ **17** *vi* ~ **à** harm.

nuisible /nɥizibl/ *adj* harmful (à to).

nuit /nɥi/ *nf* night; **cette** ~ tonight; (hier) last night; **il fait** ~ it is dark; ~ **blanche** sleepless night; **la** ~, **de** ~ at night; ~ **de noces** wedding night.

nul, ~**le** /nyl/ *adj* (aucun) no; (zéro) nil; (qui ne vaut rien) useless; (non valable) null; (contrat) void; (testament) invalid; **match** ~ draw; ~ **en sciences** no good at science; **nulle part** nowhere; ~ **autre** no one else. ● *pron* no one. **nullement**

adv not at all. **nullité** *nf* uselessness; (personne) nonentity.

numérique /nymerik/ *adj* numerical; (montre, horloge) digital.

numériser /nymerize/ *vt* digitize.

numéro /nymero/ *nm* number; (de journal) issue; (spectacle) act; ~ **de téléphone** telephone number; ~ **vert** freephone number. **numéroter 1** *vt* number.

nuque /nyk/ *nf* nape (of the neck).

nurse /nœrs/ *nf* nanny.

nutritif, -ive /nytritif, -v/ *adj* nutritious; (valeur) nutritional.

. . . .

Oo

. . . .

oasis /ɔazis/ *nf* oasis.

obéir /ɔbeir/ **2** *vt* ~ **à** obey. ● *vi* obey. **obéissance** *nf* obedience. **obéissant,** ~**e** *adj* obedient.

obèse /ɔbɛz/ *adj* obese.

objecter /ɔbʒɛkte/ **1** *vt* object.

objectif, -ive /ɔbʒɛktif, -v/ *adj* objective. ● *nm* objective; (Photo) lens.

objection /ɔbʒɛksjɔ̃/ *nf* objection; **soulever des** ~**s** raise objections.

objet /ɔbʒɛ/ *nm* (chose) object; (sujet) subject; (but) purpose, object; **être** *ou* **faire l'**~ **de** be the subject of; ~ **d'art** objet d'art; ~**s trouvés** lost property; (US) lost and found.

obligation /ɔbligasjɔ̃/ *nf* obligation; (Comm) bond; **être dans l'**~ **de** be under obligation to.

obligatoire /ɔbligatwar/ *adj* compulsory. **obligatoirement** *adv* (par règlement) of necessity; (inévitablement) inevitably.

obligeance /ɔbliʒɑ̃s/ *nf* **avoir l'**~ **de faire** be kind enough to do.

obliger /ɔbliʒe/ **40** *vt* compel, force (**à faire** to do); (aider) oblige; **être obligé de** have to (**de** for).

oblique /ɔblik/ *adj* oblique; **regard** ~ sidelong glance; **en** ~ at an angle.

oblitérer /ɔblitere/ **14** *vt* (timbre) cancel.

obnubilé, ~**e** /ɔbnybile/ *adj* obsessed.

obscène /ɔpsɛn/ *adj* obscene.

obscur, ~**e** /ɔpskyr/ *adj* dark; (confus, humble) obscure; (vague) vague.

obscurcir /ɔpskyrsir/ **2** *vt* make dark; (fig) obscure. □ **s'**~ *vpr* (ciel) darken.

obscurité /ɔpskyrite/ *nf* dark-(ness); (de passage, situation) obscurity.

obsédant, ~**e** /ɔpsedɑ̃, -t/ *adj* (problème) nagging; (musique, souvenir) haunting.

obsédé, ~**e** /ɔpsede/ *nm, f* ~ (sexuel) sex maniac; ~ **du ski/jazz** ski/jazz freak.

obséder /ɔpsede/ **14** *vt* obsess.

obsèques /ɔpsɛk/ *nfpl* funeral.

observateur, -trice /ɔpservatœr, -tris/ *adj* observant. ● *nm, f* observer.

observation /ɔpservasjɔ̃/ *nf* observation; (remarque) remark, comment; (reproche) criticism; (obéissance) observance; **en** ~ under observation.

observer /ɔpserve/ **1** *vt* (regarder) observe; (surveiller) watch, observe; (remarquer) notice, observe; **faire** ~ **qch** point sth out (**à** to).

obsession /ɔpsesjɔ̃/ *nf* obsession.

obstacle /ɔpstakl/ *nm* obstacle; (pour cheval) fence, jump; (pour athlète; hurdle; **faire ~ à** stand in the way of, obstruct.

obstétrique /ɔpstetRik/ nf obstetrics (+ sg).

obstiné, **~e** /ɔpstine/ adj obstinate.

obstiner (s') /(s)ɔpstine/ **1** vpr persist (à in).

obstruction /ɔpstRyksjɔ̃/ nf obstruction; (de conduit) blockage.

obstruer /ɔpstRye/ **1** vt obstruct.

obtenir /ɔptəniR/ **58** vt get, obtain. **obtention** nf obtaining.

obus /ɔby/ nm shell.

occasion /ɔkazjɔ̃/ nf opportunity (**de faire** of doing); (circonstance) occasion; (achat) bargain; (article non neuf) second-hand buy; **à l'~** sometimes; **d'~** second-hand. **occasionnel**, **~le** adj occasional.

occasionner /ɔkazjɔne/ **1** vt cause.

occident /ɔksidɑ̃/ nm (direction) west; **l'O~** the West.

occidental, **~e** (mpl **-aux**) /ɔksidɑ̃tal, -o/ adj western. **O~**, **~e** (mpl **-aux**) nm, f westerner.

occulte /ɔkylt/ adj occult.

occupant, **~e** /ɔkypɑ̃, -t/ nm, f occupant. ● nm (Mil) forces of occupation.

occupation /ɔkypasjɔ̃/ nf occupation.

occupé, **~e** /ɔkype/ adj busy; (place, pays) occupied; (téléphone) engaged, busy; (toilettes) engaged.

occuper /ɔkype/ **1** vt occupy; (poste) hold; (espace, temps) take up. □ **s'~** vpr (s'affairer) keep busy (**à faire** doing); **s'~ de** (personne, problème) take care of; (bureau, firme) be in charge of; (se mêler) **occupe-toi de tes affaires** mind your own business.

occurrence: en l'~ /ɑ̃lɔkyRɑ̃s/

loc in this case.

océan /ɔseɑ̃/ nm ocean.

Océanie /ɔseani/ nf Oceania.

ocre /ɔkR/ adj inv ochre.

octante /ɔktɑ̃t/ adj eighty.

octet /ɔktɛ/ nm byte.

octobre /ɔktɔbR/ nm October.

octogone /ɔktɔgɔn/ nm octagon.

octroyer /ɔktRwaje/ **31** vt grant.

oculaire /ɔkylɛR/ adj témoin **~** eye-witness; **troubles ~s** eye trouble.

oculiste /ɔkylist/ nmf ophthalmologist.

odeur /ɔdœR/ nf smell.

odieux, **-ieuse** /ɔdjø, -z/ adj odious.

odorant, **~e** /ɔdɔRɑ̃, -t/ adj sweet-smelling.

odorat /ɔdɔRa/ nm sense of smell.

œil (pl **yeux**) /œj, jø/ nm eye; **à l'~** **1** for free; **à mes yeux** in my view; **faire de l'~ à** make eyes at; **faire les gros yeux à** glare at; **ouvrir l'~** keep one's eyes open; **~ poché** black eye; **fermer les yeux** shut one's eyes; (fig) turn a blind eye.

œillères /œjɛR/ nfpl blinkers.

œillet /œjɛ/ nm (plante) carnation; (trou) eyelet.

œuf (pl **~s**) /œf, ø/ nm egg; **~ à la coque/dur/sur le plat** boiled/ hard-boiled/fried egg.

œuvre /œvR/ nf (ouvrage, travail) work; **~ d'art** work of art; (**~ de bienfaisance**) charity; **être à l'~** be at work; **mettre en ~** (réforme, moyens) implement; **mise en ~** implementation. ● nm (ensemble spécifié) **l'~ entier de Beethoven** the complete works of Beethoven.

œuvrer /œvRe/ **1** vi work.

offense /ɔfɑ̃s/ nf insult.

offenser /ɔfɑ̃se/ **1** vt offend.

□ **s'~** *vpr* take offence (**de** at).

offensive /ɔfɑ̃siv/ *nf* offensive.

offert, ~e /ɔfɛr, -t/ →**OFFRIR** 21.

office /ɔfis/ *nm* office; (Relig) service; (de cuisine) pantry; **faire ~ de** act as; **d'~** without consultation, automatically; **~ du tourisme** tourist information office.

officiel, ~le /ɔfisjɛl/ *adj* official. ● *nm* official.

officier /ɔfisje/ 45 *vi* (Relig) officiate. ● *nm* officer.

officieux, -ieuse /ɔfisjø, -z/ *adj* unofficial.

offre /ɔfʀ/ *nf* offer; (aux enchères) bid; **l'~ et la demande** supply and demand; **'~s d'emploi'** 'situations vacant'.

offrir /ɔfʀiʀ/ 21 *vt* offer (**de faire** to do); (*cadeau*) give; (*acheter*) buy; **~ à boire à** (chez soi) give a drink to; (au café) buy a drink for. □ **s'~** *vpr* (se proposer) offer oneself (**comme** as); (*solution*) present itself; (s'acheter) treat oneself to.

ogive /ɔʒiv/ *nf* **~ nucléaire** nuclear warhead.

OGM (**organisation génétiquement modifié**) genetically modified organism.

oie /wa/ *nf* goose.

oignon /ɔɲɔ̃/ *nm* (légume) onion; (de fleur) bulb.

oiseau (*pl* ~**x**) /wazo/ *nm* bird.

oisif, -ive /wazif, -v/ *adj* idle.

olive /ɔliv/ *nf* & *adj inv* olive. **olivier** *nm* olive tree.

olympique /ɔlɛ̃pik/ *adj* Olympic.

ombrage /ɔ̃bʀaʒ/ *nm* shade; **prendre ~ de** take offence at. **ombragé, ~e** *adj* shady.

ombre /ɔ̃bʀ/ *nf* (pénombre) shade; (contour) shadow; (soupçon: fig) hint, shadow; **dans l'~** (*agir, rester*) behind the scenes; **faire de l'~ à**

qn be in sb's light.

ombrelle /ɔ̃bʀɛl/ *nf* parasol.

omelette /ɔmlɛt/ *nf* omelette.

omettre /ɔmɛtʀ/ 42 *vt* omit, leave out.

omnibus /ɔmnibys/ *nm* stopping ou local train.

omoplate /ɔmoplat/ *nf* shoulder blade.

on /ɔ̃/ *pron* (tu, vous) you; (nous) we; (ils, elles) they; (les gens) people, they; (quelqu'un) someone; (indéterminé) one, you; **~ dit** people say, they say, it is said; **~ m'a demandé mon avis** I was asked for my opinion.

oncle /ɔ̃kl/ *nm* uncle.

onctueux, -euse /ɔ̃ktɥø, -z/ *adj* smooth.

onde /ɔ̃d/ *nf* wave; **~s courtes/ longues** short/long wave; **sur les ~s** on the air.

on-dit /ɔ̃di/ *nm inv* **les ~** hearsay.

onduler /ɔ̃dyle/ 1 *vi* undulate; (*cheveux*) be wavy.

onéreux, -euse /ɔneʀø, -z/ *adj* costly.

ONG *abrév f* (**organisation non gouvernementale**) NGO, nongovernmental organization.

ongle /ɔ̃gl/ *nm* (finger) nail; **~ de pied** toenail; **se faire les ~s** do one's nails.

ont /ɔ̃/ →**AVOIR** 5.

ONU *abrév f* (**Organisation des Nations unies**) UN.

onze /ɔ̃z/ *adj* & *nm* eleven. **onzième** *adj* & *nmf* eleventh.

OPA *abrév f* (**offre publique d'achat**) takeover bid.

opéra /ɔpeʀa/ *nm* opera; (édifice) opera house. **opéra-comique** (*pl* **opéras-comiques**) *nm* light opera.

opérateur, -trice /ɔpeʀatœʀ,

o

-tris/ *nm, f* operator.

opération /ɔpeʀasjɔ̃/ *nf* operation; (*Comm*) deal; (*calcul*) calculation; ~ escargot slow-moving protest convoy.

opératoire /ɔpeʀatwaʀ/ *adj* (*Méd*) surgical; **bloc** ~ operating suite.

opérer /ɔpeʀe/ 14 *vt* (*personne*) operate on; (*exécuter*) carry out, make; ~ **qn d'une tumeur** operate on sb to remove a tumour; **se faire** ~ have surgery *ou* an operation. ● *vi* (*Méd*) operate; (*faire effet*) work. □ **s'**~ *vpr* (*se produire*) occur.

opiniâtre /ɔpinjɑtʀ/ *adj* tenacious.

opinion /ɔpinjɔ̃/ *nf* opinion.

opportuniste /ɔpɔʀtynist/ *nmf* opportunist.

opposant, ~e /ɔpozɑ̃, -t/ *nm, f* opponent.

opposé, ~e /ɔpoze/ *adj* (*sens, angle, avis*) opposite; (*factions*) opposing; (*intérêts*) conflicting; **être à** ~ **à** be opposed to. ● *nm* opposite; **à l'**~ **de** (*contrairement à*) contrary to, unlike.

opposer /ɔpoze/ 1 *vt* (*objets*) place opposite each other; (*personnes*) match, oppose; (*contraster*) contrast; (*résistance, argument*) put up. □ **s'**~ *vpr* (*personnes*) confront each other; (*styles*) contrast; **s'**~ **à** oppose.

opposition /ɔpozisjɔ̃/ *nf* opposition; **par** ~ **à** in contrast with; **entrer en** ~ **avec** come into conflict with; **faire** ~ **à un chèque** stop a cheque.

oppressant, ~e /ɔpʀesɑ̃, -t/ *adj* oppressive.

opprimer /ɔpʀime/ 1 *vt* oppress.

opter /ɔpte/ 1 *vi* ~ **pour** opt for.

opticien, ~ne /ɔptisjɛ̃, -ɛn/ *nm, f* optician.

optimisme /ɔptimism/ *nm* optimism.

optimiste /ɔptimist/ *nmf* optimist. ● *adj* optimistic.

option /ɔpsjɔ̃/ *nf* option.

optique /ɔptik/ *adj* (*verre*) optical. ● *nf* (*science*) optics (+ *sg*); (*perspective*) perspective.

or[1] /ɔʀ/ *nm* gold; **d'**~ golden; **en** ~ gold; (*occasion*) golden.

or[2] /ɔʀ/ *conj* now, well; (*indiquant une opposition*) and yet.

orage /ɔʀaʒ/ *nm* (*thunder*)storm.

orageux, -euse *adj* stormy.

oral, ~e (*mpl* -**aux**) /ɔʀal, -o/ *adj* oral. ● *nm* (*pl* -**aux**) oral.

orange /ɔʀɑ̃ʒ/ *adj inv* orange; (*Aut*) (*feu*) amber; (*US*) yellow. ● *nf* orange. **orangeade** *nf* orangeade. **oranger** *nm* orange tree.

orateur, -trice /ɔʀatœʀ, -tʀis/ *nm, f* speaker.

orbite /ɔʀbit/ *nf* orbit; (*d'œil*) socket.

orchestre /ɔʀkɛstʀ/ *nm* orchestra; (*de jazz*) band; (*parterre*) stalls.

ordinaire /ɔʀdinɛʀ/ *adj* ordinary; (*habituel*) usual; (*qualité*) standard; (*médiocre*) very average. ● *nm* **l'**~ the ordinary; (*nourriture*) the standard fare; **d'**~, **à l'**~ usually. **ordinairement** *adv* usually.

ordinateur /ɔʀdinatœʀ/ *nm* computer; ~ **personnel/de bureau** personal/desktop computer; ~ **portable** laptop (computer); ~ **hôte** (*Internet*) host.

ordonnance /ɔʀdɔnɑ̃s/ *nf* (*ordre, décret*) order; (*de médecin*) prescription.

ordonné, ~e /ɔʀdɔne/ *adj* tidy.

ordonner /ɔʀdɔne/ 1 *vt* order (**à qn de** sb to); (*agencer*) arrange; (*Méd*) prescribe; (*prêtre*) ordain.

ordre /ɔʀdʀ/ *nm* order; (*propreté*) tidiness; **aux** ~**s de qn** at sb's disposal; **avoir de l'~** be tidy; **en ~** tidy, in order; **de premier ~** first-rate; **d'~ officiel** of an official nature; **l'~ du jour** (programme) agenda; **mettre de l'~ dans** tidy up; **jusqu'à nouvel ~** until further notice; **un ~ de grandeur** an approximate idea.

ordure /ɔʀdyʀ/ *nf* filth; **~s** (détritus) rubbish; (US) garbage; **~s ménagères** household refuse.

oreille /ɔʀɛj/ *nf* ear.

oreiller /ɔʀeje/ *nm* pillow.

oreillons /ɔʀɛjɔ̃/ *nmpl* mumps.

orfèvre /ɔʀfɛvʀ/ *nm* goldsmith.

organe /ɔʀgan/ *nm* organ.

organigramme /ɔʀganigʀam/ *nm* organization chart; (Ordinat) flowchart.

organique /ɔʀganik/ *adj* organic.

organisateur, -trice /ɔʀganizatœʀ, -tʀis/ *nm, f* organizer.

organisation /ɔʀganizasjɔ̃/ *nf* organization.

organiser /ɔʀganize/ **1** *vt* organize. □ **s'~** *vpr* organize oneself, get organized.

organisme /ɔʀganism/ *nm* body, organism.

orge /ɔʀʒ/ *nf* barley.

orgelet /ɔʀʒəlɛ/ *nm* sty.

orgue /ɔʀg/ *nm* organ; **~ de Barbarie** barrel-organ. **orgues** *nfpl* organ.

orgueil /ɔʀgœj/ *nm* pride. **orgueilleux, -euse** *adj* proud.

orient /ɔʀjɑ̃/ *nm* (direction) east; **l'O~** the Orient.

oriental, ~e (*mpl* **-aux**) /ɔʀjɑ̃tal, -o/ *adj* eastern; (de l'Orient) oriental. **O~, ~e** (*mpl* **-aux**) *nm, f* Asian.

orientation /ɔʀjɑ̃tasjɔ̃/ *nf* direction; (tendance politique) leanings (+ *pl*); (de maison) aspect; (Sport)

orienteering; **~ professionnelle** careers advice; **~ scolaire** curriculum counselling.

orienter /ɔʀjɑ̃te/ **1** *vt* position; (personne) direct. □ **s'~** *vpr* (se repérer) find one's bearings; **s'~ vers** turn towards.

origan /ɔʀigɑ̃/ *nm* oregano.

originaire /ɔʀiʒinɛʀ/ *adj* être ~ **de** be a native of.

original, ~e (*mpl* **-aux**) /ɔʀiʒinal, -o/ *adj* original; (curieux) eccentric. ● *nm* (œuvre) original. ● *nm, f* eccentric. **originalité** *nf* originality; eccentricity.

origine /ɔʀiʒin/ *nf* origin; **à l'~** originally; **d'~** (pièce, pneu) original; **être d'~ noble** come from a noble background.

originel, ~le /ɔʀiʒinɛl/ *adj* original.

orme /ɔʀm/ *nm* elm.

ornement /ɔʀnəmɑ̃/ *nm* ornament.

orner /ɔʀne/ **1** *vt* decorate.

orphelin, ~e /ɔʀfəlɛ̃, -in/ *nm, f* orphan. ● *adj* orphaned. **orphelinat** *nm* orphanage.

orteil /ɔʀtɛj/ *nm* toe.

orthodoxe /ɔʀtɔdɔks/ *adj* orthodox.

orthographe /ɔʀtɔgʀaf/ *nf* spelling.

ortie /ɔʀti/ *nf* nettle.

os /ɔs, o/ *nm inv* bone.

OS *abrév m* ➡**OUVRIER SPÉCIALISÉ**.

osciller /ɔsile/ **1** *vi* sway; (Tech) oscillate; (hésiter) waver; (fluctuer) fluctuate.

osé, ~e /oze/ *adj* daring.

oseille /ozɛj/ *nf* (plante) sorrel.

oser /oze/ **1** *vi* dare.

osier /ozje/ *nm* wicker.

ossature /ɔsatyʀ/ *nf* skeleton,

frame.

ossements /ɔsmã/ *nmpl* bones, remains.

osseux, -euse /ɔsø, -z/ *adj* bony; (Méd) bone.

otage /ɔtaʒ/ *nm* hostage.

OTAN /ɔtã/ *abrév f* (**Organisation du traité de l'Atlantique Nord**) NATO.

otarie /ɔtaʀi/ *nf* eared seal.

ôter /ote/ **1** *vt* remove (**à qn** from sb); (déduire) take away.

otite /ɔtit/ *nf* ear infection.

ou /u/ *conj* or; ~ **bien** or else; ~ (**bien**)... ~ (**bien**)... either... or...; **vous** ~ **moi** either you or me.

où /u/ *pron* where; (dans lequel) in which; (sur lequel) on which; (auquel) at which; **d'**~ from which; (pour cette raison) hence; **par** ~ through which; **qu'il soit** wherever he may be; **juste au moment** ~ just as; **le jour** ~ the day when. ● *adv* where; **d'**~? where from?

ouate /wat/ *nf* cotton wool; (US) absorbent cotton.

oubli /ubli/ *nm* forgetfulness; (trou de mémoire) lapse of memory; (négligence) oversight; **tomber dans l'**~ sink into oblivion.

oublier /ublije/ **45** *vt* forget; (omettre) leave out, forget. □ **s'**~ *vpr* (chose) be forgotten.

ouest /wɛst/ *adj inv* (façade, côte) west; (frontière, zone) western. ● *nm* west; **l'**~ **de l'Europe** western Europe; **vent d'**~ westerly (wind); **aller vers l'**~ go west; **l'O**~ the West; **de l'O**~ western.

oui /wi/ *adv & nm inv* yes.

ouï-dire: par ~ /parwidir/ *loc* by hearsay.

ouïe /wi/ *nf* hearing; (de poisson) gill.

ouragan /uragã/ *nm* hurricane.

ourlet /urlɛ/ *nm* hem.

ours /urs/ *nm* bear; ~ **blanc** polar bear; ~ **en peluche** teddy bear.

outil /uti/ *nm* tool. **outillage** /utijaʒ/ *nm* tools (+ *pl*). **outiller** **1** *vt* equip.

outrage /utraʒ/ *nm* (grave) insult.

outrance /utrãs/ *nf* **à** ~ excessively. **outrancier, -ière** *adj* extreme.

outre /utr/ *prép* besides. ● *adv* passer ~ pay no heed; ~ **mesure** unduly; **en** ~ in addition. **outre-mer** *adv* overseas.

outrepasser /utrapase/ **1** *vt* exceed.

outrer /utre/ **1** *vt* exaggerate; (indigner) incense.

ouvert, ~e /uvɛr, -t/ *adj* open; (gaz, radio) on. ● **→OUVRIR** **21**.

ouverture /uvertyr/ *nf* opening; (Mus) overture; (Photo) aperture; ~**s** (offres) overtures; ~ **d'esprit** open-mindedness.

ouvrable /uvrabl/ *adj jour* ~ working day; **aux heures** ~**s** during business hours.

ouvrage /uvraʒ/ *nm* (travail, livre) work; (couture) (piece of) needlework.

ouvre-boîtes /uvrəbwat/ *nm inv* tin-opener.

ouvre-bouteilles /uvrəbutɛj/ *nm inv* bottle-opener.

ouvreur, -euse /uvrœr, -øz/ *nm, f* usherette.

ouvrier, -ière /uvrije, -jɛr/ *nm, f* worker; ~ **qualifié/spécialisé** skilled/unskilled worker. ● *adj* working-class; (conflit) industrial; **syndicat** ~ trade union.

ouvrir /uvrir/ **21** *vt* open (up); (gaz, robinet) turn on. ● *vi* open (up). □ **s'**~ *vpr* open (up); **s'**~ **à qn** open one's heart to sb.

ovaire /ɔvɛr/ *nm* ovary.

ovale /ɔval/ *adj & nm* oval.

ovni /ɔvni/ *abrév m* (**objet volant non-identifié**) UFO.

ovule /ɔvyl/ *nm* (à féconder) ovum; (gynécologie) pessary.

oxygène /ɔksiʒɛn/ *nm* oxygen.

oxygéner (s') /(s)ɔksiʒene/ **14** *vpr* get some fresh air.

ozone /ozon/ *nf* ozone; **la couche d'~** the ozone layer.

Pp

pacifique /pasifik/ *adj* peaceful; (*personne*) peaceable; (Géog) Pacific. **P~** *nm* **le P~** the Pacific.

pacotille /pakɔtij/ *nf* junk, rubbish.

PACS *abrév nm* (**pacte de solidarité**) contract of civil union.

pacser (se) /səpakse/ **1** *vpr* sign a contract of civil union (PACS).

pagaie /pagɛ/ *nf* paddle.

pagaille /pagaj/ *nf* **1** mess, shambles (*+ sg*).

page /paʒ/ *nf* page; **mise en ~** layout; **tourner la ~** turn over a new leaf; **être à la ~** be up to date; **~ d'accueil** (Internet) home page.

paie /pɛ/ *nf* pay.

paiement /pɛmã/ *nm* payment.

païen, ~ne /pajɛ̃, -ɛn/ *adj & nm, f* pagan.

paillasson /pajasɔ̃/ *nm* doormat.

paille /paj/ *nf* straw. ● *adj* (*cheveux*) straw-coloured.

paillette /pajɛt/ *nf* (sur robe) sequin; (de savon) flake.

pain /pɛ̃/ *nm* bread; (miche) loaf (of bread); (de savon, cire) bar; **~ d'é-**

pices gingerbread; **~ grillé** toast.

pair, ~e /pɛʀ/ *adj* (nombre) even. ● *nm* (personne) peer; **aller de ~** go together (**avec** with); **au ~** (*jeune fille*) au pair. **paire** *nf* pair.

paisible /pezibl/ *adj* peaceful.

paître /pɛtʀ/ **44** *vi* graze.

paix /pɛ/ *nf* peace; **fiche-moi la ~!** 🗊 leave me alone!

Pakistan /pakistã/ *nm* Pakistan.

palace /palas/ *nm* luxury hotel.

palais /palɛ/ *nm* palace; (Anat) palate; **~ de Justice** law courts; **~ des sports** sports stadium.

pâle /pɑl/ *adj* pale.

Palestine /palɛstin/ *nf* Palestine.

palier /palje/ *nm* (d'escalier) landing; (étape) stage.

pâlir /pɑliʀ/ **2** *vt/i* (turn) pale.

palissade /palisad/ *nf* fence.

pallier /palje/ **45** *vt* compensate for.

palmarès /palmaʀɛs/ *nm* list of prize-winners.

palme /palm/ *nf* palm leaf; (de nageur) flipper. **palmé, ~e** *adj* (*patte*) webbed.

palmier /palmje/ *nm* palm (tree).

palper /palpe/ **1** *vt* feel.

palpiter /palpite/ **1** *vi* (battre) pound; (frémir) quiver.

paludisme /palydism/ *nm* malaria.

pamplemousse /pɑ̃pləmus/ *nm* grapefruit.

panaché, ~e /panaʃe/ *adj* (bariolé, mélangé) motley; **glace ~e** mixed-flavour ice cream. ● *nm* shandy.

pancarte /pɑ̃kaʀt/ *nf* sign; (de manifestant) placard.

pané, ~e /pane/ *adj* breaded.

panier /panje/ *nm* basket; (de basket-ball) basket; **mettre au** 🗊

throw out; **~ à salade** salad shaker; (fourgon 🔢) police van.

panique /panik/ *nf* panic. **paniquer** 🔢 *vi* panic.

panne /pan/ *nf* breakdown; **être en ~** have broken down; **être en ~ sèche** have run out of petrol; **~ d'électricité** *ou* **de courant** power failure.

panneau (*pl* **~x**) /pano/ *nm* sign; (publicitaire) hoarding; (de porte) panel; (**~ d'affichage**) notice board; (**~ de signalisation**) road sign.

panoplie /panɔpli/ *nf* (jouet) outfit; (gamme) range.

pansement /pɑ̃smɑ̃/ *nm* dressing; **~ adhésif** plaster. **panser** 🔢 *vt* (*plaie*) dress; (*personne*) dress the wound(s) of; (*cheval*) groom.

pantalon /pɑ̃talɔ̃/ *nm* trousers (+ *pl*).

panthère /pɑ̃tɛʀ/ *nf* panther.

pantin /pɑ̃tɛ̃/ *nm* puppet.

pantomime /pɑ̃tɔmim/ *nf* mime; (spectacle) mime show.

pantoufle /pɑ̃tufl/ *nf* slipper.

paon /pɑ̃/ *nm* peacock.

papa /papa/ *nm* dad(dy).

pape /pap/ *nm* pope.

paperasse /papʀas/ *nf* (péj) bumf.

papeterie /papetʀi/ *nf* (magasin) stationer's shop.

papier /papje/ *nm* paper; (formulaire) form; **~s (d'identité)** (identity) papers; **~ absorbant** kitchen paper; **~ aluminium** tin foil; **~ buvard** blotting paper; **~ cadeau** wrapping paper; **~ calque** tracing paper; **~ carbone** carbon paper; **~ collant** adhesive tape; **~ hygiénique** toilet paper; **~ journal** newspaper; **~ à lettres** writing paper; **~ mâché** papier mâché; **~ peint** wallpaper; **~ de verre** sandpaper.

papillon /papijɔ̃/ *nm* butterfly; (contravention 🔢) parking-ticket; **~ de nuit** moth.

papoter /papote/ 🔢 *vi* 🔢 chatter.

paquebot /pakbo/ *nm* liner.

pâquerette /pɑkʀɛt/ *nf* daisy.

Pâques /pɑk/ *nfpl* & *nm* Easter.

paquet /pakɛ/ *nm* packet; (de cartes) pack; (colis) parcel; **un ~ de** (beaucoup 🔢) a mass of.

par /paʀ/ *prép* by; (à travers) through; (motif) out of, from; (provenance) from; **commencer/finir ~ qch** begin/end with sth; **commencer/finir ~ faire** begin by/ end up by doing; **~ an/mois** a *ou* per year/month; **~ jour** a day; **~ personne** each, per person; **~ avion** (lettre) (by) airmail; **~-ci, ~-là** here and there; **~ contre** on the other hand; **~ ici/là** this/ that way.

parachute /paʀaʃyt/ *nm* parachute. **parachutiste** *nmf* parachutist; (Mil) paratrooper.

parader /paʀade/ 🔢 *vi* show off.

paradis /paʀadi/ *nm* (Relig) heaven; (lieu idéal) paradise; **~ fiscal** tax haven.

paradoxal, ~e (*mpl* **-aux**) /paʀadɔksal, -o/ *adj* paradoxical.

paraffine /paʀafin/ *nf* paraffin wax.

parages /paʀaʒ/ *nmpl* **dans les ~** around.

paragraphe /paʀagʀaf/ *nm* paragraph.

paraître /paʀɛtʀ/ 🔢 *vi* (se montrer) appear; (sembler) seem, appear; (ouvrage) be published, come out; **faire ~** (ouvrage) bring out; **il paraît qu'ils...** apparently they...; **oui, il paraît** so I hear.

parallèle /paʀalɛl/ *adj* parallel; (illégal) unofficial. ● *nm* parallel; **faire**

le ~ make a connection. ● *nf* parallel (line).

paralyser /paʀalize/ **1** *vt* paralyse. **paralysie** *nf* paralysis.

paramètre /paʀamɛtʀ/ *nm* parameter.

parapente /paʀapɑ̃t/ *nm* paraglider; (activité) paragliding.

parapharmacie /paʀafaʀmasi/ *nf* toiletries and vitamins (*pl.*).

parapher /paʀafe/ **1** *vi* initial; (signer) sign.

parapluie /paʀaplɥi/ *nm* umbrella.

parasite /paʀazit/ *nm* parasite; ~s (radio) interference (+ *sg*).

parasol /paʀasɔl/ *nm* sunshade.

paratonnerre /paʀatɔnɛʀ/ *nm* lightning conductor *ou* rod.

paravent /paʀavɑ̃/ *nm* screen.

parc /paʀk/ *nm* park; (de bétail) pen; (de bébé) play-pen; (entrepôt) depot; ~ **de loisirs** theme park; ~ **relais** park and ride; ~ **de stationnement** car park.

parce que /paʀsk(ə)/ *conj* because.

parchemin /paʀʃəmɛ̃/ *nm* parchment.

parcmètre /paʀkmɛtʀ/ *nm* parking meter.

parcourir /paʀkuʀiʀ/ **20** *vt* travel *ou* go through; (distance) travel; (des yeux) glance at *ou* over.

parcours /paʀkuʀ/ *nm* route; (voyage) journey.

par-delà /paʀdəla/ *prép* beyond.

par-derrière /paʀdɛʀjɛʀ/ *adv* (attaquer) from behind; (critiquer) behind sb's back.

par-dessous /paʀdəsu/ *prép & adv* under (neath).

pardessus /paʀdəsy/ *nm* overcoat.

par-dessus /paʀdəsy/ *prép & adv*

over; ~ **bord** overboard; ~ **le marché** 1 into the bargain; ~ **tout** above all.

par-devant /paʀdəvɑ̃/ *adv* (passer) by the front.

pardon /paʀdɔ̃/ *nm* forgiveness; (**je vous demande**) ~! (I am) sorry!; (pour demander qch) excuse me.

pardonner /paʀdɔne/ **1** *vt* forgive; ~ **qch à qn** forgive sb for sth.

pare-brise /paʀbʀiz/ *nm inv* windscreen.

pare-chocs /paʀʃɔk/ *nm inv* bumper.

pareil, ~**le** /paʀɛj/ *adj* similar (à to); (tel) such (a); **c'est** ~ it's the same; **ce n'est pas** ~ it's not the same thing. ● *nm, f* equal. ● *adv* 1 the same.

parent, ~**e** /paʀɑ̃, -t/ *adj* related (de to). ● *nm, f* relative, relation; ~**s** (père et mère) parents; ~ **isolé** single parent; **réunion de** ~**s d'élèves** parents' evening.

parenté /paʀɑ̃te/ *nf* relationship.

parenthèse /paʀɑ̃tɛz/ *nf* bracket, parenthesis; (fig) digression.

parer /paʀe/ **1** *vt* (esquiver) parry; (orner) adorn. ● *vi* ~ **à** deal with; ~ **au plus pressé** tackle the most urgent things first.

paresse /paʀɛs/ *nf* laziness.

paresseux, -**euse** /paʀesø, -z/ *adj* lazy. ● *nm, f* lazy person.

parfait, ~**e** /paʀfɛ, -t/ *adj* perfect. **parfaitement** *adv* perfectly; (bien sûr) absolutely.

parfois /paʀfwa/ *adv* sometimes.

parfum /paʀfœ̃/ *nm* (senteur) scent; (substance) perfume, scent; (goût) flavour. **parfumé**, ~**e** *adj* fragrant; (savon) scented; (thé) flavoured.

parfumer /paʀfyme/ **1** *vt* (embaumer) scent; (gâteau) flavour.

□ **se** ~ vpr put on one's perfume.
parfumerie nf (produits) perfumes;
(boutique) perfume shop.

pari /paʀi/ nm bet.

Paris /paʀi/ npr Paris.

parisien, ~ne /paʀizjɛ̃, -ɛn/ adj
Parisian; (banlieue) Paris. **P~, ~ne**
nm, f Parisian.

parking /paʀkiŋ/ nm car park.

parlement /paʀləmɑ̃/ nm parliament.

parlementaire /paʀləmɑ̃tɛʀ/ adj
parliamentary. ● nmf Member of
Parliament.

parlementer /paʀləmɑ̃te/ **1** vi
negotiate.

parler /paʀle/ **1** vi talk (à to); ~
de talk about; **tu parles d'un avantage!** call that a benefit!; **de quoi
ça parle?** what is it about? ● vt
(langue) speak; (politique, affaires)
talk. □ **se** ~ vpr (personnes) talk (to
each other); (langue) be spoken.
● nm speech; (dialecte) dialect.

parmi /paʀmi/ prép among(st).

paroi /paʀwa/ nf wall; ~ **rocheuse**
rock face.

paroisse /paʀwas/ nf parish.

parole /paʀɔl/ nf (mot, promesse)
word; (langage) speech; **demander
la** ~ ask to speak; **prendre la** ~
(begin) to speak; **tenir** ~ keep
one's word; **croire qn sur** ~ take
sb's word for it.

parquet /paʀkɛ/ nm (parquet)
floor; **lame de** ~ floorboard; **le** ~
(Jur) prosecution.

parrain /paʀɛ̃/ nm godfather; (fig)
sponsor.

parsemer /paʀsəme/ **6** vt strew
(**de** with).

part /paʀ/ nf share, part; **à** ~ (de
côté) aside; (séparément) separate;
(excepté) apart from; **d'une** ~ on
the one hand; **d'autre** ~ on the

other hand; (de plus) moreover; **de
la** ~ **de** from; **de toutes** ~s from
all sides; **de** ~ **et d'autre** on both
sides; **faire** ~ **à qn** inform sb (**de**
of); **faire la** ~ **des choses** make al-
lowances; **prendre** ~ **à** take part
in; (joie, douleur) share; **pour ma** ~
as for me.

partage /paʀtaʒ/ nm (division) divi-
ding; (répartition) sharing out; **recevoir qch en** ~ be left in
a will.

partager /paʀtaʒe/ **40** vt divide;
(distribuer) share out; (avoir en
commun) share. □ **se** ~ **qch** vpr
share sth.

partenaire /paʀtənɛʀ/ nmf
partner.

parterre /paʀtɛʀ/ nm flower bed;
(Théât) stalls.

parti /paʀti/ nm (Pol) party; (décision) decision; (en mariage) match;
~ **pris** bias; **prendre** ~ get involved; **prendre** ~ **pour qn** side
with sb; **j'en ai pris mon** ~ I've
come to terms with that.

partial, ~e (mpl **-iaux**) /paʀsjal,
-jo/ adj biased.

participe /paʀtisip/ nm (Gram)
participle.

participant, ~e /paʀtisipɑ̃, -t/
nm, f participant (**à** in).

participation /paʀtisipasjɔ̃/ nf
participation; (financière) contribution; (d'un artiste) appearance.

participer /paʀtisipe/ **1** vi **à**
take part in, participate in; (profits,
frais) share.

particule /paʀtikyl/ nf particle.

particulier, -ière /paʀtikylje,
-jɛʀ/ adj (spécifique) particular; (bizarre) unusual; (privé) private; **rien
de** ~ nothing special. ● nm private
individual; **en** ~ in particular, particularly. **particulièrement** adv

particularly.

partie /paʀti/ *nf* part; (cartes, Sport) game; (Jur) party; **une ~ de pêche** a fishing trip; **en ~** partly, in part; **en grande ~** largely; **faire ~ de** be part of; (adhérer à) be a member of; **faire ~ intégrante de** be an integral part of.

partiel, ~le /paʀsjɛl/ *adj* partial. ● *nm* (Univ) exam based on a module.

partir /paʀtiʀ/ 46 *vi* (aux être) go; (quitter un lieu) leave, go; (tache) come out; (bouton) come off; (coup de feu) go off; (commencer) start; **~ pour le Brésil** leave for Brazil; **~ du principe que** work on the assumption that; **à ~de** from; **à ~ de maintenant** from now on.

partisan, ~e /paʀtizɑ̃, -an/ *nm, f* supporter. ● *nm* (Mil) partisan; **être ~ de** be in favour of.

partition /paʀtisjɔ̃/ *nf* (Mus) score.

partout /paʀtu/ *adv* everywhere; **~ où** wherever.

paru /paʀy/ ➡PARAÎTRE 18.

parure /paʀyʀ/ *nf* finery; (bijoux) set of jewels; (de draps) set.

parution /paʀysjɔ̃/ *nf* publication.

parvenir /paʀvəniʀ/ 58 *vi* (aux être) **~ à** reach; **~ à faire** manage to do; **faire ~** send.

parvenu, ~e /paʀvəny/ *nm, f* upstart.

pas¹ /pa/

> Pour les expressions comme **pas encore, pas mal,** etc. ➡**encore, mal** etc.

● *adverbe*
····▸ not; **ne ~** not; **je ne sais ~** I don't know; **je ne pense ~** I

don't think so; **il a aimé, moi ~** he liked it, I didn't; **~ cher/poli** cheap/impolite.

····▸ **~ du tout** not at all; **~ de chance!** tough luck!

····▸ **on a bien ri, ~ vrai?** 🆃 we had a good laugh, didn't we?

! In spoken colloquial French **ne... pas** is often shortened to **pas.** You will hear **j'ai pas compris** instead of **je n'ai pas compris** (*I didn't understand*). NB This is not correct written French.

pas² /pa/ *nm* step; (bruit) footstep; (trace) footprint; (vitesse) pace; **à deux ~ (de)** a step away (from); **marcher au ~** march; **rouler au ~** move very slowly; **à ~ de loup** stealthily; **faire les cent ~** walk up and down; **faire le premier ~** make the first move; **~ de porte** doorstep; **~ de vis** (Tech) thread.

passage /pasaʒ/ *nm* (traversée) crossing; (visite) visit; (chemin) passage; (d'une œuvre) passage; **de ~** (voyageur) visiting; (amant) casual; **la tempête a tout emporté sur son ~** the storm swept everything away; **~ clouté** pedestrian crossing; **~ interdit** (panneau) no thoroughfare; **~ à niveau** level crossing; **~ souterrain** subway.

passager, -ère /pasaʒe, -ɛʀ/ *adj* temporary. ● *nm, f* passenger; **~ clandestin** stowaway.

passant, ~e /pasɑ̃, -t/ *adj* (rue) busy. ● *nm, f* passer-by. ● *nm* (anneau) loop.

passe /pas/ *nf* pass; **bonne/ mauvaise ~** good/bad patch; **en ~ de** on the road to.

passé, ~e /pase/ *adj* (révolu) past; (dernier) last; (fané) faded; **~ de**

mode out of fashion. ● *nm* past.
● *prép* after.

passe-partout /pɑspaʀtu/ *nm inv* master-key. ● *adj inv* for all occasions.

passeport /pɑspɔʀ/ *nm* passport.

passer /pɑse/ **1** *vi* (aux être ou avoir) go past, pass; (aller) go; (venir) come; (*temps, douleur*) pass; (*film*) be on; (*couleur*) fade; ~ let through; (*occasion*) miss; ~ **devant** (à pied) walk past; (en voiture) drive past; ~ **par** go through; **où est-il passé?** where did he get to?; ~ **outre** take no notice; **passons!** let's forget about it!; **passons aux choses sérieuses** let's turn to serious matters; ~ **dans la classe supérieure** go up a year; ~ **pour un idiot** look a fool. ● *vt* (aux avoir) (franchir) pass, cross; (donner) pass, hand; (*temps*) spend; (enfiler) slip on; (*vidéo, disque*) put on; (*examen*) take, sit; (*commande*) place; (faire) ~ **le temps** while away the time; ~ **l'aspirateur** hoover; ~ **un coup de fil à qn** give sb a ring; **je vous passe Mme X** I'll put you through to Mrs X; (en donnant l'appareil) I'll pass you over to Mrs X; ~ **qch en fraude** smuggle sth. □ **se** ~ *vpr* happen, take place; (s'écouler) go by; **se** ~ **de** go without.

passerelle /pɑsʀɛl/ *nf* footbridge; (de navire) gangway; (d'avion) (passenger) footbridge; (Internet) gateway.

passe-temps /pɑstɑ̃/ *nm inv* pastime.

passif, -ive /pɑsif, -v/ *adj* passive. ● *nm* (Comm) liabilities.

passion /pɑsjɔ̃/ *nf* passion. **passionnant, ~e** *adj* fascinating.

passionné, ~e /pɑsjɔne/ *adj* passionate; **être** ~ **de** have a passion for.

passionner /pɑsjɔne/ **1** *vt* fascinate. □ **se** ~ **pour** *vpr* have a passion for.

passoire /pɑswaʀ/ *nf* (à thé) strainer; (à légumes) colander.

pastèque /pɑstɛk/ *nf* watermelon.

pasteur /pɑstœʀ/ *nm* (Relig) minister.

pastille /pɑstij/ *nf* (médicament) pastille, lozenge.

patate /patat/ *nf* **1** spud; ~ (**douce**) sweet potato.

patauger /patoʒe/ **40** *vi* splash about.

pâte /pɑt/ *nf* paste; (à gâteau) dough; (à tarte) pastry; (à frire) batter; ~**s** (**alimentaires**) pasta (+ *sg*); ~ **à modeler** Plasticine®; ~ **d'amandes** marzipan.

pâté /pɑte/ *nm* (Culin) pâté; (d'encre) blot; (de sable) sandpie; ~ **en croûte** ≈ pie; ~ **de maisons** block (of houses).

pâtée /pɑte/ *nf* feed, mash.

patente /patɑ̃t/ *nf* trade licence.

paternel, ~le /patɛʀnɛl/ *adj* paternal. **paternité** *nf* paternity.

pathétique /patetik/ *adj* moving.

patience /pasjɑ̃s/ *nf* patience. **patient, ~e** *adj* & *nm, f* patient. **patienter** **1** *vi* wait.

patin /patɛ̃/ *nm* skate; ~ **à roulettes** roller-skate.

patinage /patinaʒ/ *nm* skating. **patiner** **1** *vi* skate; (*roue*) spin. **patinoire** *nf* ice rink.

pâtisserie /pɑtisʀi/ *nf* cake shop; (gâteau) pastry; (secteur) cake making. **pâtissier, -ière** *nm, f* confectioner, pastry-cook.

patrie /patʀi/ *nf* homeland.

patrimoine /patʀimwan/ *nm* heritage.

patriote /patʀijɔt/ adj patriotic.
● nmf patriot.

patron, ~ne /patʀɔ̃, -ɔn/ nm, f
employer, boss; (propriétaire)
owner, boss; (saint) patron saint.
● nm (couture) pattern. **patronal,
~e** (mpl **-aux**) adj employers'.
patronat nm employers (+ pl).

patrouille /patʀuj/ nf patrol.

patte /pat/ nf leg; (pied) foot; (de
chat) paw; **~s** (favoris) sideburns;
marcher à quatre ~s walk on all
fours; (bébé) crawl; **~s de derrière**
hind legs.

paume /pom/ nf (de main) palm.

paumé, ~e /pome/ nm, f 🔢 misfit.

paupière /popjɛʀ/ nf eyelid.

pause /poz/ nf pause; (halte) break.

pauvre /povʀ/ adj poor. ● nmf poor
man, poor woman. **pauvreté** nf
poverty.

pavé /pave/ nm cobblestone.

pavillon /pavijɔ̃/ nm (maison)
house; (drapeau) flag.

payant, ~e /pejɑ̃, -t/ adj (hôte)
paying; **c'est ~** you have to pay to
get in.

payer /peje/ 🔢 vt/i pay; (service,
travail) pay for; **~ qch à qn** buy sb
sth; **faire ~ qn** charge sb; **il me le
paiera** he'll pay for this. □ **se ~**
vpr **se ~ qch** buy oneself sth; **se ~
la tête de** make fun of.

pays /pei/ nm country; (région) region; **du ~** local.

paysage /peizaʒ/ nm landscape.

paysan, ~ne /peizã, -an/ nm, f
farmer, country person; (péj) peasant. ● adj (agricole) farming; (rural)
country.

Pays-Bas /peibɑ/ nmpl les ~ the
Netherlands.

PCV abrév m (**paiement contre vérification**) **téléphoner en ~** reverse the charges.

PDG abrév m (**président-directeur
général**) chairman and managing
director.

péage /peaʒ/ nm toll; (lieu)
tollgate.

peau (pl **~x**) /po/ nf skin; (cuir)
hide; **~ de chamois** shammy (leather); **~de mouton** sheepskin; **être
bien/mal dans sa ~** be/not be at
ease with oneself.

pêche /pɛʃ/ nf (fruit) peach; (activité) fishing; (poissons) catch; **~ à
la ligne** angling.

péché /peʃe/ nm sin.

pêcher /peʃe/ vt (poisson) catch;
(dénicher 🔢) dig up. ● vi fish. **pêcheur** nm fisherman; (à la ligne)
angler.

pécuniaire /pekynjɛʀ/ adj financial.

pédagogie /pedagɔʒi/ nf education.

pédale /pedal/ nf pedal.

pédalo ® /pedalo/ nm pedal boat.

pédant, ~e /pedã, -t/ adj pedantic.

pédestre /pedɛstʀ/ adj **faire de la
randonnée ~** go walking ou
hiking.

pédiatre /pedjatʀ/ nmf paediatrician.

pédicure /pedikyʀ/ nmf chiropodist.

peigne /pɛɲ/ nm comb.

peigner /peɲe/ 🔢 vt comb; (personne) comb the hair of. □ **se ~** vpr
comb one's hair.

peignoir /pɛɲwaʀ/ nm dressing gown.

peindre /pɛ̃dʀ/ 🔢 vt paint.

peine /pɛn/ nf sadness, sorrow; (effort, difficulté) trouble; (Jur) sentence; **avoir de la ~** feel sad; **faire
de la ~ à** hurt; **ce n'est pas la ~
de sonner** you don't need to ring

the bell; **j'ai de la ∼ à le croire** I find it hard to believe; **se donner** ou **prendre la ∼ de faire** go to the trouble of doing; **∼ de mort** death penalty. ● adv à ∼ hardly.

peiner /pene/ **1** vi struggle. ● vt sadden.

peintre /pɛtr/ nm painter; **∼ en bâtiment** house painter.

peinture /pɛtyr/ nf painting; (matière) paint; **∼ à l'huile** oil painting.

péjoratif, -ive /peʒɔratif, -v/ adj pejorative.

pelage /pəlaʒ/ nm coat, fur.

pêle-mêle /pɛlmɛl/ adv in a jumble.

peler /pəle/ **6** vt/i peel.

pèlerinage /pɛlrinaʒ/ nm pilgrimage.

pelle /pɛl/ nf shovel; (d'enfant) spade.

pellicule /pelikyl/ nf film; **∼s** (cheveux) dandruff.

pelote /pəlɔt/ nf (of wool) ball.

peloton /p(ə)lɔtɔ̃/ nm platoon; (Sport) pack; **∼ d'exécution** firing squad.

pelotonner (se) /(sə)plətɔne/ **1** vpr curl up.

pelouse /p(ə)luz/ nf lawn.

peluche /p(ə)lyʃ/ nf (matière) plush; (jouet) cuddly toy; **en ∼** (lapin, chien) fluffy.

pénal, ∼e (mpl **-aux**) /penal, -o/ adj penal. **pénaliser** **1** vt penalize. **pénalité** nf penalty.

penchant /pɑ̃ʃɑ̃/ nm inclination; (goût) liking (pour for).

pencher /pɑ̃ʃe/ **1** vt tilt; **∼ pour** favour. ● vi lean (over), tilt. □ **se ∼** vpr lean (forward); **se ∼ sur** (problème) examine.

pendaison /pɑ̃dɛzɔ̃/ nf hanging.

pendant¹ /pɑ̃dɑ̃/ prép (au cours

de) during; (durée) for; **∼ que** while.

pendant², ∼e /pɑ̃dɑ̃, -t/ adj hanging; **jambes ∼es** with one's legs dangling. ● nm (contrepartie) matching piece (**de** to); **∼ d'oreille** drop earring.

pendentif /pɑ̃dɑ̃tif/ nm pendant.

penderie /pɑ̃dri/ nf wardrobe.

pendre /pɑ̃dr/ **3** vt/i hang. □ **se ∼** vpr hang (**à** from); (se tuer) hang oneself.

pendule /pɑ̃dyl/ nf clock. ● nm pendulum.

pénétrer /penetre/ **14** vi **∼ (dans)** enter; **faire ∼ une crème** rub a cream in. ● vt penetrate.

pénible /penibl/ adj (travail) hard; (nouvelle) painful; (enfant) tiresome.

péniche /peniʃ/ nf barge.

pénitence /penitɑ̃s/ nf (Relig) penance; (punition) punishment; **faire ∼** repent.

pénitentiaire /penitɑ̃sjɛr/ adj (établissement) penal.

pénombre /penɔ̃br/ nf half-light.

pensée /pɑ̃se/ nf (idée) thought; (fleur) pansy.

penser /pɑ̃se/ **1** vt/i think; **∼ à** (réfléchir à) think about; (se souvenir de, prévoir) think of; **∼ faire** think of doing; **faire ∼ à** remind one of.

pensif, -ive /pɑ̃sif, -v/ adj pensive.

pension /pɑ̃sjɔ̃/ nf (Scol) boarding school; (repas, somme) board; (allocation) pension; **∼ de famille** guest house; **∼ alimentaire** (Jur) alimony. **pensionnaire** nmf (Scol) boarder; (d'hôtel) guest. **pensionnat** nm boarding school.

pente /pɑ̃t/ nf slope; **en ∼** sloping.

Pentecôte /pɑ̃tkot/ nf **la ∼** Whitsun.

pénurie /penyri/ nf shortage.

pépin /pepɛ̃/ nm (graine) pip; (ennui) hitch.

pépinière /pepinjɛʀ/ nf (tree) nursery.

perçant, ~e /pɛʀsɑ̃, -t/ adj (cri) shrill; (regard) piercing.

perce-neige /pɛʀsənɛʒ/ nm or f inv snowdrop.

percepteur /pɛʀsɛptœʀ/ nm tax inspector.

percer /pɛʀse/ **10** vt pierce; (avec perceuse) drill; (mystère) penetrate. ● vi break through; (dent) come through. **perceuse** nf drill.

percevoir /pɛʀsəvwaʀ/ **52** vt perceive; (impôt) collect.

perche /pɛʀʃ/ nf (bâton) pole.

percher (se) /(sə)pɛʀʃe/ **1** vpr perch.

percolateur /pɛʀkɔlatœʀ/ nm coffee machine.

percuter /pɛʀkyte/ **1** vt (véhicule) crash into.

perdant, ~e /pɛʀdɑ̃, -t/ adj losing. ● nm, f loser.

perdre /pɛʀdʀ/ **3** vt/i lose; (gaspiller) waste; **~ ses poils** (chat) moult. **□ se ~** vpr get lost; (rester inutilisé) go to waste.

perdrix /pɛʀdʀi/ nf partridge.

perdu, ~e /pɛʀdy/ adj lost; (endroit) isolated; (balle) stray; **c'est du temps ~** it's a waste of time.

père /pɛʀ/ nm father; **~ de famille** father, family man; **~ spirituel** father figure; **le ~ Noël** Santa Claus.

perfection /pɛʀfɛksjɔ̃/ nf perfection.

perfectionner /pɛʀfɛksjɔne/ **1** vt (technique) perfect; (art) refine. **□ se ~** vpr improve; **se ~ en anglais** improve one's English.

perforer /pɛʀfɔʀe/ **1** vt perforate; (billet, bande) punch.

performance /pɛʀfɔʀmɑ̃s/ nf performance.

perfusion /pɛʀfyzjɔ̃/ nf drip; **sous ~** on a drip.

péridurale /peʀidyʀal/ nf epidural.

péril /peʀil/ nm peril; **à tes risques et ~s** at your own risk.

périlleux, -euse /peʀijø, -z/ adj perilous.

périmé, ~e /peʀime/ adj (produit) past its use-by date; (désuet) outdated.

période /peʀjɔd/ nf period.

périodique /peʀjɔdik/ adj periodic(al). ● nm (journal) periodical.

péripétie /peʀipesi/ nf (unexpected) event, adventure.

périphérique /peʀifeʀik/ adj peripheral. ● nm (boulevard) ~ ring road.

périple /peʀipl/ nm journey.

périr /peʀiʀ/ **2** vi perish, die.

perle /pɛʀl/ nf (d'huître) pearl; (de verre) bead.

permanence /pɛʀmanɑ̃s/ nf permanence; (Scol) study room; **de ~** on duty; **en ~** permanently; **assurer une ~** keep the office open.

permanent, ~e /pɛʀmanɑ̃, -t/ adj permanent; (constant) constant; **formation ~e** continuous education. **permanente** nf (coiffure) perm.

permettre /pɛʀmɛtʀ/ **42** vt allow; **~ à qn de** allow sb to. **□ se ~** vpr (achat) afford; **se ~ de faire** take the liberty of doing.

permis, ~e /pɛʀmi, -z/ adj allowed. ● nm licence, permit; **~ (de conduire)** driving licence.

permission /pɛʀmisjɔ̃/ nf permission; **en ~** (Mil) on leave.

Pérou /peʀu/ nm Peru.

perpendiculaire /pɛʀpɑ̃dikylɛʀ/ adj & nf perpendicular.

perpétuité /pɛʀpetɥite/ nf à ~ for life.

perplexe /pɛʀplɛks/ adj perplexed.

perquisition /pɛʀkizisjɔ̃/ nf (police) search.

perron /pɛʀɔ̃/ nm (front) steps.

perroquet /pɛʀɔkɛ/ nm parrot.

perruche /pɛʀyʃ/ nf budgerigar.

perruque /pɛʀyk/ nf wig.

persécuter /pɛʀsekyte/ **1** vt persecute.

persévérance /pɛʀseveʀɑ̃s/ nf perseverance. **persévérer** **14** vi persevere.

persienne /pɛʀsjɛn/ nf (outside) shutter.

persil /pɛʀsi/ nm parsley.

persistance /pɛʀsistɑ̃s/ nf persistence. **persistant, ~e** adj persistent; (feuillage) evergreen.

persister /pɛʀsiste/ **1** vi persist (à faire in doing).

personnage /pɛʀsɔnaʒ/ nm character; (personne célèbre) personality.

personnalité /pɛʀsɔnalite/ nf personality.

personne /pɛʀsɔn/ nf person; ~s people. ● pron nobody, no-one; **je n'ai vu ~** I didn't see anybody.

personnel, ~le /pɛʀsɔnɛl/ adj personal; (égoïste) selfish. ● nm staff.

perspective /pɛʀspɛktiv/ nf (art, point de vue) perspective; (vue) view; (éventualité) prospect.

perspicace /pɛʀspikas/ adj shrewd. **perspicacité** nf shrewdness.

persuader /pɛʀsɥade/ **1** vt persuade (de faire to do).

persuasif, -ive /pɛʀsɥazif, -v/ adj persuasive.

perte /pɛʀt/ nf loss; (ruine) ruin; **à ~ de vue** as far as the eye can see; **~ de** (temps, argent) waste of; **~ sèche** total loss; **~s** (Méd) discharge.

pertinent, ~e /pɛʀtinɑ̃, -t/ adj pertinent.

perturbateur, -trice /pɛʀtyʀbatœʀ, -tʀis/ nm, f disruptive element. **perturbation** nf disruption. **perturber** **1** vt disrupt; (personne) perturb.

pervers, ~e /pɛʀvɛʀ, -s/ adj (dépravé) perverted; (méchant) wicked. **pervertir** /pɛʀvɛʀtiʀ/ **2** vt pervert.

pesant, ~e /pəzɑ̃, -t/ adj heavy. **pesanteur** /pəzɑ̃tœʀ/ nf heaviness; **la ~** (force) gravity.

pesée /pəze/ nf weighing; (effort) pressure.

pèse-personne (pl ~s) /pɛzpɛʀsɔn/ nm (bathroom) scales.

peser /pəze/ **6** vt/i weigh; ~ **sur** bear upon.

pessimiste /pesimist/ adj pessimistic. ● nmf pessimist.

peste /pɛst/ nf plague; (personne 🄸) pest.

pet /pɛ/ nm 🄸 fart 🄸.

pétale /petal/ nm petal.

Pétanque See ▷BOULES.

pétard /petaʀ/ nm banger.

péter /pete/ **14** vi 🄸 fart 🄸, go bang; (casser) snap.

pétillant, ~e /petijɑ̃, -t/ adj (boisson) sparkling; (personne) bubbly.

pétiller /petije/ **1** vi (feu) crackle; (champagne, yeux) sparkle; ~ **d'intelligence** sparkle with intelligence.

petit, ~e /p(ə)ti, -t/ adj small;

(avec nuance affective) little; (jeune) young, small; (défaut) minor; (mesquin) petty; **en ~** in miniature; **~ à ~** little by little; **un ~ peu** a little bit; **~ ami** boyfriend; **~e amie** girlfriend; **~es annonces** small ads; **~e cuillère** teaspoon; **~ déjeuner** breakfast; **~ pois** garden pea. ● *nm, f* little child; (Scol) junior; **~s** (de chat) kittens; (de chien) pups. **petite-fille** (*pl* **petites-filles**) *nf* granddaughter. **petit-fils** (*pl* **petits-fils**) *nm* grandson.

pétition /petisjɔ̃/ *nf* petition.

petits-enfants /pətizɑ̃fɑ̃/ *nmpl* grandchildren.

pétrin /petrɛ̃/ *nm* **dans le ~** 🔟 in a fix 🔟.

pétrir /petriʀ/ 🔢 *vt* knead.

pétrole /petrɔl/ *nm* oil; **~ brut** crude oil.

pétrolier, -ière /petrɔlje, -jɛʀ/ *adj* oil. ● *nm* (navire) oil-tanker.

peu /pø/ *adv* (**~ de**) (quantité) little, not much; (nombre) few, not many; **~ intéressant** not very interesting; **il mange ~** he doesn't eat very much. ● *pron* few. ● *nm* little; **un ~** (de) a little; **à ~ près** more or less; **de ~** only just; **~ à ~** gradually; **~ après/avant** shortly after/before; **~ de chose** not much; **~ nombreux** few; **~ souvent** seldom; **pour ~ que** if.

peuple /pœpl/ *nm* people. **peupler** 🔟 *vt* populate.

peuplier /pøplije/ *nm* poplar.

peur /pœʀ/ *nf* fear; **avoir ~** be afraid (**de** of); **de ~ de** for fear of; **faire ~** to frighten. **peureux, -euse** *adj* fearful.

peut /pø/ ➡POUVOIR 49.

peut-être /pøtɛtʀ/ *adv* perhaps, maybe; **~ qu'il viendra** he might come.

peux /pø/ ➡POUVOIR 49.

phare /faʀ/ *nm* (tour) lighthouse; (de véhicule) headlight; **~ anti-brouillard** fog lamp.

pharmacie /faʀmasi/ *nf* (magasin) chemist's (shop), pharmacy; (science) pharmacy; (armoire) medicine cabinet. **pharmacien, ~ne** *nm, f* chemist, pharmacist.

phénomène /fenɔmɛn/ *nm* phenomenon; (personne 🔟) eccentric.

philosophe /filɔzɔf/ *nmf* philosopher. ● *adj* philosophical. **philosophie** *nf* philosophy. **philosophique** *adj* philosophical.

phobie /fɔbi/ *nf* phobia.

phonétique /fɔnetik/ *adj* phonetic. ● *nf* phonetics.

phoque /fɔk/ *nm* (animal) seal.

photo /foto/ *nf* photo; (art) photography; **prendre en ~** take a photo of; **~ d'identité** passport photograph.

photocopie /fotɔkɔpi/ *nf* photocopy. **photocopier** 45 *vt* photocopy.

photographe /fotɔgʀaf/ *nmf* photographer. **photographie** *nf* (image) photograph; (art) photography. **photographier** 45 *vt* take a photo of.

phrase /fʀɑz/ *nf* sentence.

physicien, ~ne /fizisjɛ̃, -ɛn/ *nm, f* physicist.

physique /fizik/ *adj* physical. ● *nm* physique; **au ~** physically. ● *nf* physics (+ *sg.*).

piano /pjano/ *nm* piano.

pianoter /pjanɔte/ 🔟 *vi* tinkle; **~ sur** (ordinateur) tap at.

PIB *abrév m* (**produit intérieur brut**) GDP.

pic /pik/ *nm* (outil) pickaxe; (sommet) peak; (oiseau) woodpecker; **à ~** (falaise) sheer; (couler) straight to the bottom; **tomber à ~** 🔟 come just at the right time.

P

pichet /piʃɛ/ nm jug.

picorer /pikɔʀe/ vt/i peck.

picotement /pikɔtmɑ̃/ nm tingling. **picoter** 1 vt sting; (yeux) sting.

pie /pi/ nf magpie.

pièce /pjɛs/ nf (d'habitation) room; (de monnaie) coin; (Théât) play; (pour raccommoder) patch; (écrit) document; (morceau) piece; (~ de théâtre) play; **dix euros (la ~)** ten euros each; **~ détachée** part; **~ d'identité** identity paper; **~s jointes** enclosures; (courrier électronique) attachments; **~s justificatives** written proof; **~ montée** tiered cake; **~ de rechange** spare part; **un deux-~s** a tworoom flat.

pied /pje/ nm foot; (de meuble) leg; (de lampe) base; (de verre) stem; (d'appareil photo) stand; **être ~s nus** be barefoot; **à ~** on foot; **au ~ de la lettre** literally; **avoir ~** be able to touch the bottom; **jouer au ~ de la lettre** literally; **avoir ~** be able to touch the bottom; **jouer au tennis comme un ~** 1 be hopeless at tennis; **mettre sur ~** set up; **sur un ~ d'égalité** on an equal footing; **mettre les ~s dans le plat** 1 put one's foot in it; **c'est le ~** 1 it's great. **pied-bot** (pl **pieds-bots**) nm club-foot.

piédestal /pjedɛstal/ nm pedestal.

piège /pjɛʒ/ nm trap.

piéger /pjeʒe/ 14 40 vt trap; **lettre/voiture piégée** letter/car bomb.

piercing /pirsiŋ/ nm body piercing.

pierre /pjɛʀ/ nf stone; **~ précieuse** precious stone; **~ tombale** tombstone.

piétiner /pjetine/ 1 vi (avancer lentement) shuffle along; (fig) make no headway; **~ d'impatience** hop up and down with impatience. ● vt trample (on).

piéton /pjetɔ̃/ nm pedestrian.

pieu (pl **~x**) /pjø/ nm post, stake.

pieuvre /pjœvʀ/ nf octopus.

pieux, -ieuse /pjø, -z/ adj pious.

pigeon /piʒɔ̃/ nm pigeon.

piger /piʒe/ 40 vt/i understand, get (it).

pile /pil/ nf (tas) pile; (Électr) battery; **~ ou face?** heads or tails? ● adv (s'arrêter 1) dead; **à dix heures ~** 1 at ten on the dot.

pilier /pilje/ nm pillar.

pillage /pijaʒ/ nm looting. **pillard, ~e** nm, f looter. **piller** 1 vt loot.

pilote /pilɔt/ nm (Aviat, Naut) pilot; (Auto) driver. ● adj pilot. **piloter** 1 vt (Aviat, Naut) pilot; (Auto) drive.

pilule /pilyl/ nf pill; **la ~** the pill.

piment /pimɑ̃/ nm hot pepper; (fig) spice. **pimenté, ~e** adj spicy.

pin /pɛ̃/ nm pine.

pinard /pinaʀ/ nm 1 plonk 1, cheap wine.

pince /pɛ̃s/ nf (outil) pliers (+ pl); (levier) crowbar; (de crabe) pincer; (à sucre) tongs (+ pl); **~ à épiler** tweezers (+ pl); **~ à linge** clothes peg.

pinceau (pl **~x**) /pɛ̃so/ nm paintbrush.

pincée /pɛ̃se/ nf pinch (de of).

pincer /pɛ̃se/ 10 vt pinch; (attraper 1) catch. □ **se ~** vpr catch oneself; **se ~ le doigt** catch one's finger.

pince-sans-rire /pɛ̃ssɑ̃ʀiʀ/ nmf inv **c'est un ~** he has a deadpan sense of humour.

pingouin /pɛ̃gwɛ̃/ nm penguin.

pingre /pɛ̃gʀ/ adj 1 stingy.

pintade /pɛ̃tad/ nf guinea fowl.

piocher /pjɔʃe/ 1 vt/i dig; (étudier 1) study hard, slog away (at).

pion /pjɔ̃/ nm (de jeu) counter; (aux échecs) pawn; (Scol 1) supervisor.

pipe /pip/ nf pipe; **fumer la ~** smoke a pipe.

piquant, ~e /pikɑ̃, -t/ adj (barbe) prickly; (goût) pungent; (remarque) cutting. ● nm prickle.

pique /pik/ nm (aux cartes) spades.

pique-nique (pl **~s**) /piknik/ nm picnic.

piquer /pike/ **1** vt (épine) prick; (épice) burn, sting; (abeille, ortie) sting; (serpent, moustique) bite; (enfoncer) stick; (coudre) (machine-) stitch; (curiosité) excite; (voler **1**) pinch. ● vi (avion) dive; (goût) be hot. □ **se ~** vpr prick oneself.

piquet /pikɛ/ nm stake; (de tente) peg; (de parasol) pole; **~ de grève** (strike) picket.

piqûre /pikyʁ/ nf prick; (d'abeille) sting; (de serpent) bite; (point) stitch; (Méd) injection, jab; **faire une ~ à qn** give sb an injection.

pirate /piʁat/ nm pirate; **~ informatique** computer hacker; **~ de l'air** hijacker.

pire /piʁ/ adj worse (que than); **les ~s mensonges** the most wicked lies. ● nm **le ~** the worst; **au ~** at worst.

pis /pi/ nm (de vache) udder. ● adj inv & adv worse; **aller de mal en ~** go from bad to worse.

piscine /pisin/ nf swimming pool; **~ couverte** indoor swimming-pool.

pissenlit /pisɑ̃li/ nm dandelion.

pistache /pistaʃ/ nf pistachio.

piste /pist/ nf track; (de personne, d'animal) track, trail; (Aviat) runway; (de cirque) ring; (de ski) slope; (de danse) floor; (Sport) racetrack; **~ cyclable** cycle lane.

pistolet /pistolɛ/ nm gun, pistol; (de peintre) spray-gun.

piteux, -euse /pitø, -z/ adj pitiful.

pitié /pitje/ nf pity; **il me fait ~** I feel sorry for him.

piton /pitɔ̃/ nm (à crochet) hook; (sommet pointu) peak.

pitoyable /pitwajabl/ adj pitiful.

pitre /pitʁ/ nm clown; **faire le ~** clown around.

pittoresque /pitɔʁɛsk/ adj picturesque.

pivot /pivo/ nm pivot. **pivoter** **1** vi revolve; (personne) swing round.

placard /plakaʁ/ nm cupboard; (affiche) poster. **placarder** **1** vt (affiche) post up; (mur) cover with posters.

place /plas/ nf place; (espace libre) room, space; (siège) seat, place; (prix d'un trajet) fare; (esplanade) square; (emploi) position; (de parking) space; **à la ~ de** instead of; **en ~, à sa ~** in its place; **faire à qn** give way to; **sur ~** on the spot; **remettre qn à sa ~** put sb in his place; **ça prend de la ~** it takes up a lot of room; **se mettre à la ~ de qn** put oneself in sb's shoes ou place.

placement /plasmɑ̃/ nm (d'argent) investment.

placer /plase/ **10** vt place; (invité, spectateur) seat; (argent) invest. □ **se ~** vpr (personne) take up a position.

plafond /plafɔ̃/ nm ceiling.

plage /plaʒ/ nf beach; **~ horaire** time slot.

plagiat /plaʒja/ nm plagiarism.

plaider /plede/ **1** vt/i plead. **plaidoirie** nf (defence) speech. **plaidoyer** nm plea.

plaie /plɛ/ nf wound; (personne **1**) nuisance.

plaignant, ~e /plɛɲɑ̃, -t/ nm, f plaintiff.

plaindre /plɛ̃dʁ/ **22** vt pity. □ **se ~** vpr complain (de about); **se**

de (souffrir de) complain of.

plaine /plɛn/ nf plain.

plainte /plɛt/ nf complaint; (gémissement) groan. **plaintif, -ive** adj plaintive.

plaire /plɛʀ/ 47 vi ~ à please; ça lui plaît he likes it; **elle lui plaît** he likes her; **ça me plaît de faire** I like ou enjoy doing; **ça vous plaît** please. □ **se ~** vpr **il se plaît ici** he likes it here.

plaisance /plɛzɑ̃s/ nf **la (navigation de) ~** boating.

plaisant, ~e /plɛzɑ̃, -t/ adj pleasant; (drôle) amusing.

plaisanter /plɛzɑ̃te/ 1 vi joke. **plaisanterie** nf joke. **plaisantin** nm joker.

plaisir /plezir/ nm pleasure; **faire ~ à** please; **pour le ~** for fun ou pleasure.

plan /plɑ̃/ nm plan; (de ville) map; (de livre) outline; **~ d'eau** artificial lake; **~ social** planned redundancy programme; **premier ~** foreground.

planche /plɑ̃ʃ/ nf board, plank; (gravure) plate; **~ à repasser** ironing-board; **~ à voile** windsurfing board; (Sport) windsurfing.

plancher /plɑ̃ʃe/ nm floor.

planer /plane/ 1 vi glide; **~ sur** (mystère, danger) hang over.

planète /planɛt/ nf planet.

planeur /planœʀ/ nm glider.

planifier /planifje/ 45 vt plan.

plant /plɑ̃/ nm seedling; (de légumes) patch.

plante /plɑ̃t/ nf plant; **~ d'appartement** houseplant; **~ des pieds** sole (of the foot).

planter /plɑ̃te/ 1 vt (plante) plant; (enfoncer) drive in; (tente) put up; **rester planté** 1 stand still.

plaque /plak/ nf plate; (de marbre)

slab; (insigne) badge; **~ chauffante** hotplate; **~ commémorative** plaque; **~ minéralogique** numberplate; **~ de verglas** patch of ice.

plaquer /plake/ 1 vt (bois) veneer; (aplatir) flatten; (rugby) tackle; (abandonner 1) ditch 1; **tout ~** chuck it all.

plastique /plastik/ adj & nm plastic; **en ~** plastic.

plastiquer /plastike/ 1 vt blow up.

plat, ~e /pla, -t/ adj flat. ● nm (Culin) dish; (partie de repas) course; (de la main) flat. ● **à plat** adv (poser) flat; (batterie, pneu) flat; **à ~ ventre** flat on one's face.

platane /platan/ nm plane tree.

plateau (pl ~x) /plato/ nm tray; (de cinéma) set; (de balance) pan; (Géog) plateau; **~ de fromages** cheeseboard; **~ de fruits de mer** seafood platter. **plate-bande** (pl **plates-bandes**) nf flower bed.

platine /platin/ nm platinum. ● nf (tourne-disque) turntable; **~ laser** compact disc player.

plâtre /plɑtʀ/ nm plaster; (Méd) (plaster) cast.

plein, ~e /plɛ̃, -ɛn/ adj full (de of); (total) complete. ● nm **faire le ~ (d'essence)** fill up (the tank); **à ~** fully; **à ~ temps** full-time; **en ~ air** in the open air; **en ~ milieu/visage** right in the middle/the face; **en ~ nuit** in the middle of the night. ● adv **avoir des idées ~ la tête** be full of ideas. **pleinement** adv fully.

pleurer /plœʀe/ 1 vi cry, weep (sur over); (yeux) water. ● vt mourn.

pleurnicher /plœʀniʃe/ 1 vi 1 snivel.

pleurs /plœr/ *nmpl* tears; **en ~** in tears.

pleuvoir /pløvwar/ **48** *vi* rain; (fig) rain ou shower down; **il pleut** it is raining; **il pleut à verse** *ou* **des cordes** it is pouring.

pli /pli/ *nm* fold; (de jupe) pleat; (de pantalon) crease; (lettre) letter; (habitude) habit; (**faux ~**) crease.

pliant, **~e** /plijã, -t/ *adj* folding. ● *nm* folding stool, camp-stool.

plier /plije/ **45** *vt* fold; (courber) bend; (soumettre) submit (**à** to). ● *vi* bend. □ **se ~** *vpr* fold; **se ~ à** submit to.

plinthe /plɛ̃t/ *nf* skirting-board.

plissé, **~e** /plise/ *adj* (jupe) pleated.

plisser /plise/ **1** *vt* crease; (yeux) screw up.

plomb /plɔ̃/ *nm* lead; (fusible) fuse; **~s** (de chasse) lead shot; **de** *ou* **en ~** lead. **plombage** *nm* filling.

plomberie /plɔ̃bri/ *nf* plumbing. **plombier** *nm* plumber.

plongée /plɔ̃ʒe/ *nf* diving; **en ~** (sous-marin) submerged.

plongeoir /plɔ̃ʒwar/ *nm* diving board.

plonger /plɔ̃ʒe/ **40** *vi* dive; (route) plunge. ● *vt* plunge. □ **se ~** *vpr* plunge into; **se ~ dans** (fig) (lecture) bury oneself in. **plongeur**, **-euse** *nm*, *f* diver; (de restaurant) dishwasher.

plu /ply/ →**PLAIRE 47, PLEUVOIR 48.**

pluie /plɥi/ *nf* rain; (averse) shower; **~ battante/diluvienne** driving/torrential rain.

plume /plym/ *nf* feather; (pointe) nib.

plumeau (*pl* **~x**) /plymo/ *nm* feather duster.

plumier /plymje/ *nm* pencil box.

plupart: la ~ /laplypar/ *loc* **la ~**

des (gens, cas) most; **la ~ du temps** most of the time; **pour la ~** for the most part.

pluriel, **~le** /plyrjɛl/ *adj & nm* plural.

---

plus /ply, plys, plyz/

● *adverbe de comparaison*

····▸ more (**que** than); **~ âgé/tard** older/later; **~ beau** more beautiful; **~ j'y pense...** the more I think about it...; **deux fois ~** twice as much; **deux fois ~ cher** twice as expensive.

····▸ **le ~** the most; **le ~ grand** the biggest; (de deux) the bigger.

····▸ **~ de** (pain) more; (dix jours) more than; **il est ~ de 8 heures** it is after 8 o'clock.

····▸ **de ~** more (**que** than); (en outre) moreover; **les enfants de ~ de 10 ans** children over 10 years old; **de ~ en ~** more and more.

····▸ **~ on top of that; c'est en ~** it's extra; **en ~ de** in addition to.

····▸ **~ ou moins** more or less.

····▸ **au ~ tard** at the latest.

● *adverbe de négation*

····▸ **~ ne ~** (temps) no longer, not any more; **je n'y vais ~** I don't go there any longer *ou* any more.

····▸ **~ ne ~ de** (quantité) no more; **il n'y a ~ de pain** there is no more bread.

····▸ **~ que deux jours!** only two days left!

● *préposition & nom masculin*

····▸ (maths) plus.

plusieurs /plyzjœr/ adj & pron several.

plus-value (pl ~s) /plyvaly/ nf (bénéfice) profit.

plutôt /plyto/ adv rather (**que** than).

pluvieux, -ieuse /plyvjø, -z/ adj rainy.

PME abrév f (**petites et moyennes entreprises**) SME.

PNB abrév m (**produit national brut**) GNP.

pneu /pnø/ nm tyre. **pneumatique** adj inflatable.

pneumonie /pnømɔni/ nf pneumonia; ~ **atypique** severe acute respiratory syndrome.

poche /pɔʃ/ nf pocket; (sac) bag; ~**s** (sous les yeux) bags.

pocher /pɔʃe/ **1** vt (œuf) poach.

pochette /pɔʃɛt/ nf (de documents) folder; (sac) bag, pouch; (d'allumettes) book; (de disque) sleeve; (mouchoir) pocket handkerchief.

poêle /pwal/ nf (~ **à frire**) frying-pan. ●nm stove.

poème /pɔɛm/ nm poem. **poésie** nf (poème) poem. **poète** nm poet. **poétique** adj poetic.

poids /pwa/ nm weight; ~ **coq/lourd/plume** bantamweight/heavyweight/featherweight; ~ **lourd** (camion) lorry, juggernaut; (US) truck.

poignard /pwaɲar/ nm dagger. **poignarder** **1** vt stab.

poigne /pwaɲ/ nf **avoir de la** ~ have a strong grip.

poignée /pwaɲe/ nf (de porte) handle; (quantité) handful; ~ **de main** handshake.

poignet /pwaɲɛ/ nm wrist; (de chemise) cuff.

poil /pwal/ nm hair; (pelage) fur;

(de brosse) bristle; ~**s** (de tapis) pile; à ~ 🆃 naked; ~ **à gratter** itching powder. **poilu, -e** adj hairy.

poinçon /pwɛ̃sɔ̃/ nm awl; (marque) hallmark. **poinçonner** **1** vt (billet) punch.

poing /pwɛ̃/ nm fist.

point /pwɛ̃/ nm (endroit, Sport) point; (marque visible) spot, dot; (de couture) stitch; (pour évaluer) mark; **enlever un** ~ **par faute** take a mark off for each mistake; **à** ~ (Culin) medium; (arriver) at the right time; **faire le** ~ take stock; **mettre au** ~ (photo) focus; (technique) develop; **mettre les choses au** ~ get things clear; **Camille n'est pas encore au** ~ **pour ses examens** Camille is not ready for her exams; **sur le** ~ **de** about to; **au** ~ **que** to the extent that; (~ **final**) full stop, period; **deux** ~**s** colon; ~ **d'interrogation/d'exclamation** question/exclamation mark; ~**s de suspension** suspension points; ~ **virgule** semicolon; ~ **culminant** peak; ~ **du jour** daybreak; ~ **mort** (Auto) neutral; ~ **de repère** landmark; ~ **de suture** (Méd) stitch; ~ **de vente** point of sale; ~ **de vue** point of view. ●adv (**ne**) ~ not.

pointe /pwɛ̃t/ nf point, tip; (clou) tack; (de grille) spike; (fig) touch (**de** of); **de** ~ (industrie) high-tech; **en** ~ pointed; **heure de** ~ peak hour; **sur la** ~ **des pieds** on tiptoe.

pointer /pwɛ̃te/ **1** vt (cocher) tick off; (diriger) point, aim. ● vi (employé) (en arrivant) clock in; (en sortant) clock out. ☐ **se** ~ vpr 🆃 turn up.

pointillé /pwɛ̃tije/ nm dotted line.

pointilleux, -euse /pwɛ̃tijø, -z/ adj fastidious, particular.

pointu, -e /pwɛ̃ty/ adj pointed; (aiguisé) sharp.

pointure /pwɛtyʀ/ nf size.

poire /pwaʀ/ nf pear.

poireau (pl ~x) /pwaʀo/ nm leek.

poirier /pwaʀje/ nm pear tree.

pois /pwa/ nm pea; (motif) dot; **robe à ~** polka dot dress.

poison /pwazɔ̃/ nm poison.

poisseux, -euse /pwasø, -z/ adj sticky.

poisson /pwasɔ̃/ nm fish; **~ rouge** goldfish; **~ d'avril** April fool; **les P~s** Pisces. **poissonnerie** nf fish shop. **poissonnier, -ière** nm, f fishmonger.

poitrine /pwatʀin/ nf chest; (seins) bosom.

poivre /pwavʀ/ nm pepper. **poivré, ~e** adj peppery. **poivrière** nf pepper-pot.

poivron /pwavʀɔ̃/ nm sweet pepper.

polaire /pɔlɛʀ/ adj polar. ● nf (veste) fleece.

pôle /pol/ nm pole.

polémique /pɔlemik/ nf debate. ● adj controversial.

poli, ~e /pɔli/ adj (personne) polite.

police /pɔlis/ nf (force) police (+ pl); (discipline) (law and) order; (d'assurance) policy.

policier, -ière /pɔlisje, -jɛʀ/ adj police; (roman) detective. ● nm policeman.

polir /pɔliʀ/ **2** vt polish.

politesse /pɔlitɛs/ nf politeness; (parole) polite remark.

politicien, ~ne /pɔlitisjɛ̃, -ɛn/ nm, f (péj) politician.

politique /pɔlitik/ adj political; **homme ~** politician. ● nf politics; (ligne de conduite) policy.

pollen /pɔlɛn/ nm pollen.

polluant, ~e /pɔlɥɑ̃, -t/ adj polluting. ● nm pollutant.

polluer /pɔlɥe/ **1** vt pollute. **pollution** nf pollution.

polo /pɔlo/ nm (Sport) polo; (vêtement) polo shirt.

Pologne /pɔlɔɲ/ nf Poland.

polonais, ~e /pɔlɔnɛ, -z/ adj Polish. ● nm (Ling) Polish. **P~, ~e** nm, f Pole.

poltron, ~ne /pɔltʀɔ̃, -ɔn/ adj cowardly. ● nm, f coward.

polygame /pɔligam/ nmf polygamist.

polyvalent, ~e /pɔlivalɑ̃, -t/ adj varied; (personne) versatile.

pommade /pɔmad/ nf ointment.

pomme /pɔm/ nf apple; (d'arrosoir) rose; **~ d'Adam** Adam's apple; **~ de pin** pine cone; **~ de terre** potato; **~s frites** chips; (US) French fries; **tomber dans les ~s** **1** pass out.

pommette /pɔmɛt/ nf cheekbone.

pommier /pɔmje/ nm apple tree.

pompe /pɔ̃p/ nf pump; (splendeur) pomp; **~ à incendie** fire engine; **~s funèbres** undertaker's (+ sg).

pomper /pɔ̃pe/ **1** vt pump; (copier **1**) copy, crib; **~ l'air à qn** **1** get on sb's nerves.

pompier /pɔ̃pje/ nm fireman.

pomponner (se) /(sə)pɔ̃pɔne/ **1** vpr get dolled up.

poncer /pɔ̃se/ **10** vt sand.

ponctuation /pɔ̃ktɥasjɔ̃/ nf punctuation.

ponctuel, ~le /pɔ̃ktɥel/ adj punctual.

pondre /pɔ̃dʀ/ **3** vt/i lay.

poney /pɔnɛ/ nm pony.

pont /pɔ̃/ nm bridge; (de navire) deck; (de graissage) ramp; **faire le ~** get an extended weekend; **~ aérien** airlift. **pont-levis** (pl **ponts-**

levis) nm drawbridge.

populaire /pɔpylɛʀ/ adj popular; (expression) colloquial; (quartier, origine) working-class. **popularité** nf popularity.

population /pɔpylasjɔ̃/ nf population.

porc /pɔʀ/ nm pig; (viande) pork.

porcelaine /pɔʀsəlɛn/ nf china, porcelain.

porc-épic (pl porcs-épics) /pɔʀkepik/ nm porcupine.

porcherie /pɔʀʃəʀi/ nf pigsty.

pornographie /pɔʀnɔgʀafi/ nf pornography.

port /pɔʀ/ nm port, harbour; **à bon ~** safely; **~ maritime** seaport; (transport) carriage; (d'armes) carrying; (de barbe) wearing.

portable /pɔʀtabl/ nm (Ordinat) laptop (computer); (telephone) mobile (phone).

portail /pɔʀtaj/ nm gate.

portatif, -ive /pɔʀtatif, -v/ adj portable.

porte /pɔʀt/ nf door; (passage) doorway; (de jardin, d'embarquement) gate; **mettre à la ~** throw out; **~ d'entrée** front door.

porté, ~e /pɔʀte/ adj **~ à** inclined to; **~ sur** keen on.

porte-avions /pɔʀtavjɔ̃/ nm inv aircraft carrier.

porte-bagages /pɔʀtbagaʒ/ nm inv (de vélo) carrier.

porte-bonheur /pɔʀtbɔnœʀ/ nm inv lucky charm.

porte-clefs /pɔʀtəkle/ nm inv key ring.

porte-documents /pɔʀtdɔkymɑ̃/ nm inv briefcase.

portée /pɔʀte/ nf (d'une arme) range; (de voûte) span; (d'animaux) litter; (impact) significance; (Mus)

stave; **à ~ de (la) main** within (arm's) reach; **hors de ~ (de)** out of reach (of); **à la ~ de qn** at sb's level.

porte-fenêtre (pl portes-fenêtres) /pɔʀtfənɛtʀ/ nf French window.

portefeuille /pɔʀtəfœj/ nm wallet; (de ministre) portfolio.

porte-jarretelles /pɔʀtʒaʀtɛl/ nm inv suspender belt.

portemanteau (pl ~x) /pɔʀtmɑ̃to/ nm coat ou hat stand.

porte-monnaie /pɔʀtmɔnɛ/ nm inv purse.

porte-parole /pɔʀtpaʀɔl/ nm inv spokesperson.

porter /pɔʀte/ **1** vt carry; (vêtement, bague) wear; (fruits, responsabilité, nom) bear; (coup) strike; (amener) bring; (inscrire) enter. ● vi (bruit) carry; (coup) hit home; **~ sur** rest on; (concerner) be about. □ se ~ vpr **bien se ~** be ou feel well; **se ~ candidat** stand as a candidate.

porteur, -euse /pɔʀtœʀ, -øz/ nm, f (de nouvelles) bearer; (Méd) carrier. ● nm (Rail) porter.

portier /pɔʀtje/ nm doorman.

portière /pɔʀtjɛʀ/ nf door.

porto /pɔʀto/ nm port (wine).

portrait /pɔʀtʀɛ/ nm portrait. **portrait-robot** (pl portraits-robots) nm identikit®, photofit®.

portuaire /pɔʀtɥɛʀ/ adj port.

portugais, ~e /pɔʀtygɛ, -z/ adj Portuguese. ● nm (Ling) Portuguese. **P~, ~e** nm, f Portuguese.

Portugal /pɔʀtygal/ nm Portugal.

pose /poz/ nf installation; (attitude) pose; (Photo) exposure.

posé, ~e /poze/ adj calm, serious.

poser /poze/ **1** vt put (down); (installer) install, put in; (fondations) lay; (*question*) ask; (*problème*) pose; ~ **sa candidature** apply (à for). ● *vi* (*modèle*) pose. □ **se** ~ *vpr* (*avion, oiseau*) land; (*regard*) fall; (se présenter) arise.

positif, -ive /pozitif, -v/ *adj* positive.

position /pozisjɔ̃/ *nf* position; **prendre** ~ take a stand.

posologie /pozolɔʒi/ *nf* dosage.

posséder /posede/ [14] *vt* (*propriété*) own, possess; (*diplôme*) have.

possessif, -ive /posesif, -v/ *adj* possessive.

possession /posesjɔ̃/ *nf* possession; **prendre** ~ **de** take possession of.

possibilité /posibilite/ *nf* possibility.

possible /posibl/ *adj* possible; **dès que** ~ as soon as possible; **le plus tard** ~ as late as possible. ● *nm* ~ what is possible; **faire son** ~ do one's utmost.

postal, ~e (*mpl* **-aux**) /postal, -o/ *adj* postal.

poste /post/ *nf* (*service*) post; (bureau) post office; ~ **aérienne** airmail; **mettre à la** ~ post; ~ **restante** poste restante. ● *nm* (lieu, emploi) post; (de radio, télévision) set; (*téléphone*) extension (number); ~ **d'essence** petrol station; ~ **d'incendie** fire point; ~ **de pilotage** cockpit; ~ **de police** police station; ~ **de secours** first-aid post.

poster[1] /poste/ [1] *vt* (*lettre, personne*) post.

poster[2] /postɛʀ/ *nm* poster.

postérieur, ~e /posteʀjœʀ/ *adj* later; (*partie*) back; ~ **à** after. ● *nm* [1] posterior.

posthume /postym/ *adj* posthumous.

postiche /postiʃ/ *adj* false.

postier, -ière /postje, -jɛʀ/ *nm, f* postal worker.

post-scriptum /postskʀiptɔm/ *nm inv* postscript.

postuler /postyle/ [1] *vt*/*i* apply (à for); (*principe*) postulate.

pot /po/ *nm* pot; (en plastique) carton; (en verre) jar; (chance [1]) luck; (boisson [1]) drink; ~ **catalytique** catalytic converter; ~ **d'échappement** exhaust pipe.

potable /potabl/ *adj* **eau** ~ drinking water.

potage /potaʒ/ *nm* soup.

potager, -ère /potaʒe, -ɛʀ/ *adj* vegetable. ● *nm* vegetable garden.

pot-au-feu /potofø/ *nm inv* (plat) stew.

pot-de-vin (*pl* **pots-de-vin**) /podvɛ̃/ *nm* bribe.

poteau (*pl* ~**x**) /poto/ *nm* post; (télégraphique) pole; ~ **indicateur** signpost.

potelé, ~e /potle/ *adj* plump.

potentiel, ~le /potɑ̃sjɛl/ *adj* & *nm* potential.

poterie /potʀi/ *nf* pottery; (objet) piece of pottery. **potier** *nm* potter.

potins /potɛ̃/ *nmpl* gossip (+ *sg*).

potiron /potiʀɔ̃/ *nm* pumpkin.

pou (*pl* ~**x**) /pu/ *nm* louse.

poubelle /pubɛl/ *nf* dustbin.

pouce /pus/ *nm* thumb; (de pied) big toe; (mesure) inch.

poudre /pudʀ/ *nf* powder; (~ à canon) gunpowder; **en** ~ (lait) powdered; (*chocolat*) drinking.

poudrier /pudʀije/ *nm* (powder) compact.

pouf /puf/ *nm* pouffe.

poulailler /pulaje/ *nm* henhouse.

poulain /pulɛ̃/ *nm* foal; (*protégé*) protégé.

poule /pul/ *nf* hen; (Culin) fowl;

(femme ⊠) tart.

poulet /pulɛ/ nm chicken.

pouliche /pulif/ nf filly.

poulie /puli/ nf pulley.

pouls /pu/ nm pulse.

poumon /pumɔ̃/ nm lung.

poupe /pup/ nf stern.

poupée /pupe/ nf doll.

pour /puʀ/ prép for; (envers) to; (à la place de) on behalf of; (comme) as; ~ cela for that reason; ~ cent per cent; ~ de bon for good; ~ faire (in order to) do; ~ que so that; ~ moi (à mon avis) as for me; trop poli ~ too polite to; ~ ce qui est de as for; être ~ be in favour. ● nm inv le ~ et le contre the pros and cons.

pourboire /puʀbwaʀ/ nm tip.

pourcentage /puʀsɑ̃taʒ/ nm percentage.

pourparlers /puʀpaʀle/ nmpl talks.

pourpre /puʀpʀ/ adj & nm crimson; (violet) purple.

pourquoi /puʀkwa/ conj & adv why. ● nm inv le ~ et le comment the why and the wherefore.

pourra, pourrait /puʀa, puʀɛ/ ➡POUVOIR 49.

pourri, ~e /puʀi/ adj rotten. **pourrir** ② vt/i rot. **pourriture** nf rot.

poursuite /puʀsɥit/ nf pursuit (de of); ~s (Jur) legal action (+ sg).

poursuivre /puʀsɥivʀ/ 57 vt pursue; (continuer) continue (with); ~ (en justice) take to court; (droit civil) sue. ● vi continue. □ se ~ vpr continue.

pourtant /puʀtɑ̃/ adv yet.

pourvoir /puʀvwaʀ/ 63 vi ~ à provide for; **pourvu de** supplied with.

pourvu que /puʀvyk(ə)/ conj (condition) provided (that); (souhait) let us hope (that).

pousse /pus/ nf growth; (bourgeon) shoot.

poussé, ~e /puse/ adj (études) advanced; (enquête) thorough.

poussée /puse/ nf pressure; (coup) push; (de prix) upsurge; (Méd) attack.

pousser /puse/ ❶ vt push; (cri) let out; (soupir) heave; (continuer) continue; (exhorter) urge (à to); (forcer) drive (à to). ● vi push; (grandir) grow; faire ~ (cheveux) let grow; (plante) grow. □ se ~ vpr move over ou up; **pousse-toi!** move over!

poussette /pusɛt/ nf pushchair.

poussière /pusjɛʀ/ nf dust. **poussiéreux, -euse** adj dusty.

poussin /pusɛ̃/ nm chick.

poutre /putʀ/ nf beam; (en métal) girder.

pouvoir /puvwaʀ/ 49 v aux (possibilité) can, be able; (permission, éventualité) may, can; il peut/pouvait/pourrait venir he can/could/might come; je n'ai pas pu I couldn't; j'ai pu faire (réussi à) I managed to do; je n'en peux plus I am exhausted; il se peut que it may be that. ● nm power; (gouvernement) government; au ~ in power; ~s publics authorities.

prairie /pʀeʀi/ nf meadow.

praticien, ~ne /pʀatisjɛ̃, -ɛn/ nm, f practitioner.

pratiquant, ~e /pʀatikɑ̃, -t/ adj practising. ● nm, f churchgoer.

pratique /pʀatik/ adj practical. ● nf practice; (expérience) experience; la ~ du golf/du cheval golfing/riding. **pratiquement** adv (en pratique) in practice; (presque) practically.

pratiquer /pratike/ **1** vt/i practise; (Sport) play; (faire) make.

pré /pre/ nm meadow.

pré-affranchi, ~e /preafrɑ̃ʃi/ adj postage-paid.

préalable /prealabl/ adj preliminary, prior. ● nm precondition; au ~ first.

préambule /preɑ̃byl/ nm preamble.

préavis /preavi/ nm notice.

précaire /prekɛR/ adj precarious. **précarité** nf (d'emploi) insecurity.

précaution /prekosjɔ̃/ nf (mesure) precaution; (prudence) caution.

précédent, ~e /presedɑ̃, -t/ adj previous. ● nm precedent.

précéder /presede/ **14** vt/i precede.

précepteur, -trice /preseptœR, -tRis/ nm, f (private) tutor.

prêcher /preʃe/ **1** vt/i preach.

précieux, -ieuse /presjø, -z/ adj precious.

précipitamment /presipitamɑ̃/ adv hastily. **précipitation** nf haste.

précipiter /presipite/ **1** vt throw, precipitate; (hâter) hasten. □ se ~ vpr (se dépêcher) rush (sur at, on to); (se jeter) throw oneself; (s'accélérer) speed up.

précis, ~e /presi, -z/ adj precise, specific; (mécanisme) accurate; **dix heures ~es** ten o'clock sharp. ● nm summary.

préciser /presize/ **1** vt specify; **précisez votre pensée** could you be more specific. □ se ~ vpr become clear(er). **précision** nf precision; (détail) detail.

précoce /prekɔs/ adj (enfant) precocious.

préconiser /prekɔnize/ **1** vt advocate.

précurseur /prekyRsœR/ nm forerunner.

prédicateur /predikatœR/ nm preacher.

prédilection /predilɛksjɔ̃/ nf preference.

prédire /predir/ **37** vt predict.

prédominer /predɔmine/ **1** vi predominate.

préface /prefas/ nf preface.

préfecture /prefɛktyR/ nf prefecture; ~ de police police headquarters.

préféré, ~e /prefere/ adj & nm, f favourite.

préférence /preferɑ̃s/ nf preference; de ~ preferably.

préférentiel, ~le /preferɑ̃sjɛl/ adj preferential.

préférer /prefere/ **14** vt prefer (à to); ~ faire prefer to do; **je ne préfère pas** I'd rather not; **j'aurais préféré ne pas savoir** I wish I hadn't found out.

préfet /prefɛ/ nm prefect; ~ de police prefect ou chief of police.

préfixe /prefiks/ nm prefix.

préhistorique /preistɔRik/ adj prehistoric.

préjudice /preʒydis/ nm harm, prejudice; **porter** ~ à harm.

préjugé /preʒyʒe/ nm prejudice; **être plein de ~s** be very prejudiced.

prélasser (se) /(sə)prelase/ **1** vpr loll (about).

prélèvement /prelɛvmɑ̃/ nm deduction; (de sang) sample. **prélever** **6** vt deduct (sur from); (sang) take.

préliminaire /preliminɛR/ adj & nm preliminary; ~s (sexuels) foreplay.

prématuré, ~e /prematyRe/ adj

premature. ● *nm* premature baby.

premier, -ière /prəmje, -jɛʀ/ *adj* first; (*rang*) front, first; (*enfance*) early; (*nécessité, souci*) prime; (*qualité*) top, prime; **de ~ ordre** first-rate; **~ ministre** Prime Minister. ● *nm, f* first (one). ● *nm* (*date*) first; (*étage*) first floor; **en ~** first. **première** *nf* (Rail) first class; (*exploit jamais vu*) first; (*cinéma*, Théât) première; (Aut) (*vitesse*) first (gear). **premièrement** *adv* firstly.

prémunir /pʀemyniʀ/ ② *vt* protect (**contre** against).

prenant, ~e /pʀənɑ̃, -t/ *adj* (*activité*) engrossing; (*enfant*) demanding.

prénatal, ~e (*mpl* **~s**) /pʀenatal/ *adj* antenatal.

prendre /pʀɑ̃dʀ/ ⑳ *vt* take; (*attraper*) catch, get; (*acheter*) get; (*repas*) have; (*engager, adopter*) take on; (*poids*) put on; (*chercher*) pick up; **qu'est-ce qui te prend?** what's the matter with you? ● *vi* (*liquide*) set; (*feu*) catch; (*vaccin*) take. □ **se ~** *vpr* **se ~ pour** think one is; **s'en ~ à** attack; (*rendre responsable*) blame; **s'y ~** set about (it).

preneur, -euse /pʀənœʀ, -øz/ *nm, f* buyer; **être ~** be willing to buy; **trouver ~** find a buyer.

prénom /pʀenɔ̃/ *nm* first name.

prénommer /pʀenɔme/ ① *vt* call. □ **se ~** *vpr* be called.

préoccupation /pʀeɔkypasjɔ̃/ *nf* (*souci*) worry; (*idée fixe*) preoccupation.

préoccuper /pʀeɔkype/ ① *vt* worry; (*absorber*) preoccupy. □ **se ~ de** *vpr* think about.

préparation /pʀepaʀasjɔ̃/ *nf* preparation. **préparatoire** *adj* preparatory.

préparer /pʀepaʀe/ ① *vt* prepare;

(*repas, café*) make; **plats préparés** ready-cooked meals. □ **se ~** vpr prepare oneself (**à** for); (*s'apprêter*) get ready; (*être proche*) be brewing.

préposé, ~e /pʀepoze/ *nm, f* employee; (*des postes*) postman, postwoman.

préposition /pʀepozisjɔ̃/ *nf* preposition.

préretraite /pʀeʀətʀɛt/ *nf* early retirement.

près /pʀɛ/ *adv* near, close; **~ de** near (to), close to; (*presque*) nearly; **à cela ~** except that; **de ~** closely.

présage /pʀezaʒ/ *nm* omen.

presbyte /pʀɛsbit/ *adj* long-sighted, far-sighted.

prescrire /pʀɛskʀiʀ/ ㉚ *vt* prescribe.

préséance /pʀeseɑ̃s/ *nf* precedence.

présence /pʀezɑ̃s/ *nf* presence; (Scol) attendance.

présent, ~e /pʀezɑ̃, -t/ *adj* present. ● *nm* (*temps, cadeau*) present; **à ~** now.

présentateur, -trice /pʀezɑ̃tatœʀ, -tʀis/ *nm, f* presenter.

présentation /pʀezɑ̃tasjɔ̃/ *nf* (*de personne*) introduction; (*exposé*) presentation.

présenter /pʀezɑ̃te/ ① *vt* present; (*personne*) introduce (**à** to); (*montrer*) show. ● *vi* **bien** have a pleasing appearance. □ **se ~** vpr introduce oneself (**à** to); (*aller*) go; (*apparaître*) appear; (*candidat*) come forward; (*occasion*) arise; **se ~ à** (*examen*) sit for; (*élection*) stand for; **se ~ bien** look good.

préservatif /pʀezɛʀvatif/ *nm* condom.

préserver /pʀezɛʀve/ ① *vt* protect.

présidence /prezidãs/ nf (d'État) presidency; (de société) chairmanship.

président, ~e /prezidã, -t/ nm, f president; (de société, comité) chairman, chairwoman; **~directeur général** managing director.

présidentiel, ~le /prezidãsjɛl/ adj presidential.

présider /prezide/ **1** vt preside.

présomptueux, -euse /prezɔ̃ptɥø, -z/ adj presumptuous.

presque /prɛsk(ə)/ adv almost, nearly; **~ jamais** hardly ever; **~ rien** hardly anything; **~ pas (de)** hardly any.

presqu'île /prɛskil/ nf peninsula.

pressant, ~e /prɛsã, -t/ adj pressing, urgent.

presse /prɛs/ nf (journaux, appareil) press.

pressentiment /prɛsãtimã/ nm premonition. **pressentir** 🔢 vt have a premonition of.

pressé, ~e /prese/ adj in a hurry; (orange, citron) freshly squeezed.

presser /prese/ **1** vt squeeze, press; (appuyer sur, harceler) press; (hâter) hasten; (inciter) urge (**de** to). ● vi (temps) press; (affaire) be pressing. □ **se ~** vpr (se hâter) hurry; (se grouper) crowd.

pressing /prɛsiŋ/ nm (teinturerie) dry-cleaner's.

pression /prɛsjɔ̃/ nf pressure; (bouton) press-stud.

prestance /prɛstãs/ nf (imposing) presence.

prestation /prɛstasjɔ̃/ nf allowance; (d'artiste) performance.

prestidigitation /prɛstidiʒitasjɔ̃/ nf conjuring.

prestige /prɛstiʒ/ nm prestige.

prestigieux, -leuse adj prestigious.

présumé, e /prezyme/ adj alleged.

présumer /prezyme/ **1** vt presume; **~ que** assume that; **~ de** overrate.

prêt, ~e /prɛ, -t/ adj ready (**à qch** for sth, **à faire** to do). ● nm loan. **prêt-à-porter** nm inv ready-to-wear clothes.

prétendre /pretãdr/ **3** vt claim (**que** that); (vouloir) intend; **on le prétend riche** he is said to be very rich. **prétendu, ~e** adj so-called. **prétendument** adv supposedly, allegedly.

prétentieux, -leuse /pretãsjø, -z/ adj pretentious.

prêter /prete/ **1** vt lend (**à** to); (attribuer) attribute; **~ son aide à qn** give sb some help; **~ attention** pay attention; **~ serment** take an oath. ● vi **~ à** lead to.

prêteur, -euse /pretœr, -øz/ nm, f (money-)lender; **~ sur gages** pawnbroker.

prétexte /pretɛkst/ nm pretext, excuse.

prêtre /prɛtr/ nm priest.

preuve /prœv/ nf proof; **des ~s** evidence (+ sg); **faire ~ de** show; **faire ses ~s** prove oneself.

prévaloir /prevalwar/ 🔢 vi prevail.

prévenant, ~e /prevnã, -t/ adj thoughtful.

prévenir /prevnir/ 🔢 vt (menacer) warn; (informer) tell; (médecin) call; (éviter, anticiper) prevent.

préventif, -ive /prevãtif, -v/ adj preventive.

prévention /prevãsjɔ̃/ nf prevention; **faire de la ~** take preventive action; **~ routière** road safety.

prévenu, ~e /prevny/ nm, f defendant.

prévisible /pʀevizibl/ adj predictable. **prévision** nf prediction; (météorologique) forecast.

prévoir /pʀevwaʀ/ [63] vt foresee; (temps) forecast; (organiser) plan (for); (envisager) allow (for); **prévu pour** (jouet) designed for; **comme prévu** as planned.

prévoyance /pʀevwajɑ̃s/ nf foresight. **prévoyant, ~e** adj farsighted.

prier /pʀije/ [45] vi pray to; (demander à) ask (de to); **je vous en prie** please; (il n'y a pas de quoi) don't mention it.

prière /pʀijɛʀ/ nf prayer; (demande) request; **~ de** (vous êtes prié de) will you please.

primaire /pʀimɛʀ/ adj primary.

prime /pʀim/ nf free gift; (d'employé) bonus; (subvention) subsidy; (d'assurance) premium.

primé, ~e /pʀime/ adj prizewinning.

primeurs /pʀimœʀ/ nfpl early fruit and vegetables.

primevère /pʀimvɛʀ/ nf primrose.

primitif, -ive /pʀimitif, -v/ adj primitive; (d'origine) original. ● nm, f primitive.

primordial, ~e /pʀimɔʀdjal/ (mpl **-iaux** /-jo/) adj essential.

prince /pʀɛ̃s/ nm prince. **princesse** nf princess.

principal, ~e /pʀɛ̃sipal/ (mpl **-aux**) /-o/ adj main, principal. ● nm headmaster; (chose) main thing.

principe /pʀɛ̃sip/ nm principle; **en ~** in theory; (d'habitude) as a rule.

printanier, -ière /pʀɛ̃tanje, -jɛʀ/ adj spring(-like).

printemps /pʀɛ̃tɑ̃/ nm spring.

prioritaire /pʀijɔʀitɛʀ/ adj prior-

ity; **être ~** have priority. **priorité** nf priority; (Auto) right of way.

Priorité à droite Except at roundabouts, and unless there are other indications or regulations in force, French drivers must always give way to traffic approaching from the right.

pris, ~e /pʀi, -z/ adj (place) taken; (personne, journée) busy; (nez) stuffed up; **~ de** (peur, fièvre) stricken with; **~ de panique** panicstricken. ● ➡PRENDRE 50.

prise /pʀiz/ nf hold, grip; (animal attrapé) catch; (Mil) capture; (~ de courant) (mâle) plug; (femelle) socket; **~ multiple** multiplug adapter; **avoir ~ sur qn** have a hold over sb; **aux ~s avec** to grapple with; **~ de conscience** awareness; **~ de contact** first contact, initial meeting; **~ de position** stand; **~ de sang** blood test.

prisé, ~e /pʀize/ adj popular.

prison /pʀizɔ̃/ nf prison, jail; (réclusion) imprisonment. **prisonnier, -ière** nm, f prisoner.

privation /pʀivasjɔ̃/ nf deprivation; (sacrifice) hardship.

privatiser /pʀivatize/ [1] vt privatize.

privé /pʀive/ adj private. ● nm (Comm) private sector; (Scol) private schools (+ pl); **en ~** in private.

priver /pʀive/ [1] vt **~ de** deprive of. □ se **~ (de)** vpr go without.

privilège /pʀivilɛʒ/ nm privilege. **privilégié, ~e** nm, f privileged person.

prix /pʀi/ nm price; (récompense) prize; **à tout ~** at all costs; **au ~ de** (fig) at the expense of; **~ coûtant, ~ de revient** cost price; **à ~ fixe** set price.

probabilité /pʀɔbabilite/ nf probability. **probable** adj probable, likely. **probablement** adv probably.

probant, ~e /pʀɔbɑ̃, -t/ adj convincing, conclusive.

problème /pʀɔblɛm/ nm problem.

procédé /pʀɔsede/ nm process; (manière d'agir) practice.

procéder /pʀɔsede/ **14** vi proceed; **à** carry out.

procès /pʀɔsɛ/ nm (criminel) trial; (civil) lawsuit, proceedings (+ pl).

processus /pʀɔsesys/ nm process; **~ de paix** peace process.

procès-verbal (pl **procès-verbaux**) /pʀɔsɛvɛʀbal, -o/ nm minutes (+ pl); (contravention) ticket.

prochain, ~e /pʀɔʃɛ̃, -ɛn/ adj (suivant) next; (proche) imminent; (avenir) near. ● nm fellow man. **prochainement** adv soon.

proche /pʀɔʃ/ adj near, close; (avoisinant) neighbouring; (parent, ami) close; **~ de** close ou near to; **de ~ en ~** gradually; **dans un ~ avenir** in the near future; **être ~** (imminent) be approaching. ● nm close relative; (ami) close friend.

Proche-Orient /pʀɔʃɔʀjɑ̃/ nm Near East.

proclamation /pʀɔklamasjɔ̃/ nf declaration, proclamation. **proclamer** **1** vt declare, proclaim.

procuration /pʀɔkyʀasjɔ̃/ nf proxy.

procurer /pʀɔkyʀe/ **1** vt bring (à to). □ **se ~** vpr obtain.

procureur /pʀɔkyʀœʀ/ nm public prosecutor.

prodige /pʀɔdiʒ/ nm (fait) marvel; (personne) prodigy; **enfant ~ musicien ~** child/musical prodigy. **prodigieux, -ieuse** adj tremendous, prodigious.

prodigue /pʀɔdig/ adj wasteful;

fils ~ prodigal son.

producteur, -trice /pʀɔdyktœʀ, -tʀis/ adj producing. ● nm, f producer. **productif, -ive** adj productive. **production** nf production; (produit) product. **productivité** nf productivity.

produire /pʀɔdɥiʀ/ **17** vt produce. □ **se ~** vpr (survenir) happen; (acteur) perform.

produit /pʀɔdɥi/ nm product; **~s** (de la terre) produce (+ sg) ; **~ chimique** chemical; **~s alimentaires** foodstuffs; **~ de consommation** consumer goods; **~ intérieur brut** gross domestic product; **~ national brut** gross national product.

proéminent, ~e /pʀɔeminɑ̃, -t/ adj prominent.

profane /pʀɔfan/ adj secular. ● nmf lay person.

proférer /pʀɔfeʀe/ **14** vt utter.

professeur /pʀɔfesœʀ/ nm teacher; (Univ) lecturer; (avec chaire) professor.

profession /pʀɔfesjɔ̃/ nf occupation; **~ libérale** profession.

professionnel, ~le /pʀɔfesjɔnɛl/ adj professional; (école) vocational. ● nm, f professional.

profil /pʀɔfil/ nm profile.

profit /pʀɔfi/ nm profit; **au ~ de** in aid of. **profitable** adj profitable.

profiter /pʀɔfite/ **1** vi **~ à** benefit; **~ de** take advantage of.

profond, ~e /pʀɔfɔ̃, -d/ adj deep; (sentiment, intérêt) profound; (causes) underlying; **au plus ~ de** in the depths of. **profondément** adv deeply; (différent, triste) profoundly; (dormir) soundly. **profondeur** nf depth.

progéniture /pʀɔʒenityʀ/ nf offspring.

progiciel /pʀɔʒisjɛl/ nm (Ordinat)

p

package.

programmation /prɔgramasjɔ̃/ nf programming.

programme /prɔgram/ nm programme; (Scol) (d'une matière) syllabus; (général) curriculum; (Ordinat) program. ● vt (ordinateur, appareil) program; (émission) schedule. **programmeur, -euse** nm, f computer programmer.

progrès /prɔgrɛ/ nm & nmpl progress; **faire des ~** make progress. **progresser** 1 vi progress. **progressif, -ive** adj progressive. **progression** nf progression.

prohibitif, -ive /prɔibitif, -v/ adj prohibitive.

proie /prwa/ nf prey; **en ~ à** tormented by.

projecteur /prɔʒɛktœr/ nm floodlight; (Mil) searchlight; (cinéma) projector.

projectile /prɔʒɛktil/ nm missile.

projection /prɔʒɛksjɔ̃/ nf projection; (séance) show.

projet /prɔʒɛ/ nm plan; (ébauche) draft; **~ de loi** bill.

projeter /prɔʒte/ 38 vt (prévoir) plan (de to); (film) project, show; (jeter) hurl, project.

prolétaire /prɔletɛr/ nmf proletarian.

prologue /prɔlog/ nm prologue.

prolongation /prɔlɔ̃gasjɔ̃/ nf extension; **~s** (football) extra time.

prolonger /prɔlɔ̃ʒe/ 40 vt extend. □ **se ~** vpr go on.

promenade /prɔmnad/ nf walk; (à bicyclette, à cheval) ride; (en auto) drive, ride; **faire une ~** go for a walk.

promener /prɔmne/ 6 vt take for a walk; **~ son regard sur** cast an eye over. □ **se ~** vpr walk; (aller) **se ~** go for a walk. **prome-**

neur, **-euse** nm, f walker.

promesse /prɔmɛs/ nf promise.

prometteur, -euse /prɔmɛtœr, -øz/ adj promising.

promettre /prɔmɛtr/ 42 vt/i promise. ● vi be promising. □ **se ~ de** vpr resolve to.

promoteur /prɔmɔtœr/ nm (immobilier) property developer.

promotion /prɔmɔsjɔ̃/ nf promotion; (Univ) year; (Comm) special offer.

prompt, ~e /prɔ̃, -t/ adj swift.

promu, ~e /prɔmy/ adj **être ~** be promoted.

prôner /prone/ 1 vt extol.

pronom /prɔnɔ̃/ nm pronoun. **pronominal, ~e** (mpl -aux) adj pronominal.

prononcé, ~e /prɔnɔ̃se/ adj strong.

prononcer /prɔnɔ̃se/ 10 vt pronounce; (discours) make. □ **se ~** vpr (mot) be pronounced; (personne) make a decision (**pour** in favour of). **prononciation** nf pronunciation.

pronostic /prɔnɔstik/ nm forecast; (Méd) prognosis.

propagande /prɔpagɑ̃d/ nf propaganda.

propager /prɔpaʒe/ 40 vt spread. □ **se ~** vpr spread.

prophète /prɔfɛt/ nm prophet. **prophétie** nf prophecy.

propice /prɔpis/ adj favourable.

proportion /prɔpɔrsjɔ̃/ nf proportion; (en mathématiques) ratio; **toutes ~s gardées** relatively speaking. **proportionné, ~e** adj proportionate (**à** to). **proportionnel, ~le** adj proportional. **proportionnellement** adv proportionately.

propos /prɔpo/ nm intention; (sujet) subject; **à ~** at the right time; (dans un dialogue) by the way; **à ~ de** about; **à tout ~ at** every possible occasion. ● *nmpl* (paroles) remarks.

proposer /pʀɔpoze/ **1** *vt* suggest, propose; (offrir) offer. **□ se ~** *vpr* volunteer (**pour** to). **proposition** *nf* proposal; (affirmation) proposition; (Gram) clause.

propre /pʀɔpʀ/ *adj* (non sali) clean; (soigné) neat; (honnête) decent; (à soi) own; (sens) literal; **~ à** (qui convient) suited to; (spécifique) particular to. ● *nm* **mettre au ~** write out again neatly; **c'est du ~!** (ironique) well done!

proprement /pʀɔpʀəmã/ *adv* (avec soin) neatly; (au sens strict) strictly; **le bureau ~ dit** the office itself.

propreté /pʀɔpʀəte/ *nf* cleanliness.

propriétaire /pʀɔpʀijetɛʀ/ *nmf* owner; (Comm) proprietor; (qui loue) landlord, landlady.

propriété /pʀɔpʀijete/ *nf* property; (droit) ownership.

propulser /pʀɔpylse/ **1** *vt* propel.

proroger /pʀɔʀɔʒe/ **40** *vt* (contrat) defer; (passeport) extend.

proscrire /pʀɔskʀiʀ/ **30** *vt* proscribe.

proscrit, ~e /pʀɔskʀi, -t/ *adj* proscribed. ● *nm, f* (exilé) exile.

prose /pʀoz/ *nf* prose.

prospectus /pʀɔspɛktys/ *nm* leaflet.

prospère /pʀɔspɛʀ/ *adj* flourishing, thriving. **prospérer** **14** *vi* thrive, prosper. **prospérité** *nf* prosperity.

prosterner (se) /(sə)pʀɔstɛʀne/ **1** *vpr* prostrate oneself; **prosterné devant** prostrate before.

prostituée /pʀɔstitɥe/ *nf* prostitute. **prostitution** *nf* prostitution.

protecteur, -trice /pʀɔtɛktœʀ,

-tʀis/ *nm, f* protector. ● *adj* protective.

protection /pʀɔtɛksjɔ̃/ *nf* protection.

protégé, ~e /pʀɔteʒe/ *nm, f* protégé.

protéger /pʀɔteʒe/ **40** *vt* protect. **□ se ~** *vpr* protect oneself.

protéine /pʀɔtein/ *nf* protein.

protestant, ~e /pʀɔtɛstã, -t/ *adj & nm, f* Protestant.

protestation /pʀɔtɛstasjɔ̃/ *nf* protest. **protester** **1** *vt/i* protest.

protocole /pʀɔtɔkɔl/ *nm* protocol.

protubérant, ~e /pʀɔtybeʀã, -t/ *adj* protruding.

proue /pʀu/ *nf* bow, prow.

prouesse /pʀuɛs/ *nf* feat, exploit.

prouver /pʀuve/ **1** *vt* prove.

provenance /pʀɔvnãs/ *nf* origin; **en ~ de** from.

provençal, ~e (*mpl* **-aux**) /pʀɔvãsal, -o/ *adj & nm, f* Provençal.

provenir /pʀɔvniʀ/ **58** *vi* **~ de** come from.

proverbe /pʀɔvɛʀb/ *nm* proverb.

province /pʀɔvɛ̃s/ *nf* province; **de ~** provincial; **la ~** the provinces (+ *pl*). **provincial, ~e** (*mpl* **-iaux**) *adj & nm, f* provincial.

proviseur /pʀɔvizœʀ/ *nm* headmaster, principal.

provision /pʀɔvizjɔ̃/ *nf* supply, store; (sur un compte) credit (balance); (acompte) deposit; **~s** (vivres) food shopping.

provisoire /pʀɔvizwaʀ/ *adj* provisional.

provocant, ~e /pʀɔvɔkã, -t/ *adj* provocative. **provocation** *nf* provocation. **provoquer** **1** *vt* cause; (sexuellement) arouse; (défier) provoke.

proxénète /pʀɔksenɛt/ nm pimp, procurer.

proximité /pʀɔksimite/ nf proximity; à ~ de close to.

prude /pʀyd/ adj prudish.

prudemment /pʀydamã/ adv (conduire) carefully; (attendre) cautiously. **prudence** nf caution. **prudent**, ~e adj (au volant) careful; (à agir) cautious; (sage) wise.

prune /pʀyn/ nf plum.

pruneau (pl ~x) /pʀyno/ nm prune.

prunelle /pʀynɛl/ nf (pupille) pupil; (fruit) sloe.

prunier /pʀynje/ nm plum tree.

psaume /psom/ nm psalm.

pseudonyme /psødɔnim/ nm pseudonym.

psychanalyse /psikanaliz/ nf psychoanalysis. **psychanalyste** nmf psychoanalyst.

psychiatre /psikjatʀ/ nmf psychiatrist. **psychiatrie** nf psychiatry. **psychiatrique** adj psychiatric.

psychique /psiʃik/ adj mental, psychological.

psychologie /psikɔlɔʒi/ nf psychology. **psychologique** adj psychological. **psychologue** nmf psychologist.

pu /py/ →**POUVOIR** 49.

puant, ~e adj stinking.

pub /pyb/ nf 1 la ~ advertising; une ~ an advert.

puberté /pybɛʀte/ nf puberty.

public, -que /pyblik/ adj public. ● nm public; (assistance) audience; (Scol) state schools (+ pl); en ~ in public.

publication /pyblikasjɔ̃/ nf publication.

publicitaire /pyblisitɛʀ/ adj pub-

licity. **publicité** nf publicity, advertising; (annonce) advertisement.

publier /pyblije/ 45 vt publish.

publiquement /pyblikmã/ adv publicly.

puce /pys/ nf flea; (électronique) chip; **marché aux** ~**s** flea market.

pudeur /pydœʀ/ nf modesty.

pudibond, ~e /pydibɔ̃, -d/ adj prudish.

pudique /pydik/ adj modest.

puer /pye/ 1 vi stink. ● vt stink of.

puéricultrice /pyeʀikyltʀis/ nf pediatric nurse.

puéril, ~e /pyeʀil/ adj puerile.

puis /pɥi/ adv then.

puiser /pɥize/ 1 vt draw (**dans** from). ● vi ~ **dans qch** dip into sth.

puisque /pɥisk(ə)/ conj since, as.

puissance /pɥisãs/ nf power; **en** ~ potential.

puissant, ~e /pɥisã, -t/ adj powerful.

puits /pɥi/ nm well; (de mine) shaft.

pull(-over) /pyl(ɔvɛʀ)/ nm pullover, jumper.

pulpe /pylp/ nf pulp.

pulsation /pylsasjɔ̃/ nf (heart-) beat.

pulvériser /pylveʀize/ 1 vt pulverize; (liquide) spray.

punaise /pynɛz/ nf (insecte) bug; (clou) drawing pin.

punch[1] /pɔ̃ʃ/ nm (boisson) punch.

punch[2] /pœnʃ/ nm **avoir du** ~ have drive.

punir /pyniʀ/ 2 vt punish. **punition** nf punishment.

pupille[1] /pypij/ nf (de l'œil) pupil. ● nmf (enfant) ward.

pupitre /pypitʀ/ nm (Scol) desk; ~ **à musique** music stand.

pur /pyʀ/ adj pure; (whisky) neat.

purée /pyʀe/ nf purée; (de pommes de terre) mashed potatoes (+ pl).

pureté /pyʀte/ nf purity.

purgatoire /pyʀgatwaʀ/ nm purgatory.

purge /pyʀʒ/ nf purge. **purger** 40 vt (Pol, Méd) purge; (peine: Jur) serve.

purifier /pyʀifje/ 45 vt purify.

puritain, ~e /pyʀitɛ̃, -ɛn/ nm, f puritan. ● adj puritanical.

pur-sang /pyʀsɑ̃/ nm inv (cheval) thoroughbred.

pus /py/ nm pus.

putain /pytɛ̃/ nf p whore.

puzzle /pœzl/ nm jigsaw (puzzle).

P-V abrév m (**procès-verbal**) ticket, traffic fine.

pyjama /piʒama/ nm pyjamas (+ pl); un ~ a pair of pyjamas.

pylône /pilon/ nm pylon.

Pyrénées /piʀene/ nfpl les ~ the Pyrenees.

pyromane /piʀɔman/ nmf arsonist.

• • • • • • • • • • • • • • • • • • •

Qq

QG abrév m (**quartier général**) HQ.

QI abrév m (**quotient intellectuel**) IQ.

qu' /k/ ⇒QUE.

quadriller /kadʀije/ 1 vt (armée) take control of; (police) spread one's net over; **papier quadrillé** squared paper.

quadrupède /kadʀypɛd/ nm quadruped.

quadruple /kadʀypl/ adj quadruple. ● nm le ~ de four times. **quadrupler** 1 vt/i quadruple.

quai /ke/ nm (de gare) platform; (de port) quay; (de rivière) bank.

qualification /kalifikasjɔ̃/ nf qualification; (compétence pratique) skills (+ pl).

qualifié, ~e /kalifje/ adj (diplômé) qualified; (main-d'œuvre) skilled.

qualifier /kalifje/ 45 vt qualify; (décrire) describe (**de** as). □ **se** ~ vpr qualify (**pour** for).

qualité /kalite/ nf quality; (titre) occupation; (fonction) position; **en sa** ~ **de** in his or her capacity as.

quand /kɑ̃/ adv when; ~ **même** all the same. ● conj when; (toutes les fois que) whenever; ~ **bien même** even if.

quant à /kɑ̃ta/ prép as for.

quantité /kɑ̃tite/ nf quantity; **une** ~ **de** a lot of; **des** ~**s** (**de**) masses ou lots (of).

quarantaine /kaʀɑ̃tɛn/ nf (Méd) quarantine; **une** ~ (**de**) about forty; **avoir la** ~ be in one's forties.

quarante /kaʀɑ̃t/ adj & nm forty.

quart /kaʀ/ nm quarter; (Naut) watch; **onze heures moins le** ~ quarter to eleven; ~ (**de litre**) quarter litre; ~ **de finale** quarter-final; ~ **d'heure** quarter of an hour; ~ **de tour** ninety-degree turn.

quartier /kaʀtje/ nm area, district; (zone ethnique) quarter; (de lune, pomme, bœuf) quarter; (d'une orange) segment; ~**s** (Mil) quarters; **de** ~, **du** ~ local; ~ **général** headquarters; **avoir** ~

p
q

libre be free.

quasiment /kazimã/ adv almost, practically.

quatorze /katɔʀz/ adj & nm fourteen.

quatre /katʀ(ə)/ adj & nm four. **quatre-vingt(s)** adj & nm eighty. **quatre-vingt-dix** adj & nm ninety.

quatre-quatre /katʀkatʀ/ nm four-wheel drive.

quatrième /katʀijɛm/ adj & nmf fourth. ● nf (Auto) fourth gear.

quatuor /kwatɥɔʀ/ nm quartet.

---

que, qu' /kə, k/

qu' before vowel or mute h.

● conjunction

····▸ that; **je crains ~...** I'm worried that...

····▸ (souhait, volonté) **je veux ~ tu viennes** I want you to come; **~ tu viennes ou non** whether you come or not; **qu'il entre** let him come in.

····▸ (comparaison) than; **plus grand ~ toi** taller than you.

● pronom interrogatif

····▸ what; **~ voulez-vous manger?** what would you like to eat?

● pronom relatif

····▸ (personne) whom, that; **l'homme ~ j'ai rencontré** the man (whom) I met.

····▸ (chose) that, which; **le cheval ~ Nick m'a offert** the horse (which) Nick gave me.

● adverbe

····▸ **que c'est joli!** it's so pretty!; **~ de monde!** what a lot of people!

Québec /kebɛk/ nm Quebec.

---

quel, quelle (pl **quel-(le)s**) /kɛl/

● adjectif interrogatif

····▸ which, what; **~ auteur a écrit...?** which writer wrote...?; **~ jour sommes-nous?** what day is it today?

● adjectif exclamatif

····▸ what; **~ idiot!** what an idiot!; **quelle horreur!** that's horrible!

● adjectif relatif

····▸ **~ que soit son âge** whatever his age; **quelles que soient tes raisons** whatever your reasons; **~ que soit le gagnant** whoever the winner is.

quelconque /kɛlkɔ̃k/ adj any, some; (banal) ordinary; (médiocre) poor, second rate.

quelque /kɛlkə/ adj some; **~s** a few, some. ● adv (environ), about, some; **et ~** 🔢 and a bit; **~ chose** something; (dans les phrases interrogatives) anything; **~ part** somewhere; **~ peu** somewhat.

quelquefois /kɛlkəfwa/ adv sometimes.

quelques-uns, -unes /kɛlkəzœ̃, -yn/ pron some, a few.

quelqu'un /kɛlkœ̃/ pron someone, somebody; (dans les phrases interrogatives) anyone, anybody.

querelle /kəʀɛl/ nf quarrel. **quereller (se)** 🔢 vpr quarrel. **querelleur, -euse** adj quarrelsome.

question /kɛstjɔ̃/ nf question; (affaire) matter, question; **poser une ~** ask a question; **en ~** in question; **il est ~ de** (cela concerne) it is about; (on parle de) there is talk of; **il n'en est pas ~** it is out of the question; **pas ~!** no way!

q

questionnaire /kɛstjɔnɛr/ nm questionnaire.

questionner /kɛstjɔne/ **1** vt question.

quête /kɛt/ nf (Relig) collection; (recherche) search; **en ~ de** in search of.

queue /kø/ nf tail; (de poêle) handle; (de fruit) stalk; (de fleur) stem; (file) queue; (US) line; (de train) rear; **faire la ~** queue (up); (US) line up; **~ de cheval** ponytail; **faire une ~ de poisson à qn** (Auto) cut in front of sb.

qui /ki/

● *pronom interrogatif*

····▸ (sujet) who; **~ a fait ça?** who did that?

····▸ (complément) whom; **à ~ est ce livre?** whose book is this?

● *pronom relatif*

····▸ (personne sujet) who; **c'est Isabelle qui vient d'appeler** it's Isabelle who's just called.

····▸ (autres cas) that, which; **qu'est-ce ~ te prend?** what is the matter with you?; **invite ~ tu veux** invite whoever you want; **~ que ce soit** whoever it is, anybody.

quiche /kiʃ/ nf quiche.

quiconque /kikɔ̃k/ pron whoever; (n'importe qui) anyone.

quille /kij/ nf (de bateau) keel; (jouet) skittle.

quincaillerie /kɛ̃kɑjʀi/ nf hardware; (magasin) hardware shop. **quincaillier, -ière** nm, f hardware dealer.

quintal (pl **-aux**) /kɛ̃tal, -o/ nm quintal, one hundred kilos.

quinte /kɛ̃t/ nf ~ **de toux** coughing fit.

quintuple /kɛ̃typl/ adj quintuple. ● nm **le ~ de** five times. **quintupler** **1** vt/i quintuple, increase fivefold.

quinzaine /kɛ̃zɛn/ nf **une ~ (de)** about fifteen.

quinze /kɛ̃z/ adj & nm inv fifteen; ~ **jours** two weeks.

quiproquo /kipʀɔko/ nm misunderstanding.

quittance /kitɑ̃s/ nf receipt.

quitte /kit/ adj quits (**envers** with); ~ **à faire** even if it means doing.

quitter /kite/ **1** vt leave; (vêtement) take off; **ne quittez pas!** hold the line, please! □ **se ~** vpr part.

qui-vive /kiviv/ nm inv **être sur le ~** be alert.

quoi /kwa/ pron what; (après une préposition) which; **de ~ vivre** (assez) enough to live on; **de ~ écrire** something to write with; ~ **qu'il dise** whatever he says; ~ **que ce soit** anything; **il n'y a pas de ~ my pleasure; **il n'y a pas de ~ s'inquiéter** there's nothing to worry about.

quoique /kwak(ə)/ conj although, though.

quota /kɔta/ nm quota.

quote-part (pl **quotes-parts**) /kɔtpaʀ/ nf share.

quotidien, -ne /kɔtidjɛ̃, -ɛn/ adj daily; (banal) everyday. ● nm daily (paper); (vie quotidienne) everyday life. **quotidiennement** adv daily.

q

Rr

rabâcher /ʀabaʃe/ **1** vt keep repeating.

rabais /ʀabɛ/ nm reduction, discount. **rabaisser 1** vt (déprécier) belittle; (réduire) reduce.

rabat-joie /ʀabaʒwa/ nm inv killjoy.

rabattre /ʀabatʀ/ **11** vt (chapeau, visière) pull down; (refermer) shut; (diminuer) reduce; (déduire) take off; (col, drap) turn down. **□ se ~** vpr (se refermer) close; (véhicule) cut back in; **se ~ sur** make do with.

rabot /ʀabo/ nm plane.

rabougri, ~e /ʀabugʀi/ adj stunted.

racaille /ʀakɑj/ nf rabble.

raccommoder /ʀakɔmɔde/ **1** vt mend; (personnes **1**) reconcile.

raccompagner /ʀakɔ̃paɲe/ **1** vt see ou take back (home).

raccord /ʀakɔʀ/ nm link; (de papier peint) join; (retouche) touch-up. **raccorder 1** vt connect, join.

raccourci /ʀakuʀsi/ nm short cut; **en ~** in short.

raccourcir /ʀakuʀsiʀ/ **2** vt shorten. ● vi get shorter.

raccrocher /ʀakʀɔʃe/ **11** vt hang back up; (passant) grab hold of; (relier) connect; **le combiné** or **le téléphone** hang up. ● vi hang up. **□ se ~ à** vpr cling to; (se relier à) be connected to ou with.

race /ʀas/ nf race; (animale) breed; **de ~** (chien) pedigree; (cheval) thoroughbred.

racheter /ʀaʃte/ **6** vt buy (back); (acheter encore) buy more; (nouvel objet) buy another; (société) buy

out; **~ des chaussettes** buy new socks. **□ se ~** vpr make amends.

racial, ~e (mpl **-iaux**) /ʀasjal, -o/ adj racial.

racine /ʀasin/ nf root; **~ carrée/ cubique** square/cube root.

racisme /ʀasism/ nm racism. **raciste** adj & nmf racist.

racket /ʀakɛt/ nm racketeering.

raclée /ʀakle/ nf **1** thrashing.

racler /ʀakle/ **11** vt scrape. **□ se ~** vpr **se ~ la gorge** clear one's throat.

racolage /ʀakɔlaʒ/ nm soliciting.

raconter /ʀakɔ̃te/ **11** vt (histoire) tell; (vacances) tell about; (vie, épisode) describe; **~ à qn que** tell sb that, say to sb that; **qu'est-ce que tu racontes?** what are you talking about?

radar /ʀadaʀ/ nm radar; (automatique) speed camera.

radeau (pl **~x**) /ʀado/ nm raft.

radiateur /ʀadjatœʀ/ nm radiator; (électrique) heater.

radiation /ʀadjasjɔ̃/ nf radiation.

radical, ~e (mpl **-aux**) /ʀadikal, -o/ adj radical. ● nm (pl **-aux**) radical.

radieux, -ieuse /ʀadjø, -z/ adj radiant.

radin, ~e /ʀadɛ̃, -in/ adj **1** stingy **1**.

radio /ʀadjo/ nf radio; **à la ~** on the radio; (radiographie) X-ray.

radioactif, -ive /ʀadjoaktif, -v/ adj radioactive. **radioactivité** nf radioactivity.

radiocassette /ʀadjokasɛt/ nf radio cassette player.

radiodiffuser /ʀadjodifyze/ **11** vt broadcast.

radiographie /ʀadjɔgʀafi/ nf (photographie) X-ray.

radiomessageur /Radjɔmesa-ʒœR/ nm pager.

radis /Radi/ nm radish; **ne pas avoir un ~** 🔲 be broke.

radoter /Radote/ 🔳 vi 🔲 talk drivel.

radoucir (se) /(sə)Radusir/ 🔳 vpr (humeur) improve; (temps) become milder.

rafale /Rafal/ nf (de vent) gust; (de mitraillette) burst.

raffermir /RafɛRmiR/ 🔳 vt strengthen. □ **se ~** vpr become stronger.

raffiné, **~e** /Rafine/ adj refined. **raffinement** nm refinement.

raffiner /Rafine/ 🔳 vt refine. **raffinerie** nf refinery.

raffoler /Rafole/ 🔳 vt 🔲 **~ de** be crazy about.

raffut /Rafy/ nm 🔲 din.

rafle /Rafl/ nf (police) raid.

rafraîchir /RafReʃiR/ 🔳 vt cool (down); (mur) give a fresh coat of paint to; (personne, mémoire) refresh. □ **se ~** vpr (boire) refresh oneself; (temps) get cooler. **rafraîchissant**, **~e** adj refreshing.

rafraîchissement /RafReʃismɑ̃/ nm (boisson) cold drink; **~s** refreshments.

ragaillardir /RagajaRdiR/ 🔳 vt 🔲 cheer up.

rage /Raʒ/ nf rage; (maladie) rabies; **faire ~** (bataille, incendie) rage; (maladie) be rife; **~ de dents** raging toothache. **rageant**, **~e** adj infuriating.

ragots /Rago/ nmpl 🔲 gossip.

ragoût /Ragu/ nm stew.

raid /Rɛd/ nm (Mil) raid; (Sport) trek.

raide /Rɛd/ adj stiff; (côte) steep; (corde) tight; (cheveux) straight. ● adv (monter, descendre) steeply.

raideur nf stiffness; steepness.

raidir /RediR/ 🔳 vt (corps) tense. □ **se ~** vpr tense up; (position) harden; (corde) tighten.

raie /Rɛ/ nf (ligne) line; (bande) strip; (de cheveux) parting; (poisson) skate.

raifort /RefɔR/ nm horseradish.

rail /Raj/ nm rail, track; **le ~** (transport) rail.

raisin /Rɛzɛ̃/ nm **le ~** grapes; **~ sec** raisin; **un grain de ~** a grape.

raison /Rɛzɔ̃/ nf reason; **à ~ de** at the rate of; **avec ~** rightly; **avoir ~** be right (**de faire** to do); **avoir ~ de qn** get the better of sb; **donner ~ à** prove right; **en ~ de** because of; **~ de plus** all the more reason; **perdre la ~** lose one's mind.

raisonnable /Rɛzɔnabl/ adj reasonable, sensible.

raisonnement /Rɛzɔnmɑ̃/ nm reasoning; (propositions) argument.

raisonner /Rɛzɔne/ 🔳 vi think. ● vt (personne) reason with.

rajeunir /RaʒœniR/ 🔳 vt **~ qn** make sb (look) younger; (moderniser) modernize; (Méd) rejuvenate. ● vi (personne) look younger.

rajuster /RaʒystE/ 🔳 vt straighten; (salaires) (re)adjust.

ralenti, **~e** /Rälɑ̃ti/ adj slow. ● nm (au cinéma) slow motion; **tourner au ~** tick over, idle.

ralentir /Rälɑ̃tiR/ 🔳 vt/i slow down. □ **se ~** vpr slow down.

ralentisseur /Rälɑ̃tisœR/ nm speed ramp.

râler /Rɑle/ 🔳 vi groan; (protester 🔲) moan.

rallier /Ralje/ 45 vt rally; (rejoindre) rejoin. □ **se ~** vpr rally; **se ~ à** (avis) come round to; (parti) join.

rallonge /Ralɔ̃ʒ/ nf (de table) leaf; (de fil électrique) extension lead.

rallonger 40 vt lengthen; (*séjour, fil, table*) extend.

rallumer /Ralyme/ **1** vt (*feu*) relight; (*lampe*) switch on again; (*ranimer*: fig) revive.

rallye /Rali/ nm rally.

ramassage /Ramasaʒ/ nm (*cueillette*) gathering; (*d'ordures*) collection; ~ **scolaire** school bus service.

ramasser /Ramase/ **1** vt pick up; (*récolter*) gather; (*recueillir, rassembler*) collect. □ **se** ~ vpr huddle up, curl up.

rame /Ram/ nf (*aviron*) oar; (*train*) train.

ramener /Ramne/ **1** vt (*rapporter, faire revenir*) bring back; (*reconduire*) take back; ~ à (*réduire à*) reduce to. □ **se** ~ vpr **1** turn up; **se** ~ à (*problème*) come down to.

ramer /Rame/ **1** vi row.

ramollir /Ramɔlir/ **2** vt soften. □ **se** ~ vpr become soft.

ramoneur /Ramɔnœr/ nm (chimney) sweep.

rampe /Rãp/ nf banisters; (*pente*) ramp; ~ **d'accès** (Auto) slip road; ~ **de lancement** launching pad.

ramper /Rãpe/ **1** vi crawl.

rancard /Rãkar/ nm **1** date.

rancart /Rãkar/ nm **mettre** ou **jeter au** ~ **1** scrap.

rance /Rãs/ adj rancid.

rancœur /Rãkœr/ nf resentment.

rançon /Rãsɔ̃/ nf ransom. **rançonner** **1** vt rob, extort money from.

rancune /Rãkyn/ nf grudge; **sans** ~! no hard feelings! **rancunier, -ière** adj vindictive.

randonnée /Rãdɔne/ nf walk, ramble; **la** ~ **à cheval** pony trekking; **faire une** ~ go walking ou rambling.

rang /Rã/ nm row; (*hiérarchie, condition*) rank; **se mettre en** ~ line up; **au premier** ~ in the first row; (fig) at the forefront; **de second** ~ (péj) second-rate.

rangée /Rãʒe/ nf row.

rangement /Rãʒmã/ nm (*de pièce*) tidying (up); (*espace*) storage space.

ranger /Rãʒe/ 40 vt put away; (*chambre*) tidy (up); (*disposer*) place. □ **se** ~ vpr (*véhicule*) park; (*s'écarter*) stand aside; (*conducteur*) pull over; (*s'assagir*) settle down; **se** ~ à (*avis*) accept.

ranimer /Ranime/ **1** vt revive; (Méd) resuscitate. □ **se** ~ vpr come round.

rapace /Rapas/ nm bird of prey.
● adj grasping.

rapatriement /Rapatrimã/ nm repatriation. **rapatrier** 45 vt repatriate.

rap /Rap/ nm rap (music).

râpe /Rɑp/ nf (Culin) grater; (*lime*) rasp.

râpé, ~e /Rɑpe/ adj (*vêtement*) threadbare; (*fromage*) grated.

râper /Rɑpe/ **1** vt grate; (*bois*) rasp.

rapide /Rapid/ adj fast, rapid. ● nm (*train*) express train; (*cours d'eau*) rapids (+ pl). **rapidement** adv fast, rapidly. **rapidité** nf speed.

rappel /Rapɛl/ nm recall; (*deuxième avis*) reminder; (*de salaire*) back pay; (Méd) booster; (*de diplomate*) recall; (*de réservistes*) call-up; (Théât) curtain call.

rappeler /Raple/ 38 vt (*par téléphone*) call back; (*réserviste*) call up; (*diplomate*) recall; (*évoquer*) recall; ~ **qch à qn** remind sb of sth. □ **se** ~ vpr remember, recall.

rappeur, -euse /Rapœœːr, -øz/

nmf rapper.

rapport /RapɔR/ *nm* connection; (compte-rendu) report; (profit) yield; ~s (relations) relations; **en ~ avec** (accord) in keeping with; **mettre/se mettre en ~ avec** put/get in touch with; **par ~ à** (comparé à) compared with; (vis-à-vis de) with regard to; ~s (sexuels) intercourse.

rapporter /RapɔRte/ **1** *vt* (ici) bring back; (là-bas) take back; turn; (profit) bring in; (dire, répéter) report. ● *vi* (Comm) bring in a good return; (moucharder **1**) tell tales. □ **se ~ à** *vpr* relate to.

rapporteur, -euse /RapɔRtœR, -øz/ *nm, f* (mouchard) tell-tale. ● *nm* protractor.

rapprochement /RapRɔʃmã/ *nm* reconciliation; (Pol) rapprochement; (rapport) connection; (comparaison) parallel.

rapprocher /RapRɔʃe/ *vt* move closer (de to); (réconcilier) bring together; (comparer) compare; (date, rendez-vous) bring forward. □ **se ~** *vpr* get or come closer (de to); (personnes, pays) come together; (s'apparenter) be close (de to).

rapt /Rapt/ *nm* abduction.

raquette /Raket/ *nf* (de tennis) racket; (de ping-pong) bat.

rare /RaR/ *adj* rare; (insuffisant) scarce. **rarement** *adv* rarely, seldom. **rareté** *nf* rarity; scarcity.

ras, ~e /Ra, Raz/ *adv* **coupé ~** cut short. ● *adj* (herbe, poil) short; **à ~ de terre** very close to the ground; **en avoir ~ le bol 1** be really fed up; **~e campagne** open country; **à ~ bord** to the brim.

raser /Raze/ **1** *vt* shave; (cheveux, barbe) shave off; (frôler) skim; (abattre) raze. □ **se ~** *vpr* shave.

rasoir /RazwaR/ *nm* razor. ● *adj inv* **1** boring.

rassasier /Rasazje/ **45** *vt* satisfy, fill up; **être rassasié de** have had enough of.

rassemblement /Rasãbləmã/ *nm* gathering; (manifestation) rally.

rassembler /Rasãble/ **1** *vt* gather; (forces, courage) summon up; (idées) collect. □ **se ~** *vpr* gather.

rassis, ~e /Rasi, -z/ *adj* (pain) stale.

rassurer /RasyRe/ **1** *vt* reassure. □ **se ~** *vpr* reassure oneself; **rassure-toi** don't worry.

rat /Ra/ *nm* rat.

rate /Rat/ *nf* spleen.

raté, ~e /Rate/ *nm, f* (personne) failure. ● *nm* **avoir des ~s** (voiture) backfire.

râteau (*pl* ~**x**) /Rato/ *nm* rake.

râtelier /Ratəlje/ *nm* hayrack; (dentier **1**) dentures.

rater /Rate/ **1** *vt* (train, rendez-vous, cible) miss; (gâcher) make a mess of, spoil; (examen) fail. ● *vi* fail.

ratio /Rasjo/ *nm* ratio.

rationaliser /Rasjɔnalize/ **1** *vt* rationalize.

rationnel, ~le /Rasjɔnɛl/ *adj* rational.

rationnement /Rasjɔnmã/ *nm* rationing.

ratisser /Ratise/ **1** *vt* rake; (fouiller) comb.

rattacher /Rataʃe/ **1** *vt* (lacets) tie up again; (ceinture de sécurité, collier) refasten; (relier) link; (incorporer) join.

rattrapage /RatRapaʒ/ *nm* (Comm) adjustment; **cours de ~** remedial lesson.

rattraper /RatRape/ **1** *vt* catch;

(rejoindre) catch up with; (retard, erreur) make up for. □ se ~ vpr catch up; (se dédommager) make up for it; se ~ à catch hold of.

rature /ʀatyʀ/ nf deletion.

rauque /ʀok/ adj raucous, harsh.

ravager /ʀavaʒe/ **40** vt devastate, ravage.

ravages /ʀavaʒ/ nmpl **faire des** ~ wreak havoc.

ravaler /ʀavale/ **1** vt (façade) clean; (colère) swallow.

ravi, ~e /ʀavi/ adj delighted (que that).

ravin /ʀavɛ̃/ nm ravine.

ravir /ʀaviʀ/ **2** vt delight; ~ qch à qn rob sb of sth.

ravissant, ~e /ʀavisɑ̃, -t/ adj beautiful.

ravisseur, -euse /ʀavisœʀ, -øz/ nm, f kidnapper.

ravitaillement /ʀavitajmɑ̃/ nm provision of supplies (de to); (denrées) supplies; ~ **en essence** refuelling.

ravitailler /ʀavitaje/ **1** vt provide with supplies; (avion) refuel. □ se ~ vpr stock up.

raviver /ʀavive/ **1** vt revive; (feu, colère) rekindle.

rayé, ~e /ʀeje/ adj striped.

rayer /ʀeje/ **31** vt scratch; (biffer) cross out; '~ **la mention inutile**' 'delete as appropriate'.

rayon /ʀejɔ̃/ nm ray; (étagère) shelf; (de magasin) department; (de roue) spoke; (de cercle) radius; ~ **d'action** range; ~ **de miel** honeycomb; ~ **X** X-ray; **en connaître un** ~ ꞮͰ know one's stuff **1**.

rayonnement /ʀejɔnmɑ̃/ nm (éclat) radiance; (influence) influence; (radiations) radiation. **rayonner** **1** vi radiate; (de joie) beam; (se déplacer) tour around (from a

central point).

rayure /ʀejyʀ/ nf scratch; (dessin) stripe; à ~s striped.

raz-de-marée /ʀɑdmaʀe/ nm inv tidal wave; ~ **électoral** electoral landslide.

réacteur /ʀeaktœʀ/ nm jet engine; (nucléaire) reactor.

réaction /ʀeaksjɔ̃/ nf reaction; ~ **en chaîne** chain reaction; **moteur à** ~ jet engine.

réagir /ʀeaʒiʀ/ **2** vi react; ~ **sur** have an effect on.

réalisateur, -trice /ʀealizatœʀ, -tʀis/ nm, f (au cinéma) director; (TV) producer.

réalisation /ʀealizasjɔ̃/ nf (de rêve) fulfilment; (œuvre) achievement; (TV, cinéma) production; **projet en** ~ project in progress.

réaliser /ʀealize/ **1** vt carry out; (effort, bénéfice, achat) make; (rêve) fulfil; (film) direct; (capital) realize; (se rendre compte de) realize. □ se ~ vpr be fulfilled.

réalisme /ʀealism/ nm realism.

réaliste /ʀealist/ adj realistic. ● nmf realist.

réalité /ʀealite/ nf reality.

réanimation /ʀeanimasjɔ̃/ nf resuscitation; **service de** ~ intensive care. **réanimer** **1** vt resuscitate.

réarmement /ʀeaʀmamɑ̃/ nm rearmament.

rébarbatif, -ive /ʀebaʀbatif, -v/ adj forbidding, off-putting.

rebelle /ʀabɛl/ adj rebellious; (soldat) rebel; ~ **à** resistant to. ● nmf rebel.

rébellion /ʀebɛljɔ̃/ nf rebellion.

rebondir /ʀabɔ̃diʀ/ **2** vi bounce; rebound; (fig) get moving again.

rebondissement /ʀabɔ̃dismɑ̃/ nm (new) development.

rebord /ʀəbɔʀ/ nm edge; ~ de la fenêtre window ledge ou sill.

rebours: à ~ /aʀəbuʀ/ loc (compter, marcher) backwards.

rebrousse-poil: à ~ /aʀəbʀuspwal/ loc the wrong way; (fig) prendre qn à ~ to rub sb up the wrong way.

rebrousser /ʀəbʀuse/ **1** vt ~ chemin turn back.

rebut /ʀəby/ nm mettre ou jeter au ~ scrap.

rebutant, ~e /ʀəbytɑ̃, -t/ adj off-putting.

recaler /ʀəkale/ **1** vt **1** fail; se faire ~, être recalé fail.

recel /ʀəsɛl/ nm receiving.

receler /ʀəsəle/ **6** vt (objet volé) receive; (cacher) conceal.

récemment /ʀesamɑ̃/ adv recently.

recensement /ʀəsɑ̃smɑ̃/ nm census; (inventaire) inventory. **recenser** **1** vt (population) take a census of; (objets) list.

récent, ~e /ʀesɑ̃, -t/ adj recent.

récépissé /ʀesepise/ nm receipt.

récepteur /ʀesɛptœʀ/ nm receiver.

réception /ʀesɛpsjɔ̃/ nf reception; (de courrier) receipt. **réceptionniste** nmf receptionist.

récession /ʀesesjɔ̃/ nf recession.

recette /ʀəsɛt/ nf (Culin) recipe; (argent) takings; ~s (Comm) receipts.

receveur, -euse /ʀəs(ə)vœʀ, -øz/ nm, f (de bus) conductor; ~ des contributions tax collector.

recevoir /ʀəs(ə)vwaʀ/ **52** vt receive, get; (client, malade) see; (invités) welcome, receive; être reçu à un examen pass an exam.

rechange: de ~ /dəʀɑ̃ʒ/ loc (roue, vêtements) spare; (solution) alternative.

réchapper /ʀeʃape/ **1** vt/i ~ de come through, survive.

recharge /ʀəʃaʀʒ/ nf (de stylo) refill.

réchaud /ʀeʃo/ nm stove.

réchauffement /ʀeʃofmɑ̃/ nm (de température) rise (de in); le ~ de la planète global warming.

réchauffer /ʀeʃofe/ **1** vt warm up. □ se ~ vpr warm oneself up; (temps) get warmer.

rêche /ʀɛʃ/ adj rough.

recherche /ʀəʃɛʀʃ/ nf search (de for); (raffinement) meticulousness; ~(s) (Univ) research; (enquête) investigations; ~ d'emploi job-hunting.

recherché, ~e /ʀəʃɛʀʃe/ adj in great demand; (style) original, recherché (péj); ~ pour meurtre wanted for murder.

rechercher /ʀəʃɛʀʃe/ **1** vt search for.

rechute /ʀəʃyt/ nf (Méd) relapse; faire une ~ have a relapse.

récidiver /ʀesidive/ **1** vi commit a second offence.

récif /ʀesif/ nm reef.

récipient /ʀesipjɑ̃/ nm container.

réciproque /ʀesipʀɔk/ adj mutual, reciprocal.

réciproquement /ʀesipʀɔkmɑ̃/ adv each other; et ~ and vice versa.

récit /ʀesi/ nm (compte-rendu) account, story; (histoire) story.

réciter /ʀesite/ **1** vt recite.

réclamation /ʀeklamasjɔ̃/ nf complaint; (demande) claim.

réclame /ʀeklam/ nf advertisement; faire de la ~ advertise; en ~ on offer.

réclamer /ʀeklame/ **1** vt call for, demand. ● vi complain.

reclus, ~e /ʀəkly, -z/ nm, f recluse.

● adj reclusive.

réclusion /ʀeklyzjɔ̃/ nf imprisonment.

récolte /ʀekɔlt/ nf (action) harvest; (produits) crop, harvest; (fig) crop. **récolter** 🚹 vt harvest, gather; (fig) collect, get.

recommandation /ʀəkɔmɑ̃dasjɔ̃/ nf recommendation.

recommandé /ʀəkɔmɑ̃de/ nm registered letter; **envoyer en** ~ send by registered post.

recommander /ʀəkɔmɑ̃de/ 🚹 vt recommend.

recommencer /ʀəkɔmɑ̃se/ 🔟 vt (reprendre) begin ou start again; (refaire) repeat. ● vi start ou begin again; **ne recommence pas** don't do it again.

récompense /ʀekɔ̃pɑ̃s/ nf reward; (prix) award. **récompenser** 🚹 vt reward (de for).

réconcilier /ʀekɔ̃silje/ 45 vt reconcile. □ **se** ~ vpr become reconciled (avec with).

reconduire /ʀəkɔ̃dɥiʀ/ 17 vt see home; (à la porte) show out; (renouveler) renew.

réconfort /ʀekɔ̃fɔʀ/ nm comfort.

reconnaissance /ʀəkɔnɛsɑ̃s/ nf gratitude; (fait de reconnaître) recognition; (Mil) reconnaissance. **reconnaissant, ~e** adj grateful (de for).

reconnaître /ʀəkɔnɛtʀ/ 18 vt recognize; (admettre) admit (que that); (Mil) reconnoitre; (enfant, tort) acknowledge. □ **se** ~ vpr (s'orienter) know where one is; (l'un l'autre) recognize each other.

reconstituer /ʀəkɔ̃stitɥe/ 🚹 vt reconstitute; (crime) reconstruct; (époque) recreate.

reconversion /ʀəkɔ̃vɛʀsjɔ̃/ nf (de main-d'œuvre) redeployment.

recopier /ʀəkɔpje/ 45 vt copy out.

record /ʀəkɔʀ/ nm & a inv record.

recouper /ʀəkupe/ 🚹 vt confirm. □ **se** ~ vpr check, tally, match up.

recourbé, ~e /ʀəkuʀbe/ adj curved; (nez) hooked.

recourir /ʀəkuʀiʀ/ 20 vi to ~ à (expédient, violence) resort to; (remède, méthode) have recourse to.

recours /ʀəkuʀ/ nm resort; **avoir** ~ **à** have recourse to, resort to; **avoir** ~ **à qn** turn to sb.

recouvrer /ʀəkuvʀe/ 🚹 vt recover.

recouvrir /ʀəkuvʀiʀ/ 21 vt cover.

récréation /ʀekʀeasjɔ̃/ nf recreation; (Scol) break; (US) recess.

recroqueviller (se) /(sə)ʀəkʀɔkvije/ 🚹 vpr curl up.

recrudescence /ʀəkʀydesɑ̃s/ nf new outbreak.

recrue /ʀəkʀy/ nf recruit.

recrutement /ʀəkʀytmɑ̃/ nm recruitment. **recruter** 🚹 vt recruit.

rectangle /ʀɛktɑ̃gl/ nm rectangle. **rectangulaire** adj rectangular.

rectifier /ʀɛktifje/ 45 vt correct, rectify.

recto /ʀɛkto/ nm **au** ~ on the front of the page.

reçu, ~e /ʀəsy/ adj accepted; (candidat) successful. ● nm receipt. ● →**RECEVOIR** 52.

recueil /ʀəkœj/ nm collection.

recueillement /ʀəkœjmɑ̃/ nm meditation.

recueillir /ʀəkœjiʀ/ 25 vt collect; (prendre chez soi) take in. □ **se** ~ vpr meditate.

recul /ʀəkyl/ nm retreat; (éloignement) distance; (déclin) decline; **avoir un mouvement de** ~ recoil; **être en** ~ be on the decline; **avec**

le ∼ with hindsight.

reculé, ∼e /Rəkyle/ *adj* (*région*) remote.

reculer /Rəkyle/ **1** *vt* move back; (*véhicule*) reverse; (*différer*) postpone. ● *vi* move back; (*voiture*) reverse; (*armée*) retreat; (*régresser*) fall; (*céder*) back down; ∼ **devant** (fig) shrink from. □ **se** ∼ *vpr* move back.

récupération /Rekyperasjɔ̃/ *nf* (de l'organisme, de dette) recovery; (d'objets) salvage.

récupérer /Rekypere/ **14** *vt* recover; (*vieux objets*) salvage. ● *vi* recover.

récurer /RekyRe/ **1** *vt* scour; **poudre à** ∼ scouring powder.

récuser /Rekyze/ **1** *vt* challenge. □ **se** ∼ *vpr* state that one is not qualified to judge.

recyclage /Rəsiklaʒ/ *nm* (de personnel) retraining; (de matériau) recycling.

recycler /Rəsikle/ **1** *vt* (*personne*) retrain; (*chose*) recycle. □ **se** ∼ *vpr* retrain.

rédacteur, -trice /RedaktœR, -tRis/ *nm, f* author, writer; (de journal, magazine) editor.

rédaction /Redaksjɔ̃/ *nf* writing; (Scol) essay, composition; (personnel) editorial staff.

redevable /Rədvabl/ *adj* **être** ∼ **à qn de** (*argent*) owe sb; (fig) be indebted to sb for.

redevance /Rədvɑ̃s/ *nf* (de télévision) licence fee; (de téléphone) rental charge.

rédiger /Rediʒe/ **40** *vt* write; (*contrat*) draw up.

redire /RədiR/ **27** *vt* repeat; **avoir** ou **trouver à** ∼ **à** find fault with.

redondant, ∼e /Rədɔ̃dɑ̃, -t/ *adj*

superfluous.

redonner /Rədɔne/ **1** *vt* (*rendre*) give back; (*donner davantage*) give more; (*donner de nouveau*) give again.

redoubler /Rəduble/ **1** *vt* increase; (*classe*) repeat; ∼ **de prudence** be even more careful. ● *vi* (Scol) repeat a year; (*s'intensifier*) intensify.

redoutable /Rədutabl/ *adj* formidable.

redouter /Rədute/ **1** *vt* dread.

redressement /RədRɛsmɑ̃/ *nm* (reprise) recovery; ∼ **judiciaire** receivership.

redresser /RədRese/ **1** *vt* straighten (out ou up); (*situation*) right, redress; (*économie, entreprise*) turn around. □ **se** ∼ *vpr* (*personne*) straighten (oneself) up; (se remettre debout) stand up; (*pays, économie*) recover.

réduction /Redyksjɔ̃/ *nf* reduction.

réduire /RedɥiR/ **17** *vt* reduce (**à** to). □ **se** ∼ *vpr* be reduced ou cut; **se** ∼ **à** (revenir à) come down to.

réduit, ∼e /Redɥi, -t/ *adj* (*objet*) small-scale; (limité) limited. ● *nm* cubbyhole.

rééducation /Reedykasjɔ̃/ *nf* (de handicapé) rehabilitation; (Méd) physiotherapy. **rééduquer** **1** *vt* (*personne*) rehabilitate; (*membre*) restore normal movement to.

réel, ∼le /Reɛl/ *adj* real. ● *nm* reality. **réellement** *adv* really.

réexpédier /Reɛkspedje/ **45** *vt* forward; (*retourner*) send back.

refaire /RəfɛR/ **33** *vt* do again; (*erreur, voyage*) make again; (*réparer*) do up, redo.

réfectoire /RefɛktwaR/ *nm* refectory.

référence /ʀefeʀɑ̃s/ nf reference.

référendum /ʀefeʀɛ̃dɔm/ nm referendum.

référer /ʀefeʀe/ 14 vi en ~ à consult. □ se ~ à vpr refer to, consult.

refermer /ʀəfɛʀme/ 1 vt close (again). □ se ~ vpr close (again).

réfléchi, ~e /ʀefleʃi/ adj (personne) thoughtful; (verbe) reflexive.

réfléchir /ʀefleʃiʀ/ 2 vi think (à, sur about). ● vt reflect. □ se ~ vpr be reflected.

reflet /ʀəflɛ/ nm reflection; (nuance) sheen.

refléter /ʀəflete/ 14 vt reflect. □ se ~ vpr be reflected.

réflexe /ʀeflɛks/ adj reflex. ● nm reflex; (réaction) reaction.

réflexion /ʀefleksjɔ̃/ nf (pensée) thought, reflection; (remarque) remark, comment; à la ~ on second thoughts.

refluer /ʀəflye/ 1 vi flow back; (foule) retreat; (inflation) go down.

reflux /ʀəfly/ nm (marée) ebb, tide.

réforme /ʀefɔʀm/ nf reform. **réformer** 1 vt reform; (soldat) invalid out.

refouler /ʀəfule/ 1 vt (larmes) hold back; (désir) repress; (souvenir) suppress.

refrain /ʀəfʀɛ̃/ nm chorus; le même ~ the same old story.

refréner /ʀəfʀene/ 14 vt curb, check.

réfrigérateur /ʀefʀiʒeʀatœʀ/ nm refrigerator.

refroidir /ʀəfʀwadiʀ/ 2 vt/i cool (down). □ se ~ vpr (personne, temps) get cold. **refroidissement** nm cooling; (rhume) chill.

refuge /ʀəfyʒ/ nm refuge; (chalet) mountain hut.

réfugié, ~e /ʀefyʒje/ nm, f refugee. **réfugier (se)** 45 vpr take refuge.

refus /ʀəfy/ nm refusal; **ce n'est pas de ~** I wouldn't say no.

refuser /ʀəfyze/ 1 vt refuse (de to); (client, spectateur) turn away; (recaler) fail; (à un poste) turn down. ● vi refuse; (à qn (évidence) reject; **se ~ à** faire refuse to do.

regain /ʀəgɛ̃/ nm ~ de renewal ou revival of; (Comm) rise.

régal (pl ~s) /ʀegal/ nm treat, delight.

régaler /ʀegale/ 1 vt ~ qn de treat sb to. □ se ~ vpr (de nourriture) **je me régale** it's delicious.

regard /ʀəgaʀ/ nm (expression, coup d'œil) look; (vue) eye; (yeux) eyes; ~ fixe stare; **au ~ de** with regard to; **en ~ de** compared with.

regardant, ~e /ʀəgaʀdɑ̃, -t/ adj ~ avec son argent careful with money; **peu ~ (sur)** not fussy (about).

regarder /ʀəgaʀde/ 1 vt look at; (observer) watch; (considérer) consider; (concerner) concern; ~ fixement stare at; ~ à think about, pay attention to. ● vi look. □ se ~ vpr (soi-même) look at oneself; (personnes) look at each other.

régate /ʀegat/ nf regatta.

régie /ʀeʒi/ nf ~ d'État public corporation; (radio, TV) control room; (au cinéma) production; (Théât) stage management.

régime /ʀeʒim/ nm (organisation) system; (Pol) regime; (Méd) diet; (de moteur) speed; (de bananes) bunch; **se mettre au ~** go on a diet; **à ce ~** at this rate.

régiment /ʀeʒimɑ̃/ nm regiment.

région /ʀeʒjɔ̃/ nf region. **régional, ~e** (mpl **-aux**) adj regional.

Région The largest administrative unit in France, consisting of a number of *départements*. Each has its own *Conseil régional* (regional council) which has responsibilities in education and economic planning.
▷**Département**.

régir /ʀeʒiʀ/ **2** vt govern.

régisseur /ʀeʒisœʀ/ nm (Théât) stage manager; ~ **de plateau** (TV) floor manager; (au cinéma) studio manager.

registre /ʀəʒistʀ/ nm register.

réglage /ʀeglaʒ/ nm adjustment; (de moteur) tuning.

règle /ʀɛgl/ nf rule; (instrument) ruler; ~**s** (de femme) period; **en ~** in order.

réglé, ~**e** /ʀegle/ adj (vie) ordered; (arrangé) settled; (papier) ruled.

règlement /ʀɛgləmɑ̃/ nm (règles) regulations; (solution) settlement; (paiement) payment. **réglementaire** adj (uniforme) regulation. **réglementation** nf regulation, rules. **réglementer** **1** vt regulate, control.

régler /ʀegle/ **14** vt settle; (machine) adjust; (programmer) set; (facture) settle; (personne) settle up with; ~ **son compte à** **1** settle a score with.

réglisse /ʀeglis/ nf liquorice.

règne /ʀɛɲ/ nm reign; (végétal, animal, minéral) kingdom.

regret /ʀəgʀɛ/ nm regret; **à** ~ with regret.

regretter /ʀəgʀete/ **1** vt regret; (personne) miss; (pour s'excuser) be sorry.

regrouper /ʀəgʀupe/ **1** vt group **ou** bring together. □ **se** ~ vpr gather **ou** group together.

régularité /ʀegylaʀite/ nf regularity; (de rythme, progrès) steadiness; (de surface, écriture) evenness.

régulier, -ière /ʀegylje, -jɛʀ/ adj regular; (qualité, vitesse) steady, even; (ligne, paysage) even; (légal) legal; (honnête) honest.

rehausser /ʀaose/ **1** vt raise; (faire valoir) enhance.

rein /ʀɛ̃/ nm kidney; ~**s** (dos) small of the back.

reine /ʀɛn/ nf queen.

réinsertion /ʀeɛ̃sɛʀsjɔ̃/ nf reintegration.

réintégrer /ʀeɛ̃tegʀe/ **14** vt (lieu) return to; (Jur) reinstate; (personne) reintegrate.

réitérer /ʀeiteʀe/ **14** vt repeat.

rejaillir /ʀəʒajiʀ/ **2** vi ~ **sur** splash back onto; ~ **sur qn** (succès) reflect on sb.

rejet /ʀəʒɛ/ nm rejection; ~**s** (déchets) waste.

rejeter /ʀəʒte/ **38** vt throw back; (refuser) reject; (déverser) discharge; ~ **une faute sur qn** shift the blame for a mistake onto sb.

rejoindre /ʀəʒwɛ̃dʀ/ **22** vt go back to, rejoin; (rattraper) catch up with; (rencontrer) join, meet up with. □ **se** ~ vpr (personnes) meet up; (routes) join, meet.

réjoui, ~**e** /ʀeʒwi/ adj joyful.

réjouir /ʀeʒwiʀ/ **2** vt delight. □ **se** ~ vpr be delighted (**de** at). **réjouissances** nfpl festivities. **réjouissant**, ~**e** adj cheering.

relâche /ʀəlɑʃ/ nm (repos) break, rest; **faire** ~ (Théât) be closed.

relâcher /ʀəlɑʃe/ **1** vt slacken; (personne) release; (discipline) relax. □ **se** ~ vpr slacken.

relais /ʀəlɛ/ nm (Sport) relay; (hôtel) hotel; (intermédiaire) inter-

r

mediary; **prendre le ~ de** take over from.

relancer /rǝlɑ̃se/ **10** vt boost, revive; (renvoyer) throw back.

relatif, -ive /rǝlatif, -v/ adj relative; **~ à** relating to.

relation /rǝlasjɔ̃/ nf relationship; (ami) acquaintance; (personne puissante) connection; **~s** relations; **~s extérieures** foreign affairs; **en ~ avec qn** in touch with sb.

relativement /rǝlativmɑ̃/ adv relatively; **~ à** in relation to.

relativité /rǝlativite/ nf relativity.

relax /Rǝlaks/ adj inv **1** laid-back.

relaxer (se) /(sǝ)Rǝlakse/ **1** vpr relax.

relayer /Rǝleje/ **31** vt relieve; (émission) relay. □ **se ~** vpr take over from one another.

reléguer /Rǝlege/ **14** vt relegate.

relent /Rǝlɑ̃/ nm stink; (fig) whiff.

relève /Rǝlɛv/ nf relief; **prendre ou assurer la ~** take over (de from).

relevé, ~e /Rǝlve/ adj spicy. ● nm (de compteur) reading; (facture) bill; **~ bancaire, ~ de compte** bank statement; **faire le ~ de** list.

relever /Rǝlve/ **6** vt pick up; (personne tombée) help up; (remonter) raise; (col) turn up; (compteur) read; (défi) accept; (relayer) relieve; (remarquer, noter) note; (plat) spice up; (rebâtir) rebuild; **~ de** come within the competence of (Méd) recover from. □ **se ~** vpr (personne) get up (again); (pays, économie) recover.

relief /Rǝljɛf/ nm relief; **mettre en ~** highlight.

relier /Rǝlje/ **45** vt link (up) (à to); (livre) bind.

religieux, -ieuse /Rǝliʒjø, -z/ adj religious. ● nm, f monk, nun.

religion /Rǝliʒjɔ̃/ nf religion.

reliure /RǝljyR/ nf binding.

reluire /RǝlɥiR/ **17** vi shine.

remaniement /Rǝmanimɑ̃/ nm revision; **~ ministériel** cabinet reshuffle.

remarquable /Rǝmarkabl/ adj remarkable.

remarque /Rǝmark/ nf remark; (par écrit) comment.

remarquer /Rǝmarke/ **1** vt notice; (dire) say; **faire ~** point out (à to); **se faire ~** draw attention to oneself; **remarque(z)** mind you.

remblai /Rɑ̃blɛ/ nm embankment.

remboursement /Rɑ̃buRsǝmɑ̃/ nm (d'emprunt, dette) repayment; (Comm) refund.

rembourser /Rɑ̃buRse/ **1** vt (dette, emprunt) repay; (billet, frais) refund; (client) give a refund to; (ami) pay back.

remède /Rǝmɛd/ nm remedy; (médicament) medicine.

remédier /Rǝmedje/ **45** vi **~ à** remedy.

remerciements /RǝmɛRsimɑ̃/ nmpl thanks. **remercier** /45/ vt thank (de for); (licencier) dismiss.

remettre /RǝmɛtR/ **42** vt put back; (vêtement) put back on; (donner) hand over; (devoir, démission) hand in; (faire fonctionner) switch back on; (restituer) give back; (différer) put off; (ajouter) add; (se rappeler) remember; **~ en cause ou en question** call into question. □ **se ~** vpr (guérir) recover; **se ~ au tennis** take up tennis again; **se ~ au travail** get back to work; **se ~ à faire** start doing again; **s'en ~ à** leave it to.

remise /Rǝmiz/ nf (abri) shed; (rabais) discount; (transmission) handing over; (ajournement) postponement; **~ en cause ou en question**

calling into question; ~ **des prix** prizegiving; ~ **des médailles** medals ceremony; ~ **de peine** remission.

remontant /ʀəmɔ̃tɑ̃/ nm tonic.

remontée /ʀəmɔ̃te/ nf ascent; (d'eau, de prix) rise; ~ **mécanique** ski lift.

remonte-pente (pl ~**s**) /ʀəmɔ̃tpɑ̃t/ nm ski tow.

remonter /ʀəmɔ̃te/ **1** vi go ou come (back) up; (prix, niveau) rise (again); (revenir) go back (à to); ~ **dans le temps** go back in time. ● vt (rue, escalier) go ou come (back) up; (relever) raise; (montre) wind up; (objet démonté) put together again; (personne) buck up.

remontoir /ʀəmɔ̃twaʀ/ nm winder.

remords /ʀəmɔʀ/ nm remorse; **avoir du** ou **des** ~ feel remorse.

remorque /ʀəmɔʀk/ nf trailer; **en** ~ **on tow. remorquer 1** vt tow.

remous /ʀəmu/ nm eddy; (de bateau) backwash; (fig) turmoil.

rempart /ʀɑ̃paʀ/ nm rampart.

remplaçant, ~e /ʀɑ̃plasɑ̃, -t/ nm, f replacement; (joueur) reserve, substitute.

remplacement /ʀɑ̃plasmɑ̃/ nm replacement; **faire des** ~ do supply teaching. **remplacer 10** vt replace.

rempli, ~e /ʀɑ̃pli/ adj full (**de**) (journée) busy.

remplir /ʀɑ̃pliʀ/ **2** vt fill (up); (formulaire) fill in ou out; (condition) fulfil; (devoir, tâche, rôle) carry out. □ **se** ~ vpr fill (up). **remplissage** nm filling; (de texte) padding.

remporter /ʀɑ̃pɔʀte/ **1** vt take back; (victoire) win.

remuant, ~e /ʀəmɥɑ̃, -t/ adj boisterous.

remue-ménage /ʀəmymenaʒ/ nm inv commotion, bustle.

remuer /ʀəmɥe/ **1** vt move; (thé, café) stir; (passé) rake up. ● vi move; (gigoter) fidget. □ **se** ~ vpr move.

rémunération /ʀemyneʀasjɔ̃/ nf payment.

renaissance /ʀənɛsɑ̃s/ nf rebirth.

renard /ʀənaʀ/ nm fox.

renchérir /ʀɑ̃ʃeʀiʀ/ **2** vi (dans une vente) raise the bidding; ~ **sur** go one better than. ● vt increase, put up.

rencontre /ʀɑ̃kɔ̃tʀ/ nf meeting; (de routes) junction; (Mil) encounter; (match) match; (US) game.

rencontrer /ʀɑ̃kɔ̃tʀe/ **1** vt meet; (heurter) hit; (trouver) find. □ **se** ~ vpr meet.

rendement /ʀɑ̃dmɑ̃/ nm yield; (travail) output.

rendez-vous /ʀɑ̃devu/ nm appointment; (d'amoureux) date; (lieu) meeting-place; **prendre** ~ **(avec)** make an appointment (with).

rendormir (se) /(sə)ʀɑ̃dɔʀmiʀ/ **46** vpr go back to sleep.

rendre /ʀɑ̃dʀ/ **3** vt give back, return; (donner en retour) return; (monnaie) give; (justice) dispense; (jugement) pronounce; ~ **heureux/possible** make happy/possible; (vomir **1**) vomit; ~ **compte de** report on; ~ **service (à)** help; ~ **visite à** visit. ● vi (terres) yield; (activité) be profitable. □ **se** ~ vpr (capituler) surrender; (aller) go (à to); **se** ~ **utile** make oneself useful.

rêne /ʀɛn/ nf rein.

renfermé, ~e /ʀɑ̃fɛʀme/ adj withdrawn. ● nm **sentir le** ~ smell musty.

renflé, ~e /ʀɑ̃fle/ adj bulging.

renforcer /ʀɑ̃fɔʀse/ **10** vt

r

reinforce.

renfort /ʀɑ̃fɔʀ/ nm reinforcement; **à grand ~ de** with a great deal of.

renier /ʀənje/ **45** vt (personne, œuvre) disown; (foi) renounce.

renifler /ʀənifle/ **1** vt/i sniff.

renne /ʀɛn/ nm reindeer.

renom /ʀənɔ̃/ nm renown; (réputation) reputation. **renommé, ~e** adj famous. **renommée** nf (célébrité) fame; (réputation) reputation.

renoncement /ʀənɔ̃smɑ̃/ nm renunciation.

renoncer /ʀənɔ̃se/ **10** vi **~ à** (habitude, ami) give up; (entrer à nouveau); (revenu) come back in; (élèves) go back (to school); **~ à faire** abandon the idea of doing.

renouer /ʀənwe/ **1** vt tie up (again); (amitié) renew; **~ avec qn** get back in touch with sb; (après une dispute) make up with sb.

renouveau (pl ~x) /ʀənuvo/ nm revival.

renouveler /ʀənuvle/ **38** vt renew; (réitérer) repeat; (remplacer) replace. □ **se ~** vpr be renewed; (incident) recur, happen again.

renouvellement /ʀənuvɛlmɑ̃/ nm renewal.

rénovation /ʀenɔvasjɔ̃/ nf (d'édifice) renovation; (d'institution) reform.

renseignement /ʀɑ̃sɛɲ(ə)mɑ̃/ nm ~(s) information; (bureau des) ~s information desk; (service des) ~s téléphoniques directory enquiries.

renseigner /ʀɑ̃seɲe/ **1** vt inform, give information to. □ **se ~** vpr enquire, make enquiries, find out.

rentabilité /ʀɑ̃tabilite/ nf profitability. **rentable** adj profitable.

rente /ʀɑ̃t/ nf (private) income; (pension) annuity. **rentier, -ière** nm, f person of private means.

rentrée /ʀɑ̃tʀe/ nf return; (revenu) income; **la ~ (des classes)** the start of the new school year; **faire sa ~** make a comeback.

Rentrée The start of the new school year at the beginning of September, used as a major marketing opportunity by stores and supermarkets. The concept of the *rentrée* also extends to literary, political and other activities which resume after the holiday period. *La rentrée parlementaire*, for example, signals the return of Parliament after the summer recess.

rentrer /ʀɑ̃tʀe/ **1** vi (aux être) go ou come back home, return home; (entrer) go ou come in; (entrer à nouveau) go ou come back in; (revenu) come back in; (élèves) go back (to school); **~ dans** (heurter) smash into; **tout est rentré dans l'ordre** everything is back to normal; **~ dans ses frais** break even. ● vt (aux avoir) bring in; (griffes) draw in; (vêtement) tuck in.

renverser /ʀɑ̃vɛʀse/ **1** vt knock over ou down; (piéton) knock down; (liquide) upset, spill; (mettre à l'envers) turn upside down; (gouvernement) overthrow; (inverser) reverse. □ **se ~** vpr (véhicule) overturn; (verre, vase) fall over.

renvoi /ʀɑ̃vwa/ nm return; (d'employé) dismissal; (d'élève) expulsion; (report) postponement; (dans un livre, fichier) cross-reference; (rot) burp.

renvoyer /ʀɑ̃vwaje/ **32** vt send back, return; (employé) dismiss; (élève) expel; (ajourner) postpone; (référer) refer; (réfléchir) reflect.

repaire /ʀəpɛʀ/ nm den.

répandre /ʁepɑ̃dʁ/ **3** vt (liquide) spill; (étendre, diffuser) spread; (odeur) give off. □ **se** ~ vpr spread; (liquide) spill; **se** ~ **en injures** let out a stream of abuse.

répandu, ~**e** /ʁepɑ̃dy/ adj widespread.

réparateur, -trice /ʁepaʁatœʁ, -tʁis/ nm engineer. **réparation** nf repair; (compensation) compensation. **réparer 1** vt repair, mend; (faute) make amends for; (remédier à) put right.

repartie /ʁəpaʁti/ nf retort; **avoir de la** ~ always have a ready reply.

repartir 1 vi start again; (voyageur) set off again; (s'en retourner) go back; (secteur économique) pick up again.

répartir /ʁepaʁtiʁ/ **2** vt distribute; (partager) share out; (étaler) spread. **répartition** nf distribution.

repas /ʁəpɑ/ nm meal.

repassage /ʁəpasaʒ/ nm ironing.

repasser /ʁəpase/ **1** vi come ou go back; ~ **devant qch** go past sth again. ● vt (linge) iron; (examen) retake, resist; (film) show again.

repêcher /ʁəpeʃe/ **1** vt recover, fish out; (candidat) allow to pass.

repentir¹ /ʁəpɑ̃tiʁ/ nm repentance.

repentir² (se) /(sə)ʁəpɑ̃tiʁ/ **2** vpr repent (**de** of); **se** ~ **de** (regretter) regret.

répercuter /ʁepeʁkyte/ **1** vt (bruit) send back. □ **se** ~ vpr echo; **se** ~ **sur** have repercussions on.

repère /ʁəpɛʁ/ nm mark; (jalon) marker; (événement) landmark; (référence) reference point.

repérer /ʁəpeʁe/ **14** vt locate, spot. □ **se** ~ vpr get one's bearings.

répertoire /ʁepeʁtwaʁ/ nm (artistique) repertoire; (liste) directory;

~ **téléphonique** telephone directory; (personnel) telephone book.

répertorier **45** vt index.

répéter /ʁepete/ **14** vt repeat; (Théât) rehearse. ● vi rehearse. □ **se** ~ vpr be repeated; (personne) repeat oneself.

répétition /ʁepetisjɔ̃/ nf repetition; (Théât) rehearsal.

répit /ʁepi/ nm respite, break.

replier /ʁəplije/ **45** vt fold (up); (ailes, jambes) tuck in. □ **se** ~ vpr withdraw (**sur soi-même** into oneself).

réplique /ʁeplik/ nf reply; (riposte) retort; (objection) objection; (Théât) line; (copie) replica. **répliquer 1** vt/i reply; (riposter) retort; (objecter) answer back.

répondeur /ʁepɔ̃dœʁ/ nm answering machine.

répondre /ʁepɔ̃dʁ/ **3** vt (injure, bêtise) reply with; ~ **que** answer ou reply that; ~ **à** (être conforme à) answer; (affection, sourire) return; (avances, appel, critique) respond to; ~ **de** answer for. ● vi answer, reply; (être insolent) answer back; (réagir) respond (**à** to).

réponse /ʁepɔ̃s/ nf answer, reply; (fig) response.

report /ʁəpɔʁ/ nm (transcription) transfer; (renvoi) postponement.

reportage /ʁəpɔʁtaʒ/ nm report; (par écrit) article.

reporter¹ /ʁəpɔʁte/ **1** vt take back; (ajourner) put off; (transcrire) transfer. □ **se** ~ **à** vpr refer to.

reporter² /ʁəpɔʁtɛʁ/ nm reporter.

repos /ʁəpo/ nm rest; (paix) peace. **reposant,** ~**e** adj restful.

reposer /ʁəpoze/ **1** vt put down again; (délasser) rest. ● vi rest (**sur** on); **laisser** ~ (pâte) leave to stand. □ **se** ~ vpr rest;

r

se ~ **sur** rely on.

repousser /ʀəpuse/ **1** vt push back; (écarter) push away; (dégoûter) repel; (décliner) reject; (recommencer) resume; (redire) repeat; (modifier) alter; (blâmer) reprimand; ~ **du pain** take some more bread; **on ne m'y reprendra pas** I won't be caught out again. ● vi (recommencer) resume; (affaires) pick up. □ **se** ~ vpr (se ressaisir) pull oneself together; (se corriger) correct oneself.

reprendre /ʀəpʀɑ̃dʀ/ **50** vt take back; (confiance, conscience) regain; (souffle) get back; (évadé) recapture; (recommencer) resume; (redire) repeat; (modifier) alter; (blâmer) reprimand; ~ **du pain** take some more bread; **on ne m'y reprendra pas** I won't be caught out again. ● vi (recommencer) resume; (affaires) pick up. □ **se** ~ vpr (se ressaisir) pull oneself together; (se corriger) correct oneself.

représailles /ʀəpʀezɑj/ nfpl reprisals.

représentant, ~e /ʀəpʀezɑ̃tɑ̃, -t/ nm, f representative.

représentation /ʀəpʀezɑ̃tasjɔ̃/ nf representation; (Théât) performance.

représenter /ʀəpʀezɑ̃te/ **1** vt represent; (figures) depict, show; (pièce de théâtre) perform. □ **se** ~ vpr (s'imaginer) imagine.

répression /ʀepʀesjɔ̃/ nf repression; (d'élan) suppression.

réprimande /ʀepʀimɑ̃d/ nf reprimand.

réprimer /ʀepʀime/ **1** vt (peuple) repress; (sentiment) suppress; (fraude) crack down on.

reprise /ʀəpʀiz/ nf resumption; (Théât) revival; (TV) repeat; (de tissu) darn, mend; (essor) recovery; (Comm) part-exchange, trade-in; **à plusieurs ~s** on several occasions.

repriser /ʀəpʀize/ **1** vt darn, mend.

reproche /ʀəpʀɔʃ/ nm reproach; **faire des ~s à** find fault with.

reprocher /ʀəpʀɔʃe/ **1** vt ~ **qch à qn** reproach ou criticize sb for sth.

reproducteur, -trice /ʀəpʀɔdyktœʀ, -tʀis/ adj reproductive.

reproduire /ʀəpʀɔdɥiʀ/ **17** vt reproduce; (répéter) repeat. □ **se** ~ vpr reproduce; (se répéter) recur.

reptile /ʀɛptil/ nm reptile.

repu, ~e /ʀəpy/ adj satiated, replete.

républicain, ~e /ʀepyblikɛ̃, -ɛn/ adj & nm, f republican.

république /ʀepyblik/ nf republic; ~ **populaire** people's republic.

répudier /ʀepydje/ **45** vt repudiate; (droit) renounce.

répugnance /ʀepyɲɑ̃s/ nf repugnance; (hésitation) reluctance; **avoir de la** ~ **pour** loathe. **répugnant, ~e** adj repulsive.

répugner /ʀepyɲe/ **1** vt be repugnant to, disgust; ~ **à** (effort, violence) be averse to; ~ **à faire** be reluctant to do.

répulsion /ʀepylsjɔ̃/ nf repulsion.

réputation /ʀepytasjɔ̃/ nf reputation.

réputé, ~e /ʀepyte/ adj renowned (pour for); (école, compagnie) reputable; ~ **pour être** reputed to be.

requérir /ʀəkeʀiʀ/ **7** vt require, demand.

requête /ʀəkɛt/ nf request; (Jur) petition.

requin /ʀəkɛ̃/ nm shark.

requis, ~e /ʀəki, -z/ adj (exigé) required; (nécessaire) necessary.

RER abrév m (réseau express régional) Parisian rapid transit rail system.

rescapé, ~e /ʀɛskape/ nm, f survivor. ● adj surviving.

rescousse /ʀɛskus/ nf **à la** ~ to

the rescue.

réseau /(pl →x) /Rezo/ nm network; ~ **local** local area network, LAN; le ~ **des →x** (Ordinat) Internet.

réservation /RezɛRvasjɔ̃/ nf reservation, booking.

réserve /RezɛRv/ nf reserve; (restriction) reservation, reserve; (indienne) reservation; (entrepôt) store-room; **en** ~ in reserve; **les** ~**s** (Mil) the reserves.

réserver /RezɛRve/ **1** vt reserve; (place) book, reserve. □ **se** ~ vpr **se** ~ **qch** save sth for oneself; **se** ~ **pour** save oneself for; **se** ~ **le droit de** reserve the right to.

réservoir /RezɛRvwaR/ nm tank; (lac) reservoir.

résidence /Rezidɑ̃s/ nf residence; ~ **secondaire** second home; ~ **universitaire** hall of residence.

résident, ~**e** /Rezidɑ̃, -t/ nm, f resident; (étranger) foreign resident.

résider /Rezide/ **1** vi reside; ~ **dans qch** (difficulté) lie in.

résigner (se) /(sə)Rezipe/ **1** vpr **se** ~ **à faire** resign oneself to doing.

résilier /Rezilje/ **45** vt terminate.

résine /Rezin/ nf resin.

résistance /Rezistɑ̃s/ nf resistance; (fil électrique) element. **résistant**, ~**e** adj tough.

résister /Reziste/ **1** vi resist; ~ **à** (agresseur, assaut, influence, tentation) resist; (corrosion, chaleur) withstand.

résolu, ~**e** /Rezɔly/ adj resolute; **à faire** determined to do. ● **→RÉSOUDRE 53.**

résolution /Rezɔlysjɔ̃/ nf (fermeté) resolution; (d'un problème) solving.

résonner /Rezɔne/ **1** vi resound.

résorber /RezɔRbe/ **1** vt reduce.

□ **se** ~ vpr be reduced.

résoudre /RezudR/ **53** vt solve; (crise, conflit) resolve. □ **se** ~ **à** vpr (se décider) resolve to; (se résigner) resign oneself.

respect /Rɛspɛ/ nm respect. **respectabilité** nf respectability.

respecter /Rɛspɛkte/ **1** vt respect; **faire** ~ (loi, décision) enforce.

respectueux, -**euse** /Rɛspɛktɥø, -z/ adj respectful; ~ **de l'environnement** environmentally friendly.

respiration /RɛspiRasjɔ̃/ nf breathing; (haleine) breath. **respiratoire** adj respiratory, breathing.

respirer /RɛspiRe/ **1** vi breathe; (se reposer) catch one's breath. ● vt breathe (in); (exprimer) radiate.

resplendir /Rɛsplɑ̃diR/ **2** vi shine (de with). **resplendissant**, ~**e** adj brilliant, radiant.

responsabilité /Rɛspɔ̃sabilite/ nf responsibility; (légale) liability.

responsable /Rɛspɔ̃sabl/ adj responsible (**de** for); ~ **de** (chargé de) in charge of. ● nmf person in charge; (coupable) person responsible.

resquiller /Rɛskije/ **1** vi **1** (dans le train) fare-dodge; (au spectacle) get in without paying; (dans la queue) jump the queue.

ressaisir (se) /(sə)RəseziR/ **2** vpr pull oneself together; (équipe sportive, valeurs boursières) make a recovery.

ressemblance /Rəsɑ̃blɑ̃s/ nf resemblance.

ressemblant, ~**e** /Rəsɑ̃blɑ̃, -t/ adj **être** ~ (portrait) be a good likeness.

ressembler /Rəsɑ̃ble/ **1** vi ~ **à** resemble, look like. □ **se** ~ vpr be alike; (physiquement) look alike.

ressentiment /ʀəsɑ̃timɑ̃/ nm resentment.

ressentir /ʀəsɑ̃tiʀ/ 46 vt feel. □ se ~ de vpr feel the effects of.

resserrer /ʀəseʀe/ 1 vt tighten; (contracter) compress; (vêtement) take in. □ se ~ vpr tighten; (route) narrow; (se regrouper) move closer together.

ressort /ʀəsɔʀ/ nm (objet) spring; (fig) energy; être du ~ de be the province of; (Jur) be within the jurisdiction of; en dernier ~ as a last resort.

ressortir /ʀəsɔʀtiʀ/ 46 vi go ou come back out; (se voir) stand out; (film, disque) be re-released; faire ~ bring out; il ressort que it emerges that. ● vt take out again; (redire) come out with again; (disque, film) re-release.

ressortissant, ~e /ʀəsɔʀtisɑ̃, -t/ nm, f national.

ressource /ʀəsuʀs/ nf resource; ~s resources; à bout de ~ at one's wits' end.

ressusciter /ʀesysite/ 1 vi come back to life. ● vt bring back to life; (fig) revive.

restant, ~e /ʀɛstɑ̃, -t/ adj remaining. ● nm remainder.

restaurant /ʀɛstɔʀɑ̃/ nm restaurant.

restauration /ʀɛstɔʀasjɔ̃/ nf restoration; (hôtellerie) catering.

restaurer /ʀɛstɔʀe/ 1 vt restore. □ se ~ vpr eat.

reste /ʀɛst/ nm rest; (d'une soustraction) remainder; ~s remains (de of); (nourriture) leftovers; un ~ de poulet some left-over chicken; au ~, du ~ moreover, besides.

rester /ʀɛste/ 1 vi (aux être) stay, remain; (subsister) be left, remain; il reste du pain there is some

bread left (over); il me reste du pain I have some bread left (over); il me reste à it remains for me to; en ~ à go no further than; en ~ là stop there.

restituer /ʀɛstitɥe/ 1 vt (rendre) return; (recréer) reproduce; (rétablir) reconstruct.

restreindre /ʀɛstʀɛ̃dʀ/ 22 vt restrict. □ se ~ vpr (dans les dépenses) cut back.

restriction /ʀɛstʀiksjɔ̃/ nf restriction.

résultat /ʀezylta/ nm result.

résulter /ʀezylte/ 1 vi ~ de result from, be the result of.

résumé /ʀezyme/ nm summary; en ~ in short; (pour finir) to sum up. **résumer** 1 vt summarize.

résurrection /ʀezyʀɛksjɔ̃/ nf resurrection; (renouveau) revival.

rétablir /ʀetabliʀ/ 2 vt restore; (personne) restore to health. □ se ~ vpr (ordre, silence) be restored; (guérir) recover. **rétablissement** nm restoration; (de malade, monnaie) recovery.

retard /ʀətaʀ/ nm lateness; (sur un programme) delay; (infériorité) backwardness; avoir du ~ be late; (montre) be slow; en ~ late; (retardé) behind; en ~ sur l'emploi du temps behind schedule; rattraper ou combler son ~ catch up; prendre du ~ fall behind.

retardataire /ʀətaʀdatɛʀ/ nmf latecomer. ● adj late.

retarder /ʀətaʀde/ 1 vt ~ qn/qch delay sb/sth, hold sb/sth up; (par rapport à une heure convenue) make sb/sth late; (montre) put back. ● vi (montre) be slow; (personne) be out of touch.

retenir /ʀətniʀ/ 58 vt hold back; (souffle, attention, prisonnier) hold;

(*eau, chaleur*) retain, hold; (*larmes*) hold back; (*garder*) keep; (*retarder*) detain, hold up; (*réserver*) book; (*se rappeler*) remember; (*déduire*) deduct; (*accepter*) accept. □ **se ~** *vpr* (*se contenir*) restrain oneself; **se ~ à** hold on to; **se ~ de faire** stop oneself from doing.

rétention /Retɑ̃sjɔ̃/ *nf* retention.

retentir /Rɑtɑ̃tiʀ/ 🄱 *vi* ring out, resound; **~ sur** have an impact on. **retentissant**, **~e** *adj* resounding. **retentissement** *nm* (*effet*) effect.

retenue /Rɑtny/ *nf* restraint; (*somme*) deduction; (*Scol*) detention.

réticent, **~e** /Retisɑ̃, -t/ *adj* (*hésitant*) hesitating; (*qui rechigne*) reluctant; (*réservé*) reticent.

rétine /Retin/ *nf* retina.

retiré, **~e** /Rɑtiʀe/ *adj* (*vie*) secluded; (*lieu*) remote.

retirer /Rɑtiʀe/ 🄱 *vt* (*sortir*) take out; (*ôter*) take off; (*argent, offre, candidature*) withdraw; (*écarter*) (*main, pied*) collect, pick up; (*avantage*) derive; **~ à qn** take away from sb. □ **se ~** *vpr* withdraw, retire.

retombées /Rɑtɔ̃be/ *nfpl* (*conséquences*) effects; **~ radioactives** nuclear fall-out.

retomber /Rɑtɔ̃be/ 🄱 *vi* (*faire une chute*) fall again; (*retourner au sol*) land, come down; **~ dans** (*erreur*) fall back into.

retouche /Rɑtuʃ/ *nf* alteration; (*de photo, tableau*) retouch.

retour /Rɑtuʀ/ *nm* return; **être de ~** be back (**de** from); **~ en arrière** flashback; **par ~ du courrier** by return of post; **en ~** in return.

retourner /Rɑtuʀne/ 🄱 *vt* (*aux avoir*) turn over; (*vêtement*) turn inside out; (*maison*) turn upside

down; (*lettre, compliment*) return; (*émouvoir* 🄱) shake, upset. ● *vi* (*aux être*) go back, return. □ **se ~** *vpr* turn round; (*dans son lit*) twist and turn; **s'en ~** go back; **se ~ contre** turn against.

retrait /Rɑtʀɛ/ *nm* withdrawal; (*des eaux*) receding; **être (situé) en ~ (de)** be set back (from).

retraite /Rɑtʀɛt/ *nf* retirement; (*pension*) (retirement) pension; (*fuite, refuge*) retreat; **mettre à la ~** pension off; **prendre sa ~** retire.

retraité, **~e** /Rɑtʀete/ *adj* retired. ● *nm, f* (old-age) pensioner.

retrancher /Rɑtʀɑ̃ʃe/ 🄱 *vt* remove; (*soustraire*) deduct, subtract. □ **se ~** *vpr* (Mil) entrench oneself; **se ~ derrière** take refuge behind.

retransmettre /Rɑtʀɑ̃smɛtʀ/ 🄸🄸 *vt* broadcast.

rétrécir /Retʀesiʀ/ 🄲 *vt* make narrower; (*vêtement*) take in. ● *vi* (*tissu*) shrink; (*rue*) narrow. □ **se ~** *vpr* (*rue*) narrow.

rétribution /Retʀibysjɔ̃/ *nf* payment.

rétroactif, **-ive** /Retʀoaktif, -v/ *adj* retrospective; **augmentation à effet ~** backdated pay rise.

retrousser /Rɑtʀuse/ 🄱 *vt* pull up; (*manche*) roll up.

retrouvailles /Rɑtʀuvɑj/ *nfpl* reunion.

retrouver /Rɑtʀuve/ 🄱 *vt* find (again); (*rejoindre*) meet (again); (*forces, calme*) regain; (*lieu*) be back in; (*se rappeler*) remember. □ **se ~** *vpr* find oneself (back); (*se réunir*) meet (again); (*être présent*) be found; **s'y ~** (s'orienter, comprendre) find one's way; (*rentrer dans ses frais* 🄱) break even.

rétroviseur /Retʀovizœʀ/ *nm* (Auto) (rear-view) mirror.

réunion /Reynjɔ̃/ *nf* meeting; (ren-

contre) gathering; (après une séparation) réunion; (d'objets) collection.

réunir /reynir/ **2** vt gather, collect; (rapprocher) bring together;
(convoquer) call together; (raccorder) join; (qualités) combine. □ **se**
~ vpr meet.

réussi, ~e /reysi/ adj successful.

réussir /reysir/ **2** vi succeed, be
successful; ~ **à faire** succeed in
doing, manage to do; ~ **à un examen** pass an exam; ~ **à qn** (méthode) work well for sb; (climat,
mode de vie) agree with sb. ● vt
(vie) make a success of.

réussite /reysit/ nf success; (jeu)
patience.

revaloir /rəvalwar/ **60** vt **je vous
revaudrai cela** (en mal) I'll pay you
back for this; (en bien) I'll repay you
some day.

revanche /rəvɑ̃ʃ/ nf revenge;
(Sport) return ou revenge match;
en ~ on the other hand.

rêvasser /rɛvase/ **1** vi daydream.

rêve /rɛv/ nm dream; **faire un** ~
have a dream.

réveil /revɛj/ nm waking up, (fig)
awakening; (pendule) alarm clock.

réveillé, ~e /reveje/ adj awake.

réveille-matin /revɛjmatɛ̃/ nm
inv alarm clock.

réveiller /reveje/ **1** vt wake (up);
(sentiment, souvenir) awaken; (curiosité) arouse. □ **se** ~ vpr wake up.

réveillon /revɛjɔ̃/ nm (Noël)
Christmas Eve; (nouvel an) New
Year's Eve. **réveillonner** **1** vi see
Christmas ou the New Year in.

révéler /revele/ **14** vt reveal. □ **se**
~ vpr be revealed; **se** ~ **facile** turn
out to be easy, prove easy.

revendeur, -euse /rəvɑ̃dœr, -øz/
nm, f dealer, stockist; ~ **de drogue**

drug dealer.

revendication /rəvɑ̃dikasjɔ̃/ nf
claim. **revendiquer** **1** vt claim.

revendre /rəvɑ̃dr/ **3** vt sell
(again); **avoir de l'énergie à** ~
have energy to spare.

revenir /rəvnir/ **58** vi (aux être)
come back, return (à to); ~ **à** (activité) go back to; (se résumer à)
come down to; (échoir à) fall to; ~
à 100 euros cost 100 euros; ~ **de**
(maladie, surprise) get over; ~ **sur
ses pas** retrace one's steps; **faire** ~
(Culin) brown; **ça me revient!** now
I remember!; **je n'en reviens pas!**
1 I can't get over it!

revenu /rəvny/ nm income; (de
l'État) revenue.

rêver /rɛve/ **1** vt/i dream (à of; **de
faire** of doing).

réverbère /reverber/ nm
street lamp.

révérence /reverɑ̃s/ nf reverence;
(salut d'homme) bow; (salut de
femme) curtsy.

rêverie /rɛvri/ nf daydream; (activité) daydreaming.

revers /rəver/ nm reverse; (de
main) back; (d'étoffe) wrong side;
(de veste) lapel; (de pantalon) turn-
up; (de manche) cuff; (tennis) backhand; (fig) set-back.

revêtement /rəvɛtmɑ̃/ nm covering; (de route) surface; ~ **de sol**
floor covering. **revêtir** **61** vt cover;
(habit) put on; (prendre, avoir)
assume.

rêveur, -euse /rɛvœr, -øz/ adj
dreamy. ● nm, f dreamer.

réviser /revize/ **1** vt revise; (machine, véhicule) service. **révision** nf
revision; service.

revivre /rəvivr/ **62** vi come alive
again. ● vt relive.

révocation /revɔkasjɔ̃/ nf repeal;

(d'un fonctionnaire) dismissal.

revoir¹ /RəVWAR/ 63 vt see (again); (réviser) revise.

revoir² /RəVWAR/ nm au ∼ goodbye.

révolte /Revɔlt/ nf revolt. **révolté, ∼e** nm, f rebel.

révolter /Revɔlte/ 1 vt appal, revolt. □ **se** ∼ vpr revolt.

révolu, ∼e /Revɔly/ adj past; **avoir 21 ans** ∼**s** be over 21 years of age.

révolution /Revɔlysjɔ̃/ nf revolution. **révolutionnaire** adj & nmf revolutionary. **révolutionner** 1 vt revolutionize.

revolver /RevɔlvɛR/ nm revolver, gun.

révoquer /Revɔke/ 1 vt repeal; (fonctionnaire) dismiss.

revue /Rəvy/ nf (examen, défilé) review; (magazine) magazine; (spectacle) variety show.

rez-de-chaussée /Redʃose/ nm inv ground floor; (US) first floor.

RF abrév f (**République Française**) French Republic.

rhinocéros /RinɔseRɔs/ nm rhinoceros.

rhubarbe /RybaRb/ nf rhubarb.

rhum /Rɔm/ nm rum.

rhumatisme /Rymatism/ nm rheumatism.

rhume /Rym/ nm cold; ∼ **des foins** hay fever.

ri /Ri/ →**RIRE** 54.

ricaner /Rikane/ 1 vi snigger.

riche /Riʃ/ adj rich (en in). ● nmf rich man, rich woman.

richesse /Riʃɛs/ nf wealth; (de sol, décor) richness; ∼**s** wealth; (ressources) resources.

ride /Rid/ nf wrinkle; (sur l'eau) ripple.

rideau (pl ∼**x**) /Rido/ nm curtain;

(métallique) shutter; (fig) screen.

ridicule /Ridikyl/ adj ridiculous. ● nm (d'une situation) absurdity; (le grotesque) **le** ∼ ridicule. **ridiculiser** 1 vt ridicule.

rien /Rjɛ̃/ pron nothing; (quoi que ce soit) anything; **ne** ∼**l** I don't mention it!; ∼ **de bon** nothing good; **elle n'a** ∼ **dit** she didn't say anything; ∼ **d'autre/de plus** nothing else/more; ∼ **du tout** nothing at all; ∼ **que** (seulement) just, only; **trois fois** ∼ next to nothing; **il n'y est pour** ∼ he has nothing to do with it; ∼ **à faire!** (c'est impossible) it's no good!; (refus) no way! 1. ● nm **un** ∼ **de** a touch of; **être puni pour un** ∼ be punished for the slightest thing; **se disputer pour un** ∼ fight over nothing; **en** ∼ **de temps** in next to no time.

rieur, -euse /RijœR, -øz/ adj cheerful; (yeux) laughing.

rigide /Riʒid/ adj rigid.

rigolade /Rigɔlad/ nf fun.

rigoler /Rigɔle/ 1 vi laugh; (s'amuser) have some fun; (plaisanter) joke.

rigolo, ∼te /Rigɔlo, -ɔt/ adj 1 funny. ● nm, f 1 joker.

rigoureux, -euse /RiguRø, -z/ adj rigorous; (hiver) harsh; (sévère) strict; (travail, recherches) meticulous.

rigueur /RigœR/ nf rigour; **à la** ∼ at a pinch; **être de** ∼ be obligatory; **tenir** ∼ **à qn de qch** bear sb a grudge for sth.

rime /Rim/ nf rhyme.

rimer /Rime/ 1 vi rhyme (**avec** with); **cela ne rime à rien** it makes no sense.

rinçage /Rɛ̃saʒ/ nm rinse; (action) rinsing.

rincer /Rɛ̃se/ 10 vt rinse.

riposte /Ripɔst/ nf retort.

riposter /Ripɔste/ **1** vt retaliate; **~ à** (*attaque*) counter; (*insulte*) reply to. ● vt retort (**que** that).

rire /RiR/ 54 vi laugh (**de** at); (plaisanter) joke; (s'amuser) have fun; **c'était pour ~** it was a joke. ● nm laugh; **des ~s** laughter.

risée /Rize/ nf **la ~ de** the laughing stock of.

risque /Risk/ nm risk. **risqué, ~e** adj risky; (osé) daring.

risquer /Riske/ **1** vt risk (**de faire** of doing); (être passible de) face; **il risque de pleuvoir** it might rain; **tu risques de te faire mal** you might hurt yourself. □ **se ~ à/ dans** vpr venture to/into.

ristourne /RistuRn/ nf discount.

rite /Rit/ nm rite; (habitude) ritual. **rituel, ~le** adj & nm ritual.

rivage /Rivaʒ/ nm shore.

rival, ~e (mpl **-aux**) /Rival, -o/ adj & nm, f rival. **rivaliser** **1** vi compete (avec with). **rivalité** nf rivalry.

rive /Riv/ nf (de fleuve) bank; (de lac) shore.

riverain, ~e /RivRɛ̃, -ɛn/ adj riverside. ● nm, f riverside resident; (d'une rue) resident.

rivière /RivjɛR/ nf river.

riz /Ri/ nm rice. **rizière** nf paddy field.

robe /Rɔb/ nf (de femme) dress; (de juge) robe; (de cheval) coat; **~ de chambre** dressing-gown.

robinet /Rɔbinɛ/ nm tap; (US) faucet.

robot /Rɔbo/ nm robot; **~ ménager** food processor.

robuste /Rɔbyst/ adj robust.

roche /Rɔʃ/ nf rock.

rocher /Rɔʃe/ nm rock.

rock /Rɔk/ nm (Mus) rock.

rodage /Rɔdaʒ/ nm **en ~** (Auto) running in.

roder /Rɔde/ **1** vt (Auto) run in; **être rodé** (personne) have got the hang of things.

rôder /Rode/ **1** vi roam; (suspect) prowl.

rogne /Rɔɲ/ nf **1** anger; **en ~** in a temper.

rogner /Rɔɲe/ **1** vt trim; **~ sur** cut down on.

rognon /Rɔɲɔ̃/ nm (Culin) kidney.

roi /Rwa/ nm king; **les R~ mages** the Magi; **la fête des R~** Twelfth Night.

rôle /Rol/ nm role, part.

roller /RɔlɛR/ nm (patin) rollerblade®; (activité) rollerblading.

romain, ~e /Rɔmɛ̃, -ɛn/ adj Roman. **R~, ~e** nm, f Roman. **romaine** nf (laitue) cos.

roman /Rɔmɑ̃/ nm novel; (genre) fiction.

romance /Rɔmɑ̃s/ nf ballad.

romancier, -ière /Rɔmɑ̃sje, -jɛR/ nm, f novelist.

romanesque /Rɔmanɛsk/ adj romantic; (fantastique) fantastic; (récit) fictional; **œuvres ~s** novels, fiction.

romantique /Rɔmɑ̃tik/ adj & nmf romantic. **romantisme** nm romanticism.

rompre /Rɔ̃pR/ **3** vt break; (relations) break off. ● vi (se séparer) break up; **~ avec** (fiancé) break up with; (parti) break away from; (tradition) break with. □ **se ~** vpr break.

ronce /Rɔ̃s/ nf bramble.

rond, ~e /Rɔ̃, -d/ adj round; (gras) plump; (ivre) **1** drunk. ● nm (cercle) ring; (tranche) slice; **en ~** in a circle; **il n'a pas un ~** **1** he hasn't got a penny.

ronde /Rɔ̃d/ *nf* (de policier) beat; (de soldat, gardien) watch; (Mus) semibreve.

rondelle /Rɔ̃dɛl/ *nf* (Tech) washer; (tranche) slice.

rondement /Rɔ̃dmɑ̃/ *adv* promptly; (franchement) frankly.

rondeur /Rɔ̃dœʀ/ *nf* roundness; (franchise) frankness; (embonpoint) plumpness.

rondin /Rɔ̃dɛ̃/ *nm* log.

rond-point (*pl* ronds-points) /Rɔ̃pwɛ̃/ *nm* roundabout; (US) traffic circle.

ronfler /Rɔ̃fle/ **1** *vi* snore; (moteur) purr.

ronger /Rɔ̃ʒe/ **40** *vt* gnaw (at); (vers, acide) eat into. □ se ~ les ongles bite one's nails.

rongeur /Rɔ̃ʒœʀ/ *nm* rodent.

ronronner /Rɔ̃Rɔne/ **1** *vi* purr.

rosbif /Rɔsbif/ *nm* roast beef.

rose /Roz/ *nf* rose. ● *adj & nm* pink.

rosé, **~e** /Roze/ *adj* pinkish. ● *nm* rosé.

roseau (*pl* ~x) /Rozo/ *nm* reed.

rosée /Roze/ *nf* dew.

rosier /Rozje/ *nm* rose bush.

rossignol /Rɔsiɲɔl/ *nm* nightingale.

rotatif, -ive /Rɔtatif, -v/ *adj* rotary.

roter /Rɔte/ **1** *vi* **1** burp.

rôti /Roti/ *nm* joint; (cuit) roast; ~ de porc roast pork.

rotin /Rɔtɛ̃/ *nm* (rattan) cane.

rôtir /Rotir/ **2** *vt* roast.

rôtissoire /Rotiswar/ *nf* roasting spit.

rotule /Rɔtyl/ *nf* kneecap.

rouage /Rwaʒ/ *nm* (Tech) wheel; les ~s the works; (d'une organisation: fig) wheels.

roucouler /Rukule/ **1** *vi* coo.

roue /Ru/ *nf* wheel; ~ dentée cog

(wheel); ~ de secours spare wheel.

rouer /Rwe/ **1** *vt* ~ de coups thrash.

rouge /Ruʒ/ *adj* red; (fer) red-hot. ● *nm* red; (vin) red wine; (fard) blusher; ~ à lèvres lipstick. ● *nmf* (Pol) red. **rouge-gorge** (*pl* rouges-gorges) *nm* robin.

rougeole /Ruʒɔl/ *nf* measles (+ *sg*). **rouget** /Ruʒɛ/ *nm* red mullet.

rougeur /Ruʒœʀ/ *nf* redness; (tache) red blotch.

rougir /Ruʒir/ **2** *vi* turn red; (de honte) blush.

rouille /Ruj/ *nf* rust. **rouillé**, **~e** *adj* rusty.

rouiller /Ruje/ **1** *vi* rust. □ se ~ *vpr* get rusty.

rouleau (*pl* ~x) /Rulo/ *nm* roll; (outil, vague) roller; ~ à pâtisserie rolling pin; ~ compresseur steamroller.

roulement /Rulmɑ̃/ *nm* rotation; (bruit) rumble; (alternance) rotation; (de tambour) roll; ~ à billes ballbearing; **travailler par ~** work in shifts.

rouler /Rule/ **1** *vt* roll; (ficelle, manches) roll up; (pâte) roll out; (duper **1**) cheat. ● *vi* (véhicule, train) go, travel; (conducteur) drive. □ se ~ dans *vpr* (herbe) roll in; (couverture) roll oneself up in.

roulette /Rulɛt/ *nf* (de meuble) castor; (de dentiste) drill; (jeu) roulette; **comme sur des ~s** very smoothly.

roulotte /Rulɔt/ *nf* caravan.

roumain, **~e** /Rumɛ̃, -ɛn/ *adj* Romanian. **R~**, **~e** *nm, f* Romanian.

Roumanie /Rumani/ *nf* Romania.

rouquin, **~e** /Rukɛ̃, -in/ **1** *adj* redhaired. ● *nm, f* redhead.

rouspéter /Ruspete/ **14** *vi* **1** grumble, moan.

rousse /Rus/ →**ROUX**.

roussir /RusiR/ ② *vt* scorch. ● *vi* turn brown.

route /Rut/ *nf* road; (Naut, Aviat) route; (direction) way; (voyage) journey; (chemin: fig) path; **en ~** on the way; **en ~!** let's go!; **mettre en ~** start; **~ nationale** trunk road, main road; **se mettre en ~** set out.

routier, -ière /Rutje, -jɛʀ/ *adj* road. ● *nm* long-distance lorry ou truck driver; (restaurant) transport café; (US) truck stop.

routine /Rutin/ *nf* routine.

roux, rousse /Ru, Rus/ *adj* red, russet; (*personne*) red-haired; (*chat*) ginger. ● *nm, f* redhead.

royal, ~e (*mpl* **-aux**) /Rwajal, -jo/ *adj* royal; (*cadeau*) fit for a king.

royaume /Rwajom/ *nm* kingdom.

Royaume-Uni /Rwajomyni/ *nm* United Kingdom.

royauté /Rwajote/ *nf* royalty.

RTT *abrév f* (**réduction du temps de travail**) reduction in working hours.

ruban /Rybɑ̃/ *nm* ribbon; (de chapeau) band; **~ adhésif** sticky tape; **~ magnétique** magnetic tape.

rubéole /Rybeɔl/ *nf* German measles (+ *sg*).

rubis /Rybi/ *nm* ruby.

rubrique /RybRik/ *nf* heading; (article) column.

ruche /Ryʃ/ *nf* beehive.

rude /Ryd/ *adj* (au toucher) rough; (pénible) tough; (grossier) coarse; (fameux ①) tremendous.

rudement /Rydmɑ̃/ *adv* (*frapper*) hard; (*traiter*) harshly; (très ①) really.

rudimentaire /Rydimɑ̃tɛʀ/ *adj* rudimentary.

rue /Ry/ *nf* street.

ruée /Rye/ *nf* rush.

ruer /Rye/ ① *vi* (*cheval*) buck. □ **se ~ vpr** rush (**dans** into; **vers** towards); **se ~ sur** pounce on.

rugby /Rygbi/ *nm* rugby.

rugir /Ryʒiʀ/ ② *vi* roar.

rugueux, -euse /Rygø, -z/ *adj* rough.

ruine /Rɥin/ *nf* ruin; **en (~s)** in ruins. **ruiner** ① *vt* ruin.

ruisseau (*pl* **~x**) /Rɥiso/ *nm* stream; (rigole) gutter.

rumeur /RymœR/ *nf* (nouvelle) rumour; (son) murmur, hum.

ruminer /Rymine/ ① *vi* (*animal*) ruminate; (méditer) meditate.

rupture /RyptyR/ *nf* break; (action) breaking; (de contrat) breach; (de pourparlers) breakdown; (de relations) breaking off; (de couple, coalition) break-up.

rural, ~e (*mpl* **-aux**) /RyRal, -o/ *adj* rural.

ruse /Ryz/ *nf* cunning; **une ~** a trick, a ruse. **rusé, ~e** *adj* cunning.

russe /Rys/ *adj* Russian. ● *nm* (Ling) Russian. **R~** *nmf* Russian.

Russie /Rysi/ *nf* Russia.

rustique /Rystik/ *adj* rustic.

rythme /Ritm/ *nm* rhythm; (vitesse) rate; (de la vie) pace. **rythmique** *adj* rhythmical.

Ss

s' /s/ →**SE**.

sa /sa/ →**SON**[1].

SA *abrév f* (**société anonyme**) PLC.

sabbatique /sabatik/ *adj* (*année*) sabbatical year.

sable /sɑbl/ *nm* sand; ~s mouvants quicksands. **sabler** *vt* **❶** grit.
sablier /sɑblije/ *nm* (Culin)
eggtimer.
sablonneux, -euse /sɑblɔnø, -z/
adj sandy.
sabot /sabo/ *nm* (de cheval) hoof;
(chaussure) clog; (de frein) shoe; ~
de Denver® (wheel) clamp.
saboter /sabɔte/ **❶** *vt* sabotage;
(bâcler) botch.
sac /sak/ *nm* bag; (grand, en toile)
sack; **mettre à** ~ (maison) ransack;
(ville) sack; ~ **à dos** rucksack; ~ **à
main** handbag; ~ **de couchage**
sleeping-bag; **mettre dans le
même** ~ lump together.
saccadé, -e /sakade/ *adj* jerky.
saccager /sakaʒe/ **40** *vt* (abîmer)
wreck; (maison) ransack; (ville,
pays) sack.
saccharine /sakarin/ *nf* saccharin.
sachet /saʃɛ/ *nm* (small) bag; (d'a-
romates) sachet; ~ **de thé** teabag.
sacoche /sakɔʃ/ *nf* bag; (de vélo)
saddlebag.
sacre /sakr/ *nm* (de roi) coronation; (d'évêque) consecration.
sacré, -e *adj* sacred; (maudit **①**)
damned. **sacrement** *nm* sacrament.
sacrer **❶** *vt* crown; consecrate.
sacrifice /sakrifis/ *nm* sacrifice.
sacrifier /sakrifje/ **45** *vt* sacrifice;
~ **à** conform to. □ **se** ~ *vpr* sacrifice oneself.
sacrilège /sakrilɛʒ/ *nm* sacrilege.
● *adj* sacrilegious.
sadique /sadik/ *adj* sadistic. ● *nmf*
sadist.
sage /saʒ/ *adj* wise; (docile) good,
well behaved. ● *nm* wise man.
sage-femme (*pl* **sages-femmes**)
/saʒfam/ *nf* midwife.
sagesse /saʒɛs/ *nf* wisdom.

Sagittaire /saʒitɛr/ *nm* le ~
Sagittarius.
saignant, ~e /sɛɲɑ̃, -t/ *adj*
(Culin) rare.
saigner /seɲe/ **❶** *vt/i* bleed; ~ **du
nez** have a nosebleed.
saillant, ~e /sajɑ̃, -t/ *adj*
prominent.
sain, ~e /sɛ̃, sɛn/ *adj* healthy; (mo-
ralement) sane; ~ **et sauf** safe and
sound.
saindoux /sɛ̃du/ *nm* lard.
saint, ~e /sɛ̃, -t/ *adj* holy; (bon,
juste) saintly. ● *nm, f* saint. **Saint-
Esprit** *nm* Blessed Spirit. **sainteté** *nf*
holiness; (d'un lieu) sanctity. **Sainte
Vierge** *nf* Blessed Virgin. **Saint-
Sylvestre** *nf* New Year's Eve.
sais /sɛ/ →**SAVOIR 55**.
saisie /sezi/ *nf* (Jur) seizure; (Comput) keyboarding; ~ **de données**
data capture.
saisir /sezir/ **2** *vt* grab (hold of);
(proie) seize; (occasion, biens) seize;
(comprendre) grasp; (frapper) strike;
(Ordinat) keyboard, capture; **saisi
de** (peur) stricken by, overcome by.
□ **se** ~ *vpr* seize. **saisissant,
~e** *adj* (spectacle) gripping.
saison /sezɔ̃/ *nf* season; **la morte
~** the off season. **saisonnier, -ière**
adj seasonal.
sait /sɛ/ →**SAVOIR 55**.
salade /salad/ *nf* (plat) salad;
(plante) lettuce. **saladier** *nm*
salad bowl.
salaire /salɛr/ *nm* wages (+ *pl*);
salary.
salarié, ~e /salarje/ *adj* wage-
earning. ● *nm, f* wage earner.
sale /sal/ *adj* dirty; (mauvais) nasty.
salé, ~e /sale/ *adj* (goût) salty;
(plat) salted; (opposé à sucré) savoury; (grivois **①**) spicy; (excessif

s

1 steep. **saler** /sale/ *vt* salt.

saleté /salte/ *nf* dirtiness; (crasse) dirt; (obscénité) obscenity; ~(**s**) (camelote) rubbish; (détritus) mess.

salir /saliʀ/ **2** *vt* (make) dirty; (réputation) tarnish. □ **se** ~ *vpr* get dirty. **salissant**, ~**e** *adj* dirty; (étoffe) easily dirtied.

salive /saliv/ *nf* saliva.

salle /sal/ *nf* room; (grande, publique) hall; (de restaurant) dining room; (Théât, cinéma) auditorium; **cinéma à trois** ~**s** three-screen cinema; ~ **à manger** dining room; ~ **d'attente** waiting room; ~ **de bains** bathroom; ~ **de causette** chatroom; ~ **de séjour** living room; ~ **de classe** classroom; ~ **d'embarquement** departure lounge; ~ **d'opération** operating theatre; ~ **des ventes** saleroom.

salon /salɔ̃/ *nm* lounge; (de coiffure, beauté) salon; (exposition) show; ~ **de thé** tea-room; ~ **virtuel** chatroom.

salopette /salɔpɛt/ *nf* dungarees (+ *pl*); (d'ouvrier) overalls (+ *pl*).

saltimbanque /saltɛ̃bɑ̃k/ *nmf* (street) acrobat.

salubre /salybʀ/ *adj* healthy.

saluer /salɥe/ **1** *vt* greet; (en partant) take one's leave of; (de la tête) nod to; (de la main) wave to; (Mil) salute; (accueillir favorablement) welcome.

salut /saly/ *nm* greeting; (de la tête) nod; (de la main) wave; (Mil) salute; (rachat) salvation. ● *interj* (bonjour **1**) hello; (au revoir **1**) bye.

salutation /salytasjɔ̃/ *nf* greeting.

samedi /samdi/ *nm* Saturday.

SAMU /samy/ *abrév m* (**Service d'assistance médicale d'urgence**) ≈ mobile accident unit.

SAMU A twenty-four hour service coordinated by each *département* to send mobile medical services and staff, ambulances and helicopters to scenes of accidents and other emergencies.

sanction /sɑ̃ksjɔ̃/ *nf* sanction. **sanctionner** **1** *vt* sanction; (punir) punish.

sandale /sɑ̃dal/ *nf* sandal.

sang /sɑ̃/ *nm* blood; **se faire du mauvais** ~ **ou un** ~ **d'encre** be worried stiff. **sang-froid** *nm inv* self-control. **sanglant**, ~**e** *adj* bloody.

sangle /sɑ̃gl/ *nf* strap.

sanglier /sɑ̃glije/ *nm* wild boar.

sanglot /sɑ̃glo/ *nm* sob. **sangloter** **1** *vi* sob.

sanguin, ~**e** /sɑ̃gɛ̃, -in/ *adj* (groupe) blood.

sanguinaire /sɑ̃ginɛʀ/ *adj* bloodthirsty.

sanitaire /sanitɛʀ/ *adj* (directives) health; (conditions) sanitary; (appareils, installations) bathroom, sanitary. **sanitaires** *nmpl* bathroom.

sans /sɑ̃/ *prép* without; ~ **ça**, ~ **quoi** otherwise; ~ **arrêt** nonstop; ~ **encombre/faute/tarder** without incident/fail/delay; ~ **fin/goût/limite** endless/tasteless/limitless; ~ **importance/pareil/précédent/travail** unimportant/unparalleled/unprecedented/unemployed; **j'ai aimé mais** ~ **plus** it was good, it wasn't great.

sans-abri /sɑ̃zabʀi/ *nmf inv* homeless person.

sans-gêne /sɑ̃zɛn/ *adj inv* inconsiderate, thoughtless. ● *nm inv* thoughtlessness.

sans-papiers /sɑ̃papje/ *nm inv* illegal immigrant.

santé /sɑ̃te/ *nf* health; **à ta ou**

votre ∼! cheers!

saoul, ∼e /su, sul/ ➡**SOUL**.

sapin /sapɛ̃/ nm fir (tree); ∼ **de Noël** Christmas tree.

sarcasme /saʀkasm/ nm sarcasm. **sarcastique** adj sarcastic.

sardine /saʀdin/ nf sardine.

sas /sɑs/ nm (Naut, Aviat) airlock.

satané, ∼e /satane/ adj 🗹 damned.

satellite /satelit/ nm satellite.

satin /satɛ̃/ nm satin.

satire /satiʀ/ nf satire.

satisfaction /satisfaksjɔ̃/ nf satisfaction.

satisfaire /satisfɛʀ/ 🗓 vt satisfy.
● vi ∼ **à** fulfil. **satisfaisant**, ∼e adj (acceptable) satisfactory. **satisfait**, ∼e adj satisfied (**de** with).

saturer /satyʀe/ 🗓 vt saturate.

sauce /sos/ nf sauce; ∼ **tartare** tartar sauce. **saucière** nf sauceboat.

saucisse /sosis/ nf sausage.

saucisson /sosisɔ̃/ nm (slicing) sausage.

sauf¹ /sof/ prép except; ∼ **erreur** if I'm not mistaken; ∼ **imprévu** unless anything unforeseen happens; ∼ **avis contraire** unless otherwise stated.

sauf², **-ve** /sof, sov/ adj safe, unharmed.

sauge /soʒ/ nf (Culin) sage.

saule /sol/ nm willow; ∼ **pleureur** weeping willow.

saumon /somɔ̃/ nm salmon. ● adj inv salmon(-pink).

sauna /sona/ nm sauna.

saupoudrer /supudʀe/ 🗓 vt sprinkle (**de** with).

saut /so/ nm jump; **faire un** ∼ **chez qn** pop round to sb's (place); **le** ∼ (Sport) jumping; ∼ **en hauteur/longueur** high/long jump;

∼ **périlleux** somersault; **au** ∼ **du lit** on getting up.

sauté, ∼e /sote/ adj & nm (Culin) sauté.

saute-mouton /sotmutɔ̃/ nm inv leap-frog.

sauter /sote/ 🗓 vi jump; (exploser) blow up; (fusible) blow; (se détacher) come off; **faire** ∼ (détruire) blow up; (fusible) blow; (casser) break; ∼ **à la corde** skip; ∼ **aux yeux** be obvious; ∼ **au cou de qn** fling one's arms round sb; ∼ **sur une occasion** jump at an opportunity. ● vt jump (over); (page, classe) skip.

sauterelle /sotʀɛl/ nf grasshopper.

sautiller /sotije/ 🗓 vi hop.

sauvage /sovaʒ/ adj wild; (primitif, cruel) savage; (farouche) unsociable; (illégal) unauthorized. ● nmf unsociable person; (brute) savage.

sauve /sov/ ➡**SAUF**.²

sauvegarder /sovɡaʀde/ 🗓 vt safeguard; (Ordinat) back up.

sauver /sove/ 🗓 vt save; (d'un danger) rescue, save; (matériel) salvage. □ **se** ∼ vpr (fuir) run away; (partir 🗓) be off. **sauvetage** nm rescue. **sauveteur** nm rescuer. **sauveur** nm saviour.

savant, ∼e /savã, -t/ adj learned; (habile) skilful. ● nm scientist.

saveur /savœʀ/ nf flavour; (fig) savour.

savoir /savwaʀ/ 🗓 vt know; **elle sait conduire/nager** she can drive/ swim; **faire** ∼ **à qn** inform sb that; (**pas**) **que je sache** (not) as far as I know; **à** ∼ namely. ● nm learning.

savon /savɔ̃/ nm soap; **passer un** ∼ **à qn** 🗓 give sb a telling-off. **savonnette** nf bar of soap.

savourer /savuʀe/ 🗓 vt savour. **savoureux**, **-euse** adj tasty.

(fig) spicy.

scandale /skãdal/ *nm* scandal; (tapage) uproar; (en public) noisy scene; **faire** ~ shock people; **faire un** ~ make a scene. **scandaleux, -euse** *adj* scandalous. **scandaliser** ◼ *vt* scandalize, shock.

scander /skãde/ ◼ *vt* (vers) scan; (slogan) chant.

scandinave /skãdinav/ *adj* Scandinavian. **S~** *nmf* Scandinavian.

Scandinavie /skãdinavi/ *nf* Scandinavia.

scarabée /skaRabe/ *nm* beetle.

sceau (*pl* ~**x**) /so/ *nm* seal.

scélérat /selera/ *nm* scoundrel.

sceller /sele/ ◼ *vt* seal.

scène /sɛn/ *nf* scene; (estrade, art dramatique) stage; **mettre en** ~ (*pièce*) stage; (*film*) direct; **mise en** ~ direction; ~ **de ménage** domestic dispute.

scepticisme /sɛptisism/ *nm* scepticism.

sceptique /sɛptik/ *adj* sceptical. ● *nmf* sceptic.

schéma /ʃema/ *nm* diagram. **schématique** *adj* schematic; (sommaire) sketchy. **schématiser** ◼ *vt* simplify.

schizophrène /skizofRɛn/ *adj* & *nmf* schizophrenic.

sciatique /sjatik/ *adj* (nerf) sciatic. ● *nf* sciatica.

scie /si/ *nf* saw.

sciemment /sjamã/ *adv* knowingly.

science /sjãs/ *nf* science; (savoir) knowledge.

science-fiction /sjãsfiksjõ/ *nf* science fiction.

scientifique /sjãtifik/ *adj* scientific. ● *nmf* scientist.

scier /sje/ ◖◗ *vt* saw.

scintiller /sɛ̃tije/ ◼ *vi* glitter; (étoile) twinkle.

scission /sisjõ/ *nf* split.

sclérose /skleRoz/ *nf* sclerosis; ~ **en plaques** multiple sclerosis.

scolaire /skoleR/ *adj* school. **scolarisé, -e** *adj* going to school. **scolarité** *nf* schooling.

score /skoR/ *nm* score.

scorpion /skoRpjõ/ *nm* scorpion; le **S~** Scorpio.

scotch /skotʃ/ *nm* (boisson) Scotch (whisky); (ruban adhésif)® Sellotape®.

scout, ~**e** /skut/ *nm* & *adj* scout.

scrupule /skRypyl/ *nm* scruple. **scrupuleux, -euse** *adj* scrupulous.

scruter /skRyte/ ◼ *vt* examine, scrutinize.

scrutin /skRytɛ̃/ *nm* (vote) ballot; (élections) polls (+ *pl*).

sculpter /skylte/ ◼ *vt* sculpt, carve. **sculpteur** *nm* sculptor. **sculpture** *nf* sculpture.

SDF *abrév m* (**sans domicile fixe**) homeless person.

---

se, s' /sə, s/

s' before vowel or mute h.

● *pronom*
••••▸ himself, (féminin) herself; (indéfini) oneself; (non humain) itself; (au pluriel) themselves; ~ **laver les mains** wash one's hands; (réciproque) each other, one another; **ils se détestent** they hate each other.

❗ The translation of **se** will vary according to which verb it is associated with. You should therefore refer to the verb to find it. For example, **se promener**, **se taire** will be treated respectively under **promener** and **taire**.

séance | séjour

séance /seɑ̃s/ *nf* session; (Théât, cinéma) show; ~ **de pose** sitting; ~ **tenante** forthwith.

seau (*pl* ~**x**) /so/ *nm* bucket, pail.

sec, sèche /sɛk, sɛʃ/ *adj* dry; (*fruits*) dried; (*coup, bruit*) sharp; (*cœur*) hard; (*whisky*) neat. ● *nm* à ~ (sans eau) dry; (sans argent) broke; **au ~** in a dry place.

sèche-cheveux /sɛʃʃəvø/ *nm inv* hairdrier.

sèchement /sɛʃmɑ̃/ *adv* drily.

sécher /seʃe/ 14 *vt/i* dry; (*cours* 1) skip; (ne pas savoir 1) be stumped. □ **se** ~ *vpr* dry oneself. **sécheresse** *nf* (de climat) dryness; (temps sec) drought. **séchoir** *nm* drier.

second, ~e /səgɔ̃, -d/ *adj & nm, f* second. ● *nm* (adjoint) second in command; (étage) second floor. **secondaire** *adj* secondary. **seconde** *nf* (instant) second; (vitesse) second gear.

seconder /səgɔ̃de/ 1 *vt* assist.

secouer /səkwe/ 1 *vt* shake; (*poussière, torpeur*) shake off. □ **se** ~ *vpr* 1 (se dépêcher) get a move on; (réagir) shake oneself up.

secourir /səkuʀiʀ/ 20 *vt* assist, help. **secouriste** *nmf* first-aid worker.

secours /səkuʀ/ *nm* assistance, help; **au** ~! help!; **de** ~ (sortie) emergency; (équipe, opération) rescue. ● *nmpl* (Méd) first aid.

secousse /səkus/ *nf* jolt, jerk; (séisme) tremor.

secret, -ète /səkʀɛ, -t/ *adj* secret. ● *nm* secret; (discrétion) secrecy; **le** ~ **professionnel** professional confidentiality; ~ **de Polichinelle** open secret; **en** ~ in secret, secretly.

secrétaire /səkʀetɛʀ/ *nmf* secretary; ~ **de direction** personal assistant. ● *nm* (meuble) writing desk; ~ **d'État** junior minister.

secrétariat /səkʀetaʀja/ *nm* secretarial work; (bureau) secretariat.

sectaire /sɛktɛʀ/ *adj* sectarian.

secte /sɛkt/ *nf* sect.

secteur /sɛktœʀ/ *nm* area; (Comm) sector; (circuit: Électr) mains (+ *pl*).

section /sɛksjɔ̃/ *nf* section; (Scol) stream; (Mil) platoon. **sectionner** 1 *vt* sever.

sécuriser /sekyʀize/ 1 *vt* reassure.

sécurisé, e /sekyʀize/ *adj* (Ordinat) secure; **une ligne** ~**e** a secure line.

sécurité /sekyʀite/ *nf* security; (absence de danger) safety; **en** ~ safe, secure; **Sécurité sociale** *nf* social security, social security services; ~ **des frontières** homeland security.

sédatif /sedatif/ *nm* sedative.

sédentaire /sedɑ̃tɛʀ/ *adj* sedentary.

séducteur, -trice /sedyktœʀ, -tʀis/ *adj* seductive. ● *nm, f* seducer. **séduction** *nf* seduction; (charme) charm.

séduire /seduiʀ/ 17 *vt* charm; (plaire à) appeal to; (sexuellement) seduce. **séduisant, ~e** *adj* attractive.

ségrégation /segʀegasjɔ̃/ *nf* segregation.

seigle /sɛgl/ *nm* rye.

seigneur /sɛɲœʀ/ *nm* lord; **le S**~ the Lord.

sein /sɛ̃/ *nm* breast; **au** ~ **de** within.

séisme /seism/ *nm* earthquake.

seize /sɛz/ *adj & nm* sixteen.

séjour /seʒuʀ/ *nm* stay; (pièce) living room. **séjourner** 1 *vi* stay.

sel /sɛl/ nm salt; (piquant) spice.

sélectif, -ive /selɛktif, -v/ adj selective.

sélection /selɛksjɔ̃/ nf selection. **sélectionner** ① vt select.

selle /sɛl/ nf saddle; ~s (Méd) stools.

sellette /sɛlɛt/ nf **sur la** ~ (personne) in the hot seat.

selon /səlɔ̃/ prép according to; ~ **que** depending on whether.

semaine /səmɛn/ nf week; **en** ~ during the week.

sémantique /semɑ̃tik/ adj semantic. ● nf semantics.

semblable /sɑ̃blabl/ adj similar (à to). ● nm fellow (creature).

semblant /sɑ̃blɑ̃/ nm **faire** ~ **de** pretend to; **un** ~ **de** a semblance of.

sembler /sɑ̃ble/ ① vi seem (à to; que that); **il me semble que** it seems to me that.

semelle /səmɛl/ nf sole; ~ **compensée** wedge heel.

semence /s(ə)mɑ̃s/ nf seed.

semer /s(ə)me/ ⑥ vt (graine, doute) sow; (jeter, parsemer) strew; (personne ①) lose; ~ **la panique** spread panic.

semestre /səmɛstʀ/ nm half year; (Univ) semester. **semestriel, ~le** adj (revue) biannual; (examen) end-of-semester.

séminaire /seminɛʀ/ nm (Relig) seminary; (Univ) seminar.

semi-remorque /s(ə)miʀ(ə)mɔʀk/ nm articulated lorry.

semis /s(ə)mi/ nm seedling.

semoule /s(ə)mul/ nf semolina.

sénat /sena/ nm senate. **sénateur** nm senator.

sénile /senil/ adj senile.

senior /senjɔʀ/ adj (âgé) senior; (mode, publication) for senior citizens. ● nmf senior citizen.

sens /sɑ̃s/ nm (Méd) sense; (signification) meaning, sense; (direction) direction; **à mon** ~ to my mind; **à** ~ **unique** (rue) one-way; **ça n'a pas de** ~ it doesn't make sense; ~ **commun** common sense; ~ **giratoire** roundabout; ~ **interdit** no-entry sign; (rue) one-way street; **dans le** ~ **des aiguilles d'une montre** clockwise; **dans le** ~ **inverse des aiguilles d'une montre** anticlockwise; ~ **dessus dessous** upside down; ~ **devant derrière** back to front.

sensation /sɑ̃sasjɔ̃/ nf feeling, sensation; **faire** ~ create a sensation. **sensationnel, ~le** adj sensational.

sensé, ~e /sɑ̃se/ adj sensible.

sensibiliser /sɑ̃sibilize/ ① vt ~ **l'opinion** increase people's awareness (à qch to sth).

sensibilité /sɑ̃sibilite/ nf sensitivity. **sensible** adj sensitive (à to); (appréciable) noticeable. **sensiblement** adv noticeably.

sensoriel, ~le /sɑ̃sɔʀjɛl/ adj sensory.

sensualité /sɑ̃sɥalite/ nf sensuousness; sensuality. **sensuel, ~le** adj sensual.

sentence /sɑ̃tɑ̃s/ nf sentence.

senteur /sɑ̃tœʀ/ nf scent.

sentier /sɑ̃tje/ nm path.

sentiment /sɑ̃timɑ̃/ nm feeling; **faire du** ~ sentimentalize; **j'ai le** ~ **que...** I get the feeling that... **sentimental, ~e** (mpl **-aux**) adj sentimental.

sentir /sɑ̃tiʀ/ ⑯ vt feel; (odeur) smell; (pressentir) sense; ~ **la lavande** smell of lavender; **je ne**

peux pas le ~ 🔢 I can't stand him.
● vi smell. □ se ~ vpr se ~ **fier/
mieux** feel proud/better.

séparation /sepaʀasjɔ̃/ nf separation.

séparatiste /sepaʀatist/ adj & nmf separatist.

séparé, ~e /sepaʀe/ adj separate; (conjoints) separated.

séparer /sepaʀe/ ❶ vt separate; (en deux) split. □ se ~ vpr separate, part (de from); (se détacher) split; se ~ **de** (se défaire de) part with.

sept /sɛt/ adj & nm seven.

septante /sɛptɑ̃t/ adj & nm seventy.

septembre /sɛptɑ̃bʀ/ nm September.

septentrional, ~e (mpl -**aux**) /sɛptɑ̃tʀijɔnal, -o/ adj northern.

septième /sɛtjɛm/ adj & nmf seventh.

sépulture /sepyltyʀ/ nf burial; (lieu) burial place.

séquelles /sekɛl/ nfpl (maladie) after-effects; (fig) aftermath.

séquence /sekɑ̃s/ nf sequence.

séquestrer /sekɛstʀe/ ❶ vt confine (illegally).

sera, serait /sɔʀa, sɔʀɛ/ →**ÊTRE** ❹.

serbe /sɛʀb/ adj Serbian. **S~** nmf Serbian.

Serbie /sɛʀbi/ nf Serbia.

serein, ~e /sɔʀɛ̃, -ɛn/ adj serene.

sérénité /seʀenite/ nf serenity.

sergent /sɛʀʒɑ̃/ nm sergeant.

série /seʀi/ nf series (+ sg); (d'objets) set; de ~ (véhicule etc.) standard; **fabrication** ou **production en ~** mass production.

sérieusement /seʀjøzmɑ̃/ adv seriously.

sérieux, -ieuse /seʀjø, -z/ adj serious; (digne de confiance) reliable;

(chances, raison) good. ● nm seriousness; **garder son ~** keep a straight face; **prendre au ~** take seriously.

serin /sɔʀɛ̃/ nm canary.

seringue /sɔʀɛ̃g/ nf syringe.

serment /sɛʀmɑ̃/ nm oath; (promesse) vow.

sermon /sɛʀmɔ̃/ nm sermon. **sermonner** /sɛʀmɔne/ ❶ vt lecture.

séropositif, -ive /seʀɔpozitif, -v/ adj HIV positive.

serpent /sɛʀpɑ̃/ nm snake; ~ **à sonnettes** rattlesnake.

serpillière /sɛʀpijɛʀ/ nf floorcloth.

serre /sɛʀ/ nf (de jardin) greenhouse; (griffe) claw.

serré, ~e /seʀe/ adj (habit, nœud, écrou) tight; (personnes) packed, crowded; (lutte, mailles) close; (écriture) cramped; (cœur) heavy.

serrer /seʀe/ ❶ vt (saisir) grip; (presser) squeeze; (vis, corde, ceinture) tighten; (poing, dents) clench; ~ **qn dans ses bras** hug sb; ~ **les rangs** close ranks; ~ **qn** (vêtement) be tight on sb; ~ **qn de près** follow sb closely; ~ **la main à** shake hands with. ● vi ~ **à droite** keep over to the right. □ **se** ~ vpr (se rapprocher) squeeze (up).

serrure /seʀyʀ/ nf lock. **serrurier** nm locksmith.

servante /sɛʀvɑ̃t/ nf (maid) servant.

serveur, -euse /sɛʀvœʀ, -øz/ nm, f (homme) waiter; (femme) waitress. ● nm (Ordinat) server.

serviable /sɛʀvjabl/ adj helpful.

service /sɛʀvis/ nm service; (fonction, temps de travail) duty; (pourboire) service (charge); (dans une société) department; (~ **non**) **compris** service (not) included; **être de ~** be on duty; **pendant le ~**

s

(when) on duty; **rendre** ~ **à qn** be a help to sb; ~ **d'ordre** stewards (+ pl); ~ **après-vente** after-sales service; ~ **militaire** military service; **les** ~**s secrets** the secret service (+ sg).

serviette /sɛʀvjɛt/ *nf* (de toilette) towel; (cartable) briefcase; (~ **de table**) serviette, napkin; (~ **hygiénique** sanitary towel.

servir /sɛʀviʀ/ 46 *vt/i* serve; (être utile) be of use, serve; ~ **qn** (à table) wait on sb; **ça sert à** (outil, récipient) it is used for; **ça ne sert à/de** I use it to/as; **ça ne sert à rien** (action) it's pointless; ~ **de** serve as, be used as; ~ **à qn de guide** act as a guide for sb. □ **se** ~ *vpr* (à table) help oneself (**de** to); ~ **de** use. **serviteur** *nm* servant.

ses /se/ **⇒SON**[1].

session /sesjɔ̃/ *nf* session.

seuil /sœj/ *nm* doorstep; (entrée) doorway; (fig) threshold.

seul, ~e /sœl/ *adj* alone, on one's own; (unique) only; **un** ~ **exemple** only one example; **pas un** ~ **ami** not a single friend; **lui** ~ **le sait** only he knows; **dans le** ~ **but de** with the sole aim of; **parler tout** ~ talk to oneself; **faire qch tout** ~ do sth on one's own. ● *nm*, **f le** ~**la** ~**e** the only one. **seulement** *adv* only.

sève /sɛv/ *nf* sap.

sévère /sevɛʀ/ *adj* severe. **sévérité** *nf* severity.

sévices /sevis/ *nmpl* physical abuse.

sévir /seviʀ/ 2 *vi* (fléau) rage; ~ **contre** punish.

sevrer /səvʀe/ 6 *vt* wean.

sexe /sɛks/ *nm* sex; (organes) genitals (+ pl). **sexiste** *adj* sexist. **sexualité** *nf* sexuality. **sexuel, ~le** *adj* sexual.

shampooing /ʃɑ̃pwɛ̃/ *nm*

shampoo.

shérif /ʃeʀif/ *nm* sheriff.

short /ʃɔʀt/ *nm* shorts (+ pl).

si (**s'** before il, ils) /si, s/ *conj* if; (interrogation indirecte) if, whether; ~ **on allait se promener?** what about a walk?; **s'il vous** *ou* **te plaît** please; ~ **oui** if so; ~ **seulement** if only. ● *adv* (tellement) so; (oui) yes; **un** ~ **bon repas** such a good meal; ~ **habile qu'il soit** however skilful he may be; ~ **bien que** with the result that.

sida /sida/ *nm* (Méd) Aids.

sidérurgie /sideʀyʀʒi/ *nf* steel industry.

siècle /sjɛkl/ *nm* century; (époque) age.

siège /sjɛʒ/ *nm* seat; (Mil) siege; ~ **éjectable** ejector seat; ~ **social** head office, headquarters (+ pl). **siéger** 14 40 *vi* (assemblée) sit.

sien, ~ne /sjɛ̃, -ɛn/ *pron* **le** ~, **la** ~**ne**, **les** (~**ne**)**s** (homme) his; (femme) hers; (chose) its; **les** ~**s** (famille) one's family.

sieste /sjɛst/ *nf* nap, siesta.

sifflement /sifləmɑ̃/ *nm* whistling; **un** ~ a whistle.

siffler /sifle/ 1 *vi* whistle; (avec un sifflet) blow one's whistle; (serpent, gaz) hiss. ● *vt* (air) whistle; (acteur) hiss.

sifflet /sifle/ *nm* whistle; ~**s** (huées) boos.

sigle /sigl/ *nm* acronym.

signal (pl **-aux**) /siɲal, -o/ *nm* signal; ~ **sonore** (de répondeur) tone.

signalement /siɲalmɑ̃/ *nm* description.

signaler /siɲale/ 1 *vt* indicate; (par une sonnerie, un écriteau) signal; (dénoncer, mentionner) report; (faire remarquer) point out.

signalisation /siɲalizasjɔ̃/ *nf* signalling; signposting; (signaux) signals (+ pl).

signataire /siɲatɛʀ/ nmf signatory.

signature /siɲatyʀ/ nf signature; (action) signing; ~ **électronique** digital signature.

signe /siɲ/ nm sign; (de ponctuation) mark; **faire ~ à qn** wave at sb; (contacter) contact; **faire ~ à qn de** beckon sb to; **faire ~ que non** shake one's head; **faire ~ que oui** nod.

signer /siɲe/ **1** vt sign. □ **se ~** vpr (Relig) cross oneself.

signet /siɲɛ/ nm (pour livre, Internet) bookmark; ~**s favoris** (Internet) hotlist.

significatif, -ive /siɲifikatif, -v/ adj significant.

signification /siɲifikasjɔ̃/ nf meaning. **signifier** **45** vt mean, signify; (faire connaître) make known (à to).

silence /silɑ̃s/ nm silence; (Mus) rest; **garder le ~** keep silent.

silencieux, -ieuse /silɑ̃sjø, -z/ adj silent. ● nm silencer.

silex /silɛks/ nm inv flint.

silhouette /silwɛt/ nf outline, silhouette.

sillon /sijɔ̃/ nm furrow; (de disque) groove.

sillonner /sijɔne/ **1** vt crisscross.

similaire /similɛʀ/ adj similar. **similitude** nf similarity.

simple /sɛ̃pl/ adj simple; (non double) single. ● nm ~ **dames/ messieurs** ladies'/men's singles (+ pl). **simple d'esprit** nmf simpleton. **simplement** adv simply. **simplicité** nf simplicity; (naïveté) simpleness.

simplification /sɛ̃plifikasjɔ̃/ nf simplification. **simplifier** **45** vt simplify.

simpliste /sɛ̃plist/ adj simplistic.

simulacre /simylakʀ/ nm pretence, sham.

simulation /simylasjɔ̃/ nf simulation. **simuler** **1** vt simulate.

simultané, ~e /simyltane/ adj simultaneous.

sincère /sɛ̃sɛʀ/ adj sincere. **sincérité** nf sincerity.

singe /sɛ̃ʒ/ nm monkey; (grand) ape. **singer** **40** vt mimic, ape.

singulier, -ière /sɛ̃gylje, -jɛʀ/ adj peculiar, remarkable; (Gram) singular. ● nm (Gram) singular.

sinistre /sinistʀ/ adj sinister. ● nm disaster; (incendie) blaze; (dommages) damage.

sinistré, ~e /sinistʀe/ adj stricken. ● nm, f disaster victim.

sinon /sinɔ̃/ conj (autrement) otherwise; (sauf) except (**que** that); **difficile ~ impossible** difficult if not impossible.

sinueux, -euse /sinɥø, -z/ adj winding; (fig) tortuous.

sirène /siʀɛn/ nf (appareil) siren; (femme) mermaid.

sirop /siʀo/ nm (de fruits, Méd) syrup; (boisson) cordial.

sismique /sismik/ adj seismic.

site /sit/ nm site; ~ **touristique** place of interest; ~ **Internet** or **Web** Web site.

sitôt /sito/ adv ~ **entré** immediately after coming in; ~ **que** as soon as; **pas de ~** not for a while.

situation /sitɥasjɔ̃/ nf situation; (emploi) job, position; ~ **de famille** marital status.

situé, ~e /sitɥe/ adj situated.

situer /sitɥe/ **1** vt situate, locate. □ **se ~** vpr (se trouver) be situated.

six /sis/ (/si/ before consonant, /siz/ before vowel) adj & nm six. **sixième**

adj & nmf sixth.

sketch (*pl* **-es**) /skɛtʃ/ *nm* (Théât) sketch.

ski /ski/ *nm* (matériel) ski; (Sport) skiing; **faire du ~** ski; **~ de fond** cross-country skiing; **~ nautique** water skiing. **skier** 45 *vi* ski.

slave /slav/ *adj* Slav; (Ling) Slavonic.

slip /slip/ *nm* (d'homme) underpants (+ *pl*); (de femme) knickers (+ *pl*); **~ de bain** (swimming) trunks (+ *pl*); (du bikini) bikini bottom.

slogan /slɔgɑ̃/ *nm* slogan.

Slovaquie /slɔvaki/ *nf* Slovakia.

Slovénie /slɔveni/ *nf* Slovenia.

smoking /smɔkiŋ/ *nm* dinner jacket.

SNCF *abrév f* (**Société nationale des Chemins de fer français**) French national railway company.

snob /snɔb/ *nmf* snob. ● *adj* snobbish. **snobisme** *nm* snobbery.

sobre /sɔbr/ *adj* sober.

social, ~e (*mpl* **-iaux**) /sɔsjal, -jo/ *adj* social.

socialisme /sɔsjalism/ *nm* socialism. **socialiste** *nmf* & *a* socialist.

société /sɔsjete/ *nf* society; (entreprise) company; **~ point com** dot-com.

socle /sɔkl/ *nm* (de colonne, statue) plinth; (de lampe) base.

socquette /sɔkɛt/ *nf* ankle sock.

soda /sɔda/ *nm* fizzy drink.

sœur /sœr/ *nf* sister.

soi /swa/ *pron* oneself; **derrière ~** behind one; **en ~** in itself; **aller de ~** be obvious.

soi-disant /swadizɑ̃/ *adj inv* so-called. ● *adv* supposedly.

soie /swa/ *nf* silk.

soif /swaf/ *nf* thirst; **avoir ~** be thirsty; **donner ~** make one

thirsty.

soigné, ~e /swaɲe/ *adj* (apparence) tidy, neat; (travail) carefully done.

soigner /swaɲe/ **1** *vt* (s'occuper de) look after, take care of; (tenue, style) take care over; (maladie) treat. □ **se ~** *vpr* look after oneself.

soigneusement /swaɲøzmɑ̃/ *adv* carefully. **soigneux, -euse** *adj* careful (**de** about); (ordonné) tidy.

soi-même /swamɛm/ *pron* oneself.

soin /swɛ̃/ *nm* (ordre) tidiness; **~s** care; (Méd) treatment; **avec ~** carefully; **avoir** *ou* **prendre ~ de qn** take care of sb; **faire** *ou* **prendre ~ de faire** take care of sb to do; **premiers ~s** first aid (+ *sg*).

soir /swar/ *nm* evening; **à ce ~** see you tonight.

soirée /sware/ *nf* evening; (réception) party.

soit /swa/ *conj* (à savoir) that is to say; **~...** either... or. ● →**ÊTRE** 4.

soixante /swasɑ̃t/ *adj & nm* sixty. **soixante-dix** *adj & nm* seventy.

soja /sɔʒa/ *nm* (graines) soya beans (+ *pl*); (plante) soya.

sol /sɔl/ *nm* ground; (de maison) floor; (terrain agricole) soil.

solaire /sɔlɛr/ *adj* solar; (huile, filtre) sun.

soldat /sɔlda/ *nm* soldier.

solde¹ /sɔld/ *nf* (salaire) pay.

solde² /sɔld/ *nm* (Comm) balance; **les ~s** the sales; **~s** (écrit en vitrine) sale; **en ~** (acheter) at sale price.

solder /sɔlde/ **1** *vt* sell off at sale price; (compte) settle. □ **se ~ par** *vpr* (aboutir à) end in.

sole /sɔl/ *nf* (poisson) sole.

soleil /sɔlɛj/ *nm* sun; (fleur) sunflower; **il y a du ~** it's sunny.

solennel, ∼**le** /sɔlanɛl/ adj solemn.

solfège /sɔlfɛʒ/ nm musical theory.

solidaire /sɔlidɛʀ/ adj (mécanismes) interdependent; (collègues) (mutually) supportive; **être** ∼ **de qn** support sb. **solidarité** nf solidarity.

solide /sɔlid/ adj solid; (personne) strong. ● nm solid.

solidifier /sɔlidifje/ 45 vt solidify. □ **se** ∼ vpr solidify.

solitaire /sɔlitɛʀ/ adj solitary. ● nmf (personne) loner. **solitude** nf solitude.

solliciter /sɔlisite/ 1 vt seek; (faire appel à) call upon; **être très sollicité** be very much in demand.

sollicitude /sɔlisityd/ nf concern.

solo /sɔlo/ nm & a inv (Mus) solo.

solution /sɔlysjɔ̃/ nf solution.

solvable /sɔlvabl/ adj solvent.

solvant /sɔlvɑ̃/ nm solvent.

sombre /sɔ̃bʀ/ adj dark; (triste) sombre.

sombrer /sɔ̃bʀe/ 1 vi sink (**dans** into).

sommaire /sɔmɛʀ/ adj (exécution) summary; (description) rough. ● nm contents (+ pl); **au** ∼ on the programme.

sommation /sɔmasjɔ̃/ nf (Mil) warning; (Jur) notice.

somme /sɔm/ nf sum; **en** ∼, **toute** in short; **faire la** ∼ **de** add (up), total (up). ● nm nap.

sommeil /sɔmɛj/ nm sleep; **avoir** ∼ be ou feel sleepy; **en** ∼ (projet) put on ice. **sommeiller** 1 vi doze; (fig) lie dormant.

sommelier /sɔmalje/ nm wine steward.

sommer /sɔme/ 1 vt summon.

sommes /sɔm/ →ÊTRE 4.

sommet /sɔmɛ/ nm top; (de montagne) summit; (de triangle) apex; (gloire) height.

sommier /sɔmje/ nm bed base.

somnambule /sɔmnɑ̃byl/ nm sleepwalker.

somnifère /sɔmnifɛʀ/ nm sleeping pill.

somnolent, ∼**e** /sɔmnɔlɑ̃, -t/ adj drowsy. **somnoler** 1 vi doze.

somptueux, -**euse** /sɔ̃ptɥø, -z/ adj sumptuous.

son[1], **sa** (**son** before vowel or mute h) (pl **ses**) /sɔ̃, sa, sɔ̃, se/ adj (homme) his; (femme) her; (chose) its; (indéfini) one's.

son[2] /sɔ̃/ nm (bruit) sound; (de blé) bran; **baisser le** ∼ turn the volume down.

sondage /sɔ̃daʒ/ nm ∼ (**d'opinion**) (opinion) poll.

sonde /sɔ̃d/ nf (de forage) drill; (Méd) (d'évacuation) catheter; (d'examen) probe.

sonder /sɔ̃de/ 1 vt (population) poll; (explorer) sound; (terrain) drill; (intentions) sound out.

songe /sɔ̃ʒ/ nm dream.

songer /sɔ̃ʒe/ 40 vt ∼ **que** think that; ∼ **à** think about. **songeur**, -**euse** adj pensive.

sonné, ∼**e** /sɔne/ adj (étourdi) groggy; 1 crazy.

sonner /sɔne/ 1 vt/i ring; (clairon, glas) sound; (heure) strike; (domestique) ring for; **midi sonné** well past noon; ∼ **de** (clairon) sound, blow.

sonnerie /sɔnʀi/ nf ringing; (de clairon) sounding; (sonnette) bell.

sonnet /sɔnɛ/ nm sonnet.

sonnette /sɔnɛt/ nf bell.

sonore /sɔnɔʀ/ adj resonant; (onde, effets) sound; (rire) resounding.

sonorisation /sɔnɔʀizasjɔ̃/ nf

5

(matériel) public address system.

sonorité /sɔnɔrite/ nf resonance; (d'un instrument) tone.

sont /sɔ̃/ ➡ÊTRE 4.

sophistiqué, ~e /sɔfistike/ adj sophisticated.

sorcellerie /sɔrsɛlri/ nf witchcraft. **sorcier** nm (guérisseur) witch doctor; (maléfique) sorcerer. **sorcière** nf witch.

sordide /sɔrdid/ adj sordid; (lieu) squalid.

sort /sɔr/ nm (destin, hasard) fate; (condition) lot; (maléfice) spell; **tirer** (qch) **au** ~ draw lots for sth.

sortant, ~e /sɔrtɑ̃, -t/ adj (président etc.) outgoing.

sorte /sɔrt/ nf sort, kind; **de** ~ **que** so that; **en quelque** ~ in a way; **de la** ~ in this way; **faire en** ~ **que** make sure that.

sortie /sɔrti/ nf exit; (promenade, dîner) outing; (déclaration 1) remark; (parution) publication; (de disque, film) release; (d'un ordinateur) output; ~**s** (argent) outgoings.

sortilège /sɔrtilɛʒ/ nm (magic) spell.

sortir /sɔrtir/ 46 vi (aux être) go out, leave; (venir) come out; (aller au spectacle) go out; (livre, film) come out; (plante) come up; ~ **de** (pièce) leave; (milieu social) come from; (limites) go beyond; ~ **du commun** ou **de l'ordinaire** be out of the ordinary. ● vt (aux avoir) take out; (livre, modèle) bring out; (dire 1) come out with; ~ **qn de** get sb out of (where); **être sorti d'affaire** be in the clear. □ **s'en** ~ vpr cope, manage.

sosie /sɔzi/ nm double.

sot, ~**te** /so, sɔt/ adj silly.

sottise /sɔtiz/ nf silliness; (action,

remarque) foolish thing; **faire des** ~**s** be naughty.

sou /su/ nm 1 ~**s** money; **sans le** ~ without a penny; **près de ses** ~**s** tight-fisted.

soubresaut /subrəso/ nm (sudden) start.

souche /suʃ/ nf (d'arbre) stump; (de famille) stock; (de carnet) counterfoil.

souci /susi/ nm (inquiétude) worry; (préoccupation) concern; (plante) marigold; **se faire du** ~ worry.

soucier (se) /(sə)susje/ 45 vpr se ~ **de** care about. **soucieux, -ieuse** adj concerned (**de** about).

soucoupe /sukup/ nf saucer; ~ **volante** flying saucer.

soudain, ~e /sudɛ̃, -ɛn/ adj sudden. ● adv suddenly.

soude /sud/ nf soda.

souder /sude/ 1 vt weld, solder; **famille très soudée** close-knit family. □ **se** ~ vpr (os) knit (together).

soudoyer /sudwaje/ 31 vt bribe.

souffle /sufl/ nm (haleine) breath; (respiration) breathing; (explosion) blast; (vent) breath of air; **le** ~ **coupé** out of breath; **à couper le** ~ breathtaking.

souffler /sufle/ 1 vi blow; (haleter) puff. ● vt (bougie) blow out; (poussière, fumée) blow; (verre) blow; (par explosion) destroy; (chuchoter) whisper; ~ **la réplique à** prompt. **souffleur, -euse** nm, f (Théât) prompter.

souffrance /sufrɑ̃s/ nf suffering; **en** ~ (affaire) pending. **souffrant,** ~e adj unwell.

souffrir /sufrir/ 21 vi suffer (**de** from). ● vt (endurer) suffer; **il ne peut pas le** ~ he cannot stand ou bear him.

soufre /sufr/ nm sulphur.

souhait /swɛ/ *nm* wish; **à tes ∼s!** bless you!; **paisible à ∼** incredibly peaceful. **souhaitable** *adj* desirable.

souhaiter /swete/ **1** *vt* ∼ **qch à qn** wish sb sth; ∼ **que/faire** hope that/to do; ∼ **la bienvenue à qn** welcome sb.

soûl, ∼e /su, sul/ *adj* drunk. ● *nm* **tout son ∼** as much as one can.

soulagement /sulaʒmɑ̃/ *nm* relief. **soulager** 40 *vt* relieve.

soûler /sule/ **1** *vt* make drunk. □ **se** ∼ *vpr* get drunk.

soulèvement /sulɛvmɑ̃/ *nm* uprising.

soulever /sulve/ **6** *vt* lift, raise; (*question, poussière*) raise; (*enthousiasme*) arouse; (*foule*) stir up. □ **se** ∼ *vpr* lift ou raise oneself up; (*se révolter*) rise up.

soulier /sulje/ *nm* shoe.

souligner /suliɲe/ **1** *vt* underline; (*yeux*) outline; (*taille*) emphasize.

soumettre /sumɛtr/ 42 *vt* (assujettir) subject (à to); (présenter) submit (à to). □ **se** ∼ *vpr* submit (à to). **soumis, ∼e** *adj* submissive. **soumission** *nf* submission.

soupape /supap/ *nf* valve.

soupçon /supsɔ̃/ *nm* suspicion; **un** ∼ **de** (un peu de) a touch of. **soupçonner** **1** *vt* suspect. **soupçonneux, -euse** *adj* suspicious.

soupe /sup/ *nf* soup.

souper /supe/ **1** *vi* have supper. ● *nm* supper.

soupeser /supəze/ **1** *vt* judge the weight of; (fig) weigh up.

soupière /supjɛr/ *nf* (soup) tureen.

soupir /supir/ *nm* sigh; **pousser un** ∼ heave a sigh.

soupirer /supire/ **1** *vi* sigh.

souple /supl/ *adj* supple; (*règlement, caractère*) flexible. **souplesse**

nf suppleness; (de règlement) flexibility.

source /surs/ *nf* (de rivière, origine) source; (eau) spring; **prendre sa** ∼ **à** rise in; **de** ∼ **sûre** from a reliable source; ∼ **thermale** hot spring.

sourcil /sursi/ *nm* eyebrow.

sourciller /sursije/ **1** *vi* **sans** ∼ without batting an eyelid.

sourd, ∼e /sur, -d/ *adj* deaf; (*bruit, douleur*) dull; **faire la** ∼ **e oreille** turn a deaf ear. ● *nm, f* deaf person.

sourd-muet (*pl* **sourds-muets**), **sourde-muette** (*pl* **sourdes-muettes**) /surmɥe, surdmɥet/ *adj* deaf and dumb. ● *nm, f* deafmute.

souricière /surisjɛr/ *nf* mousetrap; (fig) trap.

sourire /surir/ 54 *vi* smile (à at); ∼ **à** (fortune) smile on. ● *nm* smile; **garder le** ∼ keep smiling.

souris /suri/ *nf* mouse; **des** ∼ mice.

sournois, ∼e /surnwa, -z/ *adj* sly, underhand.

sous /su/ *prép* under, beneath; ∼ **la main** handy; ∼ **la pluie** in the rain; ∼ **peu** shortly; ∼ **terre** underground.

sous-alimenté, ∼e /suzalimɑ̃te/ *adj* undernourished.

souscription /suskripsjɔ̃/ *nf* subscription. **souscrire** 30 *vi* ∼ **à** subscribe to.

sous-entendre /suzɑ̃tɑ̃dr/ **3** *vt* imply. **sous-entendu** *nm* innuendo, insinuation.

sous-estimer /suzɛstime/ **1** *vt* underestimate.

sous-jacent, ∼e /suʒasɑ̃, -t/ *adj* underlying.

sous-marin, ∼e /sumarɛ̃, -in/ *adj* underwater; (*plongée*) deep-sea. ● *nm* submarine.

soussigné, ∼e /susiɲe/ adj & nm, f undersigned.

sous-sol /susɔl/ nm (cave) basement.

sous-titre /sutitʀ/ nm subtitle.

soustraction /sustʀaksjɔ̃/ nf (déduction) subtraction.

soustraire /sustʀɛʀ/ 29 vt (déduire) subtract; (retirer) take away (à from). □ **se** ∼ **à** vpr escape from.

sous-traitant /sutʀɛtɑ̃/ nm subcontractor.

sous-verre /suvɛʀ/ nm inv glass mount.

sous-vêtement /suvɛtmɑ̃/ nm underwear.

soute /sut/ nf (de bateau) hold; ∼ **à charbon** coal-bunker.

soutenir /sutniʀ/ 59 vt support; (effort, rythme) sustain; (résister à) withstand; ∼ **que** maintain that.

soutenu, ∼e /sutny/ adj (constant) sustained; (style) formal.

souterrain, ∼e /suteʀɛ̃, -ɛn/ adj underground. ● nm underground passage.

soutien /sutjɛ̃/ nm support.

soutien-gorge /sutjɛ̃gɔʀʒ/ nm bra. (pl **soutiens-gorge**)

soutirer /sutiʀe/ 1 vt ∼ **à qn** extract from sb.

s **souvenir**[1] /suvniʀ/ nm memory, recollection; (objet) memento; (cadeau) souvenir; **en** ∼ **de** in memory of.

souvenir[2] (se) /(sə)suvniʀ/ 59 vpr **se** ∼ **de** remember; **se** ∼ **que** remember that.

souvent /suvɑ̃/ adv often.

souverain, ∼e /suvʀɛ̃, -ɛn/ adj sovereign. ● nm, f sovereign.

soviétique /sɔvjetik/ adj Soviet.

soyeux, **-euse** /swajø, -z/ adj silky.

spacieux, **-ieuse** /spasjø, -z/ adj spacious.

sparadrap /spaʀadʀa/ nm (sticking) plaster.

spatial, ∼e (mpl **-iaux**) /spasjal, -jo/ adj space.

speaker, ∼ine /spikœʀ, -kʀin/ nm, f announcer.

spécial, ∼e (mpl **-iaux**) /spesjal, -jo/ adj special; (bizarre) odd. **spécialement** adv (exprès) specially; (très) especially.

spécialiser (se) /saspesjalize/ 1 vpr specialize (dans in). **spécialiste** nmf specialist. **spécialité** nf speciality; (US) specialty.

spécifier /spesifje/ 45 vt specify.

spécifique /spesifik/ adj specific.

spécimen /spesimen/ nm specimen.

spectacle /spɛktakl/ nm show; (vue) sight, spectacle.

spectaculaire /spɛktakylɛʀ/ adj spectacular.

spectateur, **-trice** /spɛktatœʀ, -tʀis/ nm, f (Sport) spectator; (témoin oculaire) onlooker; **les** ∼**s** (Théât) the audience (+ sg).

spectre /spɛktʀ/ nm (revenant) spectre; (images) spectrum.

spéculateur, **-trice** /spekylatœʀ, -tʀis/ nm, f speculator. **spéculation** nf speculation. **spéculer** 1 vi speculate.

spéléologie /speleɔlɔʒi/ nf cave exploration, pot-holing.

spermatozoïde /spɛʀmatozɔid/ nm spermatozoon. **sperme** nm sperm.

sphère /sfɛʀ/ nf sphere.

spirale /spiʀal/ nf spiral.

spirituel, ∼le /spiʀitɥɛl/ adj spiritual; (amusant) witty.

spiritueux /spiʀitɥø/ nm (alcool) spirit.

splendeur /splɑ̃dœʀ/ nf splendour. **splendide** adj splendid.

sponsoriser /spɔ̃sɔʀize/ **1** vt sponsor.

spontané, ~e /spɔ̃tane/ adj spontaneous. **spontanéité** nf spontaneity.

sport /spɔʀ/ adj inv (vêtements) casual. ● nm sport; **veste/voiture de ~** sports jacket/car.

sportif, -ive /spɔʀtif, -v/ adj (personne) sporty; (physique) athletic; (résultats) sports. ● nm, f sportsman, sportswoman.

spot /spɔt/ nm spotlight; (~ **publicitaire**) ad.

square /skwaʀ/ nm small public garden.

squatter /skwate/ **1** vt squat in.

squelette /skəlɛt/ nm skeleton. **squelettique** adj skeletal.

SRAS abrév m (**syndrome respiratoire aigu sévère**) SARS.

SSII abrév f (**société de services et d'ingénierie informatiques**) computer services company

stabiliser /stabilize/ **1** vt stabilize. **stable** adj stable.

stade /stad/ nm (Sport) stadium; (phase) stage.

stage /staʒ/ nm (cours) course; (professionnel) placement. **stagiaire** nmf course member; (apprenti) trainee.

stagner /stagne/ **1** vi stagnate.

stand /stɑ̃d/ nm stand; (de fête foraine) stall.

standard /stɑ̃daʀ/ nm switchboard. ● adj inv standard. **standardiser** **1** vt standardize.

standardiste /stɑ̃daʀdist/ nmf switchboard operator.

standing /stɑ̃diŋ/ nm status, standing; **de ~** (hôtel) luxury.

starter /staʀtɛʀ/ nm (Auto) choke.

station /stasjɔ̃/ nf station; (halte) stop; **~ debout** standing position; **~ de taxis** taxi rank; **~ balnéaire/de ski** seaside/ski resort; **~ thermale** spa.

stationnaire /stasjɔnɛʀ/ adj stationary.

stationnement /stasjɔnmɑ̃/ nm parking. **stationner** **1** vi park.

station-service (pl **stations-service**) /stasjɔ̃sɛʀvis/ nf service station.

statique /statik/ adj static.

statistique /statistik/ nf statistic; (science) statistics (+ sg.) ● adj statistical.

statue /staty/ nf statue.

statuer /statɥe/ **1** vi **~ sur** give a ruling on.

statut /staty/ nm status. **statutaire** adj statutory.

sténo /steno/ nf (sténographie) shorthand. **sténodactylo** nf shorthand typist. **sténographie** nf shorthand.

stéréo /steʀeo/ nf & adj inv stereo.

stéréotype /steʀeotip/ nm stereotype.

stérile /steʀil/ adj sterile.

stérilet /steʀilɛ/ nm coil, IUD.

stérilisation /steʀilizasjɔ̃/ nf sterilization. **stériliser** **1** vt sterilize.

stéroïde /steʀɔid/ adj & nm steroid.

stimulant /stimylɑ̃/ nm stimulus; (médicament) stimulant.

stimulateur /stimylatœʀ/ nm **~ cardiaque** (Méd) pacemaker.

stimuler /stimyle/ **1** vt stimulate.

stipuler /stipyle/ **1** vt stipulate.

stock /stɔk/ nm stock. **stocker** **1** vt stock.

stoïque /stɔik/ adj stoical. ● nmf stoic.

stop /stɔp/ *interj* stop. ● *nm* stop sign; (feu arrière) brake light; **faire du ~** 🔟 hitch-hike. **stopper** 🔟 *vt/i* stop.

store /stɔr/ *nm* blind; (de magasin) awning.

strapontin /strapɔ̃tɛ̃/ *nm* folding seat, jump seat.

stratégie /strateʒi/ *nf* strategy. **stratégique** *adj* strategic.

stress /strɛs/ *nm* stress. **stressant, ~e** *adj* stressful. **stressé, ~e** *adj* stressed. **stresser** 🔟 *vt* put under stress.

strict /strikt/ *adj* strict; (tenue, vérité) plain; **le ~ minimum** the bare minimum. **strictement** *adv* strictly.

strident, ~e /stridɑ̃, -t/ *adj* shrill.

strophe /strɔf/ *nf* stanza, verse.

structure /stryktyr/ *nf* structure.

studieux, -ieuse /stydjø, -z/ *adj* studious.

studio /stydjo/ *nm* (d'artiste, de télévision) studio; (logement) studio flat.

stupéfaction /stypefaksjɔ̃/ *nf* amazement. **stupéfait, ~e** *adj* amazed.

stupéfiant, ~e /stypefjɑ̃, -t/ *adj* astounding. ● *nm* drug, narcotic. **stupéfier** /stypefje/ 45 *vt* amaze.

stupeur /stypœr/ *nf* amazement; (Méd) stupor.

stupide /stypid/ *adj* stupid. **stupidité** *nf* stupidity.

style /stil/ *nm* style.

styliste /stilist/ *nmf* fashion designer.

stylo /stilo/ *nm* pen; **~ (à) bille** ballpoint pen; **~ (à) encre** fountain pen.

su /sy/ ⇒**SAVOIR** 59.

suave /sɥav/ *adj* sweet.

subalterne /sybaltɛrn/ *adj & nmf*

subordinate.

subconscient /sypkɔ̃sjɑ̃/ *nm* subconscious.

subir /sybir/ 🔟 *vt* be subjected to; (traitement, expériences) undergo.

subit, ~e /sybi, -t/ *adj* sudden.

subjectif, -ive /sybʒɛktif, -v/ *adj* subjective.

subjonctif /sybʒɔ̃ktif/ *nm* subjunctive.

subjuguer /sybʒyge/ 🔟 *vt* (charmer) captivate.

sublime /syblim/ *adj* sublime.

submerger /sybmɛrʒe/ 40 *vt* submerge; (fig) overwhelm.

subordonné, ~e /sybɔrdɔne/ *adj & nm, f* subordinate.

subside /sybzid/ *nm* grant.

subsidiaire /sybzidjɛr/ *adj* subsidiary; **question ~** tiebreaker.

subsistance /sybzistɑ̃s/ *nf* subsistence. **subsister** 🔟 *vi* subsist; (durer, persister) exist.

substance /sypstɑ̃s/ *nf* substance.

substantiel, ~le /sypstɑ̃sjɛl/ *adj* substantial.

substantif /sypstɑ̃tif/ *nm* noun.

substituer /sypstitɥe/ 🔟 *vt* substitute (à for). □ **se ~ à** *vpr* (remplacer) substitute for. **substitut** *nm* substitute; (jur) deputy public prosecutor.

subtil, ~e /syptil/ *adj* subtle.

subtiliser /syptilize/ 🔟 *vt* **~ qch (à qn)** steal sth (from sb).

subvenir /sybvənir/ 59 *vi* **~ à** provide for.

subvention /sybvɑ̃sjɔ̃/ *nf* subsidy. **subventionner** 🔟 *vt* subsidize.

subversif, -ive /sybvɛrsif, -v/ *adj* subversive.

suc /syk/ *nm* juice.

succédané /syksedane/ *nm* substitute (de for).

succéder /syksede/ **14** vi ~ à succeed. □ se ~ vpr succeed one another.

succès /sykse/ nm success; à ~ (film, livre) successful; **avoir du** ~ be a success.

successeur /syksesœr/ nm successor. **successif, -ive** adj successive. **succession** nf succession; (jur) inheritance.

succinct, ~e /syksɛ̃, -t/ adj succinct.

succomber /sykɔ̃be/ **1** vi die; ~ à succumb to.

succulent, ~e /sykylɑ̃, -t/ adj delicious.

succursale /sykyrsal/ nf (Comm) branch.

sucer /syse/ **10** vt suck.

sucette /sysɛt/ nf (bonbon) lollipop; (tétine) dummy; (US) pacifier.

sucre /sykr/ nm sugar; ~ **d'orge** barley sugar; ~ **en poudre** caster sugar; ~ **glace** icing sugar; ~ **roux** brown sugar.

sucré /sykre/ adj sweet; (additionné de sucre) sweetened. **sucrer** **1** vt sugar, sweeten. **sucreries** nfpl sweets.

sucrier, -ière /sykrije, -jɛr/ adj sugar. ● nm (récipient) sugar-bowl.

sud /syd/ nm sugar. ~ nm south. ● adj inv south; (partie) southern.

sud-est /sydɛst/ nm south-east.

sud-ouest /sydwɛst/ nm southwest.

Suède /syɛd/ nf Sweden.

suédois, ~e /syedwa, -z/ adj Swedish. ● nm (Ling) Swedish. **S~, ~e** nm, f Swede.

suer /sye/ **1** vt/i sweat; **faire** ~ **qn** **1** get on sb's nerves.

sueur /sɥœr/ nf sweat; **en** ~ covered in sweat.

suffire /syfir/ **57** vi be enough (à qn for sb); **il suffit de compter** all you have to do is count; **une goutte suffit** a drop is enough; ~ à (besoin) satisfy. □ **se** ~ vpr se ~ **à soi-même** be self-sufficient.

suffisamment /syfizamɑ̃/ adv sufficiently; ~ **de qch** enough of sth. **suffisance** nf (vanité) conceit. **suffisant, ~e** adj sufficient; (vaniteux) conceited.

suffixe /syfiks/ nm suffix.

suffoquer /syfɔke/ **1** vt/i choke, suffocate.

suffrage /syfraʒ/ nm (voix: Pol) vote; (système) suffrage.

suggérer /sygʒere/ **14** vt suggest. **suggestion** nf suggestion.

suicidaire /sɥisidɛr/ adj suicidal. **suicide** nm suicide. **suicider (se)** **1** vpr commit suicide.

suinter /sɥɛ̃te/ **1** vi ooze.

suis /sɥi/ ⇒ÊTRE **4**, ⇒SUIVRE **57**.

Suisse /sɥis/ nf Switzerland. ● nmf Swiss. **suisse** adj Swiss.

suite /sɥit/ nf continuation, rest; (d'un film) sequel; (série) series; (appartement, escorte) suite; (résultat) consequence; **à la** ~, **de** ~ (successivement) in a row; **à la** ~ **de** (derrière) behind; **à la** ~ **de, par** ~ **de** (en conséquence) as a result of; **faire** ~ **(à)** follow; **par la** ~ afterwards; **à votre lettre du** ~ further to your letter of the; **des** ~**s de** as a result of.

suivant¹, ~e /sɥivɑ̃, -t/ adj following, next. ● nm, f following ou next person.

suivant² /sɥivɑ̃/ prép (selon) according to.

suivi, ~e /sɥivi/ adj (effort) steady, sustained; (cohérent) consistent; **peu/très** ~ (cours) poorly/well attended.

suivre /sɥivʀ/ 57 vt/i follow; (comprendre) follow; (accompagner) follow; forward. □ se ~ vpr follow each other.

sujet, ~te /syʒɛ, -t/ adj ~ à liable ou subject to. ● nm (d'un royaume) subject; (question) subject; (motif) cause; (Gram) subject; au ~ de about.

super /sypɛʀ/ nm (essence) fourstar. ● adj inv 1 (très) great. ● adv 1 ultra, really.

superbe /sypɛʀb/ adj superb.

supérette /sypeʀɛt/ nf minimarket.

superficie /sypɛʀfisi/ nf area.

superficiel, ~le /sypɛʀfisjɛl/ adj superficial.

superflu /sypɛʀfly/ adj superfluous. ● nm (excédent) surplus.

supérieur, ~e /sypeʀjœʀ/ adj (plus haut) upper; (quantité, nombre) greater (à than); (études, principe) higher (à than); (meilleur, hautain) superior (à to). ● nm, f superior. **supériorité** nf superiority.

superlatif, -ive /sypɛʀlatif, -v/ adj & nm superlative.

supermarché /sypɛʀmaʀʃe/ nm supermarket.

superposer /sypɛʀpoze/ 1 vt superimpose; **lits superposés** bunk beds.

superproduction /sypɛʀpʀɔdyksjɔ̃/ nf (film) blockbuster.

superpuissance /sypɛʀpɥisɑ̃s/ nf superpower.

superstitieux, -ieuse /sypɛʀstisjø, -z/ adj superstitious.

superviser /sypɛʀvize/ 1 vt supervise.

suppléant, ~e /sypleɑ̃, -t/ nmf & adj (professeur) ~ supply teacher; (juge) ~ deputy (judge).

suppléer /syplee/ 15 vt (remplacer) fill in for. ● vi ~ à (compenser) make up for.

supplément /syplemɑ̃/ nm (argent) extra charge; (de frites, légumes) extra portion; en ~ extra; un ~ de (travail) additional; **payer un ~** pay a supplement. **supplémentaire** adj extra, additional.

supplice /syplis/ nm torture.

supplier /syplije/ 45 vt beg, beseech (de to).

support /sypɔʀ/ nm support; (Ordinat) medium.

supportable /sypɔʀtabl/ adj bearable.

supporter[1] /sypɔʀte/ 1 vt (privations) bear; (personne) put up with; (structure) Ordinat) support; **il ne supporte pas les enfants/de perdre** he can't stand children/losing.

supporter[2] /sypɔʀtɛʀ/ nm (Sport) supporter.

supposer /sypoze/ 1 vt suppose; (impliquer) imply; **à ~ que** supposing that.

suppression /sypʀesjɔ̃/ nf (de taxe) abolition; (de sanction) lifting; (de mot) deletion. **supprimer** 1 vt (allocation) withdraw; (contrôle) lift; (train) cancel; (preuve) suppress.

suprématie /sypʀemasi/ nf supremacy.

suprême /sypʀɛm/ adj supreme.

sur /syʀ/ prép on, upon; (pardessus) over; (au sujet de) about, on; (proportion) out of; (mesure) by; ~ la photo in the photograph; **mettre/jeter** ~ put/throw on to; ~ mesure made to measure; ~ place on the spot; ~ ce, je pars with that, I must go; ~ le moment at the time.

sûr /syʀ/ adj certain, sure; (sans danger) safe; (digne de confiance) reliable; (main) steady; (jugement) sound; **être ~ de soi** self-confident; **j'en étais ~!** I knew it!

surabondance /syʀabɔ̃dɑ̃s/ nf overabundance.

surcharge /syʀʃaʀʒ/ nf overloading; (poids) excess load. **surcharger** ◻ vt overload; (texte) alter.

surchauffer /syʀʃofe/ ◻ vt overheat.

surcroît /syʀkʀwa/ nm increase (de in); **de ~** in addition.

surdité /syʀdite/ nf deafness.

surélever /syʀelve/ ◻ vt raise.

sûrement /syʀmɑ̃/ adv certainly; (sans danger) safely; **il a ~ oublié** he must have forgotten.

surenchère /syʀɑ̃ʃɛʀ/ nf higher bid. **surenchérir** ◻ vi bid higher (**sur** than).

surestimer /syʀɛstime/ ◻ vt overestimate.

sûreté /syʀte/ nf safety; (de pays) security; (d'un geste) steadiness; **être en ~** be safe; **S~ (nationale)** police (+ pl).

surexcité, ~e /syʀɛksite/ adj very excited.

surf /sœʀf/ nm surfing.

surface /syʀfas/ nf surface; **faire ~** (sous-marin, fig) surface; **en ~** on the surface.

surfait, ~e /syʀfɛ, -t/ adj overrated.

surfer /sœʀfe/ ◻ vi go surfing; **~ sur l'Internet** surf the Internet.

surgelé, ~e /syʀʒəle/ adj (deep-)frozen; **aliments ~s** frozen food.

surgir /syʀʒiʀ/ ◻ vi appear (suddenly); (difficulté) crop up.

sur-le-champ /syʀləʃɑ̃/ adv right away.

surlendemain /syʀlɑ̃dmɛ̃/ nm le **~** two days later; **le ~ de** two days after.

surligneur /syʀliɲœʀ/ nm highlighter (pen).

surmenage /syʀmənaʒ/ nm overwork.

surmonter /syʀmɔ̃te/ ◻ vt (vaincre) overcome, surmount; (être au-dessus de) surmount, top.

surnaturel, ~le /syʀnatyʀɛl/ adj supernatural.

surnom /syʀnɔ̃/ nm nickname. **surnommer** ◻ vt nickname.

surpeuplé, ~e /syʀpœple/ adj overpopulated.

surplomber /syʀplɔ̃be/ ◻ vt/i overhang.

surplus /syʀply/ nm surplus.

suprenant, ~e /syʀpʀənɑ̃, -t/ adj surprising. **surprendre** ◻ vt (étonner) surprise; (prendre au dépourvu) catch, surprise; (entendre) overhear. **surpris, ~e** adj surprised (de at).

surprise /syʀpʀiz/ nf surprise.

surréaliste /syʀʀealist/ adj & nmf surrealist.

sursaut /syʀso/ nm start, jump; **en ~** with a start; **~ de** (regain) burst of. **sursauter** ◻ vi start, jump.

sursis /syʀsi/ nm reprieve; (Mil) deferment; **deux ans (de prison) avec ~** a two-year suspended sentence.

surtaxe /syʀtaks/ nf surcharge.

surtout /syʀtu/ adv especially; (avant tout) above all; **~ pas** certainly not.

surveillance /syʀvejɑ̃s/ nf watch; (d'examen) supervision; (de la police) surveillance. **surveillant, ~e** nm, f (de prison) warder; (au lycée) supervisor (in charge of discipline). **surveiller** ◻ vt watch; (travaux, élèves) supervise.

survenir /syʀvəniʀ/ ◻ vi occur, take place; (personne) turn up.

s

survêtement /syʀvɛtmɑ̃/ nm (Sport) tracksuit.

survie /syʀvi/ nf survival.

survivant, ~e /syʀvivɑ̃, -t/ adj surviving. ● nm, f survivor.

survivre /syʀvivʀ/ 63 vi survive; ~ à (conflit) survive; (personne) outlive.

survoler /syʀvɔle/ 1 vt fly over; (livre) skim through.

sus: en ~ /āsys/ loc in addition.

susceptible /sysɛptibl/ adj touchy; ~ de faire likely to do.

susciter /sysite/ 1 vt (éveiller) arouse; (occasionner) create.

suspect, ~e /syspɛ, -ɛkt/ adj (individu, faits) suspicious; (témoignage) suspect; ~ de suspected of. ● nm, f suspect. **suspecter** 1 vt suspect.

suspendre /syspɑ̃dʀ/ 3 vt (accrocher) hang (up); (interrompre, destituer) suspend; **suspendu à** hanging from. □ **se** ~ à vpr hang from.

suspens: en ~ /āsyspɑ̃/ loc (affaire) outstanding; (dans l'indécision) in suspense.

suspense /syspɛns/ nm suspense.

suture /sytyʀ/ nf point de ~ stitch.

svelte /svɛlt/ adj slender.

S.V.P. abrév (s'il vous plaît) please.

syllabe /silab/ nf syllable.

symbole /sɛ̃bɔl/ nm symbol. **symboliser** 1 vt symbolize.

symétrie /simetʀi/ nf symmetry.

sympa /sɛ̃pa/ adj inv 1 nice; **sois** ~ be a pal.

sympathie /sɛ̃pati/ nf (goût) liking; (compassion) sympathy; **avoir de la ~ pour** like. **sympathique** adj nice, pleasant. **sympathisant, ~e** nm, f sympathizer. **sympathiser** 1 vi get on well (avec with).

symphonie /sɛ̃fɔni/ nf symphony.

symptôme /sɛ̃ptom/ nm symptom.

synagogue /sinagɔg/ nf synagogue.

synchroniser /sɛ̃kʀɔnize/ 1 vt synchronize.

syncope /sɛ̃kɔp/ nf (Méd) blackout.

syndic /sɛ̃dik/ nm ~ (d'immeuble) property manager.

syndicaliste /sɛ̃dikalist/ nmf (trade-)unionist. ● adj (trade-) union.

syndicat /sɛ̃dika/ nm (trade) union; ~ d'initiative tourist office.

syndiqué, ~e /sɛ̃dike/ adj être ~ be a (trade-)union member.

synonyme /sinɔnim/ adj synonymous. ● nm synonym.

syntaxe /sɛ̃taks/ nf syntax.

synthèse /sɛ̃tɛz/ nf synthesis. **synthétique** adj synthetic.

synthé(tiseur) /sɛ̃te(tizœʀ)/ nm synthesizer.

systématique /sistematik/ adj systematic.

système /sistɛm/ nm system; **le ~ D** 1 resourcefulness.

Tt

t' /t/ ⇒TE.

ta /ta/ ⇒TON[1].

tabac /taba/ nm tobacco; (magasin) tobacconist's shop.

table /tabl/ nf table; à ~! dinner is ready!; ~ de nuit bedside table; ~ des matières table of contents; ~ à repasser ironing board; ~ roulante (tea-)trolley; (US) (serving) cart.

tableau /pl ~x/ /tablo/ nm picture; (peinture) painting; (panneau) board; (graphique) chart; (Scol) blackboard; ~ **d'affichage** noticeboard; ~ **de bord** dashboard.

tablette /tablɛt/ nf shelf; ~ **de chocolat** bar of chocolate.

tableur /tablœʀ/ nm spreadsheet.

tablier /tablije/ nm apron; (de pont) platform; (de magasin) shutter.

tabou /tabu/ nm & adj taboo.

tabouret /tabuʀɛ/ nm stool.

tache /taʃ/ nf mark, spot; (salissure) stain; **faire ~ d'huile** spread; ~ **de rousseur** freckle.

tâche /taʃ/ nf task, job.

tacher /taʃe/ **1** vt stain. □ **se ~** vpr (personne) get oneself dirty.

tâcher /taʃe/ **1** vi ~ **de faire** try to do.

tacheté, ~e /taʃte/ adj spotted.

tact /takt/ nm tact.

tactique /taktik/ adj tactical. ● nf (Mil) tactics; **une ~** a tactic.

taie /tɛ/ nf ~ **(d'oreiller)** pillowcase.

taille /tɑj/ nf (milieu du corps) waist; (hauteur) height; (grandeur) size; **de ~** sizeable; **être de ~ à faire** be up to doing.

taille-crayons /tɑjkʀɛjɔ̃/ nm inv pencil-sharpener.

tailler /tɑje/ **1** vt cut; (arbre) prune; (crayon) sharpen; (vêtement) cut out. □ **se ~** vpr **1** clear off.

tailleur /tajœʀ/ nm (costume) woman's suit; (couturier) tailor; **en ~** cross-legged; ~ **de pierre** stonecutter.

taire /tɛʀ/ **47** vt not to reveal; **faire ~** silence. □ **se ~** vpr be silent ou quiet; (devenir silencieux) fall silent.

talc /talk/ nm talcum powder.

talent /talɑ̃/ nm talent. **talentueux, -euse** adj talented, gifted.

talon /talɔ̃/ nm heel; (de chèque) stub.

tambour /tɑ̃buʀ/ nm drum; (d'église) vestibule.

Tamise /tamiz/ nf Thames.

tampon /tɑ̃pɔ̃/ nm (de bureau) stamp; (ouate) wad, pad; (~ **hygiénique**) tampon.

tamponner /tɑ̃pɔne/ **1** vt (document) stamp; (véhicule) crash into; (plaie) swab.

tandem /tɑ̃dɛm/ nm (vélo) tandem; (personnes: fig) duo.

tandis que /tɑ̃dik(ə)/ conj while.

tanière /tanjɛʀ/ nf den.

tant /tɑ̃/ adv (travailler, manger) so much; ~ **de** (quantité) so much; (nombre) so many; ~ **que** as long as; **en ~ que** as; ~ **mieux!** all the better!; ~ **pis!** too bad!

tante /tɑ̃t/ nf aunt.

tantôt /tɑ̃to/ adv sometimes.

tapage /tapaʒ/ nm din.

tape /tap/ nf slap. **tape-à-l'œil** adj inv flashy, tawdry.

taper /tape/ **1** vt hit; (prendre **1**) scrounge; ~ **(à la machine)** type. ● vi (cogner) bang; (soleil) beat down; ~ **dans** (puiser dans) dig into; ~ **sur** hit; ~ **sur l'épaule de qn** tap sb on the shoulder. □ **se ~** vpr (corvée **1**) get stuck with **1**.

tapis /tapi/ nm carpet; (petit) rug; ~ **de bain** bathmat; ~ **roulant** (pour objets) conveyor belt; (pour piétons) moving walkway.

tapisser /tapise/ **1** vt (wall) paper; (fig) cover (**de** with). **tapisserie** nf tapestry; (papier peint) wallpaper.

taquin, ~e /takɛ̃, -in/ adj fond of teasing. ● nm, f tease(r).

tard /taʀ/ adv late; **au plus ~** at the latest; **plus ~** later; **sur le ~** late in life.

tarder /taʀde/ **1** vi (être lent à venir) be a long time coming; **~ (à faire)** take a long time (doing), delay (doing); **sans (plus) ~** without (further) delay; **il me tarde de** I'm longing to.

tardif, -ive /taʀdif, -v/ adj late.

tare /taʀ/ nf (défaut) defect.

tarif /taʀif/ nm rate; (de train, taxi) fare; **plein ~** full price.

tarir /taʀiʀ/ **2** vt/i dry up. □ **se ~** vpr dry up.

tarte /taʀt/ nf tart. ● adj inv (ridicule **1**) ridiculous.

tartine /taʀtin/ nf slice of bread; **~ de beurre** slice of bread and butter. **tartiner 1** vt spread.

tartre /taʀtʀ/ nm (de bouilloire) fur, scale; (sur les dents) tartar.

tas /ta/ nm pile, heap; **un** ou **des ~ de 1** lots of.

tasse /tas/ nf cup; **~ à thé** teacup.

tasser /tase/ **1** vt pack, squeeze; (terre) pack (down). □ **se ~** vpr (terrain) sink; (se serrer) squeeze up.

tâter /tate/ **1** vt feel; (opinion: fig) sound out. ● vi **~ de** try out.

tatillon, ~ne /tatijɔ̃, -jɔn/ adj finicky.

tâtonnements /tatɔnmɑ̃/ nmpl (essais) trial and error (+ sg). **tâtons: à ~** /atatɔ̃/ loc **avancer à ~** grope one's way along.

tatouage /tatwaʒ/ nm (dessin) tattoo.

taupe /top/ nf mole.

taureau (pl **~x**) /tɔʀo/ nm bull; **le T~** Taurus.

taux /to/ nm rate.

taxe /taks/ nf tax.

taxi /taksi/ nm taxi(-cab); (personne **1**) taxi driver.

taxiphone ® /taksifɔn/ nm pay phone.

Tchécoslovaquie /tʃekɔslɔvaki/ nf Czechoslovakia.

tchèque /tʃɛk/ adj Czech; **République ~** Czech Republic. **T~** nmf Czech.

te, t' /tə, t/ pron you; (indirect) (to) you; (réfléchi) yourself.

technicien, ~ne /tɛknisjɛ̃, -ɛn/ nm, f technician.

technique /tɛknik/ adj technical. ● nf technique.

techno /tɛkno/ nf (Mus) techno.

technologie /tɛknɔlɔʒi/ nf technology.

teindre /tɛ̃dʀ/ **22** vt dye. □ **se ~** vpr **se ~ les cheveux** dye one's hair.

teint /tɛ̃/ nm complexion.

teinte /tɛ̃t/ nf shade. **teinter 1** vt (verre) tint; (bois) stain.

teinture /tɛ̃tyʀ/ nf (produit) dye.

teinturier, -ière /tɛ̃tyʀje, -jɛʀ/ nm, f dry-cleaner.

tel, ~le /tɛl/ adj such; **un ~ livre** such a book; **~ que** such as, like; (ainsi que) (just) as; **~ ou ~** such-and-such; **~ quel** (just) as it is.

télé /tele/ nf **1** TV; **~ réalité** nf reality TV.

télécharger /teleʃaʀʒe/ **40** vt (Ordinat) download.

télécommande /telekɔmɑ̃d/ nf remote control.

télécommunications /telekɔmynikasjɔ̃/ nfpl telecommunications.

téléconférence /telekɔ̃feʀɑ̃s/ nf teleconferencing.

télécopie /telekɔpi/ nf fax. **télécopieur** nm fax machine.

téléfilm /telefilm/ nm TV film.

télégramme /telegʀam/ nm telegram.

télégraphier /telegʀafje/ **45** vt/i ∼ (à) cable.

téléguidé, ∼e /telegide/ adj radiocontrolled.

télématique /telematik/ nf telematics (+ sg).

téléphérique /teleferik/ nm cable car.

téléphone /telefɔn/ nm (tele-) phone; ∼ **à carte** cardphone. **téléphoner** **1** vt/i ∼ (à) (tele)phone.

téléphonie /telefɔni/ nf telephony; ∼ **mobile** mobile telephony. **téléphonique** adj (tele)phone.

télé-réalité /telerealite/ nf reality TV.

téléserveur /teleseʀvœʀ/ nm (Internet) remote server.

télésiège /telesjɛʒ/ nm chairlift.

téléski /teleski/ nm ski tow.

téléspectateur, -trice /telespɛktatœʀ, -tʀis/ nm, f (tv) viewer.

télévente /televɑ̃t/ nf telesales (+ pl).

télévisé, ∼e /televize/ adj (débat) televised; **émission ∼e** television programme. **télévision** nf television.

télex /telɛks/ nm telex.

tellement /tɛlmɑ̃/ adv (tant) so much; (si) so; ∼ **de** (quantité) so much; (nombre) so many.

téméraire /temeʀɛʀ/ adj (personne) reckless.

témoignage /temwaɲaʒ/ nm testimony, evidence; (récit) account; ∼ **de** (marque) token of.

témoigner /temwaɲe/ **1** vi testify (**de** to). ● vt (montrer) show; ∼ **que** testify that.

témoin /temwɛ̃/ nm witness; (Sport) baton; **être ∼ de** witness;

∼ **oculaire** eyewitness.

tempe /tɑ̃p/ nf (Anat) temple.

tempérament /tɑ̃peʀamɑ̃/ nm temperament, disposition.

température /tɑ̃peʀatyʀ/ nf temperature.

tempête /tɑ̃pɛt/ nf storm; ∼ **de neige** snowstorm.

temple /tɑ̃pl/ nm temple; (protestant) church.

temporaire /tɑ̃pɔʀɛʀ/ adj temporary.

temps /tɑ̃/ nm (notion) time; (Gram) tense; (étape) stage; **à ∼ partiel/plein** part-/full-time; **ces derniers ∼** lately; **dans le ∼** at one time; **dans quelque ∼** in a while; **de ∼ en ∼** from time to time; ∼ **d'arrêt** pause; **avoir tout son ∼** have plenty of time; (météo) weather; ∼ **de chien** filthy weather; **quel ∼ fait-il?** what's the weather like?

tenace /tanas/ adj stubborn.

tenaille /tanaj/ nf pincers (+ pl).

tendance /tɑ̃dɑ̃s/ nf tendency; (évolution) trend; **avoir ∼ à** tend to.

tendon /tɑ̃dɔ̃/ nm tendon.

tendre¹ /tɑ̃dʀ/ **3** vt stretch; (piège) set; (bras) stretch out; (main) hold out; (cou) crane; ∼ **qch à qn** hold sth out to sb; ∼ **l'oreille** prick up one's ears. ● vi ∼ **à** tend to.

tendre² /tɑ̃dʀ/ adj tender; (couleur, bois) soft. **tendresse** nf tenderness.

tendu, ∼e /tɑ̃dy/ adj (corde) tight; (personne, situation) tense.

ténèbres /tenɛbʀ/ nfpl darkness.

teneur /tanœʀ/ nf content.

tenir /taniʀ/ **59** vt hold; (pari, promesse, hôtel) keep; (place) take up; (propos) utter; (rôle) play; ∼ **de** (avoir reçu de) have got from; ∼

t

pour regard as; ~ **chaud** keep warm; ~ **compte de** take into account; ~ **le coup** hold out; ~ **tête à** stand up to. ● *vi* hold; ~ **à** be attached to; ~ **à faire** be anxious to do; ~ **bon** stand firm; ~ **dans** fit into; ~ **de qn** take after sb; **tiens!** (surprise) hey! □ **se** ~ *vpr* (debout) stand; (avoir lieu) be held; **se** ~ **à** hold on to; **s'en** ~ **à** se limiter à) confine oneself to.

tennis /tenis/ *nm* tennis; ~ **de table** table tennis. ● *nmpl* (chaussures) sneakers.

ténor /tenɔʀ/ *nm* tenor.

tension /tɑ̃sjɔ̃/ *nf* tension; **avoir de la** ~ have high blood pressure.

tentation /tɑ̃tasjɔ̃/ *nf* temptation.

tentative /tɑ̃tativ/ *nf* attempt.

tente /tɑ̃t/ *nf* tent.

tenter /tɑ̃te/ 🔳 *vt* (allécher) tempt; (essayer) try (**de faire** to do).

tenture /tɑ̃tyʀ/ *nf* curtain; ~**s** draperies.

tenu, ~**e** /təny/ *adj* **bien** ~ well kept; ~ **de** required. ● →**TENIR** 🔢.

tenue /təny/ *nf* (habillement) dress; (de maison) upkeep; (conduite) (good) behaviour; (maintien) posture; ~ **de soirée** evening dress.

Tergal ® /tɛʀgal/ *nm* Terylene®.

terme /tɛʀm/ *nm* (mot) term; (date limite) time-limit; (fin) end; **né avant** ~ premature; **à long/court** ~ long-/short-term; **en bons** ~**s** on good terms (**avec** with).

terminaison /tɛʀminɛzɔ̃/ *nf* (Gram) ending.

terminal, ~**e** (*mpl* -**aux**) /tɛʀminal, -o/ *adj* terminal. ● *nm* terminal. **terminale** *nf* (Scol) ≈ sixth form; (US) twelfth grade.

terminer /tɛʀmine/ 🔳 *vt/i* finish; (discours) end, finish. □ **se** ~ *vpr* end (**par** with).

terne /tɛʀn/ *adj* dull, drab.

ternir /tɛʀniʀ/ 🔳 *vt/i* tarnish. □ **se** ~ *vpr* tarnish.

terrain /teʀɛ̃/ *nm* ground; (parcelle) piece of land; (à bâtir) plot; ~ **d'aviation** airfield; ~ **de camping** campsite; ~ **de golf** golf course; ~ **de jeu** playground; ~ **vague** waste ground.

terrasse /teʀas/ *nf* terrace; **à la** ~ (d'un café) outside (a café).

terrasser /teʀase/ 🔳 *vt* (adversaire) knock down; (maladie) strike down.

terre /tɛʀ/ *nf* (planète, matière) earth; (étendue, pays) land; (sol) ground; **à** ~ (Naut) ashore; **par** ~ (dehors) on the ground; (dedans) on the floor; ~ (**cuite**) terracotta; **la** ~ **ferme** dry land; ~ **glaise** clay.

terreau (*pl* ~**x**) *nm* compost.

terre-plein (*pl* **terres-pleins**) *nm* platform; (de route) central reservation.

terrestre /teʀɛstʀ/ *adj* (animaux) land; (de notre planète) of the Earth.

terreur /teʀœʀ/ *nf* terror.

terrible /teʀibl/ *adj* terrible; (formidable 🔳) terrific.

terrier /teʀje/ *nm* (trou) burrow; (chien) terrier.

terrifier /teʀifje/ 🔢 *vt* terrify.

territoire /teʀitwaʀ/ *nm* territory.

terroir /teʀwaʀ/ *nm* land; **du** ~ local.

terroriser /teʀɔʀize/ 🔳 *vt* terrorize.

terrorisme /teʀɔʀism/ *nm* terrorism. **terroriste** *nmf* terrorist.

tertiaire /teʀsjɛʀ/ *adj* (secteur) service.

tes /te/ →**TON**¹.

test /tɛst/ *nm* test.

testament /tɛstamɑ̃/ *nm* (Jur) will;

(politique, artistique) testament; **Ancien/Nouveau T~** Old/New Testament.

tétanos /tetanos/ nm tetanus.

têtard /tɛtaʀ/ nm tadpole.

tête /tɛt/ nf head; (visage) face; (cheveux) hair; **à la ~ de** at the head of; **à ~ reposée** at one's leisure; **de ~** (calculer) in one's head; **faire la ~** sulk; **tenir ~ à qn** stand up to sb; **il n'en fait qu'à sa ~** he does just as he pleases; **en ~** (Sport) in the lead; **faire une ~** (au football) head the ball; **une forte ~** a rebel; **la ~ la première** head first; **de la ~ aux pieds** from head to toe.

tête-à-tête /tɛtatɛt/ nm inv tête-à-tête; **en ~** in private.

tétée /tete/ nf feed.

tétine /tetin/ nf (de biberon) teat; (sucette) dummy; (US) pacifier.

têtu, ~e /tety/ adj stubborn.

texte /tɛkst/ nm text; (de leçon) subject; (morceau choisi) passage.

texteur /tɛkstœʀ/ nm (Ordinat) word-processor.

textile /tɛkstil/ nm & adj textile.

texto /tɛksto/ nm text message.

TGV abrév m (**train à grande vitesse**) TGV, high-speed train.

thé /te/ nm tea.

théâtre /teatʀ/ nm theatre; (d'un crime) scene; **faire du ~** act.

théière /tejɛʀ/ nf teapot.

thème /tɛm/ nm theme; (traduction: Scol) prose.

théorie /teoʀi/ nf theory. **théorique** adj theoretical.

thérapie /teʀapi/ nf therapy.

thermique /tɛʀmik/ adj thermal.

thermomètre /tɛʀmɔmɛtʀ/ nm thermometer.

thermos® /tɛʀmos/ nm ou f Thermos® (flask).

thermostat /tɛʀmɔsta/ nm thermostat.

thèse /tɛz/ nf thesis.

thon /tɔ̃/ nm tuna.

thym /tɛ̃/ nm thyme.

tibia /tibja/ nm shinbone.

tic /tik/ nm (contraction) tic, twitch; (manie) habit.

ticket /tikɛ/ nm ticket.

tiède /tjɛd/ adj lukewarm; (nuit) warm.

tiédir /tjediʀ/ 2 vt/i (faire) ~ warm up.

tien, ~ne /tjɛ̃, -ɛn/ pron le ~, la ~ne, les ~(ne)s yours; à la ~ne! cheers!

tiens, tient /tjɛ̃/ ➔TENIR 59.

tiercé /tjɛʀse/ nm place-betting.

tiers, tierce /tjɛʀ, tjɛʀs/ adj third. ● nm (fraction) third; (personne) third party. **tiers-monde** nm Third World.

tige /tiʒ/ nf (Bot) stem, stalk; (en métal) shaft, rod.

tigre /tigʀ/ nm tiger.

tigresse /tigʀɛs/ nf tigress.

tilleul /tijœl/ nm lime tree.

timbre /tɛ̃bʀ/ nm stamp; (sonnette) bell; (de voix) tone. **~ poste** (pl **~s poste**) nm postage stamp. **timbrer** 1 vt stamp.

timide /timid/ adj shy, timid. **timidité** nf shyness.

timoré, ~e /timɔʀe/ adj timorous.

tintement /tɛ̃tmɑ̃/ nm (de sonnette) ringing; (de clés) jingling.

tique /tik/ nf tick.

tir /tiʀ/ nm (Sport) shooting; (action de tirer) firing; (feu, rafale) fire; ~ à l'arc archery; ~ au pigeon clay pigeon shooting.

tirage /tiʀaʒ/ nm (de photo) printing; (de journal) circulation; (de livre) edition; (Ordinat) hard copy; (de cheminée) draught; ~ au sort draw.

tire-bouchon (pl ~s) /tiʀbuʃɔ̃/ nm corkscrew.

tirelire /tiʀliʀ/ nf piggy bank.

tirer /tiʀe/ **1** vt pull; (langue) stick out; (conclusion, trait, rideaux) draw; (coup de feu) fire; (gibier) shoot; (photo) print; ~ **de** (sortir) take ou get out of; (extraire) extract from; (plaisir, nom) derive from; ~ **parti de** take advantage of; ~ **profit de** profit from; **se faire** ~ **l'oreille** get told off. ● vi shoot, fire (**sur** at); ~ **sur** (corde) pull at; (couleur) verge on; ~ **à sa fin** be drawing to a close; ~ **au clair** clarify; ~ **au sort** draw lots (for). □ **se** ~ vpr **1** clear off; **se** ~ **de** get out of; **s'en** ~ (en réchapper) pull through; (réussir **1**) cope.

tiret /tiʀe/ nm dash.

tireur /tiʀœʀ/ nm gunman; ~ **d'élite** marksman; ~ **isolé** sniper.

tiroir /tiʀwaʀ/ nm drawer. **tiroir-caisse** (pl **tiroirs-caisses**) nm till, cash register.

tisane /tizan/ nf herbal tea.

tissage /tisaʒ/ nm weaving. **tisser** **1** vt weave. **tisserand** nm weaver.

tissu /tisy/ nm fabric, material; (biologique) tissue; **un** ~ **de mensonges** (fig) a pack of lies.

tissu-éponge (pl **tissus-éponge**)

nm towelling.

titre /titʀ/ nm title; (diplôme) qualification; (Comm) bond; ~s (droits) claims; **(gros)** ~s headlines; **à** ~ **d'exemple** as an example; **à juste** ~ rightly; **à** ~ **privé** in a private capacity; **à double** ~ on two accounts; ~ **de propriété** title deed.

tituber /titybe/ **1** vi stagger.

titulaire /titylɛʀ/ adj être ~ be a permanent staff member; **être** ~ **de** hold; ~ **de** (permis) holder. ● nmf (de permis) holder.

titulariser **1** vt give permanent status to.

toast /tost/ nm (pain) piece of toast; (canapé, allocution) toast.

toboggan /tɔbɔgɑ̃/ nm (de jeu) slide; (Auto) flyover.

toi /twa/ pron you; (réfléchi) yourself; **dépêche-**~ hurry up.

toile /twal/ nf cloth; (tableau) canvas; ~ **d'araignée** cobweb; ~ **de fond** (fig) backdrop; **la** ~ (Internet) the Web.

toilette /twalɛt/ nf (habillement) outfit; ~s (cabinets) toilet(s); **de** ~ (articles, savon) toilet; **faire sa** ~ have a wash.

toi-même /twamɛm/ pron yourself.

toit /twa/ nm roof; ~ **ouvrant** (Auto) sunroof.

toiture /twatyʀ/ nf roof.

tôle /tol/ nf (plaque) iron sheet; ~ **ondulée** corrugated iron.

tolérant, ~e /tɔleʀɑ̃, -t/ adj tolerant. **tolérer** **14** vt tolerate.

tomate /tɔmat/ nf tomato.

tombe /tɔ̃b/ nf grave; (pierre) gravestone.

tombeau (pl ~x) /tɔ̃bo/ nm tomb.

tomber /tɔ̃be/ **1** vi (aux être) fall; (fièvre, vent) drop; **faire** ~ knock over; (gouvernement) bring down; **laisser** ~ (objet, amoureux) drop;

tombola | toujours

(*collègue*) let down; (*activité*) give up; **laisse** ~! **[i]** forget it!; ~ **à l'eau** (*projet*) fall through; ~ **bien** ou **à point** come at the right time; ~ **en panne** break down; ~ **en syncope** faint; ~ **sur** (*trouver*) run across.

tombola /tɔ̃bɔla/ *nf* tombola; (US) lottery.

tome /tɔm/ *nm* volume.

ton[1], **ta** (**ton** *before vowel or mute h*) (*pl* **tes**) /tɔ̃, ta, tɔ̃n, te/ *adj* your.

ton[2] /tɔ̃/ *nm* (*hauteur de voix*) pitch; **d'un** ~ **sec** drily; **de bon** ~ in good taste.

tonalité /tɔnalite/ *nf* (Mus) key; (*de téléphone*) dialling tone; (US) dial tone.

tondeuse /tɔ̃døz/ *nf* (*à moutons*) shears (+ *pl*); (*à cheveux*) clippers (+ *pl*); ~ **à gazon** lawn-mower. **tondre** **[3]** *vt* (*herbe*) mow; (*mouton*) shear; (*cheveux*) clip.

tonne /tɔn/ *nf* tonne.

tonneau (*pl* ~**x**) /tɔno/ *nm* barrel; (*en voiture*) somersault.

tonnerre /tɔnɛʀ/ *nm* thunder.

tonton /tɔ̃tɔ̃/ *nm* **[i]** uncle.

tonus /tɔnys/ *nm* energy.

torche /tɔʀʃ/ *nf* torch.

torchon /tɔʀʃɔ̃/ *nm* (*pour la vaisselle*) tea towel.

tordre /tɔʀdʀ/ **[3]** *vt* twist. □ **se** ~ *vpr* **se** ~ **la cheville** twist one's ankle; **se** ~ **de douleur** writhe in pain; **se** ~ (**de rire**) split one's sides.

tordu, -e /tɔʀdy/ *adj* twisted, bent; (*esprit*) warped, twisted.

torpille /tɔʀpij/ *nf* torpedo.

torrent /tɔʀɑ̃/ *nm* torrent.

torride /tɔʀid/ *adj* torrid; (*chaleur*) scorching.

torse /tɔʀs/ *nm* chest; (Anat) torso.

tort /tɔʀ/ *nm* wrong; **avoir** ~ be wrong (**de faire** to do); **donner** ~ **à** prove wrong; **être dans son** ~ be in the wrong; **faire (du)** ~ **à** harm; **à** ~ wrongly; **à** ~ **et à travers** without thinking.

torticolis /tɔʀtikɔli/ *nm* stiff neck.

tortiller /tɔʀtije/ **[1]** *vt* twist, twirl. □ **se** ~ *vpr* wriggle.

tortionnaire /tɔʀsjɔnɛʀ/ *nm* torturer.

tortue /tɔʀty/ *nf* tortoise; (*d'eau*) turtle.

tortueux, -euse /tɔʀtɥø, -z/ *adj* (*chemin*) twisting; (*explication*) tortuous.

torture /tɔʀtyʀ/ *nf* torture. **torturer** **[1]** *vt* torture.

tôt /to/ *adv* early; **au plus** ~ at the earliest; **le plus** ~ **possible** as soon as possible; ~ **ou tard** sooner or later; **ce n'est pas trop** ~! it's about time!

total, -e (*mpl* **-aux**) /tɔtal, -o/ *adj* total. ● *nm* (*pl* **-aux**) total; **au** ~ all in all. **totalement** *adv* totally. **totaliser** **[1]** *vt* total. **totalitaire** *adj* totalitarian.

totalité /tɔtalite/ *nf* **la** ~ **de** all of.

touche /tuʃ/ *nf* (*de piano*) key; (*de peinture*) touch; (**ligne de**) ~ (Sport) touchline.

toucher /tuʃe/ **[1]** *vt* touch; (*émouvoir*) move, touch; (*contacter*) get in touch with; (*cible*) hit; (*argent*) draw; (*chèque*) cash; (*concerner*) affect. ● *vi* ~ **à** touch; (*question*) touch on; (*fin, but*) approach; **je vais lui en** ~ **deux mots** I'll talk to him about it. □ **se** ~ *vpr* (*lignes*) touch. ● *nm* (*sens*) touch.

touffe /tuf/ *nf* (*de poils, d'herbe*) tuft; (*de plantes*) clump.

toujours /tuʒuʀ/ *adv* always; (*encore*) still; (*de toute façon*) anyway;

pour ~ for ever; ~ est-il que the fact remains that.

toupet /tupɛ/ *nm* (culot 🔢) cheek, nerve.

tour /tur/ *nf* tower; (immeuble) tower block; (échecs) rook; ~ **de contrôle** control tower. ● *nm* (mouvement, succession, tournure) turn; (excursion) trip; (à pied) walk; (en auto) drive; (artifice) trick; (circonférence) circumference; (Tech) lathe; ~ **(de piste)** lap; **à** ~ **de rôle** in turn; **à mon** ~ when it is my turn; **c'est mon** ~ it is my turn to; **faire le** ~ **de** go round; (question) survey; ~ **d'horizon** overview; ~ **de potier** potter's wheel; ~ **de taille** waist measurement; (ligne) waistline.

Tour de France The race for professional cyclists held annually in July since 1903, when it was created by Henri Desgrange (1865-1940). Renowned for its mountain stages, it covers approximately 4,800 km (3,000 miles) over a three-week period, finishing triumphantly on the *Champs Élysées*. Throughout the *Tour*, the previous day's leader wears the coveted *maillot jaune* (yellow jersey).

tourbillon /turbijɔ̃/ *nm* whirlwind; (d'eau) whirlpool; (fig) swirl.

tourisme /turism/ *nm* tourism; **faire du** ~ do some sightseeing.

touriste /turist/ *nmf* tourist. **touristique** *adj* tourist; (route) scenic.

tourmenter /turmɑ̃te/ *vt* torment. □ **se** ~ *vpr* worry.

tournant, ~**e** /turnɑ̃, -t/ *adj* (qui pivote) revolving. ● *nm* bend; (fig) turning-point.

tourne-disque (*pl* ~**s**)

/turnədisk/ *nm* record-player.

tournée /turne/ *nf* (de facteur, au café) round; **c'est ma** ~ I'll buy this round; (d'artiste) tour.

tourner /turne/ 🔢 *vt* turn; (film) shoot, make; ~ **le dos à** turn one's back on; ~ **en dérision** mock. ● *vi* turn; (toupie, tête) spin; (moteur, usine) run; ~ **autour de** go round; (personne, maison) hang around; (terre) revolve round; (question) centre on; ~ **de l'œil** 🔢 faint; **mal** ~ (affaire) turn out badly. □ **se** ~ *vpr* turn.

tournesol /turnəsɔl/ *nm* sunflower.

tournevis /turnəvis/ *nm* screwdriver.

tournoi /turnwa/ *nm* tournament.

tourte /turt/ *nf* pie.

tourterelle /turtərɛl/ *nf* turtle dove.

Toussaint /tusɛ̃/ *nf* **la** ~ All Saints' Day.

tousser /tuse/ 🔢 *vi* cough.

tout, ~**e** (*pl* **tous**, **toutes**) /tu, tut/ *nm* (ensemble) whole; **en** ~ in all; **pas du** ~! not at all! ● *adj* all; (n'importe quel) any; ~ **le pays** the whole country, all the country; ~**e la nuit/journée** the whole night/ day; ~ **un paquet** a whole pack; **tous les jours** every day; **tous les deux ans** every two years; ~ **le monde** everyone; **tous les deux**, **toutes les deux** both of them; **tous les trois** all three (of them). ● *pron* everything; anything; **tous** /tus/, **toutes** all; **tout ensemble** all together; **prends** ~ take everything; ~ **ce que tu veux** everything you want. ● *adv* (très) very; (entièrement) all; ~ **au bout** right at the end/beginning; ~ **en marchant** while walking; ~ **à coup** all of a sudden; ~ **à fait** quite, completely; ~ **à l'heure** in a moment; (passé) a moment ago; ~ **au ou le long de** throughout; ~ **au plus/moins** at most/least; ~ **de même** all the same; ~ **de suite** straight away; ~ **entier** whole; ~ **neuf** brand new; ~ **nu** stark naked.

tout-à-l'égout *nm inv* main drainage.

toutefois /tutfwa/ *adv* however.

tout(-)terrain /tuterɛ̃/ *adj inv* all terrain.

toux /tu/ *nf* cough.

toxicomane /tɔksikɔman/ *nmf* drug addict.

toxique /tɔksik/ *adj* toxic.

trac /trak/ *nm* **le** ~ nerves; (Théât) stage fright.

tracas /traka/ *nm* worry.

trace /tras/ *nf* (traînée, piste) trail; (d'animal, de pneu) tracks; ~**s de pas** footprints.

tracer /trase/ [10] *vt* draw; (écrire) write; (route) open up.

trachée-artère /traʃearter/ *nf* windpipe.

tracteur /traktœr/ *nm* tractor.

tradition /tradisjɔ̃/ *nf* tradition. **~le** *adj* traditional.

traducteur, -trice /tradyktœr, -tris/ *nm, f* translator. **traduction** *nf* translation.

traduire /traduir/ [17] *vt* translate; ~ **en justice** take to court.

trafic /trafik/ *nm* (commerce, circulation) traffic.

trafiquant, ~e /trafikɑ̃, -t/ *nm, f* trafficker; (d'armes, de drogues) dealer.

trafiquer /trafike/ [1] *vi* traffic. ● *vt* [1] (moteur) fiddle with.

tragédie /traʒedi/ *nf* tragedy. **tragique** *adj* tragic.

trahir /trair/ [2] *vt* betray. **trahi-**

son *nf* betrayal; (Mil) treason.

train /trɛ̃/ *nm* (Rail) train; (allure) pace; **aller bon** ~ walk briskly; **en** ~ **de faire** (busy) doing; ~ **d'atterrissage** undercarriage; ~ **électrique** *(jouet)* electric train set; ~ **de vie** lifestyle.

traîne /trɛn/ *nf* (de robe) train; **à la** ~ lagging behind.

traîneau *(pl* ~**x)** /trɛno/ *nm* sleigh.

traînée /trɛne/ *nf* (trace) trail; (longue) streak; (femme: péj) slut.

traîner /trɛne/ [1] *vt* drag (along); ~ **les pieds** drag one's feet. ● *vi* (pendre) trail; (rester en arrière) trail behind; (flâner) hang about; (*papiers, affaires*) lie around; ~ **(en longueur)** drag on. □ **se** ~ *vpr* (par terre) crawl.

traire /trer/ [29] *vt* milk.

trait /trɛ/ *nm* line; (en dessinant) stroke; (caractéristique) feature, trait; ~**s** (du visage) features; **avoir** ~ **à** relate to; **d'un** ~ (boire) in one gulp; ~ **d'union** hyphen; (fig) link.

traite /trɛt/ *nf* (de vache) milking; (Comm) draft; **d'une (seule)** ~ in one go, at a stretch.

traité /trete/ *nm* (pacte) treaty; (ouvrage) treatise.

traitement /trɛtmɑ̃/ *nm* treatment; (salaire) salary; ~ **de données** data processing; ~ **de texte** word processing.

traiter /trete/ [1] *vt* treat; (*affaire*) deal with; (*données, produit*) process; ~ **qn de lâche** call sb a coward. ● *vi* deal (**avec** with); ~ **de** (*sujet*) deal with.

traiteur /tretœr/ *nm* caterer; (boutique) delicatessen.

traître, -esse /trɛtr, -ɛs/ *adj* treacherous. ● *nm, f* traitor.

trajectoire /traʒɛktwar/ *nf* path.

trajet /tʀaʒɛ/ nm (voyage) journey; (itinéraire) route.

trame /tʀam/ nf (de tissu) weft.

tramway /tʀamwɛ/ nm tram; (US) streetcar.

tranchant, ~e /tʀɑ̃ʃɑ̃, -t/ adj sharp; (fig) cutting. ● nm cutting edge; à double ~ two-edged.

tranche /tʀɑ̃ʃ/ nf (rondelle) slice; (bord) edge; (d'âge, de revenu) bracket.

tranchée /tʀɑ̃ʃe/ nf trench.

trancher /tʀɑ̃ʃe/ 1 vt cut; (question) decide; (contraster) contrast (sur with).

tranquille /tʀɑ̃kil/ adj quiet; (esprit) at rest; (conscience) clear; être/ laisser ~ be/leave in peace; tiens-toi ~! be quiet! **tranquillisant** nm tranquillizer. **tranquilliser** 1 vt reassure. **tranquillité** nf (peace and) quiet; (d'esprit) peace of mind.

transcription /tʀɑ̃skʀipsjɔ̃/ nf transcription; (copie) transcript. **transcrire** 30 vt transcribe.

transe /tʀɑ̃s/ nf en ~ in a trance.

transférer /tʀɑ̃sfeʀe/ 14 vt transfer.

transfert /tʀɑ̃sfɛʀ/ nm transfer; ~ d'appel (au téléphone) call diversion.

transformation /tʀɑ̃sfɔʀmasjɔ̃/ nf change; transformation.

transformer /tʀɑ̃sfɔʀme/ 1 vt change; (radicalement) transform; (vêtement) alter. □ se ~ vpr change; (radicalement) be transformed; (se) ~ en turn into.

transgénique /tʀɑ̃sʒenik/ adj genetically modified.

transiger /tʀɑ̃siʒe/ 40 vi compromise.

transiter /tʀɑ̃zite/ 1 vt/i ~ par pass through.

transitif, -ive /tʀɑ̃zitif, -v/ adj transitive.

translucide /tʀɑ̃slysid/ adj translucent.

transmettre /tʀɑ̃smɛtʀ/ 42 vt (savoir, maladie) pass on; (ondes) transmit; (à la radio) broadcast. **transmission** nf transmission; (radio) broadcasting.

transparence /tʀɑ̃spaʀɑ̃s/ nf transparency. **transparent**, ~e adj transparent.

transpercer /tʀɑ̃spɛʀse/ 10 vt pierce.

transpiration /tʀɑ̃spiʀasjɔ̃/ nf perspiration. **transpirer** 1 vi perspire.

transplanter /tʀɑ̃splɑ̃te/ 1 vt (Bot, Méd) transplant.

transport /tʀɑ̃spɔʀ/ nm transpor-t(ation); durant le ~ in transit; les ~s transport (+ sg); les ~s en commun public transport (+ sg). **transporter** /tʀɑ̃spɔʀte/ 1 vt transport; (à la main) carry. **transporteur** nm haulier; (US) trucker.

transversal, ~e (mpl ~aux) /tʀɑ̃svɛʀsal, -o/ adj cross, transverse.

trapu, ~e /tʀapy/ adj stocky.

traumatisant, ~e /tʀomatizɑ̃, -t/ adj traumatic. **traumatiser** vt 1 traumatize. **traumatisme** nm trauma.

travail (pl ~aux) /tʀavaj, -o/ nm work; (emploi, tâche) job; (façonnage) working; **travaux** work (+ sg); (routiers) roadworks; ~ à la chaîne production line work; **travaux dirigés** (Scol) practical; **travaux forcés** hard labour; **travaux manuels** handicrafts; **travaux ménagers** housework.

travailler /tʀavaje/ 1 vi work; (se déformer) warp. ● vt (façonner) work; (étudier) work at ou on.

travailleur, -euse /tʀavajœʀ, -øz/ *nm, f* worker. ● *adj* hardworking.

travailliste /tʀavajist/ *adj* Labour. ● *nmf* Labour party member.

travers /tʀavɛʀ/ *nm* (défaut) failing; **à ~** through; **au ~ (de)** through; **de ~** (*chapeau, nez*) crooked; (*regarder*) askance; **j'ai avalé de ~** it went down the wrong way; **en ~ (de)** across.

traversée /tʀavɛʀse/ *nf* crossing.

traverser /tʀavɛʀse/ **1** *vt* cross; (*transpercer*) go (right) through; (*période, forêt*) go *ou* pass through.

traversin /tʀavɛʀsɛ̃/ *nm* bolster.

travesti /tʀavɛsti/ *nm* transvestite.

trébucher /tʀebyʃe/ **1** *vi* stumble, trip (over); **faire ~** trip (up).

trèfle /tʀɛfl/ *nm* (plante) clover; (*cartes*) clubs.

treillis /tʀeji/ *nm* trellis; (en métal) wire mesh; (tenue militaire) combat uniform.

treize /tʀɛz/ *adj & nm* thirteen.

Treizième mois An addition to an employee's salary, equal to his/her usual monthly payment, which some employees receive at the end of the calendar year.

---

tréma /tʀema/ *nm* diaeresis.

tremblement /tʀɑ̃bləmɑ̃/ *nm* shaking; **~ de terre** earthquake.

trembler **1** *vi* shake, tremble; (*lumière, voix*) quiver.

tremper /tʀɑ̃pe/ **1** *vt/i* soak; (*plonger*) dip; (*acier*) temper; **faire ~** soak; **~ dans** (fig) be mixed up in. **□ se ~** *vpr* (se baigner) have a dip.

tremplin /tʀɑ̃plɛ̃/ *nm* springboard.

trente /tʀɑ̃t/ *adj & nm* thirty; **se mettre sur son ~ et un** dress up;

tous les ~-six du mois once in a blue moon.

trépied /tʀepje/ *nm* tripod.

très /tʀɛ/ *adv* very; **~ aimé/estimé** much liked/esteemed.

trésor /tʀezɔʀ/ *nm* treasure; **le T~ public** the revenue department.

trésorerie /tʀezɔʀʀi/ *nf* (bureaux) accounts department; (du Trésor public) revenue office; (*argent*) funds (+ *pl*); (gestion) accounts (+ *pl*). **trésorier, -ière** *nm, f* treasurer.

tressaillement /tʀɛsajmɑ̃/ *nm* quiver; start.

tresse /tʀɛs/ *nf* braid, plait.

trêve /tʀɛv/ *nf* truce; (fig) respite; **~ de plaisanteries** that's enough joking.

tri /tʀi/ *nm* (classement) sorting; (sélection) selection; **faire le ~ de** (classer) sort; (choisir) select; **centre de ~** sorting office.

triangle /tʀijɑ̃gl/ *nm* triangle.

tribal, ~e (*mpl* **-aux**) /tʀibal, -o/ *adj* tribal.

tribord /tʀibɔʀ/ *nm* starboard.

tribu /tʀiby/ *nf* tribe.

tribunal (*mpl* **-aux**) /tʀibynal, -o/ *nm* court.

tribune /tʀibyn/ *nf* (de stade) grandstand; (d'orateur) rostrum; (débat) forum; (d'église) gallery.

tribut /tʀiby/ *nm* tribute.

tributaire /tʀibytɛʀ/ *adj* **~ de** dependent on.

tricher /tʀiʃe/ **1** *vi* cheat. **tricheur, -euse** *nm, f* cheat.

tricolore /tʀikɔlɔʀ/ *adj* three-coloured; (*écharpe*) red, white and blue; (*équipe*) French.

tricot /tʀiko/ *nm* (activité) knitting; (pull) sweater; **en ~** knitted; **~ de corps** vest; (US) under-

t

shirt. **tricoter** ∎ vt/i knit.

trier /tʀije/ वि vt (classer) sort; (choisir) select.

trimestre /tʀimɛstʀ/ nm quarter; (Scol) term. **trimestriel, ~le** adj quarterly; (bulletin) end-of-term.

tringle /tʀɛ̃gl/ nf rail.

trinquer /tʀɛ̃ke/ ∎ vi clink glasses.

triomphant, ~e /tʀijɔ̃fɑ̃, -t/ adj triumphant. **triomphe** nm triumph. **triompher** ∎ vi triumph (de over); (jubiler) be triumphant.

tripes /tʀip/ nfpl (mets) tripe (+ sg); (entrailles 集) guts.

triple /tʀipl/ adj triple, treble. ● nm le ~ three times as much (de as). **triplés, -es** nm, fpl triplets.

tripot /tʀipo/ nm gambling den.

tripoter /tʀipote/ ∎ vt 集 (personne) grope; (objet) fiddle with.

trisomique /tʀizɔmik/ adj être ~ have Down's syndrome.

triste /tʀist/ adj sad; (rue, temps, couleur) dreary; (lamentable) dreadful. **tristesse** nf sadness; dreariness.

trivial, ~e (mpl **-iaux**) /tʀivjal, -jo/ adj coarse.

troc /tʀɔk/ nm exchange; (Comm) barter.

trognon /tʀɔɲɔ̃/ nm (de fruit) core.

trois /tʀwa/ adj & nm three; **hôtel ~ étoiles** three-star hotel. **troisième** adj & nmf third.

trombone /tʀɔ̃bɔn/ nm (Mus) trombone; (agrafe) paperclip.

trompe /tʀɔ̃p/ nf (d'éléphant) trunk; (Mus) horn.

tromper /tʀɔ̃pe/ ∎ vt deceive, mislead; (déjouer) elude. □ **se ~** vpr be mistaken; **se ~ de route/d'heure** take the wrong road/get the time wrong.

trompette /tʀɔ̃pɛt/ nf trumpet.

trompeur, -euse /tʀɔ̃pœʀ, -øz/ adj (apparence) deceptive.

tronc /tʀɔ̃/ nm trunk; (boîte) collection box.

tronçon /tʀɔ̃sɔ̃/ nm section.

tronçonneuse /tʀɔ̃sɔnøz/ nf chain saw.

trône /tʀon/ nm throne. **trôner** ∎ vi (vase) have pride of place (sur on).

trop /tʀo/ adv (grand, loin) too; (boire, marcher) too much; ~ **(de)** quantité) too much; (nombre) too many; **ce serait ~ beau** one should be so lucky; **de ~, en ~** too much; too many; **il a bu un verre de ~** he's had one too many; **se sentir de ~** feel one is in the way.

trophée /tʀɔfe/ nm trophy.

tropical, ~e (mpl **-aux**) /tʀɔpikal, -o/ adj tropical. **tropique** nm tropic.

trop-plein (pl **~s**) /tʀɔplɛ̃/ nm excess; (dispositif) overflow.

troquer /tʀɔke/ ∎ vt exchange; (Comm) barter (contre for).

trot /tʀo/ nm trot; **aller au ~** trot. **trotter** ∎ vi trot.

trotteuse /tʀɔtøz/ nf (de montre) second hand.

trottoir /tʀɔtwaʀ/ nm pavement; (US) sidewalk; ~ **roulant** moving walkway.

trou /tʀu/ nm hole; (moment) gap; (lieu: péj) dump; ~ **(de mémoire)** memory lapse; ~ **de serrure** keyhole; **faire son** ~ carve one's niche.

trouble /tʀubl/ adj (eau, image) unclear; (louche) shady. ● nm (émoi) emotion; **~s** (Pol) disturbances; (Méd) disorder (+ sg). **troubler** /tʀuble/ ∎ vt disturb; (eau) make cloudy; (inquiéter) trouble.

□ **se** ~ *vpr* (*personne*) become flustered.

trouer /tʀue/ **1** *vt* make a hole ou holes in; **mes chaussures sont trouées** my shoes have got holes in them.

troupe /tʀup/ *nf* troop; (d'acteurs) company.

troupeau (*pl* ~**x**) /tʀupo/ *nm* herd; (de moutons) flock.

trousse /tʀus/ *nf* case, bag; **aux** ~**s de** hot on sb's heels; ~ **de toilette** toilet bag.

trousseau (*pl* ~**x**) /tʀuso/ *nm* (de clefs) bunch; (de mariée) trousseau.

trouver /tʀuve/ **1** *vt* find; (penser) think; **il est venu me** ~ he came to see me. □ **se** ~ *vpr* (être) be; (se sentir) feel; **il se trouve que** it happens that; **si ça se trouve** maybe; **se** ~ **mal** faint.

truand /tʀyɑ̃/ *nm* gangster.

truc /tʀyk/ *nm* (moyen) way; (artifice) trick; (chose 🔲) thing. **trucage** *nm* (cinéma) special effect.

truffe /tʀyf/ *nf* (champignon, chocolat) truffle; (de chien) nose.

truffer /tʀyfe/ **1** *vt* (fig) fill, pack (**de** with).

truie /tʀyi/ *nf* (animal) sow.

truite /tʀyit/ *nf* trout.

truquer /tʀyke/ **1** *vt* fix, rig; (*photo*) fake; (*résultats*) fiddle.

tsar /tsaʀ/ *nm* tsar, czar.

tu /ty/ *pron* (parent, ami, enfant) you. ➡**TAIRE 47**.

tuba /tyba/ *nm* (Mus) tuba; (Sport) snorkel.

tube /tyb/ *nm* tube.

tuberculose /tybɛʀkyloz/ *nf* tuberculosis.

tuer /tɥe/ **1** *vt* kill; (d'une balle) shoot, kill; (épuiser) exhaust; ~ **par**

balles shoot dead. □ **se** ~ *vpr* kill oneself; (*accident*) be killed.

tuerie /tyʀi/ *nf* killing.

tue-tête: **à** ~ /atytɛt/ *loc* at the top of one's voice.

tuile /tɥil/ *nf* tile; (malchance 🔲) (stroke of) bad luck.

tulipe /tylip/ *nf* tulip.

tumeur /tymœʀ/ *nf* tumour.

tumulte /tymylt/ *nm* commotion; (désordre) turmoil.

tunique /tynik/ *nf* tunic.

Tunisie /tynizi/ *nf* Tunisia.

tunnel /tynɛl/ *nm* tunnel.

turbo /tyʀbo/ *adj* turbo. ● *nf* (voiture) turbo.

turbulent, ~**e** /tyʀbylɑ̃, -t/ *adj* boisterous, turbulent.

turc, **-que** /tyʀk/ *adj* Turkish. ● *nm* (Ling) Turkish. **T**~, **-que** Turk.

turfiste /tyʀfist/ *nmf* racegoer.

Turquie /tyʀki/ *nf* Turkey.

tutelle /tytɛl/ *nf* (Jur) guardianship; (fig) protection.

tuteur, **-trice** /tytœʀ, -tʀis/ *nm*, *f* (Jur) guardian. ● *nm* (bâton) stake.

tutoiement /tytwamɑ̃/ *nm* use of the 'tu' form. **tutoyer 31** *vt* address using the 'tu' form.

tuyau (*pl* ~**x**) /tɥijo/ *nm* pipe; (conseil 🔲) tip; ~ **d'arrosage** hosepipe.

TVA *abrév f* (**taxe à la valeur ajoutée**) VAT.

tympan /tɛ̃pɑ̃/ *nm* ear-drum.

type /tip/ *nm* (genre, traits) type; (individu 🔲) bloke, guy; **le** ~ **même de** a classic example of. ● *adj inv* typical.

typique /tipik/ *adj* typical.

tyran /tiʀɑ̃/ *nm* tyrant. **tyrannie** *nf* tyranny. **tyranniser** **1** *vt* oppress, tyrannize.

Uu

UE *abrév f* (**Union européenne**) European Union.

Ukraine /ykʀɛn/ *nf* Ukraine.

ulcère /ylsɛʀ/ *nm* (Méd) ulcer.

ULM *abrév m* (**ultraléger motorisé**) microlight.

ultérieur, ~e /ylteʀjœʀ/ *adj* later. **ultérieurement** *adv* later.

ultime /yltim/ *adj* final.

---

un, une /œ̃, yn/

● *déterminant*

⋯▸ a; (devant voyelle) an; ~ **animal** an animal; ~ **jour** one day; **pas ~arbre** not a single tree; **il fait ~ froid!** it's so cold!

● *pronom*

⋯▸ one; **l'~ d'entre nous** one of us; **les ~s croient que...** some believe...

⋯▸ **la une** the front page.

⋯▸ **j'en veux une** I want one.

● *adjectif*

⋯▸ one, a, an; **j'ai ~ garçon et deux filles** I have a ou one boy and two girls; **il est une heure** it is one o'clock.

● *nom masculin & féminin*

⋯▸ ~ **par** ~ one by one.

---

unanime /ynanim/ *adj* unanimous.

unanimité /ynanimite/ *nf* unanimity; **à l'~** unanimously.

uni, ~e /yni/ *adj* united; (*couple*) close; (*surface*) smooth; (*tissu*) plain.

unième /ynjɛm/ *adj* -first; **vingt et ~** twenty-first; **cent ~** one

hundred and first.

unifier /ynifje/ **45** *vt* unify.

uniforme /ynifɔʀm/ *nm* uniform.
● *adj* uniform. **uniformiser** **1** *vt* standardize. **uniformité** *nf* uniformity.

unilatéral, ~e (*mpl* **-aux**) /ynilateʀal, -o/ *adj* unilateral.

union /ynjɔ̃/ *nf* union; **l'U ~ européenne** the European Union.

unique /ynik/ *adj* (*seul*) only; (*prix, voie*) one; (*incomparable*) unique; **enfant ~** only child; **sens ~** one-way street. **uniquement** *adv* only, solely.

unir /yniʀ/ **2** *vt* unite. □ **s'~** *vpr* unite, join.

unité /ynite/ *nf* unit; (*harmonie*) unity; ~ **centrale** (Ordinat) processor.

univers /ynivɛʀ/ *nm* universe.

universel, ~le /ynivɛʀsɛl/ *adj* universal.

universitaire /ynivɛʀsitɛʀ/ *adj* (*résidence*) university; (*niveau*) academic. ● *nmf* academic.

université /ynivɛʀsite/ *nf* university.

uranium /yʀanjɔm/ *nm* uranium.

urbain, ~e /yʀbɛ̃, -ɛn/ *adj* urban. **urbanisme** *nm* town planning.

urgence /yʀʒɑ̃s/ *nf* (*cas*) emergency; (*de situation, tâche*) urgency; **d'~** (*mesure*) emergency; (*transporter*) urgently; **les ~s** casualty (+ *sg*). **urgent, ~e** *adj* urgent.

urine /yʀin/ *nf* urine. **urinoir** *nm* urinal.

urne /yʀn/ *nf* (*électorale*) ballot box; (*vase*) urn; **aller aux ~s** go to the polls.

urticaire /yʀtikɛʀ/ *nf* hives (+ *pl*), urticar.

us /ys/ *nmpl* **les ~ et coutumes** habits and customs.

usage /yza/ *nm* use; (coutume) custom; (de langage) usage; **à l'~ de** for; **d'~** (habituel) customary; **faire ~** de make use of.

usagé, ~e /yzaʒe/ *adj* worn.

usager /yzaʒe/ *nm* user.

usé, ~e /yze/ *adj* worn (out); (banal) trite.

user /yze/ **1** *vt* wear (out). ● *vi* **~ de** use. □ **s'~** *vpr* (tissu) wear (out).

usine /yzin/ *nf* factory, plant; **~ sidérurgique** ironworks (+ *pl*).

usité, ~e /yzite/ *adj* common.

ustensile /ystɑ̃sil/ *nm* utensil.

usuel, ~le /yzɥɛl/ *adj* ordinary, everyday.

usure /yzyʁ/ *nf* (détérioration) wear (and tear).

utérus /yteʁys/ *nm* womb, uterus.

utile /ytil/ *adj* useful.

utilisable /ytilizabl/ *adj* usable.

utilisation /ytfuze use. **utiliser 1** *vt* use.

utopie /ytɔpi/ *nf* Utopia; (idée) Utopian idea. **utopique** *adj* Utopian.

UV¹ *abrév f* **(unité de valeur)** course unit.

UV² *abrév mpl* **(ultraviolets)** ultraviolet rays; **faire des ~** use a sunbed.

Vv

va /va/ ➡**ALLER 8**.

vacance /vakɑ̃s/ *nf* (poste) vacancy.

vacances /vakɑ̃s/ *nfpl* holiday(s); (US) vacation; **en ~** on holiday; **~ d'été, grandes ~** summer holidays. **vacancier, -ière** *nm, f* holidaymaker; (US) vacationer.

vacant, ~e /vakɑ̃, -t/ *adj* vacant.

vacarme /vakaʁm/ *nm* din.

vaccin /vaksɛ̃/ *nm* vaccine. **vacciner 1** *vt* vaccinate.

vache /vaʃ/ *nf* cow. ● *adj* (méchant 🛈) nasty.

vaciller /vasije/ **1** *vi* sway, wobble; (lumière) flicker; (hésiter) falter; (santé, mémoire) fail.

vadrouiller /vadʁuje/ **1** *vi* 🛈 wander about.

va-et-vient /vaevjɛ̃/ *nm inv* toing and froing; (de personnes) comings and goings; **faire le ~** go to and fro; (interrupteur) two-way switch.

vagabond, ~e /vagabɔ̃, -d/ *nm, f* vagrant.

vagin /vaʒɛ̃/ *nm* vagina.

vague /vag/ *adj* vague. ● *nm* regarder dans le ~ stare into space; **il est resté dans le ~** he was vague about it. ● *nf* wave; **~ de fond** ground swell; **~ de froid** cold spell; **~ de chaleur** heatwave.

vaillant, ~e /vajɑ̃, -t/ *adj* brave; (vigoureux) strong.

vaille /vaj/ ➡**VALOIR 60**.

vain, ~e /vɛ̃, vɛn/ *adj* vain, futile; **en ~** in vain.

vaincre /vɛ̃kʁ/ **59** *vt* defeat; (surmonter) overcome. **vaincu, ~e** *nm, f* (Sport) loser. **vainqueur** *nm* victor; (Sport) winner.

vais /vɛ/ ➡**ALLER 8**.

vaisseau (*pl* **~x**) /vɛso/ *nm* ship; (veine) vessel; **~ spatial** spaceship.

vaisselle /vɛsɛl/ *nf* crockery; (à laver) dishes; **faire la ~** do the washing-up, wash the dishes; **liquide ~** washing-up liquid.

valable /valabl/ *adj* valid; (de qualité) worthwhile.

valet /valɛ/ *nm* (aux cartes) jack; (**~ de chambre**) manservant.

valeur /valœʀ/ *nf* value; (mérite) worth, value; ~s (Comm) stocks and shares; **avoir de la** ~ be valuable; **prendre/perdre de la** ~ go up/down in value; **objets de** ~ valuables; **sans** ~ worthless.

valide /valid/ *adj* (personne) fit; (billet) valid. **valider 1** *vt* validate.

valise /valiz/ *nf* (suit) case; **faire ses** ~s pack (one's bags).

vallée /vale/ *nf* valley.

valoir /valwaʀ/ 60 *vi* (mériter) be worth; (égaler) be as good as; (être valable) apply; **faire** ~ (mérite, qualité) emphasize; (terrain) cultivate; (droit) assert; **se faire** ~ put oneself forward; **se faire** ~ cher/100 euros be worth a lot/100 euros; **que vaut ce vin?** what's this wine like?; **ne rien** ~ be useless *ou* no good; **ça ne me dit rien qui vaille** I don't like the sound of that; ~ **la peine** *or* **le coup 1** be worth it; **il vaut/vaudrait mieux faire** it is would be better to do. ● *vt* ~ **qch à qn** (éloges, critiques) earn sb sth; (admiration) win sb sth. □ **se** ~ *vpr* (être équivalents) be as good as each other; **ça se vaut** it's all the same.

valoriser /valɔʀize/ 1 *vt* add value to; (produit) promote; (profession) make attractive; (région, ressources) develop.

valse /vals/ *nf* waltz.

vandale /vɑ̃dal/ *nmf* vandal.

vanille /vanij/ *nf* vanilla.

vanité /vanite/ *nf* vanity. **vaniteux, -euse** *adj* vain, conceited.

vanne /van/ *nf* (d'écluse) sluicegate; (propos 1) dig 1.

vantard, ~e /vɑ̃taʀ, -d/ *adj* boastful. ● *nm, f* boaster.

vanter /vɑ̃te/ 1 *vt* praise. □ **se** ~ *vpr* boast (**de** about); **se** ~ **de faire** pride oneself on doing.

vapeur /vapœʀ/ *nf* (eau) steam; (brume, émanation) steam; ~s fumes; **à** ~ (bateau, locomotive) steam; **faire cuire à la** ~ steam.

vaporisateur /vapɔʀizatœʀ/ *nm* spray, atomizer. **vaporiser 1** *vt* spray.

varappe /vaʀap/ *nf* rock-climbing.

variable /vaʀjabl/ *adj* variable; (temps) changeable.

varicelle /vaʀisɛl/ *nf* chickenpox.

varié, ~e /vaʀje/ *adj* (non monotone, étendu) varied; (divers) various; **sandwichs** ~s a selection of sandwiches.

varier /vaʀje/ 45 *vt/i* vary.

variété /vaʀjete/ *nf* variety; **spectacle de** ~s variety show.

vase /vaz/ *nm* vase. ● *nf* silt, mud.

vaseux, -euse /vazø, -z/ *adj* (confus 1) woolly, hazy.

vaste /vast/ *adj* vast, huge.

vaurien, ~ne /voʀjɛ̃, -ɛn/ *nm, f* good-for-nothing.

vautour /votuʀ/ *nm* vulture.

vautrer (se) /(sə)votʀe/ 1 *vpr* sprawl; **se** ~ **dans** (vice, boue) wallow in.

veau (pl ~x) /vo/ *nm* calf; (viande) veal; (cuir) calfskin.

vécu, ~e /veky/ *adj* (réel) true, real. ➞VIVRE 62.

vedette /vədɛt/ *nf* (artiste) star; **en** ~ (objet) in a prominent position; (personne) in the limelight; **joueur** ~ star player; (bateau) launch.

végétal (mpl **-aux**) /veʒetal, -o/ *adj* plant. ● *nm* (pl **-aux**) plant.

végétalien, ~ne /veʒetaljɛ̃, -ɛn/ *adj & nm, f* vegan.

végétarien, ~ne /veʒetaʀjɛ̃, -ɛn/ *adj & nm, f* vegetarian.

végétation /veʒetasjɔ̃/ *nf* vegetation; ~s (Méd) adenoids.

véhicule /veikyl/ nm vehicle.

veille /vej/ nf (état) wakefulness; (jour précédent) the day before; **la ~ de Noël** Christmas Eve; **à la ~ de** on the eve of; **la ~ au soir** the previous evening.

veillée /veje/ nf evening (gathering).

veiller /veje/ **1** vi stay up; (monter la garde) be on watch. ● vt (malade) watch over; **~ à** attend to; **~ sur** watch over.

veilleur /vɛjœʀ/ nm **~ de nuit** night-watchman.

veilleuse /vɛjøz/ nf night light; (de véhicule) sidelight; (de réchaud) pilot light; **mettre qch en ~** put sth on the back burner.

veine /vɛn/ nf (Anat) vein; (nervure, filon) vein; (chance **I**) luck; **avoir de la ~** **I** be lucky.

véliplanchiste /veliplɑ̃ʃist/ nmf windsurfer.

vélo /velo/ nm bike; (activité) cycling; **faire du ~** go cycling; **~ tout terrain** mountain bike.

vélomoteur /velomotœʀ/ nm moped.

velours /v(ə)luʀ/ nm velvet; **~ côtelé** corduroy.

velouté, ~e /vəlute/ adj smooth. ● nm (Culin) **~ d'asperges** cream of asparagus soup.

vendanges /vɑ̃dɑ̃ʒ/ nfpl grape harvest.

vendeur, -euse /vɑ̃dœʀ, -øz/ nm, f shop assistant; (marchand) salesman, saleswoman; (Jur) vendor, seller.

vendre /vɑ̃dʀ/ **3** vt sell; **à ~** for sale. □ se **~** vpr (être vendu) be sold; (trouver acquéreur) sell; **se ~ bien** sell well.

vendredi /vɑ̃dʀədi/ nm Friday; **V~ saint** Good Friday.

vénéneux, -euse /venenø, -z/ adj poisonous.

vénérer /venere/ **14** vt revere.

vénérien, -en /venerjɛ̃, -ɛn/ adj **maladie ~ne** venereal disease.

vengeance /vɑ̃ʒɑ̃s/ nf revenge, vengeance.

venger /vɑ̃ʒe/ **40** vt avenge. □ se **~** vpr take ou get one's revenge (**de qch** for sth; **de qn** on sb).

vengeur, -eresse /vɑ̃ʒœʀ, -ɔʀɛs/ adj vengeful. ● nm, f avenger.

venimeux, -euse /vənimø, -z/ adj poisonous, venomous.

venin /vənɛ̃/ nm venom.

venir /vəniʀ/ **58** vi (aux être) come (**de** from); **faire ~** qn send for sb, call sb; **en ~ à** come to; **en ~ aux mains** come to blows; **où veut-elle en ~?** what is she driving at?; **il m'est venu à l'esprit** ou **à l'idée que** it occurred to me that; **s'il venait à pleuvoir** if it should rain; **dans les jours à ~** in the next few days. ● v aux **~ de faire** have just done; **il vient/venait d'arriver** he has/had just arrived; **~ faire** come to do; **viens voir** come and see.

vent /vɑ̃/ nm wind; **il fait du ~** it is windy; **être dans le ~** **I** be trendy.

vente /vɑ̃t/ nf sale; **~ (aux enchères)** auction; **en ~** on ou for sale; **mettre qch en ~** put sth up for sale; **~ de charité** (charity) bazaar; **~ au détail/en gros** retailing/ wholesaling; **équipe de ~** sales team.

ventilateur /vɑ̃tilatœʀ/ nm fan, ventilator. **ventiler** **1** vt ventilate.

ventouse /vɑ̃tuz/ nf suction pad; (pour déboucher) plunger.

ventre /vɑ̃tʀ/ nm stomach; (d'animal) belly; (utérus) womb; **avoir le ~** have a paunch.

v

venu, ~e /vəny/ adj bien ~ (à propos) apt, timely; mal ~ badly timed; il serait mal ~ de faire it wouldn't be a good idea to do. ● →VENIR 59

venue /vəny/ nf coming.

ver /vɛʀ/ nm worm; (dans la nourriture) maggot; (du bois) woodworm; ~ luisant glow-worm; ~ à soie silkworm; ~ solitaire tapeworm; ~ de terre earthworm.

verbal, ~e (mpl -aux) /vɛʀbal, -o/ adj verbal.

verbe /vɛʀb/ nm verb.

verdir /vɛʀdiʀ/ 2 vi turn green.

véreux, **-euse** /veʀø, -z/ adj wormy; (malhonnête) shady.

verger /vɛʀʒe/ nm orchard.

verglas /vɛʀɡla/ nm black ice.

véridique /veʀidik/ adj true.

vérification /veʀifikasjɔ̃/ nf check(ing), verification.

vérifier /veʀifje/ 45 vt check, verify; (confirmer) confirm.

véritable /veʀitabl/ adj true, real; (authentique) real.

vérité /veʀite/ nf truth; (de tableau, roman) realism; en ~ in fact, actually.

Verlan A form of French slang which reverses the order of syllables in many common words. The term itself is derived from the word l'envers the syllables of which are reversed to create vers-l'en (verlan). Single syllable words are also converted so femme becomes meuf, mec becomes keum, etc.

---

vermine /vɛʀmin/ nf vermin.

verni, ~e /vɛʀni/ adj (chaussures) patent (leather); (chanceux 🔢) lucky.

vernir /vɛʀniʀ/ 2 vt varnish. □ se ~ vpr se ~ les ongles apply nail polish.

vernis /vɛʀni/ nm varnish; (de poterie) glaze; ~ à ongles nail polish.

verra, **verrait** /vɛʀa, vɛʀɛ/ →VOIR 64.

verre /vɛʀ/ nm glass; (de lunettes) lens; ~ à vin wine glass; prendre ou boire un ~ have a drink; ~ de contact contact lens; ~ dépoli frosted glass.

verrière /vɛʀjɛʀ/ nf (toit) glass roof; (paroi) glass wall.

verrou /vɛʀu/ nm bolt; sous les ~s behind bars.

verrouillage /vɛʀujaʒ/ nm ~ central or centralisé (des portes) central locking.

verrue /vɛʀy/ nf wart; ~ plantaire verruca.

vers¹ /vɛʀ/ prép towards; (aux environs de) (temps) about; (lieu) near, around; (période) towards; ~ le soir towards evening.

vers² /vɛʀ/ nm (poésie) line of verse.

versatile /vɛʀsatil/ adj unpredictable, volatile.

verse: à ~ /avɛʀs/ loc in torrents.

Verseau /vɛʀso/ nm le ~ Aquarius.

versement /vɛʀsəmã/ nm payment; (échelonné) instalment.

verser /vɛʀse/ 1 vt/i pour; (larmes, sang) shed; (payer) pay. ● vi pour; (voiture) overturn; ~ dans (fig) lapse into.

version /vɛʀsjɔ̃/ nf version; (traduction) translation.

verso /vɛʀso/ nm back (of the page); voir au ~ see overleaf.

vert, ~e /vɛʀ, -t/ adj green; (vieillard) sprightly. ● nm green; les ~s the Greens.

vertèbre /vɛʁtɛbʀ/ *nf* vertebra; **se déplacer une ~** slip a disc.

vertical, ~e (*mpl* **-aux**) /vɛʁtikal, -o/ *adj* vertical.

vertige /vɛʁtiʒ/ *nm* dizziness; **~s** dizzy spells; **avoir le ~** feel dizzy. **vertigineux, -euse** *adj* dizzy; (très grand) staggering.

vertu /vɛʁty/ *nf* virtue; **en ~ de** in accordance with. **vertueux, -euse** *adj* virtuous.

verveine /vɛʁvɛn/ *nf* verbena.

vessie /vesi/ *nf* bladder.

veste /vɛst/ *nf* jacket.

vestiaire /vɛstjɛʀ/ *nm* cloakroom; (Sport) changing-room; (US) locker-room.

vestibule /vɛstibyl/ *nm* hall; (Théât, d'hôtel) foyer.

vestige /vɛstiʒ/ *nm* (objet) relic; (trace) vestige.

veston /vɛstɔ̃/ *nm* jacket.

vêtement /vɛtmɑ̃/ *nm* article of clothing; **~s** clothes, clothing.

vétéran /veteʁɑ̃/ *nm* veteran.

vétérinaire /veteʀinɛʀ/ *nmf* vet, veterinary surgeon, (US) veterinarian.

vêtir /vetiʀ/ **61** *vt* dress. □ **se ~** *vpr* dress.

veto /veto/ *nm inv* veto.

vêtu, ~e /vety/ *adj* dressed (de in).

veuf, veuve /vœf, -vœf/ *adj* widowed. ● *nm, f* widower, widow.

veuille /vœj/ →**VOULOIR 64**.

veut, veux /vø/ →**VOULOIR 64**.

vexation /vɛksasjɔ̃/ *nf* humiliation.

vexer /vɛkse/ **1** *vt* upset, hurt. □ **se ~** *vpr* be upset, be hurt.

viable /vjabl/ *adj* viable; (projet) feasible.

viande /vjɑ̃d/ *nf* meat.

vibrer /vibʀe/ **1** *vi* vibrate; **faire ~** (âme, foules) stir.

vicaire /vikɛʀ/ *nm* curate.

vice /vis/ *nm* (moral) vice; (physique) defect.

vicier /visje/ **45** *vt* contaminate; (air) pollute.

vicieux, -ieuse /visjø, -z/ *adj* depraved. ● *nm, f* pervert.

victime /viktim/ *nf* victim; (d'un accident) casualty.

victoire /viktwaʀ/ *nf* victory; (Sport) win. **victorieux, -ieuse** *adj* victorious; (équipe) winning.

vidange /vidɑ̃ʒ/ *nf* emptying; (Auto) oil change; (tuyau) waste pipe ou outlet.

vide /vid/ *adj* empty. ● *nm* (absence, manque) vacuum, void; (espace) space; (trou) gap; (sans air) vacuum; **à ~** empty; **emballé sous ~** vacuum packed; **suspendu dans le ~** dangling in space.

vide-greniers /vidgʀənje/ *nm inv* bric-a-brac sale.

vidéo /video/ *adj inv* video; **jeu ~** video game. ● *nf* video.

vidéocassette *nf* video (tape).

vidéoclip *nm* music video.

vidéoconférence *nf* videoconferencing; (séance) videoconference.

vidéodisque *nm* videodisc. **vidéophone** *nm* videophone.

vide-ordures /vidɔʀdyʀ/ *nm inv* rubbish chute.

vidéothèque /videotɛk/ *nf* video library.

vider /vide/ **1** *vt* empty; (poisson) gut; (expulser 🔲) throw out. □ **se ~** *vpr* empty.

vie /vi/ *nf* life; (durée) lifetime; **à ~, pour la ~** for life; **donner la ~ à** give birth to; **en ~** alive; **la ~ est chère** the cost of living is high.

vieil /vjɛj/ →**VIEUX**.

vieillard /vjɛjaʀ/ nm old man.

vieille /vjɛj/ →**VIEUX.**

vieillesse /vjɛjɛs/ nf old age.

vieillir /vjejiʀ/ **2** vi grow old, age; (mot, idée) become old-fashioned. ● vt age. **vieillissement** nm ageing.

viens, vient /vjɛ̃/ →**VENIR 59.**

vierge /vjɛʀʒ/ nf virgin; **la V∼** Virgo. ● adj virgin; (feuille, cassette) blank; (cahier, pellicule) unused, new.

vieux (vieil before vowel or mute h), **vieille** (mpl **vieux**) /vjø, vjɛj/ adj old. ● nm, f old man, old woman; **petit ∼** little old man; **les ∼** old people; **vieille fille** (péj) spinster; **∼ garçon** old bachelor. **vieux jeu** adj inv old-fashioned.

vif, vive /vif, viv/ adj (animé) lively; (émotion, vent) keen; (froid) biting; (lumière) bright; (douleur, contraste, parole) sharp; (souvenir, style, teint) vivid; (succès, impatience) great; **brûler/enterrer ∼** burn/bury alive; **de vive voix** personally. ● nm **à ∼** (plaie) open; **avoir les nerfs à ∼** be on edge; **blessé au ∼** cut to the quick.

vigie /viʒi/ nf lookout.

vigilant, ∼e /viʒilɑ̃, -t/ adj vigilant.

Vigipirate /viʒipiʀat/ nm government public security measures.

vigne /viɲ/ nf (plante) vine; (vignoble) vineyard. **vigneron, ∼ne** nm, f wine-grower.

vignette /viɲɛt/ nf (étiquette) label; (Auto) road tax disc.

vignoble /viɲɔbl/ nm vineyard.

vigoureux, -euse /viguʀø, -z/ adj vigorous, sturdy.

vigueur /vigœʀ/ nf vigour; **être; entrer en ∼** (loi) be/come into force; **en ∼** current.

VIH abrév m (**virus immuno-**

déficitaire humain) HIV.

vilain, ∼e /vilɛ̃, -ɛn/ adj (mauvais) nasty; (laid) ugly. ● nm, f naughty boy, naughty girl.

villa /villa/ nf detached house.

village /vilaʒ/ nm village.

villageois, ∼e /vilaʒwa, -z/ adj village. ● nm, f villager.

ville /vil/ nf town; (importante) city; **∼ d'eaux** spa.

vin /vɛ̃/ nm wine; **∼ d'honneur** reception.

vinaigre /vinɛgʀ/ nm vinegar. **vinaigrette** nf oil and vinegar dressing, vinaigrette.

vingt /vɛ̃/ (/vɛ̃t/ before vowel and in numbers 22-29) adj & nm twenty.

vingtaine /vɛ̃tɛn/ nf **une ∼ (de)** about twenty.

vingtième /vɛ̃tjɛm/ adj & nmf twentieth.

vinicole /vinikɔl/ adj wine(-producing).

viol /vjɔl/ nm (de femme) rape; (de lieu, loi) violation.

violemment /vjɔlamɑ̃/ adv violently.

violence /vjɔlɑ̃s/ nf violence; (acte) act of violence. **violent, ∼e** adj violent.

violer /vjɔle/ **1** vt rape; (lieu, loi) violate.

violet, ∼te /vjɔlɛ, -t/ adj purple. ● nm purple. **violette** nf violet.

violon /vjɔlɔ̃/ nm violin; **∼ d'Ingres** hobby.

violoncelle /vjɔlɔ̃sɛl/ nm cello.

vipère /vipɛʀ/ nf viper, adder.

virage /viʀaʒ/ nm bend; (en ski) turn; (changement d'attitude: fig) change of course.

virée /viʀe/ nf **1** trip, tour; (en voiture) drive; (à vélo) ride.

virement /viʀmɑ̃/ nm (Comm)

(credit) transfer; ~ **automatique** standing order.

virer /viʀe/ **1** *vi* turn; ~ **de bord** tack; (fig) do a U-turn; ~ **au rouge** turn red. ● *vt* (*argent*) transfer; (*expulser* **1**) throw out; (*élève*) expel; (*licencier* **1**) fire.

virgule /viʀgyl/ *nf* comma; (*dans un nombre*) (decimal) point.

viril, ~e /viʀil/ *adj* virile.

virtuel, ~le /viʀtɥɛl/ *adj* (*potentiel*) potential; (*mémoire, réalité*) virtual.

virulent, ~e /viʀylɑ̃, -t/ *adj* virulent.

virus /viʀys/ *nm* virus.

vis¹ /vi/ →VIVRE **62**, →VOIR **63**.

vis² /vis/ *nf* screw.

visa /viza/ *nm* visa.

visage /vizaʒ/ *nm* face.

vis-à-vis /vizavi/ *prép* ~ **de** (en face de) opposite; (à l'égard de) in relation to; (comparé à) compared to, beside. ● *nm inv* (*personne*) person opposite; **en** ~ opposite each other.

visée /vize/ *nf* aim; **avoir des** ~**s sur** have designs on.

viser /vize/ **1** *vt* (*cible, centre*) aim at; (*poste, résultats*) aim for; (*concerner*) be aimed at; (*document*) stamp; ~ **à** aim at; (*mesure, propos*) be aimed at; ~ **à faire** aim to do. ● *vi* aim.

viseur /vizœʀ/ *nm* (*d'arme*) sights (+ *pl*); (Photo) viewfinder.

visière /vizjɛʀ/ *nf* (*de casquette*) peak; (*de casque*) visor.

vision /vizjɔ̃/ *nf* vision.

visite /vizit/ *nf* visit; (*pour inspecter*) inspection; (*personne*) visitor; **heures de** ~ visiting hours; ~ **guidée** guided tour; ~ **médicale** medical; **rendre** ~ **à**, **faire une** ~ **à** pay a visit; **être en** ~ **(chez qn)** be

visiting (*sb*); **avoir de la** ~ have visitors.

visiter /vizite/ **1** *vt* visit; (*appartement*) view. **visiteur, -euse** *nm, f* visitor.

visser /vise/ *vt* screw (on).

visuel, ~le /vizɥɛl/ *adj* visual. ● *nm* (Ordinat) visual display unit, VDU.

vit /vi/ →VIVRE **62**, →VOIR **63**.

vital, ~e (*mpl* -**aux**) /vital, -o/ *adj* vital.

vitamine /vitamin/ *nf* vitamin.

vite /vit/ *adv* fast, quickly; (*tôt*) soon; ~**!** quick!; **faire** ~ be quick; **au plus** ~, **le plus** ~ **possible** as quickly as possible.

vitesse /vites/ *nf* speed; (*régime: Auto*) gear; **à toute** ~ at top speed; **en** ~ in a hurry, quickly; **boîte à cinq** ~**s** five-speed gearbox.

viticole /vitikɔl/ *adj* (*industrie*) wine; (*région*) wine-producing. **viticulteur** *nm* wine-grower.

vitrage /vitʀaʒ/ *nm* (*vitres*) windows; **double** ~ double glazing.

vitrail (*pl* -**aux**) /vitʀaj, -o/ *nm* stained-glass window.

vitre /vitʀ/ *nf* (*window*) pane; (*de véhicule*) window.

vitrine /vitʀin/ *nf* (*shop*) window; (*meuble*) display cabinet.

vivace /vivas/ *adj* (*plante*) perennial; (*durable*) enduring.

vivacité /vivasite/ *nf* liveliness; (*agilité*) quickness; (*d'émotion, d'intelligence*) keenness; (*de souvenir, style, teint*) vividness.

vivant, ~e /vivɑ̃, -t/ *adj* (*example, symbole*) living; (*en vie*) alive, living; (*actif, vif*) lively. ● *nm* **un bon** ~ a bon viveur; **de son** ~ in his lifetime; **les** ~**s** the living.

vive¹ /viv/ →VIF.

vive² /viv/ interj ~ **le roi!** long live the king!

vivement /vivmɑ̃/ adv (fortement) strongly; (vite, sèchement) sharply; (avec éclat) vividly; (beaucoup) greatly; ~ **la fin!** I'll be glad when it's the end!

vivier /vivje/ nm fish pond; (artificiel) fish tank.

vivifier /vivifje/ 48 vt invigorate.

vivre /vivʀ/ 83 vi live; ~ **de** (nourriture) live on; ~ **encore** be still alive; **faire** ~ (famille) support. ● vt (vie) live; (période, aventure) live through.

vivres /vivʀ/ nmpl supplies.

VO abrév f (**version originale**) en ~ in the original language.

vocabulaire /vɔkabylɛʀ/ nm vocabulary.

vocal, ~e (mpl -**aux**) /vɔkal, -o/ adj vocal.

vœu (pl ~**x**) /vø/ nm (souhait) wish; (promesse) vow; **meilleurs** ~**x** best wishes.

vogue /vɔg/ nf fashion, vogue; **en** ~ in fashion ou vogue.

voguer /vɔge/ 1 vi sail.

voici /vwasi/ prép here is, this is; (au pluriel) here are, these are; **me** ~ here I am; ~ **un an** (temps passé) a year ago; ~ **un an que** it is a year since.

voie /vwa/ nf (route) road; (partie de route) lane; (chemin) way; (moyen) means, way; (rails) track; (quai) platform; **en** ~ **de** in the process of; **en** ~ **de développement** (pays) developing; **espèce en** ~ **de disparition** endangered species; **par la** ~ **des airs** by air; **par** ~ **orale** orally; **sur la bonne/ mauvaise** ~ (fig) on the right/ wrong track; **montrer la** ~ lead the way; ~ **de dégagement** slip-

road; ~ **ferrée** railway; (US) railroad; **V** ~ **lactée** Milky Way; ~ **navigable** waterway; ~ **publique** public highway; ~ **sans issue** (sur panneau) no through road; (fig) dead end.

voilà /vwala/ prép there is, that is; (au pluriel) there are, those are; (voici) there is, here is are; **le** ~ there he is; ~**!** right!; (en offrant qch) there you are!; ~ **un an** (temps passé) a year ago; ~ **un an que** it is a year since; **tu en veux?** en ~ do you want some? here you are; **en** ~ **des histoires!** what a fuss!; **et** ~ **que** and then.

voilage /vwalaʒ/ nm net curtain.

voile /vwal/ nf (de bateau) sail; (Sport) sailing. ● nm voil; (tissu) léger) net.

voilé, ~e /vwale/ adj (allusion, femme) veiled; (flou) hazy.

voiler /vwale/ 1 vt (dissimuler) veil; (déformer) buckle. □ **se** ~ vpr (devenir flou) become hazy; (se déformer) (roue) buckle.

voilier /vwalje/ nm sailing ship.

voir /vwaʀ/ 84 vt see; **faire** ~ **qch à qn** show sth to sb; **laisser** ~ show; **avoir quelque chose à** ~ **avec** have something to do with; **ça n'a rien à** ~ that's got nothing to do with it; **je ne peux pas le** ~ 1 I can't stand him; **je n'y vois rien** I cannot see; **je vais le** ~ be able to see; **je n'y vois rien** I cannot see; ~ **trouble** have blurred vision; **voyons** let's now see now; **voyons, soyez sages!** come on now, behave yourselves! □ **se** ~ vpr (dans la glace) see oneself; (être visible) show; (se produire) be seen; (se trouver) find oneself; (se fréquenter, se rencontrer) see each other; (être vu) be seen.

voire /vwaʀ/ adv or even, not to say.

voirie /vwaʀi/ *nf* (service) highway maintenance.

voisin, ∼e /vwazɛ̃, -in/ *adj* (de voisinage) neighbouring; (proche) nearby; (adjacent) next (**de** to); (semblable) similar (**de** to). ● *nm, f* neighbour; **le ∼** the man next door, the neighbour. **voisinage** *nm* neighbourhood; (proximité) proximity.

voiture /vwatyʀ/ *nf* (motor) car; (wagon) coach, carriage; **en ∼!** all aboard!; **∼ bélier** ramraiding car; **∼ à cheval** horse-drawn carriage; **∼ de course** racing car; **∼ école** driving school car; **∼ d'enfant** pram; (US) baby carriage; **∼ de tourisme** saloon car.

voix /vwa/ *nf* voice; (suffrage) vote; **à ∼ basse** in a whisper.

vol /vɔl/ *nm* (d'avion, d'oiseau) flight; (groupe d'oiseaux) flock, flight; (délit) theft; (hold-up) robbery; **∼ à l'étalage** shoplifting; **∼ à la tire** pickpocketing; **à ∼ d'oiseau** as the crow flies; **de haut ∼** high-ranking; **∼ libre** hang-gliding; **∼ à voile** gliding.

volaille /vɔlɑj/ *nf* **la ∼** (poules) poultry; **une ∼** a fowl.

volant /vɔlɑ̃/ *nm* (steering-)wheel; (de jupe) flounce; (de badminton) shuttlecock; **donner un coup de ∼** turn the wheel sharply.

volcan /vɔlkɑ̃/ *nm* volcano.

volée /vɔle/ *nf* flight; (oiseaux) flight, flock; (de coups, d'obus, au tennis) volley; **à toute ∼** hard; **à la ∼** in flight, in mid-air.

voler /vɔle/ **1** *vi* (oiseau) fly; (dérober) steal (**à** from). ● *vt* steal; **∼ qn** rob sb; **il ne l'a pas volé** he deserved it.

volet /vɔlɛ/ *nm* (de fenêtre) shutter; (de document) (folded *ou* tear-off) section; **trié sur le ∼** hand-picked.

voleur, -euse /vɔlœʀ, -øz/ *nm, f* thief; **au ∼!** stop thief! ● *adj* thieving.

volley-ball /vɔlebol/ *nm* volleyball.

volontaire /vɔlɔ̃tɛʀ/ *adj* (délibéré) voluntary; (opiniâtre) determined. ● *nmf* volunteer. **volontairement** *adv* voluntarily; (exprès) intentionally.

volonté /vɔlɔ̃te/ *nf* (faculté, intention) will; (souhait) wish; (énergie) willpower; **à ∼** (comme on veut) as required; **du vin à ∼** unlimited wine; **bonne ∼** goodwill; **mauvaise ∼** ill will.

volontiers /vɔlɔ̃tje/ *adv* (de bon gré) with pleasure, willingly, gladly; (admettre) readily.

volt /vɔlt/ *nm* volt.

volte-face /vɔltafas/ *nf inv* (fig) U-turn; **faire ∼** do a U-turn.

voltige /vɔltiʒ/ *nf* acrobatics (+ *pl*).

volume /vɔlym/ *nm* volume.

volumineux, -euse /vɔlyminø, -z/ *adj* bulky; (livre, dossier) thick.

volupté /vɔlypte/ *nf* voluptuousness.

vomi /vɔmi/ *nm* vomit.

vomir /vɔmiʀ/ **2** *vt* vomit; (fig) belch out. ● *vi* be sick, vomit.

vomissement /vɔmismɑ̃/ *nm* vomiting; **∼s du matin** morning sickness.

vont /vɔ̃/ **→ALLER 8**.

vorace /vɔʀas/ *adj* voracious.

vos /vo/ **→VOTRE**.

votant, ∼e /vɔtɑ̃, -t/ *nm, f* voter.

vote /vɔt/ *nm* (action) voting; (suffrage) vote; **∼ d'une loi** passing of a bill; **∼ par correspondance/procuration** postal/proxy vote.

voter /vɔte/ **1** *vi* vote. ● *vt* vote

v

for; (adopter) pass; (crédits) vote.

votre (pl **vos**) /vɔtʀ, vo/ adj your.

vôtre /votʀ/ pron le ou la ~, les ~s yours.

vouer /vwe/ **1** vt (vie, temps) dedicate (à to); **voué à l'échec** doomed to failure.

vouloir /vulwaʀ/ **84** vt (exiger) want (**faire** to do); (souhaiter) want; **que veux-tu boire?** what would you like to drink?; **je voudrais bien y aller** I'd really like to go; **je veux bien venir** I'm happy to come; **comme tu voudras** as you wish; (accepter) **veuillez vous asseoir** please sit down; **veuillez patienter** (au téléphone) please hold the line; (signifier) ~ **dire** mean; **qu'est-ce que cela veut dire?** what does that mean?; **en** ~ **à qn** bear a grudge against sb. □ **s'en** ~ vpr regret; **je m'en veux de lui avoir dit** I really regret having told her.

voulu, ~**e** /vuly/ adj (délibéré) intentional; (requis) required.

vous /vu/ pron (sujet, complément) you; (indirect) (to) you; (réfléchi) yourself; (pluriel) yourselves; (l'un l'autre) each other. **vous-même** pron yourself. **vous-mêmes** pron yourselves.

voûte /vut/ nf (plafond) vault; (porche) archway.

vouvoiement /vuvwamã/ nm use of the 'vous' form. **vouvoyer** **31** vt address using the 'vous' form.

voyage /vwajaʒ/ nm trip (déplacement) journey; (par mer) voyage; ~**(s)** (action) travelling; ~ **d'affaires** business trip; ~ **d'études** study trip; ~ **de noces** honeymoon; ~ **organisé** (package) tour.

voyager /vwajaʒe/ **40** vi travel.

voyageur, -euse /vwajaʒœʀ, -øz/ nm, f traveller; (passager) passenger;

~ **de commerce** travelling salesman.

voyant, ~**e** /vwajã, -t/ adj gaudy. ● nm (signal) (warning) light.

voyelle /vwajɛl/ nf vowel.

voyou /vwaju/ nm hooligan.

vrac /vʀak/ loc (pêle-mêle) haphazardly; (sans emballage) loose; (en gros) in bulk.

vrai, ~**e** /vʀɛ/ adj true; (authentique) real. ● nm truth; **à** ~ **dire** to tell the truth; **pour de** ~ for real. **vraiment** adv really.

vraisemblable /vʀɛsɑ̃blabl/ adj (probable) likely; (excuse, histoire) plausible. **vraisemblablement** adv probably. **vraisemblance** nf likelihood, plausibility.

vrombir /vʀɔ̃biʀ/ **2** vi roar.

VRP abrév m (**voyageur représentant placier**) rep, representative.

VTC abrév m (**vélo tous chemins**) hybrid bike.

VTT abrév m (**vélo tout terrain**) mountain bike.

vu, ~**e** /vy/ adj; bien ~ well thought of; **ce serait plutôt mal** ~ it wouldn't go down well; **bien** ~**!** good point! ● prép in view of; ~ **que** seeing that. ● →**VOIR** **84**.

vue /vy/ nf (spectacle) sight; (vision) (eye) sight; (panorama, idée, image, photo) view; **avoir en** ~ have in mind; **à** ~ (tirer) on sight; (payable) at sight; **de** ~ by sight; **perdre de** ~ lose sight of; **en** ~ (proche) in sight; (célèbre) in the public eye; **en** ~ **de faire** with a view to doing; **à** ~ **d'œil** visibly; **avoir des** ~**s sur** have designs on.

vulgaire /vylgɛʀ/ adj (grossier) vulgar; (ordinaire) common.

vulnérable /vylneʀabl/ adj vulnerable.

Ww

wagon /vagɔ̃/ nm (de voyageurs) carriage; (de marchandises) wagon. **wagon-lit** (pl **wagons-lits**) nm sleeper. **wagon-restaurant** (pl **wagons-restaurants**) nm restaurant car.

walkman® /wokman/ nm personal stereo, walkman®.

Wallon A regional Romance language spoken in southern Belgium (*Wallonie*) by approximately 600,000 *Wallons*. It belongs to the same linguistic family as the French language, and is sometimes considered a French dialect. *Wallon* should not be confused with Belgian French, which differs from the French of France in pronunciation and vocabulary only.

waters /watɛʀ/ nmpl toilets.
watt /wat/ nm watt.
wc /(dubla)vese/ nmpl toilet (+ sg).
Web /wɛb/ nm Web; **un site** ~ a website; **une page** ~ web page.
webcam /wɛbkam/ nf webcam.
webmestre /wɛbmɛstʀ/ nm webmaster.
week-end /wikɛnd/ nm weekend.
whisky (pl **-ies**) /wiski/ nm whisky.

Xx

xénophobe /gzenɔfɔb/ adj xenophobic. ● nmf xenophone.
xérès /gzeʀes/ nm sherry.
xylophone /ksilɔfɔn/ nm xylophone.

Yy

y /i/
● *adverbe*
····▸ there; (dessus) on it; (pluriel) on them; (dedans) in it; (pluriel) in them; **j'**~ **vais** I'm on my way; **n'**~ **va pas** don't go; **du lait? il n'**~ **en a pas** milk? there's none; **tu n'**~ **arriveras jamais** you'll never manage it.
● *pronom*
····▸ **s'**~ **habituer** get used to it.
····▸ **s'**~ **attendre** expect it.
····▸ ~ **penser** think about it.
····▸ **être pour qch** have sth to do with it.

yaourt /jauʀ(t) / nm yoghurt.
yaourtière nf yoghurt-maker.
yard /jaʀd/ nm yard (= 91,44 cm).
yen /'jɛn/ nm yen.
yeux /jø/ ➡ **ŒIL.**
yoga /jɔga/ nm yoga.
yougoslave /'jugɔslav/ adj Yugoslav. **Y~** nmf Yugoslav.
Yougoslavie /'jugɔslavi/ nf

Yugoslavia.

yo-yo® /'jojo/ *nm inv* yo-yo®.

• •

Zz

• •

zapper /zape/ **1** *vi* (à la télévision) channel-hop.

zèbre /zɛbʀ/ *nm* zebra.

zèle /zɛl/ *nm* zeal.

zéro /zeʀo/ *nm* nought, zero; (température) zero; (Sport) nil; (tennis) love; (personne) nonentity; **partir de ~** start from scratch; **repartir à ~** start all over again.

zeste /zɛst/ *nm* peel; **un ~ de** (fig)

a touch of.

zézayer /zezeje/ **31** *vi* lisp.

zigzag /zigzag/ *nm* zigzag; **en ~** winding.

zinc /zɛ̃g/ *nm* (métal) zinc; (comptoir **1**) bar.

zizanie /zizani/ *nf* discord; **semer la ~** put the cat among the pigeons.

zizi /zizi/ *nm* **1** willy.

zodiaque /zɔdjak/ *nm* zodiac.

zona /zona/ *nm* (Méd) shingles (+ *sg*).

zone /zon/ *nf* zone, area; (banlieue pauvre) slums; **~ bleue** restricted parking zone; **~ euro** eurozone.

zoo /zo(o)/ *nm* zoo.

zoom /zum/ *nm* zoom lens.

zut /zyt/ *interj* **1** damn **1**.

Phrasefinder

Key phrases

yes, please
no, thank you
sorry
excuse me
you're welcome
hello/goodbye
how are you?
nice to meet you

Asking questions

do you speak English/French?
what's your name?
where are you from?
how much is it?
how far is it?
where is...?
can I have...?
would you like...?

Statements about yourself

my name is...
I'm English
I'm French
I don't speak French/English
  very well
I'm here on holiday
I live near Sheffield
I'm a student

Emergencies

can you help me?
I'm lost
I'm ill
call an ambulance
watch out!

Phrases-clés

oui, s'il vous plaît
non merci
désolé/-e
excusez-moi
de rien
bonjour/au revoir
comment allez-vous?
enchanté/-e!

Poser des questions

parlez-vous anglais/français?
comment vous appelez-vous?
d'où venez-vous?
combien ça coûte?
c'est loin d'ici?
où est...?
est-ce que je peux avoir...?
voulez-vous...?

Parler de soi

je m'appelle...
je suis anglais/-e
je suis français/-e
je ne parle pas très bien
  français/anglais
je suis en vacances ici
j'habite près de Sheffield
je suis étudiant/-e

Urgences

pouvez-vous m'aider?
je me suis perdu/-e
je suis malade
appelez une ambulance
attention!

❶ Going Places

On the road	Par la route
where's the nearest petrol station/filling station (US)?	où se trouve la station-service la plus proche?
what's the best way to get there?	quel est le meilleur chemin pour y aller?
I've got a puncture	j'ai crevé
I'd like to hire a bike/car	je voudrais louer un vélo/une voiture
I'm looking for somewhere to park	je cherche un endroit pour me garer
there's been an accident	il y a eu un accident
my car's broken down	ma voiture est en panne
the car won't start	la voiture ne démarre pas

By rail	Par le train
where can I buy a ticket?	où est-ce que je peux acheter un billet?
what time is the next train to Paris?	à quelle heure est le prochain train pour Paris?
do I have to change?	est-ce qu'il y a un changement?
can I take my bike on the train?	est-ce que je peux prendre mon vélo dans le train?
which platform for the train to Bath?	de quel quai part le train pour Bath?
there's a train to London at 10 o'clock	il y a un train pour Londres à 10 heures
a single/return to Nice, please	un aller/aller-retour pour Nice, s'il vous plaît
I'd like an all-day ticket	je voudrais un billet valable toute la journée
I'd like to reserve a seat	je voudrais réserver une place

At the airport	Par avion
when's the next flight to Paris/Rome?	quand part le prochain avion pour Paris/Rome?
what time do I have to check in?	à quelle heure est-ce que je dois me présenter à l'enregistrement?
where do I check in?	où est le comptoir d'enregistrement?
I'd like to confirm my flight	je voudrais confirmer mon vol
I'd like a window seat	je voudrais une place côté fenêtre
I want to change/cancel my reservation	je voudrais modifier/annuler ma réservation

Getting there	Trouver son chemin
could you tell me the way to the castle?	pourriez-vous m'indiquer la route pour aller au château?
how long will it take to get there?	combien de temps est-ce qu'il faut pour y arriver?
how far is it from here?	c'est loin d'ici?
which bus do I take for the cathedral?	quel bus est-ce que je dois prendre pour aller à la cathédrale?
can you tell me where to get off?	pouvez-vous me dire où je dois descendre?
how much is the fare to the town centre/center (US)?	quel est le prix d'un billet pour le centre-ville?
what time is the last bus?	à quelle heure est le dernier bus?
how do I get to the airport?	comment est-ce que je fais pour aller à l'aéroport?
where's the nearest underground/subway (US) station?	où est la station de métro la plus proche?
can you call me a taxi, please?	pouvez-vous m'appeler un taxi, s'il vous plaît?
take the first turning right	prenez la première rue à droite
turn left at the traffic lights	prenez à gauche aux feux
just past the church	juste après l'église

❷ Keeping in touch

On the phone	Au téléphone
where can I buy a phone card?	où est-ce que je peux acheter une carte de téléphone?
may I use your phone?	est-ce que je peux utiliser votre téléphone?
do you have a mobile?	avez-vous un portable?
what is the code for Lyons/ St Albans?	quel est l'indicatif pour Lyon/ St Albans?
I want to make a phone call	je veux téléphoner
I'd like to reverse the charges/ to call collect (US)	je voudrais appeler en PCV
the line's engaged/busy (US)	la ligne est occupée
there's no answer	ça ne répond pas
hello, this is Danielle	allô, c'est Danielle
is Alistair there, please?	est-ce qu'Alistair est là, s'il vous plaît?
who's calling?	qui est à l'appareil?
sorry, wrong number	désolé/-e, vous faites erreur
just a moment, please	un instant, s'il vous plaît
would you like to hold?	vous patientez?
please tell him/her I called	pourriez-vous lui dire que j'ai appelé?
I'd like to leave a message for him/her	j'aimerais lui laisser un message
I'll try again later	je réessaierai plus tard
can he/she ring me back?	est-ce qu'il/elle peut me rappeler?
my home number is...	mon numéro personnel est le...
my business number is...	mon numéro professionnel est le...
my fax number is...	mon numéro de télécopie est le...
we were cut off	on a été coupé

'Vous' is used when being generally polite (e.g. a child to a teacher, a customer to a shopkeeper, a tourist asking directions). When speaking to a friend or a member of the family, 'tu' is used instead of 'vous'.

Writing | Écrire

what's your address?	quelle est votre adresse?
here's my business card	voici ma carte de visite
where is the nearest post office?	où est le bureau de poste le plus proche?
could I have a stamp for France/Italy, please?	je voudrais un timbre pour la France/l'Italie, s'il vous plaît
I'd like to send a parcel/a telegram	je voudrais envoyer un paquet/un télégramme

On line | En ligne

are you on the Internet?	êtes-vous sur Internet?
what's your e-mail address?	quelle est votre adresse électronique?
we could send it by e-mail	nous pourrions l'envoyer par courrier électronique
I'll e-mail it to you on Thursday	je vous l'envoie jeudi par courrier électronique
I looked it up on the Internet	j'ai vérifié sur Internet
the information is on their website	l'information se trouve sur leur site Internet

Meeting up | Se retrouver

what shall we do this evening?	qu'est-ce qu'on fait ce soir?
where shall we meet?	où est-ce qu'on se retrouve?
I'll see you outside the café at 6 o'clock	on se retrouve à 6 heures devant le café
see you later	à tout à l'heure
I can't today, I'm busy	je ne peux pas aujourd'hui, je suis occupé/-e

❸ Food and Drink

Booking a table

can you recommend a good restaurant?

I'd like to reserve a table for four

a reservation for tomorrow evening at eight o'clock

I booked a table for two

Réserver une table

pouvez-vous me recommander un bon restaurant?

je voudrais réserver une table pour quatre personnes

une réservation pour demain soir à huit heures

j'ai réservé une table pour deux

Ordering

could we see the menu/wine list?

do you have a vegetarian/children's menu?

what would you recommend?

I'd like a white/black coffee

... an expresso,

... a decaffeinated coffee

... a tea/a herbal tea

... a liqueur

could I have the bill, (*Amer*) check?

we'd like to pay separately

Passer commande

est-ce qu'on pourrait voir la carte/la carte des vins?

est-ce que vous avez un menu végétarien/enfant?

Que (nous) conseillez-vous?

J'aimerais un café/un café noir

... un expresso, .

... un café décaféiné

... un thé/une infusion

... un digestif

l'addition, s'il vous plaît

on voudrait payer séparément

You will hear

Désirez-vous un apéritif?

Souhaitez-vous commander?

Désirez-vous une entrée?

Quel plat avez-vous choisi?

Je (vous) conseille le/la...

Souhaitez-vous prendre un dessert?

Désirez-vous un café/un digestif?

Anything else?

Bon appétit!

On vous dira

Would you like an aperitif?

Are you ready to order?

Would you like a starter?

What will you have for the main course?

I can recommend the ...

Would you like a dessert?

Would you like coffee?/a liqueur?

Désirez-vous autre chose?

Enjoy your meal!

Menu

Starters

hors d'œuvres	hors d'œuvres
omelette	omelette
soup	soupe

Fish

bass	perche
cod	cabillaud
eel	anguille
hake	colin
herring	hareng
monkfish	lotte
mullet	mulet
mussels	moules
oysters	huîtres
prawns	crevettes roses
salmon	saumon
sardines	sardines
shrimps	crevettes grises
sole	sole
squid	cal(a)mar
trout	truite
tuna	thon
turbot	turbot

Meat

beef	bœuf
chicken	poulet
duck	canard
goose	oie
guinea fowl	pintade
hare	lièvre
kidneys	rognons
lamb	agneau
liver	foie
pork	porc
rabbit	lapin
steak	bifteck
veal	veau
wild boar	sanglier

La carte/Le menu

Entrées

hors d'œuvres	hors d'oeuvres
omelette	omelette
soupe	soup

Poisson

anguille	eel
cabillaud	cod
cal(a)mar	squid
colin	hake
crevettes grises	shrimp
crevettes roses	prawns
hareng	herring
huîtres	oysters
lotte	monkfish
moules	mussels
mulet	mullet
perche	bass
sardines	sardines
saumon	salmon
sole	sole
thon	tuna
truite	trout
turbot	turbot

Viande

agneau	lamb
bifteck	steak
bœuf	beef
canard	duck
foie	liver
lapin	rabbit
lièvre	hare
oie	goose
pintade	guinea fowl
porc	pork
poulet	chicken
rognons	kidneys
sanglier	wild boar
veau	veal

❸ Food and Drink

Vegetables

		Légumes	
artichoke	artichaut	artichauts	artichoke
asparagus	asperges	asperges	asparagus
aubergine	aubergine	aubergines	aubergine
cabbage	chou	carottes	carrot
carrot	carrotte	céleri	celery
cauliflower	chou-fleur	champignons	mushrooms
celery	céleri	chou	cabbage
courgettes	courgettes	chou-fleur	cauliflower
endives	endives	courgettes	courgettes
green beans	haricots verts	endives	endives
mushrooms	champignons	épinards	spinach
onions	oignons	haricots verts	green beans
peas	petits pois	oignons	onions
pepper	poivron	petits pois	peas
potatoes	pommes de terre	poivrons	peppers
spinach	épinards	pommes de terre	potatoes

The way it's cooked

		La cuisson	
fried	poêlé	à la vapeur	steamed
grilled	grillé	à point	medium rare
medium rare	à point	bien cuit	well done
pureed	mixé	bleu	very rare
rare	saignant	cuit à l'étouffée	stewed
roast	rôti	grillé	grilled
steamed	à la vapeur	mixé	pureed
stewed	cuit à l'étouffée	poêlé	fried
very rare	bleu	rôti	roast
well done	bien cuit	saignant	rare

Desserts and cheese

		Fromages et desserts	
cheese board	plateau de fromages	fruit	fruit
		glace	ice cream
fruit	fruit	plateau de fromages	cheese board
ice cream	glace		
pie	tarte (recouverte de pâte)	sorbet	sorbet
		tarte	tart
sorbet	sorbet	tarte (recouverte de pâte)	pie
tart	tarte		

Sundries

bread	pain
butter	beurre
herbs	herbes
mayonnaise	mayonnaise
mustard	moutarde
olive oil	huile d'olive
pepper	poivre
salt	sel
sauce	sauce
seasoning	assaisonnement
vinegar	vinaigre

Drinks

beer	bière
bottle	bouteille
carbonated	gazeux
half-bottle	demi-bouteille
liqueur	digestif
mineral water	eau minérale
red wine	vin rouge
rosé	rosé
soft drinks	boissons non alcoolisées
still	plat, non gazeux
table wine	vin de table
white wine	vin blanc
wine	vin

Divers

assaisonnement	seasoning
beurre	butter
herbes	herbs
huile d'olive	olive oil
mayonnaise	mayonnaise
moutarde	mustard
pain	bread
poivre	pepper
sauce	sauce
sel	salt
vinaigre	vinegar

Boissons

bière	beer
boissons non alcoolisées	soft drinks
bouteille	bottle
demi-bouteille	half-bottle
digestif	liqueur
eau minérale	mineral water
gazeux	carbonated
plat	still
rosé	rosé
vin	wine
vin blanc	white wine
vin de table	table wine
vin rouge	red wine

❹ Places to stay

Camping | Camper

can we pitch our tent here?	est-ce qu'on peut planter notre tente ici?
can we park our caravan here?	est-ce qu'on peut mettre notre caravane ici?
what are the facilities like?	le camping est-il bien équipé?
how much is it per night?	c'est combien par nuit?
where do we park the car?	où est-ce qu'on peut garer la voiture?
we're looking for a campsite	on cherche un camping
this is a list of local campsites	c'est une liste des campings de la région
we go on a camping holiday every year	nous partons camper chaque année pour les vacances

At the hotel | À l'hôtel

I'd like a double/single room with bath	je voudrais une chambre double/simple avec bain
we have a reservation in the name of Milne	nous avons une réservation au nom de Milne
we'll be staying three nights, from Friday to Sunday	nous resterons trois nuits, de vendredi à dimanche
how much does the room cost?	combien coûte la chambre?
I'd like to see the room, please	je voudrais voir la chambre, s'il vous plaît
what time is breakfast?	à quelle heure est le petit déjeuner?
bed and breakfast	chambres d'hôtes
we'd like to stay another night	on voudrait rester une nuit de plus
please call me at 7:30	réveillez-moi à 7h30
are there any messages for me?	est-ce qu'il y a des messages pour moi?

Hostels

could you tell me where the youth hostel is?

what time does the hostel close?

I'm staying in a hostel

I know a really good hostel in Dublin

I'd like to go backpacking in Australia

Rooms to let

I'm looking for a room with a reasonable rent

I'd like to rent an apartment for a few weeks

where do I find out about rooms to let?

what's the weekly rent?

I'm staying with friends at the moment

I rent an apartment on the outskirts of town

the room's fine – I'll take it

the deposit is one month's rent in advance

Auberges de jeunesse

pourriez-vous me dire où se trouve l'auberge de jeunesse?

à quelle heure ferme l'auberge de jeunesse?

je loge à l'auberge de jeunesse

je connais une très bonne auberge de jeunesse à Dublin

j'aimerais bien aller faire de la randonnée en Australie

Locations

je cherche une chambre à louer avec un loyer raisonnable

je voudrais louer un appartement pendant quelques semaines

où est-ce que je peux me renseigner sur des chambres à louer?

quel est le montant du loyer pour la semaine?

je loge chez des amis pour le moment

je loue un appartement en banlieue

la chambre est bien – je la prends

l'acompte correspond à un mois de loyer payable d'avance

❺ Shopping and money

At the bank	À la banque
I'd like to change some money	je voudrais changer de l'argent
I want to change some francs into pounds	je veux changer des francs en livres
do you take Eurocheques?	acceptez-vous les Eurochèques?
what's the exchange rate today?	quel est le taux de change aujourd'hui?
I prefer traveller's cheques/ traveler's checks (US) to cash	je préfère les chèques de voyage à l'argent liquide
I'd like to transfer some money from my account	je voudrais retirer de l'argent sur mon compte
I'll get some money from the cash machine	je vais retirer de l'argent au distributeur
I usually pay by direct debit	d'habitude, je paye par prélèvement automatique

Finding the right shop	Trouver le bon magasin
where's the main shopping district?	où se trouve le principal quartier commerçant?
where's a good place to buy sunglasses?	quel est le meilleur endroit pour acheter des lunettes de soleil?
where can I buy batteries/ postcards?	où est-ce que je peux acheter des piles/cartes postales?
where's the nearest chemist/ bookshop?	où est la pharmacie/librairie la plus proche?
is there a good food shop around here?	est-ce qu'il y a une bonne épicerie près d'ici?
what time do the shops open/ close?	à quelle heure ouvrent/ ferment les magasins?
where did you get those?	où les avez-vous trouvés?
I'm looking for presents for my family	je cherche des cadeaux pour ma famille
we'll do all our shopping on Saturday	nous ferons toutes nos courses samedi

Are you being served?	**On s'occupe de vous?**
how much does that cost?	combien ça coûte?
can I try it on?	est-ce que je peux l'essayer?
can you keep it for me?	pouvez-vous me le/la garder?
do you have this in another colour/ color (US)?	est-ce que vous avez ce modèle-ci dans une autre couleur?
I'm just looking	je regarde
I'll think about it	je vais réfléchir
I need a bigger/smaller size	il me faut une taille au-dessus/au-dessous
I take a size 10/a medium	je fais du 38/il me faut une taille moyenne
it doesn't suit me	ça ne me va pas
could you wrap it for me, please?	pourriez-vous l'emballer, s'il vous plaît?
do you take credit cards?	est-ce que vous acceptez les cartes de crédit?
can I pay by cheque/check (US)?	est-ce que je peux payer par chèque?
I'm sorry, I don't have any change	je suis désolé/-e mais je n'ai pas de monnaie
I'd like a receipt, please	je voudrais un reçu, s'il vous plaît

Changing things	**Faire un échange**
can I have a refund?	j'aimerais être remboursé/-e
can you mend it for me?	est-ce que vous pouvez me le/la réparer?
can I speak to the manager?	je voudrais parler au responsable
it doesn't work	ça ne marche pas
I'd like to change it, please	je voudrais l'échanger, s'il vous plaît
I bought this here yesterday	je l'ai acheté/-e ici hier

❻ Sport and leisure

Keeping fit	Rester en bonne santé
where can we play football/squash?	où est-ce qu'on peut jouer au football/squash?
where is the sports centre/center (US)?	où se trouve le centre sportif?
what's the charge per day?	quel est le prix pour la journée?
is there a reduction for children/a student discount?	est-ce qu'il y a des réductions enfants/étudiants?
I'm looking for a swimming pool/tennis court	je cherche une piscine/un court de tennis
you have to be a member	vous devez être membre
I play tennis on Mondays	je joue au tennis le lundi
I would like to go fishing/riding	je voudrais aller à la pêche/monter à cheval
I want to do aerobics	je veux faire de l'aérobic
I love swimming/snowboarding	j'adore nager/faire du snowboard
we want to hire skis/rollerblades	nous voulons louer des skis/rollers

Watching sport	Le sport en spectateur
is there a football match on Saturday?	est-ce qu'il y a un match de foot samedi?
which teams are playing?	quelles sont les équipes qui jouent?
where can I get tickets?	où est-ce que je peux acheter des billets?
I'd like to see a rugby/football match	je voudrais voir un match de rugby/foot
my favourite/favorite (US) team is...	mon équipe préférée est...
let's watch the match on TV	regardons le match à la télé

Going to the cinema/theatre/club	**Aller au cinéma/théâtre/en boîte**
what's on?	qu'est-ce qu'il y a au programme?
when does the box office open/close?	à quelle heure ouvre/ferme le guichet?
what time does the concert/performance start?	à quelle heure commence le concert/ la représentation?
when does it finish?	à quelle heure ça finit?
are there any seats left for tonight?	est-ce qu'il y a encore des places pour ce soir?
how much are the tickets?	combien coûtent les billets?
where can I get a programme/program (US)?	où est-ce que je peux me procurer un programme?
I want to book tickets for tonight's performance	je veux réserver des places pour la représentation de ce soir
I'll book seats in the circle/in the stalls	je vais réserver des places au balcon/à l'orchestre
we'd like to go to a club	on voudrait aller en boîte
I go clubbing every weekend	je vais en boîte tous les week-ends

Hobbies	**Passe-temps**
do you have any hobbies?	est-ce que vous avez des passe-temps?
what do you do at the weekend?	que faites-vous le week-end?
I like yoga/listening to music	j'aime le yoga/écouter de la musique
I spend a lot of time surfing the Net	je passe beaucoup de temps à surfer sur l'Internet
I read a lot	je lis beaucoup
I collect comic strips	je collectionne les bandes dessinées

❼ Good timing

Telling the time

could you tell me the time?

what time is it?

it's 2 o'clock

at about 8 o'clock

at 9 o'clock tomorrow

from 10 o'clock onwards

it starts at 8 p.m.

at 5 o'clock in the morning/afternoon

it's five past/quarter past/
half past one

it's twenty-five to/quarter to/
five to one

a quarter of an hour

Exprimer l'heure

pourriez-vous me dire l'heure?

quelle heure est-il?

il est 2 heures

vers 8 heures

à 9 heures demain

à partir de 10 heures

ça commence à 20 heures

à 5 heures du matin/de l'après-midi

il est une heure cinq/et quart/
et demie

il est une heure moins
vingt-cinq/le quart/cinq

un quart d'heure

Days and dates

Sunday, Monday, Tuesday,
Wednesday, Thursday, Friday,
Saturday

January, February, March,
April, May, June, July,
August, September, October,
November, December

what's the date today?

it's the second of June

what day is it? it's Monday

we meet up every Monday

she comes on Tuesdays

we're going away in August

on November 8th

Jours et dates

dimanche, lundi, mardi,
mercredi, jeudi, vendredi,
samedi

janvier, février, mars,
avril, mai, juin, juillet,
août, septembre, octobre,
novembre, décembre

on est le combien aujourd'hui?

on est le deux juin

on est quel jour? on est lundi

on se réunit tous les lundis

elle vient le mardi

nous partons en août

le 8 novembre

Public holidays and special days	Jours fériés
Bank holiday	jour férié
long weekend	week-end prolongé
New Year's Day (1 Jan)	le Jour de l'an
St Valentine's Day (14 Feb)	la Saint-Valentin
Shrove Tuesday/Pancake Day	Mardi gras
Ash Wednesday	le mercredi des Cendres
Mother's Day	la fête des Mères
Palm Sunday	le dimanche des Rameaux
Good Friday	vendredi saint
Easter Day	Pâques
Easter Monday	le lundi de Pâques
Ascension Day	l'Ascension
Pentecost/Whitsun	la Pentecôte
Whit Monday	le lundi de Pentecôte
Father's Day	la fête des Pères
St John the Baptist's Day (24 Jun)	la Saint-Jean
Independence day (4 Jul)	la fête de l'Indépendance (aux États-Unis)
Bastille day (14 July)	le 14 juillet
Halloween (31 Oct)	Halloween (soir des fantômes et des sorcières)
All Saints' Day (1 Nov)	la Toussaint
Guy Fawkes Day/Bonfire Night (5 Nov)	fête de la Conspiration des Poudres avec feux de joie et feux d'artifice
Remembrance Sunday	le jour du Souvenir
Thanksgiving	le jour d'Action de grâces
Christmas Day (25 Dec)	Noël
Boxing Day (26 Dec)	le lendemain de Noël
New Year's Eve (31 Dec)	la Saint-Sylvestre

❽ Conversion charts/Conversion

Length/Longueur

inches/pouces	0.39	3.9	7.8	11.7	15.6	19.7	39
cm/centimètres	1	10	20	30	40	50	100

Distance/Distance

miles/miles	0.62	6.2	12.4	18.6	24.9	31	62
km/kilomètres	1	10	20	30	40	50	100

Weight/Poids

pounds/livres	2.2	22	44	66	88	110	220
kg/kilogrammes	1	10	20	30	40	50	100

Capacity/Contenance

gallons/gallons	0.22	2.2	4.4	6.6	8.8	11	22
litres/litres	1	10	20	30	40	50	100

Temperature/Température

°C	0	5	10	15	20	25	30	37	38	40
°F	32	41	50	59	68	77	86	98.4	100	104

Clothing and shoe sizes/Tailles et pointures

Women's clothing sizes/Tailles femme

UK	8	10	12	14	16	18
US	6	8	10	12	14	16
France	36	38	40	42	44	46

Men's clothing sizes/Tailles homme

UK/US	36	38	40	42	44	46
France	46	48	50	52	54	56

Men's and women's shoes/Pointures homme et femme

UK women	4	5	6	7	7.5	8			
UK men				6	7	8	9	10	11
US	6.5	7.5	8.5	9.5	10.5	11.5	12.5	13.5	14.5
France	37	38	39	40	41	42	43	44	45

a /eɪ, ə/ *determiner*

an avant voyelle ou h muet.

➡ For expressions such as **make a noise, make a fortune** → **noise, fortune.**

····➤ un/une. **~ tree** un arbre; **~ chair** une chaise.

····➤ (per) **two euros ~ kilo** deux euros le kilo; **three times ~ day** trois fois par jour.

❗ When talking about what people do or are, **a** is not translated into French: **she's a teacher** elle est professeur; **he's a widower** il est veuf.

aback /əˈbæk/ *adv* **taken ~** déconcerté.

abandon /əˈbændən/ *vt* abandonner. ● *n* abandon *m*.

abate /əˈbeɪt/ *vi* (*flood, fever*) baisser; (*storm*) se calmer. ● *vt* diminuer.

abbey /ˈæbɪ/ *n* abbaye *f*.

abbot /ˈæbət/ *n* abbé *m*.

abbreviate /əˈbriːvɪeɪt/ *vt* abréger. **abbreviation** *n* abréviation *f*.

abdicate /ˈæbdɪkeɪt/ *vt/i* abdiquer.

abdomen /ˈæbdəmən/ *n* abdomen *m*.

abduct /əbˈdʌkt/ *vt* enlever. **abductor** *n* ravisseur/-euse *m/f*.

abhor /əbˈhɔː(r)/ *vt* (*pt* **abhorred**) exécrer.

abide /əˈbaɪd/ *vt* supporter; **~ by**

respecter.

ability /əˈbɪlətɪ/ *n* capacité *f* (**to do** à faire); (*talent*) talent *m*.

abject /ˈæbdʒekt/ *adj* (*state*) misérable; (*coward*) abject.

ablaze /əˈbleɪz/ *adj* en feu.

able /ˈeɪbl/ *adj* (*skilled*) compétent; **be ~ to do** pouvoir faire; (*know how to*) savoir faire. **ably** *adv* avec compétence.

abnormal /æbˈnɔːml/ *adj* anormal. **abnormality** *n* anomalie *f*.

aboard /əˈbɔːd/ *adv* à bord. ● *prep* à bord de.

abode /əˈbəʊd/ *n* demeure *f*; **of no fixed ~** sans domicile fixe.

abolish /əˈbɒlɪʃ/ *vt* abolir.

Aborigine /æbəˈrɪdʒənɪ/ *n* aborigène *mf* (d'Australie).

abort /əˈbɔːt/ *vt* faire avorter; (*Comput*) abandonner. ● *vi* avorter.

abortion /əˈbɔːʃn/ *n* avortement *m*; **have an ~** se faire avorter.

abortive /əˈbɔːtɪv/ *adj* (*attempt*) avorté; (*coup*) manqué.

about /əˈbaʊt/ *adv* (*approximately*) environ; **~ the same** à peu près pareil; **there was no-one ~** il n'y avait personne. ● *prep* **it's ~ ...** il s'agit de ...; **what I like ~ her** is ce que j'aime chez elle c'est; **to wander ~ the streets** errer dans les rues; **how/what ~ some tea?** et si on prenait un thé?; **what ~ you?** et toi? ● *adj* **be ~ to do** être sur le point de faire; **be up and ~** être debout. **~-face, ~-turn** *n* (*fig*) volte-face *f inv*.

above /əˈbʌv/ *prep* au-dessus de;

he is not ∼ **lying** il n'est pas incapable de mentir; ∼ **all** surtout. ● adv **the apartment** ∼ l'appartement du dessus; **see** ∼ voir ci-dessus. ∼**-board** adj honnête. ∼**-mentioned** adj susmentionné.

abrasive /əˈbreɪsɪv/ adj abrasif; (manner) mordant. ● n abrasif m.

abreast /əˈbrest/ adv de front; **keep** ∼ **of** se tenir au courant de.

abroad /əˈbrɔːd/ adv à l'étranger.

abrupt /əˈbrʌpt/ adj (sudden, curt) brusque; (steep) abrupt. **abruptly** adv (suddenly) brusquement; (curtly) avec brusquerie.

abscess /ˈæbses/ n abcès m.

abseil /ˈæbseɪl/ vi descendre en rappel.

absence /ˈæbsəns/ n absence f; (lack) manque m; **in the** ∼ **of** faute de.

absent /ˈæbsənt/ adj absent.

absentee /æbsənˈtiː/ n absent/-e m/f.

absent-minded adj distrait.

absolute /ˈæbsəluːt/ adj (monarch, majority) absolu; (chaos, idiot) véritable. **absolutely** adv absolument.

absolve /əbˈzɒlv/ vt ∼ **sb of sth** décharger qn de qch.

absorb /əbˈzɔːb/ vt absorber.

abstain /əbˈsteɪn/ vi s'abstenir (from de).

abstract[1] /ˈæbstrækt/ adj abstrait. ● n (summary) résumé m; **in the** ∼ dans l'abstrait.

abstract[2] /əbˈstrækt/ vt tirer.

absurd /əbˈsɜːd/ adj absurde.

abundance /əˈbʌndəns/ n abondance f. **abundant** adj abondant. **abundantly** adv (entirely) tout à fait.

abuse[1] /əˈbjuːz/ vt (position) abuser de; (person) maltraiter; (insult) injurier.

abuse[2] /əˈbjuːs/ n (misuse) abus m (of de); (cruelty) mauvais traitement m; (insults) injures fpl.

abusive /əˈbjuːsɪv/ adj (person) grossier; (language) injurieux.

abysmal /əˈbɪzml/ adj épouvantable.

abyss /əˈbɪs/ n abîme m.

academic /ækəˈdemɪk/ adj (career) universitaire; (year) académique; (scholarly) intellectuel; (theoretical) théorique. ● n universitaire mf.

academy /əˈkædəmɪ/ n (school) école f; (society) académie f.

accelerate /əkˈseləreɪt/ vi (speed up) s'accélérer; (Auto) accélérer. **accelerator** n accélérateur m.

accent[1] /ˈæksent/ n accent m.

accent[2] /ækˈsent/ vt accentuer.

accept /əkˈsept/ vt accepter. **acceptable** adj acceptable. **acceptance** n (of offer) acceptation f; (of proposal) approbation f.

access /ˈækses/ n accès m. **accessible** adj accessible.

accessory /əkˈsesərɪ/ adj accessoire. ● n (Jur) complice mf (to de).

accident /ˈæksɪdənt/ n accident m; (chance) hasard m; **by** ∼ par hasard. **accidental** adj (death) accidentel; (meeting) fortuit. **accidentally** adv accidentellement; (by chance) par hasard.

acclaim /əˈkleɪm/ vt applaudir. ● n louanges fpl.

acclimatize /əˈklaɪmətaɪz/ vt/i (s')acclimater (to à).

accommodate /əˈkɒmədeɪt/ vt loger; (adapt to) s'adapter à; (satisfy) satisfaire. **accommodating** adj accommodant. **accommodation** n logement m.

accompaniment /əˈkʌmpənɪmənt/ n accompagnement m

m. **accompany** *vt* accompagner.

accomplice /ə'kʌmplɪs/ *n* complice *mf* (**in, to** de).

accomplish /ə'kʌmplɪʃ/ *vt* accomplir; (*objective*) réaliser. **accomplished** *adj* très compétent. **accomplishment** *n* (feat) réussite *f*; (talent) talent *m*.

accord /ə'kɔːd/ *vi* concorder (**with** avec). ● *vt* accorder (**sb sth** qch à qn). ● *n* accord *m*; **of my own ~** de moi-même.

accordance /ə'kɔːdəns/ *n* **in ~ with** conformément à.

according /ə'kɔːdɪŋ/ *adv* **~ to** (*principle, law*) selon; (*person, book*) d'après. **accordingly** *adv* en conséquence.

accordion /ə'kɔːdɪən/ *n* accordéon *m*.

accost /ə'kɒst/ *vt* aborder.

account /ə'kaʊnt/ *n* (Comm) compte *m*; (description) compte-rendu *m*; **on ~ of** à cause de; **on no ~** en aucun cas; **take into ~** tenir compte de; **it's of no ~** peu importe. □ **~ for** (explain) expliquer; (represent) représenter. **accountability** *n* responsabilité *f*. **accountable** *adj* responsable (**for** de; **to** envers).

accountancy /ə'kaʊntənsɪ/ *n* comptabilité *f*. **accountant** *n* comptable *mf*. **accounts** *npl* comptabilité *f*, comptes *mpl*.

accumulate /ə'kjuːmjʊleɪt/ *vt/i* (s')accumuler.

accuracy /'ækjərəsɪ/ *n* (of figures) justesse *f*; (of aim) précision *f*; (of forecast) exactitude *f*. **accurate** *adj* juste, précis. **accurately** *adv* exactement, précisément.

accusation /ækju'zeɪʃn/ *n* accusation *f*.

accuse /ə'kjuːz/ *vt* accuser; **the ~d**

l'accusé/-e *m/f*.

accustomed /ə'kʌstəmd/ *adj* accoutumé; **become ~ to** s'accoutumer à.

ace /eɪs/ *n* (card, person) as *m*.

ache /eɪk/ *n* douleur *f*. ● *vi* (person) avoir mal; **my leg ~s** ma jambe me fait mal.

achieve /ə'tʃiːv/ *vt* (aim) atteindre; (result) obtenir; (ambition) réaliser. **achievement** *n* (feat) réussite *f*; (fulfilment) réalisation *f* (**of** de).

acid /'æsɪd/ *adj* & *n* acide (*m*). **acidity** *n* acidité *f*. **~ rain** pluies *fpl* acides.

acknowledge /ək'nɒlɪdʒ/ *vt* (error, authority) reconnaître. (letter) accuser réception de. **acknowledgement** *n* reconnaissance *f*.

acne /'æknɪ/ *n* acné *f*.

acorn /'eɪkɔːn/ *n* (Bot) gland *m*.

acoustic /ə'kuːstɪk/ *adj* acoustique. **acoustics** *npl* acoustique *f*.

acquaint /ə'kweɪnt/ *vt* **~ sb with sth** mettre qn au courant de qch; **be ~ed with** (person) connaître. (fact) savoir. **acquaintance** *n* connaissance *f*.

acquire /ə'kwaɪə(r)/ *vt* acquérir; (habit) prendre.

acquit /ə'kwɪt/ *vt* (pt **acquitted**) (Jur) acquitter. **acquittal** *n* acquittement *m*.

acre /'eɪkə(r)/ *n* acre *f*, ≈ demi-hectare *m*.

acrid /'ækrɪd/ *adj* âcre.

acrimonious /ækrɪ'məʊnɪəs/ *adj* acrimonieux.

acrobat /'ækrəbæt/ *n* acrobate *mf*. **acrobatics** *npl* acrobaties *fpl*.

acronym /'ækrənɪm/ *n* acronyme *m*.

across /ə'krɒs/ *adv* & *prep* (side to side) d'un côté à l'autre (de); (on other side) de l'autre côté (**from**

a

de); **go** or **walk** ~ traverser; **lie** ~ **the bed** se coucher dans le lit; ~ **the world** partout dans le monde.

act /ækt/ n acte m; (Jur, Pol) loi f; **put on an** ~ jouer la comédie. ● vi agir; (Theat) jouer; ~ **as** servir de. ● vt (part, role) jouer.

acting /'æktɪŋ/ n (Theat) jeu m. ● adj (temporary) intérimaire.

action /'ækʃn/ n action f; (Mil) combat m; **out of** ~ hors service; **take** ~ agir.

activate /'æktɪveɪt/ vt (machine) faire démarrer; (alarm) déclencher.

active /'æktɪv/ adj actif; (volcano) en activité; **take an** ~ **interest in** s'intéresser activement à. **activist** n activiste mf. **activity** n activité f.

actor /'æktə(r)/ n acteur m. **actress** n actrice f.

actual /'æktʃʊəl/ adj réel; **the** ~ **words** les mots exacts; **in the** ~ **house** (the house itself) dans la maison elle-même. **actuality** n réalité f. **actually** adv (in fact) en fait; (really) vraiment.

acute /ə'kjuːt/ adj (anxiety) vif; (illness) aigu; (shortage) grave; (mind) pénétrant.

ad /æd/ n (TV) pub f 🔢; **small** ~ petite annonce f.

AD abbr (**Anno Domini**) ap. J.-C.

adamant /'ædəmənt/ adj catégorique.

adapt /ə'dæpt/ vt/i (s')adapter (**to** à). **adaptability** n adaptabilité f. **adaptable** adj souple. **adaptation** n adaptation f. **adaptor** n (Electr) adaptateur m.

add /æd/ vt/i ajouter (**to** à); (in maths) additionner. □ ~ **up** (facts, figures) s'accorder; ~ **sth up** additionner qch; ~ **up to** s'élever à.

adder /'ædə(r)/ n vipère f.

addict /'ædɪkt/ n toxicomane mf; (fig) accro mf 🔢.

addicted /ə'dɪktɪd/ adj **be** ~ avoir une dépendance (**to** à); (fig) être accro 🔢 (**to** à). **addiction** n (Med) dépendance f (**to** à); passion f (**to** pour). **addictive** adj qui crée une dépendance.

addition /ə'dɪʃn/ n (item) ajout m; (in maths) addition f; **in** ~ en plus. **additional** adj supplémentaire.

additive /'ædɪtɪv/ n additif m.

address /ə'dres/ n adresse f; (speech) discours m. ● vt (letter) mettre l'adresse sur; (crowd) s'adresser à; ~ **sth to** adresser qch à. **addressee** n destinataire mf.

adequate /'ædɪkwət/ adj suffisant; (satisfactory) satisfaisant.

adhere /əd'hɪə(r)/ vi (lit, fig) adhérer (**to** à); ~ **to** (policy) observer.

adjacent /ə'dʒeɪsnt/ adj contigu; ~ **to** attenant à.

adjective /'ædʒɪktɪv/ n adjectif m.

adjoin /ə'dʒɔɪn/ vt être contigu à. **adjoining** adj (room) voisin.

adjourn /ə'dʒɜːn/ vt (trial) ajourner; **the session was** ~ed la séance a été levée. ● vi s'arrêter; (Parliament) lever la séance; ~ **to** passer à.

adjust /ə'dʒʌst/ vt (level, speed) régler; (price) ajuster; (clothes) rajuster. ● vt/i ~ (**oneself**) **to** s'adapter à. **adjustable** adj réglable. **adjustment** n (of rates) rajustement m; (of control) réglage m; (of person) adaptation f.

ad lib /æd 'lɪb/ vt/i (pt ad libbed) improviser.

administer /əd'mɪnɪstə(r)/ vt administrer.

administration /ədmɪnɪ'streɪʃn/ n administration f. **administrative** adj administratif. **administrator** n administrateur/-trice m/f.

admiral /ˈædmərəl/ n amiral m.

admiration /ˌædməˈreɪʃn/ n admiration f. **admire** vt admirer. **admirer** n admirateur/-trice m/f.

admission /ədˈmɪʃn/ n (to a place) entrée f; (confession) aveu m.

admit /ədˈmɪt/ vt (pt **admitted**) (acknowledge) reconnaître, admettre. (crime) avouer; (new member) admettre; ∼ **to** reconnaître. **admittance** n entrée f. **admittedly** adv il est vrai.

ado /əˈduː/ n **without more** ∼ sans plus de cérémonie.

adolescence /ˌædəˈlesns/ n adolescence f. **adolescent** n & a adolescent/-e m/f .

adopt /əˈdɒpt/ vt adopter. **adopted** adj (child) adoptif. **adoption** n adoption f. **adoptive** adj adoptif.

adorable /əˈdɔːrəbl/ adj adorable. **adoration** n adoration f. **adore** vt adorer.

adorn /əˈdɔːn/ vt orner.

adrift /əˈdrɪft/ adj & adv à la dérive.

adult /ˈædʌlt/ adj & n adulte (mf).

adultery /əˈdʌltərɪ/ n adultère m.

adulthood /ˈædʌlthʊd/ n âge m adulte.

advance /ədˈvɑːns/ vt (sum) avancer; (tape, career) faire avancer; (interests) servir. ● vi (lit) avancer; (progress) progresser. ● n avance f; (progress) progrès m; **in∼** à l'avance. **advanced** adj avancé; (studies) supérieur.

advantage /ədˈvɑːntɪdʒ/ n avantage m; **take** ∼ **of** profiter de; (person) exploiter. **advantageous** adj avantageux.

adventure /ədˈventʃə(r)/ n aventure f.

adventurer /ədˈventʃərə(r)/ n aventurier-ière m/f. **adventurous** adj

aventureux.

adverb /ˈædvɜːb/ n adverbe m.

adverse /ˈædvɜːs/ adj défavorable.

advert /ˈædvɜːt/ n annonce f; (TV) pub f 🔲.

advertise /ˈædvətaɪz/ vt faire de la publicité pour; (car, house, job) mettre une annonce pour. ● vi faire de la publicité; (for staff) passer une annonce. **advertisement** n publicité f; (in newspaper) annonce f. **advertiser** n annonceur m. **advertising** n publicité f.

advice /ədˈvaɪs/ n conseils mpl; **some** ∼, **a piece of** ∼ un conseil.

advise /ədˈvaɪz/ vt conseiller; (inform) aviser; ∼ **against** déconseiller. **adviser** n conseiller/-ère m/f. **advisory** adj consultatif.

advocate[1] /ˈædvəkət/ n (Jur) avocat m; (supporter) partisan m.

advocate[2] /ˈædvəkeɪt/ vt recommander.

aerial /ˈeərɪəl/ adj aérien. ● n antenne f.

aerobics /eəˈrəʊbɪks/ n aérobic m.

aeroplane /ˈeərəpleɪn/ n avion m.

aerosol /ˈeərəsɒl/ n bombe f aérosol.

aesthetic /iːsˈθetɪk/ adj esthétique.

afar /əˈfɑː(r)/ adv **from** ∼ de loin.

affair /əˈfeə(r)/ n (matter) affaire f; (romance) liaison f.

affect /əˈfekt/ vt affecter.

affection /əˈfekʃn/ n affection f. **affectionate** adj affectueux.

affinity /əˈfɪnətɪ/ n affinité f.

afflict /əˈflɪkt/ vt affliger.

affluence /ˈæfluəns/ n richesse f.

afford /əˈfɔːd/ vt avoir les moyens d'acheter; (provide) fournir; **can you** ∼ **the time?** avez-vous le temps?

afloat /əˈfləʊt/ adj & adv

(boat) à flot.

afoot /əˈfʊt/ adv sth is ~ il se prépare qch.

afraid /əˈfreɪd/ adj be ~ (frightened) avoir peur (of, to de; that que); (worried) craindre (that que); I'm ~ I can't come je suis désolé mais je ne peux pas venir.

Africa /ˈæfrɪkə/ n Afrique f.

African /ˈæfrɪkən/ n Africain/-e m/f.
● adj africain.

after /ˈɑːftə(r)/ adv & prep après; soon ~ peu après; be ~ sth rechercher qch; ~ all après tout.
● conj après que; ~ doing après avoir fait.

aftermath /ˈɑːftəmæθ/ n conséquences fpl (of de).

afternoon /ɑːftəˈnuːn/ n aprèsmidi m or f inv; in the ~ (dans) l'après-midi.

after: ~ shave n après-rasage m. ~ thought n pensée f après coup.

afterwards /ˈɑːftəwədz/ adv après, par la suite.

again /əˈɡeɪn/ adv encore; ~ and ~ à plusieurs reprises; start ~ recommencer; she never saw him ~ elle ne l'a jamais revu.

against /əˈɡeɪnst/ prep contre; ~ the law illégal.

age /eɪdʒ/ n âge m; (era) ère f, époque f; I've been waiting for ~s j'attends depuis des heures. ● vt/i (pres p **ageing**) vieillir.

aged[1] /ˈeɪdʒd/ adj ~ **six** âgé de six ans.

aged[2] /ˈeɪdʒɪd/ adj âgé.

ageism /ˈeɪdʒɪzəm/ n discrimination f en raison de l'âge.

agency /ˈeɪdʒənsi/ n agence f.

agenda /əˈdʒendə/ n ordre m du jour; (fig) programme m.

agent /ˈeɪdʒənt/ n agent m.

aggravate /ˈæɡrəveɪt/ vt (make worse) aggraver; (annoy) exaspérer. **aggravation** n (worsening) aggravation f; (annoyance) ennuis mpl.

aggression /əˈɡreʃn/ n agression f. **aggressive** adj agressif. **aggressiveness** n agressivité f. **aggressor** n agresseur m.

agitate /ˈædʒɪteɪt/ vt agiter.

ago /əˈɡəʊ/ adv il y a; **a month** ~ il y a un mois; **long** ~ il y a longtemps; **how long** ~? il y a combien de temps?

agonize /ˈæɡənaɪz/ vi se tourmenter (over à propos de). **agonized** adj angoissé. **agonizing** adj déchirant. **agony** n douleur f atroce; (mental) angoisse f.

agree /əˈɡriː/ vi être d'accord (on sur; with avec); ~ to consentir à; ~ with (approve of) approuver. ● vt être d'accord (that sur le fait que); (admit) convenir (that que); (date, solution) se mettre d'accord sur.

agreeable /əˈɡriːəbl/ adj agréable; be ~ (willing) être d'accord.

agreed /əˈɡriːd/ adj (time, place) convenu; **we're** ~ nous sommes d'accord.

agreement /əˈɡriːmənt/ n accord m; in ~ d'accord.

agricultural /æɡrɪˈkʌltʃərəl/ adj agricole. **agriculture** n agriculture f.

aground /əˈɡraʊnd/ adv run ~ (ship) s'échouer.

ahead /əˈhed/ adv (in front) en avant, devant; (in advance) à l'avance; **be 10 points** ~ avoir 10 points d'avance; ~ **of time** en avance; **go** ~! allez-y!

aid /eɪd/ vt aider. ● n aide f; **in** ~ **of** au profit de.

aide /eɪd/ n aide m/f.

Aids /eɪdz/ n (Med) sida m.

aim /eɪm/ vt (gun) braquer (**at** sur); **be** ~ **ed at sb** (campaign, remark) viser qn. ● vi ~ **for/at sth** viser qch; ~ **to do** avoir l'intention de faire. ● n but m; **take** ~ viser. **aimless** adj sans but.

air /eə(r)/ n air m; **by** ~ par avion; **on the** ~ à l'antenne. ● vt aérer; (views) exprimer. ● adj (base, disaster) aérien; (pollution, pressure) atmosphérique. ~ **bed** n matelas m pneumatique. ~ **conditioning** n climatisation f. ~**craft** n inv avion m. ~**craft carrier** n porteavions m inv. ~**field** n terrain m d'aviation. ~ **force** n armée f de l'air. ~ **freshener** n désodorisant m d'atmosphère. ~ **hostess** n hôtesse f de l'air. ~**lift** vt transporter par pont aérien. ~**line** n compagnie f aérienne. ~**liner** n avion m de ligne. ~**lock** n (in pipe) bulle f d'air; (chamber) sas m. ~**mail** n (**by**) ~**mail** par avion. ~**plane** n (US) avion m. ~**port** n aéroport m. ~ **raid** n attaque f aérienne. ~-**tight** adj hermétique. ~ **traffic controller** n contrôleur/-euse m/f aérien/-ne. ~**waves** npl ondes fpl.

airy /'eərɪ/ adj (**-ier, -iest**) (room) clair et spacieux.

aisle /aɪl/ n (of church) allée f centrale; (in train) couloir m.

ajar /ə'dʒɑː(r)/ adv & adj entrouvert.

akin /ə'kɪn/ adj ~ **to** semblable à.

alarm /ə'lɑːm/ n alarme f; (clock) réveil m; (feeling) frayeur f. ● vt inquiéter. ~ **clock** n réveil m.

alas /ə'læs/ interj hélas.

Albania /æl'beɪnɪə/ n Albanie f.

album /'ælbəm/ n album m.

alcohol /'ælkəhɒl/ n alcool m.

alcoholic /ælkə'hɒlɪk/ adj alcoolique; (drink) alcoolisé. ● n alcoolique mf.

ale /eɪl/ n bière f.

alert /ə'lɜːt/ adj alerte; (watchful) vigilant. ● n alerte f; **on the** ~ sur le qui-vive. ● vt alerter; ~ **sb to** prévenir qn de. **alertness** n vivacité f; vigilance f.

A-level /'eɪlevl/ n ≈ baccalauréat m.

algebra /'ældʒɪbrə/ n algèbre f.

Algeria /æl'dʒɪərɪə/ n Algérie f.

alias /'eɪlɪəs/ n (pl ~**es**) faux nom m. ● prep alias.

alibi /'ælɪbaɪ/ n alibi m.

alien /'eɪlɪən/ n & a étranger/-ère (m/f) (**to** à).

alienate /'eɪlɪəneɪt/ vt éloigner.

alight /ə'laɪt/ adj en feu, allumé.

alike /ə'laɪk/ adj semblable. ● adv de la même façon; **look** ~ se ressembler.

alive /ə'laɪv/ adj vivant; ~ **to** conscient de; ~ **with** grouillant de.

---

all /ɔːl/

● **pronoun**

····▸ (everything) tout; **is that** ~? c'est tout?; **that was** ~ (**that**) **he said** c'est tout ce qu'il a dit; **I ate it** ~ j'ai tout mangé.

> ❗ Use the translation **tous** for a group of masculine or mixed gender people or objects and **toutes** for a group of feminine gender: **we were all delighted** nous étions tous ravis; **'where are the cups?'—'they're all in the kitchen'** où sont les tasses?'-'elles sont toutes dans la cuisine'.

● **determiner**

····▸ tout/toute/tous/toutes; ~

the time tout le temps; ~ his life toute sa vie; ~ of us nous tous; ~ (the) women toutes les femmes.
● adverb
····▸ (completely) tout; they were ~ alone ils étaient tout seuls; tell me ~ about it raconte-moi tout; ~ for tout à fait pour; not ~ that well pas si bien que ça; ~ too bien trop.

! When the adjective that follows is in the feminine and begins with a consonant, the translation is toute/toutes: she was all alone elle était toute seule.

allege /ə'ledʒ/ vt prétendre. ~d adj présumé; **allegedly** adv prétendument.

allergic /ə'lɜːdʒɪk/ adj allergique (to à). **allergy** n allergie f.

alleviate /ə'liːvɪeɪt/ vt alléger.

alley /'ælɪ/ n (street) ruelle f.

alliance /ə'laɪəns/ n alliance f.

allied /'ælaɪd/ adj allié.

alligator /'ælɪgeɪtə(r)/ n alligator m.

allocate /'æləkeɪt/ vt (funds) affecter; (time) accorder; (task) assigner.

allot /ə'lɒt/ vt (pt allotted) (money) attribuer; (task) assigner. **allotment** n attribution f; (land) parcelle f de terre.

all-out /'ɔːlaʊt/ adj (effort) acharné; (strike) total.

allow /ə'laʊ/ vt (authorize) autoriser à; (let) laisser; (enable) permettre; (concede) accorder; ~ for tenir compte de.

allowance /ə'laʊəns/ n allocation f; make ~s for sth tenir compte de

qch; make ~s for sb essayer de comprendre qn.

alloy /'ælɔɪ/ n alliage m.

all right /ɔːl'raɪt/ adj (not bad) pas mal; **are you ~?** ça va?; **is it ~ if ...?** est-ce que ça va si ...? ● adv (see) bien; (function) comme il faut.
● interj d'accord.

ally[1] /'ælaɪ/ n allié/-e m/f.

ally[2] /ə'laɪ/ vt allier; ~ oneself with s'allier avec.

almighty /ɔːl'maɪtɪ/ adj toutpuissant; (very great) formidable.

almond /'ɑːmənd/ n amande f. ~ tree n amandier m.

almost /'ɔːlməʊst/ adv presque; he ~ died il a failli mourir.

alone /ə'ləʊn/ adj & adv seul.

along /ə'lɒŋ/ prep le long de; walk ~ the beach marcher sur la plage.
● adv come ~ venir; walk ~ marcher; push/pull sth ~ pousser/tirer qch; all ~ (time) depuis le début; ~ with avec.

alongside /ə'lɒŋsaɪd/ adv à côté; come ~ (Naut) accoster. ● prep (next to) à côté de; (all along) le long de.

aloof /ə'luːf/ adj distant.

aloud /ə'laʊd/ adv à haute voix.

alphabet /'ælfəbet/ n alphabet m. **alphabetical** adj alphabétique.

alpine /'ælpaɪn/ adj (landscape) alpestre; (climate) alpin.

already /ɔːl'redɪ/ adv déjà.

alright /ɔːl'raɪt/ a & adv ⇒ALL RIGHT.

Alsatian /æl'seɪʃn/ n (dog) berger m allemand.

also /'ɔːlsəʊ/ adv aussi.

altar /'ɔːltə(r)/ n autel m.

alter /'ɔːltə(r)/ vt/i changer; (building) transformer; (garment) retoucher. **alteration** n changement m;

(to building) transformation *f*; (to garment) retouche *f*.

alternate¹ /ˈɔːltənət/ *vt/i* alterner.

alternate² /ˈɔːltɜːnət/ *adj* en alternance; **on ~ days** un jour sur deux. **alternately** *adv* alternativement.

alternative /ɔːlˈtɜːnətɪv/ *adj* autre; (*solution*) de rechange. ● *n* (specified option) alternative *f*; (possible option) choix *m*. **alternatively** *adv* sinon.

alternator /ˈɔːltəneɪtə(r)/ *n* alternateur *m*.

although /ɔːlˈðəʊ/ *conj* bien que.

altitude /ˈæltɪtjuːd/ *n* altitude *f*.

altogether /ɔːltəˈɡeðə(r)/ *adv* (completely) tout à fait; (on the whole) tout compte fait.

aluminium /æljʊˈmɪnjəm/ *n* aluminium *m*.

always /ˈɔːlweɪz/ *adv* toujours.

am /æm/ ➡BE.

a.m. /eɪem/ *adv* du matin.

amalgamate /əˈmælɡəmeɪt/ *vt/i* (merge) fusionner; (*metals*) (s')amalgamer.

amateur /ˈæmətə(r)/ *n & adj* amateur (*m*).

amaze /əˈmeɪz/ *vt* stupéfaire. **amazed** *adj* stupéfait. **amazement** *n* stupéfaction *f*. **amazing** *adj* stupéfiant; (great) exceptionnel.

ambassador /æmˈbæsədə(r)/ *n* ambassadeur *m*.

amber /ˈæmbə(r)/ *n* ambre *m*; (Auto) orange *m*.

ambiguity /æmbɪˈɡjuːətɪ/ *n* ambiguïté *f*.

ambiguous /æmˈbɪɡjʊəs/ *adj* ambigu.

ambition /æmˈbɪʃn/ *n* ambition *f*. **ambitious** *adj* ambitieux.

ambulance /ˈæmbjʊləns/ *n* ambulance *f*.

ambush /ˈæmbʊʃ/ *n* embuscade *f*. ● *vt* tendre une embuscade à.

amenable /əˈmiːnəbl/ *adj* obligeant; **~ to** (responsive) sensible à.

amend /əˈmend/ *vt* modifier.

amendment *n* (to rule) amendement *m*.

amends /əˈmendz/ *npl* **make ~** réparer son erreur.

amenities /əˈmiːnətɪz/ *npl* équipements *mpl*.

America /əˈmerɪkə/ *n* Amérique *f*.

American /əˈmerɪkən/ *n* Américain/-e *m/f*. ● *adj* américain.

American dream Cette expression désigne un principe américain selon lequel la réussite, en particulier financière et sociale, est accessible à quiconque travaille avec acharnement. Pour les immigrants, s'y ajoute le rêve de liberté et d'égalité.

---

amiable /ˈeɪmɪəbl/ *adj* aimable.

amicable /ˈæmɪkəbl/ *adj* amical.

amid(st) /əˈmɪd(st)/ *prep* au milieu de.

amiss /əˈmɪs/ *adj* **there is something ~** il y a quelque chose qui ne va pas.

ammonia /əˈməʊnɪə/ *n* (gas) ammoniac *m*; (solution) ammoniaque *f*.

ammunition /æmjʊˈnɪʃn/ *n* munitions *fpl*.

amnesty /ˈæmnəstɪ/ *n* amnistie *f*.

among(st) /əˈmʌŋ(st)/ *prep* parmi; (affecting a group) chez; **be ~ the poorest** être un des plus pauvres; **be ~ the first** être dans les premiers.

amorous /ˈæmərəs/ *adj* amoureux.

amount /əˈmaʊnt/ *n* quantité *f*; (total) montant *m*; (sum of money) somme f. ● vi ~ to (add up to) s'élever à; (be equivalent to) revenir à.

amp /æmp/ n ampère m.

amphibian /æmˈfɪbɪən/ n amphibie m.

ample /ˈæmpl/ adj (resources) largement suffisant; (proportions) généreux.

amplifier /ˈæmplɪfaɪə(r)/ n amplificateur m.

amputate /ˈæmpjʊteɪt/ vt amputer.

amuse /əˈmjuːz/ vt amuser.

amusement /əˈmjuːzmənt/ n (mirth) amusement m; (diversion) distraction f. ~ **arcade** n salle f de jeux.

an /æn, ən/ →A.

anaemia /əˈniːmɪə/ n anémie f.

anaesthetic /ænɪsˈθetɪk/ n anesthésique m.

analyse /ˈænəlaɪz/ vt analyser. **analysis** n (pl **-yses**) analyse f. **analyst** n analyste mf.

anarchist /ˈænəkɪst/ n anarchiste mf.

anatomical /ænəˈtɒmɪkl/ adj anatomique. **anatomy** n anatomie f.

ancestor /ˈænsestə(r)/ n ancêtre m.

anchor /ˈæŋkə(r)/ n ancre f. ● vt mettre à l'ancre. ● vi jeter l'ancre.

anchovy /ˈæntʃəvɪ/ n anchois m.

ancient /ˈeɪnʃənt/ adj ancien.

ancillary /ænˈsɪlərɪ/ adj auxiliaire.

and /ænd, ənd/ conj et; **two hundred** ~ **sixty** deux cent soixante; **go** ~ **see him** allez le voir; **richer** ~ **richer** de plus en plus riche.

anew /əˈnjuː/ adv (once more) encore, de nouveau; (in a new way) à nouveau.

angel /ˈeɪndʒl/ n ange m.

anger /ˈæŋɡə(r)/ n colère f. ● vt

mettre en colère, fâcher.

angle /ˈæŋɡl/ n angle m. ● vi pêcher (à la ligne); ~ **for** (fig) quêter.

angler n pêcheur/-euse m/f.

Anglo-Saxon /æŋɡləʊˈsæksn/ adj anglo-saxon. ● n Anglo-Saxon/-ne m/f.

angry /ˈæŋɡrɪ/ adj (**-ier**, **-iest**) fâché, en colère; **get** ~ se fâcher, se mettre en colère (**with** contre); **make sb** ~ mettre qn en colère.

anguish /ˈæŋɡwɪʃ/ n angoisse f.

animal /ˈænɪml/ n & adj animal (m).

animate¹ /ˈænɪmət/ adj (person) vivant; (object) animé.

animate² /ˈænɪmeɪt/ vt animer.

aniseed /ˈænɪsiːd/ n anis m.

ankle /ˈæŋkl/ n cheville f. ~ **sock** n socquette f.

annex /əˈneks/ vt annexer.

annex /ˈæneks/ n annexe f.

anniversary /ænɪˈvɜːsərɪ/ n anniversaire m.

announce /əˈnaʊns/ vt annoncer (**that** que). **announcement** n (spoken) annonce f; (written) avis m. **announcer** n (radio, TV) speaker/-ine m/f.

annoy /əˈnɔɪ/ vt agacer, ennuyer. **annoyance** n contrariété f. **annoyed** adj fâché (**with** contre); **get** ~**ed** se fâcher. **annoying** adj ennuyeux.

annual /ˈænjʊəl/ adj annuel. ● n publication f annuelle. **annually** adv (earn, produce) par an; (do, inspect) tous les ans.

annul /əˈnʌl/ vt (pt **annulled**) annuler.

anonymity /ænəˈnɪmətɪ/ n anonymat m. **anonymous** adj anonyme.

anorak /ˈænəræk/ n anorak m.

another /əˈnʌðə(r)/ det & pron un/-e autre; ~ **coffee** (one more) encore un café; ~ **ten minutes** encore dix minutes, dix minutes de plus; **can I have ~?** est-ce que je peux en avoir une tasse?

answer /'ɑːnsə(r)/ *n* réponse *f*; (solution) solution *f*; (phone) **there's no ~** ça ne répond pas. ● *vt* répondre; (prayer) exaucer; **~ the door** ouvrir la porte. ● *vi* répondre. □ ~ **back** répondre; **~ for** répondre de; **~ to** (superior) dépendre de; (description) répondre à. **answerable** *adj* responsable (**for** de; **to** devant). **answering machine** *n* répondeur *m*.

ant /ænt/ *n* fourmi *f*.

antagonism /æn'tægənizəm/ *n* antagonisme *m*. **antagonize** *vt* provoquer l'hostilité de.

Antarctic /æn'tɑːktɪk/ *n* **the ~** l'Antarctique *m*. ● *adj* antarctique.

antenatal /æntɪ'neɪtl/ *adj* prénatal.

antenna /æn'tenə/ *n* (*pl* -**ae**) (of insect) antenne *f*; (*pl* -**as**; aerial: US) antenne *f*.

anthem /'ænθəm/ *n* (Relig) motet *m*; (of country) hymne *n* national.

anthrax /'ænθræks/ *n* charbon *m*.

antibiotic /æntɪbaɪ'ɒtɪk/ *n & adj* antibiotique (*m*).

antibody /'æntɪbɒdɪ/ *n* anticorps *m*.

anticipate /æn'tɪsɪpeɪt/ *vt* (foresee, expect) prévoir, s'attendre à.

anticipation /æntɪsɪ'peɪʃn/ *n* attente *f*; **in ~ of** en prévision de, en attente de.

anticlimax /æntɪ'klaɪmæks/ *n* (let-down) déception *f*.

anticlockwise /æntɪ'klɒkwaɪz/ *adv & adj* dans le sens inverse des aiguilles d'une montre.

antics /'æntɪks/ *npl* pitreries *fpl*.

antifreeze /'æntɪfriːz/ *n* antigel *m*.

antiquated /'æntɪkweɪtɪd/ *adj*

(idea) archaïque; (building) vétuste.

antique /æn'tiːk/ *adj* (old) ancien; (old-style) à l'ancienne. ● *n* objet *m* ancien, antiquité *f*. **~ dealer** *n* antiquaire *mf*. **~ shop** *n* magasin *m* d'antiquités.

anti-Semitic /æntɪsɪ'mɪtɪk/ *adj* antisémite.

antiseptic /æntɪ'septɪk/ *adj & n* antiseptique (*m*).

antisocial /æntɪ'səʊʃl/ *adj* asocial, antisocial; (reclusive) sauvage.

antlers /'æntləz/ *npl* bois *mpl*.

anxiety /æŋ'zaɪətɪ/ *n* (worry) anxiété *f*; (eagerness) impatience *f*.

anxious /'æŋkʃəs/ *adj* (troubled) anxieux; (eager) impatient (**to** de).

any /'enɪ/ *det* (some) du, de l', de la, des; (after negative) de, d'; (every) tout; (no matter which) n'importe quel; **at ~ moment** à tout moment; **have you ~ water?** avez-vous de l'eau? ● *pron* (no matter which one) n'importe lequel; (any amount of it or them) en; **I do not have ~** je n'en ai pas; **did you see ~ of them?** en avez-vous vu? ● *adv* (a little) un peu; **do you have ~ more?** en avez-vous encore?; **do you have ~ more tea?** avez-vous encore du thé?; **I don't do it ~ more** je ne le fais plus.

anybody /'enɪbɒdɪ/ *pron* (no matter who) n'importe qui; (somebody) quelqu'un; (after negative) personne; **he did not see ~** il n'a vu personne.

anyhow /'enɪhaʊ/ *adv* (anyway) de toute façon; (carelessly) n'importe comment.

anyone /'enɪwʌn/ *pron* →**ANYBODY.**

anything /'enɪθɪŋ/ *pron* (no matter what) n'importe quoi; (something) quelque chose; (after negative) rien;

he did not see ~ il n'a rien vu; ~ but nullement; ~ you do tout ce que tu fais.

anyway /'enɪweɪ/ adv de toute façon.

anywhere /'enɪweə(r)/ adv (no matter where) n'importe où; (somewhere) quelque part; (after negative) nulle part; **he does not go** ~ il ne va nulle part; ~ **you go** partout où tu vas, où que tu ailles; ~ **else** partout ailleurs.

apart /ə'pɑːt/ adv (on or to one side) à part; (separated) séparé; (into pieces) en pièces; ~ **from** à part, excepté; **ten metres** ~ à dix mètres l'un de l'autre; **come** ~ (break) tomber en morceaux; (machine) se démonter; **legs** ~ les jambes écartées; **keep** ~ séparer; **take** ~ démonter.

apartment /ə'pɑːtmənt/ n (US) appartement m.

ape /eɪp/ n singe m. ● vt singer.

aperitif /ə'perətɪf/ n apéritif m.

apex /'eɪpeks/ n sommet m.

apologetic /əpɒlə'dʒetɪk/ adj (tone) d'excuse; **be** ~ s'excuser.

apologetically adv en s'excusant.

apologize /ə'pɒlədʒaɪz/ vi s'excuser (for de; to auprès de).

apology /ə'pɒlədʒɪ/ n excuses fpl.

apostrophe /ə'pɒstrəfɪ/ n apostrophe f.

appal /ə'pɔːl/ vt (pt **appalled**) horrifier. **appalling** adj épouvantable.

apparatus /æpə'reɪtəs/ n appareil m.

apparent /ə'pærənt/ adj apparent. **apparently** adv apparemment.

appeal /ə'piːl/ n appel m; (attractiveness) attrait m, charme m. ● vi (Jur) faire appel; ~ **to sb** (beg) faire appel à qn; (attract) plaire à qn; ~ **to sb for sth** demander qch à qn.

appealing adj (attractive) attirant.

appear /ə'pɪə(r)/ vi apparaître. (arrive) se présenter; (seem, be published) paraître. (Theat) jouer; ~ **on TV** passer à la télé. **appearance** n apparition f; (aspect) apparence f.

appease /ə'piːz/ vt apaiser.

appendix /ə'pendɪks/ n (pl -ices) appendice m.

appetite /'æpɪtaɪt/ n appétit m.

appetizer /'æpɪtaɪzə(r)/ n (snack) amuse-gueule m inv; (drink) apéritif m.

appetizing /'æpɪtaɪzɪŋ/ adj appétissant.

applaud /ə'plɔːd/ vt/i applaudir; (decision) applaudir à. **applause** n applaudissements mpl.

apple /'æpl/ n pomme f; ~**-tree** n pommier m.

appliance /ə'plaɪəns/ n appareil m.

applicable /'æplɪkəbl/ adj valable; **if** ~ le cas échéant.

applicant /'æplɪkənt/ n candidat/-e m/f (for à).

application /æplɪ'keɪʃn/ n application f; (request, form) demande f; (for job) candidature f.

apply /ə'plaɪ/ vt appliquer. ● vi ~ **to** (refer) s'appliquer à; (ask) s'adresser à; ~ **for** (job) postuler pour; (grant) demander; ~ **oneself to** s'appliquer à.

appoint /ə'pɔɪnt/ vt (to post) nommer; (fix) désigner; **well-~ed** bien équipé.

appointment /ə'pɔɪntmənt/ n nomination f; (meeting) rendez-vous m inv; (job) poste m; **make an** ~ prendre rendez-vous (with avec).

appraisal /ə'preɪzl/ n évaluation f. **appraise** vt évaluer.

appreciate /ə'priːʃɪeɪt/ vt (like) apprécier; (understand) comprendre; (be grateful for) être reconnais-

sant de. ● vi prendre de la valeur.
appreciation n appréciation f;
(gratitude) reconnaissance f; (rise)
augmentation f. **appreciative** adj
reconnaissant; (audience) enthousiaste.

apprehend /æprɪ'hend/ vt (arrest)
appréhender; (understand) comprendre. **apprehension** n (arrest)
appréhension f; (fear) crainte f.

apprehensive /æprɪ'hensɪv/ adj
inquiet; **be ~ of** craindre.

apprentice /ə'prentɪs/ n apprenti
m. ● vt mettre en apprentissage.

approach /ə'prəʊtʃ/ vt (s')approcher de; (accost) aborder; (with request) s'adresser à. ● vi (s')approcher. ● n approche f; **an ~ to**
(problem) une façon d'aborder;
(person) une démarche auprès de.
approachable adj abordable.

appropriate[1] /ə'prəʊprɪeɪt/ vt
s'approprier.

appropriate[2] /ə'prəʊprɪət/ adj
approprié, propre. **appropriately**
adv à propos.

approval /ə'pruːvl/ n approbation
f; **on ~** à or sous condition.

approve /ə'pruːv/ vt approuver.
● vi **~ of** approuver. **approving** adj
approbateur.

approximate[1] /ə'prɒksɪmeɪt/ vi
~ to se rapprocher de.

approximate[2] /ə'prɒksɪmət/ adj
approximatif. **approximately** adv
environ. **approximation** n approximation f.

apricot /'eɪprɪkɒt/ n abricot m.

April /'eɪprɪl/ n avril m. **~ Fools
Day** n le premier avril.

apron /'eɪprən/ n tablier m.

apt /æpt/ adj (suitable) approprié;
be ~ to avoir tendance à.

aptitude /'æptɪtjuːd/ n aptitude f.

aptly /'æptlɪ/ adv à propos.

Aquarius /ə'kweərɪəs/ n Verseau m.

aquatic /ə'kwætɪk/ adj aquatique;
(Sport) nautique.

Arab /'ærəb/ n Arabe mf. ● adj
arabe.

Arabian /ə'reɪbɪən/ adj d'Arabie.

Arabic /'ærəbɪk/ adj & n (Ling)
arabe (m).

arbitrary /'ɑːbɪtrərɪ/ adj arbitraire.

arbitrate /'ɑːbɪtreɪt/ vi arbitrer. **arbitration** n arbitrage m. **arbitrator**
n médiateur/-trice m/f.

arcade /ɑː'keɪd/ n (shops) galerie f;
(arches) arcades fpl.

arch /ɑːtʃ/ n arche f; (of foot) voûte
f plantaire. ● vt/i (s')arquer. ● adj
(playful) malicieux.

archaeological /ɑːkɪə'lɒdʒɪkl/
adj archéologique. **archaeologist** n
archéologue mf. **archaeology** n archéologie f.

archbishop /ɑːtʃ'bɪʃəp/ n archevêque m.

archery /'ɑːtʃərɪ/ n tir m à l'arc.

architect /'ɑːkɪtekt/ n architecte
mf; (of plan) artisan m. **architectural** adj architectural. **architecture**
n architecture f.

archives /'ɑːkaɪvz/ npl archives fpl.

archway /'ɑːtʃweɪ/ n voûte f.

Arctic /'ɑːktɪk/ n the **~** l'Arctique
m. ● adj (climate) arctique; (expedition) polaire; (conditions) glacial.

ardent /'ɑːdnt/ adj ardent.

are /ɑː(r)/ ➡BE.

area /'eərɪə/ n (region) région f;
(district) quartier m; (fig) domaine
m; (in geometry) aire f; **parking/picnic ~** aire f de parking/de pique-nique.

arena /ə'riːnə/ n arène f.

aren't /ɑː(r)nt/ ➡ARE NOT.

Argentina /ɑːdʒən'tiːnə/ n

Argentine f.

arguable /'ɑːgjuəbl/ adj discutable. **arguably** adv selon certains.

argue /'ɑːgjuː/ vi (quarrel) se disputer; (reason) argumenter. ● vt (debate) discuter; ~ that alléguer que.

argument /'ɑːgjʊmənt/ n dispute f; (reasoning) argument m; (discussion) débat m. **argumentative** adj ergoteur.

Aries /'eəriːz/ n Bélier m.

arise /ə'raɪz/ vi (pt arose; pp arisen) (problem) survenir; (question) se poser; ~ from résulter de.

aristocrat /'ærɪstəkræt/ n aristocrate mf.

arithmetic /ə'rɪθmətɪk/ n arithmétique f.

ark /ɑːk/ n (Relig) arche f.

arm /ɑːm/ n bras m; ~ in arm bras dessus bras dessous. ● vt armer; ~ed robbery vol m à main armée.

armament /'ɑːməmənt/ n armement m.

arm: /ɑːm/ ~band n brassard m. ~chair n fauteuil m.

armour /'ɑːmə(r)/ n armure f. **armoured** adj blindé. **armoury** n arsenal m.

armpit /'ɑːmpɪt/ n aisselle f.

arms /ɑːmz/ npl (weapons) armes fpl. ~ dealer n trafiquant m d'armes.

army /'ɑːmɪ/ n armée f.

aroma /ə'rəʊmə/ n arôme m. **aromatic** adj aromatique.

arose /ə'rəʊz/ ➡ARISE.

around /ə'raʊnd/ adv (tout) autour; (here and there) çà et là. ● prep autour de; ~ here par ici.

arouse /ə'raʊz/ vt (awaken, cause) éveiller; (excite) exciter.

arrange /ə'reɪndʒ/ vt arranger; (time, date) fixer; ~ to

s'arranger pour.

arrangement /ə'reɪndʒmənt/ n arrangement m; (agreement) entente f; **make** ~s prendre des dispositions.

array /ə'reɪ/ n **an** ~ **of** (display) un étalage impressionnant de.

arrears /ə'rɪəz/ npl arriéré m; **in** ~ (rent) arriéré; **he is in** ~ il a des retards dans ses paiements.

arrest /ə'rest/ vt arrêter; (attention) retenir. ● n arrestation f; **under** ~ en état d'arrestation.

arrival /ə'raɪvl/ n arrivée f; **new** ~ nouveau venu m, nouvelle venue f.

arrive /ə'raɪv/ vi arriver; **at** (destination) arriver à; (decision) parvenir à.

arrogance /'ærəgəns/ n arrogance f.

arrow /'ærəʊ/ n flèche f.

arse /ɑːs/ n ⊠ cul m ⊠.

arson /'ɑːsn/ n incendie m criminel. **arsonist** n incendiaire mf.

art /ɑːt/ n art m; (fine arts) beaux-arts mpl.

artery /'ɑːtərɪ/ n artère f.

art gallery n (public) musée m (d'art); (private) galerie f (d'art).

arthritis /ɑːˈθraɪtɪs/ n arthrite f.

artichoke /'ɑːtɪtʃəʊk/ n artichaut m.

article /'ɑːtɪkl/ n article m; ~ **of clothing** vêtement m.

articulate /ɑːˈtɪkjʊlət/ adj (person) capable de s'exprimer clairement; (speech) distinct.

articulated lorry n semiremorque m.

artificial /ɑːtɪˈfɪʃl/ adj artificiel.

artist /'ɑːtɪst/ n artiste mf.

arts /ɑːts/ npl **the** ~ les arts mpl; (Univ) lettres fpl.

artwork /'ɑːtwɜːk/ n (of book)

illustrations *fpl*.

as /æz/, /əz/ *conj* comme; (while) pendant que; (over gradual period of time) au fur et à mesure que; ~ **she grew older** au fur et à mesure qu'elle vieillissait; **do** ~ **I say** fais ce que je dis; ~ **usual** comme d'habitude. ● *prep* ~ **a mother** en tant que mère; ~ **a gift** en cadeau; ~ **from Monday** à partir de lundi; ~ **for,** ~ **to** quant à; ~ **if** comme si; **you look** ~ **if you're tired** vous avez l'air d'être fatigué. ● *adv* ~ **tall** ~ aussi grand que; ~ **much** ~, ~ **many** autant que; ~ **soon** ~ aussitôt que; ~ **well** ~ aussi bien que; ~ **wide** ~ **possible** aussi large que possible.

asbestos /əz'bestɒs/ *n* amiante *f*.

ascend /ə'send/ *vt* gravir. ● *vi* monter.

ascertain /æsə'teɪn/ *vt* établir (**that** que).

ash /æʃ/ *n* cendre *f*; ~**(-tree)** frêne *m*.

ashamed /ə'ʃeɪmd/ *adj* **be** ~ avoir honte (**of** de).

ashore /ə'ʃɔː(r)/ *adv* à terre.

ashtray /'æʃtreɪ/ *n* cendrier *m*.

Asia /'eɪʃə/ *n* Asie *f*.

Asian /'eɪʃn/ *n* Asiatique *mf*. ● *adj* asiatique.

aside /ə'saɪd/ *adv* de côté; ~ **from** à part. ● *n* aparté *m*.

ask /ɑːsk/ *vt/i* demander; (a question) poser; (invite) inviter; ~ **sb sth** demander qch à qn; ~ **sb to do** demander à qn de faire; ~ **about** (thing) se renseigner sur; (person) demander des nouvelles de; ~ **for** demander.

asleep /ə'sliːp/ *adj* endormi; (numb) engourdi. ● *adv* **fall** ~ s'endormir.

asparagus /ə'spærəgəs/ *n*(plant)

asperge *f*; (Culin) asperges *fpl*.

aspect /'æspekt/ *n* aspect *m*; (direction) orientation *f*.

asphyxiate /əs'fɪksɪeɪt/ *vt/i* (s')asphyxier.

aspire /ə'spaɪə(r)/ *vi* aspirer (**to**; **to do** à faire).

aspirin /'æspərɪn/ *n* aspirine® *f*.

ass /æs/ *n* âne *m*; (person Ⅱ) idiot/-e *m/f*.

assail /ə'seɪl/ *vt* attaquer. **assailant** *n* agresseur *m*.

assassin /ə'sæsɪn/ *n* assassin *m*. **assassinate** *vt* assassiner. **assassination** *n* assassinat *m*.

assault /ə'sɔːlt/ *n* (Mil) assaut *m*; (Jur) agression *f*. ● *vt* (person: Jur) agresser.

assemble /ə'sembl/ *vt*(construct) assembler; (gather) rassembler. ● *vi* se rassembler.

assembly /ə'semblɪ/ *n* assemblée *f*. ~ **line** *n* chaîne *f* de montage.

assent /ə'sent/ *n* assentiment *m*. ● *vi* consentir.

assert /ə'sɜːt/ *vt* affirmer; (rights) revendiquer. **assertion** *n* affirmation *f*. **assertive** *adj* assuré.

assess /ə'ses/ *vt* évaluer; (payment) déterminer le montant de. **assessment** *n* évaluation *f*. **assessor** *n* (valuer) expert *m*.

asset /'æset/ *n* (advantage) atout *m*; (financial) bien *m*; ~ **s** (Comm) actif *m*.

assign /ə'saɪn/ *vt* (allot) assigner; ~ **sb to** (appoint) affecter qn à.

assignment /ə'saɪnmənt/ *n* (task) mission *f*; (diplomatic) poste *m*; (academic) devoir *m*.

assist /ə'sɪst/ *vt/i* aider. **assistance** *n* aide *f*.

assistant /ə'sɪstənt/ *n* aide *mf*; (in shop) vendeur/-euse *m/f*. ● *adj* (manager) adjoint.

associate¹ /əˈsəʊʃɪət/ n & adj associé/-e (m/f).

associate² /əˈsəʊʃɪeɪt/ vt associer. ● vi ~ **with** fréquenter. **association** n association f.

assorted /əˈsɔːtɪd/ adj divers; (foods) assorti.

assortment /əˈsɔːtmənt/ n assortiment m; (of people) mélange m.

assume /əˈsjuːm/ vt supposer; (power, attitude) prendre; (role, burden) assumer.

assurance /əˈʃɔːrəns/ n assurance f.

assure /əˈʃɔː(r)/ vt assurer.

asterisk /ˈæstərɪsk/ n astérisque m.

asthma /ˈæsmə/ n asthme m.

astonish /əˈstɒnɪʃ/ vt étonner.

astound /əˈstaʊnd/ vt stupéfier.

astray /əˈstreɪ/ adv go ~ s'égarer; lead ~ égarer.

astride /əˈstraɪd/ adv & prep à califourchon (sur).

astrologer /əˈstrɒlədʒə(r)/ n astrologue mf. **astrology** n astrologie f.

astronaut /ˈæstrənɔːt/ n astronaute mf.

astronomer /əˈstrɒnəmə(r)/ n astronome mf.

asylum /əˈsaɪləm/ n asile m.

---

at /æt, ət/
● preposition

➡️ For expressions such as **laugh at, look at** ➡️**laugh, look**.

····▸ (in position or place) à; he's ~ **his desk** il est à son bureau; she's ~ **work/school** elle est au travail/à l'école.

····▸ (at someone's house or business) chez; ~**Mary's/the dentist's** chez Mary/le dentiste.

····▸ (in times, ages) à; ~ **four o'clock** à quatre heures; ~ **two years of age** à l'âge de deux ans.

····▸ (in email addresses) arobase f

ate &/eɪt/ ➡**EAT**.

atheist /ˈeɪθɪɪst/ n athée mf.

athlete /ˈæθliːt/ n athlète mf. **athletic** adj athlétique. **athletics** npl athlétisme m; (US) sports mpl.

Atlantic /ətˈlæntɪk/ adj atlantique. ● n the ~ **(Ocean)** l'Atlantique m.

atlas /ˈætləs/ n atlas m.

atmosphere /ˈætməsfɪə(r)/ n (air) atmosphère f; (mood) ambiance f. **atmospheric** adj atmosphérique; d'ambiance.

atom /ˈætəm/ n atome m.

atrocious /əˈtrəʊʃəs/ adj atroce.

atrocity /əˈtrɒsətɪ/ n atrocité f.

attach /əˈtætʃ/ vt/i (s')attacher; (letter) joindre (**to** à).

attaché /əˈtæʃeɪ/ n (Pol) attaché/-e m/f. ~ **case** n attaché-case m.

attached /əˈtætʃt/ adj be ~ **to** (like) être attaché à; **the** ~ **letter** la lettre ci-jointe.

attachment /əˈtætʃmənt/ n (accessory) accessoire m; (affection) attachement m; (e-mail) pièces fpl jointes.

attack /əˈtæk/ n attaque f; (Med) crise f. ● vt attaquer.

attain /əˈteɪn/ vt atteindre (à); (gain) acquérir.

attempt /əˈtempt/ vt tenter. ● n tentative f; **an** ~ **on sb's life** un attentat contre qn.

attend /əˈtend/ vt assister à; (class) suivre; (school, church) aller à. ● vi assister; ~ (to) (look after) s'occuper de. **attendance** n présence f; (people) assistance f.

attendant /əˈtendənt/ n employé/-e m/f. ● adj associé.

attention /əˈtenʃn/ n attention f; ~! (Mil) garde-à-vous! **pay** ~ faire or prêter attention (**to** à).

attentive /əˈtentɪv/ adj attentif; (considerate) attentionné. **attentively** adv attentivement. **attentiveness** n attention f.

attest /əˈtest/ vt/i ~ (**to**) attester.

attic /ˈætɪk/ n grenier m.

attitude /ˈætɪtjuːd/ n attitude f.

attorney /əˈtɜːnɪ/ n (US) avocat/ -e m/f.

attract /əˈtrækt/ vt attirer. **attraction** n attraction f; (charm) attrait m.

attractive /əˈtræktɪv/ adj attrayant, séduisant. **attractively** adv agréablement. **attractiveness** n attrait m, beauté f.

attribute[1] /əˈtrɪbjuːt/ vt ~ to attribuer à.

attribute[2] /ˈætrɪbjuːt/ n attribut m.

aubergine /ˈəʊbəʒiːn/ n aubergine f.

auction /ˈɔːkʃn/ n vente f aux enchères. ● vt vendre aux enchères. **auctioneer** n commissaire priseur m.

audacious /ɔːˈdeɪʃəs/ adj audacieux.

audience /ˈɔːdɪəns/ n (theatre, radio) public m; (interview) audience f.

audiovisual /ɔːdɪəʊˈvɪʒʊəl/ adj audiovisuel.

audit /ˈɔːdɪt/ n vérification f des comptes. ● vt vérifier.

audition /ɔːˈdɪʃn/ n audition f. ● vt/i auditionner (**for** pour).

auditor /ˈɔːdɪtə(r)/ n commissaire m aux comptes.

August /ˈɔːɡəst/ n août m.

aunt /ɑːnt/ n tante f.

auspicious /ɔːˈspɪʃəs/ adj favorable.

Australia /ɒˈstreɪlɪə/ n Australie f.

Australian /ɒˈstreɪlɪən/ n Australien/-ne m/f. ● adj australien.

Austria /ˈɒstrɪə/ n Autriche f.

Austrian /ˈɒstrɪən/ n Autrichien/-ne m/f. ● adj autrichien.

authentic /ɔːˈθentɪk/ adj authentique.

author /ˈɔːθə(r)/ n auteur m.

authoritarian /ɔːˌθɒrɪˈteərɪən/ adj autoritaire.

authoritative /ɔːˈθɒrətətɪv/ adj (credible) qui fait autorité; (manner) autoritaire.

authority /ɔːˈθɒrətɪ/ n autorité f; (permission) autorisation f.

authorization /ɔːθəraɪˈzeɪʃn/ n autorisation f. **authorize** vt autoriser.

autistic /ɔːˈtɪstɪk/ adj (person) autiste; (response) autistique.

autograph /ˈɔːtəɡrɑːf/ n autographe m. ● vt signer, dédicacer.

automate /ˈɔːtəmeɪt/ vt automatiser.

automatic /ɔːtəˈmætɪk/ adj automatique. ● n (Auto) voiture f automatique.

automobile /ˈɔːtəməbiːl/ n (US) auto(mobile) f.

autonomous /ɔːˈtɒnəməs/ adj autonome.

autumn /ˈɔːtəm/ n automne m.

auxiliary /ɔːɡˈzɪlɪərɪ/ adj & n auxiliaire (m/f); ~ (**verb**) auxiliaire m.

avail /əˈveɪl/ vt ~ oneself of profiter de. ● n of no ~ inutile; **to no** ~ sans résultat.

availability /əveɪləˈbɪlətɪ/ n disponibilité f. **available** adj disponible.

avenge /əˈvendʒ/ vt venger; ~ **oneself** se venger (**on** de).

avenue /ˈævənjuː/ n avenue f; (line of approach:fig) voie f.

average /ˈævərɪdʒ/ n moyenne f; **on** ~ en moyenne. ● adj moyen. ● vt faire la moyenne de; (produce, do) faire en moyenne.

aviary /ˈeɪvɪərɪ/ n volière f.

avocado /ævəˈkɑːdəʊ/ n avocat m.

avoid /əˈvɔɪd/ vt éviter. **avoidance** n (of injuries) prévention f; (of responsibility) refus m.

await /əˈweɪt/ vt attendre.

awake /əˈweɪk/ vt/i (pt **awoke**; pp **awoken**) (s')éveiller. ● adj **be** ~ ne pas dormir, être (r)éveillé.

award /əˈwɔːd/ vt (grant) attribuer; (prize) décerner; (points) accorder. ● n récompense f; prix m; (scholarship) bourse f; **pay** ~ augmentation f (de salaire).

aware /əˈweə(r)/ adj (well-informed) averti; **be** ~ **of** (danger) être conscient de; (fact) savoir; **become** ~ **of** prendre conscience de. **awareness** n conscience f.

away /əˈweɪ/ adv (far) (au) loin; (absent) absent, parti; ~ **from** loin de; **move** ~ s'écarter; (to new home) déménager; **six kilometres** ~ à six kilomètres (de distance); **take** ~ emporter; **he was snoring** ~ il ronflait. ● adj & n ~ (**match**) match m à l'extérieur.

awe /ɔː/ n crainte f (révérencielle).

awe-inspiring /ˈɔːɪnspaɪərɪŋ/ adj impressionnant.

awesome /ˈɔːsəm/ adj redoutable.

awful /ˈɔːfl/ adj affreux. **awfully** adv (badly) affreusement; (very 🆃) rudement.

awkward /ˈɔːkwəd/ adj difficile; (inconvenient) inopportun; (clumsy)

maladroit; (embarrassing) gênant; (embarrassed) gêné. **awkwardly** adv maladroitement; avec gêne. **awkwardness** n maladresse f; (discomfort) gêne f.

awning /ˈɔːnɪŋ/ n auvent m; (of shop) store m.

awoke, **awoken** ➡**AWAKE**.

axe /æks/ n hache f. ● vt (pres p **axing**) réduire; (eliminate) supprimer; (employee) renvoyer.

axis /ˈæksɪs/ n (pl **axes**) axe m.

axle /ˈæksl/ n essieu m.

Bb

BA abbr ➡**BACHELOR OF ARTS**.

babble /ˈbæbl/ vi babiller; (stream) gazouiller. ● n babillage m.

baby /ˈbeɪbɪ/ n bébé m. ~ **carriage** n (US) voiture f d'enfant. ~**-sit** vi faire du babysitting, garder des enfants. ~**-sitter** n baby-sitter mf.

bachelor /ˈbætʃələ(r)/ n célibataire m. **B**~ **of Arts** licencié/-e m/f ès lettres.

back /bæk/ n (of person, hand, page, etc.) dos m; (of house) derrière m; (of vehicle) arrière m; (of room) fond m; (of chair) dossier m; (in football) arrière m; **at the** ~ **of the book** à la fin du livre; **in** ~ **of** (US) derrière. ● adj (leg, wheel) arrière inv; (door, gate) de derrière; (taxes) arriéré. ● adv en arrière, en arrière; (returned) de retour, rentré; **come** ~ revenir; **give** ~ rendre; **take** ~ reprendre; **I want it** ~ je veux le récupérer. ● vt (support) appuyer; (bet on) miser sur; (vehicle) faire reculer. ● vi (of person, vehicle) reculer. ~ **down** céder; ~**out** se désister; (Auto) sortir en marche arrière; ~ **up** (support) appuyer. ~**ache** n mal m de dos. ~**-bencher** n (Pol) député m. ~**bone** n colonne f vertébrale. ~**date** vt antidater. ~**fire** vi (Auto) pétarader; (fig) mal tourner. ~**gammon** n trictrac m.

background /'bækgraund/ n fond m, arrière-plan m; (context) contexte m; (environment) milieu m; (experience) formation f. ● adj (music, noise) de fond.

backhand /'bækhænd/ n revers m. **backhander** /'bækrŋ/ n (bribe) pot-de-vin m.

backing /'bækɪŋ/ n soutien m.

back: ~**lash** n retour m de bâton; réaction f violente (**against** contre). ~**log** n retard m. ~**number** n vieux numéro m. ~**pack** n sac m à dos. ~**side** n (buttocks 🗎) derrière m. ~**stage** adj & adv dans les coulisses. ~**stroke** n dos m crawlé. ~**track** vi rebrousser chemin; (change one's opinion) faire marche arrière.

backup /'bækʌp/ n soutien m; (Comput) sauvegarde f. ● adj de secours; (Comput) de sauvegarde.

backward /'bækwəd/ adj (step etc.) en arrière; (retarded) arriéré.

backwards /'bækwəd/ adv en arrière; (walk) à reculons; (read) à l'envers; **go** ~ **and forwards** aller et venir.

bacon /'beɪkən/ n lard m; (in rashers) bacon m.

bacteria /bæk'tɪərɪə/ npl bactéries fpl.

bad /bæd/ adj (**worse, worst**) mauvais; (wicked) méchant; (ill) malade; (accident) grave; (food) gâté; **feel** ~ se sentir mal; **go** ~ se gâter; ~ **language** gros mots mpl; **too** ~! tant pis!; (I'm sorry) dommage!

badge /bædʒ/ n badge m; (coat

of arms) insigne m.

badger /'bædʒə(r)/ n blaireau m. ● vt harceler.

badly /'bædlɪ/ adv mal; (hurt) gravement; **want** ~ avoir grande envie de.

badminton /'bædmɪntn/ n badminton m.

bad-tempered adj irritable.

baffle /'bæfl/ vt déconcerter.

bag /bæg/ n sac m; ~ **s** (luggage) bagages mpl; (under eyes 🗎) valises fpl; ~**s of** plein de.

baggage /'bægɪdʒ/ n bagages mpl; ~ **reclaim** réception f des bagages.

baggy /'bægɪ/ adj large.

bagpipes /'bægpaɪps/ npl cornemuse f.

bail /beɪl/ n caution f; **on** ~ sous caution; (cricket) bâtonnet m. ● vt mettre en liberté provisoire.

bailiff /'beɪlɪf/ n huissier m.

bait /beɪt/ n appât m. ● vt appâter; (fig) tourmenter.

bake /beɪk/ vt faire cuire au four; ~ **a cake** faire un gâteau. ● vi cuire; (person) faire du pain. **baked beans** npl haricots mpl blancs à la tomate. **baked potato** n pomme f de terre en robe des champs.

baker n boulanger/-ère m/f. **bakery** n boulangerie f.

balance /'bæləns/ n équilibre m; (scales) balance f; (outstanding sum: Comm) solde m; (of payments, of trade) balance f; (remainder) restant m. ● vt mettre en équilibre; (weigh up also Comm) balancer; (budget) équilibrer; (to compensate) contrebalancer. ● vi être en équilibre.

balcony /'bælkənɪ/ n balcon m.

bald /bɔːld/ adj chauve; (tyre) lisse; (fig) simple.

balk /bɔːk/ vt contrecarrer. ● vi ~

at reculer devant.

ball /bɔːl/ n (golf, tennis, etc.) balle f; (football) ballon m; (billiards) bille f; (of wool) pelote f; (sphere) boule f; (dance) bal m.

ballet /'bæleɪ/ n ballet m.

balloon /bə'luːn/ n ballon m.

ballot /'bælət/ n scrutin m. ● vt consulter par vote (on sur). ~ **box** n urne f. ~ **paper** n bulletin m de vote.

ballpoint pen n stylo m (à) bille.

ban /bæn/ vt (pt banned) interdire; ~ **sb from** exclure qn de; ~ **sb from doing** interdire à qn de faire. ● n interdiction f (on de).

banal /bə'nɑːl/ adj banal.

banana /bə'nɑːnə/ n banane f.

band /bænd/ n (strip, group of people) bande f; (pop group) groupe m; (brass band) fanfare f. ● vi ~ **together** se réunir.

bandage /'bændɪdʒ/ n bandage m. ● vt bander.

B and B abbr ▸BED AND BREAKFAST.

bandit /'bændɪt/ n bandit m.

bandstand /'bændstænd/ n kiosque m à musique.

bang /bæŋ/ n (blow, noise) coup m; (explosion) détonation f; (of door) claquement m. ● vt/i taper; (door) claquer; ~ **one's head** se cogner la tête. ● interj vlan m. ● adv ↓; ~ **in the middle** en plein milieu; ~ **on time** à l'heure pile.

banger /'bæŋə(r)/ n (firework) pétard m; (Culin) saucisse f; (old) ~ (car ↓) guimbarde f.

banish /'bænɪʃ/ vt bannir.

banister /'bænɪstə(r)/ n rampe f d'escalier.

bank /bæŋk/ n (Comm) banque f; (of river) rive f; (of sand) banc m. ● vt mettre en banque. ● vi (Aviat)

virer; ~ **with** avoir un compte à; ~ **on** compter sur. ~ **account** n compte m en banque. ~ **card** n carte f bancaire. ~ **holiday** n jour m férié.

banking /'bæŋkɪŋ/ n opérations fpl bancaires; (as career) la banque.

Bank holiday Jour chômé où les banques sont fermées au Royaume-Uni, en général à l'occasion d'une fête religieuse ou civile (Christmas Day, Easter Monday, May Day, etc.). La plupart tombe un lundi: par exemple, le spring bank holiday, qui coïncide avec la Pentecôte, tombe le dernier lundi de mai ou le premier lundi de juin.

banknote /'bæŋknəʊt/ n billet m de banque.

bankrupt /'bæŋkrʌpt/ adj be ~ être en faillite; go ~ faire faillite. ● n failli/-e m/f. ● vt mettre en faillite. **bankruptcy** n faillite f.

bank statement n relevé m de compte.

banner /'bænə(r)/ n bannière f.

baptism /'bæptɪzəm/ n baptême m. **baptize** vt baptiser.

bar /bɑː(r)/ n (of metal) barre f; (on window, cage) barreau m; (of chocolate) tablette f; (pub) bar m; (counter) comptoir m; (Mus) mesure f; (fig) obstacle m; ~ **of soap** savonnette f; **the** ~ (Jur) le barreau. ● vt (pt barred) (obstruct) barrer; (prohibit) interdire; (exclude) exclure. ● prep sauf.

barbecue /'bɑːbɪkjuː/ n barbecue m. ● vt faire au barbecue.

barbed wire n fil m de fer barbelé.

barber /'bɑːbə(r)/ n coiffeur m (pour hommes).

bar code n code m (à) barres.

bare /beə(r)/ adj nu; (cupboard) vide. ● vt mettre à nu. ~**foot** adj nu-pieds inv, pieds nus. **barely** adv à peine.

bargain /'bɑːgɪn/ n (deal) marché m; (cheap thing) occasion f. ● vi négocier; (haggle) marchander; **not** ~ **for** ne pas s'attendre à.

barge /bɑːdʒ/ n péniche f. ● vi ~ **in** interrompre; (into room) faire irruption.

bark /bɑːk/ n (of tree) écorce f; (of dog) aboiement m. ● vi aboyer.

barley /'bɑːlɪ/ n orge f.

bar: ~**maid** n serveuse f. ~**man** n (pl -**men**) barman m.

barn /bɑːn/ n grange f.

barracks /'bærəks/ npl caserne f.

barrel /'bærəl/ n tonneau m; (of oil) baril m; (of gun) canon m.

barren /'bærən/ adj stérile.

barricade /bærɪ'keɪd/ n barricade f. ● vt barricader.

barrier /'bærɪə(r)/ n barrière f; **ticket** ~ guichet m.

barrister /'bærɪstə(r)/ n avocat m.

bartender /'bɑːtendə(r)/ n (US) barman m.

barter /'bɑːtə(r)/ n troc m. ● vt troquer (**for** contre).

base /beɪs/ n base f. ● vt baser (**on** sur; **in** à). ● adj ignoble. **baseball** n base-ball m.

basement /'beɪsmənt/ n sous-sol m.

bash /bæʃ/ ▣ vt cogner; ~**ed in** enfoncé. ● n coup m violent; **have a** ~ **at** s'essayer à.

basic /'beɪsɪk/ adj fondamental, élémentaire; **the** ~**s** l'essentiel m. **basically** adv au fond.

basil /'bæzl/ n basilic m.

basin /'beɪsn/ n (for liquids) cuvette

f; (for food) bol m; (for washing) lavabo m; (of river) bassin m.

basis /'beɪsɪs/ n (pl **bases**) base f.

bask /bɑːsk/ vi se prélasser (**in** à).

basket /'bɑːskɪt/ n corbeille f; (with handle) panier m. **basketball** n basket(- ball) m.

Basque /bæsk/ n (person) Basque mf; (Ling) basque m. ● adj basque.

bass¹ /beɪs/ adj (voice, part) de basse; (sound, note) grave. ● n (pl **basses**) basse f.

bass² /bæs/ n inv (freshwater fish) perche f; (sea) bar m.

bassoon /bə'suːn/ n basson m.

bastard /'bɑːstəd/ n (illegitimate) bâtard/-e m/f; (insult ▣) salaud m ▣.

bat /bæt/ n (cricket etc.) batte f; (table tennis) raquette f; (animal) chauve-souris f. ● vt (pt **batted**) (ball) frapper; **not** ~ **an eyelid** ne pas sourciller.

batch /bætʃ/ n (of cakes, people) fournée f; (of goods, text also Comput) lot m.

bath /bɑːθ/ n (pl -**s**) bain m; (tub) baignoire f; **have a** ~ prendre un bain; (swimming) ~**s** piscine f. ● vt donner un bain à.

bathe /beɪð/ vt baigner. ● vi se baigner; (US) prendre un bain.

bathing /'beɪðɪŋ/ n baignade f. ~**costume** n maillot m de bain.

bath: ~**robe** n (US) robe f de chambre. ~**room** n salle f de bains.

baton /'bætn/ n (policeman's) matraque f; (Mus) baguette f.

batter /'bætə(r)/ vt battre. ● n (Culin) pâte f (à frire).

battery /'bætərɪ/ n (Mil, Auto) batterie f; (of torch, radio) pile f.

battle /'bætl/ n bataille f; (fig) lutte

baulk | beat

f. ● *vi* se battre. **~field** *n* champ *m* de bataille.

baulk /bɔːk/ *vt/i* ➡BALK.

bay /beɪ/ *n* (Bot) laurier *m*; (Geog, Archit) baie *f.*; (area) aire *f.*; (bark) aboiement *m*; **keep** or **hold at ~** tenir à distance. ● *vi* aboyer. **~leaf** *n* feuille *f* de laurier. **~ window** *n* fenêtre *f* en saillie.

bazaar /bəˈzɑː(r)/ *n* (shop, market) bazar *m*; (sale) vente *f.*

BC *abbr* (**before Christ**) avant J.-C.

BBS *abbr* (**Bulletin Board System**) (Internet) babillard *m* électronique, BBS *m*.

---

be /biː/

present **am, is, are**; *past* **was, were**; *past participle* **been**.

● *intransitive verb*
····▸ être; **I am tired** je suis fatigué; **it's me** c'est moi.
····▸ (feelings) avoir; **I am hot** j'ai chaud; **he is hungry/thirsty** il a faim/soif; **her hands are cold** elle a froid aux mains.
····▸ (age) avoir; **I am 15** j'ai 15 ans.
····▸ (weather) faire; **it's warm** il fait chaud; **it's 25°** il fait 25°.
····▸ (health) **how are you?** comment allez-vous or comment vas-tu?
····▸ (visit) **I've never been to Italy** je ne suis jamais allé en Italie.

● *auxiliary verb*
····▸ (in tenses) **I am working** je travaille; **he was writing to his mother** il écrivait à sa mère; **she is to do it at once** (obligation) elle doit le faire tout de suite.

····▸ (in passives) **he was killed** il a été tué; **the window has been fixed** on a réparé la fenêtre.

····▸ (in tag questions) **their house is lovely, isn't it?** leur maison est très jolie, n'est-ce pas?

····▸ (in short answers) '**I am a painter**'—'**are you?**' 'je suis peintre'—'ah oui?'; '**are you a doctor?**'—'**yes, I am**' 'êtes-vous médecin?'—'oui'; '**you're not going out**'—'**yes I am**' 'tu ne sors pas'—'si'.

---

beach /biːtʃ/ *n* plage *f.*

beacon /ˈbiːkən/ *n* (lighthouse) phare *m*; (marker) balise *f.*

bead /biːd/ *n* perle *f.*

beak /biːk/ *n* bec *m.*

beaker /ˈbiːkə(r)/ *n* gobelet *m.*

beam /biːm/ *n* (timber) poutre *f.*; (of light) rayon *m*; (of torch) faisceau *m.* ● *vi* rayonner. ● *vt* (broadcast) transmettre.

bean /biːn/ *n* haricot *m.*

bear /beə(r)/ *n* ours *m.* ● *vt* (*pt* **bore**; *pp* **borne**) (carry, show, feel) porter; (endure, sustain) supporter; (child) mettre au monde. ● *vi* **~ left** (go) prendre à gauche; **~ in mind** tenir compte de. **~ out** confirmer; **~ up** tenir le coup. **bearable** *adj* supportable.

beard /bɪəd/ *n* barbe *f.*

bearer /ˈbeərə(r)/ *n* porteur/-euse *m/f.*

bearing /ˈbeərɪŋ/ *n* (behaviour) maintien *m*; (relevance) rapport *m*; **get one's ~s** s'orienter.

beast /biːst/ *n* bête *f.*; (person) brute *f.*

beat /biːt/ *vt/i* (*pt* **beat**; *pp* **beaten**) battre; **~ a retreat** battre en retraite; ~ **it!** dégage! 🆒; **it ~s me** 🆒 ça me dépasse. ● n (of drum, heart) battement m; (Mus) mesure f; (of policeman) ronde f. ~ **off** repousser; ~ **up** tabasser. **beating** n raclée f.

beautiful /'bjuːtɪfl/ adj beau.

beauty /'bjuːtɪ/ n beauté f. ~**parlour** n institut m de beauté. ~**spot** n grain m de beauté; (place) site m pittoresque.

beaver /'biːvə(r)/ n castor m.

became /bɪ'keɪm/ ⟹**BECOME.**

because /bɪ'kɒz/ conj parce que; ~ **of** à cause de.

become /bɪ'kʌm/ vt/i (pt **became**, pp **become**) devenir; (befit) convenir à; **what has ~ of her?** qu'est-ce qu'elle est devenue?

bed /bed/ n lit m; (layer) couche f; (of sea) fond m; (of flowers) parterre m; **go to ~** (aller) se coucher. ● vi (pt **bedded**) ~ **down** se coucher. **bed and breakfast** n chambre f avec petit déjeuner, chambre f d'hôte. ~ **bug** n punaise f. ~**clothes** npl couvertures fpl.

bedding /'bedɪŋ/ n literie f.

bed: ~**ridden** adj cloué au lit. ~**room** n chambre f (à coucher). ~**side** n chevet m. ~**sit**, ~**sitter** n chambre f meublée, studio m. ~**spread** n dessus m de lit. ~**time** n heure f du coucher.

bee /biː/ n abeille f. **make a ~-line for** aller tout droit vers.

beech /biːtʃ/ n hêtre m.

beef /biːf/ n bœuf m. ~**burger** n hamburger m.

beehive /'biːhaɪv/ n ruche f.

been /biːn/ ⟹**BE.**

beer /bɪə(r)/ n bière f.

beetle /'biːtl/ n scarabée m.

beetroot /'biːtruːt/ n inv betterave f.

before /bɪ'fɔː(r)/ prep (time) avant; (place) devant; **the day ~ yesterday** avant-hier. ● adv avant; (already) déjà; **the day ~** la veille. ● conj ~ **leaving** avant de partir; ~ **I forget** avant que j'oublie. **beforehand** adv à l'avance.

beg /beg/ vt (pt **begged**) (food, money, favour) demander (**from** à); ~ **sb to do** supplier qn de faire. ● vi mendier; **it is going ~ging** personne n'en veut.

began /bɪ'gæn/ ⟹**BEGIN.**

beggar /'begə(r)/ n mendiant/-e m/f.

begin /bɪ'gɪn/ vt/i (pt **began**, pp **begun**, pres p **beginning**) commencer (**to do** à faire). **beginner** n débutant/-e m/f. **beginning** n commencement m, début m.

begun /bɪ'gʌn/ ⟹**BEGIN.**

behalf /bɪ'hɑːf/ n **on ~ of** (act, speak, campaign) pour; (phone, write) de la part de.

behave /bɪ'heɪv/ vi se conduire; (oneself) se conduire bien.

behaviour /bɪ'heɪvjə(r)/, (US) **behavior** n comportement m (**towards** envers).

behead /bɪ'hed/ vt décapiter.

behind /bɪ'haɪnd/ prep derrière; (in time) en retard sur. ● adv derrière; (late) en retard; **leave ~** oublier. ● n (buttocks 🆒) derrière m 🆒.

beige /beɪʒ/ adj & n beige (m).

being /'biːɪŋ/ n (person) être m.

belch /beltʃ/ vi avoir un renvoi. ● vt ~ **out** (smoke) s'échapper. ● n renvoi m.

Belgian /'beldʒən/ n Belge mf. ● adj belge. **Belgium** n Belgique f.

belief /bɪ'liːf/ n conviction f; (trust) confiance f; (faith: Relig) foi f.

believe /bɪ'liːv/ vt/i croire; ~ **in** croire à; (deity) croire en.

believer n croyant/-e m/f.

bell /bel/ n cloche f; (small) clochette f; (on door) sonnette f.

belly /'belɪ/ n ventre m. ~ **button** n nombril m.

belong /bɪ'lɒŋ/ vi ~ **to** appartenir à; (club) être membre de.

belongings /bɪ'lɒŋɪŋz/ npl affaires fpl.

beloved /bɪ'lʌvɪd/ adj & n bien-aimé/-e (m/f).

below /bɪ'ləʊ/ prep sous, au-dessous de; (fig) indigne de. ● adv en dessous; (on page) ci-dessous.

belt /belt/ n ceinture f; (Tech) courroie f; (fig) zone f. ● vt (hit ⊞) rosser. ● vi (rush ⊞) ~ **in/out** entrer/ sortir à toute vitesse.

beltway /'beltweɪ/ n (US) périphérique m.

bemused /bɪ'mjuːzd/ adj perplexe.

bench /bentʃ/ n banc m; the ~ (Jur) la magistrature (assise).

bend /bend/ vt (pt bend) (knee, arm, wire) plier; (head, back) courber. ● vi (road) tourner; (person) se pencher. ● n courbe f; (in road) virage m; (of arm, knee) pli m.

beneath /bɪ'niːθ/ prep sous, au-dessous de; (fig) indigne de. ● adv en dessous.

benefactor /'benɪfæktə(r)/ n bienfaiteur/-trice m/f.

beneficial /benɪ'fɪʃl/ adj bénéfique.

benefit /'benɪfɪt/ n avantage m; (allowance) allocation f. ● vt (be useful to) profiter à; (do good to) faire du bien à. ● vi profiter; ~ **from** tirer profit de.

benign /bɪ'naɪn/ adj (kindly) bienveillant; (Med) bénin.

bent /bent/ →BEND. ● n (talent)

aptitude f; (inclination) penchant m. ● adj tordu; ⊠ corrompu; ~ **on doing** décidé à faire.

bequest /bɪ'kwest/ n legs m.

bereaved /bɪ'riːvd/ adj endeuillé; the ~ la famille endeuillée. **bereavement** n deuil m.

berry /'berɪ/ n baie f.

berserk /bə'sɜːk/ adj fou furieux.

berth /bɜːθ/ n (in train, ship) couchette f; (anchorage) mouillage m; **give a wide ~ to** éviter. ● vi mouiller.

beside /bɪ'saɪd/ prep à côté de; ~ **oneself** hors de soi; ~ **the point** sans rapport.

besides /bɪ'saɪdz/ prep en plus de. ● adv en plus.

besiege /bɪ'siːdʒ/ vt assiéger.

best /best/ adj meilleur; the ~ **book** le meilleur livre; **the ~ part** of la plus grande partie de; **the ~ thing is** te mieux est de. ● adv (the) ~ (behave, play) le mieux. ● n the ~ le meilleur, la meilleure; **do one's ~** faire de son mieux; **make the ~ of** s'accommoder de. ~ **man** n témoin. ~**-seller** n bestseller m, livre m à succès.

bet /bet/ n pari m. ● vt/i (pt **bet** or **betted**, pres p **betting**) parier (on sur).

betray /bɪ'treɪ/ vt trahir.

better /'betə(r)/ adj meilleur; the ~ **part** of la plus grande partie de; **get ~** s'améliorer; (recover) se remettre. ● adv mieux; **I had ~ go** je ferais mieux de partir. ● vt (improve) améliorer; (do better than) surpasser. ● n **get the ~ of** l'emporter sur; **so much the ~** tant mieux. ~ **off** (richer) plus riche; **he is/would be ~ off at home** il est/serait mieux chez lui.

betting shop n bureau m

du PMU.

between /bɪ'twiːn/ prep entre.
● adv in ~ au milieu.

beverage /'bevərɪdʒ/ n boisson f.

beware /bɪ'weə(r)/ vi prendre
garde (of à).

bewilder /bɪ'wɪldə(r)/ vt déconcerter.

beyond /bɪ'jɒnd/ prep au-delà de;
(control, reach) hors de; (besides)
excepté. ● adv au-delà; **it is ~ me**
ça me dépasse.

bias /'baɪəs/ n (inclination) tendance f; (prejudice) parti m pris. ● vt
(pt **biased**) influer sur. **biased** adj
partial.

bib /bɪb/ n bavoir m.

Bible /'baɪbl/ n Bible f.

biceps /'baɪseps/ n biceps m.

bicycle /'baɪsɪkl/ n vélo m, bicyclette f. ● adj (bell, chain) de vélo;
(pump, clip) à vélo.

bid /bɪd/ n (at auction) enchère f;
(attempt) tentative f. ● vt/i (pt
bade, pp **bidden** or **bid**, pres p **bidding**) (offer) offrir, mettre une enchère (**for** pour); ~ **sb good
morning** dire bonjour à qn; ~ **sb
farewell** faire ses adieux à qn.

bidding /'bɪdɪŋ/ n (at auction) enchères fpl; **he did my** ~ il a fait ce
que je lui ai dit.

bifocals /baɪ'fəʊklz/ npl verres mpl
à double foyer.

big /bɪg/ adj (**bigger**, **biggest**)
grand; (in bulk) gros.

bike /baɪk/ n vélo m.

bikini /bɪ'kiːnɪ/ n bikini m.

bilberry /'bɪlbrɪ/ n myrtille f.

bilingual /baɪ'lɪŋgwəl/ adj bilingue.

bill /bɪl/ n (invoice) facture f; (in
hotel, for gas) note f; (in restaurant)
addition f; (of sale) acte m; (Pol)

projet m de loi; (banknote: US) billet
m de banque; (Theat) **on the** ~ à
l'affiche; (of bird) bec m. ● vt (person: Comm) envoyer la facture à.
~**board** n panneau m d'affichage.

billet /'bɪlɪt/ n cantonnement m.
● vt (pt **billeted**) cantonner (**on**
chez).

billiards /'bɪljədz/ n billard m.

billion /'bɪlɪən/ n billion m; (US)
milliard m.

bin /bɪn/ n (for rubbish) poubelle f;
(for storage) casier m.

bind /baɪnd/ vt (pt **bound**) attacher; (book) relier; **be bound by**
être tenu par. ● n (bore) corvée f.

binding /'baɪndɪŋ/ n reliure f. ● adj
(agreement, contract) qui lie.

binge /bɪndʒ/ n (drinking) beuverie
f; (eating) gueuleton m.

binoculars /bɪ'nɒkjʊləz/ npl jumelles fpl.

biochemistry /baɪəʊ'kemɪstrɪ/ n
biochimie f.

biodegradable /baɪəʊdɪ
'greɪdəbl/ adj biodégradable.

biographer /baɪ'ɒgrəfə(r)/ n biographe mf. **biography** n biographie f.

biological /baɪə'lɒdʒɪkl/ adj biologique.

biologist /baɪ'ɒlədʒɪst/ n biologiste mf.

biology /baɪ'ɒlədʒɪ/ n biologie f.

bioterrorism /baɪə'terərɪzm/ n
bioterrorisme m.

birch /bɜːtʃ/ n (tree) bouleau m;
(whip) fouet m.

bird /bɜːd/ n oiseau m; (girl 🗊)
nana f.

Biro® /'baɪərəʊ/ n stylo m à bille,
bic® m.

birth /bɜːθ/ n naissance f; **give** ~
accoucher. ~ **certificate** n acte m

de naissance. ~**control** n contraception f. ~**day** n anniversaire m. ~**mark** n tache f de naissance. ~**rate** n taux m de natalité.

biscuit /'bɪskɪt/ n biscuit m; (US) petit pain m (au lait).

bishop /'bɪʃəp/ n évêque m.

bit /bɪt/ →BITE. ● n morceau m; (of horse) mors m; (of tool) mèche f; **a ~** (a little) un peu; (Comput) bit m.

bitch /bɪtʃ/ n chienne f; (woman ✗) garce f ✗. ● vi dire du mal (about m).

bite /baɪt/ vt/i (pt **bit**; pp **bitten**) mordre; **~ one's nails** se ronger les ongles. ● n morsure f; (by insect) piqûre f; (mouthful) bouchée f; **have a ~** manger un morceau.

bitter /'bɪtə(r)/ adj amer; (weather) glacial. ● n bière f. **bitterly** adv amèrement; **it is ~ly cold** il fait un temps glacial.

bizarre /bɪ'zɑ:(r)/ adj bizarre.

black /blæk/ adj noir; **~ and blue** couvert de bleus. ● n (colour) noir m; B~ (person) Noir/-e m/f. ● vt noircir; (goods) boycotter. ~**berry** n mûre f. ~**bird** n merle m. ~**board** n tableau m noir. ~**currant** n cassis m.

blacken /'blækən/ vt/i noircir.

black: **~ eye** n œil m poché. ~**head** n point m noir. **~ ice** n verglas m. **~ leg** n jaune m.

blacklist /'blæklɪst/ n liste f noire. ● vt mettre à l'index.

blackmail /'blækmeɪl/ n chantage m. ● vt faire chanter. **blackmailer** n maître-chanteur m.

black: **~ market** n marché m noir. ~**out** n panne f de courant; (Med) syncope f. **~ pudding** n boudin m. **~ sheep** n brebis f galeuse. ~**smith** n forgeron m. ~**spot** n point m noir.

bladder /'blædə(r)/ n vessie f.

blade /bleɪd/ n (of knife) lame f; (of propeller, oar) pale f; **~ of grass** brin m d'herbe.

blame /bleɪm/ vt accuser; **~ sb for sth** reprocher qch à qn; **he is to ~** il est responsable (for de). ● n responsabilité f (for de).

bland /blænd/ adj (insipid) fade.

blank /blæŋk/ adj (page) blanc; (screen) vide; (cheque) en blanc; **to look ~** avoir l'air ébahi. ● n blanc m; **~ (cartridge)** cartouche f à blanc.

blanket /'blæŋkɪt/ n couverture f; (layer) couche f.

blasphemous /'blæsfəməs/ adj blasphématoire; (person) blasphémateur.

blast /blɑ:st/ n explosion f; (wave of air) souffle m; (of wind) rafale f; (noise from siren etc.) coup m. ● vt (blow up) faire sauter. **~ off** décoller. ~**furnace** n haut-fourneau m. **~ off** n lancement m.

blatant /'bleɪtnt/ adj (obvious) flagrant; (shameless) éhonté.

blaze /bleɪz/ n feu m; (accident) incendie m. ● vt **a trail** faire œuvre de pionnier. ● vi (fire) brûler; (sky, eyes) flamboyer.

bleach /bli:tʃ/ n (for cleaning) eau f de Javel; (for hair, fabric) décolorant m. ● vt/i blanchir; (hair) décolorer.

bleak /bli:k/ adj (landscape) désolé; (outlook, future) sombre.

bleed /bli:d/ vt/i (pt **bled**) saigner.

bleep /bli:p/ n bip m.

blemish /'blemɪʃ/ n imperfection f; (on fruit, reputation) tache f. ● vt entacher.

blend /blend/ vt mélanger. ● vi se fondre ensemble; **to ~ with** se marier à. ● n mélange m. **blender** n mixeur n, mixer n.

bless /bles/ vt bénir; **be ~ed with** jouir de; **~ you!** à vos souhaits! **blessed** adj (holy) saint; (damned 🗉) sacré. **blessing** n bénédiction f; (benefit) avantage m; (stroke of luck) chance f.

blew /blu:/ ➡BLOW.

blight /blaɪt/ n (disease: Bot) rouille f; (fig) plaie f.

blind /blaɪnd/ adj aveugle (**to** à); (corner, bend) sans visibilité. ● vt aveugler. ● n (on window) store m; **the ~s** les aveugles mpl.

blindfold /'blaɪndfəʊld/ adj **be ~** avoir les yeux bandés. ● adv les yeux bandés. ● n bandeau m. ● vt bander les yeux à.

blindness /'blaɪndnɪs/ n (Med) cécité f; (fig) aveuglement m.

blind spot n (Auto) angle m mort.

blink /blɪŋk/ vi cligner des yeux; (light) clignoter.

bliss /blɪs/ n délice m. **blissful** adj délicieux.

blister /'blɪstə(r)/ n ampoule f; (on paint) cloque f. ● vi cloquer.

blitz /blɪts/ n (Aviat) raid m éclair. ● vt bombarder.

blob /blɒb/ n (drop) (grosse) goutte f; (stain) tache f.

block /blɒk/ n bloc m; (buildings) pâté m de maisons; (in pipe) obstruction f; ~ (of flats) immeuble m; ~ **letters** majuscules fpl. ● vt bloquer.

blockade /blɒ'keɪd/ n blocus m. ● vt bloquer.

blockage /'blɒkɪdʒ/ n obstruction f.

blockbuster n gros succès m.

bloke /bləʊk/ n 🗉 type m.

blond /blɒnd/ adj & n blond (m).

blonde /blɒnd/ adj & n blonde (f).

blood /blʌd/ n sang m. ● adj (donor, bath) de sang; (bank, poisoning) du sang; (group, vessel) sanguin. **~-pressure** n tension f artérielle. **~shed** n effusion f de sang. **~shot** adj injecté de sang. **~stream** n sang m. ~ **test** n prise f de sang.

bloody /'blʌdɪ/ adj (-ier, -iest) sanglant; 🗷 sacré. ● adv 🗷 vachement 🗉. **~-minded** adj 🗉 hargneux, obstiné.

bloom /blu:m/ n fleur f. ● vi fleurir; (person) s'épanouir.

blossom /'blɒsəm/ n fleur(s) f (pl). ● vi fleurir; (person) s'épanouir.

blot /blɒt/ n tache f. ● vt (pt **blotted**) tacher; (dry) sécher; ~ **out** effacer.

blotch /blɒtʃ/ n tache f.

blouse /blaʊz/ n chemisier m.

blow /bləʊ/ vt/i (pt **blew**; pp **blown**) souffler; (fuse) (faire) sauter; (squander 🗷) claquer; (opportunity) rater; ~ **one's nose** se moucher; ~ **a whistle** siffler. ● n coup m. □ ~ **away** or **off** emporter; ~ **out** souffler; ~ **over** passer; ~ **up** (faire) sauter; (tyre) gonfler; (Photo) agrandir.

blow-dry n brushing m. ● vt faire un brushing à.

blown /bləʊn/ ➡BLOW.

bludgeon /'blʌdʒən/ n matraque f. ● vt matraquer.

blue /blu:/ adj bleu; (movie) porno. ● n bleu m; **come out of the ~** être inattendu; **have the ~s** avoir le cafard. **~bell** n jacinthe f des bois. **~print** n projet m.

bluff /blʌf/ vt/i bluffer. ● n bluff m; **call sb's ~** dire chiche à qn. ● adj (person) carré.

blunder /'blʌndə(r)/ vi faire une bourde; (move) avancer à tâtons. ● n gaffe f.

blunt /blʌnt/ adj (knife) émoussé; (person) brusque. ● vt émousser.
bluntly adv carrément.

blur /blɜ:(r)/ n image f floue. ● vt (pt **blurred**) brouiller.

blurb /blɜ:b/ n résumé m publicitaire.

blush /blʌʃ/ vi rougir. ● n rougeur f.
blusher n fard m à joues.

blustery /blʌstərɪ/ adj ~ **wind** bourrasque f.

boar /bɔ:(r)/ n sanglier m.

board /bɔ:d/ n planche f; (for notices) tableau m; (food) pension f; **full** ~ pension f complète; **half** ~ demipension f; (committee) conseil m; ~ **of directors** conseil m d'administration; **go by the** ~ tomber à l'eau; **on** ~ à bord. ● vt (bus, train) monter dans; (Naut) monter à bord (de); ~ **with** être en pension chez.

boarding-school n école f privée avec internat.

boast /bəʊst/ vi se vanter (**about** de). ● vt s'enorgueillir de. ● n vantardise f.

boat /bəʊt/ n bateau m; (small) canot m; **in the same** ~ logé à la même enseigne.

bode /bəʊd/ vi ~ **well/ill** être de bon/mauvais augure.

bodily /bɒdɪlɪ/ adj (need, well-being) physique; (injury) corporel. ● adv physiquement; (in person) en personne.

body /bɒdɪ/ n corps m; (mass) masse f; (organization) organisme m; ~ **part** n partie f de corps; ~(**work**) (Auto) carrosserie f; **the main** ~ of le gros de. ~**building** n culturisme m. ~**guard** n garde m du corps.

bog /bɒg/ n marais m. ● vt (pt **bogged**) **get** ~**ged down**

s'enliser dans.

bogus /bəʊgəs/ adj faux.

boil /bɔɪl/ n furoncle m; **bring to the** ~ porter à ébullition. ● vt/i bouillir. ~ **down to** se ramener à; ~ **over** déborder. **boiled** adj (egg) à la coque; (potatoes) à l'eau.

boiler /bɔɪlə(r)/ n chaudière f; ~ **suit** bleu m (de travail).

boisterous /bɔɪstərəs/ adj tapageur; (child) turbulent.

bold /bəʊld/ adj hardi; (cheeky) effronté; (type) gras.

Bolivia /bəˈlɪvɪə/ n Bolivie f.

bollard /bɒlɑ:d/ n (on road) balise f.

bolt /bəʊlt/ n (on door) verrou m; (for nut) boulon m; (lightning) éclair m. ● vt (door) verrouiller; (food) engouffrer. ● vi s'emballer.

bomb /bɒm/ n bombe f; ~ **scare** alerte f à la bombe. ● vt bombarder.

bomber /bɒmə(r)/ n (aircraft) bombardier m; (person) plastiqueur m.

bombshell /bɒmʃel/ n **be a** ~ tomber comme une bombe.

bond /bɒnd/ n (agreement) engagement m; (link) lien m; (Comm) obligation f; **bon** m; **in** ~ (entreposé) en douane.

bone /bəʊn/ n os m; (of fish) arête f. ● vt désosser. ~**dry** adj tout à fait sec.

bonfire /bɒnfaɪə(r)/ n feu m; (for celebration) feu m de joie.

bonnet /bɒnɪt/ n (hat) bonnet m; (of vehicle) capot m.

bonus /bəʊnəs/ n prime f.

bony /bəʊnɪ/ adj (**-ier, -iest**) (thin) osseux; (fish) plein d'arêtes.

boo /bu:/ interj hou. ● vt/i huer. ● n huée f.

booby trap /bu:bɪtræp/ n mécanisme *m* piégé. ● *vt* (*pt*) **-trapped**) piéger.

book /bʊk/ *n* livre *m*; (*exercise*) cahier *m*; (of tickets etc.) carnet *m*; **~s** (Comm) comptes *mpl.* ● *vt* (reserve) réserver; (driver) dresser un PV à; (*player*) prendre le nom de; (write down) inscrire. ● *vi* retenir des places; (**fully**) **~ed** complet. **~case** *n* bibliothèque *f.* **booking-office** *n* guichet *m.* **~keeping** *n* comptabilité *f.* **booklet** *n* brochure *f.* **~maker** *n* bookmaker *m.* **~mark** *n* (for book, Internet) signet *m.* **~seller** *n* libraire *mf.* **~shop** *n* librairie *f.* **~stall** *n* kiosque *m* (à journaux).

boom /buːm/ *vi* (gun, wind, etc.) gronder; (*trade*) prospérer. ● *n* grondement *m*; (Comm) boom *m*, prospérité *f.*

boost /buːst/ *vt* stimuler; (*morale*) remonter; (*price*) augmenter; (*publicize*) faire de la réclame pour.

boot /buːt/ *n* (knee-length) botte *f*; (anklelength) chaussure *f* (montante); (for walking) chaussure *f* de marche; (Sport) chaussure *f* de sport; (of vehicle) coffre *m*; **get the ~** *fam* se faire virer. ● *vt/i* **~ up** (Comput) amorcer.

booth /buːð/ *n* (for telephone) cabine *f*; (at fair) baraque *f.*

booze /buːz/ *vi* *fam* boire (beaucoup). ● *n* *fam* alcool *m.*

border /'bɔːdə(r)/ *n* (edge) bord *m*; (frontier) frontière *f*; (in garden) bordure *f.* ● *vi* **~ on** être voisin de, avoisiner.

bore /bɔː(r)/ *vt* ennuyer; be **~ed** s'ennuyer; **⇒BEAR.** ● *vi* (Tech) forer. ● *n* raseur/-euse *m/f*; (thing) ennui *m.* **boredom** *n* ennui *m.* **boring** *adj* ennuyeux.

born /bɔːn/ *adj* né; be **~** naître.

borne /bɔːn/ **⇒BEAR.**

borough /'bʌrə/ *n* municipalité *f.*

borrow /'bɒrəʊ/ *vt* emprunter (from à).

Bosnia /'bɒznɪə/ *n* Bosnie *f.*

Bosnian /'bɒznɪən/ *adj* bosniaque. ● *n* Bosniaque.

bosom /'bʊzəm/ *n* poitrine *f*; **~friend** ami/-e *m/f* intime.

boss /bɒs/ *n* 🔲 patron/-ne *m/f.* ● *vt* **~ (about)** 🔲 mener par le bout du nez.

bossy /'bɒsɪ/ *adj* autoritaire.

botch /bɒtʃ/ *vt* bâcler, saboter.

both /bəʊθ/ *det* les deux; **~ the books** les deux livres. ● *pron* tous/toutes (les) deux, l'un/-e et l'autre; **we ~ agree** nous sommes tous les deux d'accord; **I bought ~ (of them)** j'ai acheté les deux; **I saw ~ of you** je vous ai vus tous les deux; **~ Paul and Anne** (et) Paul et Anne. ● *adv* à la fois.

bother /'bɒðə(r)/ *vt* (annoy, worry) ennuyer; (disturb) déranger. ● *vi* se déranger; **don't ~ (calling)** ce n'est pas la peine (d'appeler); **don't ~ about us** ne t'inquiète pas pour nous; **I can't be ~ed** j'ai la flemme 🔲. ● *n* ennui *m*; (effort) peine *f*; **it's no ~** ce n'est rien.

bottle /'bɒtl/ *n* bouteille *f*; (for baby) biberon *m.* ● *vt* mettre en bouteille. **~ up** contenir. **~ bank** *n* collecteur *m* (de verre usagé). **~neck** *n* (traffic jam) embouteillage *m.* **~opener** *n* ouvre-bouteilles *m inv.*

bottom /'bɒtəm/ *n* fond *m*; (of hill, page, etc.) bas *m*; (buttocks) derrière *m* 🔲. ● *adj* inférieur, du bas.

bought /bɔːt/ **⇒BUY.**

bounce /baʊns/ *vi* rebondir; (*person*) faire des bonds, bondir; (*cheques* 🔲) être refusé. ● *vt* faire rebondir. ● *n* rebond *m.*

bound /baʊnd/ vi (leap) bondir; **~ed by** limité de; →**BIND.** ● n bond m. ● adj **be ~ for** être en route pour, aller vers; **~ to** (obliged) obligé de; (certain) sûr de.

boundary /ˈbaʊndrɪ/ n limite f.

bounds /baʊndz/ npl limites fpl; **out of ~** être interdit d'accès.

bout /baʊt/ n période f; (Med) accès m; (boxing) combat m.

bow¹ /bəʊ/ n (weapon) arc m; (of violin) archet m; (knot) nœud m.

bow² /baʊ/ n salut m; (of ship) proue f. ● vt/i (s')incliner.

bowels /ˈbaʊəlz/ npl intestins mpl; (fig) profondeurs fpl.

bowl /bəʊl/ n (for washing) cuvette f; (for food) bol m; (for soup) assiette f creuse. ● vt/i (cricket) lancer; **~ over** bouleverser.

bowler /ˈbəʊlə(r)/ n (cricket) lanceur m; **~ (hat)** (chapeau) melon m.

bowling /ˈbəʊlɪŋ/ n (ten-pin) bowling m; (on grass) jeu m de boules. **~alley** n bowling m.

bow tie n nœud m papillon.

box /bɒks/ n boîte f; (cardboard) carton m; (Theat) loge f; **the ~** 🖵 la télé. ● vt mettre en boîte; **~ sb's ears** gifler qn; **~ in** enfermer.

boxing /ˈbɒksɪŋ/ n boxe f. ● adj de boxe. **B~ Day** n le lendemain de Noël.

box office n guichet m.

boy /bɔɪ/ n garçon m; **~ band** boys band m.

boycott /ˈbɔɪkɒt/ vt boycotter. ● n boycottage m.

boyfriend /ˈbɔɪfrend/ n (petit) ami m.

bra /brɑː/ n soutien-gorge m.

brace /breɪs/ n (fastener) attache f; (dental) appareil m; (tool) vilbrequin m; **~s** (for trousers) bretelles fpl.

● vt soutenir; **~ oneself** rassembler ses forces.

bracket /ˈbrækɪt/ n (for shelf etc.) tasseau m; (group) tranche f; **in ~s** entre parenthèses. ● vt mettre entre parenthèses or crochets.

braid /breɪd/ n (trimming) galon m; (of hair) tresse f.

brain /breɪn/ n cerveau m; **~s** (fig) intelligence f. ● vt assommer. **brainless** adj stupide. **~wash** vt faire subir un lavage de cerveau à. **~wave** n idée f géniale, trouvaille f. **brainy** adj (-ier, -iest) doué.

brake /breɪk/ n (Auto also fig) frein m. ● vt/i freiner. **~ light** n feu m stop.

bran /bræn/ n son m.

branch /brɑːntʃ/ n (of tree) branche f; (of road) embranchement m; (Comm) succursale f; (of bank) agence f. ● vi **~ (off)** bifurquer.

brand /brænd/ n marque f. ● vt **~ sb as sth** désigner qn comme qch.

brand-new /brænd'njuː/ adj tout neuf.

brandy /ˈbrændɪ/ n cognac m.

brass /brɑːs/ n cuivre m; **get down to ~ tacks** en venir aux choses sérieuses; **the ~** (Mus) les cuivres mpl; **top ~** 🅇 galonnés mpl.

brat /bræt/ n 🅇 môme mf 🅇.

brave /breɪv/ adj courageux; (smile) brave. ● n (American Indian) brave m. ● vt braver. **bravery** n courage m.

brawl /brɔːl/ n bagarre f. ● vi se bagarrer.

Brazil /brə'zɪl/ n Brésil m.

breach /briːtʃ/ n (of copyright, privilege) violation f; (in relationship) rupture f; (gap) brèche f. ● vt ouvrir une brèche dans.

bread /bred/ n pain m; **~ and but-**

ter tartine f. **~bin**, (US) **~box** n boîte f à pain. **~crumbs** npl chapelure f.

breadth /bretθ/ n largeur f.

bread-winner /'bredwɪnə(r)/ n soutien m de famille.

break /breɪk/ vt (pt **broke**, pp **broken**) casser; (smash into pieces) briser; (vow, silence, rank, etc.) rompre; (law) violer; (a record) battre; (news) révéler; (journey) interrompre; (heart, strike, ice) briser; **~ one's arm** se casser le bras. ● vi (se) casser; se briser. ● n cassure f, rupture f; (in relationship, continuity) rupture f; (interval) interruption f; (at school) récréation f, récré f; (for coffee) pause f; (luck 🆃) chance f. **~ away from** se détacher; **~ down** (collapse) s'effondrer; (negotiations) échouer; (machine) tomber en panne; vt (door) enfoncer; (analyse) analyser; **~ even** rentrer dans ses frais; **~ into** cambrioler; **~ off** (se) détacher; (suspend) rompre; (stop talking) s'interrompre; **~ out** (fire, war, etc.) éclater; **~ up** (end) (faire) cesser; (couple) rompre; (marriage) (se) briser; (crowd) (se) disperser; (schools) entrer en vacances. **breakable** adj fragile. **breakage** n casse f.

breakdown /'breɪkdaʊn/ n (Tech) panne f; (Med) dépression f; (of figures) analyse f. ● adj (Auto) de dépannage.

breakfast /'brekfəst/ n petit déjeuner m.

break /breɪk/: **~-in** n cambriolage m. **~through** n percée f.

breast /brest/ n sein m; (chest) poitrine f. **~-feed** vt (pt **-fed**) allaiter. **~-stroke** n brasse f.

breath /breθ/ n souffle m, haleine f; **out of ~** à bout de souffle; **under one's ~** tout bas.

breathalyser® /'breθəlaɪzə(r)/ n alcootest m.

breathe /bri:ð/ vt/i respirer. **~ in** inspirer; **~ out** expirer.

breathless /'breθlɪs/ adj à bout de souffle.

breathtaking /'breθteɪkɪŋ/ adj à vous couper le souffle.

bred /bred/ ➡BREED.

breed /bri:d/ vt (pt **bred**) élever; (give rise to) engendrer. ● vi se reproduire. ● n race f.

breeze /bri:z/ n brise f.

brew /bru:/ vt (beer) brasser; (tea) faire infuser. ● vi (beer) fermenter; (tea) infuser; (fig) se préparer. ● n décoction f. **brewer** n brasseur m. **brewery** n brasserie f.

bribe /braɪb/ n pot-de-vin m. ● vt soudoyer. **bribery** n corruption f.

brick /brɪk/ n brique f. **~layer** n maçon m.

bridal /'braɪdl/ adj (dress) de mariée; (car, chamber) des mariés.

bride /braɪd/ n mariée f. **~groom** n marié m. **~smaid** n demoiselle f d'honneur.

bridge /brɪdʒ/ n pont m; (Naut) passerelle f; (of nose) arête f; (card game) bridge m. ● vt **~ a gap** combler une lacune.

bridle /'braɪdl/ n bride f. ● vt brider. **~path** n piste f cavalière.

brief /bri:f/ adj bref. ● n instructions fpl; (Jur) dossier m. ● vt donner des instructions à.

briefcase /'bri:fkeɪs/ n serviette f.

briefs /bri:fs/ npl slip m.

bright /braɪt/ adj brillant, vif; (day, room) clair; (cheerful) gai; (clever) intelligent.

brighten /'braɪtn/ vt égayer. ● vi (weather) s'éclaircir; (face) s'éclairer.

brilliant /'brɪlɪənt/ adj (student,

career) brillant; (*light*) éclatant; (*very good* **1**) super.

brim /brɪm/ n bord m. ● vi (pt **brimmed**); ~ **over** déborder (**with** de).

bring /brɪŋ/ vt (pt **brought**) (*thing*) apporter; (*person, vehicle*) amener; ~ **to bear** (*pressure etc.*) exercer. ~ **about** provoquer; ~ **back** (return with) rapporter; (*colour, shine*) redonner; ~ **down** faire tomber; (shoot down, knock down) abattre; ~ **forward** avancer; ~ **off** réussir; ~ **out** (take out) sortir; (show) faire ressortir; (book) publier; ~ **round** faire revenir à soi; ~ **up** (*child*) élever; (Med) vomir; (*question*) aborder.

brink /brɪŋk/ n bord m.

brisk /brɪsk/ adj vif.

bristle /'brɪsl/ n poil m. ● vi se hérisser; **bristling with** hérissé de.

Britain /'brɪtn/ n Grande-Bretagne f.

British /'brɪtɪʃ/ adj britannique; **the** ~ les Britanniques mpl.

Briton /'brɪtn/ n Britannique mf.

Brittany /'brɪtəni/ n Bretagne f.

brittle /'brɪtl/ adj fragile.

broad /brɔːd/ adj large; (*choice, range*) grand. ~ **bean** n fève f.

broadband /'brɔːdbænd/ adj à haut débit. ● n ADSL m haut débit m.

broadcast /'brɔːdkɑːst/ vt/i (pt **broadcast**) diffuser; (*person*) parler à la television ou à la radio. ● n émission f.

broadly /'brɔːdlɪ/ adv en gros.

broad-minded /brɔːd'maɪndɪd/ adj large d'esprit.

broccoli /'brɒkəlɪ/ n inv brocoli m.

brochure /'brəʊʃə(r)/ n brochure f.

broke /brəʊk/ →**BREAK**. ● adj

(penniless **▣**) fauché.

broken /'brəʊkən/ →**BREAK**. ● adj ~ **English** mauvais anglais m.

bronchitis /brɒŋ'kaɪtɪs/ n bronchite f.

bronze /brɒnz/ n bronze m.

brooch /brəʊtʃ/ n broche f.

brood /bruːd/ n nichée f, couvée f. ● vi méditer tristement.

broom /bruːm/ n balai m.

broth /brɒθ/ n bouillon m.

brothel /'brɒθl/ n maison f close.

brother /'brʌðə(r)/ n frère m. ~**hood** n fraternité f. ~ **-in-law** n (pl ~**s-in-law**) beau-frère m.

brought /brɔːt/ →**BRING**.

brow /braʊ/ n front m; (of hill) sommet m.

brown /braʊn/ adj (*object*) marron; (*hair*) brun. ~ **bread** pain m complet; ~ **sugar** sucre m roux. ● n marron m; brun m. ● vt/i brunir; (Culin) (faire) dorer.

Brownie /'braʊnɪ/ n jeannette f.

browse /braʊz/ vi flâner; (*animal*) brouter. ● vt (Comput) naviguer.

browser /'braʊzə/ n (Comput) navigateur m.

bruise /bruːz/ n bleu m; (of knee, arm etc.) faire un bleu à; (*fruit*) abîmer.

brush /brʌʃ/ n brosse f; (skirmish) accrochage m; (bushes) broussailles fpl. ● vt brosser. ~ **against** frôler; ~ **aside** (dismiss) repousser; (move) écarter; ~ **up (on)** se remettre à.

Brussels /'brʌslz/ n Bruxelles. ~ **sprouts** npl choux mpl de Bruxelles.

brutal /'bruːtl/ adj brutal.

brute /bruːt/ n brute f; **by** ~ **force** par la force.

BSE abbr (Bovine Spongiform Encephalopathy) encéphalopathie f spongiforme bovine, ESB f.

bubble /'bʌbl/ n bulle f; **blow** ∼**s** faire des bulles. ● vi bouillonner; ∼ **over** déborder. ∼ **bath** n bain m moussant.

buck /bʌk/ n mâle m; (US, ▣) dollar m; **pass the** ∼ rejeter la responsabilité (**to** sur). ● vi (horse) ruer; ∼ **up** ▣ prendre courage; (hurry ▣) se grouiller ▣.

bucket /'bʌkɪt/ n seau m (of de).

buckle /'bʌkl/ n boucle f. ● vt/i (fasten) (se) boucler; (bend) voiler.

bud /bʌd/ n bourgeon m. ● vi (pt **budded**) bourgeonner.

Buddhism /'budɪzəm/ n bouddhisme m.

budding /'bʌdɪŋ/ adj (talent) naissant; (athlete) en herbe.

budge /bʌdʒ/ vt/i (faire) bouger.

budgerigar /'bʌdʒərɪɡɑː(r)/ n perruche f.

budget /'bʌdʒɪt/ n budget m. ● vi ∼ **for** prévoir (dans son budget).

buff /bʌf/ n (colour) chamois m; ▣ fanatique mf.

buffalo /'bʌfələʊ/ n (pl **-oes** or **-o** buffle m; (US) bison m.

buffer /'bʌfə(r)/ n tampon m; ∼ **zone** zone f tampon.

buffet¹ /'bʊfeɪ/ n (meal, counter) buffet m; ∼ **car** buffet m.

buffet² /'bʌfɪt/ n (blow) soufflet m. ● vt (pt **buffeted**) souffleter.

bug /bʌg/ n (bedbug) punaise f; (any small insect) bestiole f; (germ) microbe m; (stomachache ▣) ennuis mpl gastriques; (device) micro m; (defect) défaut m; (Comput) bogue f, bug m. ● vt (pt **bugged**) mettre les micros dans; ▣ embêter.

buggy /'bʌgɪ/ n poussette f.

build /bɪld/ vt/i (pt **built**) bâtir, construire. ● n carrure f. ∼ **up** (increase) augmenter, monter;

(accumulate) (s')accumuler. **builder** n entrepreneur m en bâtiment; (workman) ouvrier m du bâtiment.

building /'bɪldɪŋ/ n (structure) bâtiment m; (dwelling) immeuble m. ∼ **society** n caisse f d'épargne.

build-up /'bɪldʌp/ n accumulation f; (fig) publicité f.

built /bɪlt/ ⟶BUILD.

built-in /bɪlt'ɪn/ adj encastré.

built-up area n agglomération f, zone f urbanisée.

bulb /bʌlb/ n (Bot) bulbe m; (Electr) ampoule f.

Bulgaria /bʌl'geərɪə/ n Bulgarie f.

Bulgarian /bʌl'geərɪən/ n (person) Bulgare mf; (Ling) bulgare m. ● adj bulgare.

bulge /bʌldʒ/ n renflement m. ● vi se renfler, être renflé; **be bulging with** être gonflé or bourré de.

bulimia /bju:'lɪmɪə/ n boulimie f.

bulk /bʌlk/ n volume f; **in** ∼ (buy, sell) en gros; (transport) en vrac; **the** ∼ **of** la majeure partie de.

bull /bʊl/ n taureau m. ∼**dog** n bouledogue m. ∼**doze** vt raser au bulldozer.

bullet /'bʊlɪt/ n balle f.

bulletin /'bʊlətɪn/ n bulletin m.

bullet-proof /'bʊlɪtpru:f/ adj (vest) pare-balles inv; (vehicle) blindé.

bullfight /'bʊlfaɪt/ n corrida f.

bullion /'bʊlɪən/ n or m or argent m en lingots.

bullring /'bʊlrɪŋ/ n arène f.

bull's-eye /'bʊlzaɪ/ n mille m.

bully /'bʊlɪ/ n (child) petite brute f; (adult) tyran m. ● vt maltraiter.

bum /bʌm/ n ▣ derrière m ▣; (US, ▣) vagabond/-e m/f.

bumble-bee /'bʌmblbiː/ n bourdon m.

bump /bʌmp/ n (swelling) bosse f;

(on road) bosse f. ● vt/i cogner, heurter. ~ **along** cahoter; ~ **into** (hit) rentrer dans; (meet) tomber sur.

bumper /'bʌmpə(r)/ n pare-chocs m inv. ● adj exceptionnel.

bumpy /'bʌmpɪ/ adj (road) accidenté.

bun /bʌn/ n (cake) petit pain m; (hair) chignon m.

bunch /bʌntʃ/ n (of flowers) bouquet m; (of keys) trousseau m; (of people) groupe m; (of bananas) régime m; ~ **of grapes** grappe f de raisin.

bundle /'bʌndl/ n paquet m. ● vt mettre en paquet; (push) fourrer.

bung /bʌŋ/ n bouchon m. ● vt (stop up) boucher; (throw 🗙) flanquer 🅣.

bunion /'bʌnjən/ n (Med) oignon m.

bunk /bʌŋk/ n (on ship, train) couchette f. ~**-beds** npl lits mpl superposés.

buoy /bɔɪ/ n bouée f. ● vt ~ **up** (hearten) soutenir, encourager.

buoyancy /'bɔɪənsɪ/ n (of floating object) flottabilité f; (cheerfulness) gaieté f.

burden /'bɜːdn/ n fardeau m. ● vt ennuyer (**with** de).

bureau /'bjʊərəʊ/ n (pl **-eaux** bureau m.

bureaucracy /bjʊə'rɒkrəsɪ/ n bureaucratie f.

burglar /'bɜːglə(r)/ n cambrioleur m; ~ **alarm** alarme f. **burglarize** vt (US) cambrioler. **burglary** n cambriolage m. **burgle** vt cambrioler.

Burgundy /'bɜːgəndɪ/ n (wine) bourgogne m.

burial /'berɪəl/ n enterrement m.

burn /bɜːn/ vt/i (pt **burned** or **burnt**) brûler. ● n brûlure f. ~

down être réduit en cendres.
burner n (on cooker) brûleur m; (on computer) graveur m. **burning** adj en flammes; (fig) brûlant.

burnt /bɜːnt/ ➡**BURN**.

burp /bɜːp/ n 🅣 rot m. ● vi 🅣 roter.

burrow /'bʌrəʊ/ n terrier m. ● vt creuser.

bursar /'bɜːsə(r)/ n intendant/-e m/f. **bursary** n bourse f.

burst /bɜːst/ vt/i (pt **burst** (balloon, bubble) crever; (pipe) (faire) éclater. ● n explosion f; (of laughter) éclat m; (surge) élan m. ~ **into** (room) faire irruption dans; ~ **into tears** fondre en larmes; ~ **out** ~ **out laughing** éclater de rire; ~ **with** be ~**ing** with déborder de.

bury /'berɪ/ vt (person etc.) enterrer; (hide, cover) enfouir; (engross, thrust) plonger.

bus /bʌs/ n (pl **buses**) (auto)bus m. ● vt transporter en bus. ● vi (pt **bussed**) prendre l'autobus.

bush /bʊʃ/ n (shrub) buisson m; (land) brousse f.

business /'bɪznɪs/ n (task, concern) affaire f; (commerce) affaires fpl; (line of work) métier m; (shop) commerce m; **he has no** ~ **to** il n'a pas le droit de; **mean** ~ être sérieux; **that's none of your** ~! ça ne vous regarde pas! ~**like** adj sérieux. ~**man** n homme m d'affaires.

busker /'bʌskə(r)/ n musicien/-ne m/f des rues.

bus-stop n arrêt m d'autobus.

bust /bʌst/ n (statue) buste m; (bosom) poitrine f. ● vt/i (pt **busted** or **bust**) (burst 🗙) crever; (break 🗙) (se) casser. ● adj (broken, finished 🗙) fichu; **go** ~ 🗙 faire faillite.

bustle /'bʌsl/ vi s'affairer. ● n affairement *m*, remue-ménage *m*.

busy /'bɪzɪ/ *adj* (**-ier, -iest**) (*person*) occupé; (*street*) animé; (*day*) chargé. ● *vt* ~ **oneself with** s'occuper à.

but /bʌt/ *conj* mais. ● *prep* sauf; ~ **for** sans; **nobody** ~ personne d'autre que; **nothing** ~ rien que. ● *adv* (only) seulement.

butcher /'bʊtʃə(r)/ *n* boucher *m*. ● *vt* massacrer.

butler /'bʌtlə(r)/ *n* maître *m* d'hôtel.

butt /bʌt/ *n* (of gun) crosse *f*; (of cigarette) mégot *m*; (of joke) cible *f*; (barrel) tonneau *m*; (US, 🔲) derrière *m* 🔲. ● *vi* ~ **in** interrompre.

butter /'bʌtə(r)/ *n* beurre *m*. ● *vt* beurrer. ~**-bean** *n* haricot *m* blanc. ~**cup** *n* bouton-d'or *m*.

butterfly /'bʌtəflaɪ/ *n* papillon *m*.

buttock /'bʌtək/ *n* fesse *f*.

button /'bʌtn/ *n* bouton *m*. ● *vt*/*i* ~ (**up**) (se) boutonner.

buttonhole /'bʌtnhəʊl/ *n* boutonnière *f*. ● *vt* accrocher.

buy /baɪ/ *vt* (*pt* **bought**) acheter (from); ~ **sth for sb** acheter qch à qn, prendre qch pour qn; (believe 🔲) croire, avaler.

buzz /bʌz/ *n* bourdonnement *m*. ● *vi* bourdonner. **buzzer** *n* sonnerie *f*.

by /baɪ/ *prep* par, de; (near) à côté de; (before) avant; (means) en, à, par; ~ **bike** à vélo; ~ **car** en auto; ~ **day** de jour; ~ **the kilo** au kilo; ~ **running** en courant; ~ **sea** par mer; ~ **that time** à ce moment-là; ~ **the way** à propos; ~ **oneself** tout seul. ● *adv* **close** ~ tout près; **and large** dans l'ensemble.

bye(-bye) /'baɪbaɪ/ *interj* 🔲 au revoir, salut 🔲.

by-election *n* élection *f* partielle.

Byelorussia /bjeləʊ'rʊʃə/ *n* Biélo-

russie *f*.

by-law /'baɪlɔː/ *n* arrêté *m* municipal.

bypass /'baɪpɑːs/ *n* (Auto) rocade *f*; (Med) pontage *m*. ● *vt* contourner.

by-product *n* dérivé *m*; (fig) conséquence *f*.

byte /baɪt/ *n* octet *m*.

Cc

cab /kæb/ *n* taxi *m*; (of lorry, train) cabine *f*.

cabbage /'kæbɪdʒ/ *n* chou *m*.

cabin /'kæbɪn/ *n* (hut) cabane *f*; (in ship, aircraft) cabine *f*.

cabinet /'kæbɪnɪt/ *n* petit placard *m*; (glassfronted) vitrine *f*; (Pol) cabinet *m*.

cable /'keɪbl/ *n* câble *m*. ● *vt* câbler. ~**-car** *n* téléphérique *m*. ~ **television** *n* télévision *f* par câble.

cache /kæʃ/ *n* (hoard) cache *f*; (place) cachette *f*.

cackle /'kækl/ *n* (of hen) caquet *m*; (laugh) ricanement *m*. ● *vi* caqueter; (laugh) ricaner.

cactus /'kæktəs/ *n* (*pl* **-ti** or ~**es**) cactus *m*.

cadet /kə'det/ *n* élève *m* officier.

Caesarean /sɪ'zeərɪən/ *adj* ~ (**section**) césarienne *f*.

café /'kæfeɪ/ *n* café *m*, snack-bar *m*.

caffeine /'kæfiːn/ *n* caféine *f*.

cage /keɪdʒ/ *n* cage *f*. ● *vt* mettre en cage.

cagey /'keɪdʒɪ/ *adj* réticent.

cagoule /kə'guːl/ *n* K-way® *m*.

cajole /kə'dʒəʊl/ *vt* ~ **sb into doing sth** amener qn à faire qch par la cajolerie.

cake /keɪk/ n gâteau m; (of soap) pain m. ● vi former une croûte (**on** sur).

calculate /'kælkjʊleɪt/ vt calculer; (estimate) évaluer. **calculated** adj délibéré; (risk) calculé. **calculating** adj calculateur. **calculation** n calcul m. **calculator** n calculatrice f.

calculus /'kælkjʊləs/ n (pl **-li** or ∼**es**) calcul m.

calendar /'kælɪndə(r)/ n calendrier m.

calf /kɑːf/ n (pl **calves**) (young cow or bull) veau m; (of leg) mollet m.

calibre /'kælɪbə(r)/ n calibre m.

call /kɔːl/ vt/i appeler; (loudly) crier; he's ∼ed John il s'appelle john; ∼ sb stupid traiter qn d'imbécile. ● n appel m; (of bird) cri m; (visit) visite f; **make/pay a** ∼ rendre visite à; **be on** ∼ être de garde; ∼ **box** cabine f téléphonique. ∼ **centre** n centre m d'appels. ∼ **back** rappeler; (visit) repasser. ∼ **for** (help) appeler à; (demand) demander; (require) exiger; (collect) passer prendre; ∼ **in** passer. ∼ **off** annuler. ∼ **on** (visit) rendre visite à; (urge) demander à (**to do** de faire). ∼ **out (to)** appeler. ∼ **round** venir. ∼ **up** appeler.

calling /'kɔːlɪŋ/ n vocation f.

callous /'kæləs/ adj inhumain.

calm /kɑːm/ adj calme. ● n calme m. ● vt/i ∼ (**down**) (se) calmer.

calorie /'kælərɪ/ n calorie f.

camcorder /'kæmkɔːdə(r)/ n caméscope® m.

came /keɪm/ ➙COME.

camel /'kæml/ n chameau m.

camera /'kæmərə/ n appareil(-photo) m; (TV, cinema) caméra f; **in** ∼ à huis clos. ∼**man** n (pl **-men**) cadreur m, cameraman m.

camouflage /'kæməflɑːʒ/ n camouflage m. ● vt camoufler.

camp /kæmp/ n camp m. ● vi camper.

campaign /kæm'peɪn/ n campagne f. ● vi faire campagne.

camper /'kæmpə(r)/ n campeur/-euse m/f; ∼ (**-van**) n camping-car m.

camping /'kæmpɪŋ/ n camping m; **go** ∼ faire du camping.

campsite /'kæmpsaɪt/ n camping m.

campus /'kæmpəsɪz/ n (pl ∼**es**) campus m.

---

can¹ /kæn, kən/

infinitive **be able to**; present **can**; present negative **can't, cannot** (formal); past **could**; past participle **been able to**

● auxiliary verb
····▸ pouvoir; **where** ∼ **I buy stamps?** où est-ce que je peux acheter des timbres?; **she can't come** elle ne peut pas venir.

····▸ (be allowed to) pouvoir; ∼ **I smoke?** est-ce que je peux fumer?

····▸ (know how to) savoir; **she** ∼ **swim** elle sait nager; **he can't drive** il ne sait pas conduire.

····▸ (with verbs of perception),**I** ∼ **hear you** je t'entends; ∼ **they see us?** est-ce qu'ils nous voient?

can² /kæn/ n (for food) boîte f; (of petrol) bidon m. ● vt (pt **canned**) mettre en conserve.

Canada /'kænədə/ *n* Canada *m.*

Canadian /kə'neɪdɪən/ *n* Canadien/-ne *m/f.* ● *adj* canadien.

canal /kə'næl/ *n* canal *m.*

canary /kə'neərɪ/ *n* canari *m.*

cancel /'kænsl/ *vt/i* (*pt* **cancelled**) (call off, revoke) annuler; (cross out) barrer; (a stamp) oblitérer; ~ **out** (se) neutraliser. **cancellation** *n* annulation *f.*

cancer /'kænsə(r)/ *n* cancer *m;* **have** ~ avoir un cancer.

Cancer /'kænsə(r)/ *n* Cancer *m.*

cancerous /'kænsərəs/ *adj* cancéreux.

candid /'kændɪd/ *adj* franc.

candidate /'kændɪdət/ *n* candidat/-e *m/f.*

candle /'kændl/ *n* bougie *f;* (in church) cierge *m.* ~**stick** *n* bougeoir *m.*

candy /'kændɪ/ *n* (US) bonbon(s) *m(pl).* ~**-floss** *n* barbe *f* à papa.

cane /keɪn/ *n* canne *f;* (for baskets) rotin *m;* (for punishment) badine *f.* ● *vt* donner des coups de badine à.

canister /'kænɪstə(r)/ *n* boîte *f.*

cannabis /'kænəbɪs/ *n* cannabis *m.*

cannibal /'kænɪbl/ *n* cannibale *mf.*

cannon /'kænən/ *n* (*pl* ~ *or* ~**s**) canon *m.* ~**-ball** *n* boulet *m* de canon.

cannot ➡CAN NOT.

canoe /kə'nu:/ *n* canoë *m.* ● *vi* faire du canoë. **canoeist** *n* canoéiste *mf.*

canon /'kænən/ *n* (clergyman) chanoine *m;* (rule) canon *m.*

can-opener *n* ouvre-boîtes *m inv.*

canopy /'kænəpɪ/ *n* dais *m;* (for bed) baldaquin *m.*

can't ➡CAN NOT.

canteen /kæn'ti:n/ *n* (restaurant) cantine *f;* (flask) bidon *m.*

canter /'kæntə(r)/ *n* petit galop *m.* ● *vi* aller au petit galop.

canvas /'kænvəs/ *n* toile *f.*

canvass /'kænvəs/ *vt/i* (Comm, Pol) faire du démarchage (auprès de); ~ **opinion** sonder l'opinion.

canyon /'kænjən/ *n* cañon *m.*

cap /kæp/ *n* (hat) casquette *f;* (of bottle, tube) bouchon *m;* (of beer or milk bottle) capsule *f;* (of pen) capuchon *m;* (for toy gun) amorce *f.* ● *vt* (*pt* **capped**) couronner.

capability /keɪpə'bɪlətɪ/ *n* capacité *f.*

capable /'keɪpəbl/ *adj* (person) compétent; ~ **of doing** capable de faire.

capacity /kə'pæsətɪ/ *n* capacité *f;* **in my** ~ **as a doctor** en ma qualité de médecin.

cape /keɪp/ *n* (cloak) cape *f;* (Geog) cap *m.*

caper /'keɪpə(r)/ *vi* gambader. ● *n* (leap) cabriole *f;* (funny film) comédie *f;* (Culin) câpre *f.*

capital /'kæpɪtl/ *adj* (*letter*) majuscule; (*offence*) capital. ● *n* (town) capitale *f;* (money) capital *m;* ~ **(letter)** majuscule *f.*

capitalism /'kæpɪtəlɪzəm/ *n* capitalisme *m.*

capitalize /'kæpɪtəlaɪz/ *vi* ~ **on** tirer parti de.

> *i* **Capitol Hill** Ce quartier historique de Washington D.C. abrite le bâtiment du Capitole, dans lequel se réunit le Congrès depuis 1800, la cour suprême fédérale, plus haute instance judiciaire des États-Unis, et la bibliothèque du Congrès, l'une des plus grandes au monde. Par métonymie, *the Capitol* ou *the Hill* font référence au Congrès.
> ▷CONGRESS

capitulate /kə'pɪtʃʊleɪt/ vi capituler.

Capricorn /'kæprɪkɔːn/ n Capricorne m.

capsize /kæp'saɪz/ vt/i (faire) chavirer.

capsule /'kæpsjuːl/ n capsule f.

captain /'kæptɪn/ n capitaine m.

caption /'kæpʃn/ n (under photo) légende f; (subtitle) sous-titre m.

captivate /'kæptɪveɪt/ vt captiver.

captive /'kæptɪv/ adj & n captif/-ive (m/f.) **captivity** n captivité f.

capture /'kæptʃə(r)/ vt (person, animal) capturer; (moment, likeness) saisir. ● n capture f.

car /kɑː(r)/ n voiture f. ● adj (industry, insurance) automobile; (accident, phone) de voiture; (journey, chase) en voiture.

caravan /'kærəvæn/ n caravane f.

carbohydrate /kɑːbə'haɪdreɪt/ n hydrate m de carbone.

carbon /'kɑːbən/ n carbone m.

carburettor /'kɑːbərettər/ n carburateur m.

card /kɑːd/ n carte f.

cardboard /'kɑːdbɔːd/ n carton m.

cardiac /'kɑːdiæk/ adj cardiaque; ~ **arrest** arrêt m du cœur.

cardigan /'kɑːdɪgən/ n cardigan m.

carer /'keərə(r)/ n (relative) personne ayant un parent handicapé ou un malade à charge; (professional) aide f à la domicile.

cardinal /'kɑːdɪnl/ adj (sin) capital; (rule) fondamental; (number) cardinal. ● n cardinal m.

card index n fichier m.

care /keə(r)/ n (attention) soin m, attention f; (worry) souci m; (looking after) soins mpl; **take ~ of** (deal with) s'occuper de; (be careful with) prendre soin de; **take ~ to do sth**

faire bien attention à faire qch. ● vi ~ **about** s'intéresser à; ~ **for** s'occuper de; (invalid) soigner; ~ **to do** vouloir faire; **I don't ~** ça m'est égal.

career /kə'rɪə(r)/ n carrière f. ● vi ~ **in/out** entrer/sortir à toute vitesse.

carefree /'keəfriː/ adj insouciant.

careful /'keəfl/ adj prudent; (research, study) méticuleux; **(be) ~!** (fais) attention! **carefully** adv avec soin; (cautiously) prudemment.

careless /'keəlɪs/ adj négligent; (work) bâclé.

caress /kə'res/ n caresse f. ● vt caresser.

caretaker /'keəteɪkə(r)/ n concierge mf. ● adj (president) par intérim.

car ferry n ferry m.

cargo /'kɑːgəʊ/ n (pl ~es) chargement m; (Naut) cargaison f.

Caribbean /kærɪ'biːən/ adj des Caraïbes, des Antilles. ● n the ~ (sea) la mer des Antilles; (islands) les Antilles fpl.

caring /'keərɪŋ/ adj affectueux.

carnation /kɑː'neɪʃn/ n œillet m.

carnival /'kɑːnɪvl/ n carnaval m.

carol /'kærəl/ n chant m de Noël.

carp /kɑːp/ n inv carpe f. ● vi maugréer.

car-park n parc m de stationnement, parking m.

carpenter /'kɑːpəntə(r)/ n (joiner) menuisier m; (builder) charpentier m. **carpentry** n menuiserie f; (structural) charpenterie f.

carpet /'kɑːpɪt/ n (fitted) moquette f; (loose) tapis m. ● vt (pt **carpeted**) mettre de la moquette dans.

carriage /'kærɪdʒ/ n (rail) wagon m; (ceremonial) carrosse m; (of goods) transport m; (cost) port m.

carriageway /ˈkærɪdʒweɪ/ n chaussée f.

carrier /ˈkærɪə(r)/ n transporteur m; (Med) porteur/-euse m/f; **~ (bag)** sac m en plastique.

carrot /ˈkærət/ n carotte f.

carry /ˈkærɪ/ vt/i porter; (goods) transporter; (involve) comporter; (motion) voter; **be carried away** s'emballer. □ **~ off** emporter; (prize) remporter; **~ on** (continue) continuer; (business) conduire; (conversation) mener; **~ out** (order, plan) exécuter; (duty) remplir; (experiment, operation, repair) effectuer.

~-cot n portebébé m.

car sharing n covoiturage m.

cart /kɑːt/ n charrette f. ● vt (heavy bag 🔢) trimballer 🔢.

carton /ˈkɑːtn/ n (box) boîte f; (of yoghurt, cream) pot m; (of cigarettes) cartouche f.

cartoon /kɑːˈtuːn/ n dessin m humoristique; (cinema) dessin m animé; (strip cartoon) bande f dessinée.

cartridge /ˈkɑːtrɪdʒ/ n cartouche f.

carve /kɑːv/ vt tailler; (meat) découper.

car-wash n lavage m automatique.

cascade /kæˈskeɪd/ n cascade f. ● vi tomber en cascade.

case /keɪs/ n cas m; (Jur) affaire f; (suitcase) valise f; (crate) caisse f; (for spectacles) étui m; (just in) **in ~** au cas où; **in ~ he comes** au cas où il viendrait; **in ~ of fire** en cas d'incendie; **in any ~** de toute façon; **the ~ for sth** les arguments mpl en faveur de qch; **the ~ for the defence** la défense.

cash /kæʃ/ n espèces fpl, argent m; **in ~** en espèces. ● adj (price) comptant. ● vt encaisser; **~ in (on)** profiter de. **~-back** n retrait m

d'argent à la caisse. **~ desk** n caisse f. **~ dispenser** n distributeur m de billets.

cashew /ˈkæʃuː/ n cajou m.

cash flow n marge f brute d'autofinancement.

cashier /kæˈʃɪə(r)/ n caissier/-ière m/f.

cashmere /kæʃˈmɪə(r)/ n cachemire m.

cash: ~point n distributeur m de billets. **~ point card** n carte f de retrait. **~ register** n caisse f enregistreuse.

casino /kəˈsiːnəʊ/ n casino m.

casket /ˈkɑːskɪt/ n (box) coffret m; (coffin) cercueil m.

casserole /ˈkæsərəʊl/ n (pan) daubière f; (food) ragoût m.

cassette /kəˈset/ n cassette f.

cast /kɑːst/ vt (pt cast) (object, glance) jeter; (shadow) projeter; (metal) couler; **~ (off)** (shed) se dépouiller de; **~ one's vote** voter; **~ iron** fonte f. ● n (cinema, Theat, TV) distribution f; (Med) plâtre m.

castaway /ˈkɑːstəweɪ/ n naufragé/-e m/f

cast-iron adj de fonte; (fig) en béton.

castle /ˈkɑːsl/ n château m; (chess) tour f.

cast-offs npl vieux vêtements mpl.

castor /ˈkɑːstə(r)/ n (wheel) roulette f.

castrate /kæˈstreɪt/ vt châtrer.

casual /ˈkæʒʊəl/ adj (informal) décontracté; (remark) désinvolte; (acquaintance) de passage; (work) temporaire. **casually** adv (remark) d'un air détaché; (dress) simplement.

casualty /ˈkæʒʊəltɪ/ n victime f; (part of hospital) urgences fpl.

c

cat /kæt/ n chat m; (feline) félin m.

catalogue /'kætəlɒg/ n catalogue m. ● vt dresser un catalogue de.

catalyst /'kætəlɪst/ n catalyseur m.

catalytic /kætə'lɪtɪk/ adj ∼ converter pot m catalytique.

catapult /'kætəpʌlt/ n lance-pierres m inv. ● vt projeter.

cataract /'kætərækt/ n (Med, Geog) cataracte f.

catarrh /kə'tɑː(r)/ n catarrhe m.

catastrophe /kə'tæstrəfi/ n catastrophe f.

catch /kætʃ/ vt (pt caught) attraper; (bus, plane) prendre; (understand) saisir; ∼ sb doing surprendre qn en train de faire; ∼ fire prendre feu; (seize) apercevoir; ∼ sb's attention/eye attirer l'attention de qn. ● vi (get stuck) se prendre (in dans); (start to burn) prendre. ● n (fastening) fermeture f; (drawback) piège m; (in sport) prise f. ∼ on devenir populaire. ∼ out prendre de court. ∼ up rattraper son retard; ∼ up with sb rattraper qn.

catching /'kætʃɪŋ/ adj contagieux.

catchment /'kætʃmənt/ n ∼ area (School) secteur m.

catch-phrase n formule f favorite.

catchy /'kætʃɪ/ adj entraînant.

category /'kætəgərɪ/ n catégorie f.

cater /'keɪtə(r)/ vi organiser des réceptions; ∼ for/to (guests) accueillir; (needs) pourvoir à; (reader) s'adresser à. **caterer** n traiteur m.

caterpillar /'kætəpɪlə(r)/ n chenille f.

cathedral /kə'θiːdrəl/ n cathédrale f.

catholic /'kæθəlɪk/ adj éclectique. **Catholic** adj & n catholique (mf). **Catholicism** n catholicisme m.

Catseye® n plot m rétroréfléchissant.

cattle /'kætl/ npl bétail m.

caught /kɔːt/ →CATCH.

cauliflower /'kɒlɪflaʊə(r)/ n chou-fleur m.

cause /kɔːz/ n cause f; (reason) raison f, motif m. ● vt causer; ∼ sth to grow/move faire pousser/bouger qch.

causeway /'kɔːzweɪ/ n chaussée f.

caution /'kɔːʃn/ n prudence f; (warning) avertissement m. ● vt avertir. **cautious** adj prudent. **cautiously** adv prudemment.

cave /keɪv/ n grotte f. ● vi ∼ in s'effondrer; (agree) céder. ∼man n (pl -men) homme m des cavernes.

cavern /'kævən/ n caverne f.

caviare /'kævɪɑː(r)/ n caviar m.

caving /'keɪvɪŋ/ n spéléologie f.

CCTV abbr (closed circuit television) télévision f en circuit fermé.

CD abbr (compact disc) disque m compact, CD m.

CD-ROM /siːdiː'rɒm/ n disque m optique compact, CD-ROM m.

cease /siːs/ vt/i cesser. ∼-fire n cessez-le-feu m inv.

cedar /'siːdə(r)/ n cèdre m.

cedilla /sɪ'dɪlə/ n cédille f.

ceiling /'siːlɪŋ/ n plafond m.

celebrate /'selɪbreɪt/ vt (occasion) fêter; (Easter, mass) célébrer. ● vi faire la fête. **celebrated** adj célèbre. **celebration** n fête f.

celebrity /sɪ'lebrətɪ/ n célébrité f.

celery /'selərɪ/ n céleri m.

cell /sel/ n cellule f; (Electr) élément m.

cellar /'selə(r)/ n cave f.

cellist /'tʃelɪst/ n violoncelliste mf. **cello** /'tʃeləʊ/ n violoncelle m.

cellphone /'selfəʊn/ n (téléphone

m) portable.

Celt /kelt/ *n* Celte *mf.*

cement /sɪ'ment/ *n* ciment *m.* ● *vt* cimenter. **~-mixer** *n* bétonnière *f.*

cemetery /'semətrɪ/ *n* cimetière *n.*

censor /'sensə(r)/ *n* censeur *m.* ● *vt* censurer.

censure /'senʃə(r)/ *n* censure *f.* ● *vt* critiquer.

census /'sensəs/ *n* recensement *m.*

cent /sent/ *n* cent *m.*

centenary /sen'ti:nərɪ/ *n* centenaire *m.*

centigrade /'sentɪgreɪd/ *adj* centigrade.

centilitre, (US) **centiliter** /'sentɪli:tə(r)/ *n* centilitre *m.*

centimetre, (US) **centimeter** /'sentɪmi:tə(r)/ *n* centimètre *m.*

centipede /'sentɪpi:d/ *n* millepattes *m inv.*

central /'sentrəl/ *adj* central; ~ **heating** chauffage *m* central; ~ **locking** fermeture *f* centralisée des portes. **centralize** *vt* centraliser. **centrally** *adv* (situated) au centre.

centre /'sentə(r)/, (US) **center** *n* centre *m.* ● *vt* (*pt* **centred**) centrer. ● *vi* ~ **on** tourner autour de.

century /'sentʃərɪ/ *n* siècle *m.*

ceramic /sɪ'ræmɪk/ *adj* (*art*) céramique; (*object*) en céramique.

cereal /'sɪərɪəl/ *n* céréale *f.*

ceremonial /serɪ'məʊnɪəl/ *adj* (*dress*) de cérémonie. ● *n* cérémonial *m.* **ceremony** *n* cérémonie *f.*

certain /'sɜ:tn/ *adj* certain; **for** ~ avec certitude; **make** ~ **of** s'assurer de. **certainly** *adv* certainement. **certainty** *n* certitude *f.*

certificate /sə'tɪfɪkət/ *n* certificat *m.*

certify /'sɜ:tɪfaɪ/ *vt* certifier.

cesspit, cesspool /'sespɪt, 'sespu:l/ *n* fosse *f* d'aisances.

chafe /tʃeɪf/ *vt/i* frotter (contre).

chagrin /'ʃægrɪn/ *n* dépit *m.*

chain /tʃeɪn/ *n* chaîne *f;* ~ **reaction** réaction *f* en chaîne; ~ **store** magasin *m* à succursales multiples. ● *vt* enchaîner. **~-smoke** *vi* fumer sans arrêt.

chair /tʃeə(r)/ *n* chaise *f;* (armchair) fauteuil *m;* (Univ) chaire *f;* (chairperson) président/-e *m/f.* ● *vt* (preside over) présider. **~man** *n* (*pl* **-men**) président/-e *m/f.* **~woman** *n* (*pl* **-women**) présidente *f.*

chalk /tʃɔ:k/ *n* craie *f.*

challenge /'tʃælɪndʒ/ *n* défi *m;* (opportunity) challenge *m.* ● *vt* (summon) défier (**to do** de faire); (question truth of) contester. **challenger** *n* (Sport) challenger *m.* **challenging** *adj* stimulant.

chamber /'tʃeɪmbə(r)/ *n* (old use) chambre *f.* **~maid** *n* femme *f* de chambre. **~ music** *n* musique *f* de chambre. **~-pot** *n* pot *m* de chambre.

champagne /ʃæm'peɪn/ *n* champagne *m.*

champion /'tʃæmpɪən/ *n* champion/-ne *m/f.* ● *vt* défendre. **championship** *n* championnat *m.*

chance /tʃɑ:ns/ *n* (luck) hasard *m;* (opportunity) occasion *f;* (likelihood) chances *fpl;* (risk) risque *m;* **by** ~ par hasard; **by any** ~ par hasard; ~**s are that** il est probable que. ● *adj* fortuit. ● *vt* ~ **doing** prendre le risque de faire; ~ **it** tenter sa chance.

chancellor /'tʃɑ:nsələ(r)/ *n* chancelier *m;* **C~ of the Exchequer** Chancelier de l'échiquier.

chandelier /ʃændə'lɪə(r)/ *n* lustre *m.*

change /tʃeɪndʒ/ vt (alter) changer; (exchange) échanger (**for** contre). (money) changer; ~ **trains/ one's dress** changer de train/de robe; ~ **one's mind** changer d'avis. ● vi changer; (change clothes) se changer; ~ **into** se transformer en; ~ **over** passer (**to** à). ● n changement m; (money) monnaie f; **a** ~ **for the better** une amélioration; **a** ~ **for the worse** un changement en pire; **a** ~ **of clothes** des vêtements de rechange; **for a** ~ pour changer. **changeable** adj changeant. **changing room** n (in shop) cabine f d'essayage; (Sport) vestiaire m.

channel /'tʃænl/ n (for liquid, information) canal m; (TV) chaîne f; (groove) rainure f ● vt (pt **channelled**) canaliser. **C~** n the (English) **C~** la Manche; **the C~ tunnel** le tunnel sous la Manche; **the C~ Islands** les îles fpl Anglo-Normandes

chant /tʃɑːnt/ n (Relig) mélopée f; (of demonstrators) chant m scandé. ● vt/i scander; (Relig) psalmodier.

chaos /'keɪɒs/ n chaos m.

chap /tʃæp/ n (man 🔲) type m 🔲

chapel /'tʃæpl/ n chapelle f.

chaplain /'tʃæplɪn/ n aumônier m.

chapped /tʃæpt/ adj gercé.

chapter /'tʃæptə(r)/ n chapitre m.

char /tʃɑː(r)/ vt (pt **charred**) carboniser.

character /'kærəktə(r)/ n caractère m; (in novel, play) personnage m; **of good** ~ de bonne réputation.

characteristic /kærəktə'rɪstɪk/ adj & n caractéristique (f).

charcoal /'tʃɑːkəʊl/ n charbon m de bois; (art) fusain m.

charge /tʃɑːdʒ/ n (fee) frais mpl; (Mil) charge f; (Jur) inculpation f; (task, custody) charge f; **in** ~ **of**

responsable de; **take** ~ **of** prendre en charge, se charger de. ● vt (customer) faire payer; (enemy, gun) charger; (Jur) inculper (**with** de); ~ **£20 an hour** prendre 20 livres de l'heure; ~ **card** carte f d'achat. ● vi faire payer; (bull) foncer; (person) se précipiter.

charisma /kə'rɪzmə/ n charisme m. **charismatic** adj charismatique.

charitable /'tʃærɪtəbl/ adj charitable. **charity** n charité f; (organization) organisation f caritative.

charm /tʃɑːm/ n charme m; (trinket) amulette f. ● vt charmer. **charming** adj charmant.

chart /tʃɑːt/ n (graph) graphique m; (table) tableau m; (map) carte f. ● vt (route) porter sur la carte.

charter /'tʃɑːtə(r)/ n charte f; ~ (**flight**) charter m. ● vt affréter; ~**ed accountant** expert-comptable m.

chase /tʃeɪs/ vt poursuivre; ~ **away** or **off** chasser. ● vi courir (**after** après). ● n chasse f.

chassis /'ʃæsɪ/ n châssis m.

chastise /tʃæ'staɪz/ vt châtier.

chat /tʃæt/ n conversation f; (on Internet) causette f, bavardage m; **have a** ~ bavarder; ~ **show** talk-show m. ~**room** n salle f de causette, salle f de bavardage. ● vi (pt **chatted**) bavarder. ~ **up** 🔲 draguer 🔲

chatter /'tʃætə(r)/ n bavardage m. ● vi bavarder; **his teeth are** ~**ing** il claque des dents. ~**box** n bavard/-e m/f.

chatty /'tʃætɪ/ adj bavard.

chauffeur /'ʃəʊfə(r)/ n chauffeur m.

chauvinist /'ʃəʊvɪnɪst/ n chauvin/-e f; macho m.

cheap /tʃiːp/ adj bon marché inv;

(*fare, rate*) réduit; (*joke, gimmick*) facile; **~er** meilleur marché *inv.*

cheapen *vt* déprécier. **cheaply** *adv* à bas prix.

cheat /tʃiːt/ *vi* tricher. ● *vt* tromper. ● *n* tricheur/-euse *m/f.*

check /tʃek/ *vt/i* vérifier; (*tickets, rises, inflation*) contrôler; (*stop*) arrêter; (*tick off:* US) cocher. ● *n* contrôle *m;* (*curb*) frein *m;* (*chess*) échec *m;* (*pattern*) carreaux *mpl;* (*bill:* US) addition *f;* (*cheque:* US) chèque *m.* **~ in** remplir la fiche; (*at airport*) enregistrer; **~ out** partir; **~ sth out** vérifier qch. **~ up** vérifier. **~ up on** (*story*) vérifier; (*person*) faire une enquête sur.

check: **~-in** *n* enregistrement *m.* **checking account** *n* (US) compte *m* courant. **~-list** *n* liste *f* de contrôle. **~mate** *n* échec et mat *mae.* **~-out** *n* caisse *f.* **~-point** *n* contrôle *m.* **~-up** *n* examen *m* médical.

cheek /tʃiːk/ *n* joue *f;* (*impudence*) culot *m* 🔲. **cheeky** *adj* effronté.

cheer /tʃɪə(r)/ *n* gaieté *f;* **~s** acclamations *fpl;* (*when drinking*) à la vôtre. ● *vt/i* applaudir; **~ sb (up)** (*gladden*) remonter le moral à qn; **~ up** prendre courage. **cheerful** *adj* joyeux. **cheerfulness** *n* gaieté *f.*

cheerio /tʃɪərɪˈəʊ/ *interj* 🔲 salut 🔲.

cheese /tʃiːz/ *n* fromage *m.*

cheetah /ˈtʃiːtə/ *n* guépard *m.*

chef /ʃef/ *n* chef *m.*

chemical /ˈkemɪkl/ *adj* chimique. ● *n* produit *m* chimique.

chemist /ˈkemɪst/ *n* pharmacien/-ne *m/f;* (*scientist*) chimiste *mf;* **~'s (shop)** pharmacie *f.* **chemistry** *n* chimie *f.*

cheque /tʃek/ *n* chèque *m.* **~-book** *n* chéquier *m.* **~ card** *n* carte *f* bancaire.

chequered /ˈtʃekəd/ *adj* (*pattern*) à damiers; (fig) en dents de scie.

cherish /ˈtʃerɪʃ/ *vt* chérir; (*hope*) caresser.

cherry /ˈtʃerɪ/ *n* cerise *f;* (*tree, wood*) cerisier *m.*

chess /tʃes/ *n* échecs *mpl.* **~-board** *n* échiquier *m.*

chest /tʃest/ *n* (Anat) poitrine *f;* (*box*) coffre *m;* **~ of drawers** commode *f.*

chestnut /ˈtʃesnʌt/ *n* (nut) marron *m,* châtaigne *f;* (*tree*) marronnier *m;* (*sweet*) châtaignier *m.*

chew /tʃuː/ *vt* mâcher.

chic /ʃiːk/ *adj* chic *inv.*

chick /tʃɪk/ *n* poussin *m.*

chicken /ˈtʃɪkɪn/ *n* poulet *m.* ● *adj* 🔲 froussard. ● *vi* **~ out** se dégonfler. **~-pox** varicelle *f.*

chick-pea /ˈtʃɪkpiː/ *n* pois *m* chiche.

chicory /ˈtʃɪkərɪ/ *n* (*for salad*) endive *f;* (*in coffee*) chicorée *f.*

chief /tʃiːf/ *n* chef *m.* ● *adj* principal. **chiefly** *adv* principalement.

chilblain /ˈtʃɪlbleɪn/ *n* engelure *f.*

child /tʃaɪld/ *n* (*pl* **children**) enfant *mf.* **~birth** *n* accouchement *m.* **childhood** *n* enfance *f.* **childish** *adj* puéril. **childless** *adj* sans enfants. **childlike** *adj* enfantin. **~-minder** *n* nourrice *f.*

Chile /ˈtʃɪlɪən/ *n* Chili *m.*

chill /tʃɪl/ *n* froid *m;* (Med) refroidissement *m.* ● *adj* froid. ● *vt* (*person*) faire frissonner; (*wine*) rafraîchir; (*food*) mettre à refroidir.

chilli /ˈtʃɪlɪ/ *n* (*pl* **-es**) piment *m.*

chilly /ˈtʃɪlɪ/ *adj* froid; **it's ~** il fait froid.

chime /tʃaɪm/ *n* carillon *m.* ● *vt/i* carillonner.

chimney /ˈtʃɪmnɪ/ *n* cheminée *f.*

~-sweep n ramoneur m.

chimpanzee /tʃɪmpən'zi:/ n chimpanzé m.

chin /tʃɪn/ n menton m.

china /'tʃaɪnə/ n porcelaine f.

China /'tʃaɪnə/ n Chine f.

Chinese /tʃaɪ'ni:z/ n (person) Chinois/-e m/f; (Ling) chinois m. ● adj chinois.

chip /tʃɪp/ n (on plate) ébréchure f; (piece) éclat m; (of wood) copeau m; (Culin) frite f; (Comput) puce f; (potato) ~s (US) chips fpl. ● vt/i (pt **chipped**) (s')ébrécher; ~ **in** 🔢 dire son mot; (with money) contribuer.

chiropodist /kɪ'rɒpədɪst/ n pédicure mf.

chirp /tʃɜ:p/ n pépiement m. ● vi pépier. **chirpy** adj gai.

chisel /'tʃɪzl/ n ciseau m. ● vt (pt **chiselled**) ciseler.

chit /tʃɪt/ n note f; (voucher) bon m.

chitchat /'tʃɪttʃæt/ n 🔢 bavardage m.

chivalrous /'ʃɪvəlrəs/ adj galant.

chives /tʃaɪvz/ npl ciboulette f.

chlorine /'klɔ:ri:n/ n chlore m.

choc ice /'tʃɒkaɪs/ n esquimau m.

chock-a-block /tʃɒkə'blɒk/ adj plein à craquer.

chocolate /'tʃɒklət/ n chocolat m.

choice /tʃɔɪs/ n choix m. ● adj de choix.

choir /'kwaɪə(r)/ n chœur m. **~boy** n jeune choriste m.

choke /tʃəʊk/ vt/i (s')étrangler; ~ **(up)** boucher. ● n starter m.

cholesterol /kə'lestərɒl/ n cholestérol m.

choose /tʃu:z/ vt/i (pt **chose**, pp **chosen**) choisir; ~ **to do** décider de faire. **choosy** adj difficile.

chop /tʃɒp/ vt/i (pt **chopped**) (wood) couper; (food) hacher.

chopping board planche f à découper; ~ **down** abattre. ● n (meat) côtelette f. **chopper** n hachoir m. 🔢 hélico m f.

choppy /'tʃɒpɪ/ adj (sea) agité.

chopstick /'tʃɒpstɪk/ n baguette f (chinoise).

chord /kɔ:d/ n (Mus) accord m.

chore /tʃɔ:(r)/ n (routine) tâche f; (unpleasant) corvée f.

chortle /'tʃɔ:tl/ n gloussement m. ● vi glousser.

chorus /'kɔ:rəs/ n chœur m; (of song) refrain m.

chose, chosen /tʃəʊz, 'tʃəʊzən/ ➡CHOOSE.

Christ /kraɪst/ n le Christ.

christen /'krɪsn/ vt baptiser. **christening** n baptême m.

Christian /'krɪstʃən/ adj & n chrétien/-ne (m/f). ~ **name** nom m de baptême. **Christianity** n christianisme m.

Christmas /'krɪsməs/ n Noël m; ~ **Day**/**Eve** le jour/la veille de Noël. ● adj (card, tree) de Noël.

chronic /'krɒnɪk/ adj (situation, disease) chronique; (bad 🔢) nul.

chronicle /'krɒnɪkl/ n chronique f.

chronological /krɒnə'lɒdʒɪkl/ adj chronologique.

chrysanthemum /krɪ'sæn θəməm/ n chrysanthème m.

chubby /'tʃʌbɪ/ adj (-ier, -iest) potelé.

chuck /tʃʌk/ vt 🔢 lancer; ~ **away** or **out** 🔢 balancer.

chuckle /'tʃʌkl/ n gloussement m. ● vi glousser.

chuffed /tʃʌft/ adj 🔢 vachement content f.

chunk /tʃʌŋk/ n morceau m. **chunky** adj (sweater, jewellery) gros; (person) costaud.

church /tʃɜːtʃ/ n église f. **~ goer** n pratiquant/-e m/f; **~yard** n cimetière m.

churn /tʃɜːn/ n baratte f; (milk-can) bidon m. ● vt baratter; **~ out** produire en série.

chute /ʃuːt/ n toboggan m; (for rubbish) vide-ordures m inv.

chutney /'tʃʌtnɪ/ n condiment m aigredoux.

cider /'saɪdə(r)/ n cidre m.

cigar /sɪ'gɑː(r)/ n cigare m.

cigarette /sɪgə'ret/ n cigarette f; **~ end** mégot m.

cinder /'sɪndə(r)/ n cendre f.

cinema /'sɪnəmə/ n cinéma m.

cinnamon /'sɪnəmən/ n cannelle f.

circle /'sɜːkl/ n cercle m; (Theat) balcon m. ● vt (go round) tourner autour de; (word, error) encercler. ● vi tourner en rond.

circuit /'sɜːkɪt/ n circuit m. **~-board** n carte f de circuit imprimé. **~-breaker** n disjoncteur m.

circuitous /sɜː'kjuːɪtəs/ adj indirect.

circular /'sɜːkjʊlə(r)/ adj & n circulaire (f).

circulate /'sɜːkjʊleɪt/ vt/i (faire) circuler. **circulation** n circulation f; (of newspaper) tirage m.

circumcise /'sɜːkəmsaɪz/ vt circoncire.

circumference /sə'kʌmfərəns/ n circonférence f.

circumflex /'sɜːkəmfleks/ n circonflexe m.

circumstance /'sɜːkəmstəns/ n circonstance f; **~s** (financial) situation f; **under no ~s** en aucun cas.

circus /'sɜːkəs/ n cirque m.

cistern /'sɪstən/ n réservoir m.

citizen /'sɪtɪzn/ n citoyen/-ne m/f; (of town) habitant/-e m/f. **citizen-**

ship n nationalité f.

citrus /'sɪtrəs/ adj **~ fruit(s)** agrumes mpl; **~ tree** citrus m.

city /'sɪtɪ/ n (grande) ville f.

> **ⓘ**
> **The City** Quartier londonien des affaires et de la finance, la *City* est le siège des grandes banques, des compagnies d'assurance et de la plupart des sociétés d'agents de change. 500 000 personnes viennent y travailler chaque jour.

civic /'sɪvɪk/ adj (official) municipal; (pride, duty) civique.

civil /'sɪvl/ adj civil. **~ disobedience** n résistance f passive. **~ engineer** n ingénieur m des travaux publics.

civilian /sɪ'vɪlɪən/ adj & n civil/-e (m/f).

civilization /sɪvəlaɪ'zeɪʃn/ n civilisation f. **civilize** vt civiliser.

civil: ~ law n droit m civil. **~ liberties** npl libertés fpl individuelles. **~ rights** npl droits mpl civils. **~ servant** n fonctionnaire mf. **~ service** n fonction f publique. **~ war** n guerre f civile.

claim /kleɪm/ vt (demand) revendiquer; (assert) prétendre. ● n revendication f; (assertion) affirmation f; (for insurance) réclamation f; (right) droit m. **claimant** n (of benefits) demandeur/-euse m/f.

clairvoyant /kleə'vɔɪənt/ n voyant/-e m/f.

clam /klæm/ n palourde f.

clamber /'klæmbə(r)/ vi grimper.

clammy /'klæmɪ/ adj (**-ier, -iest**) moite.

clamour /'klæmə(r)/ n clameur f. ● vi **~ for** réclamer.

clamp /klæmp/ n valet m; (Med)

pince *f*; (wheel) ∼ sabot *m* de Denver. ● *vt* cramponner; (*jaw*) serrer; (*car*) mettre un sabot de Denver à; ∼ **down on** faire de la répression contre.

clan /klæn/ *n* clan *m*.

clang /klæŋ/ *n* son *m* métallique.

clap /klæp/ *vt/i* (*pt* **clapped**) applaudir; (*put forcibly*) mettre; ∼ **one's hands** frapper dans ses mains. ● *n* applaudissement *m*; (of thunder) coup *m*.

claret /'klærət/ *n* bordeaux *m* rouge.

clarification /klærɪfɪ'keɪʃn/ *n* clarification *f*. **clarify** *vt/i* (se) clarifier.

clarinet /klærə'net/ *n* clarinette *f*.

clarity /'klærətɪ/ *n* clarté *f*.

clash /klæʃ/ *n* choc *m*; (fig) conflit *m*. ● *vi* (*metal objects*) s'entrechoquer; (*armies*) s'affronter; (*meetings*) avoir lieu en même temps; (*colours*) jurer.

clasp /klɑːsp/ *n* (*fastener*) fermoir *m*. ● *vt* serrer.

class /klɑːs/ *n* classe *f*. ● *vt* classer; ∼ **sb/sth as** assimiler qn/qch à.

classic /'klæsɪk/ *adj* & *n* classique (*m*). ∼**s** (Univ) lettres *fpl* classiques. **classical** *adj* classique.

classified /'klæsɪfaɪd/ *adj* (*information*) secret; ∼ (**ad**) petite annonce *f*.

classroom /'klɑːsrʊm/ *n* salle *f* de classe.

clatter /'klætə(r)/ *n* cliquetis *m*. ● *vi* cliqueter.

clause /klɔːz/ *n* clause *f*; (Gram) proposition *f*.

claw /klɔː/ *n* (of animal, small bird) griffe *f*; (of bird of prey) serre *f*; (of lobster) pince *f*. ● *vt* griffer.

clay /kleɪ/ *n* argile *f*.

clean /kliːn/ *adj* propre; (shape, stroke) net. ● *adv* complètement.

● *vt* nettoyer; ∼ **one's teeth** se brosser les dents. ● *vi* ∼ **up** faire le nettoyage. **cleaner** *n* (at home) femme *f* de ménage; (industrial) agent *m* de nettoyage; (of clothes) teinturier/-ière *m/f*. **cleanliness** *n* propreté *f*. **cleanly** *adv* proprement; (sharply) nettement.

cleanse /klenz/ *vt* nettoyer; (fig) purifier.

clean-shaven *adj* glabre.

clear /klɪə(r)/ *adj* (*explanation*) clair; (*need*, *sign*) évident; (*glass*) transparent; (*profit*) net; (*road*) dégagé; **make sth** ∼ être très clair sur qch; ∼ **of** (away from) à l'écart de. ● *adv* complètement; **stand** ∼ **of** s'éloigner de. ● *vt* (free) dégager (**of** de). (*table*) débarrasser; (*building*) évacuer; (*cheque*) compenser; (jump over) franchir; (*debt*) liquider; (Jur) disculper. ● *vi* (*fog*) se dissiper; (*cheque*) être compensé. ∼ **away** or **off** (remove) enlever. ∼ **off** or **out** 🅣 décamper. ∼ **out** (clean) nettoyer. ∼ **up** (tidy) ranger; (*weather*) s'éclaircir.

clearance /'klɪərəns/ *n* (*permission*) autorisation *f*; (*space*) espace *m*; ∼ **sale** liquidation *f*.

clear-cut *adj* net.

clearing /'klɪərɪŋ/ *n* clairière *f*.

clearly /'klɪəlɪ/ *adv* clairement.

clef /klef/ *n* (Mus) clé *f*.

cleft /kleft/ *n* fissure *f*.

clench /klentʃ/ *vt* serrer.

clergy /'klɜːdʒɪ/ *n* clergé *m*. ∼**man** *n* (*pl* **-men**) ecclésiastique *m*.

cleric /'klerɪk/ *n* clerc *m*. **clerical** *adj* (Relig) clérical; (*staff*, *work*) de bureau.

clerk /klɑːk/ *n* employé/-e *m/f* de bureau; (US) (*sales*) ∼ vendeur/-euse *m/f*.

clever | cloud

clever /'klevə(r)/ *adj* intelligent; (skilful) habile.

click /klɪk/ *n* déclic *m*; (Comput) clic *m*. ● *vi* faire un déclic; (people 🔲) sympathiser; (Comput) cliquer (on sur.) ● *vt* (heels, tongue) faire claquer.

client /'klaɪənt/ *n* client/-e *m/f.*

clientele /kliːənˈtel/ *n* clientèle *f.*

cliff /klɪf/ *n* falaise *f.*

climate /'klaɪmət/ *n* climat *m.*

climax /'klaɪmæks/ *n* (of story, contest) point *m* culminant; (sexual) orgasme *m.*

climb /klaɪm/ *vt* grimper; (steps) monter; (tree, ladder) grimper à; (mountain) faire l'ascension de. ● *vi* grimper; ~ **into** (car) monter dans; ~ **into bed** se mettre au lit. ● *n* (of mountain) escalade *f*; (steep hill, rise) montée *f*. ~ **down** (fig) reculer. **climber** *n* (Sport) alpiniste *mf.*

clinch /klɪntʃ/ *vt* (deal) conclure; (victory, order) décrocher.

cling /klɪŋ/ *vi* (pt **clung**) se cramponner (**to** à.) (stick) coller. ~**film** *n* scellofrais® *m.*

clinic /'klɪnɪk/ *n* centre *m* médical; (private) clinique *f.* **clinical** *adj* clinique.

clink /klɪŋk/ *n* tintement *m.* ● *vt/i* (faire) tinter.

clip /klɪp/ *n* (for paper) trombone *m*; (for hair) barrette *f*; (for tube) collier *m*; (of film) extrait *m.* ● *vt* (pt **clipped**) (fasten) attacher (**to** à.) cut) couper.

clippers /'klɪpəz/ *npl* tondeuse *f*; (for nails) coupe-ongles *m inv.*

clipping /'klɪpɪŋ/ *n* (from press) coupure *f* de presse.

cloak /kləʊk/ *n* cape *f*; (man's) houppelande *f.* ~**room** *n* vestiaire *m*; (toilet) toilettes *fpl.*

clobber /'klɒbə(r)/ *n* 🔲 attirail *m.*

● *vt* (hit 🔲) tabasser 🔲.

clock /klɒk/ *n* pendule *f*; (large) horloge *f.* ● *vi* ~ **on/in** or **off/out** pointer; ~ **up** (miles) faire. ~**tower** *n* beffroi *m.* ~**wise** *adj* & *adv* dans le sens des aiguilles d'une montre.

clockwork /'klɒkwɜːk/ *n* mécanisme *m.* ● *adj* mécanique.

clog /klɒg/ *n* sabot *m.* ● *vt/i* (pt **clogged**) (se) boucher.

cloister /'klɔɪstə(r)/ *n* cloître *m.*

clone /kləʊn/ *n* clone *m.* ● *vt* cloner.

close¹ /kləʊs/ *adj* (friend, relative) proche (**to** de); (link, collaboration) étroit; (examination) minutieux; (result, match) serré; (weather) lourd; ~ **together** (crowded) serrés; ~ **by**, ~ **at hand** tout près; **have a** ~ **shave** l'échapper belle; **keep a** ~ **watch on** surveiller de près. ● *adv* près. ● *n* (street) impasse *f.*

close² /kləʊz/ *vt* fermer; (meeting, case) mettre fin à. ● *vi* se fermer; (shop) fermer; (meeting, play) prendre fin. ● *n* fin *f.*

closely /'kləʊslɪ/ *adv* (follow) de près. **closeness** *n* proximité *f.*

closet /'klɒzɪt/ *n* (US) placard *m.*

close-up *n* gros plan *m.*

closure /'kləʊʒə(r)/ *n* fermeture *f.*

clot /klɒt/ *n* (of blood) caillot *m*; (in sauce) grumeau *m.* ● *vt/i* (pt **clotted**) (se) coaguler.

cloth /klɒθ/ *n* (fabric) tissu *m*; (duster) chiffon *m*; (table-cloth) nappe *f.*

clothe /kləʊð/ *vt* vêtir.

clothes /kləʊðz/ *npl* vêtements *mpl.* ~**hanger** *n* cintre *m.* ~**line** *n* corde *f* à linge.

clothing /'kləʊðɪŋ/ *n* vêtements *mpl.*

cloud /klaʊd/ *n* nuage *m.* ● *vi* ~

over se couvrir (de nuages); (face) s'assombrir. **cloudy** adj (sky) couvert; (liquid) trouble.

clout /klaʊt/ n (blow) coup m de poing; (power) influence f. ● vt frapper.

clove /kləʊv/ n clou m de girofle; ~ of garlic gousse f d'ail.

clover /'kləʊvə(r)/ n trèfle m.

clown /klaʊn/ n clown m. ● vi faire le clown.

club /klʌb/ n (group) club m; (weapon) massue f; (golf) ~ club m (de golf); ~s (cards) trèfle m. ● vt/i (pt clubbed) matraquer. ~ together cotiser.

cluck /klʌk/ vi glousser.

clue /kluː/ n indice m; (in crossword) définition f; I haven't a ~ je n'en ai pas la moindre idée.

clump /klʌmp/ n massif m.

clumsy /'klʌmzɪ/ adj (-ier, -iest) maladroit; (tool) peu commode.

clung /klʌŋ/ ⇒CLING.

cluster /'klʌstə(r)/ n (of people, islands) groupe m; (of flowers, berries) grappe f. ● vi se grouper.

clutch /klʌtʃ/ vt (hold) serrer fort; (grasp) saisir. ● vi ~ at (try to grasp) essayer de saisir. ● n (Auto) embrayage m; (of eggs) couvée f; (of people) groupe m.

clutter /'klʌtə(r)/ n désordre m. ● vt ~ (up) encombrer.

coach /kəʊtʃ/ n autocar m; (of train) wagon m; (horse-drawn) carrosse m; (Sport) entraîneur/-euse m/f. ● vt (team) entraîner; (pupil) donner des leçons particulières à.

coal /kəʊl/ n charbon m. ~field n bassin m houiller. ~mine n mine f de charbon.

coarse /kɔːs/ adj grossier.

coast /kəʊst/ n côte f. ● vi (car, bicycle) descendre en roue libre.

coastal adj côtier.

coast: ~guard n (person) garde-côte m; (organization) gendarmerie f maritime. ~line n littoral m.

coat /kəʊt/ n manteau m; (of animal) pelage m; (of paint) couche f; ~ of arms armoiries fpl. ● vt enduire, couvrir; (with chocolate) enrober (with de). **coating** n couche f.

coax /kəʊks/ vt cajoler.

cob /kɒb/ n (of corn) épi m.

cobbler /'kɒblə(r)/ n cordonnier m.

cobblestones /'kɒblstəʊnz/ npl pavés mpl.

cobweb /'kɒbweb/ n toile f d'araignée.

cocaine /kəʊ'keɪn/ n cocaïne f.

cock /kɒk/ n (rooster) coq m. (oiseau) mâle m. ● vt (gun) armer; (ears) dresser.

cockerel /'kɒkrəl/ n jeune coq m.

cockle /'kɒkl/ n (Culin) coque f.

cock: ~pit n poste m de pilotage. ~roach n cafard m. ~tail n cocktail m.

cocky /'kɒkɪ/ adj (-ier, -iest) trop sûr de soi.

cocoa /'kəʊkəʊ/ n cacao m.

coconut /'kəʊkənʌt/ n noix f de coco.

COD abbr (cash on delivery) envoi m contre remboursement.

cod /kɒd/ n inv morue f; ~-liver oil huile f de foie de morue.

code /kəʊd/ n code m. ● vt coder.

coerce /kəʊ'ɜːs/ vt contraindre.

coexist /kəʊɪg'zɪst/ vi coexister.

coffee /'kɒfɪ/ n café m. ~ bar n café m. ~ bean m grain m de café. ~pot n cafetière f. ~table n table f basse.

coffin /'kɒfɪn/ n cercueil m.

cog /kɒg/ n pignon m; (fig) rouage m.

cognac /'kɒnjæk/ n cognac m.

coil /kɔɪl/ vt/i (s')enrouler. ● n (of rope) rouleau m; (of snake) anneau m; (contraceptive) stérilet m.

coin /kɔɪn/ n pièce f (de monnaie). ● vt (word) inventer.

coincide /kəʊɪn'saɪd/ vi coïncider. **coincidence** n coïncidence f. **coincidental** adj dû à une coïncidence.

colander /'kʌləndə(r)/ n passoire f.

cold /kəʊld/ adj froid; (person) be or feel ~ avoir froid; **it is** ~ il fait froid; **get** ~ **feet** avoir les jetons 🔲; **~-blooded** (lit) à sang froid; (fig) sans pitié. ● n froid m; (Med) rhume m; ~ **sore** bouton de fièvre. **coldness** n froideur f.

coleslaw /'kəʊlslɔː/ n salade f de chou cru.

colic /'kɒlɪk/ n coliques fpl.

collaborate /kə'læbəreɪt/ vi collaborer.

collapse /kə'læps/ vi s'effondrer; (person) s'écrouler; (fold) se plier. ● n effondrement m.

collar /'kɒlə(r)/ n col m; (of dog) collier m; ~-**bone** n clavicule f.

collateral /kə'lætərəl/ n nantissement m.

colleague /'kɒliːg/ n collègue mf.

collect /kə'lekt/ vt rassembler; (pick up) ramasser; (call for) passer prendre; (money, fare) encaisser; (taxes, rent) percevoir; (as hobby) collectionner. ● vi se rassembler; (dust) s'amasser. ● adv **call** ~ (US) appeler en PCV. **collection** n collection f; (of money) collecte f; (in church) quête f; (of mail) levée f. **collective** /kə'lektɪv/ adj collectif.

collector /kə'lektə(r)/ n (as hobby) collectionneur/-euse m/f; (of taxes) percepteur m; (of rent, debt) encaisseur m.

college /'kɒlɪdʒ/ n (for higher edu-cation) établissement m d'enseigne-ment supérieur; (within university) collège m; **be at** ~ faire des études supérieures.

collide /kə'laɪd/ vi entrer en colli-sion (with avec).

colliery /'kɒlɪərɪ/ n houillère f.

collision /kə'lɪʒn/ n collision f.

colloquial /kə'ləʊkwɪəl/ adj fami-lier. **colloquialism** n expression f fa-milière.

Colombia /kə'lɒmbɪə/ n Co-lombie f.

colon /'kəʊlən/ n (Gram) deux-points m inv; (Anat) côlon m.

colonel /'kɜːnl/ n colonel m.

colonial /kə'ləʊnɪəl/ adj & n colonial/-e (m/f).

colour, (US) **color** /'kʌlə(r)/ n couleur f; ~**-blind** adj daltonien. ● adj (photo) en couleur; (TV set) couleur inv. ● vt colorer; (with crayon) colo-rier. **coloured** adj de couleur. **col-ourful** adj aux couleurs vives; (fig) haut en couleur. **colouring** n (of skin) teint m; (in food) colorant m.

colt /kəʊlt/ n poulain m.

column /'kɒləm/ n colonne f.

coma /'kəʊmə/ n coma m.

comb /kəʊm/ n peigne m. ● vt peig-ner; ~ **one's hair** se peigner; ~ **a place** passer un lieu au peigne fin.

combat /'kɒmbæt/ n combat m. ● vt (pt combated) combattre.

combination /kɒmbɪ'neɪʃn/ n combinaison f.

combine[1] /kəm'baɪn/ vt/i (se) combiner; (s')unir.

combine[2] /'kɒmbaɪn/ n (Comm) groupe m; ~ **harvester** moissonneuse-batteuse f.

come /kʌm/ vi (pt **came**, pp **come**) venir; (bus, letter) arriver; (postman) passer; ~ **and look!** viens voir!; ~

in (*size, colour*) exister en; **when it ~s to** lorsqu'il s'agit de. **~ about** survenir. **~ across** (*meaning*) passer; **~ across sth** tomber sur qch. **~ away** (*leave*) partir; (*come off*) se détacher. **~ back** revenir. **~ by** obtenir. **~ down** descendre; (*price*) baisser; **~ forward** se présenter. **~ in** entrer; **~ in useful** être utile. **~ in for** recevoir. **~ into** (*money*) hériter de. **~ off** (*succeed*) réussir; (*fare*) s'en tirer; (*detach*) se détacher. **~ on** (*actor*) entrer en scène; (*light*) s'allumer; (*improve*) faire des progrès; **~ on!** allez!. **~ out** sortir. **~ round** reprendre connaissance; (*change mind*) changer d'avis; **~ through** s'en tirer. **~ to** reprendre connaissance; **~ to sth** (*amount*) revenir à qch; (*decision, conclusion*) arriver à qch. **~ up** (*problem*) être soulevé; (*opportunity*) se présenter; (*sun*) se lever; **~ up against** heurter à. **~ up with** trouver.
comedian /kəˈmiːdɪən/ *n* comique *m*.
comedy /ˈkɒmədɪ/ *n* comédie *f*.
comfort /ˈkʌmfət/ *n* confort *m*; (*consolation*) réconfort *m*. ● *vt* consoler. **comfortable** adj (*chair, car*) confortable; (*person*) à l'aise; (*wealthy*) aisé.
comfortably /ˈkʌmftəblɪ/ *adv* confortablement; **~ off** aisé.
comfy /ˈkʌmfɪ/ *adj* ⊞ =**COMFORTABLE**.
comic /ˈkɒmɪk/ *adj* comique. ● *n* (*person*) comique *m*; (*book*), **~ strip** bande *f* dessinée.
coming /ˈkʌmɪŋ/ *n* arrivée *f*; **~s and goings** allées et venues *fpl*. ● *adj* à venir.
comma /ˈkɒmə/ *n* virgule *f*.
command /kəˈmɑːnd/ *n* (*authority*) commandement *m*; (*order*) ordre *m*; (*mastery*) maîtrise *f*. ● *vt*

ordonner à (**to do** faire); (*be able to use*) disposer de; (*respect*) inspirer. **commandeer** *vt* réquisitionner. **commander** *n* commandant *m*. **commanding** *adj* imposant. **commandment** *n* commandement *m*.
commando /kəˈmɑːndəʊ/ *n* commando *m*.
commemorate /kəˈmeməreɪt/ *vt* commémorer.
commence /kəˈmens/ *vt/i* commencer.
commend /kəˈmend/ *vt* (*praise*) louer; (*entrust*) confier.
commensurate /kəˈmenʃərət/ *adj* proportionné.
comment /ˈkɒment/ *n* commentaire *m*. ● *vi* faire des commentaires; **~ on** commenter. **commentary** *n* commentaire *m*; (*radio, TV*) reportage *m*. **commentate** *vi* faire un reportage. **commentator** *n* commentateur/-trice *m/f*.
commerce /ˈkɒmɜːs/ *n* commerce *m*.
commercial /kəˈmɜːʃl/ *adj* commercial; (*traveller*) de commerce. ● *n* publicité *f*.
commiserate /kəˈmɪzəreɪt/ *vi* compatir (**with** avec).
commission /kəˈmɪʃn/ *n* commission *f*; (*order for work*) commande *f*; **out of ~** hors service. ● *vt* (*order*) commander; (*Mil*) nommer officier; **~ to do** charger de faire. **commissioner** *n* préfet *m* (de police); (*in EU*) membre *m* de la Commission européenne.
commit /kəˈmɪt/ *vt* (*pt* **committed**) commettre; (*entrust*) confier; **~ oneself** s'engager; **~ perjury** se parjurer; **~ suicide** se suicider; **~ to memory** apprendre par cœur.
commitment *n* engagement *m*.

committee /kə'mɪtɪ/ n comité m.

commodity /kə'mɒdətɪ/ n article m.

common /'kɒmən/ adj (shared by all) commun (**to** à); (usual) courant; (vulgar) vulgaire, commun; **in** ~ en commun; ~ **people** le peuple; ~ **sense** bon sens m. ● n terrain m communal; **the C**~**s** Chambre f des Communes.

commoner /'kɒmənə(r)/ n roturier/-ière m/f.

common law n droit m coutumier.

commonly /'kɒmənlɪ/ adv communément.

commonplace /'kɒmənpleɪs/ adj banal. ● n banalité f.

common-room n salle f de détente.

Commonwealth /'kɒmənwelθ/ n the ~ le Commonwealth m.

Commonwealth of Nations Association de nations ayant pour la plupart fait partie de l'empire britannique et qui maintiennent une coopération avec la Grande-Bretagne en matière d'économie, de culture et d'éducation. Des championnats d'athlétisme, les *Commonwealth Games* ont lieu tous les quatre ans. Le mot *Commonwealth* figure dans le nom officiel de quelques États américains (*Kentucky, Virginia, Pennsylvania, Massachusetts*).

commotion /kə'məʊʃn/ n (noise) vacarme m; (disturbance) agitation f.

communal /'kɒmjʊnl/ adj (shared) commun; (life) collectif.

commune /'kɒmjuːn/ n (group) communauté f.

communicate /kə'mjuːnɪkeɪt/ vt/i communiquer. **communication**

n communication f. **communicative** adj communicatif.

communion /kə'mjuːnɪən/ n communion f.

Communism /'kɒmjʊnɪzəm/ n communisme m. **Communist** adj & n communiste (m/f).

community /kə'mjuːnətɪ/ n communauté f.

commute /kə'mjuːt/ vi faire la navette. ● vt (Jur) commuer. **commuter** n navetteur/-euse m/f.

compact /kəm'pækt/ adj compact; (lady's case) poudrier m.

compact disc n disque m compact. ~ **player** n platine f laser.

companion /kəm'pænɪən/ n compagnon/-agne m/f. **companionship** n camaraderie f.

company /'kʌmpənɪ/ n (companionship, firm) compagnie f; (guests) invités/-es m/fpl.

comparative /kəm'pærətɪv/ adj (study, form) comparatif; (comfort) relatif.

compare /kəm'peə(r)/ vt comparer (**with, to** à). ~**d with** par rapport à. ● vi être comparable. **comparison** n comparaison f.

compartment /kəm'pɑːtmənt/ n compartiment m.

compass /'kʌmpəs/ n (for direction) boussole f; (scope) portée f; **a pair of** ~**es** un compas.

compassionate /kəm'pæʃənət/ adj compatissant.

compatible /kəm'pætəbl/ adj compatible.

compel /kəm'pel/ vt (pt **compelled**) contraindre. **compelling** adj irrésistible.

compensate /'kɒmpenseɪt/ vt/i (financially) dédommager (**for** de). ~ **for sth** compenser qch. **compensation** n compensation f; (financial) dédommagement m.

compete /kəm'piːt/ vi concourir; ~ **with** rivaliser avec.

competent /'kɒmpɪtənt/ adj compétent.

competition /kɒmpə'tɪʃn/ n (contest) concours m; (Sport) compétition f; (Comm) concurrence f.

competitive /kəm'petɪtɪv/ adj (prices) compétitif; (person) qui a l'esprit de compétition.

competitor /kəm'petɪtə(r)/ n concurrent/-e m/f.

compile /kəm'paɪl/ vt (list) dresser; (book) rédiger.

complacency /kəm'pleɪsnsɪ/ n suffisance f.

complain /kəm'pleɪn/ vi se plaindre (about, of de). **complaint** n plainte f; (official) réclamation f; (illness) maladie f.

complement /'kɒmplɪmənt/ n complément m. ● vt compléter. **complementary** adj complémentaire.

complete /kəm'pliːt/ adj complet; (finished) achevé; (downright) parfait. ● vt achever; (a form) remplir. **completely** adv complètement. **completion** n achèvement m.

complex /'kɒmpleks/ adj complexe. ● n (Psych) complexe m.

complexion /kəm'plekʃn/ n (of face) teint m; (fig) caractère m.

compliance /kəm'plaɪəns/ n (agreement) conformité f.

complicate /'kɒmplɪkeɪt/ vt compliquer. **complicated** adj compliqué. **complication** n complication f.

compliment /'kɒmplɪmənt/ n compliment m. ● vt complimenter. **complimentary** adj (offert) à titre gracieux; (praising) flatteur.

comply /kəm'plaɪ/ vi ~ **with** se conformer à, obéir à.

component /kəm'pəʊnənt/ n (of machine) pièce f; (chemical substance) composant m; (element: fig) composante f. ● adj constituant.

compose /kəm'pəʊz/ vt composer; ~ **oneself** se calmer. **composed** adj calme. **composer** n (Mus) compositeur m. **composition** n composition f.

composure /kəm'pəʊʒə(r)/ n calme m.

compound /'kɒmpaʊnd/ n (substance, word) composé m; (enclosure) enclos m. ● adj composé.

comprehend /kɒmprɪ'hend/ vt comprendre. **comprehension** n compréhension f.

comprehensive /kɒmprɪ'hensɪv/ adj étendu, complet; (insurance) tous risques inv. ~ **school** n collège m d'enseignement secondaire.

compress /kəm'pres/ vt comprimer.

comprise /kəm'praɪz/ vt comprendre, inclure.

compromise /'kɒmprəmaɪz/ n compromis m. ● vt compromettre. ● vi transiger, arriver à un compromis.

compulsive /kəm'pʌlsɪv/ adj (Psych) compulsif; (liar, smoker) invétéré.

compulsory /kəm'pʌlsərɪ/ adj obligatoire.

compute /kəm'pjuːt/ vt calculer.

computer /kəm'pjuːt/ n ordinateur m; ~ **science** informatique f. **computerize** vt informatiser.

comrade /'kɒmreɪd/ n camarade mf.

con[1] /kɒn/ vt (pt) **conned** ⊠ rouler ⊠. escroquer (**out of** de.) ● n ⊠ escroquerie f.

con[2] /kɒn/ ➡ **PRO**.

conceal /kən'siːl/

dissimuler (**from** à.).

concede /kən'si:d/ *vt* concéder.
● *vi* céder.

conceited /kən'si:tɪd/ *adj* vaniteux.

conceive /kən'si:v/ *vt/i* concevoir; ~ **of** concevoir.

concentrate /'kɒnsntreɪt/ *vt/i* (se) concentrer. **concentration** *n* concentration *f*.

concept /'kɒnsept/ *n* concept *m*.

conception /kən'sepʃn/ *n* conception *f*.

concern /kən'sɜ:n/ *n* (interest, business) affaire *f*; (worry) inquiétude *f*; (firm: Comm) entreprise *f*, affaire *f*. ● *vt* concerner; ~ **oneself with, be** ~**ed with** s'occuper de. **concerned** *adj* inquiet. **concerning** *prep* en ce qui concerne.

concert /'kɒnsət/ *n* concert *m*.

concession /kən'seʃn/ *n* concession *f*.

conciliation /kənsɪlɪ'eɪʃn/ *n* conciliation *f*.

concise /kən'saɪs/ *adj* concis.

conclude /kən'klu:d/ *vt* conclure.
● *vi* se terminer. **conclusion** *n* conclusion *f*. **conclusive** *adj* concluant.

concoct /kən'kɒkt/ *vt* confectionner; (invent: fig) fabriquer. **concoction** *n* mélange *m*.

concourse /'kɒŋkɔ:s/ *n* (Rail) hall *m*.

concrete /'kɒŋkri:t/ *n* béton *m*.
● *adj* de béton; (fig) concret. ● *vt* bétonner.

concur /kən'kɜ:(r)/ *vi* (*pt* **concurred**) être d'accord.

concurrently /kən'kʌrəntlɪ/ *adv* simultanément.

concussion /kən'kʌʃn/ *n* commotion *f* (cérébrale).

condemn /kən'dem/ *vt*
condamner.

condensation /kɒndən'seɪʃn/ *n* (on walls) condensation *f*; (on windows) buée *f*. **condense** *vt/i* (se) condenser.

condition /kən'dɪʃn/ *n* condition *f*; **on** ~ **that** à condition que. ● *vt* conditionner. **conditional** *adj* conditionnel.

conditioner /kən'dɪʃənə(r)/ *n* après-shampooing *m*.

condolences /kən'dəʊlənsɪz/ *npl* condoléances *fpl*.

condom /'kɒndɒm/ *n* préservatif *m*.

condone /kən'dəʊn/ *vt* pardonner, fermer les yeux sur.

conducive /kən'dju:sɪv/ *adj* ~ **to** favorable à.

conduct¹ /'kɒndʌkt/ *n* conduite *f*.

conduct² /kən'dʌkt/ *vt* conduire; (*orchestra*) diriger. **conductor** *n* chef *m* d'orchestre; (of bus) receveur *m*; (on train: US) chef *m* de train; (Electr) conducteur *m*. **conductress** *n* receveuse *f*.

cone /kəʊn/ *n* cône *m*. (of icecream) cornet *m*.

confectioner /kən'fekʃənə(r)/ *n* confiseur/-euse *m/f*. **confectionery** *n* confiserie *f*.

confer /kən'fɜ:(r)/ *vt/i* (*pt* **conferred**) conférer.

conference /'kɒnfərəns/ *n* conférence *f*.

confess /kən'fes/ *vt/i* avouer; (Relig) (se) confesser. **confession** *n* confession *f*; (of crime) aveu *m*.

confide /kən'faɪd/ *vt* confier. ● *vi* ~ **in** se confier à.

confidence /'kɒnfɪdəns/ *n* (trust) confiance *f*. (boldness) confiance *f* en soi; (secret) confidence *f*; **in** ~ en confidence. **confident** *adj* sûr.

confidential /kɒnfɪ'denʃl/ adj confidentiel.

configuration /kənfɪgə'reɪʃn/ n configuration f. ● **configure** vt configurer.

confine /kən'faɪn/ vt enfermer; (limit) limiter; ~**d** space espace m réduit; ~**d to** limité à.

confirm /kən'fɜːm/ vt confirmer. **confirmed** adj (bachelor) endurci; (smoker) invétéré.

confiscate /'kɒnfɪskeɪt/ vt confisquer.

conflict[1] /'kɒnflɪkt/ n conflit m.

conflict[2] /kən'flɪkt/ vi (statements, views) être en contradiction (with avec.) (appointments) tomber en même temps (with que). **conflicting** adj contradictoire.

conform /kən'fɔːm/ vt/i (se) conformer.

confound /kən'faʊnd/ vt confondre.

confront /kən'frʌnt/ vt affronter; ~ with confronter avec.

confuse /kən'fjuːz/ vt (bewilder) troubler; (mistake, confound) confondre; **become** ~**d** s'embrouiller; **I am** ~**d** je m'y perds. **confusing** adj déroutant. **confusion** n confusion f.

congeal /kən'dʒiːl/ vt/i (se) figer.

congested /kən'dʒestɪd/ adj (road) embouteillé; (passage) encombré; (Med) congestionné. **congestion** n (traffic) encombrement(s) m(pl); (Med) congestion f.

congratulate /kən'grætʃuleɪt/ vt féliciter (on de). **congratulations** npl félicitations fpl.

congregate /'kɒngrɪgeɪt/ vi se rassembler. **congregation** n assemblée f.

congress /'kɒngres/ n congrès m. **C** ~ (US) le Congrès.

Congress Le Congrès est le corps législatif des États-Unis composé de la Chambre des représentants (House of Representatives) qui compte 435 membres, et du Sénat (Senate) qui compte 100 sénateurs, deux par État. Pour devenir loi, un projet de loi doit être approuvé par les deux chambres, et ratifié par le président. ▷ **CAPITOL**.

conjugate /'kɒndʒʊgeɪt/ vt conjuguer. **conjugation** n conjugaison f.

conjunction /kən'dʒʌŋkʃn/ n (Ling) conjonction f. **in** ~**with** conjointement avec.

conjunctivitis /kəndʒʌŋktɪ'vaɪtɪs/ n conjonctivite f.

conjure /kʌn'dʒə(r)/ vi faire des tours de passe-passe. ~ **up** faire apparaître. **conjuror** n prestidigitateur/-trice m/f.

con man 🗙 escroc m.

connect /kə'nekt/ vt/i (se) relier; (in mind) faire le rapport entre; (install, wire up to mains) brancher; ~ **with** (of train) assurer la correspondance avec; ~**ed** (plug, event) lié; **be** ~**ed with** avoir rapport à.

connection /kə'nekʃn/ n rapport m. (Rail) correspondance f; (phone call) communication f; (Electr) contact m; (joining piece) raccord m; ~**s** (Comm) relations fpl.

connive /kə'naɪv/ vi ~ **at** se faire le complice de.

conquer /'kɒŋkə(r)/ vt vaincre; (country) conquérir. **conqueror** n conquérant m.

conquest /'kɒŋkwest/ n conquête f.

conscience /'kɒnʃəns/ n conscience f. **conscientious** adj consciencieux.

conscious /'kɒnʃəs/ adj conscient; (deliberate) voulu. **consciously** adv consciemment. **consciousness** n conscience f; (Med) connaissance f.

conscript /'kɒnskrɪpt/ n appelé m.

consecutive /kən'sekjʊtɪv/ adj consécutif.

consensus /kən'sensəs/ n consensus m.

consent /kən'sent/ vi consentir (to à). ● n consentement m.

consequence /'kɒnsɪkwəns/ n conséquence f. **consequently** adv par conséquent.

conservation /kɒnsə'veɪʃn/ n préservation f. ~ **area** zone f protégée. **conservationist** n défenseur m de l'environnement.

conservative /kən'sɜːvətɪv/ adj conservateur; (estimate) minimal.

Conservative Party n parti m conservateur.

conservatory /kən'sɜːvətrɪ/ n (greenhouse) serre f; (room) véranda f.

conserve /kən'sɜːv/ vt conserver; (energy) économiser.

consider /kən'sɪdə(r)/ vt considérer; (allow for) tenir compte de; (possibility) envisager (**doing** de faire).

considerable /kən'sɪdərəbl/ adj considérable; (much) beaucoup de.

considerate /kən'sɪdərət/ adj prévenant, attentionné. **consideration** n considération f. (respect) égard(s) m(pl)

considering /kən'sɪdərɪŋ/ prep compte tenu de.

consignment /kən'saɪnmənt/ n envoi m.

consist /kən'sɪst/ vi consister (**of** en; **in doing** à faire).

consistency /kən'sɪstənsɪ/ n (of liquids) consistance f. (of argument) cohérence f.

consistent /kən'sɪstənt/ adj cohérent; ~ **with** conforme à.

consolation /kɒnsə'leɪʃn/ n consolation f.

consolidate /kən'sɒlɪdeɪt/ vt/i (se) consolider.

consonant /'kɒnsənənt/ n consonne f.

conspicuous /kən'spɪkjʊəs/ adj (easily seen) en évidence; (showy) voyant; (noteworthy) remarquable.

conspiracy /kən'spɪrəsɪ/ n conspiration f.

constable /'kʌnstəbl/ n agent m de police, gendarme m.

constant /'kɒnstənt/ adj (questions) incessant; (unchanging) constant; (friend) fidèle. ● n constante f. **constantly** adv constamment.

constellation /kɒnstə'leɪʃn/ n constellation f.

constipation /kɒnstɪ'peɪʃn/ n constipation f.

constituency /kən'stɪtjʊənsɪ/ n circonscription f électorale.

constituent /kən'stɪtjʊənt/ adj constitutif. ● n élément m constitutif; (Pol) électeur/-trice m/f.

constitution /kɒnstɪ'tjuːʃn/ n constitution f.

constrain /kən'streɪn/ vt contraindre. **constraint** n contrainte f.

constrict /kən'strɪkt/ vt (flow) comprimer; (movement) gêner.

construct /kən'strʌkt/ vt construire. **construction** n construction f. **constructive** adj constructif.

consulate /'kɒnsjʊlət/ n consulat m.

consult /kən'sʌlt/ vt consulter. ● vi ~ **with** conférer avec. **consultant** n conseiller/-ère m/f. (Med) spécialiste m/f. **consultation** n consultation f.

consume /kən'sju:m/ vt consommer; (destroy) consumer. **consumer** n consommateur/-trice m/f.

consummate /'kɒnsəmeɪt/ vt consommer.

consumption /kən'sʌmpʃn/ n consommation f; (Med) phtisie f.

contact /'kɒntækt/ n contact m; (person) relation f. ● vt contacter. ~ **lenses** npl lentilles fpl (de contact).

contagious /kən'teɪdʒəs/ adj contagieux.

contain /kən'teɪn/ vt contenir; ~ **oneself** se contenir. **container** n récipient m. (for transport) conteneur m.

contaminate /kən'tæmɪneɪt/ vt contaminer.

contemplate /'kɒntəmpleɪt/ vt (gaze at) contempler; (think about) envisager.

contemporary /kən'tempərəri/ adj & n contemporain/-e (m/f).

contempt /kən'tempt/ n mépris m. **contemptible** adj méprisable. **contemptuous** adj méprisant.

contend /kən'tend/ vt soutenir. ● vi ~ **with** (compete) rivaliser avec; (face) faire face à. **contender** n adversaire mf.

content[1] /'kɒntent/ n (of letter) contenu m. (amount) teneur f; ~**s** contenu m.

content[2] /kən'tent/ adj satisfait. ● vt contenter. **contented** adj satisfait. **contentment** n contentement m.

contest[1] /'kɒntest/ n (competition) concours m. (struggle) lutte f.

contest[2] /kən'test/ vt contester; (compete for or in) disputer. **contestant** n concurrent/-e m/f.

context /'kɒntekst/ n contexte m.

continent /'kɒntɪnənt/ n continent m; **the C** ~ l'Europe f (conti-

nentale). **continental** adj continental, européen. **continental quilt** n couette f.

contingency /kən'tɪndʒənsɪ/ n éventualité f. ~ **plan** plan m d'urgence.

continual /kən'tɪnjʊəl/ adj continuel.

continuation /kəntɪnjʊ'eɪʃn/ n continuation f. (after interruption) reprise f; (new episode) suite f.

continue /kən'tɪnju:/ vt/i continuer; (resume) reprendre. **continued** adj continu.

continuous /kən'tɪnjʊəs/ adj continu. **continuously** adv (without a break) sans interruption; (repeatedly) continuellement.

contort /kən'tɔ:t/ vt tordre; ~ **oneself** se contorsionner.

contour /'kɒntʊə(r)/ n contour m.

contraband /'kɒntrəbænd/ n contrebande f.

contraception /kɒntrə'sepʃn/ n contraception f. **contraceptive** adj & n contraceptif (m).

contract[1] /'kɒntrækt/ n contrat m.

contract[2] /kən'trækt/ vt/i (se) contracter. **contraction** n contraction f.

contractor /kən'træktə(r)/ n entrepreneur/-euse m/f.

contradict /kɒntrə'dɪkt/ vt contredire. **contradictory** adj contradictoire.

contrary[1] /'kɒntrərɪ/ adj contraire (to à). ● n contraire m. **on the** ~ au contraire. ● adv ~ **to** contrairement à.

contrary[2] /kən'treərɪ/ adj entêté.

contrast[1] /'kɒntrɑ:st/ n contraste m.

contrast[2] /kən'trɑ:st/ vt/i contraster.

contravention /kɒntrə'venʃn/ n

infraction f.

contribute /kən'trɪbjuːt/ vt donner. ● vi ~ **to** contribuer à; (take part) participer à; (newspaper) collaborer à. **contribution** n contribution f. **contributor** n collaborateur/-trice m/f.

contrive /kən'traɪv/ vt imaginer; ~ **to** trouver moyen de faire.

control /kən'trəʊl/ vt (pt **controlled**) (firm) diriger; (check) contrôler; (restrain) maîtriser. ● n contrôle m. (mastery) maîtrise f. ~**s** commandes fpl. (knobs) boutons mpl; **have under** ~ (event) avoir en main; **in** ~ **of** maître de. ~ **tower** n tour f de contrôle.

controversial /kɒntrə'vɜːʃl/ adj discutable, discuté. **controversy** n controverse f.

conurbation /kɒnɜː'beɪʃn/ n agglomération f, conurbation f.

convalesce /kɒnvə'les/ vi être en convalescence.

convene /kən'viːn/ vt convoquer. ● vi se réunir.

convenience /kən'viːnɪəns/ n commodité f. ~**s** toilettes fpl. **all modern** ~**s** tout le confort moderne; **at your** ~ quand cela vous conviendra, à votre convenance. ~ **foods** npl plats mpl tout préparés.

convenient /kən'viːnɪənt/ adj commode, pratique; (time) bien choisi; **be** ~ **for** convenir à.

convent /'kɒnvənt/ n couvent m.

convention /kən'venʃn/ n (assembly, agreement) convention f. (custom) usage m. **conventional** adj conventionnel.

conversation /kɒnvə'seɪʃn/ n conversation f. **conversational** adj (tone) de la conversation; (French) de tous les jours.

converse[1] /kən'vɜːs/ vi s'entrete-nir, converser (**with** avec).

converse[2] /'kɒnvɜːs/ adj & n inverse (m). **conversely** adv inversement.

conversion /kən'vɜːʃn/ n conversion f.

convert[1] /kən'vɜːt/ vt convertir; (house) aménager. ● vi ~ **into** se transformer en.

convert[2] /'kɒnvɜːt/ n converti/-e m/f.

convertible /kən'vɜːtəbl/ adj convertible. ● n (car) décapotable f.

convey /kən'veɪ/ vt (wishes, order) transmettre; (goods, people) transporter; (idea, feeling) communiquer. **conveyor belt** n tapis m roulant.

convict[1] /kən'vɪkt/ vt déclarer coupable.

convict[2] /'kɒnvɪkt/ n prisonnier/-ière m/f.

conviction /kən'vɪkʃn/ n (Jur) condamnation f. (opinion) conviction f.

convince /kən'vɪns/ vt convaincre.

convoke /kən'vəʊk/ vt convoquer.

convoy /'kɒnvɔɪ/ n convoi m.

convulse /kən'vʌls/ vt convulser; (fig) bouleverser; **be** ~**d with laughter** se tordre de rire.

cook /kʊk/ vt/i (faire) cuire; (of person) faire la cuisine; ~ **up** 🅸 fabriquer. ● n cuisinier/-ière m/f. **cooker** n (stove) cuisinière f. **cookery** n cuisine f.

cookie /'kʊkɪ/ n (US) biscuit m.

cooking /'kʊkɪŋ/ n cuisine f. ● adj de cuisine.

cool /kuːl/ adj frais; (calm) calme; (unfriendly) froid. ● n fraîcheur f. (calmness 🅸) sang-froid m; **in the** ~ au frais. ● vt/i rafraîchir. ~ **box** n glacière f.

coolly /'kuːllɪ/ adv calmement, froidement.

coop /ku:p/ n poulailler m. ● vt ~ **up** enfermer.

cooperate /kəʊˈɒpəreɪt/ vi coopérer. **co-operation** f coopération f.

cooperative /kəʊˈɒpərətɪv/ adj coopératif. ● n coopérative f.

coordinate /kəʊˈɔːdɪnət/ vt coordonner.

cop /kɒp/ vt (pt **copped**) 🅽 piquer. ● n (policeman) 🅽 flic m. ~ **out** 🅽 se dérober.

cope /kəʊp/ vi s'en sortir 🅽, se débrouiller; ~ **with** (problem) faire face à.

copper /ˈkɒpə(r)/ n cuivre m. (coin) sou m; 🅽 flic m. ● adj de cuivre.

copulate /ˈkɒpjʊleɪt/ vi s'accoupler.

copy /ˈkɒpɪ/ n copie f. (of book, newspaper) exemplaire m; (print: Photo) épreuve f. ● vt/i copier.

copyright /ˈkɒpɪraɪt/ n droit m d'auteur, copyright m.

copy-writer n rédacteur-concepteur m, rédactrice-conceptrice f.

cord /kɔːd/ n (petite) corde f; (of curtain, pyjamas) cordon m; (Electr) cordon m électrique; (fabric) velours m côtelé.

cordial /ˈkɔːdɪəl/ adj cordial. ● n (drink) sirop m.

corduroy /ˈkɔːdərɔɪ/ n velours m côtelé.

core /kɔː(r)/ n (of apple) trognon m; (of problem) cœur m; (Tech) noyau m. ● vt (apple) évider.

cork /kɔːk/ n liège m. (for bottle) bouchon m. ● vt boucher. **cork-screw** n tire-bouchon m.

corn /kɔːn/ n blé m. (maize: US) maïs m; (seed) grain m; (hard skin) cor m.

cornea /ˈkɔːnɪə/ n cornée f.

corner /ˈkɔːnə(r)/ n coin m; (bend

in road) virage m; (football) corner m. ● vt coincer, acculer; (market) accaparer. ● vi prendre un virage.

cornflour /ˈkɔːnflaʊə(r)/ n farine f de maïs.

cornice /ˈkɔːnɪs/ n corniche f.

corny /ˈkɔːnɪ/ adj (**-ier, -iest**) (joke) éculé.

corollary /kəˈrɒlərɪ/ n corollaire m.

coronary /ˈkɒrənrɪ/ n infarctus m.

coronation /kɒrəˈneɪʃn/ n couronnement m.

corporal /ˈkɔːpərəl/ n caporal m. ~**punishment** n châtiment m corporel.

corporate /ˈkɔːpərət/ adj (ownership) en commun; (body) constitué.

corporation /kɔːpəˈreɪʃn/ n (Comm) société f.

corpse /kɔːps/ n cadavre m.

corpuscle /ˈkɔːpʌsl/ n globule m.

correct /kəˈrekt/ adj (right) exact, juste, correct; (proper) correct; **you are** ~ vous avez raison. ● vt corriger.

correction /kəˈrekʃn/ n correction f.

correlate /ˈkɒrɪleɪt/ vt/i (faire) correspondre.

correspond /kɒrɪˈspɒnd/ vi correspondre. **correspondence** n correspondance f.

corridor /ˈkɒrɪdɔː(r)/ n couloir m.

corrode /kəˈrəʊd/ vt/i (se) corroder.

corrugated /ˈkɒrəgeɪtɪd/ adj ondulé; ~ **iron** tôle f ondulée.

corrupt /kəˈrʌpt/ adj corrompu. ● vt corrompre. **corruption** n corruption f.

Corsica /ˈkɔːsɪkə/ n Corse f.

cosh /kɒʃ/ n matraque f. ● vt matraquer.

cosmetic | courier

cosmetic /kɒzˈmetɪk/ n produit m de beauté. ● adj cosmétique; (fig, pej) superficiel. ~ **surgery** n chirurgie f esthétique

cosmopolitan /kɒzməˈpɒlɪtn/ adj & n cosmopolite (mf).

cosmos /ˈkɒzmɒs/ n cosmos m.

cost /kɒst/ vt (pt **cost**) coûter. (pt **costed**) établir le prix de. ● n coût m. ~**s** (Jur) dépens mpl. **at all** ~ à tout prix; **to one's** ~ à ses dépens; ~ **price** prix m de revient; ~ **of living** coût m de la vie. ~**-effective** adj rentable.

costly /ˈkɒstlɪ/ adj (**-ier, -iest**) coûteux; (valuable) précieux.

costume /ˈkɒstjuːm/ n costume m. (for swimming) maillot m. ~ **jewellery** npl bijoux mpl de fantaisie.

cosy /ˈkəʊzɪ/ adj (**-ier, -iest**) confortable, intime.

cot /kɒt/ n lit m d'enfant; (camp-bed: US) lit m de camp.

cottage /ˈkɒtɪdʒ/ n petite maison f de campagne; (thatched) chaumière f. ~ **pie** n hachis m Parmentier.

cotton /ˈkɒtn/ n coton m. (for sewing) fil m (à coudre). ● vi ~ **on** ⊠ piger. ~ **wool** n coton m hydrophile.

couch /kaʊtʃ/ n canapé m. ● vt (express) formuler.

cough /kɒf/ vi tousser. ● n toux f. ~ **up** ⊠ cracher, payer.

could /kʊd/ →**CAN'**.

couldn't →**COULD NOT**.

council /ˈkaʊnsl/ n conseil m. ~ **house** n maison f louée par la municipalité, ≈ H.L.M. m or f.

councillor /ˈkaʊnsələ(r)/ n conseiller/-ère m/f municipal/-e.

counsel /ˈkaʊnsl/ n conseil m. ● n inv (Jur) avocat/-e m/f. **counsellor** n conseiller/-ère m/f.

count /kaʊnt/ vt/i compter. ● n (numerical record) décompte m. (nobleman) comte m. ~ **on** compter sur.

counter /ˈkaʊntə(r)/ n comptoir m. (in bank) guichet m; (token) jeton m. ● adv ~ **to** à l'encontre de. ● adj opposé. ● vt opposer; (blow) parer. ● vi riposter.

counteract /kaʊntəˈrækt/ vt neutraliser.

counterbalance /ˈkaʊntəbæləns/ n contrepoids m. ● vt contrebalancer.

counterfeit /ˈkaʊntəfɪt/ adj & n faux (m). ● vt contrefaire.

counterfoil /ˈkaʊntəfɔɪl/ n souche f.

counter-productive /kaʊntəprəˈdʌktɪv/ adj qui produit l'effet contraire.

countess /ˈkaʊntɪs/ n comtesse f.

countless /ˈkaʊntlɪs/ adj innombrable.

country /ˈkʌntrɪ/ n (land, region) pays m. (homeland) patrie f; (countryside) campagne f.

countryman /ˈkʌntrɪmən/ n (pl **-men**) campagnard m; (fellow citizen) compatriote m.

countryside /ˈkʌntrɪsaɪd/ n campagne f.

county /ˈkaʊntɪ/ n comté m.

coup /kuː/ n (achievement) joli coup m. (Pol) coup m d'état.

couple /ˈkʌpl/ n (people, animals) couple m. **a** ~ **of** (two or three) deux ou trois. ● vt/i (s')accoupler.

coupon /ˈkuːpɒn/ n coupon m; (for shopping) bon m or coupon m de réduction.

courage /ˈkʌrɪdʒ/ n courage m.

courgette /kʊəˈʒet/ n courgette f.

courier /ˈkʊərɪə(r)/ n messager/-ère m/f; (for tourists) guide m.

course /kɔːs/ n cours m; (for training) stage m; (series) série f; (Culin) plat m; (for golf) terrain m; (at sea) itinéraire m. ~ **change** = changer de cap; ~ **(of action)** façon f de faire; **during the** ~ **of** pendant; **in due** ~ en temps utile; **of** ~ bien sûr.

court /kɔːt/ n cour f; (tennis) court m; **go to** ~ aller devant les tribunaux. ● vt faire la cour à; (danger) rechercher.

courteous /ˈkɜːtɪəs/ adj courtois.

courtesy /ˈkɜːtəsɪ/ n courtoisie f; **by** ~ **of** avec la permission de.

courthouse /ˈkɔːthaʊs/ n (US) palais m de justice.

court-martial vt (pt **-martialled**) faire passer en conseil de guerre. ● n cour f martiale.

court: ~room n salle f de tribunal. **~shoe** n escarpin m. **~yard** n cour f.

cousin /ˈkʌzn/ n cousin/-e m/f. **first** ~ **cousin/-e** m/f germain/-e.

cove /kəʊv/ n anse f, crique f.

covenant /ˈkʌvənənt/ n convention f.

cover /ˈkʌvə(r)/ vt couvrir. ● n (for bed, book) couverture f; (lid) couvercle m; (for furniture) housse f; (shelter) abri m; **take** ~ se mettre à l'abri. ~ **up** cacher; (crime) couvrir; **~up for** couvrir.

coverage /ˈkʌvərɪdʒ/ n reportage m.

covering /ˈkʌvərɪŋ/ n enveloppe f. ~ **letter** lettre f d'accompagnement.

covert /ˈkʌvət/ adj (activity) secret; (threat) voilé; (look) dérobé.

cover-up n opération f de camouflage.

cow /kaʊ/ n vache f.

coward /ˈkaʊəd/ n lâche mf.

cowboy /ˈkaʊbɔɪ/ n cow-boy m.

cowshed /ˈkaʊʃed/ n étable f.

coy /kɔɪ/ adj (faussement) timide, qui fait le or la timide.

cozy US =**COSY**.

crab /kræb/ n crabe m. **~-apple** n pomme f sauvage.

crack /kræk/ n fente f; (in glass) fêlure f; (noise) craquement m; (joke 🗷) plaisanterie f. ● adj 🗉 d'élite. ● vt/i (break partially) (se) fêler; (split) (se) fendre; (nut) casser; (joke) raconter; (problem) résoudre; **get** ~**ing** 🗉 s'y mettre. ~ **down on** 🗉 sévir contre. ~ **up** 🗉 craquer.

cracker /ˈkrækə(r)/ n (Culin) biscuit m (salé); (for Christmas) diablotin f.

crackle /ˈkrækl/ vi crépiter. ● n crépitement m.

cradle /ˈkreɪdl/ n berceau m. ● vt bercer.

craft /krɑːft/ n métier m artisanal; (technique) art m; (boat) bateau m.

craftsman n (pl **-men**) artisan m.

craftsmanship n art m.

crafty /ˈkrɑːftɪ/ adj (**-ier, -iest**) rusé.

crag /kræg/ n rocher m à pic.

cram /kræm/ vt/i (pt **crammed**). (for an exam) bachoter (for pour;) ~ **into** (pack) (s')entasser dans; ~ **with** (fill) bourrer de.

cramp /kræmp/ n crampe f.

cramped /kræmpt/ adj à l'étroit.

cranberry /ˈkrænbərɪ/ n canneberge f.

crane /kreɪn/ n grue f. ● vt (neck) tendre.

crank /kræŋk/ n excentrique mf. (Tech) manivelle f.

crap /kræp/ n (nonsense 🗷) conneries fpl 🗷; (faeces 🗷) merde f 🗷.

crash /kræʃ/ n accident m; (noise) fracas m; (of thunder) coup m; (of firm) faillite *f.* ● *vt/i* avoir un accident (avec); (of plane) s'écraser; (two vehicles) se percuter; ~ **into** rentrer dans. ~ **course** *n* cours *m* intensif. ~-**helmet** *n* casque *m* (anti-choc). ~-**land** *vi* atterrir en catastrophe.

crate /kreɪt/ *n* cageot *m.*

cravat /krə'væt/ *n* foulard *m.*

crave /kreɪv/ *vt/i* ~ **for** désirer ardemment. **craving** *n* envie *f* irrésistible.

crawl /krɔːl/ *vi* (insect) ramper; (vehicle) se traîner; **be** ~**ing with** grouiller de. ● *n* (pace) pas *m.* (swimming) crawl *m.*

crayfish /'kreɪfɪʃ/ *n inv* écrevisse *f.*

crayon /'kreɪən/ *n* craie *f* grasse.

craze /kreɪz/ *n* engouement *m.*

crazy /'kreɪzɪ/ *adj* (-**ier, -iest**) fou; ~ **about** (person) fou de; (thing) fana or fou de.

creak /kriːk/ *n* grincement *m.* ● *vi* grincer.

cream /kriːm/ *n* crème *f.* ● *adj* crème *inv.* ● *vt* écrémer.

crease /kriːs/ *n* pli *m.* ● *vt/i* (se) froisser.

create /kriː'eɪt/ *vt* créer. **creation** *n* création *f.* **creative** *adj* (person) créatif; (process) créateur. **creator** *n* créateur-trice *f.*

creature /'kriːtʃə(r)/ *n* créature *f.*

crèche /kreʃ/ *n* garderie *f.*

credentials /krɪ'denʃlz/ *npl* (identity) pièces *fpl* d'identité; (competence) références *fpl.*

credibility /kredə'bɪlətɪ/ *n* crédibilité *f.*

credit /'kredɪt/ *n* (credence) crédit *m.* (honour) honneur *m*; **in** ~ créditeur; ~**s** (cinema) générique *m.* ● *adj* (balance) créditeur. ● *vt* croire; (Comm) créditer; ~ **sb with** attribuer à qn. ~ **card** *n* carte *f* de cré-

dit. ~ **note** *n* avoir *m.*

creditor /'kredɪtə(r)/ *n* créancier/-ière *m/f.*

creditworthy /'kredɪtwɜːðɪ/ *adj* solvable.

creed /kriːd/ *n* credo *m.*

creek /kriːk/ *n* (US) ruisseau *m.* **up the** ~ ⚠ dans le pétrin ⚠.

creep /kriːp/ *vi* (*pt* **crept**) (insect, cat) ramper; (fig) se glisser. ● *n* (person ⚠) pauvre type *m* ⚠. **give sb the** ~**s** faire frissonner qn. **creeper** *n* liane *f.*

cremate /krɪ'meɪt/ *vt* incinérer. **cremation** *n* incinération *f.* **crematorium** *n* (*pl* -**ia**) crématorium *m.*

crêpe /kreɪp/ *n* crêpe *m.* ~ **paper** *n* papier *m* crépon.

crept /krept/ →**CREEP.**

crescent /'kresnt/ *n* croissant *m*; (of houses) rue *f* en demi-lune.

cress /kres/ *n* cresson *m.*

crest /krest/ *n* crête *f.* (coat of arms) armoiries *fpl.*

cretin /'kretɪn/ *n* crétin-e *m/f.*

crevice /'krevɪs/ *n* fente *f.*

crew /kruː/ *n* (of plane, ship) équipage *m*; (gang) équipe *f.* ~ **cut** *n* coupe *f* en brosse. ~ **neck** *n* (col) ras du cou *m.*

crib /krɪb/ *n* lit *m* d'enfant. ● *vt/i* (*pt* **cribbed**) copier.

cricket /'krɪkɪt/ *n* (Sport) cricket *m.* (insect) grillon *m.*

crime /kraɪm/ *n* crime *m*; (minor) délit *m*; (acts) criminalité *f.*

criminal /'krɪmɪnl/ *adj* & *n* criminel/-le (*m/f*).

crimson /'krɪmzn/ *adj* & *n* cramoisi (*m*).

cringe /krɪndʒ/ *vi* reculer; (fig) s'humilier.

crinkle /'krɪŋkl/ *vt/i* (cloth) (se)

froisser. ● n pli m.

cripple /'krɪpl/ n infirme mf. ● vt estropier; (fig) paralyser.

crisis /'kraɪsɪs/ n (pl **crises**) crise f.

crisp /krɪsp/ adj (Culin) croquant; (air, reply) vif. **crisps** npl chips fpl.

criss-cross /'krɪskrɒs/ adj entre-croisé. ● vt/i (s')entrecroiser.

criterion /kraɪ'tɪərɪən/ n (pl **-ia**) critère m.

critic /'krɪtɪk/ n critique m. **critical** adj critique. **critically** adv d'une ma-nière critique; (ill) gravement.

criticism /'krɪtɪsɪzəm/ n critique f.

criticize /'krɪtɪsaɪz/ vt/i critiquer.

croak /krəʊk/ n (bird) croassement m; (frog) coassement m. ● vi croas-ser; coasser.

Croatia /krəʊ'eɪʃə/ n Croatie f.

Croatian /krəʊ'eɪʃn/ n Croate mf. ● adj Croate.

crochet /'krəʊʃeɪ/ n crochet m. ● vt faire du crochet.

crockery /'krɒkərɪ/ n vaisselle f.

crocodile /'krɒkədaɪl/ n croco-dile m.

crook /krʊk/ n (criminal 🆃) escroc m; (stick) houlette f.

crooked /'krʊkɪd/ adj tordu; (winding) tortueux; (askew) de tra-vers; (dishonest: fig) malhonnête.

crop /krɒp/ n récolte f; (fig) quan-tité f. ● vt (pt **cropped**) couper. ● vi ~ **up** se présenter.

cross /krɒs/ n croix f; (hybrid) hy-bride m. ● vt/i traverser; (legs, ani-mals) croiser; (cheque) barrer; (paths) se croiser; ~ **sb's mind** venir à l'esprit de qn. ● adj en co-lère, fâché (**with** contre). **talk at ~ purposes** parler sans se compren-dre. □ ~ **off** or **out** rayer. ~-**check** vt vérifier (pour confirmer).

~-**country** (running) n cross m.

~-**examine** vt faire subir un contre-interrogatoire à. ~-**eyed** adj be ~-**eyed** loucher. ~-**fire** n feux mpl croisés.

crossing /'krɒsɪŋ/ n (by boat) tra-versée f; (on road) passage m clouté.

crossly /'krɒslɪ/ adv avec colère.

cross: ~-**reference** n renvoi m. ~-**roads** n carrefour m. ~-**word** n mots mpl croisés.

crotch /krɒtʃ/ n (of garment) en-trejambes m inv.

crouch /kraʊtʃ/ vi s'accroupir.

crow /krəʊ/ n corbeau m; **as the ~ flies** à vol d'oiseau. ● vi (of cock) chanter; (fig) jubiler. ~-**bar** n pied-de-biche m.

crowd /kraʊd/ n foule f. **crowded** adj plein.

crown /kraʊn/ n couronne f; (top part) sommet m. ● vt couronner.

Crown Court n Cour f d'assises.

crucial /'kru:ʃl/ adj crucial.

crucifix /'kru:sɪfɪks/ n crucifix m.

crucify /'kru:sɪfaɪ/ vt crucifier.

crude /kru:d/ adj (raw) brut; (rough, vulgar) grossier.

cruel /'krʊəl/ adj (**crueller, cruel-lest**) cruel.

cruise /kru:z/ n croisière f. ● vi (ship) croiser; (tourists) faire une croisière; (vehicle) rouler; **cruising speed** vitesse f de croisière.

crumb /krʌm/ n miette f.

crumble /'krʌmbl/ vt/i (s')effriter; (bread) (s')émietter; (collapse) s'é-crouler.

crumple /'krʌmpl/ vt/i (se) froisser.

crunch /krʌntʃ/ vt croquer. ● n (event) moment m critique; **when it comes to the ~** quand ça devient sérieux.

crusade /kruːˈseɪd/ n croisade f.
crusader n (knight) croisé m; (fig) militant/-e m/f.

crush /krʌʃ/ vt écraser; (clothes) froisser. ● n (crowd) presse f; **a ~ on** ⊠ le béguin pour.

crust /krʌst/ n croûte f. **crusty** adj croustillant.

crutch /krʌtʃ/ n béquille f; (crotch) entrejambes m inv.

crux /krʌks/ n **the ~ of** (problem) le point crucial de.

cry /kraɪ/ n cri m. ● vi (weep) pleurer; (call out) crier. □ ~ **off** se décommander.

crying /ˈkraɪɪŋ/ adj (need) urgent; **a ~ shame** une vraie honte. ● n pleurs mpl.

cryptic /ˈkrɪptɪk/ adj énigmatique.

crystal /ˈkrɪstl/ n cristal m.
~-clear adj parfaitement clair.

cub /kʌb/ n petit m; **Cub** (Scout) louveteau m.

Cuba /ˈkjuːbə/ n Cuba f.

cube /kjuːb/ n cube m. **cubic** adj cubique; (metre) cube.

cubicle /ˈkjuːbɪkl/ n (in room, hospital) box m; (at swimming-pool) cabine f.

cuckoo /ˈkʊkuː/ n coucou m.

cucumber /ˈkjuːkʌmbə(r)/ n concombre m.

cuddle /ˈkʌdl/ vt câliner. ● vi (kiss and) ~ s'embrasser. ● n caresse f.
cuddly adj câlin; **cuddly toy** peluche f.

cue /kjuː/ n signal m; (Theat) réplique f; (billiards) queue f.

cuff /kʌf/ n manchette f; **off the ~** impromptu. ● vt gifler. **~-link** n bouton m de manchette.

cul-de-sac /ˈkʌldəsæk/ n (pl **culs-**

de-sac) impasse f.

cull /kʌl/ vt (select) choisir; (kill) massacrer.

culminate /ˈkʌlmɪneɪt/ vi ~ **in** se terminer par. **culmination** n point m culminant.

culprit /ˈkʌlprɪt/ n coupable mf.

cult /kʌlt/ n culte m.

cultivate /ˈkʌltɪveɪt/ vt cultiver. **cultivation** n culture f.

cultural /ˈkʌltʃərəl/ adj culturel.

culture /ˈkʌltʃə(r)/ n culture f. **cultured** adj cultivé.

cumbersome /ˈkʌmbəsəm/ adj encombrant.

cunning /ˈkʌnɪŋ/ adj rusé. ● n astuce f; ruse f.

cup /kʌp/ n tasse f; (prize) coupe f; **Cup final** finale f de la coupe.

cupboard /ˈkʌbəd/ n placard m.

cup-tie n match m de coupe.

curate /ˈkjʊərət/ n vicaire m.

curator /kjʊəˈreɪtə(r)/ n (of museum) conservateur m.

curb /kɜːb/ n (restraint) frein m; (of path) (US) bord m du trottoir. ● vt (desires) refréner; (price increase) freiner.

cure /ˈkjʊə(r)/ vt guérir; (fig) éliminer; (Culin) fumer; (in brine) saler. ● n (recovery) guérison f; (remedy) remède m.

curfew /ˈkɜːfjuː/ n couvre-feu m.

curiosity /kjʊərɪˈɒsɪtɪ/ n curiosité f. **curious** adj curieux.

curl /kɜːl/ vt/i (hair) boucler. ● n boucle f. □ ~**up** se pelotonner; (shrivel) se racornir.

curler /ˈkɜːlə(r)/ n bigoudi m.

curly /ˈkɜːlɪ/ adj (-ier, -iest) bouclé.

currant /ˈkʌrənt/ n raisin m de Corinthe.

currency /ˈkʌrənsɪ/ n (money)

monnaie f; (of word) fréquence f;
foreign ∼ devises fpl étrangères.

current /'kʌrənt/ adj (term, word)
usité; (topical) actuel; (year) en
cours. ● n courant m. ∼ **account** n
compte m courant. ∼ **events** npl
l'actualité f

currently /'kʌrəntlɪ/ adv actuellement.

curriculum /kə'rɪkjʊləm/ n (pl
-la) programme m scolaire. ∼ **vitae**
n curriculum vitae m.

curry /'kʌrɪ/ n curry m. ● vt ∼ **favour with** chercher les bonnes grâces de.

curse /kɜːs/ n (spell) malédiction f;
(swearword) juron m. ● vt maudire.
● vi (swear) jurer.

cursor /'kɜːsə(r)/ n curseur m.

curt /kɜːt/ adj brusque.

curtain /'kɜːtn/ n rideau m.

curve /kɜːv/ n courbe f. ● vi (line)
s'incurver; (edge) se recourber;
(road) faire une courbe. ● vt
courber.

cushion /'kʊʃn/ n coussin m. ● vt
(a blow) amortir; (fig) protéger.

custard /'kʌstəd/ n crème f anglaise; (set) flan m.

custody /'kʌstədɪ/ n (of child)
garde f; (Jur) détention f préventive.

custom /'kʌstəm/ n coutume f;
(patronage: Comm) clientèle f. **customary** adj habituel.

customer /'kʌstəmə(r)/ n client/-e
m/f; (person 🄸) type m.

customize /'kʌstəmaɪz/ vt person-
naliser.

custom-made adj fait sur
mesure.

customs /'kʌstəmz/ npl douane f.
● adj douanier. ∼ **officer** n douanier m.

cut /kʌt/ vt/i (pt **cut**, pres p **cutting**)

vt couper; (hedge) tailler; (prices) réduire. ● vi couper. ● n (wound) coupure f; (of clothes) coupe f; (in surgery) incision f; (share) part f; (in
prices) réduction f. □ ∼ **back** vi
faire des économies. vt réduire. ∼
down (on) réduire. ∼ **in** (in conversation) intervenir. ∼ **off** couper;
(tide, army) isoler; ∼ **out** découper; (leave out) supprimer; vi (engine) s'arrêter. ∼ **short** (visit)
écourter. ∼ **up** couper; (carve) découper.

cutback /'kʌtbæk/ n réduction f.

cute /kjuːt/ adj 🄸 mignon.

cutlery /'kʌtlərɪ/ n couverts mpl.

cutlet /'kʌtlɪt/ n côtelette f.

cut-price adj à prix réduit.

cutting /'kʌtɪŋ/ adj cinglant. ● n
(from newspaper) coupure f; (plant)
bouture f.

CV abbr →CURRICULUM VITAE.

cyanide /'saɪənaɪd/ n cyanure m.

cyberspace /'saɪbəspeɪs/ n cyberspace m.

cycle /'saɪbəspeɪs/ n cycle m; (bicycle) vélo m. ● vi aller à vélo.

cycling /'saɪklɪŋ/ n cyclisme m. ∼
shorts npl cycliste m.

cyclist /'saɪklɪst/ n cycliste mf.

cylinder /'sɪlɪndə(r)/ n cylindre m.

cymbal /'sɪmbl/ n cymbale f.

cynic /'sɪnɪk/ n cynique mf. **cynical**
adj cynique. **cynicism** n cynisme m.

cypress /'saɪprəs/ n cyprès m.

Cypriot /'sɪprɪət/ n Cypriote m/f.
● adj cypriote.

Cyprus /'saɪprəs/ n Chypre f.

cyst /sɪst/ n kyste m.

czar /zɑː(r)/ n tsar m.

Czech /tʃek/ n (person) Tchèque mf;
(Ling) tchèque m. ∼ **Republic** n République f tchèque.

Dd

dab /dæb/ vt (pt **dabbed**) tamponner; ~ **sth on** appliquer qch par petites touches. ● n touche f.

dabble /'dæbl/ vi ~ **in sth** faire qch en amateur.

dad /dæd/ n 🔟 papa m. **daddy** n 🔟 papa m.

daffodil /'dæfədɪl/ n jonquille f.

daft /dɑːft/ adj bête.

dagger /'dægə(r)/ n poignard m.

> **Dáil Éireann** Ces mots de gaélique irlandais, que l'on prononce /dɔɪl 'ɜː(ə)n/ désignent la Chambre des représentants au parlement de la République d'Irlande. Les 166 députés qui la composent représentent 42 circonscriptions électorales et sont élus par un système de scrutin à la représentation proportionnelle pour cinq ans.

daily /'deɪlɪ/ adj quotidien. ● adv tous les jours. ● n (newspaper) quotidien m.

dainty /'deɪntɪ/ adj (**-ier**, **-iest**) (lace, food) délicat; (shoe, hand) mignon.

dairy /'deərɪ/ n (on farm) laiterie f; (shop) crémerie f. ● adj (farm, cow, product) laitier; (butter) fermier.

daisy /'deɪzɪ/ n pâquerette f.

dam /dæm/ n barrage m.

damage /'dæmɪdʒ/ n (to property) dégâts mpl; (Med) lésions fpl; **to do sth** ~ (cause, trade) porter atteinte à; ~**s** (Jur) dommages-intérêts mpl. ● vt (property) endommager; (health) nuire à; (reputation) porter

atteinte à. **damaging** adj (to health) nuisible; (to reputation) préjudiciable.

damn /dæm/ vt (Relig) damner; (condemn: fig) condamner. ● interj 🔟 zut 🔟, merde 🔀. ● n **not give/ care a** ~ **about** se ficher de 🔟. ● adj fichu 🔟. ● adv franchement.

damp /dæmp/ n humidité f. ● adj humide. **dampen** vt (lit) humecter; (fig) refroidir. **dampness** n humidité f.

dance /dɑːns/ vt/i danser. ● n danse f; (gathering) bal m; ~ **hall** dancing m. **dancer** n danseur/-euse m/f.

dandelion /'dændɪlaɪən/ n pissenlit m.

dandruff /'dændrʌf/ n pellicules fpl.

Dane /deɪn/ n Danois/-e m/f.

danger /'deɪndʒə(r)/ n danger m; (risk) risque m; **be in** ~ **of** risquer de. **dangerous** adj dangereux.

dangle /'dæŋgl/ vt (object) balancer; (legs) laisser pendre. ● vi (object) se balancer (**from** à).

Danish /'deɪnɪʃ/ n (Ling) danois m. ● adj danois.

dare /deə(r)/ vt oser ((**to) do** faire); ~ **sb to do** défier qn de faire. ● n défi m. **daring** adj audacieux.

dark /dɑːk/ adj (day, colour, suit, mood, warning) sombre; (hair, eyes, skin) brun; (street, thought) noir. ● n noir m; (nightfall) tombée f de la nuit; **in the** ~ (fig) dans le noir. **darken** vt/i (sky) (s')obscurcir; (mood) (s')assombrir. **darkness** n obscurité f. ~**-room** n chambre f noire.

darling /'dɑːlɪŋ/ adj & n chéri/-e (m/f).

dart /dɑːt/ n fléchette f; ~**s** (game) fléchettes fpl. ● vi ~ **in/away**

entrer/filer comme une flèche.

dash /dæʃ/ vi se précipiter; ~ **off** se sauver. ● vt (hope) anéantir; ~ **sth against** projeter qch contre. ● n course f folle; (of liquid) goutte f; (of colour) touche f; (in punctuation) tiret m.

dashboard /ˈdæʃbɔːd/ n tableau m de bord.

data /ˈdeɪtə/ npl données fpl. ~**base** n base f de données. ~ **capture** n saisie f de données. ~ **processing** n traitement m des données. ~ **protection** n protection f de l'information.

date /deɪt/ n date f; (meeting) rendezvous m; (fruit) datte f; **out of** ~ (old-fashioned) démodé; (passport) périmé; **to** ~ à ce jour; **up to** ~ (modern) moderne; (list) à jour. ● vt/i dater; (go out with) sortir avec; ~ **from** dater de. **dated** adj démodé.

daughter /ˈdɔːtə(r)/ n fille f. ~-**in-law** n (pl ~**s-in-law**) belle-fille f.

daunt /dɔːnt/ vt décourager.

dawdle /ˈdɔːdl/ vi flâner, traînasser ▣.

dawn /dɔːn/ n aube f. ● vi (day) se lever; **it** ~**ed on me that** je me suis rendu compte que.

day /deɪ/ n jour m; (whole day) journée f; (period) époque f; **the** ~ **before** la veille; **the following** or **next** ~ le lendemain. ~**break** n aube f.

daydream /ˈdeɪdriːm/ n rêves mpl. ● vi rêvasser (about de).

day: ~**light** n jour m. ~**time** n journée f. ~ **trader** spéculateur m à la journée, scalpeur m.

daze /deɪz/ vt in a ~ (from blow) étourdi; (from drug) hébété. **dazed** adj (by blow) abasourdi; (by news) ahuri.

dazzle /ˈdæzl/ vt éblouir.

dead /ded/ adj mort; (numb) engourdi. ● adv complètement; **in** ~ **centre** au beau milieu; **stop** ~ s'arrêter net. ● n **in the** ~ **of** au cœur de; **the** ~ les morts. **deaden** vt (sound, blow) amortir; (pain) calmer. ~ **end** n impasse f. ~**line** n date f limite. ~**lock** n impasse f.

deadly /ˈdedlɪ/ adj (-**ier**, -**iest**) mortel; (weapon) meurtrier.

deaf /def/ adj sourd. **deafen** vt assourdir. **deafness** n surdité f.

deal /diːl/ vt (pt **dealt**) donner; (blow) porter. ● vi (trade) être en activité; ~ **in** être dans le commerce de. ● n affaire f; (cards) donne f; **a great** or **good** ~ beaucoup (of de). ~ **with** (handle, manage) s'occuper de; (be about) traiter de. **dealer** n marchand/-e m/f; (agent) concessionnaire mf. **dealings** npl relations f.

dear /dɪə(r)/ adj cher; ~ **Sir/Madam** Monsieur/Madame. ● n **(my)** ~ mon chéri/ma chérie m/f. ● adv cher. ● interj **oh** ~! oh mon Dieu!

death /deθ/ n mort f; ~ **penalty** peine f de mort.

debatable /dɪˈbeɪtəbl/ adj discutable.

debate /dɪˈbeɪt/ n (formal) débat m; (informal) discussion f. ● vt (formally) débattre de; (informally) discuter.

debit /ˈdebɪt/ n débit m. ● adj (balance) débiteur. ● vt (pt **debited**) débiter.

debris /ˈdebriː/ n débris mpl; (rubbish) déchets mpl.

debt /det/ n dette f; **be in** ~ avoir des dettes.

debug /diːˈbʌg/ vt (Comput) déboguer.

decade /ˈdekeɪd/ n décennie f.

decadent /'dekədənt/ adj décadent.

decaffeinated /di:'kæfɪneɪtɪd/ adj décaféiné.

decay /dɪ'keɪ/ vi (vegetation) pourrir; (tooth) se carier; (fig) décliner. ● n pourriture f; (of tooth) carie f; (fig) déclin m.

deceased /dɪ'si:st/ adj décédé. ● n défunt/-e m/f.

deceit /dɪ'si:t/ n tromperie f. **deceitful** adj trompeur.

deceive /dɪ'si:v/ vt tromper.

December /dɪ'sembə(r)/ n décembre m.

decent /'di:snt/ adj (respectable) comme il faut; (adequate) convenable; (good) bon; (kind) gentil; (not indecent) décent. **decently** adv convenablement.

deception /dɪ'sepʃn/ n tromperie f. **deceptive** adj trompeur.

decide /dɪ'saɪd/ vt/i décider (**to do** de faire); (question) régler; ~ **on** se décider pour. **decided** adj (firm) résolu; (clear) net. **decidedly** adv nettement.

decimal /'desɪml/ adj décimal. ● n décimale f; ~ **point** virgule f.

decipher /dɪ'saɪfə(r)/ vt déchiffrer.

decision /dɪ'sɪʒn/ n décision f.

decisive /dɪ'saɪsɪv/ adj (conclusive) décisif; (firm) décidé.

deck /dek/ n pont m; (of cards: US) jeu m; (of bus) étage m. ~-**chair** n chaise f longue.

declaration /deklə'reɪʃn/ n déclaration f. **declare** vt déclarer.

decline /dɪ'klaɪn/ vt/i refuser; (fall) baisser. ● n (waning) déclin m; (drop) baisse f; **in** ~ sur le déclin.

decode /di:'kəʊd/ vt décoder.

decommission /di:kə'mɪʃn/vt (arms) mettre hors service; (reactor) démanteler.

decompose /di:kəm'pəʊz/ vt/i (se) décomposer.

decor /'deɪkɔ:(r)/ n décor m.

decorate /'dekəreɪt/ vt décorer; (room) refaire, peindre. **decoration** n décoration f. **decorative** adj décoratif.

decorator /'dekəreɪtə(r)/ n peintre m; (interior) ~ décorateur/-trice m/f.

decoy /'di:kɔɪ/ n (person, vehicle) leurre m; (for hunting) appeau m.

decrease¹ /dɪ'kri:s/ vt/i diminuer.

decrease² /'di:kri:s/ n diminution f.

decree /dɪ'kri:/ n (Pol, Relig) décret m; (Jur) jugement m. ● vt (pt **decreed**) décréter.

decrepit /dɪ'krepɪt/ adj (building) délabré; (person) décrépit.

dedicate /'dedɪkeɪt/ vt dédier; ~ oneself to se consacrer à.

dedicated /'dedɪkeɪtɪd/ adj dévoué; ~ **line** (Internet) ligne f spécialisée.

dedication /dedɪ'keɪʃn/ n dévouement m; (in book) dédicace f.

deduce /dɪ'dju:s/ vt déduire.

deduct /dɪ'dʌkt/ vt déduire; (from wages) retenir.

deed /di:d/ n acte m.

deem /di:m/ vt considérer.

deep /di:p/ adj profond; (mud, carpet) épais. ● adv profondément; ~ **in thought** absorbé dans ses pensées. **deepen** vt/i (admiration, concern) augmenter.

deep-freeze n congélateur m. ● vt congeler.

deep vein thrombosis n thrombose f veineuse profonde.

deer /dɪə(r)/ n inv cerf m; (doe) biche f.

deface /dɪ'feɪs/ vt dégrader.

default | deliberate

default /dɪˈfɔːlt/ vi (Jur) ~ **(on payments)** ne pas régler ses échéances. ● n (on payments) non-remboursement m; **by** ~ par défaut; **win by** ~ gagner par forfait. ● adj (Comput) par défaut.

defeat /dɪˈfiːt/ vt vaincre; (thwart) faire échouer. ● n défaite f.

defect[1] /ˈdiːfekt/ n défaut m.

defect[2] /dɪˈfekt/ vi faire défection; ~ **to** passer à.

defective /dɪˈfektɪv/ adj défectueux.

defector /dɪˈfektə(r)/ n transfuge mf.

defence /dɪˈfens/ n défense f.

defend /dɪˈfend/ vt défendre. **defendant** n (Jur) accusé/-e m/f. **defender** défenseur m.

defensive /dɪˈfensɪv/ adj défensif. ● n défensive f.

defer /dɪˈfɜː(r)/ vt (pt **deferred**) (postpone) reporter; (judgement) suspendre; (payment) différer.

deference /ˈdefərəns/ n déférence f. **deferential** adj déférent.

defiance /dɪˈfaɪəns/ n défi m; **in** ~ **of** contre. **defiant** adj rebelle. **defiantly** adv avec défi.

deficiency /dɪˈfɪʃənsɪ/ n insuffisance f; (fault) défaut m.

deficient /dɪˈfɪʃnt/ adj insuffisant; **be** ~ **in** manquer de.

deficit /ˈdefɪsɪt/ n déficit m.

define /dɪˈfaɪn/ vt définir.

definite /ˈdefɪnɪt/ adj (exact) précis; (obvious) net; (firm) ferme; (certain) certain. **definitely** adv certainement; (clearly) nettement.

definition /defɪˈnɪʃn/ n définition f.

deflate /dɪˈfleɪt/ vt dégonfler.

deflect /dɪˈflekt/ vt (missile) dévier; (criticism) détourner.

deforestation /diːfɒrɪˈsteɪʃn/ n déforestation f.

deform /dɪˈfɔːm/ vt déformer.

defraud /dɪˈfrɔːd/ vt (client, employer) escroquer; (state, customs) frauder; ~ **sb of sth** escroquer qch à qn.

defrost /diːˈfrɒst/ vt dégivrer.

deft /deft/ adj adroit.

defunct /dɪˈfʌŋkt/ adj défunt.

defuse /diːˈfjuːz/ vt désamorcer.

defy /dɪˈfaɪ/ vt défier; (attempts) résister à.

degenerate[1] /dɪˈdʒenəreɪt/ vi dégénérer (into en).

degenerate[2] /dɪˈdʒenərət/ adj & n dégénéré/-e (m/f).

degrade /dɪˈɡreɪd/ vt (humiliate) humilier; (damage) dégrader.

degree /dɪˈɡriː/ n degré m; (Univ) diplôme m universitaire; (Bachelor's degree) licence f; **to such a** ~ **that** à tel point que.

dehydrate /diːˈhaɪdreɪt/ vt/i (se) déshydrater.

deign /deɪn/ vt ~ **to do** daigner faire.

dejected /dɪˈdʒektɪd/ adj découragé.

delay /dɪˈleɪ/ vt (flight) retarder; (decision) différer; ~ **doing** attendre pour faire. ● n (of plane, post) retard m; (time lapse) délai m.

delegate[1] /ˈdelɪɡət/ n délégué /-e m/f.

delegate[2] /ˈdelɪɡeɪt/ vt déléguer. **delegation** n délégation f.

delete /dɪˈliːt/ vt supprimer; (Comput) effacer; (with pen) barrer. **deletion** n suppression f; (with line) rature f.

deliberate[1] /dɪˈlɪbəreɪt/ vi délibérer.

deliberate[2] /dɪˈlɪbərət/ adj délibéré; (*steps, manner*) mesuré. **deliberately** adv (*do, say*) exprès; (*sarcastically, provocatively*) délibérément.

delicacy /'delɪkəsɪ/ n délicatesse f; (*food*) mets m raffiné.

delicate /'delɪkət/ adj délicat.

delicatessen /delɪkə'tesn/ n épicerie f fine.

delicious /dɪ'lɪʃəs/ adj délicieux.

delight /dɪ'laɪt/ n joie f, plaisir m. ● vt ravir. ● vi ~ **in** prendre plaisir à. **delighted** adj ravi. **delightful** adj charmant/-e.

delinquent /dɪ'lɪŋkwənt/ adj & n délinquant/-e (m/f).

delirious /dɪ'lɪrɪəs/ adj délirant.

deliver /dɪ'lɪvə(r)/ vt (*message*) remettre; (*goods*) livrer; (*speech*) faire; (*baby*) mettre au monde; (*rescue*) délivrer. **delivery** n (*of goods*) livraison f; (*of mail*) distribution f; (*of baby*) accouchement m.

delude /dɪ'luːd/ vt tromper; ~ oneself se faire des illusions.

deluge /'deljuːdʒ/ n déluge m. ● vt submerger (**with** de).

delusion /dɪ'luːʒn/ n illusion f.

delve /delv/ vi fouiller.

demand /dɪ'mɑːnd/ vt (*request, require*) demander; (*forcefully*) exiger. ● n (*request*) demande f; (*pressure*) exigence f; **in** ~ très demandé; **on** ~ à la demande. **demanding** adj exigeant.

demean /dɪ'miːn/ vt ~ oneself s'abaisser.

demeanour, (US)**demeanor** /dɪ'miːnə(r)/ n comportement m.

demented /dɪ'mentɪd/ adj fou.

demise /dɪ'maɪz/ n disparition f.

demo /'deməʊ/ n (demonstration 🔲) manif f 🔲.

democracy /dɪ'mɒkrəsɪ/ n démocratie f.

democrat /'deməkræt/ n démocrate mf. **democratic** adj démocratique.

demolish /dɪ'mɒlɪʃ/ vt démolir.

demon /'diːmən/ n démon m.

demonstrate /'demənstreɪt/ vt démontrer; (*concern, skill*) manifester. ● vi (Pol) manifester. **demonstration** n démonstration f; (Pol) manifestation f. **demonstrative** adj démonstratif. **demonstrator** n manifestant/-e m/f.

demoralize /dɪ'mɒrəlaɪz/ vt démoraliser.

demote /diː'məʊt/ vt rétrograder.

den /den/ n (of lion) antre m; (room) tanière f.

denial /dɪ'naɪəl/ n (of rumour) démenti m; (of rights) négation f; (of request) rejet m.

denim /'denɪm/ n jean m; ~s (jeans) jean m.

Denmark /'denmɑːk/ n Danemark m.

denomination /dɪnɒmɪ'neɪʃn/ n (Relig) confession f; (money) valeur f.

denounce /dɪ'naʊns/ vt dénoncer.

dense /dens/ adj dense. **densely** adv (*packed*) très. **density** n densité f.

dent /dent/ n bosse f. ● vt cabosser.

dental /'dentl/ adj dentaire; ~ **floss** fil m dentaire; ~ **surgeon** chirurgien-dentiste m.

dentist /'dentɪst/ n dentiste mf. **dentistry** n médecine f dentaire.

dentures /'dentʃəz/ npl dentier m.

deny /dɪ'naɪ/ vt nier (that que); (*rumour*) démentir; ~ **sb sth** refuser qch à qn.

deodorant /diː'əʊdərənt/ n déodorant m.

depart /dɪ'pɑːt/ vi partir; ~ **from**

(deviate) s'éloigner de.

department /dɪˈpɑːtmənt/ n (in shop) rayon m; (in hospital, office) service m; (Univ) département m; D~ of Health ministère m de la Santé; ~ **store** grand magasin m.

departure /dɪˈpɑːtʃə(r)/ n départ m; a ~ **from** (custom, truth) une entorse à.

depend /dɪˈpend/ vi dépendre (**on** de). ~ **on** (rely on) compter sur; **it** (**all**) ~s ça dépend; ~**ing on** the season suivant la saison. **dependable** adj (person) digne de confiance. **dependant** n personne f à charge. **dependence** n dépendance f.

dependent /dɪˈpendənt/ adj dépendant; **be** ~ **on** dépendre de.

depict /dɪˈpɪkt/ vt (describe) dépeindre; (in picture) représenter.

deplete /dɪˈpliːt/ vt réduire.

deport /dɪˈpɔːt/ vt expulser.

depose /dɪˈpəʊz/ vt déposer.

deposit /dɪˈpɒzɪt/ vt (pt **deposited**) déposer. ● n (in bank) dépôt m; (on house) versement m initial; (on holiday) acompte m; (against damage) caution f; (on bottle) consigne f; (of mineral) gisement m. ~ **account** compte m de dépôt. **depositor** n (Comm) déposant-e m/f.

depot /ˈdepəʊ/ n dépôt m; (US) gare f.

depreciate /dɪˈpriːʃɪeɪt/ vt/i (se) déprécier.

depress /dɪˈpres/ vt déprimer. **depressing** adj déprimant. **depression** n dépression f; (Econ) récession f.

deprivation /deprɪˈveɪʃn/ n privation f.

deprive /dɪˈpraɪv/ vt ~ **of** priver de. **deprived** adj démuni.

depth /depθ/ n profondeur f; (of

knowledge, ignorance) étendue f; (of colour, emotion) intensité f.

deputize /ˈdepjʊtaɪz/ vi ~ **for** remplacer.

deputy /ˈdepjʊtɪ/ n adjoint-e m/f. ● adj adjoint; ~ **chairman** vice-président m.

derail /dɪˈreɪl/ vt faire dérailler. **derailment** n déraillement m.

deranged /dɪˈreɪndʒd/ adj dérangé.

derelict /ˈderəlɪkt/ adj abandonné.

deride /dɪˈraɪd/ vt ridiculiser. **derision** n moqueries fpl. **derisory** adj dérisoire.

derivative /dəˈrɪvətɪv/ adj & n dérivé (m).

derive /dɪˈraɪv/ vt ~ **sth from** tirer qch de. ● vi ~ **from** découler de.

derogatory /dɪˈrɒgətrɪ/ adj (word) péjoratif; (remark) désobligeant.

descend /dɪˈsend/ vt/i descendre; **be** ~**ed from** descendre de. **descendant** n descendant-e m/f. **descent** n descente f; (lineage) origine f.

describe /dɪˈskraɪb/ vt décrire; ~ **sb as** sth qualifier qn de qch. **description** n description f. **descriptive** adj descriptif.

desert[1] /ˈdezət/ n désert m.

desert[2] /dɪˈzɜːt/ vt/i abandonner; (cause) déserter. **deserted** adj désert. **deserter** n déserteur m.

deserts /dɪˈzɜːts/ npl **get one's** ~ avoir ce qu'on mérite.

deserve /dɪˈzɜːv/ vt mériter (**to** de). **deservedly** adv à juste titre. **deserving** adj (person) méritant; (action) louable.

design /dɪˈzaɪn/ n (sketch) plan m; (idea) conception f; (pattern) motif m; (art of designing) design m; (aim) dessein m. ● vt (sketch) dessiner;

(devise, intend) concevoir.

designate /'dezıgneıt/ vt désigner.

designer /dı'zaınə(r)/ n conceptateur/-trice m/f; (of fashion, furniture) créateur/-trice m/f. ● adj (clothes) de haute couture; (sunglasses, drink) de dernière mode.

desirable /dı'zaıərəbl/ adj (outcome) souhaitable; (person) désirable.

desire /dı'zaıə(r)/ n désir m. ● vt désirer.

desk /desk/ n bureau m; (of pupil) pupitre m; (in hotel) réception f; (in bank) caisse f.

desolate /'desələt/ adj (place) désolé; (person) affligé.

despair /dı'speə(r)/ n désespoir m. ● vi désespérer (of de).

desperate /'despərət/ adj désespéré; (criminal) prêt à tout; **be ~ for** avoir désespérément besoin de. **desperately** adv désespérément; (worried) terriblement; (ill) gravement.

desperation /despə'reıʃn/ n désespoir m; **in ~** en désespoir de cause.

despicable /dı'spıkəbl/ adj méprisable.

despise /dı'spaız/ vt mépriser.

despite /dı'spaıt/ prep malgré.

despondent /dı'spɒndənt/ adj découragé.

dessert /dı'zɜːt/ n dessert m. **~spoon** n cuillère f à dessert.

destination /destı'neıʃn/ n destination f.

destiny /'destını/ n destin m.

destitute /'destıtjuːt/ adj sans ressources.

destroy /dı'strɔı/ vt détruire; (animal) abattre. **destroyer** n (warship) contre-torpilleur m.

destruction /dı'strʌkʃn/ n destruction f. **destructive** adj destructeur.

detach /dı'tætʃ/ vt détacher; **~ed house** maison f (individuelle).

detail /'diːteıl/ n détail m; **go into ~** entrer dans les détails. ● vt (plans) exposer en détail.

detain /dı'teın/ vt retenir; (in prison) placer en détention. **detainee** n détenu/-e m/f.

detect /dı'tekt/ vt (error, trace) déceler; (crime, mine, sound) détecter. **detection** n détection f. **detective** n inspecteur/-trice m/f; (private) détective m.

detention /dı'tenʃn/ n détention f; (School) retenue f.

deter /dı'tɜː(r)/ vt (pt **deterred**) dissuader (from de).

detergent /dı'tɜːdʒənt/ adj & n détergent (m).

deteriorate /dı'tıərıəreıt/ vi se détériorer.

determine /dı'tɜːmın/ vt déterminer; **~ to do** se résoudre de faire. **determined** adj (person) décidé; (air) résolu.

deterrent /dı'terənt/ n moyen m de dissuasion. ● adj (effect) dissuasif.

detest /dı'test/ vt détester.

detonate /'detəneıt/ vt/i (faire) détoner. **detonation** n détonation f. **detonator** n détonateur m.

detour /'diːtʊə(r)/ n détour m.

detract /dı'trækt/ vi **~ from** (success, value) porter atteinte à; (pleasure) diminuer.

detriment /'detrımənt/ n **to the ~ of** au détriment de. **detrimental** adj nuisible (**to** à).

devalue /diː'væljuː/ vt dévaluer.

devastate /'devəsteıt/ vt (place) ravager; (person) accabler.

develop /dı'veləp/ vt (plan) élaborer; (mind, body) développer; (land) mettre en valeur; (illness) attraper; (habit) prendre. ● vi (child, country, plot, business) se développer; (hole, crack) se former.

development /dɪ'veləpmənt/ n développement m; (housing) ~ lotissement m; (new) ~ fait m nouveau.

deviate /'diːvɪeɪt/ vi dévier; ~ **from** (norm) s'écarter de.

device /dɪ'vaɪs/ n appareil m; (means) moyen m; (bomb) engin m explosif.

devil /'devl/ n diable m.

devious /'diːvɪəs/ adj (person) retors.

devise /dɪ'vaɪz/ vt (scheme) concevoir; (product) inventer.

devoid /dɪ'vɔɪd/ adj ~ of dépourvu de.

devolution /diːvə'luːʃn/ n (Pol) régionalisation f.

devote /dɪ'vəʊt/ vt consacrer (to à). **devoted** adj dévoué. **devotion** n dévouement m; (Relig) dévotion f.

devour /dɪ'vaʊə(r)/ vt dévorer.

devout /dɪ'vaʊt/ adj fervent.

dew /djuː/ n rosée f.

diabetes /daɪə'biːtiːz/ n diabète m.

diabolical /daɪə'bɒlɪkl/ adj diabolique; (bad 🔢) atroce.

diagnose /'daɪəgnəʊz/ vt diagnostiquer. **diagnosis** n (pl -oses) diagnostic m.

diagonal /daɪ'ægənl/ adj diagonal. ● n diagonale f.

diagram /'daɪəgræm/ n schéma m.

dial /'daɪəl/ n cadran m. ● vt (pt dialled) (number) faire; (person) appeler; **dialling code** indicatif m; **dialling tone** tonalité f.

dialect /'daɪəlekt/ n dialecte m.

dialogue /'daɪəlɒg/ n dialogue m.

diameter /daɪ'æmɪtə(r)/ n diamètre m.

diamond /'daɪəmənd/ n diamant m; (shape) losange m; (baseball) terrain m; ~s (cards) carreau m.

diaper /'daɪəpə(r)/ n (US) couche f.

diaphragm /'daɪəfræm/ n diaphragme m.

diarrhoea, (US) **diarrhea** /daɪə'rɪə/ n diarrhée f.

diary /'daɪərɪ/ n (for appointments) agenda m; (journal) journal m intime.

dice /daɪs/ n inv dé m. ● vt (food) couper en dés.

dictate /dɪk'teɪt/ vt/i dicter.

dictation /dɪk'teɪʃn/ n dictée f.

dictator /dɪk'teɪtə(r)/ n dictateur m. **dictatorship** n dictature f.

dictionary /'dɪkʃənrɪ/ n dictionnaire m.

did /dɪd/ ⇒DO.

didn't /'dɪdnt/ ⇒DID NOT.

die /daɪ/ vi (pres p **dying**) mourir; (plant) crever; **be dying to do** mourir d'envie de faire. □ ~ **down** diminuer. ⇒ **out** disparaître.

diesel /'diːzl/ n gazole m; ~ **engine** moteur m diesel.

diet /'daɪət/ n (usual food) alimentation f; (restricted) régime m. ● vi être au régime. **dietary** adj alimentaire. **dietician** n diététicien/-ne m/f.

differ /'dɪfə(r)/ vi différer (from de).

difference /'dɪfrəns/ n différence f; (disagreement) différend m. **different** adj différent (from, to de).

differentiate /dɪfə'renʃɪeɪt/ vt différencier; ● vi faire la différence (between entre).

differently /'dɪfrəntlɪ/ adv différemment (from de).

difficult /'dɪfɪkəlt/ adj difficile.

difficulty n difficulté f.

diffuse[1] /dɪˈfjuːs/ adj diffus.

diffuse[2] /dɪˈfjuːz/ vt diffuser.

dig /dɪɡ/ vt/i (pt **dug**; pres p **digging**) (excavate) creuser; (in garden) bêcher. ● n (poke) coup m de coude; (remark) pique f [1]; (Archeol) fouilles fpl. □ ~ **up** déterrer.

digest /daɪˈdʒest/ vt/i digérer. **digestible** adj digestible. **digestion** n digestion f.

digger /ˈdɪɡə(r)/ n excavateur m.

digit /ˈdɪdʒɪt/ n chiffre m. ● **digitize** vt numériser.

digital /ˈdɪdʒɪtl/ adj (clock) à affichage numérique; (display, recording) numérique. ~ **audio tape** n cassette f audionumérique. ~ **camera** n appareil m photo numérique.

dignified /ˈdɪɡnɪfaɪd/ adj digne.

dignitary /ˈdɪɡnɪtərɪ/ n dignitaire m.

dignity /ˈdɪɡnətɪ/ n dignité f.

digress /daɪˈɡres/ vi faire une digression.

dilapidated /dɪˈlæpɪdeɪtɪd/ adj délabré.

dilate /daɪˈleɪt/ vt/i (se) dilater.

dilemma /daɪˈlemə/ n dilemme m.

diligent /ˈdɪlɪdʒənt/ adj appliqué.

dilute /daɪˈljuːt/ vt diluer.

dim /dɪm/ adj (**dimmer, dimmest**) (weak) faible; (dark) sombre; (indistinct) vague; [1] stupide. ● vt/i (pt **dimmed**) (light) baisser.

dime /daɪm/ n (US) (pièce f de) dix cents.

dimension /dɪˈmenʃn/ n dimension f.

diminish /dɪˈmɪnɪʃ/ vt/i diminuer.

dimple /ˈdɪmpl/ n fossette f.

din /dɪn/ n vacarme m.

dine /daɪn/ vi dîner. **diner** n dîneur/-euse m/f; (US) restaurant m

à service rapide.

dinghy /ˈdɪŋɡɪ/ n dériveur m.

dingy /ˈdɪndʒɪ/ adj (**-ier, -iest**) minable.

dining room /ˈdaɪnɪŋrʊm/n salle f à manger.

dinner /ˈdɪnə(r)/ n (evening meal) dîner m; (lunch) déjeuner m; **have** ~ dîner. ~**-jacket** n smoking m. ~ **party** n dîner m.

dinosaur /ˈdaɪnəsɔː(r)/ n dinosaure m.

dip /dɪp/ vt/i (pt **dipped**) plonger; ~ **into** (book) feuilleter; (savings) puiser dans; ~ **one's headlights** se mettre en code. ● n (slope) déclivité f; (in sea) bain m rapide.

diploma /dɪˈpləʊmə/ n diplôme m (en in).

diplomacy /dɪˈpləʊməsɪ/ n diplomatie f. **diplomat** n diplomate mf. **diplomatic** adj (Pol) diplomatique; (tactful) diplomate.

dire /daɪə(r)/ adj affreux; (need, poverty) extrême.

direct /daɪˈrekt/ adj direct. ● adv directement. ● vt diriger; (letter, remark) adresser; (a play) mettre en scène; ~ **sb to** indiquer à qn le chemin de; (order) signifier à qn de.

direction /daɪˈrekʃn/ n direction f; (Theat) mise f en scène; ~**s** indications fpl; **ask** ~**s** demander le chemin; ~**s for use** mode m d'emploi.

directly /daɪˈrektlɪ/ adv directement; (at once) tout de suite. ● conj dès que.

director /daɪˈrektə(r)/ n directeur/-trice m/f; (Theat) metteur m en scène.

directory /daɪˈrektərɪ/ n (phone book) annuaire m. ~ **enquiries** npl renseignements mpl téléphoniques.

dirt /dɜːt/ n saleté f; (earth) terre f; ~ **cheap** ⊠ très bon marché inv.

~-track n (Sport) cendrée f.

dirty /ˈdɜːtɪ/ adj (-ier, -iest) sale; (word) grossier; **get ~** se salir. ● vt/ i (se) salir.

disability /dɪsəˈbɪlətɪ/ n handicap m.

disable /dɪsˈeɪbl/ vt rendre infirme. **disabled** adj handicapé.

disadvantage /dɪsədˈvɑːntɪdʒ/ n désavantage m. **disadvantaged** adj défavorisé.

disagree /dɪsəˈgriː/ vi ne pas être d'accord (**with** avec). **~ with sb** (food, climate) ne pas convenir à qn. **disagreement** n désaccord m; (quarrel) différend m.

disappear /dɪsəˈpɪə(r)/ vi disparaître. **disappearance** n disparition f (of de).

disappoint /dɪsəˈpɔɪnt/ vt décevoir. **disappointment** n déception f.

disapproval /dɪsəˈpruːvl/ n désapprobation f (of de).

disapprove /dɪsəˈpruːv/ vi **~ (of)** désapprouver.

disarm /dɪsˈɑːm/ vt/i désarmer. **disarmament** n désarmement m.

disarray /dɪsəˈreɪ/ n désordre m.

disaster /dɪˈzɑːstə(r)/ n désastre m. **disastrous** adj désastreux.

disband /dɪsˈbænd/ vi disperser. ● vt dissoudre.

disbelief /dɪsbɪˈliːf/ n incrédulité f.

disc /dɪsk/ n disque m; (Comput) →DISK.

discard /dɪsˈkɑːd/ vt se débarrasser de; (beliefs) abandonner.

discharge /dɪsˈtʃɑːdʒ/ vt (unload) décharger; (liquid) déverser; (duty) remplir; (dismiss) renvoyer; (prisoner) libérer. ● vi (of pus) s'écouler.

disciple /dɪˈsaɪpl/ n disciple m.

disciplinary /ˈdɪsɪplɪnərɪ/ adj disciplinaire.

discipline /ˈdɪsɪplɪn/ n discipline f.

● vt discipliner; (punish) punir.

disc jockey n disc-jockey m, animateur m.

disclaimer /dɪsˈkleɪmə(r)/ n démenti m.

disclose /dɪsˈkləʊz/ vt révéler. **disclosure** n révélation f (of de).

disco /ˈdɪskəʊ/ n (club 🎵) discothèque f; (event) soirée f disco.

discolour /dɪsˈkʌlə(r)/ vt/i (se) décolorer.

discomfort /dɪsˈkʌmfət/ n gêne f.

disconcert /dɪskənˈsɜːt/ vt déconcerter.

disconnect /dɪskəˈnekt/ vt détacher; (unplug) débrancher; (cut off) couper.

discontent /dɪskənˈtent/ n mécontentement m.

discontinue /dɪskənˈtɪnjuː/ vt (service) supprimer; (production) arrêter.

discord /ˈdɪskɔːd/ n discorde f; (Mus) discordance f.

discount¹ /ˈdɪskaʊnt/ n remise f; (on minor purchase) rabais m.

discount² /dɪsˈkaʊnt/ vt (advice) ne pas tenir compte de; (possibility) écarter.

discourage /dɪsˈkʌrɪdʒ/ vt décourager.

discourse /ˈdɪskɔːs/ n discours m.

discourteous /dɪsˈkɜːtɪəs/ adj peu courtois.

discover /dɪsˈkʌvə(r)/ vt découvrir. **discovery** n découverte f.

discreet /dɪˈskriːt/ adj discret.

discrepancy /dɪsˈkrepənsɪ/ n divergence f.

discretion /dɪˈskreʃn/ n discrétion f.

discriminate /dɪˈskrɪmɪneɪt/ vt/i distinguer; **~ against** faire de la discrimination contre. **discriminat-**

ing adj qui a du discernement. **discrimination** n discernement m; (bias) discrimination f.

discus /'dɪskəs/ n disque m.

discuss /dɪ'skʌs/ vt (talk about) discuter de; (in writing) examiner. **discussion** n discussion f.

disdain /dɪs'deɪn/ n dédain m.

disease /dɪ'ziːz/ n maladie f.

disembark /dɪsɪm'bɑːk/ vt/i débarquer.

disenchanted /dɪsɪn'tʃɑːntɪd/ adj désabusé.

disentangle /dɪsɪn'tæŋgl/ vt démêler.

disfigure /dɪs'fɪgə(r)/ vt défigurer.

disgrace /dɪs'greɪs/ n (shame) honte f; (disfavour) disgrâce f. ● vt déshonorer. **disgraced** adj (in disfavour) disgracié. **disgraceful** adj honteux.

disgruntled /dɪs'grʌntld/ adj mécontent.

disguise /dɪs'gaɪz/ vt déguiser. ● n déguisement m; in ~ déguisé.

disgust /dɪs'gʌst/ n dégoût m. ● vt dégoûter.

dish /dɪʃ/ n plat m; the ~es (crockery) la vaisselle. ● vt ~ out distribuer; ~ up servir.

dishcloth /'dɪʃklɒθ/ n lavette f; (for drying) torchon m.

dishearten /dɪs'hɑːtn/ vt décourager.

dishevelled /dɪ'ʃevld/ adj échevelé.

dishonest /dɪs'ɒnɪst/ adj malhonnête.

dishonour, (US) **dishonor** /dɪs'ɒnə(r)/ n déshonneur m.

dishwasher /'dɪʃwɒʃə(r)/ n lave-vaisselle m inv.

disillusion /dɪsɪ'luːʒn/ vt désabuser. **disillusionment** n désillusion f.

disincentive /dɪsɪn'sentɪv/ n be

a ~ to décourager.

disinclined /dɪsɪn'klaɪnd/ adj ~ to peu disposé à.

disinfect /dɪsɪn'fekt/ vt désinfecter. **disinfectant** n désinfectant m.

disintegrate /dɪs'ɪntɪgreɪt/ vt/i (se) désintégrer.

disinterested /dɪs'ɪntrəstɪd/ adj désintéressé.

disjointed /dɪs'dʒɔɪntɪd/ adj (talk) décousu.

disk /dɪsk/ n (US) ➡DISC; (Comput) disque m. ~ **drive** n drive m, lecteur m de disquettes.

diskette /dɪs'ket/ n disquette f.

dislike /dɪs'laɪk/ n aversion f. ● vt ne pas aimer.

dislocate /'dɪsləkeɪt/ vt (limb) disloquer.

dislodge /dɪs'lɒdʒ/ vt (move) déplacer; (drive out) déloger.

disloyal /dɪs'lɔɪəl/ adj déloyal (to envers).

dismal /'dɪzməl/ adj morne, triste.

dismantle /dɪs'mæntl/ vt démonter, défaire.

dismay /dɪs'meɪ/ n consternation f (at devant). ● vt consterner.

dismiss /dɪs'mɪs/ vt renvoyer; (appeal) rejeter; (from mind) écarter. **dismissal** n renvoi m.

dismount /dɪs'maʊnt/ vi descendre, mettre pied à terre.

disobedient /dɪsə'biːdɪənt/ adj désobéissant.

disobey /dɪsə'beɪ/ vt désobéir à. ● vi désobéir.

disorder /dɪs'ɔːdə(r)/ n désordre m; (ailment) trouble(s) m(pl). **disorderly** adj désordonné.

disorganized /dɪs'ɔːgənaɪzd/ adj désorganisé.

disown /dɪs'əʊn/ vt renier.

disparaging /dɪ'spærɪdʒɪŋ/ adj

d

désobligeant.

dispassionate /dɪˈspæʃənət/ adj impartial; (unemotional) calme.

dispatch /dɪˈspætʃ/ vt (send, complete) expédier; (troops) envoyer. ● n expédition f, envoi m; (report) dépêche f.

dispel /dɪˈspel/ vt (pt dispelled) dissiper.

dispensary /dɪˈspensəri/ n (in hospital) pharmacie f; (in pharmacy) officine f.

dispense /dɪˈspens/ vt distribuer; (medicine) préparer. ● vi ~ with se passer de. **dispenser** n (container) distributeur m.

disperse /dɪˈspɜːs/ vt/i (se) disperser.

display /dɪˈspleɪ/ vt montrer, exposer; (feelings) manifester. ● n exposition f; manifestation f; (Comm) étalage m; (of computer) visuel m.

displeased /dɪsˈpliːzd/ adj mécontent (with de).

disposable /dɪˈspəʊzəbl/ adj jetable.

disposal /dɪˈspəʊzl/ n (of waste) évacuation f; at sb's ~ à la disposition de qn.

dispose /dɪˈspəʊz/ vt disposer. ● vi ~ of se débarrasser de; well ~d to bien disposé envers.

disposition /dɪspəˈzɪʃn/ n disposition f; (character) naturel m.

disprove /dɪsˈpruːv/ vt réfuter.

dispute /dɪˈspjuːt/ vt contester. ● n discussion f; (Pol) conflit m; in ~ contesté.

disqualify /dɪsˈkwɒlɪfaɪ/ vt rendre inapte; (Sport) disqualifier; ~ from driving retirer le permis à.

disquiet /dɪsˈkwaɪət/ n inquiétude f. **disquieting** adj inquiétant.

disregard /dɪsrɪˈɡɑːd/ vt ne pas tenir compte de. ● n

indifférence f (for à).

disrepair /dɪsrɪˈpeə(r)/ n délabrement m.

disreputable /dɪsˈrepjʊtəbl/ adj peu recommandable.

disrepute /dɪsrɪˈpjuːt/ n discrédit m.

disrespect /dɪsrɪˈspekt/ n manque m de respect. **disrespectful** adj irrespectueux.

disrupt /dɪsˈrʌpt/ vt (disturb, break up) perturber; (plans) déranger. **disruption** n perturbation f. **disruptive** adj perturbateur.

dissatisfied /dɪˈsætɪsfaɪd/ adj mécontent.

dissect /dɪˈsekt/ vt disséquer.

disseminate /dɪˈsemɪneɪt/ vt diffuser.

dissent /dɪˈsent/ vi différer (from de). ● n dissentiment m.

dissertation /dɪsəˈteɪʃn/ n mémoire m.

disservice /dɪsˈsɜːvɪs/ n do a ~ to sb rendre un mauvais service à qn.

dissident /ˈdɪsɪdənt/ adj & n dissident/-e (m/f).

dissimilar /dɪˈsɪmɪlə(r)/ adj dissemblable, différent.

dissipate /ˈdɪsɪpeɪt/ vt/i (se) dissiper. **dissipated** adj (person) dissolu.

dissolve /dɪˈzɒlv/ vt/i (se) dissoudre.

dissuade /dɪˈsweɪd/ vt dissuader.

distance /ˈdɪstəns/ n distance f; from a ~ de loin; in the ~ au loin. **distant** adj éloigné, lointain; (relative) éloigné; (aloof) distant.

distaste /dɪsˈteɪst/ n dégoût m. **distasteful** adj désagréable.

distil /dɪsˈtɪl/ vt (pt distilled) distiller.

distinct /dɪˈstɪŋkt/ adj distinct; (definite) net; as ~ from par opposition à. **distinction** n distinction f; (in exam) mention f très bien. **distinctive** adj distinctif.

distinguish /dɪˈstɪŋgwɪʃ/ vt/i distinguer.

distort /dɪˈstɔːt/ vt déformer. **distortion** n distorsion f; (of facts) déformation f.

distract /dɪˈstrækt/ vt distraire. **distracted** adj (distraught) éperdu. **distracting** adj gênant. **distraction** n (lack of attention, entertainment) distraction f.

distraught /dɪˈstrɔːt/ adj éperdu.

distress /dɪˈstres/ n douleur f; (poverty, danger) détresse f. ● vt peiner. **distressing** adj pénible.

distribute /dɪˈstrɪbjuːt/ vt distribuer.

district /ˈdɪstrɪkt/ n région f; (of town) quartier m.

distrust /dɪsˈtrʌst/ n méfiance f. ● vt se méfier de.

disturb /dɪˈstɜːb/ vt déranger; (alarm, worry) troubler. **disturbance** n dérangement m (of de); (noise) tapage m. **disturbances** npl (Pol) troubles mpl. **disturbed** adj troublé; (psychologically) perturbé. **disturbing** adj troublant.

disused /dɪsˈjuːzd/ adj désaffecté.

ditch /dɪtʃ/ n fossé m. ● vt ⊠ abandonner.

ditto /ˈdɪtəʊ/ adv idem.

dive /daɪv/ vi plonger; (rush) se précipiter. ● n plongeon m; (of plane) piqué m; (place ⊠) bouge m. **diver** n plongeur/-euse m/f.

diverge /daɪˈvɜːdʒ/ vi diverger. **divergent** adj divergent.

diverse /daɪˈvɜːs/ adj divers.

diversion /daɪˈvɜːʃn/ n détournement m; (distraction) diversion f; (of traffic) déviation f. **divert** vt détourner; (traffic) dévier.

divide /dɪˈvaɪd/ vt/i (se) diviser.

dividend /ˈdɪvɪdend/ n dividende m.

divine /dɪˈvaɪn/ adj divin.

diving: ~**-board** n plongeoir m. ~**-suit** n scaphandre m.

division /dɪˈvɪʒn/ n division f.

divorce /dɪˈvɔːs/ n divorce m (from avec). ● vt/i divorcer (d'avec).

divulge /daɪˈvʌldʒ/ vt divulguer.

DIY abbr ⇒**DO-IT-YOURSELF**.

dizziness /ˈdɪzɪnɪs/ n vertige m.

dizzy /ˈdɪzɪ/ adj (-**ier**, -**iest**) vertigineux; **be** or **feel** ~ avoir le vertige.

do /duː/

present **do**, **does**; present negative **don't**, **do not**; past **did**; past participle **done**

● *transitive and intransitive verb*

┈┈► faire; **she is doing her homework** elle fait ses devoirs.

┈┈► (progress, be suitable) aller; **how are you doing?** comment ça va?

┈┈► (be enough) suffire; **will five dollars** ~? cinq dollars, ça suffira?

● *auxiliary verb*

┈┈► (in questions) ~ **you like Mozart?** aimes-tu Mozart?, est-ce que tu aimes Mozart?; **did your sister phone?** est-ce que ta sœur a téléphoné?, ta sœur a-t-elle téléphoné?

┈┈► (in negatives) **I don't like Mozart** je n'aime pas Mozart.

┈┈► (emphatic uses) **I** ~ **like your dress** j'aime beaucoup ta robe; **I ~ think you should go** je pense vraiment que tu devrais y aller.

••••> (referring back to another verb) **I live in Orford and so does Lily** j'habite à Orford et Lily aussi; **she gets paid more than I ~** elle est payée plus que moi; **'I don't like carrots'—'neither ~ I'** 'je n'aime pas les carottes'—'moi non plus'.

••••> (imperatives) **don't shut the door** ne ferme pas la porte; **~ be quiet** tais-toi!

••••> (short questions and answers) **you like fish, don't you?** tu aimes le poisson, n'est-ce pas?; **Lola didn't phone, did she?** Lola n'a pas téléphoné par hasard?; **'does he play tennis?'—'no he doesn't/yes he does'** 'est-ce qu'il joue au tennis?'—'non/ oui'; **'Marion didn't say that'—'yes she did'** 'Marion n'a pas dit ça'—'si'.

□ **do away with** supprimer. **do up** (fasten) fermer; (house) refaire; **do with it's to ~ with** c'est à propos de; **it's nothing to ~ with** ça n'a rien à voir avec. **do without** se passer de.

docile /ˈdəʊsaɪl/ adj docile.

dock /dɒk/ n (Jur) banc m des accusés; dock m. ● vi arriver au port. ● vt mettre à quai; (wages) faire une retenue sur.

doctor /ˈdɒktə(r)/ n médecin m, docteur m; (Univ) docteur m. ● vt (cat) châtrer; (fig) altérer.

doctorate /ˈdɒktərət/ n doctorat m.

document /ˈdɒkjʊmənt/ n docu-

ment m. **documentary** adj & n documentaire (m). **documentation** n documentation f.

dodge /dɒdʒ/ vt esquiver. ● vi faire un saut de côté. ● n mouvement m de côté.

dodgems /ˈdɒdʒəmz/ npl autos fpl tamponneuses.

dodgy /ˈdɒdʒɪ/ adj (-ier, -iest) (🆃: difficult) épineux, délicat; (untrustworthy) louche 🆃.

doe /dəʊ/ n (deer) biche f.

does /dʌz/ ➔DO.

doesn't ➔DOES NOT.

dog /dɒg/ n chien m. ● vt (pt dogged) poursuivre. **~-collar** n col m romain. **~-eared** adj écorné.

dogged /ˈdɒgɪd/ adj obstiné.

dogma /ˈdɒgmə/ n dogme m. **dogmatic** adj dogmatique.

dogsbody /ˈdɒgzbɒdɪ/ n bonne f à tout faire.

do-it-yourself /duːɪtjɔːˈself/ n bricolage m.

doldrums /ˈdɒldrəmz/ npl **be in the ~** (person) avoir le cafard.

dole /dəʊl/ vt **~ out** distribuer. ● n 🆃 indemnité f de chômage; **on the ~** 🆃 au chômage.

doll /dɒl/ n poupée f. ● vt **~ up** 🆃 bichonner.

dollar /ˈdɒlə(r)/ n dollar m.

dollop /ˈdɒləp/ n (of food 🆃) gros morceau m.

dolphin /ˈdɒlfɪn/ n dauphin m.

domain /dəˈmeɪn/ n domaine m.

dome /dəʊm/ n dôme m.

domestic /dəˈmestɪk/ adj familial; (trade, flights) intérieur; (animal) domestique. **domesticated** adj (animal) domestiqué.

domestic science n arts mpl ménagers.

dominant /ˈdɒmɪnənt/ adj

dominate | down:

dominant.

dominate /'dɒmɪneɪt/ vt/i dominer. **domination** n domination f.

domineering /dɒmɪ'nɪərɪŋ/ adj dominateur.

domino /'dɒmɪnəʊ/ n (pl **-es**) domino m; **-es** (game) dominos mpl.

donate /dəʊ'neɪt/ vt faire don de. **donation** n don m.

done /dʌn/ ➡DO.

donkey /'dɒŋkɪ/ n âne m. **~ work** n travail m pénible.

donor /'dəʊnə(r)/ n donateur/-trice m/f; (of blood) donneur/-euse m/f.

don't ➡DO NOT.

doodle /'duːdl/ vi griffonner.

doom /duːm/ n (ruin) ruine f; (fate) destin m. ● vt be **~ed to** être destiné ou condamné à; **~ed (to failure)** voué à l'échec.

door /dɔː(r)/ n porte f; (of vehicle) portière f, porte f. **~bell** n sonnette f. **~man** n (pl **-men**) portier m. **~mat** n paillasson m. **~step** n pas m de (la) porte, seuil m. **~way** n porte f.

dope /dəʊp/ n 🖾 cannabis m; (idiot 🖾) imbécile mf. ● vt doper. **dopey** adj (foolish 🖾) imbécile.

dormant /'dɔːmənt/ adj en sommeil.

dormitory /'dɔːmɪtrɪ/ n dortoir m; (Univ, US) résidence f.

dosage /'dəʊsɪdʒ/ n dose f; (on label) posologie f.

dose /dəʊs/ n dose f.

dot /dɒt/ n point m; **on the ~** 🖾 à l'heure pile.

dot-com /dɒt'kɒm/ n (société) point com f. **~ millionaire** n millionaire mf de l'Internet. **~ shares** npl actions fpl des sociétés point com.

dote /dəʊt/ vi **~ on** adorer.

dotted /'dɒtɪd/ adj (fabric) à pois;

~ line pointillé m; **~ with** parsemé de.

double /'dʌbl/ adj double; (room, bed) pour deux personnes; **~ the size** deux fois plus grand. ● adv deux fois; **pay ~** payer le double. ● n double m; (stuntman) doublure f; **~s** (tennis) double m; **at** or **on the ~** au pas de course. ● vt/i doubler; (fold) plier en deux. **~-bass** n (Mus) contrebasse f. **~-check** vt revérifier. **~ chin** n double menton m. **~-cross** vt tromper. **~-decker** n autobus m à impériale.

doubt /daʊt/ n doute m. ● vt douter de; **~ if** or **that** douter que. **doubtful** adj incertain, douteux; (person) qui a des doutes. **doubtless** adv sans doute.

dough /dəʊ/ n pâte f; (money 🖾) fric m 🖾.

doughnut /'dəʊnʌt/ n beignet m.

douse /daʊs/ vt arroser; (light, fire) éteindre.

dove /dʌv/ n colombe f.

Dover /'dəʊvə(r)/ n Douvres.

dowdy /'daʊdɪ/ adj (**-ier, -iest**) (clothes) sans chic, monotone; (person) sans élégance.

down /daʊn/ adv en bas; (of sun) couché; (lower) plus bas; **come** or **go ~** descendre; **go ~ to the post office** aller à la poste; **~ under** aux antipodes; **~ with** à bas. ● prep en bas de; (along) le long de. ● vt (knock down, shoot down) abattre; (drink) vider. ● n (fluff) duvet m.

down: **~-and-out** n clochard/-e m/f. **~-cast** adj démoralisé. **~-fall** n chute f. **~grade** vt déclasser. **~-hearted** adj découragé.

downhill /daʊn'hɪl/ adv **go ~** descendre; (pej) baisser.

down: **~load** n (Comput) télécharger. **~-market** adj bas de

gamme. **~ payment** n acompte m.
~pour n grosse averse f.

downright /ˈdaʊnraɪt/ adj (utter)
véritable; (honest) franc. ● adv carrément.

downstairs /daʊnˈstɛəz/ adv en
bas. ● adj d'en bas.

down: **~stream** adv en aval.
~-to-earth adj pratique.

Downing Street Célèbre
rue de Londres où se trouvent la résidence officielle
du Premier ministre au n°10 et
celle du Chancelier de l'Échiquier
au n°11. Les médias emploient
souvent Number 10 Downing Street
ou Downing Street pour désigner le
Premier ministre ou le gouvernement britannique.

downtown /ˈdaʊntaʊn/ adj (US)
du centre-ville; **~ Boston** le centre
de Boston.

downward /ˈdaʊnwəd/ adj & adv,
downwards adv vers le bas.

doze /dəʊz/ vi s'assoupir, somnoler; **~ off**
s'assoupir. ● n somme m.

dozen /ˈdʌzn/ n douzaine f; **a ~
eggs** une douzaine d'œufs; **~s of**
[1] des dizaines de.

Dr abbr (**Doctor**) Docteur.

drab /dræb/ adj terne.

draft /drɑːft/ n (outline) brouillon
m; (Comm) traite f. **the ~** (Mil, US)
la conscription; **a ~ treaty** un projet de traité; (US) ⇒**DRAUGHT.** ● vt
faire le brouillon de; (draw up)
rédiger.

drag /dræg/ vt/i (pt **dragged**) traîner; (river) draguer; (pull away) arracher; **~ on** s'éterniser. ● n (task [1])
corvée f; (person [1]) raseur/-euse
m/f. **in ~** en travesti.

dragon /ˈdrægən/ n dragon m.

drain /dreɪn/ vt (land) drainer; (ve-

getables) égoutter; (tank, glass)
vider; (use up) épuiser; **~ (off)** (liquid) faire écouler. ● vi **~ (off)** (of
liquid) s'écouler. ● n (sewer) égout
m; **~(-pipe)** tuyau m d'écoulement;
a ~ on une ponction sur.

draining-board n égouttoir m.

drama /ˈdrɑːmə/ n art m dramatique, théâtre m; (play, event) drame
m. **dramatic** adj (situation) dramatique; (increase) spectaculaire.

dramatist n dramaturge m. **dramatize** vt adapter pour la scène; (fig)
dramatiser.

drank /dræŋk/ ⇒**DRINK.**

drape /dreɪp/ vt draper. **drapes** npl
(US) rideaux mpl.

drastic /ˈdræstɪk/ adj sévère.

draught /drɑːft/ n courant m d'air;
~s (game) dames fpl. **~ beer** n
bière f pression.

draughty /ˈdrɑːftɪ/ adj plein de
courants d'air.

draw /drɔː/ vt (pt **drew**; pp
drawn) (picture) dessiner; (line) tracer; (pull) tirer; (attract) attirer. ● vi
dessiner; (Sport) faire match nul;
(come, move) venir. ● n (Sport)
match m nul; (in lottery) tirage m au
sort. □ **~ back** reculer. **~ near**
(s')approcher (to de). **~ out**
(money) retirer. **~ up** vi (stop) s'arrêter; vt (document) dresser; (chair)
approcher.

drawback /ˈdrɔːbæk/ n inconvénient m.

drawbridge /ˈdrɔːbrɪdʒ/ n pont-
levis m.

drawer /ˈdrɔː(r)/ n tiroir m.

drawing /ˈdrɔːɪŋ/ n dessin m.
~-board n planche f à dessin.
~-pin n punaise f. **~-room** n
salon m.

drawl /drɔːl/ n voix f traînante.

drawn /drɔːn/ ⇒**DRAW.** ● adj (fea-

tures) tiré; (*match*) nul.

dread /drɛd/ n terreur f, crainte f.
● vt redouter. **dreadful** adj épouvantable, affreux. **dreadfully** adv
terriblement.

dream /driːm/ n rêve m. ● vt/i (pt
dreamed or **dreamt**) rêver; ~ **up**
imaginer. ● adj (ideal) de ses rêves.

dreary /ˈdrɪərɪ/ adj (**-ier, -iest**)
triste; (boring) monotone.

dredge /drɛdʒ/ vt (river) draguer;
~ **sth up** (fig) exhumer.

dregs /drɛgz/ npl lie f.

drench /drɛntʃ/ vt tremper.

dress /drɛs/ n robe f; (clothing)
tenue f. ● vt/i (s')habiller; (food) assaisonner; (wound) panser; ~ **up** as
se déguiser en; **get ~ed** s'habiller.
~ **circle** n premier balcon m.

dresser /ˈdrɛsə(r)/ n (furniture)
buffet m; **be a stylish** ~ s'habiller
avec chic.

dressing /ˈdrɛsɪŋ/ n (sauce) assaisonnement m; (bandage) pansement m. ~**-gown** n robe f de
chambre. ~**-room** n (Sport) vestiaire m; (Theat) loge f. ~**-table** n
coiffeuse f.

dressmaker /ˈdrɛsmeɪkə(r)/ n
couturière f. **dressmaking** n couture f.

dress rehearsal n répétition f
générale.

dressy /ˈdrɛsɪ/ adj (**-ier, -iest**)
chic inv.

drew /druː/ ➡**DRAW**.

dribble /ˈdrɪbl/ vi (liquid) dégouliner; (person) baver; (football)
dribbler.

dried /draɪd/ adj (fruit) sec.

drier /ˈdraɪə(r)/ n séchoir m.

drift /drɪft/ vi aller à la dérive; (pile
up) s'amonceler; ~ **towards** glisser
vers. ● n dérive f, amoncellement m;
(of events) tournure f; (meaning)

sens m; **snow** ~ congère f. **drift-
wood** n bois m flotté.

drill /drɪl/ n (tool) perceuse f; (for
teeth) roulette f; (training) exercice
m; (procedure 🔲) marche f à suivre;
(pneumatic) ~ marteau m piqueur.
● vt percer; (train) entraîner. ● vi
être à l'exercice.

drink /drɪŋk/ vt/i (pt **drank**; pp
drunk) boire. ● n (liquid) boisson f;
(glass of alcohol) verre m; **a** ~ **of
water** un verre d'eau. **drinking
water** n eau f potable.

drip /drɪp/ vi (pt **dripped**) (é)gout-
ter; (washing) s'égoutter. ● n
goutte f; (person 🔀) lavette f.

drip-dry vt laisser égoutter. ● adj
sans essorage.

drive /draɪv/ vt (pt **drove**; pp
driven) (vehicle) conduire; (sb
somewhere) chasser, pousser; (machine) actionner; ~ **mad** rendre
fou. ● vi conduire. ● n promenade f
en voiture; (private road) allée f;
(fig) énergie f; (Psych) instinct m;
(Pol) campagne f; (Auto) traction f;
(golf, Comput) drive m; **it's a two-
hour** ~ il y a deux heures de route;
lefthand ~ conduite f à gauche.
□ ~ **at** en venir à.

drivel /ˈdrɪvl/ n bêtises fpl.

driver /ˈdraɪvə(r)/ n conducteur/
trice m/f, chauffeur m. ~**'s license** n
(US) permis m de conduire.

driving /ˈdraɪvɪŋ/ n conduite f;
take one's ~ **test** passer son permis. ● adj (rain) battant; (wind) cinglant. ~ **licence** n permis m de
conduire. ~ **school** n auto-école f.

drizzle /ˈdrɪzl/ n bruine f. ● vi
bruiner.

drone /drəʊn/ n (of engine) ronronnement m; (of insects) bourdonnement m. ● vi ronronner; bourdonner.

drool /druːl/ vi baver (**over** sur).

d

droop /druːp/ vi pencher, tomber.

drop /drɒp/ n goutte f; (fall, lowering) chute f. ● vt/i (pt **dropped**) (laisser) tomber; (decrease, lower) baisser; ~ (**off**) (person from car) déposer; ~ **a line** écrire un mot (to à). □ ~ **in** passer (on chez). ~ **off** (doze) s'assoupir. ~ **out** se retirer (of de); (of student) abandonner.

dropout /'drɒpaʊt/ n marginal/-e m/f; raté/-e m/f.

droppings /'drɒpɪŋz/ npl crottes fpl.

drought /draʊt/ n sécheresse f.

drove /drəʊv/ →DRIVE.

droves /drəʊvz/ npl foules fpl.

drown /draʊn/ vt/i (se) noyer.

drowsy /'draʊzɪ/ adj somnolent; be or **feel** ~ avoir envie de dormir.

drug /drʌg/ n drogue f; (Med) médicament m. ● vt (pt **drugged**) droguer. ~ **addict** n drogué/-e m/f. **drugstore** n (US) drugstore m.

drum /drʌm/ n tambour m; (for oil) bidon m; ~**s** batterie f. ● vi (pt **drummed**) tambouriner. ● vt ~ **into sb** répéter sans cesse à qn; ~ **up** (support) susciter; (business) créer. **drummer** n tambour m; (in pop group) batteur m.

drumstick /'drʌmstɪk/ n baguette f de tambour; (of chicken) pilon m.

drunk /drʌŋk/ →DRINK. ● adj ivre; **get** ~ s'enivrer. ● n ivrogne/-esse m/f. **drunkard** n ivrogne/-esse m/f. **drunken** adj ivre. **drunkenness** n ivresse f.

dry /draɪ/ adj (**drier, driest**) sec; (day) sans pluie; **be** or **feel** ~ avoir soif. ● vt/i (faire) sécher; ~ **up** (dry dishes) essuyer la vaisselle; (of supplies) (se) tarir; (be silent **⊞**) se taire. ~**-clean** vt nettoyer à sec. ~**-cleaner** n teinturier m. ~ **run** n galop m d'essai.

DTD abbr (Document Type Definition) DTD f.

dual /'djuːəl/ adj double. ~ **carriageway** n route f à quatre voies. ~**-purpose** adj qui fait double emploi.

dub /dʌb/ vt (pt **dubbed**) (film) doubler (**into** en); (nickname) surnommer.

dubious /'djuːbɪəs/ adj (pej) douteux; be ~ **about** avoir des doutes sur.

duck /dʌk/ n canard m. ● vi se baisser subitement. ● vt (head) baisser; (person) plonger dans l'eau.

duct /dʌkt/ n conduit m.

dud /dʌd/ adj (tool **⊞**) mal fichu; (coin **⊞**) faux; (cheque **⊞**) sans provision. ● n **be a** ~ (not work **⊞**) ne pas marcher.

due /djuː/ adj (owing) dû; (expected) attendu; (proper) qui convient; ~ **to** à cause de; (caused by) dû à; **she's** ~ **to leave now** il est prévu qu'elle parte maintenant; **in** ~ **course** (at the right time) en temps voulu; (later) plus tard. ● adv ~ **east** droit vers l'est. ● n dû m; ~**s** droits mpl; (of club) cotisation f.

duel /'djuːəl/ n duel m.

duet /djuː'et/ n duo m.

dug /dʌg/ →DIG.

duke /djuːk/ n duc m.

dull /dʌl/ adj ennuyeux; (colour) terne; (weather) maussade; (sound) sourd. ● vt (pain) atténuer; (shine) ternir.

duly /'djuːlɪ/ adv comme il convient; (as expected) comme prévu.

dumb /dʌm/ adj muet; (stupid **⊞**) bête. □ ~ **down** (course, TV coverage) baisser le niveau intellectuel de.

dumbfound /dʌm'faʊnd/ vt sidérer, ahurir.

dummy /'dʌmɪ/ n (of tailor) mannequin m; (of baby) sucette f. ● adj factice. ~ **run** n galop m d'essai.

dump /dʌmp/ vt déposer; (get rid of T) se débarrasser de. ● n tas m d'ordures; (refuse tip) décharge f; (Mil) dépôt m; (dull place T) trou m T; **be in the** ~s T avoir le cafard.

dune /dju:n/ n dune f.

dung /dʌŋ/ n (excrement) bouse f, crotte f; (manure) fumier m.

dungarees /dʌŋɡə'ri:z/ npl salopette f.

dungeon /'dʌndʒən/ n cachot m.

duplicate[1] /'dju:plɪkət/ n double m. ● adj identique.

duplicate[2] /'dju:plɪkeɪt/ vt faire un double de; (on machine) polycopier.

durable /'djʊərəbl/ adj (tough) résistant; (enduring) durable.

duration /djʊ'reɪʃn/ n durée f.

during /'djʊərɪŋ/ prep pendant.

dusk /dʌsk/ n crépuscule m.

dusky /'dʌskɪ/ adj (-ier, -iest) foncé.

dust /dʌst/ n poussière f. ● vt/i épousseter; (sprinkle) saupoudrer (with de). ~**bin** n poubelle f.

duster /'dʌstə(r)/ n chiffon m.

dust: ~**man** n (pl -men) éboueur m. ~**pan** n pelle f (à poussière).

dusty /'dʌstɪ/ adj (-ier, -iest) poussiéreux.

Dutch /dʌtʃ/ adj néerlandais; **go** ~ partager les frais. ● n (Ling) néerlandais m. ~**man** n Néerlandais m. ~**woman** n Néerlandaise f.

dutiful /'dju:tɪfl/ adj obéissant.

duty /'dju:tɪ/ n devoir m; (tax) droit m; (official) fonction f; **on** ~ de service. ~**-free** adj hors-taxe.

duvet /'du:veɪ/ n couette f.

dwarf /dwɔ:f/ n nain/-e m/f. ● vt rapetisser.

dwell /dwel/ vi (pt dwelt) demeurer; ~ **on** s'étendre sur. **dweller** n habitant/-e m/f. **dwelling** n habitation f.

dwindle /'dwɪndl/ vi diminuer.

dye /daɪ/ vt teindre. ● n teinture f.

dying /'daɪɪŋ/ adj mourant; (art) qui se perd.

dynamic /daɪ'næmɪk/ adj dynamique.

dynamite /'daɪnəmaɪt/ n dynamite f.

dysentery /'dɪsəntrɪ/ n dysenterie f.

dyslexia /dɪs'leksɪə/ n dyslexie f. **dyslexic** adj & n dyslexique (m/f).

Ee

each /i:tʃ/ det chaque inv; ~ **one** chacun/-e m/f; ● pron chacun/-e m/f; **oranges at 30p** ~ des oranges à 30 pence pièce.

each other pron l'un/l'une l'autre, les uns/les unes les autres; **know** ~ se connaître; **love** ~ s'aimer.

eager /'i:gə(r)/ adj impatient (**to** de); (person, acceptance) enthousiaste; ~ **for** avide de.

eagle /'i:gl/ n aigle m.

ear /ɪə(r)/ n oreille f; (of corn) épi m. ~**ache** n mal m à l'oreille. ~**drum** n tympan m.

earl /ɜ:l/ n comte m.

early /'ɜ:lɪ/ adv (-ier, -iest) tôt, de bonne heure; (ahead of time) en avance; **as I said earlier** comme je l'ai déjà dit. ● adj (attempt, years) premier; (hour) matinal; (fruit) pré-

coce; (*retirement*) anticipé; **have an
~ dinner** dîner tôt; **in ~ summer**
au début de l'été; **at the earliest**
au plus tôt.

earmark /'ɪəmɑːk/ *vt* désigner (for
pour).

earn /ɜːn/ *vt* gagner; (*interest*:
Comm) rapporter.

earnest /'ɜːnɪst/ *adj* sérieux; **in ~**
sérieusement.

earnings /'ɜːnɪŋz/ *npl* salaire *m*;
(*profits*) gains *mpl*.

ear: **~phones** *npl* casque *m*.
~-ring *n* boucle *f* d'oreille. **~shot**
n **within/in ~shot** à portée
de voix.

earth /ɜːθ/ *n* terre *f*; **why/how/
where on~...?** pourquoi/
comment/où diable...? ● *vt* (Electr)
mettre à la terre. **earthenware** *n*
faïence *f*. **~quake** *n* tremblement *m*
de terre.

ease /iːz/ *n* facilité *f*; (*comfort*)
bien-être *m*; **at ~** à l'aise; (Mil) au
repos; **with ~** facilement. ● *vt*
(*pain, pressure*) atténuer; (*congestion*) réduire; (*transition*) faciliter.
● *vi* (*pain, pressure*) s'atténuer; (*congestion, rain*) diminuer.

easel /'iːzl/ *n* chevalet *m*.

east /iːst/ *n* est *m*; **the E~** (Orient)
l'Orient *m*. ● *adj* (*side, coast*) est;
(*wind*) d'est. ● *adv* à l'est.

Easter /'iːstə(r)/ *n* Pâques *m*; **~
egg** œuf *m* de Pâques.

easterly /'iːstəlɪ/ *adj* (*wind*) d'est;
(*direction*) de l'est.

eastern de l'est; **~ France** l'est de
la France.

eastward /'iːstwəd/ *adj* (*side*) est
inv; (*journey*) vers l'est.

easy /'iːzɪ/ *adj* (-**ier, -iest**) facile; **go
~ with** 🅃 y aller doucement avec;
take it ~ ne te fatigue pas.
~-going *adj* accommodant.

eat /iːt/ *vt*/*i* (*pt* **ate**; *pp* **eaten**) manger; **~ into** ronger.

eavesdrop /'iːvzdrɒp/ *vi* (*pt*
-dropped) écouter aux portes.

ebb /eb/ *n* reflux *m*. ● *vi* descendre;
(*fig*) décliner.

EC *abbr* (**European Commission**)
CE *f*.

eccentric /ɪk'sentrɪk/ *adj* & *n* excentrique (*mf*).

echo /'ekəʊ/ *n* (*pl* **-oes**) écho *m*.
● *vt* répercuter; (*idea, opinion*) reprendre. ● *vi* retentir, résonner (**to,
with** de).

eclipse /ɪ'klɪps/ *n* éclipse *f*. ● *vt*
éclipser.

ecological /iːkə'lɒdʒɪkl/ *adj* écologique.

ecology /ɪ'kɒlədʒɪ/ *n* écologie *f*.

e-commerce /'iːkɒmɜːs/ *n* commerce *m* électronique, commerce *m*
en ligne.

economic /iːkə'nɒmɪk/ *adj* économique; (*profitable*) rentable; **~
refugee** réfugié/-e *m*/*f* économique.

economical *adj* économique; (*person*) économe. **economics** *n* économie *f*, sciences *fpl* économiques.
economist *n* économiste *mf*.

economize /ɪ'kɒnəmaɪz/ *vi* ~
(**on**) économiser.

economy /ɪ'kɒnəmɪ/ *n* économie *f*.
~-class syndrome *n* syndrome *m*
de la classe économique.

ecosystem /'iːkəʊsɪstəm/ *n* éco-
système *m*.

ecstasy /'ekstəsɪ/ *n* extase *f*; (*drug*)
ecstasy *m*.

edge /edʒ/ *n* bord *m*; (*of town*)
abords *mpl*; (*of knife*) tranchant *m*;
have the ~ on 🅃 l'emporter sur;
on ~ énervé. ● *vt* (*trim*) border.
● *vi* ~ **forward** avancer doucement.

edgeways /'edʒweɪz/ *adv* **I can't**

get a word in ~ je n'arrive pas à placer un mot.

edgy /'edʒɪ/ *adj* énervé.

edible /'edɪbl/ *adj* comestible.

Edinburgh Festival Festival international des Arts qui se déroule tous les étés à Édimbourg (Écosse) depuis 1947. Pendant trois semaines, au programme du festival institutionnel et du festival parallèle (*Fringe festival*), se côtoient les plus grands noms de la musique, de la danse, du théâtre, les artistes d'avant-garde et les nouveaux talents.

edit /'edɪt/ *vt* (*pt* **edited**) (*newspaper, page*) être le rédacteur/la rédactrice de; (*check*) réviser; (*cut*) couper; (TV, cinema) monter.

edition /ɪ'dɪʃn/ *n* édition *f*.

editor /'edɪtə(r)/ *n* (*writer*) rédacteur/-trice *m/f*; (*of works, anthology*) éditeur/-trice *m/f*; (TV, cinema) monteur/-teuse *m/f*; **the** ~ **(in chief)** le rédacteur en chef.

editorial /edɪ'tɔːrɪəl/ *adj* de la rédaction. ● *n* éditorial *m*.

educate /'edʒukeɪt/ *vt* instruire; (*mind, public*) éduquer. **educated** *adj* instruit. **education** *n* éducation *f*; (*schooling*) études *fpl*. **educational** *adj* éducatif; (*establishment, method*) d'enseignement.

eel /iːl/ *n* anguille *f*.

eerie /'ɪərɪ/ *adj* (**-ier, -iest**) sinistre.

effect /ɪ'fekt/ *n* effet *m*; **come into** ~ entrer en vigueur; **in** ~ effectivement; **take** ~ agir. ● *vt* effectuer.

effective /ɪ'fektɪv/ *adj* efficace; (*actual*) effectif. **effectively** *adv* efficacement; (*in effect*) en réalité. **effectiveness** *n* efficacité *f*.

effeminate /ɪ'femɪnət/ *adj* efféminé.

effervescent /efə'vesnt/ *adj* effervescent.

efficiency /ɪ'fɪʃnsɪ/ *n* efficacité *f*; (*of machine*) rendement *m*. **efficient** *adj* efficace. **efficiently** *adv* efficacement.

effort /'efət/ *n* efforts *mpl*; **make an** ~ faire un effort; **be worth the** ~ en valoir la peine. **effortless** *adj* facile.

effusive /ɪ'fjuːsɪv/ *adj* expansif.

e.g. /iːˈdʒiː/ *abbr* par ex.

egg /eg/ *n* œuf *m*. ● *vt* ~ **on** pousser. ~**-cup** *n* coquetier *m*. ~**-plant** *n* (US) aubergine *f*. ~**shell** *n* coquille *f* d'œuf.

ego /'iːgəʊ/ *n* amour-propre *m*; (Psych) moi *m*. **egotism** *n* égotisme *m*. **egotist** *n* égotiste *mf*.

Egypt /'iːdʒɪpt/ *n* Égypte *f*.

eiderdown /'aɪdədaʊn/ *n* édredon *m*.

eight /eɪt/ *adj & n* huit (*m*). **eighteen** *adj & n* dix-huit (*m*). **eighth** *adj & n* huitième (*mf*). **eighty** *adj & n* quatre-vingts (*m*).

either /'aɪðə/ *det & pron* l'un/une ou l'autre; (*with negative*) ni l'un/une ni l'autre; **you can take** ~ tu peux prendre n'importe lequel/laquelle. ● *adv* non plus. ● *conj* ~**...or** ou (bien)...ou (bien); (*with negative*) ni...ni.

eject /ɪ'dʒekt/ *vt* (*troublemaker*) expulser; (*waste*) rejeter.

elaborate[1] /ɪ'læbərət/ *adj* compliqué.

elaborate[2] /ɪ'læbəreɪt/ *vt* élaborer. ● *vi* préciser; ~ **on** s'étendre sur.

elastic /ɪ'læstɪk/ *adj & n* élastique (*m*); ~ **band** élastique *m*. **elasticity** *n* élasticité *f*.

elated /ɪ'leɪtɪd/ *adj* transporté de joie.

elbow /'elbəʊ/ n coude m; ~ **room** espace m vital.

elder /'eldə(r)/ adj & n aîné/-e (m/f); (tree) sureau m.

elderly /'eldəlɪ/ adj âgé; **the** ~ **les** personnes fpl âgées.

eldest /'eldɪst/ adj & n aîné/-e (m/f).

elect /ɪ'lekt/ vt élire; ~ **to do** choisir de faire. ● adj (president etc.) futur. **election** n élection f. **elector** n électeur/-trice m/f. **electoral** adj électoral. **electorate** n électorat m.

electric /ɪ'lektrɪk/ adj électrique; ~ **blanket** couverture f chauffante. **electrical** adj électrique. **electrician** n électricien/-ne m/f. **electricity** n électricité f. **electrify** vt électrifier; (excite) électriser. **electrocute** vt électrocuter.

electronic /ɪlek'trɒnɪk/ adj électronique. ~ **publishing** n éditique f. **electronics** n électronique f.

elegance /'elɪgəns/ n élégance f. **elegant** adj élégant.

element /'elɪmənt/ n élément m; (of heater etc.) résistance f. **elementary** adj élémentaire.

elephant /'elɪfənt/ n éléphant m.

elevate /'elɪveɪt/ vt élever. **elevation** n élévation f. **elevator** n (US) ascenseur m.

eleven /ɪ'levn/ adj & n onze (m). **eleventh** adj & n onzième (mf).

elicit /ɪ'lɪsɪt/ vt obtenir (from de).

eligible /'elɪdʒəbl/ adj admissible (for à); **be** ~ **for** (entitled to) avoir droit à.

eliminate /ɪ'lɪmɪneɪt/ vt éliminer.

elm /elm/ n orme m.

elongate /'iːlɒŋgeɪt/ vt allonger.

elope /ɪ'ləʊp/ vi s'enfuir (with avec). **elopement** n fugue f (amoureuse).

eloquence /'eləkwəns/ n éloquence f.

else /els/ adv d'autre; **somebody/nothing** ~ quelqu'un/rien d'autre; **everybody** ~ tous les autres; **somewhere/something** ~ autre part/chose; **or** ~ ou bien. **elsewhere** adv ailleurs.

elude /ɪ'luːd/ vt échapper à.

elusive /ɪ'luːsɪv/ adj insaisissable.

email /'iːmeɪl/ n (medium) courrier m électronique; (item) e-mail m, mél m; ~ **sb** envoyer un e-mail à qn; ~ **sth** envoyer qch par courrier électronique.

emancipate /ɪ'mænsɪpeɪt/ vt émanciper.

embankment /ɪm'bæŋkmənt/ n (of river) quai m; (of railway) remblai m.

embark /ɪm'bɑːk/ vt embarquer. ● vi (Naut) embarquer; ~ **on** (journey) entreprendre; (campaign, career) se lancer dans.

embarrass /ɪm'bærəs/ vt plonger dans l'embarras; **be/feel** ~**ed** être/se sentir gêné. **embarrassment** n confusion f, gêne f.

embassy /'embəsɪ/ n ambassade f.

embed /ɪm'bed/ vt (pt **embedded**) enfoncer (**in** dans).

embellish /ɪm'belɪʃ/ vt embellir.

embers /'embəz/ npl braises fpl.

embezzle /ɪm'bezl/ vt détourner (from de). **embezzlement** n détournement m de fonds.

emblem /'embləm/ n emblème m.

embodiment /ɪm'bɒdɪmənt/ n incarnation f. **embody** vt incarner; (legally) incorporer.

emboss /ɪm'bɒs/ vt (metal) repousser; (paper) gaufrer.

embrace /ɪm'breɪs/ vt (person) étreindre; (religion) embrasser; (include) comprendre. ● n étreinte f.

embroider /ɪm'brɔɪdə(r)/ vt broder. **embroidery** n broderie f.

embryo /'embriəʊ/ n embryon m.

emerald /'emərəld/ n émeraude f.

emerge /ɪ'mɜːdʒ/ vi (person) sortir (from de); it ~d that il est apparu que. **emergence** n apparition f.

emergency /ɪ'mɜːdʒənsɪ/ n (crisis) crise f; (urgent case: Med) urgence f; in an ~ en cas d'urgence. ● adj d'urgence; ~ exit n sortie f de secours; ~ landing n atterrissage m forcé. ~ room n (US) salle f des urgences.

emigrant /'emɪgrənt/ n émigrant/-e m/f. **emigrate** vi émigrer.

eminence /'emɪnəns/ n éminence f. **eminent** adj éminent.

emission /ɪ'mɪʃn/ n émission f.

emit /ɪ'mɪt/ vt (pt emitted) émettre.

emotion /ɪ'məʊʃn/ n émotion f. **emotional** adj (development) émotif; (reaction) émotionel; (film, scene) émouvant.

emotive /ɪ'məʊtɪv/ adj qui soulève les passions.

emperor /'empərə(r)/ n empereur m.

emphasis /'emfəsɪs/ n accent m; lay ~ on mettre l'accent sur. **emphasize** vt mettre l'accent sur. **emphatic** adj catégorique; (manner) énergique.

empire /'empaɪə(r)/ n empire m.

employ /ɪm'plɔɪ/ vt employer. **employee** n employé/-e m/f; **employer** n employeur/-euse m/f.

employment /ɪm'plɔɪmənt/ n emploi m; find ~ trouver du travail.

empower /ɪm'paʊə(r)/ vt autoriser (to do à faire).

empty /'emptɪ/ adj (-ier, -iest) vide; (street) désert; (promise) vain; on an ~ stomach à jeun. ● vt/i (se) vider. ~-handed adj les mains vides.

emulate /'emjʊleɪt/ vt imiter.

enable /ɪ'neɪbl/ vt ~ sb to permettre à qn de.

enamel /ɪ'næml/ n émail m. ● vt (pt enamelled) émailler.

encase /ɪn'keɪs/ vt revêtir, recouvrir (in de).

enchant /ɪn'tʃɑːnt/ vt enchanter.

enclose /ɪn'kləʊz/ vt entourer; (land) clôturer; (with letter) joindre. **enclosed** adj (space) clos; (with letter) ci-joint. **enclosure** n enceinte f; (with letter) pièce f jointe.

encompass /ɪn'kʌmpəs/ vt inclure.

encore /'ɒŋkɔː(r)/ interj & n bis (m).

encounter /ɪn'kaʊntə(r)/ vt rencontrer. ● n rencontre f.

encourage /ɪn'kʌrɪdʒ/ vt encourager.

encroach /ɪn'krəʊtʃ/ vi ~ upon empiéter sur.

encyclopedia /ɪnsaɪklə'piːdɪə/ n encyclopédie f. **encyclopaedic** adj encyclopédique.

end /end/ n fin f; (farthest part) bout m; come to an ~ prendre fin; ~-product produit m fini; in the ~ finalement; no ~ of □ énormément de; on ~ (upright) debout; (in a row) de suite; put an ~ to mettre fin à. ● vt (marriage) mettre fin à; ~ one's days finir ses jours. ● vi se terminer; ~ up doing finir par faire.

endanger /ɪn'deɪndʒə(r)/ vt mettre en danger.

endearing /ɪn'dɪərɪŋ/ adj attachant.

endeavour, (US) **endeavor** /ɪn'devə(r)/ n (attempt) tentative f; (hard work) effort m. ● vi faire tout son possible (to do pour faire).

ending /'endɪŋ/ n fin f.

endive /'endɪv/ n chicorée f.

endless /'endlɪs/ adj interminable; (supply) inépuisable; (patience) infini.

endorse /ɪn'dɔːs/ vt (candidate, decision) appuyer; (product, claim) approuver; (cheque) endosser.

endurance /ɪn'djʊərəns/ n endurance f.

endure /ɪn'djʊə(r)/ vt supporter. ● vi durer. **enduring** adj durable.

enemy /'enəmɪ/ n & adj ennemi/-e (m/f).

energetic /enə'dʒetɪk/ adj énergique. **energy** n énergie f.

enforce /ɪn'fɔːs/ vt (rule, law) appliquer, faire respecter; (silence, discipline) imposer (on à); ~d forcé.

engage /ɪn'geɪdʒ/ vt (staff) engager; (attention) retenir; be ~d in se livrer à. ● vi ~ in se livrer à. **engaged** adj fiancé; (busy) occupé; **get** ~d se fiancer. **engagement** n fiançailles fpl; (meeting) rendezvous m; (undertaking) engagement m.

engaging /ɪn'geɪdʒɪŋ/ adj attachant, engageant.

engine /'endʒɪn/ n moteur m; (of train) locomotive f; (of ship) machines fpl. ~**-driver** n mécanicien m.

engineer /endʒɪ'nɪə(r)/ n ingénieur m; (repairman) technicien m; (on ship) mécanicien m. ● vt (contrive) manigancer.

engineering /endʒɪ'nɪərɪŋ/ n ingénierie f; (industry) mécanique f; **civil** ~ génie m civil.

England /'ɪŋɡlənd/ n Angleterre f.

English /'ɪŋɡlɪʃ/ adj anglais. ● n (Ling) anglais m; **the** ~ les Anglais mpl. ~**-man** n Anglais m. ~**-speaking** adj anglophone. ~**woman** n Anglaise f.

engrave /ɪn'greɪv/ vt graver.

engrossed /ɪn'ɡrəʊst/ adj absorbé (in dans).

engulf /ɪn'ɡʌlf/ vt engouffrer.

enhance /ɪn'hɑːns/ vt (prospects, status) améliorer; (price, value) augmenter.

enjoy /ɪn'dʒɔɪ/ vt aimer (doing faire); (benefit from) jouir de; ~ oneself s'amuser; ~ your meal! bon appétit! **enjoyable** adj agréable. **enjoyment** n plaisir m.

enlarge /ɪn'lɑːdʒ/ vt agrandir. ● vi s'agrandir; (pupil) se dilater; ~ on s'étendre sur. **enlargement** n agrandissement m.

enlighten /ɪn'laɪtn/ vt éclairer (on sur). **enlightenment** n instruction f; (information) éclaircissement m.

enlist /ɪn'lɪst/ vt (person) recruter; (fig) obtenir. ● vi s'engager.

enmity /'enmɪtɪ/ n inimitié f.

enormous /ɪ'nɔːməs/ adj énorme. **enormously** adv énormément.

enough /ɪ'nʌf/ adv & n assez; **have** ~ of en avoir assez de. ● det assez de; ~ **glasses/time** assez de verres/de temps.

enquire →INQUIRE. **enquiry** →INQUIRY.

enrage /ɪn'reɪdʒ/ vt mettre en rage, rendre furieux.

enrol /ɪn'rəʊl/ vt/i (pt enrolled) (s')inscrire. **enrolment** n inscription f.

ensure /ɪn'ʃɔː(r)/ vt garantir; ~ **that** (ascertain) s'assurer que.

entail /ɪn'teɪl/ vt entraîner.

entangle /ɪn'tæŋɡl/ vt emmêler.

enter /'entə(r)/ vt (room, club, phase) entrer dans; (note down, register) inscrire; (data) entrer, saisir. ● vi entrer (into dans); ~ **for** s'inscrire à.

enterprise /'entəpraɪz/ n entreprise f; (boldness) initiative f. **enterprising** adj entreprenant.

entertain /entə'teɪn/ vt amuser, divertir; (guests) recevoir; (ideas) considérer. **entertainer** n artiste mf. **entertaining** adj divertissant. **entertainment** n divertissement m; (performance) spectacle m.

enthral /ɪn'θrɔːl/ vt (pt enthralled) captiver.

enthusiasm /ɪn'θjuːzɪæzəm/ n enthousiasme m (for pour).

enthusiast /ɪn'θjuːzɪæst/ n passionné/-e m/f (for de). **enthusiastic** adj (supporter) enthousiaste; **be ∼ic about** être enthousiasmé par. **enthusiastically** adv avec enthousiasme.

entice /ɪn'taɪs/ vt attirer; ∼ **sb to do** entraîner qn à faire.

entire /ɪn'taɪə(r)/ adj entier. **entirely** adv entièrement. **entirety** n **in its ∼ty** en entier.

entitle /ɪn'taɪtl/ vt donner droit à (to sth à qch; to do de faire); (book) intitulé; **be ∼d to sth** avoir droit à qch.

entrance¹ /'entrəns/ n (entering, way in) entrée f (to de); (right to enter) admission f. ● adj (charge, exam) d'entrée.

entrance² /ɪn'trɑːns/ vt transporter.

entrant /'entrənt/ n (Sport) concurrent/-e m/f; (in exam) candidat/-e m/f.

entrenched /ɪn'trentʃt/ adj (opinion) inébranlable; (Mil) retranché.

entrepreneur /ɒntrəprə'nɜː(r)/ n entrepreneur/-euse m/f.

entrust /ɪn'trʌst/ vt confier; ∼ **sb with sth** confier qch à qn.

entry /'entrɪ/ n entrée f; ∼**form** fiche f d'inscription.

envelop /ɪn'veləp/ vt (pt enveloped) envelopper.

envelope /'envələʊp/ n

enveloppe f.

envious /'envɪəs/ adj envieux (of de).

environment /ɪn'vaɪərənmənt/ n (ecological) environnement m; (social) milieu m. **environmental** adj du milieu; de l'environnement. **environmentalist** n écologiste mf.

envisage /ɪn'vɪzɪdʒ/ vt prévoir (doing de faire).

envoy /'envɔɪ/ n envoyé/-e m/f.

envy /'envɪ/ n envie f. ● vt envier; ∼ **sb sth** envier qch à qn.

epic /'epɪk/ n épopée f. ● adj épique.

epidemic /epɪ'demɪk/ n épidémie f.

epilepsy /'epɪlepsɪ/ n épilepsie f.

episode /'epɪsəʊd/ n épisode m.

epitome /ɪ'pɪtəmɪ/ n modèle m. **epitomize** vt incarner.

equal /'iːkwəl/ adj à n égal/-e (m/f); ∼ **opportunities/rights** égalité f des chances/droits; ∼ **to** (task) à la hauteur de. ● vt (pt equalled) égaler. **equality** n égalité f. **equalize** vt/i égaliser. **equalizer** n (goal) but m égalisateur. **equally** adv (divide) en parts égales; (just as) tout aussi.

equanimity /ekwə'nɪmɪtɪ/ n sérénité f.

equate /ɪ'kweɪt/ vt assimiler (with à). **equation** n équation f.

equator /ɪ'kweɪtə(r)/ n équateur m.

equilibrium /iːkwɪ'lɪbrɪəm/ n équilibre m.

equip /ɪ'kwɪp/ vt (pt equipped) équiper (with de). **equipment** n équipement m.

equity /'ekwɪtɪ/ n équité f.

equivalence /ɪ'kwɪvələns/ n équivalence f.

era /'ɪərə/ n ère f, époque f.

eradicate /ɪ'rædɪkeɪt/ vt éliminer; (disease) éradiquer.

erase /ɪ'reɪz/ vt effacer. **eraser** n (rubber) gomme f.

erect /ɪ'rekt/ adj droit. ● vt ériger. **erection** n érection f.

erode /ɪ'rəʊd/ vt éroder; (fig) saper. **erosion** n érosion f.

erotic /ɪ'rɒtɪk/ adj érotique.

errand /'erənd/ n commission f, course f.

erratic /ɪ'rætɪk/ adj (behaviour, person) imprévisible; (performance) inégal.

error /'erə(r)/ n erreur f.

erupt /ɪ'rʌpt/ vi (volcano) entrer en éruption; (fig) éclater.

escalate /'eskəleɪt/ vt intensifier. ● vi (conflict) s'intensifier. **escalation** n intensification f. **escalator** n escalier m mécanique, escalator® m.

escapade /'eskəpeɪd/ n frasque f.

escape /ɪ'skeɪp/ vt échapper à. ● vi s'enfuir, s'évader; (gas) fuir. ● n fuite f, évasion f; (of gas etc.) fuite f; **have a lucky** or **narrow** ~ l'échapper belle.

escapism /ɪ'skeɪpɪzəm/ n évasion f (du réel).

escort¹ /'eskɔːt/ n (guard) escorte f; (companion) compagnon/ compagne m/f.

escort² /ɪ'skɔːt/ vt escorter.

Eskimo /'eskɪməʊ/ n Esquimau/-de m/f.

especially /ɪ'speʃəlɪ/ adv en particulier.

espionage /'espɪənɑːʒ/ n espionnage m.

espresso /e'spresəʊ/ n (café) express m.

essay /'eseɪ/ n (in literature) essai m; (School) rédaction f; (Univ) dissertation f.

essence /'esns/ n essence f.

essential /ɪ'senʃl/ adj essentiel; **the** ~s l'essentiel m. **essentially** adv essentiellement.

establish /ɪ'stæblɪʃ/ vt établir; (business) fonder.

establishment /ɪ'stæblɪʃmənt/ n (process) instauration f; (institution) établissement m; **the E**~ l'ordre m établi.

estate /ɪ'steɪt/ n (house and land) domaine m; (possessions) biens mpl; (housing estate) cité f; ~ **agent** n agent m immobilier. ~ **car** n break m.

esteem /ɪ'stiːm/ n estime f.

esthetic /es'θetɪk/ adj (US) ➡AES-THETIC.

estimate¹ /'estɪmət/ n (calculation) estimation f; (Comm) devis m.

estimate² /'estɪmeɪt/ vt évaluer; ~ **that** estimer que. **estimation** n (esteem) estime f; (judgment) opinion f.

Estonia /ɪ'stəʊnɪə/ n Estonie f.

estuary /'estʃʊərɪ/ n estuaire m.

eternal /ɪ'tɜːnl/ adj éternel.

eternity /ɪ'tɜːnətɪ/ n éternité f.

ethic /'eθɪk/ n éthique f. ~s moralité f. **ethical** adj éthique.

ethnic /'eθnɪk/ adj ethnique. ~ **cleansing** nettoyage m ethnique.

EU abbr **European Union** UE f, Union f européenne.

euphoria /juː'fɔːrɪə/ n euphorie f.

euro /'jʊərəʊ/ n euro m. ~ **zone** zone f euro.

Europe /'jʊərəp/ n Europe f.

European /jʊərə'pɪən/ adj & n européen/-ne (m/f); ~ **Community** Communauté f européenne.

eurosceptic /'jʊərəʊskeptɪk/ n eurosceptique m/f.

euthanasia /ˈjuːrəʊˈskeptik/ n euthanasie f.

evacuate /ɪˈvækjʊeɪt/ vt évacuer.

evade /ɪˈveɪd/ vt (blow) esquiver; (question) éluder.

evaluation /ɪvæljʊˈeɪʃn/ n évaluation f.

evaporate /ɪˈvæpəreɪt/ vi s'évaporer; **∼d milk** lait m condensé.

evasion /ɪˈveɪʒn/ n fuite f (of de vant); (excuse) faux-fuyant m; **tax ∼** évasion f fiscale. **evasive** adj évasif.

eve /iːv/ n veille f (of de).

even /ˈiːvn/ adj (surface, voice, contest) égal; (teeth, hem) régulier; (number) pair; **get ∼with** se venger de. ● adv même; **∼ better/**etc. (still) encore mieux/etc.; **∼ so** quand même. □ **∼ out** (differences) s'atténuer; **∼ sth out** (inequalities) réduire qch; **∼ up** équilibrer.

evening /ˈiːvnɪŋ/ n soir m; (whole evening, event) soirée f.

evenly /ˈiːvnlɪ/ adv (spread, apply) uniformément; (breathe) régulièrement; (equally) en parts égales.

event /ɪˈvent/ n événement m; (Sport) épreuve f; **in the ∼ of** en cas de. **eventful** adj mouvementé.

eventual /ɪˈventʃʊəl/ adj (outcome, decision) final; (aim) à long terme. **eventuality** n éventualité f. **eventually** adv finalement; (in future) un jour ou l'autre.

ever /ˈevə(r)/ adv jamais; (at all times) toujours.

evergreen /ˈevəɡriːn/ n arbre m à feuilles persistantes.

everlasting /evəˈlɑːstɪŋ/ adj éternel.

ever since prep & adv depuis.

every /ˈevrɪ/ adj **∼ house/window** toutes les maisons/les fenêtres; **∼ time/minute** chaque fois/minute; **∼ day** tous les jours; **∼ other day**

tous les deux jours. **everybody** pron tout le monde. **everyday** adj quotidien. **everyone** pron tout le monde. **everything** pron tout. **everywhere** adv partout; **∼where he goes** partout où il va.

evict /ɪˈvɪkt/ vt expulser (**from** de).

evidence /ˈevɪdəns/ n (proof) preuves fpl (**that** que; **of, for** de); (testimony) témoignage m; (traces) trace f (**of** de); **give ∼** témoigner; **be in ∼** être visible. **evident** adj manifeste. **evidently** adv (apparently) apparemment; (obviously) manifestement.

evil /ˈiːvl/ adj malfaisant. ● n mal m.

evoke /ɪˈvəʊk/ vt évoquer.

evolution /iːvəˈluːʃn/ n évolution f.

evolve /ɪˈvɒlv/ vi évoluer. ● vt élaborer.

ewe /juː/ n brebis f.

ex- /eks/ pref ex-, ancien.

exact /ɪɡˈzækt/ adj exact; **the ∼ opposite** exactement le contraire. ● vt exiger (**from** de). **exactly** adv exactement.

exaggerate /ɪɡˈzædʒəreɪt/ vt/i exagérer.

exalted /ɪɡˈzɔːltɪd/ adj élevé.

exam /ɪɡˈzæm/ n ✗ examen m.

examination /ɪɡzæmɪˈneɪʃn/ n examen m.

examine /ɪɡˈzæmɪn/ vt examiner; (witness) interroger. **examiner** n examinateur-trice m/f.

example /ɪɡˈzɑːmpl/ n exemple m; **for ∼** par exemple; **make an ∼ of** punir pour l'exemple.

exasperate /ɪɡˈzæspəreɪt/ vt exaspérer.

excavate /ˈekskəveɪt/ vt fouiller. **excavations** npl fouilles fpl.

exceed /ɪkˈsiːd/ vt dépasser. **exceedingly** adv extrêmement.

excel /ɪk'sel/ vi (pt **excelled**) exceller (**at, in** en; **at doing** à faire). ● vt surpasser.

excellence /'eksələns/ n excellence f. **excellent** adj excellent.

except /ɪk'sept/ prep sauf, excepté; ~ **for** à part. ● vt excepter. **excepting** prep sauf, excepté.

exception /ɪk'sepʃn/ n exception f; **take** ~ **to** s'offusquer de. **exceptional** adj exceptionnel.

excerpt /'eksɔ:pt/ n extrait m.

excess[1] /ɪk'ses/ n excès m.

excess[2] /'ekses/ adj excès; ~ **weight** excès m de poids; ~ **baggage** excédent m de bagages.

excessive /ɪk'sesɪv/ adj excessif.

exchange /ɪks'tʃeɪndʒ/ vt échanger (**for** contre). ● n échange m; (between currencies) change m; ~ **rate** taux m de change; **telephone** ~ **central** m téléphonique.

Exchequer /ɪks'tʃekə(r)/ n (Pol) ministère m britannique des finances.

excise /'eksaɪz/ n excise f, taxe f.

excite /ɪk'saɪt/ vt exciter; (enthuse) enthousiasmer. **excited** adj excité; **get** ~**d** s'exciter. **excitement** n excitation f. **exciting** adj passionnant.

exclaim /ɪk'sklaɪm/ vt s'exclamer.

exclamation /eksklə'meɪʃn/ n exclamation f; ~ **mark** or **point** (US) point m d'exclamation.

exclude /ɪk'sklu:d/ vt exclure.

exclusive /ɪk'sklu:sɪv/ adj (club) fermé; (rights) exclusif; (news item) en exclusivité; ~ **of meals** repas non compris. **exclusively** adv exclusivement.

excruciating /ɪk'skru:ʃɪeɪtɪŋ/ adj atroce.

excursion /ɪk'skɜ:ʃn/ n excursion f.

excuse[1] /ɪk'skju:z/ vt excuser; ~ from (exempt) dispenser de; ~ **me!** excusez-moi, pardon!

excuse[2] /ɪk'skju:s/ n (reason) excuse f; (pretext) prétexte m (**for sth** à qch; **for doing** pour faire).

ex-directory /eksdaɪ'rektərɪ/ adj sur liste rouge.

execute /'eksɪkju:t/ vt exécuter. **executioner** n bourreau m.

executive /ɪg'zekjʊtɪv/ n (person) cadre m; (committee) exécutif m. ● adj exécutif.

exemplary /ɪg'zemplərɪ/ adj exemplaire.

exemplify /ɪg'zemplɪfaɪ/ vt illustrer.

exempt /ɪg'zempt/ adj exempt (**from** de). ● vt exempter.

exercise /'eksəsaɪz/ n exercice m; ~ **book** cahier m. ● vt exercer; (restraint, patience) faire preuve de. ● vi faire de l'exercice.

exert /ɪg'zɜ:t/ vt exercer; ~ **oneself** se fatiguer. **exertion** n effort m.

exhaust /ɪg'zɔ:st/ vt épuiser. ● n (Auto) pot m d'échappement. **exhaustive** /ɪg'zɔ:stɪv/ adj exhaustif.

exhibit /ɪg'zɪbɪt/ vt exposer; (fig) manifester. ● n objet m exposé.

exhibition /eksɪ'bɪʃn/ n exposition f; (of skill) démonstration f. **exhibitionist** n exhibitionniste mf.

exhibitor /ɪg'zɪbɪtə(r)/ n exposant/-e mf.

exhilarate /ɪg'zɪlərət/ vt griser.

exile /'eksaɪl/ n exil m; (person) exilé/-e mf. ● vt exiler.

exist /ɪg'zɪst/ vi exister. **existence** n existence f; **be in** ~**ence** exister. **existing** adj actuel.

exit /'eksɪt/ n sortie f. ● vt/i (also Comput) sortir (de).

exodus /'eksədəs/ n exode m.

exonerate /ɪɡ'zɒnəreɪt/ vt disculper.

exotic /ɪɡ'zɒtɪk/ adj exotique.

expand /ɪk'spænd/ vt étendre; (workforce) accroître. ● vi se développer; (population) s'accroître; (metal) se dilater.

expanse /ɪk'spæns/ n étendue f.

expansion /ɪk'spænʃn/ n développement m; (Pol, Comm) expansion f.

expatriate /eks'pætrɪət/ adj & n expatrié/-e (m/f).

expect /ɪk'spekt/ vt s'attendre à; (suppose) supposer; (demand) exiger; (baby) attendre.

expectancy /ɪk'spektənsɪ/ n attente f.

expectant /ɪk'spektənt/ adj ∼ mother future maman f.

expectation /ekspek'teɪʃn/ n (assumption) prévision f; (hope) aspiration f; (demand) exigence f.

expedient /ɪk'spiːdɪənt/ adj opportun. ● n expédient m.

expedition /ekspɪ'dɪʃn/ n expédition f.

expel /ɪk'spel/ vt (pt **expelled**) expulser; (pupil) renvoyer.

expend /ɪk'spend/ vt consacrer.

expenditure /ɪk'spendɪtʃə(r)/ n dépenses fpl.

expense /ɪk'spens/ n frais mpl; at sb's ∼ aux frais de qn; ∼ **account** frais mpl de représentation. **expensive** adj cher; (tastes) de luxe. **expensively** adv luxueusement.

experience /ɪk'spɪərɪəns/ n expérience f. ● vt (undergo) connaître; (feel) éprouver; ∼**d** expérimenté.

experiment /ɪk'sperɪmənt/ n expérience f. ● vi expérimenter, faire des essais.

expert /'ekspɜːt/ n spécialiste mf. ● adj spécialisé, expert. **expertise** n compétence f. **expertly** adv de

manière experte.

expire /ɪk'spaɪə(r)/ vi expirer; ∼**d** périmé. **expiry** n expiration f.

explain /ɪk'spleɪn/ vt expliquer. **explanation** n explication f. **explanatory** adj explicatif.

explicit /ɪk'splɪsɪt/ adj explicite.

explode /ɪk'spləʊd/ vt/i (faire) exploser.

exploit[1] /'eksplɔɪt/ n exploit m.

exploit[2] /ɪk'splɔɪt/ vt exploiter.

exploration /eksplə'reɪʃn/ n exploration f. **exploratory** adj (talks) exploratoire. **explore** vt explorer; (fig) étudier. **explorer** n explorateur/-trice m/f.

explosion /ɪk'spləʊʒn/ n explosion f. **explosive** adj & n explosif (m).

exponent /ɪk'spəʊnənt/ n avocat/-e m/f (of de).

export[1] /ɪk'spɔːt/ vt exporter.

export[2] /'ekspɔːt/ n (process) exportation f; (product) produit m d'exportation.

expose /ɪk'spəʊz/ vt exposer; (disclose) révéler.

exposure /ɪk'spəʊʒə(r)/ n révélation f; (Photo) pose f; **die of** ∼ mourir de froid.

express /ɪk'spres/ vt exprimer. ● adj exprès. ● adv **send sth** ∼ envoyer qch en exprès. ● n (train) rapide m. **expression** n expression f. **expressive** adj expressif. **expressly** adv expressément.

exquisite /'ekskwɪzɪt/ adj exquis.

extend /ɪk'stend/ vt (visit) prolonger; (house) agrandir; (range) élargir; (arm, leg) étendre. ● vi (stretch) s'étendre; (in time) se prolonger. **extension** n (of line, road) prolongement m; (of visa, loan) prorogation f; (building) addition f; (phone number) poste m; (cable) rallonge f.

extensive /ɪk'stensɪv/ adj vaste;

(study) approfondi; (damage) considérable. **extensively** adv (much) beaucoup; (very) très.

extent /ɪk'stent/ n (size, scope) étendue f; (degree) mesure f; **to some ~** dans une certaine mesure; **to such an ~ that** à tel point que.

extenuating /ɪk'stenjueɪtɪŋ/ adj atténuant.

exterior /ɪk'stɪərɪə(r)/ adj & n extérieur (m).

exterminate /ɪk'stɜːmɪneɪt/ vt exterminer.

external /ɪk'stɜːnl/ adj extérieur; (cause, medical use) externe.

extinct /ɪk'stɪŋkt/ adj (species) disparu; (volcano, passion) éteint.

extinguish /ɪk'stɪŋgwɪʃ/ vt éteindre. **extinguisher** n extincteur m.

extol /ɪk'stəʊl/ vt (pt extolled) louer, chanter les louanges de.

extort /ɪk'stɔːt/ vt extorquer (**from** à). **extortion** n (Jur) extorsion f. **extortionate** adj exorbitant.

extra /'ekstrə/ adj supplémentaire; **~ charge** supplément m; **~ time** (football) prolongation f; **~ strong** extrafort. ● adv encore; plus. ● n supplément m; (cinema) figurant/-e m/f.

extract[1] /ɪk'strækt/ vt sortir (from de); (tooth) extraire; (promise) arracher.

extract[2] /'ekstrækt/ n extrait m.

extra-curricular /ekstrəkə 'rɪkjʊlə(r)/ adj parascolaire.

extradite /'ekstrədaɪt/ vt extrader.

extramarital /ekstrə'mærɪtl/ adj extraconjugal.

extramural /ekstrə'mjʊərəl/ adj (Univ) hors faculté.

extraordinary /ɪk'strɔːdnrɪ/ adj extraordinaire.

extravagance /ɪk'strævəgəns/ n prodigalité f. **extravagant** adj (person) dépensier; (claim) extravagant.

extreme /ɪk'striːm/ adj & n extrême (m). **extremely** adv extrêmement. **extremist** n extrémiste mf. **extremity** n extrémité f.

extricate /'ekstrɪkeɪt/ vt dégager.

extrovert /'ekstrəvɜːt/ n extraverti/-e m/f.

exuberance /ɪg'zjuːbərəns/ n exubérance f.

exude /ɪg'zjuːd/ vt (charm) respirer; (smell) exhaler.

eye /aɪ/ n œil m (pl yeux); **keep an ~ on** surveiller. ● vt (pt eyed; pres p eyeing) regarder. **~ball** n globe m oculaire. **~brow** n sourcil m. **~-catching** adj attrayant. **~lash** n cil m. **~lid** n paupière f. **~-opener** n révélation f. **~-shadow** n ombre f à paupières. **~sight** n vue f. **~sore** n horreur f. **~witness** n témoin m oculaire.

Ff

fable /'feɪbl/ n fable f.

fabric /'fæbrɪk/ n (cloth) tissu m.

fabulous /'fæbjʊləs/ adj fabuleux; (marvellous 🅸) formidable.

face /feɪs/ n visage m, figure f; (expression) air m; (appearance, dignity) face f; (of clock) cadran m; (Geol) face f; (of rock) paroi f; **in the ~ of** face à; **make a (funny) ~** faire la grimace; **~ to ~** face à face. ● vt être en face de; (risk) devoir affronter; (confront) faire face à; (deal with) **I can't ~ him** je n'ai pas le courage de le voir. ● vi (person) regarder; (chair) être tourné vers; (window) donner sur; **~ up to**

faire face à; **~d with** face à.

facelift /'feɪslɪft/ n lifting m; **give a ~ to** donner un coup de neuf à.

face value n valeur f nominale; **take sth at~** prendre qch au pied de la lettre.

facial /'feɪʃl/ adj (hair) du visage; (injury) au visage. ● n soin m du visage.

facility /fə'sɪlətɪ/ n (building) complexe m; (feature) fonction f; **facilities** (equipment) équipements mpl.

facsimile /fæk'sɪməlɪ/ n facsimilé n.

fact /fækt/ n fait m; **as a matter of ~, in ~** en fait; **know for a ~ that** savoir de source sûre que; **owing/due to the ~ that** étant donné que.

factor /'fæktə(r)/ n facteur m.

factory /'fæktərɪ/ n usine f.

factual /'fæktʃʊəl/ adj (account, description) basé sur les faits; (evidence) factuel.

faculty /'fæklti/ n faculté f.

fade /feɪd/ vi (sound) s'affaiblir; (memory) s'effacer; (flower) se faner; (material) se décolorer; (colour) passer.

fail /feɪl/ vi échouer; (grow weak) (s'af)faiblir; (run short) manquer; (engine) tomber en panne. ● vt (exam) échouer à; **~ to do** (not do) ne pas faire; (not be able) ne pas réussir à faire; **without ~** à coup sûr.

failing /'feɪlɪŋ/ n défaut m; **~ that/this** sinon.

failure /'feɪljə(r)/ n échec m; (person) raté·e m/f; (breakdown) panne f; **~ to do** (inability) incapacité f de faire.

faint /feɪnt/ adj léger, faible; **feel ~** (ill) se sentir mal; **I haven't the ~est idea** je n'en ai pas la moindre

idée. ● vi s'évanouir. ● n évanouissement m; **~-hearted** adj timide.

fair /feə(r)/ n foire f. ● adj (hair, person) blond; (skin) clair; (weather) beau; (amount, quality) raisonnable; (just) juste, équitable. ● adv (play) loyalement.

fairground n champ m de foire.

fairly /'feəlɪ/ adv (justly) équitablement; (rather) assez.

fairness /'feənɪs/ n justice f.

fairy /'feərɪ/ n fée f; **~ story, ~-tale** n conte m de fées.

faith /feɪθ/ n (belief) foi f; (confidence) confiance f.

faithful /'feɪθfl/ adj fidèle.

fake /feɪk/ n (forgery) faux m; (person) imposteur m; **it is a ~** c'est un faux. ● adj faux. ● vt (signature) contrefaire; (results) falsifier; (illness) feindre.

falcon /'fɔːlkən/ n faucon m.

fall /fɔːl/ vi (pt fell; pp fallen) tomber; **~ short** être insuffisant. ● n chute f; (autumn: US) automne m; **Niagara F~s** chutes fpl du Niagara. ▫ **~ back on** se rabattre sur. **~ behind** prendre du retard. **~ down or over** tomber. **~ for** (person ⊡) tomber amoureux de; (a trick ⊡) se laisser prendre à. **~ in** (Mil) se mettre en rangs. **~ off** (decrease) diminuer. **~ out** se brouiller (with avec). **~ over** tomber (with terre). **~ through** (plans) tomber à l'eau.

fallacy /'fæləsɪ/ n erreur f.

false /fɔːls/ adj faux. **~ teeth** npl dentier m.

falter /'fɔːltə(r)/ vi (courage) faiblir; (when speaking) hésiter ⊡.

fame /feɪm/ n renommée f; **famed** adj célèbre (for pour).

familiar /fə'mɪlɪə(r)/ adj familier; **be ~ with** connaître.

family /ˈfæməlɪ/ n famille f.

famine /ˈfæmɪn/ n famine f.

famished /ˈfæmɪʃt/ adj affamé.

famous /ˈfeɪməs/ adj célèbre (**for** pour).

fan /fæn/ n (mechanical) ventilateur m; (hand-held) éventail m; (of person) fan mf 🗌, admirateur/-trice m/f; (enthusiast) fervent/-e m/f, passionné/-e m/f. ● vt (pt **fanned**) (face) éventer; (fig) attiser. ● vi ~ **out** se déployer en éventail.

fanatic /fəˈnætɪk/ n fanatique mf.

fan belt n courroie f de ventilateur.

fancy /ˈfænsɪ/ n (whim, fantasy) fantaisie f; **take a** ~**to sb** se prendre d'affection pour qn; **it took my** ~ ça m'a plu. ● adj (buttons etc.) fantaisie inv; (prices) extravagant; (impressive) impressionnant. ● vt s'imaginer; (want 🗌) avoir envie de; (like 🗌) aimer. ~ **dress** n déguisement m.

fang /fæŋ/ n (of dog) croc m; (of snake) crochet m.

fantasize /ˈfæntəsaɪz/ vi fantasmer.

fantastic /fænˈtæstɪk/ adj fantastique.

fantasy /ˈfæntəsɪ/ n fantaisie f; (daydream) fantasme m.

fanzine /ˈfænziːn/ n magazine n des fans, fanzine m.

FAQ abbr (**Frequently Asked Questions**) (Internet) FAQ f, foire f aux questions.

far /fɑː(r)/ adv loin; (much) beaucoup; (very) très; ~ **away**, ~ **off** au loin; **as** ~ **as** (up to) jusqu'à; **as** ~**as I know** autant que je sache; **by** ~ de loin; ~ **from** loin de. ● adj lointain; (end, side) autre. ~**away** adj lointain.

farce /fɑːs/ n farce f.

fare /feə(r)/ n (price du) billet m;

(food) nourriture f. ● vi (progress) aller; (manage) se débrouiller.

Far East n Extrême-Orient m.

farewell /feəˈwel/ interj & n adieu (m).

farm /fɑːm/ n ferme f. ● vt cultiver; ~ **out** céder en sous-traitance. ● vi être fermier. **farmer** n fermier m. ~**house** n ferme f. **farming** n agriculture f. ~**yard** n basse-cour f.

fart /fɑːt/ 🗌 vi péter 🗌. ● n pet m 🗌.

farther /ˈfɑːðə(r)/ adv plus loin. ● adj plus éloigné.

farthest /ˈfɑːðɪst/ adv le plus loin. ● adj le plus éloigné.

fascinate /ˈfæsɪneɪt/ vt fasciner.

Fascism /ˈfæʃɪzəm/ n fascisme m.

fashion /ˈfæʃn/ n (current style) mode f; (manner) façon f; **in** ~ à la mode; **out of** ~ démodé. ● vt façonner. **fashionable** adj à la mode.

fast /fɑːst/ adj rapide; (colour) grand teint inv; (firm) fixe, solide; **be** ~ (of a clock) avancer. ● adv vite; (firmly) ferme; **be** ~ **asleep** dormir d'un sommeil profond. ● vi jeûner. ● n jeûne m.

fasten /ˈfɑːsn/ vt/i (s')attacher. **fastener**, **fastening** n attache f, fermeture f.

fast food n fast-food m. restauration f rapide.

fat /fæt/ n graisse f; (on meat) gras m. ● adj (**fatter**, **fattest**) gros, gras; (meat) gras; (profit) gros; **a** ~ **lot** 🗌 bien peu (of de).

fatal /ˈfeɪtl/ adj mortel; (fateful, disastrous) fatal. **fatality** n mort m. **fatally** adv mortellement.

fate /feɪt/ n sort m. **fateful** adj fatidique.

father /ˈfɑːðə(r)/ n père m. ~**hood** n paternité f. ~**-in-law** n (pl ~**s-inlaw**) beau-père m.

fathom /ˈfæðəm/ n brasse f (= 1.8 m). ● vt ~(out) comprendre.

fatigue /fəˈtiːg/ n épuisement m; (Tech) fatigue f. ● vt fatiguer.

fatten /ˈfætn/ vt/i engraisser. **fattening** adj qui fait grossir.

fatty /ˈfætɪ/ adj (food) gras; (tissue) adipeux.

faucet /ˈfɔːsɪt/ n (US) robinet m.

fault /fɔːlt/ n (defect, failing) défaut m; (blame) faute f; (Geol) faille f; at ~ fautif; **find** ~ **with** critiquer. ● vt ~ **sth/sb** prendre en défaut qn/qch. **faulty** adj défectueux.

favour, (US) **favor** /ˈfeɪvə(r)/ n faveur f; **do sb a** ~ rendre service à qn; **in** ~ **of** pour. ● vt favoriser; (support) être en faveur de; (prefer) préférer. **favourable** adj favorable.

favourite /ˈfeɪvərɪt/ adj & n favori/-te (m/f).

fawn /fɔːn/ n (animal) faon m; (colour) beige m foncé. ● vi ~ **on** flagorner.

fax /fæks/ n fax m, télécopie f. ● vt faxer, envoyer par télécopie. ~ **machine** n fax m, télécopieur m; (for public use) Publifax® m.

FBI abbr (**Federal Bureau of Investigation**) (US) Police f judiciaire fédérale.

fear /fɪə(r)/ n crainte f, peur f; (fig) risque m; **for** ~ **of/that** de peur de/que. ● vt craindre.

feasible /ˈfiːzəbl/ adj faisable; (likely) plausible.

feast /fiːst/ n festin m; (Relig) fête f. ● vi festoyer. ● vt régaler (**on** de).

feat /fiːt/ n exploit m.

feather /ˈfeðə(r)/ n plume f. ● vt ~ **one's nest** s'enrichir.

feature /ˈfiːtʃə(r)/ n caractéristique f; (of person, face) trait m; (film) long métrage m; (article) article m de fond. ● vt (advert) représenter;

(give prominence to) mettre en vedette. ● vi figurer (**in** dans).

February /ˈfebruərɪ/ n février m.

fed /fed/ ➡**FEED**. ● adj **be ~ up** ⊺ en avoir marre ⊺ (**with** de).

federal /ˈfedərəl/ adj fédéral.

fee /fiː/ n (for entrance) prix m; ~(**s**) (of doctor) honoraires mpl; (of actor, artist) cachet m; (for tuition) frais mpl; (for enrolment) droits mpl.

feeble /ˈfiːbl/ adj faible.

feed /fiːd/ vt (pt **fed**) nourrir, donner à manger à; (suckle) allaiter; (supply) alimenter. ● vi se nourrir (**on** de). ~ **in information** rentrer des données. ● n nourriture f; (of baby) tétée f.

feedback /ˈfiːdbæk/ n réaction (s) f(pl); (Med, Tech) feed-back m.

feel /fiːl/ vt (pt **felt**) (touch) tâter; (be conscious of) sentir; (emotion) ressentir; (experience) éprouver; (think) estimer. ● vi (tired, lonely) se sentir; ~ **hot/thirsty** avoir chaud/ soif; ~ **as if** avoir l'impression que; ~ **awful** (ill) se sentir malade; ~ **like** (want ⊺) avoir envie de.

feeler /ˈfiːlə(r)/ n antenne f; **put out** ~**s** tâter le terrain.

feeling /ˈfiːlɪŋ/ n (emotion) sentiment m; (physical) sensation f; (impression) impression f.

feet /fiːt/ ➡**FOOT**.

feign /feɪn/ vt feindre.

fell /fel/ ➡**FALL**. ● vt (cut down) abattre.

fellow /ˈfeləʊ/ n compagnon m, camarade m; (of society) membre m; (man ⊺) type m ⊺. ~**-countryman** n compatriote m. ~**-passenger** n compagnon m de voyage.

fellowship /ˈfeləʊʃɪp/ n camaraderie f; (group) association f.

felony /ˈfelənɪ/ n crime m.

felt /felt/ **→FEEL.** ● n feutre m. ∼**-tip** n feutre m.

female /ˈfiːmeɪl/ adj (animal) femelle; (voice, sex) féminin. ● n femme f; (animal) femelle f.

feminine /ˈfemənɪn/ adj & n féminin (m). **femininity** n féminité f. **feminist** n féministe mf.

fence /fens/ n barrière f; **sit on the** ∼ ne pas prendre position. ● vt ∼ **(in)** clôturer. ● vi (Sport) faire de l'escrime. **fencing** n escrime f.

fend /fend/ vi ∼ **for oneself** se débrouiller tout seul. ● vt ∼ **off** (blow, attack) parer.

fender /ˈfendə(r)/ n (for fireplace) garde-cendre m; (mudguard: US) garde-boue m inv.

ferment[1] /ˈfɜːment/ n ferment m; (excitement: fig) agitation f.

ferment[2] /fəˈment/ vt/i (faire) fermenter.

fern /fɜːn/ n fougère f.

ferocious /fəˈrəʊʃəs/ adj féroce.

ferret /ˈferɪt/ n (animal) furet m. ● vi ∼ **about** fureter. ● vt ∼ **out** dénicher.

ferry /ˈferɪ/ n (long-distance) ferry m; (short-distance) bac m. ● vt transporter.

fertile /ˈfɜːtaɪl/ adj fertile; (person, animal) fécond. **fertilizer** n engrais m.

festival /ˈfestɪvl/ n festival m; (Relig) fête f.

festive /ˈfestɪv/ adj de fête, gai; ∼ **season** période f des fêtes. **festivity** n réjouissances fpl.

fetch /fetʃ/ vt (go for) aller chercher; (bring person) amener; (bring thing) apporter; (be sold for) rapporter.

fête /feɪt/ n fête f; (church) kermesse f. ● vt fêter.

fetish /ˈfetɪʃ/ n (object) fétiche m;

(Psych) obsession f.

feud /fjuːd/ n querelle f.

fever /ˈfiːvə(r)/ n fièvre f. **feverish** adj fiévreux.

few /fjuː/ det peu de; **a** ∼ **houses** quelques maisons; **quite a** ∼ **people** un bon nombre de personnes. ● pron quelques-uns/ quelques-unes.

fewer /ˈfjuːə(r)/ det moins de; **be** ∼ être moins nombreux (**than** que). **fewest** det le moins de.

fiancé /fɪˈɒnseɪ/ n fiancé m. **fiancée** n fiancée f.

fibre, (US) **fiber** /ˈfaɪbə(r)/ n fibre f. ∼**-glass** n fibre f de verre.

fiction /ˈfɪkʃn/ n fiction f; **(works of)** ∼ romans mpl. **fictional** adj fictif.

fiddle /ˈfɪdl/ n ① violon m; (swindle ①) combine f. ● vi ✕ frauder. ● vt ① falsifier; ∼ **with** ① tripoter ①.

fidget /ˈfɪdʒɪt/ vi gigoter sans cesse.

field /fiːld/ n champ m; (Sport) terrain m; (fig) domaine m. ● vt (ball: cricket) bloquer.

fierce /fɪəs/ adj féroce; (storm, attack) violent.

fiery /ˈfaɪərɪ/ adj (-**ier, -iest**) (hot) ardent; (spirited) fougueux.

fifteen /fɪfˈtiːn/ adj & n quinze (m).

fifth /fɪfθ/ adj & n cinquième (mf).

fifty /ˈfɪftɪ/ adj & n cinquante (m).

fig /fɪg/ n figue f.

fight /faɪt/ vi (pt **fought**) se battre; (struggle: fig) lutter; (quarrel) se disputer. ● vt se battre avec; (evil: fig) lutter contre. ● n (struggle) lutte f; (quarrel) dispute f; (brawl) bagarre f; (Mil) combat m. □ ∼ **back** se défendre (**against** contre). ∼**off** surmonter. ∼**over** se disputer qch. **fighter** n (determined person) lutteur/-euse m/f; (plane) avion m de chasse. **fighting** n combats mpl.

figment /'fɪgmənt/ n a ~ of the imagination un produit de l'imagination.

figure /'fɪgə(r)/ n (number) chiffre m; (diagram) figure f; (shape) forme f; (body) ligne f; ~s arithmétique f. ● vt s'imaginer. ● vi (appear) figurer; **that** ~s (US, ⊞) c'est logique; ~ out comprendre; ~ of speech façon f de parler.

file /faɪl/ n (tool) lime f; dossier m, classeur m; (Comput) fichier m; (row) file f. ● vt limer; (papers) classer; (Jur) déposer. □ ~ in entrer en file. ~ past défiler devant.

filing cabinet n classeur m.

fill /fɪl/ vt/i (se) remplir. ● have had one's ~ en avoir assez. □ ~ in (form) remplir. ~ out prendre du poids. ~ up (Auto) faire le plein (de carburant); (bath, theatre) (se) remplir.

fillet /'fɪlɪt/ n filet m. ● vt découper en filets.

filling /'fɪlɪŋ/ n (of tooth) plombage m; (of sandwich) garniture f. ~ station n station-service f.

film /fɪlm/ n film m; (Photo) pellicule f. ● vt filmer. ~-goer n cinéphile mf. ~star n vedette f de cinéma.

filter /'fɪltə(r)/ n filtre m; (traffic signal) flèche f. ● vt/i filtrer; (of traffic) suivre la flèche. ~ coffee n café m filtre.

filth /fɪlθ/ n crasse f. **filthy** adj crasseux.

fin /fɪn/ n (of fish, seal) nageoire f; (of shark) aileron m.

final /'faɪnl/ adj dernier; (conclusive) définitif. ● n (Sport) finale f.

finale /fɪ'nɑːlɪ/ n (Mus) finale m.

finalize /'faɪnəlaɪz/ vt mettre au point, fixer.

finally /'faɪnəlɪ/ adv (lastly, at last) enfin, finalement; (once and for all) définitivement.

finance /'faɪnæns/ n finance f. ● adj financier. ● vt financer. **financial** adj financier.

find /faɪnd/ vt (pt found) trouver; (sth lost) retrouver. ~ out vt trouvaille f; vi se renseigner (about sur). **findings** npl conclusions fpl.

fine /faɪn/ adj fin; (excellent) beau; ~ arts beaux-arts mpl. ● n amende f. ● vt condamner à une amende.

finger /'fɪŋgə(r)/ n doigt m. ● vt palper. ~nail n ongle m. ~print n empreinte f digitale. ~tip n bout m du doigt.

finish /'fɪnɪʃ/ vt/i finir; ~ doing finir de faire; ~ up doing finir par faire; ~ up se retrouver à. ● n fin f; (of race) arrivée f; (appearance) finition f.

finite /'faɪnaɪt/ adj fini.

Finland /'fɪnlənd/ n Finlande f. **Finn** n Finlandais(-e m/f.

Finnish /'fɪnɪʃ/ adj finlandais. ● n (Ling) finnois m.

fir /fɜː(r)/ n sapin m.

fire /'faɪə(r)/ n (element) feu m; (blaze) incendie m; (heater) radiateur m; **set** ~ **to** mettre le feu à. ● vt (bullet) tirer; (dismiss) renvoyer; (fig) enflammer. ● vi tirer (at sur). ~ a gun tirer un coup de revolver/de fusil. ~ alarm n alarme f incendie. ~arm n arme f à feu. ~ brigade n pompiers mpl. ~ engine n voiture f de pompiers. ~ escape n escalier m de secours. ~ extinguisher n extincteur m. ~ man n (pl -men) pompier m. ~place n cheminée f. ~ station n caserne f de pompiers. ~wall n mur m coupe-feu; (Internet) pare-feu m inv. ~wood n bois m de chauffage.

∼**work** n feu m d'artifice.

firing squad n peloton m d'exécution.

firm /fɜːm/ n entreprise f, société f. ● adj ferme; (belief) solide.

first /fɜːst/ adj premier; **at** ∼ **hand** de première main; **at** ∼ **sight** à première vue; ∼ **of all** tout d'abord. ● n premier/-ière m/f. ● adv d'abord, premièrement; (arrive) le premier, la première; **at** ∼ d'abord. ∼ **aid** n premiers soins mpl. ∼**-class** adj de première classe. ∼ **floor** n premier étage m; (US) rez-de-chaussée m inv. ∼ **gear** n première (vitesse) f. **F**∼ **Lady** n (US) épouse f du Président.

firstly /ˈfɜːstlɪ/ adv premièrement.

first name n prénom m.

fish /fɪʃ/ n poisson m; ∼ **shop** poissonnerie f. ● vi pêcher; ∼ **for** (cod) pêcher; ∼ **out** (from water) repêcher; (take out 🔟) sortir. **fisherman** n (pl -**men**) pêcheur m.

fishing /ˈfɪʃɪŋ/ n pêche f; **go** ∼ aller à la pêche. ∼ **rod** n canne f à pêche.

fishmonger /ˈfɪʃmʌŋgə(r)/ n poissonnier/-ière m/f.

fist /fɪst/ n poing m.

fit /fɪt/ n accès m, crise f; **be a good** ∼ (dress) être à la bonne taille. ● adj (**fitter, fittest**) en bonne santé; (proper) convenable; (good enough) bon; (able) capable; **in no** ∼ **state to do** pas en état de faire. ● vt/i (pt **fitted**) (into space) aller; (install) poser. ∼ **in** vt caser; vi (newcomer) s'intégrer. ∼ **out,** ∼ **up** équiper.

fitness /ˈfɪtnɪs/ n forme f; (of remark) justesse f.

fitted /ˈfɪtɪd/ adj (wardrobe) encastré. ∼ **carpet** n moquette f.

fitting /ˈfɪtɪŋ/ adj approprié. ● n es-

sayage m. ∼ **room** n cabine f d'essayage.

five /faɪv/ adj & n cinq (m).

fix /fɪks/ vt (make firm, attach, decide) fixer; (mend) réparer; (deal with) arranger; ∼ **sb up with sth** trouver qch à qn.

fixture /ˈfɪkstʃə(r)/ n (Sport) match m; ∼**s** (in house) installations fpl.

fizz /fɪz/ vi pétiller. ● n pétillement m. **fizzy** adj gazeux.

flabbergast /ˈflæbəgɑːst/ vt sidérer.

flabby /ˈflæbɪ/ adj flasque.

flag /flæg/ n drapeau m; (Naut) pavillon m. ● vt (pt **flagged**) ∼ (**down**) faire signe de s'arrêter à. ● vi (weaken) faiblir; (sick person) s'affaiblir. ∼**-pole** n mât m. ∼**stone** n dalle f.

flake /fleɪk/ n flocon m; (of paint, metal) écaille f. ● vi s'écailler.

flamboyant /flæmˈbɔɪənt/ adj (colour) éclatant; (manner) extravagant.

flame /fleɪm/ n flamme f; **burst into** ∼**s** exploser; **go up in** ∼**s** brûler. ● vi flamber.

flamingo /fləˈmɪŋgəʊ/ n flamant m (rose).

flammable /ˈflæməbl/ adj inflammable.

flan /flæn/ n tarte f; (custard tart) flan m.

flank /flæŋk/ n flanc m. ● vt flanquer.

flannel /ˈflænl/ n (material) flannelle f; (for face) gant m de toilette.

flap /flæp/ vi (pt **flapped**) battre. ● vt ∼ **its wings** battre des ailes. ● n (of pocket) rabat m; (of table) abattant m.

flare /fleə(r)/ vi ∼ **up** (fighting) éclater. ● n flamboiement m; (Mil) fusée f éclairante; (in skirt) évasement m. **flared** adj évasé.

flash /flæʃ/ vi briller; (on and off) clignoter; ~ **past** passer à toute vitesse. ● vt faire briller; (aim torch) diriger (**at** sur); (flaunt) étaler; ~ **one's headlights** faire un appel de phares. ● n (of news, camera) flash m; **in a** ~ en un éclair. ~**back** n retour m en arrière. ~**light** n lampe f de poche.

flask /flɑːsk/ n (for chemicals) flacon m; (for drinks) thermos® m or f inv.

flat /flæt/ adj (**flatter, flattest**) plat; (tyre) à plat; (refusal) catégorique; (fare, rate) fixe. ● adv (say) carrément. ● n (rooms) appartement m; (tyre Ⓐ) crevaison f; (Mus) bémol m.

flat out adv (drive) à toute vitesse; (work) d'arrache-pied.

flatten /ˈflætn/ vt/i (s')aplatir.

flatter /ˈflætə(r)/ vt flatter.

flaunt /flɔːnt/ vt étaler, afficher.

flavour, (US) **flavor** /ˈfleɪvə(r)/ n goût m; (of ice-cream) parfum m. ● vt parfumer (**with** à), assaisonner (**with** de). **flavouring** n arôme m artificiel.

flaw /flɔː/ n défaut m.

flea /fliː/ n puce f. ~ **market** n marché m aux puces.

fleck /flek/ n petite tache f.

fled /fled/ ⇒**FLEE**.

flee /fliː/ vt/i (pt **fled**) fuir.

fleece /fliːs/ n toison f; (garment) polaire f. ● vt plumer.

fleet /fliːt/ n (Naut, Aviat) flotte f; **a** ~ **of vehicles** (in reserve) parc m; (on road) convoi m.

fleeting /ˈfliːtɪŋ/ adj très bref.

Flemish /ˈflemɪʃ/ adj flamand. ● n (Ling) flamand m.

flesh /fleʃ/ n chair f; **one's (own)**

~ **and blood** la chair de sa chair.

flew /fluː/ ⇒**FLY**.

flex /fleks/ vt (knee) fléchir; (muscle) faire jouer. ● n (Electr) fil m.

flexible /ˈfleksəbl/ adj flexible.

flexitime /ˈfleksitaɪm/ n horaire m variable.

flick /flɪk/ n petit coup m. ● vt donner un petit coup à; ~ **through** feuilleter.

flight /flaɪt/ n (of bird, plane) vol m; ~ **of stairs** escalier m; (fleeing) fuite f; **take** ~ prendre la fuite. ~**deck** n poste m de pilotage.

flimsy /ˈflɪmzɪ/ adj (**-ier, -iest**) (pej) mince, peu solide.

flinch /flɪntʃ/ vi (wince) broncher; (draw back) reculer.

fling /flɪŋ/ vt (pt **flung**) jeter.

flint /flɪnt/ n (rock) silex m.

flip /flɪp/ vt (pt **flipped**) donner un petit coup à; ~ **through** feuilleter. ● n chiquenaude f.

flippant /ˈflɪpənt/ adj désinvolte.

flipper /ˈflɪpə(r)/ n (of seal) nageoire f; (of swimmer) palme f.

flirt /flɜːt/ vi flirter. ● n flirteur/-euse m/f.

float /fləʊt/ vt/i (faire) flotter. ● n flotteur m; (cart) char m.

flock /flɒk/ n (of sheep) troupeau m; (of people) foule f. ● vi affluer.

flog /flɒg/ vt (pt **flogged**) (beat) fouetter; (sell Ⓐ) vendre.

flood /flʌd/ n inondation f; (fig) flot m. ● vt inonder. ● vi (building) être inondé; (river) déborder; (people: fig) affluer.

floodlight /ˈflʌdlaɪt/ n projecteur m. ● vt (pt **floodlit**) illuminer.

floor /flɔː(r)/ n sol m, plancher m; (for dancing) piste f; (storey) étage m. ● vt (knock down) terrasser; (baffle) stupéfier. ~**board** n planche f

flop /flɒp/ vi (pt **flopped**) (drop) s'affaler; (fail) échouer; (head) tomber. ● n ▣ échec m, fiasco m.

floppy /'flɒpɪ/ adj lâche, flasque. **~ (disk)** n disquette f.

florist /'flɒrɪst/ n fleuriste mf.

flounder /'flaʊndə(r)/ vi (animal, person) se débattre (in dans); (economy) stagner. ● n flet m; (US) poisson m plat.

flour /'flaʊə(r)/ n farine f.

flourish /'flʌrɪʃ/ vi prospérer. ● vt brandir. ● n geste m élégant.

flout /flaʊt/ vt se moquer de.

flow /fləʊ/ vi couler; (circulate) circuler; (traffic) s'écouler; (hang loosely) flotter; **~ in** affluer; **~ into** (of river) se jeter dans. ● n (of liquid, traffic) écoulement m; (of tide) flux m; (of orders, words: fig) flot m. **~ chart** n organigramme m.

flower /'flaʊə(r)/ n fleur f. ● vi fleurir.

flown /fləʊn/ →**FLY**.

flu /fluː/ n grippe f.

fluctuate /'flʌktjʊeɪt/ vi varier.

fluent /'fluːənt/ adj (style) aisé; **be ~ (in a language)** parler (une langue) couramment.

fluff /flʌf/ n peluche(s) f(pl). (down) duvet m.

fluid /'fluːɪd/ adj & n fluide (m).

fluke /fluːk/ n coup m de chance.

flung /flʌŋ/ →**FLING**.

fluoride /'flɔːraɪd/ n fluor m.

flush /flʌʃ/ vi rougir. ● vt nettoyer à grande eau; **~ the toilet** tirer la chasse d'eau; (in blush) rouger; (fig) excitation f. ● adj **~ with** (level with) au ras de. □ **~ out** chasser.

fluster /'flʌstə(r)/ n énerver.

flute /fluːt/ n flûte f.

flutter /'flʌtə(r)/ vi voleter; (of wings) battre. ● n (wings) batte-

ment m; (fig) agitation f; (bet ▣) pari m.

flux /flʌks/ n changement m continuel.

fly /flaɪ/ n mouche f; (of trousers) braguette f. ● vi (pt **flew**; pp **flown**) voler; (passengers) voyager en avion; (flag) flotter; (rush) filer. ● vt (aircraft) piloter; (passengers, goods) transporter par avion; (flag) arborer. □ **~ off** s'envoler.

flyer /'flaɪə(r)/ n (person) aviateur m; (circular) prospectus m.

flying /'flaɪŋ/ adj (saucer) volant; **with ~ colours** haut la main; **~ start** excellent départ m; **~ visit** visite f éclair (adj inv). ● n (activity) aviation f.

flyover /'flaɪəʊvə(r)/ n pont m (routier).

foal /fəʊl/ n poulain m.

foam /fəʊm/ n écume f, mousse f; **~ (rubber)** caoutchouc m mousse. ● vi écumer, mousser.

focus /'fəʊkəs/ n (pl **~es** or **-ci**) foyer m; (fig) centre m; **be in/out of ~** être/ne pas être au point. ● vt/i (faire) converger; (instrument) mettre au point; (with camera) faire la mise au point (**on** sur); (fig) (se) concentrer. **~ group** groupe m de discussion.

fodder /'fɒdə(r)/ n fourrage m.

foe /fəʊ/ n ennemi/-e m/f.

foetus /'fiːtəs/ n fœtus m.

fog /fɒg/ n brouillard m. ● vt/i (pt **fogged**) (window) (s')embuer.

foggy /'fɒgɪ/ adj brumeux; **it is ~** il fait du brouillard.

foil /fɔɪl/ n (tin foil) papier m d'aluminium; (deterrent) repoussoir m. ● vt (thwart) déjouer.

fold /fəʊld/ vt/i (paper, clothes) (se) plier; (arms) croiser; (fail) s'effondrer. ● n pli m; (for sheep) parc m à moutons; (Relig) bercail m. **folder** n (file) chemise f; (leaflet) dépliant m. **folding** adj pliant.

foliage /ˈfəʊlɪɪdʒ/ n feuillage m.

folk /fəʊk/ n gens mpl; ~**s** parents mpl. ● adj (dance) folklorique; (music) folk.

folklore /ˈfəʊklɔː(r)/ n folklore m.

follow /ˈfɒləʊ/ vt/i suivre; **it ~s that** il s'ensuit que; ~ **suit** en faire autant; ~ **up** (letter) donner suite à. **follower** n partisan m.

following /ˈfɒləʊɪŋ/ n partisans mpl. ● adj suivant; ~ **day** lendemain. ● prep à la suite de.

fond /fɒnd/ adj (loving) affectueux; (hope) cher; **be** ~ **of** aimer.

fondle /ˈfɒndl/ vt caresser.

fondness /ˈfɒndnɪs/ n affection f; (for things) attachement m.

food /fuːd/ n nourriture f; **French** ~ la cuisine française. ● adj alimentaire. ~ **processor** n robot m (ménager).

fool /fuːl/ n idiot/-e m/f. ● vt duper. ● vi ~ **around** faire l'idiot; **foolish** adj idiot.

foot /fʊt/ n (pl **feet**) pied m; (measure) pied m (=30.48 cm); (of stairs, page) bas m; **on** ~ à pied; **on** or **to one's feet** debout; **under sb's feet** dans les jambes de qn. ● vt (bill) payer.

foot-and-mouth disease n fièvre f aphteuse.

football /ˈfʊtbɔːl/ n (ball) ballon m; (game) football m. **footballer** n footballeur m.

foot: ~**bridge** n passerelle f; ~**hold** n prise f.

footing /ˈfʊtɪŋ/ n **on an equal** ~ sur un pied d'égalité; **be on a friendly** ~ **with sb** avoir des rapports amicaux avec qn; **lose one's** ~ perdre pied.

foot: ~**note** n note f (en bas de la page). ~**path** n (in countryside) sentier m; (in town) chemin m. ~**print** n empreinte f (de pied). ~**step** n pas m. ~**wear** n chaussures fpl.

for /fɔː(r)/

● preposition

····▸ pour; ~ **me** pour moi; **music** ~ **dancing** de la musique pour danser; **what is it** ~? ça sert à quoi?

····▸ (with a time period that is still continuing) depuis; **I've been waiting** ~ **two hours** j'attends depuis deux heures; **I haven't seen him** ~ **ten years** je ne l'ai pas vu depuis dix ans.

····▸ (with a time period that has ended) pendant; **I waited** ~ **two hours** j'ai attendu pendant deux heures.

····▸ (with a future time period) pour; **I'm going to Paris** ~ **six weeks** je vais à Paris pour six semaines.

····▸ (with distances) pendant; **I drove** ~ **50 kilometres** j'ai roulé pendant 50 kilomètres.

forbid /fəˈbɪd/ vt (pt **forbade**, pp **forbidden**) interdire, défendre (**sb to do** à qn de faire). ~ **sb sth** interdire or défendre qch à qn; **you are forbidden to leave** il vous est interdit de partir. **forbidding** adj menaçant.

force /fɔːs/ n force f; **come into** ~ entrer en vigueur; **the** ~**s** les forces fpl armées. ● vt forcer. □ ~ **into** faire entrer de force. ~ **on** imposer à. **forced** adj forcé.

force-feed vt (pt **-fed**) (person)

nourrir de force; (*animal*) gaver.

forceful /ˈfɔːsfl/ *adj* énergique.

ford /fɔːd/ *n* gué *m*. ● *vt* passer à gué.

forearm /ˈfɔːrɑːm/ *n* avant-bras *m inv*.

forecast /ˈfɔːkɑːst/ *vt* (*pt* forecast) prévoir. ● *n* weather ~ météo *f*.

forecourt /ˈfɔːkɔːt/ *n* (of garage) devant *m*; (of station) cour *f*.

forefinger /ˈfɔːfɪŋɡə(r)/ *n* index *m*.

forefront /ˈfɔːfrʌnt/ *n* at/in the ~ of à la pointe de.

foregone /ˈfɔːɡɒn/ *adj* it's a ~ conclusion c'est couru d'avance.

foreground /ˈfɔːɡraʊnd/ *n* premier plan *m*.

forehead /ˈfɒrɪd/ *n* front *m*.

foreign /ˈfɒrən/ *adj* étranger; (*trade*) extérieur; (*travel*) à l'étranger. **foreigner** *n* étranger/-ère *m/f*.

foreman /ˈfɔːmən/ *n* (*pl* **-men**) contremaître *m*.

foremost /ˈfɔːməʊst/ *adj* le plus éminent. ● *adv* first and ~ tout d'abord.

forensic /fəˈrensɪk/ *adj* médico-légal; ~ **medicine** médecine *f* légale.

foresee /fɔːˈsiː/ *vt* (*pt* **-saw.** *pp* **-seen**) prévoir.

forest /ˈfɒrɪst/ *n* forêt *f*. **forestry** *n* sylviculture *f*.

foretaste /ˈfɔːteɪst/ *n* avant-goût *m*.

forever /fəˈrevə(r)/ *adv* toujours.

foreword /ˈfɔːwɜːd/ *n* avant-propos *m inv*.

forfeit /ˈfɔːfɪt/ *n* (penalty) peine *f*; (in game) gage *m*. ● *vt* perdre.

forgave /fəˈɡeɪv/ →**FORGIVE**.

forge /fɔːdʒ/ *n* forge *f*. ● *vt* (metal, friendship) forger; (copy) contrefaire, falsifier. ● *vi* ~ ahead aller de l'a-

vant, avancer. **forger** *n* faussaire *m*.

forgery *n* faux *m*, contrefaçon *f*.

forget /fəˈɡet/ *vt*/*i* (*pt* forgot. *pp* forgotten) oublier; ~ **oneself** s'oublier. **forgetful** *adj* distrait. ~**-menot** *n* myosotis *m*.

forgive /fəˈɡɪv/ *vt* (*pt* forgave. *pp* forgiven) pardonner (sb for sth qch à qn).

fork /fɔːk/ *n* fourchette *f*; (for digging) fourche *f*; (in road) bifurcation *f*. ● *vi* (road) bifurquer; ~ **out** Ⓣ payer. **forked** *adj* fourchu. ~**-lift truck** *n* chariot *m* élévateur.

form /fɔːm/ *n* forme *f*; (document) formulaire *m*; (School) classe *f*; **on** ~ en forme. ● *vt*/*i* (se) former.

formal /ˈfɔːml/ *adj* officiel, en bonne et due forme; (*person*) compassé, cérémonieux; (*dress*) de cérémonie; (*denial*, *grammar*) formel; (*language*) soutenu. **formality** *n* cérémonial *m*; (requirement) formalité *f*.

format /ˈfɔːmæt/ *n* format *m*. ● *vt* (*pt* formatted) (disk) formater.

former /ˈfɔːmə(r)/ *adj* ancien; (first of two) premier. ● *n* the ~ celui-là, celle-là. **formerly** *adv* autrefois.

formula /ˈfɔːmjʊlə/ *n* (*pl* **-ae** or **-as**) formule *f*. **formulate** *vt* formuler.

fort /fɔːt/ *n* (Mil) fort *m*; **to hold the** ~ s'occuper de tout.

forth /fɔːθ/ *adv* from this day ~ à partir d'aujourd'hui; **and so** ~ et ainsi de suite; **go back and** ~ aller et venir.

forthcoming /fɔːθˈkʌmɪŋ/ *adj* à venir, prochain; (sociable Ⓣ) communicatif.

forthright /ˈfɔːθraɪt/ *adj* direct.

forthwith /fɔːθˈwɪθ/ *adv* sur-le-champ.

fortnight /ˈfɔːtnaɪt/ *n* quinze jours

mpl, quinzaine f.

fortnightly /ˈfɔːtnaɪtlɪ/ adj bimensuel. ● adv tous les quinze jours.

fortunate /ˈfɔːtʃənət/ adj heureux; **be** ~ avoir de la chance. **fortunately** adv heureusement.

fortune /ˈfɔːtʃuːn/ n fortune f; **make a** ~ faire fortune; **have the good** ~ **to** avoir la chance de. ~**-teller** n diseur/-euse m/f de bonne aventure.

forty /ˈfɔːtɪ/ adj & n quarante (m). ~ **winks** un petit somme.

forward /ˈfɔːwəd/ adj en avant; (advanced) précoce; (bold) effronté. ● n (Sport) avant m. ● adv en avant; **come** ~ se présenter; **go** ~ avancer. ● vt (letter, e-mail) faire suivre; (goods) expédier; (fig) favoriser. **forwardness** n précocité f. **forwards** adv en avant.

fossil /ˈfɒsl/ n & adj fossile (m).

foster /ˈfɒstə(r)/ vt (promote) encourager; (child) élever. ● adj (child, parent) adoptif; (family, home) de placement.

fought /fɔːt/ →FIGHT.

foul /faʊl/ adj (smell, weather) infect; (place, action) immonde; (language) ordurier. ● n (football) faute f. ● vt souiller, encrasser; ~ **up** 🔲 gâcher. ~**-mouthed** adj grossier.

found /faʊnd/ →FIND. ● vt fonder. **foundation** n fondation f; (basis) fondement m; (make-up) fond m de teint. **founder** n fondateur/-trice m/f.

fountain /ˈfaʊntɪn/ n fontaine f; ~**-pen** n stylo m à encre.

four /fɔː(r)/ adj & n quatre (m).

fourteen /fɔːˈtiːn/ adj & n quatorze (m).

fourth /fɔːθ/ adj & n quatrième (m).

four-wheel drive n (car)

fortnightly | freedom

quatre-quatre m.

fowl /faʊl/ n (one bird) poulet m; (group) volaille f.

fox /fɒks/ n renard m. ● vt (baffle) mystifier; (deceive) tromper.

fraction /ˈfrækʃn/ n fraction f.

fracture /ˈfræktʃə(r)/ n fracture f. ● vt/i (se) fracturer.

fragile /ˈfrædʒaɪl/ adj fragile.

fragment /ˈfrægmənt/ n fragment m.

fragrance /ˈfreɪɡrəns/ n parfum m.

frail /freɪl/ adj frêle.

frame /freɪm/ n (of building, boat) charpente f; (of picture) cadre m; (of window) châssis m; (of spectacles) monture f. ~ **of mind** humeur f. ● vt encadrer; (fig) formuler; (Jur, 🔲) monter un coup contre. ~**work** n structure f; (context) cadre m.

France /frɑːns/ n France f.

franchise /ˈfræntʃaɪz/ n (Pol) droit m de vote; (Comm) franchise f.

frank /fræŋk/ adj franc. ● vt affranchir. **frankly** adv franchement.

frantic /ˈfræntɪk/ adj frénétique. ~ **with** fou de.

fraternity /frəˈtɜːnətɪ/ n (bond) fraternité f; (group, club) confrérie f.

fraud /frɔːd/ n (deception) fraude f; (person) imposteur m. **fraudulent** adj frauduleux.

fray /freɪ/ n the ~ la bataille. ● vt/i (s')effilocher.

freckle /ˈfrekl/ n tache f de rousseur.

free /friː/ adj libre; (gratis) gratuit; (lavish) généreux; ~ **(of charge)** gratuit(ement); **a** ~ **hand** carte f blanche. ● vt (pt **freed**) libérer; (clear) dégager.

freedom /ˈfriːdəm/ n liberté f.

free: ~ **enterprise** n la libre entreprise. ~ **kick** n coup m franc. ~**lance** adj & n free-lance (mf), indépendant/-e (m/f).

freely /ˈfriːlɪ/ adv librement.

Freemason /ˈfriːmeɪsn/ n francmaçon m.

Freenet /ˈfriːnet/ n (Comput) Libertel m.

free: ~**phone**, ~ **number** n numéro m vert. ~**range** adj (eggs) de ferme.

Freeware /ˈfriːweə(r)/ n (Comput) Gratuiciel m.

freeway /ˈfriːweɪ/ n (US) autoroute f.

freeze /friːz/ vt/i (pt **froze**. pp **frozen**) geler; (Culin) (se) congeler; (wages) bloquer. ● n gel m. blocage m; ~**dried** adj lyophilisé.

freezer /ˈfriːzə(r)/ n congélateur m.

freezing /ˈfriːzɪŋ/ adj glacial; **below** ~ au-dessous de zéro.

freight /freɪt/ n fret m.

French /frentʃ/ adj français. ● n (Ling) français m; **the** ~ les Français mpl; ~ **bean** n haricot m vert; ~ **fries** npl frites fpl; ~**man** n Français m; ~**speaking** adj francophone; ~ **window** n porte-fenêtre f; ~**woman** n Française f.

frenzied /ˈfrenzɪd/ adj frénétique. **frenzy** n frénésie f.

frequent[1] /ˈfriːkwənt/ adj fréquent.

frequent[2] /frɪˈkwent/ vt fréquenter.

fresco /ˈfreskəʊ/ n fresque f.

fresh /freʃ/ adj frais; (different, additional) nouveau; (cheeky 🅸) culotté.

freshen /ˈfreʃn/ vi (weather) fraîchir. ~ **up** (person) se rafraîchir.

freshly /ˈfreʃlɪ/ adv nouvellement.

freshness /ˈfreʃnɪs/ n fraîcheur f.

freshwater /ˈfreʃwɔːtə(r)/ adj d'eau douce.

friction /ˈfrɪkʃn/ n friction f.

Friday /ˈfraɪdɪ/ n vendredi m.

fridge /frɪdʒ/ n frigo m.

fried /fraɪd/ ➔**FRY**. ● adj frit; ~ **eggs** œufs mpl sur le plat.

friend /frend/ n ami/-e m/f. **friendly** adj (**-ier, -iest**) amical, gentil. **friendship** n amitié f.

frieze /friːz/ n frise f.

fright /fraɪt/ n peur f; (person, thing) horreur f.

frighten /ˈfraɪtn/ vt effrayer; ~ **off** faire fuir. **frightened** adj effrayé; **be** ~**ed** avoir peur (of de). **frightening** adj effrayant.

frill /frɪl/ n (trimming) fanfreluche f; **with no** ~**s** très simple.

fringe /frɪndʒ/ n (edging, hair) frange f; (of area) bordure f; (of society) marge f ~ **benefits** npl avantages mpl sociaux.

frisk /frɪsk/ vt (search) fouiller.

fritter /ˈfrɪtə(r)/ n beignet m. ● vt ~ **away** gaspiller.

frivolity /frɪˈvɒlɪtɪ/ n frivolité f.

frizzy /ˈfrɪzɪ/ adj crépu.

fro ➔**TO AND FRO**.

frog /frɒg/ n grenouille f; **a** ~ **in one's throat** un chat dans la gorge.

frolic /ˈfrɒlɪk/ vi (pt **frolicked**) s'ébattre. ● n ébats mpl.

from /frɒm/ prep de; (with time, prices) à partir de, de; (habit, conviction) par; (according to) d'après; **take** ~ **sb** prendre à qn; **take** ~ **one's pocket** prendre dans sa poche.

front /frʌnt/ n (of car, train) avant m; (of garment, building) devant m; (Mil, Pol) front m; (of book, pamphlet) début m; (appearance: fig) façade f. ● adj de devant, avant inv; (first) premier; ~ **door** porte f d'entrée; **in** ~ **(of)** devant. **frontage** n façade f.

frontier /ˈfrʌntɪə(r)/ n frontière f.

frost /frɒst/ n gel m, gelée f; (on glass) givre m. ● vt/i (se) givrer. ~**bite** n gelure f.

frosty /ˈfrɒstɪ/ adj (weather, welcome) glacial; (window) givré.

froth /frɒθ/ n (on beer) mousse f; (on water) écume f. ● vi mousser, écumer.

frown /fraʊn/ vi froncer les sourcils; ~ **on** désapprouver. ● n froncement m de sourcils.

froze /frəʊz/ ⇒FREEZE.

frozen /ˈfrəʊzn/ ⇒FREEZE. ● adj congelé.

fruit /fruːt/ n fruit m; (collectively) fruits mpl. **fruitful** adj (discussions) fructueux. ~ **machine** n machine f à sous.

frustrate /frʌˈstreɪt/ vt (plan) faire échouer; (person: Psych) frustrer; (upset 🔢) exaspérer. **frustration** n (Psych) frustration f; (disappointment) déception f.

fry /fraɪ/ vt/i (pt **fried**) (faire) frire. **frying-pan** n poêle f (à frire).

FTP abbr (**File Transfer Protocol**) (Internet) protocole m FTP.

fudge /fʌdʒ/ n caramel m mou. ● vt (issue) esquiver.

fuel /ˈfjuːəl/ n combustible m; (for car engine) carburant m. ● vt (pt **fuelled**) alimenter en combustible.

fugitive /ˈfjuːdʒətɪv/ n & a fugitif/-ive (m/f).

fulfil /fʊlˈfɪl/ vt (pt **fulfilled**) accomplir, réaliser; (condition) remplir; ~ **oneself** s'épanouir. **fulfilling** adj satisfaisant. **fulfilment** n réalisation f, épanouissement m.

full /fʊl/ adj plein de; (bus,

hotel) complet; (programme) chargé; (skirt) ample; **be** ~ **(up)** n'avoir plus faim; **at** ~ **speed** à toute vitesse. ● n in ~ intégralement; **to the** ~ complètement. ~ **back** n (Sport) arrière m. ~ **moon** n pleine lune f. ~ **name** n nom m et prénom m. ~**scale** adj (drawing etc.) grandeur nature inv; (fig) de grande envergure. ~ **stop** n point m. ~**time** adj & adv à plein temps.

fully /ˈfʊlɪ/ adv complètement; ~ **fledged** (member, citizen) à part entière.

fume /fjuːm/ vi rager. **fumes** npl émanations fpl, vapeurs fpl.

fun /fʌn/ n amusement m; **be** ~ être chouette; **for** ~ pour rire; **make** ~ **of** se moquer de.

function /ˈfʌŋkʃn/ n (purpose, duty) fonction f; (event) réception f. ● vi fonctionner.

fund /fʌnd/ n fonds m. ● vt fournir les fonds pour.

fundamental /fʌndəˈmentl/ adj fondamental. **fundamentalist** n intégriste mf.

funeral /ˈfjuːnərəl/ n enterrement m. ● adj funèbre.

funfair /ˈfʌnfeə(r)/n fête f foraine.

fungus /ˈfʌŋɡəs/ n (pl **-gi**) (plant) champignon m; (mould) moisissure f.

funnel /ˈfʌnl/ n (for pouring) entonnoir m; (of ship) cheminée f.

funny /ˈfʌnɪ/ adj (**-ier, -iest**) drôle; (odd) bizarre.

fur /fɜː(r)/ n (for garment) fourrure f; (on animal) poils mpl; (in kettle) tartre m.

furious /ˈfjʊərɪəs/ adj furieux.

furnace /ˈfɜːnɪs/ n fourneau m.

furnish /ˈfɜːnɪʃ/ vt (room) meubler; (supply) fournir. **furnishings** npl ameublement m.

furniture /'fɜːnɪtʃə(r)/ n meubles mpl, mobilier m.

furry /'fɜːrɪ/ adj (animal) à fourrure; (toy) en peluche.

further /'fɜːðə(r)/ adj plus éloigné; (additional) supplémentaire. ● adv plus loin; (more) davantage. ● vt avancer. ~ **education** n formation f continue.

furthermore /fɜːðə'mɔː(r)/ adv en outre, de plus.

furthest /'fɜːðɪst/ adj le plus éloigné. ● adv le plus loin.

fury /'fjʊərɪ/ n fureur f.

fuse /fjuːz/ vt/i (melt) fondre; (unite: fig) fusionner; ~ **the lights** faire sauter les plombs. ● n (of plug) fusible m; (of bomb) amorce f.

fuss /fʌs/ n (when upset) histoire(s) f(pl); (when excited) agitation f; **make a ~** faire des histoires. s'agiter; (about food) faire des chichis; **make a ~ of** faire grand cas de. ● vi s'agiter. **fussy** adj (finicky) tatillon; (hard to please) difficile.

future /'fjuːtʃə(r)/ adj futur. ● n avenir m; (Gram) futur m; **in ~** à l'avenir.

fuzzy /'fʌzɪ/ adj (hair) crépu; (photograph) flou; (person 🆃) à l'esprit confus.

Gg

Gaelic /'geɪlɪk/ n gaélique m.

gag /gæg/ n (on mouth) bâillon m; (joke) blague f. ● vt (pt **gagged**) bâillonner.

gain /geɪn/ vt (respect, support) gagner; (speed, weight) prendre. ● vi (of clock) avancer. ● n (increase)

augmentation f (**in** de); (profit) gain m.

galaxy /'gæləksɪ/ n galaxie f.

gale /geɪl/ n tempête f.

gallery /'gælərɪ/ n galerie f; (art) ~ musée m.

Gallic /'gælɪk/ adj français.

gallon /'gælən/ n gallon m (imperial = 4.546 litres; Amer. = 3.785 litres).

gallop /'gæləp/ n galop m. ● vi (pt **galloped**) galoper.

galore /gə'lɔː(r)/ adv (prizes, bargains) en abondance; (drinks, sandwiches) à gogo 🆃.

gamble /'gæmbl/ vt/i jouer. ~ **on** miser sur. ● n (venture) entreprise f risquée; (bet) pari m; (risk) risque m. **gambling** n jeu m.

game /geɪm/ n jeu m; (football) match m; (tennis) partie f; (animals, birds) gibier m. ● adj (brave) courageux. ~ **for** prêt à. ~**keeper** n gardechasse m.

gammon /'gæmən/ n jambon m.

gang /gæŋ/ n (of youths) bande f; (of workmen) équipe f. ● vi ~ **up** se liguer (**on, against** contre).

gangmaster n gangmaster m, chef m d'équipe d'ouvriers saisonniers.

gangway /'gæŋweɪ/ n passage m; (aisle) allée f; (of ship) passerelle f.

gaol /dʒeɪl/ n & vt ➡JAIL.

Gap Year La prise d'une
année sabbatique est une pratique répandue chez les jeunes britanniques avant d'entrer à l'université. Certains trouvent un stage dans une entreprise et en profitent pour mettre de l'argent de côté pour leurs études, mais beaucoup partent travailler ou étudier à l'étranger ou faire le tour du monde.

gap | genetics

gap /gæp/ n trou m, vide m; (in time) intervalle m; (in education) lacune f; (difference) écart m.

gape /geɪp/ vi rester bouche bée. **gaping** adj béant.

garage /ˈgærɑːʒ/ n garage m. ● vt mettre au garage.

garbage /ˈgɑːbɪdʒ/ n (US) ordures fpl.

garden /ˈgɑːdn/ n jardin m. ● vi jardiner. **gardener** n jardinier/-ière m/f. **gardening** n jardinage m.

gargle /ˈgɑːgl/ vi se gargariser.

garish /ˈgeərɪʃ/ adj (clothes) tape-à-l'œil.

garland /ˈgɑːlənd/ n guirlande f.

garlic /ˈgɑːlɪk/ n ail m.

garment /ˈgɑːmənt/ n vêtement m.

garnish /ˈgɑːnɪʃ/ vt garnir (with de). ● n garniture f.

garter /ˈgɑːtə(r)/ n jarretière f.

gas /gæs/ n (pl ~es) gaz m; (Med) anesthésie f; (petrol: US) essence f. ● adj (mask, pipe) à gaz. ● vt asphyxier; (Mil) gazer.

gash /gæʃ/ n entaille f. ● vt entailler.

gasoline /ˈgæsəliːn/ n (petrol: US) essence f.

gasp /gɑːsp/ vi haleter; (in surprise: fig) avoir le souffle coupé. ● n halètement m.

gate /geɪt/ n (in garden, airport) porte f; (of field, level crossing) barrière f. **~way** n porte f; (Internet) passerelle f.

gather /ˈgæðə(r)/ vt (people, objects) rassembler; (pick up) ramasser; (flowers) cueillir; (fig) comprendre; **~ speed** prendre de la vitesse; (sewing) froncer. ● vi (people) se rassembler; (pile up) s'accumuler. **gathering** n réunion f.

gauge /geɪdʒ/ n jauge f, indicateur m. ● vt (speed, distance) jauger; (reaction, mood) évaluer.

gaunt /gɔːnt/ adj décharné.

gauze /gɔːz/ n gaze f.

gave /geɪv/ ➡GIVE.

gay /geɪ/ adj (joyful) gai; (homosexual) gay inv. ● n gay m/f.

gaze /geɪz/ vi ~ (at) regarder (fixement). ● n regard m (fixe).

GB abbr ➡GREAT BRITAIN.

gear /gɪə(r)/ n (equipment) matériel m; (Tech) engrenage m; (Auto) vitesse f; **in** ~ en prise. **out of** ~ au point mort. ● vt **to be geared to** s'adresser à. **~box** n (Auto) boîte f de vitesses. **~lever**, (US) **~shift** n levier m de vitesse.

geese /giːs/ ➡GOOSE.

gel /dʒel/ n (for hair) gel m.

gem /dʒem/ n pierre f précieuse.

Gemini /ˈdʒemɪnaɪ/ n Gémeaux mpl.

gender /ˈdʒendə(r)/ n (Ling) genre m; (of person) sexe m.

gene /dʒiːn/ n gène m. **~ library** n génothèque f.

general /ˈdʒenrəl/ adj général. ● n général m; **in** ~ en général.

general election n élections fpl législatives.

generalization /dʒenrəlaɪˈzeɪʃn/ n généralisation f. **generalize** vt/i généraliser.

general practitioner n (Med) généraliste m.

generate /ˈdʒenəreɪt/ vt produire.

generation /dʒenəˈreɪʃn/ n génération f.

generator /ˈdʒenəreɪtə(r)/ n (Electr) groupe m électrogène.

generosity /dʒenəˈrɒsətɪ/ n générosité f. **generous** adj généreux; (plentiful) copieux.

genetics /dʒɪˈnetɪks/ n génétique f.

Geneva /dʒɪˈniːvə/ n Genève.

genial /ˈdʒiːnɪəl/ adj affable, sympathique.

genitals /ˈdʒenɪtlz/ npl organes mpl génitaux.

genius /ˈdʒiːnɪəs/ n (pl **~es**) génie m.

genome /ˈdʒiːnəʊm/ n génome m.

gentle /ˈdʒentl/ adj (mild, kind) doux; (pressure, breeze) léger; (reminder, hint) discret.

gentleman /ˈdʒentlmən/ n (pl **-men**) (man) monsieur m; (well-bred) gentleman m.

gently /ˈdʒentlɪ/ adv doucement.

gents /dʒents/ npl (toilets) toilettes fpl; (on sign) 'Messieurs'.

genuine /ˈdʒenjʊɪn/ adj (reason, motive) vrai; (jewel, substance) véritable; (person, belief) sincère.

geography /dʒɪˈɒɡrəfɪ/ n géographie f.

geology /dʒɪˈɒlədʒɪ/ n géologie f.

geometry /dʒɪˈɒmɪtrɪ/ n géométrie f.

geriatric /dʒerɪˈætrɪk/ adj gériatrique.

germ /dʒɜːm/ n (Med) microbe m.

German /ˈdʒɜːmən/ n (person) Allemand/-e m/f; (Ling) allemand m. ● adj allemand.

German measles n rubéole f.

Germany /ˈdʒɜːmənɪ/ n Allemagne f.

gesture /ˈdʒestʃə(r)/ n geste m.

---

get /get/

past **got**; past participle **got**, **gotten** (US); present participle **getting**

● transitive verb
····▸ recevoir. **we got a letter**

nous avons reçu une lettre.

····▸ (obtain) **I got a job in Paris** j'ai trouvé un travail à Paris. **I'll ~ sth to eat at the airport** je mangerai qch à l'aéroport.

····▸ (buy) acheter. **~ sb a present** acheter un cadeau à qn.

····▸ (achieve) obtenir. **he got it right** il a obtenu le bon résultat. **~ good grades** avoir de bonnes notes.

····▸ (fetch) chercher. **go and ~ a chair** va chercher une chaise.

····▸ (transport) prendre. **we can ~ the bus** on peut prendre le bus.

····▸ (understand 𝐈) comprendre. **now let me ~ this right** alors si je comprends bien...

····▸ (experience) **~ a surprise** être surpris. **~ a shock** avoir un choc.

····▸ (illness) **~ measles** attraper la rougeole. **~ a cold** s'enrhumer.

····▸ (ask or persuade) **~ him to call me** dis-lui de m'appeler. **I'll ~ her to help me** je lui demanderai de m'aider.

····▸ (cause to be done) **~ a TV repaired** faire réparer une télévision. **~ one's hair cut** se faire couper les cheveux.

● intransitive verb
····▸ devenir. **he's getting old** il vieillit; **it's getting late** il se fait tard.

····▸ (in passives) **~ married** se marier. **~ hurt** être blessé.

····▸ (arrive) arriver. **~ to the airport** arriver à l'aéroport. □ **~ about** (person) se déplacer. **~ along** (manage) se

débrouiller; (progress) avancer.
~ **along with** s'entendre avec.
~ **at** (reach) atteindre; (imply)
vouloir dire; (escape) s'échapper. ~ **back** vi revenir. ● vt récupérer. ~ **by** vi (manage) se débrouiller. ● vt (pass) passer. ~ **down** vt/i descendre. ● vt (depress) déprimer. ~ **in** entrer. ~ **into** (car) monter dans; (dress) mettre. ~ **off** vt (bus) descendre; (remove) enlever. ● vi (from bus) descendre; (leave) partir; (Jur) être acquitté. ~ **on** vi (to bus) monter; (succeed) réussir. ● vt (bus) monter. ~ **on with** (person) s'entendre avec; (job) attaquer. ~ **out** sortir. ~ **out of** (fig) se soustraire. ~ **over** (illness) se remettre de. ~ **round** (rule) contourner; (person) entortiller. ~ **through** vi passer; (on phone) ~ **through to sb** avoir qn. ● vt traverser. ~ **up** se lever. ~ **up** to faire.

getaway /ˈgetəweɪ/ n fuite f.

ghastly /ˈgɑːstlɪ/ adj (**-ier, -iest**) affreux.

gherkin /ˈgɜːkɪn/ n cornichon m.

ghetto /ˈgetəʊ/ n ghetto m.

ghost /gəʊst/ n fantôme m.

giant /ˈdʒaɪənt/ n & adj géant (m).

gibberish /ˈdʒɪbərɪʃ/ n baragouin m, charabia m.

giblets /ˈdʒɪblɪts/ npl abats mpl.

giddy /ˈgɪdɪ/ adj (**-ier, -iest**) vertigineux. **be** or **feel** ~ avoir le vertige.

gift /gɪft/ n (present) cadeau m; (ability) don m.

gifted /ˈgɪftɪd/ adj doué.

gift wrap n papier m cadeau.

gigantic /dʒaɪˈgæntɪk/ adj gigantesque.

giggle /ˈgɪgl/ vi ricaner (sottement), glousser. ● n ricanement m; **the** ~**s** le fou rire.

gimmick /ˈgɪmɪk/ n truc m.

gin /dʒɪn/ n gin m.

ginger /ˈdʒɪndʒə(r)/ n gingembre m. ● adj (hair) roux. ~ **beer** n boisson f gazeuse au gingembre. ~**bread** n pain m d'épices.

gingerly /ˈdʒɪndʒəlɪ/ adv avec précaution.

giraffe /dʒɪˈrɑːf/ n girafe f.

girl /gɜːl/ n (child) (petite) fille f; (young woman) (jeune) fille f. ~ **band** n girls band m. ~**friend** n amie f; (of boy) petite amie f.

giro /ˈdʒaɪrəʊ/ n virement m bancaire; (cheque) mandat m.

gist /dʒɪst/ n essentiel m.

give /gɪv/ vt (pt **gave**; pp **given**) donner; (gesture) faire; (laugh, sigh) pousser; ~ **sb sth** donner qch à qn. ● vi donner; (yield) céder; (stretch) se détendre. ● n élasticité f. ▢ ~ **away** (donner); (secret) trahir; ~ **back** rendre. ~ **in** (yield) céder (to à). ~ **off** (heat, fumes) dégager; (signal, scent) émettre. ~ **out** vt distribuer. ~ **over** (devote) consacrer; (stop ⚀) cesser; ~ **up** vt/i (renounce) renoncer (à); (yield) céder. ~ **oneself up** se rendre. ~ **way** céder; (collapse) s'effondrer.

given /ˈgɪvn/ ➞GIVE. ● adj donné. ~ **name** n prénom m.

glad /glæd/ adj content. **gladly** adv avec plaisir.

glamorous /ˈglæmərəs/ adj séduisant, ensorcelant.

glamour, (US) **glamor** /ˈglæmə(r)/ n enchantement m, séduction f.

g

glance /glɑːns/ n coup m d'œil.
● vi ~ **at** jeter un coup d'œil à.

gland /glænd/ n glande f.

glare /gleə(r)/ vi briller très fort. ~
at regarder d'un air furieux. ● n (of
lights) éclat m (aveuglant); (stare:
fig) regard m furieux. **glaring** adj
(dazzling) éblouissant; (obvious)
flagrant.

glass /glɑːs/ n verre m. **glasses** npl
(spectacles) lunettes fpl.

glaze /gleɪz/ vt (door) vitrer; (pottery) vernisser. ● n vernis m.

gleam /gliːm/ n lueur f. ● vi luire.

glide /glaɪd/ vi glisser; (of plane)
planer. **glider** n planeur m.

glimpse /glɪmps/ n (insight)
aperçu m; **catch a ~ of** entrevoir.

glitter /ˈglɪtə(r)/ vi scintiller. ● n
scintillement m.

global /ˈgləʊbl/ adj (world-wide)
mondial; (allembracing) global. ~-
warming n réchauffement m de la
planète.

globalization /gləʊbəlaɪˈzeɪʃən/
n globalisation f.

globe /gləʊbəlaɪˈzeɪʃən/ n globe m.

gloom /gluːm/ n obscurité f; (sadness: fig) tristesse f. **gloomy** adj
triste; (pessimistic) pessimiste.

glorious /ˈglɔːrɪəs/ adj splendide;
(deed, hero) glorieux.

glory /ˈglɔːrɪ/ n gloire f; (beauty)
splendeur f. ● vi ~ **in** être très
fier de.

gloss /glɒs/ n lustre m, brillant m.
● adj brillant. ● vi ~ **over** (make
light of) glisser sur; (cover up) dissimuler.

glossary /ˈglɒsərɪ/ n glossaire m.

glossy /ˈglɒsɪ/ adj brillant.

glove /glʌv/ n gant m. ~ **compartment** n (Auto) boîte f à gants.

glow /gləʊ/ vi (fire) rougeoyer;

(person, eyes) rayonner. ● n rou-
geoiement m, éclat m. **glowing** adj
(report) enthousiaste.

glucose /ˈgluːkəʊs/ n glucose m.

glue /gluː/ n colle f. ● vt (pres p glu-
ing) coller.

GM abbr (genetically modified)
transgénique.

gnaw /nɔː/ vt/i ronger.

GNP abbr (**Gross National Product**)
produit m national brut, PNB m.

---

go /gəʊ/

present go, goes; *past* went; *past
participle* gone

● *intransitive verb*

····▶ aller; ~ **to school/town/
market** aller à l'école/en ville/
au marché. ~ **for a swim/
walk** aller nager/se promener.

····▶ (leave) s'en aller. **I must be
~ing** il faut que je m'en aille.

····▶ (vanish) **the money's gone**
il n'y a plus d'argent. **my
bike's gone** mon vélo n'est
plus là.

····▶ (work, function) marcher. **is
the car ~ing?** est-ce que la
voiture marche?

····▶ (become) devenir. ~ **blind**
devenir aveugle. ~ **pale/red**
pâlir/rougir.

····▶ (turn out, progress) aller.
how's it going? comment ça
va? **how did the exam ~ ?**
comment s'est passé l'examen?

····▶ (in future tenses) **be ~ing
to do** aller faire.

● *noun*

····▶ (turn) tour m; (try) essai m;

have a ~! essaie!; **full of ~** 🆔 dynamique.

□ **go across** traverser. **go after** poursuivre. **go away** partir. ~ **away!** va-t'en!, allez-vous-en! **go back** retourner. ~ **back in** rentrer. ~ **back to work** reprendre le travail. **go down** (quality, price) baisser; (person) descendre; (sun) se coucher. **go in** entrer. **go in for** (exam) se présenter à. **go off** (leave) partir; (bomb) exploser; (alarm clock) sonner; (milk) tourner; (light) s'éteindre. **go on** (continue) continuer; (light) s'allumer; ~ **on doing** continuer à faire. **what's ~ing on?** qu'est-ce qui se passe? **go out** sortir; (light, fire) s'éteindre. **go over** vérifier. **go round** (be enough) être assez. ~ **round to see sb** passer voir qn. **go through** (check) examiner; (search) fouiller; ~ **through a difficult time** traverser une période difficile. **go together** aller ensemble. **go under** (sink) couler; (fail) échouer. **go up** (person) monter; (price, salary) augmenter. **go without** ne pas se passer de.

go-ahead /'gəʊəhed/ n feu m vert. ● adj dynamique.

goal /gəʊl/ n but m. ~**keeper** n gardien m de but. ~**post** n poteau m de but.

goat /gəʊt/ n chèvre f.

gobble /'gɒbl/ vt engouffrer.

go-between /'gəʊbɪtwiːn/ n intermédiaire mf.

god /gɒd/ n dieu m. ~**child** n (pl -children) filleul/-e m/f. ~**daughter** n filleule f.

goddess /'gɒdɪs/ n déesse f.

god: ~**father** n parrain m.

~**mother** n marraine f. ~**send** n aubaine f. ~**son** n filleul m.

goggles /'gɒglz/ npl lunettes fpl (protectrices).

going /'gəʊɪŋ/ n **it is slow/hard ~** c'est lent/difficile. ● adj (price, rate) actuel.

go-kart /'gəʊkɑːt/ n kart m.

gold /gəʊld/ n or m. ● adj en or, d'or.

golden /'gəʊldən/ adj en or, d'or; (in colour) doré; (opportunity) unique.

gold: ~**fish** n poisson m rouge. ~**plated** adj plaqué or. ~**smith** n orfèvre m.

golf /gɒlf/ n golf m. ~**course** n terrain m de golf.

gone /gɒn/ ⇒**GO**. ● adj parti. ~ **six o'clock** six heures passées. **the butter's all ~** il n'y a plus de beurre.

good /gʊd/ adj (better, best) bon; (weather) beau; (well-behaved) sage; **as ~ as** (almost) pratiquement. **that's ~ of you** c'est gentil (de ta part). **be ~ with** savoir s'y prendre avec. **feel ~** se sentir bien. **it is ~ for you** ça vous fait du bien. ● n bien; **do ~** faire du bien. **is it any ~?** est-ce que c'est bien? **it's no ~** ça ne vaut rien. **it is no ~ shouting** ça ne sert à rien de crier. **for ~** pour toujours. ~ **afternoon** interj bonjour. ~**bye** interj & n au revoir (m inv). ~ **evening** interj bonsoir. **G~ Friday** n Vendredi m saint. ~**looking** adj beau. ~ **morning** interj bonjour. ~**natured** adj gentil.

goodness /'gʊdnɪs/ n bonté f; **my ~!** mon Dieu!

goodnight interj bonsoir, bonne nuit.

goods /gʊdz/ npl marchandises fpl.

goodwill /gʊd'wɪl/ n bonne volonté f.

google® /'gu:gl/vt/i chercher sur (le moteur de recherche) Google®, googler.

goose /gu:s/ n (pl **geese**) oie f.
gooseberry n groseille f à maquereau. ~**pimples** npl chair f de poule.

gorge /gɔ:dʒ/ n (Geog) gorge f. ● vt ~ oneself se gaver (**on** de).

gorgeous /'gɔ:dʒəs/ adj magnifique, splendide, formidable.

gorilla /gə'rɪlə/ n gorille m.

gory /'gɔ:rɪ/ adj (-**ier**, -**iest**) sanglant; (horrific: fig) horrible.

gospel /'gɒspl/ n évangile m; **the** G~ l'Évangile m.

gossip /'gɒsɪp/ n bavardages mpl, commérages mpl; (person) bavard·e m/f. ● vi bavarder.

got /gɒt/ ➞**GET**. ● **have** ~ avoir. **have** ~ **to** do devoir faire.

govern /'gʌvn/ vt/i gouverner. **governess** n gouvernante f. **government** n gouvernement m. **governor** n gouverneur m.

gown /gaʊn/ n robe f; (of judge, teacher) toge f.

GP abbr ➞**GENERAL PRACTITIONER**.

GPS abbr (Global Positioning System) GPS m.

grab /ɡræb/ vt (pt **grabbed**) saisir.

grace /ɡreɪs/ n grâce f. ● vt (honour) honorer; (adorn) orner. **graceful** adj gracieux.

gracious /'ɡreɪʃəs/ adj (kind) bienveillant; (elegant) élégant.

grade /ɡreɪd/ n catégorie f; (of goods) qualité f; (on scale) grade m; (school mark) note f; (class: US) classe f. ● vt classer; (school work) noter. ~ **school** n (US) école f primaire.

gradual /'ɡrædʒʊəl/ adj progressif, graduel. **gradually** adv progressivement, peu à peu.

graduate¹ /'ɡrædʒʊət/ n (Univ) diplômé·e m/f.

graduate² /'ɡrædʒʊeɪt/ vi obtenir son diplôme. ● vt graduer. **graduation** n remise f des diplômes.

graffiti /ɡrə'fi:tɪ/ npl graffiti mpl.

graft /ɡrɑ:ft/ n (Med, Bot) greffe f; (work) boulot m. ● vt greffer (**on** to sur); (work) trimer.

grain /ɡreɪn/ n (seed, quantity, texture) grain m; (in wood) fibre f.

gram /ɡræm/ n gramme m.

grammar /'ɡræmə(r)/ n grammaire f.

grand /ɡrænd/ adj magnifique; (duke, chorus) grand.

grandad /'ɡrændæd/ n 🅸 papy m.

grand: ~**child** n (girl) petite-fille f; (boy) petit-fils m; **her** ~**children** ses petits-enfants mpl. ~**daughter** n petite-fille f. ~**father** n grand-père m. ~**ma** n ➞**GRANNY**. ~**mother** n grandmère f. ~**parents** npl grandsparents mpl. ~**piano** n piano m à queue. ~**son** n petit-fils m. ~**stand** n tribune f.

granny /'ɡrænɪ/ n 🅸 mémé f, mamie f.

grant /ɡrɑ:nt/ vt (permission) accorder; (request) accéder à; (admit) admettre (**that** que); **take sth for** ~**ed** considérer qch comme une chose acquise. ● n subvention f; (Univ) bourse f.

granule /'ɡrænju:l/ n (of sugar, salt) grain m; (of coffee) granulé m.

grape /ɡreɪp/ n grain m de raisin. ~**s** raisin(s) m (pl).

grapefruit /'ɡreɪpfru:t/ n inv pamplemousse m.

graph /ɡrɑ:f/ n graphique m.

graphic /'ɡræfɪk/ adj (arts) graphique; (fig) vivant, explicite. **graphics** npl (Comput) graphiques mpl.

grasp /ɡrɑ:sp/ vt saisir. ● n (hold)

prise *f*: (strength of hand) poigne *f*: (reach) portée *f*; (fig) compréhension *f*.

grass /grɑːs/ *n* herbe *f*. **∼hopper** *n* sauterelle *f*. **∼land** *n* prairie *f*.

grass roots *npl* peuple *m*. ● *adj* (movement) populaire; (support) de base.

grate /greɪt/ *n* (hearth) âtre *m*; (fire basket) grille *f*. ● *vt* râper. ● *vi* grincer.

grateful /ˈɡreɪtfl/ *adj* reconnaissant.

grater /ˈɡreɪtə(r)/ *n* râpe *f*.

gratified /ˈɡrætɪfaɪd/ *adj* très heureux. **gratify** *vt* faire plaisir à.

grating /ˈɡreɪtɪŋ/ *n* (bars) grille *f*; (noise) grincement *m*.

gratitude /ˈɡrætɪtjuːd/ *n* reconnaissance *f*.

gratuity /ɡrəˈtjuːətɪ/ *n* (tip) pourboire *m*; (bounty; Mil) prime *f*.

grave¹ /ɡreɪv/ *n* tombe *f*. ● *adj* (serious) grave.

grave² /ɡrɑːv/ *adj* ∼ accent accent *m* grave.

gravel /ˈɡrævl/ *n* graviers *mpl*.

grave: **∼stone** *n* pierre *f* tombale. **∼yard** *n* cimetière *m*.

gravity /ˈɡrævətɪ/ *n* (seriousness) gravité *f*; (force) pesanteur *f*.

gravy /ˈɡreɪvɪ/ *n* jus *m* (de viande).

gray /ɡreɪ/ *adj & n* ➡GREY.

graze /ɡreɪz/ *vi* (eat) paître. ● *vt* (touch) frôler; (scrape) écorcher. ● *n* écorchure *f*.

grease /ɡriːs/ *n* graisse *f*. ● *vt* graisser. **greasy** *adj* graisseux.

great /ɡreɪt/ *adj* grand; (very good 🔢) génial 🔢, formidable 🔢; (grandfather, grandmother) arrière.

Great Britain *n* Grande-Bretagne *f*.

greatly /ˈɡreɪtlɪ/ *adv* (very) très;

(much) beaucoup.

Greece /ɡriːs/ *n* Grèce *f*.

greed /ɡriːd/ *n* avidité *f*; (for food) gourmandise *f*. **greedy** *adj* avide; gourmand.

Greek /ɡriːk/ *n* (person) Grec/-que *m/f*; (Ling) grec *m*. ● *adj* grec.

green /ɡriːn/ *adj* vert; (fig) naïf. ● *n* vert *m*; (grass) pelouse *f*; (golf) green *m*. **∼s** légumes *mpl* verts. **∼grocer** *n* marchand/-e *m/f* de fruits et légumes.

Green Card Document qui permet à un étranger de vivre et de travailler aux États-Unis, et qui lui donne les mêmes droits que ceux d'un citoyen américain, à l'exception du droit de vote. Les services d'immigration américains distribuent 50 000 green cards par an au moyen d'une loterie à laquelle participent des millions de candidats.

---

greenhouse *n* serre *f*; ∼ **effect** effet *m* de serre.

greet /ɡriːt/ *vt* (welcome) accueillir; (address politely) saluer. **greeting** *n* accueil *m*.

greetings /ˈɡriːtɪŋz/ *interj* salutations 🔢 ● *npl* (Christmas) vœux *mpl*. ∼ **card** *n* carte *f* de vœux.

grew /ɡruː/ ➡GROW.

grey /ɡreɪ/ *adj* gris; (fig) triste; **go** ∼ (hair, person) grisonner. ● *n* gris *m*. **∼hound** *n* lévrier *m*.

grid /ɡrɪd/ *n* grille *f*; (network; Electr) réseau *m*.

grief /ɡriːf/ *n* chagrin *m*; **come to** ∼ (person) avoir un malheur; (fail) tourner mal.

grievance /ˈɡriːvns/ *n* griefs *mpl*.

grieve /ɡriːv/ *vt/i* (s')affliger; ∼ **for** pleurer.

grill /grɪl/ n (cooking device) gril m; (food) grillade f; (Auto) calandre f. ● vt/i (faire) griller; (interrogate) mettre sur la sellette.

grim /grɪm/ adj sinistre.

grimace /grɪˈmeɪs/ n grimace f. ● vi grimacer.

grime /graɪm/ n crasse f.

grin /grɪn/ vi (pt **grinned**) sourire. ● n (large) sourire m.

grind /graɪnd/ vt (pt **ground**) (grain) écraser; (coffee) moudre; (sharpen) aiguiser; ∼ **one's teeth** grincer des dents. ● vi ∼ **to a halt** s'immobiliser. ● n corvée f.

grip /grɪp/ vt (pt **gripped**) saisir; (interest) passionner. ● n prise f; (strength of hand) poigne f; **come to** ∼**s with** en venir aux prises avec.

grisly /ˈgrɪzlɪ/ adj (**-ier, -iest**) (remains) macabre; (sight) horrible.

gristle /ˈgrɪsl/ n cartilage m.

grit /grɪt/ n (for roads) sable m; (fig) courage m. ● vt (pt **gritted**) (road) sabler; (teeth) serrer.

groan /grəʊn/ vi gémir. ● n gémissement m.

grocer /ˈgrəʊsə(r)/ n (person) épicier/-ière m/f; (shop) épicerie f. **groceries** npl (shopping) courses fpl; (goods) épicerie f. **grocery** n (shop) épicerie f.

groin /grɔɪn/ n aine f.

groom /gruːm/ n marié m; (for horses) palefrenier/-ière m/f. ● vt (horse) panser; (fig) préparer.

groove /gruːv/ n (for door etc.) rainure f; (in record) sillon m.

grope /grəʊp/ vi tâtonner. ∼ **for** chercher à tâtons.

gross /grəʊs/ adj (behaviour) vulgaire; (Comm) brut. ● n inv grosse f.

grotto /ˈgrɒtəʊ/ n (pl ∼**es**) grotte f.

grouch /graʊtʃ/ vi (grumble 🗊) rouspéter, râler.

ground[1] /graʊnd/ n terre f, sol m; (area) terrain m; (reason) raison f; (Electr, US) masse f; ∼**s** terres fpl, parc m; (of coffee) marc m; **on the** ∼ **par terre.** lose ∼ perdre du terrain. ● vt/i (Naut) échouer; (aircraft) retenir au sol.

ground[2] /graʊnd/ ⟶GRIND. ● adj ∼ **beef** (US) bifteck m haché.

ground: ∼ **floor** n rez-de-chaussée m inv. ∼**work** n travail m préparatoire.

group /gruːp/ n groupe m. ● vt/i (se) grouper. ∼**ware** n (Comput) logiciel m de groupe.

grovel /ˈgrɒvl/ vi (pt **grovelled**) ramper.

grow /grəʊ/ vi (pt **grew**; pp **grown**) (person) grandir; (plant) pousser; (become) devenir; (crime) augmenter. ● vt cultiver. ∼ **up** devenir adulte, grandir. **grower** n cultivateur/-trice m/f.

growl /graʊl/ vi (dog) gronder; (person) grogner. ● n grognement m.

grown /grəʊn/ ⟶GROW. ● adj adulte. ∼**-up** adj & n adulte (mf).

growth /grəʊθ/ n (of person, plant) croissance f; (in numbers) accroissement m; (of hair, tooth) pousse f; (Med) grosseur f, tumeur f.

grudge /grʌdʒ/ vt ∼ **doing** faire à contrecœur. ∼ **sb sth** (success, wealth) en vouloir à qn de qch. ● n rancune f; **have a** ∼ **against** en vouloir à.

grumble /ˈgrʌmbl/ vi ronchonner, grogner (at après).

grumpy /ˈgrʌmpɪ/ adj (**-ier, -iest**) grincheux, grognon.

grunt /grʌnt/ vi grogner. ● n grognement m.

guarantee /gærən'tiː/ n garantie f. ● vt garantir.

guard /gɑːd/ vt protéger; (watch) surveiller. ● vi **against** se protéger contre. ● n (Mil) garde f; (person) garde m; (on train) chef m de train.

guardian /'gɑːdɪən/ n gardien/-ne m/f; (of orphan) tuteur/-trice m/f.

guess /ges/ vt/i deviner; (suppose) penser. ● n conjecture f.

guest /gest/ n invité/-e m/f; (in hotel) client/-e m/f. **~house** n pension f. **~room** n chambre f d'amis.

guidance /'gaɪdns/ n (advice) conseils mpl; (information) information f.

guide /gaɪd/ n (person, book) guide m; (girl) guide f. ● vt guider. **~book** n guide m. **~ dog** n chien m d'aveugle. **~line** n indication f; (advice) conseils mpl.

guillotine /'gɪlətiːn/ n (for execution) guillotine f; (for paper) massicot m.

guilt /gɪlt/ n culpabilité f. **guilty** adj coupable.

guinea-pig /'gɪnɪpɪg/ n (animal) cochon m d'Inde; (fig) cobaye m.

guitar /gɪ'tɑː(r)/ n guitare f.

gulf /gʌlf/ n (part of sea) golfe m; (hollow) gouffre m.

gull /gʌl/ n mouette f, (larger) goéland m.

gullible /'gʌləbl/ adj crédule.

gully /'gʌlɪ/ n (ravine) ravin m; (drain) rigole f.

gulp /gʌlp/ vt **~ (down)** avaler en vitesse. ● vi (from fear etc.) avoir la gorge serrée. ● n gorgée f.

gum /gʌm/ n (Anat) gencive f; (glue) colle f; (for chewing) chewing-gum m. ● vt (pt **gummed**) gommer.

gun /gʌn/ n (pistol) revolver m; (rifle) fusil m; (large) canon m. ● vt

(pt **gunned**) **~ down** abattre. **~ fire** n fusillade f. **~powder** n poudre f à canon. **~shot** n coup m de feu.

gurgle /'gɜːgl/ n (of water) gargouillement m; (of baby) gazouillis m. ● vi (water) gargouiller; (baby) gazouiller.

gush /gʌʃ/ vi **~ (out)** jaillir. ● n jaillissement m.

gust /gʌst/ n rafale f; (of smoke) bouffée f.

gut /gʌt/ n (belly 🗊) ventre m. ● vt (pt **gutted**) (fish) vider; (of fire) dévaster. **gutted** adj 🗊 abattu.

guts /gʌts/ npl 🗊 (insides of human) tripes fpl 🗊; (insides of animal, building) entrailles fpl; (courage) cran m 🗊.

gutter /'gʌtə(r)/ n (on roof) gouttière f; (in street) caniveau m.

guy /gaɪ/ n (man 🗊) type m.

gym /dʒɪm/ n (place) gymnase m; (activity) gym(nastique) f.

gymnasium /dʒɪm'neɪzɪəm/ n gymnase m.

gymnastics /dʒɪm'næstɪks/ npl gymnastique f.

gynaecologist /gaɪnə'kɒlədʒɪst/ n gynécologue mf.

gypsy /'dʒɪpsɪ/ n bohémien/-ne m/f.

· ·

Hh

· ·

habit /'hæbɪt/ n habitude f; (costume: Relig) habit m; **be in/get into the ~ of** avoir/prendre l'habitude.

habitual /hə'bɪtʃʊəl/ adj (usual) habituel; (smoker, liar) invétéré.

hack /hæk/ n (writer) écrivaillon m

g
h

● vi (Comput) pirater; ~ **into** s'introduire dans. ● vt tailler. **hacker** n (Comput) pirate m informatique.

hackneyed /'hæknɪd/ adj rebattu.

had /hæd/ →HAVE.

haddock /'hædək/ n inv églefin m.

haemorrhage /'hemərɪdʒ/ n hémorragie f.

haggard /'hægəd/ adj (person) exténué; (face, look) défait.

haggle /'hægl/ vi marchander; ~ **over sth** discuter du prix de qch.

hail /heɪl/ n grêle f. ● vt (greet) saluer; (taxi) héler. ● vi grêler; ~ **from** venir de. ~**stone** n grêlon m.

hair /heə(r)/ n (on head) cheveux mpl; (on body, of animal) poils mpl; (single strand on head) cheveu m; (on body) poil m. ~**brush** n brosse f à cheveux. ~**cut** n coupe f de cheveux. ~**do** n Ⅰ coiffure f. ~**dresser** n coiffeur/-euse m/f. ~**drier** n séchoir m (à cheveux). ~**pin** n épingle f à cheveux. ~ **remover** n dépilatoire m. ~**style** n coiffure f.

hairy /'heərɪ/ adj (-ier, -iest) poilu; (terrifying) Ⅰ horrifiant.

half /hɑ:f/ n (pl **halves**) (part) moitié f; (fraction) demi m; ~ **a dozen** une demi-douzaine; ~ **an hour** une demi-heure; **four and a** ~ quatre et demi; **an hour and a** ~ une heure et demie; ~ **and half** moitié moitié; **in** ~ en deux. ● adj demi; ~ **price** à moitié prix. ● adv à moitié. ~**back** n (Sport) demi m. ~**hearted** adj tiède. ~**mast** n à ~**mast** en berne. ~**term** n vacances fpl de demi-trimestre. ~**time** n mi-temps f. ~**way** adv à mi-chemin. ~**wit** n imbécile mf.

hall /hɔ:l/ n (in house) entrée f; (corridor) couloir m; (in airport) hall m; (for events) salle f. ~ **of residence** résidence f universitaire.

hallmark /'hɔ:lmɑ:k/ n (on gold) poinçon m; (fig) caractéristique f.

hallo →HELLO.

Hallowe'en /hæləʊ'i:n/ n la veille de la Toussaint.

halt /hɔ:lt/ n arrêt m; (temporary) suspension f; (Mil) halte f. ● vt (proceedings) interrompre; (arms sales, experiments) mettre fin à. ● vi (vehicle) s'arrêter; (army) faire halte.

halve /hɑ:v/ vt (time) réduire de moitié; (fruit) couper en deux.

ham /hæm/ n jambon m.

hamburger /'hæmbɜ:gə(r)/ n hamburger m.

hammer /'hæmə(r)/ n marteau m. ● vt/i marteler; ~ **sth into sth** enfoncer qch dans qch; ~ **sth out** (agreement) parvenir à qch.

hammock /'hæmək/ n hamac m.

hamper /'hæmpə(r)/ n panier m. ● vt gêner.

hamster /'hæmstə(r)/ n hamster m.

hand /hænd/ n main f; (of clock) aiguille f; (writing) écriture f; (worker) ouvrier/-ière m/f; (cards) jeu m; **give sb a** ~ donner un coup de main à qn; **at** ~ proche; **on** ~ disponible; **on the one** ~...**on the other** ~ d'une part...d'autre part; **to** ~ à portée de la main. ● vt ~ **sb sth**, ~ **sth to sb** donner qch à qn. □ ~**in** or **over** remettre; ~ **out** distribuer. ~**bag** n sac m à main. ~**baggage** n bagages mpl à main. ~**book** n manuel m. ~**brake** n frein m à main. ~**cuffs** npl menottes fpl.

handicap /'hændɪkæp/ n handicap m. ● vt (pt **handicapped**) handicaper.

handkerchief /'hæŋkətʃɪf/ n (pl ~**s**) mouchoir m.

handle /'hændl/ n (of door, bag) poignée f; (of implement) manche m; (of cup, bucket) anse f; (of frying pan) queue f. ● vt (manage) manier; (deal with) traiter; (touch) manipuler.

handout /'hændaʊt/ n document m; (leaflet) prospectus m; (money) aumône f.

hands-free kit n kit m mains libres conducteur.

handshake /'hændʃeɪk/ n poignée f de main.

handsome /'hænsəm/ adj (good looking) beau; (generous) généreux.

handwriting /'hændraɪtɪŋ/ n écriture f.

handy /'hændɪ/ adj (-ier, -iest) (book, skill) utile; (size, shape, tool) pratique; (person) doué. **~man** n (pl **-men**) bricoleur m.

hang /hæŋ/ vt (pt **hung**) (from hook, hanger) accrocher; (from rope) suspendre; (pt **hanged**) (person) pendre. ● vi (from hook) être accroché; (from rope) être suspendu; (person) être pendu. ● n **get the ~ of doing** 🄸 piger comment faire 🄸. □ **~ about** traîner; **~ on** 🄸 hold out) tenir; (wait) attendre; **~ on to sth** s'agripper à qch; **~ out** vi 🄸 (live) crécher 🄸; (spend time) passer son temps; vt (washing) étendre; **~ up** (telephone) raccrocher.

hanger /'hæŋə(r)/ n (for clothes) cintre m.

hang-gliding /'hæŋglaɪdɪŋ/ n vol m libre.

hangover /'hæŋəʊvə(r)/ n gueule f de bois 🄸.

hang-up /'hæŋʌp/ n 🄸 complexe m.

haphazard /hæp'hæzəd/ adj peu méthodique.

happen /'hæpən/ vi arriver, se passer; **~ to sb** arriver à qn; **it so ~s that** il se trouve que.

happily /'hæpɪlɪ/ adv joyeusement; (fortunately) heureusement.

happiness /'hæpɪnɪs/ n bonheur m.

happy /'hæpɪ/ adj (-ier, -iest) heureux; **I'm not ~ about it** je ne suis pas content; **~ medium** juste milieu m.

harass /'hærəs/ vt harceler. **harassment** n harcèlement m.

harbour, (US) **harbor** /'hɑːbə(r)/ n port m. ● vt (shelter) héberger.

hard /hɑːd/ adj dur; (difficult) difficile, dur; (evidence, fact) solide; **find it ~to** do avoir du mal à faire; **~ on sb** dur envers qn. ● adv (work) dur; (pull, hit, cry) fort; (think, study) sérieusement. **~board** n aggloméré m. **~ copy** n (Comput) tirage m. **~ disk** n disque m dur.

hardly /'hɑːdlɪ/ adv à peine; (expect, hope) difficilement; **~ ever** presque jamais.

hardship /'hɑːdʃɪp/ n (poverty) privations fpl; (ordeal) épreuve f.

hard: **~ shoulder** n bande f d'arrêt d'urgence. **~ up** adj 🄸 fauché 🄸. **~ware** n (Comput) matériel m; hardware m; (goods) quincaillerie f. **~working** adj travailleur.

hardy /'hɑːdɪ/ adj (-ier, -iest) résistant.

hare /heə(r)/ n lièvre m.

harm /hɑːm/ n mal m; **there is no ~ in** il n'y a pas de mal à. ● vt (person) faire du mal à; (object) endommager. **harmful** adj nuisible. **harmless** adj inoffensif.

harmony /'hɑːmənɪ/ n harmonie f.

harness /'hɑːnɪs/ n harnais m. ● vt (horse) harnacher; (use) exploiter.

harp /hɑːp/ n harpe f. ● vi **~ on (about)** rabâcher.

harrowing /'hærəʊɪŋ/ adj (experience) atroce; (story) déchirant.

harsh /hɑːʃ/ adj (punishment) sé-

vère; (*person*) dur; (*light*) cru; (*voice*)
rude; (*chemical*) corrosif. **harshness**
n dureté f.

harvest /'hɑːvɪst/ n récolte f; the
wine ~ les vendanges fpl. ● vt
(*corn*) moissonner; (*vegetables*) récolter.

has /hæz/ →HAVE.

hassle /'hæsl/ n complications fpl.
● vt 🔲 talonner (*about* à propos
de); (*worry*) stresser.

haste /heɪst/ n hâte f; in ~ à la
hâte; **make** ~ se dépêcher.

hasty /'heɪstɪ/ adj (**-ier, -iest**) pré-
cipité.

hat /hæt/ n chapeau m.

hatch /hætʃ/ n (Aviat) panneau m
mobile; (Naut) écoutille f; (*for food*)
passeplats m inv. ● vt/i (*eggs*) (faire)
éclore.

hate /heɪt/ n haine f. ● vt détester;
(*violently*) haïr; (*sport, food*) avoir
horreur de.

hatred /'heɪtrɪd/ n haine f.

haughty /'hɔːtɪ/ adj (**-ier, -iest**)
hautain.

haul /hɔːl/ vt tirer. ● n (*by thieves*)
butin m; (*by customs*) saisie f; **it will
be a long** ~ l'étape sera longue;
long/short ~ (*transport*) long/court
courrier m. **haulage** n transport m
routier. **haulier** n (firm) société f de
transports routiers.

haunt /hɔːnt/ vt hanter. ● n lieu m
de prédilection.

have /hæv/

● *present* have, has;
● *past* had;
● *past participle* had

● *transitive verb*
····▸ (possess) avoir; **I** ~ (got) a
car j'ai une voiture; **they** ~

(got) problems ils ont des problèmes.

····▸ (do sth) ~ a try essayer; ~
a bath prendre un bain.

····▸ ~ sth done faire faire qch; ~
your hair cut se faire couper les cheveux.

● *auxiliary verb*
····▸ (in perfect tenses) avoir;
être; **I** ~ seen him je l'ai vu;
she had fallen elle était
tombée.

····▸ (in tag questions) you've
seen her, haven't you? tu l'as
vue, n'est-ce pas?; you haven't
seen her, ~you? tu ne l'as pas
vue, par hasard?

····▸ (in short answers) 'you've
never met him'—'yes I ~' 'tu
ne l'as jamais rencontré'—
'mais si!'

····▸ (must) ~ to devoir; **I** ~ to
go je dois partir; you don't ~
to do it tu n'es pas obligé de
le faire.

➡ For expressions such as
have a walk, have din-
ner →walk, dinner.

haven /'heɪvn/ n refuge m; (fig)
havre m.

havoc /'hævək/ n dévastation f.

hawk /hɔːk/ n faucon m.

hay /heɪ/ n foin m; ~ fever rhume
m des foins.

haywire /'heɪwaɪə(r)/ adj go ~
(*plans*) dérailler; (*machine*) se détraquer.

hazard /'hæzəd/ n risque m; ~
(warning) lights feux mpl de détresse. ● vt hasarder.

haze /heɪz/ n brume f.

hazel /'heɪzl/ n (bush) noisetier m.

~**nut** n noisette f.

hazy /'heɪzɪ/ adj (-**ier**, -**iest**) (misty) brumeux; (fig) vague.

he /hi:/ pron il; (emphatic) lui; **here ~ is** le voici.

head /hed/ n tête f; (leader) chef m; (of beer) mousse f; **~s or tails?** pile ou face? ● vt (list) être en tête de; (team) être à la tête de; (chapter) intituler; ~ **the ball** faire une tête. ● vi **~ for** se diriger vers.

headache /'hedeɪk/ n mal m de tête; **have a ~** avoir mal à la tête.

heading /'hedɪŋ/ n titre m; (subject category) rubrique f.

head: ~**lamp**, ~**light** n phare m. ~**line** n gros titre m. ~**master** n directeur m. ~**mistress** n directrice f. ~ **office** n siège m social. ~**on** adj & adv de front. ~**phones** npl casque m. ~**quarters** npl siège m social; (Mil) quartier m général. ~ **rest** n (Auto) repose-tête m inv. ~**strong** adj têtu.

heal /hi:l/ vt/i guérir.

health /helθ/ n santé f. ~ **centre** n centre m médico-social. ~ **food** n produits mpl diététiques. ~ **insurance** n assurance f maladie.

healthy /'helθɪ/ adj (person, plant, skin, diet) sain; (air) salutaire.

heap /hi:p/ n tas m; ~**s of** 🔲 un tas de. ● vt ~ (**up**) entasser.

hear /hɪə(r)/ vt (pt **heard**) entendre; (news, rumour) apprendre; (lecture, broadcast) écouter. ● vi entendre; ~ **from** recevoir des nouvelles de; ~ **of** or **about** entendre parler de.

hearing /'hɪərɪŋ/ n ouïe f; (of case) audience f; **give sb a ~** écouter qn. ~**aid** n prothèse f auditive.

hearse /hɜ:s/ n corbillard m.

heart /hɑ:t/ n cœur m; ~**s** (cards) cœur m; **at ~** au fond; **by ~** par

cœur; **be ~-broken** avoir le cœur brisé; **lose ~** perdre courage. ~ **attack** n crise f cardiaque. ~**burn** n brûlures fpl d'estomac. ~**felt** adj sincère.

hearth /hɑ:θ/ n foyer m.

heartily /'hɑ:tɪlɪ/ adv (greet) chaleureusement; (laugh, eat) de bon cœur.

hearty /'hɑ:tɪ/ adj (-**ier**, -**iest**) (sincere) chaleureux; (meal) solide.

heat /hi:t/ n chaleur f; (contest) épreuve f éliminatoire. ● vt (house) chauffer; ~ (**up**) (food) faire chauffer; (reheat) réchauffer. **heated** adj (fig) passionné; (lit) (pool) chauffé.

heater n appareil m de chauffage.

heather /'heðə(r)/ n bruyère f.

heating /'hi:tɪŋ/ n chauffage m.

heave /hi:v/ vt (lift) hisser; (pull) traîner péniblement; ~ **a sigh** pousser un soupir. ● vi (pull) tirer de toutes ses forces; (retch) avoir un haut-le-cœur.

heaven /'hevn/ n ciel m.

heavily /'hevɪlɪ/ adv lourdement; (smoke, drink) beaucoup.

heavy /'hevɪ/ adj (-**ier**, -**iest**) lourd; (cold, work) gros; (traffic) dense. ~ **goods vehicle** n poids m lourd. ~**-handed** adj maladroit. ~**weight** n poids m lourd.

Hebrew /'hi:bru:/ n (person) Hébreu m; (Ling) hébreu m. ● adj hébreu; (Ling) hébraïque.

hectic /'hektɪk/ adj (activity) intense; (period, day) mouvementé.

hedge /hedʒ/ n haie f. ● vi (in answering) se dérober.

hedgehog /'hedʒhɒg/ n hérisson m.

heel /hi:l/ n talon m.

hefty /'heftɪ/ adj (-**ier**, -**iest**) (person) costaud 🔲; (object) pesant.

height /haɪt/ n hauteur f; (of person) taille f; (of plane, mountain) altitude f; (of fame, glory) apogée m; (of joy, folly, pain) comble m.

heir /eə(r)/ n héritier/-ière m/f. **heiress** n héritière f. **heirloom** n objet m de famille.

held /held/ ➡HOLD.

helicopter /'helɪkɒptə(r)/ n hélicoptère m.

hell /hel/ n enfer m.

hello /hə'ləʊ/ interj bonjour!; (on phone) allô!

helmet /'helmɪt/ n casque m.

help /help/ vt/i aider (to do à faire); ~ (sb) with the housework aider qn à porter un sac/à faire le ménage; ~ oneself se servir; he can't ~ it ce n'est pas de sa faute. ● n aide f. ● interj au secours!
helper n aide f. **helpful** adj utile; (person) serviable. **helping** n portion f. **helpless** adj impuissant.

hem /hem/ n ourlet m. ● vt (pt hemmed) faire un ourlet à; ~ in cerner.

hen /hen/ n poule f.

hence /hens/ adv (for this reason) d'où; (from now) d'ici. **henceforth** adv désormais.

hepatitis /hepə'taɪtɪs/ n hépatite f.

her /hɜː(r)/ pron la, l'; (indirect object) lui; it's ~ c'est elle; for ~ pour elle. ● adj son, sa; pl ses.

herb /hɜːb/ n herbe f; ~s (Culin) fines herbes fpl.

herd /hɜːd/ n troupeau m.

here /hɪə(r)/ adv ici; ~! (take this) tiens!; tenez!; ~ is, ~ are voici; I'm ~ je suis là. **hereabouts** adv par ici. **hereafter** adv après; (in book) ci-après. **hereby** adv par le présent acte; (in letter) par la présente.

herewith /hɪəwɪð/ adv ci-joint.

heritage /'herɪtɪdʒ/ n patrimoine

m. ~ **tourism** n tourisme m culturel.

hernia /'hɜːnɪə/ n hernie f.

hero /'hɪərəʊ/ n (pl ~es) héros m.

heroic /hɪ'rəʊɪk/ adj héroïque.

heroin /'herəʊɪn/ n héroïne f.

heroine /'herəʊɪn/ n héroïne f.

heron /'herən/ n héron m.

herring /'herɪŋ/ n hareng m.

hers /hɜːz/ pron le sien, la sienne, les sien(ne)s; it is ~ c'est à elle or le sien or la sienne.

herself /hɜː'self/ pron (emphatic) elle-même; (reflexive) se; **proud of ~** fière d'elle; **by ~** toute seule.

hesitate /'hezɪteɪt/ vi hésiter. **hesitation** n hésitation f.

heterosexual /hetərə'sekʃʊəl/ adj & n hétérosexuel/-le (m/f).

hexagon /'heksəgən/ n hexagone m.

heyday /'heɪdeɪ/ n apogée m.

HGV abbr ➡HEAVY GOODS VEHICLE.

hi /haɪ/ interj ☐ salut! ☐.

hiccup /'hɪkʌp/ n hoquet m; (the) ~s le hoquet. ● vi hoqueter.

hide /haɪd/ vt (pt hid; pp hidden) cacher (from à). ● vi se cacher (from de); **go into hiding** se cacher. ● n (skin) peau f.

hideous /'hɪdɪəs/ adj (monster, object) hideux; (noise) affreux.

hiding /'haɪdɪŋ/ n **go into** ~ se cacher; **give sb a** ~ administrer une correction à qn.

hierarchy /'haɪəraːkɪ/ n hiérarchie f.

hi-fi /'haɪfaɪ/ n (chaîne f) hi-fi f inv.

high /haɪ/ adj haut; (price, number) élevé; (priest, speed) grand; (voice) aigu; **in the** ~ **season** en pleine saison. ● n a (new) ~ un niveau record. ● adv haut. ~**brow** adj & n intellectuel/-le (m/f). ~ **chair** n chaise f haute. **~ court** n cour f suprême. **higher education** n enseignement m supérieur. **~-jump** n saut m en hauteur. **~-level** adj à haut niveau.

highlight /'haɪlaɪt/ n (best moment) point m fort; **~s** (in hair) reflet m; (artificial) mèches fpl; (Sport) résumé m. ● vt (emphasize) souligner.

highly /'haɪlɪ/ adv extrêmement; (paid) très bien; **speak/think ~ of** dire/penser beaucoup de bien de.

Highness /'haɪnɪs/ n Altesse f.

high: **~-rise (building)** n tour f. **~ school** n lycée m. **~-speed** adj (train) à grande vitesse; (film) ultrarapide. **~ street** n rue f principale. **~-tech** adj de pointe.

highway /'haɪweɪ/ n route f nationale; (US) autoroute f; **~ code** code m de la route.

hijack /'haɪdʒæk/ vt détourner. ● n détournement m. **hijacker** n pirate m (de l'air).

hike /haɪk/ n randonnée f; **price ~** hausse f de prix. ● vi faire de la randonnée.

hilarious /hɪ'leərɪəs/ adj désopilant.

hill /hɪl/ n colline f; (slope) côte f. **hilly** adj vallonné.

him /hɪm/ pron le, l'; (indirect object) lui; **it's ~** c'est lui; **for ~** pour lui.

himself /hɪm'self/ pron (emphatic) lui-même; (reflexive) se; **proud of ~** fier de lui; **by ~** tout seul.

hind /haɪnd/ adj de derrière.

hinder /'hɪndə(r)/ vt (hamper) gêner; (prevent) empêcher. **hindrance** n obstacle m, gêne f.

hindsight /'haɪndsaɪt/ n **with ~** rétrospective.

Hindu /hɪn'du:/ n Hindou/-e m/f. ● adj hindou.

hinge /hɪndʒ/ n charnière f. ● vi **~ on** dépendre de.

hint /hɪnt/ n allusion f; (of spice, accent) pointe f; (of colour) touche f; (advice) conseil m. ● vt laisser entendre. ● vi **~ at** faire allusion à.

hip /hɪp/ n hanche f.

hippopotamus /hɪpə'pɒtəməs/ n (pl **~es**) hippopotame m.

hire /'haɪə(r)/ vt (thing) louer; (person) engager. ● n location f; **~-car** n voiture f de location. **~-purchase** n achat m à crédit.

his /hɪz/ adj son, sa, pl ses. ● pron le sien, la sienne, les sien(ne)s; **it is ~** c'est à lui or le sien or la sienne.

hiss /hɪs/ n sifflement m. ● vt/i siffler.

history /'hɪstrɪ/ n histoire f; **make ~** entrer dans l'histoire.

hit /hɪt/ vt (pt **hit**; pres p **hitting**) frapper; (collide with) heurter; (find) trouver; (affect, reach) toucher. ● vi **~ on** (find) tomber sur; **~ it off** s'entendre bien (**with** avec). ● n (blow) coup m; (fig) succès m; (song) tube m 🔊; (on Internet) (visite) visite f, accès m; (result) page f trouvée, résultat m.

hitch /hɪtʃ/ vt (fasten) accrocher; **~ up** remonter. ● n (snag) anicroche f. **~-hike** vi faire du stop 🔊. **~-hiker** n auto-stoppeur/-euse m/f.

hi-tech /'haɪtek/ adj

de pointe.

HIV abbr (**human immunodeficiency virus**) VIH m.

hive /haɪv/ n ruche f. ● vt ~ **off** séparer; (industry) céder.

HIV-positive adj séropositif.

hoard /hɔːd/ vt amasser; (supplies) stocker. ● n trésor m; (of provisions) provisions fpl.

hoarse /hɔːs/ adj enroué.

hoax /həʊks/ n canular m.

hobby /ˈhɒbɪ/ n passe-temps m inv.

hockey /ˈhɒkɪ/ n hockey m.

hog /hɒg/ n cochon m. ● vt (pt hogged) 🔢 monopoliser.

hold /həʊld/ vt (pt held) tenir; (contain) contenir; (conversation, opinion) avoir; (shares, record, person) détenir; ~ (**the line**), **please** ne quittez pas. ● vi (rope, weather) tenir. ● n prise f; **get** ~ **of** attraper; (ticket) se procurer; (person) (by phone) joindre; **on** ~ en attente. □ ~ **back** (contain) retenir; (hide) cacher; ~ **down** (job) garder; (person) tenir; (costs) limiter; ~ **on** (stand firm) tenir bon; (wait) attendre; ~ **on to** (keep) garder; (cling to) se cramponner à; ~ **out** vt (offer) offrir; vi (resist) tenir le coup; ~ **up** (support) soutenir; (delay) retarder; (rob) attaquer.

holder /ˈhəʊldə(r)/ n détenteur/-trice m/f; (of passport, post) titulaire mf; (for object) support m.

holding /ˈhəʊldɪŋ/ n participation f.

hold-up /ˈhəʊldɪŋ/ n retard m; (of traffic) embouteillage m; (robbery) hold-up m inv.

hole /həʊl/ n trou m.

holiday /ˈhɒlɪdeɪ/ n vacances fpl; (public) jour m férié; (time off) congé m. ● vi passer ses vacances. ● adj de vacances. ~-**maker** n

vacancier/-ière m/f.

Holland /ˈhɒlənd/ n Hollande f.

hollow /ˈhɒləʊ/ adj creux; (fig) faux. ● n creux m. ● vt creuser.

holly /ˈhɒlɪ/ n houx m.

holy /ˈhəʊlɪ/ adj (-**ier**, -**iest**) saint; (water) bénit; **H**~ **Ghost**, **H**~ **Spirit** Saint-Esprit m.

homage /ˈhɒmɪdʒ/ n hommage m.

home /həʊm/ n (place to live) logement m; maison f; (institution) maison f; (family base) foyer m; (country) pays m. ● adj de la maison, du foyer; (of family) de famille; (Pol) intérieur; (match, visit) à domicile. ● adv (**at**) à la maison, chez soi; **come** or **go** ~ rentrer; (from abroad) rentrer dans son pays; **feel at** ~ **with** être à l'aise avec. ~ **computer** n ordinateur m, PC m.

homeland /ˈhəʊmlænd/ n patrie f; ~ **security** n sécurité f des frontières.

homeless /ˈhəʊmlɪs/ adj sans abri. ● n the ~ les sans-abri mpl.

homely /ˈhəʊmlɪ/ adj (-**ier**, -**iest**) (cosy) accueillant; (simple) sans prétention; (person: US) sans attraits.

home: ~-**made** adj (fait) maison. **H**~ **Office** n ministère m de l'Intérieur. ~ **page** n (Internet) page f d'accueil. **H**~ **Secretary** n Ministre m de l'Intérieur. ~**sick** adj **be** ~**sick** avoir le mal du pays. ~**work** n devoirs mpl.

homosexual /hɒməˈsekʃʊəl/ adj & n homosexuel/-le (m/f).

honest /ˈɒnɪst/ adj (truthful) intègre; (trustworthy) honnête; (sincere) franc. **honestly** adv honnêtement; franchement. **honesty** n honnêteté f.

honey /ˈhʌnɪ/ n miel m; (person 🔢) chéri/-e m/f. ~**moon** n voyage m de noces; (fig) lune f de miel.

honk /hɒŋk/ vi klaxonner.

honorary /ˈɒnərərɪ/ adj (person) honoraire; (degree) honorifique.

honour, (US) **honor** /ˈɒnə(r)/ n honneur m. ● vt honorer.

hood /hʊd/ n capuchon m; (on car, pram) capote f; (car engine cover: US) capot m.

hoof /huːf/ n (pl ∼s) sabot m.

hook /hʊk/ n crochet m; (on garment) agrafe f; (for fishing) hameçon m; **off the ∼** tiré d'affaire; (phone) décroché. ● vt accrocher.

hoot /huːt/ n (of owl) (h)ululement m; (of car) coup m de klaxon. ● vi (owl) (h)ululer; (car) klaxonner; (jeer) huer.

hoover /ˈhuːvə(r)/ vt ∼ **a room** passer l'aspirateur dans une pièce.

Hoover® /ˈhuːvə(r)/ n aspirateur m.

hop /hɒp/ vi (pt **hopped**) sauter (à cloche-pied); ∼ **in!** 🅸 vas-y, monte! ● n bond m; ∼s houblon m.

hope /həʊp/ n espoir m. ● vt/i espérer; ∼ **for** espérer avoir; **I** ∼ **so** je l'espère.

hopeful /ˈhəʊpfl/ adj (news, sign) encourageant; (person) plein d'espoir; (mood) optimiste. **hopefully** adv (with luck) avec un peu de chance; (with hope) avec optimisme.

hopeless /ˈhəʊplɪs/ adj désespéré; (useless: fig) nul 🅸.

horizon /həˈraɪzn/ n horizon m.

horizontal /hɒrɪˈzɒntl/ adj horizontal.

hormone /ˈhɔːməʊn/ n hormone f.

horn /hɔːn/ n corne f; (of car) klaxon® m; (Mus) cor m.

horoscope /ˈhɒrəskəʊp/ n horoscope m.

horrible /ˈhɒrɪbl/ adj horrible.

horrid /ˈhɒrɪd/ adj horrible.

horrific /həˈrɪfɪk/ adj horrifiant.

horrify /ˈhɒrɪfaɪ/ vt horrifier.

horror /ˈhɒrə(r)/ n horreur f. ● adj (film, story) d'épouvante.

horse /hɔːs/ n cheval m. ∼**back** n **on** ∼**back** à cheval. ∼**chestnut** n marron m (d'Inde). ∼**man** n (pl -**men**) cavalier m. ∼**power** n puissance f (en chevaux). ∼**race** n course f de chevaux. ∼**radish** n raifort m. ∼**shoe** n fer m à cheval. ∼ **show** n concours m hippique.

hose /həʊz/ n tuyau m. ● vt arroser. ∼**pipe** n tuyau m.

hospitable /hɒˈspɪtəbl/ adj hospitalier.

hospital /ˈhɒspɪtl/ n hôpital m.

host /həʊst/ n (to guests) hôte m; (on TV) animateur m; (Internet) ordinateur m hôte; **a** ∼ **of** une foule de; (Relig) hostie f.

hostage /ˈhɒstɪdʒ/ n otage m; **hold sb** ∼ garder qn en otage.

hostel /ˈhɒstl/ n foyer m; **(youth)** ∼ auberge f (de jeunesse).

hostess /ˈhəʊstɪs/ n hôtesse f.

hostile /ˈhɒstaɪl/ adj hostile.

hot /hɒt/ adj (hotter, hottest) chaud; (Culin) épicé; **be** or **feel** ∼ avoir chaud; **it is** ∼ il fait chaud; **in** ∼ **water** 🅸 dans le pétrin. ● vt/i (pt **hotted**) ∼ **up** 🅸 chauffer. ∼ **air balloon** n montgolfière f. ∼ **dog** n hot-dog m.

hotel /həʊˈtel/ n hôtel m.

hot: ∼**headed** adj impétueux. ∼ **list** n (Internet) signets mpl favoris. ∼**plate** n plaque f chauffante. ∼ **water bottle** n bouillotte f.

hound /haʊnd/ n chien m de chasse. ● vt poursuivre.

hour /aʊə(r)/ n heure f.

hourly /ˈaʊəlɪ/ adj horaire; **on an** ∼ **basis** à l'heure. ● adv toutes les heures.

house¹ /haʊs/ n maison f; (Pol) Chambre f; **on the ~** aux frais de la maison.

house² /haʊz/ vt loger; (of building) abriter.

household /'haʊshəʊld/ n (house, family) ménage m. ● adj ménager.

house: ~keeper n gouvernante f. **~-proud** adj méticuleux. **~-warming** n pendaison f de crémaillère. **~wife** n (pl **-wives**) ménagère f. **~work** n travaux mpl ménagers.

housing /'haʊzɪŋ/ n logement m; **~ association** service m de logement; **~ development** cité f; (smaller) lotissement m.

hover /'hɒvə(r)/ vi (bird) voleter; (vacillate) vaciller. **hovercraft** n aéroglisseur m.

how /haʊ/ adv comment; **~ are you?** comment allez-vous?; **~ long/tall is...?** quelle est la longueur/hauteur de...?; **~ many?**, **~ much?** combien?; **~ pretty!** comme or que c'est joli!; **~ about a walk?** si on faisait une promenade?; **~ do you do?** (greeting) enchanté.

however /haʊˈevə(r)/ adv (nevertheless) cependant; **~ hard I try** j'ai beau essayer; **~ much it costs** quel que soit le prix; **~ young/poor he is** si jeune/pauvre soit-il; **~ you like** comme tu veux.

howl /haʊl/ n hurlement m. ● vi hurler.

HP abbr ➡HIRE-PURCHASE.

hp abbr ➡HORSEPOWER.

HQ abbr ➡HEADQUARTERS.

hub /hʌb/ n moyeu m; (fig) centre m.

hug /hʌg/ vt (pt **hugged**) serrer dans ses bras. ● n étreinte f; give

sb a **~** serrer qn dans ses bras.

huge /hjuːdʒ/ adj énorme.

hull /hʌl/ n (of ship) coque f.

hum /hʌm/ vt/i (pt **hummed**) (person) fredonner; (insect) bourdonner; (engine) ronronner. ● n bourdonnement m; ronronnement m.

human /'hjuːmən/ adj humain. ● n humain m. **~ being** n être m humain.

humane /hjuːˈmeɪn/ adj (person) humain; (act) d'humanité; (killing) sans cruauté.

humanitarian /hjuːmænɪ'teərɪən/ adj humanitaire.

humanity /hjuːˈmænətɪ/ n humanité f.

humble /'hʌmbl/ adj humble.

humid /'hjuːmɪd/ adj humide.

humiliate /hjuːˈmɪlɪeɪt/ vt humilier.

humorous /'hjuːmərəs/ adj humoristique; (person) plein d'humour.

humour, (US) **humor** /'hjuːmə(r)/ n humour m; (mood) humeur f. ● vt amadouer.

hump /hʌmp/ n bosse f. ● vt ▱ porter.

hunchback /'hʌntʃbæk/ n bossu/-e m/f.

hundred /'hʌndrəd/ adj & n cent (m); **two ~ and one** deux cent un; **~s of** des centaines de. **hundredth** adj & n centième (mf).

hung /hʌŋ/ ➡HANG.

Hungarian /hʌŋˈgeərɪən/ n (person) Hongrois/-e m/f; (Ling) hongrois m. ● adj hongrois. **Hungary** n Hongrie f.

hunger /'hʌŋgə(r)/ n faim f. ● vi **~ for** avoir faim de.

hungry /'hʌŋgrɪ/ adj (**-ier**, **-iest**) affamé; **be ~** avoir faim.

hunt /hʌnt/ vt/i chasser; ~ **for** chercher. ● n chasse f. **hunter** n chasseur m. **hunting** n chasse f.

hurdle /'hɜːdl/ n (Sport) haie f; (fig) obstacle m.

hurricane /'hʌrɪkən/ n ouragan m.

hurry /'hʌrɪ/ vi se dépêcher; ~ **out** sortir précipitamment. ● vt (work) terminer à la hâte; (person) bousculer. ● n hâte f; **in a** ~ pressé.

hurt /hɜːt/ vt/i (pt **hurt**) faire mal (à); (injure, offend) blesser. ● adj blessé. ● n blessure f.

hurtle /'hɜːtl/ vi ~ **down** dévaler; ~ **along a road** foncer sur une route.

husband /'hʌzbənd/ n mari m.

hush /hʌʃ/ vt faire taire; ~ **up** (news) étouffer. ● n silence m. ● interj chut!

husky /'hʌskɪ/ adj (-**ier**, -**iest**) enroué. ● n husky m.

hustle /'hʌsl/ vt (push, rush) bousculer. ● vi (hurry) se dépêcher; (work: US) se démener. ● n ~ **and bustle** agitation f.

hut /hʌt/ n cabane f.

hyacinth /'haɪəsɪnθ/ n jacinthe f.

hydrant /'haɪdrənt/ n (fire) ~ bouche f d'incendie.

hydraulic /haɪ'drɔːlɪk/ adj hydraulique.

hydroelectric /haɪdrəʊ'lektrɪk/ adj hydroélectrique.

hydrogen /'haɪdrədʒən/ n hydrogène m; ~ **bomb** bombe f à hydrogène.

hyena /haɪ'iːnə/ n hyène f.

hygiene /'haɪdʒiːn/ n hygiène f. **hygienic** adj hygiénique.

hymn /hɪm/ n cantique m; (fig) hymne m.

hype /haɪp/ n 🔢 battage m publicitaire. ● vt ~ **(up)** (film, book) faire du battage pour.

hyperactive /haɪpər'æktɪv/ adj hyperactif.

hyperlink /'haɪpəlɪŋk/ n hyperlien m.

hypermarket /'haɪpəmɑːkɪt/ n hypermarché m.

hypertext /'haɪpətekst/ n hypertexte m.

hyphen /'haɪfn/ n trait m d'union.

hypnosis /hɪp'nəʊsɪs/ n hypnose f.

hypocrisy /hɪ'pɒkrəsɪ/ n hypocrisie f. **hypocrite** n hypocrite mf. **hypocritical** adj hypocrite.

hypothesis /haɪ'pɒθəsɪs/ n (pl -**ses**) hypothèse f.

hysteria /hɪ'stɪərɪə/ n hystérie f. **hysterical** adj hystérique.

hysterics /hɪ'sterɪks/ npl crise f de nerfs; **be in** ~ rire aux larmes.

     h
     i

Ii

I /aɪ/ pron je, j'; (stressed) moi.

ice /aɪs/ n glace f; (on road) verglas m. ● vt (cake) glacer. ● vi ~ **(up)** (window) se givrer; (river) geler. ~**box** n (US) réfrigérateur m. ~**-cream** n glace f. ~**-cube** n glaçon m. ~ **hockey** n hockey m sur glace.

Iceland /'aɪslənd/ n Islande f. **Icelander** n Islandais/-e m/f. **Icelandic** adj & n islandais (m).

ice: ~ **lolly** n glace f (sur bâtonnet). ~ **rink** n patinoire f. ~ **skate** n patin m à glace.

icicle /'aɪsɪkl/ n stalactite f (de glace).

icing /'aɪsɪŋ/ n (sugar) glaçage m.

icy /'aɪsɪ/ adj (**-ier, -iest**) (hands, wind) glacé; (road) verglacé; (manner, welcome) glacial.

ID /ɪd/ n pièce f d'identité; ~ **card** carte f d'identité.

idea /aɪ'dɪə/ n idée f.

ideal /aɪ'diːəl/ adj idéal. ● n idéal m.

identical /aɪ'dentɪkl/ adj identique.

identification /aɪdentɪfɪ'keɪʃn/ n identification f; (papers) pièce f d'identité.

identify /aɪ'dentɪfaɪ/ vt identifier. ● vi ~ **with** s'identifier à.

identikit /aɪ'dentɪkɪt/ n ~ **picture** portraitrobot m.

identity /aɪ'dentətɪ/ n identité f; ~ **theft** vol m d'identité.

ideological /aɪdɪə'lɒdʒɪkl/ adj idéologique.

idiom /'ɪdɪəm/ n (phrase) idiome m; (language) parler m, langue f. **idiomatic** adj idiomatique.

idiosyncrasy /ɪdɪə'sɪŋkrəsɪ/ n particularité f.

idiot /'ɪdɪət/ n idiot/-e m/f. **idiotic** adj idiot.

idle /'aɪdl/ adj (lazy) paresseux; (doing nothing) oisif; (boast, threat) vain. ● vi (engine) tourner au ralenti. ● vt ~ **away** gaspiller.

idol /'aɪdl/ n idole f. **idolize** vt idolâtrer.

idyllic /ɪ'dɪlɪk/ adj idyllique.

i.e. abbr c-à-d, c'est-à-dire.

if /ɪf/ conj si.

ignite /ɪg'naɪt/ vt/i (s')enflammer.

ignition /ɪg'nɪʃn/ n (Auto) allumage m; ~ (**switch**) contact m; ~ **key** clé f de contact.

ignorance /'ɪgnərəns/ n ignorance f. **ignorant** adj ignorant (of de). **ignorantly** adv par ignorance.

ignore /ɪg'nɔː(r)/ vt (person) igno-

rer; (mistake, remark) ne pas relever; (feeling, fact) ne pas tenir compte de.

ill /ɪl/ adj malade. ● adv mal. ● n mal m. ~-**advised** adj malavisé. ~ **at ease** adj mal à l'aise. ~-**bred** adj mal élevé.

illegal /ɪ'liːgl/ adj illégal.

illegible /ɪ'ledʒəbl/ adj illisible.

illegitimate /ɪlɪ'dʒɪtɪmət/ adj illégitime.

ill: ~-**fated** adj malheureux. ~ **feeling** n ressentiment m.

illiterate /ɪ'lɪtərət/ adj & n analphabète (mf).

illness /'ɪlnɪs/ n maladie f.

ill-treat vt maltraiter.

illuminate /ɪ'luːmɪnent/ vt éclairer; (decorate with lights) illuminer. **illumination** n éclairage m. illumination f.

illusion /ɪ'luːʒn/ n illusion f.

illustrate /'ɪləstrent/ vt illustrer. **illustration** n illustration f. **illustrative** adj qui illustre.

image /'ɪmɪdʒ/ n image f; (of firm, person) image f de marque. **imagery** n images fpl.

imaginable /ɪ'mædʒɪnəbl/ adj imaginable. **imaginary** adj imaginaire. **imagination** n imagination f. **imaginative** adj plein d'imagination.

imagine /ɪ'mædʒɪn/ vt (s')imaginer (that que). ~ **being rich** s'imaginer riche.

imbalance /ɪm'bæləns/ n déséquilibre m.

imitate /'ɪmɪtent/ vt imiter.

immaculate /ɪ'mækjʊlət/ adj impeccable.

immaterial /ɪmə'tɪərɪəl/ adj sans importance (to pour; that que).

immature /ɪmə'tjʊə(r)/ adj (person) immature; (*plant*) qui n'est pas arrivé à maturité.

immediate /ɪˈmiːdɪət/ *adj* immédiat.

immediately /ɪˈmiːdɪətlɪ/ *adv* immédiatement. ● *conj* dès que.

immense /ɪˈmens/ *adj* immense. **immensely** *adv* extrêmement, immensément. **immensity** *n* immensité *f*.

immerse /ɪˈmɜːs/ *vt* plonger (**in** dans). **immersion** *n* immersion *f*; **immersion heater** chauffe-eau *m* *inv* électrique.

immigrant /ˈɪmɪɡrənt/ *n* & *adj* immigré/-e (*m/f*). (newly-arrived) immigrant/-e (*m/f*). **Immigrate** *vi* immigrer. **immigration** *n* immigration *f*.

imminent /ˈɪmɪnənt/ *adj* imminent.

immobilizer /ɪˈməʊbɪlaɪzə(r)/ *n* système *m* antidémarrage.

immoral /ɪˈmɒbɪlaɪzə(r)/ *adj* immoral.

immortal /ɪˈmɔːtl/ *adj* immortel.

immune /ɪˈmjuːn/ *adj* immunisé (**from, to** contre); (*reaction, system*) immunitaire. **immunity** *n* immunité *f*. **immunization** *n* immunisation *f*. **immunize** *vt* immuniser.

impact /ˈɪmpækt/ *n* impact *m*.

impair /ɪmˈpeə(r)/ *vt* (*performance*) affecter; (*ability*) affaiblir.

impart /ɪmˈpɑːt/ *vt* communiquer, transmettre.

impartial /ɪmˈpɑːʃl/ *adj* impartial.

impassable /ɪmˈpɑːsəbl/ *adj* (*barrier*) infranchissable; (*road*) impraticable.

impassive /ɪmˈpæsɪv/ *adj* impassible.

impatience /ɪmˈpeɪʃns/ *n* impatience *f*. **impatient** *adj* impatient; **get impatient** s'impatienter. **impa-**

tiently *adv* impatiemment.

impeccable /ɪmˈpekəbl/ *adj* impeccable.

impede /ɪmˈpiːd/ *vt* entraver.

impediment /ɪmˈpedɪmənt/ *n* entrave *f*; **speech ~** défaut *m* d'élocution.

impending /ɪmˈpendɪŋ/ *adj* imminent.

imperative /ɪmˈperətɪv/ *adj* urgent. ● *n* impératif *m*.

imperfect /ɪmˈpɜːfɪkt/ *adj* incomplet; (*faulty*) défectueux. ● *n* (Gram) imparfait *m*. **imperfection** *n* imperfection *f*.

imperial /ɪmˈpɪərɪəl/ *adj* impérial; (*measure*) conforme aux normes britanniques. **imperialism** *n* impérialisme *m*.

impersonal /ɪmˈpɜːsənl/ *adj* impersonnel.

impersonate /ɪmˈpɜːsəneɪt/ *vt* se faire passer pour; (*mimic*) imiter.

impertinent /ɪmˈpɜːtɪnənt/ *adj* impertinent.

impervious /ɪmˈpɜːvɪəs/ *adj* imperméable (**to** à).

impetuous /ɪmˈpetʃʊəs/ *adj* impétueux.

impetus /ˈɪmpɪtəs/ *n* impulsion *f*.

impinge /ɪmˈpɪndʒ/ *vi* **~ on** affecter; (encroach) empiéter sur.

implement /ˈɪmplɪmənt/ *n* instrument *m*; (*tool*) outil *m*. ● *vt* exécuter, mettre en application; (*software*) implanter. **implementation** *n* mise *f* en application.

implicit /ɪmˈplɪsɪt/ *adj* (*implied*) implicite (**in** dans); (*unquestioning*) absolu.

imply /ɪmˈplaɪ/ *vt* (assume, mean) impliquer; (insinuate) laisser entendre.

impolite /ɪmpəˈlaɪt/ *adj* impoli.

import[1] /ɪm'pɔːt/ vt importer.

import[2] /'ɪmpɔːt/ n (article) importation f; (meaning) signification f.

importance /ɪm'pɔːtns/ n importance f. **important** adj important.

impose /ɪm'pəʊz/ vt imposer (**on** sb à qn; **on** sth sur qch). ● vi s'imposer; ~ **on** sb abuser de la bienveillance de qn. **imposing** adj imposant.

impossible /ɪm'pɒsəbl/ adj impossible. ● **the** ~ l'impossible m.

impotent /'ɪmpətənt/ adj impuissant.

impound /ɪm'paʊnd/ vt confisquer, saisir.

impoverish /ɪm'pɒvərɪʃ/ vt appauvrir.

impractical /ɪm'præktɪkl/ adj peu réaliste.

impregnable /ɪm'pregnəbl/ adj imprenable.

impress /ɪm'pres/ vt impressionner; ~ **sth on** sb faire bien comprendre qch à qn. **impression** n impression f. **impressionable** adj impressionnable. **impressive** adj impressionnant.

imprint[1] /'ɪmprɪnt/ n empreinte f.

imprint[2] /ɪm'prɪnt/ vt (fix) graver (**on** dans); (print) imprimer.

imprison /ɪm'prɪzn/ vt emprisonner.

improbable /ɪm'prɒbəbl/ adj (not likely) improbable; (incredible) invraisemblable.

improper /ɪm'prɒpə(r)/ adj (unseemly) malséant; (dishonest) irrégulier.

improve /ɪm'pruːv/ vt/i (s')améliorer. **improvement** n amélioration f.

improvise /'ɪmprəvaɪz/ vt/i improviser.

impudent /'ɪmpjʊdənt/ adj impudent.

impulse /'ɪmpʌls/ n impulsion f; **on** ~ sur un coup de tête. **impulsive** adj impulsif. **impulsively** adv par impulsion.

impurity /ɪm'pjʊərəti/ n impureté f.

in /ɪn/ prep (inside, within) dans; (expressing place, position) à, en; (expressing time) en, dans; ~ **the box/garden** dans la boîte/le jardin; ~ **Paris/school** à Paris/l'école; ~ **town** en ville; ~ **the country** à la campagne; ~ **English** en anglais; ~ **India** en Inde; ~ **japan** au japon; ~ **winter** en hiver; ~ **spring** au printemps; ~ **an hour** (at end of) au bout d'une heure; ~ **an hour('s time)** dans une heure; ~ **(the space of) an hour** en une heure; ~ **doing** en faisant; ~ **the evening** le soir; **one** ~ **ten** un sur dix; ~ **between** entre les deux; (time) entretemps; ~ **a firm voice** d'une voix ferme; ~ **blue** en bleu; ~ **ink** à l'encre; ~ **uniform** en uniforme; ~ **a skirt** en jupe; ~ **a whisper** en chuchotant; ~ **a loud voice** d'une voix forte; **the best** ~ le meilleur de; **we are** ~ **for** on va avoir; **have it** ~ **for** sb **🄸** avoir qn dans le collimateur. ● adv (inside) dedans; (at home) là, à la maison; (in fashion) à la mode; **come** ~ entrer; **run** ~ entrer en courant.

inability /ɪnə'bɪləti/ n incapacité f (**to do** de faire).

inaccessible /ɪnæk'sesəbl/ adj inaccessible.

inaccurate /ɪn'ækjʊrət/ adj inexact.

inactive /ɪn'æktɪv/ adj inactif. **inactivity** n inaction f.

inadequate /ɪn'ædɪkwət/ adj insuffisant.

inadvertently /ɪnəd'vɜːtəntli/ adv par mégarde.

inadvisable /ˌɪnəd'vaɪzəbl/ adj inopportun, à déconseiller.

inane /ɪ'neɪn/ adj idiot, débile.

inanimate /ɪn'ænɪmət/ adj inanimé.

inappropriate /ˌɪnə'prəʊprɪət/ adj inopportun; (term) inapproprié.

inarticulate /ˌɪnɑː'tɪkjʊlət/ adj qui a du mal à s'exprimer.

inasmuch as /ˌɪnəz'mʌtʃəz/ adv dans la mesure où; (because) vu que.

inaugurate /ɪ'nɔːgjʊreɪt/ vt (open, begin) inaugurer; (person) investir.

inborn /ˈɪnbɔːn/ adj inné.

inbred /ɪn'bred/ adj (inborn) inné.

Inc. abbr (**incorporated**) S.A.

incapable /ɪn'keɪpəbl/ adj incapable (**of doing** de faire).

incapacitate /ˌɪnkə'pæsɪteɪt/ vt immobiliser.

incense¹ /ˈɪnsens/ n encens m.

incense² /ɪn'sens/ vt mettre en fureur.

incentive /ɪn'sentɪv/ n motivation f; (payment) prime f.

incessant /ɪn'sesnt/ adj incessant. **incessantly** adv sans cesse.

incest /ˈɪnsest/ n inceste m. **incestuous** adj incestueux.

inch /ɪntʃ/ n pouce m (=2.54 cm.). ● vi **~ towards** se diriger petit à petit vers.

incidence /ˈɪnsɪdəns/ n fréquence f.

incident /ˈɪnsɪdənt/ n incident m. **incidental** adj secondaire. **incidentally** adv à propos; (by chance) par la même occasion.

incinerate /ɪn'sɪnəreɪt/ vt incinérer. **incinerator** n incinérateur m.

incite /ɪn'saɪt/ vt inciter, pousser.

inclination /ˌɪnklɪ'neɪʃn/ n (ten-

dency) tendance f; (desire) envie f.

incline¹ /ɪn'klaɪn/ vt/i (s')incliner; **be ~d to** avoir tendance à.

incline² /ˈɪnklaɪn/ n pente f.

include /ɪn'kluːd/ vt comprendre, inclure. **including** prep (y) compris. **inclusion** n inclusion f.

inclusive /ɪn'kluːsɪv/ adj & adv inclus; **~ of delivery** livraison comprise.

income /ˈɪnkʌm/ n revenus mpl; **~ tax** impôt m sur le revenu.

incoming /ˈɪnkʌmɪŋ/ adj (tide) montant; (tenant, government) nouveau; (call) qui vient de l'extérieur.

incompatible /ˌɪnkəm'pætɪbl/ adj incompatible.

incompetent /ɪn'kɒmpɪtənt/ adj incompétent.

incomplete /ˌɪnkəm'pliːt/ adj incomplet.

incomprehensible /ɪnˌkɒmprɪ'hensəbl/ adj incompréhensible.

inconceivable /ˌɪnkən'siːvəbl/ adj inconcevable.

inconclusive /ˌɪnkən'kluːsɪv/ adj peu concluant.

incongruous /ɪn'kɒŋgrʊəs/ adj déconcertant, surprenant.

inconsiderate /ˌɪnkən'sɪdərət/ adj (person) peu attentif à autrui; (act) maladroit.

inconsistent /ˌɪnkən'sɪstənt/ adj (argument) incohérent; (performance) inégal; (behaviour) changeant; **~ with** en contradiction avec.

inconspicuous /ˌɪnkən'spɪkjʊəs/ adj qui passe inaperçu.

incontinent /ɪn'kɒntɪnənt/ adj incontinent.

inconvenience /ˌɪnkən'viːnɪəns/ n dérangement m; (drawback) inconvénient m. ● vt déranger. **inconvenient** adj incommode; **if it's not inconvenient for you** si cela ne vous dérange pas.

incorporate /ɪnˈkɔːpəreɪt/ vt incorporer (**into** dans); (contain) comporter.

incorrect /ɪnkəˈrekt/ adj incorrect.

increase[1] /ˈɪŋkriːs/ n augmentation f (**in**, **of** de). be on the ~ être en progression.

increase[2] /ɪnˈkriːs/ vt/i augmenter. **increasing** adj croissant. **increasingly** adv de plus en plus.

incredible /ɪnˈkredəbl/ adj incroyable.

incriminate /ɪnˈkrɪmɪneɪt/ vt incriminer. **incriminating** adj compromettant.

incubate /ˈɪŋkjʊbeɪt/ vt (eggs) couver. **incubation** n incubation f. **incubator** n couveuse f.

incur /ɪnˈkɜː(r)/ vt (pt **incurred**) (penalty, anger) encourir; (debts) contracter.

indebted /ɪnˈdetɪd/ adj ~ to sb redevable à qn (**for** de); (grateful) reconnaissant à qn.

indecent /ɪnˈdiːsnt/ adj indécent.

indecisive /ɪndɪˈsaɪsɪv/ adj indécis; (ending) peu concluant.

indeed /ɪnˈdiːd/ adv en effet; (emphatic) vraiment.

indefinite /ɪnˈdefɪnət/ adj vague; (period, delay) illimité. **indefinitely** adv indéfiniment.

indelible /ɪnˈdeləbl/ adj indélébile.

indemnity /ɪnˈdemnətɪ/ n (protection) assurance f; (payment) indemnité f.

indent /ɪnˈdent/ vt (text) renfoncer. **indentation** n (dent) marque f.

independence /ɪndɪˈpendəns/ n indépendance f. **independent** adj indépendant. **independently** adv de façon indépendante; **independently of** indépendamment de.

index /ˈɪndeks/ n (pl ~**es**) (in

book) index m; (in library) catalogue m; (in economy) indice m; ~ card fiche f; ~ (**finger**) index m. ● vt classer. ~-**linked** adj indexé.

India /ˈɪndɪə/ n Inde f.

Indian /ˈɪndɪən/ n Indien/-ne m/f. ● adj indien.

indicate /ˈɪndɪkeɪt/ vt indiquer. **indication** n indication f.

indicative /ɪnˈdɪkətɪv/ adj & n indicatif (m).

indicator /ˈɪndɪkeɪtə(r)/ n (pointer) aiguille f; (on vehicle) clignotant m; (board) tableau m.

indict /ɪnˈdaɪt/ vt inculper. **indictment** n accusation f.

indifferent /ɪnˈdɪfrənt/ adj indifférent; (not good) médiocre.

indigenous /ɪnˈdɪdʒɪnəs/ adj indigène.

indigestible /ɪndɪˈdʒestəbl/ adj indigeste. **indigestion** n indigestion f.

indignant /ɪnˈdɪɡnənt/ adj indigné.

indirect /ɪndɪˈrekt/ adj indirect. **indirectly** adv indirectement.

indiscreet /ɪndɪˈskriːt/ adj indiscret. **indiscretion** n indiscrétion f.

indiscriminate /ɪndɪˈskrɪmɪnət/ adj sans distinction. **indiscriminately** adv sans distinction.

indisputable /ɪndɪˈspjuːtəbl/ adj indiscutable.

individual /ɪndɪˈvɪdʒʊəl/ adj individuel; (tuition) particulier. ● n individu m. **individualist** n individualiste m/f. **individuality** n individualité f. **individually** adv individuellement.

indoctrinate /ɪnˈdɒktrɪneɪt/ vt endoctriner. **indoctrination** n endoctrinement m.

indolent /ˈɪndələnt/ adj indolent.

Indonesia /ɪndəʊˈniːzjə/ n Indonésie f.

indoor /ˈɪndɔː(r)/ adj (clothes) d'intérieur; (pool, court) couvert. **indoors** adv à l'intérieur.

induce /ɪnˈdjuːs/ vt (influence) persuader; (stronger) inciter (**to do** à faire). **inducement** n (financial) récompense f; (incentive) motivation f.

induction /ɪnˈdʌkʃn/ n (Electr) induction f; (inauguration) installation f.

indulge /ɪnˈdʌldʒ/ vt (person, whim) céder à; (child) gâter. ● vi ~ **in** se livrer à. **indulgence** n indulgence f; (treat) plaisir m. **indulgent** adj indulgent.

industrial /ɪnˈdʌstrɪəl/ adj industriel; (accident) du travail; ~ **action** grève f; ~ **dispute** conflit m social. **industrialist** n industriel/-le m/f. **industrialized** adj industrialisé.

industrious /ɪnˈdʌstrɪəs/ adj diligent.

industry /ˈɪndəstrɪ/ n industrie f; (zeal) zèle m.

inebriated /ɪˈniːbrɪeɪtɪd/ adj ivre.

inedible /ɪnˈedɪbl/ adj immangeable.

ineffective /ɪnɪˈfektɪv/ adj inefficace.

inefficient /ɪnɪˈfɪʃnt/ adj inefficace; (person) incompétent.

ineligible /ɪnˈelɪdʒəbl/ adj inéligible; **be** ~ **for** ne pas avoir droit à.

inept /ɪˈnept/ adj incompétent; (tactless) maladroit.

inequality /ɪnɪˈkwɒlətɪ/ n inégalité f.

inescapable /ɪnɪˈskeɪpəbl/ adj indéniable.

inevitable /ɪnˈevɪtəbl/ adj inévitable.

inexcusable /ɪnɪkˈskjuːzəbl/ adj inexcusable.

inexhaustible /ɪnɪgˈzɔːstəbl/ adj inépuisable.

inexpensive /ɪnɪkˈspensɪv/ adj pas cher.

inexperience /ɪnɪkˈspɪərɪəns/ n inexpérience f. **inexperienced** adj inexpérimenté.

infallible /ɪnˈfæləbl/ adj infaillible.

infamous /ˈɪnfəməs/ adj (person) tristement célèbre; (deed) infâme.

infancy /ˈɪnfənsɪ/ n petite enfance f; **in its** ~ (fig) à ses débuts mpl. **infant** n (baby) bébé m; (at school) enfant m/f. **infantile** adj infantile.

infatuated /ɪnˈfætʃʊeɪtɪd/ adj ~ **with** entiché de. **infatuation** n engouement m.

infect /ɪnˈfekt/ vt contaminer; ~ **sb with sth** transmettre qch à qn. **infection** n infection f. **infectious** adj contagieux.

infer /ɪnˈfɜː(r)/ vt (pt **inferred**) (deduce) déduire.

inferior /ɪnˈfɪərɪə(r)/ adj inférieur (**to** à). (work, product) de qualité inférieure. ● n inférieur/-e m/f. **inferiority** n infériorité f.

inferno /ɪnˈfɜːnəʊ/ n (hell) enfer m; (blaze) brasier m.

infertile /ɪnˈfɜːtaɪl/ adj infertile.

infest /ɪnˈfest/ vt infester (**with** de).

infidelity /ɪnfɪˈdelətɪ/ n infidélité f.

infighting /ˈɪnfaɪtɪŋ/ n conflits mpl internes.

infinite /ˈɪnfɪnət/ adj infini. **infinitely** adv infiniment. **infinitive** n infinitif m. **infinity** n infinité f.

infirm /ɪnˈfɜːm/ adj infirme. **infirmary** n hôpital m; (sick-bay) infirmerie f. **infirmity** n infirmité f.

inflame /ɪnˈfleɪm/ vt enflammer. **inflammable** adj inflammable. **inflammation** n inflammation f. **inflammatory** adj incendiaire.

inflatable /ɪnˈfleɪtəbl/ adj gonflable. **inflate** vt (lit, fig) gonfler.

inflation /ɪnˈfleɪʃn/ n inflation f.

inflection /ɪnˈflekʃn/ n (of word root) flexion f; (of vowel, voice) inflexion f.

inflict /ɪnˈflɪkt/ vt infliger (on à).

influence /ˈɪnflʊəns/ n influence f; under the ~ (drunk 🄸) éméché. ● vt (person) influencer; (choice) influer sur. **influential** adj (powerful) influent; (theory, artist) très suivi.

influenza /ɪnflʊˈenzə/ n grippe f.

influx /ˈɪnflʌks/ n afflux m.

inform /ɪnˈfɔːm/ vt informer (of de). **keep ~ed** tenir au courant.

informal /ɪnˈfɔːml/ adj (simple) simple, sans façons; (unofficial) officieux; (colloquial) familier. **informality** n simplicité f. **informally** adv (dress) en tenue décontractée; (speak) en toute simplicité.

informant /ɪnˈfɔːmənt/ n indicateur/-trice m/f.

information /ɪnfəˈmeɪʃn/ n renseignements mpl, informations fpl; **some ~** un renseignement. **~ superhighway** n autoroute f de l'information. **~ technology** n informatique f.

informative /ɪnˈfɔːmətɪv/ adj (book) riche en renseignements; (visit) instructif.

informer /ɪnˈfɔːmə(r)/ n indicateur/-trice m/f.

infrequent /ɪnˈfriːkwənt/ adj rare.

infringe /ɪnˈfrɪndʒ/ vt (rule) enfreindre; (rights) ne pas respecter. **infringement** n infraction f.

infuriate /ɪnˈfjʊərieɪt/ vt exaspérer.

ingenuity /ɪndʒɪˈnjuːɪti/ n ingéniosité f.

ingot /ˈɪŋgət/ n lingot m.

ingrained /ɪnˈgreɪnd/ adj (hatred) enraciné; (dirt) bien incrusté.

ingratiate /ɪnˈgreɪʃieɪt/ vt ~ oneself with se faire bien voir de.

ingredient /ɪnˈgriːdɪənt/ n ingrédient m.

inhabit /ɪnˈhæbɪt/ vt habiter. **inhabitable** adj habitable. **inhabitant** n habitant/-e m/f.

inhale /ɪnˈheɪl/ vt inhaler; (smoke) avaler. **inhaler** n inhalateur m.

inherent /ɪnˈhɪərənt/ adj inhérent (in à). **inherently** adv en soi, par sa nature.

inherit /ɪnˈherɪt/ vt hériter de; ~ sth from sb hériter qch de qn. **inheritance** n héritage m.

inhibit /ɪnˈhɪbɪt/ vt (restrain) inhiber; (prevent) entraver.

inhospitable /ɪnhɒˈspɪtəbl/ adj inhospitalier.

inhuman /ɪnˈhjuːmən/ adj inhumain.

initial /ɪˈnɪʃl/ n initiale f. ● vt (pt initialled) parapher. ● adj initial.

initiate /ɪˈnɪʃieɪt/ vt (project) mettre en œuvre; (talks) amorcer; (person) initier (into à). **initiation** n initiation f; (start) amorce f.

initiative /ɪˈnɪʃətɪv/ n initiative f.

inject /ɪnˈdʒekt/ vt injecter (into dans). (new element: fig) insuffler (into à). **injection** n injection f, piqûre f.

injure /ˈɪndʒə(r)/ vt blesser; (damage) nuire à. **injury** n blessure f.

injustice /ɪnˈdʒʌstɪs/ n injustice f.

ink /ɪŋk/ n encre f.

inkling /ˈɪŋklɪŋ/ n petite idée f.

inland /ˈɪnlənd/ adj intérieur; **I~ Revenue** service m des impôts britannique.

in-laws /ˈɪnlɔːz/ npl (parents) beaux-parents mpl; (family) belle-famille f.

inlay¹ /ɪnˈleɪ/ vt (pt inlaid) incruster (with de); (on wood) marqueter.

inlay² /ˈɪnleɪ/ n incrustation f; (on

wood) marqueterie f.

inlet /'mlet/ n bras m de mer; (Tech) arrivée f.

inmate /'ɪnmeɪt/ n (of asylum) interné/-e m/f; (of prison) détenu /-e m/f.

inn /ɪn/ n auberge f.

innate /ɪ'neɪt/ adj inné.

inner /'ɪnə(r)/ adj intérieur; ∼ **city** quartiers mpl déshérités; ∼ **tube** chambre f à air.

innocent /'ɪnəsnt/ adj & n innocent/-e (m/f).

innocuous /ɪ'nɒkjʊəs/ adj inoffensif.

innovate /'ɪnəveɪt/ vi innover.

innuendo /ɪnjuː'endəʊ/ n (pl ∼es) insinuations fpl; (sexual) allusions fpl grivoises.

innumerable /ɪ'njuːmərəbl/ adj innombrable.

inoculate /ɪ'nɒkjʊleɪt/ vt vacciner (**against** contre).

inopportune /ɪn'ɒpətjuːn/ adj inopportun.

in-patient /'ɪnpeɪʃnt/ n malade mf hospitalisé/-e.

input /'ɪnpʊt/ n (of energy) alimentation f (**of** en); (contribution) contribution f; (data) données fpl; (computer process) saisie f des données. ● vt (data) saisir.

inquest /'ɪŋkwest/ n enquête f.

inquire /ɪn'kwaɪə(r)/ vi se renseigner (**about, into** sur). ● vt demander.

inquiry /ɪn'kwaɪərɪ/ n demande f de renseignements; (inquest) enquête f.

inquisitive /ɪn'kwɪzətɪv/ adj curieux.

inroad /'ɪnrəʊd/ n **make** ∼s **into** faire une avancée sur.

insane /ɪn'seɪn/ adj fou; (Jur)

aliéné. **insanity** n folie f; (Jur) aliénation f mentale.

inscribe /ɪn'skraɪb/ vt inscrire. **inscription** n inscription f.

inscrutable /ɪn'skruːtəbl/ adj énigmatique.

insect /'ɪnsekt/ n insecte m. **insecticide** n insecticide m.

insecure /ɪnsɪ'kjʊə(r)/ adj (person) qui manque d'assurance; (job) précaire; (lock, property) peu sûr. **insecurity** n (of person) manque m d'assurance; (of situation) insécurité f.

insensitive /ɪn'sensətɪv/ adj insensible; (remark) indélicat.

inseparable /ɪn'seprəbl/ adj inséparable (**from** de).

insert /ɪn'sɜːt/ vt insérer (**in** dans).

in-service /ɪn'sɜːvɪs/ adj (training) continu.

inshore /ɪn'ʃɔː(r)/ adj côtier.

inside /ɪn'saɪd/ n intérieur m; ∼**s** 🄸 entrailles fpl. ● adj intérieur. ● adv à l'intérieur; **go** ∼ entrer. ● prep à l'intérieur de; (of time) en moins de; ∼ **out** à l'envers; (thoroughly) à fond.

insight /'ɪnsaɪt/ n (perception) perspicacité f; (idea) aperçu m.

insignia /ɪn'sɪgnɪə/ npl insigne m.

insignificant /ɪnsɪg'nɪfɪkənt/ adj (cost, difference) négligeable; (person) insignifiant.

insincere /ɪnsɪn'sɪə(r)/ adj peu sincère.

insinuate /ɪn'sɪnjʊeɪt/ vt insinuer.

insist /ɪn'sɪst/ vt/i insister (**that** pour que). ∼ **on** exiger; ∼ **on doing** vouloir à tout prix faire. **insistence** n insistance f. **insistent** adj insistant. **insistently** adv avec insistance.

insofar as /ɪnsəʊ'fɑːəz/ adv dans la mesure où.

insolent /'ɪnsələnt/ adj insolent.

insolvent /ɪn'sɒlvənt/ adj insolvable.

insomnia /ɪn'sɒmnɪə/ n insomnie f. **insomniac** n insomniaque mf.

inspect /ɪn'spekt/ vt (school, machinery) inspecter; (tickets) contrôler. **inspection** n inspection f; (of passport, ticket) contrôle m. **inspector** n inspecteur/-trice m/f; (on bus) contrôleur/-euse m/f.

inspiration /ɪnspə'reɪʃn/ n inspiration f. **inspire** vt inspirer.

install /ɪn'stɔːl/ vt installer.

instalment /ɪn'stɔːlmənt/ n (payment) versement m; (of serial) épisode m.

instance /'ɪnstəns/ n exemple m; (case) cas m; **for ~** par exemple; **in the first ~** en premier lieu.

instant /'ɪnstənt/ adj immédiat; (food) instantané. ● n instant m. **instantaneous** adj instantané. **instantly** adv immédiatement.

instead /ɪn'sted/ adv plutôt; **~ of doing** au lieu de faire; **~ of sb** à la place de qn.

instep /'ɪnstep/ n cou-de-pied m.

instigate /'ɪnstɪgeɪt/ vt (attack) lancer; (proceedings) engager.

instil /ɪn'stɪl/ vt (pt **instilled**) inculquer; (fear) insuffler.

instinct /'ɪnstɪŋkt/ n instinct m. **instinctive** adj instinctif.

institute /'ɪnstɪtjuːt/ n institut m. ● vt instituer; (proceedings) engager. **institution** n institution f; (school, hospital) établissement m.

instruct /ɪn'strʌkt/ vt (teach) instruire; (order) ordonner; **~ sb in sth** enseigner qch à qn; **~ sb to do** donner l'ordre à qn de faire. **instruction** n instruction f. **instructions** npl (for use) mode m d'emploi. **instructive** adj instructif.

instructor n (skiing, driving) moniteur/-trice m/f.

instrument /'ɪnstrəmənt/ n instrument m.

instrumental /ɪnstrə'mentl/ adj instrumental; **be ~ in** contribuer à. **instrumentalist** n instrumentaliste mf.

insubordinate /ɪnsə'bɔːdɪnət/ adj insubordonné.

insufficient /ɪnsə'fɪʃnt/ adj insuffisant.

insular /'ɪnsjʊlə(r)/ adj (Geog) insulaire; (mind, person: fig) borné.

insulate /'ɪnsjʊleɪt/ vt (room, wire) isoler.

insulin /'ɪnsjʊlɪn/ n insuline f.

insult[1] /ɪn'sʌlt/ vt insulter.

insult[2] /'ɪnsʌlt/ n insulte f.

insurance /ɪn'ʃɔːrəns/ n assurance f (against contre).

insure /ɪn'ʃɔː(r)/ vt assurer; **~ that** (US) s'assurer que.

intact /ɪn'tækt/ adj intact.

intake /'ɪnteɪk/ n (of food) consommation f; (School, Univ) admissions fpl.

integral /'ɪntɪgrəl/ adj intégral (to à).

integrate /'ɪntɪgreɪt/ vt/i (s')intégrer (with à; into dans).

integrity /ɪn'tegrətɪ/ n intégrité f.

intellect /'ɪntəlekt/ n intelligence f. **intellectual** adj & n intellectuel/-le (m/f).

intelligence /ɪn'telɪdʒəns/ n intelligence f; (Mil) renseignements mpl. **intelligent** adj intelligent. **intelligently** adv intelligemment.

intend /ɪn'tend/ vt (outcome) vouloir; **~ to do** avoir l'intention de faire. **intended** adj (result) voulu; (visit) projeté.

intense /ɪn'tens/ adj intense; (person) sérieux. **intensely** adv (very) extrêmement.

intensify /ɪn'tensɪfaɪ/ vt/i (s')intensifier.

intensive /ɪn'tensɪv/ adj intensif; **in ~ care** en réanimation.

intent /ɪn'tent/ n intention f. ● adj absorbé; **~ on doing** résolu à faire.

intention /ɪn'tenʃn/ n intention f. **intentional** adj intentionnel.

intently /ɪn'tentlɪ/ adv attentivement.

interact /ɪntər'ækt/ vi (factors) agir l'un sur l'autre; (people) communiquer. **interactive** adj (TV, video) interactif.

intercept /ɪntə'sept/ vt intercepter.

interchange /'ɪntətʃeɪndʒ/ n (road junction) échangeur m; (exchange) échange m.

interchangeable /ɪntə'tʃeɪndʒəbl/ adj interchangeable.

intercom /'ɪntəkɒm/ n interphone® m.

interconnected /ɪntəkə'nektɪd/ adj (parts) raccordé; (problems) lié.

intercourse /'ɪntəkɔːs/ n rapports mpl.

interest /'ɪntrəst/ n intérêt m; **~ rate** taux m d'intérêt. ● vt intéresser (**in** à). **interested** adj intéressé; **be ~ed in** s'intéresser à. **interesting** adj intéressant.

interface /'ɪntəfeɪs/ n interface f.

interfere /ɪntə'fɪə(r)/ vi se mêler des affaires des autres; **~ in** se mêler de; **~ with** (freedom) empiéter sur; (tamper with) toucher. **interference** n ingérence f; (sound, light waves) brouillage m; (radio) parasites mpl.

interim /'ɪntərɪm/ n **in the ~** entre-temps. ● adj (government) provisoire; (payment) intermédiaire.

interior /ɪn'tɪərɪə(r)/ n intérieur m.

● adj intérieur.

interjection /ɪntə'dʒekʃn/ n interjection f.

interlock /ɪntə'lɒk/ vt/i (Tech) (s')emboîter, (s')enclencher.

interlude /'ɪntəluːd/ n intervalle m; (Theat, Mus) intermède m.

intermediary /ɪntə'miːdɪərɪ/ adj & n intermédiaire (mf).

intermediate /ɪntə'miːdɪət/ adj intermédiaire; (exam, level) moyen.

intermission /ɪntə'mɪʃn/ n (Theat) entracte m.

intermittent /ɪntə'mɪtənt/ adj intermittent.

intern[1] /ɪn'tɜːn/ vt interner.

intern[2] /'ɪntɜːn/ n (US) stagiaire mf; (Med) interne mf.

internal /ɪn'tɜːnl/ adj interne; (domestic, Pol) intérieur; **I~ Revenue** (US) service m des impôts américain.

international /ɪntə'næʃnəl/ adj international.

Internet /'ɪntənet/ n Internet m; **on the ~** sur Internet; **~ access** accès à Internet; **~ service provider** fournisseur m d'accès Internet.

interpret /ɪn'tɜːprɪt/ vt interpréter (**as** comme). ● vi faire l'interprète. **interpretation** n interprétation f. **interpreter** n interprète mf.

interrelated /ɪntərɪ'leɪtɪd/ adj interdépendant, lié.

interrogate /ɪn'terəgeɪt/ vt interroger. **interrogative** adj & n (Ling) interrogatif (m).

interrupt /ɪntə'rʌpt/ vt/i interrompre. **interruption** n interruption f.

intersect /ɪntə'sekt/ vt/i (lines, roads) (se) croiser. **intersection** n intersection f.

interspersed /ɪntə'spɜːst/ adj parsemé (**with** de).

i

intertwine /ɪntəˈtwaɪn/ vt/i (s')entrelacer.

interval /ˈɪntəvl/ n intervalle m; (Theat) entracte m.

intervene /ɪntəˈviːn/ vi intervenir; (of time) s'écouler (between entre); (happen) arriver.

interview /ˈɪntəvjuː/ n (for job) entretien m; (by a journalist) interview f. ● vt (candidate) faire passer un entretien à; (celebrity) interviewer.

intestine /ɪnˈtestɪn/ n intestin m.

intimacy /ˈɪntɪməsɪ/ n intimité f.

intimate¹ /ˈɪntɪmət/ vt (state) annoncer; (hint) laisser entendre.

intimate² /ˈɪntɪmət/ adj intime. **intimately** adv intimement.

intimidate /ɪnˈtɪmɪdeɪt/ vt intimider.

into /ˈɪntuː/, /ˈɪntə/ prep (put, go, fall) dans; (divide, translate, change) en; be ~ jazz être fana du jazz 🔟; 8 ~ 24 is 3 24 divisé par 8 égale 3.

intolerant /ɪnˈtɒlərənt/ adj intolérant.

intonation /ɪntəˈneɪʃn/ n intonation f.

intoxicate /ɪnˈtɒksɪkeɪt/ vt enivrer. **intoxicated** adj ivre. **intoxication** n ivresse f.

intractable /ɪnˈtræktəbl/ adj (person) intraitable; (problem) rebelle.

intranet /ˈɪntrənet/ n (Comput) intranet m.

intransitive /ɪnˈtrænsətɪv/ adj intransitif.

intravenous /ɪntrəˈviːnəs/ adj (Med) intraveineux.

intricate /ˈɪntrɪkət/ adj complexe.

intrigue /ɪnˈtriːg/ vt intriguer. ● n intrigue f. **intriguing** adj fascinant; (curious) curieux.

intrinsic /ɪnˈtrɪnzɪk/ adj intrinsèque (to à).

introduce /ɪntrəˈdjuːs/ vt (person, idea, programme) présenter; (object, law) introduire (into dans). **introduction** n introduction f; (of person) présentation f. **introductory** adj (words) préliminaire.

introvert /ˈɪntrəvɜːt/ n introverti/-e m/f.

intrude /ɪnˈtruːd/ vi (person) s'imposer (on sb à qn), déranger. **intruder** n intrus/-e m/f. **intrusion** n intrusion f.

intuition /ɪntjuːˈɪʃn/ n intuition f. **intuitive** adj intuitif.

inundate /ˈɪnʌndeɪt/ vt inonder (with de).

invade /ɪnˈveɪd/ vt envahir.

invalid¹ /ˈɪnvəliːd/ n malade mf; (disabled) infirme mf.

invalid² /ɪnˈvælɪd/ adj (passport) pas valable; (claim) sans fondement. **invalidate** vt (argument) infirmer; (claim) annuler.

invaluable /ɪnˈvæljʊəbl/ adj inestimable.

invariable /ɪnˈveərɪəbl/ adj invariable. **invariably** adv invariablement.

invasion /ɪnˈveɪʒn/ n invasion f.

invent /ɪnˈvent/ vt inventer. **invention** n invention f. **inventive** adj inventif. **inventor** n inventeur/-trice m/f.

inventory /ˈɪnvəntrɪ/ n inventaire m.

invert /ɪnˈvɜːt/ vt (order) intervertir; (image, values) renverser; ~ed commas guillemets mpl.

invest /ɪnˈvest/ vt investir; (time, effort) consacrer. ● vi faire un investissement; ~ in (buy) s'acheter.

investigate /ɪnˈvestɪgeɪt/ vt examiner; (crime) enquêter sur. **investigation** n investigation f. **investi-**

gator n (police) enquêteur/ -euse m/f.

investment /ɪn'vestmənt/ n investissement m; **emotional ~** engagement m personnel. **investor** n investisseur/-euse m/f; (in shares) actionnaire m/f.

invigilate /ɪn'vɪdʒɪleɪt/ vi (exam) surveiller. **invigilator** n surveillant/ -e m/f.

invigorate /ɪn'vɪgəreɪt/ vt revigorer.

invisible /ɪn'vɪzəbl/ adj invisible.

invitation /ɪnvɪ'teɪʃn/ n invitation f. **invite** vt inviter; (ask for) demander. **inviting** adj engageant.

invoice /'ɪnvɔɪs/ n facture f. ● vt facturer.

involuntary /ɪn'vɒləntrɪ/ adj involontaire.

involve /ɪn'vɒlv/ vt impliquer; (person) faire participer (in à). **involved** adj (complex) compliqué; (at stake) en jeu; (in work) participer à; (crime) être mêlé à. **involvement** n participation f (in à).

inward /'ɪnwəd/ adj (feeling) intérieur. **inwardly** adv intérieurement. **inwards** adv vers l'intérieur.

iodine /'aɪədiːn/ n iode m; (antiseptic) teinture f d'iode.

iota /aɪ'əʊtə/ n iota m; **not one ~ of** pas un grain de.

IOU /aɪəʊ'juː/ n (I owe you) reconnaissance f de dette.

IQ abbr (**Intelligence quotient**) QI m.

Iran /ɪ'rɑːn/ n Iran m.

Iraq /ɪ'rɑːk/ n Irak m.

irate /aɪ'reɪt/ adj furieux.

IRC abbrev (**Internet Relay Chat**) (Internet) conversation f IRC.

Ireland /'aɪələnd/ n Irlande f.

Irish /'aɪərɪʃ/ n & adj irlandais (m).

~man n Irlandais m. **~woman** n Irlandaise f.

iron /'aɪən/ n fer m; (appliance) fer m (à repasser). ● adj (will) de fer; (bar) en fer. ● vt repasser.

ironic /aɪ'rɒnɪk/ adj ironique.

iron: ironing-board n planche f à repasser. **~monger** n quincaillier m.

irony /'aɪrənɪ/ n ironie f.

irrational /ɪ'ræʃənl/ adj irrationnel; (person) pas raisonnable.

irregular /ɪ'regjʊlə(r)/ adj irrégulier.

irrelevant /ɪ'reləvnt/ adj hors de propos.

irreplaceable /ɪrɪ'pleɪsəbl/ adj irremplaçable.

irresistible /ɪrɪ'zɪstəbl/ adj irrésistible.

irrespective /ɪrɪ'spektɪv/ adj **~ of** sans tenir compte de.

irresponsible /ɪrɪ'spɒnsəbl/ adj irresponsable.

irreverent /ɪ'revərənt/ adj irrévérencieux.

irrigate /'ɪrɪgeɪt/ vt irriguer.

irritable /'ɪrɪtəbl/ adj irritable.

irritate /'ɪrɪteɪt/ vt irriter. **irritating** adj irritant.

is /ɪz/ →BE.

ISDN abbr (integrated services digital network) RNIS n, réseau m numérique à intégration de services.

Islam /ɪz'lɑːm/ n (faith) islam m; (Muslims) Islam m. **Islamic** adj islamique.

island /'aɪlənd/ n île f.

isle /aɪl/ n île f.

isolate /'aɪsəleɪt/ vt isoler. **isolation** n isolement m.

Israel /'ɪzreɪl/ n Israël m.

Israeli /ɪz'reɪlɪ/ n Israélien/-ne m/f. ● adj israélien.

issue /ˈɪʃuː/ n question f; (outcome) résultat m; (of magazine) numéro m; (of stamps) émission f; (offspring) descendance f; **at** ~ en cause. ● vt distribuer; (stamps) émettre; (book) publier; (order) délivrer. ● vi ~ **from** provenir de.

it /ɪt/
● pronoun
····▸ (subject) il, elle; **'where's the book/chair?'— '~'s in the kitchen'** 'où est le livre/la chaise?'—'il/elle est dans la cuisine'.
····▸ (object) le, la, l'; ~**'s my book and I want** ~ c'est mon livre et je le veux; **I liked his shirt, did you notice** ~? sa chemise m'a plu, l'as-tu remarquée?; **give** ~ **to me** donne-le-moi.
····▸ (with preposition) **we talked a lot about** ~ on en a beaucoup parlé; **Elliott went to** ~ Elliott y est allé.
····▸ (impersonal) il; ~**'s raining** il pleut; ~ **will snow** il va neiger.

IT abbr →**INFORMATION TECHNOLOGY**.

Italian /ɪˈtæljən/ n (person) Italien/-ne m/f; (Ling) italien m. ● adj italien.

italics /ɪˈtælɪks/ npl italique m.

Italy /ˈɪtəlɪ/ n Italie f.

itch /ɪtʃ/ n démangeaison f. ● vi démanger; **my arm** ~**es** j'ai le bras qui me démange; **be** ~**ing to do** mourir d'envie de faire.

item /ˈaɪtəm/ n article m; (on agenda) point m.

itemize /ˈaɪtəmaɪz/ vt détailler; ~**d bill** facture f détaillée.

itinerary /aɪˈtɪnərərɪ/ n itinéraire m.

its /ɪts/ det son, sa; pl ses.

it's →**IT IS, IT HAS**.

itself /ɪtˈself/ pron lui-même, elle-même; (reflexive) se.

ivory /ˈaɪvərɪ/ n ivoire m; ~ **tower** tour f d'ivoire.

ivy /ˈaɪvɪ/ n lierre m.

The Ivy League Ce terme désigne les huit universités les plus prestigieuses de la côte est des États-Unis (Harvard, Yale, Columbia, Cornell, Dartmouth, Brown, Princeton, Pennsylvania). Elles doivent ce nom au lierre qui pousse sur les bâtiments des plus anciennes d'entre elles. Ces universités sont réputées tant dans les domaines académiques que sportifs.

Jj

jab /dʒæb/ vt (pt **jabbed**) ~ **sth into sth** planter qch dans qch. ● n coup m; (injection) piqûre f.

jack /dʒæk/ n (Auto) cric m; (cards) valet m; (Electr) jack m. ● vt ~ **up** soulever avec un cric.

jacket /ˈdʒækɪt/ n veste f, veston m; (of book) jaquette f.

jackknife /ˈdʒæknaɪf/ n couteau m pliant. ● vi (lorry) se mettre en portefeuille.

jackpot /ˈdʒækpɒt/ n gros lot m; **hit the** ~ gagner le gros lot.

jade /dʒeɪd/ n (stone) jade m.

jaded /ˈdʒeɪdɪd/ adj (tired) fatigué;

(bored) blasé.

jagged /'dʒægɪd/ adj (rock) déchiqueté; (knife) dentelé.

jail /dʒeɪl/ n prison f. ● vt mettre en prison.

jam /dʒæm/ n confiture f; (traffic) ~ embouteillage m. ● vt/i (pt **jammed**) (wedge) (se) coincer; (cram) (s')entasser; (street) encombrer; (radio) brouiller.

Jamaica /dʒə'meɪkə/ n Jamaïque f.

jam-packed adj 🄸 bondé; ~ **with** bourré de.

jangle /'dʒæŋgl/ n tintement m. ● vt/i (faire) tinter.

janitor /'dʒænɪtə(r)/ n (US) gardien m.

January /'dʒænjʊərɪ/ n janvier m.

Japan /dʒə'pæn/ n Japon m.

Japanese /dʒæpə'niːz/ n (person) Japonais/-e m/f; (Ling) japonais m. ● adj japonais.

jar /dʒɑː(r)/ n pot m, bocal m. ● vi (pt **jarred**) rendre un son discordant; (colours) détonner. ● vt ébranler.

jargon /'dʒɑːgən/ n jargon m.

jaundice /'dʒɔːndɪs/ n jaunisse f.

javelin /'dʒævlɪn/ n javelot m.

jaw /dʒɔː/ n mâchoire f.

jay /dʒeɪ/ n geai m.

jazz /dʒæz/ n jazz m. ● vt ~ **up** (dress) rajeunir; (event) ranimer.

jealous /'dʒeləs/ adj jaloux. **jealousy** n jalousie f.

jeans /dʒiːnz/ npl jean m.

jeer /dʒɪə(r)/ n vt/i ~ (at) huer. ● n huée f.

jelly /'dʒelɪ/ n gelée f; ~**fish** n méduse f.

jeopardize /'dʒepədaɪz/ vt (career, chance) compromettre; (lives) mettre en péril.

jerk /dʒɜːk/ n secousse f; (fool 🄲)

crétin m 🄸. ● vt tirer brusquement. ● vi tressaillir. **jerky** adj saccadé.

jersey /'dʒɜːzɪ/ n (garment) pullover m; (fabric) jersey m.

jet /dʒet/ n (plane, stream) jet m; (mineral) jais m; ~ **lag** décalage m horaire.

jettison /'dʒetɪsn/ vt jeter pardessus bord; (Aviat) larguer; (fig) rejeter.

jetty /'dʒetɪ/ n jetée f.

Jew /dʒuː/ n juif/juive m/f.

jewel /'dʒuːəl/ n bijou m. **jeweller** n bijoutier/-ière m/f. **jeweller('s)** n (shop) bijouterie f. **jewellery** n bijoux mpl.

Jewish /'dʒuːɪʃ/ adj juif.

jibe /dʒaɪb/ n moquerie f.

jigsaw /'dʒɪgsɔː/ n puzzle m.

jingle /'dʒɪŋgl/ vt/i (faire) tinter. ● n tintement m; (advertising) refrain m publicitaire, sonal m.

jinx /dʒɪŋks/ n (person) portemalheur m inv, (fig) sort m.

jitters /'dʒɪtəz/ npl **have the** ~ 🄸 être nerveux. **jittery** adj nerveux.

job /dʒɒb/ n emploi m; (post) poste m; **out of a** ~ sans emploi; **it is a good** ~ **that** heureusement que; **just the** ~ tout à fait ce qu'il faut. ~ **centre** n bureau m des services nationaux de l'emploi. **jobless** adj sans emploi.

jockey /'dʒɒkɪ/ n jockey m.

jog /dʒɒg/ n **go for a** ~ aller faire un jogging. ● vt (pt **jogged**) heurter; (memory) rafraîchir. ● vi faire du jogging. **jogging** n jogging m.

join /dʒɔɪn/ vt (attach) réunir, joindre; (club) devenir membre de; (company) entrer dans; (army) s'engager dans; (queue) se mettre dans; ~ **sb** (in activity) se joindre à qn; (meet) rejoindre qn. ● vi (become member) adhérer; (pieces) se joindre; (roads) se rejoindre. ● n raccord m. □ ~ **in** participer à; ~ **in sth** participer à qch; ~ **up** (Mil) s'engager; ~ **sth up** relier qch. **joiner** n menuisier/-ière m/f.

joint /dʒɔɪnt/ adj (action) collectif; (measures, venture) commun; (winner) ex aequo inv; (account) joint; ~ **author** coauteur m. ● n (join) joint m; (Anat) articulation f; (Culin) rôti m; **out of** ~ déboîté.

joke /dʒəʊk/ n plaisanterie f; (trick) farce f; **it's no** ~ ce n'est pas drôle. ● vi plaisanter. **joker** n blagueur/ -euse m/f; (cards) joker m.

jolly /dʒɒlɪ/ adj (**-ier, -iest**) (person) enjoué; (tune) joyeux. ● adv 🔢 drôlement.

jolt /dʒəʊlt/ vt secouer. ● vi cahoter. ● n secousse f; (shock) choc m.

jostle /dʒɒsl/ vt/i (se) bousculer.

jot /dʒɒt/ vt (pt jotted) ~ (**down**) noter.

journal /dʒɜːnl/ n journal m. **journalism** n journalisme m. **journalist** n journaliste m/f.

journey /dʒɜːnɪ/ n (trip) voyage m; (short or habitual) trajet m. ● vi voyager.

joy /dʒɔɪ/ n joie f. **joyful** adj joyeux. **joy:** ~**riding** n rodéo m à la voiture volée. ~**stick** n (Comput) manette f; (Aviat) manche m à balai.

jubilant /dʒuːbɪlənt/ adj (person) exultant; (mood) réjoui.

Judaism /dʒuːdeɪɪzəm/ n judaïsme m.

judge /dʒʌdʒ/ n juge m. ● vt juger; (distance) estimer; **judging by/from** à en juger par. **judg(e)ment** n jugement m.

judicial /dʒuːdɪʃl/ adj judiciaire. **judiciary** n magistrature f.

judo /dʒuːdəʊ/ n judo m.

jug /dʒʌg/ n (glass) carafe f; (pot

tery) pichet m.

juggernaut /dʒʌgənɔːt/ n (lorry) poids m lourd.

juggle /dʒʌgl/ vt/i jongler (avec). **juggler** n jongleur/-euse m/f.

juice /dʒuːs/ n jus m. **juicy** adj juteux; (details 🔢) croustillant.

jukebox /dʒuːkbɒks/ n jukebox m.

July /dʒuːlaɪ/ n juillet m.

jumble /dʒʌmbl/ vt mélanger. ● n (of objects) tas m; (of ideas) fouillis m; ~ **sale** vente f de charité.

jumbo /dʒʌmbəʊ/ n (also ~ **jet**) gros-porteur m.

jump /dʒʌmp/ vt sauter; ~ **the lights** passer au feu rouge; ~ **the queue** passer devant tout le monde. ● vi sauter; (in surprise) sursauter; (price) monter en flèche; ~ **at** (opportunity) sauter sur. ● n saut m, bond m; (increase) bond m.

jumper /dʒʌmpə(r)/ n pull(-over) m; (dress: US) robe f chasuble.

jump-leads npl câbles mpl de démarrage.

jumpy /dʒʌmpɪ/ adj nerveux.

junction /dʒʌŋkʃn/ n (of roads) carrefour m; (on motorway) échangeur m.

June /dʒuːn/ n juin m.

jungle /dʒʌŋgl/ n jungle f.

junior /dʒuːnɪə(r)/ adj (young) jeune; (in rank) subalterne; (school) primaire. ● n cadet/-te m/f; (School) élève m/f du primaire.

junk /dʒʌŋk/ n bric-à-brac m inv; (poor quality) camelote f; ~ **food** nourriture f industrielle.

junkie /dʒʌŋkɪ/ n 🔢 drogué/ -e m/f.

junk: ~ **mail** n prospectus mpl. ~**-shop** n boutique f de bric-à-brac.

jurisdiction /dʒʊərɪsdɪkʃn/ n

compétence f; (Jur) juridiction f.

juror /'dʒʊərə(r)/ n juré m.

jury /'dʒʊərɪ/ n jury m.

just /dʒʌst/ adj (fair) juste. ● adv (immediately, slightly) juste; (simply) tout simplement; (exactly) exactement; **he has/had ~ left** il vient/venait de partir; **have ~ missed** avoir manqué de peu; **I'm ~ leaving** je suis sur le point de partir; **it's ~ a cold** ce n'est qu'un rhume; **~ as tall/well as** tout aussi grand/bien que; **~ listen!** écoutez donc!; **it's ~ ridiculous** c'est vraiment ridicule.

justice /'dʒʌstɪs/ n justice f; **J~ of the Peace** juge m de paix.

justification /dʒʌstɪfɪ'keɪʃn/ n justification f. **justify** vt justifier.

jut /dʒʌt/ vi (pt **jutted**) (~ **out**) s'avancer en saillie.

juvenile /'dʒuːvənaɪl/ adj (childish) puéril; (offender) mineur; (delinquent) jeune. ● n jeune mf; (Jur) mineur/-e m/f.

juxtapose /dʒʌkstə'pəʊz/ vt juxtaposer.

· ·

Kk

kangaroo /kæŋgə'ruː/ n kangourou m.

karate /kə'rɑːtɪ/ n karaté m.

kebab /kɪ'bæb/ n brochette f.

keel /kiːl/ n (of ship) quille f. ● vi ~ **over** (bateau) chavirer; (person) s'écrouler.

keen /kiːn/ adj (interest, wind, feeling) vif; (mind, analysis) pénétrant; (edge, appetite) aiguisé; (eager) enthousiaste; **be ~ on** être passionné de; **be ~ to do** or **on doing** tenir beaucoup à faire. **keenly** adv vivement. **keenness** n enthousiasme m.

keep /kiːp/ vt (pt **kept**) garder; (promise, shop, diary) tenir; (family) faire vivre; (animals) élever; (rule) respecter; (celebrate) célébrer; (delay) retenir; **~ sth clean/warm** garder qch propre/au chaud; **~ sb in/out** empêcher qn de sortir/d'entrer; **~ sb from doing** empêcher qn de faire. ● vi (food) se conserver; **~ (on)** continuer (**doing** à faire). ● n pension f; (of castle) donjon m. □ **~ down** rester allongé; **~ sth down** limiter qch; **~ your voice down!** baisse ta voix!; **~ to** (road) ne pas s'écarter de; (rules) respecter; **~ up** (car, runner) suivre; (rain) continuer; **~ up with sb** (in speed) aller aussi vite que; (class, inflation, fashion, news) suivre.

keeper /'kiːpə(r)/ n gardien/-ne m/f.

keepsake /'kiːpseɪk/ n souvenir m.

kennel /'kenl/ n niche f.

kept /kept/ ➡**KEEP.**

kerb /kɜːb/ n bord m du trottoir.

kernel /'kɜːnl/ n amande f; **~ of truth** fond m de vérité.

kettle /'ketl/ n bouilloire f.

key /kiː/ n clé f; (of computer, piano) touche f. ● adj (industry, figure) clé (inv). ● vt ~ **(in)** saisir. **~board** n clavier m. **~hole** n trou m de serrure. **~pad** n (of telephone) clavier m numérique. **~-ring** n porte-clés m inv **~stroke** n (Comput) frappe f.

khaki /'kɑːkɪ/ adj kaki inv.

kick /kɪk/ vt/i donner un coup de pied (à); (horse) botter. ● n coup m de pied; (of gun) recul m; **get a ~ out of doing** ① prendre plaisir à faire. □ **~ out** ① virer ①.

kick-off *n* coup *m* d'envoi.

kid /kɪd/ *n* (goat, leather) chevreau *m*; (child 🔟) gosse *mf* 🔟. ● *vt/i* (*pt* **kidded**) blaguer.

kidnap /'kɪdnæp/ *vt* (*pt* **kidnapped**) enlever. **kidnapping** *n* enlèvement *m*.

kidney /'kɪdnɪ/ *n* rein *m*; (Culin) rognon *m*.

kill /kɪl/ *vt* tuer; (rumour: fig) arrêter. ● *n* mise *f* à mort. **killer** *n* tueur/-euse *m/f*. **killing** *n* meurtre *m*.

kiln /kɪln/ *n* four *m*.

kilo /'kiːləʊ/ *n* kilo *m*.

kilobyte /'kɪləbaɪt/ *n* kilo-octet *m*.

kilogram /'kɪləgræm/ *n* kilogramme *m*.

kilometre, (US) **kilometer** /'kɪləmiːtə(r)/ *n* kilomètre *m*.

kilowatt /'kɪləwɒt/ *n* kilowatt *m*.

kin /kɪn/ *n* parents *mpl*.

kind /kaɪnd/ *n* genre *m*, sorte *f*; in ~ en nature; ~ of (somewhat 🔟) assez. ● *adj* gentil, bon.

kindergarten /'kɪndəgɑːtn/ *n* jardin *m* d'enfants.

kindle /'kɪndl/ *vt/i* (s')allumer.

kindly /'kaɪndlɪ/ *adj* (**-ier, -iest**) (person) gentil; (interest) bienveillant. ● *adv* avec gentillesse; **would you ~ do** auriez-vous l'amabilité de faire.

kindness /'kaɪndnɪs/ *n* bonté *f*.

king /kɪŋ/ *n* roi *m*. **kingdom** *n* royaume *m*; (Bot) règne *m*. ~**fisher** *n* martin-pêcheur *m*. ~**size(d)** *adj* géant.

kiosk /'kiːɒsk/ *n* kiosque *m*; **telephone** ~ cabine *f* téléphonique; (Internet) borne *f* interactive, kiosque *m*.

kiss /kɪs/ *n* baiser *m*. ● *vt/i* (s')embrasser.

kit /kɪt/ *n* (clothing) affaires *fpl*; (set of tools) trousse *f*; (for assembly) kit *m*. ● *vt* (*pt* **kitted**) ~ **out** équiper.

kitchen /'kɪtʃɪn/ *n* cuisine *f*.

kite /kaɪt/ *n* (toy) cerf-volant *m*; (bird) milan *m*.

kitten /'kɪtn/ *n* chaton *m*.

kitty /'kɪtɪ/ *n* (fund) cagnotte *f*.

knack /næk/ *n* tour *m* de main (**of doing** pour faire).

knead /niːd/ *vt* pétrir.

knee /niː/ *n* genou *m*. ~**cap** *n* rotule *f*.

kneel /niːl/ *vi* (*pt* **knelt**) ~ (**down**) se mettre à genoux; (in prayer) s'agenouiller.

knew /njuː/ →**KNOW**.

knickers /'nɪkəz/ *npl* petite culotte *f*, slip *m*.

knife /naɪf/ *n* (*pl* **knives**) couteau *m*. ● *vt* poignarder.

knight /naɪt/ *n* chevalier *m*; (chess) cavalier *m*. ● *vt* anoblir. ~**hood** *n* titre *m* de chevalier.

knit /nɪt/ *vt/i* (*pt* **knitted** or **knit**) tricoter; (bones) (se) souder. **knitting** *n* tricot *m*. **knitwear** *n* tricots *mpl*.

knob /nɒb/ *n* bouton *m*.

knock /nɒk/ *vt/i* cogner; (criticize 🔟) critiquer; ~ **sth off/out** faire tomber qch. ● *n* coup *m*. □ ~ **down** (chair, pedestrian) renverser; (demolish) abattre; (reduce) baisser; ~ **off** (stop work 🔟) arrêter de travailler; ~ **£ 10 off** faire une réduction de 10 livres; ~ **it off!** 🔟 ça suffit!; ~ **out** assommer; ~ **over** renverser; ~ **up** (meal) préparer en vitesse.

knockout /'nɒkaʊt/ *n* (boxing) knock-out *m*.

knot /nɒt/ *n* nœud *m*. ● *vt* (*pt* **knotted**) nouer.

know /nəʊ/ *vt/i* (*pt* **knew**; *pp*

known (*answer, reason, language*)
savoir (**that** que); (*person, place,
name, rule, situation*) connaître; (recognize) reconnaître; **to do**
savoir faire; **~ about** (*event*) être au
courant de; (*subject*) s'y connaître
en; **~ of** (from experience) connaître; (from information) avoir entendu parler de. **~-how** n savoirfaire m inv.

knowingly /'nəʊɪŋlɪ/ adv (intentionally) délibérément; (meaningfully) d'un air entendu.

knowledge /'nɒlɪdʒ/ n connaissance f; (learning) connaissances fpl.
knowledgeable adj savant.

knuckle /'nʌkl/ n jointure f, articulation f.

Koran /kə'rɑːn/ n Coran m.

Korea /kə'rɪə/ n Corée f.

kosher /'kəʊʃə(r)/ adj casher inv.

• •

Ll

• •

lab /læb/ n Ⅰ labo m.

label /'leɪbl/ n étiquette f. • vt (pt
labelled) étiqueter.

laboratory /lə'bɒrətrɪ/ n laboratoire m.

laborious /lə'bɔːrɪəs/ adj laborieux.

labour, (US) **labor** /'leɪbə(r)/ n travail m; (workers) main-d'œuvre f; in
~ en train d'accoucher. • vi peiner
(**to do** à faire). • vt trop insister sur.

Labour /'leɪbə(r)/ n le parti travailliste. • adj travailliste.

laboured /'leɪbəd/ adj laborieux.

labourer /'leɪbərə(r)/ n ouvrier/-ière m/f; (on farm) ouvrier/-ière m/f.

agricole.

lace /leɪs/ n dentelle f; (of shoe)
lacet m. • vt (shoe) lacer; (drink)
arroser.

lacerate /'læsəreɪt/ vt lacérer.

lack /læk/ n manque m; **for ~ of**
faute de. • vt manquer de; **be**
~ing manquer (**in** de).

lad /læd/ n garçon m, gars m.

ladder /'lædə(r)/ n échelle f; (in
stocking) maille f filée. • vt/i (stocking) filer.

laden /'leɪdn/ adj chargé (**with** de).

ladle /'leɪdl/ n louche f.

lady /'leɪdɪ/ n (pl **ladies**) dame f; **ladies and gentlemen** mesdames et
messieurs; **young ~** jeune femme
or fille f. **~bird** n coccinelle f.

ladylike /'leɪdɪlaɪk/ adj distingué.

lag /læg/ vi (pt **lagged**) traîner. • vt
(pipes) calorifuger. • n (interval) décalage m.

lager /'lɑːgə(r)/ n bière f blonde.

lagoon /lə'guːn/ n lagune f.

laid /leɪd/ ⇒LAY¹. **~ back** adj décontracté.

lain /leɪn/ ⇒LIE².

lake /leɪk/ n lac m.

lamb /læm/ n agneau m; **leg of ~**
gigot m d'agneau.

lame /leɪm/ adj boiteux.

lament /lə'ment/ n lamentation f.
• vt/i se lamenter (sur).

laminated /'læmɪneɪtɪd/ adj
laminé.

lamp /læmp/ n lampe f. **~post** n
réverbère m. **~shade** n abat-jour
m inv.

lance /lɑːns/ vt (Med) inciser.

land /lænd/ n terre f; (plot) terrain
m; (country) pays m. • adj terrestre;
(policy, reform) agraire. • vt/i débarquer; (aircraft) (se) poser, (faire) atterrir; (fall) tomber; (obtain) décro-

k
l

cher; (a blow) porter; ~ **up** se retrouver.

landing /'lændɪŋ/ n débarquement m; (Aviat) atterrissage m; (top of stairs) palier m. **~-stage** n débarcadère m.

land: **~lady** n propriétaire f; (of pub) patronne f. **~lord** n propriétaire m; (of pub) patron m. **~mark** n (point de) repère m. **~mine** n mine f terrestre.

landscape /'lænskeɪp/ n paysage m. ● vt aménager.

landslide /'lænslaɪd/ n glissement m de terrain; (Pol) raz-de-marée m inv (électoral).

lane /leɪn/ n (path, road) chemin m; (strip of road) voie f; (of traffic) file f; (Aviat) couloir m.

language /'læŋgwɪdʒ/ n langue f; (speech, style) langage m. ~ **engineering** n ingénierie f des langues. ~ **laboratory** n laboratoire m de langue.

lank /læŋk/ adj (hair) plat.

lanky /'læŋkɪ/ adj (-ier, -iest) grand et maigre.

lantern /'læntən/ n lanterne f.

lap /læp/ n genoux mpl; (Sport) tour m (de piste). ● vi (pt **lapped**) (waves) clapoter. □ ~ **up** laper.

lapel /la'pel/ n revers m.

lapse /læps/ vi (decline) se dégrader; (expire) se périmer; ~ **into** retomber dans. ● n défaillance f, erreur f; (of time) intervalle m.

laptop /'læptɒp/ n (Comput) portable m.

lard /lɑːd/ n saindoux m.

larder /'lɑːdə(r)/ n garde-manger m inv.

large /lɑːdʒ/ adj grand, gros; **at** ~ en liberté; **by and** ~ en général. **largely** adv en grande mesure.

lark /lɑːk/ n (bird) alouette f; (bit of

fun 🔢) rigolade f. ● vi 🔢 rigoler.

larva /'lɑːvə/ n (pl **-vae**) larve f.

laryngitis /ˌlærɪn'dʒaɪtɪs/ n laryngite f.

laser /'leɪzə(r)/ n laser m. ~ **printer** n imprimante f laser. ~ **treatment** n (Med) laserothérapie f.

lash /læʃ/ vt fouetter. ● n coup m de fouet; (eyelash) cil m. □ ~ **out** (spend) dépenser follement; ~ **out against** attaquer.

lass /læs/ n jeune fille f.

lasso /læ'suː/ n lasso m.

last /lɑːst/ adj dernier; **the** ~ **straw** le comble; **the** ~ **word** le mot de la fin; **on its** ~ **legs** sur le point de rendre l'âme; ~ **night** hier soir. ● adv en dernier; (most recently) la dernière fois. ● n dernier/-ière m/f; (remainder) reste m; **at** (**long**) ~ enfin. ● vi durer. **~-ditch** adj ultime. **lasting** adj durable. **lastly** adv en dernier lieu. **~-minute** adj de dernière minute.

latch /lætʃ/ n loquet m.

late /leɪt/ adj (not on time) en retard; (former) ancien; (hour, fruit) tardif; **the** ~ **Mrs X** feu Mme X. ● adv (not early) tard; (not on time) en retard; **in** ~ **July** fin juillet; **of** ~ dernièrement. **lately** adv dernièrement. **latest** adj ➡LATE; (last) dernier.

lathe /leɪð/ n tour m.

lather /'lɑːðə(r)/ n mousse f. ● vt savonner. ● vi mousser.

Latin /'lætɪn/ n (Ling) latin m. ● adj latin. ~ **America** n Amérique f latine.

latitude /'lætɪtjuːd/ n latitude f.

latter /'lætə(r)/ adj dernier. ● n **the** ~ celui-ci, celle-ci.

Latvia /'lætvɪə/ n Lettonie f.

laudable /'lɔːdəbl/ adj louable.

laugh /lɑːf/ vi rire (**at** de). ● n rire

m. **laughable** *adj* ridicule.

laughing stock *n* risée *f.*

laughter /'lɑːftə(r)/ *n* (act) rire *m*; (sound of laughs) rires *mpl.*

launch /lɔːntʃ/ *vt* (rocket) lancer; (boat) mettre à l'eau; ~ (**out**) **into** se lancer dans. ● *n* lancement *m*; (boat) vedette *f.* **launching pad** *n* aire *f* de lancement.

launderette /'lɔːndrəmæt/ *n* laverie *f* automatique.

laundry /'lɔːndrɪ/ *n* (place) blanchisserie *f*; (clothes) linge *m.*

laurel /'lɒrəl/ *n* laurier *m.*

lava /'lɑːvə/ *n* lave *f.*

lavatory /'lævətrɪ/ *n* toilettes *fpl.*

lavender /'lævəndə(r)/ *n* lavande *f.*

lavish /'lævɪʃ/ *adj* (person) généreux; (lush) somptueux. ● *vt* prodiguer (**on** à). **lavishly** *adv* luxueusement.

law /lɔː/ *n* loi *f*; (profession, subject of study) droit *m*; ~ **and order** l'ordre public. ~-**abiding** *adj* respectueux des lois. ~-**court** *n* tribunal *m.*

lawful /'lɔːfl/ *adj* légal.

lawn /lɔːn/ *n* pelouse *f,* gazon *m.* ~-**mower** *n* tondeuse *f* à gazon.

lawsuit /'lɔːsuːt/ *n* procès *m.*

lawyer /'lɔːjə(r)/ *n* avocat *m.*

lax /læks/ *adj* (government) laxiste; (security) relâché.

laxative /'læksətɪv/ *n* laxatif *m.*

lay¹ /leɪ/ *adj* (non-clerical) laïque; (worker) non-initié. ● *vt* (*pt* **laid**) poser, mettre; (trap) tendre; (table) mettre; (plan) former; (eggs) pondre. ● *vi* pondre; ~ **waste** ravager. □ ~ **aside** mettre de côté; ~ **down** (dé)poser; (condition) (im-)poser; ~ **off** *vt* (worker) licencier; *vi* ▯ arrêter; ~ **on** (provide) fournir; ~ **out** (design) dessiner; (display) disposer; (money) dépenser.

lay² /leɪ/ →LIE³.

lay-by /'leɪbaɪ/ *n* (*pl* ~**s**) aire *f* de repos.

layer /'leɪə(r)/ *n* couche *f.*

layman /'leɪmən/ *n* (*pl* -**men**) profane *m.*

layout /'leɪaʊt/ *n* disposition *f.*

laze /leɪz/ *vi* paresser. **laziness** *n* paresse *f,* **lazy** *adj* (-**ier**, -**iest**) paresseux.

lead¹ /liːd/ *vt*/*i* (*pt* **led**) mener; (team) mener; (life) mener; (induce) amener; ~ **to** conduire à, mener à. ● *n* avance *f*; (clue) indice *m*; (leash) laisse *f*; (Theat) premier rôle *m*; (wire) fil *m*; **in the** ~ en tête. □ ~ **away** emmener; ~ **up to** (come to) en venir à; (precede) précéder.

lead² /led/ *n* plomb *m*; (of pencil) mine *f.*

leader /'liːdə(r)/ *n* chef *m*; (of country, club) dirigeant/-e *m/f*; (leading article) éditorial *m.* **leadership** *n* direction *f.*

lead-free *adj* (petrol) sans plomb.

leading /'liːdɪŋ/ *adj* principal.

leaf /liːf/ *n* (*pl* **leaves**) feuille *f*; (of table) rallonge *f.* ● *vi* ~ **through** feuilleter.

leaflet /'liːflɪt/ *n* prospectus *m.*

leafy /'liːfɪ/ *adj* feuillu.

league /liːg/ *n* ligue *f*; (Sport) championnat *m*; **in** ~ **with** de mèche avec.

leak /liːk/ *n* fuite *f.* ● *vi* fuir; (news: fig) s'ébruiter. ● *vt* répandre; (fig) divulguer.

lean¹ /liːn/ *adj* maigre. ● *n* (of meat) maigre *m.*

lean² /liːn/ *vt*/*i* (*pt* **leaned** or **leant**) (rest) (s')appuyer; (slope) pencher. □ ~ **out** se pencher à l'extérieur; ~ **over** (of person) se pencher.

leaning /'liːnɪŋ/ *adj* penché. ● *n* tendance *f.*

leap /liːp/ vi (pt **leaped** or **leapt**) bondir. ● n bond m. ~ **year** n année f bissextile.

learn /lɜːn/ vt/i (pt **learned** or **learnt**) apprendre (**to do** à faire). **learned** adj érudit. **learner** n débutant/-e m/f. **learning curve** n courbe f d'apprentissage.

lease /liːs/ n bail m. ● vt louer à bail.

leash /liːʃ/ n laisse f.

least /liːst/ adj **the ~** (smallest amount of) le moins de; (slightest) le or la moindre. ● n le moins. ● adv le moins; (with adjective) le or la moins; **at ~** au moins.

leather /ˈleðə(r)/ n cuir m.

leave /liːv/ vt (pt **left**) laisser; (depart from) quitter; (person) laisser tranquille; **be left** (over) rester. ● n (holiday) congé m; (consent) permission f; **take one's ~** prendre congé (of de); **on ~** (Mil) en permission. □ **~ alone** (thing) ne pas toucher; (person) laisser tranquille; **~ behind** laisser; **~ out** omettre.

Lebanon /ˈlebanan/ n Liban m.

lecture /ˈlektʃə(r)/ n cours m, conférence f; (rebuke) réprimande f. ● vt/i faire un cours or une conférence (à); (rebuke) réprimander. **lecturer** n conférencier/-ière m/f; (Univ) enseignant/-e m/f.

led /led/ →**LEAD**[1].

ledge /ledʒ/ n (window) rebord m; (rock) saillie f.

ledger /ˈledʒə(r)/ n grand livre m.

leech /liːtʃ/ n sangsue f.

leek /liːk/ n poireau m.

leer /lɪə(r)/ vi **~** (at) lorgner. ● n regard m sournois.

leeway /ˈliːweɪ/ n (fig) liberté f d'action; (Naut) dérive f.

left /left/ →**LEAVE**. ● adj gauche. ● adv à gauche. ● n gauche f.

~-hand adj à or de gauche.

~-handed adj gaucher.

left luggage (**office**) n consigne f.

left-overs npl restes mpl.

left-wing adj de gauche.

leg /leg/ n jambe f; (of animal) patte f; (of table) pied m; (of chicken) cuisse f; (of lamb) gigot m; (of journey) étape f.

legacy /ˈlegəsɪ/ n legs m.

legal /ˈliːgl/ adj légal; (affairs) juridique.

legend /ˈledʒənd/ n légende f.

leggings /ˈlegɪŋz/ npl (for woman) caleçon m.

legible /ˈledʒəbl/ adj lisible.

legionnaire /liːdʒəˈneə(r)/ n légionnaire m.

legislation /ledʒɪsˈleɪʃn/ n (body of laws) législation f; (law) loi f. **legislature** n corps m législatif.

legitimate /lɪˈdʒɪtɪmət/ adj légitime.

leisure /ˈleʒə(r)/ n loisirs mpl; **at one's ~** à tête reposée. ● adj (centre) de loisirs.

leisurely /ˈleʒəlɪ/ adj lent. ● adv sans se presser.

lemon /ˈlemən/ n citron m.

lemonade /leməˈneɪd/ n (fizzy) limonade f; (still) citronnade f.

lend /lend/ vt (pt **lent**) prêter; (credibility) conférer; **~ itself to** se prêter à.

length /leŋθ/ n longueur f; (in time) durée f; (section) morceau m; **at ~** (at last) enfin; (at great) longuement.

lengthen /ˈleŋθən/ vt/i (s')allonger.

lengthways /ˈleŋθweɪz/ adv dans le sens de la longueur.

lengthy /ˈleŋθɪ/ adj long.

lenient /ˈliːnɪənt/ adj indulgent.

lens /lenz/ n lentille f; (of spectacles) verre m; (Photo) objectif m.

lent /lent/ ➡LEND.

Lent /lent/ n Carême m.

lentil /'lentl/ n lentille f.

Leo /'li:əʊ/ n Lion m.

leopard /'lepəd/ n léopard m.

leotard /'li:ətɑ:d/ n body m.

leprosy /'leprəsɪ/ n lèpre f.

lesbian /'lezbɪən/ n lesbienne f.
● adj lesbien.

less /les/ adj (in quantity) moins de (than que). ● adv, n & prep moins; ~ than (with numbers) moins de; ~ work ~ than travailler moins que; ten pounds ~ dix livres de moins; ~ and ~ de moins en moins.

lessen vt/i diminuer. **lesser** adj moindre.

lesson /'lesn/ n leçon f.

let /let/ vt (pt let; pres p letting) laisser; (lease) louer. ● v aux ~ us do, ~'s do faisons; ~ him do qu'il fasse; ~ me know the results informe-moi des résultats. ● n location f. □ ~ **down** baisser; (deflate) dégonfler; (fig) décevoir; ~ go of lâcher; vi lâcher prise; ~ **sb in/out** laisser or faire entrer/sortir qn; ~ a dress out élargir une robe; ~ **one-self in for** (task) s'engager à; (trouble) s'attirer; ~ **off** (explode, fire) faire éclater or partir; (excuse) dispenser; (not punish) ne pas punir; ~ **up** 🆘 s'arrêter.

let-down n déception f.

lethal /'li:θl/ adj mortel; (weapon) meurtrier.

letter /'letə(r)/ n lettre f. ~**-bomb** n lettre f piégée. ~**-box** n boîte f à or aux lettres.

lettering /'letərɪŋ/ n (letters) caractères mpl.

lettuce /'letɪs/ n laitue f, salade f.

let-up /'letʌp/ n répit m.

leukaemia /lu:'ki:mɪə/ n leucémie f.

level /'levl/ adj plat, uni; (on surface) horizontal; (in height) au même niveau (**with** que); (in score) à égalité. ● n niveau m; (spirit) ~ niveau m à bulle; **be on the** ~ 🆘 être franc. ● vt (pt **levelled**) niveler; (aim) diriger. □ ~ **crossing** n passage m à niveau. ~**-headed** adj équilibré.

lever /'li:və(r)/ n levier m. ● vt soulever au moyen d'un levier.

leverage /'li:vərɪdʒ/ n influence f.

levy /'levɪ/ vt (tax) prélever. ● n impôt m.

lexicon /'leksɪkən/ n lexique m.

liability /laɪə'bɪlətɪ/ n responsabilité f; 🆘 handicap m; **liabilities** (debts) dettes fpl.

liable /'laɪəbl/ adj **be** ~ **to do** avoir tendance à faire, pouvoir faire; ~ **to** (illness) sujet à; (fine) passible de; ~ **for** responsable de.

liaise /lɪ'eɪz/ vi 🆘 faire la liaison. **liaison** n liaison f.

liar /'laɪə(r)/ n menteur/-euse m/f.

libel /'laɪbl/ n diffamation f. ● vt (pt **libelled**) diffamer.

liberal /'lɪbərəl/ adj libéral; (generous) généreux, libéral.

Liberal /'lɪbərəl/ adj & n (Pol) libéral/-e (m/f).

liberate /'lɪbəreɪt/ vt libérer.

liberty /'lɪbətɪ/ n liberté f; **at** ~ **to** libre de; **take liberties** prendre des libertés.

Libra /'li:brə/ n Balance f.

librarian /laɪ'breərɪən/ n bibliothécaire mf.

library /'laɪbrərɪ/ n bibliothèque f.

libretto /lɪ'bretəʊ/ n livret m.

lice /laɪs/ ➡LOUSE.

licence, (US) **license** /'laɪsns/ n permis m; (for television) redevance *f*; (Comm) licence *f*; (liberty: fig) licence *f.* **~ plate** n plaque *f* minéralogique.

license /'laɪsns/ *vt* accorder un permis à, autoriser.

lick /lɪk/ *vt* lécher; (defeat 🔳) rosser; (fig) **a ~ of paint** un petit coup de peinture. ● *n* coup *m* de langue.

lid /lɪd/ *n* couvercle *m*.

lie¹ /laɪ/ *n* mensonge *m*. ● *vi* (*pt* **lied**; *pres p* **lying**) (tell lies) mentir.

lie² /laɪ/ *vi* (*pt* **lay**; *pp* **lain**; *pres p* **lying**) s'allonger; (remain) rester; (be) se trouver, être; (in grave) reposer; **be lying** être allongé. □ **~ down** s'allonger; **~ in** faire la grasse matinée; **~ low** se cacher.

lieutenant /lef'tenənt/ *n* lieutenant *m*.

life /laɪf/ *n* (*pl* **lives**) vie *f.* **~belt** *n* bouée *f* de sauvetage. **~boat** *n* canot *m* de sauvetage. **~buoy** *n* bouée *f* de sauvetage. **~coach** *n* conseiller/ère *m/f* en développement personnel. **~ cycle** *n* cycle *m* de vie. **~guard** *n* sauveteur *m.* **~insurance** *n* assurance-vie *f.* **~jacket** *n* gilet *m* de sauvetage.

lifeless /'laɪflɪs/ *adj* inanimé.

lifelike /'laɪflaɪk/ *adj* très ressemblant.

life: **~long** *adj* de toute la vie. **~ sentence** *n* condamnation *f* à perpétuité. **~-size(d)** *adj* grandeur nature *inv.* **~ story** *n* vie *f.* **~style** *n* style *m* de vie. **~ support machine** *n* appareil *m* de respiration artificielle.

lifetime /'laɪftaɪm/ *n* vie *f*; **in one's ~** de son vivant.

lift /lɪft/ *vt* lever; (steal 🔳) voler. ● *vi* (of fog) se lever. ● *n* (in building) ascenseur *m*; **give a ~ to** emmener (en voiture). **~-off** *n* (Aviat)

décollage *m*.

light /laɪt/ *n* lumière *f*; (lamp) lampe *f*; (for fire, on vehicle) feu *m*; (headlight) phare *m*; **bring to ~** révéler; **come to ~** être révélé; **have you got a ~?** vous avez du feu? ● *adj* (not dark) clair; (not heavy) léger. ● *vt* (*pt* **lit** or **lighted**) allumer; (room) éclairer; (match) frotter. □ **~ up** *vi* s'allumer; *vt* (room) éclairer. **~ bulb** *n* ampoule *f.*

lighten /'laɪtn/ *vt* (give light to) éclairer; (make brighter) éclaircir; (make less heavy) alléger.

lighter /'laɪtə(r)/ *n* briquet *m*; (for stove) allume-gaz *m inv.*

light: **~-headed** *adj* (dizzy) qui a un vertige; (frivolous) étourdi. **~-hearted** *adj* gai. **~house** *n* phare *m.*

lighting /'laɪtɪŋ/ *n* éclairage *m.*

lightly /'laɪtlɪ/ *adv* légèrement.

lightning /'laɪtnɪŋ/ *n* éclair *m*, foudre *f.* ● *adj* (visit) éclair *inv.*

lightweight /'laɪtweɪt/ *adj* léger. ● *n* (boxing) poids *m* léger.

light year *n* année *f* lumière.

like¹ /laɪk/ *adj* semblable, pareil; **be ~-minded** avoir les mêmes sentiments. ● *prep* comme. ● *conj* 🔳 comme. ● *n* pareil *m*; **the ~s of** you les gens comme vous.

like² /laɪk/ *vt* aimer (bien); **I should ~** je voudrais, j'aimerais; **would you ~?** voudriez-vous?, voudrais-tu?; **~s** goûts *mpl.* **likeable** *adj* sympathique.

likelihood /'laɪklɪhʊd/ *n* probabilité *f.*

likely /'laɪklɪ/ *adj* (**-ier, -iest**) probable. ● *adv* probablement; **he is ~ to do** il fera probablement; **not ~!** 🔳 pas question!

likeness /'laɪknɪs/ *n* ressemblance *f.*

likewise /'laɪkwaɪz/ adv également.

liking /'laɪkɪŋ/ n (for thing) penchant m; (for person) affection f.

lilac /'laɪlək/ n lilas m. ● adj lilas inv.

Lilo® /'laɪləʊ/ n matelas m pneumatique.

lily /'lɪlɪ/ n lis m, lys m.

limb /lɪm/ n membre m.

limber /'lɪmbə(r)/ vi ~ up faire des exercices d'assouplissement.

limbo /'lɪmbəʊ/ n be in ~ (forgotten) être tombé dans l'oubli.

lime /laɪm/ n (fruit) citron m vert; ~(-tree) tilleul m.

limelight /'laɪmlaɪt/ n in the ~ en vedette.

limestone /'laɪmstəʊn/ n calcaire m.

limit /'lɪmɪt/ n limite f. ● vt limiter.

limited company n société f anonyme.

limp /lɪmp/ vi boiter. ● n have a ~ boiter. ● adj mou.

line /laɪn/ n ligne f; (track) voie f; (wrinkle) ride f; (row) rangée f, file f; (of poem) vers m; (rope) corde f; (of goods) gamme f; (queue: US) queue f; be in ~ for avoir de bonnes chances de; **hold the** ~ ne quittez pas; **in** ~ **with** en accord avec; **stand in** ~ faire la queue. ● vt (paper) régler; (streets) border; (garment) doubler; (fill) remplir, garnir. □ ~ **up** (s')aligner; (in queue) faire la queue; ~ **sth up** prévoir qch. ~ **dancing** danse f en ligne.

linen /'lɪnɪn/ n (sheets) linge m; (material) lin m.

liner /'laɪnə(r)/ n paquebot m.

linesman /'laɪnzmən/ n (football) juge m de touche; (tennis) juge m de ligne.

linger /'lɪŋgə(r)/ vi s'attarder; (smells) persister.

linguist /'lɪŋgwɪst/ n linguiste mf.
linguistics n linguistique f.

lining /'laɪnɪŋ/ n doublure f.

link /lɪŋk/ n lien m; (of chain) maillon m. ● vt relier; (relate) (re)lier; ~ **up** (of roads) se rejoindre.
linkage n lien m. **links** n inv terrain m de golf. **~-up** n liaison f.

lino /'laɪnəʊ/ n lino m.

lion /'laɪən/ n lion m. **lioness** n lionne f.

lip /lɪp/ n lèvre f; (edge) rebord m; **pay** ~**-service to** n'approuver que pour la forme. ~**-read** vt/i lire sur les lèvres. ~**salve** n baume m pour les lèvres. ~**stick** n rouge m (à lèvres).

liquid /'lɪkwɪd/ n & adj liquide (m).

liquidation /lɪkwɪ'deɪʃn/ n liquidation f; **go into** ~ déposer son bilan.

liquidize /'lɪkwɪdaɪz/ vt passer au mixeur. **liquidizer** n mixeur m.

liquor /'lɪkə(r)/ n alcool m.

liquorice /'lɪkərɪs/ n réglisse f.

lisp /lɪsp/ n zézaiement m; **with a** ~ en zézayant. ● vi zézayer.

list /lɪst/ n liste f. ● vt dresser la liste de. ● vi (ship) gîter.

listen /'lɪsn/ vi écouter; ~ **to**, ~ **in (to)** écouter. **listener** n auditeur/-trice m/f.

listless /'lɪstlɪs/ adj apathique.

lit /lɪt/ →LIGHT.

liter /'liːtər/ →LITRE.

literal /'lɪtərəl/ adj (meaning) littéral; (translation) mot à mot. **literally** adv littéralement; mot à mot.

literary /'lɪtərəri/ adj littéraire.

literate /'lɪtərət/ adj qui sait lire et écrire.

literature /'lɪtrətʃə(r)/ n littérature f; (brochures) documentation f.

Lithuania /lɪθju:'eɪnɪə/ n

Lituanie f.

litigation /lɪtɪ'geɪʃn/ n litiges mpl.

litre, (US) **liter** /'liːtə(r)/ n litre m.

litter /'lɪtə(r)/ n (rubbish) détritus mpl, papiers mpl; (animals) portée f. ● vt éparpiller; (make untidy) laisser des détritus dans; **~ed with** jonché de. **~bin** n poubelle f.

little /'lɪtl/ adj petit; (not much) peu de. ● n peu m; **a ~** un peu (de). ● adv peu.

live[1] /laɪv/ adj vivant; (wire) sous tension; (broadcast) en direct; **be a ~ wire** être très dynamique.

live[2] /lɪv/ vt/i vivre; (reside) habiter, vivre; **~ it up** mener la belle vie. □ **~ down** faire oublier; **~ on** (feed oneself on) vivre de; (continue) survivre; **~ up to** se montrer à la hauteur de.

livelihood /'laɪvlɪhʊd/ n moyens mpl d'existence.

lively /'laɪvlɪ/ adj (-ier, -iest) vif, vivant.

liven /'laɪvn/ vt/i **~ up** (s')animer; (cheer up) s'égayer.

liver /'lɪvə(r)/ n foie m.

livestock /'laɪvstɒk/ n bétail m.

livid /'lɪvɪd/ adj livide; (angry) furieux.

living /'lɪvɪŋ/ adj vivant. ● n vie f; **make a ~** gagner sa vie; **~ conditions** conditions fpl de vie. **~-room** n salle f de séjour.

lizard /'lɪzəd/ n lézard m.

load /ləʊd/ n charge f; (loaded goods) chargement m, charge f; (weight, strain) poids m; **~s of** 🔢 des tas de 🔢. ● vt charger.

loaf /ləʊf/ n (pl **loaves**) pain m. ● vi **~ (about)** fainéanter.

loan /ləʊn/ n prêt m; (money borrowed) emprunt m. ● vt prêter.

loathe /ləʊð/ vt détester (**doing** faire). **loathing** n dégoût m.

lobby /'lɒbɪ/ n entrée f, vestibule m; (Pol) lobby m, groupe m de pression. ● vt faire pression sur.

lobster /'lɒbstə(r)/ n homard m.

local /'ləʊkl/ adj local; (shops) du quartier; **~ government** administration f locale. ● n personne f du coin; (pub 🔢) pub m du coin.

localization /ləʊklaɪ'zeɪʃn/ n localisation f.

locally /'ləʊklɪ/ adv localement; (nearby) dans les environs.

locate /ləʊ'keɪt/ vt (situate) situer; (find) repérer.

location /ləʊ'keɪʃn/ n emplacement m; **on ~** (cinema) en extérieur.

lock /lɒk/ n (of door) serrure f; (on canal) écluse f; (of hair) mèche f. ● vt/i fermer à clef; (wheels: Auto) (se) bloquer. □ **~ in** or **up** (person) enfermer; **~ out** (by mistake) enfermer dehors.

locker /'lɒkə(r)/ n casier m.

locket /'lɒkɪt/ n médaillon m.

locksmith /'lɒksmɪθ/ n serrurier m.

locum /'ləʊkəm/ n (doctor) remplaçant/-e mf.

lodge /lɒdʒ/ n (house) pavillon m (de gardien ou de chasse); (of porter) loge f. ● vt (accommodate) loger; (money, complaint) déposer. ● vi être logé (**with** chez); (become fixed) se loger. **lodger** n locataire mf, pensionnaire mf. **lodgings** n logement m.

loft /lɒft/ n grenier m.

lofty /'lɒftɪ/ adj (-ier, -iest) (tall, noble) élevé; (haughty) hautain.

log /lɒg/ n (of wood) bûche f; **~(-book)** (Naut) journal m de bord; (Auto) ≈ carte f grise. ● vt (pt **logged**) noter; (distance) parcourir. □ **~ on** (Comput) se connecter; **~**

off (Comput) se déconnecter.

logic /'lɒdʒɪk/ adj logique. **logical** adj logique.

logistics /lə'dʒɪstɪks/ n logistique f.

loin /lɔɪn/ n (Culin) filet m; ~s reins mpl.

loiter /'lɔɪtə(r)/ vi traîner.

loll /lɒl/ vi se prélasser.

lollipop /'lɒlɪpɒp/ n sucette f.

London /'lʌndən/ n Londres. **Londoner** n Londonien/-ne m/f.

lone /ləʊn/ adj solitaire.

lonely (**-ier, -iest**) solitaire; (person) seul, solitaire.

long /lɒŋ/ adj long; **how** ~ **is?** quelle est la longueur de?; (in time) quelle est la durée de?; **how** ~? combien de temps?; **a** ~ **time** longtemps. ● adv longtemps; **he will not be** ~ il n'en a pas pour longtemps; **as** or **so** ~ **as** pourvu que; **before** ~ avant peu; **I no** ~ **do** je ne le fais plus. ● vi avoir bien or très envie (**for, to** de); ~ **for sb** se languir de qn. ~**-distance** adj (flight) sur long parcours; (phone call) interurbain; (runner) de fond. ~ **face** n grimace f. ~**hand** n écriture f courante.

longing /'lɒŋɪŋ/ n envie f (**for** de); (nostalgia) nostalgie f (**for** de).

longitude /'lɒndʒɪtjuːd/ n longitude f.

long: ~ **jump** n saut m en longueur. ~**-range** adj (missile) à longue portée; (forecast) à long terme. ~**-sighted** adj presbyte. ~**-standing** adj de longue date. ~**-term** adj à long terme. ~ **wave** n grandes ondes fpl. ~**-winded** adj verbeux.

loo /luː/ n 🔢 toilettes fpl.

look /lʊk/ vi regarder; (seem) avoir l'air; ~ **like** ressembler à, avoir l'air de. ● n regard m; (appearance) air

m, aspect m; (**good**) ~**s** beauté f. □ ~ **after** s'occuper de, soigner; ~ **at** regarder; ~ **back on** repenser à; ~ **down on** mépriser; ~ **for** chercher; ~ **forward to** attendre avec impatience; ~ **in on** passer voir; ~ **into** examiner; ~ **out** faire attention; ~ **out for** (person) guetter; (symptoms) guetter l'apparition de; ~ **round** se retourner; ~ **up** (word) chercher; (visit) passer voir; ~ **up to** respecter.

lookout /'lʊkaʊt/ n (Mil) poste m de guet; (person) guetteur m; **be on the** ~ **for** rechercher.

loom /luːm/ vi surgir; (war) menacer; (interview) être imminent. ● n métier m à tisser.

loony /'luːnɪ/ n & adj 🔢 fou, folle (mf).

loop /luːp/ n boucle f. ● vt boucler. ~**hole** n lacune f.

loose /luːs/ adj (knot) desserré; (page) détaché; (clothes) ample, lâche; (tooth) qui bouge; (lax) relâché; (not packed) en vrac; (inexact) vague; (pej) immoral; **at a** ~ **end** désœuvré; **come** ~ bouger.

loosely adv sans serrer; (roughly) vaguement. **loosen** vt (slacken) desserrer; (untie) défaire.

loot /luːt/ n butin m. ● vt piller.

lord /lɔːd/ n seigneur m; (British title) lord m; **the L**~ le Seigneur; (**good**) **L**~**!** mon Dieu!

lorry /'lɒrɪ/ n camion m.

lose /luːz/ vt/i (pt **lost**) perdre; **get lost** se perdre. **loser** n perdant/-e m/f.

loss /lɒs/ n perte f; **be at a** ~ être perplexe; **be at a** ~ **to** être incapable de; **heat** ~ déperdition f de chaleur.

lost /lɒst/ ➜**LOSE.** ● adj perdu. ~ **property** n objets mpl trouvés.

lot /lɒt/ n the ~ (le) tout m; (people) tous mpl, toutes fpl; a ~ (of), ~s (of) ☐ beaucoup (de); quite a ~ (of) ☐ pas mal (de); (fate) sort m; (at auction) lot m; (land) lotissement m.

lotion /ˈləʊʃn/ n lotion f.

lottery /ˈlɒtərɪ/ n loterie f.

loud /laʊd/ adj bruyant, fort. ● adv fort; **out** ~ tout haut. **loudly** adv fort. ~**speaker** n haut-parleur m.

lounge /laʊndʒ/ vi paresser. ● n salon m.

louse /laʊs/ n (pl **lice**) pou m.

lousy /ˈlaʊzɪ/ adj (-ier, -iest) ☐ infect.

lout /laʊt/ n rustre m.

lovable /ˈlʌvəbl/ adj adorable.

love /lʌv/ n amour m; (tennis) zéro m; **in** ~ amoureux (**with** de); **make** ~ faire l'amour. ● vt (person) aimer; (like greatly) aimer (beaucoup) (**to do** faire). ~ **affair** n liaison f amoureuse. ~ **life** n vie f amoureuse.

lovely /ˈlʌvlɪ/ adj (-ier, -iest) joli; (delightful ☐) très agréable.

lover /ˈlʌvə(r)/ n (male) amant m; (female) maîtresse f; (devotee) amateur m (**of** de).

loving /ˈlʌvɪŋ/ adj affectueux.

low /ləʊ/ adj & adv bas; ~ **in sth** à faible teneur en qch. ● n (low pressure) dépression f; **reach a (new)** ~ atteindre son niveau le plus bas. ● vi meugler. ~**calorie** adj basses-calories. ~**cut** adj décolleté.

lower /ˈləʊə(r)/ adj & adv ►LOW. ● vt baisser; ~ **oneself** s'abaisser.

low: ~**fat** adj (diet) sans matières grasses; (cheese) allégé. ~**key** adj modéré; (discreet) discret. ~**lands** npl plaine(s) f(pl). ~**lying** adj à faible altitude.

loyal /ˈlɔɪəl/ adj loyal (**to** envers).

loyalty /ˈlɔɪəltɪ/ n fidélité f. ~**card** n carte f de fidélité.

lozenge /ˈlɒzɪndʒ/ n (shape) losange m; (tablet) pastille f.

LP n (disque m) 33 tours m.

Ltd. abbr (**Limited**) SA.

lubricant /ˈluːbrɪkənt/ n lubrifiant m. **lubricate** vt lubrifier.

luck /lʌk/ n chance f; **bad** ~ malchance f; **good** ~! bonne chance!

luckily /ˈlʌkɪlɪ/ adv heureusement.

lucky /ˈlʌkɪ/ adj (-ier, -iest) qui a de la chance, heureux; (event) heureux; (number) qui porte bonheur; **it's** ~ **that** heureusement que.

ludicrous /ˈluːdɪkrəs/ adj ridicule.

lug /lʌg/ vt (pt **lugged**) traîner.

luggage /ˈlʌgɪdʒ/ n bagages mpl. ~**rack** n porte-bagages m inv.

lukewarm /luːkˈwɔːm/ adj tiède.

lull /lʌl/ vt he ~ed them into thinking that il leur a fait croire que. ● n accalmie f.

lullaby /ˈlʌləbaɪ/ n berceuse f.

lumber /ˈlʌmbə(r)/ n bois m de charpente. ● vt ☐ ~ **sb with** (chore) coller à qn ☐. ~**jack** n bûcheron m.

luminous /ˈluːmɪnəs/ adj lumineux.

lump /lʌmp/ n morceau m; (swelling on body) grosseur f; (in liquid) grumeau m. ● vt ~ **together** réunir. ~ **sum** n somme f globale.

lunacy /ˈluːnəsɪ/ n folie f.

lunar /ˈluːnə(r)/ adj lunaire.

lunatic /ˈluːnətɪk/ n fou/folle m/f.

lunch /lʌntʃ/ n déjeuner m. ● vi déjeuner.

luncheon /ˈlʌntʃən/ n déjeuner m. ~ **voucher** n chèque-repas m.

lung /lʌŋ/ n poumon m.

lunge /lʌndʒ/ vi bondir (**at** sur; **forward** en avant).

lurch /lɜːtʃ/ n leave in the ~ planter là, laisser en plan. ● vi (person) tituber.

lure /lʊə(r)/ vt appâter, attirer. ● n (attraction) attrait m, appât m.

lurid /ˈlʊərɪd/ adj choquant, affreux; (gaudy) voyant.

lurk /lɜːk/ vi se cacher; (in ambush) s'embusquer; (prowl) rôder; (suspicion, danger) menacer.

luscious /ˈlʌʃəs/ adj appétissant.

lush /lʌʃ/ adj luxuriant.

lust /lʌst/ n luxure f.

Luxemburg /ˈlʌksəmbɜːg/ n Luxembourg m.

luxurious /lʌɡˈzjʊərɪəs/ adj luxueux.

luxury /ˈlʌkʃərɪ/ n luxe m. ● adj de luxe.

lying /ˈlaɪɪŋ/ ⇒LIE¹, ⇒LIE². ● n mensonges mpl.

lyric /ˈlɪrɪk/ adj lyrique. **lyrical** /ˈlɪrɪkl/ adj lyrique. **lyrics** npl paroles fpl.

• •

Mm

• •

MA abbr ⇒MASTER OF ARTS.

mac /mæk/ n 🇬🇧 imper m.

machine /məˈʃiːn/ n machine f. ● vt (sew) coudre à la machine; (Tech) usiner. **~-gun** n mitrailleuse f.

mackerel /ˈmækrəl/ n inv maquereau m.

mackintosh /ˈmækɪntɒʃ/ n imperméable m.

mad /mæd/ adj (**madder, maddest**) fou; (foolish) insensé; (dog) enragé; (angry 🇬🇧) furieux; **be ~ about** se passionner pour; (person)

être fou de; **drive sb ~** exaspérer qn; **like ~** comme un fou. **~ cow disease** n maladie f de la vache folle.

madam /ˈmædəm/ n madame f; (unmarried) mademoiselle f.

made /meɪd/ ⇒MAKE.

madly /ˈmædlɪ/ adv (interested, in love) follement; (frantically) comme un fou.

madman /ˈmædmən/ n (pl **-men**) fou m.

madness /ˈmædnɪs/ n folie f.

magazine /ˌmæɡəˈziːn/ n revue f; (of gun) magasin m.

maggot /ˈmæɡət/ n (in fruit) ver m, (for fishing) asticot m.

magic /ˈmædʒɪk/ n magie f. ● adj magique.

magician /məˈdʒɪʃn/ n magicien-ne m/f.

magistrate /ˈmædʒɪstreɪt/ n magistrat m.

magnet /ˈmæɡnɪt/ n aimant m. **magnetic** /mæɡˈnetɪk/ adj magnétique.

magnificent /mæɡˈnɪfɪsnt/ adj magnifique.

magnify /ˈmæɡnɪfaɪ/ vt grossir; (sound) amplifier; (fig) exagérer. **magnifying glass** n loupe f.

magpie /ˈmæɡpaɪ/ n pie f.

mahogany /məˈhɒɡənɪ/ n acajou m.

maid /meɪd/ n (servant) bonne f; (in hotel) femme f de chambre.

maiden /ˈmeɪdn/ n (old use) jeune fille f. ● adj (aunt) célibataire; (voyage) premier. **~ name** n nom m de jeune fille.

mail /meɪl/ n (postal service) poste f; (letters) courrier m; (armour) cotte f de mailles. ● adj (bag, van) postal. ● vt envoyer par la poste. **~ box** n boîte f aux lettres; (Comput) boîte f aux lettres électronique. **mailing**

list n liste f d'adresses. **~man** n (pl **-men**) (US) facteur m. **~ order** n vente f par correspondance. **~ shot** n publipostage m.

main /meɪn/ adj principal; a **~ road** une grande route. ● n (water/ gas) **~** conduite f d'eau/de gaz; **the ~s** (Electr) le secteur; **in the ~** en général. **~frame** n unité f centrale. **~land** n continent m. **~stream** n tendance f principale, ligne f.

maintain /meɪn'teɪn/ vt (continue, keep, assert) maintenir; (house, machine, family) entretenir; (rights) soutenir.

maintenance /'meɪntənəns/ n (care) entretien m; (continuation) maintien m; (allowance) pension f alimentaire.

maisonette /meɪzə'net/ n duplex m.

maize /meɪz/ n maïs m.

majestic /mə'dʒestɪk/ adj majestueux.

majesty /'mædʒəstɪ/ n majesté f.

major /'meɪdʒə(r)/ adj majeur. ● n commandant m. ● vi **~ in** (Univ, US) se spécialiser en.

majority /mə'dʒɒrətɪ/ n majorité f; **the ~ of people** la plupart des gens. ● adj majoritaire.

make /meɪk/ vt/i (pt made) faire; (manufacture) fabriquer; (friends) se faire; (money) gagner; (decision) prendre; (place, position) arriver à; (cause to be) rendre; **~ sb do sth** faire faire qch à qn; **be made of** être fait de; **~ oneself at home** se mettre à l'aise; **~ sb happy** rendre qn heureux; **~ it** arriver; (succeed) réussir; **I ~ it two o'clock** j'ai deux heures; **I ~ it 150** d'après moi, ça fait 150; **I cannot ~ anything of it** je n'y comprends rien; **can you ~ Friday?** vendredi, c'est possible?; **~ as if to** faire mine de. ● n (brand) marque f. □ **~ do** (manage) se débrouiller (with avec); **~ for** se diriger vers; (cause) tendre à créer; **~ good** vi réussir; vt compenser; (repair) réparer; **~ off** filer (with avec); **~ out** distinguer; (understand) comprendre; (draw up) faire; (assert) prétendre; **~ up** vt faire, former; (story) inventer; (deficit) combler; vi se réconcilier; **~ up for** compenser; (time) rattraper; **~ up one's mind** se décider.

make-believe adj feint, illusoire. ● n fantaisie f.

maker /'meɪkə(r)/ n fabricant m.

makeshift /'meɪkʃɪft/ adj improvisé.

make-up /'meɪkʌp/ n maquillage m; (of object) constitution f; (Psych) caractère m.

malaria /mə'leərɪə/ n paludisme m.

Malaysia /mə'leɪzɪə/ n Malaisie f.

male /meɪl/ adj (voice, sex) masculin; (Bot, Tech) mâle. ● n mâle m.

malfunction /mæl'fʌŋkʃn/ n mauvais fonctionnement m. ● vi mal fonctionner.

malice /'mælɪs/ n méchanceté f. **malicious** adj méchant.

malignant /mə'lɪgnənt/ adj malveillant; (tumour) malin.

mall /mɔːl/ n (shopping) **~** (in suburbs) centre m commercial; (in town) galerie f marchande.

malnutrition /mælnjuː'trɪʃn/ n sousalimentation f.

Malta /'mɔːltə/ n Malte f.

mammal /'mæml/ n mammifère m.

mammoth /'mæməθ/ n mammouth m. ● adj (task) gigantesque; (organization) géant.

man /mæn/ n (pl **men**) homme m; (in sports team) joueur m; (chess) pièce f. ~ **to man** d'homme à homme. ● vt (pt **manned**) (desk) tenir; (ship) armer; (guns) servir; (be on duty at) être de service à.

manage /'mænɪdʒ/ vt (project, organization) diriger; (shop, affairs) gérer; (handle) manier; **I could ~ another drink** 🅵 je prendrais bien encore un verre; **can you ~ Friday?** vendredi, c'est possible? ● vi se débrouiller; ~ **to do** réussir à faire. **manageable** adj (tool, size, person) maniable; (job) faisable.

management /'mænɪdʒmənt/ n (managers) direction f; (of shop) gestion f.

manager /'mænɪdʒə(r)/ n directeur/-trice m/f; (of shop) gérant/-e m/f; (of actor) impresario m.

mandate /'mændeɪt/ n mandat m.

mandatory /'mændətərɪ/ adj obligatoire.

mane /meɪn/ n crinière f.

mango /'mæŋgəʊ/ n (pl ~**es**) mangue f.

manhandle /'mænhændl/ vt maltraiter, malmener.

man: ~**hole** n regard m. ~**hood** n âge m d'homme; (quality) virilité f.

maniac /'meɪnɪæk/ n maniaque mf, fou m, folle f.

manicure /'mænɪkjʊə(r)/ n manicure f. ● vt soigner, manucurer.

manifest /'mænɪfest/ adj manifeste. ● vt manifester.

manipulate /mə'nɪpjʊleɪt/ vt (tool, person) manipuler.

mankind /mæn'kaɪnd/ n genre m humain.

manly /'mænlɪ/ adj viril.

man-made /'mænmeɪd/ adj (fibre) synthétique; (pond) artificiel; (disaster)

d'origine humaine.

manned // adj (spacecraft) habité.

manner /'mænə(r)/ n manière f; (attitude) attitude f; (kind) sorte f; ~**s** (social behaviour) manières fpl.

mannerism /'mænərɪzəm/ n particularité f; (quirk) manie f.

manoeuvre /mə'nu:və(r)/ n manœuvre f. ● vt/i manœuvrer.

manor /'mænə(r)/ n manoir m.

manpower /'mænpaʊə(r)/ n main-d'œuvre f.

mansion /'mænʃn/ n (in countryside) demeure f; (in town) hôtel m particulier.

manslaughter /'mænslɔːtə(r)/ n homicide m involontaire.

mantelpiece /'mæntlˌself/ n (manteau m de) cheminée f.

manual /'mænjʊəl/ adj (labour) manuel; (typewriter) mécanique. ● n (handbook) manuel m.

manufacture /mænjʊ'fæktʃə(r)/ vt fabriquer. ● n fabrication f.

manure /mə'njʊə(r)/ n fumier m.

many /'menɪ/ adj & n beaucoup (de); **a great** or **good** ~ un grand nombre (de); ~ **a** bien des.

map /mæp/ n carte f; (of streets) plan m. ● vt (pt **mapped**) faire la carte de; ~ **out** (route) tracer; (arrange) organiser.

mar /mɑː(r)/ vt (pt **marred**) gâcher.

marble /'mɑːbl/ n marbre m; (for game) bille f.

March /mɑːtʃ/ n mars m.

march /mɑːtʃ/ vi (Mil) marcher (au pas). ● vt ~ **off** (lead away) emmener. ● n marche f.

margin /'mɑːdʒɪn/ n marge f.

marginal /'mɑːdʒɪnl/ adj marginal; (increase) léger, faible; (seat: Pol) disputé.

marinate /'mærɪneɪt/ vt faire

mariner (**in** dans).

marine /məˈriːn/ adj marin. ● n (shipping) marine f; (sailor) fusilier m marin.

marital /ˈmærɪtl/ adj conjugal. ~ **status** n situation f de famille.

mark /mɑːk/ n (currency) mark m; (stain) tache f; (trace) marque f; (School) note f; (target) but m. ● vt marquer; (exam) corriger; ~ **out** délimiter; (person) désigner; ~ **time** marquer le pas.

marker /ˈmɑːkə(r)/ n (pen) marqueur m; (tag) repère m; (School, Univ) examinateur/-trice m/f.

market /ˈmɑːkɪt/ n marché m; **on the** ~ en vente. ● vt (sell) vendre; (launch) commercialiser. ~ **research** n étude f de marché.

marmalade /ˈmɑːməleɪd/ n confiture f d'oranges.

maroon /məˈruːn/ n bordeaux m inv. ● adj bordeaux inv.

marooned /məˈruːnd/ adj abandonné; (snowbound) bloqué.

marquee /mɑːˈkiː/ n grande tente f; (of circus) chapiteau m; (awning: US) auvent m.

marriage /ˈmærɪdʒ/ n mariage m (**to** avec).

married /ˈmærɪd/ adj marié (**to** à); (life) conjugal; **get** ~ se marier (**to** avec).

marrow /ˈmærəʊ/ n (of bone) moelle f; (vegetable) courge f.

marry /ˈmærɪ/ vt épouser; (give or unite in marriage) marier. ● vi se marier.

marsh /mɑːʃ/ n marais m.

marshal /ˈmɑːʃl/ n maréchal m; (at event) membre m du service d'ordre. ● vt (pt **marshalled**) rassembler.

martyr /ˈmɑːtə(r)/ n martyr/-e m/f. ● vt martyriser.

marvel /ˈmɑːvl/ n merveille f. ● vi (pt **marvelled**) s'émerveiller (**at** de).

marvellous /ˈmɑːvələs/ adj merveilleux.

marzipan /ˈmɑːzɪpæn/ n pâte f d'amandes.

masculine /ˈmæskjʊlɪn/ adj & n masculin (m).

mash /mæʃ/ n (potatoes ⊞) purée f. ● vt écraser. **mashed potatoes** npl purée f (de pommes de terre).

mask /mɑːsk/ n masque m. ● vt masquer.

Mason /ˈmeɪsn/ n franc-maçon m.

masonry /ˈmeɪsnrɪ/ n maçonnerie f.

mass /mæs/ n (Relig) messe f; masse f; **the** ~**es** les masses fpl. ● vt/i (se) masser.

massacre /ˈmæsəkə(r)/ n massacre m. ● vt massacrer.

massage /ˈmæsɑːʒ/ n massage m. ● vt masser.

massive /ˈmæsɪv/ adj (large) énorme; (heavy) massif.

mass media n médias mpl.

mass-produce vt fabriquer en série.

mast /mɑːst/ n (on ship) mât m; (for radio, TV) pylône m.

master /ˈmɑːstə(r)/ n maître m; (in secondary school) professeur m; **M**~ **of Arts** titulaire mf d'une maîtrise ès lettres. ● vt maîtriser.

masterpiece /ˈmɑːstəpiːs/ n chef-d'œuvre m.

mastery /ˈmɑːstərɪ/ n maîtrise f.

mat /mæt/ n (petit) tapis m; (at door) paillasson m.

match /mætʃ/ n (for lighting fire) allumette f; (Sport) match m; (equal) égal/-e m/f; (marriage) mariage m; (sb to marry) parti m; **be a**

~ **for** pouvoir tenir tête à. ● *vt* opposer; (go with) aller avec; (cups) assortir; (equal) égaler. ● *vi* (be alike) être assorti. **matchbox** *n* boîte *f* à allumettes.

matching /'mætʃɪŋ/ *adj* assorti.

mate /meɪt/ *n* camarade *mf*; (of animal) compagnon *m*, compagne *f*; (assistant) aide *mf*; (chess) mat *m*. ● *vt/i* (s')accoupler (**with** avec).

material /mə'tɪərɪəl/ *n* matière *f*; (fabric) tissu *m*; (documents, for building) matériau(x) *m*(*pl*); ~**s** (equipment) matériel *m*. ● *adj* matériel; (fig) important. **materialistic** *adj* matérialiste.

materialize /mə'tɪərɪəlaɪz/ *vi* se matérialiser, se réaliser.

maternal /mə'tɜːnl/ *adj* maternel.

maternity /mə'tɜːnətɪ/ *n* maternité *f*. ● *adj* (clothes) de grossesse. ~ **hospital** *n* maternité *f*. ~ **leave** *n* congé *m* maternité.

mathematics /mæθə'mætɪks/ *n* & *npl* mathématiques *fpl*.

maths /mæθs/, (US) **math** /mæθs/ *n* maths *fpl*.

mating /'meɪtɪŋ/ *n* accouplement *m*.

matrimony /'mætrɪmənɪ/ *n* mariage *m*.

matron /'meɪtrən/ *n* (married, elderly) dame *f* âgée; (in hospital) infirmière *f* en chef.

matt /mæt/ *adj* mat.

matter /'mætə(r)/ *n* (substance) matière *f*; (affair) affaire *f*; **as a** ~ **of fact** en fait; **what is the** ~? qu'est-ce qu'il y a? ● *vi* importer; **it does not** ~ ça ne fait rien; **no** ~ **what happens** quoi qu'il arrive.

mattress /'mætrɪs/ *n* matelas *m*.

mature /mə'tjʊə(r)/ *adj* (psychologically) mûr; (plant) adulte. ● *vt/i* (se) mûrir. **maturity** *n* maturité *f*.

mauve /məʊv/ *adj* & *n* mauve (*m*).

maverick /'mævərɪk/ *n* non-conformiste *mf*.

maximize /'mæksɪmaɪz/ *vt* porter au maximum.

maximum /'mæksɪməm/ *adj* & *n* (*pl* **-ima**) maximum (*m*).

may /meɪ/

past **might**

● *auxiliary verb*

····> (possibility) **they** ~ **be able to come** ils pourront peut-être venir; **she** ~ **not have seen him** elle ne l'a peut-être pas vu; **it** ~**rain** il risque de pleuvoir; **'will you come?'—'I might'** 'tu viendras?' —'peut-être'.

····> (permission) **you** ~ **leave** vous pouvez partir; ~ **I smoke?** puis-je fumer?

····> (wish) ~ **he be happy** qu'il soit heureux.

May /meɪ/ *n* mai *m*.

maybe /'meɪbɪ/ *adv* peut-être.

mayhem /'meɪhem/ *n* (havoc) ravages *mpl*.

mayonnaise /meɪə'neɪz/ *n* mayonnaise *f*.

mayor /meə(r)/ *n* maire *m*.

maze /meɪz/ *n* labyrinthe *m*.

Mb *abbr* (**megabyte**) (Comput) Mo.

me /miː/ *pron* me, m'; (after prep.) moi; (indirect object) me, m'; **he knows** ~ il me connaît.

meadow /'medəʊ/ *n* pré *m*.

meagre /'miːgə(r)/ *adj* maigre.

meal /miːl/ *n* repas *m*; (grain) farine *f*.

m

mean /miːn/ adj (poor) misérable; (miserly) avare; (unkind) méchant; (average) moyen. ● n milieu m; (average) moyenne f; **in the ~time** en attendant. ● vt (pt **meant**) vouloir dire, signifier; (involve) entraîner; **I ~ that!** je suis sérieux; **be meant for** être destiné à; **~ to do** avoir l'intention de faire.

meaning /miːnɪŋ/ n sens m, signification f. **meaningful** adj significatif. **meaningless** adj dénué de sens.

means /miːnz/ n moyen(s) m (pl); **by ~ of sth** au moyen de qch. ● npl (wealth) moyens mpl financiers; **by all ~** certainement; **by no ~** nullement.

meant /ment/ →MEAN.

meantime /miːntaɪm/, **meanwhile** adv en attendant.

measles /miːzlz/ n rougeole f.

measure /meʒə(r)/ n mesure f; (ruler) règle f. ● vt/i mesurer; **~up to** être à la hauteur de. **measurement** n mesures fpl.

meat /miːt/ n viande f. **meaty** adj de viande; (fig) substantiel.

mechanic /mɪkænɪk/ n mécanicien/-ne mf.

mechanical /mɪkænɪkl/ adj mécanique.

mechanism /mekənɪzəm/ n mécanisme m.

medal /medl/ n médaille f.

meddle /medl/ vi (interfere) se mêler (**in** de); (tinker) toucher (**with** à).

media /miːdɪə/ n →MEDIUM. ● npl **the~** les média mpl; **talk to the ~** parler à la presse.

median /miːdɪən/ adj médian. ● n médiane f.

mediate /miːdɪeɪt/ vi servir d'intermédiaire.

medical /medɪkl/ adj médical;

(student) en médecine. ● n visite f médicale.

medication /medɪkeɪʃn/ n médicaments mpl.

medicine /medsn/ n (science) médecine f; (substance) médicament m.

medieval /medɪiːvl/ adj médiéval.

mediocre /miːdɪəʊkə(r)/ adj médiocre.

meditate /medɪteɪt/ vt/i méditer.

Mediterranean /medɪtəreɪnɪən/ adj méditerranéen. ● n **the ~** la Méditerranée f.

medium /miːdɪəm/ n (pl **media**) (mid-point) milieu m; (for transmitting data) support m; (pl **mediums**) (person) médium m. ● adj moyen.

medley /medlɪ/ n mélange m; (Mus) potpourri m.

meet /miːt/ vt (pt **met**) rencontrer; (see again) retrouver; (be introduced to) faire la connaissance de; (face) faire face à; (requirement) satisfaire. ● vi se rencontrer; (see each other again) se retrouver; (in session) se réunir.

meeting /miːtɪŋ/ n réunion f; (between two people) rencontre f.

megabyte /megəbaɪt/ n (Comput) mégaoctet m.

melancholy /melənkəlɪ/ n mélancolie f. ● adj mélancolique.

mellow /meləʊ/ adj (fruit) mûr; (sound, colour) moelleux, doux; (person) mûri. ● vt/i (mature) mûrir; (soften) (s')adoucir.

melody /melədɪ/ n mélodie f.

melon /melən/ n melon m.

melt /melt/ vt/i (faire) fondre.

member /membə(r)/ n membre m. **M~ of Parliament** n député m. **membership** n adhésion f; (members) membres mpl; (fee) cotisation f.

memento /mɪˈmentəʊ/ n (pl ~es) (object) souvenir m.

memo /ˈmeməʊ/ n note f.

memoir /ˈmemwɑː(r)/ n (record, essay) mémoire m.

memorandum /meməˈrændəm/ n note f.

memorial /məˈmɔːrɪəl/ n monument m. ● adj commémoratif.

memorize /ˈmeməraɪz/ vt apprendre par cœur.

memory /ˈmeməri/ n (mind, in computer) mémoire f; (thing remembered) souvenir m; **from ~** de mémoire; **in ~ of** à la mémoire de.

men /men/ ➔MAN.

menace /ˈmenəs/ n menace f; (nuisance) peste f. ● vt menacer.

mend /mend/ vt réparer; (darn) raccommoder; **~ one's ways** s'amender; **● n** raccommodage m; **on the ~** en voie de guérison.

meningitis /menɪnˈdʒaɪtɪs/ n méningite f.

menopause /ˈmenəpɔːz/ n ménopause f.

mental /ˈmentl/ adj mental; (hospital) psychiatrique.

mentality /menˈtælətɪ/ n mentalité f.

mention /ˈmenʃn/ vt mentionner; **don't ~it!** il n'y a pas de quoi, je vous en prie! ● n mention f.

menu /ˈmenjuː/ n (food, on computer) menu m; (list) carte f.

MEP abbr (**Member of the European Parliament**) député m au Parlement européen.

mercenary /ˈmɜːsɪnərɪ/ adj & n mercenaire (m.)

merchandise /ˈmɜːtʃəndaɪz/ n marchandises fpl.

merchant /ˈmɜːtʃənt/ n marchand m. ● adj (ship, navy) marchand. **~**

bank n banque f de commerce.

merciful /ˈmɜːsɪfl/ adj miséricordieux.

mercury /ˈmɜːkjʊrɪ/ n mercure m.

mercy /ˈmɜːsɪ/ n pitié f; **at the ~** of à la merci de.

mere /mɪə(r)/ adj simple. **merest** adj moindre.

merge /mɜːdʒ/ vt/i (se) mêler (**with** à); (companies: Comm) fusionner. **merger** n fusion f.

mermaid /ˈmɜːmeɪd/ n sirène f.

merrily /ˈmerɪlɪ/ adv (happily) joyeusement; (unconcernedly) avec insouciance.

merry /ˈmerɪ/ adj (-ier, -iest) gai; **make ~** faire la fête. **~-go-round** n manège m.

mesh /meʃ/ n maille f; (fabric) tissu m à mailles; (network) réseau m.

mesmerize /ˈmezməraɪz/ vt hypnotiser.

mess /mes/ n désordre m, gâchis m; (dirt) saleté f; (Mil) mess m; **make a ~ of** gâcher. **● vi ~ up** gâcher.; vi **~ about** s'amuser; (dawdle) traîner; **~ with** (tinker with) tripoter.

message /ˈmesɪdʒ/ n message m.

messenger /ˈmesɪndʒə(r)/ n messager/-ère m/f.

messy /ˈmesɪ/ adj (-ier, -iest) en désordre; (dirty) sale.

met /met/ ➔MEET.

metal /ˈmetl/ n métal m. ● adj de métal. **metallic** adj métallique; (paint, colour) métallisé.

metallurgy /mɪˈtælədʒɪ/ n métallurgie f.

metaphor /ˈmetəfə(r)/ n métaphore f.

meteor /ˈmiːtɪə(r)/ n météore m.

meteorite /ˈmiːtɪəraɪt/ n météorite m.

meteorology /miːtɪəˈrɒlədʒɪ/ n

météorologie f.

meter /'miːtə(r)/ n compteur m; (US) ➡METRE.

method /'meθəd/ n méthode f.

methylated spirit(s) /'meθəleɪtɪd 'spɪrɪt(s)/ n alcool m à brûler.

meticulous /mɪ'tɪkjʊləs/ adj méticuleux.

metre, (US) **meter** /'miːtə(r)/ n mètre m.

metric /'metrɪk/ adj métrique.

metropolis /mə'trɒpəlɪs/ n métropole f. **metropolitan** adj métropolitain.

mew /mjuː/ n miaulement m. ● vi miauler.

mews /mjuːz/ npl appartements mpl chic aménagés dans d'anciennes écuries.

Mexico /'meksɪkəʊ/ n Mexique m.

miaow /miː'aʊ/ n & vi ➡MEW.

mice /maɪs/ ➡MOUSE.

mickey /'mɪkɪ/ n take the ~ out of 🄸 se moquer de.

microchip /'maɪkrəʊtʃɪp/ n puce f; circuit m intégré.

microlight /'maɪkrəʊlaɪt/ n ULM m.

microprocessor /'maɪkrəʊ prəʊsesə(r)/ n microprocesseur m.

microscope /'maɪkrəskəʊp/ n microscope m.

microwave /'maɪkrəweɪv/ n micro-onde f; ~ (oven) four m à micro-ondes. ● vt passer au four à micro-ondes.

mid /mɪd/ adj in ~ air en plein ciel; in ~ March à la mi-mars; ~ afternoon milieu m de l'après-midi; he's in his ~ twenties il a environ vingt-cinq ans.

midday /mɪd'deɪ/ n midi m.

middle /'mɪdl/ adj (door, shelf) du milieu; (size) moyen. ● n milieu m; in the ~ of au milieu de. ~-aged adj d'âge mûr. **M~ Ages** n Moyen âge m. ~ **class** n classe f moyenne. **M~ East** n Moyen-Orient m.

midge /mɪdʒ/ n moucheron m.

midget /'mɪdʒɪt/ n nain/-e m/f. ● adj minuscule.

midnight /'mɪdnaɪt/ n minuit f; it's ~ il est minuit.

midst /mɪdst/ n in the ~ of au beau milieu de; in our ~ parmi nous.

midsummer /mɪd'sʌmə(r)/ n milieu m de l'été; (solstice) solstice m d'été.

midway /mɪd'weɪ/ adv ~ between/along à mi-chemin entre/le long de.

midwife /'mɪdwaɪf/ n (pl -wives) sagefemme f.

might[1] /maɪt/ v aux I ~ have been killed! j'aurais pu être tué; you ~ try doing sth vous pourriez faire qch; ➡MAY.

might[2] /maɪt/ n puissance f.

mighty /'maɪtɪ/ adj (huge) 🄸) énorme. ● adv 🄸 vachement 🄸.

migrant /'maɪgrənt/ adj & n (bird) migrateur (m); (worker) migrant/-e (m/f).

migrate /maɪ'greɪt/ vi émigrer. **migration** n migration f.

mild /maɪld/ adj (surprise, taste, tobacco, attack) léger; (weather, cheese, soap, person) doux; (case, infection) bénin.

mile /maɪl/ n mile m (= 1,6 km); walk for ~s marcher pendant des kilomètres; ~ better 🄸 bien meilleur. **mileage** n nombre m de miles, kilométrage m.

milestone /'maɪlstəʊn/ n (lit) borne f; (fig) étape f importante.

military /'mɪlɪtrɪ/ *adj* militaire.

militia /mɪ'lɪʃə/ *n* milice *f*.

milk /mɪlk/ *n* lait *m*. ● *vt* (*cow*) traire; (*fig*) pomper.

milkman /'mɪlkmən/ *n* (*pl* **-men**) laitier *m*.

milky /'mɪlkɪ/ *adj* (*skin, colour*) laiteux; (*tea*) au lait; **M— Way** Voie *f* lactée.

mill /mɪl/ *n* moulin *m*; (*factory*) usine *f*. ● *vt* moudre. ● *vi* ~ **around** grouiller.

millennium /mɪ'lenɪəm/ *n* (*pl* ~**s**) millénaire *m*.

millimetre, (US) **millimeter** /'mɪlɪmiːtə(r)/ *n* millimètre *m*.

million /'mɪljən/ *n* million *m*; **a** ~ **pounds** un million de livres. **millionaire** *n* millionnaire *m*.

millstone /'mɪlstəʊn/ *n* meule *f*; (*fig*) boulet *m*.

mime /maɪm/ *n* (*actor*) mime *mf*; (*art*) mime *m*. ● *vt/i* mimer.

mimic /'mɪmɪk/ *vt* (*pt* **mimicked**) imiter. ● *n* imitateur/-trice *m/f*.

mince /mɪns/ *vt* hacher; **not to** ~ **matters** ne pas mâcher ses mots. ● *n* viande *f* hachée.

mind /maɪnd/ *n* esprit *m*; (*sanity*) raison *f*; (*opinion*) avis *m*; **be on sb's** ~ préoccuper qn; **bear that in** ~ ne l'oubliez pas; **change one's** ~ changer d'avis; **make up one's** ~ se décider (**to** à). ● *vt* (*have charge of*) s'occuper de; (*heed*) faire attention à; **I do not** ~ **the noise** le bruit ne me dérange pas; **I don't** ~ ça m'est égal; **would you** ~ **checking?** je peux vous demander de vérifier?

minder /'maɪndə(r)/ *n* (*bodyguard*) garde *m* de corps; (*child*) ~ nourrice *f*.

mindless /'maɪndlɪs/ *adj* (*programme*) bête; (*work*) abrutissant;

(*vandalism*) gratuit.

mine /maɪn/ *n* mine *f*. ● *vt* extraire; (Mil) miner. ● *pron* le mien, la mienne, les mien(ne)s; **the blue car is** ~ la voiture bleue est la mienne or à moi.

minefield /'maɪnfiːld/ *n* (lit) champ *m* de mines; (fig) terrain *m* miné.

miner /'maɪnə(r)/ *n* mineur *m*.

mineral /'mɪnərəl/ *n* & *adj* minéral (*m*); ~ **water** eau *f* minérale.

minesweeper /'maɪnswiːpə(r)/ *n* (ship) dragueur *m* de mines.

mingle /'mɪŋgl/ *vt/i* (se) mêler (**with** à).

minibus /'mɪnɪbʌs/ *n* minibus *m*.

minicab /'mɪnɪkæb/ *n* taxi *m* (*non agréé*).

minimal /'mɪnɪml/ *adj* minimal.

minimize /'mɪnɪmaɪz/ *vt* minimiser; (Comput) réduire.

minimum /'mɪnɪməm/ *adj* & *n* (*pl* **-ima**) minimum (*m*).

minister /'mɪnɪstə(r)/ *n* ministre *m*. **ministerial** *adj* ministériel. **ministry** *n* ministère *m*.

mink /mɪŋk/ *n* vison *m*.

minor /'maɪnə(r)/ *adj* (*change, surgery*) mineur; (*injury, burn*) léger; (*road*) secondaire. ● *n* (Jur) mineur/-e *m/f*.

minority /maɪ'nɒrətɪ/ *n* minorité *f*; **in the** ~ en minorité. ● *adj* minoritaire.

mint /mɪnt/ *n* (Bot, Culin) menthe *f*; (*sweet*) bonbon *m* à la menthe; (*fortune* 🔢) fortune *f*. ● *vt* frapper; **in** ~ **condition** à l'état neuf.

minus /'maɪnəs/ *prep* moins; (*without* 🔢) sans. ● *n* moins *m*; (*drawback*) inconvénient *m*.

minute[1] /'mɪnɪt/ *n* minute *f*; ~**s** (*of meeting*) compte-rendu *m*.

minute² /mar'nju:t/ adj (object)
minuscule; (risk, variation) minime.

miracle /'mɪrəkl/ n miracle m.

mirror /'mɪrə(r)/ n miroir m, glace
f; (Auto) rétroviseur m. ● vt refléter.

misbehave /mɪsbɪ'heɪv/ vi se conduire mal.

miscalculation /mɪskælkjʊ
'leɪʃn/ n (lit) erreur f de calcul; (fig)
mauvais calcul m.

miscarriage /'mɪskærɪdʒ/ n
fausse couche f; ~ **of justice** erreur
f judiciaire.

miscellaneous /mɪsə'leɪnɪəs/ adj
divers.

mischief /'mɪstʃɪf/ n (playfulness)
espièglerie f; (by children) bêtises
fpl. **mischievous** adj espiègle; (malicious) méchant.

misconduct /mɪs'kɒndʌkt/ n
mauvaise conduite f.

misconstrue /mɪskən'stru:/ vt
mal interpréter.

miser /'maɪzə(r)/ n avare m.

miserable /'mɪzrəbl/ adj (sad)
malheureux; (wretched) misérable;
(performance, result) lamentable.

misery /'mɪzərɪ/ n (unhappiness)
souffrance f; (misfortune) misère f;
(person 🔢) rabat-joie mf inv.

misfit /'mɪsfɪt/ n inadapté/-e m/f.

misfortune /mɪs'fɔ:tʃu:n/ n malheur m.

misgiving /mɪs'gɪvɪŋ/ n (doubt)
doute m; (apprehension) crainte f.

misguided /mɪs'gaɪdɪd/ adj (foolish) imprudent; (mistaken) erroné;
be ~ (person) se tromper.

mishap /'mɪshæp/ n incident m.

misjudge /mɪs'dʒʌdʒ/ vt (distance,
speed) mal évaluer; (person)

mal juger.

mislay /mɪs'leɪ/ vt (pt **mislaid**)
égarer.

mislead /mɪs'li:d/ vt (pt **misled**)
tromper. **misleading** adj trompeur.

misplace /mɪs'pleɪs/ vt mal ranger; (lose) égarer. **misplaced** adj
(fear, criticism) déplacé.

misprint /'mɪsprɪnt/ n coquille f,
faute f typographique.

misread /mɪs'ri:d/ vt (pt **misread**)
mal lire; (intentions) mal interpréter.

miss /mɪs/ vt/i manquer; (bus) rater;
he ~**es her**/Paris elle/Paris lui
manque; **you're** ~**ing the point** tu
n'as rien compris; ~ **sth out** omettre qch; ~ **out on sth** laisser passer
qch. ● n coup m manqué; **it was a
near** ~ on l'a échappé belle.

Miss /mɪs/ n Mademoiselle f; ~
Smith (written) Mlle Smith.

misshapen /mɪs'ʃeɪpən/ adj
difforme.

missile /'mɪsaɪl/ n (Mil) missile m;
(thrown) projectile m.

mission /'mɪʃn/ n mission f. **missionary** n missionnaire m.

misspell /mɪs'spel/ vt (pt **misspelt**
or **misspelled**) mal écrire.

mist /mɪst/ n brume f; (on window)
buée f. ● vt/i (s')embuer.

mistake /mɪ'steɪk/ n erreur f; **by**
~ par erreur; **make a** ~ faire une
erreur. ● vt (pt **mistook**, pp **mistaken**) (meaning) mal interpréter; ~
for prendre pour.

mistaken /mɪ'steɪkən/ adj (enthusiasm) mal placé; **be** ~ avoir tort.

mistletoe /'mɪsltəʊ/ n gui m.

mistreat /mɪs'tri:t/ vt maltraiter.

mistress /'mɪstrɪs/ n maîtresse f.

misty /'mɪstɪ/ adj (**-ier, -lest**) brumeux; (window) embué.

misunderstanding /mɪsʌndə

'stændɪŋ/ n malentendu m.

misuse /mɪs'juːz/ vt (word) mal employer; (power) abuser de; (equipment) faire mauvais usage de.

mitten /'mɪtn/ n moufle f.

mix /mɪks/ n mélange m. ● vt mélanger; (drink) préparer; (cement) malaxer. ● vi se mélanger (with avec, à); (socially) être sociable; ~ **with sb** fréquenter qn. □ ~ **up** (confuse) confondre; (jumble up) mélanger; **get ~ed up in** se trouver mêlé à.

mixed /mɪkst/ adj (school) mixte; (collection, diet) varié; (nuts, sweets) assorti.

mixer /'mɪksə(r)/ n (Culin) batteur m électrique; **be a good ~** être sociable; ~ **tap** mélangeur m.

mixture /'mɪkstʃə(r)/ n mélange m.

mix-up /'mɪksʌp/ n confusion f (over sur).

moan /məʊn/ n gémissement m. ● vi gémir; (complain 🔢) râler 🔢.

mob /mɒb/ n (crowd) foule f; (gang) gang m; **the M~** la Mafia. ● vt (pt **mobbed**) assaillir.

mobile /'məʊbaɪl/ adj mobile; ~ **phone** téléphone m portable. ● n mobile m.

mobilize /'məʊbɪlaɪz/ vt/i mobiliser.

mock /mɒk/ vt/i se moquer (de). ● adj faux.

mockery /'mɒkərɪ/ n moquerie f; **a ~ of** une parodie de.

mock-up n maquette f.

mode /məʊd/ n mode m.

model /'mɒdl/ n (Comput, Auto) modèle m; (scale representation) maquette f; (person showing clothes) mannequin m. ● adj modèle; (car) modèle réduit inv; (railway) miniature. ● vt (pt **modelled**)

modeler; (clothes) présenter. ● vi être mannequin; (pose) poser.

modelling n métier m de mannequin.

modem /'məʊdem/ n modem m.

moderate /'mɒdərət/ adj & n modéré/-e (m/f).

moderation /mɒdə'reɪʃn/ n modération f; **in ~** avec modération.

modern /'mɒdn/ adj moderne; ~ **languages** langues fpl vivantes.

modernize vt moderniser.

modest /'mɒdɪst/ adj modeste.

modesty n modestie f.

modification /mɒdɪfɪ'keɪʃn/ n modification f. **modify** vt modifier.

module /'mɒdjuːl/ n module m.

moist /mɔɪst/ adj (soil) humide; (skin, palms) moite; (cake) moelleux.

moisten vt humecter. **moisture** n humidité f. **moisturizer** n crème f hydratante.

molar /'məʊlə(r)/ n molaire f.

mold (US) →**MOULD.**

mole /məʊl/ n grain m de beauté; (animal) taupe f.

molecule /'mɒlɪkjuːl/ n molécule f.

molest /mə'lest/ vt (pester) importuner; (sexually) agresser sexuellement.

moment /'məʊmənt/ n (short time) instant m; (point in time) moment m. **momentarily** adv momentanément; (soon: US) très bientôt.

momentary adj momentané.

momentum /mə'mentəm/ n élan m.

monarch /'mɒnək/ n monarque m.

monarchy n monarchie f.

Monday /'mʌndeɪ/ n lundi m.

monetary /'mʌnɪtrɪ/ adj monétaire.

money /'mʌnɪ/ n argent m; **make**

m

~ (*person*) gagner de l'argent; (*business*) rapporter de l'argent. **~box** n tirelire f. **~ order** n mandat m postal.

monitor /'mɒnɪtə(r)/ n dispositif m de surveillance; (Comput) moniteur m. ● vt surveiller; (*broadcast*) être à l'écoute de.

monk /mʌŋk/ n moine m.

monkey /'mʌŋkɪ/ n singe m.

monopolize /mə'nɒpəlaɪz/ vt monopoliser. **monopoly** n monopole m.

monotonous /mə'nɒtənəs/ adj monotone. **monotony** n monotonie f.

monsoon /mɒn'suːn/ n mousson f.

monster /'mɒnstə(r)/ n monstre m. **monstrous** adj monstrueux.

month /mʌnθ/ n mois m.

monthly /'mʌnθlɪ/ adj mensuel. ● adv (*pay*) au mois; (*publish*) tous les mois. ● n (*periodical*) mensuel m.

monument /'mɒnjʊmənt/ n monument m.

moo /muː/ vi meugler.

mood /muːd/ n humeur f; **in a good/bad** ~ de bonne/mauvaise humeur. **moody** adj d'humeur changeante.

moon /muːn/ n lune f.

moonlight /'muːnlaɪt/ n clair m de lune. **moonlighting** n 🔢 travail m au noir.

moor /mɔː(r)/ n lande f. ● vt amarrer.

mop /mɒp/ n balai m à franges; ~ **of hair** crinière f 🔢. ● vt (pt **mopped**) ~ éponger.

moped /'məʊped/ n vélomoteur m.

moral /'mɒrəl/ adj moral. ● n morale f. ● ~s moralité f.

morale /mə'rɑːl/ n moral m.

morbid /'mɔːbɪd/ adj morbide.

more /mɔː(r)/ adv plus; ~ **serious** plus sérieux; **work** ~ travailler plus; **sleep** ~ **and** ~ dormir de plus en plus; **once** ~ une fois de plus; **I don't go there any** ~ je n'y vais plus; ~ **or less** plus ou moins. ● det plus de; **a little** ~ **wine** un peu plus de vin; ~ **bread** encore un peu de pain; **there's no** ~ **bread** il n'y a plus de pain; **nothing** ~ rien de plus. ● pron plus; **cost** ~ **than** coûter plus cher que; **I need** ~ **of it** il m'en faut davantage.

moreover /mɔː'rəʊvə(r)/ adv de plus.

morning /'mɔːnɪŋ/ n matin m; (*whole morning*) matinée f.

Morocco /mə'rɒkəʊ/ n Maroc m.

morsel /'mɔːsl/ n morceau m.

mortal /'mɔːtl/ adj & n mortel/-le (m/f).

mortgage /'mɔːɡɪdʒ/ n emprunt-logement m. ● vt hypothéquer.

mortuary /'mɔːtʃərɪ/ n morgue f.

mosaic /məʊ'zeɪɪk/ n mosaïque f.

mosque /mɒsk/ n mosquée f.

mosquito /məs'kiːtəʊ/ n (pl ~**es**) moustique m.

moss /mɒs/ n mousse f.

most /məʊst/ det (*nearly all*) la plupart de; ~ **people** la plupart des gens; **the** ~ **votes/money** le plus de voix/d'argent. ● n le plus. ● pron la plupart; ~ **of us** la plupart d'entre nous; ~ **of the money** la plus grande partie de l'argent; **the** ~ **I can do is ...** tout ce que je peux faire c'est ... ● adv (*the*) ~ **beautiful house/hotel in Oxford** la maison la plus belle/l'hôtel le plus beau d'Oxford; ~ **interesting** très intéressant; **what I like** ~ (*of all*) ce que j'aime le plus c'est. **mostly** adv surtout.

moth /mɒθ/ n papillon m de nuit; (in cloth) mite f.

mother /'mʌðə(r)/ n mère f. ● vt (lit) materner; (fig) dorloter.
motherhood n maternité f. **~-in-law** n (pl **~s-in-law**) belle-mère f. **~-of-pearl** n nacre f. **M~'s Day** n la fête des mères. **~-to-be** n future maman f. **~ tongue** n langue f maternelle.

motion /'məʊʃn/ n mouvement m; (proposal) motion f. **~ picture** (US) film m. ● vt/i **~ (to) sb to** faire signe à qn de. **motionless** adj immobile.

motivate /'məʊtɪveɪt/ vt motiver.

motive /'məʊtɪv/ n motif m; (Jur) mobile m.

motor /'məʊtə(r)/ n moteur m; (car) auto f. ● adj (industry, insurance, vehicle) automobile; (activity, disorder; Med) moteur. **~bike** n moto f. **~ car** n auto f. **~cyclist** n motocycliste mf. **~ home** n autocaravane f.

motorist /'məʊtərɪst/ n automobiliste mf.

motorway /'məʊtəweɪ/ n autoroute f.

mottled /'mɒtld/ adj tacheté.

motto /'mɒtəʊ/ n (pl **-es**) devise f.

mould /məʊld/ n (shape) moule m; (fungus) moisissure f. ● vt mouler; (influence) former. **moulding** n moulure f. **mouldy** adj moisi.

mount /maʊnt/ n (hill) mont m; (horse) monture f. ● vt (stairs) gravir; (platform, horse, bike) monter sur; (jewel, picture, campaign, exhibit) monter. ● vi monter; (number, toll) augmenter; (concern) grandir.

mountain /'maʊntɪn/ n montagne f. **~ bike** (vélo) tout terrain m, VTT m. **mountaineer** n alpiniste mf.

mourn /mɔːn/ vt/i **~ (for)** pleurer.

mournful adj mélancolique.
mourning n deuil m.

mouse /maʊs/ n (pl **mice**) souris f. **~trap** n souricière f.

mouth /maʊθ/ n bouche f; (of dog, cat) gueule f; (of cave, tunnel) entrée f. **mouthful** n bouchée f. **~wash** n eau f dentifrice. **~watering** adj appétissant.

move /muːv/ vt (object) déplacer; (limb, head) bouger; (emotionally) émouvoir; **~ house** déménager. ● vi bouger; (vehicle) rouler; (change address) déménager; (act) agir. ● n mouvement m; (in game) coup m; (player's turn) tour m; (step, act) manœuvre f; (house change) déménagement m; **on the ~** en mouvement. □ **~ back** reculer; **~ in** emménager; **~ in with** (on person) s'installer avec; (vehicle) se mettre en route; (vehicle) repartir; (time) passer; **~ sth on** faire avancer qch; **~ sb on** faire circuler qn; **~ over** or **up** se pousser.

movement /'muːvmənt/ n mouvement m.

movie /'muːvɪ/ n (US) film m; **the ~s** le cinéma.

moving /'muːvɪŋ/ adj (vehicle) en marche; (part, target) mobile; (staircase) roulant; (touching) émouvant.

mow /məʊ/ vt (pp **mowed** or **mown**) (lawn) tondre; (hay) couper; **~ down** faucher. **mower** n tondeuse f.

MP abbr →MEMBER OF PARLIAMENT.

Mr /'mɪstə(r)/ n (pl **Messrs**) **~ Smith** Monsieur or M. Smith; **~ President** Monsieur le Président.

Mrs /'mɪsɪz/ n (pl **Mrs**) **~ Smith** Madame or Mme Smith.

Ms /məz/ n Mme.

much /mʌtʃ/ adv beaucoup; **too ~** trop; **very ~** beaucoup; **I like them**

as ~ **as you** (**do**) je les aime autant que toi. ● *pron* beaucoup; **not** ~ **pas** grand-chose; **he didn't say** ~ il n'a pas dit grand-chose; **I ate so** ~ **that** j'ai tellement mangé que. ● *det* beaucoup de; **too** ~ **money** trop d'argent; **how** ~ **time is left?** combien de temps reste-t-il?

muck /mʌk/ *n* saletés *fpl*; (*manure*) fumier *m*. □ ~ **about** 𝕋 faire l'imbécile. **mucky** *adj* sale.

mud /mʌd/ *n* boue *f*.

muddle /'mʌdl/ *n* (mix-up) malentendu *m*; (*mess*) pagaille *f* 𝕋; **get into a** ~ s'embrouiller. □ ~ **through** se débrouiller. □ ~ **up** embrouiller.

muddy /'mʌdɪ/ *adj* couvert de boue.

muffle /'mʌfl/ *vt* emmitoufler; (*bell*) assourdir; (*voice*) étouffer.

mug /mʌg/ *n* grande tasse *f*; (for beer) chope *f*; (face 𝕋) gueule *f* 𝕏; (fool 𝕋) poire *f* 𝕏. ● *vt* (*pt* **mugged**) agresser. **mugger** *n* agresseur *m*.

muggy /'mʌgɪ/ *adj* lourd.

mule /mjuːl/ *n* mulet *m*.

multicoloured /mʌltɪˈkʌləd/ *adj* multicolore.

multiple /'mʌltɪpl/ *adj & n* multiple (*m*); ~ **sclerosis** sclérose *f* en plaques.

multiplication /mʌltɪplɪˈkeɪʃn/ *n* multiplication *f*. **multiply** *vt/i* (se) multiplier.

multistorey /mʌltɪˈstɔːrɪ/ *adj* (car park) à niveaux multiples.

mum /mʌm/ *n* maman *f*.

mumble /'mʌmbl/ *vt/i* marmonner.

mummy /'mʌmɪ/ *n* (mother 𝕋) maman *f*; (embalmed body) momie *f*.

mumps /mʌmps/ *n* oreillons *mpl*.

munch /mʌntʃ/ *vt* mâcher.

mundane /mʌnˈdeɪn/ *adj* terre-à-terre.

municipal /mjuːˈnɪsɪpl/ *adj* municipal.

mural /'mjʊərəl/ *adj* mural. ● *n* peinture *f* murale.

murder /'mɜːdə(r)/ *n* meurtre *m*. ● *vt* assassiner. **murderer** *n* meurtrier *m*, assassin *m*.

murky /'mɜːkɪ/ *adj* (-ier, -iest) (*water*) glauque; (*past*) trouble.

murmur /'mɜːmə(r)/ *n* murmure *m*. ● *vt/i* murmurer.

muscle /'mʌsl/ *n* muscle *m*. ● *vi* ~ **in** s'imposer (**on** dans).

muscular /'mʌskjʊlə(r)/ *adj* (*tissue, disease*) musculaire; (*body, person*) musclé.

museum /mjuːˈzɪəm/ *n* musée *m*.

mushroom /'mʌʃrʊm/ *n* champignon *m*. ● *vi* (town) proliférer; (demand) s'accroître rapidement.

music /'mjuːzɪk/ *n* musique *f*.

musical /'mjuːzɪkl/ *adj* (person) musicien; (*voice*) mélodieux; (*accompaniment*) musical; (*instrument*) de musique. ● *n* comédie *f* musicale.

musician /mjuːˈzɪʃn/ *n* musicien/ -ne *m/f*.

Muslim /'mʊzlɪm/ *n* Musulman/-e *m/f*. ● *adj* musulman.

mussel /'mʌsl/ *n* moule *f*.

must /mʌst/ *v aux* devoir; **you** ~ **go** vous devez partir, il faut que vous partiez; **she** ~ **be consulted** il faut la consulter; **he** ~ **be old** il doit être vieux; **I** ~ **have done it** j'ai dû le faire. ● *n* **be a** ~ 𝕋 être indispensable.

mustard /'mʌstəd/ *n* moutarde *f*.

musty /'mʌstɪ/ *adj* (-ier, -iest) (*room*) qui sent le renfermé;

(*smell*) de moisi.

mute /mjuːt/ *adj & n* muet/-te (*m/f*). **muted** *adj* (*colour*) sourd; (*response*) tiède; (*celebration*) mitigé.

mutilate /ˈmjuːtɪleɪt/ *vt* mutiler.

mutter /ˈmʌtə(r)/ *vt/i* marmonner.

mutton /ˈmʌtn/ *n* mouton *m*.

mutual /ˈmjuːtʃʊəl/ *adj* (*reciprocal*) réciproque; (*common*) commun; (*consent*) mutuel. **mutually** *adv* mutuellement.

muzzle /ˈmʌzl/ *n* (*snout*) museau *m*; (*device*) muselière *f*; (*of gun*) canon *m*. ● *vt* museler.

my /maɪ/ *adj* mon, ma, *pl* mes.

myself /maɪˈself/ *pron* (*reflexive*) me, m'; **I've hurt ~** je me suis fait mal; (*emphatic*) moi-même; **I did it ~** je l'ai fait moi-même; (*after preposition*) moi, moi-même; **I am proud of ~** je suis fier de moi.

mysterious /mɪˈstɪərɪəs/ *adj* mystérieux.

mystery /ˈmɪstərɪ/ *n* mystère *m*.

mystic /ˈmɪstɪk/ *adj & n* mystique (*mf*). **mystical** *adj* mystique.

myth /mɪθ/ *n* mythe *m*. **mythical** *adj* mythique. **mythology** *n* mythologie *f*.

••••••••••••••••••••••••••••••••

Nn

••••••••••••••••••••••••••••••••

nag /næg/ *vt/i* (*pt* **nagged**) critiquer; (*pester*) harceler. **nagging** *adj* persistant.

nail /neɪl/ *n* clou *m*; (*of finger, toe*) ongle *m*; **on the ~** sans tarder, tout de suite. ● *vt* clouer. **~ polish** *n* vernis *m* à ongles.

naïve /naɪˈiːv/ *adj* naïf.

naked /ˈneɪkɪd/ *adj* nu; **to the ~**

eye à l'œil nu.

name /neɪm/ *n* nom *m*; (*fig*) réputation *f*. ● *vt* nommer; (*terms*) fixer; **be ~d after** porter le nom de.

namely /ˈneɪmlɪ/ *adv* à savoir.

nanny /ˈnænɪ/ *n* nurse *f*.

nap /næp/ *n* somme *m*.

nape /neɪp/ *n* nuque *f*.

napkin /ˈnæpkɪn/ *n* serviette *f*.

nappy /ˈnæpɪ/ *n* couche *f*.

narcotic /nɑːˈkɒtɪk/ *adj & n* narcotique (*m*).

narrative /ˈnærətɪv/ *n* récit *m*.

narrator *n* narrateur/-trice *m/f*.

narrow /ˈnærəʊ/ *adj* étroit. ● *vt/i* (se) rétrécir; (*limit*) (se) limiter; **~ down the choices** limiter les choix. **~-minded** *adj* à l'esprit étroit; (*ideas*) étroit.

nasal /ˈneɪzl/ *adj* nasal.

nasty /ˈnɑːstɪ/ *adj* (**-ier, -iest**) mauvais, désagréable; (*malicious*) méchant.

nation /ˈneɪʃn/ *n* nation *f*.

national /ˈnæʃənl/ *adj* national. ● *n* ressortissant/-e *m/f*.

nationality /næʃəˈnælətɪ/ *n* nationalité *f*.

nationalize /ˈnæʃənəlaɪz/ *vt* nationaliser.

nationally /ˈnæʃnəlɪ/ *adv* à l'échelle nationale.

m
n

National Trust Association caritative britannique fondée en 1895 pour assurer la protection de certains édifices ou parties de littoral menacés par l'industrialisation. Cette association est aujourd'hui le premier propriétaire foncier britannique car elle a acquis ou reçu en dons depuis sa création de nombreux sites et bâtiments; la plupart sont ouverts au public.

native /'neɪtɪv/ n (local inhabitant) autochtone mf; (non-European) indigène mf; **be a ~ of** être originaire de. ● adj indigène; (country) natal; (inborn) inné; **~ language** langue f maternelle; **~ speaker of French** personne f de langue maternelle française.

natural /'nætʃrəl/ adj naturel.

naturally /'nætʃrəlɪ/ adv (normally, of course) naturellement; (by nature) de nature.

nature /'neɪtʃə(r)/ n nature f.

naughty /'nɔːtɪ/ adj (**-ier, -iest**) vilain, méchant; (indecent) grivois.

nausea /'nɔːsɪə/ n nausée f. **nauseous** adj (smell) écœurant.

nautical /'nɔːtɪkl/ adj nautique.

naval /'neɪvl/ adj (battle) naval; (officer) de marine.

navel /'neɪvl/ n nombril m.

navigate /'nævɪgeɪt/ vt (sea) naviguer sur; (ship) piloter. ● vi naviguer. **navigation** n navigation f.

navy /'neɪvɪ/ n marine f. ● adj ~ **(blue)** bleu inv marine.

near /nɪə(r)/ adv près; **draw ~** (s')approcher (**to** de). ● prep près de. ● adj proche; **~ to** près de. ● vt approcher de.

nearby /nɪə'baɪ/ adj proche. ● adv à proximité.

nearly /'nɪəlɪ/ adv presque; **I ~ forgot** j'ai failli oublier; **not ~ as pretty as** loin d'être aussi joli que.

nearness /'nɪənɪs/ n proximité f.

nearside /'nɪəsaɪd/ adj (Auto) du côté du passager.

neat /niːt/ adj soigné, net; (room) bien rangé; (clever) habile; (drink) sec. **neatly** adv avec soin; habilement.

necessarily /nesə'serəlɪ/ adv nécessairement.

necessary /'nesəsərɪ/ adj nécessaire.

necessitate /nɪ'sesɪteɪt/ vt nécessiter.

necessity /nɪ'sesətɪ/ n nécessité f; (thing) chose f indispensable.

neck /nek/ n cou m; (of dress) encolure f. **~ and neck** à égalité. **~lace** n collier m. **~line** n encolure f. **~tie** n cravate f.

nectarine /'nektərɪn/ n brugnon m, nectarine f.

need /niːd/ n besoin m. ● vt avoir besoin de; (demand) demander; **you ~ not come** vous n'êtes pas obligé de venir.

needle /'niːdl/ n aiguille f.

needless /'niːdlɪs/ adj inutile.

needlework /'niːdlwɜːk/ n couture f; (object) ouvrage m (à l'aiguille).

needy /'niːdɪ/ adj (**-ier, -iest**) nécessiteux. ● n **the ~** les indigents.

negative /'negətɪv/ adj négatif. ● n (of photograph) négatif m; (word: Gram) négation f; **in the ~** (answer) par la négative; (Gram) à la forme négative.

neglect /nɪ'glekt/ vt négliger, laisser à l'abandon; **~ to do** négliger de faire. ● n manque m de soins; **(state of) ~** abandon m.

negligent /'neglɪdʒənt/ adj négligent.

negotiate /nɪ'gəʊʃɪeɪt/ vt/i négocier. **negotiation** n négociation f.

neigh /neɪ/ n hennissement m. ● vi hennir.

neighbour, (US) **neighbor** /'neɪbə(r)/ n voisin/-e mf. **neighbourhood** n voisinage m, quartier m; **in the ~hood of** aux alentours de. **neighbouring** adj voisin. **neighbourly** adj amical.

neither /'naɪðə(r)/ adj & pron

aucun/-e des deux, ni l'un/-e ni l'autre. ● adv ni; ~ **big nor small** ni grand ni petit. ● conj (ne) non plus; ~ **am I coming** je ne viendrai pas non plus.

nephew /'nefjuː/ n neveu m.

nerve /nɜːv/ n nerf m; (courage) courage m; (calm) sang-froid m; (impudence 🗉) culot m; ~**s** (before exams) trac m. **~-racking** adj éprouvant.

nervous /'nɜːvəs/ adj nerveux; **be or feel ~** (afraid) avoir peur; **~ breakdown** dépression f nerveuse. **nervousness** n nervosité f; (fear) crainte f.

nest /nest/ n nid m. ● vi nicher. **~-egg** n pécule m.

nestle /'nesl/ vi se blottir.

net /net/ n filet m; (Comput) net m, Internet m. ● vt (pt **netted**) prendre au filet. ● adj (weight) net. **~ball** n netball m.

Netherlands /'neðələndz/ n the ~ les Pays-Bas mpl.

netiquette /'netɪket/ n nétiquette f.

Netsurfer /'netɪket/ n Internaute mf.

nettle /'netl/ n ortie f.

network /'netwɜːk/ n réseau m.

neurotic /njʊəˈrɒtɪk/ adj & n névrosé/-e (m/f).

neuter /'njuːtə(r)/ adj & n neutre (m). ● vt (castrate) castrer.

neutral /'njuːtrəl/ adj neutre; ~ **(gear)** (Auto) point m mort.

never /'nevə(r)/ adv (ne) (ne) jamais; **he ~ refuses** il ne refuse jamais; **I ~ saw him** 🗉 je ne l'ai pas vu; ~ **again** plus jamais; ~ **mind** (don't worry) ne vous en faites pas; (it doesn't matter) peu importe.

nevertheless /nevəðə'les/ adv néanmoins, toutefois.

new /njuː/ adj nouveau; (brand-new) neuf. **~-born** adj nouveau-né. **~-comer** n nouveau venu m, nouvelle venue f.

newly /'njuːlɪ/ adv nouvellement. **~-weds** npl jeunes mariés mpl.

news /njuːz/ n nouvelle(s) f(pl); (radio, press) informations fpl; (TV) actualités fpl, informations fpl. ~ **agency** n agence f de presse. **~agent** n marchand/-e m/f de journaux. **~caster** n présentateur/-trice m/f. **~group** n (Internet) forum m de discussion. **~letter** n bulletin m. **~paper** n journal m.

new year n nouvel an m. **New Year's Day** n le jour de l'an. **New Year's Eve** n la Saint-Sylvestre.

New Zealand /njuːˈziːlənd/ n Nouvelle-Zélande f.

next /nekst/ adj prochain; (adjoining) voisin; (following) suivant; ~ **to** à côté de; ~ **door** à côté (à **to** de). ● adv la prochaine fois; (afterwards) ensuite. ● n suivant/-e m/f; (e-mail) message m suivant. **~-door** adj d'à côté. ~ **of kin** parent m le plus proche.

nib /nɪb/ n plume f.

nibble /'nɪbl/ vt/i grignoter.

nice /naɪs/ adj agréable, bon; (kind) gentil; (pretty) joli; (respectable) bien inv; (subtle) délicat. **nicely** adv agréablement; gentiment; (well) bien.

nicety /'naɪsətɪ/ n subtilité f.

niche /niːʃ/ n (recess) niche f; (fig) place f, situation f.

nick /nɪk/ n petite entaille f; **be in good/bad ~** 🗉 être en bon/ mauvais état. ● vt (steal, arrest 🗉) piquer.

nickel /'nɪkl/ n (metal) nickel m; (US) pièce f de cinq cents.

nickname /'nɪkneɪm/ n surnom m. ● vt surnommer.

n

nicotine /'nɪkəti:n/ n nicotine f.

niece /ni:s/ n nièce f.

niggling /'nɪglɪŋ/ adj (person) tatillon; (detail) insignifiant.

night /naɪt/ n nuit f. (evening) soir
m. ● adj de nuit. ~**cap** n boisson f
(avant d'aller se coucher). ~**club** n
boîte f de nuit. ~**dress** n chemise f
de nuit. ~**fall** n tombée f de la
nuit. **nightie** n chemise f de nuit.

nightingale /'naɪtɪŋgeɪl/ n rossignol m.

nightly /'naɪtlɪ/ adj & adv (de) chaque nuit or soir.

night /naɪt/: ~**mare** n cauchemar
m. ~**time** n nuit f.

nil /nɪl/ n (Sport) zéro m. ● adj
(chances, risk) nul.

nimble /'nɪmbl/ adj agile.

nine /naɪn/ adj & n neuf (m).

nineteen /naɪn'ti:n/ adj & n dix-
neuf (m).

ninety /'naɪntɪ/ adj & n quatre-
vingt-dix (m).

ninth /naɪnθ/ adj & n neuvième
(mf).

nip /nɪp/ vt/i (pt nipped) (pinch)
pincer; (rush ⛀) courir; ~ **out**/
back sortir/rentrer rapidement. ● n
pincement m.

nipple /'nɪpl/ n mamelon m; (of
baby's bottle) tétine f.

nippy /'nɪpɪ/ adj (-ier, -iest) (air)
piquant; (car) rapide.

nitrogen /'naɪtrədʒən/ n azote m.

no /nəʊ/ det aucun/-e; pas de; ~
man aucun homme; ~ **money**/
time pas d'argent/de temps; ~
one ⟶NOBODY; ~ **smoking**/**entry**
défense de fumer/d'entrer; ~ **way!**
⛀ pas question! ● adv non. ● n (pl
noes) non m inv.

nobility /nəʊ'bɪlətɪ/ n noblesse f.

noble /'nəʊbl/ adj noble. ~**man** n

(pl -men) noble m.

nobody /'nəʊbədɪ/ pron (ne) personne; **he knows** ~ il ne connaît
personne. ● n nullité f.

nocturnal /nɒk'tɜ:nl/ adj
nocturne.

nod /nɒd/ vt/i (pt nodded); ~
(one's head) faire un signe de tête;
~ **off** s'endormir. ● n signe m de
tête.

noise /nɔɪz/ n bruit m; **make a** ~
faire du bruit. **noisily** adv bruyam-
ment. **noisy** adj (-ier, -iest)
bruyant.

no man's land n no man's
land m.

nominal /'nɒmɪnl/ adj symbolique,
nominal; (value) nominal.

nominate /'nɒmɪneɪt/ vt nommer;
(put forward) proposer.

none /nʌn/ pron aucun/-e; ~ **of us**
aucun-e de nous; **I have** ~ je n'en
ai pas.

non-existent /nɒnɪg'zɪstənt/ adj
inexistant.

nonplussed /nɒn'plʌst/ adj
perplexe.

nonsense /'nɒnsns/ n absurdi-
tés fpl.

non-smoker /nɒn'sməʊkə(r)/ n
non-fumeur m.

non-stick adj antiadhésif.

non-stop /nɒn'stɒp/ adj (train,
flight) direct. ● adv sans arrêt.

noodles /'nu:dlz/ npl nouilles fpl.

noon /nu:n/ n midi m.

nor /nɔ:(r)/ adv ni. ● conj (ne) non
plus; ~ **shall I come** je ne viendrai
pas non plus.

norm /nɔ:m/ n norme f.

normal /'nɔ:ml/ adj normal.

Norman /'nɔ:mən/ n Normand/-e
m/f. ● adj (village) normand; (arch)
roman.

north /nɔːθ/ n nord m. ● adj nord inv, du nord. ● adv vers le nord.

North America n Amérique f du Nord.

north-east /nɔːθˈiːst/ n nord-est m.

northerly /ˈnɔːðəlɪ/ adj (wind, area) du nord; (point) au nord.

northern /ˈnɔːðən/ adj (accent) du nord; (coast) nord. **northerner** n habitant/-e m/f du nord.

northward /ˈnɔːθwəd/ adj (side) nord inv; (journey) vers le nord.

north-west /nɔːθˈwest/ n nord-ouest m.

Norway /ˈnɔːweɪ/ n Norvège f.

Norwegian /nɔːˈwiːdʒən/ n (person) Norvégien/-ne m/f; (language) norvégien m. ● adj norvégien.

nose /nəʊz/ n nez m. ● vi ~ about fouiner.

nosedive /ˈnəʊzdaɪv/ n piqué m. ● vi descendre en piqué.

nostalgia /nɒˈstældʒə/ n nostalgie f.

nostril /ˈnɒstrɪl/ n narine f; (of horse) naseau m.

nosy /ˈnəʊzɪ/ adj (-ier, -iest) Ⅰ curieux, indiscret.

not /nɒt/ adv (ne) pas; I do ~ know je ne sais pas; ~ at all pas du tout; ~ yet pas encore; I suppose ~ je suppose que non.

notably /ˈnəʊtəblɪ/ adv notamment.

notch /nɒtʃ/ n entaille f. ● vt ~ up (score) marquer.

note /nəʊt/ n note f; (banknote) billet m; (short letter) mot m. ● vt noter; (notice) remarquer. ~**book** n carnet m.

nothing /ˈnʌθɪŋ/ pron (ne) rien; he eats ~ il ne mange rien; ~ else rien d'autre; ~ much pas grand-chose; for ~ pour rien, gratis. ● n

rien m; (person) nullité f. ● adv nullement.

notice /ˈnəʊtɪs/ n avis m, annonce f; (poster) affiche f; (advance) ~ préavis m; at short ~ dans des délais très brefs; give in one's ~ donner sa démission; take ~ faire attention (of à). ● vt remarquer, observer. **noticeable** adj visible. ~**board** n tableau m d'affichage.

notify /ˈnəʊtɪfaɪ/ vt (inform) aviser; (make known) notifier.

notion /ˈnəʊʃn/ n idée f, notion f.

notorious /nəʊˈtɔːrɪəs/ adj (criminal) notoire; (district) mal famé; (case) tristement célèbre.

notwithstanding /nɒtwɪθ-ˈstændɪŋ/ prep malgré m. ● adv néanmoins.

nought /nɔːt/ n zéro m.

noun /naʊn/ n nom m.

nourish /ˈnʌrɪʃ/ vt nourrir. **nourishing** adj nourrissant. **nourishment** n nourriture f.

novel /ˈnɒvl/ n roman m. ● adj nouveau. **novelist** n romancier/-ière m/f. **novelty** n nouveauté f.

November /nəˈvembə(r)/ n novembre m.

now /naʊ/ adv maintenant. ● conj maintenant que; just ~ maintenant; (a moment ago) tout à l'heure; ~ and again, ~ and then de temps à autre.

nowadays /ˈnaʊədeɪz/ adv de nos jours.

nowhere /ˈnəʊweə(r)/ adv nulle part.

nozzle /ˈnɒzl/ n (tip) embout m; (of hose) jet m.

nuclear /ˈnjuːklɪə(r)/ adj nucléaire.

nude /njuːd/ adj nu. ● n nu/-e m/f; in the ~ tout nu.

nudge /nʌdʒ/ vt pousser du coude. ● coup m de coude.

nudism /'njuːdɪzəm/ n nudisme m.
nudity n nudité f.

nuisance /'njuːsns/ n (thing, event) ennui m; (person) peste f; **be a ~** être embêtant.

null /nʌl/ adj nul.

numb /nʌm/ adj engourdi (with par). ● vt engourdir.

number /'nʌmbə(r)/ n nombre m; (of ticket, house, page) numéro m; (written figure) chiffre m; **a ~ of people** plusieurs personnes. ● vt numéroter; (count, include) compter. **~-plate** n plaque f d'immatriculation.

numeral /'njuːmərəl/ n chiffre m.

numerate /'njuːmərət/ adj qui sait compter.

numerical /njuː'merɪkl/ adj numérique.

numerous /'njuːmərəs/ adj nombreux.

nun /nʌn/ n religieuse f.

nurse /nɜːs/ n infirmier/-ière m/f; (nanny) nurse f. ● vt soigner; (hope) nourrir.

nursery /'nɜːsərɪ/ n (room) chambre f d'enfants; (for plants) pépinière f; **(day) ~** crèche f; **~ rhyme** n comptine f; **~ school** n (école) maternelle f.

nursing home n maison f de retraite.

nut /nʌt/ n (walnut, Brazil nut) noix f; (hazelnut) noisette f; (peanut) cacahuète f; (Tech) écrou m. **~crackers** npl casse-noix m inv.

nutmeg /'nʌtmeg/ n muscade f.

nutrient /'njuːtrɪənt/ n substance f nutritive.

nutritious /njuː'trɪʃəs/ adj nutritif.

nuts /nʌts/ adj (crazy 🄸) cinglé.

nutshell /'nʌtʃel/ n coquille f de noix; **in a ~** en un mot.

nylon /'naɪlɒn/ n nylon m.

Oo

oak /əʊk/ n chêne m.

OAP abbr **old-age pensioner** retraité/-e m/f.

oar /ɔː(r)/ n rame f.

oath /əʊθ/ n (promise) serment m; (swearword) juron m.

oats /əʊts/ npl avoine f.

obedience /ə'biːdɪəns/ n obéissance f. **obedient** adj obéissant. **obediently** adv docilement.

obese /əʊ'biːs/ adj obèse.

obey /ə'beɪ/ vt/i obéir (à).

object¹ /'ɒbdʒɪkt/ n (thing) objet m; (aim) but m; (Gram) complément m d'objet; **money is no ~** l'argent n'est pas un problème.

object² /əb'dʒekt/ vi protester. ● vt **~ that** objecter que; **~ to** (behaviour) désapprouver; (plan) protester contre. **objection** n objection f; (drawback) inconvénient m.

objective /əb'dʒektɪv/ adj & n objectif (m)

obligation /ɒblɪ'geɪʃn/ n devoir m.

obligatory /ə'blɪgətrɪ/ adj obligatoire.

oblige /ə'blaɪdʒ/ vt obliger (to do à faire).

oblivion /ə'blɪvɪən/ n oubli m. **oblivious** adj inconscient (to, of de).

oblong /'ɒblɒŋ/ adj oblong. ● n rectangle m.

obnoxious /əb'nɒkʃəs/ adj odieux.

oboe /'əʊbəʊ/ n hautbois m.

obscene /əb'siːn/ adj obscène.

obscure /əb'skjuə(r)/ adj obscur.
● vt obscurcir; (conceal) cacher.

observance /əb'zɜ:vəns/ n (of law) respect m; (of sabbath) observance f. **observant** adj observateur.

observation /ɒbzə'veɪʃn/ n observation f.

observe /əb'zɜ:v/ vt observer; (remark) remarquer.

obsess /əb'ses/ vt obséder. **obsession** n obsession f. **obsessive** adj (person) maniaque; (thought) obsédant; (illness) obsessionnel.

obsolete /'ɒbsəli:t/ adj dépassé.

obstacle /'ɒbstəkl/ n obstacle m.

obstinate /'ɒbstənət/ adj obstiné.

obstruct /əb'strʌkt/ vt (road) bloquer; (view) cacher; (progress) gêner. **obstruction** n (act) obstruction f; (thing) obstacle m; (in traffic) encombrement m.

obtain /əb'teɪn/ vt obtenir. ● vi avoir cours. **obtainable** adj disponible.

obvious /'ɒbvɪəs/ adj évident. **obviously** adv manifestement.

occasion /ə'keɪʒn/ n occasion f; (big event) événement m; on ~ à l'occasion.

occasional /ə'keɪʒənl/ adj (event) qui a lieu de temps en temps; the ~ letter une lettre de temps en temps. **occasionally** adv de temps à autre.

occupation /ɒkjʊ'peɪʃn/ n (activity) occupation f; (job) métier m, profession f. **occupational therapy** n ergothérapie f.

occupier /'ɒkjʊpaɪə(r)/ n occupant/-e m/f.

occupy /'ɒkjʊpaɪ/ vt occuper.

occur /ə'kɜ:(r)/ vi (pt occurred) se produire; (arise) se présenter; ~ to sb venir à l'esprit de qn.

occurrence /ə'kʌrəns/ n (event)

fait m; (instance) occurrence f.

ocean /'əʊʃn/ n océan m.

Oceania /əʊʃɪ'eɪnɪə/ n Océanie f.

o'clock /ə'klɒk/ adv it is six ~ il est six heures; at one ~ à une heure.

October /ɒk'təʊbə(r)/ n octobre m.

octopus /'ɒktəpəs/ n (pl) ~es pieuvre f.

odd /ɒd/ adj bizarre; (number) impair; (left over) qui reste; (sock) dépareillé; write the ~ article écrire un article de temps en temps; ~ jobs menus travaux mpl; twenty ~ vingt et quelques. **oddity** n bizarrerie f.

odds /ɒdz/ npl chances fpl; (in betting) cote f (on de); at ~ en désaccord; it makes no ~ ça ne fait rien; ~ and ends des petites choses.

odour, (US) **odor** /'əʊdə(r)/ n odeur f. **odourless** adj inodore.

of /ɒv/

o

⇒ For expressions such as **of course, consist of** → **course, consist.**

● preposition
····▸ de; a photo ~ the dog une photo du chien; the king ~ the beasts le roi des animaux; (made) ~ gold en or; it's kind ~ you c'est très gentil de votre part; some ~ us quelques-uns d'entre nous; ~ it/them en; have you heard ~ it? est-ce que tu en as entendu parler?

off /ɒf/ adv be ~ partir, s'en aller; I'm ~ je m'en vais; 30 metres ~ à 30 mètres; a month ~ dans un mois. ● adj (gas, water) coupé; (tap) fermé; (light, TV) éteint; (party, match) annulé; (bad) (food) avarié; (milk) tourné; **Friday is my day ~** je ne travaille pas le vendredi; **25% ~** 25% de remise. ● prep **3 metres ~ the ground** 3 mètres (au-dessus) du sol; **just ~ the kitchen** juste à côté de la cuisine; **that is ~ the point** là n'est pas la question.

offal /'ɒfl/ n abats mpl.

offence /ə'fens/ n (Jur) infraction f; **give ~ to** offenser; **take ~** s'offenser (**at** de).

offend /ə'fend/ vt offenser; **be ~ed** s'offenser (**at** de). ● vi (Jur) commettre une infraction. **offender** n délinquant/-e m/f.

offensive /ə'fensɪv/ adj (remark) injurieux; (language) grossier; (smell) repoussant; (weapon) offensif. ● n offensive f.

offer /'ɒfə(r)/ vt (pt **offered**) offrir. ● n offre f; **on ~** en promotion.

offhand /ɒf'hænd/ adj désinvolte. ● adv à l'improviste.

office /'ɒfɪs/ n bureau m; (duty) fonction f; **in ~** au pouvoir. ● adj de bureau.

officer /'ɒfɪsə(r)/ n (army) officier m; (police ~) policier m; (government ~) fonctionnaire m/f.

official /ə'fɪʃl/ adj officiel. ● n (civil servant) fonctionnaire m/f; (of party, union) officiel/-le m/f; (of police, customs) agent m.

off: **~-licence** n magasin m de vins et spiritueux. **~-line** adj autonome; (switched off) déconnecté; (Comput) hors connexion. **~-load** vt (stock) écouler; (Comput) décharger. **~-peak** adj (call) au tarif réduit; (travel) en période creuse. **~-putting** adj rebutant. **~-set** vt (pt **-set**. pres p **-setting**) compenser. **~shore** adj (out to sea) au large, en mer; (towards the sea) de terre; **an**

~ breeze une brise de terre. ● adv (funds) hors-lieu inv. **~side** adj (Sport) hors jeu inv; (Auto) du côté du conducteur. **~spring** n inv progéniture f.

often /'ɒfn/ adv souvent; **how ~ do you meet?** vous vous voyez tous les combien?; **every so ~** de temps en temps.

oil /ɔɪl/ n (for lubrication, cooking) huile f; (for fuel) pétrole m; (for heating) mazout m. ● vt huiler. **~ field** n gisement m pétrolifère. **~-painting** n peinture f à l'huile. **~skins** npl ciré m. **~-tanker** n pétrolier m.

oily /'ɔɪlɪ/ adj graisseux.

ointment /'ɔɪntmənt/ n pommade f.

OK, okay /əʊ'keɪ/ adj d'accord; **is it ~ if...?** ça va si...?; **feel ~** aller bien.

old /əʊld/ adj vieux; (person) vieux, âgé; (former) ancien; **how ~ is he?** quel âge a-t-il?; **he is eight years ~** il a huit ans; **~er, ~est** aîné. **~ age** n vieillesse f. **~-age pensioner** n retraité/-e m/f. **~-fashioned** adj démodé; (person) vieux jeu inv. **~ man** n vieillard m, vieux m. **~ woman** n vieille f.

olive /'ɒlɪv/ n olive f; **~ oil** huile f d'olive. ● adj olive inv.

Olympic /ə'lɪmpɪk/ adj olympique.

~ Games npl Jeux mpl olympiques.

omelette /ˈɒmlɪt/ n omelette f.

omen /ˈəʊmən/ n augure m.

ominous /ˈɒmɪnəs/ adj (presence, cloud) menaçant; (sign) de mauvais augure.

omission /əˈmɪʃn/ n omission f.

omit vt (pt **omitted**) omettre.

on /ɒn/ prep sur; **~** the table sur la table; **put the key ~ it** mets la clé dessus; **~ 22 March** le 22 mars; **~ Monday** lundi; **~ TV** à la télé; **~ video** en vidéo; **be ~ steroids** prendre des stéroïdes; **~ arriving** en arrivant. ● adj (TV, oven, light) allumé; (dishwasher, radio) en marche; (tap) ouvert; (lid) mis; **the match is still ~** le match aura lieu quand même; **the news is ~ in 10 minutes** les informations sont dans 10 minutes. ● adv **have sth ~** porter qch; **20 years ~** 20 ans plus tard; **from that day ~** à partir de ce jour-là; **further ~** plus loin; **~ and off** (occasionally) de temps en temps; **go ~ and ~** (a person) parler pendant des heures.

once /wʌns/ adv une fois; (formerly) autrefois. ● conj une fois que; **all at ~** tout d'un coup.

oncoming /ˈɒnkʌmɪŋ/ adj (vehicle) qui approche.

one /wʌn/ det & n un/-e (m/f). ● pron un/-e m/f; (impersonal) on; **~ (and only)** seul (et unique); **a big ~** un grand/une grande; **this/that ~** celui-ci/-là, celle-ci/-là; **another** l'un/-e l'autre. **~-off** adj 🇬🇧 unique, exceptionnel. **~self** pron soi-même; (reflexive) se. **~-way** adj (street) à sens unique; (ticket) simple.

ongoing /ˈɒngəʊɪŋ/ adj (process) continu; **be ~** être en cours.

onion /ˈʌnjən/ n oignon m.

on-line /ɒnˈlaɪn/ adj & adv en ligne.

onlooker /ˈɒnlʊkə(r)/ n spectateur/-trice m/f.

only /ˈəʊnlɪ/ adj seul; **~ son** fils unique. ● adv & adj seulement; **he is ~ six** il n'a que six ans.

onset /ˈɒnset/ n début m.

onward(s) /ˈɒnwəd(z)/ adv en avant.

open /ˈəʊpən/ adj ouvert; (view) dégagé; (free to all) public; (undisguised) manifeste; (question) en attente; **in the ~ air** en plein air. ● vt/i (door) (s')ouvrir; (shop, play) ouvrir; **~ out** or **up** (s')ouvrir. **~-ended** adj (stay) de durée indéterminée; (debate, question) ouvert. **~-heart** adj (surgery) à cœur ouvert.

opening /ˈəʊpnɪŋ/ n (of book) début m; (of exhibition, shop) ouverture f; (of film) première f; (in market) débouché m; (job) poste m (disponible).

open: **~-minded** adj **be ~-minded** avoir l'esprit ouvert. **~-plan** adj paysagé.

> ### Open University *i*
> Organisme britannique d'enseignement universitaire à distance. Les étudiants de tous âges travaillent chez eux et suivent les cours à la télévision ou sur Internet; ils envoient leurs travaux à leur directeur d'études (tutor) qu'ils peuvent rencontrer lors de stages en été. Les diplômes obtenus ont la même valeur que ceux délivrés par les universités traditionnelles.

opera /ˈɒprə/ n opéra m.

operate /ˈɒpəreɪt/ vt/i opérer; (Tech) (faire) fonctionner; **~ on** (Med) opérer; **operating theatre** salle f d'opération.

operation /ɒpəˈreɪʃn/ n opération f; **have an ~** se faire opérer; **in ~** (plan) en vigueur; (mine) en service.

operative /ˈɒpərətɪv/ n employé/-e m/f. ● adj (law) en vigueur.

operator /ˈɒpəreɪtə(r)/ n opérateur/-trice m/f; (telephonist) standardiste m/f.

opinion /əˈpɪnɪən/ n opinion f, avis m. **opinionated** adj qui a des avis sur tout.

opponent /əˈpəʊnənt/ n adversaire m/f.

opportunity /ɒpəˈtjuːnətɪ/ n occasion f (to do de faire).

oppose /əˈpəʊz/ vt s'opposer à; **as ~d to** par opposition à. **opposing** adj opposé.

opposite /ˈɒpəzɪt/ adj (direction, side) opposé; (building) d'en face. ● n contraire m. ● adv en face. ● prep **~ (to)** en face de.

opposition /ɒpəˈzɪʃn/ n opposition f.

oppress /əˈpres/ vt opprimer. **oppressive** adj (cruel) oppressif; (heat) oppressant.

opt /ɒpt/ vi **~ for** opter pour; **~ out** refuser de participer (of à); **~ to do** choisir de faire.

optical /ˈɒptɪkl/ adj optique. **~ illusion** n illusion f d'optique. **~ scanner** n lecteur m optique.

optician /ɒpˈtɪʃn/ n opticien/-ne m/f.

optimism /ˈɒptɪmɪzəm/ n optimisme m. **optimist** n optimiste m/f. **optimistic** adj optimiste.

option /ˈɒpʃn/ n option f; (choice) choix m.

optional /ˈɒpʃənl/ adj facultatif; **~ extras** accessoires mpl en option.

or /ɔː(r)/ conj ou; (with negative) ni.

oral /ˈɔːrəl/ n & adj oral (m).

orange /ˈɒrɪndʒ/ n (fruit) orange f; (colour) orange m. ● adj (colour) orange inv.

orbit /ˈɔːbɪt/ n orbite f. ● vt décrire une orbite autour de.

orchard /ˈɔːtʃəd/ n verger m.

orchestra /ˈɔːkɪstrə/ n orchestre m.

orchid /ˈɔːkɪd/ n orchidée f.

ordeal /ɔːˈdiːl/ n épreuve f.

order /ˈɔːdə(r)/ n ordre m; (Comm) commande f; **in ~** (tidy) en ordre; (document) en règle; **in ~ that** pour que; **in ~ to** pour. ● vt ordonner; (goods) commander; **~ sb to** ordonner à qn de.

orderly /ˈɔːdəlɪ/ adj (tidy) ordonné; (not unruly) discipliné. ● n (Mil) planton m; (Med) aide-soignant/-e m/f.

ordinary /ˈɔːdənrɪ/ adj (usual) ordinaire; (average) moyen.

ore /ɔː(r)/ n minerai m.

organ /ˈɔːgən/ n organe m; (Mus) orgue m.

organic /ɔːˈgænɪk/ adj organique; (produce) biologique.

organization /ɔːgənaɪˈzeɪʃn/ n organisation f.

organize /ˈɔːgənaɪz/ vt organiser.

organizer /ˈɔːgənaɪzə(r)/ n organisateur/-trice m/f; **electronic ~** agenda m électronique.

orgasm /ˈɔːgæzəm/ n orgasme m.

Orient /ˈɔːrɪənt/ n **the ~** l'Orient m. **oriental** adj oriental.

origin /ˈɒrɪdʒɪn/ n origine f.

original /əˈrɪdʒənl/ adj original; (inhabitant) premier; (member) originaire. **originality** n originalité f. **originally** adv (at the outset) à l'origine.

originate /əˈrɪdʒɪneɪt/ vi (plan) prendre naissance; **~ from** provenir de; (person) venir de. ● vt être l'auteur de. **originator** n (of idea) auteur m; (of invention) créateur/-trice m/f.

ornament /'ɔːnəmənt/ n (decoration) ornement m; (object) objet m décoratif.

orphan /'ɔːfn/ n orphelin/-e m/f. ● vt rendre orphelin. **orphanage** n orphelinat m.

orthopaedic /ɔːθə'piːdɪk/ adj orthopédique.

ostentatious /ɒsten'teɪʃəs/ adj tape-à-l'œil inv.

osteopath /'ɒstɪəpæθ/ n ostéopathe m/f.

ostrich /'ɒstrɪtʃ/ n autruche f.

other /'ʌðə(r)/ adj autre; **the ~ one** l'autre m/f. ● n & pron autre m/f; (some) **~s** d'autres. ● adv **~ than** (apart from) à part; (otherwise than) autrement que. **otherwise** adv autrement.

otter /'ɒtə(r)/ n loutre f.

ouch /aʊtʃ/ interj aïe!

ought /ɔːt/ v aux devoir; **you ~ to stay** vous devriez rester; **he ~ to succeed** il devrait réussir; **I ~ to have done it** j'aurais dû le faire.

ounce /aʊns/ n once f (= 28.35 g).

our /'aʊə(r)/ adj notre, pl nos.

ours /'aʊəz/ poss le or la nôtre, les nôtres.

ourselves /aʊə'selvz/ pron (reflexive) nous; (emphatic) nous-mêmes; (after preposition) for ~ pour nous, pour nous-mêmes.

out /aʊt/ adv dehors; **he's ~** il est sorti; **further ~** plus loin; **be ~** (book) être publié; (light) être éteint; (sun) briller; (flower) être épanoui; (tide) être bas; (player) être éliminé; ~ **of** hors de; **go/walk/get ~ of** sortir de; ~ **of pity** par pitié; **made ~ of** fait de; **5**

~ **of 6** 5 sur 6. **~break** n (of war) déclenchement m; (of violence, boils) éruption f. **~burst** n explosion f. **~cast** n paria m. **~class** vt surclasser. **~come** n résultat m. **~cry** n tollé m. **~dated** adj démodé. **~door** adj (activity) de plein air; (pool) en plein air. **~doors** adv dehors.

outer /'aʊtə(r)/ adj extérieur; ~ **space** espace m extra-atmosphérique.

outfit /'aʊtfɪt/ n (clothes) tenue f.

outgoing /'aʊtgəʊɪŋ/ adj (minister, tenant) sortant; (sociable) ouvert. **outgoings** npl dépenses fpl.

outgrow /aʊt'grəʊ/ vt (pt **-grew**, pp **-grown**) (clothes) devenir trop grand pour; (habit) dépasser.

outing /'aʊtɪŋ/ n sortie f.

outlaw /'aʊtlɔː/ n hors-la-loi m inv. ● vt déclarer illégal.

outlet /'aʊtlet/ n (for water, gas) tuyau m de sortie; (for goods) débouché m; (for feelings) exutoire m.

outline /'aʊtlaɪn/ n contour m; (of plan) grandes lignes fpl; (of essay) plan m. ● vt tracer le contour de; (summarize) exposer brièvement.

out: **~live** vt survivre à. **~look** n perspective f. **~number** vt surpasser en nombre. ~ **of date** adj démodé; (expired) périmé. ~ **of hand** adj incontrôlable. ~ **of order** adj en panne. ~ **of work** adj sans travail. **~patient** n malade m/f externe.

output /'aʊtpʊt/ n rendement m; (Comput) sortie f. ● vt/i (Comput) sortir.

outrage /'aʊtreɪdʒ/ n (anger) indignation f; (atrocity) attentat m; (scandal) outrage m. ● vt (morals) outrager; (person) scandaliser. **outrageous** adj scandaleux.

outright /'aʊtraɪt/ adv (completely) catégoriquement; (killed) sur le coup. ● adj (majority) absolu; (ban) catégorique; (hostility) pur et simple.

outset /'autset/ n début m.

outside /aut'saɪd/ n extérieur m. ● adv dehors. ● prep en dehors de; (in front of) devant. ● adj extérieur. **outsider** n étranger/-ère m/f; (Sport) outsider m.

out: ~ **skirts** npl périphérie f. ~**spoken** adj franc. ~**standing** adj exceptionnel; (not settled) en suspens.

outward /'autwəd/ adj & adv vers l'extérieur; (sign) extérieur. (journey) d'aller. **outwards** adv vers l'extérieur.

oval /'əʊvl/ n & adj ovale (m).

Oval Office Symbole même de la présidence américaine, le bureau ovale du président des États-Unis est situé dans l'aile ouest de la Maison-Blanche et a été inauguré en 1909. Le goût des pièces de forme ovale remonte à la présidence de George Washington (1789-1797) qui donnait des réceptions à son domicile de Philadelphie dans un salon ovale.

ovary /'əʊvərɪ/ n ovaire m.

oven /'ʌvn/ n four m.

over /'əʊvə(r)/ prep (across) pardessus; (above) au-dessus de; (covering) sur; (more than) plus de; it's ~ **the road** c'est de l'autre côté de la rue; ~ **here**/there par ici/là; **children** ~ **six** les enfants de plus de six ans; ~ **the weekend** pendant le weekend; **all** ~ **the house** partout dans la maison. ● adj, adv (term) terminé; (war) fini; **get sth** ~ **with** en finir avec qch;

ask sb ~ inviter qn; ~ **and** ~ **(again)** à plusieurs reprises; **five times** ~ cinq fois de suite.

overall /əʊvər'ɔːl/ adj global, d'ensemble; (length) total. ● adv globalement.

overalls /'əʊvərɔːls/ npl combinaison f.

over: /'əʊvə(r)/ ~**board** adv pardessus bord. ~**cast** adj couvert. ~**charge** vt faire payer trop cher à. ~**coat** n pardessus m.

overcome /əʊvə'kʌm/ vt (pt **-came**, pp **-come**) (enemy) vaincre; (difficulty, fear) surmonter; ~**by** accablé de.

overcrowded /əʊvə'kraʊdɪd/ adj bondé; (country) surpeuplé.

overdo /əʊvə'duː/ vt (pt **-did**, pp **-done**) (Culin) trop cuire; ~ **it** (overwork) en faire trop.

over: ~ **dose** n surdose f, overdose f. ~**draft** n découvert m. ~**draw** vt (pt **-drew**, pp **-drawn**) faire un découvert sur. ~ **due** adj en retard; (bill) impayé.

overflow¹ /əʊvə'fləʊ/ vi déborder.

overflow² /'əʊvəfləʊ/ n (outlet) trop-plein m. ~ **car park** n parking m de délestage.

overhaul /əʊvə'hɔːl/ vt réviser.

overhead¹ /əʊvə'hed/ adv au-dessus; (in sky) dans le ciel.

overhead² /'əʊvəhed/ adj aérien; ~ **projector** rétroprojecteur m. **overheads** npl frais mpl généraux.

over: ~**hear** vt (pt **-heard**) entendre par hasard. ~**lap** vt/i (pt **-lapped**) (se) chevaucher. ~**leaf** adv au verso. ~**load** vt surcharger. ~**look** vt (building) donner sur; (miss) ne pas voir.

overnight¹ /əʊvə'naɪt/ adv dans la nuit; (instantly: fig) du jour au lendemain.

overnight² /'əʊvənaɪt/ adj (train) de nuit; (stay) d'une nuit; (fig) soudain.

over: ~**power** vt (thief) maîtriser; (army) vaincre; (fig) accabler. ~**priced** adj trop cher. ~**rate** vt surestimer. ~**react** vi réagir de façon excessive. ~**riding** adj (consideration) numéro un; (importance) primordial. ~**rule** vt (decision) annuler.

overrun /əʊvə'rʌn/ vt (pt **-ran**, pp **-run**; pres p **-running**) (country) envahir; (budget) dépasser. ● vi (meeting) durer plus longtemps que prévu.

overseas /əʊvə'siːz/ adj étranger. ● adv outre-mer, à l'étranger.

over: ~**see** vt (pt **-saw**, pp **-seen**) surveiller. ~**sight** n omission f. ~**sleep** vi (pt **-slept**) se réveiller trop tard. ~**take** vt/i (pt **-took**, pp **-taken**) dépasser; (Auto) doubler. ~**time** n heures fpl supplémentaires. ~**turn** vt/i (se) renverser. ~**weight** adj trop gros.

overwhelm /əʊvə'welm/ vt (enemy) écraser; (shame) accabler. **overwhelmed** adj (with offers, calls) submergé (with, by de); (with shame, work) accablé; (by sight) ébloui. **overwhelming** adj (heat, grief) accablant; (defeat, victory) écrasant; (urge) irrésistible.

overwork /əʊvə'wɜːk/ vt/i (se) surmener. ● n surmenage m.

owe /əʊ/ vt devoir. **owing** adj dû; **owing to** en raison de.

owl /aʊl/ n hibou m.

own /əʊn/ adj propre. ● pron **my** ~ le mien, la mienne; **a house of one's** ~ sa propre maison; **on one's** ~ tout seul. ● vt posséder; ~ **up (to)** 🔢 avouer. **owner** n propriétaire mf. **ownership** n propriété f; (of land) possession f.

oxygen /'ɒksɪdʒən/ n oxygène m.

oyster /'ɔɪstə(r)/ n huître f.

ozone /'əʊzəʊn/ n ozone m; ~ **layer** couche f d'ozone.

Pp

PA abbr ➡ **PERSONAL ASSISTANT.**

pace /peɪs/ n pas m; (speed) allure f; **keep** ~ **with** suivre. ● vi (room) arpenter. ● vi ~ **(up and down)** faire les cent pas.

Pacific /pə'sɪfɪk/ n ~ **(Ocean)** océan m Pacifique.

pack /pæk/ n paquet m; (Mil) sac m; (of hounds) meute f; (of thieves) bande f; (of lies) tissu m. ● vt (into case) mettre dans une valise; (into box, crate) emballer; (for sale) conditionner; (crowd) remplir complètement; ~ **one's suitcase** faire sa valise. ● vi faire ses valises; ~ **into** (cram) s'entasser dans; ~ **off** expédier; **send** ~**ing** envoyer promener.

package /'pækɪdʒ/ n paquet m; (Comput) progiciel m; ~ **deal** offre f globale; ~ **holiday** voyage m organisé. ● vt empaqueter.

packed /pækt/ adj (crowded) bondé; ~ **lunch** repas m froid.

packet /'pækɪt/ n paquet m.

packing /'pækɪŋ/ n (action, material) emballage m.

pad /pæd/ n (of paper) bloc m; (to protect) protection f; (for ink) tampon m; **(launch)** ~ rampe f de lancement. ● vt (pt **padded**) rembourrer; (text: fig) délayer. ● vi (pt **padded**) (walk) marcher à pas feutrés. **padding** n rembourrage m.

paddle /'pædl/ n pagaie f. ● vt ~ a canoe pagayer. ● vi patauger.

padlock /'pædlɒk/ n cadenas m. ● vt cadenasser.

paediatrician /piːdjə'trɪʃən/ n pédiatre mf.

pagan /'peɪgən/ adj & n païen/-ne (m/f).

page /peɪdʒ/ n (of book) page f. ● vt (on pager) rechercher; (over speaker) faire appeler. **pager** n radiomessageur m.

pain /peɪn/ n douleur f; ~s efforts mpl; be in ~ souffrir; take ~s to se donner du mal pour. ● vt (grieve) peiner. **painful** adj douloureux; (laborious) pénible. ~-**killer** n analgésique m. **painless** adj (operation) indolore; (death) sans souffrance; (trouble-free) sans peine. **painstaking** adj minutieux.

paint /peɪnt/ n peinture f; ~s (in tube, box) couleurs fpl. ● vt/i peindre. ~ **brush** n pinceau m. **painter** n peintre m. **painting** n peinture f. ~**work** n peintures fpl.

pair /peə(r)/ n paire f; (of people) couple m; a ~ of trousers un pantalon. ● vi ~ off former un couple.

pajamas /pə'dʒɑːməz/ npl (US) ➔PYJAMAS.

Pakistan /pɑːkɪ'stɑːn/ n Pakistan m.

palace /'pælɪs/ n palais m.

palatable /'pælətəbl/ adj (food) savoureux; (solution) acceptable.

palate n palais m.

pale /peɪl/ adj pâle. ● vi pâlir.

Palestine /'pæləstaɪn/ n Palestine f.

pallid /'pælɪd/ adj pâle.

palm /pɑːm/ n (of hand) paume f; (tree) palmier m; (symbol) palme f. □ ~ **off** 1 ~ sth off as faire passer qch pour; ~ **sth off on sb** refiler qch à qn 1.

palpitate /'pælpɪteɪt/ vi palpiter.

paltry /'pɔːltrɪ/ adj (-ier, -iest) dérisoire, piètre.

pamper /'pæmpə(r)/ vt choyer.

pamphlet /'pæmflɪt/ n brochure f.

pan /pæn/ n casserole f; (for frying) poêle f.

pancake /'pænkeɪk/ n crêpe f.

pandemonium /pændɪ'məʊnɪəm/ n tohu-bohu m.

pander /'pændə(r)/ vi ~ **to** (person, taste) flatter bassement.

pane /peɪn/ n carreau m, vitre f.

panel /'pænl/ n (of door) panneau m; (of experts, judges) commission f; (on discussion programme) invités mpl; **(instrument)** ~ tableau m de bord.

pang /pæŋ/ n serrement m au cœur; ~**s of conscience** remords mpl.

panic /'pænɪk/ n panique f. ● vt/i (pt **panicked**) (s')affoler. ~-**stricken** adj pris de panique, affolé.

pansy /'pænzɪ/ n (Bot) pensée f.

pant /pænt/ vi haleter.

panther /'pænθə(r)/ n panthère f.

pantomime /'pæntəmaɪm/ n (show) spectacle m de Noël; (mime) mime m.

pantry /'pæntrɪ/ n garde-manger m inv.

pants /pænts/ npl (underwear) slip

m; (trousers: US) pantalon m.

paper /'peɪpə(r)/ n papier m; (newspaper) journal m; (exam) épreuve f; (essay) exposé m; (wallpaper) papier m peint; (identity) ~s papiers mpl (d'identité); **on** ~ par écrit. ● vt (room) tapisser. ~**back** n livre m de poche. ~**clip** n trombone m. ~ **feed tray** n (Comput) bac m d'alimentation en papier. ~**work** n (work) travail m administratif; (documentation) documents mpl.

par /pɑː(r)/ n **be below** ~ ne pas être en forme; **on a** ~ **with** (performance) comparable à; (person) l'égal de; (golf) par m.

parachute /'pærəʃuːt/ n parachute m. ● vi descendre en parachute.

parade /pə'reɪd/ n (procession) parade f; (Mil) défilé m. ● vi défiler. ● vt faire étalage de.

paradise /'pærədaɪs/ n paradis m.

paradox /'pærədɒks/ n paradoxe m.

paraffin /'pærəfɪn/ n pétrole m (lampant); (wax) paraffine f.

paragliding /'pærəglaɪdɪŋ/ n parapente m.

paragon /'pærəgən/ n modèle m.

paragraph /'pærəgrɑːf/ n paragraphe m.

parallel /'pærəlel/ adj parallèle. ● n parallèle m; (maths) parallèle f.

Paralympics /pærə'lɪmpɪks/ npl **the** ~ les jeux paralympiques.

paralyse /'pærəlaɪz/ vt paralyser. **paralysis** n paralysie f.

paramedic /'pærə'medɪk/ n auxiliaire mf médical/-e.

parameter /pə'ræmɪtə(r)/ n paramètre m.

paramount /'pærəmaʊnt/ adj suprême.

paranoia /pærə'nɔɪə/ n paranoïa f.

paranoid adj paranoïaque; (Psych) paranoïde.

paraphernalia /pærəfə'neɪlɪə/ n attirail m.

parasol /'pærəsɒl/ n ombrelle f; (on table, at beach) parasol m.

paratrooper /'pærətruːpə(r)/ n (Mil) parachutiste mf.

parcel /'pɑːsl/ n paquet m.

parchment /'pɑːtʃmənt/ n parchemin m.

pardon /'pɑːdn/ n pardon m; (Jur) grâce f; **I beg your** ~ je vous demande pardon. ● vt (pt **pardoned**) pardonner (sb for sth qch à qn); (Jur) gracier.

parent /'peərənt/ n parent m.

parenthesis /pə'renθəsɪs/ n (pl -theses) parenthèse f.

parenthood /'peərənthʊd/ n (fatherhood) paternité f; (motherhood) maternité f.

Paris /'pærɪs/ n Paris.

parish /'pærɪʃ/ n (Relig) paroisse f; (municipal) commune f.

park /pɑːk/ n parc m. ● vt/i (se) garer; (remain parked) stationner. ~ **and ride** n relais. ~

parking /'pɑːkɪŋ/ n stationnement m; **no** ~ stationnement interdit. ~ **lot** n (US) parking m. ~ **meter** n parcmètre m. ~ **ticket** n (fine) contravention f, PV m ①.

parliament /'pɑːləmənt/ n parlement m. **parliamentary** adj parlementaire.

Parliament Corps législatif britannique composé de la Chambre des communes (*House of Commons*) et de la Chambre des lords (*House of Lords*) qui siègent au Palais de Westminster. Le souverain convoque et dissout le Parlement, ouvre chaque session parlementaire et signe les textes de lois. ▷**SCOTTISH PARLIAMENT**, ▷**WELSH ASSEMBLY**, ▷**DÁIL**

parlour, (US) **parlor** /'pɑːlə(r)/ *n* salon *m*.

parody /'pærədɪ/ *n* parodie *f.* ● *vt* parodier.

parole /pə'rəʊl/ *n* **on ~** en liberté conditionnelle.

parrot /'pærət/ *n* perroquet *m*.

parry /'pærɪ/ *vt* (Sport) parer; (question) éluder. ● *n* parade *f.*

parsley /'pɑːslɪ/ *n* persil *m*.

parsnip /'pɑːsnɪp/ *n* panais *m*.

part /pɑːt/ *n* partie *f*; (of serial) épisode *m*; (of machine) pièce *f*; (Theat) rôle *m*; (side in dispute) parti *m*; **in ~** en partie; **on the ~ of** de la part de; **take ~** in participer à. ● *adj* partiel. ● *adv* en partie. ● *vt/i* (separate) (se) séparer; **~ with** se séparer de.

part-exchange *n* reprise *f*; **take sth in ~** reprendre qch.

partial /'pɑːʃl/ *adj* partiel; (biased) partial; **be ~ to** avoir un faible pour.

participant /pɑː'tɪsɪpənt/ *n* participant/-e *m/f.* **participate** *vi* participer (**in** à). **participation** *n* participation *f.*

participle /'pɑːtɪsɪpl/ *n* participe *m*.

particular /pə'tɪkjʊlə(r)/ *n* détail *m*; **~s** détails *mpl*; **in ~** en particulier. ● *adj* particulier; (fussy) difficile; (careful) méticuleux; **that ~** man cet homme-là. **particularly** *adv* particulièrement.

parting /'pɑːtɪŋ/ *n* séparation *f*; (in hair) raie *f.* ● *adj* d'adieu.

partition /pɑː'tɪʃn/ *n* (of room) cloison *f*; (Pol) partition *f.* ● *vt* (room) cloisonner; (country)

partager.

partly /'pɑːtlɪ/ *adv* en partie.

partner /'pɑːtnə(r)/ *n* (in professional) associé·e *m/f*; (economic, sporting) partenaire *m/f*; (spouse) époux/-se *m/f*; (unmarried) partenaire *mf.* **partnership** *n* association *f.*

partridge /'pɑːtrɪdʒ/ *n* perdrix *f.*

part-time *adj & adv* à temps partiel.

party /'pɑːtɪ/ *n* fête *f*; (formal) réception *f*; (group) groupe *m*; (Pol) parti *m*; (Jur) partie *f.*

pass /pɑːs/ *vt/i* (*pt* **passed**) passer; (overtake) dépasser; (in exam) réussir; (approve) (candidate) admettre; (invoice) approuver; (remark) faire; (judgement) prononcer; (law, bill) adopter; **~ (by)** (building) passer devant; (person) croiser. ● *n* (permit) laisser-passer *m inv*; (ticket) carte *f* d'abonnement; (Geog) col *m*; (Sport) passe *f*; **~ (mark)** (in exam) moyenne *f.* **~ away** mourir; **~ out** (faint) s'évanouir; **~ sth out** distribuer qch; **~ over** (overlook) délaisser; **~ up** (forego) laisser passer.

passage /'pæsɪdʒ/ *n* (way through, text) passage *m*; (voyage) traversée *f*; (corridor) couloir *m*.

passenger /'pæsɪndʒə(r)/ *n* (in car, plane, ship) passager/-ère *m/f*; (in train, bus, tube) voyageur/-euse *m/f.*

passer-by /pɑːsə'baɪ/ *n* (*pl* **passers-by**) passant/-e *m/f.*

passing /'pɑːsɪŋ/ *adj* (motorist) qui passe; (whim) passager; (reference) en passant.

passion /'pæʃn/ *n* passion *f.* **passionate** *adj* passionné.

passive /'pæsɪv/ *adj* passif.

passport /'pɑːspɔːt/ *n* passeport *m*.

password /'pɑːswɜːd/ *n* mot *m*

de passe.

past /pɑːst/ adj (times, problems) passé; (president) ancien; **the ~ months** ces derniers mois. ● n passé m. ● prep (beyond) après; **walk/go ~ sth** passer devant qch; **10 ~ 6** six heures dix; **it's ~ 11** il est 11 heures passées. ● adv **go/walk ~** passer.

pasta /'pæstə/ n pâtes fpl (alimentaires).

paste /peɪst/ n (glue) colle f; (dough) pâte f; (of fish, meat) pâté m; (jewellery) strass m. ● vt coller.

pasteurize /'pɑːstʃəraɪz/ vt pasteuriser.

pastime /'pɑːstaɪm/ n passe-temps m inv.

pastry /'peɪstrɪ/ n (dough) pâte f; (tart) pâtisserie f.

pat /pæt/ vt (pt **patted**) tapoter. ● n petite tape f.

patch /pætʃ/ n pièce f; (over eye) bandeau m; (spot) tache f; (of snow, ice) plaque f; (of vegetables) carré m; **bad ~** période f difficile. □ **~ up** (trousers) rapiécer; (quarrel) résoudre.

patent /'peɪtnt/ adj (obvious) manifeste; (patented) breveté; **~ leather** cuir m verni. ● n brevet m. ● vt faire breveter.

path /pɑːθ/ n (pl **-s**) sentier m, chemin m; (in park) allée f; (of rocket) trajectoire f.

pathetic /pə'θetɪk/ adj misérable; (bad 🄸) lamentable.

patience /'peɪʃns/ n patience f.

patient /'peɪʃnt/ adj patient. ● n patient/-e m/f. **patiently** adv patiemment.

patriotic /pætrɪ'ɒtɪk/ adj patriotique; (person) patriote.

patrol /pə'trəʊl/ n patrouille f; **~ car** voiture f de police. ● vt/i pa-

trouiller (dans).

patron /'peɪtrən/ n (of the arts) mécène m; (customer) client/-e m/f.
patronage n clientèle f; (support) patronage m. **patronize** vt (person) traiter avec condescendance; (establishment) fréquenter.

patter /'pætə(r)/ n (of steps) bruit m; (of rain) crépitement m.

pattern /'pætn/ n motif m, dessin m; (for sewing) patron m; (for knitting) modèle m.

paunch /pɔːntʃ/ n ventre m.

pause /pɔːz/ n pause f. ● vi faire une pause; (hesitate) hésiter.

pave /peɪv/ vt paver; **~ the way** ouvrir la voie (**for** à).

pavement /'peɪvmənt/ n trottoir m; (US) chaussée f.

paving stone n pavé m.

paw /pɔː/ n patte f. ● vt (animal) donner des coups de patte à; (touch 🄸) peloter 🄸.

pawn /pɔːn/ n pion m. ● vt mettre en gage. **~-broker** n prêteur-euse m/f sur gages. **~-shop** n mont-de-piété m.

pay /peɪ/ vt (pt **paid**) payer; (interest) rapporter; (compliment, attention) faire; (visit, homage) rendre. ● vi payer; (business) rapporter; **~ for sth** payer qch. ● n salaire m; **~ rise** augmentation f (de salaire); **~ back** rembourser; **~ in** déposer; **~ off** (loan) rembourser; (worker) congédier; (succeed) être payant; **~ out** payer, débourser.

payable /'peɪəbl/ adj payable; **~ to** (cheque) à l'ordre de.

payment /'peɪmənt/ n paiement m; (regular) versement m; (reward) récompense f.

payroll /'peɪrəʊl/ n fichier m des salaires; **be on the ~ of** être employé par.

PC *abbr* ➡PERSONAL COMPUTER.

PDA *abbr* (personal digital assistant) assistant *m* personnel numérique.

PE *abbr* (**physical education**) éducation *f* physique, EPS *f*.

pea /piː/ *n* (petit) pois *m*.

peace /piːs/ *n* paix *f*; **~ of mind** tranquillité *f* d'esprit. **peaceful** *adj* (tranquil) paisible; (peaceable) pacifique.

peach /piːtʃ/ *n* pêche *f*.

peacock /ˈpiːkɒk/ *n* paon *m*.

peak /piːk/ *n* (of mountain) pic *m*; (of cap) visière *f*; (maximum) maximum *m*; (on graph) sommet *m*; (of career) apogée *m*; (of fitness) meilleur *m*; **~ hours** heures *fpl* de pointe.

peal /piːl/ *n* (of bells) carillon *m*; (of laughter) éclat *m*.

peanut /ˈpiːnʌt/ *n* cacahuète *f*; **~s** (money) 🔲 clopinettes *fpl* 🔲.

pear /peə(r)/ *n* poire *f*.

pearl /pɜːl/ *n* perle *f*.

peasant /ˈpeznt/ *n* paysan/-ne *m/f*.

peat /piːt/ *n* tourbe *f*.

pebble /ˈpebl/ *n* caillou *m*; (on beach) galet *m*.

peck /pek/ *vt/i* (food) picorer; (attack) donner des coups de bec (à). ● *n* coup *m* de bec; **a ~ on the cheek** une bise.

peckish /ˈpekɪʃ/ *adj* **be ~** 🔲 avoir faim.

peculiar /pɪˈkjuːlɪə(r)/ *adj* (odd) bizarre; (special) particulier (**to** à). **peculiarity** *n* bizarrerie *f*.

pedal /ˈpedl/ *n* pédale *f*. ● *vi* pédaler.

pedantic /pɪˈdæntɪk/ *adj* pédant.

peddle /ˈpedl/ *vt* colporter; (drugs) faire du trafic de.

pedestrian /pɪˈdestrɪən/ *n* piéton *m*. ● *adj* (precinct, street) piétonnier; (fig) prosaïque; **~ crossing** passage *m* pour piétons.

pedigree /ˈpedɪɡriː/ *n* (of animal) pedigree *m*; (of person) ascendance *f*. ● *adj* (dog) de pure race.

pee /piː/ *vi* 🔲 faire pipi 🔲.

peek /piːk/ *vi* & *n* ➡PEEP.

peel /piːl/ *n* (on fruit) peau *m*; (removed) épluchures *fpl*. ● *vt* (fruit, vegetables) éplucher; (prawn) décortiquer. ● *vi* (of skin) peler; (of paint) s'écailler.

peep /piːp/ *vi* jeter un coup d'œil (furtif) (**at** à). ● *n* coup *m* d'œil (furtif). **~hole** *n* judas *m*.

peer /pɪə(r)/ *vi* **~ (at)** regarder fixement. ● *n* (equal, noble) pair *m*. **peerage** *n* pairie *f*.

peg /peɡ/ *n* (for clothes) pince *f* à linge; (to hang coats) patère *f*; (for tent) piquet *m*. ● *vt* (*pt* **pegged**) (clothes) accrocher avec des pinces; (prices) indexer.

pejorative /pɪˈdʒɒrətɪv/ *adj* péjoratif.

pelican /ˈpelɪkən/ *n* pélican *m*; **~ crossing** passage *m* pour piétons.

pellet /ˈpelɪt/ *n* (round mass) boulette *f*; (for gun) plomb *m*.

pelt /pelt/ *vt* bombarder (**with** de). ● *n* (skin) peau *f*.

pelvis /ˈpelvɪs/ *n* (Anat) bassin *m*.

pen /pen/ *n* stylo *m*; (for sheep) enclos *m*; (for baby, cattle) parc *m*.

penal /ˈpiːnl/ *adj* pénal. **penalize** *vt* pénaliser.

penalty /ˈpenltɪ/ *n* peine *f*; (fine) amende *f*; (in football) penalty *m*.

penance /ˈpenəns/ *n* pénitence *f*.

pence /pens/ ➡PENNY.

pencil /ˈpensl/ *n* crayon *m*. ● *vt* (*pt* **pencilled**) crayonner; **~ in** noter provisoirement. **~-sharpener** *n* taille-crayons *m inv*.

pending /'pendɪŋ/ adj (matter) en souffrance; (Jur) en instance. ● prep (until) en attendant.

penetrate /'penɪtreɪt/ vt pénétrer; (silence, defences) percer; (organization) infiltrer. ● vi pénétrer. **penetrating** adj pénétrant.

pen-friend n correspondant/ -e m/f.

penguin /'peŋgwɪn/ n manchot m, pingouin m.

pen: ~knife n (pl **-knives**) canif m. **~name** n pseudonyme m.

penniless /'penɪlɪs/ adj sans le sou.

penny /'penɪ/ n (pl **pennies** or **pence**) (unit of currency) penny m; (small amount) centime m.

pension /'penʃn/ n (from state) pension f; (from employer) retraite f; **~ scheme** plan m de retraite. **~ off** mettre à la retraite. **pensioner** n retraité/-e m/f.

pensive /'pensɪv/ adj songeur.

penthouse /'penthaʊs/ n appartement m de luxe (au dernier étage).

penultimate /pen'ʌltɪmət/ adj avant-dernier.

people /'piːpl/ n/pl gens mpl, personnes fpl; **English ~** les Anglais mpl; **~ say** on dit. ● n peuple m. ● vt peupler. **~ carrier** n monospace m.

pepper /'pepə(r)/ n poivre m; (vegetable) poivron m. ● vt (Culin) poivrer.

peppermint /'pepəmɪnt/ n (plant) menthe f poivrée; (sweet) bonbon m à la menthe.

per /pɜː(r)/ prep par; **~ annum** par an; **~ cent** pour cent; **~ kilo** le kilo; **ten km ~ hour** dix km à l'heure.

percentage /pə'sentɪdʒ/ n pourcentage m.

perception /pə'sepʃn/ n perception f. **perceptive** adj perspicace.

perch /pɜːtʃ/ n (of bird) perchoir m. ● vi (se) percher.

perennial /pə'renɪəl/ adj perpétuel; (plant) vivace.

perfect[1] /pə'fekt/ vt perfectionner.

perfect[2] /'pɜːfɪkt/ adj parfait. ● n (Ling) parfait m. **perfectly** adv parfaitement.

perfection /pə'fekʃn/ n perfection f; **to ~** à la perfection.

perforate /'pɜːfəreɪt/ vt perforer.

perform /pə'fɔːm/ vt (task) exécuter; (function) remplir; (operation) procéder à; (play) jouer; (song) chanter. ● vi (actor, musician, team) jouer; **~ well/badly** (candidate, business) avoir de bons/de mauvais résultats. **performance** n interprétation f; (of car, team) performance f; (show) représentation f; (fuss) histoire f. **performer** n artiste mf.

perfume /'pɜːfjuːm/ n parfum m.

perhaps /pə'hæps/ adv peut-être.

peril /'perəl/ n péril m. **perilous** adj périlleux.

perimeter /pə'rɪmɪtə(r)/ n périmètre m.

period /'pɪərɪəd/ n période f; (era) époque f; (lesson) cours m; (Gram) point m; (Med) règles fpl. ● adj d'époque. **periodical** n périodique m.

peripheral /pə'rɪfərəl/ adj (vision, suburb) périphérique; (issue) annexe. ● n (Comput) périphérique m.

perish /'perɪʃ/ vi périr; (rubber) se détériorer.

perjury /'pɜːdʒərɪ/ n faux témoignage m.

perk /pɜːk/ n ⬜ avantage m. ● vt/i **~ up** ⬜ (se) remonter. **perky** adj ⬜ gai.

perm /pɜːm/ n permanente f. **to have one's hair ~ed** se faire faire une permanente.

permanent /'pɜːmənənt/ adj permanent. **permanently** adv (happy) en permanence; (employed) de façon permanente.

permissible /pə'mɪsɪbl/ adj permis.

permission /pə'mɪʃn/ n permission f.

permissive /pə'mɪsɪv/ adj libéral; (pej) permissif.

permit[1] /pə'mɪt/ vt (pt permitted) permettre (sb to à qn de), autoriser (sb to qn à).

permit[2] /'pɜːmɪt/ n permis m.

perpendicular /pɜːpən'dɪkjʊlə(r)/ adj perpendiculaire.

perpetrator /'pɜːpɪtreɪtə(r)/ n auteur m.

perpetuate /pə'petjʊeɪt/ vt perpétuer.

perplexed /pə'plekst/ adj perplexe.

persecute /'pɜːsɪkjuːt/ vt persécuter.

perseverance /pɜːsɪ'vɪərəns/ n persévérance f. **persevere** vi persévérer.

persist /pə'sɪst/ vi persister (in doing à faire). **persistence** n persistance f. **persistent** adj (cough, snow) persistant; (obstinate) obstiné; (noise, pressure) continuel.

person /'pɜːsn/ n personne f; in ~ en personne.

personal /'pɜːsənl/ adj (life, problem, opinion) personnel; (safety, freedom, insurance) individuel. ~ **ad** n petite annonce f. ~ **assistant** n secrétaire mf de direction. ~ **computer** n ordinateur m (personnel), microordinateur m.

personality /pɜːsə'nælətɪ/ n personnalité f; (star) vedette f.

personal: ~ **organizer** n agenda

m. ~ **stereo** n baladeur m.

personnel /pɜːsə'nel/ n personnel m.

perspiration /pɜːspɪ'reɪʃn/ n (sweat) sueur f; (sweating) transpiration f. **perspire** vi transpirer.

persuade /pə'sweɪd/ vt persuader (to de). **persuasion** n persuasion f. **persuasive** adj persuasif.

pertinent /'pɜːtɪnənt/ adj pertinent.

perturb /pə'tɜːb/ vt troubler.

Peru /pə'ruː/ n Pérou m.

pervasive /pə'veɪsɪv/ adj (smell) pénétrant; (feeling) envahissant.

perverse /pə'vɜːs/ adj (desire) pervers; (refusal, attitude) illogique. **perversion** n perversion f.

pervert[1] /pə'vɜːt/ vt (truth) travestir; (values) fausser; (justice) entraver.

pervert[2] /'pɜːvɜːt/ n pervers-e m/f.

pessimist /'pesɪmɪst/ n pessimiste mf. **pessimistic** adj pessimiste.

pest /pest/ n (insect) insecte m nuisible; (animal) animal m nuisible; (person 🔟) enquiquineur/-euse m/f 🔟.

pester /'pestə(r)/ vt harceler.

pet /pet/ n animal m de compagnie; (favourite) chouchou/-te m/f. ● adj (theory, charity) favori; ~ **hate** bête f noire; ~ **name** petit nom m. ● vt (pt petted) caresser; (spoil) chouchouter 🔟.

petal /'petl/ n pétale m.

peter /'piːtə(r)/ vi ~ **out** (conversation) tarir; (supplies) s'épuiser.

petite /pə'tiːt/ adj (woman) menue.

petition /pə'tɪʃn/ n pétition f. ● vt adresser une pétition à.

petrol /'petrəl/ n essence f. ~ **bomb** n cocktail m molotov. ~ **station** n station-service f. ~ **tank** n réservoir m d'essence.

petticoat /'petɪkəʊt/ n jupon m.

petty /'petɪ/ adj (-ier, -iest) (minor) petit; (mean) mesquin; ~ **cash** petite caisse f.

pew /pju:/ n banc m (d'église).

pharmacist /'fɑ:məsɪst/ n pharmacien/-ne m/f. **pharmacy** n pharmacie f.

phase /feɪz/ n phase f. ● vt ~ **in/out** introduire/supprimer peu à peu.

PhD abbr (**Doctor of Philosophy**) doctorat m.

pheasant /'feznt/ n faisan/-e m/f.

phenomenon /fə'nɒmɪnən/ n (pl **-ena**) phénomène m.

phew /fju:/ interj ouf.

philosopher /fɪ'lɒsəfə(r)/ n philosophe m/f. **philosophical** adj philosophique; (resigned) philosophe. **philosophy** n philosophie f.

phlegm /flem/ n (Med) mucosité f.

phobia /'fəʊbɪə/ n phobie f.

phone /fəʊn/ n téléphone m; **on the** ~ au téléphone. ● vt (person) téléphoner à; ~ **England** téléphoner en Angleterre. ● vi téléphoner; ~ **back** rappeler. ~ **book** n annuaire m. ~ **booth**, ~ **box** n cabine f téléphonique. ~ **call** n coup m de fil ①. ~**card** n télécarte f. ~**-in** n émission f à ligne ouverte. ~ **number** n numéro m de téléphone.

phonetic /fə'netɪk/ adj phonétique.

phoney /'fəʊnɪ/ adj (-ier, -iest) ① faux. ● n (person) charlatan m; **it's a** ~ c'est un faux.

photocopier /'fəʊtəʊkɒpɪə(r)/ n photocopieuse f.

photocopy /'fəʊtəʊkɒpɪ/ n photocopie f. ● vt photocopier.

photograph /'fəʊtəgrɑːf/ n pho-

tographie f. ● vt photographier.

photographer n photographe m/f.

phrase /freɪz/ n expression f; (idiom) locution f. ● vt exprimer, formuler. ~**-book** n guide m de conversation.

physical /'fɪzɪkl/ adj physique.

physicist /'fɪzɪsɪst/ n physicien/-ne m/f.

physics /'fɪzɪks/ n physique f.

physiotherapist /fɪzɪəʊ-'θerəpɪst/ n kinésithérapeute m/f. **physiotherapy** n kinésithérapie f.

physique /fɪ'ziːk/ n physique m.

piano /pɪ'ænəʊ/ n piano m.

pick /pɪk/ n choix m; (best) meilleur/-e m/f; (tool) pioche f. ● vt choisir; (flower) cueillir; (lock) crocheter; ~ **a quarrel with** chercher querelle à; ~ **one's nose** se curer le nez. □ ~ **on** harceler; ~ **out** choisir; (identify) distinguer; ~ **up** vt ramasser; (sth fallen) relever; (weight) soulever; (habit, passenger, speed) prendre; (learn) apprendre; vi s'améliorer.

pickaxe /'pɪkæks/ n pioche f.

picket /'pɪkɪt/ n (striker) gréviste m/f; (stake) piquet m; ~ (**line**) piquet m de grève. ● vt (pt **picketed**) installer un piquet de grève devant.

pickle /'pɪkl/ n conserves fpl au vinaigre; (gherkin) cornichon m. ● vt conserver dans du vinaigre.

pick-up /'pɪkʌp/ n (stylus-holder) lecteur m; (on guitar) capteur m; (collection) ramassage m; (improvement) reprise f.

picnic /'pɪknɪk/ n pique-nique m. ● vi (pt **picnicked**) pique-niquer.

pictorial /pɪk'tɔːrɪəl/ adj (magazine) illustré; (record) graphique.

picture /'pɪktʃə(r)/ n image f; (painting) tableau m; (photograph) photo f; (drawing) dessin m; (film)

p

film m; (fig) description f; **the ~s** le cinéma. ● vt s'imaginer; **be ~d** (shown) être représenté.

picturesque /pɪktʃəˈresk/ adj pittoresque.

pie /paɪ/ n (sweet) tarte f; (savoury) tourte f.

piece /piːs/ n morceau m; (of string, ribbon) bout m; (of currency, machine) pièce f; **a ~ of advice/furniture** un conseil/meuble; **go to ~s** (fig) s'effondrer; **take to ~s** démonter.

pier /pɪə(r)/ n jetée f.

pierce /pɪəs/ vt percer.

pig /pɪg/ n porc m, cochon m.

pigeon /ˈpɪdʒɪn/ n pigeon m. **~-hole** n casier m.

pig-headed adj entêté.

pigsty /ˈpɪgstaɪ/ n porcherie f.

pigtail /ˈpɪgteɪl/ n natte f.

pike /paɪk/ n inv (fish) brochet m.

pile /paɪl/ n (heap) tas m; (stack) pile f; (of carpet) poil m; **~s of** 🄸 un tas de 🄸. ● vt **~ (up)** entasser. ● vi **~ into** s'engouffrer dans; **~ up** (snow, leaves) s'entasser; (debts, work) s'accumuler. **~-up** n (Auto) carambolage m.

pilgrim /ˈpɪlgrɪm/ n pèlerin m. **pilgrimage** n pèlerinage m.

pill /pɪl/ n pilule f.

pillar /ˈpɪlə(r)/ n pilier m. **~-box** n boîte f aux lettres.

pillion /ˈpɪliən/ n siège m de passager; **ride ~** monter en croupe.

pillow /ˈpɪləʊ/ n oreiller m. **~case** n taie f d'oreiller.

pilot /ˈpaɪlət/ n pilote m. ● adj pilote. ● vt (pt **piloted**) piloter. **~-light** n veilleuse f.

pimple /ˈpɪmpl/ n bouton m.

pin /pɪn/ n épingle f; (of plug) fiche f; (for wood, metal) goujon m; (in

surgery) broche f; **have ~s and needles** avoir des fourmis. ● vt (pt **pinned**) épingler, attacher; (trap) coincer; **~ sb down** (fig) forcer qn à se décider; **~ up** accrocher.

pinafore /ˈpɪnəfɔːr/ n tablier m.

pincers /ˈpɪnsəz/ npl tenailles fpl.

pinch /pɪntʃ/ vt pincer; (steal 🄸) piquer. ● vi (be too tight) serrer. ● n (mark) pinçon m; (of salt) pincée f; **at a ~** à la rigueur.

pine /paɪn/ n (tree) pin m. ● vi **~ (away)** dépérir; **~ for** languir après.

pineapple /ˈpaɪnæpl/ n ananas m.

pinecone /ˈpaɪnkəʊn/ n pomme f de pin.

pink /pɪŋk/ adj & n rose (m).

pinpoint /ˈpɪnpɔɪnt/ vt (problem, cause, location) indiquer; (time) déterminer.

pint /paɪnt/ n pinte f (GB = 0.57 litre; US = 0.47 litre).

pin-up /ˈpɪnʌp/ n 🄸 pin-up f inv 🄸

pioneer /paɪəˈnɪə(r)/ n pionnier m. ● vt **~ the use of** être le premier à utiliser.

pious /ˈpaɪəs/ adj pieux.

pip /pɪp/ n (seed) pépin m; (sound) top m.

pipe /paɪp/ n tuyau m; (to smoke) pipe f; (Mus) chalumeau m; **~s** cornemuse f. ● vt transporter par tuyau. □ **~ down** se taire.

pipeline /ˈpaɪplaɪn/ n oléoduc m; **in the ~** en cours.

piping /ˈpaɪpɪŋ/ n tuyauterie f; **~ hot** fumant.

pirate /ˈpaɪərət/ n pirate m. ● vt pirater.

Pisces /ˈpaɪsiːz/ n Poissons mpl.

pistol /ˈpɪstl/ n pistolet m.

pit /pɪt/ n fosse f; (mine) puits m; (quarry) carrière f; (for orchestra) fosse f; (of stomach) creux m; (of cherry: US) noyau m. ● vt (pt **pitted**) marquer; (fig) opposer; ~ oneself **against** se mesurer à.

pitch /pɪtʃ/ n (Sport) terrain m; (of voice, note) hauteur f; (degree) degré m; (Mus) ton m; (tar) brai m. ● vt jeter; (tent) planter. ● vi (ship) tanguer. □ ~ **in** 🇬🇧 contribuer.

pitfall /'pɪtfɔːl/ n écueil m.

pitiful /'pɪtɪfl/ adj pitoyable. **pitiless** adj impitoyable.

pit stop n arrêt m mécanique.

pittance /'pɪtns/ n **earn a** ~ gagner trois fois rien.

pity /'pɪtɪ/ n pitié f; (regrettable fact) dommage m; **take** ~ **on** avoir pitié de; **what a** ~! quel dommage! ● vt avoir pitié de.

pivot /'pɪvət/ n pivot m. ● vi (pt **pivoted**) pivoter.

placard /'plækɑːd/ n affiche f.

place /pleɪs/ n endroit m, lieu m; (house) maison f; (seat, rank) place f; **at** or **to my** ~ chez moi; **change** ~s changer de place; **in the first** ~ d'abord; **out of** ~ déplacé; **take** ~ avoir lieu. ● vt placer; (order) passer; (remember) situer; **be** ~**d** (in race) se placer. ~-**mat** n set m.

placid /'plæsɪd/ adj placide.

plagiarism /'pleɪdʒərɪzəm/ n plagiat m. **plagiarize** vt/i plagier.

plague /pleɪg/ n (bubonic) peste f; (epidemic) épidémie f; (of ants, locusts) invasion f. ● vt harceler.

plaice /pleɪs/ n inv carrelet m.

plain /pleɪn/ adj (obvious) clair; (candid) franc; (simple) simple; (not pretty) sans beauté; (not patterned) uni; ~ **chocolate** chocolat m noir; **in** ~ **clothes** en civil. ● adv franchement. ● n plaine f. **plainly** adv clairement; franchement; simplement.

plaintiff /'pleɪntɪf/ n (Jur)

plaignant/-e m/f.

plaintive /'pleɪntɪv/ adj plaintif.

plait /plæt/ vt tresser. ● n natte f.

plan /plæn/ n project m, plan m; (diagram) plan m. ● vt (pt **planned**) projeter (**to do** de faire); (timetable, day) organiser; (economy, work) planifier. ● vi prévoir; ~ **on** s'attendre à.

plane /pleɪn/ n (level) plan m; (aeroplane) avion m; (tool) rabot m. ● adj plan. ● vt raboter.

planet /'plænɪt/ n planète f.

plank /plæŋk/ n planche f.

planning /'plænɪŋ/ n (of economy, work) planification f; (of holiday, party) organisation f; (of town) urbanisme m; **family** ~ planning m familial; ~ **permission** permis m de construire.

plant /plɑːnt/ n plante f; (Tech) matériel m; (factory) usine f. ● vt planter; (bomb) placer.

plaster /'plɑːstə(r)/ n plâtre m; (adhesive) sparadrap m. ● vt plâtrer; (cover) couvrir (**with** de).

plastic /'plæstɪk/ adj en plastique; (art, substance) plastique; ~ **surgery** chirurgie f esthétique. ● n plastique m.

plate /pleɪt/ n assiette f; (of metal) plaque f; (silverware) argenterie f; (in book) gravure f. ● vt (metal) plaquer.

plateau /'plætəʊ/ n (pl ~x) plateau m; (fig) palier m.

platform /'plætfɔːm/ n (stage) estrade f; (for speaking) tribune f; (Rail) quai m; (Pol) plate-forme f.

platoon /plə'tuːn/ n (Mil) section f.

play /pleɪ/ vt/i jouer; (instrument) jouer de; (record) mettre; (game) jouer à; (opponent) jouer contre; (match) disputer; ~ **safe** ne pas prendre de risques. ● n jeu m;

(Theat) pièce f. □ ~ **down** minimiser; ~**on** (fears) exploiter; ~ **up** 🔟 commencer à faire des siennes 🔟; ~ **up sth** mettre l'accent sur qch.

playful /'pleifl/ adj (remark) taquin; (child) joueur.

play: ~**ground** n cour f de récréation. ~**group**, ~**school** n garderie f

playing /'pleɪɪŋ/ n (Sport) jeu m; (Theat) interprétation f. ~**card** n carte f à jouer. ~**field** n terrain m de sport.

play: ~**pen** n parc m (pour bébé). ~**wright** n auteur m dramatique.

plc abbr (**public limited company**) SA.

plea /pli:/ n (for mercy, tolerance) appel m; (for food, money) demande f; (reason) excuse f; **make a ~ of guilty** plaider coupable.

plead /pli:d/ vt/i supplier; (Jur) plaider.

pleasant /'pleznt/ adj agréable.

please /pli:z/ vt/i plaire (à), faire plaisir (à); ~ **oneself**, **do as one ~s** faire ce qu'on veut. ● adv s'il vous en te plaît. **pleased** adj content (**with** de). **pleasing** adj agréable.

pleasure /'pleʒə(r)/ n plaisir m; **with ~** avec plaisir; **my ~** je vous en prie.

pleat /pli:t/ n pli m. ● vt plisser.

pledge /pledʒ/ n (token) gage m; (promise) promesse f. ● vt promettre; (pawn) mettre en gage.

plentiful /'plentifl/ adj abondant.

plenty /'plenti/ n abondance f; ~ (**of**) (a great deal) beaucoup de; (enough) assez (de).

pliers /'plaɪəz/ npl pinces fpl.

plight /plaɪt/ n détresse f.

plinth /plɪnθ/ n socle m.

plod /plɒd/ vi (pt **plodded**) avancer péniblement.

plonk /plɒŋk/ n 🔟 pinard m 🔟.

plot /plɒt/ n (conspiracy) complot m; (of novel) intrigue f; ~ (**of land**) terrain m. ● vt/i (pt **plotted**) (plan) comploter; (mark out) tracer.

plough /plaʊ/ n charrue f. ● vt/i labourer. □ ~ **back** réinvestir; ~ **through** avancer péniblement dans.

plow /plaʊ/ n & vt/i (US)
→PLOUGH.

ploy /plɔɪ/ n stratagème m.

pluck /plʌk/ vt (flower, fruit) cueillir; (bird) plumer; (eyebrows) épiler; (strings: Mus) pincer; ~ **up courage** prendre son courage à deux mains. **plucky** adj courageux.

plug /plʌg/ n (for sink) bonde f; (Electr) fiche f, prise f. ● vt (pt **plugged**) (hole) boucher; (publicize 🔟) faire du battage autour de. □ ~ **in** brancher. ~**hole** n bonde f.

plum /plʌm/ n prune f. ~ **pudding** (plum-)pudding m.

plumber /'plʌmə(r)/ n plombier m.

plume /plu:m/ n (of feathers) panache m.

plummet /'plʌmɪt/ vi tomber, plonger.

plump /plʌmp/ adj potelé, dodu.

plunge /plʌndʒ/ vt/i (dive, thrust) plonger; (fall) tomber. ● n plongeon m; (fall) chute f; **take the ~** se jeter à l'eau. **plunger** n (for sink) ventouse f.

plural /'plʊərəl/ adj pluriel; (noun) au pluriel; (ending) du pluriel. ● n pluriel m.

plus /plʌs/ prep plus; **ten ~** plus de dix. ● adj (Electr & fig) positif. ● n signe m plus; (fig) atout m.

ply /plaɪ/ vt (tool) manier; (trade) exercer. ● vi faire la navette; ~ **sb with drink** offrir continuellement à boire à qn.

plywood /'plaɪwʊd/ n contreplaqué m.

p.m. /piː'em/ adv de l'après-midi or du soir.

pneumatic drill /njuːˈmætɪk drɪl/ n marteaupiqueur m.

pneumonia /njuːˈməʊnɪə/ n pneumonie f.

PO abbr ➞POST OFFICE.

poach /pəʊtʃ/ vt/i (game) braconner; (staff) débaucher; (Culin) pocher.

PO Box n boîte f postale.

pocket /'pɒkɪt/ n poche f; be out of ~ avoir perdu de l'argent. ● adj de poche. ● vt empocher. **~-book** n (notebook) carnet m; (wallet: US) portefeuille m; (handbag: US) sac m à main. **~-money** n argent m de poche.

pod /pɒd/ n (peas) cosse f; (vanilla) gousse f.

podgy /'pɒdʒɪ/ adj (-ier, -iest) dodu.

poem /'pəʊɪm/ n poème m. **poet** n poète m. **poetic** adj poétique. **poetry** n poésie f.

point /pɔɪnt/ n (position) point m; (tip) pointe f; (decimal point) virgule f; (remark) remarque f; **good ~s** qualités fpl; **on the ~ of** sur le point de; **~ in time** moment m; **~ of view** point m de vue; **to the ~** pertinent; **what is the ~?** à quoi bon? ● vt (aim) braquer; (show) indiquer; **~ out** signaler; ~ vi indiquer du doigt; ~ **out that, make the ~ that** faire remarquer que. **~-blank** adj & adv à bout portant.

pointed /'pɔɪntɪd/ adj (sharp) pointu; (window) en pointe; (remark) lourd de sens.

pointless /'pɔɪntlɪs/ adj inutile.

poise /pɔɪz/ n (confidence) assurance f; (physical elegance) aisance f.

poison /'pɔɪzn/ n poison m. ● vt empoisonner. **poisonous** adj (substance) toxique; (plant) vénéneux; (snake) venimeux.

poke /pəʊk/ vt/i (push) pousser; (fire) tisonner; (thrust) fourrer; ~ **fun at** se moquer de. ● n (petit) coup m. ~ **out** (head) sortir.

poker /'pəʊkə(r)/ n (for fire) tisonnier m; (cards) poker m.

Poland /'pəʊlənd/ n Pologne f.

polar /'pəʊlə(r)/ adj polaire.

pole /pəʊl/ n (stick) perche f; (for flag) mât m; (Geog) pôle m.

Pole /pəʊl/ n Polonais/-e m/f.

pole-vault n saut m à la perche.

police /pəˈliːs/ n police f. ● vt faire la police dans. ~ **constable** n agent m de police. ~**man** n (pl -**men**) agent m de police. ~ **station** n commissariat m de police. ~**woman** n (pl -**women**) femme-agent f.

policy /'pɒləsɪ/ n (insurance) police f (d'assurance).

polish /'pɒlɪʃ/ vt polir; (shoes, floor) cirer. ● n (for shoes) cirage m; (for floor) encaustique f; (for nails) vernis m; (shine) poli m; (fig) raffinement m. □ ~ **off** finir en vitesse; ~ **up** (language) perfectionner.

Polish /'pəʊlɪʃ/ adj polonais. ● n (Ling) polonais m.

polished /'pɒlɪʃt/ adj raffiné.

polite /pəˈlaɪt/ adj poli.

political /pəˈlɪtɪkl/ adj politique.

politician /pɒlɪˈtɪʃn/ n homme m politique, femme f politique.

politics /'pɒlətɪks/ n politique f.

poll /pəʊl/ n (vote casting) scrutin m; (survey) sondage m; **go to the ~s** aller aux urnes. ● vt (votes) obtenir.

p

pollen /'pɒlən/ n pollen m.

polling booth n isoloir m.

polling station n bureau m de vote.

pollution /pə'luːʃn/ n pollution f.

polo /'pəʊləʊ/ n polo m. ~ **neck** n col m roulé.

pomegranate /'pɒmɪɡrænɪt/ n grenade f.

pomp /pɒmp/ n pompe f.

pompous /'pɒmpəs/ adj pompeux.

pond /pɒnd/ n étang m; (artificial) bassin m; (stagnant) mare f.

ponder /'pɒndə(r)/ vt/i réfléchir (à), méditer (sur).

pong /pɒŋ/ n (stink 🔢) puanteur f. ● vi 🔢 puer.

pony /'pəʊnɪ/ n poney m. ~**tail** n queue f de cheval.

poodle /'puːdl/ n caniche m.

pool /puːl/ n (puddle) flaque f; (pond) étang m; (of blood) mare f; (for swimming) piscine f; (fund) fonds m commun; (of ideas) réservoir m; (snooker) billard m américain; ~**s** pari m mutuel sur le football. ● vt mettre en commun.

poor /pɔː(r)/ adj (not wealthy) pauvre; (not good) médiocre, mauvais.

poorly /'pɔːlɪ/ adj malade. ● adv mal.

pop /pɒp/ n (noise) pan m; (music) pop m. ● adj pop inv. ● vt/i (pt **popped**) (burst) crever; (put) mettre; ~ **in/out/off** entrer/sortir/ partir. □ ~ **up** surgir. ~**up** fenêtre f pop-up.

pope /pəʊp/ n pape m.

poppy /'pɒpɪ/ n pavot m; (wild) coquelicot m.

popular /'pɒpjʊlə(r)/ adj populaire; (in fashion) en vogue; **be** ~ **with** plaire à.

population /pɒpjʊ'leɪʃn/ n population f.

porcelain /'pɔːsəlɪn/ n porcelaine f.

porcupine /'pɔːkjʊpaɪn/ n porc-épic m.

pork /pɔːk/ n porc m.

pornography /pɔː'nɒɡrəfɪ/ n pornographie f.

port /pɔːt/ n (harbour) port m; (left: Naut) bâbord m; ~ **of call** escale f; (wine) porto m.

portable /'pɔːtəbl/ adj portable.

porter /'pɔːtə(r)/ n (carrier) porteur m; (doorkeeper) portier m.

portfolio /pɔːt'fəʊlɪəʊ/ n (Pol, Comm) portefeuille m.

portion /'pɔːʃn/ n (at meal) portion f; (part) partie f.

portrait /'pɔːtreɪt/ n portrait m.

portray /pɔː'treɪ/ vt représenter.

Portugal /'pɔːtjʊɡl/ n Portugal m.

Portuguese /pɔːtʃʊ'ɡiːz/ n (Ling) portugais m; (person) Portugais/-e m/f. ● adj portugais.

pose /pəʊz/ vt/i poser; ~ **as** (expert) se poser en. ● n pose f.

poser /'pəʊzə(r)/ n (person) frimeur/-euse m/f; (puzzle) colle f.

posh /pɒʃ/ adj 🔢 chic inv.

position /pə'zɪʃn/ n position f; (job, state) situation f. ● vt placer.

positive /'pɒzətɪv/ adj positif; (sure) sûr, certain; (real) réel, vrai.

possess /pə'zes/ vt posséder.

possession /pə'zeʃn/ n possession f; **take** ~ **of** prendre possession de.

possessive /pə'zesɪv/ adj possessif.

possible /'pɒsəbl/ adj possible.

possibly /'pɒsəblɪ/ adv peut-être; **if I** ~ **can** si cela m'est possible; **I cannot** ~ **leave** il m'est impossible de partir.

post /pəʊst/ n (pole) poteau m;

(station, job) poste m; (mail service) poste f; (letters) courrier m. ● adj postal. ● vt (letter) poster; keep ~ed tenir au courant; ~ (up) (a notice) afficher; (appoint) affecter.

postage /'pəʊstɪdʒ/ n affranchissement m; tarif m postal.

postal /'pəʊstl/ adj postal. ~ **order** n mandat m.

post: ~**box** n boîte f aux lettres. ~**card** n carte f postale. ~ **code** n code m postal.

poster /'pəʊstə(r)/ n (for information) affiche f; (for decoration) poster m.

postgraduate /pəʊst'grædʒʊət/ n étudiant/-e m/f de troisième cycle.

posthumous /'pɒstjʊməs/ adj posthume.

post: ~**man** n (pl -**men**) facteur m. ~**mark** n cachet m de la poste.

post-mortem /pəʊst'mɔːtəm/ n autopsie f.

post office n poste f.

postpone /pə'spəʊn/ vt remettre.

postscript /'pəʊsskrɪpt/ n (to letter) postscriptum m inv.

posture /'pɒstʃə(r)/ n posture f. ● vi prendre des poses.

pot /pɒt/ n pot m; (drug [!]) hasch m; **go to** [!] aller à la ruine; **take** ~ **luck** tenter sa chance. ● vt (plants) mettre en pot.

potato /pə'teɪtəʊ/ n (pl ~**es**) pomme f de terre.

pot-belly n bedaine f.

potential /pə'tenʃl/ adj & n potentiel (m).

pothole /'pɒthəʊl/ n (in rock) caverne f; (in road) nid m de poule. **pot-holing** n spéléologie f.

potter /'pɒtə(r)/ n potier m. ● vi bricoler. **pottery** n (art) poterie f; (objects) poteries fpl.

potty /'pɒtɪ/ adj (-**ier**, -**iest**) (crazy [x]) toqué. ● n pot m.

pouch /paʊtʃ/ n poche f; (for tobacco) blague f.

poultry /'pəʊltrɪ/ n volailles fpl.

pounce /paʊns/ vi bondir (**on** sur). ● n bond m.

pound /paʊnd/ n (weight) livre f (= 454 g); (money) livre f; (for dogs, cars) fourrière f. ● vt (crush) piler; (bombard) pilonner. ● vi frapper fort; (of heart) battre fort; (walk) marcher à pas lourds.

pour /pɔː(r)/ vt verser. ● vi couler, ruisseler (**from** de); (rain) pleuvoir à torrents. □ ~ **in/out** (people) arriver/sortir en masse; ~ **off** or **out** vider. **pouring rain** n pluie f torrentielle.

pout /paʊt/ vi faire la moue.

poverty /'pɒvətɪ/ n misère f, pauvreté f.

powder /'paʊdə(r)/ n poudre f. ● vt poudrer.

power /'paʊə(r)/ n (strength) puissance f; (control) pouvoir m; (energy) énergie f; (Electr) courant m. ● vt (engine) faire marcher; (plane) propulser; ~**ed by** (engine) propulsé par; (generator) alimenté par. ~ **cut** n coupure f de courant.

powerful /'paʊəfl/ adj puissant.

powerless /'paʊəlɪs/ adj impuissant.

power: ~**point** n prise f de courant. ~**station** n centrale f électrique.

practical /'præktɪkl/ adj pratique. ~ **joke** n farce f.

practice /'præktɪs/ n (procedure) pratique f; (of profession) exercice m; (Sport) entraînement m; **in** ~ (in fact) en pratique; (well-trained) en forme; **out of** ~ rouillé; **put into** ~ mettre en pratique.

practise | premium

504

practise /'præktɪs/ vt/i (musician, typist) s'exercer (à); (Sport) s'entraîner (à); (put into practice) pratiquer; (profession) exercer.

practitioner /præk'tɪʃənə(r)/ n praticien/-ienne m/f; **dental ~** dentiste mf.

praise /preɪz/ vt faire l'éloge de; (God) louer. ● n éloges mpl, louanges fpl.

pram /præm/ n landau m.

prance /prɑːns/ vi caracoler.

prawn /prɔːn/ n crevette f rose.

pray /preɪ/ vi prier. **prayer** n prière f.

preach /priːtʃ/ vt/i prêcher; **~ at** or to prêcher.

precarious /prɪ'keərɪəs/ adj précaire.

precaution /prɪ'kɔːʃn/ n précaution f.

precede /prɪ'siːd/ vt précéder.

precedence /'presɪdəns/ n (in importance) priorité f; (in rank) préséance f.

precedent /'presɪdənt/ n précédent m.

precinct /'priːsɪŋkt/ n quartier m commerçant; (pedestrian area) zone f piétonne; (district: US) circonscription f.

precious /'preʃəs/ adj précieux.

precipitate /prɪ'sɪpɪteɪt/ vt (person, event, chemical) précipiter.

précis /'preɪsiː/ n résumé m.

precise /prɪ'saɪs/ adj précis; (careful) méticuleux. **precision** n précision f.

precocious /prɪ'kəʊʃəs/ adj précoce.

preconceived /priːkən'siːvd/ adj préconçu.

predator /'predətə(r)/ n prédateur m.

predicament /prɪ'dɪkəmənt/ n situation f difficile.

predict /prɪ'dɪkt/ vt prédire. **predictable** adj prévisible. **prediction** n prédiction f.

predispose /priːdɪ'spəʊz/ vt prédisposer (**to do** à faire).

predominant /prɪ'dɒmɪnənt/ adj prédominant.

pre-empt /priː'empt/ vt (anticipate) anticiper; (person) devancer.

preface /'prefɪs/ n (to book) préface f; (to speech) préambule m.

prefect /'priːfekt/ n (pupil) élève m/f chargé/-e de la discipline; (official) préfet m.

prefer /prɪ'fɜː(r)/ vt (pt **preferred**) préférer (**to do** faire). **preferably** adv de préférence. **preference** n préférence f. **preferential** adj préférentiel.

prefix /'priːfɪks/ n préfixe m.

pregnancy /'pregnənsɪ/ n grossesse f. **pregnant** adj (woman) enceinte; (animal) pleine; (pause) éloquent.

prehistoric /priːhɪ'stɒrɪk/ adj préhistorique.

prejudge /priː'dʒʌdʒ/ vt (issue) préjuger de; (person) juger d'avance.

prejudice /'predʒʊdɪs/ n préjugé/-s) m(pl); (harm) préjudice m. ● vt (claim) porter préjudice à; (person) léser. **prejudiced** adj partial; (person) qui a des préjugés.

premature /'premətjʊə(r)/ adj prématuré.

premeditated /priː'medɪteɪtɪd/ adj prémédité.

premises /'premɪsɪz/ npl locaux mpl; **on the ~** sur place.

premium /'priːmɪəm/ n (insurance) prime f; **be at a ~** être précieux.

preoccupied /priːˈɒkjʊpaɪd/ adj préoccupé.

preparation /ˌprepəˈreɪʃn/ n préparation f; ~s préparatifs mpl.

preparatory /prɪˈpærətrɪ/ adj préparatoire. ~ **school** n école f primaire privée; (US) école f secondaire privée.

prepare /prɪˈpeə(r)/ vt/i (se) préparer (for à); be ~d for (expect) s'attendre à; ~d to prêt à.

preposition /ˌprepəˈzɪʃn/ n préposition f.

preposterous /prɪˈpɒstərəs/ adj absurde, ridicule.

prep school n →PREPARATORY SCHOOL.

prerequisite /priːˈrekwɪzɪt/ n condition f préalable.

prescribe /prɪˈskraɪb/ vt prescrire.

prescription /prɪˈskrɪpʃn/ n (Med) ordonnance f.

presence /ˈprezns/ n présence f; ~ of mind présence f d'esprit.

present[1] /ˈpreznt/ adj présent. ● n présent m; (gift) cadeau m; at ~ à présent; for the ~ pour le moment.

present[2] /prɪˈzent/ vt présenter; (film, concert) donner; ~ sb with offrir à qn. **presentation** n présentation f. **presenter** n présentateur/-trice m/f.

preservation /ˌprezəˈveɪʃn/ n (of food) conservation f; (of wildlife) préservation f.

preservative /prɪˈzɜːvətɪv/ n (Culin) agent m de conservation.

preserve /prɪˈzɜːv/ vt préserver; (Culin) conserver. ● n réserve f; (fig) domaine m; (jam) confiture f.

presidency /ˈprezɪdənsɪ/ n présidence f.

president /ˈprezɪdənt/ n président/-e m/f.

press /pres/ vt/i (button) appuyer (sur); (squeeze) presser; (iron) repasser; (pursue) poursuivre; be ~ed for (time) manquer de; ~ for sth faire pression pour avoir qch; ~ sb to do sth pousser qn à faire qch; ~ on continuer (with sth qch). ● n (newspapers, machine) presse f; (for wine) pressoir m. ~ **cutting** n coupure f de presse.

pressing /ˈpresɪŋ/ adj pressant.

press: ~ **release** n communiqué m de presse. ~-**stud** n boutonpression m. ~-**up** n pompe f.

pressure /ˈpreʃə(r)/ n pression f. ● vt faire pression sur. ~-**cooker** n cocotte-minute f. ~ **group** n groupe m de pression.

pressurize /ˈpreʃəraɪz/ vt (cabin) pressuriser; (person) faire pression sur.

prestige /preˈstiːʒ/ n prestige m.

presumably /prɪˈzjuːməblɪ/ adv vraisemblablement.

presume /prɪˈzjuːm/ vt (suppose) présumer.

pretence, (US) **pretense** /prɪˈtens/ n feinte f, simulation f; (claim) prétention f; (pretext) prétexte m.

pretend /prɪˈtend/ vt/i faire semblant (to do de faire); ~ to (lay claim to) prétendre à.

pretentious /prɪˈtenʃəs/ adj prétentieux.

pretext /ˈpriːtekst/ n prétexte m.

pretty /ˈprɪtɪ/ adj (-ier, -iest) joli. ● adv assez; ~ **much** presque.

prevail /prɪˈveɪl/ vi (be usual) prédominer; (win) prévaloir; ~ on persuader (to do de faire). **prevailing** adj actuel; (wind) dominant.

prevalent /ˈprevələnt/ adj répandu.

prevent /prɪˈvent/ vt empêcher (from doing de faire). **prevention**

P

n prévention *f.* **preventive** *adj* préventif.

preview /ˈpriːvjuː/ *n* avant-première *f;* (fig) aperçu *m.*

previous /ˈpriːvɪəs/ *adj* précédent, antérieur; ~ **to** avant. **previously** *adv* auparavant.

prey /preɪ/ *n* proie *f;* **bird of** ~ rapace *m.* ● *vi* ~ **on** faire sa proie de; (worry) préoccuper.

price /praɪs/ *n* prix *m.* ● *vt* fixer le prix de. **priceless** *adj* inestimable; (amusing 🆃) impayable 🆃.

prick /prɪk/ *vt* (with pin) piquer; ~ **up one's ears** dresser l'oreille. ● *n* piqûre *f.*

prickle /ˈprɪkl/ *n* piquant *m.*

pride /praɪd/ *n* orgueil *m;* (satisfaction) fierté *f;* ~ **of place** place *f* d'honneur. ● *vpr* ~ **oneself on** s'enorgueillir de.

priest /priːst/ *n* prêtre *m.*

prim /prɪm/ *adj* (**primmer, primmest**) guindé, méticuleux.

primarily /ˈpraɪmərəlɪ/ *adv* essentiellement.

primary /ˈpraɪmərɪ/ *adj* (school, elections) primaire; (chief, basic) premier, fondamental. ● *n* (Pol: US) primaire *f.*

prime /praɪm/ *adj* principal, premier; (first-rate) excellent. ● *vt* (pump, gun) amorcer; (surface) apprêter. **P~ Minister** *n* Premier Ministre *m.*

primitive /ˈprɪmɪtɪv/ *adj* primitif.

primrose /ˈprɪmrəʊz/ *n* primevère *f* (jaune).

prince /prɪns/ *n* prince *m.* **princess** *n* princesse *f.*

principal /ˈprɪnsəpl/ *adj* principal. ● *n* (of school) directeur-trice *m/f.*

principle /ˈprɪnsəpl/ *n* principe *m;* **in/on** ~ en par principe.

print /prɪnt/ *vt* imprimer; (write in

capitals) écrire en majuscules; ~ed **matter** imprimés *mpl.* ● *n* (of foot) empreinte *f;* (letters) caractères *mpl;* (photograph) épreuve *f;* (engraving) gravure *f;* **in** ~ disponible; **out of** ~ épuisé. **printer** *n* (person) imprimeur *m;* (Comput) imprimante *f.*

prion /ˈpriːɒn/ *n* prion *m.*

prior /ˈpraɪə(r)/ *adj* précédent. ● *n* (Relig) prieur *m.* ~ **to** *prep* avant (de).

priority /praɪˈɒrɪtɪ/ *n* priorité *f;* **take** ~ avoir la priorité (**over** sur).

prise /praɪz/ *vt* forcer; ~ **open** ouvrir en forçant.

prison /ˈprɪzn/ *n* prison *f.* **prisoner** *n* prisonnier-ière *m/f.* ~ **officer** *n* gardien-ne *m/f* de prison.

pristine /ˈprɪstiːn/ *adj* **be in** ~ **condition** être comme neuf.

privacy /ˈprɪvəsɪ/ *n* intimité *f,* solitude *f.*

private /ˈpraɪvɪt/ *adj* privé; (confidential) personnel; (lessons, house) particulier; (ceremony) intime; **in** ~ en privé; (of ceremony) dans l'intimité. ● *n* (soldier) simple soldat *m.* **privately** *adv* en privé; dans l'intimité; (inwardly) intérieurement.

privilege /ˈprɪvəlɪdʒ/ *n* privilège *m.* **privileged** *adj* privilégié; **be ~d to** avoir le privilège de.

prize /praɪz/ *n* prix *m.* ● *vt* (value) priser.

pro /prəʊ/ *n* **the ~s and cons** le pour et le contre.

probable /ˈprɒbəbl/ *adj* probable. **probably** *adv* probablement.

probation /prəˈbeɪʃn/ *n* (testing) essai *m;* (Jur) liberté *f* surveillée.

probe /prəʊb/ *n* (device) sonde *f;* (fig) enquête *f.* ● *vt* sonder. ● *vi* ~ **into** sonder.

problem /ˈprɒbləm/ *n* problème *m.* ● *adj* difficile. **problematic** *adj* problématique.

procedure /prəˈsiːdʒə(r)/ n procédure f; (way of doing sth) démarche f à suivre.

proceed /prəˈsiːd/ vi (go) aller, avancer; (pass) passer (**to** à); (act) procéder; ~ **(with)** continuer; ~ **to do** se mettre à faire.

proceedings /prəˈsiːdɪŋz/ npl (discussions) débats mpl; (meeting) réunion f; (report) actes mpl; (Jur) poursuites fpl.

proceeds /ˈprəʊsiːdz/ npl (profits) produit m, bénéfices mpl.

process /ˈprəʊses/ n processus m; (method) procédé m; **in** ~ en cours; **in the** ~ **of doing** en train de faire. ~**or** n (Culin) robot m (ménager); (Comput) unité f centrale. ● vt (material, data) traiter.

procession /prəˈseʃn/ n défilé m.

procrastinate /prəʊˈkræstɪneɪt/ vi différer, tergiverser.

procure /prəˈkjʊə(r)/ vt obtenir.

prod /prɒd/ vt/i (pt prodded) pousser doucement. ● n petit coup m.

prodigy /ˈprɒdɪdʒɪ/ n prodige m.

produce¹ /ˈprɒdjuːs/ n produits mpl.

produce² /prəˈdjuːs/ vt/i produire; (bring out) sortir; (show) présenter; (cause) provoquer; (Theat, TV), mettre en scène; (radio) réaliser; (cinema) produire. **producer** n metteur m en scène; réalisateur m; producteur m.

product /ˈprɒdʌkt/ n produit m.

production /prəˈdʌkʃn/ n production f; (Theat, TV) mise f en scène; (radio) réalisation f.

productive /prəˈdʌktɪv/ adj productif. **productivity** n productivité f.

profession /prəˈfeʃn/ n profession f.

professional /prəˈfeʃənl/ adj professionnel; (of high quality) de professionnel; (person) qui exerce une profession libérale. ● n professionnel/-le m/f.

professor /prəˈfesə(r)/ n professeur m (titulaire d'une chaire).

proficient /prəˈfɪʃnt/ adj compétent.

profile /ˈprəʊfaɪl/ n (of face) profil m; (of body, mountain) silhouette f; (by journalist) portrait m.

profit /ˈprɒfɪt/ n profit m, bénéfice m. ● vi ~ **by** tirer profit de. **profitable** adj rentable.

profound /prəˈfaʊnd/ adj profond.

profusely /prəˈfjuːslɪ/ adv (bleed) abondamment; (apologize) avec effusion. **profusion** n profusion f.

program /ˈprəʊɡræm/ n (US) ➡**PROGRAMME**; (computer) ~ programme m. ● vt (pt programmed) programmer.

programme /ˈprəʊɡræm/ n programme m; (broadcast) émission f.

programmer /ˈprəʊɡræmə(r)/ n programmeur/-euse m/f.

programming /ˈprəʊɡræmɪŋ/ n (Comput) programmation f.

progress¹ /ˈprəʊɡres/ n progrès m (pl) (**in** ~) en cours; **make** ~ faire des progrès; ~ **report** compte-rendu m.

progress² /prəˈɡres/ vi (advance, improve) progresser.

progressive /prəˈɡresɪv/ adj progressif; (reforming) progressiste.

prohibit /prəˈhɪbɪt/ vt interdire (**sb from doing** à qn de faire).

project¹ /prəˈdʒekt/ vt projeter. ● vi (jut out) être en saillie.

project² /ˈprɒdʒekt/ n (plan) projet m; (undertaking) entreprise f; (School) dossier m.

p

projection /prəˈdʒekʃn/ n projection f; saillie f; (estimate) prévision f.

projector /prəˈdʒektə(r)/ n projecteur m.

proliferate /prəˈlɪfəreɪt/ vi proliférer.

prolong /prəˈlɒŋ/ vt prolonger.

prominent /ˈprɒmɪnənt/ adj (projecting) proéminent; (conspicuous) bien en vue; (fig) important.

promiscuous /prəˈmɪskjʊəs/ adj de mœurs faciles.

promise /ˈprɒmɪs/ n promesse f. ● vt/i promettre. **promising** adj prometteur; (person) qui promet.

promote /prəˈməʊt/ vt promouvoir; (advertise) faire la promotion de. **promotion** n promotion f.

prompt /prɒmpt/ adj rapide; (punctual) à l'heure, ponctuel. ● adv (on the dot) pile. ● vt inciter; (cause) provoquer; (Theat) souffler à. ● n (Comput) message m guide-opérateur. **prompter** n souffleur/-euse m/f. **promptly** adv rapidement; ponctuellement.

prone /prəʊn/ adj ~ to sujet à.

pronoun /ˈprəʊnaʊn/ n pronom m.

pronounce /prəˈnaʊns/ vt prononcer. **pronunciation** n prononciation f.

proof /pruːf/ n (evidence) preuve f; (test, trial copy) épreuve f; (of alcohol) teneur f en alcool. ● adj ~ against à l'épreuve de.

prop /prɒp/ n support m; (Theat) accessoire m. ● vt (pt **propped**) ~ (**up**) (support) étayer; (lean) appuyer.

propaganda /prɒpəˈgændə/ n propagande f.

propel /prəˈpel/ vt (pt **propelled**) (vehicle, ship) propulser; (person) pousser.

propeller /prəˈpelə(r)/ n hélice f.

proper /ˈprɒpə(r)/ adj correct, bon; (adequate) convenable; (real) vrai; (thorough 🔢) parfait. **properly** adv correctement, comme il faut; (adequately) convenablement.

proper noun n nom m propre.

property /ˈprɒpətɪ/ n (house) propriété f; (things owned) biens mpl, propriété f. ● adj immobilier, foncier.

prophecy /ˈprɒfəsɪ/ n prophétie f.

prophet /ˈprɒfɪt/ n prophète m.

proportion /prəˈpɔːʃn/ n (ratio, dimension) proportion f; (amount) partie f.

proposal /prəˈpəʊzl/ n proposition f; (of marriage) demande f en mariage.

propose /prəˈpəʊz/ vt proposer. ● vi faire une demande en mariage; ~ to se proposer de faire.

proposition /prɒpəˈzɪʃn/ n proposition f; (matter 🔢) affaire f ● vt 🔢 faire des propositions malhonnêtes à.

proprietor /prəˈpraɪətə(r)/ n propriétaire mf.

propriety /prəˈpraɪətɪ/ n (correct behaviour) bienséance f.

prose /prəʊz/ n prose f; (translation) thème m.

prosecute /ˈprɒsɪkjuːt/ vt poursuivre en justice.

prosecution n poursuites fpl. **prosecutor** n procureur m.

prospect[1] /'prɒspekt/ n (outlook) perspective f; (chance) espoir m.

prospect[2] /prə'spekt/ vt/i prospecter.

prospective /prə'spektɪv/ adj (future) futur; (possible) éventuel.

prospectus /prə'spektəs/ n brochure f; (Univ) livret m de l'étudiant.

prosperity /prɒ'sperətɪ/ n prospérité f. **prosperous** adj prospère.

prostitute /'prɒstɪtjuːt/ n prostituée f.

prostrate /'prɒstreɪt/ adj (prone) à plat ventre; (exhausted) prostré.

protect /prə'tekt/ vt protéger. **protection** n protection f. **protective** adj protecteur; (clothes) de protection.

protein /'prəʊtiːn/ n protéine f.

protest[1] /'prəʊtest/ n protestation f; **under~** en protestation.

protest[2] /prə'test/ vt/i protester.

Protestant /'prɒtɪstənt/ adj & n protestant/-e (m/f).

protester /prə'testə(r)/ n manifestant/-e m/f.

protocol /'prəʊtəkɒl/ n protocole m.

protrude /prə'truːd/ vi dépasser.

proud /praʊd/ adj fier, orgueilleux.

prove /pruːv/ vt prouver. ● vi (~ to be) easy se révéler facile; ~ oneself faire ses preuves. **proven** adj éprouvé.

proverb /'prɒvɜːb/ n proverbe m.

provide /prə'vaɪd/ vt fournir (sb with sth qch à qn); (allow for) prévoir; (guard against) parer à; (person) pourvoir aux besoins de.

provided /prə'vaɪdɪd/ conj ~ that

à condition que.

providing /prə'vaɪdɪŋ/ conj →PROVIDED.

province /'prɒvɪns/ n province f; (fig) compétence f.

provision /prə'vɪʒn/ n (stock) provision f; (supplying) fourniture f; (stipulation) dispositions fpl; **~s** (food) provisions fpl.

provisional /prə'vɪʒənl/ adj provisoire.

provocative /prə'vɒkətɪv/ adj provocant.

provoke /prə'vəʊk/ vt provoquer.

prow /praʊ/ n proue f.

prowess /'praʊɪs/ n prouesses fpl.

prowl /praʊl/ vi rôder.

proxy /'prɒksɪ/ n **by ~** par procuration.

prudish /'pruːdɪʃ/ adj pudibond, prude.

prune /pruːn/ n pruneau m. ● vt (cut) tailler.

pry /praɪ/ vi ~ **into** mettre son nez dans.

psalm /sɑːm/ n psaume m.

pseudonym /'sjuːdənɪm/ n pseudonyme m.

psychiatric /saɪkɪ'ætrɪk/ adj psychiatrique. **psychiatrist** n psychiatre mf. **psychiatry** n psychiatrie f.

psychic /'saɪkɪk/ adj (phenomenon) métapsychique; (person) doué de télépathie.

psychoanalyse /saɪkəʊ'ænəlaɪz/ vt psychanalyser.

psychoanalysis n psychanalyse f.

psychological /saɪkə'lɒdʒɪkl/ adj psychologique. **psychologist** n psychologue mf. **psychology** n psychologie f.

PTO abbr (**please turn over**) TSVP.

pub /pʌb/ n pub m.

Pub Au Royaume-Uni, établissement où l'on sert des boissons (alcoolisées ou non) et parfois des repas légers. Certains appartiennent à une marque de bière alors que les *free houses* sont indépendants. C'est un lieu convivial où l'on vient passer un bon moment (fléchettes, billard, jeux de groupes). Aujourd'hui, la loi leur permet d'ouvrir de 11h à 23h.

puberty /'pjuːbətɪ/ n puberté f.

public /'pʌblɪk/ adj public; (library) municipal; **in ∼** en public.

publican /'pʌblɪkən/ n patron/-ne m/f de pub.

publication /pʌblɪ'keɪʃn/ n publication f.

public house n pub m.

publicity /pʌb'lɪsətɪ/ n publicité f.

publicize /'pʌblɪsaɪz/ vt faire connaître au public.

public: **∼ relations** n relations fpl publiques. **∼ school** n école f privée; (US) école f publique. **∼ transport** n transports mpl en commun.

Public schools Mis à part l'Écosse où ce terme désigne souvent une école publique, les *public schools* britanniques sont en réalité des écoles privées qui fonctionnent souvent sur le mode de l'internat et dont les frais de scolarité sont très élevés. Ces écoles accordent cependant des bourses aux élèves brillants mais peu fortunés. Les *public schools* américaines sont des écoles publiques et la scolarité y est gratuite.▷ **STATE SCHOOL.**

publish /'pʌblɪʃ/ vt publier. **publisher** n éditeur m. **publishing** n

édition f.

pudding /'pʊdɪŋ/ n dessert m; (steamed) pudding m.

puddle /'pʌdl/ n flaque f d'eau.

puff /pʌf/ n (of smoke) bouffée f; (of breath) souffle m. ● vt/i souffler. **∼ at** (cigar) tirer sur. **∼ out** (swell) (se) gonfler.

pull /pʊl/ vt/i tirer; (muscle) se froisser; **∼ a face** faire une grimace; **∼ one's weight** faire sa part du travail; **∼ sb's leg** faire marcher qn. ● n traction f; (fig) attraction f; (influence) influence f; **give a ∼** tirer. **∼ away** (Auto) démarrer; **∼ back** or **out** (withdraw) se retirer; **∼ down** (building) démolir; **∼ in** (enter) entrer; (stop) s'arrêter; **∼ off** enlever; (fig) réussir; **∼ out** (from bag) sortir; (extract) arracher; (Auto) déboîter; **∼ over** (Auto) se ranger (sur le côté); **∼ through** s'en tirer; **∼ oneself together** se ressaisir.

pull-down menu n (Comput) menu m déroulant.

pulley /'pʊlɪ/ n poulie f.

pullover /'pʊləʊvə(r)/ n pull (-over) m.

pulp /pʌlp/ n (of fruit) pulpe f; (for paper) pâte f à papier.

pulpit /'pʊlpɪt/ n chaire f.

pulsate /pʌl'seɪt/ vi battre.

pulse /pʌls/ n (Med) pouls m.

pump /pʌmp/ n pompe f; (plimsoll) chaussure f de sport. ● vt/i pomper; (person) soutirer des renseignements à; **∼ up** gonfler.

pumpkin /'pʌmpkɪn/ n citrouille f.

pun /pʌn/ n jeu m de mots.

punch /pʌntʃ/ vt donner un coup de poing à; (ticket) poinçonner. ● n coup m de poing; (vigour 🔢) punch m; (device) poinçonneuse f; (drink) punch *m*. ~-line *n* chute *f*.

punctual /'pʌŋktʃuəl/ *adj* à l'heure; (habitually) ponctuel.

punctuation /pʌŋktʃʊ'eɪʃn/ *n* ponctuation *f*.

puncture /'pʌŋktʃə(r)/ *n* crevaison *f*. ● *vt/i* crever.

pungent /'pʌndʒənt/ *adj* âcre.

punish /'pʌnɪʃ/ *vt* punir (**for** sth de qch). **punishment** *n* punition *f*.

punk /pʌŋk/ *n* (music, fan) punk *m*; (US: 🆃) voyou *m*.

punt /pʌnt/ *n* (boat) barque *f*; (Hist) (Irish pound) livre *f* irlandaise.

puny /'pju:nɪ/ *adj* -**ier**, -**iest** chétif.

pupil /'pju:pl/ *n* (person) élève *mf*; (of eye) pupille *f*.

puppet /'pʌpɪt/ *n* marionnette *f*.

puppy /'pʌpɪ/ *n* chiot *m*.

purchase /'pɜːtʃəs/ *vt* acheter (**from** sb à qn). ● *n* achat *m*.

pure /pjʊə(r)/ *adj* pur.

purgatory /'pɜːgətrɪ/ *n* purgatoire *m*.

purge /pɜːdʒ/ *vt* purger (**of** de). ● *n* purge *f*.

purification /pjʊərɪfɪ'keɪʃn/ *n* (of water, air) épuration *f*; (Relig) purification *f*. **purify** *vt* épurer; purifier.

puritan /'pjʊərɪtən/ *n* puritain/ -e *m/f*.

purity /'pjʊərətɪ/ *n* pureté *f*.

purple /'pɜːpl/ *adj* & *n* violet (*m*).

purpose /'pɜːpəs/ *n* but *m*; (determination) résolution *f*; **on** ~ exprès; **to no** ~ sans résultat.

purr /pɜː(r)/ *n* ronronnement *m*. ● *vi* ronronner.

purse /pɜːs/ *n* porte-monnaie *m inv*; (handbag; US) sac *m* à main. ● *vt* (lips) pincer.

pursue /pə'sju:/ *vt* poursuivre.

pursuit /pə'sju:t/ *n* poursuite *f*; (hobby) activité *f*, occupation *f*.

pus /pʌs/ *n* pus *m*.

push /pʊʃ/ *vt/i* pousser; (button) appuyer sur; (thrust) enfoncer; (recommend 🆃) proposer avec insistance; **be** ~**ed for** (time) manquer de; **be** ~**ing thirty** 🆃 friser la trentaine; ~ **sb around** bousculer qn. ● *n* poussée *f*; (effort) gros effort *m*; (drive) dynamisme *m*; **give the** ~ **to** 🆃 flanquer à la porte 🆃. □ ~ **in** resquiller; ~ **on** continuer; ~ **up** (lift) relever; (prices) faire monter.

pushchair /'pʊʃtʃeə(r)/ *n* poussette *f*.

pusher /'pʊʃə(r)/ *n* revendeur/ -euse *m/f* (de drogue).

push-up *n* pompe *f*.

put /pʊt/ *vt/i* (*pt* **put**; *pres p* **putting**) mettre, placer, poser; (question) poser; ~ **the damage at a million** estimer les dégâts à un million; ~ **sth tactfully** dire qch avec tact. □ ~ **across** communiquer; ~ **away** ranger; (in hospital, prison) enfermer; ~ **back** (postpone) remettre; (delay) retarder; ~ **down** (déposer; (write) inscrire; (pay) verser; (suppress) réprimer; ~ **forward** (plan) soumettre; ~ **in** (insert) introduire; (fix) installer; (submit) soumettre; ~ **in for** faire une demande de; ~ **off** (postpone) renvoyer à plus tard; (disconcert) déconcerter; (displease) rebuter; ~ **sb off sth** dégoûter qn de qch; ~ **on** (clothes, radio) mettre; (light) allumer; (accent, weight) prendre; ~ **out** (extend; (stretch) (é)tendre; (extinguish) éteindre; (disconcert) déconcerter; (inconvenience) déranger; ~ **up** lever, remonter; (building) construire; (notice) mettre; (price) augmenter; (guest) héberger; (offer) offrir; ~ **up with** supporter.

putt /pʌt/ *vi* putter. ● *n* putt *m*.

putty /'pʌtɪ/ *n* mastic *m*.

puzzle /'pʌzl/ n énigme f; (game) casse-tête m inv; (jigsaw) puzzle m. ● vt rendre perplexe. ● vi se creuser la tête.

pyjamas /pə'dʒɑːməz/ npl pyjama m.

pylon /'paɪlən/ n pylône m.

Qq

quack /kwæk/ n (of duck) coincoin m inv; (doctor) charlatan m.

quadrangle /'kwɒdræŋgl/ (of college) n cour f.

quadruple /'kwɒdrʊpl/ adj & n quadruple (m). ● vt/i quadrupler.

quail /kweɪl/ n (bird) caille f.

quaint /kweɪnt/ adj pittoresque; (old) vieillot; (odd) bizarre.

qualification /kwɒlɪfɪ'keɪʃn/ n diplôme m; (ability) compétence f; (fig) réserve f, restriction f.

qualified /'kwɒlɪfaɪd/ adj diplômé; (able) qualifié (**to do** pour faire); (fig) conditionnel.

qualify /'kwɒlɪfaɪ/ vt qualifier; (modify) mettre des réserves à; (statement) nuancer. ● vi obtenir son diplôme (**as** de); (Sport) se qualifier; **~ for** remplir les conditions requises pour.

quality /'kwɒlətɪ/ n qualité f.

qualm /kwɑːm/ n scrupule m.

quantity /'kwɒntətɪ/ n quantité f.

quarantine /'kwɒrəntiːn/ n quarantaine f.

quarrel /'kwɒrəl/ n dispute f, querelle f. ● vi (pt quarrelled) se disputer.

quarry /'kwɒrɪ/ n (excavation) carrière f; (prey) proie f. ● vt extraire.

quart /kwɔːt/ n ≈ litre m.

quarter /'kwɔːtə(r)/ n quart m; (of year) trimestre m; (25 cents: US) quart m de dollar; (district) quartier m; ~**s** logement m; **from all ~s** de toutes parts. ● vt diviser en quatre; (troops) cantonner.

quarterly /'kwɔːtəlɪ/ adj trimestriel. ● adv tous les trois mois.

quartet /kwɔː'tet/ n quatuor m.

quartz /kwɔːts/ n quartz m. ● adj (watch) à quartz.

quash /kwɒʃ/ vt (suppress) étouffer; (Jur) annuler.

quaver /'kweɪvə(r)/ vi trembler, chevroter. ● n (Mus) croche f.

quay /kiː/ n (Naut) quai m.

queasy /'kwiːzɪ/ adj **feel ~** avoir mal au cœur.

queen /kwiːn/ n reine f; (cards) dame f.

queer /kwɪə(r)/ adj étrange; (dubious) louche; ⊠ homosexuel.

quench /kwentʃ/ vt éteindre; (thirst) étancher; (desire) étouffer.

query /'kwɪərɪ/ n question f. ● vt mettre en question.

quest /kwest/ n recherche f.

question /'kwestʃən/ n question f; **in ~** en question; **out of the ~** hors de question. ● vt interroger; (doubt) mettre en question, douter de. ~ **mark** n point m d'interrogation.

questionnaire /kwestʃə'neə(r)/ n questionnaire m.

queue /kjuː/ n queue f. ● vi (pres p queuing) faire la queue.

quibble /'kwɪbl/ vi ergoter.

quick /kwɪk/ adj rapide; (clever) vif/vive; **be ~** (hurry) se dépêcher. ● adv vite. ~ **cut to the ~** piquer au vif. **quicken** vt/i (s')accélérer.

quickly adv rapidement, vite.

~**sand** n sables mpl mouvants.

quid /kwɪd/ *n inv* 🄸 livre *f* sterling.

quiet /'kwaɪət/ *adj* (calm, still) tranquille; (silent) silencieux; (gentle) doux; (discreet) discret; **keep ~** se taire. ● *n* tranquillité *f*; **on the ~** en cachette. **quieten** *vt/i* (se) calmer.

quietly *adv* (speak) doucement; (sit) en silence.

quilt /kwɪlt/ *n* édredon *m*; (continental) ~ couette *f*.

quirk /kwɜːk/ *n* bizarrerie *f*.

quit /kwɪt/ *vt* (*pt* **quitted**) quitter; (smoking) arrêter de. ● *vi* abandonner; (resign) démissionner; ~ **doing** (US) cesser de faire.

quite /kwaɪt/ *adv* tout à fait, vraiment; (rather) assez; ~ **a few** un bon nombre (de).

quits /kwɪts/ *adj* quitte (with envers); **call it ~** en rester là.

quiver /'kwɪvə(r)/ *vi* trembler.

quiz /kwɪz/ *n* (*pl* **quizzes**) test *m*; (game) jeu-concours *m*. ● *vt* (*pt* **quizzed**) questionner.

quotation /kwəʊ'teɪʃn/ *n* citation *f*; (price) devis *m*; (stock exchange) cotation *f*; ~ **marks** guillemets *mpl*.

quote /kwəʊt/ *vt* citer; (reference, number) rappeler; (price) indiquer; (share price) coter. ● *vi* ~ **for** faire un devis pour; ~ **from** citer. ● *n* (quotation) citation *f*; (estimate) devis *m*; **in ~s** 🄸 entre guillemets.

Rr

rabbi /'ræbaɪ/ *n* rabbin *m*.

rabbit /'ræbɪt/ *n* lapin *m*.

rabies /'reɪbiːz/ *n* (disease) rage *f*.

race /reɪs/ *n* (contest) course *f*; (group) race *f*. ● *adj* racial; ~ **rela-**

tions relations *fpl* inter-raciales. ● *vt* (compete with) faire la course avec; (horse) faire courir. ● *vi* courir; (pulse) battre précipitamment; (engine) s'emballer. ~**course** *n* champ *m* de courses. ~**horse** *n* cheval *m* de course. ~**track** *n* piste *f*; (for horses) champ *m* de course.

racing /'reɪsɪŋ/ *n* courses *fpl*; ~ **car** voiture *f* de course.

racism /'reɪsɪzəm/ *n* racisme *m*. **racist** *adj* & *n* raciste (*mf*).

rack /ræk/ *n* (shelf) étagère *f*; (for clothes) portant *m*; (for luggage) compartiment *m* à bagages; (for dishes) égouttoir *m*. ● *vt* ~ **one's brains** se creuser la cervelle.

racket /'rækɪt/ *n* (Sport) raquette *f*; (noise) vacarme *m*; (swindle) escroquerie *f*; (crime) trafic *m*.

radar /'reɪdɑː(r)/ *n* & *adj* radar (*m*).

radial /'reɪdɪəl/ *n* ~ **(tyre)** pneu *m* radial.

radiate /'reɪdɪeɪt/ *vt* (happiness) rayonner de; (heat) émettre. ● *vi* rayonner (from de). **radiation** *n* (radioactivity) radiation *f* **radiator** *n* radiateur *m*.

radical /'rædɪkl/ *n* & *a* radical/-e (*mf*).

radio /'reɪdɪəʊ/ *n* radio *f*; **on the ~** à la radio. ● *vt* (message) envoyer par radio; (person) appeler par radio.

radioactive /reɪdɪəʊ'æktɪv/ *adj* radioactif.

radiographer /reɪdɪ'ɒɡrəfə(r)/ *n* manipulateur/-trice *m/f* radiographe.

radish /'rædɪʃ/ *n* radis *m*.

radius /'reɪdɪəs/ *n* (*pl* -**dii**) rayon *m*.

raffle /'ræfl/ *n* tombola *f*.

rag /ræɡ/ *n* chiffon *m*; ~**s** loques *fpl*.

rage /reɪdʒ/ *n* rage *f*, colère *f*; **be all the ~** faire fureur. ● *vi* (person) tempêter; (*storm, battle*) faire rage.

ragged /'rægɪd/ adj (*clothes*) en loques; (*person*) dépenaillé.

raid /reɪd/ n (Mil, on stock market) raid m; (by police) rafle f; (by criminals) hold-up m inv. ● vt faire un raid or une rafle or un hold-up dans. **raider** n (thief) pillard m; (Mil) commando m; (corporate) raider m.

rail /reɪl/ n (on balcony) balustrade f; (stairs) rampe f; (for train) rail m; (for curtain) tringle f; **by** ~ par chemin de fer.

railing /'reɪlɪŋ/ n (also ~s) grille f.

railway /, (US) **railroad** n chemin m de fer. ~ **line** n voie f ferrée. ~ **station** n gare f.

rain /reɪn/ n pluie f. ● vi pleuvoir. ~**bow** n arc-en-ciel m. ~**coat** n imperméable m. ~**fall** n précipitation f. ~ **forest** n forêt f tropicale.

rainy /'reɪnɪ/ adj (**-ier, -iest**) pluvieux; (*season*) des pluies.

raise /reɪz/ vt (barrier, curtain) lever; (child, cattle) élever; (question) soulever; (price, salary) augmenter. ● n (US) augmentation f.

raisin /'reɪzn/ n raisin m sec.

rake /reɪk/ n râteau m. ● vt (garden) ratisser; (search) fouiller dans. □ ~ **in** (money) amasser; ~ **up** (past) remuer.

rally /'rælɪ/ vt/i (se) rallier; (strength) reprendre; (after illness) aller mieux; ~ **round** venir en aide. ● n rassemblement m; (Auto) rallye m; (tennis) échange m.

ram /ræm/ n bélier m. ● vt (pt **rammed**) (thrust) enfoncer; (crash into) rentrer dans.

RAM abbr (**random access memory**) RAM f.

ramble /'ræmbl/ n randonnée f. ● vi faire une randonnée. □ ~ **on** discourir.

ramp /ræmp/ n (slope) rampe f; (in garage) pont m de graissage.

rampage[1] /ræm'peɪdʒ/ vi se déchaîner (**through** dans).

rampage[2] /'ræmpeɪdʒ/ n **go on the** ~ tout saccager.

ran /ræn/ ➡RUN.

rancid /'rænsɪd/ adj rance.

random /'rændəm/ adj (*fait*) au hasard. ● n **at** ~ au hasard.

rang /ræŋ/ ➡RING[2].

range /reɪndʒ/ n (of prices, products) gamme f; (of people, beliefs) variété f; (of radar, weapon) portée f; (of aircraft) autonomie f; (of mountains) chaîne f. ● vi aller; (vary) varier.

rank /ræŋk/ n rang m; (Mil) grade m. ● vt/i ~ **among** (se) classer parmi.

ransack /'rænsæk/ vt (search) fouiller; (pillage) mettre à sac.

ransom /'rænsəm/ n rançon f.

rap /ræp/ n coup m sec; (Mus) rap m. ● vi (pt **rapped**) donner des coups secs (**on** sur).

rape /reɪp/ vt violer. ● n viol m.

rapid /'ræpɪd/ adj rapide.

rapist /'reɪpɪst/ n violeur m.

rapturous /'ræptʃərəs/ adj (delight) extasié; (welcome) enthousiaste.

rare /reə(r)/ adj rare; (Culin) saignant. **rarely** adv rarement.

rascal /'rɑːskl/ n coquin/-e m/f.

rash /ræʃ/ n (Med) rougeurs fpl. ● adj irréfléchi.

raspberry /'rɑːzbrɪ/ n framboise f.

rat /ræt/ n rat m. ● vi (pt **ratted**) ~ **on** (desert) lâcher; (inform on) dénoncer.

rate /reɪt/ n (ratio, level) taux m; (speed) rythme m; (price) tarif m; (of exchange) taux m; **at any** ~ en tout cas. ● vt (value) estimer; (deserve) mériter; ~ sth highly admirer beaucoup qch. ● vi ~ as être considéré comme.

rather /'rɑːðə(r)/ adv (by preference) plutôt; (fairly) assez, plutôt; (a little) un peu; I would ~ go j'aimerais mieux partir; ~ than go plutôt que de partir.

rating /'reɪtɪŋ/ n (score, value) cote f; **the ~s** (TV) l'indice m d'écoute, l'audimat® m.

ratio /'reɪʃɪəʊ/ n proportion f.

ration /'ræʃn/ n ration f. ● vt rationner.

rational /'ræʃənl/ adj rationnel; (person) sensé.

rationalize /'ræʃnəlaɪz/ vt justifier; (organize) rationaliser.

rattle /'rætl/ vi (bottles, chains) s'entrechoquer; (window) vibrer. ● vt (bottles, chains) faire s'entrechoquer; (fig, □) énerver. ● n cliquetis m; (toy) hochet m. ~snake n serpent m à sonnette, crotale m.

rave /reɪv/ vi (enthuse) s'emballer; (in fever) délirer; (in anger) tempêter.

raven /'reɪvn/ n corbeau m.

ravenous /'rævənəs/ adj be ~ avoir une faim de loup.

ravine /rə'viːn/ n ravin m.

raving /'reɪvɪŋ/ adj ~ **lunatic** fou m furieux, folle f furieuse.

ravishing /'rævɪʃɪŋ/ adj ravissant.

raw /rɔː/ adj cru; (not processed) brut; (wound) à vif; (immature) inexpérimenté; **get a ~ deal** être mal traité; ~ **material** matière f première.

ray /reɪ/ n (of light) rayon m; ~ of hope lueur f d'espoir.

razor /'reɪzə(r)/ n rasoir m. ~**blade** n lame f de rasoir.

re /riː/ prep au sujet de; (at top of

letter) objet.

reach /riːtʃ/ vt (place, level) atteindre; (decision) arriver à; (contact) joindre; (audience, market) toucher. ● vi ~ **up/down** lever/baisser le bras; ~ **across** étendre le bras. ● n portée f; **within ~ of** à portée de; (close to) à proximité de.

react /rɪ'ækt/ vi réagir. **reaction** n réaction f. **reactor** n réacteur m.

read /riːd/ vt/i (pt **read**) lire; (study) étudier; (instrument) indiquer; ~ **about sb** lire quelque chose sur qn; ~ **out** lire à haute voix. **reader** n lecteur/-trice m/f. **reading** n lecture f; (measurement) indication f; (interpretation) interprétation f

readjust /riːə'dʒʌst/ vt rajuster. ● vi se réadapter (to à).

read-only memory, ROM n mémoire f morte.

ready /'redɪ/ adj (-ier, -iest) prêt; (quick) prompt. ~**made** adj tout fait. ~**to-wear** adj prêt-à-porter.

real /rɪəl/ adj (not imaginary) véritable, réel; (not artificial) vrai; **it's a ~ shame** c'est vraiment dommage. ~ **estate** n biens mpl immobiliers.

realism /'rɪəlɪzəm/ n réalisme m. **realistic** adj réaliste.

reality /rɪ'ælətɪ/ n réalité f. ~ **TV** n télé-réalité f.

reasonable /'riːznəbl/ adj raisonnable.

realize /'rɪəlaɪz/ vt se rendre compte de, comprendre; (fulfil, turn into cash) réaliser; (price) atteindre.

really /'rɪəlɪ/ adv vraiment.

reap /riːp/ vt (crop) recueillir; (benefits) récolter.

reappear /riːə'pɪə(r)/ vi reparaître.

rear /rɪə(r)/ n arrière m; (of person) derrière m. **Ⅰ** ● adj (seat) arrière inv;

r

(entrance) de derrière. ● vt élever.
● vi (horse) se cabrer. ~-view mirror n rétroviseur m.

reason /'ri:zn/ n raison f (**to do,
for doing** de faire); **within ~** dans
la limite du raisonnable.

reassurance /ri:ə'ʃɔːrəns/ n réconfort m. **reassure** vt rassurer.

rebate /'ri:beɪt/ n (refund) remboursement m; (discount) remise f.

rebel[1] /'rebl/ n & adj rebelle (mf).

rebel[2] /rɪ'bel/ vi (pt **rebelled**) se
rebeller. **rebellion** n rébellion f.

rebound[1] /rɪ'baʊnd/ vi rebondir;
~ on (backfire) se retourner contre.

rebound[2] /'ri:baʊnd/ n rebond m.

rebuke /rɪ'bjuːk/ vt réprimander.
● n réprimande f.

recall /rɪ'kɔːl/ vt (remember) se
souvenir de; (call back) rappeler.
● n (memory) mémoire f; (Comput,
Mil) rappel m.

recap /'ri:kæp/ vt/i (pt **recapped**)
récapituler. ● n récapitulation f.

recede /rɪ'siːd/ vi s'éloigner; **his
hair is receding** son front se dégarnit.

receipt /rɪ'siːt/ n (written) reçu m;
(of letter) réception f; **~s** (Comm)
recettes fpl.

receive /rɪ'siːv/ vt recevoir; (stolen
goods) receler. **receiver** n (telephone) combiné m; (TV) récepteur m.

recent /'ri:snt/ adj récent. **recently**
adv récemment.

receptacle /rɪ'septəkl/ n récipient m.

reception /rɪ'sepʃn/ n réception f;
give sb a warm ~ donner un accueil chaleureux à qn.

recess /rɪ'ses/ n (alcove) alcôve f;
(for door) embrasure f; (Jur, Pol) vacances fpl; (School, US) récréation f.

recession /rɪ'seʃn/ n récession f.

recharge /ri:'tʃɑːdʒ/ vt recharger.

recipe /'resəpɪ/ n recette f.

recipient /rɪ'sɪpɪənt/ n (of honour) récipiendaire mf; (of letter) destinataire mf.

reciprocate /rɪ'sɪprəkeɪt/ vt (compliment) retourner; (kindness) payer
de retour. ● vi en faire autant.

recite /rɪ'saɪt/ vi réciter.

reckless /'reklɪs/ adj imprudent.

reckon /'rekən/ vt/i calculer;
(judge) considérer; (think) penser;
~ on/with compter sur/avec. **reckoning** n (guess) estimation f; (calculation) calculs mpl.

reclaim /rɪ'kleɪm/ vt récupérer;
(flooded land) assécher.

recline /rɪ'klaɪn/ vi s'allonger;
(seat) s'incliner.

recluse /rɪ'kluːs/ n reclus/-e m/f.

recognition /rekəg'nɪʃn/ n reconnaissance f; **beyond ~** méconnaissable; **gain ~** être reconnu.

recognize /'rekəgnaɪz/ vt reconnaître.

recollect /rekə'lekt/ vt se souvenir
de, se rappeler. **recollection** n souvenir m.

recommend /rekə'mend/ vt recommander. **recommendation** n
recommandation f.

reconcile /'rekənsaɪl/ vt (people)
réconcilier; (facts) concilier; **~ oneself to** se résigner à.

recondition /ri:kən'dɪʃn/ vt remettre à neuf.

reconsider /ri:kən'sɪdə(r)/ vt réexaminer. ● vi réfléchir.

reconstruct /ri:kən'strʌkt/ vt reconstruire; (crime) faire une reconstitution de.

record[1] /rɪ'kɔːd/ vt/i (in register,
on tape) enregistrer; (in diary)

noter; ∼**that** rapporter que.

record² /'rekɔːd/ n (of events) compte-rendu m; (official) procès-verbal m; (personal, administrative) dossier m; (historical) archives fpl; (past history) réputation f; (Mus) disque m; (Sport) record m; (**criminal**) ∼ casier m judiciaire; **off the** ∼ officieusement. ● adj record inv.

recorder /rɪ'kɔːdə(r)/ n (Mus) flûte f à bec.

recording /rɪ'kɔːdɪŋ/ n enregistrement m.

record-player n tourne-disque m.

recover /rɪ'kʌvə(r)/ vt récupérer. ● vi se remettre; (economy) se redresser. **recovery** n (Med) rétablissement m; (of economy) relance f.

recreation /rekrɪ'eɪʃn/ n récréation f.

recruit /rɪ'kruːt/ n recrue f. ● vt recruter. **recruitment** n recrutement m.

rectangle /'rektæŋgl/ n rectangle m.

rectify /'rektɪfaɪ/ vt rectifier.

recuperate /rɪ'kuːpəreɪt/ vt récupérer. ● vi se rétablir.

recur /rɪ'kɜː(r)/ vi (pt recurred) se reproduire.

recycle /riː'saɪkl/ vt recycler.

red /red/ adj (**redder, reddest**) rouge; (hair) roux. ● n rouge m; **in the** ∼ en déficit. **R∼ Cross** n Croix-Rouge f. ∼**currant** n groseille f.

redecorate /riː'dekəreɪt/ vt repeindre, refaire.

redeploy /riːdɪ'plɔɪ/ vt réorganiser; (troops) répartir.

red: ∼**-handed** adj en flagrant délit. ∼**-hot** adj brûlant.

redirect /riːdɪ'rekt/ vt (traffic) dévier; (letter) faire suivre.

redness /'rednɪs/ n rougeur f.

redo /riː'duː/ vt (pt **-did**; pp **-done**) refaire.

redress /rɪ'dres/ vt (wrong) redresser; (balance) rétablir. ● n réparation f.

reduce /rɪ'djuːs/ vt réduire; (temperature) faire baisser. **reduction** n réduction f.

redundancy /rɪ'dʌndənsɪ/ n licenciement m.

redundant /rɪ'dʌndənt/ adj superflu; (worker) licencié; **make** ∼ licencier.

reed /riːd/ n (plant) roseau m.

reef /riːf/ n récif m, écueil m.

reel /riːl/ n (of thread) bobine f; (of film) bande f; (winding device) dévidoir m. ● vi chanceler. ● vt ∼ **off** réciter.

refectory /rɪ'fektrɪ/ n réfectoire m.

refer /rɪ'fɜː(r)/ vt/i (pt referred) ∼ **to** (allude to) faire allusion à; (concern) s'appliquer à; (consult) consulter; (direct) renvoyer à.

referee /refə'riː/ n (Sport) arbitre m. ● vt (pt refereed) arbitrer.

reference /'refərəns/ n référence f; (mention) allusion f; (person) personne f pouvant fournir des références; **in** or **with** ∼ **to** en ce qui concerne; (Comm) suite à.

referendum /refə'rendəm/ n (pl ∼**s**) référendum m.

refill¹ /riː'fɪl/ vt (glass) remplir à nouveau; (pen) recharger.

refill² /'riːfɪl/ n recharge f.

refine /rɪ'faɪn/ vt raffiner.

reflect /rɪ'flekt/ vt refléter; (heat, light) renvoyer. ● vi réfléchir (on à); ∼ **well/badly on sb** faire honneur/du tort à qn.

reflection /rɪ'flekʃn/ n réflexion f; (image) reflet m; **on** ∼ à la réflexion.

reflective /rɪˈflektɪv/ adj (surface) réfléchissant; (person) réfléchi.

reflector /rɪˈflektə(r)/ n (on car) catadioptre m.

reflex /ˈriːfleks/ adj & n réflexe (m).

reflexive /rɪˈfleksɪv/ adj (Gram) réfléchi.

reform /rɪˈfɔːm/ vt réformer. ● vi (person) s'amender. ● n réforme f.

refrain /rɪˈfreɪn/ n refrain m. ● vi s'abstenir (from de).

refresh /rɪˈfreʃ/ vt (drink) rafraîchir; (rest) reposer. **refreshments** npl rafraîchissements m.

refrigerate /rɪˈfrɪdʒəreɪt/ vt réfrigérer. **refrigerator** n réfrigérateur m.

refuel /ˌriːˈfjuːəl/ vt/i (pt refuelled) (se) ravitailler.

refuge /ˈrefjuːdʒ/ n refuge m; take ~ se réfugier. **refugee** n réfugié/-e m/f.

refund[1] /rɪˈfʌnd/ vt rembourser.

refund[2] /ˈriːfʌnd/ n remboursement m.

refurbish /riːˈfɜːbɪʃ/ vt remettre à neuf.

refuse[1] /rɪˈfjuːz/ vt/i refuser.

refuse[2] /ˈrefjuːs/ n ordures fpl.

regain /rɪˈgeɪn/ vt retrouver; (lost ground) regagner.

regard /rɪˈɡɑːdl/ vt considérer; as ~s en ce qui concerne. ● n égard m, estime f. in this ~ à cet égard; ~s amitiés fpl. **regarding** prep en ce qui concerne.

regardless /rɪˈɡɑːdlɪs/ adv malgré tout; ~ of sans tenir compte de.

regime /reɪˈʒiːm/ n régime m.

regiment /ˈredʒɪmənt/ n régiment m.

region /ˈriːdʒən/ n région f; in the ~ of environ.

register /ˈredʒɪstə(r)/ n registre m.

● vt (record) enregistrer; (vehicle) faire immatriculer; (birth) déclarer; (letter) recommander; (indicate) indiquer; (express) exprimer. ● vi (enrol) s'inscrire; (at hotel) se présenter; (fig) être compris.

registrar /ˌredʒɪˈstrɑː(r)/ n officier m de l'état civil; (Univ) responsable m du bureau de la scolarité.

registration /ˌredʒɪˈstreɪʃn/ n (of voter, student) inscription f; (of birth) déclaration f; ~ **(number)** (Auto) numéro m d'immatriculation.

registry office n bureau m de l'état civil.

regret /rɪˈɡret/ n regret m. ● vt (pt **regretted**) regretter (**to do** de faire). **regretfully** adv à regret.

regular /ˈreɡjʊlə(r)/ adj régulier; (usual) habituel. ● n habitué/-e m/f. **regularity** n régularité f. **regularly** adv régulièrement.

regulate /ˈreɡjʊleɪt/ vt régler. **regulation** n (rule) règlement m; (process) réglementation f.

rehabilitate /ˌriːəˈbɪlɪteɪt/ vt (in public esteem) réhabiliter; (prisoner) réinsérer.

rehearsal /rɪˈhɜːsl/ n répétition f. **rehearse** vt/i répéter.

reign /reɪn/ n règne m. ● vi régner (over sur).

reimburse /ˌriːɪmˈbɜːs/ vt rembourser.

reindeer /ˈreɪndɪə(r)/ n inv renne m.

reinforce /ˌriːɪnˈfɔːs/ vt renforcer. **reinforcement** n renforcement m; ~s renforts mpl.

reinstate /ˌriːɪnˈsteɪt/ vt (person) réintégrer; (law) rétablir.

reject[1] /ˈriːdʒekt/ n marchandise f de deuxième choix.

reject[2] /rɪˈdʒekt/ vt (offer, plea) rejeter; (goods) refuser. **rejection** n

rejoice | remnant

(personal) rejet m; (of candidate, work) refus m.

rejoice /rɪˈdʒɔɪs/ vi se réjouir.

relapse /rɪˈlæps/ n rechute f. ● vi rechuter; ~ **into** retomber dans.

relate /rɪˈleɪt/ vt raconter; (associate) associer. ● vi ~ **to** se rapporter à; (get on with) s'entendre avec. **related** adj (ideas) lié; **we are** ~**d** nous sommes parents.

relation /rɪˈleɪʃn/ n rapport m; (person) parent/-e m/f. **relationship** n relations fpl; (link) rapport m.

relative /ˈrelətɪv/ n parent/-e m/f. ● adj relatif; (respective) respectif.

relax /rɪˈlæks/ vt (grip) relâcher; (muscle) décontracter; (discipline) assouplir. ● vi (person) se détendre; (grip) se relâcher. **relaxation** n détente f. **relaxing** adj délassant.

relay¹ /ˈriːleɪ/ n (also ~ **race**) course f de relais.

relay² /ˈriːleɪ/ vt relayer.

release /rɪˈliːs/ vt (prisoner) libérer; (fastening) faire jouer; (object, hand) lâcher; (film) faire sortir; (news) publier. ● n libération f; (of film) sortie f; (new record, film) nouveauté f.

relevance /ˈreləvəns/ n pertinence f, intérêt m.

relevant /ˈreləvənt/ adj pertinent; **be** ~ **to** avoir rapport à.

reliability /rɪlaɪəˈbɪlətɪ/ n (of firm) sérieux m; (of car) fiabilité f; (of person) honnêteté f. **reliable** adj (firm) sérieux; (person, machine) fiable.

reliance /rɪˈlaɪəns/ n dépendance f.

relic /ˈrelɪk/ n vestige m; (object) relique f.

relief /rɪˈliːf/ n soulagement m (from f); (assistance) secours m; (outline) relief m; ~ **road** route f de délestage.

relieve /rɪˈliːv/ vt soulager; (help) secourir; (take over from) relayer.

religion /rɪˈlɪdʒən/ n religion f. **religious** adj religieux.

relish /ˈrelɪʃ/ n plaisir m; (Culin) condiment m. ● vt (food) savourer; (idea) se réjouir de.

relocate /riːləʊˈkeɪt/ vt muter. ● vi (company) déménager; (worker) être muté. **relocation** n délocalisation f.

reluctance /rɪˈlʌktəns/ n répugnance f.

reluctant /rɪˈlʌktənt/ adj (person) peu enthousiaste; (consent) accordé à contrecœur; ~ **to** peu disposé à. **reluctantly** adv à contrecœur.

rely /rɪˈlaɪ/ vi ~ **on** (count) compter sur; (be dependent) dépendre de.

remain /rɪˈmeɪn/ vi rester. **remainder** n reste m.

remand /rɪˈmɑːnd/ vt mettre en détention provisoire. ● n **on** ~ en détention provisoire.

remark /rɪˈmɑːk/ n remarque f. ● vt remarquer. ● vi ~ **on** faire des remarques sur. **remarkable** adj remarquable.

remedy /ˈremədɪ/ n remède m. ● vt remédier à.

remember /rɪˈmembə(r)/ vt se souvenir de, se rappeler; ~ **to do** ne pas oublier de faire. **remembrance** n souvenir m.

remind /rɪˈmaɪnd/ vt rappeler (**sb of sth** qch à qn); ~ **sb to do** rappeler à qn de faire. **reminder** n rappel m.

reminisce /remɪˈnɪs/ vi évoquer ses souvenirs.

remission /rɪˈmɪʃn/ n (Med) rémission f; (Jur) remise f.

remnant /ˈremnənt/ n reste m; (trace) vestige m; (of cloth) coupon *m*.

remodel /riːˈmɒdl/ *vt* (*pt* **remodelled**) remodeler.

remorse /rɪˈmɔːs/ *n* remords *m*.

remote /rɪˈməʊt/ *adj* (*place, time*) lointain; (*person*) distant; (*slight*) vague; **~ control** télécommande *f*.

removable /rɪˈmuːvəbl/ *adj* amovible.

removal /rɪˈmuːvl/ *n* (of employee) renvoi *m*; (of threat) suppression *f*; (of troops) retrait *m*; (of stain) détachage *m*; (from house) déménagement *m*; **~ men** déménageurs *mpl*.

remove /rɪˈmuːv/ *vt* enlever; (dismiss) renvoyer; (do away with) supprimer; (Comput) effacer.

remunerate /rɪˈmjuːnəreɪt/ *vt* rémunérer. **remuneration** *n* rémunération *f*.

render /ˈrendə(r)/ *vt* rendre.

renegade /ˈrenɪɡeɪd/ *n* renégat/-e *m/f*.

renew /rɪˈnjuː/ *vt* renouveler; (resume) reprendre. **renewable** *adj* renouvelable.

renounce /rɪˈnaʊns/ *vt* renoncer à; (disown) renier.

renovate /ˈrenəveɪt/ *vt* rénover.

renown /rɪˈnaʊn/ *n* renommée *f*.

rent /rent/ *n* loyer *m*. ● *vt* louer; **for ~** à louer. **rental** *n* prix *m* de location.

reopen /riːˈəʊpən/ *vt/i* rouvrir.

reorganize /riːˈɔːɡənaɪz/ *vt* réorganiser.

rep /rep/ *n* (Comm) représentant/-e *m/f*.

repair /rɪˈpeə(r)/ *vt* réparer. ● *n* réparation *f*; **in good/bad ~** en bon/mauvais état.

repatriate /riːˈpætrɪeɪt/ *vt* rapatrier. **repatriation** *n* rapatrie-

ment *m*.

repay /riːˈpeɪ/ *vt* (*pt* **repaid**) rembourser; (reward) récompenser. **repayment** *n* remboursement *m*.

repeal /rɪˈpiːl/ *vt* abroger. ● *n* abrogation *f*.

repeat /rɪˈpiːt/ *vt/i* répéter; (renew) renouveler; **~ itself**, **~ oneself** se répéter. ● *n* répétition *f*; (broadcast) reprise *f*.

repel /rɪˈpel/ *vt* (*pt* **repelled**) repousser.

repent /rɪˈpent/ *vi* se repentir (of de).

repercussion /riːpəˈkʌʃn/ *n* répercussion *f*.

repetition /repɪˈtɪʃn/ *n* répétition *f*.

replace /rɪˈpleɪs/ *vt* (put back) remettre; (take the place of) remplacer. **replacement** *n* remplacement *m* (of de); (person) remplaçant/-e *m/f*; (new part) pièce *f* de rechange.

replay /ˈriːpleɪ/ *n* (Sport) match *m* rejoué; (recording) répétition *f* immédiate.

replenish /rɪˈplenɪʃ/ *vt* (refill) remplir; (renew) renouveler.

replica /ˈreplɪkə/ *n* copie *f* exacte.

reply /rɪˈplaɪ/ *vt/i* répondre. ● *n* réponse *f*.

report /rɪˈpɔːt/ *vt* rapporter, annoncer (that que); (notify) signaler; (denounce) dénoncer. ● *vi* faire un rapport; **~ (on)** (news item) faire un reportage sur; **~ to** (go) se présenter chez. ● *n* rapport *m*; (in press) reportage *m*; (School) bulletin *m*. **reporter** *n* reporter *m*.

repossess /riːpəˈzes/ *vt* reprendre.

represent /reprɪˈzent/ *vt* représenter.

representation /reprɪzenˈteɪʃn/ *n* représentation *f*; **make ~s to** protester auprès de.

representative /reprɪˈzentətɪv/ adj représentatif, typique (**of** de). ● n représentant/-e m/f.

repress /rɪˈpres/ vt réprimer.

reprieve /rɪˈpriːv/ n (delay) sursis m; (pardon) grâce f. ● vt accorder un sursis à; gracier.

reprimand /ˈreprɪmɑːnd/ vt réprimander. ● n réprimande f.

reprisals /rɪˈpraɪzlz/ npl représailles fpl.

reproach /rɪˈprəʊtʃ/ vt reprocher (**sb for sth** qch à qn). ● n reproche m.

reproduce /riːprəˈdjuːs/ vt/i (se) reproduire. **reproduction** n reproduction f. **reproductive** adj reproducteur.

reptile /ˈreptaɪl/ n reptile m.

republic /rɪˈpʌblɪk/ n république f. **republican** adj & n républicain/-e (m/f).

repudiate /rɪˈpjuːdɪeɪt/ vt répudier; (contract) refuser d'honorer.

reputable /ˈrepjʊtəbl/ adj honorable, de bonne réputation.

reputation /repjʊˈteɪʃn/ n réputation f.

repute /rɪˈpjuːt/ n réputation f.

request /rɪˈkwest/ n demande f. ● vt demander (**of, from** à).

require /rɪˈkwaɪə(r)/ vt (of thing) demander; (of person) avoir besoin de; (demand, order) exiger. **required** adj requis. **requirement** n exigence f; (condition) condition f (requise).

rescue /ˈreskjuː/ vt sauver. ● n sauvetage m (**of** de); (help) secours m.

research /rɪˈsɜːtʃ/ n recherche(s) f(pl). ● vt/i faire des recherches (sur). **researcher** n chercheur/-euse m/f.

resemblance /rɪˈzembləns/ n ressemblance f. **resemble** vt

ressembler à.

resent /rɪˈzent/ vt être indigné de, s'offenser de. **resentment** n ressentiment m.

reservation /rezəˈveɪʃn/ n (doubt) réserve f; (booking) réservation f; (US) réserve f (indienne); **make a** ∼ réserver.

reserve /rɪˈzɜːv/ vt réserver. ● n (stock, land) réserve f; (Sport) remplaçant/-e m/f; **in** ∼ en réserve; **the** ∼**s** (Mil) les réserves fpl. **reserved** adj (person, room) réservé.

reshuffle /riːˈʃʌfl/ vt (Pol) remanier. ● n (Pol) remaniement m (ministériel).

residence /ˈrezɪdəns/ n résidence f; (of students) foyer m; **in** ∼ (doctor) résidant.

resident /ˈrezɪdənt/ adj résidant; **be** ∼ résider. ● n habitant/-e m/f; (foreigner) résident/-e m/f; (in hotel) pensionnaire m/f. **residential** adj résidentiel.

resign /rɪˈzaɪn/ vt abandonner; (job) démissionner de. ● vi démissionner; ∼ **oneself to** se résigner à. **resignation** n résignation f; (from job) démission f. **resigned** adj résigné.

resilience /rɪˈzɪlɪəns/ n élasticité f, ressort m.

resin /ˈrezɪn/ n résine f.

resist /rɪˈzɪst/ vt/i résister (à). **resistance** n résistance f. **resistant** adj (Med) rebelle; (metal) résistant.

resolution /rezəˈluːʃn/ n résolution f.

resolve /rɪˈzɒlv/ vt résoudre (**to do** de faire). ● n résolution f.

resort /rɪˈzɔːt/ vi ∼ **to** avoir recours à. ● n (recourse) recours m; (place) station f; **in the last** ∼ en dernier ressort.

resource /rɪˈsɔːs/ n ressource f;

r

~s (wealth) ressources *fpl*. **re-sourceful** *adj* ingénieux.

respect /rɪˈspekt/ *n* respect *m*; (aspect) égard *m*; **with ~ to** à l'égard de, relativement à. ● *vt* respecter.

respectability /rɪspektəˈbɪlətɪ/ *n* respectabilité *f*. **respectable** *adj* respectable.

respectful /rɪˈspektfl/ *adj* respectueux.

respective /rɪˈspektɪv/ *adj* respectif.

respite /ˈrespaɪt/ *n* répit *m*.

respond /rɪˈspɒnd/ *vi* répondre (**to** à); **~ to** (react to) réagir à. **response** *n* réponse *f*.

responsibility /rɪspɒnsəˈbɪlətɪ/ *n* responsabilité *f*. **responsible** *adj* responsable; (*job*) qui comporte des responsabilités.

responsive /rɪˈspɒnsɪv/ *adj* réceptif.

rest /rest/ *vt/i* (se) reposer; (lean) (s')appuyer (**on** sur); (be buried, lie) reposer; (remain) demeurer. ● *n* repos *m*; (support) support *m*; **have a ~** se reposer; **the ~** (remainder) le reste (**of** de); (other people) les autres.

restaurant /ˈrestrɒnt/ *n* restaurant *m*.

restless /ˈrestlɪs/ *adj* agité.

restoration /restəˈreɪʃn/ *n* rétablissement *m*; restauration *f*.

restore /rɪˈstɔː(r)/ *vt* rétablir; (building) restaurer; **~ sth to sb** restituer qch à qn.

restrain /rɪˈstreɪn/ *vt* contenir; **~ sb from** retenir qn de. **restrained** *adj* (moderate) mesuré; (in control of self) maître de soi.

restrict /rɪˈstrɪkt/ *vt* restreindre. **restriction** *n* restriction *f*.

rest room *n* (US) toilettes *fpl*.

result /rɪˈzʌlt/ *n* résultat *m*. ● *vi*

résulter; **~ in** aboutir à.

resume /rɪˈzjuːm/ *vt/i* reprendre.

résumé /ˈrezjuːmeɪ/ *n* résumé *m*; (of career: US) CV *m*, curriculum vitae *m*.

resurrect /rezəˈrekt/ *vt* ressusciter.

resuscitate /rɪˈsʌsɪteɪt/ *vt* réanimer.

retail /ˈriːteɪl/ *n* détail *m*. ● *adj & adv* au détail. ● *vt/i* (se) vendre (au détail). **retailer** *n* détaillant/-e *m/f*.

retain /rɪˈteɪn/ *vt* (hold back, remember) retenir; (keep) conserver.

retaliate /rɪˈtælɪeɪt/ *vi* riposter. **retaliation** *n* représailles *fpl*.

retch /retʃ/ *vi* avoir un haut-le-cœur.

retire /rɪˈtaɪə(r)/ *vi* (from work) prendre sa retraite; (withdraw) se retirer; (go to bed) se coucher. **retired** *adj* retraité. **retirement** *n* retraite *f*.

retort /rɪˈtɔːt/ *vt/i* répliquer. ● *n* réplique *f*.

retrace /riːˈtreɪs/ *vt* **~ one's steps** revenir sur ses pas.

retract /rɪˈtrækt/ *vt/i* (se) rétracter.

retrain /riːˈtreɪn/ *vt/i* (se) recycler.

retreat /rɪˈtriːt/ *vi* (Mil) battre en retraite. ● *n* retraite *f*.

retrieval /rɪˈtriːvl/ *n* (Comput) extraction *f*. **retrieve** *vt* (object) récupérer; (situation) redresser; (data) extraire.

retrospect /ˈretrəuspekt/ *n* **in ~** rétrospectivement.

return /rɪˈtɜːn/ *vi* (come back) revenir; (go back) retourner; (go home) rentrer. ● *vt* (give back) rendre; (bring back) rapporter; (send back) renvoyer; (put back) remettre. ● *n* retour *m*; (yield) rapport *m*; **~s** (Comm) bénéfices *mpl*; **in ~ for** en échange de. ~ **ticket** n aller-retour m.

reunion /riːˈjuːnɪən/ n réunion f.

reunite /riːjuːˈnaɪt/ vt réunir.

rev /rev/ n (Auto 🔲) tour m. ● vt/i (pt **revved**) ~ **(up)** (engine 🔲) (s')emballer.

reveal /rɪˈviːl/ vt révéler; (allow to appear) laisser voir.

revelation /revəˈleɪʃn/ n révélation f.

revenge /rɪˈvendʒ/ n vengeance f. ● vt venger.

revenue /ˈrevənjuː/ n revenu m.

reverberate /rɪˈvɜːbəreɪt/ vi (sound, light) se répercuter.

reverend /ˈrevərənd/ adj révérend.

reversal /rɪˈvɜːsl/ n renversement m; (of view) revirement m.

reverse /rɪˈvɜːs/ adj contraire, inverse. ● n contraire m; (back) revers m, envers m; (gear) marche f arrière. ● vt (situation, bracket) renverser; (order) inverser; (decision) annuler; ~ **the charges** appeler en PCV. ● vi (Auto) faire marche arrière.

review /rɪˈvjuː/ n (inspection, magazine) revue f; (of book) critique f. ● vt passer en revue; (situation) réexaminer; faire la critique de. **reviewer** n critique m.

revise /rɪˈvaɪz/ vt réviser; (text) revoir. **revision** n révision f.

revival /rɪˈvaɪvl/ n (of economy) reprise f; (of interest) regain m.

revive /rɪˈvaɪv/ vt (person, hopes) ranimer; (custom) rétablir. ● vi se ranimer.

revoke /rɪˈvəʊk/ vt révoquer.

revolt /rɪˈvəʊlt/ vt/i (se) révolter. ● n révolte f. **revolting** adj dégoûtant.

revolution /revəˈluːʃn/ n révolution f.

revolve /rɪˈvɒlv/ vi tourner.

revolver /rɪˈvɒlvə(r)/ n revolver m.

revolving door n porte f à tambour.

reward /rɪˈwɔːd/ n récompense f. ● vt récompenser (**for** de). **rewarding** adj rémunérateur; (worthwhile) qui (en) vaut la peine.

rewind /riːˈwaɪnd/ vt (pt **rewound**) rembobiner.

rewire /riːˈwaɪə(r)/ vt refaire l'installation électrique de.

rhetorical /rɪˈtɒrɪkl/ adj (de) rhétorique; (question) de pure forme.

rheumatism /ˈruːmətɪzəm/ n rhumatisme m.

rhinoceros /raɪˈnɒsərəs/ n (pl ~ **es**) rhinocéros m.

rhubarb /ˈruːbɑːb/ n rhubarbe f.

rhyme /raɪm/ n rime f; (poem) vers mpl. ● vt/i (faire) rimer.

rhythm /ˈrɪðəm/ n rythme m. **rhythmic(-al)** adj rythmique.

rib /rɪb/ n côte f.

ribbon /ˈrɪbən/ n ruban m; **in** ~**s** en lambeaux.

rice /raɪs/ n riz m. ~ **pudding** n riz m au lait.

rich /rɪtʃ/ adj riche.

rid /rɪd/ vt (pt **rid**; pres p **ridding**) débarrasser (**of** de); **get** ~ **of** se débarrasser de.

ridden /ˈrɪdn/ ⇒**RIDE**.

riddle /ˈrɪdl/ n énigme f. ● vt ~ **with** (bullets) cribler de; (mistakes) bourrer de.

ride /raɪd/ vi (pt **rode**; pp **ridden**) aller (à bicyclette, à cheval); (in car) rouler; (on a horse as sport) monter à cheval. ● vt (a particular horse) monter; (distance) parcourir. ● n promenade f, tour m; (distance) trajet m; **give sb a** ~ (US) prendre qn en voiture; **go for a** ~ aller faire un

r

tour (à bicyclette, à cheval). **rider** n cavalier/-ière m/f; (in horse race) jockey m; (cyclist) cycliste mf; (motorcyclist) motocycliste mf.

ridge /rɪdʒ/ n arête f, crête f.

ridiculous /rɪˈdɪkjʊləs/ adj ridicule.

riding /ˈraɪdɪŋ/ n équitation f.

rifle /ˈraɪfl/ n fusil m. ● vt (rob) dévaliser.

rift /rɪft/ n (crack) fissure f; (between people) désaccord m.

rig /rɪɡ/ vt (pt rigged) (equip) équiper; (election, match) truquer. ● n (for oil) derrick m. □ ~ out habiller; ~ up (arrange) arranger.

right /raɪt/ adj (morally) bon; (fair) juste; (best) bon, il faut; (not left) droit; **be** ~ (person) avoir raison (**to** de); (calculation, watch) être exact; **put** ~ arranger, rectifier. ● n (entitlement) droit m; (not left) droite f; (not evil) le bien; **be in the** ~ avoir raison; **on the** ~ à droite. ● vt (a wrong, sth fallen) redresser. ● adv (not left) à droite; (directly) tout droit; (exactly) bien, juste; (completely) tout à fait); ~ **away** tout de suite; ~ **now** (at once) tout de suite; (at present) en ce moment.

righteous /ˈraɪtʃəs/ adj vertueux.

rightful /ˈraɪtfl/ adj légitime.

right-handed adj droitier.

rightly /ˈraɪtlɪ/ adv correctement; (with reason) à juste titre.

right of way n (Auto) priorité f.

right wing adj de droite.

rigid /ˈrɪdʒɪd/ adj rigide.

rigorous /ˈrɪɡərəs/ adj rigoureux.

rim /rɪm/ n bord m.

rind /raɪnd/ n (on cheese) croûte f; (on bacon) couenne f; (on fruit) écorce f.

ring[1] /rɪŋ/ n (hoop) anneau m;

(jewellery) bague f; (circle) cercle m; (boxing) ring m; (wedding) ~ alliance f. ● vt entourer; (word in text) entourer d'un cercle.

ring[2] /rɪŋ/ vt/i (pt rang; pp rung) sonner; (of words) retentir; ~ **the bell** sonner. ● n sonnerie f; **give sb a** ~ donner un coup de fil à qn. □ ~ **back** rappeler; ~ **off** raccrocher; ~ **up** téléphoner (à).

ring road n périphérique m.

rink /rɪŋk/ n patinoire f.

rinse /rɪns/ vt rincer; ~ **out** rincer. ● n rinçage m.

riot /ˈraɪət/ n émeute f; (of colours) profusion f; **run** ~ se déchaîner. ● vi faire une émeute.

rip /rɪp/ vt/i (pt ripped) (se) déchirer; let ~ (not check) laisser courir; ~ **off** 🅱 rouler. ● n déchirure f.

ripe /raɪp/ adj mûr. **ripen** vt/i mûrir.

rip-off n 🅱 vol m; arnaque f 🅱.

ripple /ˈrɪpl/ n ride f, ondulation f. ● vt/i (water) (se) rider.

rise /raɪz/ vi (pt rose; pp risen) (go upwards, increase) monter, s'élever; (stand up, get up from bed) se lever; (rebel) se soulever; (sun) se lever; (water) monter; ~ **up** se soulever. ● n (slope) pente f; (increase) hausse f; (in pay) augmentation f; (progress, boom) essor m; **give** ~ **to** donner lieu à.

risk /rɪsk/ n risque m; **at** ~ menacé. ● vt risquer; ~ **doing** (venture) se risquer à faire. **risky** adj risqué.

rite /raɪt/ n rite m; **last** ~s derniers sacrements mpl.

rival /ˈraɪvl/ n rival/-e m/f. ● adj rival; (claim) opposé. ● vt (pt rivalled) rivaliser avec.

river /ˈrɪvə(r)/ n rivière f; (flowing into sea) fleuve m. ● adj (fishing, traffic) fluvial.

rivet /ˈrɪvɪt/ n (bolt) rivet m. ● vt (pt riveted) river, riveter.

Riviera /rɪvɪˈeərə/ n **the** (French) ~ la Côte d'Azur.

road /rəʊd/ n route f; (in town) rue f; (small) chemin m; **the** ~ **to** (glory: fig) le chemin de. ● adj (sign, safety) routier. ~**map** n carte f routière. ~ **rage** n violence f au volant. ~**worthy** adj en état de marche.

roam /rəʊm/ vi errer. ● vt (streets, seas) parcourir.

roar /rɔː(r)/ n hurlement m; (of lion, wind) rugissement m; (of lorry, thunder) grondement m. ● vt/i hurler; (lion, wind) rugir; (lorry, thunder) gronder; ~ **with laughter** rire aux éclats.

roast /rəʊst/ vt/i rôtir. ● n (meat) rôti m. ● adj rôti. ~ **beef** n rôti m de bœuf.

rob /rɒb/ vt (pt robbed) voler (sb of sth qch à qn); (bank, house) dévaliser; (deprive) priver (of de). **robber** n voleur/-euse m/f. **robbery** n vol m.

robe /rəʊb/ n (of judge) robe f; (dressinggown) peignoir m.

robin /ˈrɒbɪn/ n rouge-gorge m.

robot /ˈrəʊbɒt/ n robot m.

robust /rəʊˈbʌst/ adj robuste.

rock /rɒk/ n roche f; (rock face, boulder) rocher m; (hurled stone) pierre f; (sweet) sucre m d'orge; (Mus) rock m; **on the** ~**s** (drink) avec des glaçons; (marriage) en crise. ● vt/i (se) balancer; (shake) (faire) trembler; (child) bercer. ~**climbing** n varappe f.

rocket /ˈrɒkɪt/ n fusée f.

rocking-chair n fauteuil m à bascule.

rocky /ˈrɒkɪ/ adj (-ier, -iest) (ground) rocailleux; (hill) rocheux;

(shaky: fig) branlant.

rod /rɒd/ n (metal) tige f; (wooden) baguette f; (for fishing) canne f à pêche.

rode /rəʊd/ ⇒RIDE.

roe /rəʊ/ n œufs mpl de poisson.

rogue /rəʊg/ n (dishonest) bandit m; (mischievous) coquin/-e m/f.

role /rəʊl/ n rôle m.

roll /rəʊl/ vt/i rouler; ~ (**about**) (child, dog) se rouler; **be** ~**ing** (**in money**)⚀ rouler sur l'or. ● n rouleau m; (list) liste f; (bread) petit pain m; (of drum, thunder) roulement m; (of ship) roulis m. □ ~ **out** étendre; ~ **over** se retourner; ~ **up** (sleeves) retrousser.

roll-call n appel m.

roller /ˈrəʊlə(r)/ n rouleau m. ~ **blade** n patin m en ligne, roller m. ~**coaster** n montagnes fpl russes. ~**skate** n patin m à roulettes.

ROM abbr (**read-only memory**) mémoire f morte.

Roman /ˈrəʊmən/ adj & n romain/-e (m/f). ~ **Catholic** adj & n catholique (mf).

romance /rəʊˈmæns/ n (novel) roman m d'amour; (love) amour m; (affair) idylle f; (fig) poésie f.

Romania /rəʊˈmeɪnɪə/ n Roumanie f.

Romanian /rəʊˈmeɪnɪən/ adj roumain. ● n (person) Roumain/-e m/f; (language) roumain m.

romantic /rəʊˈmæntɪk/ adj (love) romantique; (of the imagination) romanesque.

roof /ruːf/ n toit m; (of mouth) palais m. ● vt recouvrir. ~**rack** n galerie f. ~**top** n toit m.

room /ruːm/ n pièce f; (bedroom) chambre f; (large hall) salle f; (space) place f; ~ **for manœuvre** marge f de manœuvre. ~**mate** n camarade *mf* de chambre.

roomy /'ruːmɪ/ *adj* spacieux; (*clothes*) ample.

root /ruːt/ *n* racine *f*; (source) origine *f*; **take** ~ prendre racine. ● *vt/i* (s')enraciner. □ ~ **about** fouiller; ~ **for** (US [T]) encourager; ~ **out** extirper.

rope /rəʊp/ *n* corde *f*; **know the** ~**s** être au courant. ● *vt* attacher; ~ **in** (*person*) enrôler.

rose /rəʊz/ *n* rose *f*. □ ● →RISE.

rosé /'rəʊzeɪ/ *n* rosé *m*.

rosy /'rəʊzɪ/ *adj* (**-ier, -iest**) rose; (hopeful) plein d'espoir.

rot /rɒt/ *vt/i* (*pt* **rotted**) pourrir. ● *n* pourriture *f*.

rota /'rəʊtə/ *n* liste *f* de service.

rotary /'rəʊtərɪ/ *adj* rotatif.

rotate /rəʊ'teɪt/ *vt/i* (faire) tourner; (change round) alterner.

rotten /'rɒtn/ *adj* pourri; (*tooth*) gâté; (bad [T]) mauvais, sale.

rough /rʌf/ *adj* (manners) rude; (to touch) rugueux; (ground) accidenté; (violent) brutal; (bad [T]) mauvais; (estimate) approximatif. ● *adv* (live) à la dure.

roughage /'rʌfɪdʒ/ *n* fibres *fpl*.

roughly /'rʌflɪ/ *adv* rudement; (approximately) à peu près.

round /raʊnd/ *adj* rond. ● *n* (circle) rond *m*; (slice) tranche *f*; (of visits, drinks) tournée *f*; (competition) partie *f*, manche *f*; (boxing) round *m*; (of talks) série *f*; ~ **of applause** applaudissements *mpl*; **go the** ~**s** circuler. ● *prep* autour de; **she lives** ~ **here** elle habite par ici; ~ **the clock** vingt-quatre heures sur vingt-quatre. ● *adv* autour; ~ **about** (nearby) par ici; (fig) à peu près; **go** or **come** ~ **to** (a *friend*) passer chez; **enough to go** ~ assez pour tout le monde. ● *vt* (object) arrondir; (corner) tourner. □ ~ **off** termi-

ner; ~ **up** rassembler.

roundabout /'raʊndəbaʊt/ *n* (in fairground) manège *m*; (for traffic) rond-point *m* (à sens giratoire). ● *adj* indirect.

round trip *n* voyage *m* aller-retour.

round-up *n* rassemblement *m*; (of suspects) rafle *f*.

route /ruːt/ *n* itinéraire *m*, parcours *m*; (Naut, Aviat) route *f*.

routine /ruː'tiːn/ *n* routine *f*. ● *adj* de routine.

row[1] /rəʊ/ *n* rangée *f*, rang *m*; **in a** ~ (consecutive) consécutif. ● *vi* ramer; (Sport) faire de l'aviron. ● *vt* ~ **a boat up the river** remonter la rivière à la rame.

row[2] /raʊ/ *n* (noise [T]) tapage *m*; (quarrel [T]) dispute *f*. ● *vi* [T] se disputer.

rowdy /'raʊdɪ/ *adj* (**-ier, -iest**) tapageur.

rowing /'rəʊɪŋ/ *n* aviron *m*. ~**-boat** *n* bateau à rames.

royal /'rɔɪəl/ *adj* royal; **royalty** *n* famille *f* royale; **royalties** droits *mpl* d'auteur.

RSI *abbr* (repetitive strain injury) TMS *m*, trouble *m* musculo-squelettique.

rub /rʌb/ *vt/i* (*pt* **rubbed**) frotter; ~ **it in** insister, en rajouter. ● *n* friction *f*. □ ~ **out** (s')effacer.

rubber /'rʌbə(r)/ *n* caoutchouc *m*; (eraser) gomme *f*. ~ **band** *n* élastique *m*. ~ **stamp** *n* tampon *m*.

rubbish /'rʌbɪʃ/ *n* (refuse) ordures *fpl*; (junk) saletés *fpl*; (fig) bêtises *fpl*.

rubble /'rʌbl/ *n* décombres *mpl*.

ruby /'ruːbɪ/ *n* rubis *m*.

rucksack /'rʌksæk/ *n* sac *m* à dos.

rude /ruːd/ *adj* impoli, grossier; (improper) indécent; (blow) brutal.

ruffle /'rʌfl/ *vt* (hair) ébouriffer;

(*clothes*) froisser; (*person*) contrarier. ● *n* (frill) ruche *f*.

rug /rʌg/ *n* petit tapis *m*.

rugby /'rʌgbɪ/ *n* rugby *m*.

rugged /'rʌgɪd/ *adj* (*surface*) rude, rugueux; (*ground*) accidenté; (*character*, *features*) rude.

ruin /'ru:ɪn/ *n* ruine *f*. ● *vt* (destroy) ruiner; (damage) abîmer; (spoil) gâter.

rule /ru:l/ *n* règle *f*; (regulation) règlement *m*; (Pol) gouvernement *m*; **as a ~** en règle générale. ● *vt* gouverner; (master) dominer; (decide) décider; **~ out** exclure. ● *vi* régner.

ruler *n* dirigeant/-e *m/f*; (measure) règle *f*.

ruling /'ru:lɪŋ/ *adj* (class) dirigeant; (*party*) au pouvoir. ● *n* décision *f*.

rum /rʌm/ *n* rhum *m*.

rumble /'rʌmbl/ *vi* gronder; (*stomach*) gargouiller. ● *n* grondement *m*; gargouillement *m*.

rumour, (US) **rumor** /'ru:mə(r)/ *n* bruit *m*, rumeur *f*; **there's a ~ that** le bruit court que.

rump /rʌmp/ *n* (of animal) croupe *f*; (of bird) croupion *m*; (steak) romsteck *m*.

run /rʌn/ *vi* (*pt* **ran**; *pp* **run**; *pres p* **running**) courir; (flow) couler; (pass) passer; (function) marcher; (melt) fondre; (extend) s'étendre; (of bus) circuler; (of play) se jouer; (last) durer; (of colour in washing) déteindre; (in election) être candidat. ● *vt* (manage) diriger; (event) organiser; (risk, race) courir; (house) tenir; (temperature, errand) faire; (Comput) exécuter. ● *n* course *f*; (journey) parcours *m*; (outing) promenade *f*; (rush) ruée *f*; (series) série *f*; (for chickens) enclos *m*; (in cricket) point *m*; **in the long ~** avec le temps; **on the ~** en fuite.

□ **~ across** rencontrer par hasard; **~ away** s'enfuir; **~ down** descendre en courant; (of vehicle) renverser; (production) réduire progressivement; (belittle) dénigrer; **~ into** (hit) heurter; **~ off** (copies) tirer; **~ out** (be used up) s'épuiser; (of lease) expirer; **~ out of** manquer de; **~ over** (of vehicle) écraser; (details) revoir; **~ through** regarder qch rapidement; **~ sth through sth** passer qch à travers qch; **~ up** (bill) accumuler.

runaway /'rʌnəweɪ/ *n* fugitif/-ive *m/f*. ● *adj* fugitif; (horse, vehicle) fou; (inflation) galopant.

rung /rʌŋ/ →RING². ● *n* (of ladder) barreau *m*.

runner /'rʌnə(r)/ *n* coureur/-euse *m/f*. **~ bean** *n* haricot *m* d'Espagne. **~-up** *n* second/-e *m/f*.

running /'rʌnɪŋ/ *n* course *f* à pied; (of business) gestion *f*; (of machine) marche *f*; **be in the ~ for** être sur les rangs pour. ● *adj* (commentary) suivi; (water) courant; **four days ~** quatre jours de suite.

runway /'rʌnweɪ/ *n* piste *f*.

rural /'rʊərəl/ *adj* rural.

rush /rʌʃ/ *vi* (move) se précipiter; (be in a hurry) se dépêcher. ● *vt* (person) bousculer; (Mil) prendre d'assaut; **~ to** envoyer d'urgence à. ● *n* ruée *f*; (haste) bousculade *f*; (plant) jonc *m*; **in a ~** pressé. **~-hour** *n* heure *f* de pointe.

Russia /'rʌʃə/ *n* Russie *f*.

Russian /'rʌʃn/ *adj* russe. ● *n* (person) Russe *mf*; (language) russe.

rust /rʌst/ *n* rouille *f*. ● *vt/i* rouiller.

rustle /'rʌsl/ *vt/i* (papers) froisser.

rusty /'rʌstɪ/ *adj* rouillé.

ruthless /'ru:θlɪs/ *adj* impitoyable.

rye /raɪ/ *n* seigle *m*.

Ss

sabbath /'sæbəθ/ n (Jewish) sabbat m; (Christian) jour m du seigneur.

sabbatical /sə'bætɪkl/ adj (Univ) sabbatique.

sabotage /'sæbətɑːʒ/ n sabotage m. ● vt saboter.

saccharin /'sækərɪn/ n saccharine f.

sack /sæk/ n (bag) sac m; **get the ~** 🔳 être renvoyé. ● vt 🔳 (plunder) saccager. **sacking** n (cloth) toile f à sac; (dismissal 🔳) renvoi m.

sacrament /'sækrəmənt/ n sacrement m.

sacred /'seɪkrɪd/ adj sacré.

sacrifice /'sækrɪfaɪs/ n sacrifice m. ● vt sacrifier.

sad /sæd/ adj (**sadder, saddest**) triste.

saddle /'sædl/ n selle f. ● vt (horse) seller.

sadist /'seɪdɪst/ n sadique mf. **sadistic** adj sadique.

sadly /'sædlɪ/ adv tristement; (unfortunately) malheureusement.

sadness /'sædnɪs/ n tristesse f.

safe /seɪf/ adj (not dangerous) sans danger; (reliable) sûr; (out of danger) en sécurité; (after accident) sain et sauf; **~ from** à l'abri de f. ● n coffre-fort m.

safeguard /'seɪfɡɑːd/ n sauvegarde f. ● vt sauvegarder.

safely /'seɪflɪ/ adv sans danger; (in safe place) en sûreté.

safety /'seɪftɪ/ n sécurité f. **~-belt** n ceinture f de sécurité. **~-pin** n épingle f de sûreté. **~-valve** n sou-

pape f de sûreté.

saffron /'sæfrən/ n safran m.

sag /sæɡ/ vi (pt sagged) (beam, mattress) s'affaisser; (flesh) être flasque.

sage /seɪdʒ/ n (herb) sauge f.

Sagittarius /sædʒɪ'teərɪəs/ n Sagittaire m.

said /sed/ →SAY.

sail /seɪl/ n voile f; (journey) tour m en bateau. ● vi (person) voyager en bateau; (as sport) faire de la voile; (set off) prendre la mer; **~ across** traverser. ● vt (boat) piloter; (sea) traverser. **sailing-boat**, **sailing-ship** n voilier m.

sailor /'seɪlə(r)/ n marin m.

saint /seɪnt/ n saint/-e m/f.

sake /seɪk/ n **for the ~ of** pour.

salad /'sæləd/ n salade f.

salaried /'sælərɪd/ adj salarié.

salary /'sælərɪ/ n salaire m.

sale /seɪl/ n vente f; **for ~** à vendre; **on ~** en vente; (reduced) en solde; **~s** (reductions) soldes mpl; **~s assistant**, (US) **~s clerk** vendeur/-euse m/f.

salesman /'seɪlzmən/ n (pl **-men**) (in shop) vendeur m; (traveller) représentant m.

saline /'seɪlaɪn/ adj salin. ● n sérum m physiologique.

saliva /sə'laɪvə/ n salive f.

salmon /'sæmən/ n inv saumon m.

salon /'sælɒn/ n salon m.

saloon /sə'luːn/ n (on ship) salon m; **~ (car)** berline f.

salt /sɔːlt/ n sel m. ● vt saler. **salty** adj salé.

salutary /'sæljʊtrɪ/ adj salutaire.

salute /sə'luːt/ n salut m. ● vt saluer. ● vi faire un salut.

salvage /'sælvɪdʒ/ n sauvetage m; (of waste) récupération f. ● vt sauver; (for re-use) récupérer.

same /seɪm/ adj même (as que). ● pron the ~ le même, la même, les mêmes; at the ~ time en même temps; the ~ (thing) la même chose.

sample /ˈsɑːmpl/ n échantillon m; (of blood) prélèvement m. ● vt essayer; (food) goûter.

sanctimonious /sæŋktɪˈməʊnɪəs/ adj (pej) supérieur.

sanction /ˈsæŋkʃn/ n sanction f. ● vt sanctionner.

sanctity /ˈsæŋktətɪ/ n sainteté f.

sanctuary /ˈsæŋktʃʊərɪ/ n (safe place) refuge m; (Relig) sanctuaire m; (for animals) réserve f.

sand /sænd/ n sable m; ~s (beach) plage f.

sandal /ˈsændl/ n sandale f.

sandpaper /ˈsændpeɪpə(r)/ n papier m de verre. ● vt poncer.

sandpit /ˈsændpɪt/ n bac m à sable.

sandwich /ˈsænwɪdʒ/ n sandwich m; ~ course cours m avec stage pratique.

sandy /ˈsændɪ/ adj (beach) de sable; (soil) sablonneux; (hair) blond roux inv.

sane /seɪn/ adj (view) sensé; (person) sain d'esprit.

sang /sæŋ/ ➡SING.

sanitary /ˈsænɪtrɪ/ adj (clean) hygiénique; (system) sanitaire; ~ towel serviette f hygiénique.

sanitation /sænɪˈteɪʃn/ n installations fpl sanitaires.

sanity /ˈsænətɪ/ n équilibre m mental; (sense) bon sens m.

sank /sæŋk/ ➡SINK.

Santa (Claus) /ˈsæntə (klɔːz)/ n le père Noël.

sapphire /ˈsæfaɪə(r)/ n saphir m.

sarcasm /ˈsɑːkæzəm/ n sarcasme m. **sarcastic** adj sarcastique.

sash /sæʃ/ n (on uniform) écharpe f; (on dress) ceinture f.

sat /sæt/ ➡SIT.

satchel /ˈsætʃəl/ n cartable m.

satellite /ˈsætəlaɪt/ n & adj satellite (m); ~ dish antenne f parabolique.

satire /ˈsætaɪə(r)/ n satire f. **satirical** adj satirique.

satisfaction /sætɪsˈfækʃn/ n satisfaction f.

satisfactory /sætɪsˈfæktərɪ/ adj satisfaisant.

satisfy /ˈsætɪsfaɪ/ vt satisfaire; (convince) convaincre.

satphone /ˈsætfəʊn/ n téléphone m satellite.

saturate /ˈsætʃəreɪt/ vt saturer. **saturated** adj (wet) trempé.

Saturday /ˈsætədeɪ/ n samedi m.

sauce /sɔːs/ n sauce f.

saucepan /ˈsɔːspən/ n casserole f.

saucer /ˈsɔːsə(r)/ n soucoupe f.

Saudi Arabia /saʊdɪ əˈreɪbɪə/ n Arabie f saoudite.

sausage /ˈsɒsɪdʒ/ n (for cooking) saucisse f; (ready to eat) saucisson m.

savage /ˈsævɪdʒ/ adj (blow, temper) violent; (attack) sauvage. ● n sauvage mf. ● vt attaquer sauvagement.

save /seɪv/ vt sauver; (money) économiser; (time) gagner; (keep) garder; ~ (sb) doing sth éviter (à qn) de faire qch. ● n (football) arrêt m. **saver** n épargnant/-e m/f. **saving** n économie f. **savings** npl économies fpl.

saviour, (US) **savior** /ˈseɪvɪə(r)/ n sauveur m.

savour, (US) **savor** /ˈseɪvə(r)/ n saveur f. ● vt savourer. **savoury** adj (tasty) savoureux; (Culin) salé.

saw /sɔː/ →SEE. ● n scie f. ● vt (pt sawed; pp sawn or sawed) scier.

sawdust /'sɔːdʌst/ n sciure f.

saxophone /'sæksəfəʊn/ n saxophone m.

say /seɪ/ vt/i (pt said) dire; (prayer) faire. ● n have a ~ dire son mot; (in decision) avoir voix au chapitre. **saying** n proverbe m.

scab /skæb/ n croûte f.

scaffolding /'skæfəldɪŋ/ n échafaudage m.

scald /skɔːld/ vt (injure, cleanse) ébouillanter. ● n brûlure f.

scale /skeɪl/ n (for measuring) échelle f; (extent) étendue f; (Mus) gamme f; (on fish) écaille f. ● on a small ~ sur une petite échelle; ~ model maquette f. ● vt (climb) escalader; ~ down réduire. **scales** npl (for weighing) balance f.

scallop /'skɒləp/ n coquille f Saint-Jacques.

scalp /skælp/ n cuir m chevelu.

scampi /'skæmpɪ/ npl (fresh) langoustines fpl; (breaded) scampi mpl.

scan /skæn/ vt (scanned) scruter; (quickly) parcourir. ● n (ultrasound) échographie f; (CAT) scanner m.

scandal /'skændl/ n scandale m; (gossip) potins mpl 🗓.

Scandinavia /skændɪ'neɪvɪə/ n Scandinavie f.

scanty /'skæntɪ/ adj (-ier, -iest) maigre; (clothing) minuscule.

scapegoat /'skeɪpgəʊt/ n bouc m émissaire.

scar /skɑː(r)/ n cicatrice f. ● vt (pt scarred) marquer.

scarce /skeəs/ adj rare. **scarcely** adv à peine.

scare /skeə(r)/ vt faire peur à; be ~d avoir peur. ● n peur f; bomb ~ alerte f à la bombe. **scarecrow** n

épouvantail m.

scarf /skɑːf/ n (pl scarves) écharpe f; (over head) foulard m.

scarlet /'skɑːlət/ adj écarlate; ~ fever scarlatine f.

scary /'skeərɪ/ adj (-ier, -iest) 🗓 qui fait peur.

scathing /'skeɪðɪŋ/ adj cinglant.

scatter /'skætə(r)/ vt (throw) éparpiller, répandre; (disperse) disperser. ● vi se disperser.

scavenge /'skævɪndʒ/ vi fouiller (dans les ordures). **scavenger** n (animal) charognard m.

scene /siːn/ n scène f; (of accident, crime) lieu m; (sight) spectacle m; **behind the** ~**s** en coulisse. **scenery** n paysage m; (Theat) décors mpl. **scenic** adj panoramique.

scent /sent/ n (perfume) parfum m; (trail) piste f. ● vt flairer; (make fragrant) parfumer.

sceptic /'skeptɪk/ n sceptique mf. **sceptical** adj sceptique. **scepticism** n scepticisme m.

schedule /'ʃedjuːl/, /'skedʒʊl/ n horaire m; (for job) planning m; **behind** ~ en retard; **on** ~ dans les temps. ● vt prévoir; ~**d flight** vol m régulier.

scheme /skiːm/ n projet m; (dishonest) combine f; **pension** ~ plan m de retraite. ● vi comploter.

schizophrenic /skɪtsəʊ'frenɪk/ adj & n schizophrène (mf).

scholar /'skɒlə(r)/ n érudit/-e m/f.

school /skuːl/ n école f; **go to** ~ aller à l'école. ● adj (age, year, holidays) scolaire. ~**boy** n élève m. ~**girl** n élève f **schooling** n scolarité f. ~**teacher** n (primary) instituteur/-trice m/f; (secondary) professeur m.

science /'saɪəns/ n science f; **teach** ~ enseigner les sciences. **scientific**

adj scientifique. **scientist** *n* scientifique *mf*.

scissors /'sɪzəz/ *npl* ciseaux *mpl*.

scold /skəʊld/ *vt* gronder.

scoop /sku:p/ *n* (shovel) pelle *f*; (measure) mesure *f*; (for ice cream) cuillère *f* à glace; (news) exclusivité *f*.

scooter /'sku:tə(r)/ *n* (child's) trottinette *f*; (motor cycle) scooter *m*.

scope /skəʊp/ *n* étendue *f*; (competence) compétence *f*; (opportunity) possibilité *f*.

scorch /skɔ:tʃ/ *vt* brûler; (iron) roussir.

score /skɔ:(r)/ *n* score *m*; (Mus) partition *f*; **on that** ~ à cet égard. ● *vt* marquer; (success) remporter. ● *vi* marquer un but; (football) marquer un point; (keep score) marquer les points. **scorer** *n* (Sport) marqueur *m*.

scorn /skɔ:n/ *n* mépris *m*. ● *vt* mépriser.

Scorpio /'skɔ:pɪəʊ/ *n* Scorpion *m*.

Scot /skɒt/ *n* écossais/-e *m*/*f*.

Scotland /'skɒtlənd/ *n* écosse *f*.

Scottish /'skɒtɪʃ/ *adj* écossais.

scoundrel /'skaʊndrəl/ *n* gredin *m*.

scour /'skaʊə(r)/ *vt* (pan) récurer; (search) parcourir. **scourer** *n* tampon *m* à récurer.

scourge /skɜːdʒ/ *n* fléau *m*.

scout /skaʊt/ *n* éclaireur *m*. ● *vi* ~ **around for** rechercher.

scowl /skaʊl/ *n* air *m* renfrogné. ● *vi* prendre un air renfrogné.

scramble /'skræmbl/ *vi* (clamber) grimper. ● *vt* (eggs) brouiller. ● *n* (rush) course *f*.

scrap /skræp/ *n* petit morceau *m*; ~**s** (of metal, fabric) déchets *mpl*; (of food) restes *mpl*; (fight 🅺) bagarre *f*. ● *vt* (*pt* **scrapped**) abandonner; (car) détruire.

scrape /skreɪp/ *vt* gratter; (damage) érafler. ● *vi* ~ **against** érafler. □ ~ **through** réussir de justesse.

scrap: ~-**paper** *n* papier *m* brouillon. ~**yard** *n* casse *f*.

scratch /skrætʃ/ *vt*/*i* (se) gratter; (with claw, nail) griffer; (graze) érafler; (mark) rayer. ● *n* (on body) égratignure *f*; (on surface) éraflure *f*; **start from** ~ partir de zéro; **up to** ~ à la hauteur. ~ **card** *n* jeu *m* de grattage.

scrawl /skrɔ:l/ *n* gribouillage *m*. ● *vt*/*i* gribouiller.

scrawny /'skrɔ:nɪ/ *adj* (-**ier**, -**iest**) décharné.

scream /skri:m/ *vt*/*i* crier. ● *n* cri *m* (perçant).

screech /skri:tʃ/ *vi* (scream) hurler; (tyres) crisser. ● *n* cri *m* strident; (of tyres) crissement *m*.

screen /skri:n/ *n* écran *m*; (folding) paravent *m*. ● *vt* masquer; (protect) protéger; (film) projeter; (candidates) filtrer; (Med) faire subir un test de dépistage. **screening** *n* (cinema) projection *f*; (Med) dépistage *m*.

screen: ~**play** *n* scénario *m*. ~

saver n protecteur m d'écran.

screw /skru:/ n vis f. ● vt visser; ~ up (eyes) plisser; (ruin 🔲) cafouiller 🔲. ~driver n tournevis m.

scribble /'skrɪbl/ vt/i griffonner. ● n griffonnage m.

script /skrɪpt/ n script m; (of play) texte m.

scroll /skrəʊl/ n rouleau m. ● vt/i (Comput) (faire) défiler. ~ bar n barre f de défilement.

scrounge /skraʊndʒ/ 🔲 vt (favour) quémander; (cigarette) piquer 🔲; ~ money from sb taper de l'argent à qn. ● vi ~ off sb vivre sur le dos de qn.

scrub /skrʌb/ n (land) broussailles fpl. ● vt/i (pt scrubbed) nettoyer (à la brosse), frotter.

scruffy /'skrʌfɪ/ adj (-ier, -iest) dépenaillé.

scrum /skrʌm/ n (rugby) mêlée f.

scruple /'skru:pl/ n scrupule m.

scrutinize /'skru:tɪnaɪz/ vt scruter. **scrutiny** n examen m minutieux.

scuba-diving /'sku:bədaɪvɪŋ/ n plongée f sousmarine.

scuffle /'skʌfl/ n bagarre f.

sculpt /skʌlpt/ vt/i sculpter. **sculptor** n sculpteur m.

sculpture /'skʌlptʃə(r)/ n sculpture f.

scum /skʌm/ n (on liquid) mousse f; (people: pej) racaille f.

scurry /'skʌrɪ/ vi se précipiter, courir (for pour chercher); ~ off se sauver.

sea /si:/ n mer f; at ~ en mer; by ~ par mer. ● adj (air) marin; (bird) de mer; (voyage) par mer. ~food n fruits mpl de mer. ~gull n mouette f.

seal /si:l/ n (animal) phoque m; (insignia) sceau m; (with wax) cachet m. ● vt sceller; cacheter; (stick down) coller. □ ~ off (area) boucler.

seam /si:m/ n (in cloth) couture f; (of coal) veine f.

search /sɜ:tʃ/ vt/i (examine) fouiller; (seek) chercher; (study) examiner; (Comput) rechercher. ● n fouille f; (quest) recherches fpl; (Comput) recherche f; in ~ of à la recherche de. ~ engine n (Internet) moteur m de recherche. ~light n projecteur m. ~warrant n mandat m de perquisition.

sea: ~shell n coquillage m. ~shore n (coast) littoral m; (beach) plage f.

seasick /'si:sɪk/ adj be ~ avoir le mal de mer.

seaside /'si:saɪd/ n bord m de la mer.

season /'si:zn/ n saison f; ~ ticket carte f d'abonnement. ● vt assaisonner. **seasonal** adj saisonnier. **seasoning** n assaisonnement m.

seat /si:t/ n siège m; (place) place f; (of trousers) fond m; **take a ~** asseyez-vous. ● vt (put) placer; the room ~s 30 la salle peut accueillir 30 personnes. ~-belt n ceinture f (de sécurité)

seaweed /'si:wi:d/ n algue f marine.

secluded /sɪ'klu:dɪd/ adj retiré.

seclusion /sɪ'klu:ʒn/ n isolement m.

second¹ /'sekənd/ adj deuxième, second; a ~ chance une nouvelle chance; **have ~ thoughts** avoir des doutes. ● n deuxième mf, second/-e m/f; (unit of time) seconde f; ~ s (food) rab m. 🔲 ● adv (in race) deuxième; (secondly) deuxièmement. ● vt (proposal) appuyer.

second² /sɪ'kɒnd/ vt (transfer) détacher (to à).

secondary /'sekəndrɪ/ adj secondaire; ~**school** lycée m, école f secondaire.

second-best n pis-aller m.

second-class adj (Rail) de deuxième classe; (post) au tarif lent.

second hand n (on clock) trotteuse f.

second-hand adj & adv (article) d'occasion; (information) de seconde main.

secondly /'sekəndlɪ/ adv deuxièmement.

second-rate adj médiocre.

secrecy /'si:krəsɪ/ n secret m.

secret /'si:krɪt/ adj secret. ● n secret m; in ~ en secret.

secretarial /sekrə'teərɪəl/ adj (work) de secrétaire.

secretary /'sekrətrɪ/ n secrétaire mf; S ~ of State ministre m; (US) ministre m des Affaires étrangères.

secrete /sɪ'kri:t/ vt (Med) sécréter; (hide) cacher.

secretive /'si:krətɪv/ adj secret. **secretly** adv secrètement.

sect /sekt/ n secte f. **sectarian** adj sectaire.

section /'sekʃn/ n partie f; (in store) rayon m; (of newspaper) rubrique f; (of book) passage m.

sector /'sektə(r)/ n secteur m.

secular /'sekjʊlə(r)/ adj (school) laïque; (art, music) profane.

secure /sɪ'kjʊə(r)/ adj (safe) sûr; (job, marriage) stable; (knot, lock) solide; (window) bien fermé; (feeling) de sécurité; (person) sécurisé. ● vt attacher; (obtain) s'assurer; (ensure) assurer.

security /sɪ'kjʊərətɪ/ n (safety) sécurité f; (for loan) caution f; ~ **guard** vigile m.

sedate /sɪ'deɪt/ adj calme. ● vt don-

ner un sédatif à. **sedative** n sédatif m.

seduce /sɪ'dju:s/ vt séduire. **seducer** n séducteur/-trice m/f. **seduction** n séduction f. **seductive** adj séduisant.

see /si:/ vt/i (pt saw; pp seen) voir; **see you** (soon)! à bientôt!; ~**ing** that vu que. ☐ ~ **out** (person) raccompagner à la porte; (deception) déceler; (person) percer à jour; ~ **sth through** mener qch à bonne fin; ~ **to** s'occuper de; ~ **to it that** veiller à ce que.

seed /si:d/ n graine f; (collectively) graines fpl; (origin: fig) germe m; (tennis) tête f de série. **seedling** n plant m.

seek /si:k/ vt (pt **sought**) chercher.

seem /si:m/ vi sembler; **he** ~**s to think** il a l'air de croire.

seen /si:n/ ⇒SEE.

seep /si:p/ vi suinter; ~ **into** s'infiltrer dans.

see-saw /'si:sɔ:/ n tapecul m. ● vi osciller.

seethe /si:ð/ vi ~ **with** (anger) bouillir de; (people) grouiller de.

segment /'segmənt/ n segment m; (of orange) quartier m.

segregate /'segrɪgeɪt/ vt séparer.

seize /si:z/ vt saisir; (territory, prisoner) s'emparer de. ● vi ~ **on** (chance) saisir; ~ **up** (engine) se gripper.

seizure /'si:ʒə(r)/ n (Med) crise f.

seldom /'seldəm/ adv rarement.

select /sɪ'lekt/ vt sélectionner. ● adj privilégié. **selection** n sélection f. **selective** adj sélectif.

self /self/ n (pl **selves**) moi m; (on cheque) moi-même. ~**-assured** adj plein d'assurance. ~**-catering** adj (holiday) en location. ~**-centred**, (US) ~**-centered** adj égocentrique.

S

~**-confident** adj sûr de soi.
~**-conscious** adj timide.
~**-contained** adj (flat) indépendant. ~**-control** n sangfroid m.
~**-defence** n autodéfense f; (jur) légitime défense f. ~**-employed** adj qui travaille à son compte.
~**-esteem** n amour-propre m.
~**-governing** adj autonome. ~**-indulgent** adj complaisant.
~**-interest** n intérêt m personnel.

selfish /'selfɪʃ/ adj égoïste.

selfless /'selflɪs/ adj désintéressé.

self: ~**-portrait** n autoportrait m.
~**-reliant** adj autosuffisant. ~**-respect** n respect m de soi. ~**-righteous** adj satisfait de soi.
~**-sacrifice** n abnégation f.
~**-satisfied** adj satisfait de soi.
~**-seeking** adj égoïste. ~**-service** n & adj libre-service (m).

sell /sel/ vt/i (pt **sold**) vendre; ~ **well** se vendre bien. □ ~ **off** liquider; ~ **out** (items) se vendre; **have sold out** avoir tout vendu.

Sellotape® /'seləteɪp/ n scotch® m.

sell-out n (betrayal) 🔲 revirement m; **be a** ~ (show) afficher complet.

semester /sɪ'mestə(r)/ n (Univ) semestre m.

semicircle /'semɪsɜːkl/ n demi-cercle m.

semicolon /semɪ'kəʊlən/ n point-virgule m.

semi-detached /semɪdɪ'tætʃt/ adj ~ **house** maison f jumelée.

semifinal /semɪ'faɪnl/ n demi-finale f.

seminar /'semɪnɑː(r)/ n séminaire m.

semolina /semə'liːnə/ n semoule f.

senate /'senɪt/ n sénat m. **senator** n sénateur m.

send /send/ vt/i (pt **sent**) envoyer.

□ ~ **away** (dismiss) renvoyer; ~ (**away** or **off**) **for** commander (par la poste); ~ **back** renvoyer; ~ **for** (person, help) envoyer chercher; ~ **up** 🔲 parodier.

senile /'siːnaɪl/ adj sénile.

senior /'siːnɪə(r)/ adj plus âgé (**to** que); (in rank) haut placé; **be** ~ **to** sb être le supérieur de qn. ● n aîné/-e m/f. ~ **citizen** personne f âgée. ~ **school** n lycée m.

sensation /sen'seɪʃn/ n sensation f. **sensational** adj sensationnel.

sense /sens/ n sens m; (mental impression) sentiment m; (common sense) bon sens m, ~**s** (mind) raison f; **there's no** ~ **in doing** cela ne sert à rien de faire; **make** ~ avoir un sens; **make** ~ **of** comprendre. ● vt (pres)sentir. **senseless** adj insensé; (Med) sans connaissance.

sensible /'sensəbl/ adj raisonnable; (clothing) pratique.

sensitive /'sensətɪv/ adj sensible (**to** à); (issue) difficile.

sensory /'sensərɪ/ adj sensoriel.

sensual /'senʃʊəl/ adj sensuel. **sensuality** n sensualité f.

sensuous /'senʃʊəs/ adj sensuel.

sent /sent/ →**SEND**.

sentence /'sentəns/ n phrase f; (punishment: Jur) peine f. ● vt ~ **to** condamner à.

sentiment /'sentɪmənt/ n sentiment m. **sentimental** adj sentimental.

sentry /'sentrɪ/ n sentinelle f.

separate[1] /'sepərət/ adj (piece) à part; (issue) autre; (sections) différent; (organizations) distinct.

separate[2] /'sepəreɪt/ vt/i (se) séparer.

separately /'sepərətlɪ/ adv séparément.

separation /sepəˈreɪʃn/ n séparation f.

September /sepˈtembə(r)/ n septembre m.

septic /ˈseptɪk/ adj (wound) infecté; ~ **tank** fosse f septique.

sequel /ˈsiːkwəl/ n suite f.

sequence /ˈsiːkwəns/ n (order) ordre m; (series) suite f; (in film) séquence f.

Serb /sɜːb/ adj serbe. ● n (person) Serbe mf; (Ling) serbe m.

Serbia /ˈsɜːbɪə/ n Serbie f.

sergeant /ˈsɑːdʒənt/ n (Mil) sergent m; (policeman) brigadier m.

serial /ˈsɪərɪəl/ n feuilleton m. ● adj (Comput) série inv.

series /ˈsɪəriːz/ n inv série f.

serious /ˈsɪərɪəs/ adj sérieux; (accident, crime) grave.

seriously /ˈsɪərɪəslɪ/ adv sérieusement; (ill) gravement; **take** ~ prendre au sérieux.

sermon /ˈsɜːmən/ n sermon m.

serpent /ˈsɜːpənt/ n serpent m.

serrated /sɪˈreɪtɪd/ adj dentelé.

serum /ˈsɪərəm/ n sérum m.

servant /ˈsɜːvənt/ n domestique mf.

serve /sɜːv/ vt/i servir; faire; (transport, hospital) desservir; ~ **as/to** servir de/à; ~ **a purpose** être utile; ~ **a sentence** (Jur) purger une peine. ● n (tennis) service m.

server /ˈsɜːvə(r)/ n serveur m; remote ~ téléserveur m.

service /ˈsɜːvɪs/ n service m; (maintenance) révision f; (Relig) office m; ~s (Mil) forces fpl armées. ● vt (car) réviser. ~**area** n (Auto) aire f de services. ~ **charge** n service m. ~ **station** n station-service f.

session /ˈseʃn/ n séance f; **be in** ~ (Jur) tenir séance.

set /set/ vt (pt) set; pres p setting placer; (table) mettre; (limit) fixer; (clock) mettre à l'heure; (example, task) donner; (TV), (cinema) situer; ~ **fire to** mettre le feu à; ~ **free** libérer; ~ **to music** mettre en musique. ● vi (sun) se coucher; (jelly) prendre; ~ **sail** partir. ● n (of chairs, stamps) série f; (of knives, keys) jeu m; (of people) groupe m; (TV), (radio) poste m; (Theat) décor m; (tennis) set m; (mathematics) ensemble m. ● adj (time, price) fixe; (procedure) bien determiné; (meal) à prix fixe; (book) au programme; ~ **against sth** opposé à; **be** ~ **on doing** tenir absolument à faire. □ ~ **about** se mettre à; ~ **back** (delay) retarder; (cost [£]) coûter; ~ **in** (take hold) s'installer, commencer; ~ **off** or **out** partir; ~ **off** (panic, riot) déclencher; (bomb) faire exploser; ~ **out** (state) présenter; (arrange) disposer; ~ **out to do sth** chercher à faire qch; ~ **up** (stall) monter; (equipment) assembler; (experiment) préparer; (company) créer; (meeting) organiser. ~**back** n revers m.

settee /seˈtiː/ n canapé m.

setting /ˈsetɪŋ/ n cadre m; (on dial) position f.

settle /ˈsetl/ vt (arrange, pay) régler; (date) fixer; (nerves) calmer. ● vi (come to rest) (bird) se poser; (dust) se déposer; (live) s'installer. □ ~ **down** se calmer; (marry etc.) se ranger; ~ **for** accepter; ~ **in** s'installer; ~ **up** (with) régler.

settlement /ˈsetlmənt/ n règlement m (de); (agreement) accord m; (place) colonie f.

settler /ˈsetlə(r)/ n colon m.

seven /ˈsevn/ adj & n sept (m).

seventeen /sevnˈtiːn/ adj & n dix-sept (m).

seventh /'sevnθ/ adj & n septième (mf).

seventy /'sevntɪ/ adj & n soixante-dix (m).

sever /'sevə(r)/ vt (cut) couper; (relations) rompre.

several /'sevrəl/ adj & pron plusieurs; ~ of us plusieurs d'entre nous.

severe /sɪ'vɪə(r)/ adj (harsh) sévère; (serious) grave.

sew /səʊ/ vt/i (pt sewed; pp sewn or sewed) coudre.

sewage /'suːɪdʒ/ n eaux fpl usées.

sewer /'suːə(r)/ n égout m.

sewing /'səʊɪŋ/ n couture f. ~-machine n machine f à coudre.

sewn /səʊn/ →SEW.

sex /seks/ n sexe m; have ~ avoir des rapports (sexuels). ● adj sexuel.

sexist adj & n sexiste (mf). **sexual** adj sexuel.

shabby /'ʃæbɪ/ adj (-ier, -iest) (place, object) miteux; (person) habillé de façon miteuse; (treatment) mesquin.

shack /ʃæk/ n cabane f.

shade /ʃeɪd/ n ombre f; (of colour, opinion) nuance f; (for lamp) abat-jour m inv; a ~ bigger légèrement plus grand. ● vt (tree) ombrager; (hat) projeter une ombre sur.

shadow /'ʃædəʊ/ n ombre f. ● vt (follow) filer. S~ Cabinet n cabinet m fantôme.

shady /'ʃeɪdɪ/ adj (-ier, -iest) ombragé; (dubious) véreux.

shaft /ʃɑːft/ n (of tool) manche m; (of arrow) tige f; (in machine) axe m; (of mine) puits m; (of light) rayon m.

shake /ʃeɪk/ vt (pt shook; pp shaken) secouer; (bottle) agiter; (belief) ébranler; ~ hands with serrer la main à; ~ one's head dire

non de la tête. ● vi trembler. ● n secousse f; give sth a ~ secouer qch. □~ off se débarrasser de. ~-up n (Pol) remaniement m.

shaky /'ʃeɪkɪ/ adj (-ier, -iest) (hand, voice) tremblant; (ladder) branlant; (weak; fig) instable.

shall /ʃæl/ v aux I ~ do je ferai; we ~ see nous verrons; ~ we go. . . ? si on allait . . . ?

shallow /'ʃæləʊ/ adj peu profond; (fig) superficiel.

shame /ʃeɪm/ n honte f; it's a ~ c'est dommage. ● vt faire honte à.

shampoo /ʃæm'puː/ n shampooing m. ● vt faire un shampooing à.

shandy /'ʃændɪgæf/ n panaché m.

shan't →SHALL NOT.

shanty /'ʃæntɪ/ n (shack) baraque f; ~ town bidonville m.

shape /ʃeɪp/ n forme f. ● vt (clay) modeler; (rock) façonner; (future; fig) déterminer; ~ sth into balls faire des boules avec qch. ● vi ~ up (plan) prendre tournure; (person) faire des progrès.

share /ʃeə(r)/ n part f; (Comm) action f. ● vt/i partager; (feature) avoir en commun. ~holder n actionnaire mf. ~ware n (Comput) logiciel m contributif.

shark /ʃɑːk/ n requin m.

sharp /ʃɑːp/ adj (knife) tranchant; (pin) pointu; (point, angle, cry) aigu; (person, mind) vif; (tone) acerbe. ● adv (stop) net; (sing, play) trop haut; six o'clock ~ six heures pile. ● n (Mus) dièse m.

sharpen /'ʃɑːpən/ vt aiguiser; (pencil) tailler.

shatter /'ʃætə(r)/ vt (glass) fracasser; (hope) briser. ● vi (glass) voler en éclats.

shave /ʃeɪv/ vt/i (se) raser. ● n have a ~ se raser. **shaver** n rasoir

~ **sb in/out** faire entrer/sortir qn. ● *vi* (be visible) se voir. ● *n* (exhibition) exposition *f*; salon *m*; (Theat) spectacle *m*; (cinema) séance *f*; (of strength) démonstration *f*; **for** ~ pour l'effet; **on** ~ exposé. ▢ ~ **off** faire le fier/la fière; ~ **sth/sb off** exhiber qch/qn; ~ **up** se voir; (appear) se montrer; ~ **sb up** ▮ faire honte à qn.

shower /ˈʃaʊə(r)/ *n* douche *f*; (of rain) averse *f*. ● *vt* ~ **with** couvrir de. ● *vi* se doucher.

showing /ˈʃəʊɪŋ/ *n* performance *f*; (cinema) séance *f*.

show-jumping *n* concours *m* hippique.

shown /ʃəʊn/ →SHOW.

show- ~**off** *n* m'as-tu-vu *mf inv.* ▮ ~**room** *n* salle *f* d'exposition.

shrank /ʃræŋk/ →SHRINK.

shrapnel /ˈʃræpnl/ *n* éclats *mpl* d'obus.

shred /ʃred/ *n* lambeau *m*; (least amount: fig) parcelle *f*. ● *vt* (*pt* **shredded** déchiqueter; (Culin) râper.

shrewd /ʃruːd/ *adj* (person) habile; (move) astucieux.

shriek /ʃriːk/ *n* hurlement *m*. ● *vt/i* hurler.

shrill /ʃrɪl/ *adj* (voice) perçant; (tone) strident.

shrimp /ʃrɪmp/ *n* crevette *f*.

shrine /ʃraɪn/ *n* (place) lieu *m* de pèlerinage.

shrink /ʃrɪŋk/ *vt/i* (*pt* **shrank**; *pp* **shrunk** rétrécir; (lessen) diminuer; ~ **from** reculer devant.

shrivel /ˈʃrɪvl/ *vt/i* (*pt* **shrivelled**) (se) ratatiner.

shroud /ʃraʊd/ *n* linceul *m*. ● *vt* (veil) envelopper.

Shrove Tuesday *n* mardi *m* gras.

shrub /ʃrʌb/ *n* arbuste *m*.

shrug /ʃrʌg/ *vt* (*pt* **shrugged** ~ **one's shoulders** hausser les épaules; ~ **sth off** ignorer qch.

shrunk /ʃrʌŋk/ →SHRINK.

shudder /ˈʃʌdə(r)/ *vi* frémir. ● *n* frémissement *m*.

shuffle /ˈʃʌfl/ *vt* (feet) traîner; (cards) battre. ● *vi* traîner les pieds.

shun /ʃʌn/ *vt* (*pt* **shunned**) fuir.

shut /ʃʌt/ *vt* (*pt* **shut**; *pres p* **shutting**) fermer. ● *vi* (door) se fermer; (shop) fermer. ▢ ~ **in** *or* ~ **up** enfermer; ~ **up** se taire; (cover) mer; ~ **up** se taire; ~ **sb up** faire taire qn.

shutter /ˈʃʌtə(r)/ *n* volet *m*; (Photo) obturateur *m*.

shuttle /ˈʃʌtl/ *n* (bus) navette *f*; ~ **service** navette *f*. ● *vi* faire la navette. ● *vt* transporter.

shuttlecock /ˈʃʌtlkɒk/ *n* (badminton) volant *m*.

shy /ʃaɪ/ *adj* timide. ● *vi* ~ **away from** se tenir à l'écart de.

sibling /ˈsɪblɪŋ/ *n* frère/sœur *m/f*.

sick /sɪk/ *adj* malade; (humour) macabre; (mind) malsain; **be** ~ (vomit) vomir; **be** ~ **of** ▮ en avoir assez *or* marre de ▮; **feel** ~ avoir mal au cœur. ~**leave** *n* congé *m* de maladie.

sickly /ˈsɪklɪ/ *adj* (**-ier, -iest**) (person) maladif; (taste, smell) écœurant.

sickness /ˈsɪknɪs/ *n* maladie *f*.

sick-pay *n* indemnité *f* de maladie.

side /saɪd/ *n* côté *m*; (of road, river) bord *m*; (of hill, body) flanc *m*; (Sport) équipe *f*; (TV ▮) chaîne *f*; **by** ~ côte à côte. ● *adj* latéral. ● *vi* ~ **with** se ranger du côté de. ~**board** *n* buffet *m*. ~**effect** *n* effet *m* secondaire. ~**light** *n* (Auto) feu *m* de position. ~**line** *n* activité *f* secondaire. ~**show** *n* attraction *f*. ~**step** *vt* (*pt* -**stepped**) éviter.

s

∼**street** n rue f latérale. ∼**track**
vt fourvoyer. ● **walk** n (US) trottoir m.

sideways /'saɪdweɪz/ adj (look) de
travers. ● adv (move) latéralement;
(look at) de travers.

siding /'saɪdɪŋ/ n voie f de garage.

sidle /'saɪdl/ vi s'avancer furtivement (up to vers).

siege /siːdʒ/ n siège m.

siesta /sɪ'estə/ n sieste f.

sieve /sɪv/ n tamis m; (for liquids)
passoire f. ● vt tamiser.

sift /sɪft/ vt tamiser. ● vi ∼ through
examiner.

sigh /saɪ/ n soupir m. ● vt/i soupirer.

sight /saɪt/ n vue f; (scene) spectacle m; (on gun) mire f. **at or on** ∼ à
vue; **catch** ∼ **of** apercevoir; **in** ∼
visible; **lose** ∼ **of** perdre de vue.
● vt apercevoir.

sightseeing /'saɪtsiːɪŋ/ n tourisme m.

sign /saɪn/ n signe m; (notice) panneau m. ● vt/i signer. □ ∼ **on** (as
unemployed) pointer au chômage;
∼ **up** (s')engager.

signal /'sɪgnl/ n signal m. ● vt (pt
signalled) (gesture) faire signe
(that que); (indicate) indiquer.

signatory /'sɪgnətrɪ/ n signataire mf.

signature /'sɪgnətʃə(r)/ n signature f; ∼ **tune** indicatif m.

significance /sɪg'nɪfɪkəns/ n importance f; (meaning) signification f.
significant adj important; (meaningful) significatif. **significantly** adv
(much) sensiblement.

signify /'sɪgnɪfaɪ/ vt signifier.

signpost /'saɪnpəʊst/ n panneau m
indicateur.

silence /'saɪləns/ n silence m. ● vt
faire taire.

silent /'saɪlənt/ adj silencieux;
(film) muet. **silently** adv silencieu-
sement.

silhouette /sɪluː'et/ n silhouette f.
● vt **be** ∼**d against** se profiler
contre.

silicon /'sɪlɪkən/ n silicium m; ∼
chip puce f électronique.

silk /sɪlk/ n soie f.

silly /'sɪlɪ/ adj (-**ier, -iest**) bête,
idiot.

silver /'sɪlvə(r)/ n argent m; (silverware) argenterie f. ● adj en argent.

similar /'sɪmɪlə(r)/ adj semblable
(to à). **similarity** n ressemblance f.
similarly adv de même.

simile /'sɪmɪlɪ/ n comparaison f.

simmer /'sɪmə(r)/ vt/i (soup) mijoter; (water) (laisser) frémir.

simple /'sɪmpl/ adj simple.

simplicity /sɪm'plɪsətɪ/ n simplicité f.

simplify /'sɪmplɪfaɪ/ vt simplifier.

simplistic /sɪm'plɪstɪk/ adj simpliste.

simply /'sɪmplɪ/ adv simplement;
(absolutely) absolument.

simulate /'sɪmjʊleɪt/ vt simuler.

simultaneous /sɪml'teɪnɪəs/ adj
simultané.

sin /sɪn/ n péché m. ● vi (pt **sinned**)
pécher.

---

since /sɪns/

● preposition

····▸ depuis; **I haven't seen him**
∼ **Monday** je ne l'ai pas vu
depuis lundi; **I've been waiting** ∼ **yesterday** j'attends depuis hier; **she had been living
in Paris** ∼ **1985** elle habitait
Paris depuis 1985.

● conjunction

····➤ (in time expressions) depuis que; ~ **she's been working here** depuis qu'elle travaille ici; ~ **she left** depuis qu'elle est partie or depuis son départ.

····➤ (because) comme; ~ **he was ill, he couldn't go** comme il était malade, il ne pouvait pas y aller.

● adverb

····➤ depuis; **he hasn't been seen** ~ on ne l'a pas vu depuis.

sincere /sɪnˈsɪə(r)/ adj sincère. **sincerely** adv sincèrement. **sincerity** n sincérité f.

sinful /ˈsɪnfl/ adj immoral; ~ **man** pécheur m.

sing /sɪŋ/ vt/i (pt **sang**; pp **sung**) chanter.

singe /sɪndʒ/ vt (pres p **singeing**) brûler légèrement; (with iron) roussir.

singer /ˈsɪŋə(r)/ n chanteur/ -euse m/f.

single /ˈsɪŋgl/ adj seul; (not double) simple; (unmarried) célibataire; (room, bed) pour une personne; (ticket) simple; **in** ~ **file** en file indienne. ● n (ticket) aller simple m; (record) 45 tours m inv; ~**s** (tennis) simple m. ● vt ~ **out** choisir.
~**-handed** adj tout seul.
~**-minded** adj tenace. ~ **parent** n parent m isolé.

singular /ˈsɪŋgjʊlə(r)/ n singulier m. ● adj (strange) singulier; (noun) au singulier.

sinister /ˈsɪnɪstə(r)/ adj sinistre.

sink /sɪŋk/ vt (pt **sank**; pp **sunk**) (boat) couler; (well) forer; (post) enfoncer. ● vi (boat) couler; (sun, level) baisser; (wall) s'effondrer. ● n (in

kitchen) évier m; (wash-basin) lavabo m. □ ~ **in** (news) faire son chemin.

sinner /ˈsɪnə(r)/ n pécheur/ -eresse m/f.

sip /sɪp/ n petite gorgée f. ● vt (pt **sipped**) boire à petites gorgées.

siphon /ˈsaɪfn/ n siphon m. ● vt ~ **off** siphonner.

sir /sɜː(r)/ n Monsieur m; **Sir** (title) Sir m.

siren /ˈsaɪərən/ n sirène f.

sirloin /ˈsɜːlɔɪn/ n aloyau m.

sister /ˈsɪstə(r)/ n sœur f; (nurse) infirmière f en chef. ~**-in-law** n (pl ~**s-in-law**) belle-sœur f.

sit /sɪt/ vt/i (pt **sat**; pres p **sitting**) (s')asseoir; (committee) siéger; ~ **(for)** (exam) se présenter à; **be** ~**ting** être assis. □ ~ **around** ne rien faire; ~ **down** s'asseoir.

site /saɪt/ n emplacement m; (building) ~ chantier m. ● vt construire.

sitting /ˈsɪtɪŋ/ n séance f; (in restaurant) service m. ~**-room** n salon m.

situate /ˈsɪtjʊeɪt/ vt situer; **be** ~**d** être situé. **situation** n situation f.

six /sɪks/ adj & n six (m).

sixteen /sɪkˈstiːn/ adj & n seize (m).

sixth /sɪksθ/ adj & n sixième (mf).

sixty /ˈsɪkstɪ/ adj & n soixante (m).

size /saɪz/ n dimension f; (of person, garment) taille f; (of shoes) pointure f; (of sum, salary) montant m; (extent) ampleur f. □ ~ **up** (person) se faire une opinion de; (situation) évaluer. **sizeable** adj assez grand.

skate /skeɪt/ n patin m; (fish) raie f. ● vi patiner.

skateboard /ˈskeɪtbɔːd/ n skateboard m, planche f à roulettes. ● vi faire du skateboard.

S

skating /'skeɪtɪŋ/ n patinage m.

skeleton /'skelɪtn/ n squelette m; ~ **staff** effectifs mpl minimums.

sketch /sketʃ/ n esquisse f; (hasty) croquis m; (Theat) sketch m. ● vt faire une esquisse ou un croquis de. ● vi faire des esquisses.

sketchy /'sketʃɪ/ adj (-ier, -iest) (details) insuffisant; (memory) vague.

skewer /'skjuːə(r)/ n brochette f.

ski /skiː/ n ski m. ● adj de ski. ● vi (pt **ski'd** ou **skied**; pres p **skiing**) skier; (go skiing) faire du ski.

skid /skɪd/ vi (pt **skidded**) déraper. ● n dérapage m.

skier /'skiːə(r)/ n skieur/-euse m/f.

skiing /'skiːɪŋ/ n ski m.

ski jump n saut m à ski.

skilful /'skɪlfl/ adj habile.

ski lift n remontée f mécanique.

skill /skɪl/ n habileté f; (craft) compétence f; ~**s** connaissances fpl. **skilled** adj (worker) qualifié; (talented) consommé.

skim /skɪm/ vt (pt **skimmed**) écumer; (milk) écrémer; (pass over) effleurer. ● vi ~ **through** parcourir.

skimpy /'skɪmpɪ/ adj (clothes) étriqué.

skin /skɪn/ n peau f. ● vt (pt **skinned**) (animal) écorcher; (fruit) éplucher.

skinny /'skɪnɪ/ adj (-ier, -iest) □ maigre.

skip /skɪp/ vi (pt **skipped**) sautiller; (with rope) sauter à la corde. ● vt (page, class) sauter. ● n petit saut m; (container) benne f.

skipper /'skɪpə(r)/ n capitaine m.

skirmish /'skɜːmɪʃ/ n escarmouche f.

skirt /skɜːt/ n jupe f. ● vt contourner. **skirting-board** n plinthe f.

skittle /'skɪtl/ n quille f.

skull /skʌl/ n crâne m.

sky /skaɪ/ n ciel m. ~-**blue** adj & n bleu ciel m inv. ~-**marshal** n garde m armé (à bord d'un avion.) ~**scraper** n gratte-ciel m inv.

slab /slæb/ n (of stone) dalle f.

slack /slæk/ adj (not tight) détendu; (person) négligent; (period) creux. ● n (in rope) mou m. ● vi se relâcher.

slacken /'slækən/ vt (rope) donner du mou à; (grip) relâcher; (pace) réduire. ● vi (grip, rope) se relâcher; (activity) ralentir; (rain) se calmer.

slam /slæm/ vt/i (pt **slammed**) (door) claquer; (throw) flanquer; (criticize □) critiquer. ● n (noise) claquement m.

slander /'slɑːndə(r)/ n (offence) diffamation f; (statement) calomnie f. ● vt calomnier; (Jur) diffamer. **slanderous** adj diffamatoire.

slang /slæŋ/ n argot m.

slant /slɑːnt/ vt/i (faire) pencher; (news) présenter sous un certain jour. ● n inclinaison f; (bias) angle m. **slanted** adj (biased) orienté; (sloping) en pente.

slap /slæp/ vt (pt **slapped**) (strike) donner une tape à; (face) gifler; (put) flanquer □. ● n claque f; (on face) gifle f. ● adv tout droit.

slapdash /'slæpdæʃ/ adj (person) brouillon □; (work) bâclé □.

slash /slæʃ/ vt (picture, tyre) taillader; (face) balafrer; (throat) couper; (fig) réduire (radicalement). ● n lacération f.

slat /slæt/ n (in blind) lamelle f; (in bed) latte f.

slate /sleɪt/ n ardoise f. ● vt □ taper sur □.

slaughter /'slɔːtə(r)/ n massacrer; (animal) abattre. ● n massacre m; abattage m.

slave /sleɪv/ n esclave mf. ● vi trimer ⊞. **slavery** n esclavage m.

sleazy /ˈsliːzɪ/ adj (-ier, -iest) ⊞ (story) scabreux; (club) louche.

sledge /sledʒ/ n luge f; (horse-drawn) traîneau m.

sleek /sliːk/ adj (hair) lisse, brillant; (shape) élégant.

sleep /sliːp/ n sommeil m; **go to ~** s'endormir. ● vi (pt **slept**) dormir; (spend the night) coucher; **~ in** faire la grasse matinée. ● vt loger.

sleeper /ˈsliːpə(r)/ n (Rail) (berth) couchette f; (on track) traverse f.

sleeping-bag n sac m de couchage.

sleeping-pill n somnifère m.

sleep-walker n somnambule mf.

sleepy /ˈsliːpɪ/ adj (-ier, -iest) somnolent; **be ~** avoir sommeil.

sleet /sliːt/ n neige f fondue.

sleeve /sliːv/ n manche f; (of record) pochette f; **up one's ~** en réserve.

sleigh /sleɪ/ n traîneau m.

slender /ˈslendə(r)/ adj (person) mince; (majority) faible.

slept /slept/ ⟹SLEEP.

slice /slaɪs/ n tranche f. ● vt couper (en tranches).

slick /slɪk/ adj (adept) habile; (insincere) roublard ⊞. ● n (oil) ~ marée f noire.

slide /slaɪd/ vt/i (pt **slid**) glisser; **~ into** (go silently) se glisser dans. ● n glissade f; (fall: fig) baisse f; (in playground) toboggan m; (for hair) barrette f; (Photo) diapositive f.

sliding /ˈslaɪdɪŋ/ adj (door) coulissant; **~ scale** échelle f mobile.

slight /slaɪt/ adj petit, léger; (slender) mince; (frail) frêle. ● vt (insult) offenser. ● n affront m. **slightest** adj moindre. **slightly** adv légèrement,

un peu.

slim /slɪm/ adj (**slimmer, slimmest**) mince. ● vi (pt **slimmed**) maigrir.

slime /slaɪm/ n dépôt m gluant; (on riverbed) vase f. **slimy** adj visqueux; (fig) servile.

sling /slɪŋ/ n (weapon, toy) fronde f; (bandage) écharpe f. ● vt (pt **slung**) jeter, lancer.

slip /slɪp/ vt/i (pt **slipped**) glisser; **~ped disc** hernie f discale; **~ sb's mind** échapper à qn. ● n (mistake) erreur f; (petticoat) combinaison f; (paper) bout m de papier; **~ of the tongue** lapsus m. **~ away** s'esquiver; □ **into** (go) se glisser dans; (clothes) mettre; □ **up** ⊞ faire une gaffe ⊞.

slipper /ˈslɪpə(r)/ n pantoufle f.

slippery /ˈslɪpərɪ/ adj glissant.

slip road n bretelle f.

slit /slɪt/ n fente f. ● vt (pt **slit**; pres p **slitting**) déchirer; **~ sth open** ouvrir qch; **~ sb's throat** égorger qn.

slither /ˈslɪðə(r)/ vi glisser.

sliver /ˈslɪvə(r)/ n (of glass) éclat m; (of soap) reste m.

slobber /ˈslɒbə(r)/ vi baver.

slog /slɒg/ ⊞ vt (pt **slogged**) (hit) frapper dur. ● vi (work) bosser ⊞. ● n (work) travail m dur.

slogan /ˈsləʊgən/ n slogan m.

slope /sləʊp/ vi être en pente; (handwriting) pencher. ● n pente f; (of mountain) flanc m.

sloppy /ˈslɒpɪ/ adj (-ier, -iest) (food) liquide; (work) négligé; (person) négligent.

slosh /slɒʃ/ vt ⊞ répandre; (hit) ⊞ frapper. ● vi clapoter.

slot /slɒt/ n fente f. ● vt/i (pt **slotted**) (s')insérer.

sloth /sləʊθ/ n paresse f.

slot-machine n distributeur m automatique; (for gambling) machine f à sous.

slouch /slaʊtʃ/ vi être avachi.

Slovakia /slə'vækɪə/ n Slovaquie f.

Slovenia /slə'viːnɪə/ n Slovénie f.

slovenly /'slʌvnlɪ/ adj débraillé.

slow /sləʊ/ adj lent; be ~ (clock) retarder; in ~ motion au ralenti. ● adv lentement. ● vt/i ralentir.

slowly adv lentement. **slowness** n lenteur f.

sludge /slʌdʒ/ n vase f.

slug /slʌg/ n (mollusc) limace f; (bullet Ⓔ) balle f; (blow Ⓔ) coup m.

sluggish /'slʌgɪʃ/ adj (person) léthargique; (circulation) lent.

slum /slʌm/ n taudis m.

slump /slʌmp/ n (Econ) effondrement m; (in support) baisse f. ● vi (demand, trade) chuter; (economy) s'effondrer; (person) s'affaler.

slung /slʌŋ/ ➡SLING.

slur /slɜː(r)/ vt/i (pt slurred) (words) mal articuler. ● n calomnie f (on sur).

slush /slʌʃ/ n (snow) neige f fondue. ~ fund n caisse f noire.

sly /slaɪ/ adj (crafty) rusé; (secretive) sournois. ● n on the ~ en cachette.

smack /smæk/ n tape f; (on face) gifle f. ● vt donner une tape à; gifler. ● vi ~ of sth sentir qch. ● adv Ⓔ tout droit.

small /smɔːl/ adj petit. ● n ~ of the back creux m des reins. ● adv (cut) menu. ~ ad n petite annonce f. ~ business n petite entreprise f. ~ change n petite monnaie f. ~-pox n variole f. ~ print n petits caractères mpl. ~ talk n banalités fpl.

smart /smɑːt/ adj élégant; (clever Ⓔ) malin, habile; (restaurant) chic

inv; (Comput) intelligent. ● vi (wound) brûler.

smarten /'smɑːtn/ vt/i ~ (up) embellir; ~ (oneself) up s'arranger.

smash /smæʃ/ vt/i (se) briser, (se) fracasser; (opponent, record) pulvériser. ● n (noise) fracas m; (blow) coup m; (car crash) collision f; (hit record Ⓔ) tube m. Ⓔ

smashing /'smæʃɪŋ/ adj Ⓔ épatant.

SME abbr (small and medium enterprises) PME.

smear /smɪə(r)/ vt (stain) tacher; (coat) enduire; (discredit: fig) diffamer. ● n tache f; (effort to discredit) propos m diffamatoire; ~ (test) frottis m.

smell /smel/ n odeur f; (sense) odorat m. ● vt/i (pt smelt or smelled) sentir; ~ of sentir. **smelly** adj qui sent mauvais.

smelt /smelt/ ➡SMELL.

smile /smaɪl/ n sourire m. ● vi sourire.

smiley /'smaɪlɪ/ n (Internet) binette f

smirk /smɜːk/ n petit sourire m satisfait.

smitten /'smɪtn/ adj (in love) fou d'amour.

smog /smɒg/ n smog m.

smoke /sməʊk/ n fumée f; have a ~ fumer. ● vt/i fumer. **smoked** adj fumé. **smokeless** adj (fuel) non polluant. **smoker** n fumeur/-euse m/f. **smoky** adj (air) enfumé.

smooth /smuːð/ adj lisse; (movement) aisé; (manners) onctueux; (flight) sans heurts. ● vt lisser; (process) faciliter.

smoothly /'smuːðlɪ/ adv (move, flow) doucement; (brake, start) en douceur; go ~ marcher bien.

smother /'smʌðə(r)/ vt (stifle) étouffer; (cover) couvrir.

smoulder /ˈsməʊldə(r)/ vi (lit) se consumer; (fig) couver.

smudge /smʌdʒ/ n trace f. ● vt/i (ink) (s')étaler.

smug /smʌg/ adj (**smugger, smuggest**) suffisant.

smuggle /ˈsmʌgl/ vt passer (en contrebande). **smuggler** n contrebandier/-ière m/f. **smuggling** n contrebande f.

smutty /ˈsmʌtɪ/ adj grivois.

snack /snæk/ n casse-croûte m inv.

snag /snæg/ n inconvénient m; (in cloth) accroc m.

snail /sneɪl/ n escargot m.

snake /sneɪk/ n serpent m.

snap /snæp/ vt/i (pt **snapped**) (whip, fingers) (faire) claquer; (break) (se) casser net; (say) dire sèchement. ● n claquement m; (Photo) photo f. ● adj soudain. □ ~ **up** (buy) sauter sur.

snapshot /ˈsnæpʃɒt/ n photo f.

snare /sneə(r)/ n piège m.

snarl /snɑːl/ vi gronder (en montrant les dents). ● n grondement m. ~-**up** n embouteillage m.

snatch /snætʃ/ vt (grab) attraper; (steal) voler; (opportunity) saisir; ~ sth from sb arracher qch à qn. ● n (theft) vol m; (short part) fragment m.

sneak /sniːk/ vi aller furtivement. ● n 🔁 rapporteur/-euse m/f.

sneer /snɪə(r)/ n sourire m méprisant. ● vi sourire avec mépris.

sneeze /sniːz/ n éternuement m. ● vi éternuer.

snide /snaɪd/ adj narquois.

sniff /snɪf/ vt/i renifler. ● n reniflement m.

snigger /ˈsnɪgə(r)/ n ricanement m. ● vi ricaner.

snip /snɪp/ vt (pt **snipped**) couper.

sniper /ˈsnaɪpə(r)/ n tireur m embusqué.

snippet /ˈsnɪpɪt/ n bribe f.

snivel /ˈsnɪvl/ vi (pt **snivelled**) pleurnicher.

snob /snɒb/ n snob mf.

snooker /ˈsnuːkə(r)/ n snooker m.

snoop /snuːp/ vi 🔁 fourrer son nez partout.

snooty /ˈsnuːtɪ/ adj (-**ier**, -**iest**) 🔁 snob inv, hautain.

snooze /snuːz/ n petit somme m. ● vi sommeiller.

snore /snɔː(r)/ n ronflement m. ● vi ronfler.

snorkel /ˈsnɔːkl/ n tuba m.

snort /snɔːt/ n grognement m. ● vi (person) grogner; (horse) s'ébrouer.

snout /snaʊt/ n museau m.

snow /snəʊ/ n neige f. ● vi neiger; be ~ed under with être submergé de.

snowball /ˈsnəʊbɔːl/ n boule f de neige. ● vi faire boule de neige.

snow: ~**board** n snowboard m. ~**boarding** n surf m des neiges. ~**bound** adj bloqué par la neige. ~**drift** n congère f. ~**drop** n perce-neige m or f inv. ~**flake** n flocon m de neige. ~**man** n (pl -**men**) bonhomme m de neige. ~**plough** n chasse-neige m inv.

snub /snʌb/ vt (pt **snubbed**) rembarrer. ● n rebuffade f.

snuffle /ˈsnʌfl/ vi renifler.

snug /snʌg/ adj (**snugger, snuggest**) (cosy) confortable; (tight) bien ajusté.

snuggle /ˈsnʌgl/ vi se pelotonner.

so /səʊ/ adv si, tellement; (thus) ainsi; ~ am I moi aussi; ~ good as aussi bon que; that is ~ c'est ça; I think ~ je pense que oui; five or ~ environ cinq; ~ as to ma-

nière à; ~ **far** jusqu'ici; ~ **long!** ▯
à bientôt!; ~ **many**, ~ **much** tant
(de); ~ **that** pour que. ● *conj* donc,
alors.

soak /səʊk/ *vt/i* (faire) tremper (**in**
dans). □ ~ **in** pénétrer; ~ **up** absorber. **soaking** *a* trempé.

soap /səʊp/ *n* savon *m*. ● *vt* savonner. ~ **opera** *n* feuilleton *m*. ~
powder *n* lessive *f*.

soar /sɔː(r)/ *vi* monter (en flèche).

sob /sɒb/ *n* sanglot *m*. ● *vi* (*pt*
sobbed) sangloter.

sober /'səʊbə(r)/ *adj* qui n'a pas bu
d'alcool; (serious) sérieux. ● *vi* ~
up dessoûler.

soccer /'sɒkə(r)/ *n* football *m*.

sociable /'səʊʃəbl/ *adj* sociable.

social /'səʊʃl/ *adj* social. ● *n* réunion *f* (amicale), fête *f*.

socialism /'səʊʃəlɪzəm/ *n* socialisme *m*. **socialist** *adj* & *n* socialiste (*mf*).

socialize /'səʊʃəlaɪz/ *vi* se mêler
aux autres; ~ **with** fréquenter.

socially /'səʊʃəlɪ/ *adv* socialement;
(meet) en société.

social: ~ **security** *n* aide *f* sociale.
~ **worker** *n* travailleur/-euse *m/f*
social/-e.

society /sə'saɪətɪ/ *n* société *f*.

sociological /səʊsɪə'lɒdʒɪkl/ *adj*
sociologique. **sociologist** *n* sociolo-
gue *mf*. **sociology** *n* sociologie *f*.

sock /sɒk/ *n* chaussette *f*. ● *vt* (hit
▯) flanquer un coup de (poing) à.

socket /'sɒkɪt/ *n* (for lamp) douille
f; (Electr) prise *f* (de courant); (of
eye) orbite *f*.

soda /'səʊdə/ *n* soude *f*; ~(**-water**)
eau *f* de Seltz.

sodden /'sɒdn/ *adj* détrempé.

sofa /'səʊfə/ *n* canapé *m*. ~ **bed** *n*
canapé-lit *m*.

soft /sɒft/ *adj* (gentle, lenient) doux;
(not hard) doux, mou; (heart, wood)
tendre; (silly) ramolli. ~ **drink** *n*
boisson *f* non alcoolisée.

soften /'sɒfn/ *vt/i* (se) ramollir;
(tone down) atténuer (s')adoucir.

soft spot *n* to have a ~ **for** sb
avoir un faible pour qn.

software /'sɒftweə(r)/ *n* logiciel *m*.

soggy /'sɒgɪ/ *adj* (**-ier, -iest**)
(ground) détrempé; (food) ramolli.

soil /sɔɪl/ *n* sol *m*, terre *f*. ● *vt/i* (se)
salir.

sold /səʊld/ ⟹SELL. ● *adj* ~ **out**
épuisé.

solder /'səʊldə(r)/ *n* soudure *f*. ● *vt*
souder.

soldier /'səʊldʒə(r)/ *n* soldat *m*.
● *vi* ~ **on** ▯ persévérer.

sole /səʊl/ *n* (of foot) plante *f*; (of
shoe) semelle *f*; (fish) sole *f*. ● *adj*
unique, seul. **solely** *adv* uniquement.

solemn /'sɒləm/ *adj* solennel.

solicitor /sə'lɪsɪtə(r)/ *n* notaire *m*;
(for court and police work) ≈
avocat/-e *m/f*.

solid /'sɒlɪd/ *adj* solide; (not hollow)
plein; (gold) massif; (mass) compact; (meal) substantiel. ● *n* solide
m; ~**s** (food) aliments *mpl* solides.

solidarity /sɒlɪ'dærətɪ/ *n* solidarité *f*.

solidify /sə'lɪdɪfaɪ/ *vt/i* (se) solidifier.

solitary /'sɒlɪtrɪ/ *adj* (alone) solitaire; (only) seul.

solo /'səʊləʊ/ *n* solo *m*. ● *adj* (Mus)
solo *inv*; (flight) en solitaire.

soluble /'sɒljʊbl/ *adj* soluble.

solution /sə'lu:ʃn/ *n* solution *f*.

solve /sɒlv/ *vt* résoudre.

solvent /'sɒlvənt/ *adj* (Comm)

solvable. ● n (dis)solvant m.

some /sʌm, səm/
● *determiner*
····▸ (unspecified amount) du/de l'/de la/des; **I have to buy ~ bread** je dois acheter du pain; **have ~ water** prenez de l'eau; **~ sweets** des bonbons.
····▸ (certain) certains/certaines; **~ people say that** certains disent que.
····▸ (unknown) un/une; **~ man came to the house** un homme est venu à la maison.
····▸ (considerable amount) **we stayed there for ~ time** nous sommes restés là assez longtemps; **it will take ~ doing** ça ne va pas être facile à faire.

➡ In front of a plural adjective *des* changes to *de*: some pretty dresses *de jolies robes*.

● *pronoun*
····▸ en; **he wants ~** il en veut; **have ~ more** reprenez-en.
····▸ (certain) certains/certaines; **~ are expensive** certains sont chers.
● *adverb*
····▸ environ; **~ 20 people** environ 20 personnes.

somebody /'sʌmbədɪ/ *pron* quelqu'un. ● n **be a ~** être quelqu'un.
somehow /'sʌmhaʊ/ *adv* d'une manière ou d'une autre; (for some reason) je ne sais pas pourquoi.
someone /'sʌmwʌn/ *pron & n* ➡SOMEBODY.
someplace /'sʌmpleɪs/ *adv* (US)

➡SOMEWHERE.
somersault /'sʌməsɔlt/ n roulade f. ● vi faire une roulade.
something /'sʌmθɪŋ/ *pron & n* quelque chose (m); **~ good** quelque chose de bon; **~ like** un peu comme.
sometime /'sʌmtaɪm/ *adv* un jour; **~ in June** en juin. ● *adj* (former) ancien.
sometimes /'sʌmtaɪmz/ *adv* quelquefois, parfois.
somewhat /'sʌmwɒt/ *adv* quelque peu, un peu.
somewhere /'sʌmweə(r)/ *adv* quelque part.
son /sʌn/ n fils m.
song /sɒŋ/ n chanson f; (of bird) chant m.
son-in-law /'sʌnɪnlɔ:/ n (pl **sons-in-law**) gendre m.
soon /su:n/ *adv* bientôt; (early) tôt; **I would ~er stay** j'aimerais mieux rester; **~ after** peu après; **~er or later** tôt ou tard.
soot /sʊt/ n suie f.
soothe /su:ð/ vt calmer.
sophisticated /sə'fɪstɪkeɪtɪd/ *adj* raffiné; (machine) sophistiqué.
sopping /'sɒpɪŋ/ *adj* trempé.
soppy /'sɒpɪ/ *adj* (-ier, -iest) 🅸 sentimental.
sorcerer /'sɔ:sərə(r)/ n sorcier m.
sordid /'sɔ:dɪd/ *adj* sordide.
sore /sɔ:(r)/ *adj* douloureux; (vexed) en rogne (at, with contre). ● n plaie f.
sorely /'sɔ:lɪ/ *adv* fortement.
sorrow /'sɒrəʊ/ n chagrin m.
sorry /'sɒrɪ/ *adj* (-ier, -iest) (regretful) désolé (to de; that que); (wretched) triste; **feel ~ for** plaindre; **~! pardon!
sort /sɔ:t/ n genre m, sorte f, espèce

🅢

f; (person ▣) type m; **what** ~ **of?** quel genre de?; **be out of** ~s ne pas être dans son assiette. ● vt ~ **(out)** (classify) trier; ~ **out** (tidy) ranger; (arrange) arranger; (problem) régler.

so-so /sǝʊ'sǝʊ/ adj & adv comme ci comme ça.

sought /sɔːt/→SEEK.

soul /sǝʊl/ n âme f.

sound /saʊnd/ n son m, bruit m. ● adj solide; (healthy) sain; (sensible) sensé. ● vt/i sonner; (seem) sembler (**as if** que); (test) sonder; ~ **out** sonder; ~ **a horn** klaxonner; ~ **like** sembler être. ~ **asleep** adj profondément endormi. ~ **barrier** n mur m du son.

soundly /'saʊndlɪ/ adv (sleep) à poings fermés; (built) solidement.

sound-proof /'saʊndpruːf/ adj insonorisé. ● vt insonoriser.

sound-track /'saʊndtræk/ n bande f sonore.

soup /suːp/ n soupe f, potage m.

sour /saʊǝ(r)/ adj aigre. ● vt/i (s')aigrir.

source /sɔːs/ n source f.

south /saʊθ/ n sud m. ● adj sud inv, du sud. ● adv vers le sud.

South Africa n Afrique f du Sud.

South America n Amérique f du Sud.

south-east n sud-est m.

southern /'sʌðǝn/ adj du sud.

southerner n habitant/-e m/f du sud.

southward /'saʊθwǝd/ adj (side) sud inv; (journey) vers le sud.

south-west n sud-ouest m.

souvenir /suːvǝ'nɪǝ(r)/ n souvenir m.

sovereign /'sɒvrɪn/ n & a souverain/-e (m/f).

sow[1] /sǝʊ/ vt (pt sowed; pp sowed or sown) (seed) semer; (land) ensemencer.

sow[2] /saʊ/ n (pig) truie f.

soya /'sɔɪǝ/ n soja m. ~ **sauce** n sauce f soja.

spa /spɑː/ n station f thermale.

space /speɪs/ n espace m; (room) place f; (period) période f. ● adj (research) spatial. ● vt ~ **(out)** espacer. ~**craft** n inv, ~**ship** n engin m spatial. ~**suit** n combinaison f spatiale.

spacious /'speɪʃǝs/ adj spacieux.

spade /speɪd/ n (for garden) bêche f; (child's) pelle f; (cards) pique m. ~**work** n (fig) travail m préparatoire.

spaghetti /spǝ'getɪ/ n spaghetti mpl.

spam /spæm/ n (Comput) multipostage n abusif.

Spain /speɪn/ n Espagne f.

span /spæn/ n (of arch) portée f; (of wings) envergure f; (of time) durée f. ● vt (pt **spanned**) enjamber; (in time) embrasser.

Spaniard /'spænjǝd/ n Espagnol/ -e m/f.

spaniel /'spænjǝl/ n épagneul m.

Spanish /'spænɪʃ/ adj espagnol. ● n (Ling) espagnol m.

spank /spæŋk/ vt donner une fessée à.

spanner /'spænǝ(r)/ n (tool) clé f (plate); (adjustable) clé f à molette.

spare /speǝ(r)/ vt (treat leniently) épargner; (do without) se passer de; (afford to give) donner, accorder. ● adj en réserve; (surplus) de trop; (tyre, shoes) de rechange; (room, bed) d'ami; **are there any** ~ **tickets?** y a-t-il encore des places? ● n ~ **(part)** pièce f de rechange. ~ **time** n loisirs mpl.

sparing /'speərɪŋ/ adj frugal. **sparingly** adv en petite quantité.

spark /spɑːk/ n étincelle f. ● vt ~ **off** (initiate) provoquer.

sparkle /'spɑːkl/ vi étinceler. ● n étincellement m. **sparkling** adj (wine) mousseux; (eyes) brillant.

spark-plug n bougie f.

sparrow /'spærəʊ/ n moineau m.

sparse /spɑːs/ adj clairsemé. **sparsely** adv (furnished) peu.

spasm /'spæzəm/ n (of muscle) spasme m; (of coughing, anger) accès m.

spat /spæt/ →SPIT.

spate /speɪt/ n a ~ of (letters) une avalanche de.

spatter /'spætə(r)/ vt éclabousser (with de).

spawn /spɔːn/ n frai m, œufs mpl. ● vt pondre. ● vi frayer.

speak /spiːk/ vi (pt spoke; pp spoken) parler. ● vt (say) dire; (language) parler. □ ~ up parler plus fort.

speaker /'spiːkə(r)/ n (in public) orateur m; (Pol) président m; (loudspeaker) baffle m; **be a French/~ good ~** parler français/bien.

spear /spɪə(r)/ n lance f.

spearmint /'spɪəmɪnt/ n menthe f verte.

special /'speʃl/ adj spécial; (exceptional) exceptionnel.

specialist /'speʃəlɪst/ n spécialiste mf.

speciality, **specialty** /speʃɪ'ælətɪ/ n spécialité f.

specialize /'speʃəlaɪz/ vi se spécialiser (in en).

specially /'speʃəlɪ/ adv spécialement.

species /'spiːʃiːz/ n inv espèce f.

specific /spə'sɪfɪk/ adj précis,

explicite.

specification /spesɪfɪ'keɪʃn/ n (of design) spécification f; (of car equipment) caractéristiques fpl. **specify** vt spécifier.

specimen /'spesɪmən/ n spécimen m, échantillon m.

speck /spek/ n (stain) (petite) tache f; (particle) grain m.

specs /speks/ npl 🔟 lunettes fpl.

spectacle /'spektəkl/ n spectacle m. **spectacles** n lunettes fpl. **spectacular** adj spectaculaire.

spectator /spek'teɪtə(r)/ n spectateur/-trice m/f.

spectrum /'spektrəm/ n (pl **-tra**) spectre m; (of ideas) gamme f.

speculate /'spekjuleɪt/ vi s'interroger (about sur); (Comm) spéculer. **speculation** n conjectures fpl; (Comm) spéculation f. **speculator** n spéculateur/-trice m/f.

speech /spiːtʃ/ n (faculty) parole f; (diction) élocution f; (dialect) langage m; (address) discours m. **speechless** adj muet (with de).

speed /spiːd/ n (of movement) vitesse f; (swiftness) rapidité f. ~ **camera** n radar m. ~ **dating®** n rencontres fpl rapides, speed dating m. ● vi (pt sped) aller vite; (pt speeded) (drive too fast) aller trop vite. □ ~ up accélérer; (of pace) s'accélérer.

speedboat /'spiːdbəʊt/ n vedette f.

speeding /'spiːdɪŋ/ n excès m de vitesse.

speed limit n limitation f de vitesse.

speedometer /spɪ'dɒmɪtə(r)/ n compteur m (de vitesse).

spell /spel/ n (magic) charme m, sortilège m; (curse) sort m; (of time) (courte) période f. ● vt/i (pt spelled or **spelt**) écrire; (mean) signifier; ~ **out** épeler; (explain) expliquer. ~**checker** n correcteur m orthographique.

spelling /'spelɪŋ/ n orthographe f. ● adj (mistake) d'orthographe.

spend /spend/ vt (pt **spent**) (money) dépenser (**on** pour); (time, holiday) passer; (energy) consacrer (**on** à). ● vi dépenser.

spent /spent/ →SPEND. ● adj (used) utilisé; (person) épuisé.

sperm /spɜːm/ n (pl **sperms** or **sperm**) sperme m.

sphere /sfɪə(r)/ n sphère f.

spice /spaɪs/ n épice f; (fig) piquant m.

spick-and-span adj impeccable.

spicy /'spaɪsɪ/ adj épicé; piquant.

spider /'spaɪdə(r)/ n araignée f.

spike /spaɪk/ n pointe f.

spill /spɪl/ vt (pt **spilled** or **spilt**) renverser, répandre. ● vi se répandre; ~ **over** déborder.

spin /spɪn/ vt/i (pt **spun**; pres p **spinning**) (wool, web) filer; (turn) (faire) tourner; (story) débiter; ~ **out** faire durer. ● n (movement, excursion) tour m.

spinach /'spɪnɪdʒ/ n épinards mpl.

spinal /'spaɪnl/ adj vertébral. ~ **cord** n moelle f épinière.

spin-drier n essoreuse f.

spine /spaɪn/ n colonne f vertébrale; (prickle) piquant m.

spin-off n avantage m accessoire; (by-product) dérivé m.

spinster /'spɪnstə(r)/ n célibataire f; (pej) vieille fille f.

spiral /'spaɪərəl/ adj en spirale; (staircase) en colimaçon. ● n spirale f. ● vi (pt **spiralled**) (prices) monter (en flèche).

spire /'spaɪə(r)/ n flèche f.

spirit /'spɪrɪt/ n esprit m; (boldness) courage m; ~s (morale) moral m; (drink) spiritueux mpl. ● vt ~ **away** faire disparaître. **spirited** adj fougueux. ~**level** n niveau m à bulle.

spiritual /'spɪrɪtʃʊəl/ adj spirituel.

spit /spɪt/ vt/i (pt **spat** or **spit**; pres p **spitting**) cracher; (of rain) crachiner; ~ **out** cracher; **the ~ting image of** le portrait craché or vivant de. ● n crachat(s) m(pl); (for meat) broche f.

spite /spaɪt/ n rancune f; **in ~ of** malgré. ● vt contrarier.

splash /splæʃ/ vt éclabousser. ● vi faire des éclaboussures; ~ (**about**) patauger. ● n (act, mark) éclaboussure f; (sound) plouf m; (of colour) tache f.

spleen /spliːn/ n (Anat) rate f.

splendid /'splendɪd/ adj magnifique, splendide.

splint /splɪnt/ n (Med) attelle f.

splinter /'splɪntə(r)/ n éclat m; (in finger) écharde f. ~ **group** n groupe m dissident.

split /splɪt/ vt/i (pt **split**; pres p **splitting**) (se) fendre; (tear) (se) déchirer; (divide) (se) diviser; (share) partager; ~ **one's sides** se tordre (de rire). ● n fente f; déchirure f; (share 🏗) part f, partage m; (quarrel) rupture f; (Pol) scission f. □ ~ **up** (couple) rompre. ~ **second** n fraction f de seconde.

splutter /'splʌtə(r)/ vi crachoter; (stammer) bafouiller; (engine) tousser.

spoil /spɔɪl/ vt (pt **spoilt** or **spoiled**) (pamper) gâter; (ruin) abîmer; (mar) gâcher, gâter. ● n ~(s) butin m. ~**sport** n trouble-fête mf inv.

spoke[1] /spəʊk/ n rayon m.

spoke[2], **spoken** →SPEAK.

spokesman /ˈspəʊksmən/ n (pl **-men**) porteparole m inv.

sponge /spʌndʒ/ n éponge f. ● vi ~ **on** vivre aux crochets de. ~-**bag** n trousse f de toilette. ~-**cake** n génoise f.

sponsor /ˈspɒnsə(r)/ n (of concert) parrain m, sponsor m; (surety) garant m; (for membership) parrain m, marraine f. ● vt parrainer, sponsoriser; (member) parrainer. **sponsorship** n patronage m; parrainage m.

spontaneous /spɒnˈteɪnɪəs/ adj spontané.

spoof /spuːf/ n ① parodie f.

spoon /spuːn/ n cuiller f, cuillère f.

spoonful /ˈspuːnfʊl/ n (pl ~**s**) cuillerée f.

sport /spɔːt/ n sport m; (**good sport**) ~ (person ①) chic type m; (~**s car/coat**) voiture/veste f de sport. ● vt (display) exhiber, arborer.

sporting /ˈspɔːtɪŋ/ adj sportif; **a** ~ **chance** une assez bonne chance.

sportsman /ˈspɔːtsmən/ n (pl **-men**) sportif m.

sporty /ˈspɔːtɪ/ adj ① sportif.

spot /spɒt/ n (mark, stain) tache f; (dot) point m; (in pattern) pois m; (drop) goutte f; (place) endroit m; (pimple) bouton m; **a** ~ **of** ① un peu de; **on the** ~ sur place; (without delay) sur le coup. ● vt (pt **spotted**) ① apercevoir. ~ **check** n contrôle m surprise.

spotless /ˈspɒtlɪs/ adj impeccable.

spotlight /ˈspɒtlaɪt/ n (lamp) projecteur m, spot m.

spotty /ˈspɒtɪ/ adj (skin) boutonneux.

spouse /spaʊz/ n époux m, épouse f.

spout /spaʊt/ n (of teapot) bec m; (of liquid) jet m; **up the** ~ (ruined ①) fichu. ● vi jaillir.

sprain /spreɪn/ n entorse f, foulure f. ● vt ~ **one's wrist** se fouler le poignet.

sprang /spræŋ/ ⇒SPRING.

sprawl /sprɔːl/ vi (town, person) s'étaler. ● n étalement m.

spray /spreɪ/ n (of flowers) gerbe f; (water) gerbe f d'eau; (from sea) embruns mpl; (device) bombe f, atomiseur m. ● vt (surface, insecticide, plant) vaporiser; (person) asperger; (crops) traiter.

spread /spred/ vt/i (pt **spread**) (stretch, extend) (s')étendre; (news, fear) (se) répandre; (illness) (se) propager; (butter) (s')étaler. ● n propagation f (of population) distribution f; (paste) pâte f à tartiner; (food) belle table f. ~-**eagled** adj bras et jambes écartés. ~**sheet** n tableur m.

spree /spriː/ n **go on a** ~ (have fun ①) faire la noce.

sprig /sprɪg/ n petite branche f.

sprightly /ˈspraɪtlɪ/ adj (-**ier**, -**est**) alerte, vif.

spring /sprɪŋ/ vi (pt **sprang**; pp **sprung**) bondir. ● vt ~ **sth on sb** annoncer qch de but en blanc à qn. ● n bond m; (device) ressort m; (season) printemps m; (of water) source f. ~ **from** provenir de; ~ **up** surgir. ~**board** n tremplin m. ~ **onion** n oignon m blanc.

springy /ˈsprɪŋɪ/ adj (-**ier**, -**iest**) élastique.

sprinkle /ˈsprɪŋkl/ vt (with liquid) arroser (**with** de); (with salt, flour) saupoudrer (**with** de); (sand) répandre. **sprinkler** n (in garden) arroseur m; (for fires) extincteur m (à déclenchement) automatique.

sprint /sprɪnt/ vi (Sport) sprinter. ● n sprint m.

sprout /spraʊt/ vt/i pousser. ●

(on plant) pousse f; (Brussels) ∼s choux mpl de Bruxelles.

spruce /spru:s/ adj pimpant. ● vt ∼ oneself up se faire beau. ● n (tree) épicéa m.

sprung /sprʌŋ/ →SPRING.

spud /spʌd/ n 🔢 patate f.

spun /spʌn/ →SPIN.

spur /spɜ:(r)/ n (of rider) éperon m; (stimulus) aiguillon m; **on the ∼ of the moment** sous l'impulsion du moment. ● vt (pt **spurred**) éperonner.

spurious /ˈspjʊəriəs/ adj faux.

spurn /spɜ:n/ vt repousser.

spurt /spɜ:t/ vi jaillir; (fig) accélérer. ● n jet m; (of energy) sursaut m.

spy /spaɪ/ n espion/-ne m/f. ● vi espionner. ● vt apercevoir.

squabble /ˈskwɒbl/ vi se chamailler. ● n chamaillerie f.

squad /skwɒd/ n (of soldiers) escouade f; (Sport) équipe f.

squadron /ˈskwɒdrən/ n (Mil) escadron m; (Aviat) escadrille f.

squalid /ˈskwɒlɪd/ adj sordide.

squander /ˈskwɒndə(r)/ vt (money, time) gaspiller.

square /skweə(r)/ n carré m; (open space in town) place f. ● adj carré; (honest) honnête; (meal) solide; (boring 🔢) ringard; **(all) ∼ (quits)** quitte; ∼ **metre** mètre m carré. ● vt (settle) régler; ∼ **up to** faire face à.

squash /skwɒʃ/ vt écraser; (crowd) serrer. ● n (game) squash m; (marrow; US) courge f; **lemon ∼** citronnade f; **orange ∼** orangeade f.

squat /skwɒt/ vi (pt **squatted**) s'accroupir; ∼ **in a house** squatteriser une maison. ● adj (dumpy) trapu. **squatter** n squatter m.

squawk /skwɔ:k/ n cri m rauque. ● vi pousser un cri rauque.

squeak /skwi:k/ n petit cri m; (of door) grincement m. ● vi crier; grincer.

squeal /skwi:l/ n cri m aigu. ● vi pousser un cri aigu; ∼ **on** (inform on 🔢) dénoncer.

squeamish /ˈskwi:mɪʃ/ adj (trop) délicat.

squeeze /skwi:z/ vt presser; (hand, arm) serrer; (extract) exprimer (**from** de); (extort) soutirer (**from** à). ● vi (force one's way) se glisser. ● n pression f; (Comm) restrictions fpl de crédit.

squid /skwɪd/ n calmar m.

squint /skwɪnt/ vi loucher; (with half-shut eyes) plisser les yeux. ● n (Med) strabisme m.

squirm /skwɜ:m/ vi se tortiller.

squirrel /ˈskwɪrəl/ n écureuil m.

squirt /skwɜ:t/ vt/i (faire) jaillir. ● n jet m.

stab /stæb/ vt (pt **stabbed**) (with knife) poignarder. ● n (of couteau); **have a ∼ at sth** essayer de faire qch.

stability /stəˈbɪlətɪ/ n stabilité f. **stabilize** vt stabiliser.

stable /ˈsteɪbl/ adj stable. ● n écurie f. ∼**-boy** n lad m.

stack /stæk/ n tas m. ● vt (∼ **up**) entasser, empiler.

stadium /ˈsteɪdɪəm/ n stade m.

staff /stɑ:f/ n personnel m; (in school) professeurs mpl; (Mil) étatmajor m; (stick) bâton m. ● vt pourvoir en personnel.

stag /stæg/ n cerf m.

stage /steɪdʒ/ n (Theat) scène f; (phase) stade m, étape f; (platform in hall) estrade f; **go on the ∼** faire du théâtre. ● vt mettre en scène; (fig) organiser. ∼ **door** n entrée f des artistes. ∼ **fright** n trac m.

stagger /ˈstægə(r)/ vi chanceler.

● vt (shock) stupéfier; (payments) échelonner. **staggering** adj stupéfiant.

stagnate /stæg'neɪt/ vi stagner.

stag night n soirée f pour enterrer une vie de garçon.

staid /steɪd/ adj sérieux.

stain /steɪn/ vt tacher; (wood) colorer. ● n tache f; (colouring) colorant m. **stained glass window** n vitrail m.

stainless steel n acier m inoxydable.

stain remover n détachant m.

stair /steə(r)/ n marche f; **the ~s** l'escalier m. **~case**, **~way** n escalier m.

stake /steɪk/ n (post) pieu m; (wager) enjeu m; **at ~** en jeu. ● vt (area) jalonner; (wager) jouer; **~ a claim to** revendiquer.

stale /steɪl/ adj pas frais; (bread) rassis; (smell) de renfermé.

stalk /stɔːk/ n (of plant) tige f. ● vi marcher de façon guindée. ● vt (hunter) chasser; (murderer) suivre.

stall /stɔːl/ n (in stable) stalle f; (in market) éventaire m; **~s** (Theat) orchestre m. ● vt/i (Auto) caler; **~ (for time)** temporiser.

stallion /'stælɪən/ n étalon m.

stamina /'stæmɪnə/ n résistance f.

stammer /'stæmə(r)/ vt/i bégayer. ● n bégaiement m.

stamp /stæmp/ vt/i **~ (one's foot)** taper du pied. ● vt (letter) timbrer. ● n (for postage, marking) timbre m; (mark: fig) sceau m. **~ out** supprimer. **~-collecting** n philatélie f.

stampede /stæm'piːd/ n fuite f désordonnée; (rush: fig) ruée f. ● vi s'enfuir en désordre; se ruer.

stand /stænd/ vi (pt **stood**) être or se tenir (debout); (rise) se lever; (be situated) se trouver; (Pol) être can-

didat (for à); **~ in line** (US) faire la queue; **~ to reason** être logique. ● vt mettre (debout); (tolerate) supporter; **~ a chance** avoir une chance. ● n (stance) position f; (Mil) résistance f; (for lamp) support m; (at fair) stand m; (in street) kiosque m; (for spectators) tribune f; (Jur, US) barre f. **make a ~** prendre position. **~ back** reculer. **~ by** or **around** ne rien faire; **~ by** (be ready) se tenir prêt; (promise, person) rester fidèle à; **~ down** se désister; **~ for** représenter; Ⓣ supporter; **~ in for** remplacer; **~ out** ressortir; **~ up** se lever; **~ up for** défendre; **~ up to** résister à.

standard /'stændəd/ n norme f; (level) niveau m (voulu); (flag) étendard m; **~ of living** niveau m de vie; **~s** (morals) principes mpl. ● adj ordinaire.

standard of living n niveau m de vie.

standby /'stændbaɪ/ adj de réserve. ● n **be a ~** être de réserve.

stand-in /'stændɪn/ n remplaçant/-e m/f.

standing /'stændɪŋ/ adj debout inv. ● n réputation f; (duration) durée f; **~ order** n prélèvement m bancaire.

standpoint /'stændpɔɪnt/ n point m de vue.

standstill /'stændstɪl/ n **at a ~** immobile; **bring/come to a ~** (s')immobiliser.

stank /stæŋk/ ➡**STINK**.

staple /'steɪpl/ n agrafe f. ● vt agrafer. ● adj principal, de base. **stapler** n agrafeuse f.

star /stɑː(r)/ n étoile f; (person) vedette f. ● vt (pt **starred**) (film) avoir pour vedette. ● vi **~ in** être la vedette de.

starch /stɑːtʃ/ n amidon m; (in food) fécule f. ● vt amidonner.

stardom /'stɑːdəm/ n célébrité f.

stare /steə(r)/ vi ~ **at** regarder fixement. ● n regard m fixe.

starfish /'stɑːfɪʃ/ n étoile f de mer.

stark /stɑːk/ adj (desolate) désolé; (severe) austère; (utter) complet; (fact) brutal. ● adv complètement.

starling /'stɑːlɪŋ/ n étourneau m.

start /stɑːt/ vt/i commencer; (machine) (se) mettre en marche; (fashion) lancer; (cause) provoquer; (jump) sursauter; (of vehicle) démarrer; ~ **to do** commencer or se mettre à faire; ~**ing tomorrow** à partir de demain. ● n commencement m, début m; (of race) départ m; (lead) avance f; (jump) sursaut m. □ ~ **off** commencer (pour faire); ~ **out** partir; ~ **up** (business) lancer. **starter** n (Auto) démarreur m; (runner) partant m; (Culin) entrée f.

starting point n point m de départ.

startle /'stɑːtl/ vt (make jump) faire tressaillir; (shock) alarmer.

starvation /stɑː'veɪʃn/ n faim f.

starve /stɑːv/ vi mourir de faim. ● vt affamer; (deprive) priver.

stash /stæʃ/ vt cacher.

state /steɪt/ n état m; (pomp) apparat m; S~ état m; **the S~s** les États-Unis; **get into a ~** s'affoler. ● adj d'état, de l'état; (school) public. ● vt affirmer (that que); (views) exprimer; (fix) fixer.

State school Environ 90% des élèves britanniques font leur scolarité dans une *state school* (école publique). L'enseignement y est gratuit et suit le programme scolaire national établi par le gouvernement. À l'entrée dans le secondaire, les élèves intègrent normalement une *comprehensive school*, ou, à l'issue d'un examen d'entrée, une *grammar school*. ▷**PUBLIC SCHOOLS**.

stately /'steɪtlɪ/ adj (**-ier, -iest**) majestueux. ~ **home** n château m.

statement /'steɪtmənt/ n déclaration f; (of account) relevé m.

statesman /'steɪtsmən/ n (pl **-men**) homme m d'état.

static /'stætɪk/ adj statique. ● n (radio, TV) parasites mpl.

station /'steɪʃn/ n (Rail) gare f; (TV) chaîne f; (Mil) poste m; (rank) condition f. ● vt poster, placer; ~**ed at** or **in** (Mil) en garnison à.

stationary /'steɪʃənrɪ/ adj immobile, stationnaire; (vehicle) à l'arrêt.

stationery /'steɪʃənrɪ/ n papeterie f.

station wagon n (US) break m.

statistic /stə'tɪstɪk/ n statistique f; ~**s** statistique f.

statue /'stætʃuː/ n statue f.

status /'steɪtəs/ n (pl ~**es**) situation f, statut m; (prestige) standing m.

statute /'stætʃuːt/ n loi f; ~**s** (rules) statuts mpl. **statutory** adj statutaire; (holiday) légal.

staunch /stɔːntʃ/ adj (friend) loyal, fidèle.

stave /steɪv/ n (Mus) portée f. ● vt ~ **off** éviter, conjurer.

stay /steɪ/ vi rester; (spend time) séjourner; (reside) loger. ● vt (hunger) tromper. ● n séjour m. □ ~ **away from** (school) ne pas aller à; ~ **behind** or **on** rester; ~ **in** rester à la maison; ~ **up** veiller, se coucher tard.

stead /sted/ n **stand sb in good ~** être utile à qn.

steadfast /'stedfɑːst/ adj ferme.

steady /'stedɪ/ adj (-ier, -iest) stable; (hand, voice) ferme; (regular) régulier; (staid) sérieux. ● vt maintenir, assurer; (calm) calmer.

steak /steɪk/ n steak m, bifteck m; (of fish) darne f.

steal /stiːl/ vt/i (pt **stole**, pp **stolen**) voler (**from** sb à qn).

steam /stiːm/ n vapeur f; (on glass) buée f. ● vt (cook) cuire à la vapeur. ● vi fumer. ~-**engine** n locomotive f à vapeur.

steamer /'stiːmə(r)/ n (Culin) cuit-vapeur m; (boat) (bateau à) vapeur m.

steel /stiːl/ n acier m; ~ **industry** sidérurgie f. ● vpr ~ **oneself** s'endurcir, se cuirasser.

steep /stiːp/ adj raide, rapide; (price: 🔢) excessif. ● vt (soak) tremper; ~**ed in** (fig) imprégné de.

steeple /'stiːpl/ n clocher m.

steer /stɪə(r)/ vt diriger; (ship) gouverner; (fig) guider. ● vi (in ship) gouverner; ~ **clear of** éviter.

steering-wheel n volant m.

stem /stem/ n tige f; (of glass) pied m. ● vi (pt **stemmed**) ~ **from** provenir de. ● vt (pt **stemmed**) (check, stop) endiguer, contenir. ~ **cell** n cellule f souche.

stench /stentʃ/ n puanteur f.

stencil /'stensɪl/ n pochoir m. ● vt (pt **stencilled**) décorer au pochoir.

step /step/ vi (pt **stepped**) marcher, aller. ● n pas m; (stair) marche f; (of train) marchepied m; (action) mesure f; ~**s** (ladder) escabeau m; **in** ~ au pas; (fig) conforme (**with** à). ~ **down** (resign) démissionner; (from ladder) descendre; ~ **forward** faire un pas en avant; ~ **in** (intervene) intervenir; ~ **up** (pressure) augmenter. ~**brother** n demi-frère m. ~**daughter** n belle-fille f.

~**father** n beau-père m. ~**ladder** n escabeau m. ~**mother** n belle-mère f. **stepping-stone** n (fig) tremplin m. ~**sister** n demi-sœur f. ~**son** n beau-fils m.

stereo /'sterɪəʊ/ n stéréo f; (record-player) chaîne f stéréo. ● adj stéréo inv.

stereotype /'sterɪətaɪp/ n stéréotype m.

sterile /'steraɪl/ adj stérile. **sterility** n stérilité f.

sterilize /'sterəlaɪz/ vt stériliser.

sterling /'stɜːlɪŋ/ n livre(s) f (pl) sterling. ● adj sterling inv; (silver) fin; (fig) excellent.

stern /stɜːn/ adj sévère. ● n (of ship) arrière m.

steroid /'stɪərɔɪd/ n stéroïde m.

stew /stjuː/ vt/i cuire à la casserole; ~**ed fruit** compote f; ~**ed tea** thé m trop infusé. ● n ragoût m.

steward /stjʊəd/ n (of club) intendant m; (on ship) steward m. **stewardess** n hôtesse f.

stick /stɪk/ vt (pt **stuck**) (glue) coller; (put 🔢) mettre; (endure 🔢) supporter. ● vi (adhere) coller, adhérer; (to pan) attacher; (remain 🔢) rester; (be jammed) être coincé; **be stuck with** sb 🔢 se farcir qn. ● n bâton m; (for walking) canne f. ~ **at** persévérer dans; ~ **out** vt (head) sortir; (tongue) tirer; vi (protrude) dépasser; ~ **to** (promise) rester fidèle à; ~ **up for** 🔢 défendre.

sticker /'stɪkə(r)/ n autocollant m.

sticky /'stɪkɪ/ adj -ier, -iest poisseux; (label, tape) adhésif.

stiff /stɪf/ adj raide; (limb, joint) ankylosé; (tough) dur; (drink) fort; (price) élevé; (manner) guindé; ~ **neck** torticolis m.

stifle /'staɪfl/ vt/i étouffer.

stiletto /str'letəʊ/ adj & n ~s, ~ **heels** talons mpl aiguille.

still /stɪl/ adj immobile; (quiet) calme, tranquille; (keep ~!) arrête de bouger! ● n silence m. ● adv encore, toujours; (even) encore; (nevertheless) tout de même.

stillborn /stɪlbɔːn/ adj mort-né.

still life n nature f morte.

stimulate /'stɪmjʊleɪt/ vt stimuler. **stimulation** n stimulation f.

stimulus /'stɪmjʊləs/ n (pl -li) (spur) stimulant m.

sting /stɪŋ/ n piqûre f; (of insect) aiguillon m. ● vt/i (pt stung) piquer.

stingy /'stɪndʒɪ/ adj (-ier, -iest) avare (with de).

stink /stɪŋk/ n puanteur f. ● vi (pt stank or stunk; pp stunk) ~ (of) puer.

stipulate /'stɪpjʊleɪt/ vt stipuler.

stir /stɜː(r)/ vt/i (pt stirred) (move) remuer; (excite) exciter; ~ up (trouble) provoquer. ● n agitation f.

stirrup /'stɪrəp/ n étrier m.

stitch /stɪtʃ/ n point m; (in knitting) maille f; (Med) point m de suture; (muscle pain) point m de côté; **be in ~es** 🔲 avoir le fou rire. ● vt coudre.

stock /stɒk/ n réserve f; (Comm) stock m; (financial) valeurs fpl; (family) souche f; (soup) bouillon m; **we're out of ~** il n'y en a plus; **take ~** (fig) faire le point; **in ~** en stock. ● adj (goods) courant. ● vt (shop) approvisionner; (sell) vendre. ● vi ~ **up** s'approvisionner (with de). ~**broker** n agent m de change. ~**cube** n bouillon-cube m. **S~ Exchange** n Bourse f.

stocking /'stɒkɪŋ/ n bas m.

stock market n Bourse f.

stockpile /'stɒkpaɪl/ n stock m. ● vt stocker; (arms) amasser.

stock-taking n (Comm) inventaire m.

stocky /'stɒkɪ/ adj (-ier, -iest) trapu.

stodgy /'stɒdʒɪ/ adj lourd.

stole, stolen ➡STEAL.

stomach /'stʌmək/ n estomac m; (abdomen) ventre m. ● vt (put up with) supporter. ~**ache** n mal m à l'estomac ou au ventre.

stone /stəʊn/ n pierre f; (pebble) caillou m; (in fruit) noyau m; (weight) 6,350 kg. ● adj de pierre; ~**cold**-**deaf** complètement froid/ sourd. ● vt (throw stones) lapider; (fruit) dénoyauter.

stony /'stəʊnɪ/ adj pierreux.

stood /stʊd/ ➡STAND.

stool /stuːl/ n tabouret m.

stoop /stuːp/ vi (bend) se baisser; (condescend) s'abaisser. ● n **have a** ~ être voûté.

stop /stɒp/ vt/i (pt stopped) arrêter (doing de faire); (moving, talking) s'arrêter; (prevent) empêcher (from de); (hole, leak) boucher; (pain, noise) cesser; (stay 🔲) rester. ● n arrêt m; (full stop) point m;~ (-over) halte f; (port of call) escale f ~ **off** s'arrêter; ~ **up** boucher.

stopgap /'stɒpgæp/ n bouche-trou m. ● adj intérimaire.

stoppage /'stɒpɪdʒ/ n arrêt m; (of work) arrêt m de travail; (of pay) retenue f.

stopper /'stɒpə(r)/ n bouchon m.

stop-watch n chronomètre m.

storage /'stɔːrɪdʒ/ n (of goods, food) emmagasinage m. ~ **heater** n radiateur m électrique à accumulation.

store /stɔː(r)/ n réserve f; (warehouse) entrepôt m; (shop) grand magasin m; (US) magasin m; **have in** ~ **for** réserver à; **set** ~ **by** attacher du prix à. ● vt (for future) mettre en réserve; (in warehouse, mind) emmagasiner. **~-room** n réserve f.

storey /'stɔːrɪ/ n étage m.

stork /stɔːk/ n cigogne f.

storm /stɔːm/ n tempête f, orage m. ● vt prendre d'assaut. ● vi (rage) tempêter.

story /'stɔːrɪ/ n histoire f; (in press) article m; (storey: US) étage m. **~-teller** n conteur/-euse m/f.

stout /staʊt/ adj corpulent; (strong) solide. ● n bière f brune.

stove /stəʊv/ n cuisinière f.

stow /stəʊ/ vt ~ **away** (put away) ranger; (hide) cacher. ● vi voyager clandestinement.

straddle /'strædl/ vt être à cheval sur, enjamber.

straggler /'stræglə(r)/ n traînard/-e m/f.

straight /streɪt/ adj droit; (tidy) en ordre; (frank) franc; ~ **face** visage m sérieux; **get sth** ~ mettre qch au clair. ● adv (in straight line) droit; (direct) tout droit; ~ **ahead** or on tout droit; ~ **away** tout de suite; ~ **off** 1 sans hésiter. ● n (Sport) ligne f droite.

straighten /'streɪtn/ vt (nail, situation) redresser; (tidy) arranger.

straightforward /streɪt'fɔːwəd/ adj honnête; (easy) simple.

straight off adj 1 sans hésiter.

strain /streɪn/ vt (rope, ears) tendre; (limb) fouler; (eyes) fatiguer; (muscle) froisser; (filter) passer; (vegetables) égoutter; (fig) mettre à l'épreuve. ● vi fournir des efforts. ● n tension f; (fig) effort m; (breed) race f; (of virus) variété f; ~s (tune: Mus) accents mpl. **strained** adj forcé; (relations) tendu. **strainer** n passoire f.

strait /streɪt/ n détroit m; ~s dé-

troit m; **be in dire ~s** être aux abois. **~-jacket** n camisole f de force.

strand /strænd/ n (thread) fil m, brin m; (of hair) mèche f.

stranded /'strændɪd/ adj (person) en rade; (ship) échoué.

strange /streɪndʒ/ adj étrange; (unknown) inconnu. **stranger** n inconnu/-e m/f.

strangle /'stræŋgl/ vt étrangler.

stranglehold /'stræŋglhəʊld/ n have a ~ on tenir à la gorge.

strap /stræp/ n (of leather) courroie f; (of dress) bretelle f; (of watch) bracelet m. ● vt (pt **strapped**) attacher.

strategic /strə'tiːdʒɪk/ adj stratégique. **strategy** n stratégie f.

straw /strɔː/ n paille f; **the last** ~ le comble.

strawberry /'strɔːbrɪ/ n fraise f.

stray /streɪ/ vi s'égarer; (deviate) s'écarter. ● adj perdu; (isolated) isolé. ● n animal m perdu.

streak /striːk/ n raie f, bande f; (trace) trace f; (period) période f; (tendency) tendance f. ● vt (mark) strier. ● vi filer à toute allure.

stream /striːm/ n ruisseau m; (current) courant m; (flow) flot m; (in school) classe f (de niveau). ● vi ruisseler (with de); (eyes, nose) couler.

streamline /'striːmlaɪn/ vt rationaliser. **streamlined** adj (shape) aérodynamique.

street /striːt/ n rue f; **~car** n (US) tramway m. **~ lamp** n réverbère m. **~ map** n indicateur m des rues.

strength /streŋθ/ n force f; (of wall, fabric) solidité f; **on the ~ of** en vertu de. **strengthen** vt renforcer, fortifier.

strenuous /'strenjʊəs/ adj (exercise) énergique; (work) ardu.

stress /stres/ n (emphasis) accent m; (pressure) pression f; (Med) stress m. ● vt souligner, insister sur.

stretch /stretʃ/ vt (pull taut) tendre; (arm, leg) étendre; (neck) tendre; (clothes) étirer; (truth) forcer; ~ **one's legs** se dégourdir les jambes. ● vi s'étendre; (person) s'étirer; (clothes) se déformer. ● n étendue f; (period) période f; (of road) tronçon m; **at a** ~ d'affilée. ● adj (fabric) extensible.

stretcher /stretʃə(r)/ n brancard m.

strew /struː/ vt (pt **strewed**;pp **strewed** or **strewn**) (scatter) répandre; (cover) joncher.

strict /strɪkt/ adj strict.

stride /straɪd/ vi (pt **strode**; pp **stridden**) faire de grands pas. ● n grand pas m.

strife /straɪf/ n conflit(s) m(pl).

strike /straɪk/ vt (pt **struck**) frapper; (blow) donner; (match) frotter; (gold) trouver. ● vi faire grève; (attack) attaquer; (clock) sonner. ● n (of workers) grève f; (Mil) attaque f; (find) découverte f; **on** ~ en grève. □ ~ **off** or **out** rayer; ~ **up** (a friendship) lier amitié (**with** avec).

striker n gréviste mf; (football) attaquant/-e mf.

string /strɪŋ/ n ficelle f; (of violin, racket) corde f; (of pearls) collier m; (of lies) chapelet m; **the** ~s (Mus) les cordes; **pull** ~s faire jouer ses relations. ● vt (pt **strung**) (thread) enfiler. **stringed** adj (instrument) à cordes.

stringent /strɪndʒənt/ adj rigoureux, strict.

stringy /strɪŋɪ/ adj filandreux.

strip /strɪp/ vt/i (pt **stripped**) (un-

dress) (se) déshabiller; (deprive) dépouiller. ● n bande f.

stripe /straɪp/ n rayure f, raie f. **striped** adj rayé.

strip light n néon m.

stripper /strɪpə(r)/ n stripteaseur/-euse m/f; (solvent) décapant.

strip-tease n strip-tease m.

strive /straɪv/ vi (pt **strove**; pp **striven**) s'efforcer (**to** de).

strode /strəʊd/ →STRIDE.

stroke /strəʊk/ vt (with hand) caresser. ● n coup m; (of pen) trait m; (swimming) nage f; (Med) attaque f, congestion f; **at a** ~ d'un seul coup.

stroll /strəʊl/ vi flâner; ~ **in** entrer tranquillement. ● n petit tour m. **stroller** n (US) poussette f.

strong /strɒŋ/ adj fort; (shoes, fabric) solide; **be fifty** ~ être fort de cinquante personnes. ~**hold** n bastion m.

strongly /strɒŋlɪ/ adv (greatly) fortement; (with energy) avec force; (deeply) profondément.

strove /strəʊv/ →STRIVE.

struck /strʌk/ →STRIKE.

structure /strʌktʃə(r)/ n (of cell, poem) structure f; (building) construction f.

struggle /strʌgl/ vi lutter, se battre. ● n lutte f; (effort) effort m; **have a** ~ to avoir du mal à.

strum /strʌm/ vt (pt **strummed**) gratter de.

strung /strʌŋ/ →STRING. ● adj ~ **up** (tense) nerveux.

strut /strʌt/ n (support) étai m. ● vi (pt **strutted**) se pavaner.

stub /stʌb/ n bout m; (counterfoil) talon m. ● vt (pt **stubbed**) ~ **one's toe** se cogner le doigt de pied. □ ~ **out** écraser.

stubble | submissive

stubble /'stʌbl/ n (on chin) barbe f de plusieurs jours; (remains of wheat) chaume f.

stubborn /'stʌbən/ adj obstiné.

stuck /stʌk/ →STICK.● adj (jammed) coincé; **I'm ~** (for answer) je sèche. **~-up** adj f/ prétentieux.

stud /stʌd/ n (on jacket) clou m; (for collar) bouton m; (stallion) étalon m; (horse farm) haras m. ● vt (pt **studded**) clouter.

student /'stju:dnt/ n (Univ) étudiant/-e m/f; (School) élève mf. ● adj (restaurant, life) universitaire.

studio /'stju:dɪəʊ/ n studio m.

studious /'stju:dɪəs/ adj (person) studieux; (deliberate) étudié.

study /'stʌdɪ/ n étude f; (office) bureau m. ● vt/i étudier.

stuff /stʌf/ n chose (s) f (pl). ● vt rembourrer; (animal) empailler; (cram) bourrer; (Culin) farcir; (block up) boucher; (put) fourrer. **stuffing** n bourre f; (Culin) farce f.

stuffy /'stʌfɪ/ adj (-ier, -iest) mal aéré; (dull 🛈) vieux jeu inv.

stumble /'stʌmbl/ vi trébucher; **~ across** or **on** tomber sur. **stumbling block** n obstacle m.

stump /stʌmp/ n (of tree) souche f; (of limb) moignon m; (of pencil) bout m.

stumped /stʌmpt/ adj embarrassé.

stun /stʌn/ vt (pt **stunned**) étourdir; (bewilder) stupéfier.

stung /stʌŋ/ →STING.

stunk /stʌŋk/ →STINK.

stunning /'stʌnɪŋ/ adj (delightful 🛈) sensationnel.

stunt /stʌnt/ vt (growth) retarder. ● n (feat 🛈) tour m de force; (trick 🛈) truc m; (dangerous) cascade f.

stupid /'stju:pɪd/ adj stupide, bête.

stupidity n stupidité f.

sturdy /'stɜːdɪ/ adj (-ier, -iest) robuste.

stutter /'stʌtə(r)/ vi bégayer. ● n bégaiement m.

sty /staɪ/ n (pigsty) porcherie f; (on eye) orgelet m.

style /staɪl/ n style m; (fashion) mode f; (sort) genre m; (pattern) modèle m; **do sth in ~** faire qch avec classe. ● vt (design) créer; **~ sb's hair** coiffer qn.

stylish /'staɪlɪʃ/ adj élégant.

stylist /'staɪlɪst/ n (of hair) coiffeur/-euse m/f.

suave /swɑːv/ adj (urbane) courtois; (smooth: pej) doucereux.

subconscious /sʌb'kɒnʃəs/ adj & n inconscient (m), subconscient (m.)

subcontract /sʌbkən'trækt/ vt sous-traiter.

subdue /səb'dju:/ vt (feeling) maîtriser; (country) subjuguer. **subdued** adj (person, mood) morose; (light) tamisé; (criticism) contenu.

subject[1] /'sʌbdʒɪkt/ adj (state) soumis; **~ to** soumis à; (liable to, dependent on) sujet à. ● n sujet m; (focus) objet m; (School,Univ) matière f; (citizen) ressortissant/-e m/f, sujet/-te m/f.

subject[2] /səb'dʒekt/ vt soumettre.

subjective /səb'dʒektɪv/ adj subjectif.

subject-matter n contenu m.

subjunctive /səb'dʒʌŋktɪv/ adj & n subjonctif (m.)

sublet /sʌb'let/ vt sous-louer.

submarine /sʌbmə'ri:n/ n sousmarin m.

submerge /səb'mɜːdʒ/ vt submerger. ● vi plonger.

submissive /səb'mɪsɪv/ adj soumis.

submit /səb'mɪt/ vt/i (pt submitted) (se) soumettre (to à).

subordinate /sə'bɔːdɪnət/ adj subalterne; (Gram) subordonné. ● n subordonné/-e m/f.

subpoena /sə'piːnə/ n (Jur) citation f, assignation f.

subscribe /səb'skraɪb/ vt/i verser (de l'argent) (to à). **~ to** (loan, theory) souscrire à; (newspaper) s'abonner à, être abonné à. **subscriber** n abonné/-e m/f. **subscription** n abonnement m; (membership dues) cotisation f.

subsequent /'sʌbsɪkwənt/ adj (later) ultérieur; (next) suivant. **subsequently** adv par la suite.

subside /səb'saɪd/ vi (land) s'affaisser; (flood, wind) baisser.

subsidiary /səb'sɪdɪərɪ/ adj accessoire. ● n (Comm) filiale f.

subsidize /'sʌbsɪdaɪz/ vt subventionner. **subsidy** n subvention f.

substance /'sʌbstəns/ n substance f.

substandard /sʌb'stændəd/ adj de qualité inférieure.

substantial /səb'stænʃl/ adj considérable; (meal) substantiel.

substitute /'sʌbstɪtjuːt/ n succédané m; (person) remplaçant/-e m/f. ● vt substituer (for à).

subtitle /'sʌbtaɪtl/ n sous-titre m.

subtle /'sʌtl/ adj subtil.

subtract /səb'trækt/ vt soustraire.

suburb /'sʌbɜːb/ n faubourg m, banlieue f; **~s** banlieue f. **suburban** adj de banlieue. **suburbia** n la banlieue.

subway /'sʌbweɪ/ n passage m souterrain; (US) métro m.

succeed /sək'siːd/ vi réussir (in doing à faire). ● vt (follow) succéder à.

success /sək'ses/ n succès m,

réussite f.

successful /sək'sesfl/ adj réussi, couronné de succès; (favourable) heureux; (in exam) reçu; **be ~ in doing** réussir à faire.

succession /sək'seʃn/ n succession f; **in ~** de suite.

successive /sək'sesɪv/ adj successif; **six ~ days** six jours consécutifs.

successor /sək'sesə(r)/ n successeur m.

such /sʌtʃ/ det & pron tel(le), tel(le)s; (so much) tant(de). ● adv si; **~ a book** un tel livre; **~ books** de tels livres; **~ courage** tant de courage; **~ a big house** une si grande maison; **~ as** comme; tel que; **as ~** en tant que tel; **there's no ~ thing** ça n'existe pas. **~-and-~** adj tel ou tel.

suck /sʌk/ vt sucer. □ **~ in** or **up** aspirer. **sucker** n (rubber pad) ventouse f; (person 🅸) dupe f.

suction /'sʌkʃn/ n succion f.

sudden /'sʌdn/ adj soudain, subit; **all of a ~** tout à coup. **suddenly** adv subitement, brusquement.

sue /suː/ vt (pres p) **suing** poursuivre (en justice).

suede /sweɪd/ n daim m.

suffer /'sʌfə(r)/ vt/i souffrir; (loss, attack) subir. **sufferer** n victime f, malade m/f. **suffering** n souffrance(s) f(pl).

sufficient /sə'fɪʃnt/ adj (enough) suffisamment de; (big enough) suffisant.

suffix /'sʌfɪks/ n suffixe m.

suffocate /'sʌfəkeɪt/ vt/i suffoquer.

sugar /'ʃʊgə(r)/ n sucre m. ● vt sucrer.

suggest /sə'dʒest/ vt suggérer. **suggestion** n suggestion f.

suicidal /suːɪ'saɪdl/ adj suicidaire.

suicide /'suːɪsaɪd/ n suicide m;

commit ~ se suicider.

suit /su:t/ n (man's) costume m; (woman's) tailleur m; (cards) couleur f. ● vt convenir à; (garment, style) aller à; (adapt) adapter.

suitable /'su:təbl/ adj qui convient (for à), convenable. **suitably** adv convenablement.

suitcase /'su:tkeɪs/ n valise f.

suite /swi:t/ n (rooms) suite f; (furniture) mobilier m.

suited /'su:tɪd/ adj (well) ~ (matched) bien assorti; ~ to fait pour, apte à.

sulk /sʌlk/ vi bouder.

sullen /'sʌlən/ adj maussade.

sultana /sʌl'tɑ:nə/ n raisin m de Smyrne, raisin m sec.

sultry /'sʌltrɪ/ adj (-ier, -iest) étouffant, lourd; (fig) sensuel.

sum /sʌm/ n somme f; (in arithmetic) calcul m. ● vt/i (pt summed) ~ up résumer, récapituler; (assess) évaluer.

summarize /'sʌməraɪz/ vt résumer.

summary /'sʌmərɪ/ n résumé m. ● adj sommaire.

summer /'sʌmə(r)/ n été m. ● adj d'été. **~time** n (season) été m.

summery /'sʌmərɪ/ adj estival.

summit /'sʌmɪt/ n sommet m; (conference) (Pol) conférence f au sommet m.

summon /'sʌmən/ vt appeler; ~ sb to a meeting convoquer qn à une réunion; ~ up (strength, courage) rassembler.

summons /'sʌmənz/ n (Jur) assignation f. ● vt assigner.

sun /sʌn/ n soleil m. ● vt (pt sunned) ~ oneself se chauffer au soleil. **~burn** n coup m de soleil.

Sunday /'sʌndeɪ/ n dimanche m. ~ school n catéchisme m.

sundry /'sʌndrɪ/ adj divers; sundries articles mpl divers; all and ~ tout le monde.

sunflower /'sʌnflaʊə(r)/ n tournesol m.

sung /sʌŋ/ →SING.

sun-glasses npl lunettes fpl de soleil.

sunk /sʌŋk/ →SINK.

sunken /'sʌŋkən/ adj (ship) submergé; (eyes) creux.

sunlight /'sʌnlaɪt/ n soleil m.

sunny /'sʌnɪ/ adj (-ier, -iest) ensoleillé.

sun: **~rise** n lever m du soleil. **~roof** n toit m ouvrant. **~ screen** n filtre m solaire. **~ set** n coucher m du soleil. **~shine** n soleil m. **~stroke** n insolation f.

sun-tan /'sʌntæn/ n bronzage m. **~ lotion** n lotion f solaire. **~ oil** n huile f solaire.

super /'su:pə(r)/ adj [1] formidable.

superb /su:'pɜ:b/ adj superbe.

superficial /su:pə'fɪʃl/ adj superficiel.

superfluous /su:'pɜ:fluəs/ adj superflu.

superimpose /su:pərɪm'pəʊz/ vt

Summer camps Les camps de vacances sont une composante importante des vacances des jeunes Américains. Souvent situés dans des parc nationaux, ces camps proposent de multiples activités de plein air (canoë, escalade, équitation, natation, ski nautique, tennis, randonnée, etc.). Des milliers d'étudiants y sont recrutés chaque année en tant que moniteurs.

s

superposer (**on** à).

superintendent /suːpərɪn
ˈtendənt/ n directeur/-trice m/f; (of
police) commissaire m.

superior /suːˈpɪərɪə(r)/ adj & n
supérieur/-e (m /f).

superlative /suːˈpɜːlətɪv/ adj suprême. ● n (Gram) superlatif m.

supermarket /ˈsuːpəmɑːkɪt/ n
supermarché m.

supersede /suːpəˈsiːd/ vt remplacer, supplanter.

superstition /suːpəˈstɪʃn/ n superstition f. **superstitious** adj superstitieux.

superstore /ˈsuːpəstɔː(r)/ n hypermarché m.

supervise /ˈsuːpəvaɪz/ vt surveiller,
diriger. **supervision** n surveillance f.
supervisor n surveillant/-e m/f;
(shop) chef m de rayon; (firm) chef
m de service.

supper /ˈsʌpə(r)/ n dîner m; (late at
night) souper m.

supple /ˈsʌpl/ adj souple.

supplement[1] /ˈsʌplɪmənt/ n supplément m. **supplementary** adj
supplémentaire.

supplement[2] /ˈsʌplɪmənt/ vt
compléter.

supplier /səˈplaɪə(r)/ n fournisseur m.

supply /səˈplaɪ/ vt fournir; (equip)
pourvoir; (feed) alimenter (**with**
en). ● n provision f; (of gas) alimentation f; **supplies** (food) vivres mpl;
(material) fournitures fpl.

support /səˈpɔːt/ vt soutenir; (family) assurer la subsistance de. ● n
soutien m, appui m; (Tech) support
m. **supporter** n partisan/-e m/f;
(Sport) supporter m. **supportive** adj
qui soutient et encourage.

suppose /səˈpəʊz/ vt/i supposer;
be ∼d to do être censé faire, de-

voir faire; **supposing he comes**
supposons qu'il vienne. **supposedly**
adv soi-disant, prétendument.

suppress /səˈpres/ vt (put an end
to) supprimer; (restrain) réprimer;
(stifle) étouffer.

supreme /suːˈpriːm/ adj suprême.

surcharge /ˈsɜːtʃɑːdʒ/ n supplément m; (tax) surtaxe f.

sure /ʃɔː(r)/ adj sûr; **make ∼ of**
s'assurer de; **make ∼ that** vérifier
que. ● adv (US 🔲) pour sûr. **surely**
adv sûrement.

surf /sɜːf/ n ressac m. ● vi faire du
surf; (Internet) surfer.

surface /ˈsɜːfɪs/ n surface f. ● adj
superficiel. ● vt revêtir. ● vi faire
surface; (fig) réapparaître.

surfer /ˈsɜːfə(r)/ n surfeur/-euse
m/f; (Internet) internaute mf.

surge /sɜːdʒ/ vi (waves, crowd) déferler; (increase) monter. ● n (wave)
vague f; (rise) montée f.

surgeon /ˈsɜːdʒən/ n chirurgien m.

surgery /ˈsɜːdʒərɪ/ n chirurgie f;
(office) cabinet m; (session) consultation f; **need ∼** devoir être opéré.

surgical /ˈsɜːdʒɪkl/ adj chirurgical.
∼ spirit n alcool m à 90 degrés.

surly /ˈsɜːlɪ/ adj (**-ier**, **-iest**) bourru.

surname /ˈsɜːneɪm/ n nom m de
famille.

surplus /ˈsɜːpləs/ n surplus m. ● adj
en surplus.

surprise /səˈpraɪz/ n surprise f. ● vt
surprendre. **surprised** adj surpris (**at**
de). **surprising** adj surprenant.

surrender /səˈrendə(r)/ vi se rendre. ● vt (hand over) remettre; (Mil)
rendre. ● n (Mil) reddition f; (of
passport) remise f.

surround /səˈraʊnd/ vt entourer;
(Mil) encercler. **surrounding** adj environnant. **surroundings** npl envi-

rons mpl; (setting) cadre m.

surveillance /sɜːˈveɪləns/ n surveillance f.

survey¹ /səˈveɪ/ vt (review) passer en revue; (inquire into) enquêter sur; (building) inspecter.

survey² /ˈsɜːveɪ/ n (inquiry) enquête f; inspection f; (general view) vue f d'ensemble.

surveyor /səˈveɪə(r)/ n expert m (géomètre).

survival /səˈvaɪvl/ n survie f.

survive /səˈvaɪv/ vt/i survivre (à). **survivor** n survivant/-e m/f.

susceptible /səˈseptəbl/ adj sensible (to à); ~ **to** (prone to) prédisposé à.

suspect¹ /səˈspekt/ vt soupçonner; (doubt) douter de.

suspect² /ˈsʌspekt/ n & adj suspect/-e m/f.

suspend /səˈspend/ vt (hang, stop) suspendre; (licence) retirer provisoirement. **suspended sentence** n condamnation f avec sursis.

suspender /səˈspendə(r)/ n jarretelle f; ~s (braces: US) bretelles fpl. ~ **belt** n porte-jarretelles m.

suspension /səˈspenʃn/ n suspension f; retrait m provisoire.

suspicion /səˈspɪʃn/ n soupçon m; (distrust) méfiance f.

suspicious /səˈspɪʃəs/ adj soupçonneux; (causing suspicion) suspect; **be** ~ **of** se méfier de. **suspiciously** adv de façon suspecte.

sustain /səˈsteɪn/ vt supporter; (effort) soutenir; (suffer) subir.

sustenance /ˈsʌstɪnəns/ n (food) nourriture f; (nourishment) valeur f nutritive.

swallow /ˈswɒləʊ/ vt/i avaler; ~ **up** (absorb, engulf) engloutir. ● n hirondelle f.

swam /swæm/ →SWIM.

swamp /swɒmp/ n marais m. ● vt (flood, overwhelm) submerger.

swan /swɒn/ n cygne m.

swap /swɒp/ vt/i (pt swapped) [T] échanger. ● n [T] échange m.

swarm /swɔːm/ n essaim m. ● vi fourmiller; ~ **into** or **round** (crowd) envahir.

swat /swɒt/ vt (pt swatted) (fly) écraser.

sway /sweɪ/ vt/i (se) balancer; (influence) influencer. ● n balancement m; (rule) empire m.

swear /sweə(r)/ vt/i (pt swore, pp sworn) jurer (**to sth** de qch); ~ **at** injurier; ~ **by sth** [T] ne jurer que par qch. ~ **-word** n juron m.

sweat /swet/ n sueur f. ● vi suer.

sweater /ˈswetə(r)/ n pull-over m.

sweat-shirt n sweat-shirt m.

swede /swiːd/ n rutabaga m.

Swede /swiːd/ n Suédois/-e m/f. **Sweden** n Suède f.

Swedish /ˈswiːdɪʃ/ adj suédois. ● n (Ling) suédois m.

sweep /swiːp/ vt/i (pt swept) (floor) balayer; (carry away) emporter, entraîner; (chimney) ramoner. ● n coup m de balai; (curve) courbe f; (movement) geste m, mouvement m; (for chimneys) ramoneur m. ~ **by** passer rapidement or majestueusement. **sweeper** n (for carpet) balai m mécanique; (football) libero m.

sweet /swiːt/ adj (not sour, pleasant) doux; (not savoury) sucré; (charming [T]) gentil; **have a** ~ **tooth** aimer les sucreries. ● n bonbon m; (dish) dessert m. ~**corn** n maïs m.

sweeten /ˈswiːtn/ vt sucrer; (fig) adoucir. **sweetener** n édulcorant m.

sweetheart /ˈswiːthɑːt/ n petit/-e ami/-e m/f; (term of endearment) chéri/-e *m/f.*

sweetly /'swiːtlɪ/ *adv* gentiment.

sweetness /'swiːtnɪs/ *n* douceur *f;* goût *m* sucré.

sweet pea *n* pois *m* de senteur.

swell /swel/ *vt/i (pt* swelled; *pp* swollen *or* swelled) (increase) grossir; (expand) (se) gonfler; (hand, face) enfler. ● *n (of sea)* houle *f.*

swelling *n* (Med) enflure *f.*

sweltering /'sweltərɪŋ/ *adj* étouffant.

swept /swept/ ➡SWEEP.

swerve /swɜːv/ *vi* faire un écart.

swift /swɪft/ *adj* rapide. ● *n* (bird) martinet *m.*

swim /swɪm/ *vi (pt* swam; *pp* swum; *pres p* swimming) nager; (be dizzy) tourner. ● *vt* traverser à la nage; (distance) nager. ● *n* baignade *f;* **go for a ~** aller se baigner. **swimmer** *n* nageur/-euse *m/f.* **swimming** *n* natation *f.*

swimming pool *n* piscine *f.*

swimsuit /'swɪmsuːt/ *n* maillot *m* (de bain).

swindle /'swɪndl/ *vt* escroquer. ● *n* escroquerie *f.*

swine /swaɪn/ *npl* (pigs) pourceaux *mpl.* ● *n inv* (person ⊞) salaud *m.*

swing /swɪŋ/ *vt/i (pt* swung) (se) balancer; (turn round) tourner; (pendulum) osciller. ● *n* balancement *m;* (seat) balançoire *f;* (of opinion) revirement *m* (towards en faveur de); (Mus) rythme *m;* **be in full ~** battre son plein. □ **~ round** (person) se retourner.

swipe /swaɪp/ *vt* (hit ⊞) frapper; (steal ⊞) piquer. **~ card** *n* carte *f* magnétique, badge *m.*

swirl /swɜːl/ *vi* tourbillonner. ● *n* tourbillon *m.*

Swiss /swɪs/ *adj* suisse. ● *n inv* Suisse *mf.*

switch /swɪtʃ/ *n* bouton *m* (électrique), interrupteur *m;* (shift) changement *m,* revirement *m.* ● *vt* (transfer) transférer; (exchange) échanger (for contre); (reverse positions of) changer de place; **~ trains** (change) changer de train. ● *vi* changer. □ **~ off** éteindre; **~ on** mettre, allumer.

switchboard /'swɪtʃbɔːd/ *n* standard *m.*

Switzerland /'swɪtsələnd/ *n* Suisse *f.*

swivel /'swɪvl/ *vt/i (pt* swivelled) (faire) pivoter.

swollen /'swəʊlən/ ➡SWELL.

swoop /swuːp/ *vi* (bird) fondre; (police) faire une descente, foncer. ● *n* (police raid) descente *f.*

sword /sɔːd/ *n* épée *f.*

swore /swɔː(r)/ ➡SWEAR.

sworn /swɔːn/ ➡SWEAR. ● *adj* (enemy) juré; (ally) dévoué.

swot /swɒt/ *vt/i (pt* swotted) (study ⊞) bûcher ⊞. ● *n* ⊞ bûcheur/-euse *m/f.*

swum /swʌm/ ➡SWIM.

swung /swʌŋ/ ➡SWING.

syllabus /'sɪləbəs/ *n (pl* ~es) (School, Univ) programme *m.*

symbol /'sɪmbl/ *n* symbole *m.* **symbolic (al)** *adj* symbolique. **symbolize** *vt* symboliser.

symmetrical /sɪ'metrɪkəl/ *adj* symétrique.

sympathetic /sɪmpə'θetɪk/ *adj* compatissant; (fig) compréhensif.

sympathize /'sɪmpəθaɪz/ *vi* **~ with** (pity) plaindre; (fig) comprendre les sentiments de. **sympathizer** *n* sympathisant/-e *m/f.*

sympathy /'sɪmpəθɪ/ *n* (pity) compassion *f;* (fig) compréhension *f;* (solidarity) solidarité *f;* (condolences) condoléances *fpl;* (affinity) affinité *f*; **be in** ~ **with** comprendre, être en accord avec.

symptom /'sɪmptəm/ *n* symptôme *m*.

synagogue /'sɪnəgɒg/ *n* synagogue *f*.

synonym /'sɪnənɪm/ *n* synonyme *m*.

synopsis /sɪ'nɒpsɪs/ *n* (*pl* **-opses**) résumé *m*.

syntax /'sɪntæks/ *n* syntaxe *f*.

synthesis /'sɪnθəsɪs/ *n* (*pl* **-theses**) synthèse *f*.

synthetic /sɪn'θetɪk/ *adj* synthétique.

syringe /sɪ'rɪndʒ/ *n* seringue *f*.

syrup /'sɪrəp/ *n* (liquid) sirop *m*; (treacle) mélasse *f* raffinée.

system /'sɪstəm/ *n* système *m*; (body) organisme *m*; (order) méthode *f*. **systematic** *adj* systématique.

systems analyst *n* analyste-programmeur/- euse *m/f*.

• •

Tt

• •

tab /tæb/ *n* (on can) languette *f*; (on garment) patte *f*; (label) étiquette *f*; (US ⚠) addition *f*; (Comput) tabulatrice *f*; (setting) tabulation *f*.

table /'teɪbl/ *n* table *f*; **at (the)** ~ à table; **lay** or **set the** ~ mettre la table. • *vt* (motion) présenter. ~**-cloth** *n* nappe *f*. ~**-mat** *n* set *m* de table. ~**spoon** *n* cuillère *f* de service.

tablet /'tæblɪt/ *n* (of stone) plaque *f*; (drug) comprimé *m*.

table tennis *n* tennis *m* de table;

ping-pong® *m*.

taboo /tə'buː/ *n* & *a* tabou (*m*).

tacit /'tæsɪt/ *adj* tacite.

tack /tæk/ *n* (nail) clou *m*; (stitch) point *m* de bâti; (course of action) voie *f*. • *vt* (nail) clouer; (stitch) bâtir; (add) ajouter. • *vi* (Naut) louvoyer.

tackle /'tækl/ *n* équipement *m*; (in soccer) tacle *m*; (in rugby) plaquage *m*. • *vt* (problem) s'attaquer à; (player) tacler, plaquer.

tact /tækt/ *n* tact *m*. **tactful** *adj* plein de tact.

tactics /'tæktɪks/ *npl* tactique *f*.

tadpole /'tædpəʊl/ *n* têtard *m*.

tag /tæg/ *n* (label) étiquette *f*. • *vt* (*pt* **tagged**) (label) étiqueter. • *vi* ~ **along** ⚠ suivre.

tail /teɪl/ *n* queue *f*; ~**s** (coat) habit *m*; ~**s!** (on coin) pile! • *vt* (follow) filer. • *vi* ~ **away** or **off** diminuer. ~**-back** *n* bouchon *m*. ~**-gate** *n* hayon *m*.

tailor /'teɪlə(r)/ *n* tailleur *m*. • *vt* (garment) façonner; (fig) adapter. ~**-made** *adj* fait sur mesure.

take /teɪk/ *vt/i* (*pt* **took**, *pp* **taken**) prendre (**from sb** à qn); (carry) emporter, porter (**to** à); (escort) emmener; (contain) contenir; (tolerate) supporter; (accept) accepter; (prize) remporter; (exam) passer; (precedence) avoir; (view) adopter; ~ **sb home** ramener qn chez lui; **be taken by** or **with** être impressionné par; **be taken ill** tomber malade; **it** ~**s time** il faut du temps pour. ▫ ~ **after** tenir de; ~ **apart** démonter; (fig) descendre en flammes ⚠; ~ **away** (object) enlever; (person) emmener; (pain) supprimer; ~ **back** reprendre; (return) rendre; (accompany) raccompagner; (statement) retirer; ~ **down** (object) descendre; (notes) prendre; ~ **in** (ob-

ject) rentrer; (*include*) inclure; (*cheat*) tromper; ~ **off** (*Aviat*) décoller; ~ **sth off** enlever qch; ~ **sb off** imiter qn; ~ **on** (*task, staff, passenger*) prendre; (*challenger*) relever le défi de; ~ **out** sortir; (*stain*) enlever; ~ **over** *vt* (*country, firm*) prendre le contrôle de; *vi* prendre le pouvoir; ~ **over from** remplacer; ~ **part** participer (in à); ~ **place** avoir lieu; ~ **to** se prendre d'amitié pour; (*activity*) prendre goût à; ~ **to doing** se mettre à faire; ~ **up** (*object*) monter; (*hobby*) se mettre à; (*occupy*) prendre; (*resume*) reprendre; ~ **up with** se lier avec. ~**away** *n* (*meal*) repas *m* à emporter. ~**off** *n* (*Aviat*) décollage *m*. ~**over** *n* (*Pol*) prise *f* de pouvoir; (*Comm*) rachat *m*.

tale /teɪl/ *n* conte *m*; (*report*) récit *m*; (*lie*) histoire *f*.

talent /'tælənt/ *n* talent *m*. **talented** *adj* doué.

talk /tɔːk/ *vt/i* parler; (*chat*) bavarder; ~ **sb into doing** persuader qn de faire; ~ **sth over** discuter de qch. ● *n* (*talking*) propos *mpl*; (*conversation*) conversation *f*; (*lecture*) exposé *m*.

talkative /'tɔːkətɪv/ *adj* bavard.

tall /tɔːl/ *adj* (*high*) haut; (*person*) grand.

tame /teɪm/ *adj* apprivoisé; (*dull*) insipide. ● *vt* apprivoiser; (*lion*) dompter.

tamper /'tæmpə(r)/ *vi* ~ **with** (*lock, machine*) tripoter; (*accounts, evidence*) trafiquer.

tan /tæn/ *vt/i* (*pt* **tanned**) bronzer; (*hide*) tanner. ● *n* bronzage *m*.

tangerine /'tændʒəriːn/ *n* mandarine *f*.

tangle /'tæŋgl/ *vt/i* ~ **(up)** s'emmêler. ● *n* enchevêtrement *m*.

tank /tæŋk/ *n* réservoir *m*; (*vat*) cuve *f*; (*for fish*) aquarium *m*; (*Mil*) char *m* (de combat).

tanker /'tæŋkə(r)/ *n* (*lorry*) camion-citerne *m*; (*ship*) navire-citerne *m*; **oil/petrol** ~ pétrolier *m*.

tantrum /'tæntrəm/ *n* crise *f* (de colère).

tap /tæp/ *n* (*for water*) robinet *m*; (*knock*) petit coup *m*; **on** ~ disponible. ● *vt* (*pt* **tapped**) (*knock*) taper (doucement); (*resources*) exploiter; (*phone*) mettre sur écoute.

tape /teɪp/ *n* bande *f* (magnétique); (*cassette*) cassette *f*; (*video*) cassette *f* vidéo; (*fabric*) ruban *m*; (*sticky*) scotch (r) *m*. ● *vt* (*record*) enregistrer; ~ **sth to sth** coller qch à qch. ~**measure** *n* mètre *m* ruban. ~ **recorder** *n* magnétophone *m*.

tapestry /'tæpəstri/ *n* tapisserie *f*.

tar /tɑː(r)/ *n* goudron *m*. ● *vt* (*pt* **tarred**) goudronner.

target /'tɑːgɪt/ *n* cible *f*; (*objective*) objectif *m*. ● *vt* (*city*) prendre pour cible; (*weapon*) diriger; (*in marketing*) viser.

tariff /'tærɪf/ *n* (*price list*) tarif *m*; (*on imports*) droit *m* de douane.

tarmac, Tarmac® /'tɑːmæk/ *n* macadam *m*; (*runway*) piste *f*.

tarpaulin /tɑː'pɔːlɪn/ *n* bâche *f*.

tarragon /'tærəgən/ *n* estragon *m*.

tart /tɑːt/ *n* tarte *f*. ● *adj* aigrelet.

task /tɑːsk/ *n* tâche *f*.

taste /teɪst/ *n* goût *m*; (*experience*) aperçu *m*. ● *vt* (*eat, enjoy*) goûter à; (*try*) goûter; (*perceive taste of*) sentir (le goût de). ● *vi* ~ **of** or **like** avoir un goût de. **tasteful** *adj* de bon goût.

tattoo /tə'tuː/ *vt* tatouer. ● *n* tatouage *m*.

tatty /'tæti/ *adj* (**-ier, -iest**) 🆃 miteux.

taught /tɔːt/ ➡TEACH.

taunt /tɔːnt/ vt railler. ● n raillerie f.

Taurus /'tɔːrəs/ n Taureau m.

tax /tæks/ n (on goods, services) taxe f; (on income) impôt m. ● vt imposer; (put to test: fig) mettre à l'épreuve. **taxable** adj imposable. **taxation** n imposition f; (taxes) impôts mpl.

tax: ~ **collector** n percepteur m. ~**deductible** adj déductible des impôts. ~ **disc** n vignette f. ~**free** adj exempt d'impôts. ~**haven** n paradis m fiscal.

taxi /'tæksɪ/ n taxi m. ● n **rank** n station f de taxi.

tax: ~**payer** n contribuable mf. ~ **relief** n dégrèvement m fiscal. ~ **return** n déclaration f d'impôts.

tea /tiː/ n (drink, meal) thé m; (children's snack) goûter m; ~ **bag** sachet m de thé.

teach /tiːtʃ/ vt (pt **taught**) apprendre (**sb sth** qch à qn); (in school) enseigner (**sb sth** qch à qn). ● vi enseigner. **teacher** n enseignant/-e m/f; (secondary) professeur m; (primary) instituteur/-trice m/f.

team /tiːm/ n équipe f; (of animals) attelage m. ● vi ~ **up** faire équipe (**with** avec).

teapot /'tiːpɒt/ n théière f.

tear[1] /teə(r)/ vt/i (pt **tore**; pp **torn**) (se) déchirer; (snatch) arracher (**from** à); (rush) aller à toute vitesse. ● n déchirure f.

tear[2] /tɪə(r)/ n larme f; **in** ~**s** en larmes. ~**gas** n gaz m lacrymogène.

tease /tiːz/ vt taquiner. ● n taquin/-e m/f.

tea: ~ **shop** n salon m de thé. ~**spoon** n petite cuillère f.

teat /tiːt/ n tétine f.

tea-towel n torchon m.

technical /'teknɪkl/ adj technique.

technician /tek'nɪʃn/ n technicien/-ne m/f.

technique /tek'niːk/ n technique f.

techno /'teknəʊ/ n (Mus) techno f.

technology /tek'nɒlədʒɪ/ n technologie f.

technophobe /teknə'fəʊb/ n technophobe mf.

teddy /'tedɪ/ adj ~ **bear** ours m en peluche.

tedious /'tiːdɪəs/ adj ennuyeux.

tee /tiː/ n (golf) tee m.

teenage /'tiːneɪdʒ/ adj (girl, boy) adolescent; (fashion) des adolescents. **teenager** n jeune mf, adolescent/-e m/f.

teens /tiːnz/ npl **in one's** ~ adolescent.

teeth /tiːθ/ ➡TOOTH.

teethe /tiːð/ vi faire ses dents.

teetotaller /tiː'təʊtələ(r)/ n personne f qui ne boit pas d'alcool.

telecommunications /telɪkəmjuːnɪ'keɪʃnz/ npl télécommunications fpl.

telecommuting /telɪkə'mjuːtɪŋ/ n télétravail m.

teleconferencing /telɪ'kɒnfərənsɪŋ/ n téléconférence f.

telegram /'telɪɡræm/ n télégramme m.

telegraph /'telɪɡrɑːf/ n télégraphe m. ● adj télégraphique.

telephone /'telɪfəʊn/ n téléphone m. ● vt (person) téléphoner à; (message) téléphoner. ● vi téléphoner. ~ **book** annuaire m. ~ **booth**, ~ **box** n cabine f téléphonique. ~ **call** n coup m de téléphone. ~ **number** n numéro m de téléphone.

telephoto /telɪ'fəʊtəʊ/ adj ~ **lens** téléobjectif m.

telescope /'telɪskəʊp/ n télescope m.

t

m. ● *vt/i* (se) télescoper.

teletext /'telɪtekst/ *n* télétexte *m.*

televise /'telɪvaɪz/ *vt* téléviser.

television /'telɪvɪʒn/ *n* télévision *f*; ~ **set** poste *m* de télévision, téléviseur *m.*

teleworking /'telɪwɜːkɪŋ/ *n* télétravail *m.*

telex /'teleks/ *n* télex *m.* ● *vt* envoyer par télex.

tell /tel/ *vt* (*pt* **told**) dire (**sb sth** qch à qn); (*story*) raconter; (*distinguish*) distinguer; ~ **sb to do sth** dire à qn de faire qch; ~ **sth from sth** voir la différence entre qch et qch. ● *vi* (*show*) avoir un effet; (*know*) savoir. □ ~ **off** 🔢 gronder.

temp /temp/ *n* intérimaire *mf.* ● *vi* faire de l'intérim.

temper /'tempə(r)/ *n* humeur *f*; (*anger*) colère *f*; **lose one's** ~ se mettre en colère.

temperament /'temprəmənt/ *n* tempérament *m.* **temperamental** *adj* capricieux.

temperature /'temprətʃə(r)/ *n* température *f*; **have a** ~ avoir de la fièvre or de la température.

temple /'templ/ *n* temple *m*; (*of head*) tempe *f.*

temporary /'temprərɪ/ *adj* temporaire, provisoire.

tempt /tempt/ *vt* tenter; ~ **sb to do sth** donner envie à qn de faire.

ten /ten/ *adj* & *n* dix (*m*).

tenacious /tɪ'neɪʃəs/ *adj* tenace.

tenancy /'tenənsɪ/ *n* location *f.* **tenant** *n* locataire *mf.*

tend /tend/ *vt* s'occuper de. ● *vi* ~ **to** (*be apt to*) avoir tendance à; (*look after*) s'occuper de. **tendency** *n* tendance *f.*

tender /'tendə(r)/ *adj* tendre; (*sore, painful*) sensible. ● *vt* offrir, donner. ● *vi* faire une soumission. ● *n*

(*Comm*) soumission *f*; **be legal** ~ (*money*) avoir cours.

tendon /'tendən/ *n* tendon *m.*

tennis /'tenɪs/ *n* tennis *m.* ● *adj* (*court, match*) de tennis.

tenor /'tenə(r)/ *n* (*meaning*) sens *m* général; (*Mus*) ténor *m.*

tense /tens/ *n* (*Gram*) temps *m.* ● *adj* tendu; ● *vt* (*muscles*) tendre, raidir. ● *vi* (*face*) se crisper.

tension /'tenʃn/ *n* tension *f.*

tent /tent/ *n* tente *f.*

tentative /'tentətɪv/ *adj* provisoire; (*hesitant*) timide.

tenth /tenθ/ *adj* & *n* dixième (*mf*).

tepid /'tepɪd/ *adj* tiède.

term /tɜːm/ *n* (*word, limit*) terme *m*; (*of imprisonment*) temps *m*; (*School*) trimestre *m*; ~**s** conditions *fpl*; **on good/bad** ~**s** en bons/ mauvais termes; **in the short/long** ~ à court/long terme; **come to** ~**s with** accepter qch; ~ **of office** (*Pol*) mandat *m.* ● *vt* appeler.

terminal /'tɜːmɪnl/ *adj* terminal; (*illness*) incurable. ● *n* (*oil, computer*) terminal *m*; (*Rail*) terminus *m*; (*Electr*) borne *f*; **air** ~ aérogare *f.*

terminate /'tɜːmɪneɪt/ *vt* mettre fin à. ● *vi* prendre fin.

terminus /'tɜːmɪnəs/ *n* (*pl* **-ni**) (*station*) terminus *m.*

terrace /'terəs/ *n* terrasse *f*; (*houses*) rangée *f* de maisons contiguës; **the** ~**s** (*Sport*) les gradins *mpl.*

terracotta /terə'kɒtə/ *n* terre *f* cuite.

terrible /'terəbl/ *adj* affreux, atroce.

terrific /tə'rɪfɪk/ *adj* (*huge*) énorme; (*great* 🔢) formidable.

terrify /'terɪfaɪ/ *vt* terrifier; **be terrified of** avoir très peur de.

territory /ˈterətrɪ/ n territoire m.

terror /ˈterə(r)/ n terreur f.

terrorism /ˈterərɪzəm/ n terrorisme m. **terrorist** n terroriste mf.

test /test/ n épreuve f; (written exam) contrôle m; (of machine, product) essai m; (of sample) analyse f; **driving ∼** examen m du permis de conduire. ● vt évaluer; (School) contrôler; (machine, product) essayer; (sample) analyser; (patience, strength) mettre à l'épreuve. ● vi **∼ for** faire une recherche de.

testament /ˈtestəmənt/ n testament m; **Old/New T∼** Ancien/Nouveau Testament m.

testicle /ˈtestɪkl/ n testicule m.

testify /ˈtestɪfaɪ/ vt/i témoigner (**to** de; **that** que).

testimony /ˈtestɪmənɪ/ n témoignage m.

test tube n éprouvette f.

tetanus /ˈtetənəs/ n tétanos m.

text /tekst/ n texte m. ● vt **∼ sb** envoyer un texto à qn. **∼book** n manuel m. **∼ message** n texto m.

texture /ˈtekstʃə(r)/ n (of paper) grain m; (of fabric) texture f.

than /ðæn/, /ðən/ conj que, qu'; (with numbers) de; **more/less ∼ ten** plus/moins de dix.

thank /θæŋk/ vt remercier; **∼ you!**, **∼s!** merci! **thankful** adj reconnaissant (**for** de). **thanks** npl remerciements mpl; **∼s to** grâce à. **Thanksgiving (Day)** n (US) jour m d'Action de Grâces.

that /ðæt/ pl **those**

● determiner

····▸ ce, cet, cette, ces; **∼ dog** ce chien; **∼ man** cet homme; **∼ woman** cette femme; **those**

books ces livres; **at ∼ moment** à ce moment-là.

! To distinguish **that/those** from **this/these**, you add -là to the noun: **I prefer that car** je préfère cette voiture-là.

● pronoun

····▸ cela, ça, ce; **what's ∼?**, **what are those?** qu'est-ce que c'est (que ça)?; **who's ∼?** qui est-ce?; **∼ is my brother** c'est or voilà mon frère; **those are my parents** ce sont mes parents.

····▸ (emphatic) celui-là, celle-là, ceux-là, celles-là; **all the dresses are nice but I like ∼/those best** toutes ces robes sont jolies mais je préfère celle-là/celles-là.

● relative pronoun

····▸ (for subject) qui; **the man ∼ stole the car** l'homme qui a volé la voiture.

····▸ (for object) que; **the girl ∼ I met** la fille que j'ai rencontrée.

! With a preposition, use lequel/laquelle/lesquels/lesquelles: **the chair ∼ I was sitting on** la chaise sur laquelle j'étais assis.
With a preposition that translates as à, use auquel/à laquelle/auxquels/auxquelles: **the girls ∼ I was talking to** les filles auxquelles je parlais.
With a preposition that translates as de, use dont: **the people ∼ I've talked about** les personnes dont j'ai parlé.

● conjunction que; **she said ∼ she would do it** elle a dit qu'elle le ferait.

t

thatched /ˈθætʃd/ adj de chaume; ~ **cottage** chaumière f.

thaw /θɔː/ vt/i (faire) dégeler; (snow) (faire) fondre. ● n dégel m.

---

the /ðə, ðiː/ determiner

····▸ le, l', la, les; ~ **dog** le chien; ~ **tree** l'arbre; ~ **chair** la chaise; **to** ~ **shops** aux magasins.

! With a preposition the translates as à: à + le = au and à + les = aux.

---

theatre /ˈθɪətə(r)/ n théâtre m.

theft /θeft/ n vol m.

their /ðeə(r)/ adj leur, pl leurs.

theirs /ðeəz/ pron le la leur, les leurs.

them /ðem, ðəm/ pron les; (after preposition) eux, elles; **(to)** ~ leur; **phone** ~! téléphone-leur!; **I know** ~ je les connais; **both of** ~ tous/ toutes les deux.

theme /θiːm/ n thème m. ~ **park** n parc m de loisirs (à thème).

themselves /ðem'selvz/ pron eux-mêmes, elles-mêmes; (reflexive) se; (after preposition) eux, elles.

then /ðen/ adv alors; (next) ensuite, puis; (therefore) alors, donc. ● adj d'alors; **from** ~ **on** dès lors.

theology /θɪˈɒlədʒɪ/ n théologie f.

theory /ˈθɪərɪ/ n théorie f.

therapy /ˈθerəpɪ/ n thérapie f.

there /ðeə(r)/ adv là; (with verb) y; (over there) là-bas; **he goes** ~ il y va; **on** ~ là-dessus; ~ **is,** ~ **are** il y a; (pointing) voilà. ● interj ~, ~! allons, allons!

therefore /ˈðeəfɔː(r)/ adv donc.

thermal /ˈθɜːml/ adj thermique.

thermometer /θəˈmɒmɪtə(r)/ n thermomètre m.

Thermos® /ˈθɜːməs/ n thermos ® m or f inv.

thermostat /ˈθɜːməstæt/ n thermostat m.

thesaurus /θɪˈsɔːrəs/ n (pl **-ri**) dictionnaire m de synonymes.

these /ðiːz/ ➡THIS.

thesis /ˈθiːsɪs/ n (pl **theses**) thèse f.

they /ðeɪ/ pron ils, elles; (emphatic) eux, elles; (people in general) on.

thick /θɪk/ adj épais; (stupid) bête; **be 6 cm** ~ avoir 6 cm d'épaisseur.

thief /θiːf/ n (pl **thieves**) voleur/- euse m/f.

thigh /θaɪ/ n cuisse f.

thin /θɪn/ adj (**thinner, thinnest**) mince; (person) maigre, mince; (sparse) clairsemé; (fine) fin. ● vt/i (pt **thinned**) ~ **(down)** (paint) diluer; (soup) allonger.

thing /θɪŋ/ n chose f; ~**s** (belongings) affaires fpl; **the best** ~ **is to** le mieux est de; **the (right)** ~ ce qu'il faut **(for sb** à qn).

think /θɪŋk/ vt/i (pt **thought**) penser **(about, of** à); (carefully) réfléchir **(about, of** à); (believe) croire; **I** ~ **so** je crois que oui; ~ **of doing** envisager de faire. □ ~ **over** bien réfléchir à; □ ~ **up** inventer.

third /θɜːd/ adj troisième. ● n troisième m/f; (fraction) tiers m. **T~ World** n tiers-monde m.

thirst /θɜːst/ n soif f.

thirsty /ˈθɜːstɪ/ adj **be** ~ avoir soif; **make** ~ donner soif à.

thirteen /θɜːˈtiːn/ adj & n treize (m).

thirty /ˈθɜːtɪ/ adj & n trente (m).

this /ðɪs/pl **these**

● determiner

┈┈▸ ce/cet/cette/ces; ～ **dog** ce chien; ～ **man** cet homme; ～ **woman** cette femme; **these books** ces livres.

❗ To distinguish from **that** and **those**, you need to add -ci after the noun: **I prefer this car** je préfère cette voiture-ci.

● pronoun

┈┈▸ ce; what's ～?, what are these? qu'est-ce que c'est?; who is ～? qui est-ce?; ～ **is the kitchen** voici la cuisine; ～ **is Sophie** je te or vous présente Sophie; **these are your things** ce sont tes affaires.

┈┈▸ (emphatic) celui-ci/celle-ci/ceux-ci/celles-ci; **all the dresses are nice but I like** ～/**these best** toutes les robes sont jolies mais je préfère celle-ci/celles-ci.

thistle /ˈθɪsl/ n chardon m.

thorn /θɔːn/ n épine f.

thorough /ˈθʌrə/ adj (detailed) approfondi; (meticulous) minutieux. **thoroughly** adv (clean, study) à fond; (very) tout à fait.

those /ðəʊz/ ▶THAT.

though /ðəʊ/ conj bien que. ● adv quand même.

thought /θɔːt/ ▶THINK. ● n pensée f, idée f. **thoughtful** adj pensif; (kind) prévenant.

thousand /ˈθaʊznd/ adj & n mille (m inv); ～**s of** des milliers de. **thousandth** adj & n millième (mf).

thread /θred/ n (yarn & fig) fil m; (of screw) pas m. ● vt enfiler; ～ **one's way** se faufiler.

threat /θret/ n menace f. **threaten**

vt/i menacer (with de).

three /θriː/ adj & n trois (m).

threw /θruː/ ▶THROW.

thrill /θrɪl/ n frisson m; (pleasure) plaisir m. ● vt transporter (de joie); **be** ～**ed** être ravi. ● vi frissonner (de joie).

thrive /θraɪv/ vi (pt **thrived** or **throve**;pp **thrived** or **thriven**) prospérer; **he** ～**s on it** cela lui réussit.

throat /θrəʊt/ n gorge f; **have a sore** ～ avoir mal à la gorge.

throb /θrɒb/ vi (pt **throbbed**) (heart) battre; (engine) vibrer. ● n (pain) élancement m; (of engine) vibration f. **throbbing** adj (pain) lancinant.

throne /θrəʊn/ n trône m.

through /θruː/ prep à travers; (during) pendant; (by means or way of, out of) par; (by reason of) grâce à, à cause de. ● adv à travers; (entirely) jusqu'au bout. ● adj (train) direct; **be** ～ (finished) avoir fini; **come** or **go** ～ (cross, pierce) traverser; **I'm putting you** ～ je vous passe votre correspondant.

throughout /θruːˈaʊt/ prep ～ **the country** dans tout le pays; ～ **the day** pendant toute la journée. ● adv (place) partout; (time) tout le temps.

throw /θrəʊ/ vt (pt **threw**; pp **thrown**) jeter, lancer; (baffle) déconcerter; ～ **a party** faire une fête. ● n jet m; (of dice) coup m. □ **away** jeter; ～ **off** (get rid of) se débarrasser de; ～ **out** jeter; (person) expulser; (reject) rejeter; ～ **up** (arms) lever; (vomit 🔢) vomir.

thrust /θrʌst/ vt (pt **thrust**) pousser. ● n poussée f.

thud /θʌd/ n bruit m sourd.

thug /θʌg/ n voyou m.

thumb /θʌm/ n pouce m. ● vt

t

(book) feuilleter; ~ a lift faire de l'autostop. ~-index n répertoire m à onglets.

thump /θʌmp/ vt/i cogner (sur); (heart) battre fort. ● n coup m.

thunder /'θʌndə(r)/ n tonnerre m. ● vi (weather, person) tonner. ~storm n orage m.

Thursday /'θɜːzdeɪ/ n jeudi m.

thus /ðʌs/ adv ainsi.

thwart /θwɔːt/ vt contrecarrer.

thyme /taɪm/ n thym m.

tick /tɪk/ n (sound) tic-tac m; (mark) coche f; (moment 🔢) instant m; (insect) tique f.● vi faire tic-tac. ● vt (~ off) cocher. □ ~ over tourner au ralenti.

ticket /'tɪkɪt/ n billet m; (for bus, cloakroom) ticket m; (label) étiquette f. ~-collector n contrôleur/-euse m/f.~-office n guichet m.

tickle /'tɪkl/ vt chatouiller; (amuse: fig) amuser.● n chatouillement m.

tidal /'taɪdl/ adj (river) à marées; ~ wave raz-de-marée m inv.

tide /taɪd/ n marée f; (of events) cours m.

tidy /'taɪdɪ/ adj (-ier,-iest) (room) bien rangé; (appearance, work) soigné; (methodical) ordonné; (amount 🔢) joli.● vt/i ~ (up) faire du rangement; ~ sth (up) ranger qch; ~ oneself up s'arranger.

tie /taɪ/ vt (pres p tying) attacher; (knot) faire; (scarf) nouer; (link) lier.● vi (in football) faire match nul; (in race) être ex aequo.● n (necktie) cravate f; (fastener) attache f; (link) lien m; (draw) match m nul. ~ down attacher; ~ in with être lié à; ~ up attacher; (money) immobiliser; (occupy) occuper.

tier /tɪə(r)/ n étage m, niveau m; (in stadium) gradin m.

tiger /'taɪgə(r)/ n tigre m.

tight /taɪt/ adj (clothes, budget) serré; (grip) ferme; (rope) tendu; (security) strict; (angle) aigu. ● adv (hold, sleep) bien; (squeeze) fort.

tighten /'taɪtn/ vt/i (se) tendre; (bolt) (se) resserrer; (control) renforcer.

tights /taɪts/ npl collant m.

tile /taɪl/ n (on wall, floor) carreau m; (on roof) tuile f. ● vt carreler; couvrir de tuiles.

till /tɪl/ n caisse f (enregistreuse).● vt (land) cultiver. ● prep & conj ➞UNTIL.

timber /'tɪmbə(r)/ n bois m (de construction); (trees) arbres mpl.

time /taɪm/ n temps m; (moment) moment m; (epoch) époque f; (by clock) heure f; (occasion) fois f; (rhythm) mesure f; ~s (multiplying) fois fpl; any ~ n'importe quand; for the ~ being pour le moment; from ~ to ~ de temps en temps; have a good ~ s'amuser; in no ~ en un rien de temps; in ~ à temps; (eventually) avec le temps; a long ~ longtemps; on ~ à l'heure; what's the ~? quelle heure est-il? ~ off du temps libre. ● vt choisir le moment de; (measure) minuter; (Sport) chronométrer. ~ limit n délai m.

timer /'taɪmə(r)/ n minuterie f; (for cooker) minuteur m.

time: ~-scale n délais mpl. ~table n horaire m. ~ zone n fuseau m horaire.

timid /'tɪmɪd/ adj timide; (fearful) peureux.

tin /tɪn/ n étain m; (container) boîte f; ~(plate) fer-blanc m. ● vt (pt tinned) mettre en boîte. ~foil n papier m d'aluminium.

tingle /'tɪŋgl/ vi picoter. ● n picotement m.

tin-opener n ouvre-boîtes m inv.

tint /tɪnt/ n teinte f; (for hair) shampooing m colorant. ● vt teinter.

tiny /'taɪnɪ/ adj (**-ier, -iest**) tout petit.

tip /tɪp/ n (of stick, pen, shoe, ski) pointe f; (of nose, finger, wing) bout m; (gratuity) pourboire m; (advice) tuyau m; (for rubbish) décharge f. ● vt/i (pt **tipped**) (tilt) pencher; (overturn) (faire) basculer; (pour) verser; (empty) déverser; (give money) donner un pourboire à. □ ∼ **off** prévenir.

tiptoe /'tɪptəʊ/ n on ∼ sur la pointe des pieds.

tire /'taɪə(r)/ vt/i (se) fatiguer; ∼ of se lasser de. ● n (US) pneu m.

tired /'taɪəd/ adj fatigué; be ∼ of en avoir assez de.

tiring /'taɪərɪŋ/ adj fatigant.

tissue /'tɪʃuː/ n tissu m; (handkerchief) mouchoir m en papier; ∼ (**paper**) papier m de soie.

tit /tɪt/ n (bird) mésange f; give ∼ for tat rendre coup pour coup.

title /'taɪtl/ n titre m. ● **deed** n titre m de propriété.

---

to /tuː, tə/

● preposition

····▸ à; ∼ **Paris** à Paris; **give the book** ∼ **Jane** donne le livre à Jane; ∼ **the office** au bureau; ∼ **the shops** aux magasins.

····▸ (with feminine countries) en; ∼ **France** en France.

····▸ (to + personal pronoun) me/te/lui/nous/vous/leur; **she gave it** ∼ **them** elle le leur a donné; **I'll say it** ∼ **her** je vais

le lui dire.

! à + le = **au**
    à + les = **aux.**

● in an infinitive

to is not translated (**to go** aller; **to sing** chanter)

····▸ (in order to) pour; **he's gone into town** ∼ **buy a shirt** il est parti en ville pour acheter une chemise.

····▸ (after adjectives) à; de; **be easy/difficult** ∼ **read** être facile/difficile à lire; **it's easy/difficult to read her writing** c'est facile/difficile de lire son écriture.

➡️ For verbal expressions using the infinitive 'to' such as **to tell sb to do sth, to help sb to do sth** →**tell, help.**

---

toad /təʊd/ n crapaud m.

toast /təʊst/ n pain m grillé, toast m; (drink) toast m. ● vt (bread) faire griller; (drink to) porter un toast à. **toaster** n grille-pain m inv.

tobacco /tə'bækəʊ/ n tabac m.

tobacconist /tə'bækənɪst/ n marchand-e m/f de tabac; ∼'s (**shop**) tabac m.

toboggan /tə'bɒgən/ n toboggan m, luge f.

today /tə'deɪ/ n & adv aujourd'hui (m).

toddler /'tɒdlə(r)/ n bébé m (qui fait ses premiers pas).

toe /təʊ/ n orteil m; (of shoe) bout m; **on one's** ∼**s** vigilant. ● vt ∼ the line se conformer.

together /tə'geðə(r)/ adv ensemble; (at same time) à la fois; ∼ **with** avec.

toilet /'tɔɪlɪt/ n toilettes fpl.

toiletries /'tɔɪlɪtrɪz/ npl articles mpl de toilette.

token /'təʊkən/ n (symbol) témoignage m; (voucher) bon m; (coin) jeton m. ● adj symbolique.

told /təʊld/ →TELL.

tolerance /'tɒlərəns/ n tolérance f.

tolerate /'tɒləreɪt/ vt tolérer.

toll /təʊl/ n péage m; death ~ nombre m de morts; take its ~ faire des ravages. ● vi (bell) sonner.

tomato /tə'mɑːtəʊ/ n (pl ~es) tomate f.

tomb /tuːm/ n tombeau m.

tomorrow /tə'mɒrəʊ/ n & adv demain (m); ~ morning/night demain matin/soir; the day after ~ après-demain.

ton /tʌn/ n tonne f (= 1016 kg); (metric) ~ tonne f (= 1000 kg); ~s of 🄸 des masses de.

tone /təʊn/ n ton m; (of radio, telephone) tonalité f. ● vt ~ down atténuer. ● vi ~ (in) s'harmoniser (with avec).

tongs /tɒŋz/ npl (for coal) pincettes fpl; (for sugar) pince f; (for hair) fer m.

tongue /tʌŋ/ n langue f.

tonic /'tɒnɪk/ n (Med) tonique m. ● adj (effect, accent) tonique; ~ (water) tonic m, Schweppes® m.

tonight /tə'naɪt/ n & adv (evening) ce soir; (night) cette nuit.

tonsil /'tɒnsl/ n amygdale f.

too /tuː/ adv trop; (also) aussi; ~ many people trop de gens; I've got ~much/many j'en ai trop; me ~ moi aussi.

took→TAKE.

tool /tuːl/ n outil m. ~bar n barre f d'outils. ~box n boîte f à outils.

toot /tuːt/ n coup m de klaxon®.

● vt/i ~ (the horn) klaxonner.

tooth /tuːθ/ n (pl teeth) dent f. ~ache n mal m de dents. ~brush n brosse f à dents. ~paste n dentifrice m. ~pick n cure-dents m inv.

top /tɒp/ n (highest point) sommet m; (upper part) haut m; (upper surface) dessus m; (lid) couvercle m; (of bottle, tube) bouchon m; (of beer bottle) capsule f; (of list) tête f; on ~ of sur; (fig) en plus de. ● adj (shelf) du haut; (step, floor) dernier; (in rank) premier; (best) meilleur; (distinguished) éminent; (maximum) maximum. ● vt (pt topped) (exceed) dépasser; (list) venir en tête de; ~ up remplir; ~ped with (dome) surmonté de; (cream) recouvert de.

topic /'tɒpɪk/ n sujet m.

topless /'tɒplɪs/ adj aux seins nus.

torch /tɔːtʃ/ n (electric) lampe f de poche; (flaming) torche f.

tore /tɔː(r)/ →TEAR¹.

torment /tɔː'ment/ vt tourmenter.

torn /tɔːn/ →TEAR¹.

torrent /'tɒrənt/ n torrent m.

tortoise /'tɔːtəs/ n tortue f. ~shell n écaille f.

torture /'tɔːtʃə(r)/ n torture f; (fig) supplice m. ● vt torturer.

Tory /'tɔːrɪ/ n a tory (mf), conservateur/-trice (m/f).

toss /tɒs/ vt (ancer; (salad) remuer; (pancake) faire sauter. ● vi se retourner; ~ a coin, ~ up tirer à pile ou face (for pour).

tot /tɒt/ n petit/-e enfant m/f; (drink) petit verre m.

total /'təʊtl/ n a total (m). ● vt (pt totalled) (add up) additionner; (amount to) se monter à.

touch /tʌtʃ/ vt toucher; (tamper with) toucher à. ● vi se toucher. ● n (sense) toucher m; (contact) contact m; (of artist, writer) touche f; **a ~of** (small amount) un petit peu de; **get in ~ with** se mettre en contact avec; **out of ~ with** déconnecté de. □ **~ down** (Aviat) atterrir; **~ up** retoucher. **~down** n atterrissage m; (Sport) essai m. **~ line** n ligne f de but; **~tone** adj (phone) à touches.

tough /tʌf/ adj (negotiator) coriace; (law) sévère; (time) difficile; (robust) robuste.

tour /tʊə(r)/ n voyage m; (visit) visite f; (by team) tournée f; **on ~** en tournée. ● vt visiter.

tourist /ˈtʊərɪst/ n touriste mf. ● adj touristique. **~ office** n syndicat m d'initiative.

tournament /ˈtɔːnəmənt/ n tournoi m.

tout /taʊt/ vi **~ (for)** racoler 🔟. ● vt (sell) revendre. ● n racoleur/-euse m/f; revendeur/-euse m/f.

tow /təʊ/ vt remorquer. ● n remorque f; **on ~** en remorque.

toward(s) /təˈwɔːd(z)/ prep vers; (of attitude) envers.

towel /ˈtaʊəl/ n serviette f.

tower /ˈtaʊə(r)/ n tour f. ● vi **~ above** dominer.

town /taʊn/ n ville f; **in ~** en ville. **~ council** n conseil m municipal. **~ hall** n mairie f.

tow: ~ path n chemin m de halage. **~ truck** n dépanneuse f.

toxic /ˈtɒksɪk/ adj toxique.

toy /tɔɪ/ n jouet m. ● vi **~ with** (object) jouer avec; (idea) caresser.

trace /treɪs/ n trace f. ● vt (person) retrouver; (cause) déterminer; (life) retracer; (draw) tracer; (with tracing paper) décalquer.

track /træk/ n (of person, car) traces fpl; (of missile) trajectoire f; (path) sentier m; (Sport) piste f;

(Rail) voie f; (on disc) morceau m; **keep ~ of** suivre. ● vt suivre la trace or la trajectoire de. □ **~ down** retrouver. **~ suit** n survêtement m.

tractor /ˈtræktə(r)/ n tracteur m.

trade /treɪd/ n commerce m; (job) métier m; (swap) échange m. ● vi faire du commerce; **~on** exploiter. ● vt échanger. ● adj (route, deficit) commercial. **~-in** n reprise f. **~ mark** n marque f (de fabrique); (registered) marque f déposée.

trader /ˈtreɪdə(r)/ n commerçant/-e m/f; (on stockmarket) opérateur/-trice m/f.

trade union n syndicat m.

trading /ˈtreɪdɪŋ/ n commerce m; (on stockmarket) transactions fpl (boursières).

tradition /trəˈdɪʃn/ n tradition f.

traffic /ˈtræfɪk/ n trafic m; (on road) circulation f. ● vi (pt **trafficked**) faire du trafic (**in** de). **~ jam** n embouteillage m. **~-lights** npl feux mpl (de circulation). **~ warden** n contractuel/-le m/f.

trail /treɪl/ vt/i traîner; (plant) ramper; (track) suivre; **~ behind** traîner. ● n (of powder) traînée f; (track) piste f; (path) sentier m.

trailer /ˈtreɪlə(r)/ n remorque f; (caravan) caravane f; (film) bande-annonce f.

train /treɪn/ n (Rail) train m; (underground) rame f; (procession) file f; (of dress) traîne f. ● vt (instruct, develop) former; (sportsman) entraîner; (animal) dresser; (ear) exercer; (aim) braquer. ● vi être formé, étudier; (Sport) s'entraîner.

trained adj (skilled) qualifié; (doctor) diplômé. **trainee** n stagiaire mf.

trainer n (Sport) entraîneur/-euse m/f. **trainers** npl (shoes) chaussures fpl de sport. **training** n formation f;

t

(Sport) entraînement m.

tram /træm/ n tram(way) m.

tramp /træmp/ vi marcher (d'un pas lourd). ● vt parcourir. ● n (vagrant) clochard/-e m/f; (sound) bruit m.

trample /'træmpl/ vt/i ∼ (on) piétiner; (fig) fouler aux pieds.

tranquil /'træŋkwɪl/ adj tranquille. **tranquillizer** n tranquillisant m.

transact /træn'zækt/ vt négocier. **transaction** n transaction f.

transcript /'trænskrɪpt/ n transcription f.

transfer[1] /træns'fɜ:(r)/ vt (pt **transferred**) transférer; (power) céder; (employee) muter. ● vi être transféré; (employee) être muté.

transfer[2] /'trænsfɜ:(r)/ n transfert m; (of employee) mutation f; (image) décalcomanie f.

transform /træns'fɔ:m/ vt transformer.

transitive /'trænzətɪv/ adj transitif.

translate /trænz'leɪt/ vt traduire. **translation** n traduction f; **translator** n traducteur/-trice m/f.

transmit /trænz'mɪt/ vt (pt **transmitted**) transmettre. **transmitter** n émetteur m.

transparency /træns'pærənsɪ/ n transparence f; (Photo) diapositive f.

transplant /træns'plɑ:nt/ n transplantation f; (Med) greffe f.

transport[1] /'trænspɔ:t/ n transporter.

transport[2] /'trænspɔ:t/ n transport m.

trap /træp/ n piège m. ● vt pt **trapped** (jam, pin down) coincer; (cut off) bloquer; (snare) prendre au piège.

trash /træʃ/ n (refuse) ordures fpl; (nonsense) idioties fpl. ∼**-can** n (US)

poubelle f.

trauma /'trɔ:mə/ n traumatisme m. **traumatic** adj traumatisant.

travel /'trævl/ vi (pt **travelled**, US **traveled**) voyager; (vehicle, bullet) aller. ● vt parcourir. ● n voyages mpl. ∼ **agency** n agence f de voyages.

traveller, (US) **traveler** /'trævlə(r)/ n voyageur/-euse m/f; ∼'s **cheque** chèque m de voyage.

trawler /'trɔ:lə(r)/ n chalutier m.

tray /treɪ/ n plateau m; (on office desk) corbeille f.

treacle /'tri:kl/ n mélasse f.

tread /tred/ vi (pt **trod**; pp **trodden**) marcher (**on** sur). ● vt fouler. ● n (sound) pas m; (of tyre) chape f.

treasure /'treʒə(r)/ n trésor m. ● vt (gift, memory) chérir; (friendship, possession) tenir beaucoup à.

treasury /'treʒərɪ/ n trésorerie f; **the T**∼ le ministère des Finances.

treat /tri:t/ vt traiter; ∼ **sb to sth** offrir qch à qn. ● n (pleasure) plaisir m; (food) gâterie f. **treatment** n traitement m.

treaty /'tri:tɪ/ n traité m.

treble /'trebl/ adj triple; ∼ **clef** clé f de sol. ● vt/i tripler. ● n (voice) soprano m.

tree /tri:/ n arbre m.

trek /trek/ n randonnée f. ● vi (pt **trekked**) ∼ **across/through** traverser péniblement; **go** ∼**king** faire de la randonnée.

tremble /'trembl/ vi trembler.

tremendous /trɪ'mendəs/ adj énorme; (excellent) formidable.

tremor /'tremə(r)/ n tremblement m; (earth) ∼ secousse f.

trench /trentʃ/ n tranchée f.

trend /trend/ n tendance f; (fashion) mode f. **trendy** adj 🆃 branché 🆃.

trespass /'trespəs/ vi s'introduire illégalement (**on** dans). **trespasser** n intrus/-e m/f.

trial /'traɪəl/ n (Jur) procès m; (test) essai m; (ordeal) épreuve f; **go on ∼** passer en jugement; **by ∼ and error** par expérience.

triangle /'traɪæŋgl/ n triangle m.

tribe /traɪb/ n tribu f.

tribunal /traɪ'bjuːnl/ n tribunal m.

tributary /'trɪbjʊtərɪ/ n affluent m.

tribute /'trɪbjuːt/ n tribut m; **pay ∼ to** rendre hommage à.

trick /trɪk/ n tour m; (dishonest) combine f; (knack) astuce f; **do the ∼** 🛈 faire l'affaire. ● vt tromper. **trickery** n ruse f.

trickle /'trɪkl/ vi dégouliner; ∼ **in/out** arriver ou partir en petit nombre. ● n filet m; (fig) petit nombre m.

tricky /'trɪkɪ/ adj (task) difficile; (question) épineux; (person) malin.

trifle /'traɪfl/ n bagatelle f; (cake) diplomate m; **a ∼** (small amount) un peu. ● vi ∼ **with** jouer avec.

trigger /'trɪgə(r)/ n (of gun) gâchette f; (of machine) manette f. ● vt ∼ **(off)** (initiate) déclencher.

trim /trɪm/ adj (trimmer, trimmest) soigné; (figure) svelte. ● vt (pt trimmed) (hair, grass) couper; (budget) réduire; (decorate) décorer. ● n (cut) coupe f d'entretien; (decoration) garniture f; **in ∼** en forme.

trinket /'trɪŋkɪt/ n babiole f.

trip /trɪp/ vt/i (pt tripped) (faire) trébucher. ● n (journey) voyage m; (outing) excursion f.

triple /'trɪpl/ adj triple. ● vt/i tripler. **triplets** npl triplés/-es m/fpl.

tripod /'traɪpɒd/ n trépied m.

trite /traɪt/ adj banal.

triumph /'traɪʌmf/ n triomphe m. ● vi triompher (**over** de).

trivial /'trɪvɪəl/ adj insignifiant.

trod, trodden /trɒd(ən)/ →TREAD.

trolley /'trɒlɪ/ n chariot m.

trombone /trɒm'bəʊn/ n (Mus) trombone m.

troop /truːp/ n bande f; ∼**s** (Mil) troupes fpl. ● vi ∼ **in/out** entrer/ sortir en bande.

trophy /'trəʊfɪ/ n trophée m.

tropic /'trɒpɪk/ n tropique m; ∼**s** tropiques mpl.

trot /trɒt/ n trot m; **on the ∼** 🛈 coup sur coup. ● vi (pt trotted) trotter.

trouble /'trʌbl/ n problèmes mpl ; ennuis mpl; (pains, effort) peine f; **be in ∼** avoir des ennuis; **go to a lot of ∼** se donner du mal; **what's the ∼?** quel est le problème? ● vt (bother) déranger; (worry) tracasser. ● vi ∼ **(oneself)** to do se donner la peine de faire. ∼**maker** n provocateur/-trice m/f. ∼**shooter** n conciliateur/-trice m/f. (Tech) expert m.

troublesome /'trʌbləsəm/ adj ennuyeux.

trousers /'traʊzəz/ npl pantalon m; **short ∼** short m.

trout /traʊt/ n inv truite f.

trowel /'traʊəl/ n (garden) déplantoir m; (for mortar) truelle f.

truant /'truːənt/ n (School) élève mf qui fait l'école buissonnière; **play ∼** sécher les cours.

truce /truːs/ n trève f.

truck /trʌk/ n (lorry) camion m; (cart) chariot m; (Rail) wagon m de marchandises. ∼**driver** n routier m.

true /truː/ adj vrai; (accurate) exact; (faithful) fidèle.

truffle /'trʌfl/ n truffe f.

truly /'truːlɪ/ adv vraiment; (faithfully) fidèlement; (truthfully) sincèrement.

trumpet /'trʌmpɪt/ n trompette f.

trunk /trʌŋk/ n (of tree, body) tronc m; (of elephant) trompe f; (box) malle f; (Auto, US) coffre m; ~s (for swimming) slip m de bain.

trust /trʌst/ n confiance f; (association) trust m; **in** ~ en dépôt. ● vt avoir confiance en; **to** ~ **sb with** confier à qn. ● vi ~ **in** or **to** s'en remettre à. **trustee** n administrateur/-trice m/f. **trustworthy** adj digne de confiance.

truth /truːθ/ n (pl -s) vérité f. **truthful** adj (account) véridique; (person) qui dit la vérité.

try /traɪ/ vt/i (pt **tried**) essayer; (be a strain on) éprouver; (Jur) juger; ~ **on** or **out** essayer; ~ **to do** essayer de faire. ● n (attempt) essai m; (rugby) essai m.

T-shirt /'tiːʃɜːt/ n tee-shirt m.

tub /tʌb/ n (for flowers) bac m; (of ice cream) pot m; (bath) baignoire f.

tube /tjuːb/ n tube m; **the** ~ m le métro.

tuberculosis /tjuːbɜːkjʊ'ləʊsɪs/ n tuberculose f.

tuck /tʌk/ n pli m. ● vt (put away, place) ranger; (hide) cacher. ● vi ~ **in** or **into** m attaquer; ~ **in** (shirt) rentrer; (blanket, person) border.

Tuesday /'tjuːzdeɪ/ n mardi m.

tug /tʌg/ vt (pt **tugged**) tirer; ~ **at/on** tirer sur. ● n (boat) remorqueur m.

tuition /tjuː'ɪʃn/ n cours mpl; (fee) frais mpl pédagogiques.

tulip /'tjuːlɪp/ n tulipe f.

tumble /'tʌmbl/ vi (fall) dégringoler. ● n chute f. ~**drier** n sèchelinge m inv.

tumbler /'tʌmblə(r)/ n verre m droit.

tummy /'tʌmɪ/ n m ventre m.

tumour /'tjuːmə(r)/ n tumeur f.

tuna /'tjuːnə/ n inv thon m.

tune /tjuːn/ n air m; **be in** ~/**out of** ~ (instrument) être/ne pas être en accord; (singer) chanter juste/faux. ● vt (engine) régler; (Mus) accorder. ● vi ~ **in (to)** (radio),TV écouter. □ ~ **up** s'accorder.

Tunisia /tjuː'nɪzɪə/ n Tunisie f.

tunnel /'tʌnl/ n tunnel m; (in mine) galerie f. ● vi (pt **tunnelled**) creuser un tunnel (**into** dans).

turf /tɜːf/ n (pl **turf** or **turves**) gazon m; **the** ~ (racing) le turf. ● vt ~ **out** m jeter dehors.

Turk /tɜːk/ n Turc m, Turque f. **Turkey** n Turquie f.

turkey /'tɜːkɪ/ n dinde f.

Turkish /'tɜːkɪʃ/ adj turc. ● n (Ling) turc m.

turn /tɜːn/ vt/i tourner; (person) se tourner; (to other side) retourner; (change) (se) transformer (**into** en); (become) devenir; (deflect) détourner; (milk) tourner. ● n tour m; (in road) tournant m; (of mind, events) tournure f; **do a good** ~ rendre service; **in** ~ à tour de rôle; **take** ~**s** se relayer. □ ~ **against** vi se retourner contre; ~ **away** vi se détourner; vt (avert) détourner; (refuse) refuser; (send back) renvoyer; ~ **back** vi (return) retourner; (vehicle) faire demi-tour; vt (fold) rabattre; ~ **down** vt (fold) rabattre; (reduce) baisser; ~ **off** (tap) éteindre; (engine) arrêter; (tap) fermer; (of driver) tourner; ~ **on** (light) allumer; (engine) allumer; (tap) ouvrir; ~ **out** vt (light) éteindre; (empty) vider; (produce) produire; vi **it** ~**s out that** il se trouve que; ~ **out well/badly** bien/mal se terminer; ~ **over** (se) retourner; ~

round (person) se retourner; ~ **up** *vi* arriver; (be found) se retrouver; *vt* (find) déterrer; (collar) remonter.

turning /'tɜːnɪŋ/ *n* rue *f*; (bend) virage *m*.

turnip /'tɜːnɪp/ *n* navet *m*.

turn-: ~**out** *n* assistance *f*. ~**over** *n* (pie) chausson *m*; (money) chiffre *m* d'affaires. ~**table** *n* (for record) platine *f*.

turquoise /'tɜːkwɔːz/ *adj* turquoise *inv*.

turtle /'tɜːtl/ *n* tortue *f* (de mer). ~**neck** *n* col *m* montant.

tutor /'tjuːtə(r)/ *n* (private) professeur *m* particulier; (Univ) (GB) chargé/-e *m/f* de travaux dirigés.

tutorial /tjuː'tɔːrɪəl/ *n* (Univ) classe *f* de travaux dirigés.

tuxedo /tʌk'siːdəʊ/ *n* (US) smoking *m*.

TV /tiː'viː/ *n* télé *f*.

tweezers /'twiːzəz/ *npl* pince *f* (à épiler).

twelfth /twelfθ/ *adj* & *n* douzième (*mf*).

twelve /twelv/ *adj* & *n* douze (*m*); ~ **(o'clock)** midi *m* or minuit *m*.

twentieth /'twentɪəθ/ *adj* & *n* vingtième (*mf*).

twenty /'twentɪ/ *adj* & *n* vingt (*m*).

twice /twaɪs/ *adv* deux fois.

twig /twɪg/ *n* brindille *f*.

twilight /'twaɪlaɪt/ *n* crépuscule *m*. ● *adj* crépusculaire.

twin /twɪn/ *n* & *a* jumeau/-elle (*m/f*). ● *vt* (*pt* **twinned**) jumeler.

twinge /twɪndʒ/ *n* (of pain) élancement *m*; (of conscience, doubt) accès *m*.

twinkle /'twɪŋkl/ *vi* (star) scintiller; (eye) pétiller. ● *n* scintillement *m*; pétillement *m*.

twinning /'twɪnɪŋ/ *n* jumelage *m*.

twist /twɪst/ *vt* tordre; (weave together) entortiller; (roll) enrouler; (distort) déformer. ● *vi* (rope) s'entortiller; (road) zigzaguer. ● *n* torsion *f*; (in rope) tortillon *m*; (in road) tournant *m*; (in play, story) coup *m* de théâtre.

twitch /twɪtʃ/ *vi* (person) trembloter; (mouth) trembler; (string) vibrer. ● *n* (tic) tic *m*; (jerk) secousse *f*.

two /tuː/ *adj* & *n* deux (*m*); **in** ~**s** par deux; **break in** ~ casser en deux.

tycoon /taɪ'kuːn/ *n* magnat *m*.

type /taɪp/ *n* type *m*, genre *m*; (print) caractères *mpl*. ● *vt/i* (write) taper (à la machine). ~**face** *n* police *f* (de caractères). ~**writer** *n* machine *f* à écrire.

typical /'tɪpɪkl/ *adj* typique.

typist /'taɪpɪst/ *n* dactylo *mf*.

tyrant /'taɪərənt/ *n* tyran *m*.

tyre /'taɪə(r)/ *n* pneu *m*.

Uu

udder /'ʌdə(r)/ *n* pis *m*, mamelle *f*.

UFO /'juːfəʊ/ *n* OVNI *m inv*.

UHT *abbr* **ultra heat treated** ~ **milk** lait *m* longue conservation.

ugly /'ʌglɪ/ *adj* (**-ier, -iest**) laid.

UK *abbr* ➡**UNITED KINGDOM.**

Ukraine /juː'kreɪn/ *n* Ukraine *f*.

ulcer /'ʌlsə(r)/ *n* ulcère *m*.

ulterior /ʌl'tɪərɪə(r)/ *adj* ultérieur; ~ **motive** arrière-pensée *f*.

ultimate /'ʌltɪmət/ *adj* dernier, ultime; (definitive) définitif; (basic) fondamental.

ultrasound /'ʌltrəsaʊnd/ *n*

ultrason m.

umbilical cord /ʌmˈbɪlɪkl kɔːd/ n cordon m ombilical.

umbrella /ʌmˈbrelə/ n parapluie m.

umpire /ˈʌmpaɪə(r)/ n arbitre m. ● vt arbitrer.

umpteenth /ʌmpˈtiːnθ/ adj 🆃 énième.

UN abbr (**United Nations**) ONU f.

unable /ʌnˈeɪbl/ adj incapable; (through circumstances) dans l'impossibilité (**to do** de faire).

unacceptable /ʌnəkˈseptəbl/ adj (suggestion) inacceptable; (behaviour) inadmissible.

unanimous /juːˈnænɪməs/ adj unanime. **unanimously** adv à l'unanimité.

unattended /ʌnəˈtendɪd/ adj sans surveillance.

unattractive /ʌnəˈtræktɪv/ adj (idea) peu attrayant; (person) peu attirant.

unauthorized /ʌnˈɔːθəraɪzd/ adj non autorisé.

unavoidable /ʌnəˈvɔɪdəbl/ adj inévitable.

unbearable /ʌnˈbeərəbl/ adj insupportable.

unbelievable /ʌnbrˈliːvəbl/ adj incroyable.

unbiased /ʌnˈbaɪəst/ adj impartial.

unblock /ʌnˈblɒk/ vt déboucher.

unborn /ʌnˈbɔːn/ adj (child) à naître; (generation) à venir.

uncalled-for /ʌnˈkɔːldfɔː(r)/ adj injustifié, déplacé.

uncanny /ʌnˈkænɪ/ adj (-ier, -iest) étrange, troublant.

uncivilized /ʌnˈsɪvɪlaɪzd/ adj barbare.

uncle /ˈʌŋkl/ n oncle m.

uncomfortable /ʌnˈkʌmftəbl/ adj (chair) inconfortable; (feeling) pénible; **feel** or **be** ~ (person) être mal à l'aise.

uncommon /ʌnˈkɒmən/ adj rare.

unconscious /ʌnˈkɒnʃəs/ adj sans connaissance, inanimé; (not aware) inconscient (**of** de). ● n inconscient m.

unconventional /ʌnkən'venʃənl/ adj peu conventionnel.

uncouth /ʌnˈkuːθ/ adj grossier.

uncover /ʌnˈkʌvə(r)/ vt découvrir.

undecided /ʌndɪˈsaɪdɪd/ adj indécis.

under /ˈʌndə(r)/ prep sous; (less than) moins de; (according to) selon. ● adv au-dessous; ~ **it/there** là-dessous. ~ **age** adj mineur. ~**cover** adj secret. ~**cut** vt (pt **-cut**; pres p **-cutting**) (Comm) vendre moins cher que. ~**dog** n (Pol) opprimé/-e m/f; (socially) déshérité/-e m/f. ~**done** adj pas assez cuit. ~**estimate** vt sous-estimer. ~**fed** adj sous-alimenté. ~**go** vt (pt **-went**; pp **-gone**) subir. ~**graduate** n étudiant/-e m/f (qui prépare la licence).

underground /ˈʌndəɡraʊnd/ adj souterrain; (secret) clandestin. ● adv sous terre. ● n (rail) métro m.

under: ~line vt souligner. ~mine vt saper.

underneath /ʌndəˈniːθ/ prep sous. ● adv (en) dessous.

under: ~pants npl slip m. ~rate vt sous-estimer.

understand /ʌndəˈstænd/ vt/i (pt -stood) comprendre.

understanding /ʌndəˈstændɪŋ/ adj compréhensif. ● n compréhension f; (agreement) entente f.

undertake /ʌndəˈteɪk/ vt (pt -took; pp -taken) entreprendre. ~taker n entrepreneur m de pompes funèbres. ~taking n (task) entreprise f; (promise) promesse f.

underwater /ʌndəˈwɔːtə(r)/ adj sous-marin. ● adv sous l'eau.

under: ~wear n sous-vêtements mpl. ~world n (of crime) milieu m, pègre f.

undo /ʌnˈduː/ vt (pt -did; pp -done) défaire, détacher; (wrong) réparer; (Comput) annuler.

undress /ʌnˈdres/ vt/i (se) déshabiller; **get** ~ed se déshabiller.

undue /ʌnˈdjuː/ adj excessif.

unearth /ʌnˈɜːθ/ vt déterrer.

uneasy /ʌnˈiːzɪ/ adj (ill at ease) mal à l'aise; (worried) inquiet; (situation) difficile.

uneducated /ʌnˈedʒʊkeɪtɪd/ adj (person) inculte; (speech) populaire.

unemployed /ʌnɪmˈplɔɪd/ adj en chômage. ● npl the ~ les chômeurs mpl.

unemployment /ʌnɪmˈplɔɪmənt/ n chômage m; ~ **benefit** allocations fpl de chômage.

uneven /ʌnˈiːvn/ adj inégal.

unexpected /ʌnɪkˈspektɪd/ adj inattendu, imprévu. **unexpectedly** adv (arrive) à l'improviste; (small, fast) étonnamment.

unfair /ʌnˈfeə(r)/ adj injuste.

unfaithful /ʌnˈfeɪθfl/ adj infidèle.

unfit /ʌnˈfɪt/ adj (Med) pas en forme; (ill) malade; (unsuitable) impropre (**for** à); ~ **to** (unable) pas en état de.

unfold /ʌnˈfəʊld/ vt déplier; (expose) exposer. ● vi se dérouler.

unforeseen /ʌnfɔːˈsiːn/ adj imprévu.

unforgettable /ʌnfəˈɡetəbl/ adj inoubliable.

unfortunate /ʌnˈfɔːtʃənət/ adj malheureux; (event) fâcheux.

ungrateful /ʌnˈɡreɪtfl/ adj ingrat.

unhappy /ʌnˈhæpɪ/ adj (-ier, -iest) (person) malheureux; (face) triste; (not pleased) mécontent (**with** de).

unharmed /ʌnˈhɑːmd/ adj indemne, sain et sauf.

unhealthy /ʌnˈhelθɪ/ adj (-ier, -iest) (climate) malsain; (person) en mauvaise santé.

unheard-of /ʌnˈhɜːdɒv/ adj inouï.

unhurt /ʌnˈhɜːt/ adj indemne.

uniform /ˈjuːnɪfɔːm/ n uniforme m. ● adj uniforme.

unify /ˈjuːnɪfaɪ/ vt unifier.

unintentional /ʌnɪnˈtenʃənl/ adj involontaire.

uninterested /ʌnˈɪntrəstɪd/ adj indifférent (**in** à).

union /ˈjuːnɪən/ n union f; (trade union) syndicat m; **U**~ **jack** drapeau m du Royaume-Uni.

unique /juːˈniːk/ adj unique.

unit /ˈjuːnɪt/ n unité f; (of furniture) élément m; ~ **trust** ~ SICAV f.

unite /juːˈnaɪt/ vt/i (s')unir.

United Kingdom n Royaume-Uni m.

United Nations npl Nations fpl Unies.

United States (of America)

u

npl états-Unis *mpl* (d'Amérique).

unity /ˈjuːnətɪ/ *n* unité *f*.

universal /juːnɪˈvɜːsl/ *adj* universel.

universe /ˈjuːnɪvɜːs/ *n* univers *m*.

university /juːnɪˈvɜːsətɪ/ *n* université *f*. ● *adj* universitaire; (*student, teacher*) d'université.

unkind /ʌnˈkaɪnd/ *adj* pas gentil, méchant.

unknown /ʌnˈnəʊn/ *adj* inconnu. ● *n* the ~ l'inconnu *m*.

unleaded /ʌnˈledɪd/ *adj* sans plomb.

unless /ənˈles/ *conj* à moins que.

unlike /ʌnˈlaɪk/ *adj* différent. ● *prep* contrairement à; (*different from*) différent de.

unlikely /ʌnˈlaɪklɪ/ *adj* improbable.

unload /ʌnˈləʊd/ *vt* décharger.

unlock /ʌnˈlɒk/ *vt* ouvrir.

unlucky /ʌnˈlʌkɪ/ *adj* **-ier, -iest** malheureux; (*number*) qui porte malheur.

unmarried /ʌnˈmærɪd/ *adj* célibataire.

unnatural /ʌnˈnætʃrəl/ *adj* pas naturel, anormal.

unnecessary /ʌnˈnesəsrɪ/ *adj* inutile.

unnoticed /ʌnˈnəʊtɪst/ *adj* inaperçu.

unofficial /ʌnəˈfɪʃl/ *adj* officieux.

unpack /ʌnˈpæk/ *vt* (*suitcase*) défaire; (*contents*) déballer. ● *vi* défaire sa valise.

unpleasant /ʌnˈpleznt/ *adj* désagréable (**to** avec).

unplug /ʌnˈplʌg/ *vt* débrancher.

unpopular /ʌnˈpɒpjʊlə(r)/ *adj* impopulaire; ~ **with** mal vu de.

unprofessional /ʌnprəˈfeʃənl/ *adj* peu professionnel.

unqualified /ʌnˈkwɒlɪfaɪd/ *adj*

non diplômé; (*success*) total; **be** ~ **to** ne pas être qualifié pour.

unravel /ʌnˈrævl/ *vt* (*pt* **unravelled**) démêler.

unreasonable /ʌnˈriːznəbl/ *adj* irréaliste.

unrelated /ʌnrɪˈleɪtɪd/ *adj* sans rapport (**to** avec).

unreliable /ʌnrɪˈlaɪəbl/ *adj* peu sérieux; (*machine*) peu fiable.

unrest /ʌnˈrest/ *n* troubles *mpl*.

unroll /ʌnˈrəʊl/ *vt* dérouler.

unruly /ʌnˈruːlɪ/ *adj* indiscipliné.

unsafe /ʌnˈseɪf/ *adj* (*dangerous*) dangereux; (*person*) en danger.

unscheduled /ʌnˈʃedjuːld/ *adj* pas prévu.

unscrupulous /ʌnˈskruːpjʊləs/ *adj* sans scrupules, malhonnête.

unsettled /ʌnˈsetld/ *adj* instable.

unsightly /ʌnˈsaɪtlɪ/ *adj* laid.

unskilled /ʌnˈskɪld/ *adj* (*worker*) non qualifié.

unsound /ʌnˈsaʊnd/ *adj* (*roof*) en mauvais état; (*investment*) douteux.

unsteady /ʌnˈstedɪ/ *adj* (*step*) chancelant; (*ladder*) instable; (*hand*) mal assuré.

unsuccessful /ʌnsəkˈsesfl/ *adj* (*result, candidate*) malheureux; (*attempt*) infructueux; **be** ~ ne pas réussir (**in doing** à faire).

unsuitable /ʌnˈsuːtəbl/ *adj* inapproprié; **be** ~ ne pas convenir.

unsure /ʌnˈʃɔː(r)/ *adj* incertain.

untidy /ʌnˈtaɪdɪ/ *adj* **-ier, -iest** (*person*) désordonné; (*room*) en désordre; (*work*) mal soigné.

untie /ʌnˈtaɪ/ *vt* (*knot, parcel*) défaire; (*person*) détacher.

until /ʌnˈtɪl/ *prep* jusqu'à; **not** ~ pas avant. ● *conj* jusqu'à ce que; **not** ~ pas avant que.

untrue /ʌnˈtruː/ *adj* faux.

unused /ʌnˈjuːst/ adj (new) neuf; (not in use) inutilisé.

unusual /ʌnˈjuːʒl/ adj exceptionnel; (strange) insolite, étrange.

unwanted /ʌnˈwɒntɪd/ adj (useless) superflu; (child) non désiré.

unwelcome /ʌnˈwelkəm/ adj fâcheux; (guest) importun.

unwell /ʌnˈwel/ adj souffrant.

unwilling /ʌnˈwɪlɪŋ/ adj peu disposé (to à); (accomplice) malgré soi.

unwind /ʌnˈwaɪnd/ vt/i (pt **unwound**) (se) dérouler; (relax Ⓘ) se détendre.

unwise /ʌnˈwaɪz/ adj imprudent.

unwrap /ʌnˈræp/ vt déballer.

up /ʌp/ adv en haut, en l'air; (sun, curtain) levé; (out of bed) levé, debout; (finished) fini; be ~ (level, price) avoir monté. ● prep (a hill) en haut de; (a tree) dans; (a ladder) sur; **come** or **go** ~ monter; ~ **in the bedroom** là-haut dans la chambre; ~ **there** là-haut; ~ **to** jusqu'à; (task) à la hauteur de; **it is** ~ **to you** ça dépend de vous (to de); **be** ~ **to sth** (able) être capable de qch; (plot) préparer qch; **be** ~ **to** (in book) en être à; **be** ~ **against** faire face à; ~ **to date** moderne; (news) récent. ● n ~**s and downs** les hauts et les bas mpl.

up-and-coming adj prometteur.

upbringing /ˈʌpbrɪŋɪŋ/ n éducation f.

update /ʌpˈdeɪt/ vt mettre à jour.

upgrade /ʌpˈɡreɪd/ vt améliorer; (person) promouvoir.

upheaval /ʌpˈhiːvl/ n bouleversement m.

uphill /ʌpˈhɪl/ adj qui monte; (fig) difficile. ● adv **go** ~ monter.

upholstery /ʌpˈhəʊlstərɪ/ n rembourrage m; (in vehicle) garniture f.

upkeep /ˈʌpkiːp/ n entretien m.

up-market adj haut-de-gamme.

upon /əˈpɒn/ prep sur.

upper /ˈʌpə(r)/ adj supérieur; **have the** ~ **hand** avoir le dessus. ● n (of shoe) empeigne f. ~ **class** n aristocratie f. ~**most** adj (highest) le plus haut.

upright /ˈʌpraɪt/ adj droit. ● n (post) montant m.

uprising /ˈʌpraɪzɪŋ/ n soulèvement m.

uproar /ˈʌprɔː(r)/ n tumulte m.

uproot /ʌpˈruːt/ vt déraciner.

upset[1] /ʌpˈset/ vt (pt **upset**; pres p **upsetting**) (overturn) renverser; (plan, stomach) déranger; (person) contrarier, affliger. ● adj peiné.

upset[2] /ˈʌpset/ n dérangement m; (distress) chagrin m.

upside-down /ʌpsaɪdˈdaʊn/ adv (lit) à l'envers; (fig) sens dessus dessous.

upstairs /ʌpˈsteəz/ adv en haut. ● adj (flat) du haut.

uptight /ʌpˈtaɪt/ adj Ⓘ tendu, coincé Ⓘ.

up-to-date adj à la mode; (records) à jour.

upward /ˈʌpwəd/ adj & adv, **upwards** adv vers le haut.

urban /ˈɜːbən/ adj urbain.

urge /ɜːdʒ/ vt conseiller vivement (to do de faire); ~ **on** encourager. ● n forte envie f.

urgency /ˈɜːdʒənsɪ/ n urgence f; (of request, tone) insistance f. **urgent** adj urgent; (request) pressant.

urinal /jʊəˈraɪnl/ n urinoir m.

urine /ˈjʊərɪn/ n urine f.

us /ʌs, əs/ pron nous; (to) ~ nous; **both of** ~ tous/toutes les deux.

US abbr →UNITED STATES.

USA abbr →UNITED STATES OF AMERICA.

use¹ /juːz/ *vt* se servir de, utiliser. (consume) consommer; ~ **up** épuiser.

use² /juːs/ *n* usage *m*, emploi *m*; **in** ~ **en** usage; **it is no** ~ **doing** ça ne sert à rien de faire; **make** ~ **of** se servir de; **of** ~ utile.

used¹ /juːzd/ *adj* (car) d'occasion.

used² /juːst/ *v aux* **he** ~ **up** il fumait (autrefois). ● *adj* ~ **to** habitué à.

useful /'juːsfl/ *adj* utile.

useless /'juːslɪs/ *adj* inutile; (person) incompétent.

user /'juːzə(r)/ *n* (of road, service) usager *m*; (of product) utilisateur/-trice *m/f*; ~-**friendly** *adj* facile d'emploi; (Comput) convivial.

usual /'juːʒl/ *adj* habituel, normal; **as** ~ comme d'habitude. **usually** *adv* d'habitude.

utility /juːˈtɪlətɪ/ *n* utilité *f*; **(public)** ~ **service** *m* public.

utmost /'ʌtməʊst/ *adj* (furthest, most intense) extrême; **the** ~ **care** le plus grand soin. ● *n* **do one's** ~ faire tout son possible.

utter /'ʌtə(r)/ *adj* complet, absolu. ● *vt* prononcer.

U-turn /juːˈtɜːn/ *n* demi-tour *m*; (fig) volteface *f inv*.

··

Vv

··

vacancy /'veɪkənsɪ/ *n* (post) poste *m* vacant; (room) chambre *f* disponible.

vacant /'veɪkənt/ *adj* (post) vacant; (seat) libre; (look) vague.

vacate /vəˈkeɪt/ *vt* quitter.

vacation /vəˈkeɪʃn/ *n* vacances *fpl*.

vaccinate /'væksɪneɪt/ *vt* vacciner.

vacuum /'vækjʊəm/ *n* vide *m*. ~ **cleaner** *n* aspirateur *m*. ~-**packed** *adj* emballé sous vide.

vagina /vəˈdʒaɪnə/ *n* vagin *m*.

vagrant /'veɪɡrənt/ *n* vagabond/ -e *m/f*.

vague /veɪɡ/ *adj* vague; (outline) flou; **be** ~ **about** ne pas préciser.

vain /veɪn/ *adj* (conceited) vaniteux; (useless) vain; **in** ~ en vain.

valentine /'væləntaɪn/ *n* ~ **(card)** carte *f* de la Saint-Valentin.

valid /'vælɪd/ *adj* (argument, ticket) valable; (passport) valide.

valley /'vælɪ/ *n* vallée *f*.

valuable /'væljʊəbl/ *adj* (object) de valeur; (help) précieux. **valuables** *npl* objets *mpl* de valeur.

valuation /væljʊˈeɪʃn/ *n* (of painting) expertise *f*; (of house) évaluation *f*.

value /'væljuː/ *n* valeur *f*; ~ **added tax** taxe *f* à la valeur ajoutée, TVA *f*. ● *vt* (appraise) évaluer; (cherish) attacher de la valeur à.

valve /vælv/ *n* (Tech) soupape *f*; (of tyre) valve *f*; (Med) valvule *f*.

van /væn/ *n* camionnette *f*.

vandal /'vændl/ *n* vandale *mf*.

vanguard /'vænɡɑːd/ *n* **in the** ~ **of** à l'avantgarde *f* de.

vanilla /vəˈnɪlə/ *n* vanille *f*.

vanish /'vænɪʃ/ *vi* disparaître.

vapour /'veɪpə(r)/ *n* vapeur *f*.

variable /'veərɪəbl/ *adj* variable.

varicose /'værɪkəʊs/ *adj* ~ **veins** varices *fpl*.

varied /'veərɪd/ *adj* varié.

variety /vəˈraɪətɪ/ *n* variété *f*; (entertainment) variétés *fpl*.

various /'veərɪəs/ *adj* divers.

varnish /'vɑːnɪʃ/ *n* vernis *m*. ● *vt*

vernir.

vary /'vɛərɪ/ vt/i varier.

vase /vɑːz/ n vase m.

vast /vɑːst/ adj (space) vaste; (in quantity) énorme.

vat /væt/ n cuve f.

VAT abbr (**value added tax**) TVA f.

vault /vɔːlt/ n (roof) voûte f; (in bank) chambre f forte; (tomb) caveau m; (jump) saut m. ● vt/i sauter.

VCR abbr ➡VIDEO CASSETTE RECORDER.

VDU abbr ➡VISUAL DISPLAY UNIT.

veal /viːl/ n veau m.

vegan /'viːgən/ adj & n végétalien-ne (m/f).

vegetable /'vedʒtəbl/ n légume m. ● adj végétal.

vegetarian /vedʒɪ'teərɪən/ adj & n végétarien-ne (m/f).

vehicle /'vɪəkl/ n véhicule m.

veil /veɪl/ n voile m.

vein /veɪn/ n (in body, rock) veine f; (on leaf) nervure f.

velvet /'velvɪt/ n velours m.

vending-machine /'vendɪŋ məˈʃiːn/ n distributeur m automatique.

veneer /vɪˈnɪə(r)/ n (on wood) placage m; (fig) vernis m.

venereal /vəˈnɪərɪəl/ adj vénérien.

venetian /vɪˈniːʃn/ adj ~ blind jalousie f.

vengeance /'vendʒəns/ n vengeance f; with a ~ de plus belle.

venison /'venɪsn/ n venaison f.

venom /'venəm/ n venin m.

vent /vent/ n bouche f, conduit m; (in coat) fente f. ● vt (anger) décharger (on sur).

ventilate /'ventɪleɪt/ vt ventiler. **ventilator** n ventilateur m.

venture /'ventʃə(r)/ n entreprise f.
● vt/i (se) risquer.

venue /'venjuː/ n lieu m.

verb /vɜːb/ n verbe m.

verbal /'vɜːbl/ adj verbal.

verdict /'vɜːdɪkt/ n verdict m.

verge /vɜːdʒ/ n bord m; on the ~ of doing sur le point de faire. ● vi ~ on friser, frôler.

verify /'verɪfaɪ/ vt vérifier.

vermin /'vɜːmɪn/ n vermine f.

versatile /'vɜːsətaɪl/ adj (person) aux talents variés; (mind) souple.

verse /vɜːs/ n strophe f; (of Bible) verset m; (poetry) vers mpl.

version /'vɜːʃn/ n version f.

versus /'vɜːsəs/ prep contre.

vertebra /'vɜːtɪbrə/ n (pl -brae) vertèbre f.

vertical /'vɜːtɪkl/ adj vertical.

vertigo /'vɜːtɪgəʊ/ n vertige m.

very /'verɪ/ adv très. ● adj (actual) même; the ~ day le jour même; at the ~ end tout à la fin; the ~ first le tout premier; ~ much beaucoup.

vessel /'vesl/ n vaisseau m.

vest /vest/ n maillot m de corps; (waistcoat: US) gilet m.

vet /vet/ n vétérinaire mf. ● vt (pt **vetted**) (candidate) examiner (de près).

veteran /'vetərən/ n vétéran m; war ~ ancien combattant m.

veterinary /'vetrɪnrɪ/ adj vétérinaire; ~ surgeon vétérinaire mf.

veto /'viːtəʊ/ n (pl **-es**) veto m; (right) droit m de veto. ● vt mettre son veto à.

vibrate /vaɪˈbreɪt/ vt/i (faire) vibrer.

vicar /'vɪkə(r)/ n pasteur m.

vice /vaɪs/ n (depravity) vice m; (Tech) étau m.

v

vicinity /vɪ'sɪnətɪ/ n environs mpl; **in the ~ of** à proximité de.

vicious /'vɪʃəs/ adj (spiteful) méchant; (violent) brutal; **~ circle** cercle m vicieux.

victim /'vɪktɪm/ n victime f.

victor /'vɪktə(r)/ n vainqueur m. **victory** n victoire f.

video /'vɪdɪəʊ/ adj (game, camera) vidéo inv. ● n (recorder) magnétoscope m; (film) vidéo f; **~ (cassette)** cassette f vidéo. **~ game** n jeu m vidéo. **~phone** n vidéophone m. ● vt enregistrer.

videotape /'vɪdɪəʊteɪp/ n bande f vidéo. ● vt (programme) enregistrer; (wedding) filmer avec une caméra vidéo.

view /vjuː/ n vue f; **in my ~** à mon avis; **in ~ of** compte tenu de; **on ~** exposé; **with a ~ to** dans le but de. ● vt (watch) regarder; (consider) considérer (**as** comme); (house) visiter. **viewer** n (TV) téléspectateur/-trice m/f.

view: ~finder n viseur m. **~point** n point m de vue.

vigilant /'vɪdʒɪlənt/ adj vigilant.

vigour, (US) **vigor** /'vɪgə(r)/ n vigueur f.

vile /vaɪl/ adj (base) vil; (bad) abominable.

villa /'vɪlə/ n pavillon m; (for holiday) villa f.

village /'vɪlɪdʒ/ n village m.

villain /'vɪlən/ n scélérat m, bandit m; (in story) méchant m.

vindictive /vɪn'dɪktɪv/ adj vindicatif.

vine /vaɪn/ n vigne f.

vinegar /'vɪnɪgə(r)/ n vinaigre m.

vineyard /'vɪnjəd/ n vignoble m.

vintage /'vɪntɪdʒ/ n (year) année f, millésime m. ● adj (wine) de grand

cru; (car) d'époque.

viola /vɪ'əʊlə/ n (Mus) alto m.

violate /'vaɪəleɪt/ vt violer.

violence /'vaɪələns/ n violence f. **violent** adj violent.

violet /'vaɪələt/ n (Bot) violette f; (colour) violet m.

violin /vaɪə'lɪn/ n violon m.

VIP abbr (**very important person**) personnalité f, VIP m.

virgin /'vɜːdʒɪn/ n (woman) vierge f.

Virgo /'vɜːgəʊ/ n Vierge f.

virtual /'vɜːtʃʊəl/ adj quasi-total; (Comput) virtuel. **virtually** adv pratiquement.

virtue /'vɜːtʃuː/ n vertu f; (advantage) mérite m; **by ~ of** en raison de.

virus /'vaɪərəs/ n virus m.

visa /'viːzə/ n visa m.

visibility /vɪzə'bɪlətɪ/ n visibilité f. **visible** adj visible.

vision /'vɪʒn/ n vision f.

visit /'vɪzɪt/ vt (pt **visited**) (person) rendre visite à; (place) visiter. ● vi être en visite. ● n (tour, call) visite f; (stay) séjour m. **visitor** n visiteur/-euse m/f; (guest) invité/-e m/f.

visual /'vɪʒʊəl/ adj visuel. **~ display unit** n visuel m, console f de visualisation.

visualize /'vɪʒʊəlaɪz/ vt se représenter; (foresee) envisager.

vital /'vaɪtl/ adj vital.

vitamin /'vɪtəmɪn/ n vitamine f.

vivacious /vɪ'veɪʃəs/ adj plein de vivacité.

vivid /'vɪvɪd/ adj (colour, imagination) vif; (description, dream) frappant.

vivisection /vɪvɪ'sekʃn/ n vivisection f.

vocabulary /vəˈkæbjʊlərɪ/ n vocabulaire m.

vocal /ˈvəʊkl/ adj vocal; (person) qui s'exprime franchement. ~ **cords** npl cordes fpl vocales.

vocation /vəʊˈkeɪʃn/ n vocation f. **vocational** adj professionnel.

voice /vɔɪs/ n voix f. ● vt (express) formuler. ~ **mail** n messagerie f vocale.

void /vɔɪd/ adj vide (of de); (not valid) nul. ● n vide m.

volatile /ˈvɒlətaɪl/ adj (person) versatile; (situation) explosif.

volcano /vɒlˈkeɪnəʊ/ n (pl ~es) volcan m.

volley /ˈvɒlɪ/ n (of blows, in tennis) volée f; (of gunfire) salve f.

volt /vəʊlt/ n (Electr) volt m. **voltage** n tension f.

volume /ˈvɒljuːm/ n volume m.

voluntary /ˈvɒləntrɪ/ adj volontaire; (unpaid) bénévole.

volunteer /vɒlənˈtɪə(r)/ n volontaire mf. ● vi s'offrir (**to do** pour faire); (Mil) s'engager comme volontaire. ● vt offrir.

vomit /ˈvɒmɪt/ vt/i (pt **vomited**) vomir. ● n vomi m.

vote /vəʊt/ n vote m; (right) droit m de vote. ● vt/i voter; ~ **sb in** élire qn. **voter** n électeur/-trice m/f. **voting** n vote m (of de); (poll) scrutin m.

vouch /vaʊtʃ/ vi ~ **for** se porter garant de.

voucher /ˈvaʊtʃə(r)/ n bon m.

vowel /ˈvaʊəl/ n voyelle f.

voyage /ˈvɔɪɪdʒ/ n voyage m (en mer).

vulgar /ˈvʌlgə(r)/ adj vulgaire.

vulnerable /ˈvʌlnərəbl/ adj vulnérable.

Ww

wad /wɒd/ n (pad) tampon m; (bundle) liasse f.

wade /weɪd/ vi ~ **through** (mud) patauger dans. (book: fig) avancer péniblement dans.

wafer /ˈweɪfə(r)/ n (biscuit) gaufrette f.

waffle /ˈwɒfl/ n (talk 🇬🇧) verbiage m; (cake) gaufre f. ● vi 🇬🇧 divaguer.

wag /wæg/ vt/i (pt **wagged**) (tail) remuer.

wage /weɪdʒ/ vt (campaign) mener; ~ **war** faire la guerre. ● n (weekly, daily) salaire m; ~**s** salaire m. ~**earner** n salarié/-e m/f.

wagon /ˈwægən/ n (horse-drawn) chariot m; (Rail) wagon m (de marchandises).

wail /weɪl/ vi gémir. ● n gémissement m.

waist /weɪst/ n taille f. ~**coat** n gilet m.

wait /weɪt/ vt/i attendre; **I can't** ~ **to start** j'ai hâte de commencer; **let's** ~ **and see** attendons voir; ~ **for** attendre; ~ **on** servir. ● n attente f.

waiter /ˈweɪtə(r)/ n garçon m, serveur m.

waiting-list n liste f d'attente.

waiting-room n salle f d'attente.

waitress /ˈweɪtrɪs/ n serveuse f.

waive /weɪv/ vt renoncer à.

wake /weɪk/ vt/i (pt **woke**; pp **woken**) ~ (**up**) (se) réveiller. ● n (track) sillage m; **in the** ~ **of** (after) à la suite de. ~ **up call** n réveil m téléphoné.

Wales /weɪlz/ n pays m de Galles.

walk /wɔːk/ vi marcher; (not ride) aller à pied; (stroll) se promener. ● vt (streets) parcourir; (distance) faire à pied; (dog) promener. ● n promenade f, tour m; (gait) démarche f; (pace) marche f, pas m; (path) allée f; **have a** ~ faire une promenade. □ ~ **out** (go away) partir; (worker) faire grève; ~ **out on** abandonner.

walkie-talkie /wɔːkɪˈtɔːkɪ/ n talkie-walkie m.

walking /ˈwɔːkɪŋ/ n marche f (à pied). ● adj (corpse, dictionary: fig) ambulant.

walkman® /ˈwɔːkmən/ n walkman® m, baladeur m.

walk: ~**-out** n grève f surprise. ~**-over** n victoire f facile.

wall /wɔːl/ n mur m; (of tunnel, stomach) paroi f. ● adj mural. **walled** adj (city) fortifié.

wallet /ˈwɒlɪt/ n portefeuille m.

wallpaper /ˈwɔːlpeɪpə(r)/ n papier m peint. ● vt tapisser.

walnut /ˈwɔːlnʌt/ n (nut) noix f; (tree) noyer m.

waltz /wɔːls/ n valse f. ● vi valser.

wander /ˈwɒndə(r)/ vi errer; (stroll) flâner; (digress) s'écarter du sujet; (in mind) divaguer.

wane /weɪn/ vi décroître.

want /wɒnt/ vt vouloir (**to do** faire); (need) avoir besoin de (**doing** d'être fait); (ask for) demander; **I** ~ **you to do it** je veux que vous le fassiez. ● vi ~ **for** manquer de. ● n

(need, poverty) besoin m; (desire) désir m; (lack) manque m; **for** ~ **of** faute de. **wanted** adj (criminal) recherché par la police.

war /wɔː(r)/ n guerre f; **at** ~ en guerre; **on the** ~**path** sur le sentier de la guerre.

ward /wɔːd/ n (in hospital) salle f; (minor: Jur) pupille mf; (Pol) division f électorale. ● vt ~ **off** (danger) prévenir.

warden /ˈwɔːdn/ n directeur/-trice m/f; (of park) gardien/-ne m/f; (traffic ~) contractuel/-le m/f.

wardrobe /ˈwɔːdrəʊb/ n (furniture) armoire f; (clothes) garde-robe f.

warehouse /ˈweəhaʊs/ n entrepôt m.

wares /weəz/ npl marchandises fpl.

warfare /ˈwɔːfeə(r)/ n guerre f.

warm /wɔːm/ adj chaud; (hearty) chaleureux; **be or feel** ~ avoir chaud; **it is** ~ il fait chaud. ● vt/i ~ (**up**) (se) réchauffer; (food) chauffer; (liven up) (s')animer; (exercise) s'échauffer.

warmth /wɔːmθ/ n chaleur f.

warn /wɔːn/ vt avertir, prévenir; ~ **sb off sth** (advise against) mettre qn en garde contre qch; (forbid) interdire qch à qn.

warning /ˈwɔːnɪŋ/ n avertissement m; (notice) avis m; **without** ~ sans prévenir. ~ **light** n voyant m. ~ **triangle** n triangle m de sécurité.

warp /wɔːp/ vt/i (wood) (se) voiler; (pervert) pervertir; (judgment) fausser.

warrant /ˈwɒrənt/ n (for arrest) mandat m (d'arrêt); (Comm) autorisation f ● vt justifier.

warranty /ˈwɒrəntɪ/ n garantie f.

wart /wɔːt/ n verrue f.

wartime /ˈwɔːtaɪm/ n **in** ~ en

wary | weakness

temps de guerre.

wary /'weərɪ/ adj (-ier, -iest) prudent.

was /wɒz, wəz/ ➡BE.

wash /wɒʃ/ vt/i (se) laver. (flow over) baigner; ~ one's hands of se laver les mains de. ● n lavage m; (clothes) lessive f; have a ~ se laver. ~ up faire la vaisselle; (US) se laver. ~-basin n lavabo m.

washer /'wɒʃə(r)/ n rondelle f.

washing /'wɒʃɪŋ/ n lessive f. ~-machine n machine f à laver. ~-powder n lessive f.

washing-up n vaisselle f. ~ liquid n liquide m vaisselle.

wash: ~-out n [T] fiasco m. ~-room n (US) toilettes fpl.

wasp /wɒsp/ n guêpe f.

wastage /'weɪstɪdʒ/ n gaspillage m.

waste /weɪst/ vt gaspiller; (time) perdre. ● vi ~ away dépérir. ● adj superflu; ~ products or matter déchets mpl. ● n gaspillage m; (of time) perte f; (rubbish) déchets mpl; lay ~ dévaster. **wasteful** adj peu économique; (person) gaspilleur.

waste: ~land n (desolate) terre f désolée; (unused) terre f inculte; (in town) terrain m vague. ~ paper n vieux papiers mpl. ~-paper basket n corbeille f (à papier).

watch /wɒtʃ/ vt/i (television) regarder; (observe) observer; (guard, spy on) surveiller; (be careful about) faire attention à. ● n (for telling time) montre f; (Naut) quart m; be on the ~ guetter; keep ~ on surveiller. ~ out (take care) faire attention (for à); ~ out for (keep watch) guetter.

water /'wɔːtə(r)/ n eau f; by ~ en bateau. ● vt arroser. ● vi (eyes) larmoyer; my/his mouth ~s l'eau

me/lui vient à la bouche. □ ~ down couper (d'eau); (tone down) édulcorer. ~-colour n (painting) aquarelle f. ~cress n cresson m (de fontaine). ~fall n chute f d'eau, cascade f. ~ heater n chauffe-eau m. **watering-can** n arrosoir m. ~-lily n nénuphar m. ~-melon n pastèque f. ~-proof adj (material) imperméable. ~ shed n (in affairs) tournant m décisif. ~-skiing n ski m nautique. ~-tight adj étanche. ~-way n voie f navigable.

watery /'wɔːtərɪ/ adj (colour) délavé; (eyes) humide; (soup) trop liquide.

wave /weɪv/ n vague f; (in hair) ondulation f; (radio) onde f; (sign) signe m. ● vt agiter. ● vi faire signe (de la main); (move in wind) flotter.

waver /'weɪvə(r)/ vi vaciller.

wavy /'weɪvɪ/ adj (line) onduleux; (hair) ondulé.

wax /wæks/ n cire f; (for skis) fart m. ● vt cirer; farter; (car) lustrer.

way /weɪ/ n (road, path) chemin m (to de); (distance) distance f (direction) direction f; (manner) façon f; (means) moyen m; ~s (habits) habitudes fpl; be in the ~ bloquer le passage; (hindrance: fig) gêner (qn); be on one's ~ être sur son or le chemin; by the ~ à propos; by the~side au bord de la route; by ~ of comme; (via) par; go out of one's ~ se donner du mal; in a ~ dans un sens; make one's ~ somewhere se rendre quelque part; push one's ~ through se frayer un passage; that ~ par là; this ~ par ici; ~ in entrée f; ~ out sortie f. ● adv [T] loin.

we /wiː/ pron nous.

weak /wiːk/ adj faible; (delicate) fragile.

weakness /'wiːknɪs/ n faiblesse f;

w

(fault) point *m* faible; **a ~ for** (liking) un faible pour.

wealth /welθ/ *n* richesse *f*; (riches, resources) richesses *fpl*; (quantity) profusion *f*.

wealthy /'welθɪ/ *adj* (-**ier, -iest**) riche. ● **the ~** les riches *mpl*.

weapon /'wepən/ *n* arme *f*; **~s of mass destruction** armes *fpl* de destruction massive.

wear /weə(r)/ *vt* (*pt* **wore**; *pp* **worn**) porter; (put on) mettre; (*expression*) avoir. ● *vi* (last) durer; **~ (out)** (s')user. ● *n* (use) usage *m*; (damage) usure *f*. **~ down** user; **~ off** (*colour, pain*) passer; **~ out** (exhaust) épuiser.

weary /'wɪərɪ/ *adj* (-**ier, -iest**) fatigué, las. ● *vi* **~** se lasser de.

weather /'weðə(r)/ *n* temps *m*; **under the ~** patraque. ● *adj* météorologique. ● *vt* (survive) réchapper de or à. **~ forecast** *n* météo *f*.

weave /wiːv/ *vt/i* (*pt* **wove**; *pp* **woven**) tisser; (*basket*) tresser; (move) se faufiler. ● *n* (style) tissage *m*.

web /web/ *n* (of spider) toile *f*; (on foot) palmure *f*.

Web /web/ *n* (Comput) Web *m*. **~cam** *n* webcam *f*. **~master** *n* administrateur *m* de site Internet. **~page** *n* page *f* Web. **~search** *n* recherche *f* sur le Web. **~site** *n* site *m* Internet.

wedding /'wedɪŋ/ *n* mariage *m*. **~ring** *n* alliance *f*.

wedge /wedʒ/ *n* (of wood) coin *m*; (under wheel) cale *f*. ● *vt* caler; (push) enfoncer; (crowd) coincer.

Wednesday /'wenzdɪ/ *n* mercredi *m*.

weed /wiːd/ *n* mauvaise herbe *f*. ● *vt/i* désherber; **~ out** extirper.

week /wiːk/ *n* semaine *f*; **a ~**

today/tomorrow aujourd'hui/demain en huit. **~day** *n* jour *m* de semaine. **~end** *n* week-end *m*, fin *f* de semaine.

weekly /'wiːklɪ/ *adv* toutes les semaines. ● *adj* & *n* (periodical) hebdomadaire (*m*).

weep /wiːp/ *vt/i* (*pt* **wept**) pleurer (**for sb** qn).

weigh /weɪ/ *vt/i* peser; **~ anchor** lever l'ancre. **~ down** lester (avec un poids); (bend) faire plier; (fig) accabler; **~ up** calculer.

weight /weɪt/ *n* poids *m*; **lose/put on ~** perdre/prendre du poids. **~-lifting** *n* haltérophilie *f*. **~ training** *n* musculation *f* en salle.

weird /wɪəd/ *adj* bizarre.

welcome /'welkəm/ *adj* agréable; (timely) opportun; **be ~** être le or la bienvenu(e), être les bienvenu(e)s; **you're ~!** il n'y a pas de quoi!; **~ to do** libre de faire. ● *interj* soyez le or la bienvenu(e), soyez les bienvenu(e)s. ● *n* accueil *m*. ● *vt* accueillir; (as greeting) souhaiter la bienvenue à; (fig) se réjouir de.

weld /weld/ *vt* souder. ● *n* soudure *f*.

welfare /'welfeə(r)/ *n* bien-être *m*; (aid) aide *f* sociale. **W~ State** *n* état-providence *m*.

well¹ /wel/ *n* puits *m*.

well² /wel/ *adv* (**better, best**) bien; **do ~** (succeed) réussir; **~ done!** bravo! ● *adj* bien *inv*; **as ~** aussi; **be ~** (healthy) aller bien. ● *interj* eh bien; (surprise) tiens.

well-behaved *adj* sage. **~-being** *n* bien-être *m inv*.

wellington /'welɪŋtən/ *n* (boot) botte *f* de caoutchouc.

well-known *adj* (bien) connu. **~-meaning** *adj* bien intentionné. **~ off** aisé, riche. **~-read** *adj* ins-

fruit. ~-**to-do** adj riche. ~-**wisher** n admirateur/-trice m/f.

Welsh /welʃ/ adj gallois. ● n (ling) gallois m.

Welsh Assembly L'Assemblée du Pays de Galles a
été établie à Cardiff en
1999, à l'issue d'un référendum
auprès de la population galloise. À
la différence du parlement écossais, elle n'a pas de réel pouvoir
législatif, mais ses 60 membres
peuvent aménager les lois natio-
nales en fonction des besoins spécifi-
ques des Gallois. ▸SCOTTISH PAR-
LIAMENT.

went /went/ ➡GO.

wept /wept/ ➡WEEP.

were /wɜː(r)/ ➡BE.

west /west/ n ouest m; **the W~**
(Pol) l'Occident m. ● adj d'ouest.
● adv vers l'ouest.

western /'westən/ adj de l'ouest;
(Pol) occidental. ● n (film) western
m. **westerner** n occidental/-e m/f.

West Indies /west 'ɪndiːz/ n Antilles fpl.

westward /'westwəd/ adj (side)
ouest inv; (journey) vers l'ouest.

wet /wet/ adj (**wetter, wettest**)
mouillé; (damp, rainy) humide;
(paint) frais; **get** ~ se mouiller. ● vt
(pt **wetted**) mouiller. ● n the ~
l'humidité f; (rain) la pluie f. ~**suit** f
combinaison f de plongée.

whale /weɪl/ n baleine f.

wharf /wɔːf/ n quai m.

what /wɒt/

● pronoun

••••➤ (in questions as object pronoun) qu'est-ce que?; ~ **are**
we going to do? qu'est-ce que
(nous) allons faire?

••••➤ (in questions as subject
pronoun) qu'est-ce qui?; ~
happened? qu'est-ce qui s'est
passé?

••••➤ (introducing clause as object) ce que; **I don't know** ~
he wants je ne sais pas ce
qu'il veut.

••••➤ (introducing clause as subject) ce qui; **tell me** ~ **hap-**
pened raconte moi ce qui s'est
passé.

••••➤ (with prepositions) quoi; ~
are you thinking about? à
quoi penses-tu?

● determiner

••••➤ quel/quelle/quels/quelles; ~
train did you catch? quel train
as-tu pris?; ~ **time is it?**
quelle heure est-il?

whatever /wɒt'evə(r)/ adj ~
book quel que soit le livre. ● pron
(no matter what) quoi que, quoi
qu'; (anything that) tout ce que or
qu'; (object) tout ce que or qu'; ~ **hap-**
pens quoi qu'il arrive; ~ **hap-**
pened? qu'est-ce qui est arrivé?; ~
the problems quels que soient les
problèmes; ~ **you want** tout ce
que vous voulez; **nothing** ~ rien
du tout.

whatsoever /wɒtsəʊ'evə(r)/ adj &
pron ➡WHATEVER.

wheat /wiːt/ n blé m, froment m.

wheel /wiːl/ n roue f; **at the** ~ (of
vehicle) au volant; (helm) au gouvernail. ● vt pousser. ● vi tourner;
~ **and deal** faire des combines.
~**barrow** n brouette f. ~**chair** n
fauteuil m roulant.

when /wen/ adv & pron quand.
● conj quand, lorsque; **the day/mo-**

ment ~ le jour/moment où.

whenever /wen'evə(r)/ *conj & adv* (at whatever time) quand; (every time that) chaque fois que.

where /weə(r)/ *adv, conj & pron* où; (whereas) alors que; (the place où) là où.

whereabouts /weərə'baʊts/ *adv* (à peu près) où. ● *n* sb's ~ l'endroit où se trouve qn.

whereas /wear'æz/ *conj* alors que.

wherever /weər'evə(r)/ *conj & adv* où que; (everywhere) partout où; (anywhere) (là) où; (emphatic where) où donc.

whether /'weðə(r)/ *conj* si; not know ~ ne pas savoir si; ~ I go or not que j'aille ou non.

which /wɪtʃ/

● *pronoun*

••••► (in questions) lequel/laquelle/lesquels/lesquelles; **there are three peaches, ~ do you want?** il y a trois pêches, laquelle veux-tu?

••••► (in questions with superlative adjective) quel/quelle/quels/quelles; ~ **(apple) is the biggest?** quelle est la plus grosse?

••••► (in relative clauses as subject) qui; **the book ~ is on the table** le livre qui est sur la table.

••••► (in relative clauses as object) que; **the book ~ Tina is reading** le livre que lit Tina.

● *determiner*

••••► quel/quelle/quels/quelles; ~ **car did you choose?** quelle voiture as-tu choisie?

whichever /wɪtʃ'evə(r)/ *adj* ~ **book** quel que soit le livre que or qui; **take** ~ **book you wish** prenez le livre que vous voulez. ● *pron* celui/celle/ceux/celles qui or que.

while /waɪl/ *n* moment m. ● *conj* (when) pendant que; (although) bien que; (as long as) tant que. ● *vt* ~ **away** (time) passer.

whilst /waɪlst/ *conj* ➞ WHILE.

whim /wɪm/ *n* caprice m.

whine /waɪn/ *vi* gémir, se plaindre. ● *n* gémissement m.

whip /wɪp/ *n* fouet m. ● *vt* (pt **whipped**) fouetter; (Culin) fouetter, battre; (seize) enlever brusquement. ● *vi* (move) aller en vitesse. □ ~ **up** exciter; (cause) provoquer; (meal 🎂) préparer.

whirl /wɜːl/ *vt/i* (faire) tourbillonner. ● *n* tourbillon m. ~**pool** *n* tourbillon m. ~**wind** *n* tourbillon m (de vent).

whisk /wɪsk/ *vt* (snatch) enlever or emmener brusquement; (Culin) fouetter. ● *n* (Culin) fouet m.

whiskers /'wɪskə(r)s/ *npl* (of animal) moustaches *fpl*; (of man) favoris *mpl*.

whisper /'wɪspə(r)/ *vt/i* chuchoter. ● *n* chuchotement m; (rumour: fig) rumeur f, bruit m.

whistle /'wɪsl/ *n* sifflement m; (instrument) sifflet m. ● *vt/i* siffler; ~ **at** or **for** siffler.

white /waɪt/ *adj* blanc. ● *n* blanc m; (person) blanc/-che m/f. ~ **coffee** *n* café m au lait. ~**collar worker** *n* employé/-e m/f de bureau. ~ **elephant** *n* projet m coûteux et peu rentable. ~ **lie** *n* pieux mensonge m. **W~ Paper** *n* livre m blanc.

whitewash /'waɪtwɒʃ/ *n* blanc m de chaux. ● *vt* blanchir à la chaux; (person: fig) blanchir.

Whitsun /'wɪtsn/ n la Pentecôte.

whiz /wɪz/ vi (pt whizzed) (through air) fendre l'air; (hiss) siffler; (rush) aller à toute vitesse. **~-kid** n jeune prodige m.

who /huː/ pron qui.

whoever /huːˈevə(r)/ pron (no matter who) qui que ce soit qui or que; (the one who) quiconque; **tell ~ you want** dites-le à qui vous voulez.

whole /həʊl/ adj entier; (intact) intact; **the ~ house** toute la maison. ● n totalité f; (unit) tout m; **on the ~** dans l'ensemble. **~foods** npl aliments mpl naturels et diététiques. **~-hearted** adj sans réserve. **~meal** adj complet.

wholesale /'həʊlseɪl/ adj (firm) de gros; (fig) systématique. ● adv (in large quantities) en gros; (fig) en masse.

wholesome /'həʊlsəm/ adj sain.

wholly /'həʊllɪ/ adv entièrement.

whom /huːm/ pron (that) que, qu'; (after prepositions & in questions) qui; **of ~** dont; **with ~** avec qui.

whooping cough /'huːpɪŋ kɒf/ n coqueluche f.

whose /huːz/ pron & a à qui, de qui; **~ hat is this?**, **~ is this hat?** à qui est ce chapeau?; **~ son are you?** de qui êtes-vous le fils?; **the man ~ hat I see** l'homme dont je vois le chapeau.

why /waɪ/ adv pourquoi; **the reason ~** la raison pour laquelle.

wicked /'wɪkɪd/ adj méchant, mauvais, vilain.

wide /waɪd/ adj large; (ocean) vaste. ● adv (fall) loin du but; **open ~** ouvrir tout grand; **~ open** grand ouvert; **~ awake** éveillé. **widely** adv (spread, spaced) largement; (travel) beaucoup; (generally) géné-ralement; (extremely) extrêmement.

widespread /'waɪdspred/ adj très répandu.

widow /'wɪdəʊ/ n veuve f. **widowed** adj (man) veuf; (woman) veuve. **widower** n veuf m.

width /wɪdθ/ n largeur f.

wield /wiːld/ vt (axe) manier; (power: fig) exercer.

wife /waɪf/ n (pl wives) femme f, épouse f.

wig /wɪg/ n perruque f.

wiggle /'wɪgl/ vt/i remuer; (hips) tortiller; (worm) se tortiller.

wild /waɪld/ adj sauvage; (sea, enthusiasm) déchaîné; (mad) fou; (angry) furieux. ● adv (grow) à l'état sauvage.

wildlife /'waɪldlaɪf/ n faune f.

---

will¹   /wɪl/

present **will**; *present negative* **won't, will not**; *past* **would**

● *auxiliary verb*

····▸ (in future tense) **he'll come** il viendra; **it ~ be sunny tomorrow** il va faire du soleil demain.

····▸ (inviting and requesting) **~ you have some coffee?** est-ce que vous voulez du café?

····▸ (making assumptions) **they won't know what's happened** ils ne doivent pas savoir ce qui s'est passé.

····▸ (in short questions and answers) **you'll come again, won't you?** tu reviendras, n'est-ce pas?; '**they won't forget**'—'**yes they ~**' 'ils n'oublieront pas'—'si'.

w

····➤ (capacity) **the lift ~ hold 12** l'ascenseur peut transporter 12 personnes.

····➤ (ability) **the car won't start** la voiture ne veut pas démarrer.

● *transitive verb* ~ **sb's death** souhaiter ardemment la mort de qn.

will² /wɪl/ *n* volonté *f*; (document) testament *m*; **at ~** quand or comme on veut.

willing /'wɪlɪŋ/ *adj* (help, offer) spontané; (helper) bien disposé; ~ **to** disposé à. **willingly** *adv* (with pleasure) volontiers; (not forced) volontairement. **willingness** *n* empressement *m* (**to do** à faire).

willow /'wɪləʊ/ *n* saule *m*.

will-power /'wɪlpaʊə(r)/ *n* volonté *f*.

win /wɪn/ *vt/i* (*pt* **won**; *pres p* **winning**) gagner; (victory, prize) remporter; (fame, fortune) acquérir, trouver; ~ **round** convaincre. ● *n* victoire *f*.

winch /wɪntʃ/ *n* treuil *m*. ● *vt* hisser au treuil.

wind¹ /wɪnd/ *n* vent *m*; (breath) souffle *m*; **get ~ of** avoir vent de; **in the ~** dans l'air. ● *vt* essouffler. ~ **farm** *n* ferme *f* d'éoliennes.

wind² /waɪnd/ *vt/i* (*pt* **wound**) (s')enrouler; (of path, river) serpenter; ~ (**up**) (clock) remonter; ~ **up** (end) (se) terminer; ~ **up in hospital** finir à l'hôpital.

windmill /'wɪndmɪl/ *n* moulin *m* à vent.

window /'wɪndəʊ/ *n* fenêtre *f*; (glass pane) vitre *f*; (in vehicle, train) vitre *f*; (in shop) vitrine *f*; (counter) guichet *m*; (Comput) fenêtre *f*. ~-**box** *n* jardinière *f*.

~-**cleaner** *n* laveur *m* de carreaux.

~-**dresser** *n* étalagiste *mf*. ~-**ledge** *n* rebord *m* de (la) fenêtre.

~-**shopping** *n* lèche-vitrines *m*.

~-**sill** *n* (inside) appui *m* de (la) fenêtre; (outside) rebord *m* de (la) fenêtre.

windscreen /'wɪndskriːn/ *n* pare-brise *m inv.* ~ **wiper** *n* essuie-glace *m*.

windshield /'wɪndʃiːld/ *n* (US) ►**WINDSCREEN**.

windsurfing /'wɪndsɜːfɪŋ/ *n* planche *f* à voile.

windy /'wɪndɪ/ *adj* (**-ier, -iest**) venteux; **it is ~** il y a du vent.

wine /waɪn/ *n* vin *m*. ~-**cellar** *n* cave *f* (à vin). ~-**glass** *n* verre *m* à vin. ~-**grower** *n* viticulteur *m*. ~-**list** *n* carte *f* des vins. ~-**tasting** *n* dégustation *f* de vins.

wing /wɪŋ/ *n* aile *f*; ~**s** (Theat) coulisses *fpl*; **under one's ~** sous son aile. ~ **mirror** *n* rétroviseur *m* extérieur.

wink /wɪŋk/ *vi* faire un clin d'œil; (light, star) clignoter. ● *n* clin *m* d'œil; clignotement.

winner /'wɪnə(r)/ *n* (of game) gagnant/-e *m*/*f*; (of fight) vainqueur *m*.

winning /'wɪnɪŋ/ ►**WIN**. ● *adj* (number, horse) gagnant; (team) victorieux; (smile) engageant. **winnings** *npl* gains *mpl*.

winter /'wɪntə(r)/ *n* hiver *m*.

wipe /waɪp/ *vt* essuyer. ● *vi* essuyer la vaisselle. ● *n* coup *m* de torchon or d'éponge. □ ~ **out** (destroy) anéantir; (remove) effacer.

wire /waɪə(r)/ *n* fil *m*; (US) télégramme *m*.

wiring /'waɪərɪŋ/ *n* (Electr) installation *f* électrique.

wisdom /'wɪzdəm/ *n* sagesse *f*.

wise /waɪz/ *adj* prudent, sage;

(look) averti.

wish /wɪʃ/ n (specific) souhait m, vœu m; (general) désir m; **best ~es** (in letter) amitiés fpl; (on greeting card) meilleurs vœux mpl. ● vt souhaiter, vouloir, désirer (**to do** faire); (bid) souhaiter. ● vi ~ **for** souhaiter; **I ~ he'd leave** je voudrais bien qu'il parte.

wishful /'wɪʃfl/ adj **it's ~ thinking** c'est prendre ses désirs pour des réalités.

wistful /'wɪstfl/ adj mélancolique.

wit /wɪt/ n intelligence f; (humour) esprit m; (person) homme m d'esprit, femme f d'esprit.

witch /wɪtʃ/ n sorcière f.

with /wɪð/ prep avec; (having) à; (because of) de; (at house of) chez; **the man ~ the beard** l'homme à la barbe; **fill ~** remplir de; **pleased/ shaking ~** content/frémissant de.

withdraw /wɪð'drɔː/ vt/i (pt **withdrew**, pp **withdrawn**) (se) retirer. **withdrawal** n retrait m.

wither /'wɪðə(r)/ vt/i (se) flétrir.

withhold /wɪð'həʊld/ vt (pt **withheld**) refuser (de donner); (retain) retenir; (conceal) cacher (**from** à).

within /wɪ'ðɪn/ prep & adv à l'intérieur (de); (in distances) à moins de; **~ a month** (before) avant un mois; **~ sight** en vue.

without /wɪ'ðaʊt/ prep sans; **~ my knowing** sans que je sache.

withstand /wɪð'stænd/ vt (pt **withstood**) résister à.

witness /'wɪtnɪs/ n témoin m; (evidence) témoignage m; **bear ~ to** témoigner à. ● vt être le témoin de, voir. **~ box, ~ stand** n barre f des témoins.

witty /'wɪtɪ/ adj (-ier, -iest) spirituel.

wives /waɪvz/ →**WIFE**.

wizard /'wɪzəd/ n magicien m; (genius: fig) génie m.

WMD abbr (weapon of mass destruction) ADM f.

woke, **woken** →**WAKE**.

wolf /wʊlf/ n (pl **wolves**) loup m. ● vt (food) engloutir.

woman /'wʊmən/ n (pl **women**) femme f; **~ doctor** femme f médecin; **~ driver** femme f au volant.

women /'wɪmɪn/ →**WOMAN**.

won /wʌn/ →**WIN**.

wonder /'wʌndə(r)/ n émerveillement m; (thing) merveille f; **it is no ~ ce or il n'est pas étonnant (that** que). ● vt se demander (**if** si). ● vi s'étonner (**at** de); (reflect) songer (**about** à).

wonderful /'wʌndəfl/ adj merveilleux.

won't /wəʊnt/ →**WILL NOT**.

wood /wʊd/ n bois m.

wooden /'wʊdn/ adj en or de bois. (stiff: fig) raide, comme du bois.

wood: **~wind** n (Mus) bois mpl. **~work** n (craft, objects) menuiserie f.

wool /wʊl/ n laine f. **woollen** adj de laine. **woollens** npl lainages mpl.

woolly /'wʊlɪ/ adj laineux; (vague) nébuleux. ● n (garment 🔲) lainage m.

word /wɜːd/ n mot m; (spoken) parole f, mot m; (promise) parole f; (news) nouvelles fpl; **by ~ of mouth** de vive voix; **give/keep one's ~** donner/tenir sa parole; **have a ~ with** parler à; **in other ~s** autrement dit. ● vt rédiger. **wording** n termes mpl.

word processing n traitement m de texte. **word processor** n machine f à traitement de texte.

wore /wɔː(r)/ →**WEAR**.

work /wɜːk/ n travail m; (product,

book) œuvre f, ouvrage m; (building work) travaux mpl; **~s** (Tech) mécanisme m; (factory) usine f. ● vi (person) travailler; (drug) agir; (Tech) fonctionner, marcher. ● vt (Tech) faire fonctionner, faire marcher; (land, mine) exploiter; (shape, hammer) travailler; **~ sb** (make work) faire travailler qn. □ **~ out** vt (solve) résoudre; (calculate) calculer; (elaborate) élaborer; vi (succeed) marcher; (Sport) s'entraîner; **~ up** vt développer; vi (to climax) monter vers; **~ed up** (person) énervé.

workaholic /wɜːkəˈhɒlɪk/ n 🔲 bourreau m de travail.

worker /ˈwɜːkə(r)/ n travailleur/-euse m/f; (manual) ouvrier/-ière m/f.

work-force n main-d'œuvre f.

working /ˈwɜːkɪŋ/ adj (day, lunch) de travail; **~s** mécanisme m; **in ~ order** en état de marche.

working class n classe f ouvrière. ● adj ouvrier.

workman /ˈwɜːkmən/ n (pl **-men**) ouvrier m.

work: **~out** n séance f de mise en forme. **~shop** n atelier m. **~-station** n poste m de travail.

world /wɜːld/ n monde m; **best in the ~** le meilleur au monde. ● adj (power) mondial; (record) du monde.

world-wide adj universel.

World Wide Web, WWW n World Wide Web m, réseau m des réseaux.

worm /wɜːm/ n ver m. ● vt **~ one's way into** s'insinuer dans.

worn /wɔːn/ →WEAR. ● adj usé. **~-out** (thing) complètement usé; (person) épuisé.

worried /ˈwʌrɪd/ adj inquiet.

worry /ˈwʌrɪ/ vt/i (s')inquiéter. ● n

souci m.

worse /wɜːs/ adj pire, plus mauvais; **be ~ off** perdre. ● adv plus mal. ● n pire m. **worsen** vt/i empirer.

worship /ˈwɜːʃɪp/ n (adoration) culte m. ● vt (pt **worshipped**) adorer. ● vi faire ses dévotions.

worst /wɜːst/ adj pire, plus mauvais. ● adv (the) **~** (sing) le plus mal. ● n **the ~ (one)** (person, object) le or la pire; **the ~ (thing)** le pire.

worth /wɜːθ/ adj **be ~** valoir; **it is ~ waiting** ça vaut la peine d'attendre; **it is ~ (one's) while** ça (en) vaut la peine. ● n valeur f; **ten pence ~ of** (pour) dix pence de. **worthless** adj qui ne vaut rien. **worthwhile** adj qui (en) vaut la peine.

worthy /ˈwɜːðɪ/ adj (**-ier, -iest**) digne (**of** de); (laudable) louable.

would /wʊd/ v aux **he ~ do/you ~ sing** (conditional tense) il ferait/tu chanterais; **he ~ have done** il aurait fait; **I ~ come every day** (used to) je venais chaque jour; **I ~ like some tea** je voudrais du thé; **~ you come here?** voulez-vous venir ici?; **he wouldn't come** il a refusé de venir. **~-be** adj soidisant.

wound[1] /wuːnd/ n blessure f. ● vt blesser; **the ~ed** les blessés mpl.

wound[2] /waʊnd/ →WIND[2].

wove, woven /wəʊv, ˈwəʊvn/ →WEAVE.

wrap /ræp/ vt (pt **wrapped**) **~ (up)** envelopper. ● vi **~ up** (dress warmly) se couvrir; **~ped up in** (engrossed) absorbé dans.

wrapping /ˈræpɪŋ/ n emballage m.

wreak /riːk/ vt **~ havoc** faire des ravages.

wreath /riːθ/ n (of flowers, leaves) couronne f.

wreck /rek/ n (sinking) naufrage m; (ship, remains, person) épave f; (vehicle) voiture f accidentée or délabrée. ● vt détruire; (ship) provoquer le naufrage de. **wreckage** n (pieces) débris mpl; (wrecked building) décombres mpl.

wrestle /ˈresl/ vi lutter, se débattre (**with** contre).

wrestling /ˈreslɪŋ/ n lutte f; (**all-in**) ~ catch m.

wriggle /ˈrɪgl/ vt/i (se) tortiller.

wring /rɪŋ/ vt (pt **wrung**) (twist) tordre; (clothes) essorer; ~ **out of** (obtain from) arracher à.

wrinkle /ˈrɪŋkl/ n (crease) pli m; (on skin) ride f. ● vt/i (se) rider.

wrist /rɪst/ n poignet m.

write /raɪt/ vt/i (pt **wrote**; pp **written**) écrire. □ ~ **back** répondre; ~ **down** noter; ~ **off** (debt) passer aux profits et pertes; (vehicle) considérer bon pour la casse; ~ **up** (from notes) rédiger.

write-off /ˈraɪtɒf/ n perte f totale.

writer /ˈraɪtə(r)/ n auteur m, écrivain m; ~ **of** auteur de.

write-up /ˈraɪtʌp/ n compte-rendu m.

writing /ˈraɪtɪŋ/ n écriture f; ~(**s**) (works) écrits mpl; **in** ~ par écrit. ~-**paper** n papier m à lettres.

written →WRITE.

wrong /rɒŋ/ adj (incorrect, mistaken) faux, mauvais. (unfair) injuste; (amiss) qui ne va pas; (clock) pas à l'heure; be ~ (person) avoir tort (**to** de); (be mistaken) se tromper; **go** ~ (err) se tromper; (turn out badly) mal tourner; **it is** ~ **to** (morally) c'est mal de; **what's** ~? qu'est-ce qui ne va pas?; **what is** ~ **with you?** qu'est-ce que vous avez?

● adv mal. ● n injustice f; (evil) mal m; **be in the** ~ avoir tort. ● vt faire (du) tort à. **wrongful** adj injustifié, injuste. **wrongly** adv à tort.

wrote /rəʊt/ →WRITE.

wrought iron /rɔːt ˈaɪən/ n fer m forgé.

wrung /rʌŋ/ →WRING.

Xmas /ˈkrɪsməs/ n Noël m.

X-ray /ˈeksreɪ/ n rayon m X; (photograph) radio (graphie) f. ● vt radiographier.

yank /jæŋk/ vt tirer brusquement. ● n coup m brusque.

yard /jɑːd/ n (measure) yard m (= 0.9144 metre). (of house) cour f; (garden: US) jardin m; (for storage) chantier m, dépôt m. ~**stick** n mesure f.

yawn /jɔːn/ vi bâiller. ● n bâillement m.

yeah /jeə/ adv 🗆 ouais.

year /jɪə(r)/ n an m, année f; **school/tax** ~ année scolaire/fiscale; **be ten** ~**s old** avoir dix ans.

yearly /ˈjɪəlɪ/ adj annuel. ● adv annuellement.

yearn /jɜːn/ vi avoir bien or très envie (**for, to** de).

w
x
y

yeast /ji:st/ n levure f.

yell /jel/ vt/i hurler. ● n hurlement m.

yellow /'jeləʊ/ adj jaune; (cowardly 🄵) froussard. ● n jaune m.

yes /jes/ adv oui; (as answer to negative question) si. ● n oui m inv.

yesterday /'jestədeɪ/ n & adv hier (m).

yet /jet/ adv encore; (already) déjà. ● conj pourtant, néanmoins.

yew /ju:/ n if m.

yield /ji:ld/ vt (produce) produire, rendre; (profit) rapporter; (surrender) céder. ● n rendement m.

yoga /'jəʊgə/ n yoga m.

yoghurt /'jɒgət/ n yaourt m.

yolk /jəʊk/ n jaune m (d'œuf).

you /ju:/ pron (familiar form) tu, pl vous; (polite form) vous; (object) te, t', pl vous; (polite) vous; (after prep.) toi, pl vous; (polite) vous; (indefinite) on; (object) vous; (to) ~ te, t', pl vous; (polite) vous; I gave ~ a pen je vous ai donné un stylo; I know ~ je te connais or je vous connais.

young /jʌŋ/ adj jeune. ● n (people) jeunes mpl; (of animals) petits mpl.

your /jɔ:(r)/ adj (familiar form) ton, ta, pl tes; (polite form, & familiar form pl.) votre, pl vos.

yours /jɔ:z/ pron (familiar form) le tien, la tienne, les tien(ne)s; (polite form, & familiar form pl.) le or la vôtre, les vôtres; ~ faithfully/sincerely je vous prie d'agréer mes salutations les meilleures.

yourself /jɔ:'self/ pron (familiar form) toi-même; (polite form) vous-même; (reflexive & after pre-

positions) te, t'; vous; proud of ~ fier de toi. **yourselves** pron vous-mêmes; (reflexive) vous.

youth /ju:θ/ n jeunesse f; (young man) jeune m. ~ **hostel** n auberge f de jeunesse.

Yugoslav /'ju:gəʊslɑ:v/ adj yougoslave. ● n Yougoslave mf.

Yugoslavia /ju:gəʊ'slɑ:vɪə/ n Yougoslavie f.

Zz

zap /zæp/ vt 🄵 (kill) descendre; (Comput) enlever.

zeal /zi:l/ n zèle m.

zebra /'zebrə/ n zèbre m. ~ **crossing** n passage m pour piétons.

zero /'zɪərəʊ/ n zéro m.

zest /zest/ n (gusto) entrain m; (spice: fig) piment m; (of orange or lemon peel) zeste m.

zip /zɪp/ n (vigour) allant m; ~(-fastener) fermeture f éclair(r). ● vt (pt zipped) fermer avec une fermeture éclair(r); (Comput) compresser. **Zip code** (US) n code m postal.

zodiac /'zəʊdɪæk/ n zodiaque m.

zone /zəʊn/ n zone f.

zoo /zu:/ n zoo m.

zoom /zu:m/ vi (rush) se précipiter. ▫ ~ **off** or **past** filer (comme une flèche). ~ **lens** n zoom m.

zucchini /zu:'ki:nɪ/ n inv (US) courgette f.

French Verbs

1 chanter

Present indicative

je	chante
tu	chantes
il	chante
nous	chantons
vous	chantez
ils	chantent

Present subjunctive

(que)	je	chante
(que)	tu	chantes
(qu')	il	chante
(que)	nous	chantions
(que)	vous	chantiez
(qu')	ils	chantent

Future indicative

je	chanterai
tu	chanteras
il	chantera
nous	chanterons
vous	chanterez
ils	chanteront

Present conditional

je	chanterais
tu	chanterais
il	chanterait
nous	chanterions
vous	chanteriez
ils	chanteraient

Imperfect indicative

je	chantais
tu	chantais
il	chantait
nous	chantions
vous	chantiez
ils	chantaient

Past participle

chanté/chantée

Pluperfect indicative

j'	avais	chanté
tu	avais	chanté
il	avait	chanté
elle	avait	chanté
nous	avions	chanté
vous	aviez	chanté
ils	avaient	chanté
elles	avaient	chanté

Perfect indicative

j'	ai	chanté
tu	as	chanté
il	a	chanté
elle	a	chanté
nous	avons	chanté
vous	avez	chanté
ils	ont	chanté
elles	ont	chanté

2 finir

Present indicative

je	finis
tu	finis
il	finit
nous	finissons
vous	finissez
ils	finissent

Future indicative

je	finirai
tu	finiras
il	finira
nous	finirons
vous	finirez
ils	finiront

Imperfect indicative

je	finissais
tu	finissais
il	finissait
nous	finissions
vous	finissiez
ils	finissaient

Perfect indicative

j'	ai	fini
tu	as	fini
il	a	fini
elles	a	fini
nous	avons	fini
vous	avez	fini
ils	ont	fini
elles	ont	fini

Present subjunctive

(que)	je	finisse
(que)	tu	finisses
(qu')	il	finisse
(que)	nous	finissions
(que)	vous	finissiez
(qu')	ils	finissent

Present conditional

je	finirais
tu	finirais
il	finirait
nous	finirions
vous	finiriez
ils	finiraient

Past participle

fini/finie

Pluperfect indicative

j'	avais	fini
tu	avais	fini
il	avait	fini
elle	avait	fini
nous	avions	fini
vous	aviez	fini
ils	avaient	fini
elles	avaient	fini

3 attendre

Present indicative

j'	attends
tu	attends
il	attend
nous	attendons
vous	attendez
ils	attendent

Future indicative

j'	attendrai
tu	attendras
il	attendra
nous	attendrons
vous	attendrez
ils	attendront

Imperfect indicative

j'	attendais
tu	attendais
il	attendait
nous	attendions
vous	attendiez
ils	attendaient

Perfect indicative

j'	ai	attendu
tu	as	attendu
il	a	attendu
elle	a	attendu
nous	avons	attendu
vous	avez	attendu
ils	ont	attendu
elles	ont	attendu

Present subjunctive

(que)	j'	attende
(que)	tu	attendes
(qu')	il	attende
(que)	nous	attendions
(que)	vous	attendiez
(qu')	ils	attendent

Present conditional

j'	attendrais
tu	attendrais
il	attendrait
nous	attendrions
vous	attendriez
ils	attendraient

Past participle

attendu/attendue

Pluperfect indicative

j'	avais	attendu
tu	avais	attendu
il	avait	attendu
elle	avait	attendu
nous	avions	attendu
vous	aviez	attendu
ils	avaient	attendu
elles	avaient	attendu

4 être

Present indicative

je	suis
tu	es
il	est
nous	sommes
vous	êtes
ils	sont

Present subjunctive

(que)	je	sois
(que)	tu	sois
(qu')	il	soit
(que)	nous	soyons
(que)	vous	soyez
(qu')	ils	soient

Future indicative

je	serai
tu	seras
il	sera
nous	serons
vous	serez
ils	seront

Present conditional

je	serais
tu	serais
il	serait
nous	serions
vous	seriez
ils	seraient

Imperfect indicative

j'	étais
tu	étais
il	était
nous	étions
vous	étiez
ils	étaient

Past participle

été (*invariable*)

Perfect indicative

j'	ai	été
tu	as	été
il	a	été
elle	a	été
nous	avons	été
vous	avez	été
ils	ont	été
elles	ont	été

Pluperfect indicative

j'	avais	été
tu	avais	été
il	avait	été
elle	avait	été
nous	avions	été
vous	aviez	été
ils	avaient	été
elles	avaient	été

5 avoir

Present indicative

j'	ai
tu	as
il	a
nous	avons
vous	avez
ils	ont

Present subjunctive

(que)	j'	aie
(que)	tu	aies
(qu')	il	ait
(que)	nous	ayons
(que)	vous	ayez
(qu')	ils	aient

Future indicative

j'	aurai
tu	auras
il	aura
nous	aurons
vous	aurez
ils	auront

Present conditional

j'	aurais
tu	aurais
il	aurait
nous	aurions
vous	auriez
ils	auraient

Imperfect indicative

j'	avais
tu	avais
il	avait
nous	avions
vous	aviez
ils	avaient

Past participle

eu/eue

Pluperfect indicative

j'	avais	eu
tu	avais	eu
il	avait	eu
elle	avait	eu
nous	avions	eu
vous	aviez	eu
ils	avaient	eu
elles	avaient	eu

Perfect indicative

j'	ai	eu
tu	as	eu
il	a	eu
elle	a	eu
nous	avons	eu
vous	avez	eu
ils	ont	eu
elles	ont	eu

[6] acheter
1 j'achète 2 j'achèterai 3 j'achetais
4 que j'achète 5 acheté

[7] acquérir
1 j'acquiers, nous acquérons,
ils acquièrent 2 j'acquerrai
3 j'acquérais 4 que j'acquière
5 acquis

[8] aller
1 je vais, tu vas, il va, nous allons,
vous allez, ils vont 2 j'irai 3 j'allais
4 que j'aille, que nous allions, qu'ils
aillent 5 allé

[9] asseoir
1 j'assois, tu assois, il assoit, nous
assoyons, vous assoyez, ils assoient
2 j'assoirai 3 j'assoyais 4 que
j'assoie, que nous assoyions, qu'ils
assoient 5 assis

[10] avancer
1 nous avançons 3 j'avançais

[11] battre
1 je bats, il bat, nous battons
2 je battrai 3 je battais 4 que je
batte 5 battu

[12] boire
1 je bois, il boit, nous buvons,
ils boivent 2 je boirai 3 je buvais
4 que je boive 5 bu

[13] bouillir
1 je bous, il bout, nous bouillons,
ils bouillent 2 je bouillirai

3 je bouillais 4 que je bouille
5 bouilli

[14] céder
1 je cède, nous cédons, ils cèdent
2 je céderai 3 je cédais 4 que je
cède 5 cédé

[15] créer
1 je crée, nous créons 2 je créerai
3 je créais 4 que je crée 5 créé

[16] conclure
1 je conclus, il conclut, nous
concluons, ils concluent 2 je
conclurai 3 je concluais 4 que je
conclue 5 conclu (but inclus)

[17] conduire
1 je conduis, nous conduisons,
2 je conduirai 3 je conduisais
4 que je conduise 5 conduit (but lui,
nui)

[18] connaître
1 je connais, il connaît, nous
connaissons 2 je connaîtrai
3 je connaissais 4 que je connaisse
5 connu

[19] coudre
1 je couds, il coud, nous cousons,
ils cousent 2 je coudrai 3 je cousais
4 que je couse 5 cousu

[20] courir
1 je cours, il court, nous courons,
ils courent 2 je courrai 3 je courais
4 que je coure 5 couru

---

1 Present Indicative 2 Future Indicative 3 Imperfect Indicative
4 Present Subjunctive 5 Past Participle

[21] couvrir

1 je couvre 2 je couvrirai 3 je couvrais 4 que je couvre 5 couvert

[22] craindre

1 je crains, il craint, nous craignons, ils craignent 2 je craindrai 3 je craignais 4 que je craigne 5 craint

[23] croire

1 je crois, il croit, nous croyons, ils croient 2 je croirai 3 je croyais, nous croyions 4 que je croie, que nous croyions 5 cru

[24] croître

1 je croîs, il croît, nous croissons 2 je croîtrai 3 je croissais 4 que je croisse 5 crû/crue (but accru, décru)

[25] cueillir

1 je cueille 2 je cueillerai 3 je cueillais 4 que je cueille 5 cueilli

[26] devoir

1 je dois, il doit, nous devons, ils doivent 2 je devrai 3 je devais 4 que je doive, que nous devions 5 dû/due

[27] dire

1 je dis, il dit, nous disons, vous dites, ils disent 2 je dirai 3 je disais 4 que je dise 5 dit

[28] dissoudre

1 je dissous, il dissout, nous dissolvons, ils dissolvent 2 je dissoudrai 3 je dissolvais 4 que je dissolve 5 dissous/dissoute

[29] distraire

1 je distrais, il distrait, nous distrayons 2 je distrairai 3 je distrayais 4 que je distraie 5 distrait

[30] écrire

1 j'écris, il écrit, nous écrivons 2 j'écrirai 3 j'écrivais 4 que j'écrive 5 écrit

[31] employer

1 j'emploie, nous employons, ils emploient 2 j'emploierai 3 j'employais, nous employions 4 que j'emploie, que nous employions 5 employé

[32] envoyer

1 j'envoie, nous envoyons, ils envoient 2 j'enverrai 3 j'envoyais, nous envoyions 4 que j'envoie, que nous envoyions 5 envoyé

[33] faire

1 je fais, nous faisons (say /fəzɔ̃/), vous faites, ils font 2 je ferai 3 je faisais (say /fəzɛ/) 4 que je fasse, que nous fassions 5 fait

[34] falloir (impersonal)

1 il faut 2 il faudra 3 il fallait 4 qu'il faille 5 fallu

[35] fuir

1 je fuis, nous fuyons 2 je fuirai 3 je fuyais, nous fuyions 4 que je fuie, que nous fuyions 5 fui

---

1 Present Indicative   2 Future Indicative   3 Imperfect Indicative
4 Present Subjunctive   5 Past Participle

[36] haïr

1 je hais, il hait, nous haïssons, ils haïssent 2 je haïrai 3 je haïssais 4 que je haïsse 5 haï

[37] interdire

1 j'interdis, vous interdisez 2 j'interdirai 3 j'interdisais 4 que j'interdise 5 interdit

[38] jeter

1 je jette, nous jetons, ils jettent 2 je jetterai 3 je jetais 4 que je jette 5 jeté

[39] lire

1 je lis, il lit, nous lisons 2 je lirai 3 je lisais 4 que je lise 5 lu

[40] manger

1 je mange, nous mangeons 2 je mangerai 3 je mangeais 4 que je mange, que nous mangions 5 mangé

[41] maudire

1 je maudis, il maudit, nous maudissons 2 je maudirai 3 je maudissais 4 que je maudisse 5 maudit

[42] mettre

1 je mets, tu mets, nous mettons 2 je mettrai 3 je mettais 4 que je mette 5 mis

[43] mourir

1 je meurs, il meurt, nous mourons 2 je mourrai 3 je mourais 4 que je meure 5 mort

[44] naître

1 je nais, il naît, nous naissons 2 je naîtrai 3 je naissais 4 que je naisse 5 né

[45] oublier

1 j'oublie, nous oublions, ils oublient 2 j'oublierai 3 j'oubliais, nous oubliions, vous oubliiez 4 que nous oubliions, que vous oubliiez 5 oublié

[46] partir

1 je pars, nous partons 2 je partirai 3 je partais 4 que je parte 5 parti

[47] plaire

1 je plais, il plaît (but il tait), nous plaisons 2 je plairai 3 je plaisais 4 que je plaise 5 plu

[48] pleuvoir *(impersonal)*

1 il pleut 2 il pleuvra 3 il pleuvait 4 qu'il pleuve 5 plu

[49] pouvoir

1 je peux, il peut, nous pouvons, ils peuvent 2 je pourrai 3 je pouvais 4 que je puisse, que nous puissions 5 pu

[50] prendre

1 je prends, il prend, nous prenons 2 je prendrai 3 je prenais 4 que je prenne 5 pris

---

1 Present Indicative **2** Future Indicative **3** Imperfect Indicative
4 Present Subjunctive **5** Past Participle

[51] prévoir

1 je prévois, il prévoit, nous prévoyons, ils prévoient **2** je prévoirai **3** je prévoyais, nous prévoyions **4** que je prévoie, que nous prévoyions **5** prévu

[52] recevoir

1 je reçois, il reçoit, nous recevons, ils reçoivent **2** je recevrai **3** je recevais **4** que je reçoive, que nous recevions **5** reçu

[53] résoudre

1 je résous, il résout, nous résolvons, ils résolvent **2** je résoudrai **3** je résolvais **4** que je résolve **5** résolu

[54] rire

1 je ris, nous rions, ils rient **2** je rirai **3** je riais, nous riions **4** que je rie, que nous riions **5** ri

[55] savoir

1 je sais, il sait, nous savons, ils savent **2** je saurai **3** je savais **4** que je sache, que nous sachions **5** su

[56] suffire

1 il suffit, ils suffisent **2** il suffira **3** il suffisait **4** qu'il suffise **5** suffi (but frit)

[57] suivre

1 je suis, il suit, nous suivons **2** je suivrai **3** je suivais **4** que je suive **5** suivi

[58] tenir

1 je tiens, il tient, nous tenons, ils tiennent **2** je tiendrai **3** je tenais **4** que je tienne, que nous tenions **5** tenu

[59] vaincre

1 je vaincs, il vainc, nous vainquons, ils vainquent **2** je vaincrai **3** je vainquais **4** que je vainque **5** vaincu

[60] valoir

1 je vaux, il vaut, nous valons **2** je vaudrai **3** je valais **4** que je vaille, que nous valions **5** valu

[61] vêtir

1 je vêts, il vêt, nous vêtons **2** je vêtirai **3** je vêtais **4** que je vête **5** vêtu

[62] vivre

1 je vis, il vit, nous vivons, ils vivent **2** je vivrai **3** je vivais **4** que je vive **5** vécu

[63] voir

1 je vois, nous voyons, ils voient **2** je verrai **3** je voyais, nous voyions **4** que je voie, que nous voyions **5** vu

[64] vouloir

1 je veux, il veut, nous voulons, ils veulent **2** je voudrai **3** je voulais **4** que je veuille, que nous voulions **5** voulu

---

1 Present Indicative **2** Future Indicative **3** Imperfect Indicative **4** Present Subjunctive **5** Past Participle

What are the equivalent tenses in English

Present indicative
je chante = I sing, I'm singing

Future indicative
je chanterai = I will sing

Imperfect indicative
je chantais = I was singing

Perfect indicative
j'ai chanté = I sang, I have sung

Pluperfect indicative
j'avais chanté = I had sung

Present subjunctive
bien que je chante = although I sing

Present conditional
si je pouvais, je chanterais
= if I could, I would sing

Past participle
chanté/chantée = sung

How to conjugate a reflexive verb

Present indicative and other simple tenses

je me lave
tu te laves
il se lave
elle se lave
nous nous lavons
vous vous lavez
ils se lavent
elles se lavent

Perfect indicative and other compound tenses

(always with auxiliary être)

je me suis lavé
tu t'es lavé
il s'est lavé
elle s'est lavée
nous nous sommes lavés
vous vous êtes lavés
ils se sont lavés
elles se sont lavées

in the negative form

je ne me lave pas
tu ne te laves pas
il ne se lave pas
elle ne se lave pas
nous ne nous lavons pas
vous ne vous lavez pas
ils ne se lavent pas
elles ne se lavent pas

in the negative form

je ne me suis pas lavé
tu ne t'es pas lavé
il ne s'est pas lavé
elle ne s'est pas lavée
nous ne nous sommes pas lavés
vous ne vous êtes pas lavés
ils ne se sont pas lavés
elles ne se sont pas lavées

Verbes irréguliers anglais

Infinitif	Prétérit	Participe passé	Infinitif	Prétérit	Participe passé
be	was	been	**drive**	drove	driven
bear	bore	borne	**eat**	ate	eaten
beat	beat	beaten	**fall**	fell	fallen
become	became	become	**feed**	fed	fed
begin	began	begun	**feel**	felt	felt
bend	bent	bent	**fight**	fought	fought
bet	bet,	bet,	**find**	found	found
	betted	betted	**flee**	fled	fled
bid	bade, bid	bidden, bid	**fly**	flew	flown
bind	bound	bound	**freeze**	froze	frozen
bite	bit	bitten	**get**	got	got, gotten US
bleed	bled	bled	**give**	gave	given
blow	blew	blown	**go**	went	gone
break	broke	broken	**grow**	grew	grown
breed	bred	bred	**hang**	hung,	hung,
bring	brought	brought		hanged	hanged
build	built	built	**have**	had	had
burn	burnt,	burnt,	**hear**	heard	heard
	burned	burned	**hide**	hid	hidden
burst	burst	burst	**hit**	hit	hit
buy	bought	bought	**hold**	held	held
catch	caught	caught	**hurt**	hurt	hurt
choose	chose	chosen	**keep**	kept	kept
cling	clung	clung	**kneel**	knelt	knelt
come	came	come	**know**	knew	known
cost	cost,	cost,	**lay**	laid	laid
	costed (vt)	costed	**lead**	led	led
cut	cut	cut	**lean**	leaned,	leaned,
deal	dealt	dealt		leant	leant
dig	dug	dug	**learn**	learnt,	learnt,
do	did	done		learned	learned
draw	drew	drawn	**leave**	left	left
dream	dreamt,	dreamt,	**lend**	lent	lent
	dreamed	dreamed	**let**	let	let
drink	drank	drunk	**lie**	lay	lain

Infinitif	Prétérit	Participe passé	Infinitif	Prétérit	Participe passé
lose	lost	lost	**spend**	spent	spent
make	made	made	**spit**	spat	spat
mean	meant	meant	**spoil**	spoilt,	spoilt,
meet	met	met		spoiled	spoiled
pay	paid	paid	**spread**	spread	spread
put	put	put	**spring**	sprang	sprung
read	read	read	**stand**	stood	stood
ride	rode	ridden	**steal**	stole	stolen
ring	rang	rung	**stick**	stuck	stuck
rise	rose	risen	**sting**	stung	stung
run	ran	run	**stride**	strode	stridden
say	said	said	**strike**	struck	struck
see	saw	seen	**swear**	swore	sworn
seek	sought	sought	**sweep**	swept	swept
sell	sold	sold	**swell**	swelled	swollen,
send	sent	sent			swelled
set	set	set	**swim**	swam	swum
sew	sewed	sewn, sewed	**swing**	swung	swung
shake	shook	shaken	**take**	took	taken
shine	shone	shone	**teach**	taught	taught
shoe	shod	shod	**tear**	tore	torn
shoot	shot	shot	**tell**	told	told
show	showed	shown	**think**	thought	thought
shut	shut	shut	**throw**	threw	thrown
sing	sang	sung	**thrust**	thrust	thrust
sink	sank	sunk	**tread**	trod	trodden
sit	sat	sat	**under-**	under-	understood
sleep	slept	slept	**stand**	stood	
sling	slung	slung	**wake**	woke	woken
smell	smelt,	smelt,	**wear**	wore	worn
	smelled	smelled	**win**	won	won
speak	spoke	spoken	**write**	wrote	written
spell	spelled,	spelled,			
	spelt	spelt			